The Book of
TOLE & DECORATIVE PAINTING

Priscilla Hauser

ACKNOWLEDGMENTS

I would like to express my gratitude to the following: Sheila Ross of Shiva, Incorporated; Bob Simmons of Robert Simmons, Incorporated; Jim Harkness of Color Photography, Incorporated; Juanita Scott, my Project Coordinator; Marynell Snow, Editor of Priscilla Hauser Publications.

I shall be forever grateful to my family, friends, students, and business associates for the encouragement, cooperation, and assistance that they have given me in all my ventures. Their love is the most precious part of my life.

Library of Congress Cataloging in Publication Data

Hauser, Priscilla.
  The Priscilla Hauser book of tole and decorative painting.

  Includes index.
  1. Tole painting.   2. Painting.   3. Design, Decorative—Plant forms.   I. Title.
TT385.H38   745.7'2   77-4767
ISBN 0-442-23236-5

Other books by Priscilla Hauser
Dimensional Glass, Book I, 1971
Dimensional Glass, Book II, 1971
Rub Out Painting, 1972
For Whom the Brush Toles, Volume I, 1973
For Whom the Brush Toles, Volume II, 1974
For Whom the Brush Toles, Volume III, 1976
Make Mine Country Style, 1975
Priscilla Hauser's Workbook (published four times a year), 1973, 1974, 1975, 1976, 1977
Priscilla Hauser's Idea Book, 1977
The Collection Series, Volume I, *Daisies*, 1977
The Collection Series, Volume II, *Strawberries*, 1977

Contents

1-1.

Priscilla Hauser

I can teach you to paint! Now wait a minute—I know what you are thinking: "That gal is nuts. I can't paint. That takes talent." If you are one of the poor misled people who believe this, please believe me when I say you are wrong. All you need to say to me is, "I wish I could." Painting is like anything else: it can be learned, and, furthermore, it is not hard. Painting is no different from cooking, sewing, or playing a musical instrument. There is a sad misconception of art in our society today, because people think that it is necessary to have talent to paint. That's nonsense!

Stop and think. If a paintbrush had been placed in your hand instead of a pencil when you were a child, you'd use that paintbrush beautifully today. Remember that a paintbrush is just another tool of communication and is not difficult to use.

As an example, my husband Jerry and I have four children. They all paint; they are not afraid of a paintbrush because they have been brought up in a home where their mother paints. We always have paints and brushes out on a table, and to our children painting is just a part of life that is fun. I must admit that none of our children can cook; I don't cook either—just paint!

How I wish I could put into words what painting can mean to you. It is a joy, it is time filled with happiness that will last your life through.

There is another mistaken idea about art: that one must study it from childhood in order to be able to paint. That is absolutely false! No matter how old you are, I *can* teach you to paint. I didn't study art in college: I studied dental hygiene, because my father felt that I should have what he called an insurance policy—a way to support a family if necessary.

It is true that painting has interested me since I was a child. When I was in the seventh grade, a dear friend of mine received a gorgeous set of bedroom furniture from her parents. It was French in design. The twin beds, dresser, and little camelback trunk were white, trimmed in gold, and roses were painted on everything. I asked my mother and father

for furniture just like it, but they felt that it was too expensive for a young girl's room.

The following Christmas my parents gave me a beautiful camelback trunk, but it was unpainted. I went to the artist who had painted my friend's furniture and asked if she would teach me to paint. Her answer was "no," but in that conversation she referred to that type of decoration as tole painting. At age 12 tole painting became a part of my vocabulary. I asked everyone I knew where I could take lessons in tole painting, but no one knew. A few decorators in town sold tole lamps and trays, but, alas, there was no one to study with.

Years later, after Jerry and I were married, I longed to paint that little trunk for our home. We moved from Dallas to Kansas City, and, to my amazement, I found classes in tole and decorative painting at the YMCA and other recreation centers. I studied there for a few short months, learning all I could about tole and decorative painting, before we moved from Kansas City to Tulsa. We bought our first home, and I began to paint the wonderful collection of junk that we'd been accumulating for years: milk cans, coffee pots, waste-paper baskets, and, yes, my little trunk, which I painted with pears and grapes and gave to my mother the following Christmas.

My painting continued. Neighbors saw what I was doing and asked me to teach them to paint. This sounded like a good way to make a little extra money. I felt that, if people paid me, I must have something to offer them, so I began trying to figure out the best ways to teach them to paint. If I have any God-given talent, it is the ability to teach. Perhaps this talent developed because I have a beautiful sister who is without sight. All of us at home communicated things to her, since she was unable to see them.

As I painted, I made notes on everything I did and began developing methods, or recipes, for painting, just as for cooking. My first class had 6 students and was held in the garage of our home. Before I realized it, my classes had grown: I had about 35 students.

One day, to my dismay, I received a telephone call from the

zoning board, telling me that I was running a business in a neighborhood that was not zoned for business, that I would have to give up my classes or find a business location. Dismayed but not defeated, I went to a local paint store. The manager was delighted to stock the artist's supplies and materials I needed and made a small studio space available to me in the back of the store. Classes continued to grow, but then the manager of the store was transferred.

This was my opportunity to make a break and open my own business without stepping on any toes. Jerry thought I had lost my mind. "What do you want to go into business for?" he asked. "You are 22 years old and don't know a thing about business. You have a young family to raise. A business is a nightmare; you'll be working day and night." That did it. When anyone tells me that I can't do something, I'll break my neck to see that it is done and done well.

I borrowed some money from my mother, who had always felt that I could succeed. Jerry found a little old house that had been an antique shop. We rented it for $50 a month, and the Little Red Tole House was born. All my students worked to establish the Little Red Tole House, but the efforts of one person in particular stand out in my mind. My long-time student and friend, Lucille DeWitt, brought her husband Don to the Tole House who, along with other students, worked day and night knocking out walls, painting, and laying floors. It was July, the temperature was 105°, and we didn't have air conditioning. I'll always be grateful to those friends. That is another wonderful thing about this world of painting. It opens the door to so many new friends, people who share a common interest.

Classes continued to grow at the Little Red Tole House, and Noreen Banes—who to this day is my right hand—joined my staff as a teacher. Money received from classes was reinvested in inventory. I had 275 students a week and was teaching three classes a day. My business demanded so much of me that I was exhausted, but I loved it. By this time my husband started to take a different view of things. In the beginning he had said that I'd never make a go of it, and I must admit that my operation was not very businesslike at times.

I'll never forget the afternoon that two men from the tax department called on me. I was teaching a class at the Tole House when they asked to speak to me in private. Frightened to death, with no idea what they wanted, I told them that I had no office but that we could go to the bathroom. They

1-2.

6

looked amazed, and I explained that the tub was covered with wood and served as a table where salesmen showed me their wares. They did not wish to go to the bathroom with me and said so. They decided to return at three when class was dismissed.

Three o'clock found a surprise birthday party for one of the students in full swing, complete with a blazing birthday cake. The tax men returned to find wall-to-wall females, with the crowd getting larger and louder by the minute. In desperation they agreed to meet me in the bathroom. One of them sat on the board covering the tub, and I tried to hide my terror by graciously lowering the lid to the toilet and offering the other man a seat. He accepted with obvious reluctance: I can't describe the look on his face. Before we had a chance to begin our talk, the door burst open, pinning me behind it, and a student shrieked, "Man in the bathroom!" Both men shot out of the bathroom with me staggering behind them. They finally gasped that they must see my records. Upon being told that the records were at my home, they heaved a sigh of relief and agreed to meet me there.

My home was no better than the Tole House. Children were running everywhere; telephones were ringing and so was the doorbell. I seated the men at the kitchen table and gave them my records. They needed more light, so I pulled a lamp across the room, leaving the cord stretched across the doorway. At that moment my poodle, Arpege, ran into the kitchen, coughed twice, and vomited on one man's shoes. He stared in horrified amazement, gagging, as I tried to clean his shoes. The final blow came when the children raced into the kitchen, hit the lamp cord, and brought the lamp crashing down. Both men beat a hasty retreat to the front porch, where they weakly explained to me that I must account for the fact that I paid no sales tax for the month of August. The answer was simple: the Tole House was closed during the month of August, and I had no sales. When I asked them if they understood, they said: "Yes, Mrs. Hauser, we understand. But we don't know if the State of Oklahoma will." I've never been bothered by any tax men since.

In the beginning my business was a total fiasco, but it was a happy and wonderful time. I couldn't afford to hire help, so I traded lessons for help from various students. In exchange for a three-hour lesson each student worked half a day. It was a riot. Each girl who worked in the shop had her own ideas of the most attractive way to arrange the merchandise, and it was moved constantly. We couldn't find anything! The customers took it all with great good nature, and we made it. More important, we had fun doing it. Jerry and the children handled the shipping from our garage, so it really was a family venture.

Students were coming from surrounding towns and even from out of state for painting classes. Many of these people wanted not only to learn to paint but also to learn my teaching methods and techniques. After much careful thought I decided that I would enjoy training teachers, and the Priscilla

Hauser National Tole Teachers Seminar School came into being. Eventually a second small house was purchased for seminar headquarters.

Today there are hundreds of Priscilla Hauser Accredited Teachers around the world, and literally thousands of students have passed through the doors of the seminar house. (A Priscilla Hauser Accredited Teacher is one who has studied the basics of tole and decorative painting with me or with members of my National Teaching Staff for at least 100 hours. The list grows with each tole and decorative-painting seminar that we teach. The teachers are listed at the back of this book.)

In 1970 I was working day and night at the Tole House, and it came as quite a jolt when I discovered that our fourth child was on the way. In the early years Jerry and I bundled the little ones in sleeping bags and took them to the Tole House so we could restock the shelves and take care of the other things that had to be done at night when there were no classes. It wasn't easy, and now we would have to cope with a little one again.

I was quite ill with that pregnancy and was forced to slow down a bit. When one of my students suggested that I should write a book about my teaching methods, I said: "Why on earth would I want to do that? I'm too busy here at the Tole House." She replied, "Just think about it, and remember, if you ever need my help, I'd like to type it for you." As my activities became more limited, her words kept coming back to me. So one day I called Marynell Snow and said, "Marynell, do you really think I could write a book?" She said: "Of course you can. There's nothing to it." Thus Priscilla Hauser Publications began. Marynell is now the editor of all my publications. The first book that I wrote was about dimensional glass painting. It sold and sold well.

Decorative painting became increasingly popular, and I felt that all people who love this hobby should unite. In October 1972 I asked all the teachers, shop owners, and seminar students I could think of to come to Tulsa for a meeting. At that meeting I founded the National Society for Tole and Decorative Painters. Today this organization has well over 8,000 members, with chapters all over the United States.

Marynell encouraged a second book and then a third. With the help of another dear friend who believed in what I was doing, money was provided to help my company grow. Priscilla Hauser Products began to appear on the market. Jerry and the children were delighted. My mother and father were so pleased with the sale of all the books that they were absolutely beside themselves. Without the support of students and family the growth of my tole and decorative-painting enterprises would not have been possible.

Today, some twenty-six books later, the dream of my life has come true with the publishing of this hardcover book. I ask you to join hands with me through its pages and to give tole and decorative painting a try. I promise that the joy it brings to you will be unending.

Introduction to Tole and Decorative Painting

Why should you learn to paint? Well, if for no other reason, for the pleasure it will bring you—and it will bring you pleasure. All it takes is desire; talent truly is not necessary. My method-painting program for tole and decorative painting was developed to teach beautiful techniques, literally step by step, and to make painting as easy as possible. Tole painting actually means the painting or decoration of tinware, but today we call it tole and decorative painting, which means the painting or decoration of any surface, be it wood, glass, tin, or whatever. In decorative painting a pattern is used, and painting is done by a method, a step-by-step technique. Tole and decorative painting is extremely popular because it *can* be learned by anyone who will take the time to read my instructions carefully, study the worksheets, and practice. Believe me, you will learn to paint, and you will love it. Supplies for tole and decorative painting are readily available at craft shops all over the world, and the number of teachers is growing steadily. You can now study right in your own home with the Priscilla Hauser Tole and Decorative Painting Television Workshop, which is currently on cable television from coast to coast.

Now take your paintbrush in hand. Look at it. Study it, work it back and forth in the palm of your hand. Pretend that the brush is a pencil; you're going to learn to use that brush just as you learned to use a pencil. Take control of your brush—don't let it take control of you. Always make yourself as comfortable as you possibly can when you begin to paint. I've always been told that you should sit in a straight chair with both feet flat on the floor, holding the brush as if it were a pencil and you were about to write a letter. This is something I never do. I sit on one foot, with my other leg propped up on another chair. I *do* hold my brush as I hold a pencil—but the most important thing is to be comfortable.

Hold your work so you can turn it as you paint; keep it in the easiest and most comfortable position to paint in and, above all, have fun.

Read and study every page of this book carefully. Read it again and again, because each time you read it, I honestly believe you'll gain a little more from it, and it will all become easier for you to do. Just relax and enjoy your painting.

TERMINOLOGY

Please take the time to read through this section, even though I do not expect you to grasp the full meaning of these terms until you put the techniques into practice. Most of them are taught in detail in the chapter on fundamentals, but reading through this section and familiarizing yourself with the basics will help you as you study.

Paint consistency refers to the thinness or thickness of the paint. It describes the way the paint feels when you mix it with turpentine or some other medium using a palette knife. Proper paint consistency is vital to good technique.

Round red-sable tole brushes are referred to as stroke brushes. They are more graceful than flat brushes, and basic brushstrokes made with them are an important part of good painting technique. Round brushes are not used for drybrush blending or for patting. As you can see in Figure 2-1, the bristles in one of the round brushes are longer than in the other brush. Either brush is perfect for tole and decorative painting, but a beginner may find the short-bristled brush a bit easier to handle. I designed it with this in mind.

The liner brush is a long-haired, round red-sable brush that is used for fine lines, scrolls, and detail. It is sometimes called a scroll brush (Figure 2-2).

Flat red-sable tole brushes are used for strokework, primarily for blending. Many different effects can be achieved with the flat brush (Figure 2-3).

Oil paints are pigments ground in oil. They dry slowly and can be blended beautifully. Some colors are opaque; others are transparent.

Transparent simply means that light can pass through.

Opaque means that light will not pass through.

Acrylic paints are water-based; they dry quickly, but blending is limited by the fast drying time.

Colorbook painting is filling in a solid area between pattern lines with one color.

Outlining is done with a round brush with a fine point or with a liner brush. Fill the brush heavily with thin paint, twist to a point, then outline, using a light touch. Using a light touch means applying as little pressure to the brush as you possibly can.

Double loading means to carry two colors side by side on the brush.

Dirty brush is sometimes used in double loading. A color is used on one side of the brush, with the dirty brush on the other side. To do this, simply fill the brush with paint, wipe the paint out of the brush, and load only one side of the brush with color.

When you double-load a brush with two colors, you must blend *in the same spot on the palette* so that the two colors will blend softly together in the middle. Figure 2-4 shows the difference between a stroke correctly blended on the palette and one in which the color is not softened by blending.

Blending or drybrush blending is the combining of two or more colors. Blending is done with flat red sable brushes. Do not dip the brush in turp while blending: wipe it often on a rag. Light pressure is usually used on the brush.

2-1.

2-4.

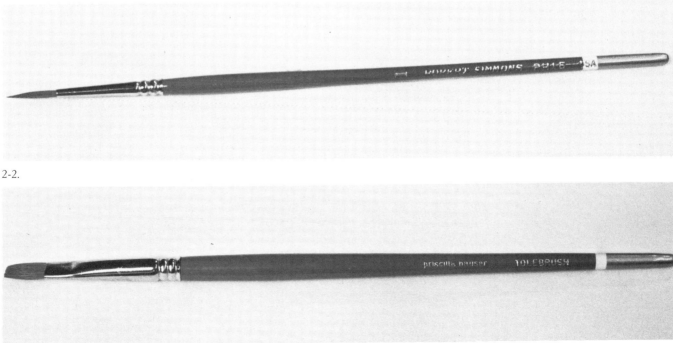

2-2.

2-3.

2-5. Lemons undercoated in white brushing acrylic.

WRONG: DARK RED   DARK RED
          RED

2-6.

RIGHT:
(DARK RED - TO RED - TO ORANGE
CREATES CONTRAST)

DARK RED   ORANGE
RED

Cross-blending describes the brushstroke direction used to pull color from one side of the subject being painted across to the other side.

Pat blending and streak blending are done with the flat red sable brush. A light touch keeps your brushstrokes from showing.

Overblending mixes all the colors that you have applied into one solid color. It can be caused by applying too much pressure on the brush or simply by blending too long. The most difficult part of blending is learning when to stop. This comes with practice. When the subject that you are blending looks good to you, stop. You want to be aware of all the colors that you have applied.

Shading is the use of light and dark colors to create effects of depth and dimension.

Tinting or rouging is a form of drybrush blending. After you have painted and blended a subject, a peach, for instance, you may want to add more pink to it. Do this by picking up a bit of the desired color on your brush and gently patting it on the desired area while the paint is wet.

To paint something that is light in color over a dark background, you may sometimes need to undercoat before painting the subject. For instance, before painting yellow lemons on a black background, undercoat the lemons carefully and neatly with a thin, smooth coat of Priscilla Hauser (ph) white brushing acrylic base coat. Let it dry thoroughly, then paint the lemons. The lemons will appear light and vivid because of the undercoating beneath them. I do not believe in undercoating unless it is absolutely necessary. You must stay exactly within the pattern lines and the paint must be perfectly smooth, or it will show through the finished painting. It is much better to learn to blend with a light touch so that undercoating is not necessary.

Contrast is the key to beautiful painting. It involves sharp differences between two or more colors used on the same subject. Contrast makes your painting look alive, not dull. If you learn to paint with contrast, your work will have zip and sparkle. It will have light and life. Contrast is beautiful (Figure 2-6)!

SUPPLIES

Before we get into the specific supplies that you will need, I want to caution you to always use care and common sense in using and storing these products. *Never* put turp in a glass: it looks like water. Always *read* and *heed* the instructions for *any* product. And for heaven's sake keep all painting supplies out of the reach of children and pets. Our dog once ate an entire tube of white oil paint. Fortunately, it didn't seem to make him sick, but the poor thing pooped white for a week!

Paints

Tole and decorative painting can be done with either oils or acrylics. The finished effect will be different due to the characteristics of the chosen medium. There are advantages to both: acrylics dry much faster; oils allow more blending. I have used acrylics very successfully, but I still prefer oils. Try painting the same pattern with both oils and acrylics. You will enjoy the variety of effects that you can achieve. If acrylics are your choice and you are satisfied with the results, by all means use them.

There are many fine paints on the market today, each with its own characteristics. My favorite brand is Shiva, but try different brands to see for yourself. Look for (1), coverage (opacity), (2) brilliance, and (3) consistency.

When you open a tube of paint and squeeze it from the tube, a great deal of oil sometimes comes out on your palette. This does not necessarily mean that the paint is bad. Oil-pigment separation can be caused by hot or cold temperatures; some pigments just do not mix as readily with oil as others do. If the *paint* is thin and runny as it comes from the tube, then it should be returned to the manufacturer.

Oil paints are fun to buy and use. Many colors are available, and it's great to experiment with as many different colors as you desire. Let me suggest some basic colors that, with proper usage, can achieve almost any color effect you wish (the letters "T" and "O" indicate which colors are transparent and which are opaque):

titanium white (O)
cadmium yellow light (O)
cadmium yellow medium (O)
cadmium orange (O)
yellow ochre (O)
Prussian blue (T)
raw sienna (T)
burnt sienna (O)
raw umber (T)
burnt umber (O)
Shiva cadmium red scarlet (O)
Shiva red crimson (O)
Shiva yellow citron (O)
cadmium red pale (O)
Shiva ferrous black (O)
brilliant yellow light (O)
Shiva leaf green (O)
Shiva violet deep (O)
Shiva ice blue (O)
sap green (T)
asphaltum (T)
olive green (T)

The Priscilla Hauser Beginning Tole Set, manufactured by Shiva, contains twelve colors in small tubes and is excellent for the beginner.

Brushes

Use only the finest red sable brushes, because your brush is your most important tool: your work will only be as good as your brush. I'll agree to skimping on almost any supplies except your brushes. There are many types of brushes available. I have designed and developed my ph tole brushes especially for tole and decorative painting. Robert Simmons, Inc., manufactures these excellent brushes. They have short handles and are made from the finest red-sable or kolinsky-squirrel hair.

You will need both flat and round red-sable brushes. If you are just beginning to paint, I recommend a #4 and #8 PH10 flat red-sable tole brush, a #3 PH20 round red-sable tole or watercolor brush, and a #1 PH15 liner brush. You should eventually get at least every other size from #00 through #16 of flat brush and #1, #3, and #5 round brushes. I use the #1 liner for striping, fine-line, and detail work, and the ph spotting brush for tiny strawberry seeds and faces.

Other supplies are:

ph tracing-paper disposable palette (this serves two needs, since it is both a disposable palette and a pad of tracing paper—I have tried using virtually every surface as a palette and find that mixing paint to the proper consistency, filling the brush, and double loading are more easily done on a tracing-paper palette—do not use a wax-coated palette pad)

palette knife with a flat blade

Shiva Signa-Turp or other odorless turpentine

white and colored chalk

white and gray graphite carbon

paper towels or rags

small jar for turp

ph brush creme and a small bar of Ivory soap for cleaning your brushes

copal medium (optional)

I'd like to explain the use of copal medium at this point. It enables you to thin tube oil colors without diminishing the

2-7.

opacity of the paint. A very small amount of paint thinned with copal will cover adequately and give a very smooth look to your painting. Since copal medium does make the paint slick, patting and blending are more difficult until you learn to use a light touch. I do not recommend it for beginners, but experienced painters will enjoy it.

There are many brands of copal medium on the market. At the present time I am using Taubes copal medium lightweight. If you use copal medium, mix it into all your colors—not just one. Sometimes I fill a small jar lid with copal medium, then dip my brush into it and then into my colors as I paint. Copal dries much faster than turp and will get sticky and tacky on the palette. When this happens, you may add more copal or thin with turp.

Copal medium is a paint extender, so you use less paint, but you cannot save your oils by placing them in the freezer, as you can if turp is used as a medium. Copal palettes do not keep.

Copal can get too old to use. If it is left exposed to air, it can become too tacky to use. If oils mixed with copal are not used within one day, particles of dried paint will form and make a mess of what you are trying to paint.

Brushes must be cleaned with extreme care after using them in copal medium, or they will be ruined. Always dispose of any turp that you have used while painting with copal.

Always clean your brushes after you have finished painting for the day. If proper care is taken, brushes will last quite a long time. To clean a brush, stroke it gently back and forth in a jar of turp. Never abuse or break the bristles. After washing the brush well in turp place a dab of ph brush creme in the palm of your hand. As you work the brush back and forth in the brush creme, you will see the paint come out of the brush. Rinse the brush in turp again and stroke it gently back and forth on a bar of Ivory soap. Leave the soap in the brush and shape it with your fingers until every hair is in place. This serves as sizing and helps keep the brush in good condition. Soap will not harm brush, turp, or paint. Before using the brush again gently rinse it in turp—*unless* the brush is to be used for dry-brush blending. In that event just flip the dry soap out of the brush with your fingers.

If you wish, eliminate the soap and leave the brush creme in the brush. Be sure to remove the creme from the brush with turp before using. Which way is best? I use both methods.

TRANSFERRING THE PATTERN

Use tracing paper and a fine-point marking pen or pencil to make a careful tracing of the pattern. You may transfer the pattern with graphite carbon or by chalking the back of the tracing. I prefer using chalk, because the lines can always be removed after an item is painted. Graphite-carbon lines sometimes show and are almost impossible to remove.

Let's talk about transferring with chalk first. If the item to be decorated is a medium to a dark color, use white chalk on the back of your tracing. If the background is white or a light color, use brown chalk. On the back side of the tracing go over the lines of the pattern firmly with chalk. Never rub chalk all over the back of the pattern. Shake off the excess dust. Center the pattern on the item to be painted, secure it with

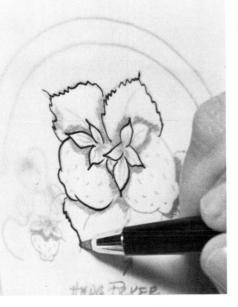

2-8. Trace the pattern carefully.

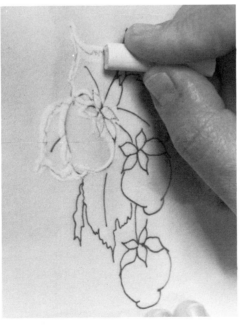

2-9. Chalk the lines on the back of the traced pattern.

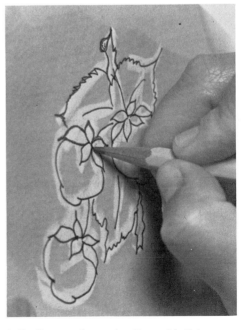

2-10. Go over the tracing lines with light pressure.

masking tape if you wish, and go over the pattern lines with a sharp-pointed pencil or stylus. Do not press hard with the pencil: you do not want to make an indentation on the surface below.

To transfer with graphite carbon, use white graphite on dark surfaces and black graphite on light backgrounds. Position the pattern on the item to be decorated and secure it with masking tape if you wish. Slip the carbon under the pattern and transfer the pattern, using light pressure on the pencil or stylus. Graphite carbon can usually be removed with turp when you are sure that your painting is completely dry. Ink-work is very difficult to do over graphite, since the carbon repels the ink.

2-11. Transferred pattern.

Fundamentals of Tole and Decorative Painting

This is the most important chapter in this book, because the basics taught in it are the foundation for good tole and decorative painting. Please, please read and understand them. Your painting success is based on them. It is possible to paint without knowing these fundamentals, but your work will never achieve the quality and beauty that it *could* have. If you wish to prove this point, read only this first paragraph, turn to the daisy lesson, and paint the very best daisy you can. Then come back and really *learn* and *practice* everything taught in this chapter. When you understand and can carry out the step-by-step instructions in this chapter, paint a second daisy. You will find your painting greatly improved, and your daisy will truly be lovely. The actual learning and practicing is a fascinating experience that will give you a skill you'll enjoy for the rest of your life! Please try. Your best efforts, combined with the painting techniques that I can teach you, are all you need to become an accomplished decorative painter. And remember, anything worthwhile takes a little time, practice, and patience.

PAINT CONSISTENCY

Proper consistency of the paint is one of the most important fundamentals. Consistency refers to the thickness or thinness of the paint. If you add a lot of turp to your paint, the consistency will be very thin. With less turp the paint will be thicker. The consistency should be different for different techniques. The paint must have a thick, creamy consistency for blending; it must be very thin for brushstroke or line-

work. Some colors come out of the tube very thick; others may be thin and oily, depending on the pigmentation in the paint. The following descriptions show you how the paint should feel and look when you mix it with turp or another medium. Before you begin to paint, you should always consider: "What consistency should my paint be in order to achieve the best results?"

1. Whipped cream—paint mixed with turp and whipped up and down with the palette knife so that it will hold peaks but still feel soft, not stiff, to the touch. Use this for daisy, rose, and violet petals.

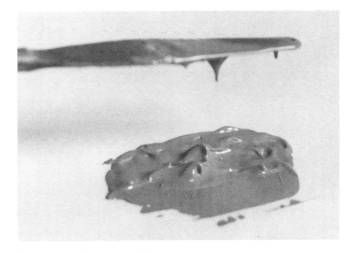

3-1. Whipped-cream consistency.

15

2. Thin—the paint should be as thin as ink so that it will flow from the brush just as ink flows from a pen. Add many drops of turp. This is the proper consistency for fine lines, curlicues, and striping.

3. Thick creamy—add very little turp. Paint should move easily when it is mixed with a palette knife but be thick and creamy, almost like soft butter. This is the consistency for drybrush blending.

4. Thin creamy—add more turp than for the thick-creamy consistency. The paint should have the consistency of mustard—thin enough to flow from the brush when you are doing strokework.

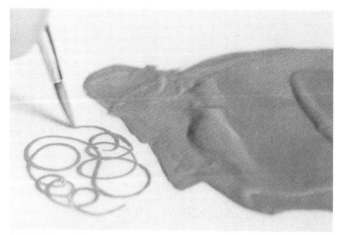

3-2. Thin as ink.

3-3. Thick-creamy consistency.

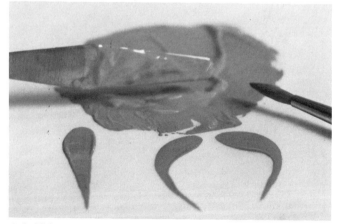

3-4. Thin-creamy consistency.

Always remember to check the consistency of your paint while you are using it. Even though the consistency may be perfect when you first set up your palette, the turp or other medium can evaporate, and, before you know it, the paint can become too thick. If this happens, beware—you'll have a real mess! The few seconds that you spend correcting this will really pay off for you. Your paint *must* be kept at the proper consistency for the technique that you are using.

LET'S BEGIN

There are two main partners involved in good tole and decorative painting: (1) basic brushstrokes with both the flat and round brush and (2) blending techniques. These partners, working together, achieve truly fine decorative painting.

Please follow my directions carefully, especially in the beginning. The way you learn in the beginning will make or break the more advanced techniques you will learn later. Tole and decorative painting can be learned. It is a technique, not a talent. I promise you that, with patience and practice, you can achieve thrilling results. And furthermore, you'll love it!

Practice is necessary, but you can practice too much. I never let my students practice on tracing paper or wax paper more than a few times. They must paint an actual project, and the sooner, the better! So what if it isn't perfect? You're learning, not perfecting. You have plenty of time to develop and perfect after you have learned "how to." If you do not like the work on your first projects, donate them to bazaars or garage sales. You will be surprised and delighted to see that someone else will like them and buy them. And each time you paint something, you will improve. I still have many of my first pieces. They're really bad, but I love them.

BASIC BRUSHSTROKES
The Round Brush

Don't ever let anyone tell you that knowledge of brushstrokes is not important to you as a decorative painter. That is sheer nonsense. Brushstrokes are vital to the total technique. Painting without them is almost like trying to sign your name without an alphabet. In tole and decorative painting your brush is more important than any other painting tool. Buy the best brushes you can and keep them in excellent condition. Without good brushes you will not paint good brushstrokes—and if your paint is not a good *thin-creamy* consistency, forget it! The consistency must be right so that the paint will flow from the brush. Many people try to paint with too thick paint. Don't be one of those people!

Always practice a few brushstrokes with the flat and the round brush each time you sit down to paint. Practice will greatly reward you; painting a few brushstrokes will also help you relax.

There are three basic round-brush strokes that must be learned. These strokes are universal. They are called by many different names, but the strokes are basically the same. These beautiful, basic strokes are easily recognized in the folk-art designs of all countries of the world:

1. polliwog, sometimes called a teardrop stroke
2. polliwog comma angled to the left, sometimes called an eyebrow stroke
3. polliwog comma angled to the right

The #3 ph round red-sable tole or watercolor brush is very versatile. It comes to a very fine point or, if pressure is applied, spreads widely apart. This brush holds a great deal of paint if it is loaded or filled properly.

To paint a polliwog, fill the brush with paint, stroking back and forth in the paint. (The paint should have a thin-creamy consistency and flow smoothly from the brush.) Touch the brush to your tracing paper, apply pressure to the brush, and start lifting and dragging, watching the hairs of the brush—turning (not twisting) the brush *slightly* to the left or right and lifting until a point is formed.

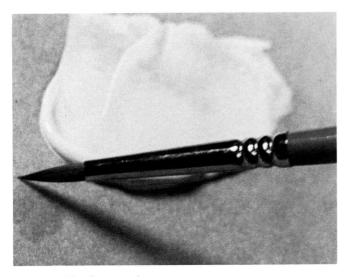

3-5. Round brush at a point.

3-6. Pressure on round brush.

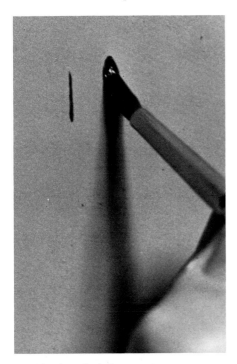

3-7. Touch and apply pressure.

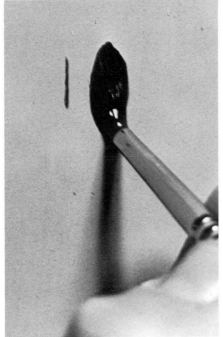

3-8. Start lifting and dragging.

3-9. Finished stroke.

17

Here are some helpful tips:

1. The stroke should look almost like an exclamation point.

2. Be sure the paint is thin enough to flow easily from the brush.

3. If your hand shakes, don't let it bother you. It will steady with practice.

4. Avoid the common mistakes shown in the illustrations.

5. Practice painting on top of the illustrations. Lay a sheet of tracing paper over the worksheet and make your strokes right over mine. Practice all the strokes on the worksheet (Figure C-1) as often as you feel like it. This will be a big help to you.

To paint a polliwog comma angled to the left, angle the point of your brush toward the left corner of your practice sheet. Touch and apply pressure. Start *lifting* and *dragging*, leaning to the *inside edge* of your brush. Lift until a point is formed. Polliwog commas are sometimes called eyebrow strokes. They will probably be easier for you to paint than the straight polliwog stroke.

The polliwog comma angled to the right is simply the reverse of the preceding stroke. Angle the point of your brush toward the right corner of your practice sheet. Touch, apply pressure, and start lifting and dragging, leading to the *inside edge* of your brush. Lift until a point is formed.

Do not twist or turn the brush for the comma strokes: just lean to the inside edge of the brush, lift, and drag until a point is formed. It is easier for a right-handed person to paint a comma stroke angled to the left, and for left-handed people to paint comma strokes angled to the right. Practice painting comma strokes in different sizes. I know that this will seem difficult to you at first, but, if you will only have patience, believe me, you *will* learn, and you will be delighted!

3-10. Touch and apply pressure.

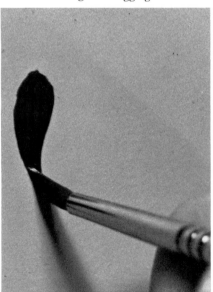

3-11. Start lifting and dragging.

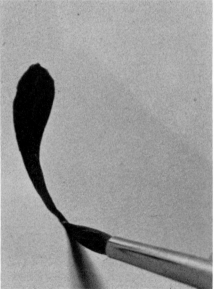

3-12. Finished stroke.

3-13. Touch and apply pressure.

3-14. Start lifting and leaning.

3-15. Finished stroke.

4-13. Press the contact paper into place, making sure that the edges stick securely.

4-15. Wipe off the excess glaze.

4-14. Apply antiquing glaze to the entire surface, including contact paper.

4-16. Remove the contact paper. Touch up the edges of the oval if needed.

Leaves

Leaves are one subject that all of us must learn to paint. In tole and decorative painting you will find leaves not only with all flowers and fruits but, as you advance, in the bouquet of daisies that the dear little girl you are painting is holding. If you are painting owls or eagles, they are probably sitting on a branch, and there are *leaves* on the branch. So get with it from the start: promise me that you will practice painting leaves whenever you have a chance. You will soon develop an enjoyable technique.

There are three types of leaves that you should learn to paint. The first leaf, which I teach to all my beginners, is the basic leaf. It is the simplest leaf to paint. Even though you will learn a more advanced and more attractive leaf later, there may be times when you are in a hurry and want to use the basic leaf. The second leaf is called the basic brush-stroke dry brush-blend leaf. The general form of this leaf can be applied to almost any type of leaf that you desire to paint. Learn to paint the Basic Leaf first, and, when you feel you have mastered it fairly well, begin to practice the second leaf. The techniques for these leaves are shown step-by-step on the color worksheet (Figure C-2). Study them carefully, then place a sheet of tracing paper over them and paint with me, stroke by stroke. With practice and patience you will learn to paint beautiful leaves, and you will enjoy doing it! The third leaf that you should learn is the turned leaf, which adds so much to any design, especially one that contains a lot of leaves. This leaf is so valuable to the decorative painter that I have included a separate color worksheet (Figure C-3) for it. Practice it, following my instructions. You will love painting these beautiful leaves.

THE BASIC LEAF

One leaf by itself is not a particularly beautiful thing, but many well-painted leaves can combine to create lovely borders and even complete designs. Leaves serve as a frame for fruits and flowers, and no two leaves are exactly the same.

In the beginning and intermediate levels of decorative painting we do not work with an established light source. We're painting designs on trays and around milk cans rather than painting a still-life design where the light is coming from one direction. Just remember to paint the leaves to the back of the design very dark; the leaves in the middle of the design should be a medium value, and the leaves to the front—or on top—a very light value. Sometimes it helps to number the leaves in the pattern. Let the #1 leaves be the dark ones, the ones to the back of the design. Let the #2 leaves be the medium value, the leaves to the middle. The leaves to the front of the design, which are the lightest, will be the #3 leaves.

Now, to help you paint dark, medium, and light leaves, I want you to mix three shades of leaf green as shown on the color worksheet (Figure C-2). To mix the dark, or #1-value, leaf green, mix a little ferrous black into Shiva leaf green until a *very* dark green is reached. (By the way, if you can't get Shiva leaf green, you can mix it by adding just a little of any black to cadmium yellow medium.) For the #2 middle-value leaves use Shiva leaf green or the mixture of black and yellow described above. For the #3 lightest leaves mix equal amounts of Shiva leaf green, Shiva yellow citron, and titanium white or brilliant yellow light. By using these three shades of leaf green you will be able to get beautiful contrast between the dark, medium, and light leaves.

Additional colors that may be blended into the #1 dark leaves are more burnt umber, burnt sienna, raw umber, and even a little ice blue. Now, I realize that ice blue is light, but it truly gives the dark leaves depth and beauty— don't be afraid to try it. For the #2 leaves you may blend in any medium-value color, such as cadmium yellow medium, Shiva yellow citron, or even a little cadmium orange. For the #3 lightest leaves you may blend in any light-value color, such as brilliant yellow light and/or titanium white, ice blue, or sometimes even a little cadmium yellow light.

As a general rule of thumb, paint your leaves with the base, or bottom, of the leaf toward you, placing the darkest shading color you are using on the left side of the leaf and the lightest shading color on the right side of the leaf. We use this rule of "dark to the left, light to the right" until much later in decorative painting when we work with an established light source.

I hope you have read and somewhat understood what I have said so far about painting leaves. I also hope you have studied the leaf worksheet (Figure C-2), as it will help you learn very easily. Now, the only way to really get the job of learning done is to practice and practice the basic leaf. The following instructions will take you through the painting of a #2 medium-value leaf. The #1 and #3 leaves are painted exactly the same way: you simply adjust the colors for the value of leaf you are painting.

Study the color worksheet (Figure C-2) carefully. Look at the contrast between leaves. It is important that you learn to include contrast *within* each leaf and contrast *between* the leaves. To paint the practice leaf on the worksheet, use a #4 ph flat red-sable tole brush and a #1 ph liner brush. The size of the brush depends, of course, on the size of the pattern.

1. Thin the paint to a thick-creamy consistency.

2. Double-load the flat brush with leaf green on one side and a touch of burnt umber on the other. Blend on the palette to soften the color.

3. Paint the left (dark) side of the leaf first. Remember that you are doing decorative—not realistic—painting. In your first year do not worry about establishing a light source. It's hard enough to learn to paint without having to worry about where the light is coming from. Touch the brush at the bottom of the leaf; paint two strokes as illustrated. Pick up more green and umber and refill the brush. Touch at the bottom of the leaf, apply pressure to the brush, hold the pressure, and pull, lifting up on the flat edge of the brush at the top point of the leaf. You may paint from the base of the leaf up, or, if it is easier for you, turn the leaf around and pull the stroke toward you, lifting up on the flat edge of the brush. Find the position most comfortable for you. It will make your painting easier. The dark area at the base of the leaf represents a shadow. If the base of the leaf does not fall under another object in your pattern, omit the dark shadow.

4. Double-load the brush with leaf green and titanium white. Blend on the palette to soften the color, then paint the right (light) side of the leaf. The white should be to the outside.

5. The two sides of the leaf are blocked in, but there is a hole left in the middle. This is the most fun part of the basic leaf. In that hole you can dab on a little leaf green and always a little yellow. To me yellow is sunshine, and it adds light and life to the leaf. Add a bit of Shiva yellow citron or any other medium-value color you choose. Wipe the brush thoroughly: *don't put it in turp!* Using a light touch, blend the leaf. Study the color worksheet (Figure C-2) carefully.

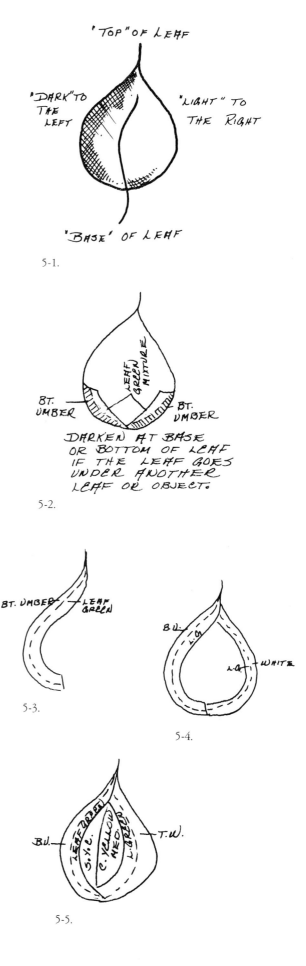

"TOP" OF LEAF

"DARK" TO THE LEFT   "LIGHT" TO THE RIGHT

"BASE" OF LEAF

5-1.

LEAF GREEN MIXTURE

BT. UMBER   BT. UMBER

DARKEN AT BASE OR BOTTOM OF LEAF IF THE LEAF GOES UNDER ANOTHER LEAF OR OBJECT.

5-2.

BT. UMBER — LEAF GREEN

5-3.

B.U. — L.G.   L.G. — WHITE

5-4.

B.U. — LEAF GREEN / S.Y.C. / C. YELLOW MEDIUM / L. GREEN — T.W.

5-5.

Here are some helpful tips on perfecting your leaf:

1. Feel free to add a touch of any color you desire to your leaves, as long as you use dark values on dark leaves, medium colors on medium leaves, and light values on your lightest leaves. For example, when I paint strawberries or apples, I blend a tiny touch of red in the leaves; if I am painting roses, I add a bit of the rose color; when I paint blue violets, of course, a touch of blue is blended into the leaves.

2. Be careful not to overblend.

3. Use a light touch. If you apply too much pressure on the brush or blend too long, all the colors will mix together, giving the leaf a solid look. You want to be aware of all the lovely colors that you have applied.

4. As you blend, be sure to wipe the brush often.

A vein is a curved line—never a straight line. It starts at the bottom of the leaf and stops short of the top. It is painted in the darkest shading color, which in this case is burnt umber. The paint must be thinned with turp so that it flows freely from the brush. You can paint the vein with a liner brush, the point of a round brush, or the flat edge of a flat brush. Some beginners find it easier to allow the leaf to dry slightly before painting the vein.

THE BASIC BRUSHSTROKE DRYBRUSH-BLEND LEAF

For this leaf use a #4 ph flat red-sable tole brush and a #1 ph liner brush. Colors are the same as for the basic leaf. For your #1, or darkest, leaves, mix Shiva leaf green with a touch of ferrous black. Other colors to blend into #1 leaves are burnt umber and titanium white or brilliant yellow light. For the #2 medium-value leaves use leaf green; colors to blend into #2 leaves are burnt umber, titanium white or brilliant yellow light, cadmium yellow medium, and Shiva yellow citron. The #3, or lightest, leaves require a mixture of equal parts of leaf green, Shiva yellow citron, and brilliant yellow light. (Color swatches are shown in Figure C-2). Other colors to blend into #3 leaves are burnt umber, brilliant yellow light, and/or ice blue or titanium white.

The following instructions tell you how to paint a #2 medium-value leaf. Paint this leaf with the base (bottom) toward you, keeping the dark color to the left and the light color to the right.

1. Thin the paint to a thick-creamy consistency.

2. Double-load the brush with leaf green and burnt umber. Blend on the palette to soften the color.

3. Paint two S strokes at the base of the leaf as shown. Double-load the brush again, touch on the flat edge of the brush, apply pressure to the flat surface of the brush, and pull in toward the bottom of the leaf. Place a second stroke on top of the first in the same manner.

4. To paint the top of the leaf, stand the brush on the flat edge, umber side up, and pull. Let the brush roll to the left.

5. Double-load the brush with leaf green and titanium white. Blend on the palette to soften the color. Study the illustration of the right and wrong ways to paint this side of the leaf (Figure 5-9), then paint two commalike strokes opposite the strokes on the other side of the leaf. When you paint these two strokes on the right-hand side of the leaf, your wrist will be in a very awkward position.

6. After the leaf is blocked in, there will be a hole in the middle. To fill in this space, dab in the colors of your choice—always medium-value. I usually apply a little leaf green, yellow to add light and life, and Shiva yellow citron.

7. Wipe the brush carefully and begin to blend, using a very light touch. Blend from the base of the leaf out or from the outside edges of the leaf in. Do as much blending as you wish but do not overblend, or you will lose all the lovely colors that you have put into the leaf.

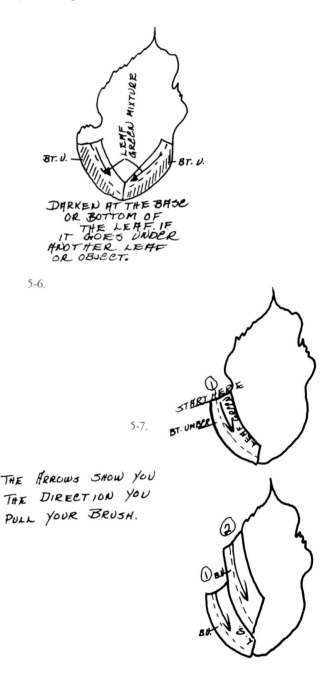

5-6.

5-7.

THE ARROWS SHOW YOU THE DIRECTION YOU PULL YOUR BRUSH.

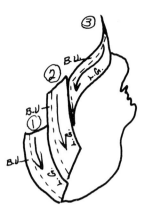

YOUR BRUSH ANGLE WILL BE
PERPENDICULAR ON STROKE
#3

5-8.

Here are some helpful tips for this type of leaf:

1. Do not paint a B on the right-hand side of the leaf. Most beginners do so when painting a leaf for the first time, perhaps because it is very comfortable to angle the brush down to the left when the brush should angle to the right. Using the proper brush angle will help you avoid this common mistake.

2. You may go back over any or all of the strokes as many times as needed to block your leaf in satisfactorily.

3. In painting a leaf stroke from the outside edge in toward the center. Never stroke from the inside of the leaf outward.

4. Work clockwise with your strokes as you block in the leaf.

5. Always remember to work for contrast *within* each leaf and *between* the individual leaves in a design. How dull it would be to paint all leaves the same!

Leaves require a lot of practice, but don't let them stump you. Go ahead and paint your flowers and fruit. In time you will find that your leaf technique improves tremendously.

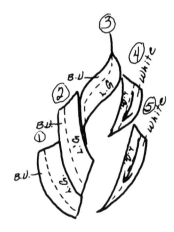

5-9.

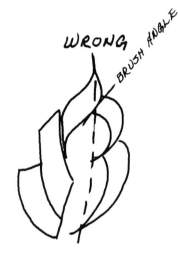

OR B.S. OR A
TOUCH OF P.B.

5-10.

TURNED LEAVES

Before you begin to paint a turned leaf, you should study it carefully to understand how it turns. On this leaf (Figure 5-11) the entire upper end is turned over the top of the leaf. If you have studied the basic leaf and the basic brushstroke drybrush-blend leaf, you know that a leaf is painted with the base or bottom toward you, placing the dark color to the left and the light color to the right. The basic brushstroke drybrush-blend leaf should be well understood before attempting turned leaves.

If the entire end of a leaf turns, then one side of the turned edge should technically be dark, and the other side light. This is one way in which it may be painted. The step-by-step photographs will be of great help to you in understanding this turned leaf.

In painting the leaf shown in the color worksheet (Figure C-3), I used a #8 ph flat red-sable tole brush. Of course, the size of the brush depends on the size of the pattern. Use any combination of colors you wish. The following suggestions may be of help to you. Use Shiva leaf green or mix a leaf green with cadmium yellow medium plus a touch of ferrous black. I also used burnt umber, titanium white, Shiva yellow citron, Prussian blue, cadmium orange, and Shiva ice blue. (You can mix ice blue with a touch of Prussian blue, a touch of burnt umber, and a lot of titanium white.) Use yellow citron, ice blue, and cadmium orange as accent colors. All colors should be mixed with turp to a creamy consistency.

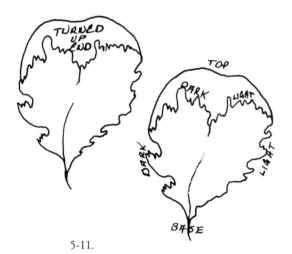

5-11.

1. Double-load a #8 flat brush with leaf green on one side of the brush and burnt umber plus a touch of Prussian blue on the other side. Blend on the palette to soften the color. Paint the first stroke. Remember that your pattern is a guide and *only* a guide. Do not worry about staying within the pattern lines exactly.

2. Place the second stroke on top of the first stroke.

3. Stand the brush on the flat edge. Let the umber edge of the third stroke touch the umber edge of the second stroke. Pull. Apply pressure on the brush as you pull, then lift back up on the flat edge at the center point of the leaf.

4. Double-load the brush with leaf green and titanium white. Blend on the palette to soften the color. Turn the leaf on its side so that the umber edge is on the bottom, or toward you. Stand the brush on the flat edge, pull, apply pressure, and lift back up on the flat edge at the center point of the leaf.

5. Paint the fifth and sixth strokes as illustrated (Figure 5-16).

6. After blocking in the edges of the leaf shadow under the turned end. On the light side shadow dark, using a little burnt umber and just a touch of Prussian blue.

7. On the dark side of the leaf you have several choices. For instance, you can shade in a darker value than the turned edge, using a little more Prussian blue. Technically speaking, it should be darker, since it is the shadow beneath the turn—but, remember, you are doing decorative painting and are not working with an established light source. You can shade lighter, using Shiva yellow citron or another light color. Still another way to shade is to blend the turned (top) section fairly lightly on what would normally be the dark side. In other words, paint the whole turned-over edge relatively light, then paint the dark shadow directly underneath the turned edge. You will find one of these leaves on the color worksheet (Figure C-3). Study it carefully.

8. After the leaf is blocked in and shadows placed as desired, add the colors of your choice to the remaining areas of the leaf. Wipe the brush, pat, and blend. Again, study the color worksheet.

5-12.

5-13.

5-14.

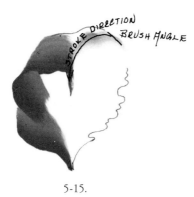

5-15.

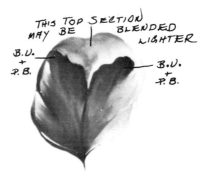

5-16.

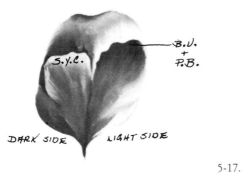

5-17.

Pears

The pear is one of the most beautiful fruits that you can paint, and I enjoy teaching students to put a great deal of color into it. If you read and follow the directions carefully and thoroughly understand the pear's construction before you begin to paint, I know that you will enjoy painting pears.

Brushes for pears are a #4 and a #8 ph flat red-sable tole brush and a #1 ph liner brush for detail work. For a yellow pear the colors are titanium white and/or brilliant yellow light, cadmium yellow medium, yellow ochre, burnt sienna, cadmium orange, Shiva yellow citron, and sometimes a touch of cadmium red pale or Shiva red crimson. For a green pear the colors are titanium white, cadmium yellow medium, Shiva leaf green (or cadmium yellow medium plus a touch of black), burnt umber, burnt sienna, Prussian blue, and Shiva yellow citron.

Let's look at the way in which a pear is put together. The top part is smaller than the bottom part. Colors are applied to both parts separately; the parts are blended separately; then the two are blended together. The yellow pear is explained in the instructions—the color setup for the green pear is given at the end of the lesson:

1. Thin the paints if necessary to a thick-creamy consistency. Fill a #4 brush with titanium white and undercoat the center of each section of the pear.

2. Wipe the brush and pick up cadmium yellow medium. Paint all the way around the white. Wipe the brush and pick up yellow ochre. Paint all around the yellow in each section.

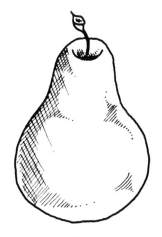

10-1.

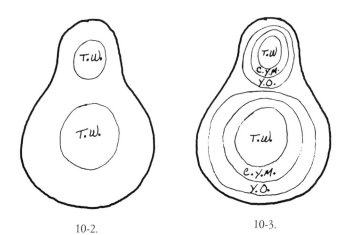

10-2.

10-3.

3. Wipe the brush and double-load with yellow ochre and burnt sienna. Blend on the palette to soften the color. With the burnt sienna to the outside, shade down the entire left (dark) side of the pear.

4. Clean the brush. Double-load with yellow ochre and Shiva yellow citron. Blend on the palette to soften the color. With the Shiva yellow citron to the outside, shade down the entire right (light) side of the pear.

5. A completely dry brush should not be used to blend the pear. Fill the #8 brush with yellow ochre, then wipe it thoroughly. (Never dip the brush in turp unless you are so instructed.) Begin to gently pat and blend the top section of the pear. Add more color if needed. Be careful not to overblend. Brushstroke direction should follow the natural lines of the fruit.

6. Wipe the brush thoroughly and begin to blend the bottom section of the pear. Follow the pear's natural curve as you blend. If needed, cross-blending may be used to pull the dark color across to the light or the light color across to the dark. After the cross-blending is completed, wipe the brush and lightly blend again, following the contour of the fruit.

7. Blend the two sections together. Wipe the #8 brush thoroughly, then gently blend from the top of the pear to the bottom, following the natural curve of the pear and using as light a touch as possible. Refer to the color worksheet (Figure C-7).

8. In blending the two sections together an indentation of dark color is needed on the left side, and an indentation of light color on the right side. This creates dimension. Place this shading where the pear sections join in a figure-3-type shape (Figure 10-10).

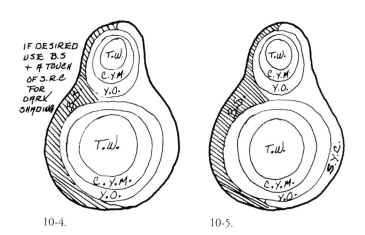

10-4.

10-5.

BLEND TOP SECTION

10-6.

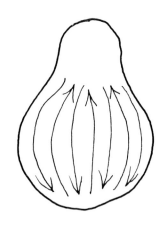

BLEND BOTTOM SECTION

10-7.

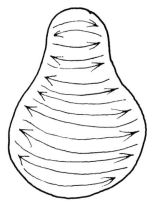

10-8.

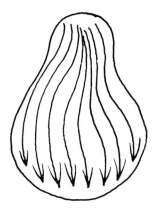

FINISH BLENDING

UP AND DOWN - FOLLOWING
THE NATURAL DIRECTION
THE PEAR GROWS.

10-9.

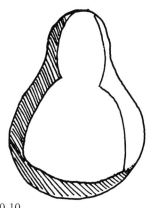

10-10.

Pears are sometimes blushed or tinted with a touch of color. The technique is almost like applying a touch of rouge to the cheeks—hence the term rouging. The color worksheet (Figure C-7) will help you add this delicate touch to your pear. The color is applied after blending is completed and while the paint is still wet. Use either cadmium red pale or Shiva red crimson. Thoroughly wipe the brush used for blending and pick up a tiny touch of color. Ever so lightly *pat* and blend this color where desired on the pear.

A point of dimension must be painted where the stem meets the pear:

1. Use burnt sienna plus a tiny touch of burnt umber thinned to a thin consistency. Fill the #1 liner brush with this dark color and paint a smile at the top of the pear.

2. Fill a #1 flat brush with burnt umber plus a touch of burnt sienna. Wipe the brush thoroughly, then carefully pull the smile down into the pear. Let the strokes follow the natural lines of the pear as illustrated (Figure 10-12).

SMILE
IS - B.S plus
A LITTLE B.U.

10-11.

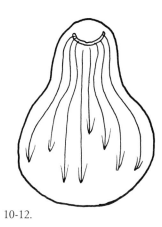

10-12.

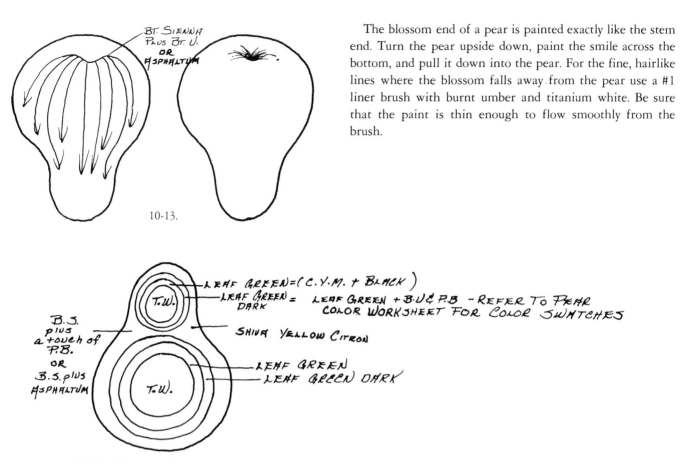

10-13.

The blossom end of a pear is painted exactly like the stem end. Turn the pear upside down, paint the smile across the bottom, and pull it down into the pear. For the fine, hairlike lines where the blossom falls away from the pear use a #1 liner brush with burnt umber and titanium white. Be sure that the paint is thin enough to flow smoothly from the brush.

10-14. Color setup for green pear.

Peaches

Peaches are among the loveliest of fruits. Their coloring can vary from soft yellow tinged with pink and yellow-green to a deep yellow tinged with cadmium red pale and burnt sienna. The many different colors in peaches require long and careful blending but must *not* be overblended.

Brushes used are #4, #6, and #8 ph flat red-sable tole brushes. Colors are titanium white, cadmium yellow light and/or medium, yellow ochre, Shiva yellow citron, Shiva red crimson, burnt sienna, and cadmium orange. Thin the paints with a few drops of turp to a thick-creamy consistency.

Note that a peach is divided into two sections. Apply colors as described, following the color worksheet (Figure C-7):

1. Using a #4 flat brush, undercoat the center of both sections with titanium white.

2. Wipe the brush and pick up cadmium yellow medium. Apply the yellow all the way around the white.

3. Wipe the brush and pick up yellow ochre. Apply it around the cadmium yellow medium.

4. Wipe the brush. Double-load with the dirty brush on one side and cadmium orange on the other. Blend on the palette to soften the color and shade down the right (light) side of the peach with cadmium orange.

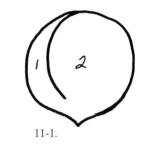

11-1.

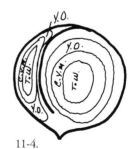

11-2.

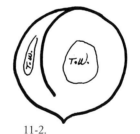

11-3.

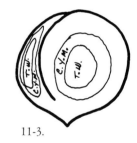

11-4.

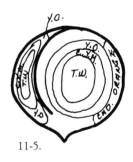

11-5.

5. Wipe the brush and double-load with yellow ochre and Shiva yellow citron. Blend on the palette to soften the color. Apply yellow citron across the bottom of the peach as illustrated (Figure 11-6).

6. Wipe the brush. Double-load with the dirty brush on one side and burnt sienna plus Shiva red crimson on the other. Blend on the palette to soften the color and apply the paint as shown (Figure 11-7).

7. Fill the #8 flat brush with titanium white, wipe it well, and begin to pat and blend. Blend up and down, following the natural lines of the fruit. Cross-blend, then blend back up and down. I like to blend each section of the peach separately, then to carefully pat and blend the two sections together. *A very light touch* is of the utmost importance. It takes a long time to blend a peach. Care must also be taken not to overblend. You need to be aware of all the beautiful colors in the peach. More of any color can be added carefully if needed. Remember, *color contrast* is vital to the beauty of the finished peach.

In a grouping of peaches you want color variation. Peaches to the back of the design should be darker; those closer to the front should be lighter. Vary your colors. Use more yellow in some peaches, more Shiva yellow citron in some, more cadmium orange in others.

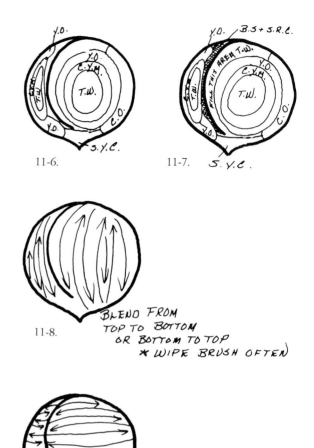

11-6.

11-7.

11-8.   BLEND FROM
TOP TO BOTTOM
OR BOTTOM TO TOP
* WIPE BRUSH OFTEN

11-9.   CAREFULLY
CROSS BLEND
EACH SECTION

Mushrooms and Grass

MUSHROOMS

I believe that the mushroom is here to stay. Like the daisy, the mushroom will never grow old to the decorative painter. Painting these interesting little fungi, with their different sizes, colors, and shapes, is intriguing. You may not be aware of the magnificent range of colors found in mushrooms and toadstools—almost any color you can imagine, from hot orange and purple to soft off-white and cream colors. You will find a little study of mushrooms and toadstools most rewarding, particularly in regard to their different shapes and colors.

As you read through this lesson, study the drawings and the color worksheet (Figure C-8). They will enable you to understand the mechanics of painting mushrooms. Once the mechanics are understood, all you need is practice. There are many different techniques for painting mushrooms. The following instructions explain basic techniques—not too easy or too difficult—an intermediate level of decorative painting. Practice these techniques, and later, if you want to study more advanced methods of mushroom painting, you will have no trouble mastering them.

Use flat brushes. The size of the brush depends on the size of the mushroom to be painted and blended. Always use as large a brush as you can handle. For the practice mushrooms use a #1 ph flat red-sable tole brush for the color setup and a #5 ph flat red-sable tole brush for drybrush blending.

For a red mushroom use titanium white, cadmium red pale, cadmium red scarlet, Shiva red crimson, cadmium orange, burnt umber, and burnt sienna. For a pink mushroom use titanium white, Naples yellow or brilliant yellow light, Venetian red, and raw umber. (This combination may not sound too great, but try it: it's beautiful!) For a white mushroom use titanium white, Naples yellow light or brilliant yellow light, raw umber for brown-gray shading, black for blue-gray shading, olive or sap green for a greenish tint, and burnt umber for brown shading. The red mushroom is used as an example in the following lesson. Color setups for the other mushrooms are given on the color worksheet (Figure C-8).

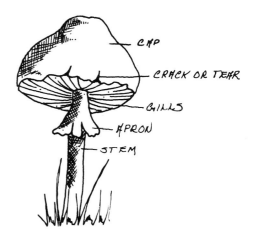

12-1. Parts of a mushroom.

Here is how to paint the mushroom cap:

1. Using a #1 flat brush, undercoat the center of the mushroom with titanium white. Wipe the brush. Pick up cadmium red pale.

2. Go all the way around the white with cadmium red pale. Wipe the brush. Pick up cadmium red scarlet.

3. Go all the way around with cadmium red scarlet.

4. Double-load the brush with cadmium red scarlet and Shiva red crimson. Blend on the palette to soften the color. Shade across the top, down the left (dark) side of the cap, and partway across the bottom.

5. Double-load the brush with Shiva red scarlet and cadmium orange or white. Blend on the palette to soften the color and shade the right (light) side and across the bottom of the mushroom cap.

6. Wipe the brush (do not clean it in turp) and begin to pat and blend. Use as large a brush as you can handle. Blend and wipe, following the natural growth direction of the mushroom. You may blend from top to bottom and/or from bottom to top. *Remember to wipe the brush often and to use light pressure.*

7. If you want to pull the dark and/or light color in from the sides of the mushroom cap, you may cross-blend. Finish blending up and down, following the natural lines of the mushroom cap. More color can be added at any time during blending.

12-2.

12-3.

12-4.

12-5.

12-6.

BLENDING FROM "TOP TO BOTTOM"

BLENDING FROM "BOTTOM TO TOP"

12-7.

CROSS BLENDING EITHER DIRECTION

FINISH BLENDING BACK UP AND DOWN FOLLOW "NATURAL DIRECTION" OF MUSHROOM

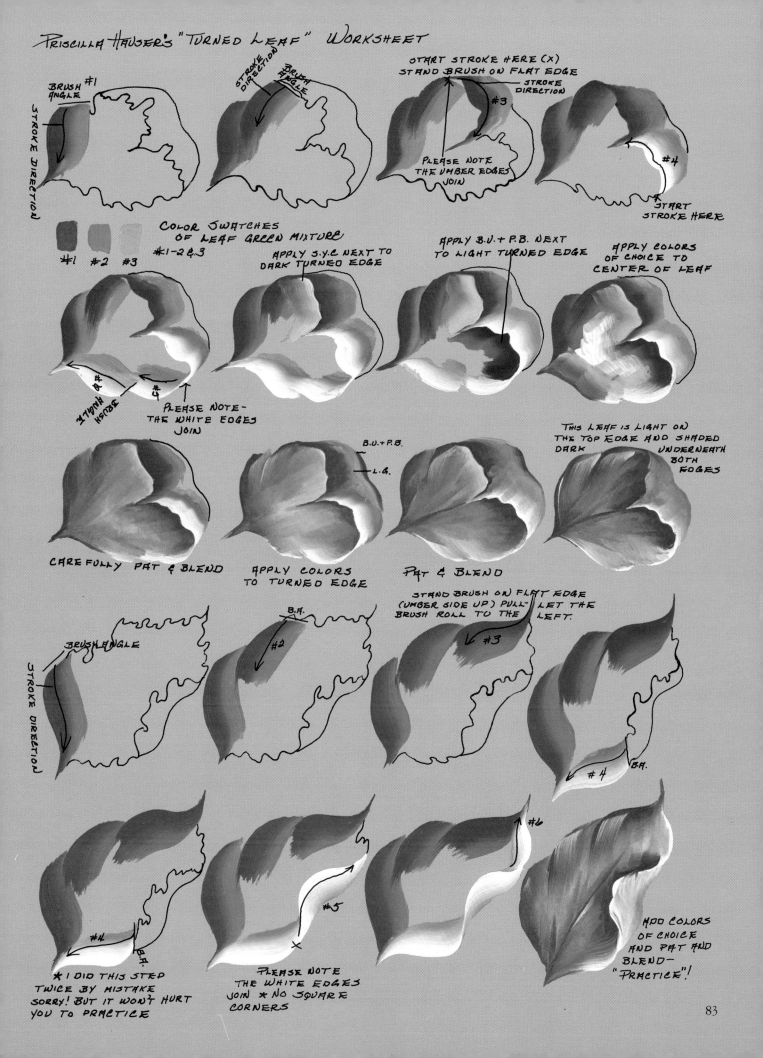

Priscilla Hauser's "Turned Leaf" Worksheet

BRUSH #1
BRUSH ANGLE
STROKE DIRECTION

STROKE DIRECTION
BRUSH ANGLE

START STROKE HERE (X)
STAND BRUSH ON FLAT EDGE
STROKE DIRECTION
#3
PLEASE NOTE THE UMBER EDGES JOIN

#4
START STROKE HERE

COLOR SWATCHES OF LEAF GREEN MIXTURE
#1-2 & 3
#1 #2 #3

APPLY S.Y.C. NEXT TO DARK TURNED EDGE

APPLY B.U. + P.B. NEXT TO LIGHT TURNED EDGE

APPLY COLORS OF CHOICE TO CENTER OF LEAF

BRUSH ANGLE #3 #4
PLEASE NOTE - THE WHITE EDGES JOIN

THIS LEAF IS LIGHT ON THE TOP EDGE AND SHADED DARK UNDERNEATH BOTH EDGES

CAREFULLY PAT & BLEND

B.U. + P.B.
L.G.
APPLY COLORS TO TURNED EDGE

PAT & BLEND

BRUSH ANGLE
STROKE DIRECTION

B.A.
#2

STAND BRUSH ON FLAT EDGE (UMBER SIDE UP) PULL - LET THE BRUSH ROLL TO THE LEFT.
#3

#4 B.A.

#4 B.A.
* I DID THIS STEP TWICE BY MISTAKE SORRY! BUT IT WON'T HURT YOU TO PRACTICE

#5
X
PLEASE NOTE THE WHITE EDGES JOIN * NO SQUARE CORNERS

#6
ADD COLORS OF CHOICE AND PAT AND BLEND - "PRACTICE"!

83

Priscilla Hauser's Daisy Worksheet

UNDERCOAT IN COLOR OF CHOICE - USE THIN PAINT. - THIS COLOR IS ASPHALTUM

TOP COAT IS "WHIPPED CREAM" CONSISTENCY

MAKE TOP COAT STROKES VERY NEAT

LINE WORK MAY BE "CAREFULLY" DONE ON PETALS IF DESIRED

CENTER

APPLY C.Y.M.

SHADE DOWN LEFT EDGE & ACROSS BOTTOM WITH B.S.

PAT & BLEND "KEEP SIENNA SHARP IN COLOR"

ADD "DOTS" — BE LOOSE NOT TIGHT WITH DOTS

LINE WORK SHOULD FLOW FROM THE SAME SPOT ON EACH PETAL. USE THIN PAINT & PRACTICE!

BLACK EYED SUSANS

UNDERCOAT WITH B.S. PLUS A TOUCH OF C.R.P. IF DESIRED.

TOP COAT — CAD. YELLOW MEDIUM

CENTER

— B.U.

C.R.P.

— T.W. OR B.Y.L.

APPLY DOTS OF C.Y.M. — T.W. - B.U - C.O.

Hauser

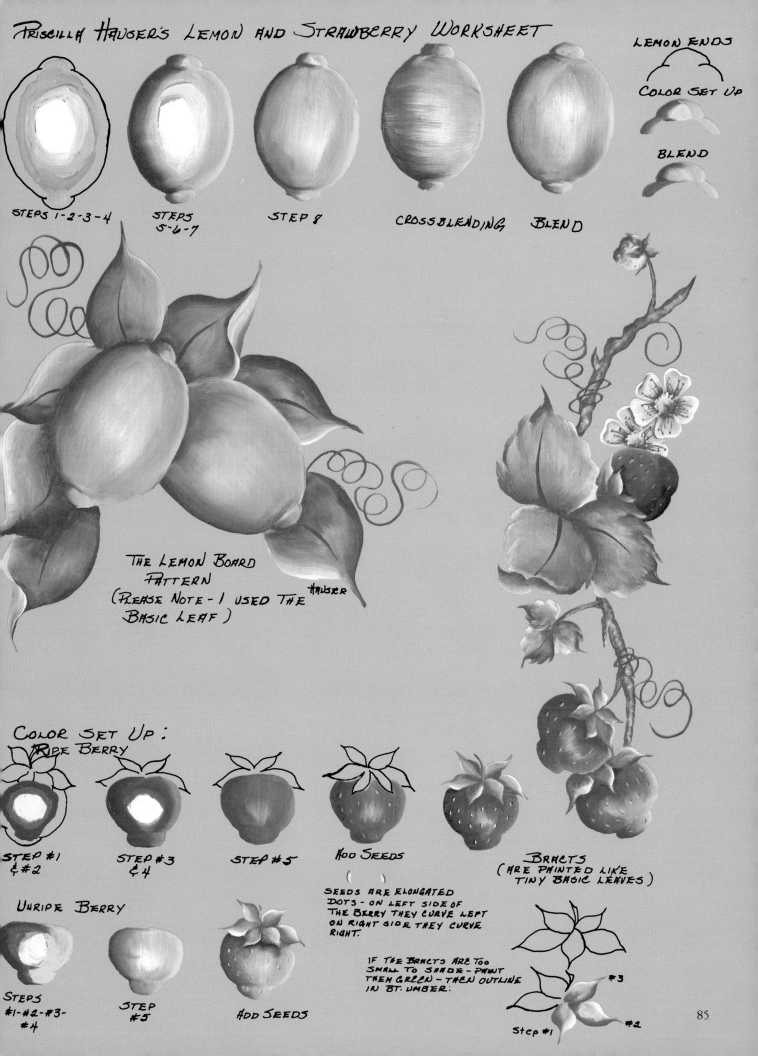

Priscilla Hauser's Lemon and Strawberry Worksheet

STEPS 1-2-3-4

STEPS 5-6-7

STEP 8

CROSSBLENDING

BLEND

LEMON ENDS

COLOR SET UP

BLEND

THE LEMON BOARD PATTERN
(PLEASE NOTE - I USED THE
BASIC LEAF)

Hauser

COLOR SET UP:
Ripe Berry

STEP #1 & #2

STEP #3 & 4

STEP #5

Add Seeds

Bracts
(ARE PAINTED LIKE TINY BASIC LEAVES)

SEEDS ARE ELONGATED
DOTS - ON LEFT SIDE OF
THE BERRY THEY CURVE LEFT
ON RIGHT SIDE THEY CURVE
RIGHT.

Unripe Berry

STEPS #1-#2-#3-#4

STEP #5

Add Seeds

IF THE BRACTS ARE TOO
SMALL TO SHADE - PAINT
THEM GREEN - THEN OUTLINE
IN BT. UMBER.

Step #1

#3

#2

85

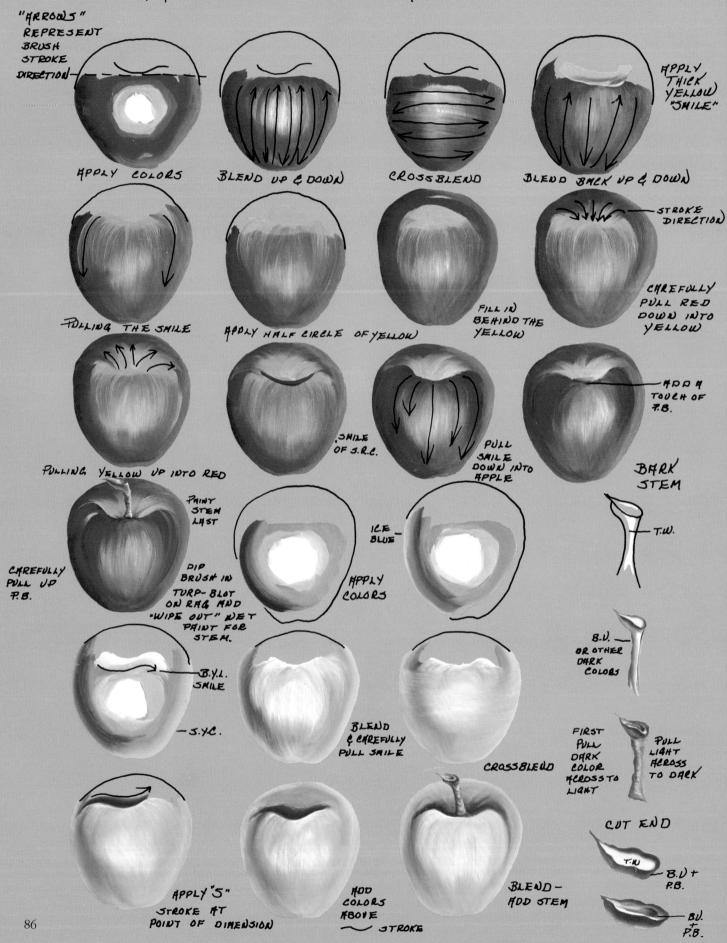

Priscilla Hauser's Red & Green Apple Worksheet

"ARROWS" REPRESENT BRUSH STROKE DIRECTION

APPLY COLORS
BLEND UP & DOWN
CROSSBLEND
BLEND BACK UP & DOWN
APPLY THICK YELLOW "SMILE"

PULLING THE SMILE
APPLY HALF CIRCLE OF YELLOW
FILL IN BEHIND THE YELLOW
STROKE DIRECTION
CAREFULLY PULL RED DOWN INTO YELLOW

PULLING YELLOW UP INTO RED
SMILE OF S.R.C.
PULL SMILE DOWN INTO APPLE
ADD A TOUCH OF P.B.

DARK STEM
T.W.

CAREFULLY PULL UP P.B.
PAINT STEM LAST
DIP BRUSH IN TURP-BLOT ON RAG AND "WIPE OUT" WET PAINT FOR STEM.
ICE BLUE
APPLY COLORS

B.U. OR OTHER DARK COLORS

B.Y.L. SMILE
S.Y.C.
BLEND & CAREFULLY PULL SMILE
CROSSBLEND
FIRST PULL DARK COLOR ACROSS TO LIGHT
PULL LIGHT ACROSS TO DARK

CUT END

APPLY "S" STROKE AT POINT OF DIMENSION
ADD COLORS ABOVE STROKE
BLEND- ADD STEM

T.W.
B.U + P.B.
B.U + P.B.

PRISCILLA HAUSER'S PEAR AND PEACH WORKSHEET

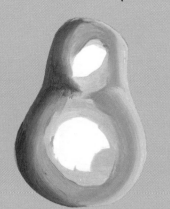

APPLY COLORS

BLEND EACH SECTION SEPARATELY

CROSSBLEND

BLEND WITH NATURAL CURVE OF PEAR – ADD "SMILE"

TRY A GREEN PEAR

THE BLOSSOM END

CAREFULLY PULL SMILE DOWN INTO PEARS

FINE LINE WORK   T.W. ACCENTS

USE B.V. & THIN PAINT.

APPLY COLORS

C.Y.M. — T.W.

Y.O —

T.W.

—C.O

1.S.Y.C.

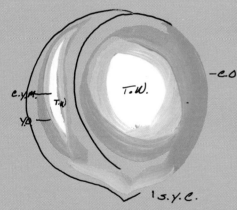

B.Y.L

B.S.+S.R.C.

BLEND & CROSSBLEND

BLEND BACK WITH THE NATURAL CURVE OF THE FRUIT

*FEEL FREE TO ADD MORE OF ANY COLOR NEEDED.

STUDY THIS & BARK.

PEACH –

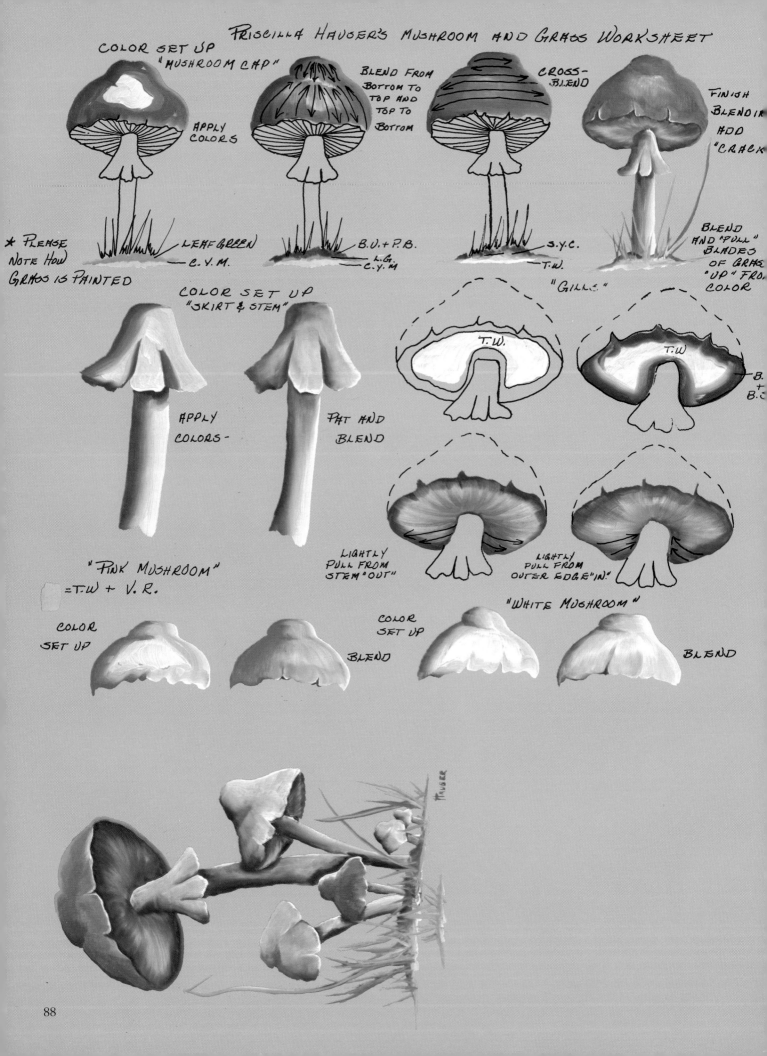

Priscilla Hauser's Mushroom and Grass Worksheet

COLOR SET UP "MUSHROOM CAP"

APPLY COLORS

BLEND FROM BOTTOM TO TOP AND TOP TO BOTTOM

CROSS-BLEND

FINISH BLENDING ADD "CRACK"

* Please note how grass is painted

LEAF GREEN — C.Y.M.

B.U. + P.B.
L.G.
C.Y.M.

S.Y.C.
T.W.

BLEND AND "PULL" BLADES OF GRASS "UP" FROM COLOR

COLOR SET UP "SKIRT & STEM"

APPLY COLORS —

PAT AND BLEND

"GILLS."

T.W.

T.W.

B. + B.C.

LIGHTLY PULL FROM STEM "OUT"

LIGHTLY PULL FROM OUTER EDGE "IN."

"PINK MUSHROOM"
= T.W + V.R.

COLOR SET UP

BLEND

COLOR SET UP

"WHITE MUSHROOM"

BLEND

88

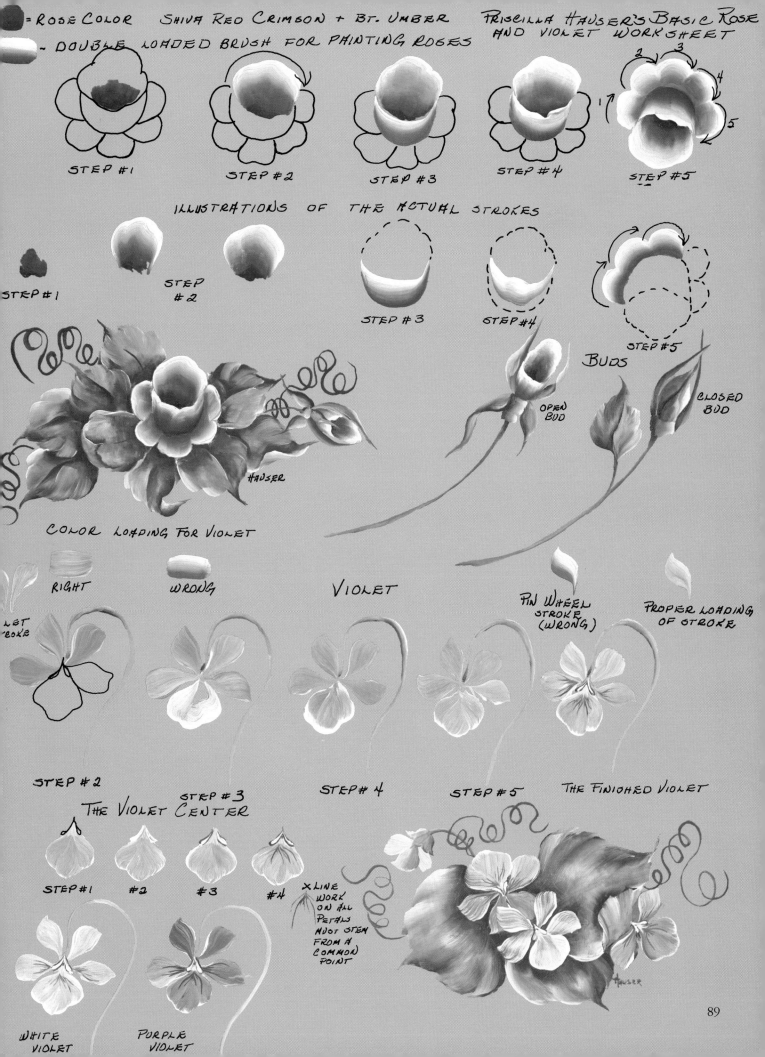

= ROSE COLOR   SHIVA RED CRIMSON + BT. UMBER   PRISCILLA HAUSER'S BASIC ROSE AND VIOLET WORKSHEET

~ DOUBLE LOADED BRUSH FOR PAINTING ROSES

STEP #1   STEP #2   STEP #3   STEP #4   STEP #5

ILLUSTRATIONS OF THE ACTUAL STROKES

STEP #1   STEP #2   STEP #3   STEP #4   STEP #5

BUDS

OPEN BUD   CLOSED BUD

HAUSER

COLOR LOADING FOR VIOLET

RIGHT   WRONG   VIOLET   PIN WHEEL STROKE (WRONG)   PROPER LOADING OF STROKE

LET ROKE

STEP #2   STEP #3   STEP #4   STEP #5   THE FINISHED VIOLET

THE VIOLET CENTER

STEP #1   #2   #3   #4   X LINE WORK ON ALL PETALS MUST STEM FROM A COMMON POINT

WHITE VIOLET   PURPLE VIOLET

HAUSER

89

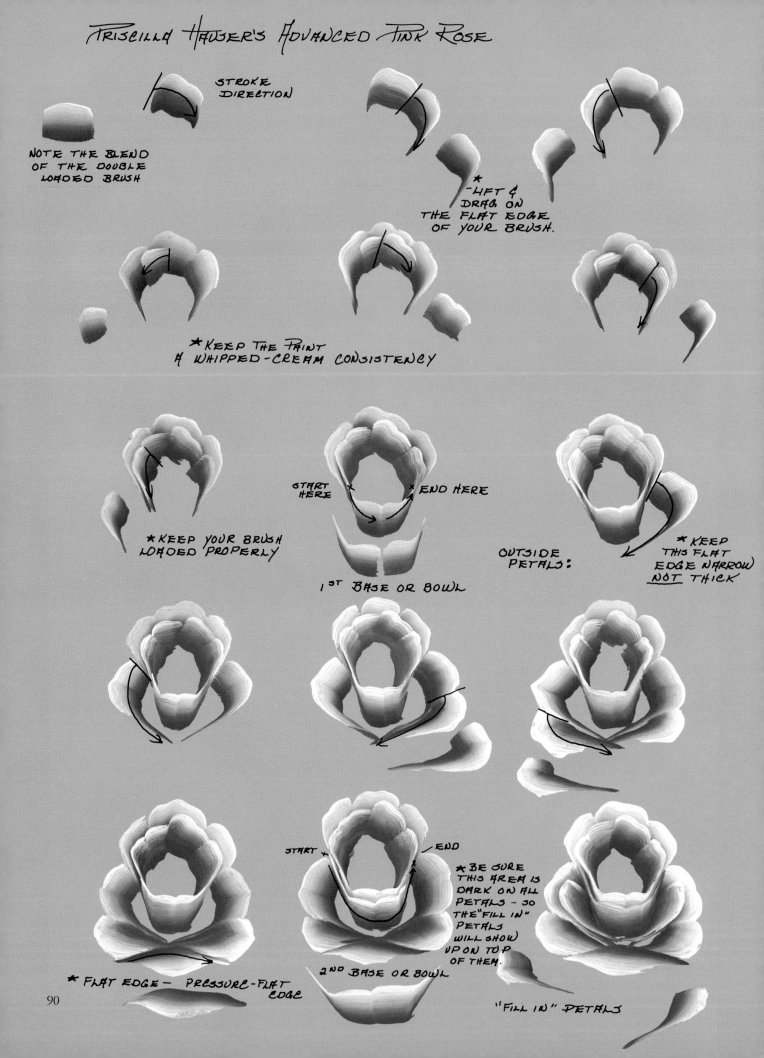

Priscilla Hauser's Advanced Pink Rose

STROKE DIRECTION

NOTE THE BLEND OF THE DOUBLE LOADED BRUSH

* -LIFT & DRAG ON THE FLAT EDGE OF YOUR BRUSH.

* KEEP THE PAINT A WHIPPED-CREAM CONSISTENCY

* KEEP YOUR BRUSH LOADED PROPERLY

START HERE   END HERE

1ST BASE OR BOWL

OUTSIDE PETALS:

* KEEP THIS FLAT EDGE NARROW NOT THICK

START   END

* BE SURE THIS AREA IS DARK ON ALL PETALS - SO THE "FILL IN" PETALS WILL SHOW UP ON TOP OF THEM.

* FLAT EDGE - PRESSURE - FLAT EDGE

2ND BASE OR BOWL

"FILL IN" PETALS

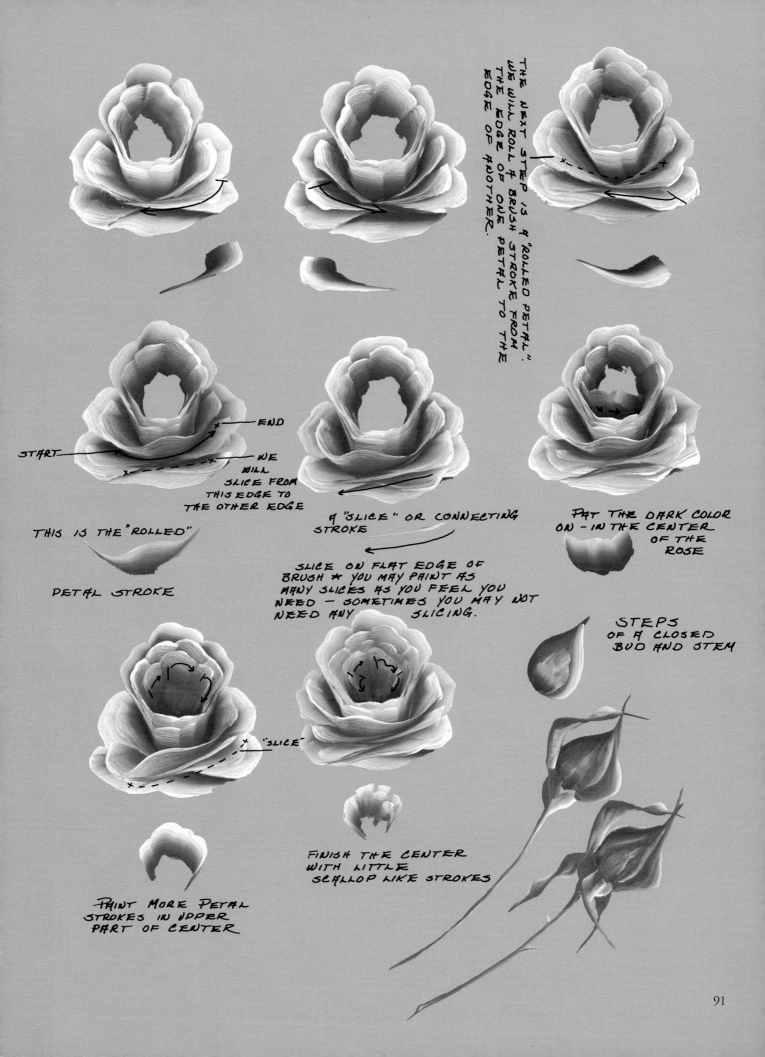

THE NEXT STEP IS A "ROLLED PETAL." WE WILL ROLL A BRUSH STROKE FROM THE EDGE OF ONE PETAL TO THE EDGE OF ANOTHER.

START

END

WE WILL SLICE FROM THIS EDGE TO THE OTHER EDGE

THIS IS THE "ROLLED"

PETAL STROKE

A "SLICE" OR CONNECTING STROKE

SLICE ON FLAT EDGE OF BRUSH ★ YOU MAY PAINT AS MANY SLICES AS YOU FEEL YOU NEED — SOMETIMES YOU MAY NOT NEED ANY SLICING.

PAT THE DARK COLOR ON - IN THE CENTER OF THE ROSE

STEPS OF A CLOSED BUD AND STEM

"SLICE"

PAINT MORE PETAL STROKES IN UPPER PART OF CENTER

FINISH THE CENTER WITH LITTLE SCALLOP LIKE STROKES

91

C-12.

C-13.

C-14.

C-12. Tin trays and wooden plaques with usable items attached. Under the strawberry hangs a little bract picker. The painted back of a muffin tin makes a darling wall hanging.

C-13. Strawberries and black-eyed-susans painted on small wooden projects are excellent for beginners. The pink rose is a little more advanced. It is painted on an oval piece of Masonite, then mounted inside an old box lid. I call it a box-lid frame.

C-14. Lap desks make beautiful gifts for friends and family. If you are planning on selling your work, you will find that a lap desk is an item that people like to buy. I glued a quote on the daisy-and-lemon lap desk, then painted around it.

C-15. The white roses are painted on a replica of an antique candle box. A little bird house is as cheery and cute as can be. Wooden hangers make charming gifts and will certainly grace a guest closet. They are even attractive in wall groupings. The board with painted apples and daisies has wooden pegs for hanging coats and sweaters.

C-16. A letter box, an old cheese box, and a darling wooden basket. The basket may be used for plants, candy, decorated eggs or even as an Easter basket—and, of course, it will last a lifetime.

C-17. Ladderback chairs are a pleasure to look at. Paint a dining-table chair for each member of your family. They will love it.

C-18. These little keepsake cabinets have shelves to house all kinds of treasures. The scene in the center of each design is done in pen-and-ink. Gold leaf was used behind the lemons. Projects like this are such fun to paint!

C-19. The tole sampler is done on a patchwork board and combines pen-and-ink and decorative painting. I stained and sealed the board, then painted each of the four sections with one of my acrylic-base-coat colors. This design can also be fabric-painted and would make a darling pillow. Use patches of real calico. The tavern sign will welcome all your guests. It is lovely in a hall grouping. A dry-measure spoon hangs from a nail on this daisy board.

C-15.

C-16.

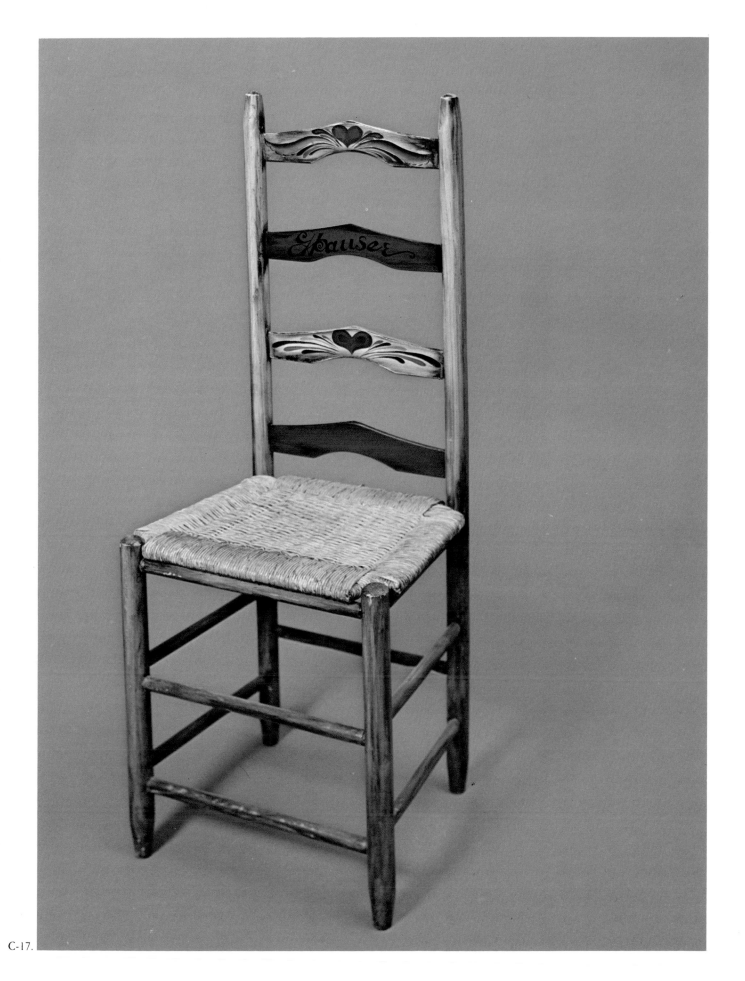

C-17.

C-18.

C-19.

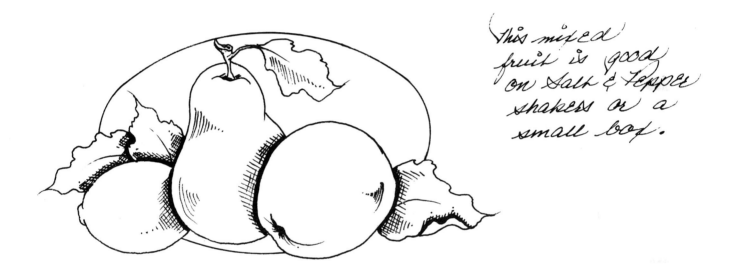

This mixed
fruit is good
on Salt & Pepper
shakers or a
small box.

16-1.

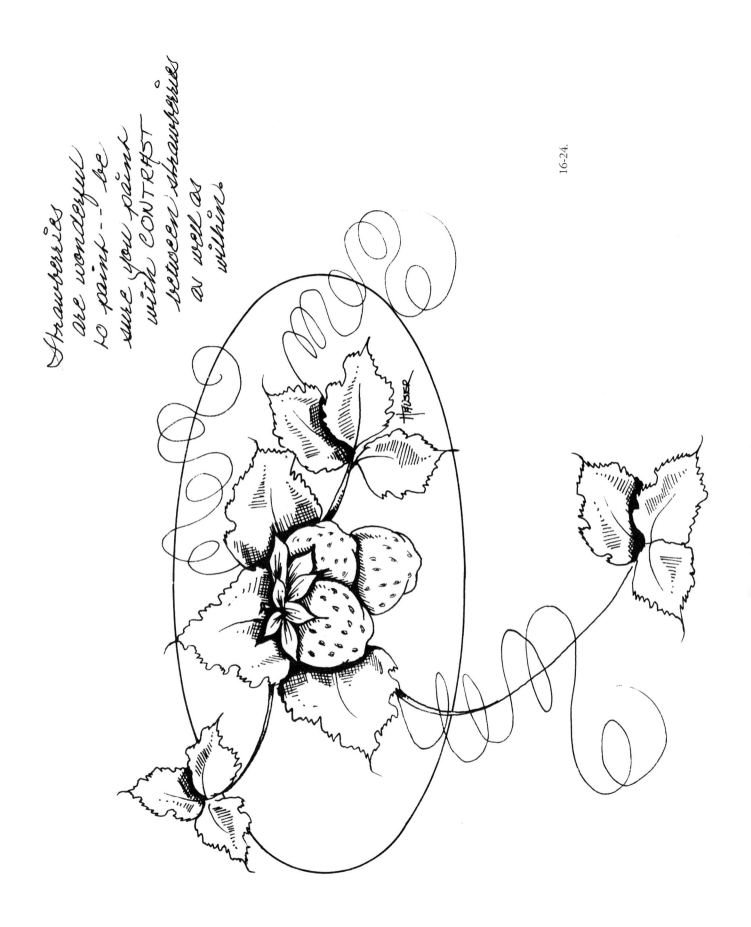

Strawberries
are wonderful
to paint -- be
sure you paint
with CONTRAST
between strawberries
as well as
within.

HAUSER

16-24.

119

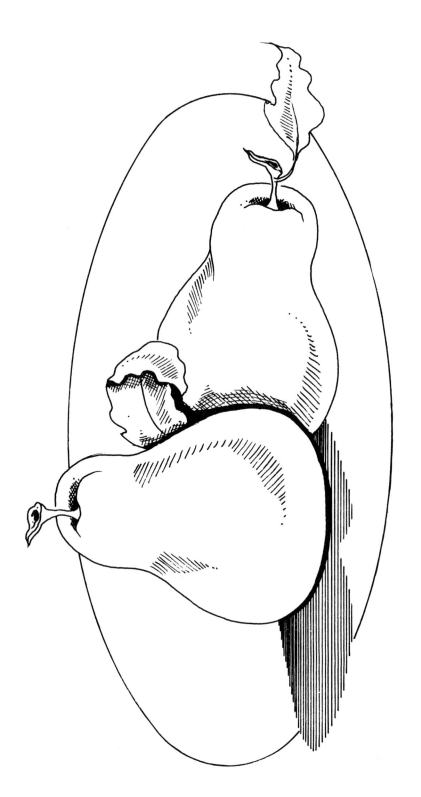

16-25.

16-40.

Try this basic rose design on a wooden hanger. It makes a charming bridal shower gift. This design lends itself well to a lap desk for small stool or even a little girl's dresser.

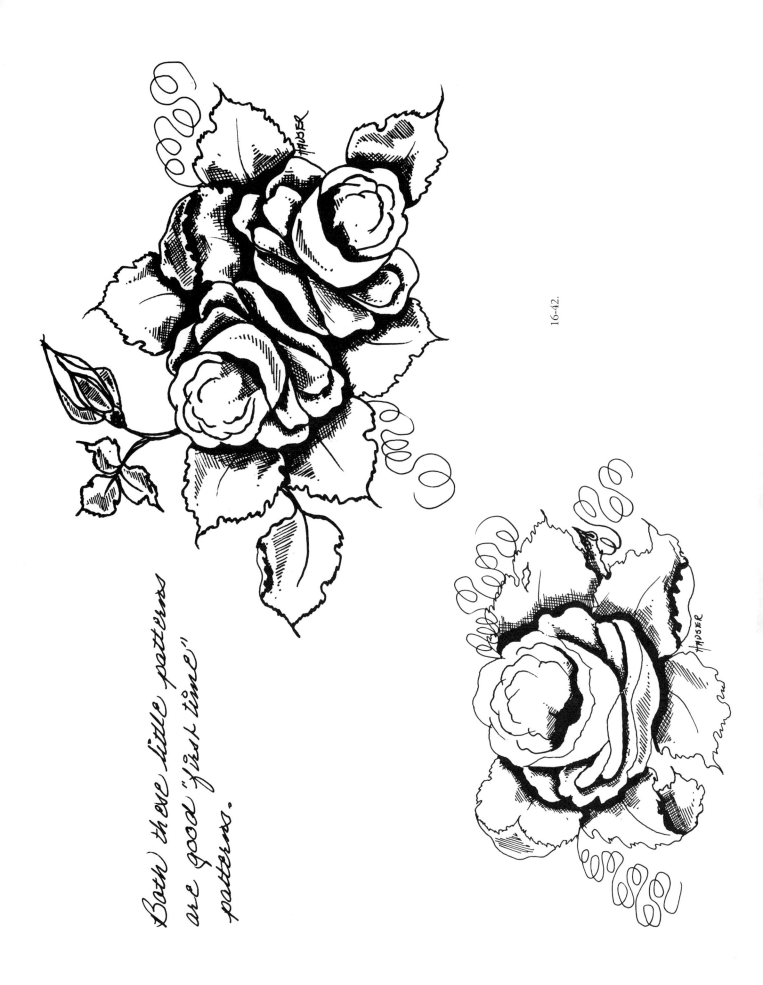

Both these little patterns are good "first time" patterns.

16-42.

137

Roses take
practice — but
are worth
every minute
of it.

16-43.

NIXONLAND

PREFACE

I N 1964, THE DEMOCRATIC PRESIDENTIAL CANDIDATE LYNDON B. JOHN-
son won practically the biggest landslide in American history, with 61.05
percent of the popular vote and 486 of 538 electoral college votes. In 1972,
the Republican presidential candidate Richard M. Nixon won a strikingly
similar landslide—60.67 percent and 520 electoral college votes. In the eight
years in between, the battle lines that define our culture and politics were
forged in blood and fire. This is a book about how that happened, and why.

At the start of 1965, when those eight years began, blood and fire weren't
supposed to *be* a part of American culture and politics. According to the
pundits, America was more united and at peace with itself than ever. Five
years later, a pretty young Quaker girl from Philadelphia, a winner of a
Decency Award from the Kiwanis Club, was cross-examined in the trial of
seven Americans charged with conspiring to start a riot at the 1968 Democratic National Convention.

"You practice shooting an M1 yourself, don't you?" the prosecutor
asked her.

"Yes, I do," she responded.

"You also practice karate, don't you?"

"Yes, I do."

"That is for the revolution, isn't it?"

"After Chicago I changed from being a pacifist to the realization that we
had to defend ourselves. A nonviolent revolution was impossible. I desperately wish it was possible."

And, several months after that, an ordinary Chicago ad salesman would
be telling *Time* magazine, "I'm getting to feel like I'd actually enjoy going
out and shooting some of these people. I'm just so goddamned mad. They're
trying to destroy everything I've worked for—for myself, my wife, and my
children."

This American story is told in four sections, corresponding to four elections: in 1966, 1968, 1970, and 1972. Politicians, always reading the cultural
winds, make their life's work convincing 50 percent plus one of their constituency that they understand their fears and hopes, can honor and redeem

them, can make them safe and lead them toward their dreams. Studying the process by which a notably successful politician achieves that task, again and again, across changing cultural conditions, is a deep way into an understanding of those fears and dreams—and especially, how those fears and dreams *change*.

The crucial figure in common to all these elections was Richard Nixon—the brilliant and tormented man struggling to forge a public language that promised mastery of the strange new angers, anxieties, and resentments wracking the nation in the 1960s. His story is the engine of this narrative. Nixon's character—his own overwhelming angers, anxieties, and resentments in the face of the 1960s chaos—sparks the combustion. But there was nothing natural or inevitable about how he did it—nothing inevitable in the idea that a president could come to power by *using* the angers, anxieties, and resentments produced by the cultural chaos of the 1960s. Indeed, he was slow to the realization. He reached it, through the 1966 election, studying others: notably, Ronald Reagan, who won the governorship of California by providing a political outlet for the outrages that, until he came along to articulate them, hadn't seemed like *voting* issues at all. If it hadn't been for the shocking defeats of a passel of LBJ liberals blindsided in 1966 by a conservative politics of "law and order," things might have turned out differently: Nixon might have run on a platform not too different from that of the LBJ liberals instead of one that cast them as American villains.

Nixon's win in 1968 was agonizingly close: he began his first term as a *minority* president. But the way he achieved that narrow victory seemed to point the way toward an entire new political alignment from the one that had been stable since FDR and the Depression. Next, Nixon bet his presidency, in the 1970 congressional elections, on the idea that an "emerging Republican majority"—rooted in the conservative South and Southwest, seething with rage over the destabilizing movements challenging the Vietnam War, white political power, and virtually every traditional cultural norm—could give him a governing majority in Congress. But when Republican candidates suffered humiliating defeats in 1970, Nixon blamed the chicanery of his enemies: *America*'s enemies, he had learned to think of them. He grew yet more determined to destroy them, because of what he was convinced was their determination to destroy *him*.

Millions of Americans recognized the balance of forces in the exact same way—that America was engulfed in a pitched battle between the forces of darkness and the forces of light. The only thing was: Americans disagreed radically over which side was which. By 1972, defining that order of battle as one between "people who identified with what Richard Nixon stood for" and "people who despised what Richard Nixon stood for" was as good a description as any other.

Richard Nixon, now, is long dead. But these sides have hardly changed.

We now call them "red" or "blue" America, and whether one or the other wins the temporary allegiances of 50 percent plus one of the electorate—or 40 percent of the electorate, or 60 percent of the electorate—has been the narrative of every election since. It promises to be thus for another generation. But the size of the constituencies that sort into one or the other of the coalitions will always be temporary.

The main character in *Nixonland* is not Richard Nixon. Its protagonist, in fact, has no name—but lives on every page. It is the voter who, in 1964, pulled the lever for the Democrat for president because to do anything else, at least that particular Tuesday in November, seemed to court civilizational chaos, and who, eight years later, pulled the lever for the Republican for exactly the same reason.

BOOK I

CHAPTER ONE

Hell in the City of Angels

Y OU MIGHT SAY THE STORY STARTS WITH A TELEVISION BROADCAST. IT issued from the Los Angeles television station KTLA, for four straight August days in 1965, culminating Sunday night, August 15, with a one-hour wrap-up. Like any well-produced TV program, the wrap-up featured its own theme music—pounding, dissonant, like the scores composer Bernard Herrmann produced for Alfred Hitchcock—and a logo, likewise jagged and blaring. It opened with a dramatic device: a voice-over redolent of the old L.A. police procedural *Dragnet*—elements familiar enough, almost, to make it feel like just another cops-and-robbers show.

"It was a hot and humid day in the city of Los Angeles, Wednesday, August eleventh, 1965," the gravelly narration began . . .

"The City of Angels is the nation's third-largest metropolis.

"Two and a half million people live here, in virtually an ideal climate, surrounded by natural beauty, and the benefits of economic prosperity.

"Within the vast metropolitan spread live 523,000 Negroes. A sixth of them reside in southeastern Los Angeles in an area that is not an abject slum in the New York or Detroit context, but nonetheless four times as congested as an average area in the rest of the city.

"The community had prided itself on its relatively harmonious racial relations, few demonstrations, no massive civil disobedience, little trouble from militant factions."

The camera tracks an ordinary-looking residential block, tree-lined and neat, a row of modest ranch houses fronted by postage-stamp lawns, suburban, almost. The angle came from a helicopter—KTLA-TV's "telecopter" was the first of its kind. The utility of the Korean War–vintage Bell 47G-5 with the camera affixed to its belly had so far been mostly prurient: shots of the swimming pool where Marlon Brando's maid had drowned; of the well that swallowed a darling little girl; of movie stars' mansions being devoured by brush fires in the Hollywood hills. Now the chopper was returned to its wartime roots. Los Angeles' black citizens were burning down their neighborhood.

When the Watts riots began, television stations sent in their mobile cars to cover it. They were stoned like a scene from Leviticus. The next day militants cautioned, or threatened, the TV crews not to come: they were all-white—the enemy. There was even fear that KTLA's shiny red helicopter might be shot down, by the same snipers peppering the firefighters who were trying to douse the burning blocks.

The risk was taken. Which was why the worst urban violence in American history ended up being shown live on TV for four straight days, virtually nonstop.

Then, that Sunday-night wrap-up: The narrator paused, the telecopter slowed to a hover at the end of the tree-lined block, lingering on a single bungalow on the corner. Its roof was gone, the insides blackened like the remains of a weekend barbecue.

The voice-over intensified:

"Then with the suddenness of a lightning bolt and all the fury of an infernal holocaust, there was HELL in the City of Angels!"

Cue the music: shrieking trumpets, pealing from television speakers in Southern California recreation rooms and dens, apartments and bars, wherever people gathered, pealing as heralds, because American politics, for those white, middle-class folks who formed the bedrock of the American political conversation, could never be the same again.

Until that week the thought that American politics was on the verge of a transformation would have been judged an absurdity by almost every expert. Indeed, its course had never seemed more certain.

Lyndon Johnson had spent 1964, the first year of his accidental presidency, redeeming the martyr: passing, with breathtaking aplomb, a liberal legislative agenda that had only known existence as wish during John F. Kennedy's lifetime. His Economic Opportunity Act of 1964—the "war on poverty"—passed nearly two to one. The beloved old general Dwight D. Eisenhower came out of retirement to campaign against the Kennedy-Johnson tax cut. But Lyndon Johnson passed that, too. And then there was the issue of civil rights.

"Let this session of Congress be known as the session which did more for civil rights than the last hundred sessions combined," Johnson intoned in his first State of the Union address. It was just five weeks after John F. Kennedy's assassination, seven months after Kennedy, alarmed by a wave of civil rights uprisings sparked in Birmingham, Alabama, had introduced the most sweeping civil rights bill since Reconstruction. It had been bogged down by Congress's recalcitrant conservative coalition of Northern Republicans and Southern Democrats. Even Martin Luther King's heroic hundreds of thousands of pilgrims marching on Washington couldn't unstick it. But President Johnson unstuck it. By June of 1964, the first session of the Eighty-eighth Congress had indeed done more for civil rights than the last hundred sessions combined: segregation in the United States in public accommodations was now illegal. "Our Constitution, the foundation of our republic, forbids it. The principles of our freedom forbid it. Morality forbids it. And the law I sign tonight forbids it," Johnson said at a ceremony carried live on all three networks.

What the ceremony marked was not merely a law but a liberal apotheosis—an apparent liberal national consensus. Johnson's approval rating even among Republicans was 74 percent. Pundits and public-opinion experts proclaimed him an exact match for the spirit of the age. So, even, did conservative businessmen: speaking before the U.S. Chamber of Commerce, the president was interrupted for applause some sixty times. They had reason to cheer. So dynamic had the American economic engine become that it was fashionable to presume that prosperity could fix any social problem. "I'm sick of all the people who talk about the things we can't do," Lyndon Johnson told an aide in one of his patented exhortations. "Hell, we're the richest country in the world, the most powerful. We can do it all." The Great Society was the name Johnson gave his ambition. It "rests on abundance and liberty for all," he said in a May 22 speech, "a society of success without squalor, beauty without barrenness, works of genius without the wretchedness of poverty." The rhetoric was incredible. Still more incredible: it seemed reasonable.

The Republican Party spent the year of the liberal apotheosis enacting the most unlikely political epic ever told: a right-wing fringe took over the party from the ground up, nominating Barry Goldwater, the radical-right senator from Arizona, while a helpless Eastern establishment-that-was-now-a-fringe looked on in bafflement. Experts, claiming the Republican tradition of progressivism was as much a part of its identity as the elephant, began talking about a party committing suicide. The Goldwaterites didn't see suicide. They saw redemption. This was part and parcel of their ideology—that Lyndon Johnson's "consensus" was their enemy in a battle for the survival of civilization. For them, the idea that calamitous liberal nonsense—ready acceptance of federal interference in the economy; Negro "civil disobedience"; the doctrine of "containing" the mortal enemy Communism when conservatives insisted it must be *beaten*—could be described as a "consensus" at all was symbol and substance of America's moral rot. They also believed the vast majority of ordinary Americans already agreed with *them*, whatever spake the polls—"crazy figures," William F. Buckley harrumphed, doctored "to say, 'Yes, Mr. President.'" It was their article of faith. And *faith*, and the uncompromising passions attending it, was key to their political makeup.

That, the experts said, was exactly what made Goldwater so frightening. Unadulterated political passion was judged a dangerous thing by the dominant ideologists of American consensus. One of the deans among them, University of California president Clark Kerr, used to give his students a piece of advice that might as well have served as these experts' motto: a man should

seek "to lend his energies to many organizations and give himself completely
to none." Lest all the competing passions crosscutting a modern, complex
society such as America's become irreconcilable, beyond compromise—a
state of affairs Kerr could only imagine degenerating into "all-out war."

Here was no idle metaphor. "I know that very often each of us did not
just disagree, we poured forth our vituperation," the Episcopal bishop of
Fond du Lac, Wisconsin, wrote in a typical expression in late 1963. "The
accumulation of this hatred expressed itself in the bullet that killed John
Kennedy." Opinion-molders warned, with the numbness of habit, against
"extremists of the left and right"—that veering too far from the center
spurred the savage beast that lurked inside every soul. Goldwater, in accepting his party's nomination, had proudly declared that "extremism in defense
of liberty is no vice." Lyndon Johnson successfully framed his reformist
agenda as something that was not ideological at all—conservative, even,
simply a pragmatic response to pressing national problems, swept forward
on ineluctable tides of material progress. "The Democrats, in nominating
Lyndon Johnson, made a rather careful decision to adhere to the rules of
American politics," political scientist Clinton Rossiter wrote. "The Republicans, in nominating Barry Goldwater, deliberately chose to ignore, to
downgrade, perhaps to change these rules."

And so in November 1964 Lyndon Johnson won the grandest presidential victory since Franklin Delano Roosevelt's in 1936. There was an old saying in Iowa, overwhelmingly Republican from time immemorial: "Iowa
would go Democrat when hell went Methodist." Hell went Methodist in
1964; or at least Iowa's seven-man delegation to the House of Representatives went five-sevenths Democratic. In Congress, Democrats now outnumbered Republicans more than two to one. A bright new class of pro-Johnson
liberals was swept in on his coattails, forty-seven in the House of Representatives alone. The right had been rendered a joke, an embarrassment, a political footnote—probably for good.

"I doubt that there has ever been so many people seeing so many things
alike on decision day," Lyndon Johnson declared in acknowledging his victory on November 5.

"These are the most hopeful times since Christ was born in Bethlehem,"
he said while lighting the White House Christmas tree.

And in his January 4, 1965, State of the Union address, he said, "We have
achieved a unity of interest among our people that is unmatched in the history of freedom."

He continued:

"I propose that we begin a massive attack on crippling and killing diseases.

"I propose that we launch a national effort to make the American city a
better and more stimulating place to live.

"I propose that we increase the beauty of America and end the poisoning of our rivers and the air that we breathe. . . .

"I propose that we eliminate every remaining obstacle to the right and the opportunity to vote.

"I propose that we honor and support the achievements of thought and the creations of art."

And he insisted that America would honor its pledge to the people of Vietnam, where, according to the public record, not a single American bomb had been dropped save in immediate retaliation for the Gulf of Tonkin incident, nor a single infantryman sent. "Our goal is peace in Southeast Asia," the president intoned. "That will come only when aggressors leave their neighbors in peace. What is at stake is the cause of freedom and in that cause America will never be found wanting. . . . To ignore aggression now would only increase the danger of a much larger war."

And that, to a vast majority of Americans, sounded perfectly reasonable. It all sounded reasonable. Johnson "is almost universally liked," the left-wing *Nation* reported that week—hinting, even, that they rather liked him, too. Even the man who wrote Barry Goldwater's 1964 convention platform, Representative Melvin Laird of Wisconsin, said it would be "suicidal" for the Republicans "to ignore the election results and try to resist any change in the party." A poll that month found that 65 percent of rank-and-file Republicans still called themselves conservatives. Should that two-thirds dominate their party's direction, warned two of the nation's most respected political scientists, "we can expect an end to the competitive two-party system."

The system wasn't all that competitive in any event. The Republican National Committee had been purged of Goldwater holdovers. One staffer, Frank Kovak, had been allowed to remain for his financial expertise. Throughout the spring Kovak surreptitiously passed the RNC's private donor lists to right-wing groups that raised funds in competition with the Republicans. Party chairman Ray Bliss found out and ordered him to stop. Kovak continued. So on June 18, two weeks after Bliss presided over a ceremonial RNC meeting meant to herald an era of Republican healing, his assistant broke into Kovak's desk. The break-in was bungled. Kovak alerted the press.

That was the Republican Party in 1965.

Lyndon Johnson took advantage of the weakened opposition. His hero was Franklin Delano Roosevelt. Now he *became* Franklin Delano Roosevelt. Actually, he outpaced him. The liberals' struggle to pass federal funding for education had been a political dry hole since the New Deal. Johnson passed it in the House in March by a margin of 263–153. He then insisted the Senate pass the same bill without a single word changed. The Elementary and Secondary Education Act passed the Senate two weeks later with only eighteen votes in opposition. He then turned the nation to dreams of immortality, proclaiming, "Heart disease, cancer, and stroke can be conquered—not in a millennium, not in a century, but in the next few onrushing decades." The down payment on the revolution was medical insurance for the elderly funded out of Social Security contributions—another stalled New Deal–era initiative, steered by Johnson past its permanent obstacle, the American Medical Association (the only major professional organization to back Barry Goldwater), by a 110-vote House margin.

And then there was civil rights.

The genesis of the Voting Rights Act of 1965 echoed the genesis of the Civil Rights Act of 1964: televised images of Southern sadism. In 1963 it had been Birmingham children set upon by fire hoses and police dogs. Now Martin Luther King, the freshly minted Nobel Peace Prize laureate, came to Selma, Alabama, a town of twenty-nine thousand, of which fifteen thousand were blacks of voting age. Only about three hundred were registered to vote.

Soon came mass arrests—including, on February 1, the detention of five hundred schoolchildren, who had been transported to a state prison farm after the warning "Sing one more freedom song and you are under arrest." When King himself was arrested, he published an open letter in the *New York Times:* "This Is Selma, Alabama. There Are More Negroes in Jail with Me Than There Are on the Voting Rolls." Soon after, troopers shot protester Jimmy Lee Jackson to death.

The stage was set. A march was planned for March 7 down U.S. Highway 80—thereabouts known as the Jefferson Davis Highway—to the state capital, Montgomery, fifty miles to the east. At the far side of the point of embarkation, the Edmund Pettus Bridge, stood rank upon rank of Sheriff Jim Clark's officers, and, outfitted in gas masks, cordons of Governor George Wallace's fearsome Alabama state troopers. The six hundred marchers, clutching sleeping bags for the five-day journey ahead, were ordered to disperse. They did not. The troopers rushed, clubs flailing, tear-gas canisters exploding, white spectators wildly cheering them on; then Jim Clark's forces, on horseback, swinging rubber tubes wrapped in barbed wire, and bullwhips, and electric cattle prods, littered the bridge with writhing black bodies splattering blood. The film ran on national TV. Over and over. On NBC, the broadcast cut into a showing of the film *Judgment at Nuremberg*—a story about what happens when ordinary citizens turn a blind eye to evil.

Federal mediators negotiated safe passage for a peaceful march a week later. The next night, local thugs beat the Reverend James Reeb, a white minister from Boston, to death (he had been watching *Judgment at Nuremberg* when his conscience directed him to travel to Selma). Lyndon Johnson was a man given to towering rages. Now he was angrier than any of his intimates had ever seen him. He prepared to give the greatest speech of his career. Outside the White House, left-wing picketers marched by bearing signs reading

LBJ, JUST YOU WAIT . . . SEE WHAT HAPPENS IN '68. The threat—redeem the martyrs or be punished at the polls—seemed viable. Answering that yearning now appeared not just a moral imperative, but a political one.

Yet no one was prepared for the moral force of the speech Lyndon Johnson gave to Congress and the nation on March 15. He wrote it himself, and delivered it over the objections of temporizing aides:

"It is wrong—deadly wrong—to deny any of your fellow Americans the right to vote in this country. . . . There is no issue of states' rights or national rights. There is only the struggle for human rights. . . . Their cause must be our cause, too. Because it is not just Negroes, but really it is all of us, who must overcome the crippling legacy of bigotry and injustice."

Then, stunningly, he raised his arms in the air and invoked the slogan of a movement that was not too long ago perceived as the preeminent irritant to America's national unity: "And . . . we . . . shall . . . overcome!"

There followed the silence of a reaction too stunned for mere applause. Martin Luther King cried. Senators cried. Southern legislators cornered LBJ's befuddled mentor, Georgia senator Richard Russell, and demanded an explanation for his protégé's betrayal of his native South. They looked like heartless old jackasses.

The next Selma procession, on March 21, was celebratory—thousands of singing marchers, ranks of glamorous celebrities in the fore, marching all the way through to Montgomery.

That night one of the white marchers, a Detroit mother of five named Viola Liuzzo, while humming "We Shall Overcome" in her car, was shot to death by the Ku Klux Klan because she was sitting next to a black man.

The martyr only seemed to intensify the nation's moral resolve. "Should we defeat every enemy, should we double our wealth and conquer the stars, and still be unequal to this issue," Lyndon Johnson had proclaimed, "then we will have failed as a people and as a nation."

He signed the Voting Rights Act of 1965 on August 6 under the Capitol dome. He intoned about the slaves, who "came in darkness and they came in chains. . . . Today, we strike away the last major shackle of those fierce and ancient bonds."

People cried. The Negro's cause was America's cause. Who could argue with that? Johnson, the *Times*' agenda-setting pundit James "Scotty" Reston avowed, was "getting everything through the Congress but the abolition of the Republican party, and he hasn't tried that yet."

The rioting in Los Angeles began five nights later. The spark came at the corner of 116th and Avalon. Two black men, brothers, were stopped by a California highway patrolman at 7:19 p.m., the driver under suspicion of drunkenness. The three scuffled; a crowd gathered. Their mother came out from her house to quarrel with the cops, then another woman joined the fight. The crowd thought the second woman was pregnant (she was wearing a barber's smock). When the cops struck the second woman—kicking a pregnant woman in the stomach?—the mob surged as one. By ten fifteen several hundred Watts residents were on the street, throwing things at white car passengers, staving in store windows, looting. Police tried to seal off the immediate area. But things had already spiraled out of control.

The images came soon afterward, raw and ubiquitous—and, because of a quirk of technology (the telecopter did not record its images on film, as most news cameras did, but via a microwave signal), *live.* KTLA fed it raw into people's homes for the next four days. As a public service, they shared the feeds with the other L.A. channels and the networks.

You would see the telecopter hovering over a hapless lone individual turning a garden hose on a fire at an army surplus store, whose exploding ammunition had already kindled adjacent drug and liquor stores, as upward of a thousand lingered to watch them burn and to harass the Good Samaritan as fire trucks approached and were turned away by a hail of bricks.

You saw fire trucks escorted by sixteen police cruisers to secure their passage, flames high enough to down power lines, the transformer in front of a furniture store about to blow, black smoke spreading second by second over a massive expanse of roof, then over the lion's share of the block, the helicopter tacking through banks of black smoke, looking for ribbons of light through which to capture the scurrying firemen below.

The reporter narrates the action in surges and lulls, like a demonic sports play-by-play:

"There is little that they can do. These buildings will be a total loss before they can get the first drop of water on the building—AND ANOTHER FIRE JUST ERUPTED ABOUT A BLOCK AWAY! . . .

"And the spectators do not seem to be concerned by what's going on. . . .

"Here are two kids running away from the fire right now! . . . *If the command center can see our picture, I would check the parking lot next to the National Dollar Store for three individuals.* . . . *AND NOW THERE'S ANOTHER BUILDING ON FIRE ON THE NORTH SIDE OF THE STREET!* . . .

"And there's another group of spectators! All they're doing is standing around and looking. They couldn't be less concerned. . . .

"And now we have orders to climb higher into the air as potshots are being taken from the ground. Rifle fire and small-arms fire. So we're pulling up and out."

Then you saw the helicopter *swof-swof* across two more miles of blazing streets, to Fifty-first and Avalon, for shots of a burning car turned on its back like a helpless scarab, the crowd guarding their treasure with a street barricade of picnic tables, park benches, and trash cans, the flames ascending heavenward.

War, breaking out in the streets of the United States of America, as if out of nowhere.

The supposed American consensus had always been clouded. The experts had just become expert at ignoring the clouds. The violent, feudal South had long been classed as a vestige, its caste-ridden folkways soon to be inundated by the flood tide of progress, hastened by the salving balm of federal intervention, just as in Selma. Social critics on the left thought the kind of violence you saw in the South might just represent the nation's future, not its past. But they, too, were ignored—seen as vestiges of the thirties, back when there wasn't a consensus.

There had been race riots in the summer of 1964 in New York, Philadelphia, New Jersey, Rochester. And then, when Goldwater lost overwhelmingly, pundits systematically breathed a sigh of relief. "White Backlash Doesn't Develop," the *New York Times* headlined. But backlash *was* developing, whatever the *Times*'s triumphant conclusion. In a statewide referendum in California, with Proposition 14, voters struck down the state's "open housing" law, which prevented property owners from discriminating against purchasers or renters on the basis of race, by a proportion of two to one—an anti-civil-rights vote of almost the same size as the day's vote for President Johnson.

A prominent liberal Southern newspaper editor, Samuel Talmadge Ragan, asserted that after the aberration of five Southern states going for Goldwater, "leaders of both parties are confident" that "elections will be decided on issues other than civil rights." It was a perverse interpretation: in Mississippi, the presidential candidate who had voted against Johnson's 1964 Civil Rights Act won 87 percent of the vote, compared to the 24.7 percent Nixon had won in 1960. Yet Ragan's conclusions ran in the most respectable outlet imaginable, the sober quarterly *American Scholar*. American scholars, like liberals everywhere in early 1965, chose to bask in the sun.

There had been violence on both sides in the presidential campaign— vandalism against campaign offices, civil rights activists and conservative partisans assaulting one another, death threats against the candidates. None of it was seen as a pattern. Watts was absorbed, six days after the passage of the Voting Rights Act, as a visitation from another planet. "How is it possible after all we've accomplished?" Lyndon Johnson cried in anguish. "How could it be? Is the world topsy-turvy?" Los Angeles radio station KNX fired its most popular call-in host. He insisted on talking about Watts. His bosses wanted him talking about anything but. In this way consensus was institutionalized.

Vietnam made the myth harder to sustain. Johnson had spent the first thirteen months of his presidency in fits of sleeplessness. Holding the line against further Communist insurgency into South Vietnam, holding it against an escalating American commitment that might bring China and

Russia actively into the fray, perhaps even forcing the threat of nuclear war: these were the Scylla and Charybdis through which Lyndon Johnson attempted to steer his Vietnam thinking. Some days it threatened to crack open his skull. Then, in January 1965, the latest in a series of South Vietnamese governmental coups led National Security Adviser McGeorge Bundy to urge that America's present course, massive aid to Saigon coupled with secret low-grade sabotage and airborne harassment, "could only lead to disastrous defeat." The election was over, Bundy reminded his boss—the election in which Johnson had run as a peace candidate even while authorizing elaborate plans not just to retaliate against Communist insurgency but to provoke a pretext to "retaliate" against.

The pretext presented itself on February 7: a deadly mortar attack on the American barracks of among the twenty-three thousand U.S. "advisers" at Pleiku, the Vietnamese Central Highlands outpost Americans had been introduced to a few months back during Bob Hope's televised USO Christmas special. ("They had a ring of security around us bigger than anything since I hit the Orpheum circuit," he quipped from the makeshift stage, brandishing his golf club.) What followed was code-named Rolling Thunder—continuous air war against North Vietnam. What followed hard upon that was the landing of two marine battalions to secure the bases from which the air raids were launched. By spring there were thirty-six hundred Rolling Thunder sorties a month and ninety thousand troops to secure them. By mid-June the pretense of defense was dropped altogether, as squads were sent out on the first major missions to "search and destroy" the enemy. They said that if you supported Goldwater, Bob Hope had quipped, America would end up in Vietnam. "I forgot to take the Goldwater sticker off my car, and here I am." Not so funny now.

Johnson lied about all of it. Just as he lied about an April incursion of twenty thousand marines into the Dominican Republic—making up a story that the ambassador phoned him from underneath his desk as Communist bullets ricocheted around the room. (A young administration defense intellectual named Daniel Ellsberg said actually the Dominican Republic was "one of the few Communist-free environments in the whole world.") By summer, plans were in place to put nearly one hundred thousand more American troops into Vietnam, though Johnson told the public the number was half that and denied any policy had changed. "Few Americans will quarrel with President Johnson's determined conclusion to hold on in Vietnam," the Newspaper of Record editorialized the day after that announcement.

Vietnam critics gathered exponentially: fourteen were arrested for blocking the entrance of the U.S. Mission to the United Nations in February; the first of one hundred campus "teach-ins" by the end of the school year came days after the first marines landed at Da Nang (at first the administration sent spokesmen to these events, but they were so rhetorically manhandled for the

gaps and contradictions in their presentations, they stopped showing up).
The biggest peace rally in the history of the republic, organized by Students
for a Democratic Society, the regnant "New Left" organization, brought
twenty thousand to D.C. on April 27. SDS discussed a "Kamikaze Plan" to
urge young men not to register for the draft in explicit violation of the 1917
Espionage Act.

But the Senate passed the president's $700 million Vietnam appropriation
that spring 88–3. The *Times* subheaded its report on the SDS protest "Holiday from Exams." According to one poll, more Americans thought such
protesters were "tools of the Communists" than disagreed with Johnson on
Vietnam.

Johnson kept on rolling out his Great Society: preschool for poor children, college prep for poor teenagers, legal services for indigent defendants,
economic redevelopment funds for lagging regions, landmark immigration
reform, a Department of Housing and Urban Development, national
endowments for the humanities and arts—even a whole new category for the
liberal agenda, environmentalism: a Highway Beautification Act, a Water
Quality Act, a Clean Air Act, bulldozed through as if the opposition from
the Big Three automakers, the advertising industry, and the chemical industry weren't even there. The Republican National Committee could hardly
raise the $200,000 each month necessary to keep its office open. The conser-
vative organizations thriving the most—such as the John Birch Society,
which had leveraged a successful membership drive out of the Goldwater
defeat—were so far out that Republican leaders wanted little to do with
them. The *Washington Post* editorialized of a party fighting off an
"attempted gigantic political kidnapping" by "fanatics": a party in smoldering ruins, ghouls the only sign of life.

Only in hindsight did the report from thirty-three-year-old Morley Safer
on August 5 from the village of Cam Ne look like a foreshadowing of Watts:
marines torching a peasant village by touching off the straw roofs with cigarette lighters, what soldiers called a "Zippo raid."

"This is what the war in Vietnam is all about," Safer narrated. "To a Vietnamese peasant whose house meant a lifetime of backbreaking labor, it will
take more than presidential promises to convince him that we are on his
side."

What wasn't on film was even worse: a South Vietnamese cameraman
persuading marines not to aim a flamethrower into the warren in which
women and children were hiding.

In America, the first antiwar mass arrests soon followed: three hundred
collared on the Capitol steps at an "Assembly of Unrepresented Peoples"
commemorating the twentieth anniversary of Hiroshima and Nagasaki.
Brigades from Berkeley's Vietnam Day Committee made the most militant
antiwar intervention yet, explicitly drawing parallels with the Germans who

defied Hitler, standing in front of barreling troop trains shipping soldiers out for Vietnam, giving way like matadors only at the last possible moment. "I felt I might die," one participant said, "and that would be okay." Others burned their draft cards even though a recently passed law made the act a federal crime. J. Edgar Hoover called them "halfway citizens who are neither morally, mentally, nor emotionally mature."

"We have achieved a unity of interest among our people that is unmatched in the history of freedom."

Turn on the TV: burning huts in Vietnam. Turn on the TV: burning buildings in Watts. Turn on the TV: one set of young people were comparing another set of young people to Nazis, and Da Nang was equated with Nagasaki.

Lyndon Johnson was being mocked. He was losing his consensus.

The most frightening Watts footage did not require a telecopter. The morning after the first day, a series of calm intervals led officials to the false hope that the worst of the riot was over. The Los Angeles Human Relations Commission called a community meeting at Athens Park, eleven blocks from ground zero. A respected black minister with a polite little mustache made an appeal to stay off the streets: "I think that the civil rights drive in America has demonstrated that violence will never be the just end to the grievances we have." He soon lost control of the meeting. A parade of locals stepped to the microphone with angrier and angrier grievances: at the police (who were known to buck themselves up before ghetto tours of duty by crying "LSMFT"—"Let's shoot a motherfucker tonight"); at their rotting homes (nine in ten Watts houses were built before 1939); at the 30 percent black unemployment rate.

Then a kid stepped up to the microphone. He was sixteen, but he looked younger.

"I'm going to tell it the way it is," he began. "I'm gonna tell you somethin'. Tonight there's gonna be another one, whether *you* like it or not."

Murmurs.

He raised his hand for attention, his face intensifying. "Wait! Wait! Listen. We, the Negro people down here, have got completely fed up. And you know what they gonna do tonight. They not gonna fight down here no more. You know where they goin'. They after the white people. They gonna congregate, they gonna caravan out to Englewood, to Marina Del Rey"—someone tried to push him away from the microphone—"and everywhere else the white man's gonna stay. They gonna do the white man *in* tonight!"

There was applause.

The human relations commissioner begged local stations not to air the clip that night. They showed it anyway. Angry whites had begun mobbing sporting-goods stores. More TV images, these ones to scare Negroes: Cau-

casians siting down the barrels of rifles, stockpiling bows and arrows, slingshots, any weapon they could lay their hands on. Race war seemed imminent.
In the integrating community of Pasadena, a little girl lay awake at night wondering whether the new family moving in down the block was going to burn
down her house while she slept, she remembered forty years later.

The terror was compounded by administrative chaos within Governor
Edmund "Pat" Brown's Democratic administration. Brown was on vacation
in the Mediterranean. Executive authority rested with his lieutenant governor, Glenn Anderson. By 7 a.m. Friday the police announced that the situation was "rather well in hand." Lieutenant Governor Anderson, by then
more worried about a situation brewing at Berkeley—student protesters
were rumored to be planning a lie-in before a troop train—jetted north for
a meeting of the University of California regents.

Within two hours the violence in Watts started up worse than before,
now in broad daylight. L.A.'s police chief, William Parker, called Pat
Brown's executive secretary to ask for the National Guard—a pro forma
request, he thought. A maelstrom of misunderstanding and recrimination
unfolded instead. Anderson, who mistrusted Parker as a blustering racist,
held off. By the time Anderson made it back to Los Angeles, Parker refused
to meet with him.

At four fifteen Parker called a press conference to fulminate against a
municipal stab in the back. Watts by then was six thousand rampaging bodies, the most violent civil disturbance since the New York City draft riots of
1863. The first National Guard units hit the streets at 7 p.m.—around the
time the first rioter was shot by police. Pat Brown learned his city was out of
control from the *Athens Daily Post.* He embarked on the twenty-four-hour
journey home, arriving back in time for a report from a French airline pilot
upon his final approach to Los Angeles International that the view looked in
no way different from the war zones he had overflown during World War II.

Situation reports, minute by minute, to the president:

Saturday, August 14, 1700 hours: *Riots are picking up tempo. No information on specific incidents such as siege of the police station and Napalm
factory.*

18:25: Defense Secretary Robert McNamara recommended LBJ dispatch
C-13 transport planes to the California National Guard and send someone
from the Department of Justice "to stay close to Brown and give advice."

19:45: *Looting reported but not verified at the Bank of America at Washington and Vermont. Also report by police that they are unable to guarantee
anyone's safety in area of 45 sq. mi. surround Watts area.*

At 1:56 a.m., the draft of an executive order was cleared by McNamara
for possible use:

*Now, therefore, by virtue of the authority vested in me by the Constitu-
tion and laws of the United States, including Chapter 15 of Title 10 of the*

*United States code, particularly section 331 and 334 thereof, it is hereby
ordered as follows:*

*Section 1. The Secretary of Defense is authorized and directed to take all
appropriate steps to suppress the insurrection, and domestic violence now in
progress in the state of California.*

*Section 2. In furtherance of the authority and direction contained in sec-
tion 1 hereof, the Secretary of Defense is authorized to use such of the armed
forces of the United States as he may deem necessary.*

*Section 3. I hereby authorize and direct the Secretary of Defense to call
into the active military service of the United States, as he may deem appropriate to carry out the purposes of this order, any or all the units of the Army
National Guard and of the Air National Guard of the State of California to
serve in active military service of the United States.*

It didn't quite come to that, though there would be occasion to consult
this document again in the years to come.

Watts was subdued once and for all Sunday morning by 12,242 National
Guardsmen, twenty-year-olds patrolling American streets in troop carriers
with .30-caliber machine guns, looking like scared doughboys from General
Pershing's expeditionary force, guarding the Harbor Freeway, a main
Southern California artery that passed directly above the rioting, the imag-
ined vector for some imminent black incursion on Greater Los Angeles.
When KTLA aired its roundup documentary "Hell in the City of Angels"
Sunday evening, they had to label the violent scenes "videotape" lest view-
ers think the uprising was still ongoing—though that reassurance was sub-
verted when they had to cut in with live footage of new rioting in nearby
Long Beach.

Cops in white helmets and the mien of Selma sheriff Jim Clark were
shown kicking backsides, poking gun barrels into suspects, shouting things
like "First one drops their hands is a dead man," stepping over prostrate bodies stripped down to their underpants. The news got out: four thousand
arrests, thirty deaths, all but five of them black—some of them mere
bystanders. (The only peace officer to die had accidentally shot himself, the
only fireman from standing next to a wall as it collapsed.)

Some whites noticed a pattern: in 1964, rioting had broken out a few
weeks after the signing of the *last* civil-rights-law-to-end-all-civil-rights-
laws. Watts wasn't even the only riot that week; in Chicago, a black neighborhood went up after an errant fire truck killed a woman. Some whites
noticed some liberal politicians seemed to be *excusing* it all. *Time* quoted Senator Robert F. Kennedy: "There is no point in telling Negroes to obey the
law. To many Negroes the law is the enemy."

But what were we left with without respect for the law? *Time* answered
that question by quoting a "husky youth": "If we don't get things changed

here, we're gonna do it again. We know the cops are scared, and now all of us have guns. Last time we weren't out to kill whites. Next time is going to be different."

Lyndon Johnson, petrified, instructed federal agencies to pump $29 million into the neighborhood—in secret, for fear of charges he was pandering to rioters, for fear that rising expectations would lead but to more chaos ("Negroes will end up pissing in the aisles of the Senate"). The Republican Policy Committee, meeting at the end of August, took a side on Watts—Chief Parker's, who argued that the civil rights movement was responsible for the violence. Congressmen's mail changed overnight: "People are saying that the Irish had their problems and the Italians had their problems, but that they didn't turn to civil disobedience," a West Pennsylvania Democrat told the president. Los Angeles' Democratic mayor, Sam Yorty, a Nixon supporter in 1960, began boasting of never having visited Watts and received a standing ovation from a businessmen's luncheon when he said of the white Sacramento guardsmen sent down to his city, "What a difference between these fine young men and the people they were sent to control!"

The president pulled in his legislative reins, signing the law authorizing the establishment of a Department of Housing and Urban Development only after arranging to stall the appointment of its designated secretary, Robert C. Weaver, who had served the federal government since his days as the New Deal's unofficial Negro ambassador, until January. Conventional wisdom converged on the president's "credibility gap" on Vietnam. Americans' doubts about their president were made flesh when he went under the knife in October for gallbladder and kidney-stone surgery. Johnson had a habit of taking on maladies when stress on him was greatest; in 1948 he passed a kidney stone right before the agonizingly close Senate race that earned him the mocking nickname Landslide Lyndon; in 1955 he had a heart attack. This time so many people presumed he was lying—that he had really suffered another heart attack—that he shocked reporters by lifting his shirt to show them where the scar was. In the *New York Review of Books,* house organ for the left-wing intelligentsia, cartoonist David Levine drew the wound in the shape of Vietnam.

Such were the political facts of life as 1966 approached.

Though one more political fact of life—one more political force of nature—should also be noted: Richard Nixon was on the road, doing what he had been doing since he had moved to New York in 1963—since moments after he was crowned the Job of American politics, the patron saint of losers, after his defeat against Pat Brown for California governor. Bookies gave him a thousand-to-one shot that he would ever succeed in politics again. Nixon didn't take the tip. He was plugging away to become leader of the free world, the tasks to check off yawning numberless and interminable.

One evening, the task was breaking into the manor grounds of a millionaire.

The "politically retired" Nixon had been traveling through 1965 giving rousing political speeches before Republican audiences in carefully selected locations. He also gave speeches to business clients in his capacity as a partner in the Wall Street firm Nixon, Mudge, Rose, Guthrie & Alexander. Occasionally the two tasks overlapped on the same trip. But not this time. He was in Miami to give a speech to the board of directors of a Minnesota-based company called Investors Diversified Services and to visit with one of the rich industrialists who was backing his presidential play, Elmer Bobst of Warner-Lambert pharmaceuticals. He had brought along a retainer for the trip, a fellow law partner, Leonard Garment; he liked to have along a cordon sanitaire to keep the celebrity-naggers at bay, the better to withdraw bubble-like within himself to prepare, which he always did obsessively for whatever task he set out to do. He had to have someone with him so he could be alone.

Nixon and Garment repaired to the mansion of Nixon's patron for drinks. Then they had dinner at Bobst's club. Then Nixon and his second were limousined off to the place they had been provided, through some favor or another, to spend the night. It was a house in a new suburban tract that was just starting to sell lots. Garment recorded what happened next in his memoirs:

"Nixon took one look at the place, and his always-operational political instincts and suspicions told him that in the morning the developers would expect to get pictures of him in the house in order to use his name and photograph for publicity purposes."

It was the tiniest possible thing. But not, for Richard Nixon, a small thing at all. To be photographed thus, under circumstances not of his own control, in a city where he hadn't advertised his presence, would dilute his political capital by some appreciable amount, though probably only Richard Nixon was sensitive enough to measure it. Nixon ordered the driver back the hour or so to the magnate's house from whence they had come. "When we arrived, after midnight, the gates were locked," Garment wrote. "A high wall surrounded the estate."

Nixon's next words were hard to forget: "Come on, Garment. It's over the wall we go."

And so over the wall they clawed, briefcases in hand. Nixon had spied a pool house with twin beds inside. It turned out to be unlocked. They would sleep there. They stayed up half the night talking. Nixon told Garment he would do anything, make any sacrifice, to get where he wanted to go. "Anything," he said, "except see a shrink."

Scaling a pool-house wall was even, in its way, routine. Another time, in 1966, Garment found himself pulled into a locked stairwell by Nixon to avoid an inconveniently milling crowd before his introduction to a Midwestern county GOP fund-raiser. The boss had a general's sensitivity to commanding time and space. He was especially meticulous about making dramatic entrances. He wouldn't sacrifice this one by appearing before the appointed hour, no matter that Garment nearly had a panic attack pounding on the fireproof doors to get out. Nixon was cool. There was political advantage to be had. If this was what it took, this was what it took. At this point in this man's life, clawing for political advantage—anywhere, anytime, by any means necessary—was Richard Nixon's way. Which was why there would come a moment, sometime in the future, when the complex set of forces unleashed by Watts, and the final rise, before the final fall, of Richard Milhous Nixon, would come to seem synonymous.

CHAPTER TWO

The Orthogonian

B Y 1966 RICHARD NIXON HAD BEEN CLAWING ALL HIS LIFE. WHENEVER a dirty job had to get done, he had been there to do it.

From the time he was a boy in the Southern California citrus groves, staying up half the night to man the creepy little potbellied orchard heaters that kept the frost from the trees but not the black smudge from the boy tending them, to stain his clothes for school the next day; from the time his father built a combination grocery and gas station and made it his second son's duty to begin each day in the dark, at 4 a.m., driving to the Los Angeles market to select the day's produce; from the time he was denied a chance to go to Harvard because he could only afford to live at home; from the time he was blacklisted from his little local college's single social club because he was too unpolished; from the time he was reduced to sharing a one-room shack without heat or indoor plumbing while working his way through Duke Law School; from the time, finishing third in his class, he trudged frantically from white-shoe Wall Street law firm to white-shoe Wall Street law firm and was shown the door at each one (he ended up practicing law back home, where, forced to handle divorce cases, he would stare at his shoes, crimson-red in embarrassment, as women related to him the problems they suffered at the marital bed). To the time, back from the war, he begged Southern California's penny-ante plutocrats, navy cap in hand, for their sufferance of his first congressional bid; to the time he trundled across California in his wood-paneled station wagon, bringing his Senate campaign into every godforsaken little burg in that state with so many scores of godforsaken little burgs.

The town he was born in, Yorba Linda, was just that sort of godforsaken burg. Frank Nixon had built a little plaster-frame house there in 1910 across from a cruddy, oversize ditch that must have shaped one of the boy's earliest indelible impressions of the world. It was, by Yorba Linda standards, a historic ditch: it brought in the freshwater that promised to make good for the first time on the Chamber of Commerce boast that this desert outpost was a fine place to grow citrus. For the children of this cactus-covered town, the Anaheim Ditch made for a bit of fun: they could swim in it, or at least wade in it. All except the Nixon boys, whose overstrict father forbade them. When Frank Nixon saw his boys in the canal, he would grab them by the scruff of the neck, haul them out, push them in, taunt them, then throw them in a few more times. One of Richard Nixon's biographers, reflecting upon the image, speculated the kid "might well have felt that his father was trying to drown him like an unwanted puppy."

For most farmers, that ditch helped bring a decent crop. Not Frank Nixon, who was filled with the kind of self-destructive abstemiousness that is sometimes labeled pride. "I won't buy fertilizer until I raise enough lemons to pay for it," he said, though in Yorba Linda's "loaf-sugar" soil—it tended to clump—you couldn't grow lemons without fertilizer. Frank and his family went bust.

California wasn't supposed to be like this. Frank had come from Indiana after a life spent collecting humiliating jobs: farmhand (upon dropping out of school in the sixth grade); streetcar motorman (his feet got frostbitten in the unheated cab); glassworker; potter; housepainter; sheep rancher; telephone-pole climber; oxcart driver; oil-field roustabout. When Dick was ten, the family moved to the Quaker outpost of Whittier, home to his mother Hannah's people. They never really approved of Frank. That didn't keep the patriarch from affecting a peacocklike sense of superiority. To the point of tedium, he would remind people that he had once met William McKinley—as if that, and not the family he was raising, was his life's great accomplishment.

Eventually Richard Nixon's loquacious father didn't do too poorly with his store. He built it in a former church, which was appropriate enough, for in this family, to toil was a sacrament. Frank, who did the store's butchering, took pride in changing his bloodstained shirts no more than once a week. Richard Nixon would ever transit between feelings of pride and feelings of shame toward his dirty-necked, lusty spitfire of a father, between apologizing for him and boasting about him, between desperately reaching for success to honor him and desperately reaching for success to repudiate him.

Dirty jobs, either way.

Richard Nixon was a serial collector of resentments. He raged for what he could not have or control. At the age of seven he so wanted a jar of pollywogs a younger boy had collected from the forbidden canal that he beaned the kid in the head with a toy hatchet (his victim bore the scar for life). He ever felt unfairly put upon: at age ten he wrote a letter to the mother he revered, rendered distant by the raising of four other often-sickly boys, for a school assignment in the voice of a pet. Addressed "My Dear Master," it spun out fantastic images of unearned persecutions: "The two dogs that you left with me are very bad to me. . . . While going through the woods one of the boys triped [sic] and fell on me. . . . He kiked [sic] me in the side. . . . I wish you would come home right now." A few months later he betrayed another foreshadowing trait: groveling to elevate his station in life. "Please consider me for the position of office boy mentioned in the Times paper," he wrote to the big-city daily his family took and which he devoured, the reactionary *Los Angeles Times*. "I am eleven years of age.... I am willing to come to your office at any time and I will accept any pay offered."

He contained his raging ambition in the discipline of debate. That was his father's influence; the surest way to Frank's heart (though there was never really any sure way) was through skill at argumentation. Frank loved to argue, sometimes to the point of driving customers from the store. The son received his first opportunity to argue competitively in the fifth grade, and his father, the sixth-grade dropout, did the research, obsessed with seeing his son whip others with words. When Dick joined the high school debate team, Frank attended every meet. Dick won often. The coach bemoaned his "ability to kind of slide around an argument instead of meeting it head on." Sometimes he broke the rules outright.

As a schoolboy he hadn't a single close friend, preferring to cloister himself up in the former church's bell tower, reading, hating to ride the school bus because he thought the other children smelled bad. At Whittier, a fine Quaker college of regional reputation unknown anywhere else, he embarked upon what might have been his most humiliating job of all: learning to be a backslapping hail-fellow-well-met. ("I had the impression he would even practice his inflection when he said 'hello,'" a reporter later observed.) The seventeen-year-old blossomed when he realized himself no longer alone in his outsiderdom: the student body was run, socially, by a circle of swells who called themselves the Franklins, and the remainder of the student body, a historian noted, "seemed resigned to its exclusion." So this most unfraternal of youth organized the remnant into a fraternity of his own. Franklins were well-rounded, graceful, moved smoothly, talked slickly. Nixon's new club, the Orthogonians, was for the strivers, those not to the manner born, the commuter students like him. He persuaded his fellows that reveling in one's unpolish was a nobility of its own. Franklins were never photographed save in black tie. Orthogonians wore shirtsleeves. "Beans, brains, and brawn" was their motto. He told them *orthogonian*—basically, "at right angles"—meant "upright," "straight shooter." Also, their enemies might have added, all elbows.

The Orthogonians' base was among Whittier's athletes. On the surface, jocks seem natural Franklins, the Big Men on Campus. But Nixon always had a gift for looking under social surfaces to see and exploit the subterranean truths that roiled underneath. It was an eminently Nixonian insight: that on every sports team there are only a couple of stars, and that if you want to win the loyalty of the team for yourself, the surest, if least glamorous, strategy is to concentrate on the nonspectacular—silent—majority. The ones who labor quietly, sometimes resentfully, in the quarterback's shadow: the linemen, the guards, the punter. Nixon himself was exemplarily nonspectacular: the 150-pounder was the team's tackle dummy, kept on squad by a loving, tough, and fatherly coach who appreciated Nixon's unceasing grit and team spirit—nursing hurt players, cheering on the listless, even organizing his own team dinners, entertaining the guests on the piano, perhaps favoring them with the Orthogonian theme song. It was his own composition.

Nixon beat a Franklin for student body president. Looking back later, acquaintances marveled at the feat of this awkward, skinny kid the yearbook called "a rather quiet chap about campus," dour and brooding, who couldn't even win a girlfriend, who attracted enemies, who seemed, a schoolmate recalled, "the man least likely to succeed in politics." They hadn't learned what Nixon was learning. Being hated by the right people was no impediment to political success. The unpolished, after all, were everywhere in the majority.

Ever-expanding circles of Orthogonians, encompassing all those who ever felt their pride wounded by the Franklins of the world, were already his constituency. Richard Nixon at their center, yet apart, as their leader. The circle could be made to expand, Richard Nixon might have realized even then. Though via a paradox: the greater their power, the more they felt oppressed. When the people who felt like losers united around their shared psychological sense of grievance, their enemies felt somehow more overwhelming, not less; even if the Franklins weren't always *really* so powerful at all, Franklin "power" often being merely a self-perpetuating effect of an Orthogonian sense of victimization. Martyrs who were not really martyrs, oppressors who were not really oppressors: a class politics for the white middle class. The keynote of the new, Nixonian politics . . . though we are getting ahead of ourselves. For first we must send Richard Nixon to law school, where he was a monk.

He had been second in his class at Whittier to a woman; as if exorcizing the shame, in law school Nixon earned the nickname Iron Butt for his marathon stints at the library. Duke's law school was brand-new, a weakling little brother to a university striving in the shadow of the Ivies, an Orthogonian institution itself. Heirs to the Duke tobacco fortune gave out scholarships to the new law school like candy to out-of-state students. The degree didn't guarantee them a decent job—as Nixon learned the hard way, when only the top two members in his class (Nixon was third) got jobs on Wall Street. Then Nixon was turned down for a job with the FBI. "List the names of any relatives now in the government service, with the degree of membership, and where employed," the application asked. "None," Nixon was forced to reply; no hope, apparently, even in the FBI, for a man without connections.

With World War II he escaped Whittier by taking a Washington job with the Office of Price Administration. Ivy Leaguers dominated the staff. They acted, he decided, just like Franklins. One of his coworkers recalled, "Because he lacked sophistication and the big-city graces, he never quite fit in"; Nixon called them "remnants of the old violent New Deal." Then he signed up for the navy, not least because going to war was what young men with political ambitions did in 1943.

And in the navy, Richard Nixon played poker.

That's not how he would later put it, running for Congress in 1946 on a made-up record of time spent "in the foxholes." In Whittier, he had been a man of no small responsibility: partner in a failed business to sell orange juice in a newfangled, frozen form; partner in the town's top law firm; assistant city attorney; organizer of his own Jaycees-like service club. He was given a position of no small responsibility as a junior navy officer, leading a Southern Combat Air Transport Command unit on the Melanesian islands in charge of unloading and reprovisioning cargo planes. It was important work—sometimes the cargo was mutilated men returning from combat duty—and Nixon did it admirably. But it wasn't dangerous work. It also made for lots of leisure time. On Green Island, Nixon set up Nick's, a makeshift beer joint where between more hazardous duty combatants dropped in for games of high-stakes poker. But playing hands across from Lieutenant Commander Nixon was hazardous, too. Much later, a former lieutenant named Stewart boasted that he had been the first person to teach Nixon poker. It may have been Stewart who had been played. Nixon likely entered the navy knowing the game, learning it in the months he worked the wheel of fortune at a carnival in Prescott, Arizona.

Some people say the best way to win at poker is to possess an iron butt: never bet a hand until you are sure you can win, even if that means folding for hours on end. You play the person, not the cards. You always give something to the mark: give him the confidence to believe he has one up on you. That is when you spring the trap.

It was, to be sure, an unglamorous way to play. The fun in gambling lies in risking the chance. Which was how people who had not mastered the endurance of the dirty job—most people—played. Which may be one of the reasons Nixon was so successful against them. Sometimes Nixon played pots as high as the price of a new car. Waiting, waiting, waiting; enduring not so much the losses as the long stretches of nonwinning; because you've only really ever finally lost when you've given up the game. At any rate he won enough money at poker to fund the greater part of his first congressional race. He knew a whole lot about winning by then.

There is one more thing to say before we launch Richard Nixon on his public career.

Nixon has been the subject of more psychobiographies than any other politician. His career vindicates one of that maligned genre's most trustworthy findings: the recipe for a successfully driven politician should include a doting mother to convince the son he can accomplish anything, and an emotionally distant father to convince the son that no accomplishment can ever be enough.

We have seen something of the father. Now, something of the mother. Nixon called Hannah Nixon a saint. People remembered her as soft-spoken and pious. But Nixon's best psychobiographer, Fawn M. Brodie, sees evidence of "repressed anger" in Hannah Nixon's makeup. History dotes upon her honesty. But that, too, doesn't quite cover it. For even while instructing her sons that lying was the most unpardonable sin, on one subject she lied often, especially later in life: on the subject of her second son.

To understand this we must explain the death of his brothers. It is another psychobiographical theme in the lives of successful men: the deaths of siblings. The first one to die was the youngest, Arthur, who came down with what might have been tubercular meningitis. Twelve-year-old Richard was given reason to believe that a concussion from a schoolyard rock thrown to Arthur's head that Richard had been unable to prevent had been a contributing factor. Older brothers are supposed to protect younger ones. Richard was convulsed by his failure, and the loss.

Then, the second brother. Richard hadn't been the favorite son. The golden boy, the one on whom great hopes were pinned, was the oldest, Harold—handsome, well-rounded, graceful: the first Franklin Richard knew. Harold became even more the center of the family universe when he came down with tuberculosis. After Hannah set up a second household for him to recuperate in the hot, dry air of Prescott, Arizona, Richard was left behind with two other brothers under the care of their slave-master father. It was the middle of the Depression. The family almost went bankrupt. Richard was sent to Arizona to help nurse the boarders Hannah brought in to help keep the family afloat. The work was endless, dirty, unrewarding, sepulchral. When Harold died, Hannah once told *Ladies' Home Journal,* Richard "sank into a deep, impenetrable silence. . . . From that time on it seemed that he was trying to be three sons in one, striving even harder than before to make up to his father and me for our loss."

Hannah would come to recast Richard in her mind as an impregnable figure of destiny, bringer of miracles. When he became famous, she began to report that Richard had been born the day of an eclipse (he wasn't), that his ragged and forlorn family had sold land upon which oil was found immediately afterward (they hadn't). The exaggerations she got away with drove home for her son the lesson that a lie unexposed does no harm, that a soul viewed as a saint can also lie. And her swooning (though she withheld praise in his presence) drove home a lesson the politician was predisposed to internalize: that he *was* a figure of destiny, impregnable. Which could only heighten the pain of the losses he had pledged himself to endure when they

came. Which made him want to win even more; though the pleasure of those
victories was dulled to the vanishing point by survivor's guilt; even as any
victory could not be enough to please his internalized father anyway. This
was an ego finely tuned to believe that it was nothing unless it was everything: one for which winning wasn't everything, it was the only thing—but
which even victory could never fully satisfy.

Richard Milhous Nixon was born to beat Horace Jeremiah Voorhis, his first
opponent for Congress. The California Twelfth District's popular five-term
congressman was rich, well-bred, a Yale Phi Beta Kappa, and a Yale Law
graduate. He had been voted the most hardworking congressman by his
peers and the most honest congressman by the press corps—even, in 1945,
the year before Nixon faced him, the best congressman west of the Mississippi. It was said that he was the model for *Mr. Smith Goes to Washington.*
If nobility was Jerry Voorhis's liability, nobody had thought to exploit it
before.

The *Los Angeles Times* suggested General George S. Patton as a good
candidate to run against him, but it never came off. A group of conservative
Southern California entrepreneurs calling themselves the Committee of 100
was so desperate for an effective opponent that they took out classified ads
in twenty-six newspapers to find one over the heads of the regular Republican organization. They came across only losers: a white supremacist, a
strange man obsessed with smog, a small-town mayor who'd run if they
guaranteed him a job if he lost.

Nixon, off in Washington for the OPA, never saw the notice. He came
recommended by the former president of Whittier College. He wore his
only decent suit of clothes—his navy uniform—to the audition. His conservative, populist speech was a hit. As was his private pledge, afterward, to
"tear Voorhis to pieces." The Committee of 100 tried to recruit California's
star political operative, Murray Chotiner, to manage Nixon's campaign. But
Chotiner supported Voorhis. He was for winners, and Nixon didn't have a
chance. He accepted only when the Committee of 100 offered him a huge
sum, though his affinity with his new client was not long in coming.
Chotiner was a spiritual Orthogonian, a back-alley brawler whose legal specialty was representing bookies. Both agreed that the problem was that not
enough voters of California's Twelfth Congressional District yet knew they
were, as it were, Orthogonians, too—that swells like Voorhis oppressed
them. Convincing them became the focus of Nixon's iron-assed will.

Nixon's success or failure in his campaigns would often turn on how well
or poorly he chose the main issue by which he framed them. Running for
Whittier student body president, he managed to become both the students'
and the administration's beau ideal by calling for an end to the campus ban
on dancing (once-a-month chaperoned affairs on campus, he assured the

administration, better vouchsafed students' virtue than jalopy runs to Los Angeles juke joints). Some twenty-six years later, barnstorming in 1958 for his party's congressional candidates, he learned what a poorly chosen issue could do. He pushed antilabor "right-to-work" laws as the Republicans' central plank, and the party suffered its worst year ever. (He hardly said an ill word about the labor movement in public again.) In 1946, the issue he chose was perfect. Actually, he didn't much choose it at all. It fell into his lap—for from Stettin in the Baltic to Trieste on the Adriatic, an Iron Curtain had descended across Europe.

American politicians straightaway heeded Winston Churchill's famous warning, delivered in Fulton, Missouri, in March 1946, about the Soviet Union's designs for a death grip on Europe. Harry Truman was equally alarmed. But Truman occupied a post that considerably straitened his political freedom of movement when it came to the emerging anticommunism issue. As the nation's chief diplomat he had to avail himself of a range of tonal responses in foreign policy, not just the martial barks of the demagogue. The suspicions of softness that resulted could easily tar unwary members of his own party with the same "quisling" brush—even Jerry Voorhis, who had proposed a bill outlawing the American Communist Party. Voorhis possessed an added vulnerability: he had once been a member of the Socialist Party. Not a Communist; but for the upright burghers of Southern California's suburbs, to whom property was as sacred as anything in the Bible, the distinction was sufficiently arcane to be moot.

Richard Nixon spoke for those upright burghers. He started his campaign agitating for the abolition of wartime price controls, a strong Republican national issue that year. But it didn't quite hit the gut—not least because Voorhis himself was lukewarm on controls. Then Nixon found his jackhammer. In his August 29 kickoff rally he announced, "I want you to know that I am your candidate primarily because there are no special strings attached to me. I have no support from any special interest or pressure group. I welcome the opposition of the PAC, with its Communist principles."

The only question was, which "PAC" did he mean?

CIO-PAC, the nonpartisan but liberal political arm of the progressive labor federation the Congress of Industrial Organizations, was the only political action committee most Americans had heard of in 1946. Soon the CIO would undertake a ruthless purge of the Communists and fellow travelers in its midst. It hadn't yet. The *Los Angeles Times* had claimed a week and a half after Churchill's Iron Curtain speech that CIO-PAC was Communist-dominated—and that they were raising $6 million (a made-up figure) for congressional elections nationwide. Nixon actually "meant" a smaller and more obscure outfit, the National Citizens Political Action Committee. Or so he would claim when pressed, which was rarely. NCPAC had endorsed Voorhis. CIO-PAC had not. Arcane distinctions, not for

Richard Nixon to call attention to. He just kept on saying "PAC." As in, "Voorhis Voted the Moscow–PAC–Henry Wallace line."

He and Chotiner were chartering the Nixon method. You didn't have to attack to attack. Better, much better, to give something to the mark: make him feel that he has one up on you. Let him pounce on your "mistake." That makes him look unduly aggressive. Then you sprang the trap, garnering the pity by making the enemy look like a self-righteous and hyperintellectual enemy of common sense. You attacked jujitsu-style, positioning yourself as the attacked, inspiring a strange sort of protective love among voters whose wounded resentments grow alongside your performance of being wounded. Your enemies appear only to have died of their own hand. Which makes you stronger.

A Voorhis supporter, in the question-and-answer session at a candidate debate, baited the trap. Why, he trilled condescendingly, had Nixon implied that Voorhis was CIO-PAC's man even though Voorhis had told CIO-PAC he wouldn't accept their endorsement even if they offered it?

Jujitsu time.

Nixon pulled out a mimeographed NCPAC bulletin and listed the names of the people who sat on the boards of *both* groups. An interlocking directorate. That most nefarious of aristocratic tricks against the plain people. The plain people stood up and cheered Nixon on.

A Nixon newspaper ad now harped on the number of times this "former registered Socialist" whose "voting record in Congress is more Socialistic and Communistic than Democratic" had "voted [CIO-PAC's] viewpoint." Three of the times, Voorhis had actually voted the opposite. That didn't deter Nixon. It was part of the method: challenged on the lie, he attacked the challenger, in tones of self-pity, for lying. Even if he had to lie to do it: "A VOTE FOR NIXON IS A VOTE AGAINST THE COMMUNIST-DOMI-NATED PAC WITH ITS GIGANTIC SLUSH FUND."

Watch opponent squirm. Repeat as necessary.

Nixon still harped on price controls and shortages; in one brilliant tactic he stockpiled household appliances for which shortages existed and sold them at cost at his campaign headquarters. The crux of his genius was how he simultaneously fused that mundane old issue with the exotic new one. The Office of Price Administration, the agency in Washington in charge of fighting inflation (which he worked for in 1945), was, he avowed, "shot through with extreme left-wingers boring from within, striving to force private enterprise into bankruptcy and thus bring about the socialization of America's basic institutions and industries." The pinko was established as but another specimen of Franklin. Nixon, on the other hand, his campaign posters labeled "One of Us."

Though not everyone agreed. "I know it's against religion to hate anybody, but I just can't help hating that Nixon," a little old lady from Whittier told pundit Stewart Alsop in 1958, her shame at her blasphemy evident. No such shame from Nixon. Nixon believed an enemy must be pulverized, never to walk again. Play your cards right and you harmed yourself not a whit in the bargain; you emerged, indeed, stronger than ever. Do the people's hating for them. Emerge as the people's champion. Except to the people who hate you more than ever.

Nixon won. At thirty-three years of age, he was now a U.S. congressman.

With Alger Hiss he but refined his accomplishment.

The story that began with an odd and lumbering Columbia University undergraduate named Whittaker Chambers receiving the holy orders of Communist Party membership in 1925, and reached its peak in the late forties in a tale of safe houses, pilfered microfilm, hidden compartments, and mysterious suicides (or were they murders?), was a spy story with the trappings of Cold War grand opera. "I have testified against him with remorse and pity" went a typically melodramatic Whittaker Chambers pronouncement about Alger Hiss, the man he claimed had once been his best friend. "But in a moment of historical jeopardy in which this nation now stands, so help me God, I could not do otherwise."

Once upon a time Whittaker Chambers dedicated his life to running an underground spying apparatus for the only cause he believed could redeem a hopelessly fallen world. Alger Hiss, one of the foreign policy establishment's glamour boys, was an accomplice. A paranoid and an apocalyptic, Chambers took a precaution: during his last months as a Red spy, he kept some of the intelligence Alger Hiss had stolen from the State Department and hid it in a safe place. In case Chambers died under mysterious circumstances, it could be proven a murder. Later, when Chambers switched sides and became an anticommunist, he kept the documents: they now could serve duty in the event of a final showdown between East and West by convincing the spineless middle classes how the enemies of freedom were preparing to destroy them.

Ten years passed. Chambers established a quiet career as a man of letters. Hiss continued his ascent up the slopes of the Establishment. Then, in 1948, Harry Truman called Congress back from its summer recess to deal with inflation and got more than he bargained for. The House Un-American Activities Committee maneuvered, characteristically, to steal the limelight, calling hearings on espionage to piggyback on a New York grand jury's recent indictment of twelve Communist leaders based on the testimony of Elizabeth Bentley, whom the New York *World-Telegram* racily labeled a "beautiful blonde." She was actually a homely brunette. But a sense of sexualized menace was a common currency of voyeuristic tabloids and voyeuristic congressional committees at the high tide of the Cold War.

Few expected anything substantial to come from HUAC, then or ever.

Some of its members were so dumb that they couldn't follow the proceedings. Others compulsively interrupted to compare Communism to venereal disease—or, in the case of Mississippi's John Rankin, to fulminate against the Jewish Communists in the ancient Levant who crucified Christ. The worst thing about HUAC, to some who took anticommunism seriously, was that it was ineffectual in building cases for the prosecution of actual Communists.

At least it put on a good show. The hearings were packed. What else was there to do on hot D.C. afternoons in August? HUAC subpoenaed Chambers. Hiss was one of the people he named as a secret Communist. But Chambers's testimony, a mealymouthed reprise of information he had given the FBI a decade earlier, had little effect. When America was introduced to him the next morning in the news, observed his biographer, he appeared as if "newly emerged from the sinister depths of the underground, his suit wrinkled, his expression haunted, his eyes averted from the camera as if in a guilty light." He was not an inspiring man. Alger Hiss's name would likely have died in obscurity had Hiss taken the advice of friends and simply ignored the charge until it blew over. But Alger Hiss fancied himself an inspiring man. He was certainly an arrogant man. He sent a telegram to HUAC demanding to testify in his defense, intending to take this absurd congressional committee on and humiliate them.

When first he testified, it seemed to work. Alger Hiss didn't duck behind the Fifth Amendment. He talked circles around his hapless interrogators. Not only had he "never followed the Communist Party line, directly or indirectly," he said, "none of my friends is a Communist." He named those friends: Supreme Court justice Oliver Wendell Holmes; Francis Bowes Sayre, legendary diplomat and son-in-law of Woodrow Wilson; former secretary of state Edward Reilly Stettinius; John Foster Dulles, presumptive secretary of state for presumptive president Thomas Dewey. Hiss reviewed the luminous career they had sponsored: clerking for the Supreme Court, yeoman's service in the New Deal's First Hundred Days, staff attorney of a congressional committee, all before the age of thirty-one; key player at the San Francisco founding convention of the United Nations by the age of forty-one ("in a class by himself," *Time* had reported of his performance there).

On the other side, his accuser: this disheveled lump, Whittaker Chambers. Hiss said he had never known anyone by the name.

The committee, awed by Hiss, sat and took it while he lectured them. He finished to thunderclaps of applause. Rankin of Mississippi led a procession of members to the witness table to apologize. Truman called HUAC's latest hearings a "red herring." Supportive journalists confided to HUAC members that unless they ignored this foolish Chambers, their committee, already weakened by the Hollywood 10 circus of the previous year, was finished. The members were ready to pack it in and spend the rest of the summer back home.

Only one member thought differently.

No one who knew of this bright young Richard Nixon's capabilities and ambitions (he had formed a group to unify the freshmen Republicans, the Chowder and Marching Club) expected that upon entering Congress the previous year he would have welcomed a place on the House Un-American Activities Committee. Actually, he lobbied for it. He had ascertained a change in the cultural winds. Once the faith of boobs, Red-hunting was now the state religion. In the Hiss case, Nixon spotted the chance to engineer his investiture as its pope.

At a meeting of the committee two days after Hiss's testimony, Nixon argued vociferously that Hiss and Chambers should face each other—that Hiss was the guilty one; and, what's more, that the committee had to pursue the case against him to the hilt if they wanted to save their honor.

With every opinion blowing the other way, why did Richard Nixon take the opposite bet? He always said it came of a hunch, a subtle suspicion that Alger Hiss was lying. He wrote, "I saw that he had never once said flatly, 'I don't know Whittaker Chambers.'" Hiss had always qualified it carefully to say, "I have never known a man by the name of Whittaker Chambers." Nixon won the argument. The case against Hiss would continue, but in fact Nixon was lying. He hadn't noticed Hiss's circumlocution on his own. He had been tipped off to look for it. When Richard Nixon joined HUAC, the savvier Red-hunters, the ones eager to separate their crusade from the crackpots, had spotted him as the cream of the crop, just as he had hoped. One of them, a sleuthing anticommunist priest, showed Nixon reports of rumors that Alger Hiss was the most influential Communist in the State Department. The omnipowerful FBI director, J. Edgar Hoover, had been impressed with Nixon, too. He may have shown Nixon tentative FBI intelligence suggesting the same thing.

Nixon did indeed harbor a hunch in that hearing room. It just wasn't a forensic one. It was political. He saw that Alger Hiss was a pitch-perfect Franklin. Everything followed from that.

Nixon later described Hiss's behavior at that first hearing vividly: "insolent," "insulting in the extreme," "almost condescending." The language was personal. Here was someone who had everything Nixon coveted: the Harvard pedigree, the affection of Supreme Court justices—"tall, elegant, handsome, and perfectly poised" to boot, Nixon recalled some thirty years after the fact. Here was someone he could hate quite productively. Someone through whom he could expand the circle of Orthogonians and place himself at their center. California had a senate race coming open in 1950. Nixon had his eye on it. Nixon didn't do all of the work to break the Hiss case—HUAC investigator Robert Stripling did more. But Nixon did plenty of the work, and plenty more to make sure that he received exclusive credit. His allies knew they might not be able to prove that Alger Hiss was a spy. But they might prove Hiss had once known Whittaker Chambers—that he had lied before Congress. Nixon took Chambers under his wing, coaxing him to produce a detailed account of quotidian details of the Hiss household as he had known it over a decade before. Over the next nine days, Nixon worked round-the-clock to corroborate it. Then, in a second interrogation of Hiss, this time in secret, Hiss unwittingly confirmed the corroboration. It came in a slew of silly details, later immortalized in American folklore like the punch-lines to a joke: the Ford roadster with the "sassy trunk" (Hiss had owned it and loaned it to Chambers), the "prothonotary warbler" (which Hiss boasted to Chambers as his proudest sighting in his bird-watching career), "Hilly and Pross" (Hiss family pet names). Under questioning, Hiss's spine unstiffened: now he acknowledged that he *might* have known the man the committee called Chambers, only under some other name. Next came the ambush. First in another private session, then in a public hearing that lasted a melodramatic nine and one-half hours, the committee brought the two together for con-frontations. Hiss buckled. The case seemed broken. Richard Nixon had bagged his man.

And yet, there was dissonance. The more mumbling and unlikely Hiss's counterclaims became, the stronger were the voices of the Establishment and some of its press, insinuating that Chambers was the guilty one: a madman, a spurned homosexual, a drunk. Chambers thought he knew why: Commu-nists in high places were pulling strings behind the scenes. Richard Nixon harbored the more prosaic theory a lifetime of resentments had prepared him for: the Establishment was protecting one of its own.

The saga that followed has been told well dozens of times before: the Hiss prosecution's reversals of fortune; the double crosses; the bungles and the near misses; the court cases; the agonies of the suicidal Whittaker Chambers, so painfully withdrawn; the arrogance of Alger Hiss, so commanding and elegant. The way Richard Nixon used them both. How the Hiss-Chambers case burned itself on the retina of a generation—not least in the incredible evidence that sealed the case: that secret microfilm Chambers had stashed away so long ago, rescued from a dusty dumbwaiter, then hid, for one dra-matic night, inside a hollowed-out pumpkin gourd.

For Richard Nixon the bottom line was this: he had beaten the Franklins, and for this the bastards would never forgive him. So, proactively, he would never forgive them.

He capped it off with one more twist of the knife.

After Harry Truman's surprise upset of Tom Dewey in November of 1948, space was opened up for fresh Republican faces. Nixon, soundly reelected in a Democratic year on the strength of his Red-hunting, was a comer. On Jan-uary 25, 1950, as Hiss was sentenced to five years in Lewisburg Penitentiary for perjury, one of Hiss's fellow foreign-policy mandarins, President Truman's moralistic secretary of state, Dean Acheson, offered his disgraced fellow

Franklin a few words of Christian charity. "I do not intend to turn my back on Alger Hiss," he said at a press conference, citing the Sermon on the Mount: "I was a stranger, and ye took me in: Naked, and ye clothed me; I was sick, and ye visited me; I was in prison, and ye came unto me."

The very next day, in the most stem-winding speech of his congressional career, Richard Nixon said that Dean Acheson's words were sacrilege. The oration was called "The Hiss Case—a Lesson for the American People." The lesson was that Alger Hiss's conviction indicted Harry Truman himself—who "threw the great power and prestige of his office against the Hiss investigation" even after it was apparent Hiss was guilty. The secretary of state (whose law firm had turned Richard Nixon down after he graduated from Duke) had thrown the power and prestige of his office behind Hiss after he had been convicted. That was just how those liberals were. They coddled traitors. They invoked the Holy Name to do so. They traduced Americans' moral values.

Ingeniously, Richard Nixon had deployed the Hiss case to make himself the debating partner of the president. He was now an undisputed leader of a leaderless Republican Party. For a man in Congress only three years, it was a stunning accomplishment.

Then two weeks later a senator from Wisconsin, also in Congress only four years, announced to the ladies of the Wheeling, West Virginia, Women's Republican Club that scores of Communists were "still working and shaping the policy at the State Department." Large tracts of Joseph McCarthy's speech were borrowed outright from Nixon's peroration. The pitch Nixon had spent years setting up, McCarthy hit out of the park. The bastard.

Though Nixon would eventually get his revenge.

In California that summer, people were telling the Republican senatorial candidate to drop the issue of Communism as yesterday's news. In the injunction, Richard Nixon spotted an opening. It gave him a chance to look brave. "I have been advised not to talk about Communism," he would begin. "But I am going to tell the people anyway."

He had put his finger to the wind: the people were more afraid than ever. China had joined the Red bloc; America was at war with North Korea (and was soon fighting Chinese troops); the Soviet Union had exploded its own nuclear bomb (the nation would soon learn that spies at Los Alamos had helped). So much, also, for Harry Truman's "red herring": his attorney general, Tom Clark, now warned that Communists "are everywhere—in factories, offices, butcher shops, on street corners, in private businesses—and each carries in himself the germs of death for society."

That kind of language helped explain the reticence of those overpolite souls who were telling Nixon to lay off the issue. To attempt to harness these foul political winds was not a fit pursuit for statesmen. Nixon wasn't hearing it. A stream of liberal Democrats fell to Red-baiting conservative Democrats in primaries that spring. George Smathers beat Florida senator Claude Pepper by accusing him of being a "sexagenarian," committing "nepotism" with his sister-in-law, openly proud of a sister who Smathers said was a "thespian." He also pointed out that Pepper had been a Harvard classmate of Alger Hiss's.

Nixon marked it well: in the fever swamps of the Red Scare, fears of sexual and political irregularity were deeply intertwined. Hints of sexualized threat suffused his Senate campaign. He promised chivalry: "I am confronted with an unusual situation. My opponent is a woman. . . . There will be no name-calling, no smears, no misrepresentations in this campaign" (which he was apparently admitting were par for the course in campaigns involving men). Then he promptly broke his pledge. Congresswoman Helen Gahagan Douglas's Franklin credentials, Hollywood chapter, came partly through her husband, the handsome, mustachioed leading man Melvyn Douglas. Though from the sound of Nixon's campaign you would think she was married to Alger Hiss. "Pink right down to her underwear," he called her, as if she were Elizabeth Bentley. That was hard to forget. So were the five hundred thousand flyers Nixon sent out that tied Douglas to Representative Vito Marcantonio, a backbencher who represented a Bronx district that was one of the poorest in the nation. The mailer, sent out on pink paper, dubbed him "the notorious Communist party-line Congressman from New York" and said Helen Gahagan Douglas "voted the same as Marcantonio 354 times."

Nixon himself had voted "exactly as" Marcantonio had in the triple digits himself. Douglas tried to point this out. It didn't matter. The explanations were complicated. The smear was simple. The more Douglas tried to wriggle free, the more she sounded like—Alger Hiss. Just as she was supposed to. On the stump, Nixon intimated the stakes: the Russians were on the verge of attacking the West Coast through Alaska, aided and abetted by a domestic fifth column, ordered by Moscow to start "a reign of terror if we ever cross swords with Russia"—power-plant sabotage, food contamination, seizing arsenals. Maybe, just maybe, he hinted, this graceful and well-spoken Helen Gahagan Douglas had something to do with that fifth column. This was not the time for nuance.

Soon enough, she wounded herself by her own hand. "Thou Shalt Not Bear False Witness," ran the headline of her full-page response ad. She thought she was playing good cards. She was actually handing another pot to Nixon. Now he could play his favorite role: the wounded innocent. Helen Gahagan Douglas *had* voted 354 times with Vito Marcantonio. And here she was citing Scripture to call *him* a liar—just like that Dean Acheson.

It was the thinnest of gruel. But deciding to pull one lever in a voting booth instead of another is not necessarily a thick decision. Richard Nixon repeated his calumnies and repeated them and repeated them until they stuck: "Don't Vote the Red Ticket, Vote the Red, White, and Blue Ticket."

"Be an American, Be for Nixon." "If You Want to Work for Uncle Sam Instead of Slave for Uncle Joe, Vote for Richard Nixon." Liberals cried foul. Nixon turned that into a recommendation: "The commies didn't like it when I smash into Truman for his attempt to cover up the Hiss case . . . but the more the commies yell, the surer I am that I'm waging an honest American campaign."

He won his honest American campaign seven points ahead of every other Republican on the ticket, in a state where Democrats outnumbered registered Republicans by a million. Richard Nixon, thirty-seven years old, was now California's senator-elect in an upset.

Though there were unexpected repercussions.

A new senator can expect to get invited to all the best Georgetown parties. At one of them, thrown by Joseph Alsop, brother and fellow columnist to Stewart Alsop, Nixon sank himself deep in a regally plush armchair, after Mrs. Alsop gathered the evidence by which she soon would indict him to the world as "wooden and stiff . . . terribly difficult to talk to . . . a terrible dancer to boot." W. Averell Harriman, son of the railroad baron, known to one and all as Ambassador for his service as Roosevelt's special envoy to Europe, wartime emissary to the Soviet Union, then ambassador to the Court of St. James's, was announced. He had traveled to California that campaign season to help Helen Gahagan Douglas. He was hard of hearing. At least that was the excuse, after he spotted Nixon, when the words tumbled from his mouth at a volume that hardly befitted a gentleman:

"I will not break bread with that man!"

He stalked out. The act was loud enough for *tout* Georgetown to hear.

Next, Richard Nixon clawed his way to his party's second-highest job. California's Republican Party in 1952, like Republican organizations elsewhere, was split between followers of the conservative Senate warhorse Robert Taft and the internationalist darling of the Republican Party's Franklins, General Eisenhower. Early in his House career Richard Nixon had received the remarkable opportunity to join the commission assembled by veteran Massachusetts representative Christian Herter to travel to Europe to assess its postwar reconstruction needs, and ended up breaking with the Republican conservative wing's deep and abiding suspicion of entangling alliances with the Old World to support the Marshall Plan. He became an Eisenhower partisan early on in the 1952 nomination maneuverings.

The new senator was already grinding out extra-credit work in the form of an endless round of fund-raising speeches for his party. He appeared as "a Republican meld of Paul Revere and Billy Sunday," wrote conservative journalist Ralph de Toledano, who followed him on the road. (Though the liberal Brooklyn congressman Emanuel Celler saw him as "an inept, naive, Piltdown statesman . . . a maladjusted purblind Throttlebottom hoax of a statesman.") Toledano was writing a book about the Hiss case that put Nixon at its center, as the story's hero. Ike read the book and liked the cut of the young man's jib. The people running the political neophyte Eisenhower's campaign also began to take notice of Nixon's efforts and soon held out for him the chance of a lifetime.

California's convention votes were pledged to a favorite son, Governor Earl Warren—whom Nixon, conveniently, hated. The delegation traveled from California to the Chicago convention in a custom train called the Earl Warren Special. Nixon boarded halfway through, at Denver. It was something a clever Hollywood screenwriter might dream up: move the plot along by introducing a new passenger who knows something—or is assumed to know something—that those already cooped up incommunicado on a speeding train do not. All the way to Chicago, Senator Nixon sedulously ambled from car to car, imparting what his interlocutors could only assume was established fact: that Eisenhower had the convention wrapped up and that loyalty to Warren was a waste. Saying so helped make it so. Eisenhower needed California to win the nomination. Nixon had been tendered a deal by Eisenhower's top managers, Tom Dewey, Herbert Brownell, and General Lucius Clay: win the Earl Warren Special's passengers away from Earl Warren after the first ballot, and they would try to make him the running mate if Eisenhower pulled out the nomination. At a close and ugly convention, involving a last-minute deal between Warren and the Eisenhower forces, Eisenhower pulled it out. And Richard Nixon got the vice-presidential nod. Eisenhower introduced him to the Republican National Convention as "a man who has a special talent and ability to ferret out any kind of subversive influence wherever it may be found and the strength and persistence to get rid of it."

Then he almost lost the job.

Eisenhower had never paid all that much attention to the man he signed off on as his number two; his sense of the man was casual enough to describe Richard Nixon as someone who "did not persecute or defame." It is hard to say when he changed his mind, or exactly how much, or even to what extent the famous news report of the liberal *New York Post* on September 18— "Secret Nixon Fund: Secret Rich Men's Trust Keeps Nixon in Style Far Beyond His Salary"—precipitated his ambivalence. What is certain is that Eisenhower was willing to cut his boy adrift, like a distant and unloving father, drowning a son.

On the campaign trail, the vice-presidential candidate had learned to marshal special vigor on a favorite Eisenhower theme: the Truman administration's alleged corruption, "gangsters getting favors from government." If the rot could "only be chopped out with a hatchet," he would say, "then let's call for a hatchet" (a psychobiographer might recall the hatchet with which young Richard smacked the pollywog boy in 1920). Soon several reporters discovered that some Southern California businessmen, of the sort that had originally boosted him on the Committee of 100, had paid for Senator Nixon's political travels in 1951 and 1952. The *Post* broke the story.

There wasn't that much to worry about, necessarily. The "secret fund" wasn't really secret; it wasn't illegal; it wasn't even, really, unethical—or anything worse than the fund the Democratic standard-bearer, Adlai Stevenson, kept for himself, as Nixon immediately suspected when Stevenson didn't join the pile-on despite his reputation for unimpeachable probity. Handled artfully—as, say, Nixon's dark maestro Murray Chotiner would have handled it—the hatchet could have boomeranged right back into Adlai Stevenson's skull. The matter certainly wasn't something to threaten kicking someone off a campaign for—not least because replacing a vice-presidential candidate halfway through might do more damage than standing fast.

The affair turned out to become another opportunity for Richard Nixon to endure a slow, soiling humiliation. The worst, in fact, of his life.

That day, September 18, Nixon was harassed about the fund by campaign crowds spiked with heckling Democrats; but he had no problem handling that. The next, a Friday, he was harassed by the *New York Herald Tribune*. And that was a crushing blow. The *Herald Tribune,* the house organ of the Wall Street wing of the Republican Party, was not an ordinary newspaper to Richard Nixon. In the Hiss case, it had been his Franklin seal of approval (and if there is one thing an Orthogonian secretly craves, it is a Franklin seal of approval). Nixon had fed their ace Washington correspondent Bert Andrews scoops in exchange for shoe-leather work that let Nixon keep control of the inquiry. Now "Tom Dewey's paper" editorialized that Richard Nixon should offer his resignation. Eisenhower hadn't even bothered to contact him to discuss the matter. Apparently, this editorial *was* Eisenhower's discussion of the matter—the signal that Nixon was supposed to resign. Nixon kept on campaigning, through the Pacific Northwest, through the heckling and the sound of rattling coins; people dressed like beggars, braying, "Nickels for poor Nixon."

He was not without his Orthogonians. A Nixon-baiter held a sign reading SHHH! ANYONE WHO MENTIONS THE $16,000 IS A COMMUNIST; Nixon's fans beat him to a pulp, jeering, naturally, "Dirty Communist!" Little consolation for the *Herald Tribune*'s death sentence, hanging there over his head. When the day's appearances were over, Nixon was left to his agony. It was made worse after he learned that Eisenhower had just told reporters, "Of what avail is it for us to carry on this crusade against this business of what has been going on in Washington if we aren't ourselves as clean as a hound's tooth?" The statement was on background. But newsmen knew enough to go on the record as quickly as possible—the radio broadcasters, immediately—with their sage predictions of Nixon's imminent resignation. Publicly, Eisenhower kept his counsel, letting Nixon twist in the wind. That ordeal continued for three full days.

Late Sunday afternoon Nixon sat in a Portland hotel suite, brooding over whether his meteoric political ascent was over. His campaign doctor massaged his aching back in an attempt to cut its Gordian knots. A wire from his mother came: she was praying for him. Nixon broke into tears. Then he went and gave a rousing after-dinner speech. Usually politicians did not campaign on the Sabbath. But Nixon tended to work harder than most candidates. This speech was to the Temple Beth Israel Men's Club, and it wasn't the Sabbath for them.

He conferred with his aides in his suite until it was Monday. At 3 a.m. he spent two hours alone, brooding, methodically reviewing his options. He decided, finally, to hang on for dear life—to figure out his own hand to play. The Eisenhower string-pullers had given him the opportunity to go on TV to explain himself. Eisenhower, for his part, still cruelly refused to indicate what Nixon should say one way or the other. It was cowardly. The tacit demand was that Nixon go on TV and resign.

So Nixon decided to fight dirty.

He was offered an open slot on Monday night, after Lucille Ball's phenomenally popular situation comedy. Nixon said that wouldn't give him enough time to prepare. Milton Berle was on Tuesdays. He was phenomenally popular, too. Nixon chose the half hour after that.

The delay proved fortunate: it gave the public time to absorb that day's report that Adlai had his own secret fund, and that a law firm and an accounting firm had completed reports confirming that Nixon's fund was aboveboard and legal.

And so, on Tuesday evening at the NBC studio in Los Angeles' El Capitan Theater, on a stage set built to look like a suburban middle-class den— Richard Nixon did what he had to do. A camera locked in on his business card, a makeshift title screen. The red light went on. The senator went live. Not even General Eisenhower, who was getting telegrams running three to one that Richard Nixon should be dumped, knew what he was going to say. The telegrams were important: Eisenhower had gone on the record that he would make his recommendation based on the number of favorable messages that Richard Nixon's little show inspired.

To understand what Richard Nixon would now do, think yourself into his shoes.

Choose the part of your past that feels most vulnerable.

Take twenty-four hours to prepare.

Wait for the red light, then look into the camera and convince the largest audience in the medium's history why your conduct regarding same supports the judgment that you are beyond reproach. In one half hour, exactly.

And do it practically without notes.

"My fellow Americans," Richard Nixon began.

"I come before you tonight as a candidate for the vice presidency and as a man whose honesty and integrity have been questioned."

And off he went: "I am sure that you have read the charges, and you have heard it, that I, Senator Nixon, took eighteen thousand dollars from a group of my supporters."

The technical value of the financial accounting that followed was highly debatable. It would be highly debated. His account of smears the press supposedly piled upon him during the Hiss case and after was even more so. This would be debated, too. The insiders on the campaign trains noticed the nice little defensive jab at Stevenson: "I would suggest that under the circumstances . . . Mr. Stevenson should come before the American people as I have." Then they marveled at the haymaker he landed upon, of all people, dear old Ike: ". . . because, remember, a man who's to be president . . . must have the confidence of all the people." It was subtle, but Nixon was reminding his padrone, this spotless man, that he also had a financial impropriety on his hands: a squirrelly tax decision he had won concerning the proceeds from his memoirs. That was the dirty part of the job. Now Eisenhower couldn't disavow Nixon without being right there on the hook with him.

That was clever. But that wasn't what delivered the masses' telegrams. What delivered the telegrams were the stories. These, too, left plenty of room for dispute. "I worked my way through college," he said—he hadn't; "I guess I'm entitled to a couple of battle stars" from the war—he wasn't; his wife "was born on St. Patrick's Day"—she was born the day *before* St. Patrick's Day.

He wound up for the conclusion with more accountancy: "I own a 1950 Oldsmobile car. . . . We have our furniture. We have no stocks and bonds of any type. . . . Now that is what we have. What do we owe? Well, in addition to the mortgages, the twenty-thousand-dollar mortgage on the house in Washington and the ten-thousand-dollar one on the house in Whittier, I owe forty-five hundred dollars to the Riggs bank in Washington, D.C., with interest four and a half percent. I owe thirty-five hundred dollars to my parents."

Admitting on national TV he owed his parents money. That had to sting.

"Well, that's about it. That's what we have and that's what we owe. It isn't very much but Pat and I have the satisfaction that every dime we've got is honestly ours." (Take *that*, Adlai Stevenson, rich man's son.)

"I should say this—that Pat doesn't have a mink coat."

(From time to time, the camera had cut away to Pat, gazing at him adoringly off to one side in an armchair, tight-lipped.)

"But she does have a respectable Republican cloth coat. And I always tell her that she'd look good in anything."

Then he brought up one more asset.

"One other thing I probably should tell you, because if I don't, they'll probably be saying this about me, too. We did get something—a gift—after the election.

"A man down in Texas heard Pat on the radio mention the fact that our two youngsters would like to have a dog. And, believe it or not, the day before we left on this campaign trip we got a message from Union Station in Baltimore saying they had a package for us. We went down to get it.

"You know what it was?

"It was a little cocker spaniel dog in a crate that he sent all the way from Texas. Black-and-white-spotted. And our little girl—Tricia, the six-year-old—named it Checkers. And you know the kids love that dog, and I just want to say this right now, that regardless of what they say about it, we're going to keep it."

It became the obsession of his adversaries, that line about the cocker spaniel in what went down in history as the "Checkers Speech." They took this part for the whole. The liberal Catholic journal *Commonweal* called it "a cheap attempt to exploit decent human motives." But Richard Nixon's people could take a part for the whole as well. They interpreted the puppy story just as Nixon intended it: as a jab at a bunch of bastards who were piling on, kicking a man when he was down, a regular guy, just because they could do it and he couldn't fight back. *What will they dream up to throw at me next? To take away my little girl's puppy dog?* They, too, had mortgages, just like Richard Nixon. They, too, had cars that were not quite as nice as they might have liked—not nice enough to impress the neighbors, certainly. They, too, had worked hard as he had, their hard work not always noticed, sometimes disparaged. The agony of having to grovel to justify oneself just to keep one's job: they had been there, too.

And they, too, would dread the prospect, as Richard Nixon had truly, truly dreaded it—he collapsed into tears once more when the ordeal was safely over—of being forced to justify their financial affairs, their financial decisions, their financial *vulnerabilities,* to their fathers, be they surrogate or otherwise, as if they weren't even really grown-ups at all.

"There goes my actor," his high school drama teacher, in whose productions Nixon had excelled, pronounced to her TV in disgust. Though this wasn't just an act. And it wasn't just sincere. It was a hustle; and it was from the heart. It was all those things, all at the same time.

And it worked.

The telegrams poured in: over 2 million of them, and according to one careful sample, only 0.4 percent of them negative. The 99.6 percent were the ones who had let themselves be drafted as Orthogonians—the ones who felt the speech in their hearts. The ones Nixon had called out to when he misquoted Abraham Lincoln: "God must have loved the common people; he made so many of them." And those so convinced—that they were common; that Nixon was common; that Nixon was being persecuted and that they, too, were somehow being persecuted because they, too, were common— were the ones who carried the day. General Eisenhower was forced to take back his errant son with open arms. Richard Nixon had won.

The people who knew it was a hustle—Ambassador Harriman's people—were flummoxed. A nickname was coined right around this time to describe these sorts of folks, affixed specifically to the man who was taken as their greatest tribune, Adlai Stevenson: eggheads. There weren't all that many televisions in America then, though the number of sets was growing exponentially, as part and parcel of America's postwar economic boom. These were the types who took pride in themselves, already, for *not* owning them. They knew enough to realize that the television commercials that exploited the cuteness of puppies were the most fiendishly effective ones. A Nixon associate would later characterize them as an effete corps of impudent snobs. They did not view themselves thus. They saw themselves as the guardians of American decency. Liberals now hated Richard Nixon. He had hit them where it hurt. "Dick Nixon," as one especially astute columnist observed of the Checkers Speech in its immediate wake, "has suddenly placed the burden of old-style Republican aloofness on the Democrats." A Stevensonian liberal could be defined as someone who quailed at that very thought—and even more, who panicked to the point of neurosis at the possibility that it was shared by 99.6 percent of Richard Nixon's audience. The whole business enraged them. It also helped define them: right then and there, hating Richard Nixon became a central part of the liberal creed.

"The man who the people of the sovereign state of California believed was actually representing them," the *Sacramento Bee* editorialized, was actually "the pet and protégé of rich Southern Californians . . . their subsidized front man, if not their lobbyist." This "kept man," chimed in the *New Republic,* was bamboozling people who were not rich into believing that he was their tribune. The pundit Walter Lippmann called it "the most demeaning experience my country has ever had to bear. . . . With all the magnification of modern electronics, simply mob law." The in-house humorist of Stevensonian liberalism, Mort Sahl, suggested a sequel. Nixon could read the Constitution aloud to his two daughters. Pat, his devoted helpmeet, could sit within camera view, gazing lovingly upon him while knitting an American flag.

Liberal intellectuals were betraying themselves in a moment of crisis for liberal ideology. They saw *themselves* as tribunes of the people, Republicans as the people's traducers. Liberals had written the New Deal social and labor legislation that let ordinary Americans win back a measure of economic security. Then liberals helped lead a war against fascism, a war conservatives opposed, and then worked to create, in the postwar reconversion, the consumer economy that built the middle class, a prosperity for ordinary laborers unprecedented in the history of the world. *Liberalism* had done that. Now history had caught them in a bind: with the boom they had helped build, ordinary laborers were becoming ever less reliably downtrodden, vulnerable to appeal from the Republicans. The pollster Samuel Lubell was the first to recognize it: "The inner dynamics of the Roosevelt coalition have shifted from those of getting to those of keeping."

Their liberal champions developed a distaste for them. One of the ways it manifested itself was in matters of style. The liberal capitalism that had created this mass middle class created, in its wake, a mass culture of consumption. And the liberals whose New Deal created this mass middle class were more and more turning their attention to critiquing the degraded mass culture of cheap sensation and plastic gadgets and politicians who seemed to cater to this lowest common denominator—public-relations-driven politicians who catered to only the basest and most sentimental emotions in men. Who resembled in certain formal respects—didn't they?—the fascists who'd won power most effectively with, as Adolf Hitler bragged, a radio microphone. Now came the boob tube, "a vast wasteland," as Adlai Stevenson's administrative assistant Newton Minow would later say, when he became FCC chair. A working class that was no longer poor, but seemed so much poorer in spirit. And its tribunes: men like . . . Richard Nixon.

That a new American common man was emerging who, thanks to men like Nixon, thought he could be a Republican—to liberals this idea that the "comfortable" class associated with Richard Nixon was a class of victims was enraging. "We do not detect any desperate impoverishment in a man who has bought two homes, even if his Oldsmobile is two years old," huffed the *New York Post.*

(*Oldsmobile:* here was a word to linger on. Not a stylish car. Kind of tacky even if it was expensive—maybe even tackier because it *was* expensive. Kind of—*common.* Though not in an Aaron Copland, "Fanfare for the Common Man," sort of way. A Richard Nixon kind of car.)

In 1950 Nixon's campaign took out ads promising "Electric clocks, Silex coffeemakers with heating units—General Electric automatic toasters—silver salt and pepper shakers, sugar and creamer sets, candy and butter dishes, etc., etc.," to everyone who answered "Win with Nixon!" when his or her phone rang. Richard Nixon was now the poster child for this deranged new politics of mass consumption. It felt divorced from any mature and reasoned and logical analysis of who *really* ran things in society, who were the real economic beneficiaries, how power really worked, elite liberals thought. This was a new style of political demagoguery, a kind of *right-wing* populism, almost. This hucksterism. Hadn't Richard Nixon worked as a carnival barker as a boy in Prescott, Arizona? Hadn't the organizer of the Committee of 100, an advertising executive, proclaimed, upon discovering Richard Nixon in 1946, "This is salable merchandise!"? They would laugh at Nixon's line from the so-called Kitchen Debate with Nikita Khrushchev in Moscow in 1959: "There are some instances where you may be ahead of us, for example, in the development of the thrust of your rockets for the investigation of outer space; there may be some instances in which we are ahead of you—in color television, for instance." Soft-drink CEO Donald Kendall would later get Nixon his job at a New York law firm in 1963 as quid pro quo for the vice president's arranging for Khrushchev to be photographed with a bottle of Pepsi. Here was something to worry the liberals: Did the American way of life they had fought for come down to *color television*? Did freedom come down to Pepsi-Cola? They would laugh when he became president and named as his chief of staff a former J. Walter Thompson advertising executive. Could freedom be sold the way Bob Haldeman had sold Disneyland and Black Flag?

Let them laugh. Richard Nixon was back on the ticket. He now turned to assailing Secretary of State Dean Acheson for his "color blindness, a form of pink eye toward the Communist threat in the United States"; Adlai Stevenson for his "Ph.D. from Dean Acheson's College of Cowardly Communist Containment"; and Acheson, Stevenson, and President Truman for having become "traitors to the high principles in which many of the nation's Democrats believe." Dwight D. Eisenhower won the election; Richard Nixon became the nation's vice president at thirty-nine years old; and Checkers became a watershed for the way Americans were coming to divide themselves.

After Checkers, to the cosmopolitan liberals, hating Richard Nixon, congratulating yourself for *seeing through* Richard Nixon and the elaborate political poker bluffs with which he hooked the sentimental rubes, was becoming part and parcel of a political identity.

And to a new suburban mass middle class that was tempting itself into Republicanism, admiring Richard Nixon was becoming part and parcel of a political identity based on seeing through the pretensions of the cosmopolitan liberals who claimed to know so much better than you (and Richard Nixon) what was best for your country. This side saw everything that was most genuine in Nixon, everything that was most brave—who saw the Checkers Speech for what it *also* actually was, not just a hustle but also an act of existential heroism: a brave refusal to let haughty "betters" have their way with him. They were no less self-congratulatory than the liberals.

Call the America they shared—the America over whose direction they struggled for the next fifty years, whose meaning they continue to contest even as this book goes to press, even as you hold it in your hands—by this name: Nixonland. Study well the man at Nixonland's center, the man from Yorba Linda. Study well those he opposed. The history that follows is their political war.

CHAPTER THREE

The Stench

IN 1953, CERTAIN OF THE MORE ELEVATED INTERPRETERS OF AMERICAN politics began to spy a becoming new dignity in Richard Nixon now that he had been inaugurated vice president. The psychology made sense. Who wanted to admit that America now had a blackguard a heartbeat away from the presidency?

President Eisenhower sent Nixon on a diplomatic mission to Asia, a region rendered strategically crucial by the deteriorating position of our allies the French against the Communist insurgency in the colony of Vietnam. Upon his return, the press greeted him as a statesman. It wasn't the first time Nixon returned from travels to find his stature enhanced; that would have been when a newly mature young man returned to Whittier after helping his mother nurse tubercular patients in Arizona. Then, when the young lawyer came back from the war to practice law in Whittier. Stature-enhancing trips to distant lands would always be a Nixon staple.

This time, however, he quickly tumbled from grace. It came of a dirty job. Joseph McCarthy had once been indulged by the Eisenhower administration as a useful, if distasteful, political asset. When he took on the army, he had to be cut loose for going too far. The task fell to the party's *other* most prominent Red-baiter. Nixon had the credibility to shiv the cur without alienating the Republicans' rank-and-file Red-baiters in the bargain. For the Republican Franklins, there was an added bonus: they could hold themselves further aloof from Richard Nixon, using the stench of the task they had just delegated to him as their excuse.

So Nixon embraced the stench. In his most-watched TV appearance since he'd introduced the world to his cocker spaniel, on March 13, 1954, he said that Joseph McCarthy just didn't play fair.

"I have heard people say, 'Well, why all this hullabaloo about being fair when you're dealing with a gang of traitors?'" he said, in his by then trademark tones of histrionic solemnity. "'After all, they're a bunch of rats.' Well, I agree they're a bunch of rats, but just remember this. When you go out to shoot rats, you have to shoot straight, because when you shoot wildly, it only means that the rat may get away more easily. You make it easier on the rat."

It was the eve of the 1954 congressional election season. On the campaign trail for his party's congressional candidates, Nixon did some wild shooting of his own. McCarthy originally claimed dozens of subversives had infiltrated the Truman administration. Nixon claimed the new Republican administration had rousted "thousands." (Eisenhower's civil service commissioner later admitted they hadn't found a single one.) Nixon also claimed that the new White House occupants had "found in the files a blueprint for socializing America." Reporters asked him for a copy. Nixon claimed he had been speaking metaphorically. Though he also claimed possession of "a secret memorandum of the Communist Party" proving "it is determined to conduct its program within the Democratic Party."

He made no mistake about whom the Communists' vector would be. Adlai Stevenson was also chasing around the country campaigning for Democratic congressional victories, in pursuit of which Nixon accused him of "attack[ing] with violent fury the economic system of the United States." Nixon hated Stevenson. He was another of his perfect enemies. Nixon's dad bragged incessantly of once having met a president; Stevenson's father, the son of a vice president, was dandled on a president's knee. Young Dick begged a newspaper for a job; Little Adlai's family owned a newspaper. Accomplishments seemed to attach themselves to Stevenson without any visible exertion on his part. The contrast couldn't be more stark.

Nixon traveled almost as many miles as the administration's political emissary in 1954 as he had as its diplomatic emissary in 1953. No national figure had ever worked so hard in an off-year election. The *Washington Post*'s Herb Block commemorated the accomplishment in a famous political cartoon. It depicted a cluster of Republican fat cats gathering around Nixon with WELCOME signs as he emerged, suitcase plastered with stickers from his many stops, from a manhole cover. He was traveling around the country — get it? — by sewer.

The next year the sewer dweller would get another opportunity to recover the mantle of statesman when President Eisenhower was struck by a heart attack. Nixon took on emergency duties. Political allies urged him to press his temporary advantage for long-term gain. Nixon avoided the temptation. His maturity impressed even his enemies. But it didn't burnish his public image. He couldn't catch the break. Now when people talked about the vice president, it was in the context of death. The president himself, fearing for his own mortality and perhaps the nation's, summoned Nixon and tried to get him to take a cabinet post. The next spring, in 1956, Eisenhower was laid up in the hospital again, losing several inches of his small intestine to an unpleasant malady called ileitis. Nixon's enemies read in the frailties of the old man's face the specter of a President Nixon. Their proliferating plots against him made "Dump Nixon" the political catch-phrase of 1956.

Nixon maneuvered his way past the threat. He once more embraced the stench.

Stevenson ran again as the Democratic candidate. The courtly type, he couldn't campaign directly against a dying war hero; instead he ran against the man who might replace him. And he did it in a singularly uncourtly fashion. He wrote his friend John Kenneth Galbraith, the (courtly) Harvard economist, "I want you to write the speeches against Nixon. You have no tendency to be fair." Galbraith acknowledged that as a "noble compliment." A private DNC memo made explicit the Democrats' 1956 strategy: dump *on* Nixon. "We are fortunate in the fact that an amazingly large segment of the population, and even of his own party, seems to dislike and mistrust him instinctively."

Went one of the Stevenson/Galbraith jeremiads: "As a citizen more than a candidate, I recoil at the prospect of Mr. Nixon as a custodian of this nation's future, as guardian of the hydrogen bomb." Ran another: "Our nation stands at a fork in the political road. In one direction lies a land of slander and scare; the land of sly innuendo, the poison pen, the anonymous phone call and hustling, pushing, shoving; the land of smash and grab and anything to win. This is Nixonland. America is something different."

Of course, saying a President Nixon would unleash the bomb was also slander and scare, and spared not the innuendo. Adlai Stevenson and his learned speechwriter had coined a useful word, *Nixonland.* They just did not grasp its full resonance. They described themselves outside its boundaries. Actually, they were citizens in good standing. Stevenson defined himself by his high-mindedness, said things like—from his 1952 acceptance speech— "What does concern me, along with thinking partisans of both parties, is not just winning this election, but *how* it is won. How well we can take advantage of this great quadrennial opportunity to debate the issues sensibly, and soberly." And yet it only stood to reason that if you believed your opponent was neither sensible nor sober and would do anything to win, and that his victory would destroy civilization, a certain insobriety was permissible to *beat* him.

Thus a more inclusive definition of Nixonland: it is the America where two separate and irreconcilable sets of apocalyptic fears coexist in the minds of two separate and irreconcilable groups of Americans. The first group, enemies of Richard Nixon, are the spiritual heirs of Stevenson and Galbraith. They take it as an axiom that if Richard Nixon and the values associated with him triumph, America itself might *end.* The second group are the people who wrote those telegrams begging Dwight D. Eisenhower to keep their hero on the 1952 Republican ticket. They believe, as did Nixon, that if the *enemies* of Richard Nixon triumph—the Alger Hisses and Helen Gahagan

Douglases, the Herblocks and hippies, the George McGoverns and all the rest—America might end. The DNC was right: an amazingly large segment of the population disliked and mistrusted Richard Nixon instinctively. What they did not acknowledge was that an amazingly large segment of the population also trusted him as their savior. "Nixonland" is what happens when these two groups try to occupy a country together. By the end of the 1960s, Nixonland came to encompass the entire political culture of the United States. It would define it, in fact, for the next fifty years.

Though we are getting ahead of ourselves.

The 1956 presidential campaign was rough on Richard Nixon. It wasn't the abuse—that he rather thrived on. It was a new task that Eisenhower thrust upon him. The president, running on a message of tail-finned peace and prosperity, commanded his pit bull just this once to "give 'em heaven." Frank Nixon's son found the advice awkward. Soothing bromides issuing from Nixonian lips tended to backfire; the image adjustment only reinforced the suspicion that Richard Nixon was only, well, *image.*

Reporters had coined a phrase to describe this purported "nice guy" in their midst: the "new Nixon." Adlai Stevenson heard that and unsheathed his dagger: "I don't wish for a moment to deprecate the vice president's new personality. . . . But I do wish that we might hear some word from him repudiating the irresponsible, the vindictive, and the malicious words so often spoken by the impostor who has been using his name all these years." Pat Nixon didn't help. Asked by a reporter if *she* had noticed a new Nixon, she replied, "He's the same. He'd never change."

Luckily when Stevenson began to gain, General Eisenhower gave Nixon license once more to breathe fire. (Nixon later recalled he felt "as if a great weight had been lifted from me.") Eisenhower was reelected in a landslide. Stevenson—who'd taken to uttering at the mealtime mention of Nixon's name, "Please! Not while I'm eating!"—wrote an anguished letter to a friend: "The world is so much more dangerous and wicked even than it was barely four years ago when we talked, that I marvel and tremble at the rapidity of this deterioration."

But Richard Nixon, you might say, did not win. For the first time since 1844, the party that won the White House captured neither house of Congress. Americans voted for the genial old general, the warm and wise national grandfather. They didn't vote for his party. Nixon, everyone knew, was the partisan on the team. *He* was blamed for the congressional losses.

In the spring of 1958 the second-term VP received another travel opportunity. They called them "goodwill tours," these Eisenhower administration junkets to shore up Cold War alliances. As regarded South and Central America, a semi-imperialist American sphere of influence since the imposi-

tion of the Monroe Doctrine, the naïveté of a hegemon lay behind the con-
ceit. Europe, after World War II, had been rewarded with the Marshall Plan:
its free nations would contribute to U.S. economic health as a prosperous
market for U.S. goods. South America's reward was NSC 144/1: instead of
direct economic aid, its leaders were to be patronizingly instructed "that
their own self-interest requires the creation of a climate which will attract
investment." South America was to be a repository of raw materials and
cheap labor. NSC 144/1 acknowledged a potential tension: "There is increasing popular demand for immediate improvement in the low living standards
of the masses, with the result that most Latin American governments are
under intense domestic political pressure to increase production and diver-
sify their economies." That was a bureaucrat's way of describing what
Guatemalan president Jacobo Arbenz Guzmán was doing: expropriating fal-
low lands of the United States Fruit Company and distributing it to landless
peasants. He modeled the program on the U.S. Homestead Act. He was
rewarded in 1954 with a CIA-led military coup.

Denizens of South America's more prestigious universities were well
versed in this history. As they were with Richard Nixon's warm and friendly
1955 visit with Arbenz's dictatorial successor, and Nixon's assertion that
"this is the first instance in history where a Communist government has been
replaced by a free one." And South America's more prestigious universities
were prominent on the itinerary of Richard Nixon in the spring of 1958.

He was harassed by Marxist demonstrators as soon as he made landfall.
It was brave when Nixon emerged from his car at the gates of the hemisphere's oldest university, in Lima, to address demonstrators bearing signs
like NIXON—MERCHANT OF WAR, NIXON PIRATE, and NIXON DOG. A thrown
rock grazed his throat.

Eisenhower dispatched a telegram: "Dear Dick, Your courage, patience,
and calmness in the demonstration directed against you by radical agitators
have brought you a new respect and admiration in our country." (The compliment felt backhanded, the implication being that he hadn't enjoyed respect
and admiration heretofore.)

In Caracas, agitators subjected his motorcade to a rain of stones. ("That
is a frightening sound, incidentally," Nixon later wrote, "the crack of rocks
against a closed car.") It looked like a mob attempt on his life. Nixon's Secret
Servicemen reached for their revolvers. Nixon displayed the kind of presence of mind for which battlefield commanders win medals: sensing that the
sound of a single shot might start a riot, he ordered the guns put away.
Rocks spiderwebbed the limousines' glass—shatterproof glass, the occupants could comfort themselves, until one of the shards socked the Venezue-
lan foreign minister in the eye. The motorcade escaped in a cloud of tear gas.
Nixon wrote, "I felt as though I had come as close as anyone could get, and
still remain alive." Eisenhower airlifted in two companies of marines and

dispatched a navy flotilla just in case. Nixon emerged a hero. His next motorcade bore him past the White House, one hundred thousand cheering bodies thronging the way. For weeks, wherever he went he got standing ovations. It was a new high in his life. For once he wasn't just a hero to Orthogonians. He was a hero to everyone.

The liberals at the *New Republic* suspected a hoax—a setup to build the popularity of the Republicans' presumptive 1960 nominee. "The nomination of Slippery Dick Nixon," they complained, "is not worth the dumbest doughface in the United States Army." The military maneuvers to protect him in the riots were code-named Operation Poor Richard. This was the embarrassing nickname Nixon had drawn in the wake of the Checkers Speech. Enemies of Richard Nixon, it seemed, lurked everywhere.

The high was promptly followed by another of his life's routine lows.

He hadn't wanted to go to South America; he had a bigger project on his plate. Everyone knew the Republican presidential nomination was his to lose. To secure his chance he would have to lead his party to a good showing in the off-year elections. But 1958 did not look to be a Republican year. A recession was in effect. Richard Nixon did everything within a vice president's puny power to loosen its grip. He joined the administration's liberal labor secretary, James Mitchell, to implore Eisenhower to cut taxes to stimulate job growth. Then Nixon had to ship out to the tropics on his goodwill trip. Eisenhower's right-wing former treasury secretary, George Humphrey, prevailed upon the president to choose fiscal conservatism instead. Nixon's temporary status as a hero upon his return from South America might prove a mess of pottage unless he could devise a strategy to *turn* 1958 into a Republican year.

It seemed like a good idea at the time for Richard Nixon to turn organized labor into a scapegoat for the nation's problems by urging antiunion right-to-work initiatives to be put on the ballot in seven states. You might not have expected Nixon's second-best solution to the problem of 1958 would be to sell out his ally for his first (Mitchell was staunchly anti-right-to-work). But Richard Nixon's ideological flexibility could be limitless. It was businessmen, not union workers, who formed the sturdiest portion of the Republican political base. Nineteen fifty-seven had been a year of dramatic televised hearings on mob racketeering in unions like the Teamsters. Nixon presumed popular disgust at unions would help the Republican candidates.

The miscalculation was severe. Right-to-work wasn't popular with a general public that understood how a strong labor movement had rocketed millions of voters into the middle class. It also further divided an already badly divided Republican Party. Traditionally the party in the White House loses a dozen or so House seats in an off-year election. This year they lost forty-seven. In Ohio and California, Democrats replaced Republicans in the statehouse. The class of Republican congressmen swept out had been the one swept in in 1946: Richard Nixon's class. And it was Richard Nixon, the *New York Times* pointed out, who "formulated the Republican campaign strategy."

Richard Nixon always had a reputation as an ugly campaigner. Now, for the first time, he had a reputation as a losing one, too.

Nineteen sixty. A presidential election lost by 0.1 votes per precinct in the United States provides the loser plenty of opportunities for reflection, a storehouse of memories to roll over in the mind's eye. Every last errant decision, each missed opportunity, every break that had it tumbled this way instead of that it would have made Richard Nixon the hero instead of the lonely man who spent the first half of 1961 alone in a Los Angeles apartment eating meals from soup cans as his girls finished out the school year back East—this torture of retrospection Richard Nixon would rewind for the rest of his life.

The memories of the Republican convention that was supposed to be his coronation—interrupted by an emergency flight to Manhattan so that the richest and most arrogant man in the world, Nelson Rockefeller, could dictate to him a rewrite of the Republican platform in exchange for his support.

Memories, from that convention, of the conservative-Republican rank and file that had so long been his champion breaking for an emotional, last-minute attempt to draft the wild-eyed, right-wing cowboy Barry Goldwater.

Memories of Eisenhower, asked if Richard Nixon, running as the candidate of experience, had come up with a single one of the administration's "major ideas," saying, "If you give me a week, I might think of one." (Eisenhower's problem coming up with one might have reflected that the projects Nixon focused on were top secret: working with the Dulles brothers to overturn regimes in Guatemala and Iran; advocating nuclear weapons to break the resistance at Dien Bien Phu.)

Memories of his mother, asked if *she* had noticed a "new Nixon," answering, "No, I never knew anyone to change so little."

Memories of Walter Cronkite, asking him on the CBS news, "There are some . . . who would say, 'I don't know what it is, but I just don't like the man; I can't put my finger on it; I just don't like him.' Would you have any idea what might inspire that kind of feeling on the part of anybody?"

Memories of Henry Luce, the imperious publisher of *Life,* getting cold feet and pulling at the last minute an article by Billy Graham that was to urge the evangelist's millions of devoted acolytes not to vote for a man just because he was "more handsome and charming."

And, above all, memories of that more handsome and charming man. Another perfect enemy.

John F. Kennedy's good fortune was not built of the kind of honest paternal toil whose signs were worn on a butcher's bloody shirt. Joseph Kennedy had been a financial speculator and a bootlegger (Richard Nixon's people didn't even drink). Richard Nixon had tried to win his future wife Pat's favor by driving her on her dates with *other* men; Kennedy blithely stole a wife seventeen years younger than Pat from her fiancé when he needed a family to display for his political career. Kennedy's 1946 congressional nomination required no supplication of social betters; Joseph Kennedy bought it, in installments, such as his $600,000 donation to the archdiocese of Boston ("Tip," Joe Kennedy told Thomas P. "Tip" O'Neill, JFK's successor in the House, "Never expect any appreciation from my boys. These kids have had so much done for them by other people that they just assume it's coming to them"). To establish a voting address in the district, Jack moved into a hotel. (Dick once lived in a hotel—during his first three months in Congress, when he couldn't find a decent family-size apartment on his congressional salary.) Then the Kennedy boys carelessly missed the filing deadline and availed themselves of a little light breaking and entering to get the papers on the pile by the opening of business the next morning. After failing to bribe the front-runner out of the race, Joseph Kennedy called in a chit with William Randolph Hearst to keep the man's name out of the newspaper. Another candidate, a city councilman named Joseph Russo, lost ground when Joe Kennedy hired a custodian with the same name to file. Jack Kennedy's opponents pinned $20 bills to their lapels—"Kennedy buttons." The joke was too cheap by more than half: the real amount of "walking around" money per Kennedy man was $50.

And they called Dick Nixon the dirty one.

They weren't unfriendly, these two young Turks of the Eightieth Congress; they weren't unlike each other. Both had lost an older brother (the charming one, the one originally destined for greatness). Both were ideologically flexible except when it came to hunting Reds; both had run as World War II veterans. When Kennedy acceded to the Senate in 1953, he drew an office across the hall from that body's constitutional officer, and they grew friendly. Though soon the corridor between their suites was a snarl of reporters, TV cameras, and swooning young Capitol Hill secretaries desperate to catch a glimpse of the bachelor senator voted the most handsome man in Congress.

In 1960, coming off his triumph outdebating the Soviet premier in Moscow, fresh from settling an epic steel strike, Nixon was the presidential election's odds-on favorite. Still he dwelled often on these matters of physical charisma. It suited his self-pity. When Walter Cronkite asked his embarrassing question about all the people who couldn't put their finger on why they disliked him, Nixon answered by granting the premise, concluding that it might be his appearance. "Oh, I get letters from women, for example, sometimes—and men—who support me," he said. "And they say, 'Why do you wear that heavy beard when you are on television?' Actually, I don't try, but I can shave within thirty seconds before I go on television and I still have a beard, unless we put some powder on, as we have done today."

A man wearing makeup. That surely was the wrong thing to say.

And everyone knows what happened next.

On Monday, September 26, the first presidential debate in the history of television was broadcast from the studios of WBBM-TV in Chicago. Kennedy was six points behind in the polls. At the studio, the challenger was the first one asked whether he would appreciate the services of a makeup artist. He refused. (He was bronzed from a recent stint campaigning in California, and his aides had already dabbed him with theatrical powder.) The champion, taking the bluff, refused in turn.

That was a problem.

In his convention acceptance speech four weeks earlier, Nixon had promised to "carry this campaign into every one of the fifty states between now and November eighth." It was a flourish designed to separate Nixon in voters' minds from enfeebled old Eisenhower. Nixon was knocking off states in the South at a handsome clip when he contracted a staph infection after banging his knee on a car door. His physicians counseled three weeks in the hospital. Newspaper editorialists urged the honorable course on his opponent: to cease campaigning for those three weeks. The Democrat sent a get-well message instead. (And they called Dick Nixon the dirty one.) Ill-advisedly, Nixon kept on knocking off states: Maryland and Indiana and Texas and California his first day out, Oregon and Idaho with a side trip up to Canada the second. The next day, between Grand Forks and Peoria, Richard Nixon caught a cold. Then as he crossed a tarmac in the rain, flew the red-eye to St. Louis, and struggled to connect with a hostile Democratic crowd of union machinists on three hours' sleep, the cold got worse. Then a scratchy-voiced peroration in New Jersey; then a hop to Roanoke for an open-air address that added another line to his crowded medical chart: a high fever, something to enjoy on the predawn flight back halfway across the continent to Omaha, Nebraska.

As the day of the debate approached, Nixon was swallowing drowsy-making antibiotics, but still losing sleep; fortifying himself against weight loss with several chocolate milk shakes a day, but still losing weight; losing color; adding choler. He looked pale, awful.

His staff offered practice sessions. Nixon barked that he already knew how to debate. He was underwhelmed by the event at any rate. "Television is not as effective as it was in 1952," he had told a journalist. "The novelty has worn off."

Kennedy prepared like a monk. The afternoon of the showdown, he capped off the last of three intensified practice sessions with a fortifying nap, piles of index cards covering him like a security blanket.

While Kennedy slept, Nixon campaigned in front of another hostile union crowd. His TV advisers became increasingly frenzied as the appointed hour approached; they were kept away from him, and weren't able to brief him on the debate format. Nixon took a single phone call of advice, from his vice-presidential candidate, Henry Cabot Lodge.

The hour arrived. For security, the candidates were driven directly inside the studio building. One wonders what distraction inspired Richard Nixon's awkward egress that ended with his smashing his bad knee once more on the car door's edge. His facial reaction was recorded for posterity: "white and pasty."

Kennedy emerged from his car looking in a producer's recollection like "a young Adonis." (That the young Adonis, but for a dangerous schedule of pharmaceuticals, was sick as an old man was for future generations to find out.) He kept his suit fresh by slipping into a robe. He walked out onto a terrace, sunlight dancing on his skin, paced back and forth, all coiled energy, punching his palm with his fist: the challenger.

In the other corner, the reigning heavyweight debating champion, weighing in at—

(Eight pounds less than it took to fill the shirt he was wearing.)

His people had begged Nixon to let them buy him a new one. He stubbornly refused. An aide had slathered a species of makeup over a portion of his face—a product called Lazy Shave, cadged at the last minute at a corner drugstore, to cover up his day's beard growth. The concession was no doubt ascribable to Herblock's infamous caricatures in the *Washington Post.* They'd rendered Nixon's "five-o'clock shadow" a national laughingstock.

In lieu of a boxing arena's bell, the sickeningly sweet strains of a jingle for Maybelline mascara. In lieu of a bout card, the smiling mug of Andy Griffith, star of the eponymous sitcom, a stalk of wheat between his lips, and the announcement that the program originally scheduled would not be seen that night.

(One wonders whether Richard Nixon's egghead enemies cringed in anticipatory dread at the irony. Andy Griffith had starred three years earlier in a film, *A Face in the Crowd,* partially inspired by the Checkers Speech, about a right-wing demagogue who harnessed the malign power of TV to cast a gullible nation under his spell with a show of slick and cynical sentimentality.)

Andy Griffith absented the screen. The panel of reporters introduced themselves. And Howard K. Smith of ABC intoned, "In this discussion, the first of a series of four joint appearances, the subject matter, it has been agreed, will be restricted to internal, or domestic, American matters." He called the Democrat to begin his opening statement; and the Democrat opened up, staring stalwartly into the camera, with a sucker punch.

And they called Dick Nixon the dirty one.

"We discuss tonight domestic issues. But I would not want that to be—

any implication to be given that this does not involve directly our struggle with Mr. Khrushchev for survival." Kennedy was bending past the breaking point the spirit of the two campaigns' formal agreement to focus the first debate on domestic issues and talking about what Nixon was not yet primed to discuss: foreign policy. The distraction was brilliant. It left Nixon with two immediate choices—calling the foul and looking as if he were ducking, or letting Kennedy get away with controlling the debate.

One thing he didn't do was counterpunch. It came, one suspected, of that phone call from Henry Cabot Lodge, the Boston Brahmin, the sort of Establishment grandee Richard Nixon had alternately been flailing against and kowtowing to his entire adult life. What Lodge told Nixon on the phone was "Erase the assassin image." Following this advice cut across every instinct that had made Richard Nixon a successful politician since 1946. But now he was running for *president*. Leader of the free world. Campaigning to join, if there was ever any way he could truly join, the *Establishment*—confidant of those mufti-clad dignitaries he met abroad, peer to the likes of Ambassador Averell Harriman. And does not every man who defines himself by his battle against the Franklins secretly wish to *be* a Franklin?

He had been campaigning as a statesman, the voice of sage experience. He would recite the number of meetings he had taken with the president (173), the times he had sat with the National Security Council (217), the countries he had visited (54), the presidents and prime ministers with whom he had had "extended discussion" (44, plus an emperor and a shah)—adding always, "incidentally, I have talked with Khrushchev." Friends advised him to smear his opponent's unpopular religion, his mendacity about his health, his loose interpretation of his marriage vows. Nixon forswore. He decided to debate as a gentleman.

Or perhaps not decided. Perhaps the only thing that coursed through Richard Nixon's head was the dull ache of stuffed sinuses, pain from his agonized knee, a heaviness born of too many chocolate milk shakes. Perhaps he wanted to fight; perhaps he just wasn't able.

Kennedy floated into an assessment of America's progress in that struggle against Communism, in rocking cadence: "I am not satisfied, as an American, with the progress we are making. . . .

"This is a great country, but I think it could be a greater country. And this is a powerful country, but it could be a more powerful country. . . .

"I'm not satisfied to have fifty percent of our steel mill capacity unused.

"I'm not satisfied when, last year, the United States had the lowest rate of economic growth of *any major industrialized society in the world*. . . .

"I'm not satisfied when we have over nine billion dollars' worth of food, some of it rotting, even though there is a hungry world"—Kennedy's intensity was mounting—"and even though four million Americans wait every month for a food package from the government which averages *five cents a day* per individual. I saw cases in West Virginia—here in the United States—where children took home part of their school lunch to feed their families. . . . I don't think we're meeting our obligations towards these Americans.

"I'm not satisfied when the Soviet Union is turning out twice as many scientists and engineers as we are.

"I'm not satisfied when many of our teachers are inadequately paid, or when our children go to school part-time shifts. I think we should have an educational system second to none.

"I'm not satisfied when I see men like Jimmy Hoffa, in charge of the largest union in the United States, still free."

(Are *you* satisfied, Dick?)

"These are all the things in our country that can make our society strong, or it can stand still. I think we can do better. . . .

"That is the obligation upon our generation. In 1933 Franklin Roosevelt said in his inaugural that this generation has a rendezvous with destiny. I think that our generation of Americans has the same rendezvous.

"The question now is, can freedom now be maintained under the most severe attack it has ever known? I think it can be. And I think that in the final analysis it depends on what *we—do—here.*"

Kennedy stabbed the podium at the words.

"I think it's time America started moving again."

He strode confidently back to his seat.

There had been a time when Richard Nixon had known just how to handle this sort of gambit. When Adlai Stevenson had made similar points in 1954, Nixon came back with, "He has attacked with violent fury the economic system of the United States." He could have put Kennedy on the defensive: "How dare he impugn all the hardworking teachers across this great land?"—something like that.

Instead, Nixon granted the point.

"The things that Senator Kennedy has said, many of us can agree with," he began his opening statement. "There is no question but that this nation cannot stand still." Though the point he was granting was a criticism of the administration of which he was an officer. "I subscribe completely to the *spirit* that Senator Kennedy has expressed tonight—the spirit that the United States *should* move ahead." His points were lugubrious, technical, as if he were rebutting in a high school debate: "We heard tonight the statement made that our growth in product last year was the lowest in the industrial world; that happened to be a recession year."

Then a glistening bead of sweat popped forth to illuminate the powderless little valley between his lower lip and chin.

"We are for programs which will see that our medical care for the aged is—are much better handled than at the present time"—the present time being that of his own administration.

At just that moment the camera cut to the face of John F. Kennedy, filling nearly every inch of the nation's tiny TV screens. It offered little to remark upon: it was without noticeable blemish. When the close-up was on Nixon, you could write a book: the discomfited fluttering of the eyelids (it made him look fey), the deeply etched lines of his jowls (one side was deeper than the other; the dimple in his tie was also off-center), the shadow of beard that bled through when he tilted his chin at the angle he used for emphasis on key points. There had been a time when Richard Nixon had known how to take advantage of his awkwardness—to make a face like Kennedy's stand in for every smooth, slick superior who had ever done an ordinary Joe wrong. That's what he had done with Alger Hiss. Not this time. This time, he kept on subscribing *completely* to the *spirit* that Senator Kennedy had expressed.

"I could give better examples," Nixon said at one point, then didn't; instead he moved to self-pity: "I know what it means to be poor, I know what it means to see people who are unemployed."

Perhaps ABC News's Bob Fleming began the question-and-answer portion out of sympathy by presenting Kennedy with a restatement of Richard Nixon's key campaign theme more aggressively than Nixon had been willing to make it: "The vice president, in his campaign, has said at times that you are naive and immature." It proved alarmingly easy to dispatch. "The vice president and I came to the Congress together, in 1946," Kennedy responded, then quickly bent things back to his will. "I think the question is, er, what are the *programs* that we advocate? What is the party record that we lead?

"I come out of the Democratic Party, which in this century has produced Woodrow Wilson and Franklin Roosevelt and Harry Truman. And which supported and sustained these programs which I've described tonight. Mr. Nixon comes out of the Republican Party. He was nominated by it. And it is a fact that through most of these last twenty-five years, the Republican leadership has opposed federal aid for education, medical care for the aged, development of the Tennessee Valley, development of our natural resources."

The camera now presented a Richard Nixon whose chin framed a single bead of sweat, like a big white pearl. Whose eyes shifted nervously before fixing into an expression that could only be described as a glower, and whose microphone, for some reason, squeaked like a chalkboard as he mustered his smug reply: "I have no comment." Then he swallowed, and the microphone picked that up—a gulp heard round the world. "I felt so sorry for Nixon's mother tonight," Mrs. Rose Kennedy later remarked.

"I think Mr. Nixon is an effective leader of his party"—(let's see Dick try to back out of that one)—"I hope he would grant me the same. The question before us is which point of view, and which party, do we want to lead the United States."

On the one hand Kennedy was up to something elementary: by inviting Nixon to confirm or deny his allegiance to the political party that had made him, Kennedy took advantage of the fact, obscured by Eisenhower's ecumenical popularity, that registered Democrats outnumbered Republicans by a great margin. On the other, he was doing something more profound—more alchemical, almost, than political. Repeatedly all evening, Kennedy held up the charge that he was *young* to the light—and rhetorically embraced it. Young, fresh, exciting, even risky: that, above all else, was the spirit that Senator Kennedy had expressed. Kennedy had just as effectively framed Nixon, about the same age he was, as the candidate of the old men—if not an old man himself—whenever Kennedy said something like (this on the Republicans' position on agriculture) "I do not therefore believe that this is a sharp enough breach with the past to give us any hope for the future."

The future. "I think we're ready to move," Kennedy said, in closing. "And it is to that great task, if we are successful, that we will address ourselves." Nixon closed sounding like a penny-pinching old shopkeeper: presidents must "not allow a dollar spent that could be better spent by the people themselves." Kennedy was spinning the emerging zeitgeist. Nixon was caught in its web. America entered the 1960s with an almost obsessive fixation on the notion of having entered a *new* decade—even a new age. The January issue of *Esquire* ran an essay by Arthur Schlesinger, "The New Mood in Politics," that began, "At periodic moments in our history, our country has paused on the threshold of a new epoch in our national life, unable for a moment to open the door, but aware that it must advance if it is to preserve its national vitality and identity. One feels that we are approaching such a moment now." *Life* ran a series taking stock of America's "national purpose." *Look,* on January 5: "How America Feels as It Enters the Soaring Sixties." These magazines were read by upward of 20 million people each week.

And how did America feel as it entered the soaring sixties? It is not too much to say: like the inheritor of a new world. The 1950s had been "a listless interlude, quickly forgotten, in which the American people collected itself for the greater exertions and higher splendors in the future," Arthur Schlesinger wrote. John Steinbeck said that month he noticed in the air "a nervous restlessness, a thirst, a yearning for something unknown." It wasn't just a Democratic mood. That same January, the *Los Angeles Times* introduced its newest political columnist: "The decade of the Sixties should be the most dynamic in the world's modern history. . . . That is why, beginning next Sunday, on our editorial pages, the *Times* will present a three-times-a-week column written especially for the *Times* by the leading conservative thinker in American public life, United States Senator Barry Goldwater." In the 1960s, even conservatives had to be "dynamic."

Nixon might subscribe to the "spirit of what Senator Kennedy said." But grant that, and he had given up everything. Kennedy made "leadership for the '60s" a slogan, made addressing his youth not just a defensive necessity but a virtue, preached *future* like it was a new religion: "The world is changing. The old ways will not do.... If we stand still here at home, we stand still around the world.... I promise you no sure solutions, no easy life.... If you are tired and don't want to move, then stay with the Republicans." EXPERIENCE COUNTS—that's what Richard Nixon's campaign posters read, below a photograph of his face. It wouldn't count as much as it used to. Just as in 1958, Richard Nixon had chosen the wrong issue on which to campaign. Kennedy styled himself the very incarnation of youth: of action, of charisma, of passion, risk-taking, stylishness and idealism and even heedlessness. Nixon, so recently the fair-haired boy of postwar politics—only four years older than Kennedy!—had let himself become the race's rumpled old man. At the ballot box it was almost a tie. On television, in retrospect, it looked as if John F. Kennedy had won in a landslide.

November 6, 1962, at the Beverly Hills Hilton, the first day of the rest of Richard Nixon's life. The first Tuesday after the first Monday in November every two years was always the first day of the rest of Richard Nixon's life. He spent this one morosely, in front of a television set, in a dressing gown and necktie. (Even in an elementary-school class photograph, he is one of only two boys wearing a necktie. "I never remember him ever getting dirty," his first-grade teacher recalled.)

H. R. "Bob" Haldeman, his campaign manager, was there, and John Ehrlichman, the logistics man; Congressman Pat Hillings, Nixon's successor in California's Twelfth District; and Murray Chotiner and a young publicist named Ron Ziegler. Pat Nixon was next door weeping. The returns were coming in. Nixon had just lost the California gubernatorial election.

Press aide Herb Klein entered. The press had just implored Klein to go upstairs and fetch his candidate for the traditional concession speech so they could file their stories and go home.

"They're all waiting," Klein said in a low grumble. "You've got to go down."

The press had recently become Nixon's enemy of first resort. Later generations would remember the media's relationship to Nixon as he had wanted people to remember it: as implacably hostile from the beginning. Not so. The *Los Angeles Times* had supported him back when he was an unknown. His working relationship with Bert Andrews of the *New York Herald Tribune* on the Hiss case helped make him a national figure. Even after the Checkers Speech, coverage of Nixon was quite balanced. Balance was the fourth estate's religion. They were even, sometimes, unbalanced in his favor. In 1960, for example, the two most powerful magazines in the country, Henry Luce's *Time* and *Life,* were practically Nixon megaphones.

But he was the sort to spy betrayal even in the midst of affection. Of all the explanations for the margin between defeat and victory in 1960, his favorite was Henry Luce's withdrawing the Billy Graham article. Meanwhile as Nixon entered the lists in California, a new kind of bestseller was sweeping the nation. Its author was no fan; the first time Theodore White boarded the Nixon campaign train, he sported a sizable KENNEDY FOR PRESIDENT button. The most flattering emotion *The Making of the President 1960* could muster toward him was pity ("One could listen to such a speech as Mr. Nixon gave in Herald Square and quibble and pick at its phraseology, but one could not look at the man who sat on the dais and deny that he had given all that was in him to this effort at the presidency and, looking at him, one could only sorrow for the man and his wife.") Nixon had lost that election by a whisper. In the book by which most people would remember it, his loss felt inevitable.

Teddy White's bestseller opened a new kind of wound. The book Richard Nixon published as 1962 approached, *Six Crises*, was an even-tempered, even introspective rehearsal of the public dramas he argued made him so fit to lead. (Write a book, Jack Kennedy once advised him, the intellectuals will love you. Nixon had written much more of *Six Crises* than Jack Kennedy ever had of *Profiles in Courage*, which Joe Kennedy had fixed to win a Pulitzer Prize.) The conclusion to Nixon's eighty-three-page account of the Hiss case, however, stuck out like a sore thumb: "For the next twelve years of my public service in Washington, I was to be subjected to an utterly unprincipled and vicious smear campaign. Bigamy, forgery, drunkenness, thievery, anti-Semitism, perjury, the whole gamut of misconduct in public office, ranging from unethical to downright criminal activities—all these were among the charges that were hurled against me, some publicly and others through whispering campaigns that were even more difficult to counteract."

Bigamy? Thievery? Forgery? It was a curious litany. He didn't marshal facts to support it because he couldn't. He had gotten across what had become, for him, the main truth: the world was out to get him, and the campaign was headquartered in the nation's newsrooms.

He held fast to it even though by the time he got around to accepting the entreaties to run for governor the press had once more crowned a New Nixon—"relaxed and quick with a wisecrack," went a typical assessment. The *Los Angeles Times* gave him a syndicated column. In initial polls he led the incumbent Pat Brown by sixteen points. There was an aura of inevitability. People assumed if he weren't a shoo-in, he wouldn't be running. What profit a man to come 120,000 votes from the White House, yet forfeit a statehouse?

The first surprise came when he announced his intentions in September 1961. A state legislator, oilman, and former USC football star, Joe Shell, so boring that a friend said "not to know Joe is to love him," decided to keep running even though he had only 2 percent in the polls. His far-right ideol-

ogy matched a mood among Republican activists. The Los Angeles County
Young Republicans' president had declared that the "difference between a
'liberal' Republican and a 'liberal' Democrat is the difference between creep-
ing socialism and galloping socialism." At a convention of the California
Republican Assembly, Nixon denounced the "nuts and kooks" of the John
Birch Society. A miscalculation; the CRA had been taken over by those selfsame nuts and kooks. Their leader averred, "I don't consider the John Birch
Society extremists. Except maybe extremely American." Shell himself
asserted that the "middle of the road is seventy-five percent socialism."
Nixon's primary victory over Shell was humiliatingly close. (President
Kennedy plunged in the knife at a press conference: "I think he emerged
from a tough one.") Shell then demanded concessions in return for delivering his supporters—some of whom hadn't trusted Nixon since he disavowed
McCarthy in 1954.

Nixon refused Shell.

Another miscalculation.

Brown accused Nixon of seeking the governorship "only as a stepping-
stone for his presidential ambitions." Nixon replied, "Not only will I not
seek the presidency in 1964, not only will I not accept a draft, I will see to it
there is no draft." There is evidence he meant it. "If I ran for governor I felt
I would have to pledge to spend the full term in Sacramento," he wrote in
one of the convincing lines in his 1978 memoirs. "That would leave someone
else to square off in 1964 against Kennedy, his money, his tactics." But
nobody believed him. Brown fans sent out postcards: "Would you buy a
used car from this man?" Shell supporters heckled him. The previous Republican governor endorsed Brown. Nixon lost the statehouse. And Nixon
blamed the press. He was especially livid at the *Los Angeles Times,* which,
under new management, was reporting on him objectively for the first time
in his political life.

Now there they were, waiting to humiliate him, in the pressroom of the
Beverly Hills Hilton.

On his TV Nixon heard Klein say, "The boss won't be down. . . . He
plans to go home and be with his family." The microphones picked up guf-
fawing from the press.

An aide beseeched Nixon, saying that the press thought he was a chicken:
"Don't let them bluff you. Go down and tell them what you think."

Another: "It looks like you're ducking."

Jules Witcover of the Newhouse papers described what happened next:
"Nixon, suddenly bristling, turned and stormed down the corridor, about
half a dozen supporters trailing him, onto a waiting elevator. . . . On the
ground floor, Nixon stepped out and started through the lobby." Someone
heard him say this loss was like being bitten by a mosquito after being bitten by a rattlesnake.

He didn't even wait for Klein to finish a sentence. Shoving him aside, Nixon grumbled into the microphone, "Now that all the members of the press are so delighted that I have lost, I'd like to make a statement of my own."

His deep-set eyes looked small, raccooned. His hands were scrunched deep into his pockets. Expectoration was observed as the words left his lips. This most disciplined of public servants broke composure, and the effect was akin to watching a train wreck.

"And as I leave the press, all I can say is this: for sixteen years, ever since the Hiss case, you've have a lot of fun—a lot of fun—that you've had an opportunity to attack me, and I think I've given as good as I've taken. . . . I leave you gentlemen now"—he smirked—"and you will write it. You will interpret it. That's your right. But as I leave you I want you to know—just think of how much you're going to be missing. You won't have Nixon to kick around anymore, because, gentlemen, this is my last press conference."

Then, honest to God, he said this: "And I hope what I have said today will at least make television, radio, the press, *recognize* that they have a right and responsibility if they're against a candidate to give him the shaft. But also recognize that if they give him the shaft"—another smirk—"to put one reporter on the campaign who will report what the candidate says now and then. Thank you, gentlemen, and good day!"

No one used words like this on TV. Nixon locked eyes with his anguished press secretary. "I gave it to them right in the behind. It had to be said, goddammit. It had to be said." *Time* quoted that, pronouncing its verdict: "Barring a miracle, his political career ended last week."

Nixon retreated into his dark imaginings: that in salons across the Eastern seaboard, champagne bottles were gushing forth. ABC broadcast a half-hour special, *The Political Obituary of Richard Nixon,* emceed by correspondent Howard K. Smith. One of the commentators was an old friend late of Lewisburg Penitentiary: the convicted perjurer Alger Hiss—doing better in polite society than Richard Nixon.

But Richard Nixon's 1978 memoirs had another convincing line. They recorded his thoughts the day of John F. Kennedy's inauguration in 1961. Nixon stood out in the cold on a Capitol balcony, turned to look in on the great hall of state one more time, then "suddenly stopped short, struck by the thought that this was not the end—that someday I would be back here. I walked as fast as I could back to the car."

He had learned something from enduring *The Political Obituary of Richard Nixon*: ABC had been deluged with eighty thousand letters of complaint. It was a lesson he would never forget: Orthogonians resented the news media as just another species of Franklin.

The front-runner for the Republican nomination was Barry Goldwater.

Kennedy was favored to swamp him. Then Kennedy introduced the most sweeping civil rights bill since Reconstruction, and the situation shifted. Columnist Stewart Alsop predicted "a political goldmine" for the candidate who dared to exploit the anti-civil-rights backlash in the blue-collar precincts of the North. That was exactly what Barry Goldwater appeared to be doing. *Look* ran the banner headline "JFK Could Lose." And in a poll of Republican leaders, only 3 percent said Nixon would make a good candidate. He was too liberal.

Then Kennedy was shot, the bottom dropped out of the United States of America, and anything that smacked of "extremism" lost its luster. Goldwater's star started fading. The field now hungered for centrists. It shook Richard Nixon out of his notional retirement for good.

In a December 6, 1963, speech, he bid fair for Goldwater's conservative supporters ("Planning an economy eventually ends in planning men's lives"). Nixon agents made inquiries in New Hampshire. His performance at the winter RNC meeting led one state chair to observe, "Most people climb aboard a bandwagon. Nixon threw himself in front of it." After the Republican moderate and ambassador to South Vietnam Henry Cabot Lodge won a surprise absentee victory in New Hampshire, Nixon told the press, "I feel that there is no man in this country who can make a case against Mr. Johnson more effectively than I can." In the spring, he made another stature-enhancing trip: to Lebanon, Malaysia, Thailand, the Philippines, Hong Kong, Taiwan, Japan, Pakistan, and Saigon, where he met with the new Republican front-runner, Henry Cabot Lodge. At the airport in New York newly christened JFK, he struck a Goldwater note on Vietnam: "There is no substitute for victory." Pennsylvania governor William Warren Scranton, considered the likely liberal successor to a compromised Nelson Rockefeller, said, "I always thought they were terribly unfair when they called him Tricky Dick. Now I don't know."

A trusted aide told Tricky Dick, back in the States, ready to make his move, that Goldwater's grassroots army had locked up the nomination. In Oregon, Nixon hired operatives to set up a clandestine campaign via fifty phone lines installed in a Portland boiler room to wire a "spontaneous" primary upset. An NBC camera crew was tipped off to the scene; Nixon's managers claimed they were working on a magazine poll; Nixon finished a dismal fourth.

As the decisive California primary approached, Nixon began pinning his hopes on a deadlocked convention. He couldn't afford to alienate anyone. Then rumors surfaced that Nixon was working with the "stop Goldwater" movement of Eastern Establishment Republicans. Nixon called Goldwater headquarters in a panic, begging to be put on the phone with the candidate. Who was on the road in the middle of nowhere. Nixon groveled to be put in contact by radio. Once connected, he feigned nonchalance, said he had called to RSVP for Goldwater's daughter's wedding the next month—and added that, by the way, he had nothing to do with any stop-Goldwater movement. The last weekend before the primary, Nixon got word that his mother was ringing doorbells for Goldwater and whisked her away to visit him in New York.

Goldwater won California. Nixon told the press he supported Goldwater for the nomination.

The next week, Nixon told Michigan Republicans, "If the party should decide on me as its candidate, Mr. Johnson would know he'd been in a fight." Then, at the National Governors' Conference in Cleveland, he lobbied for a draft of Michigan governor George Romney and announced that Goldwater's nomination would be a "tragedy" for the party. Romney declared himself uninterested. Nixon attended a breakfast for exhausted Republican governors who'd been up all night trying to broker deals to stop Goldwater.

He asked for the floor. He announced he would entertain questions. An agonizing, awkward interval passed before anyone realized that Nixon was waiting for them to ask him to run for president.

The silence, reporters learned, lasted a full fifteen seconds.

He told these same reporters he detected a "very lively interest" in his running at the breakfast.

Herblock ran a cartoon of Nixon with his arms crossed, thumbs sticking outward like a demented hitchhiker, trying to flag down two cars at once, one labeled "Pro-Goldwater," the other labeled "Anti-Goldwater."

Two weeks before the Republican National Convention, Nixon phoned the former RNC chair, and his 1960 campaign manager, Len Hall, to ask him for political advice. Hall asked him if he was finally convinced he couldn't get this nomination. Nixon finally allowed he was. Hall told him what he had to do: "Get Bill Miller"—the current RNC chair—"to switch your appearance on the convention program. Forget your Tuesday speech before the balloting. Ask to be allowed to introduce the nominee to the convention on Thursday."

And so, before the cheering throngs at the Cow Palace, eighteen years after his first election to public office, Richard Nixon delivered a paean to the man he had proclaimed four weeks before "a tragedy," whom he now said would "have the largest and most enthusiastic supporters in presidential history."

Although just in case Goldwater died piloting his plane above the Cow Palace, Nixon had set up a command center at San Francisco's St. Francis Hotel, where Bob Haldeman was poised to engineer the last-minute presidential draft.

Columnists Rowland Evans and Robert Novak told the whole sorry story in the November 1964 issue of *Esquire.* "The Unmaking of a President" began with an epigram from the nineteenth-century British poet Dante

Gabriel Rossetti: "Look in my face: my name is Might-have-been; I am also called No-more, Too-late, Farewell." Concluded the columnizing duo: "Each of his carefully calculated moves in 1964 was followed only by his own further political destruction."

But Richard Nixon was smarter than Evans and Novak, was smarter than any of them. Nobody else had the iron-assed will to do what needed to be done—to wait out the dozens and dozens of poker hands it would take before you had the cards you needed to *really* be able to collect the only bounty that mattered, in 1968. Evans and Novak didn't control that nomination, nor Howard K. Smith, nor Teddy White (in *Making of the President 1964,* he called Nixon's convention speech "nostalgically attractive")—none of those bastards who could only see how short Nixon's stack of chips was just *now.* Nelson Rockefeller didn't control that nomination, nor William Warren Scranton, nor George Romney, all of whom refused to campaign for Barry Goldwater that fall. Nor Thruston Morton, the Kentucky senator who went so far as to offer Lyndon Johnson secret advice about how to *beat* Barry Goldwater. Nixon had watched the assiduous cunning with which F. Clifton White had engineered Goldwater's nomination, by installing fanatical loyalists as functionaries at the grass roots (in early 1963 Nixon had even tried to hire Clif White for himself). Nixon was one of the few outsiders to understand what was happening: that the delegates he addressed at the Cow Palace would be controlling the nomination in 1968, even if Barry Morris Goldwater didn't win a single electoral vote in 1964.

That was why Nixon was the only Republican of national stature not to abandon the Goldwater ticket. He gave 156 speeches for Goldwater in the fall of 1964 and repeated his every-other-year ritual of campaigning for any Republican aspirant who invited him, in godforsaken burgs in thirty-six states. The liberal Republicans treated him like a leper. The Goldwater staff treated him like a leper. They did, however, learn that he could come in handy. In the middle of October, after LBJ's most trusted personal aide was caught receiving sexual favors from a retired sailor in the basement restroom of a Washington, D.C., YMCA, Nixon made it the focus of his speech: "A cloud hangs over the White House this morning because of Lyndon Johnson and his selection of men." *His selection of men.* Lyndon's johnson might as well have been right there in that men's room with Jenkins.

Dirty jobs.

The Wednesday before the election Nixon made his endorsement on national TV. Six days later, Goldwater went down in the predicted landslide. And, his enemies thanked God, Richard Nixon had gone down right there with him.

Let his enemies think it. Always give something to the mark. *He* was the one with the chits it would take to get nominated in 1968. All the other Republican heavies had refused to campaign for Goldwater altogether.

"There is a strong conservative wing of the Republican Party," Nixon told the *New York Times* in a page-one interview. "It deserves a major voice in party councils, and the liberal wing deserves a party voice, but neither can dominate or dictate. The center must lead."

Every side owed him something. Because all the other prominent Republicans had burned their bridges with conservatives.

Then he was off for another stature-enhancing trip to Asia. Then he played peacemaker at a contentious annual RNC meeting in January. Barry Goldwater introduced him as the man "who worked harder than any one person for the ticket. . . .

"Dick, I will never forget it! I know that you did it in the interest of the Republican Party and not for any selfish reasons, but if there ever comes a time I can turn those into selfish reasons, I am going to do all I can to see that it comes about."

Richard Nixon smiled sanctimoniously and said there'd be no selfishness to serve—proclaiming to a standing ovation that he was here and now calling for a moratorium on presidential politicking until after the 1966 midterm elections, promising to lead by example.

Tricky Dick.

The media was so starved for someone, anyone, to anoint as a Republican heir apparent that *Newsweek* put a backbench liberal congressman named John Lindsay on its cover as "the most exciting and important politician operating in America today" and called his entrance into the 1965 New York mayoral race "the first chapter in the making of the President, 1972." Nixon was still the butt of half the political jokes cracked in the United States. His base of presidential politicking was his law office at 20 Broad Street, around the corner from the New York Stock Exchange and all the white-shoe law firms that had rejected him in 1937. Now he was one of them—sort of.

Nixon's ambiguous stature was sanctified in an April *New York Times Magazine* profile: "Over Nominated, Under-Elected, Still a Promising Candidate." It was predictable now, this coronation as a "new Nixon" after a loss, the systole and diastole of Nixon's political heartbeat: "He is decidedly more relaxed and mellow than he appeared in his political campaign." It was a favorite man-bites-dog feature hook in 1965: can you believe people are taking Dick Nixon seriously again?

This latest new Nixon was a man-about-town, the *Times* related—feted at a testimonial dinner at the Metropolitan Club's sumptuous edifice on Sixtieth Street, member of fancy country clubs in Westchester and Long Island, serving on the boards of old-line corporations and top-line charitable foundations (his favorite was the Boys Clubs of America, which he chaired). His daughter came out at a debutante ball. His new dog was a gray French poodle. His companions were the likes of William S. Paley of CBS; Walter Thayer, publisher of the *Herald Tribune;* Eisenhower budget director Maurice Stans and Warner-Lambert's Elmer Bobst and Pepsi's Donald Kendall, and Robert Abplanalp, an entrepreneur who'd made millions in aerosol spray cans, and Bebe Rebozo, a taciturn Cuban-American real estate tycoon. Nixon dined out at the Recess Club at 60 Broad ("where he enjoys the panorama from the top floor") and the India House ("where he enjoys looking at models of old sailing ships"), made the scene at Toots Shor's, hit the Metropolitan Opera and all the hottest Broadway shows ("Naturally, they have not missed *Hello, Dolly!*"), hosted dinner parties at "21," Le Pavillon, the Colony, Delmonico's. (It must all have been a trial. "I can eat in ten minutes," he boasted in 1968. "Why waste an hour or two eating?")

The *Times* also dropped subtly embarrassing details. He "sometimes plays on the championship course at Baltusrol": because his partners were members (though he was earning more money than he ever had in his life, much more, he certainly was not *one of them*). Without exactly saying so, the *Times* enumerated an arriviste's lapses in taste: license plates reading NXN, the spinet piano upon which, "without much coaxing," he "hams it up . . . with such songs as the staples on 'Sing Along with Mitch'" (the schmaltzy TV show in which a choir sang popular ditties while a bouncing ball lined out the lyrics at the bottom of the screen), the twelve-room Fifth Avenue town house he bought adjacent to Nelson Rockefeller's—a little too tawdry, climbing like that.

Everything was political. His job itself had roots in a chit: Mudge, Stern, Baldwin, and Todd was the first firm to take Don Kendall up on his offer to throw Pepsi's international legal work to whichever firm offered Richard Nixon a job (that repaid Nixon for having Nikita Khrushchev drink Pepsi during the 1959 Kitchen Debate visit). When a columnist wrote that Nixon spent only one day a week at the law office and the rest scheming politics, Nixon wrote each of his clients individually to say it wasn't true. In fact it was only half-true. His office—a museum of political kitsch: silver plates engraved with testimonials, commemorative gavels, keys to cities, a long walnut cabinet filled with signed photographs of heads of state in the line of sight of visitors sitting across from Nixon at the polished walnut desk—was where he did his politics. The wheelhouse of his political machine.

He brought with him his longtime secretary, Rose Mary Woods, his bureaucratic second skin (they joked she was the "fifth Nixon": Pat, Dick, Tricia, Julie, just like the Beatles), a hardscrabble, working-class Chicago Irish girl who some said spotted the young senator as her own chance to make it to the White House. Her Rolodex big as a basketball, she typed up ingratiating notes to VIPs for "Dick"'s signature at every possible opportunity: J. Edgar Hoover, newspaper publisher Walter Annenberg, the third-world potentate Nixon had met on some 1955 Latin American tour who had suddenly taken sick.

Life, in a sense, was sweet. He was rich now, for the first time in his life. He had sent his firm's business through the roof. He traveled on a lifetime diplomatic passport, issued to him as the former vice president, met at every stop by an embassy control officer. He could have retired placidly. But then he wouldn't be who he was.

Clients like the Japanese trading conglomerate Mitsui provided occasions for handy trips to Asia. He stopped by Saigon in September 1965, laying down political markers in press conferences: "For the United States to negotiate a peace agreement now which would in any way reward the Communists for their aggression would not only lead to the loss of Asia but would greatly increase the risk of World War III." A trip to Finland for some industrial clients provided occasion for an "impulsive" twenty-hour train ride to Moscow.

His domestic politics now was an exquisitely couched centrism: that Republicans accept Great Society reforms, while never "carrying them to the point of intolerable federal power and expenditure." This was the GOP soup du jour, the kind of thing his new, Franklin allies at the firm appreciated. Avowals like that helped Len Garment, a fast-talking and glad-handing Jewish former jazz musician, build a New York political network. A PR flack named Bill Safire contributed a ten-page letter on how to make a two-time loser without any fixed geographical base and a lifetime of enemies fit for an unstoppable comeback. The trick, Safire said, was cleaning up his image. Which may have been how Nixon ended up in the *New York Times Magazine* as such an exemplary swell.

Fashionable opinions about such things as civil liberties and the Pill and long hair were not uncommon among the young partners at a firm like Nixon, Mudge. So was familiarity with the latest discotheques and Tom Wolfe's kandy-kolored evocations of fashion's latest "It" girl in the *Herald Tribune*. It was what a certain kind of Franklin, circa 1965, was digging. The scene was tough for Dick to make. It didn't match an Orthogonian's instincts. But then, at times an Orthogonian's instincts still came in handy — as his hip new friends soon learned to their chagrin, when he next embraced the stench in the opening move of his 1968 presidential campaign.

A speaker at an April teach-in at Rutgers University, a thirty-five-year-old history professor named Eugene Genovese, made news, proclaiming, "I am a Marxist and a socialist. Therefore, I do not fear or reject the impending Vietcong victory in Vietnam. I welcome it." American Legion types called for his hide. The board of trustees refused to fire a tenured professor for remarks made outside the classroom. The Democratic governor, Richard Hughes, a Vietnam hawk but a civil libertarian, refused to intervene. His opponent, State Senator Wayne Dumont, was so far from being a threat that advisers were telling him to stop spending money. Then the Republican sniffed out a Nixonian opportunity. Dumont made the professor the focus of his campaign — and recruited the master to help. On October 24, Nixon joined Dumont in Morristown and made as if he were still going to school on George Smathers's talk of thespians and sexagenarians.

"I do not raise the question of Professor Genovese's right to be for segregation or integration, for free love or celibacy, for Communism or anarchy— in peacetime. But the United States is at war."

(Anarchistic, multiracial Communistic orgies, in wartime, no less.)

"If anyone had welcomed a Nazi victory during World War II, there would have been no question about what to do. Leadership requires that the governor step in and put the security of the nation above the security of the individual."

The uncouth relapse into Red-baiting set the teeth of Nixon's new pals at the Recess Club on edge—a huge setback in their work reforming his "old Nixon" image. It didn't even work. Hughes won, most New Jerseyans telling pollsters they hadn't heard of Gene Genovese. William Safire got to work on damage control, drafting a speech on academic freedom for the honorary degree Nixon had been invited to receive from the University of Rochester.

Nixon wrote a long and legalistic letter to the *New York Times* that he was actually arguing for the *preservation* of academic freedom, "by defending the system of government which guarantees freedom of speech to individuals." And Len Garment realized something fundamental: the Franklins thought they had reformed him once and for all. But these artful dodgings between Nixons old and new were fundamental to who Nixon was—and Nixon saw this occasion to shock the respectable by sounding like a McCarthyite in New Jersey as an *opportunity*.

"So much for their fucking sophistication!" Nixon said one day in delight at the shocked reaction of the gentlemen of the press over something or another. "Oh, I know you and the rest of the intellectuals won't like it—the men back at the firm won't like it either—but somebody had to take them on."

The "them" was quintessentially "old Nixon." In a career full of ideological inconsistencies, it may have been his most consistent position: that calls for intellectual freedom were how the holier-than-thou covered up a will to subversion. He had given a prizewinning schoolboy speech in 1929 saying exactly the same thing: "Should the morals of this nation be offended and polluted in the name of freedom of the press? In the words of Lincoln, the individual can have no rights against the best interests of society." His maiden address in the House of Representatives argued that "the rights of free speech and free press do not carry with them the right to advocate the destruction of the very government which protects the freedom of an individual to express his views." On this the deepest instincts of his psyche coincided with the soundest principles of political demagoguery: the safe political bet was in ultimately siding with those who distrusted the intellectuals; Orthogonians over Franklins—*them*. The Genovese issue may not have helped Dumont. It helped Nixon. It assured Republican Orthogonians that despite what they had heard, he still was one of *us*. In the December Gallup poll of Republicans, Nixon was the presidential preference of 34 percent, as much as the next three names combined.

Nixon had noted the teach-ins, the protests, the marches—and the grass-roots revulsion these things were beginning to engender. Among the pundits, in all the right magazines, on TV, "youth" were being held up as some mystic fount of virtue, avatars of the soaring sixties, a uniquely idealistic generation midwifed by the martyr JFK. It was enough to make an Orthogonian cringe. The *Times Magazine* profile listed as Nixon's most burdensome liability the fact that no Republican could win the presidency without attracting Democrats, who made up the majority of registered voters. The idea of Richard Nixon luring Democratic voters frankly seemed unimaginable. But there were new currents to surf in the soaring sixties, based in the same kind of old resentments, new kinds of common people being put upon by new kinds of insolent and condescending Franklins—the new kind of liberal who seemed to be saying that Negroes who burned down their neighborhoods were somehow as innocent as they once considered Alger Hiss, and that college kids who spat on the flag were oh-so-much more with-it than *you*.

Issues to expand the circle of Orthogonians. Even, perhaps, into the Democratic coalition itself.

CHAPTER FOUR

Ronald Reagan

N INETEEN SIXTY-SIX, AND WATTS WAS THE NATION'S PREOCCUPATION. "Now and then the police cars mount the sidewalk and drive through the ruins, threading through alleyways and behind stores, their searchings darting here and there for hiding youths," the *Washington Post* reported, quoting one of those youths: "They are looking at the same old places. What they don't know is that when it comes it ain't gonna be like last time." The *Times* also quoted an L.A. cop: "There are a lot more guns out there. They looted every pawnshop and sports shop in the area last summer."

The cop repeated himself: "There are a lot more guns out there."

The meaning of Watts was fiercely debated. Militant blacks spoke of an "insurgency": "I threw the firebomb right in that front window," a youngster fondly reminisced to a CBS correspondent. "I call it getting even." A group of Berkeley radicals, the Vietnam Day Committee, appropriated Watts for their manifesto: "The Los Angeles riots in the summer of 1965 are analogous to the peasant struggle in Vietnam." Liberal technocrats reasoned, "If the Los Angeles rioting reveals the underlying weaknesses of the current federal approach to segregation, poverty, and housing, and if it stimulates some fresh thinking"—this was a Columbia professor—"it may compensate at least in part for the terrible havoc it wreaked." *Fortune* magazine, speaking for enlightened business opinion, counseled understanding, quoting Langston Hughes:

> *Negroes,*
> *Sweet and docile,*
> *Meek, humble, and kind:*
> *Beware the day*
> *They change their mind!*

But the debate was dominated by the conservatives. Their spokesman was Chief William Parker, who in press conferences, like a candidate running for office, laid out the party line: it was the civil rights movement's fault.

They were the ones who preached, "You don't have to obey the law if you think it's unjust." *They* were the ones who forced guilt-ridden passage of civil rights laws that "sanctified their acts." Chief Parker had provided this account of the riot's origins to Governor Brown's blue-ribbon panel studying Watts: "Someone threw a rock, and like monkeys in a zoo, they all started throwing rocks." He maintained that unless decent folks did something drastic, the monkeys would be visited even unto their own doorsteps—and for saying it was drowned in forty thousand congratulatory messages a month.

In March there almost was another riot, sparked by a turf war between some Mexican and black kids. Over a hundred helmeted officers promptly flooded the scene and successfully sealed off the perimeter, and what the media histrionically dubbed Watts II was over before it began, but not before the ripples from this schoolyard brawl spread to Sacramento and Washington, D.C.: state legislators said Governor Pat Brown's $61.5 million program responding to the first riots was now dead, and a planned White House conference on civil rights was indefinitely postponed. The *Los Angeles Times* columnist Paul Coates described the panicked calls he was getting from readers: "My wife just called. Said she heard five was dead. And they're spreading out all over town. This time I'm gonna get me a gun."

At his announcement in January of his candidacy for California governor, Ronald Reagan had blamed the original Watts riot on the "philosophy that in any situation the public should turn to government for the answer." Now he denounced Governor Brown. And the *New York Times*—which had last taken note of the California governor's race in mid-February, commenting on how little attention the actor Ronald Reagan had been able to garner since "his dramatic and carefully rehearsed television entry into the race" (the paper had sent its Hollywood correspondent to cover it, and he had dwelled on the living-room set with the crackling fire, and props such as the bottle Reagan waved while warning how "social tinkering had caused the layoff of 200 workers in ketchup factories")—now reported, "A withering crossfire of political accusations emerged today after Tuesday's violent outbreak." Reagan had charged that Brown had left the state despite warnings of trouble; Brown harrumphed that if he reacted to every tip he got about impending violence in Watts, he couldn't do anything else.

Brown didn't feel much need to defend himself. Surely the state would remember his political debut in the 1950s as a law-and-order district attorney, and that he was the governor who had seen to the execution of the Red Light Bandit, Caryl Chessman, after his Republican predecessors had dithered in the face of mercy pleas from everyone from Eleanor Roosevelt to Billy Graham.

Reagan's Republican primary opponent, former San Francisco mayor George Christopher, let the two fight it out among themselves. He was the primary front-runner—easily "matching oratorical skill" with Reagan, the

New York Times thought, in an article enumerating Reagan's manifold defects: his toxic ties to the far right and the Goldwater campaign; the bright, young party moderates who viewed the prospect of a Governor Reagan "with something approaching horror"; his rookie mistakes. "You know, a tree is a tree, how many more do you need to look at?" he had blundered in a speech on conservation. It was at that point that the *San Francisco Chronicle* reported that his campaign would soon "bottom out." George Christopher joked that if Brown knew what was good for him, he'd start working for Reagan.

More or less, Brown was doing exactly that. "'Bring him on' is our motto," his press secretary had scrawled on the bottom of the January 1965 gossip item that Reagan was going to run. A young assistant was sent out to scout Reagan during one of his exploratory appearances and had not been impressed:

"He will fall apart when he gets attacked from the floor and is asked leading questions, hounded, and the like. . . .

"His attacks on LBJ and Governor Brown won't make it with those who don't think the President is a dictator and those who realize the necessity of close state and federal cooperation. . . .

"The real issue always boils down to what Reagan would do as governor, and given the present situation and our close working relationship with Washington, he could do nothing."

George Christopher, a popular big-city mayor, would be hard to beat. Reagan, the know-nothing actor attacking popular government programs, would be a cinch. Thus Brown's strategy for the primary season: puff Reagan.

Pat was not the most inspiring of politicians: a "tower of Jell-O," according to the Democrats' legislative boss, Jesse Unruh. It was only what he had accomplished that was inspiring. His first legislative session, in 1959, was the most productive in California history: bold new agencies for economic development and consumer protection; top-to-bottom bureaucratic reorganization; increased social security and welfare benefits; new funding for hospitals, mental health clinics, and drug treatment; a ban on racial discrimination in hiring; massive new funding for schools; miles upon miles of highways, rail lines, tunnels, and bridges. The next year, he successfully appropriated $1.75 billion to deliver 100 million gallons of water to Southern California by 1972. He had built 1,000 of the state's 1,650 miles of freeway; ordered up the greatest college construction boom in human history—room enough for 25 percent of high school grads to attend the greatest public university system in the world, tuition-free; had added two hundred thousand jobs. And if he hadn't done it with any particular stylishness—well, what of it? Under his touch, the biggest state in the union had blossomed into a kind of bourgeois utopia. Let the actor have at him: the middle class knew better than to fall for that. He had built the ladder upon which they had climbed.

Reagan punditry fixated on whether his appearances in *Knute Rockne, All*

American and *Bedtime for Bonzo* on the late show violated equal-time provisions. An editorial cartoon depicted Goldwater directing him from a prompter's box ("Perfect, Ronald . . . enter stage right"). Picket signs materialized reading ELIZABETH TAYLOR FOR SUPERINTENDENT OF PUBLIC INSTRUCTION. A *Washington Star* columnist recorded "the air of furtive jubilation down at Lassie for Governor headquarters." *Esquire* graciously allowed that the "Republican Party isn't bankrupt, or isn't that bankrupt that it has to turn to Liberace for leadership." The *Christian Century,* unchristianly, called him Borax Boy, after the sponsor of his last TV show.

Bring him on indeed.

The pundits little noted the Reagan-friendly culture wars roiling beneath the surface of the bourgeois utopia. Only recently, the drug lysergic acid diethylamide had been rhapsodized as a therapeutic miracle; its acolytes included Cary Grant. Now it brought headlines like "Girl, 5, Eats LSD and Goes Wild" and "Thrill Drug Warps Mind, Kills." Now *Time* reported in March that it had reached "the dormitories of expensive prep schools" and "has grown into an alarming problem at UCLA and on the UC campus at Berkeley." Senator Robert F. Kennedy changed a hearing scheduled on mental retardation into an inquiry into LSD instead—one of three going on concurrently.

A group called the California League Enlisting Action Now (CLEAN) pushed an initiative forbidding judges from dismissing any pornography case. Their ads called pornographers masters of "Pavlov's conditioned response," responsible for an epidemic of "rape, perversion, and venereal disease." Other activists went to war on a textbook—Negro historian John Hope Franklin's *Land of the Free,* which, their pamphlets insisted, "destroys pride in America's past, develops a guilt complex, mocks American justice, indoctrinates toward Communism, is hostile to religious concepts, overemphasizes Negro participation in American history, projects negative thought models, criticizes business and free enterprise, plays politics, foments class hatred, slants and distorts facts," and "promotes propaganda and poppycock." The L.A. County Board of Supervisors voted "to uphold high moral standards" by censoring an exhibition by an artist named Ed Keinholz, who said he displayed his dioramas of consumer products and mannequins in sexual congress and babies without heads to comment on America's "sick society."

In the Golden State, it was a season of moral panic; and as so often, California led a national trend. The head of the nation's leading association of private schools released a statement worrying that "students have adopted 'terrifying' attitudes toward sex . . . for lack of a moral code." But others looked upon the same developments and judged them symptoms of cultural health. A psychiatry professor, for instance, spoke that same March at the

Arizona Medical Association in praise of the "beatniks" who were "urging the revision of some of our medieval customs," especially sexual ones. A writer in the *Nation* asserted that students who dropped out of school to "find themselves" were "probably in many ways, a more promising moral resource than those who stay in."

More and more Americans were forthrightly asserting visions of what a truly moral society would look like. Unfortunately, their visions were irreconcilable.

At their fringes, irreconcilable moralities begat violence.

In San Diego, a terrorist tossed a burning oil rag through the window of a San Diego civil rights group. In Pacific Palisades—where Ronald Reagan lived—fifty earnest kids marched back and forth in front of the high school carrying signs reading THERE IS NO SCIENTIFIC PROOF THAT LONG HAIR INHIBITS LEARNING, and the dean of boys dispatched the football team to break up the demonstration with what the *Los Angeles Times* described as "gridiron tactics." In Detroit a teenager shot his rabbi dead as one thousand congregants looked on, crying, "This congregation is a travesty and an abomination. It has made a mockery with its phoniness and hypocrisy."

A new antiwar group surfaced, the W.E.B. Du Bois Club. Lyndon Johnson's attorney general, Nicholas Katzenbach, ruled it a front for the Communist Party. Richard Nixon called it a "totalitarian organization" that chose its name (which one pronounced "du-BOYS Club") "not unaware of the confusion they are causing among our supporters and among many other good citizens"—who might mistake it for the venerable service organization whose board he chaired: the Boys Club. In San Francisco, a right-wing terrorist burned down the Du Bois headquarters with a Molotov cocktail. In Brooklyn, members were beaten by a mob.

Time ran a stark red sentence on its April 8 cover: "Is God Dead?" (The answer, it decided, was no, which didn't keep an angry letter-writer from fuming, "*Time*'s story is biased, pro-atheist and pro-Communist, shocking and entirely un-American.") An Oklahoma minister drummed up a movement to censure a "Southern Baptist preacher in a high government position"—White House press secretary Bill Moyers—for conduct that "brings dishonor to the work and name of our Lord Jesus Christ." Moyers's sin was getting photographed in the papers dancing the Watusi at the White House.

Then there were campuses like Berkeley—where, late in 1964, a police car rolled onto campus to dismantle a recruitment table for Mississippi voter registration that fell afoul of campus rules about where political advocacy was permitted. The squad car was promptly trapped on the main campus plaza by hundreds of students, who started climbing up on its roof and delivering inspiring speeches about the right to free speech, the necessity of defying illegitimate authority, the soul-crushing blindness of the bureaucrats. Then thousands occupied the administration building. For them the "Free Speech

Movement" was a moment of moral transcendence. To the man on the street—especially the man on the street never afforded the privilege of a college education—it was petulant brattishness. Then came the "filthy speech movement." *That* started when a couple of angry kids sat on the Student Union steps with curses scrawled on placards. A few score kids rallied to their support. But by 1966, these few score kids had become Middle America's synecdoche for "Berkeley." "All the most vociferous of them could produce was four-letter words," Illinois's Republican Senate candidate, Charles Percy, told eighteen hundred students at the University of Illinois in a speech on the New Left's "general uncleanliness." The students gave him a standing ovation.

The outrages, all of them, felt linked: the filth, the crime, "the kids," the Communists, the imprecations against revealed religion. It all had something to do with "liberalism." Pat Brown was a "liberal." And it arrived that liberalism's enemy, Ronald Reagan, wasn't doing too poorly at all. He was providing a political outlet for all the outrages—outrages that, until he came along, hadn't seemed like political issues at all.

The Associated Press's Bill Boyarsky dropped in on Reagan's walk through the blue-collar aerospace suburb of Norwalk, a formless sprawl so typical, "political reporters considered the reaction of the crowds almost as sound a test of public opinion in the area as a scientific poll." The reaction was adulation. At the Lakewood Shopping Center, grinning his modest little grin, Reagan launched into remarks about the high cost of welfare. A giant crowd had assembled—in the middle of the day, on a weekday. They went wild. Norwalk was registered three-quarters Democratic. Even Reagan seemed taken a little aback. Pat Brown, forced to campaign in the primary to put down a sudden conservative challenge from Sam Yorty for the Democratic nomination, came to Norwalk later in the month. The same people heckled him so loudly reporters couldn't phone in their stories.

Martin Luther King was in Chicago. In 1956, Eleanor Roosevelt had said that if the Windy City desegregated, it would set a lovely example for the South. Mayor Daley replied that there was no segregation in Chicago. He was still proclaiming it—even though, in 1965, after Dick Gregory led silent desegregation marches past Daley's Bridgeport house, neighborhood schoolgirls adopted a new jump-rope chant: "I'd like to be an Alabama trooper / That is what I'd truly like to be / 'Cause if I were an Alabama trooper / I could kill the niggers legally."

King had once believed impoverished Northern blacks would "benefit derivatively from the Southern struggle." Then he saw Chicago's endless ramshackle "Black Belt." In January he rented a four-room walk-up for his family in the Lawndale ("Slumdale") neighborhood. Reporters crowded each other on move-in day, noting the smell of urine, the single hall light, the rumors the block was controlled by gangs. It was King's last public relations triumph for months. Mayor Daley proved a more formidable opponent than any redneck Southern sheriff. He simply announced, "All of us are for the elimination of slums," sent out fifty building inspectors to make a show of a stand against tenements, and announced statistics on the death toll for rats like McNamara toting up body counts in Vietnam. Mayor Daley always beat the out-of-town liberals—like the previous year, when LBJ's education commissioner announced he might withhold federal funds from segregated schools in Chicago. The mayor called the president. Forthwith, the commissioner was fired.

By late March, King's campaign looked defeated, ready to retreat without a single accomplishment, a single dramatic confrontation. But King was devising a plan. It built off a congressional debate. President Johnson had introduced his proposed 1966 Civil Rights Act at the end of April. The measure at its center, Title IV, to outlaw housing discrimination, appeared dead on arrival. After all, whenever some city council somewhere passed an open-housing law—even in supposedly liberal Berkeley—citizens availed themselves of whatever means of direct democracy at their disposal to crush it. And that had been *before* Watts.

At committee hearings, the conservative opposition quoted liberal Supreme Court justice William O. Douglas in a 1963 decision: "The principle that a man's home is his castle is basic to our system of jurisprudence." The eighty-three-thousand-member National Association of Real Estate Boards transformed itself into a lobbying army, trooping to Washington to testify that Title IV was an "inherently evil" measure that "would sound the death knell of the right of private property ownership," was an unconstitutional usurpation of the marketplace, an invitation to neighborhood breakdown that would destroy the most precious asset most middle-class families possessed: the equity in their homes.

Liberals steadied their grip and harnessed their reason: hadn't conservatives said the same things during the debate over the 1964 civil rights law, and private property yet survived? And if a man leaves his castle and puts it up for sale, how could he logically claim it continued to be his castle? They pointed to Title IV as the domino that could topple the very system of racially based economic inequality itself: "Employment often depends on education," said the Democratic floor manager Manny Celler, chair of the House Judiciary Committee; "education in turn, on neighborhood schools, and housing." Clergymen testified of the imperatives of Scripture. The chairman of Time Inc. said freeing the housing market from the irrational distortions of racism would swell the nation's tax coffers. Whitney Young of the Urban League said that those revenues would immeasurably contribute to solving the very problems "attributable in substantial measure to the development of racial ghettos: crime, broken homes, racial animosity." To those who claimed it unconstitutional for the federal government to interfere with the private housing market, the bill's supporters pointed out how deeply the federal government *subsidized* the private housing market. To those who said integration brought neighborhood breakdown, they introduced social science into the *Congressional Record* ("Old concepts about neighborhood homogeneity, the relationship of changes in value to housing supply, the price mechanism as a controlling factor in family mobility, the significance of panic-selling and block-busting techniques, and property maintenance habits of nonwhite families are being revised and are no longer supported by responsible literature in the field") and the conclusions of President Eisenhower's Civil Rights Commission that integration brought lower "rates of disease, juvenile delinquency, crime, and social demoralization." Real estate tycoon James W. Rouse pointed out that he had made money hand over fist developing properties under open-occupancy laws, and that his fellow real estate professionals were working against their own interest when they fought federal regulation: if everyone worked under the same rules, *all* would be protected from unscrupulous "blockbusters" who intentionally exploited racial fears to lower property values. Attorney General Katzenbach thundered like a preacher, "The nation as a whole suffers when so many of its people are prevented from making the contribution they are able to make to the country's social and economic well-being."

To liberals, the law just made so much *sense*—how could it lose? They didn't understand that questions of who defined a "neighborhood" tended not to be fought out via the "responsible literature in the field" but in blood and fire—that opponents like North Carolina's Sam Ervin meant it when they said they'd resist open housing "as long as they have breath," and that reason played little role in neighborhoods where children sang ditties celebrating lynching.

Aggrieved constituents began flooding congressmen's mailboxes:

"This takes away a person's rights. We are people and need someone to protect us."

"'Freedom for all'—including the white race, please!"

King's theory of civil disobedience was that confrontation between irreconcilables like these was what brought social justice. Thus his strategy to unstalemate his campaign: storm the citadels of Chicago's whites-only neighborhoods, and see what happened then.

Meanwhile the birthplace of King's doctrine of civil disobedience was disproving the newspaper editor who predicted that after 1964 elections in the South "will be decided on issues other than civil rights." Alabama's constitution wouldn't let Governor George Wallace succeed himself. So he tried to ram through a constitutional amendment allowing him to run for reelection. But Alabama legislators proved unwilling to give up what slim reed of power they had over the state's de facto dictator. Wallace wasn't about to quit politics; "the only thing that counts," he would tell his children at the dinner table, waxing philosophic, "is money and power." He needed a political base to run for president in 1968. So he decided to run his cancer-ridden wife, Lurleen, for governor instead and run the state from behind the scenes. One sweltering day late in April, a week before the Democratic primary, he staged one last publicity stunt. Title VI of the 1964 Civil Rights Act outlawed federal funding for any institution practicing segregation. Administrators at two Alabama hospitals had been foolish enough to make token efforts to comply. Thus it was that, at the crack of dawn, with Wallace as witness, inmates at the state mental hospital in Mount Vernon, and the mental ward of Bryce Hospital in Tuscaloosa, were roused from their beds and shipped to the opposite institution, 140 miles away—a show of resegregating Alabama's madmen for the delectation of his political base.

Wallace wasn't Dixie's most effective segregationist. He was just the most theatrical. "If every politician is an actor, only a few are consummately talented," Norman Mailer once wrote. "Wallace is talented." Wallace pledged to sign on as Lurleen's "adviser" at $1 a year: "I'm gonna draw the water, tote in the wood, wind the clock, and put out the cat." For anyone who dared critique the ruse, he affected disgust at the attack on the honor of Southern womanhood. Lurleen's candidacy was announced mere days after she underwent surgery for the cancer that would kill her two years later. Behind the scenes, an acquaintance reported, Wallace treated her like a "whipped dog."

It was a competitive race. Civil rights groups flooded the state with voter registration drives; not for nothing had George Wallace pleaded to Lyndon Johnson a year earlier that the Voting Rights Act was the work of "malcontents," trained "in Moscow or New York." Not for nothing did the Southern Christian Leadership Conference's James Bevel tell an August 1965 convention, "There is no more civil rights movement. President Johnson signed it out of existence when he signed the voting-rights bill." Alabama's primary, under Justice Department observation in thirty-one counties, was the new law's first test. Three strong candidates joined the challenge. Lucky for George, the one he feared most, Ryan DeGraffenried, a young up-and-comer known as Alabama's JFK, died in a small-plane accident. Carl Elliot, the favorite of the Yankee pundits, pledged "a middle ground for Alabamans": he would neither "stand on the Edmund Pettus Bridge and shout, 'Never,'" nor in Negro churches "singing 'We Shall Overcome.'" The latter reference was to the contender to his left, Attorney General Richmond Flowers, who bid for the new black vote by pledging to remove the Confederate flag from the state Capitol.

The Wallaces campaigned twelve hours a day. The band would strike up "Just a Closer Walk with Thee" (Lurleen's favorite hymn, the emcee said); Lurleen would recite a 519-word text pledging "the same honesty and integrity in government that Alabamans have had in the past three years" (actually her husband ran the state on kickbacks); then George would declaim for an hour—defending the honor of the Stars and Bars ("Wherever you see the Confederate flag flying . . . you won't find college students taking up money for the Vietcong and giving blood to the Vietcong or burning their draft cards"); proposing Washington organize a combat brigade for "all the dirty beatniks that march in these shindigs," in order to "get rid of them"; and excoriating "these big Northern newspapers having a fit because my wife is a candidate for governor," who said "we should change our image to suit some Communist Hottentot ten thousand miles from here."

In Wetumpka, up in the Appalachian foothills, he roared, "I see we got the editor of the *Alabama Journal* here today."

That would be Ray Jenkins, a critic, who had just returned from a Nieman Fellowship at Harvard.

"You know, he's one of them *Hahhh*-verd-educated intellectuals that sticks his little finger up in the air when he sips tea and looks down his long nose at us ordinary Alabamans. I had a goat one time, and I fed him a copy of the *Alabama Journal*. And the poor goat died."

Ray Jenkins smiled and performed a little bow. He wasn't smiling later, when Wallace strong-armed Montgomery liquor stores into withdrawing their advertising from his paper.

Wallace never hid his national ambitions: "An Alabaman would make as good a president as somebody from New York and maybe a darn sight better than *somebody* from Texas," he would say. "We've got support in California and Wisconsin and Maryland and all over the country." The pundits' darling, Carl Elliot, boasted of his "liberal" economic record—oblivious that in Alabama the word had become a curse. There was no more middle ground in a state where Klansmen painted "Never!" over his billboards. Richmond Flowers ran his campaign into a ditch when he pointed out that Lurleen was a high school dropout. An attorney general's lapse in chivalry was apparently more disqualification for higher office than the lack of a twelfth-grade education. His support crumbled. Lurleen won in a landslide. "It was at Selma a year ago that Wallace really won Tuesday's election," pollster Sam Lubell said his surveys showed: the federally protected march was seen even by moderates as "a show of force by some foreign occupying power." "It's rubbing salt in our wounds," he quoted one. "I've become George Wallace's man."

The South was supposed to be becoming more like the rest of the country. Instead, in Georgia's gubernatorial race, polls gave a man named Lester Maddox a strong chance. His qualification for office was having chased Negroes from his Atlanta fried-chicken emporium after passage of the Civil Rights Act with a pistol and a pickax handle. In Maryland a man named George P. Mahoney was rolling up support in Baltimore blue-collar wards by calling the Congress of Racial Equality's open-housing drive a conspiracy to flood neighborhoods with welfare cheats.

These results were a harbinger. The rest of the country was becoming more like the South. The Irish in South Boston were fighting with the ruthlessness of a street gang defending their turf against a state law mandating racial balance in schools; their leader, a genteel lady named Louise Day Hicks, won reelection to the city's school committee with a staggering 65 percent of the at-large vote. In New York, John Lindsay took steps to set up a civilian board to review complaints against the police, and the Patrolman's Benevolent Association pledged to spend every penny in its treasury to defeat it. Barry Goldwater himself was touring the country to huge crowds, lecturing that conservatives would once again control the Republican National Convention. "God forbid," his liberal Republican Senate colleague Hugh Scott responded, in a minor breach of senatorial courtesy.

Democrats were falling to a tangle of angry factionalism over Vietnam. In October 1965, one hundred thousand citizens had marched against the war in New York. The theologian Reinhold Niebuhr, America's preeminent liberal anticommunist, wrote in *Christianity and Crisis* in December, "We are making South Vietnam into an American colony" and "ruining an unhappy nation in the process of 'saving' it." In February, Senator William J. Fulbright, chairman of the Foreign Relations Committee, held six days of televised hearings in which millions of Americans heard luminaries like George Kennan, architect of the doctrine of containment, say victory in Vietnam could only come "at the cost of a degree of damage to civilian life and civilian suffering, generally, for which I would not like to see this country responsible." (CBS viewers missed Kennan's musings, the network having by then returned to its regularly scheduled reruns of *The Andy Griffith Show*—explaining that the hearings "obfuscate" and "confuse" the issue.)

Small-town clergymen were marching against the war; suburban mothers were marching against the war; even soldiers were marching against the war. "The Whole Thing Was a Lie!" a Vietnam Special Forces veteran wrote in an article published in the February issue of the San Francisco–based New Left magazine *Ramparts*. Robert F. Kennedy had delivered his maiden Senate speech in 1965 urging the president to honor his brother's commitment to Vietnam, but now Washington gossip converged on the question of whether Kennedy would announce a presidential challenge to Lyndon B. Johnson on a peace platform—even as Lyndon Johnson's liberal attorney general said antiwar protesters tended "in the direction of treason."

And then, a watershed: General Lewis B. Hershey, director of the nation's Selective Service System, announced that universities must hand over class ranks to draft boards so they could cancel the deferments of college students with bad grades. At the Universities of Wisconsin and Chicago students took over administration buildings. SDS passed out an alternative draft examination: "The war in South Vietnam is supposed to be part of our policy to contain Communist Chinese aggression. How many Communist Chinese troops are actively engaged in combat in Vietnam? (A) None (B) 1,000 (C) 50,000 (D) 100,000 (E) 500,000." The correct answer, of course, was "(A) None." The United States, on the other hand, had 250,000 troops in Vietnam.

The premises by which the government sold the war were lies. That the government's critics were right didn't make it easier for everyone to accept them. It made it harder, more fundamentally subversive of a piety that Americans were raised to believe: that their government was worthy of trust. For most Americans the antiwar movement was horrifying—frightening out of all proportion to its actual influence. When New York suffered a huge blackout in November of 1965, two newsmen had the same simultaneous thought: "'The anti-Vietnam demonstrators have pulled something off.'"

History would remember the antiwar side's turn to violence years later, but neglected the pro-war side's, which was immediate. The first antiwar teach-in, at the University of Michigan, was interrupted by a bomb threat (so the organizers held an impromptu outdoor rally, three thousand people in twenty-degree weather). In Berkeley in October 1965, fifteen thousand militants marched from campus to "pacify" the Oakland Army Terminal. They were turned back by cordons of riot-helmeted police, but not before Hells Angels were allowed across police lines to crack some hippie heads. In January, the same month the pro-war anthem "The Ballad of the Green Berets" sold as fast as a Beatles record, a Texas Democrat introduced a bill in the House to outlaw antiwar demonstrations.

March saw the assaults against the Du Bois clubs in New York and San Francisco. A week later, in Richmond, Virginia, two pacifists who had been passing out antiwar literature were found shot seventeen times in the back. March 26: marchers in Oklahoma City and Boston were run off by mobs; in New York, marchers held their ground against taunts of "Kill a commie for Jesus" and phone threats that "if we march, we can be assured we will all be dead by four p.m." March 31: four draft resisters were beaten by a teenage mob while police stood by and cameramen jostled for the best angles. April: the headquarters of the Berkeley Vietnam Day Committee and the offices of two radical newspapers in New York were bombed. On the afternoon of May 16, a man walked into the Detroit office of the Socialist Workers Party asking to see books about Lenin, then told the three occupants, "You're all Communists," and fired nine shots, killing one.

The barn of a pacifist communal farm in Voluntown, Connecticut, burned down (police said nothing led them to believe the fire had been set, though the farm was constantly harassed by vigilantes after a local petition campaign failed to run the pacifists out of town). A Unitarian Church in Denver hosting a "Stop the War" meeting was vandalized with red-paint bombs. At Boston College forty-five hundred students chanting "Get off our campus!" had to be held back by mounted police from attacking protesters at a Hubert Humphrey speech. In Champaign, Illinois, leaders of peace demonstrations got stickers on their mailboxes reading, "You are in the sights of a Minuteman." In Queens, the DA seized an arsenal, to be used by the right-wing vigilante group the Minutemen in assaults on "left-wing camps in a three-state area," including mortars, bazookas, grenades, trench knives, over 150 rifles, a "half dozen garroting devices," and over a million rounds of ammunition.

Richard Nixon was gearing up to run for president in a different country from the one that had apotheosized Lyndon Johnson. The only consensus was that the consensus was long gone. Some Americans still spoke of the "soaring sixties." Sargent Shriver, the Office of Economic Opportunity director, spoke of ending poverty in ten years; intellectuals preached a cybernetic revolution, "potentially unlimited output," via "systems of machines which will require little cooperation from human beings." Acid gurus Timothy Leary and Richard Alpert, fired Harvard psychology instructors, opened a retreat "to create a new organism and a new dedication to life as art . . . the automobile is external child's play compared to the unleashing of cortical energy." Even Ronald Reagan said it in his January 1966 TV kickoff: "Our problems are many, but our capacity for solving them is limitless." *The most hopeful times since Christ was born in Bethlehem.*

Other Americans—sometimes the same Americans—were enveloped by dreads.

A social studies textbook: "In the application of biological technology— the engineering of man's biological self and his biological environment—we will face moral, ethical, psychological, and political issues, which will make those faced by the atomic scientists look like child's play."

The hottest novel: *The Crying of Lot 49,* a dystopic vision of a world in which surveillance and conspiracy lurked beneath every surface. A new book, Edward J. Epstein's *Inquest,* charged that every important conclusion reached by the commission of inquiry led by Chief Justice Earl Warren on President Kennedy's assassination was open to question; another, Mark Lane's *Rush to Judgment,* which stayed on bestseller lists for a year, wondered why commission witnesses kept dying under suspicious circumstances.

The hottest idea was that a mood of radical helplessness was blanketing the land—America was suffering an epidemic of "alienation." The Harris organization concocted an "alienation index" to measure it, based on the responses to five statements: "The rich get richer and the poor get poorer"; "What you think doesn't count very much"; "The people running the country don't really care what happens to you"; "People who have the power are out to take advantage of you"; "Left out of the things around you." Robert F. Kennedy's aides, even, felt alienated. "We suddenly found ourselves seriously discussing the possibility that the world might come to an end," one of them recalled while discussing the war. Another took to doodling Hitler mustaches on pictures of Lyndon Johnson.

"'Great Society' or Nation in Crisis: *What Are You to Believe?*" a magazine ad for *The U.S. Book of Facts, 1966,* asked. "Is America's star rising toward a great new Utopia, or sinking into a morass of overpopulation, poverty, and crime? Are we making enormous strides toward a golden era of peace and prosperity, or rapidly digging our own collective grave?"

Ronald Reagan put on a rally on Thursday, May 12, 1966, at San Francisco's Cow Palace—the very hall where, at the Republican National Convention two years earlier, conservatism was supposed to have been interred. "There is a leadership gap, and a morality and decency gap, in Sacramento," he said in the spot where confetti had once rained upon Barry Goldwater. "And there is no better illustration of that than what has been perpetrated at the University of California at Berkeley, where a small minority of beatniks, radicals, and filthy-speech advocates have brought such shame to a great university."

The mess began, Reagan explained, "when so-called 'free speech advocates,' who in truth have no appreciation of freedom, were allowed to assault and humiliate the symbol of authority, a policeman in uniform, and that was the moment when the ringleaders should have been taken by the scruff of the neck and thrown off campus—personally."

And now things had gotten worse. At a dance two months earlier, a fundraiser by Berkeley's Vietnam Day Committee, the ones who'd tried to shut down the Oakland Army Terminal, Reagan said:

"The hall was entirely dark except for the light from two movie screens.

"On these screens the nude torsos of men and women were portrayed, from time to time, in suggestive positions and movements."

Voices hushed.

"Three rock bands played simultaneously.

"The smell of marijuana was thick throughout the hall. There were signs that some of those present had taken dope.

"There were intimations of other happenings which cannot be mentioned. . . .

"This has been allowed to go on in the name of academic freedom. What in heaven's name does academic freedom have to do with rioting, with anarchy, with attempts to destroy the primary purpose of the university, which is to educate our young people?"

At which forty-five hundred people stamped their feet and pounded on the tables, disturbing the cold fried chicken and potato salad they had each paid $7.50 to consume.

Governor Pat Brown spent the evening at a $25-a-plate dinner in Sacramento. He whined about Yorty and Reagan, whose "propaganda efforts . . .

erode public confidence in government. They do create fear and strife. They do block social progress, pitting minorities against each other and against the majority." The idea that Reagan could use California's glorious, world-beating system of higher education as a cudgel against him was baffling, enraging. His reaction to the takeover of Sproul Hall had been the biggest mass arrest in California history. His opinion of these "alienated" kids was the same as that of the people whooping it up for Reagan: they were spitting on their privilege. His ability to control the campus was statutorily limited, in any event. The governor was just one of twenty-four coequal members of the Board of Regents. The charges against him didn't make any sense.

And yet it also made perfect sense. "Pat had the grays and Reagan had the black and whites," Frederick Dutton, a Bobby Kennedy aide who was Brown's closest ally on the Board of Regents, would later reflect. The next day, Yorty aped Reagan, claiming he'd seen a UCLA group distributing "material on sexual practices . . . under sanction of university authority." Why not? The state's most reliable poll had shown George Christopher with a seventeen-point edge over Reagan among self-identified moderate Republicans in mid-April. Now his lead among them was only two. And, this Friday, May 13, the bad luck was all Pat Brown's. He was ten points behind against *both* Republicans.

As American consensus transformed itself into American cacophony, the man whom Pat Brown had forced into political retirement in 1962 oiled his political machine. He had a full-time researcher and writer, a combative twenty-eight-year-old orthodox Catholic out of St. Louis named Patrick Buchanan. Brazenly, he had approached Nixon at a St. Louis party and said if he was running in 1968, he wanted to come aboard. Summoning Buchanan to New York for a grueling three-hour interview, Nixon asked him, "You're not as conservative as William F. Buckley, are you—or am I wrong?" Buchanan, who was *more* conservative than Buckley (his specialty as an editorial writer for the right-wing *St. Louis Globe-Democrat* was disseminating smears about civil rights leaders passed on by J. Edgar Hoover), artfully dodged the question: "I have a tremendous admiration for Bill Buckley."

You had to admire a kid who could play the game like that.

Nixon also had a flack on retainer, William Safire, who sported ostentatious plaid coats and an air of intellectual pretension. Other conspirators flitted in and out of Nixon's office at 20 Broad Street: young lawyers from the firm like Len Garment, Tom Evans, and John Sears; congressmen and lobbyists; advance men from the '60 campaign like Bob Haldeman and John Ehrlichman (they wouldn't commit to help until he pledged to delegate more and drink less); consultants like Edward Teller, the nuclear sage. Nixon even hired Paul Keyes from the *Jack Paar Show* to write his gags. It worked. Soon, a journalist was writing, "His jokes are less forced, his delivery is better, and, most importantly, he has learned the value of poking fun at his own foibles."

What he really needed was money. He needed it to finance the cornerstone of his master plan: a national political tour dubbed "Congress '66." Thus the most important member of the team was fund-raiser Maurice Stans. Dwight D. Eisenhower's former budget director spoke with an aristocratic accent—though he was the son of an impoverished bricklayer. As a penniless youth, he had trekked to Chicago to study business at night school: an Orthogonian. He learned more practical skills, though, as a stenographer at a sausage-casings factory. "What are friends for if you can't screw them once in a while?" his boss instructed him. He would later have occasion to plead to Senate investigators that he had put his education in the relationship between sausage-making and accountancy well behind him.

Stans thought Dick Nixon stood head and shoulders above any other man in the country. But Stans was like most Americans: he thought the notion of Richard Nixon running for president again a bit absurd. Then, one evening in September of 1965, after Nixon's latest Far Eastern trip, the Nixons and the Stanses went to the World's Fair in Queens. Watching the former vice president get mobbed by autograph seekers, Stans realized the idea of a Nixon comeback wasn't so crazy after all. And once Stans pledged himself to the effort, money came rolling in: from blue-chip CEOs like Pepsi's Donald Kendall and Warner-Lambert's Elbert Bobst; from rich right-wingers grateful Nixon had stuck with Barry Goldwater in 1964 like oilmen J. Howard Pew and Henry Salvatori and J. Paul Getty, and Walter Harnischfeger, the Milwaukee mining-equipment manufacturer and one-time Nazi sympathizer. Lila and DeWitt Wallace chipped in $8,500, though their most important contribution was space for Nixon to pontificate in their magazine, *Reader's Digest,* the most widely read monthly in America.

Nixon still pleaded cloth-coated poverty when he wrote old associates: "Dear (Insert Name Here): I am planning to spend five weeks in September and October campaigning in some of the key congressional and Senate races across the country. As usual, I am undertaking this ambitious schedule with only a very part time staff at my disposal. If you could find the time to do some volunteer advance work during that period I would greatly appreciate it.... As usual, we have no funds available for salaries for our advance men." He hit up the Republican National Committee for a free airplane because, he said, he would be working for the party's sake, not his own. Fortunately for the other 1968 contenders, RNC chair Ray Bliss, who had a keen ear for bullshit, made him rent one, out of the half million dollars raised by Stans.

The crusade began in January with a speech to the white-gloved ladies of the Women's National Republican Club at the Waldorf-Astoria (how he hated speaking to women's groups: "I will not go and talk to those shitty ass old ladies!" he once said). The next day, he appeared on the ABC Sunday

show *Issues and Answers,* and the *New York Times* nicely obliged him by
featuring his most important talking point: "I do not expect to be a candidate.
I am motivated solely by a desire to strengthen the party so that whomever
we nominate in 1968 can win."

His usual round of Lincoln's-birthday Republican fund-raising dinners
followed, run this year like a miniature presidential campaign: blocks of hotel
rooms reserved for the press; mimeographed bullet points slipped under
their doors; then on to the next city by Jetstar—the same plane "in which
James Bond was transported by the fabulous Pussy Galore in the movie version of *Goldfinger,*" wrote an agog David Broder of the *New York Times,*
who found Nixon's "wearying" pace "a source of wonder."

So did Leonard Garment. "Day after day," he wrote in his memoirs, "he
mused and muttered, fussing with details, calling here and there, soaking up
information, reacting to events, doubling back, breaking away occasionally
for a foreign trip or business meeting, ceaselessly tinkering, bobbing, weav-
ing, and maneuvering at his disciplined chess player's pace toward the 1968
endgame. This time, Nixon must have said to himself, over and over, there
must be no screwup." Garment thought to himself this must be how Olympic
decathletes trained. Trips to fifty congressional districts were already scheduled for the rest of the year. Nothing—locale, personnel, audience—was left
to chance.

Broder marveled at "the durability of his political appeal." In Cleveland
he spoke before four thousand. In Seattle the local paper reported he got the
"biggest, noisiest reception any Republican has had in years" (much bigger
than the media's darling for the nomination, Michigan governor George
Romney). Then he sat for a televised Q&A with high school students, slaying them with Paul Keyes's one-liners. ("I'm a dropout from the electoral
college. I flunked debate.") Then to Louisville, where he laid a wreath on the
grave of Abraham Lincoln's grandfather. At every stop, he heaped praise on
local GOP office seekers. The fiction was that he was doing this for them.

He was actually implementing an old Nixon technique: discredit your
opponent before he even realizes the campaign has started. Lyndon Johnson,
he told these Republican audiences, was a "political operator"—whose
"political luck has finally begun to peak." He "doesn't come across well on
television" ("and I'm an expert on that"—another Keyes one-liner). He'd
stop just short of calling the president a liar on Vietnam, then add that he
would not be speaking about the war during Johnson's "sensitive negotiating efforts with Hanoi," before extending his sympathy to the president for
all the "well-intentioned but mistaken Democrats who have taken the soft
line, the appeasement line." For we could only lose in Vietnam "if President
Johnson fails to take a strong line that will preserve the peace by refusing to
reward the aggressors."

The bad faith, in retrospect, was pungent. In his memoir, Leonard Garment later revealed that Nixon then believed—though he would only say so in private meetings with top donors—that militarily, Vietnam could not be "won," and that the only practical question was how and when and at what disadvantage the eventual withdrawal would be staged.

Every dig—at Johnson's untrustworthiness, his awkwardness, his divided party—played to a neurotic man's fears. Nixon harped on inflation—within ten months "the country will face higher prices or higher taxes, or controls on wages and prices, and perhaps all three"—baffling reporters: inflation, Evans and Novak observed, was a problem "more phantom than reality," averaging less than 2 percent a year. Every word was entirely deliberate, though what the tactic was would only later become clear. As Nixon noted in an oral history he gave in February about his foreign-policy mentor John Foster Dulles, being Machiavellian "was not necessarily bad. It could be very good."

The Du Bois Club/Boys Club flap broke in March. Len Garment, spending every spare moment preparing what the Franklins at the firm considered the most important component of Nixon's political comeback—arguing as attorney of record in a case before the Supreme Court—went through the roof. The *New Yorker*'s "Talk of the Town" had mocked Nixon: "Custom and continuity are so lacking in these quick times that it was downright heartwarming last week to hear Richard M. Nixon warning us once again about the creepy, infinitely devious ways of the Communist party." Garment thought the boss had just pissed away two years of work spent rehabilitating his post–Last Press Conference reputation—in fresh jeopardy now that the University of Rochester faculty were working to deny him a promised honorary degree because of his depredations against academic freedom in the Genovese flap. The boss was unfazed. He told Garment to stop listening to the "damned press." In the Gallup Poll, among presidential contenders, he was the leading Republican by thirteen points. Appealing to Orthogonians didn't hurt him. It helped.

On April 10 a Boston University senior sat down in front of the White House and tried and failed to do what Quaker Norman Morrison had done beneath Robert McNamara's Pentagon window the previous year: burn himself to death to protest the war. On April 15, five thousand antiwar activists marched in New York, four thousand in Berkeley. The next day Nixon spoke at Tulane University in Louisiana. He asked whether the United States should let China "blackmail us out of the Pacific." *"No!!!!!"* students roared back. Youth politics came in many stripes.

Nixon was touring the South on the eve of House deliberations on the civil rights bill. Liberal Republicans were demanding state GOP parties drop the segregationist planks in their platforms such as: "We feel segregation of the races is absolutely essential to harmonious racial relations and the continued progress of both races in the State of Mississippi." Nixon was, an unnamed prominent Republican told David Broder for a profile he was doing of George Romney, "trying to take the remnants of the Goldwater thing and give it some respectability, but it isn't going to work."

At Nixon's press conference upon arrival in Jackson, Mississippi, a national reporter asked if he was there to raise money for "segregationist candidates."

Nixon was prepared. He'd carved his response with precision:

"I will go to any state in the country to campaign for a strong two-party system, whether or not I agree with local Republicans on every issue."

It was his version of an old Dixie war cry: accusing its critics of anti-Southern bigotry. He pressed on, "I am opposed to any so-called 'segregationist plank' in the Republican platform. . . . I would fight it in the national Republican platform and speak against it." But to direct state party platforms from above was "unrealistic and unwise." Washington "cannot dictate to them."

The cleverness was sublime. He was ventriloquizing a generation of Southern lost-cause speechifying about Yankees dictating to Dixie. At a party dinner that night—the largest in Mississippi since Goldwater came to Jackson in '62—he urged *all* political parties to cease using race in favor of the "issues of the future." Language like this was a flawlessly polished diamond, glinting different colors depending from which angle light struck. To the applauding segregationists, it was a blow at the likes of Richmond Flowers, Lurleen Wallace's liberal opponent who mucked up Alabama politics by campaigning with Martin Luther King—*that* was "using" race. To another variety of Southern Republican—sophisticated, white-collar Episcopalian types who were attracted to the party to strike a blow against the dirty-necked, economically populist courthouse Democrats—"issues of the future" referred to the South's integration into the national industrial economy. Finally, for the consensus-besotted national media, it sounded as if he were heralding the de-Dixifying of Dixie. "Nixon, in the South, Bids GOP Drop Race Issue," Broder's dispatch was headlined on May 7.

The headline belied the piece's sophisticated understanding of what Nixon was up to. By June, Broder reported, "Nixon will have completed a carefully planned circuit of the 11 states of the Confederacy, begun last year." Broder had been one of the myriad reporters to realize too late what F. Clifton White had been up to in 1963. Now he grasped what Clif White grasped. Delegates from the South had comprised 279 out of the 655 needed to nominate in 1964, the biggest regional-bloc vote by far. What's more, Broder wrote, "With convention voting strength keyed to party performance in the last election, the South's relative strength in the Republican convention in 1968 is likely to be even greater because it contributed nearly all of Mr. Goldwater's electoral votes and almost all the few new Republican congressmen." *"Nixon is trying to take the remnants of the Goldwater thing and give it some respectability, but it isn't going to work.*" Actually, it might work just fine. The conventional wisdom also was that Nixon's gravest liability was his lack of a geographical base. Broder, in his calm, methodical way, shredded it. Nixon's geographical base was these eleven Southern states—"As of today," Broder concluded, "more than adequate dimensions for a serious bid."

Nixon's most important coup came at his next stop, South Carolina, where die-hard conservative Republicans had led the surprise attempted draft of Barry Goldwater at the 1960 convention. The Palmetto State's most powerful Republican was Senator Strom Thurmond, running for reelection for the first time since switching from the Democratic Party in 1964. Nixon sought an audience with Thurmond's closest political confidant, state Republican chairman Harry Dent. He learned that the beloved Dent family dog had just been run over by a car. Maybe, just maybe, dispatching a new one to the bereaved family would help his hand with Dent by some appreciable amount.

Regardless of what they might say about it, he was going to try it.

Whether because of the dog or not, Nixon got his meeting. By that time, Nixon was confident he could win the nomination. His terror was the possibility of George Wallace running as a third-party candidate, denying him enough states for an electoral college majority. Nixon flattered Dent by asking him his advice on how to handle the problem, already knowing the answer. It was, Dent said, to win the loyalty of Strom Thurmond. Then Dent told Nixon how to do it. In his press conference the next day, some Eastern Establishment reporter asked Nixon if he found it embarrassing to share a party with "ol' States' Rights Strom." Nixon responded, "Strom is no racist. Strom is a man of courage and integrity."

Richard Nixon understood what dirty-necks like Strom most deeply craved: respect from the elite. "It was like being granted absolution from purgatory by the pope of American politics," one wise interpreter of Southern politics later reflected. Because *of course* Strom Thurmond was a racist, a thoroughgoing racist gargoyle, and forevermore, he would be grateful for the absolution. And Richard Nixon was on his way. This, he told young Buchanan, was *living*. "If I had to practice law and nothing else, I would be mentally dead in two years and physically dead in four."

In the middle of May an L.A. cop stopped a black man named Leonard Deadwyler for speeding through Watts. He stuck his gun in the driver's-side window—"to attract the driver's attention," he later testified. He also claimed the car suddenly lurched forward, causing his gun to discharge. Leonard Deadwyler slumped into the lap of his wife and muttered his last words—"But she's having a baby"—as his two-year-old son looked on from the backseat. He had been speeding her to the nearest hospital, miles away; there was no hospital in Watts—an area twice the size of Manhattan.

Hundreds marched to the Seventy-seventh Precinct in protest. They dispersed peacefully—then a *Newsweek* reporter was ambushed from behind by a two-by-four. ("They stoned him with boulders a foot in diameter," the right-wing tabloid the *L.A. Herald Examiner* embellished in a story headlined "New Race Violence: Riot, Beating, in L.A. Area.") Every day, hundreds of angry Negroes clamored for entrance to the hearing over whether the cop acted properly. The *New York Times*—every broken window in Watts was a national story now—quoted a "well-dressed man" who said that if the cop was cleared, "it'll be like World War II all over again." The *Times* also ran a feature on a Los Angeles black nationalist leader, Ron Karenga, who "told an enthusiastic Negro teenager audience last night they should be prepared to defend themselves—if need be from whites." Mayor Yorty said the Communists were behind it all. Southern California clenched for the next riot.

What prevented it was an agreement between the district attorney and KTLA to televise the inquest live. One token of the city's eggshell sensitivities was that the anchorman felt compelled to remind his viewers over and over that the hearing officer referred to Deadwyler's lawyer as "Johnnie" Cochran because that was how the black lawyer preferred to be called, "no disrespect or condescension intended." The jury ruled the discharge accidental. Cochran addressed the camera on behalf of his client, pleading for peace. Race war was averted, but only in Los Angeles. In Bakersfield, two thousand Negroes at a "grits and gripes" picnic to discuss the city council's nondisbursal of federal poverty funds firebombed a school bus. Whites retaliated with a Molotov cocktail attack on the ghetto.

The gubernatorial election was June 7, one week away.

On Memorial Day weekend Ronald Reagan fulminated at a stadium rally about "arson and murder in Watts." The *Times* led its report noting that when the emcee, Chuck Connors, the television cowboy, said that you could search "from the coasts of Maine to the coasts of California" and not find another politician like Reagan, someone shouted, "Try Arizona!" The *Times* reporter was impressed that Reagan didn't take the bait: he never mentioned Barry Goldwater, and "did not sound much like the conservative hero. He only talked about the same things." That Reagan represented Goldwater's ideas without Goldwater's liabilities was precisely why his boosters backed him for governor in the first place. The Newspaper of Record's conclusion suggested their political instincts had been correct.

This San Diego speech was a typical performance. Reagan pointedly distanced himself from the "nuts and kooks of the extreme right"—though he also courted them by humoring their paranoia: after a microphone failed and was replaced by another, he joked, "How about that, we found one they didn't cut!" He worked in a reference to Vietnam that simultaneously hammered the administration and distanced him from accusations of unpatriotic meddling: "A suspicion prevails," he said—note the artful passivity—that American troops "are being denied the right to try for victory in that war." The *Times* observed how, when the subject turned to Berkeley, "he dwells on 'sexual orgies . . . so vile I cannot describe it to you.'" That got the wildest applause of all.

He spoke of outrageous taxes ("There's no more leeway for squeezing the people"), "the philosophy that only government has the answer," that under Great Society bureaucrats "we cannot remain a free society." He announced as his campaign theme the "Creative Society," where "the people have the strength and ability to confront the problems before us." (For example, since state hospitals and mental institutions were "in a sense, hotel operations," an expert committee of hotel operators could oversee them instead of "government planners.") He savaged skyrocketing welfare programs that brought migrants to the state to "loaf." The California Supreme Court had just invalidated Proposition 14, the anti-open-housing referendum passed in 1964, and Reagan didn't like that one bit: "I have never believed that majority rule has the right to impose on an individual as to what he does with his property. This has nothing to do with discrimination. It has to do with our freedom, our basic freedom." Southern California's bourgeois utopians roared. The *Times* said California Democrats "now believe Ronald Reagan has an excellent chance to be the next governor of the most populous state in the union."

Brown stubbornly kept to his strategy of aiding Reagan. George Christopher had been convicted in 1939 for violating a milk-pricing statute. The conviction, later reversed, was for the sin of setting the price too *low*—hardly a political liability when his opponents had introduced it in past campaigns, so Brown's managers advised him to leave well enough alone. Instead, Brown had the information passed on to muckraking columnist Drew Pearson. Right-wingers in Southern California, where the revelation was fresh, did their part by circulating anonymous handbills featuring Christopher with a number across his chest and the caption "Wanted." Reagan surged some more.

Christopher fought back with theatrics of his own. He flew to Eureka College in Illinois, his opponent's alma mater, where the hypocrite Reagan had once led a student strike himself. A Christopher TV documentary alerted Californians that their hero had belonged to Communist fronts. The charges didn't stick. Nothing stuck to this guy. "I disagree with almost everything he says," an exasperated Brown appointee told the *Saturday Evening Post.* "But dammit, I can't help but feel that he is basically a nice guy."

Reagan latched onto a stricture laid down by California's Republican chairman, San Diego obstetrician Gaylord Parkinson, after the divisive 1964 primary between Nelson Rockefeller and Barry Goldwater: "Thou shalt not speak ill of a fellow Republican." Christopher backed it, too, until his last-ditch dispatch from Eureka, after which Parkinson publicly censured him—making Reagan look like the candidate of Republican unity.

Ronald Reagan had been underestimated, not for the last time. He learned to count on it, cherish it, revel in it: it was his political capital.

At a rally in San Francisco's Chinatown, Brown cried that Reagan was "sailing a course that's pure Goldwater; the only difference is that Reagan's turned out the running lights." Brown meanwhile did his best to sail a course more like Reagan's, not quite getting the coordinates right: signing the nation's first law outlawing LSD, he promised it would "not hamper proper use of the drug for legitimate purposes." He put in gray— "*proper use . . . legitimate purposes*"—what Reagan rendered in black and white: "*The smell of marijuana was thick throughout the hall.*"

In the California Poll the top issues of public concern were now "crime, drugs, and juvenile delinquency." Forty-five percent credited Reagan as the candidate who would do a better job on them. He used phrases like "basic freedom," "basic principles," "basic individual rights of all citizens." He called "the one overriding issue of this campaign . . . the issue of simple morality." In a season of moral panic, it made him the star.

The leftists of the California Democratic Council, moralists in their own right, turned their back on Brown for his support of the administration on Vietnam. One of the president's favorite congressmen, Jeffrey Cohelan, was almost knocked off in a primary challenge in the district straddling Oakland and Berkeley from New Leftist magazine editor Robert Scheer. Johnson's poverty czar, Sargent Shriver, gave a speech to a conference of the Citizen's Crusade Against Poverty and was jostled off the stage by radicals: "You're lying!" they cried. "Stop listening to him!"

Moral panics from the right, moral panics from the left; poor, dumpy Pat Brown pinioned helplessly in the middle. On primary day he couldn't even get a majority, holding on to the nomination only because minor candidates diluted Yorty's tally. Yorty received 38 percent of the vote practically without campaigning, overwhelmingly winning in blue-collar areas adjacent to black neighborhoods. People started talking about running him for Senate against the liberal Republican Thomas Kuchel in 1968.

Also on the ballot in L.A. County was a $12.3 million bond issue to finally build a hospital in Watts. The hospital that would have saved Leonard Deadwyler's life.

It failed.

And, oh, yes, California Republicans, "against all counsels of common sense and prudence," in the words of the *New York Times* editorial, "insisted upon nominating actor Ronald Reagan for governor." They did it in a landslide.

*   *   *

Reagan the conquering hero was invited to address the National Press Club. Nixon briefed Senator George Murphy and a young factotum named Sandy Quinn on how to coach the neophyte for his national political coming-out. The press would bug Reagan about whether he was using California as a stepping-stone to a presidential candidacy in 1968, Nixon explained, just as they had bugged Nixon in 1962; the customary answer—Reagan had a contract with the people of California to serve out his term—"will not go over with this sophisticated group." It had not, after all, worked for Nixon—and he was the most skilled political professional in the country. The charge that Nixon was plotting to use the governorship as a stepping-stone to the presidency had stuck—it was what the slogan "Would you buy a used car from this man?" referred to. But he should at least try it, Nixon had his friends tell Reagan.

Nixon's advice bore a double agenda. First, he wanted Ronald Reagan to be in his debt should Reagan win the statehouse. At the same time, conservatives were already talking about Reagan as a presidential prospect—so Nixon stood to benefit mightily if Reagan pledged before the national political press corps not to run in 1968 (for if Reagan did run, he could claim he had accomplished what Nixon could not: beating Pat Brown).

Reagan dashed off a note thanking Nixon for "your very good suggestions," then jetted East. In Pittsburgh he was the guest of right-wing billionaire Richard Mellon Scaife. In Gettysburg his host was General Eisenhower—who said "you can bet" Reagan would be a presidential prospect if he beat Pat Brown. (The bastard, Nixon had to be thinking, kicking Dick Nixon once more.)

In Washington, Reagan met with the California congressional delegation—all except Senator Thomas Kuchel, who had been complaining that the Republican Party in California was being taken over by "fanatical" and "neo-fascist elements." Shrewdly, skillfully, Reagan refused to cop to a feud; he said his relationship with Kuchel had always been "very cordial."

Thence to the National Press Club, where he introduced the Creative Society as a "constructive alternative" to a so-called Great Society that cost Americans "an ounce of personal freedom for every ounce of federal help we get." He envisioned instead "a state government mobilizing the energies of the people . . . helping them organize their own solutions to these problems." Not a word on orgies so vile. He spoke a language Washington insiders could abide.

Came the inevitable question: are you interested in taking on LBJ in 1968?

Reagan's face sparked a boyish grin. "Wel-l-l-l"—that word, followed by a chuckle, would become the most famous in his lexicon—"gosh, it's taken me all my life to get up the nerve to do what I'm doing. That's as far as my dreams go."

And that was it. No follow-up questions, then or in the months to come. D.C.'s ink-stained wretches thought of themselves as the toughest audience in the world. Now they were applauding Ronald Reagan like schoolboys. Reagan dashed to New York for a secret meeting at 20 Broad Street. His host had to wonder who was the master, and who was the student. This Reagan was someone to watch. He was someone to learn from.

Nixon started watching Reagan very, very carefully.

Commencement season. Which had traditionally been the nation's consensus season: occasion for endless Johnsonesque bromides about the challenge of making our society even greater than it already was.

Not this year.

Richard Nixon, speaking at the University of Rochester in defiance of the faculty's successful petition not to offer him an honorary degree (he lied that "since leaving the office of vice president it has been my policy not to accept honorary degrees"), aped Reagan: "If we are to defend academic freedom from encroachment we must also defend it from its own excesses."

The president's new education commissioner, Harold Howe II, spoke at Vassar. He said the next civil rights battles would be fought in the suburbs and urban middle-class bungalow belts—"in quiet communities, in pleasant neighborhoods."

Louise Day Hicks, the school-committee member who had become a political superstar in Boston fighting to make sure no integration battles were won in *her* constituents' pleasant neighborhoods, rose to speak at a high school in the ghetto neighborhood of Roxbury. "A foul enemy of ours has been brought into this place!" a parent cried, rushing the stage, taking the microphone. "If this were a synagogue, would you have invited Hitler?"

Sargent Shriver, at Illinois Wesleyan, said Vietnam might be liberalism's front line, but "our slums, ghettos, and economically depressed areas are the rear," and we "must not win the war in Vietnam and lose the battle we are fighting in Watts, Harlem." That only pointed up the impossible contradiction dividing the liberal movement, as evinced at the graduations at Amherst and NYU—where, protesting speaker Robert McNamara, architect of this "liberal" war, liberal students walked out.

Arthur Schlesinger, speaking at Smith, said the acrimony between pro- and antiwar forces would force upon us a new dawn of McCarthyism: "The situation is worse, because fifteen years ago, liberals were determined to maintain rational discussion."

John Steinbeck pronounced himself horrified by the "fallout, drop-out, cop-out insurgency of our children and young people, the rush to stimulant as well as hypnotic drugs, the rise of narrow, ugly, and vengeful cults of all kinds, the mistrust and revolt against all authority—this in a time of plenty such as has never been known," the passing of a nation in which "the rules were understood and accepted by everyone." Horrified also was the advertising agency Deutsch & Shea, which took out a full-page ad in the *New York Times* worrying that to the class of '66, "business has become a dirty word":

"Isn't it time to say the things that need to be said about business and industry and the way things really are?

"Now?

"Before we lose another generation?"

The valedictorian at Columbia, on the other hand, said "protests and demonstrations against social injustice were as important to a student's overall education as classwork."

They called this the "generation gap": a magazine feature-writer's fancy phrase for the screaming matches that were breaking out across dinner tables around the country. The cultural war within which Ronald Reagan thrived was enveloping the nation.

CHAPTER FIVE

Long, Hot Summer

A MAIN FRONT IN THE NEW AMERICAN CONFLAGRATION WAS RACIAL. By the end of June, a young man named Stokely Carmichael, and a doctrine called Black Power, doused it with gasoline.

Early in the year a young, black Southern Nonviolent Coordinating Committee activist registering voters in Tuskegee, Alabama, stopped at a gas station for some cigarettes, asked the clerk to point him to the bathroom, and was told to use the one for coloreds out back. "Haven't you heard of the Civil Rights Act?" Sammy Younge snapped back. The clerk replied by shooting him in the head.

This sort of thing made younger civil rights activists wonder about the wisdom of the nonviolence preached by Martin Luther King. It was an old argument, watched nervously in the national press ever since 1961 when a former marine and North Carolina NAACP official named Robert Williams called for armed cadres to protect demonstrators on Second Amendment grounds. Rejection of nonviolence tended to come of an organic process: heartening civil rights gains would be followed by corrosive disappointments; disillusionment set in, calling for increasingly spectacular acts, a spiral of militancy. "If we can't sit at the table," SNCC executive director James Forman had said at a 1965 mass meeting in Montgomery, "let's knock the fucking legs off."

Few had lived the process more intimately than Forman's intense and brilliant twenty-four-year-old comrade Stokely Carmichael. Stokely had grown up in the Bronx watching white people humiliate his idealistic Trinidadian father—and seeing his father, the more he was humiliated, profess ever more faith in the American dream. In 1960, Stokely headed South after reading about the Woolworth lunch-counter sit-ins. The next year on the Freedom Rides he was beaten and went to jail for the first of twenty-six times. In 1964, after Lyndon Johnson seated the "regular" white Mississippi delegation at the Democratic convention instead of the integrated Mississippi Freedom Democratic Party, Stokely's commitment to ordinary politics ended for good. "This proves," he cried, "the liberal Democrats are just as racist as Goldwater." The next year he watched police beat demonstrators outside his Selma hotel-room window. He started screaming. He couldn't stop. He had a nervous breakdown that lasted two days.

Then 1966 was rung in with the blood of Brother Younge. The day after his funeral, SNCC's chairman, John Lewis, read out a statement at a press conference: "The murder of Samuel Younge in Tuskegee, Alabama, is no different than the murder of peasants in Vietnam, for both Younge and the Vietnamese sought, and are seeking, to secure the rights guaranteed them by law. . . . We are in sympathy with, and support, the men in this country who are unwilling to respond to a military draft which would compel them to contribute their lives to United States aggression in Vietnam in the name of the 'freedom' we find so false in this country."

Reporters' jaws began dropping. This was nothing less than a categorical break with the best president for civil rights since Abraham Lincoln. Whitney Young of the Urban League and Roy Wilkins of the National Association for the Advancement of Colored People, mainstream Negro leaders, distanced themselves in horror. Julian Bond, a SNCC activist who had won election to the Georgia legislature with 82 percent of his district's votes, was asked if he supported Lewis's statement. "Sure, I support it," he said—at which his fellow legislators labeled him a traitor and barred him from being sworn in.

Lurleen Wallace's victory seemed to render Sammy Younge's martyrdom vain. "You don't imitate white politics because white politics are corrupt," Carmichael pronounced. "Negroes have to view themselves as colonies, and right now is the time for them to quit being white men's colonies and become independent." SNCC's next convention kicked out John Lewis for being too moderate. "We need someone who can grab Lyndon Johnson by his balls and tell him to kiss our ass," one delegate said. "We need someone who can stand up to Dr. King and tell him the same thing." Lewis's replacement was Stokely Carmichael. His first move was to withdraw SNCC from the historic White House civil rights conference in June to protest America's repression "of the Third [nonwhite] World." The brackets were the *New York Times*'s, explaining a baffling new *Marxisant* locution.

Tuesday, June 7, was primary day in Mississippi, same as in California. The previous Sunday, James Meredith, decked out in a pocket protector and a pith helmet, set out on a quixotic 220-mile march from Memphis to Jackson, refusing the protection of federal marshals, to convince black voters it was safe to go to the polls. He crossed the border of the state whose university he had integrated in 1962. A farmer emptied a double-barreled shotgun into his hide. Early, inaccurate reports from the AP had it that he died. "Meredith Regrets He Was Not Armed," the *New York Times* announced the next morning.

At first the effect on a fast-dividing civil rights movement seemed salvific.

All factions flocked to Meredith's bedside and pledged to complete Meredith's march, even Stokely Carmichael. The first day, police shoved the assembled leaders off the highway and onto the shoulder; they fell together, arm in arm. SNCC's Cleveland Sellers was facedown in the mud. Carmichael leapt for one of the officers. Martin Luther King held him back. Carmichael, chastened, promised that he, too, would march in the name of nonviolence.

The march grew day by day. Of that civil rights legislation that no one was giving a chance, the *Washington Post* said, "Meredith's sacrifice might spur the bill to swift enactment." Donations to King's Southern Christian Leadership Conference had been tapering off: the left was turning their dollars to the fight against the Vietnam War. So the onrushing unity was especially heartening to King. It felt, again, like Selma: nonviolence on the march.

Stokely, however, was playing an entirely different game. He hoped to heighten, not salve, the mounting contradictions within the civil rights movement.

In negotiations over the march's manifesto, he insisted on savaging the president of the United States. Roy Wilkins and Whitney Young quit in disgust, playing into Carmichael's hands: with the moderates out of the picture, he worked to take over. For a few more days the squabbles stayed private, the images heroic. On June 9, an old man fell from a heart attack. And still they marched. They didn't have tents to sleep in at night. And still they marched. Byron de la Beckwith, the murderer of Medgar Evers, acquitted by a Mississippi jury though his fingerprints were on the murder weapon, followed them in his pickup truck, dandling a shotgun on his knee. And still they marched. Mississippi drew down twenty of the twenty-four officers it had detailed to protect the marchers from violence. And still they marched—united.

Until, that is, June 16. One thousand marchers swung into the Black Belt town of Greenwood, one of the places where SNCC had aggressively sought to register penniless sharecroppers. As soon as Stokely Carmichael set foot in town, he was arrested. The next day, a rally was organized to celebrate his release.

He mounted the speaker's platform, eyes wide. "This is the twenty-seventh time I have been arrested," he began. "I ain't going to jail no more."

The SNCC militants had been testing out a phrase among one another. Americans of African descent were known as "Negroes." SNCC militants had begun to call one another "black," the word Malcolm X had used: its starkness carried a militant charge. As did how they wore their hair: naturally kinky, covering the scalp, rather than cut short and greased down and straightened (they called the style the "natural"—the other way was phony; or the "Afro"—the other way was European). They also began telling one another that to call theirs a "freedom" movement was wishy-washy; what they really needed was *power.*

Thus the phrase Stokely Carmichael now debuted—the phrase that signaled a civil war within the civil rights movement.

"We want *black power!*"

Some in the crowd: *"That's right."*

"We want black power!"

"That's right!"

"That's right. We want black power, and we don't want to be ashamed of it. We have stayed here, and we have *begged* the president. We have *begged* the federal government. That's all we've been doin'—beggin', beggin'. It's time we stand up and take over. Every courthouse in Mississippi ought to be burned down tomorrow to get rid of the dirt in there!"

CBS cut to the crowd. Some were clearly startled. Others looked transported. It was the day a House subcommittee had referred the civil rights bill to the full Judiciary. Now the TV filled with images of Stokely Carmichael, in black shirt, sunglasses, and a tie leading marchers like a drill sergeant in his new chant with his fist in the air. The new phrase was capitalized: *Black Power.* The fist in the air became known as the "Black Power salute." Moderates tripped over themselves to repudiate the formulation—"a reverse Hitler, a reverse Ku Klux Klan," said Roy Wilkins. United Auto Workers president Walter Reuther was denied a speaking spot at the June 28 closing rally in Jackson. Charles Sim of the Deacons for Defense was not. He "has a long arrest record not connected with civil rights activities," the *Los Angeles Times* noted. They also reported that SNCC had desecrated an American flag.

The other main front in America's domestic civil war was yoked to events nine thousand miles away—where, in the hours between June 29 and June 30, Vietnam time, American planes began raining fire on fuel depots in densely populated areas near Hanoi and Haiphong. The next week, at the LBJ Ranch, the president gave a rosy status report: 86 percent of the enemy's known fuel-storage capacity had been taken out; the most recent troop surge "has been forceful and it has been effective"; hearts and minds were being won in South Vietnam via six hundred thousand new acres of irrigated land distributed to landless peasants, thirteen thousand new village health stations, ten thousand new students in U.S.-sponsored "vocational training" classes.

What he did not mention: North Vietnam maintained enough dispersed petroleum capacity to be virtually unaffected; the flow of men and matériel down the Ho Chi Minh Trail was undiminished; and the contingency he had risked to achieve these nugatory results—an errant bomb hitting some Russian ship and dragging the USSR into the war—had inspired him to confide to his daughter, "Your daddy may go down in history as having started World War III."

Lying about Vietnam: it was now a Washington way of life. The lies started with the war's ontological premise. We were supposed to be defending a "country" called "South Vietnam." But South Vietnam was not quite a country at all. Vietnamese independence fighters had begun battling the French since practically the day they stopped fighting side by side in World War II. In 1954 they fought their colonial overlords to a final defeat at the stronghold of Dien Bien Phu. It was the first military loss for a European colonial power in three hundred years. Though these stalwarts, the Vietminh, now controlled four-fifths of the country's territory, at the peace conference in Geneva they made a concession: they agreed to administer an armistice area half that size, demarcated at the seventeenth parallel (but for some last-minute haggling, it would have been the eighteenth). A government loyal to the French would administer the lands to the south. The ad hoc demarcation was to last twenty-four months, at which time the winner of an internationally supervised election in 1956 would run the entire country.

Instead, the division lasted for nineteen years. The reason was the United States, which saw to it the reunification election never took place. American intelligence knew that Ho Chi Minh, the Communist leader of the independence fighters, would have won 80 percent of the vote. The seventeenth parallel was read backward as an ordinary international boundary. If "North Vietnam" crossed it, they'd be guilty of "aggression." Meanwhile, the CIA launched a propaganda campaign to depopulate North Vietnam, whose sizable Catholic population was shipped to "South Vietnam" via the U.S. Seventh Fleet. There, they found themselves part of a citizenry that had no reason for being in history, culture, or geography; even as the U.S. pretended—then came to believe—they were a brave, independence-loving nation of long standing. Actually the great city in the South, Saigon, had been France's imperial headquarters. There, France had crowned a figurehead emperor at the tender age of twelve. During World War II, Emperor Bao Dai had collaborated with Vichy France and the Japanese. This was the man the South Vietnamese were supposed to venerate as the leader of their independent nation.

He was replaced by someone worse: a wily hustler named Ngo Dinh Diem. In 1952, Diem engineered a presidential election between himself and the emperor, with the help of U.S. government advisers, and "won" 98.2 percent of the vote. He then revived the guillotine as punishment for anyone "infringing upon the security of the state." His favorite rebuff to an insult from a political opponent was "Shoot him dead!" His sister-in-law Madame Nhu, who served as his emissary abroad, told Americans the last thing her family was interested in was "your crazy freedoms." This was the government to which the United States would now ask its citizens to pledge their lives, their fortunes, and their sacred honor. Diem was not a Communist. And that, said America, made him a democrat.

Ho Chi Minh had no special beef with the United States. He liked to quote the Declaration of Independence; on the march to Hanoi during World War II, his forces called themselves the Viet-American Army; after the war, Ho sent telegrams to President Truman offering an independent Vietnam as "a fertile field for American capital and enterprise." (Truman never answered.) The French reconquered Vietnam with what was practically an American mercenary force: 78 percent of the French army's funding came from the United States. More hawkish Americans lobbied for direct intervention; Richard Nixon, after his visit in 1953, advised Eisenhower that two or three atomic bombs would do the trick. Ho Chi Minh's supporters in South Vietnam began their guerrilla war in 1960. It led to a kind of Cold War nervous breakdown. Falter in Vietnam, Lyndon Johnson claimed in 1964, and "they may just chase you into your own kitchen."

Absurdities were propounded as gospel truth: that to interdict the flow of men supposedly pouring forth down the Ho Chi Minh Trail from North Vietnam was to make the Vietcong insurgency stop (but by March of 1966, 216,400 U.S. forces were in South Vietnam, and 13,100 North Vietnamese troops). That bringing pain to North Vietnam through bombing raids would make the insurgency stop (instead it only made North Vietnam more determined). That diplomatic pressure on China and the Soviet Union—LBJ called them the enemy's "two big brothers"—could make the insurgency stop. (But neither ever sent troops, or could tell the fiercely nationalistic insurgency what to do, and noncommunist countries sent almost as many merchant ships to North Vietnam as the Soviets.) That we could eventually arm and inspirit the South Vietnamese to defend themselves from Ho Chi Minh. (But first they had to be convinced Ho Chi Minh was an enemy. One U.S. adviser knew the effort was sunk the day he walked into his first peasant hut and saw side by side pictures of Ho and John F. Kennedy.)

The Saigon government was reckless and corrupt. The South Vietnamese army was a joke (one top officer was a double agent). Their main skill was antagonizing the local peasantry. Same, in fact, with American GIs. America's war aim in Vietnam was supposed to be to win the allegiance of its people to the government we preferred. The brass called that "winning hearts and minds." The acronym—WHAM—was all too apt. To warn VC, combat battalions took to nailing severed enemy ears to trees. Helicopter door gunners mowed down suspiciously placed figures wearing "black pajamas," what the VC wore instead of proper uniforms. Problem being, Vietnamese farmers wore black pajamas, too. One of the main methods to protect the farmers was to exile them at gunpoint to refugee camps—from villages to whom their ties were so spiritually deep their ancestors' umbilical cords were buried there.

The insurgency only grew. It grew of the efforts to stop it, an infernal machine.

It was not as if American leaders hadn't been warned. It was "the wrong war, at the wrong place, at the wrong time, and with the wrong enemy," the

World War II hero Omar Bradley had first observed in 1951. Such sage warnings tended to be ignored. When Undersecretary of State George Ball began
criticizing the commitment to South Vietnam in the early 1960s, he was shut
out of meetings. He managed to buttonhole the president nonetheless.
"Within five years," he said, "we'll have three hundred thousand men in the
paddies and jungles and never will find them again. That was the French experience." JFK came back, "George, you're just crazier than hell." Ball indeed
misjudged: the actual number of troops at the end of 1966 was 385,300.

The 1964 Special National Intelligence Estimate predicted the South Vietnamese army would *never* be an effective fighting force. Johnson's most
trusted friend in the Senate, Richard Russell, reminded him that the consensus of the intelligence agencies was that bombing the North would be little
more effective. Get out, and get out quickly, Russell advised. "I can't see anything but catastrophe for my country."

Johnson did not. In April of 1965 he explained the escalation at Johns
Hopkins University: "We must fight if we are to live in a world where every
country can shape its own destiny." Sixty million Americans watched it on
TV. But according to a memo filed by Assistant Secretary of Defense John
McNaughton a month earlier, 70 percent of the reason we were fighting was
"to avoid a humiliating U.S. defeat." Helping the people of South Vietnam
shape their own destiny he listed at 10 percent.

And by the time of the fuel-depot bombings, the horror of those who
found the lies too monstrous to abide reached a new dramatic pitch. On June
30, three soldiers, a Puerto Rican, a Negro, and an Italian-American—the
"Fort Hood Three"—gave a press conference:

"We speak as American soldiers. We have been in the army long enough
to know we are not the only GIs who feel as we do. Large numbers of men
in the service either do not understand this war or are against it. . . .

"Our man or men in Saigon have always been brutal dictators. . . .

"No one uses the word 'winning' anymore because in Vietnam it has no
more meaning. Our officers just talk about five and ten more years of war
with at least a half million of our boys into the grinder. . . .

"We have made our decision. We will not be a part of this unjust,
immoral, and illegal war. We want no part of a war of extermination. We
oppose the criminal waste of American lives and resources.

"We refuse to go to Vietnam!"

That was a Thursday. Monday was the Fourth of July. And in Southern California, everyone knew that there would be a riot over the holiday—and that
when the fires came this time, they would immolate white suburbs.

Los Angeles Times columnist Paul Coates once again reported the calls he
was receiving:

"Have you heard there's going to be a race riot in Torrance?"

"My mother-in-law goes to a beautician whose boyfriend is a cop, and he told her that the talk is that there's going to be an attack on Woodland Hills. What can we do?"

"There was a car full of them cruising around Santa Monica at two o'clock this morning. . . . Why would they be doing that if they weren't planning some kind of trouble?"

Chief Parker was in Sacramento demanding an antiriot law, claiming holiday intelligence of "urban guerrilla warfare—an absolute plan to burn and sack a city." Paul Coates concluded his column quoting a La Brea shopkeeper: "I'm not a nut, but this may be something. I just saw a skywriting plane and it was making the Greek letter omega. You know what that means? The last letter in the Greek alphabet. It means the end."

Independence Day came and went. Los Angeles didn't blow. Riots broke out in places like Des Moines and Omaha instead. In New York City, Mayor Lindsay walked the streets of Harlem night and day, begging for peace in the ninety-eight-degree heat, personally opening hydrants, getting himself photographed for the papers cavorting with squealing kids. In Miami, two factions in a beachside knife fight joined forces and attacked the police.

Other disturbances broke out in air-conditioned comfort. In Baltimore, the Congress for Racial Equality, which used to be 50 percent white, hosted as its annual convention's keynote speaker one "Lonnie X," who spoke surrounded by twenty Fruit of Islam guards. A white nun stalked out: "This is the Congress for Racial Superiority." (The next week the worst prison riot in Maryland history broke out. A spokesman blamed CORE: "If they don't stop telling these prisoners about their rights, it's going to get worse.") The NAACP met in tense L.A. Roy Wilkins pleaded that in a white-run society Black Power "can mean in the end only black death," for NAACP "moderates" as much as SNCC "militants." "Many white persons," he pointed out to the press, "distinguish very little between groups." American Nazi Party thugs soon made his point by rushing the stage during the proceedings.

That was Tuesday. On Wednesday, July 6, at another Los Angeles hotel, the National Governors' Conference opened with the traditional gala parade of the states. The *New York Times* had predicted the conclave would help Pat Brown, as host, "receive some helpful luster." It didn't work out that way. A thousand antiwar picketers disrupted his address. The scuttlebutt between sessions was whether Ronald Reagan was presidential timber, and tips on the best time to mobilize the National Guard when one of your cities was going up in flames.

Nebraska's Democratic governor, Frank Morrison, downplayed the significance of the riot he had left behind in his own state. He flew back to Omaha when it didn't go away, calling up six companies of the National Guard, pledging that the violence would have no effect on policymaking. Then he toured Omaha's Near North Side ghetto, which he had never before seen. Shell-shocked, he pronounced the neighborhood "unfit for human habitation" and announced he would open a state employment office in the inner city as soon as possible, then returned to Los Angeles and attended every conference session on economic opportunity he could find.

At the LBJ Ranch, a president whose approval rating was inching down toward 50 percent, and who newspapers were reporting was only half as popular as Senator Robert Kennedy among California Democrats, fought off a ravenous press corps.

"Mr. President, regarding racial incidents, sir, in various cities, what is your estimate of the immediate hazards in the situation, and do you have any advice for Americans in this connection?" Johnson's reply almost pleaded: "We believe that every citizen ought to have the right to have a decent home. We are doing everything we can, as quickly as we can, under our voter's rights bill, under our civil rights bills, under our housing bills, under proposals we have made in cooperation with the mayors under the able leadership of the vice president, to improve these terrible conditions that exist in the ghettos of this country."

The president had staked his political future on a nation's sympathy with the black freedom movement. But the black freedom movement was now defined by language like this, from a leaked SNCC position paper: "When we view the masses of white people . . . we view in reality 180 million racists." Johnson refused to back down: "We are going to continue as long as I am president to do everything we can to see that all citizens are treated equally and have equal opportunities." Others made a show of refusing to be intimidated by black rage. An item in the July 6, 1966, *New York Times:* "Montpelier—The Board of State Library Trustees voted 4 to 1 tonight to retain the name of Niggerhead Pond and Niggerhead Mountain in Groton State Forest." Those opposed to the name change had argued that *niggerhead* was only a logging term for a burrlike passage in a river.

A tiny piece appeared in the *Los Angeles Times* that same morning datelined Sacramento: "Shots from one or two cars filled with whites killed two Negro men in a downtown waterfront slum area Tuesday night." You would think something like that might make the front page. Instead, it was tucked deep inside the paper. Page one was monopolized by events at the state capitol: the debate over the antiriot law. Chief Parker testified, "We're talking about putting moats around our new buildings." A black witness was asked, if unemployment was 40 percent in Watts, why didn't people just move? The witness was incredulous: "The California Real Estate Association took care of that with Proposition 14." Watts assemblyman Melvin Dymally said the legislation would "be the first step in inciting riots in Los Angeles" and endorsed the call to incorporate Watts as an independent "Freedom City" with its own police force.

The legislative session was set by law to end at 5 p.m. It was now 4:38.

Then the explosion went off.

"Frightened senators and spectators glanced bewilderedly at the old gas lamps and high marble pillars and then laughed when they realized that merely a Fourth of July leftover had exploded," the *Los Angeles Times* reported, claiming, unconvincingly, that it relieved the room's tensions.

At 4:50 the solons availed themselves of an old parliamentary trick by stopping the clock on the wall. They worked through dinner, and the antiriot bill passed 30-0. Governor Brown congratulated them on "a most productive legislative session." Actually, besides the LSD ban and this semiconstitutional bit of grandstanding, they had hardly passed anything substantial at all.

The Fort Hood Three were abducted on July 7 at a church meeting by military police and held incommunicado. In the South Vietnamese coastal city of Hue, Buddhists protesting the strong-arm rule of the American-backed prime minister Nguyen Cao Ky—he had just issued an edict prescribing summary execution as a penalty for advocating peace—rampaged through the streets overturning cars, smashing shop windows, and burning down the U.S. Information Service building. It was, all told, one of the scariest weeks since President Kennedy had been shot down in Dallas. U.S. combat deaths in Vietnam hit 4,129; 115 died that week alone. In his 1966 State of the Union address in January, the president had laid out grandiose plans: a minimum wage increase, new mine and highway safety laws, child nutrition initiatives, rent supplements, federal reform of the bail system, a Model Cities program announced with the promise "that the city is not beyond the reach of redemption by men of goodwill." Just not now, Johnson told presidential assistant Joseph Califano, just not now. "We're going to have to take our time on everything except Vietnam."

In Chicago, Martin Luther King's activists inaugurated their new strategy. Chicago had an open-housing ordinance, passed in 1963—that was what let Mayor Daley say there was no segregation in Chicago. So married black couples began visiting real estate offices in bucolic white neighborhoods and asking to be shown a home. They would be told there were none available. A similarly situated white couple would make the same request and would be given the red-carpet treatment. On July 8 alone, in the neighborhood of Gage Park, the testers recorded thirty prima facie violations of the law. Chicago's power structure wasn't about to do anything about that. Doing something about it would be to torch the entire moral economy of the city as Mayor Daley and his core constituency understood it.

Chicago's white ethnics cherished their neighborhoods as they cherished their families and faith. The three seemed identical. Their parents and grandparents, summoned from Catholic Europe to work in Chicago's stockyards and factories at the turn of the century, settled in sordid tenements. Southern blacks were similarly called North to work during World War I. They worked the same factories and stockyards—last hired, first fired, and always in the dirtiest jobs—and lived in yet more dilapidated tenements. With the 1920s economic boom, white workers had the wherewithal to get the hell out of the tenements. Black workers did not.

Through no agency of their own, Chicago's white ethnics were the beneficiaries of an urban-planning miracle. The National Association of Real Estate Boards—the same group that turned itself into a political machine to lobby against open occupancy in 1966—launched an "Own Your Own Home" crusade in the 1920s to coax families into putting down payments on single-family houses of their very own; simultaneously, idealistic reformers coming out of England's Arts and Crafts movement devised a new form of cheap and felicitous housing unmatched in the history of the industrial working class: the urban "bungalow." Squat, handsome, one-and-a-half-story single-family homes in sturdy brick, garden plots out front, each a happy marriage of community-building uniformity and dignity-enhancing individuality (families could choose their own geometrically patterned brickwork, limestone trim, colorful awnings, artistic leaded glass, even custom-toned mortar); plentiful sunlight; minimal traffic (garages were in the back alley); endless ribbons of common greensward out front for children to play; each neighborhood anchored by parish church and school; all manner of citizens' bunds to join; lively neighborhood newspapers; attentive block captains under the discipline of Daley's Democratic machine attuned to their every municipal need.

When another wave of Negroes migrated to Chicago during and after World War II, however, not-so-enlightened reformers boxed them into soulless "housing projects." You could draw a map of the boundary within which the city's seven hundred thousand Negroes were allowed to live by marking an X wherever a white mob attacked a Negro. Move beyond it, and a family had to face down a mob of one thousand, five thousand, or even (in the Englewood riot of 1949, when the presence of blacks at a union meeting sparked a rumor the house was to be "sold to niggers") ten thousand bloody-minded whites. In the late 1940s, when the postwar housing shortage was at its peak, you could find ten black families living in a basement, sharing a single stove but not a single flush toilet, in "apartments" subdivided by cardboard. One racial bombing or arson happened every three weeks. The job of the mayor's Commission on Human Relations was to see that none of these incidents made it into one of the city's six daily papers. Because officially, there was no segregation in Chicago.

In the neighborhoods where they were allowed to "buy" houses, they couldn't actually buy them at all: banks would not write them mortgages, so unscrupulous businessmen sold them contracts that gave them no equity or title to the property, from which they could be evicted the first time they

were late with a payment. Or they crowded into the same dilapidated tenements the white ethnics had abandoned. Some were right across the street
from the bungalows—making a thoroughfare like Ashland Avenue about as
risky to cross as no-man's-land in World War I. White ethnics felt themselves
defending an urban middle-class paradise against Martin Luther King. And
Illinois's junior senator, seventy-four-year-old Democrat Paul Douglas, up
for reelection that fall, began getting letters like these:

"As a citizen and a taxpayer I was very upset to hear about 'Title IV' of
the so-called civil rights Bill S. 3296. This is not Civil Rights. This takes away
a person's rights. We too are people and need someone to protect us."

"We designed and built our own home and I would hate to think of being
forced to sell my lovely home to anyone just because they had the money."

"Do you or any of your friends live next door to a negro—why should
we have them pushed down our throats?"

On July 10, Martin Luther King led a rally at Soldier Field. He followed
it with a march to City Hall—where, like his namesake, Martin Luther, he
tacked the movement's open-housing and slum-clearing demands on the
mayor's doorposts. Daley shrugged, saying, "They have no programs."
"What he meant," retorted Mike Royko, the cantankerous Daley-baiting
columnist for the *Chicago Sun-Times,* "was, they had no program that didn't
include blacks moving into white neighborhoods."

It was the third straight day of ninety-degree heat in Chicago. On the
fifth day of the heat wave, Martin Luther King was enjoying dinner with his
wife, Coretta, at the home of Mahalia Jackson. He noticed something out the
window: a shrieking, angry crowd careening down the streets. "Those people," he said distractedly, "I wonder if there's a riot starting."

He rushed to Shiloh Baptist Church, site of a previously scheduled mass
meeting, muttering to himself, "I *told* Mayor Daley, I *told* Mayor Daley,
something like this would happen if something wasn't done." He pleaded
for nonviolence from the pulpit; angry young men walked out. He persuaded a police commander to sit down with and hear the grievances of those
who stayed—as, unbeknownst to the cops or to King, kids outside assembled Molotov cocktails.

The Washington papers—the ones read by legislators debating the civil
rights bill—reported the spreading Chicago violence as if it were local news:
"Youths crashed through the windows of a currency exchange, setting baskets of waste paper on fire. Firemen were stoned as they fought the flames."
"Hundreds of persons were hurling objects from windows and roofs. Police
communications and officers in the area called for more ammunition." "A
policeman, Donald Ingraham, about 31, was shot a few hours earlier as officers attempted to find a sniper in a building." Forty-two hundred National
Guardsmen were called out. Ten thousand police officers worked twelve-
hour shifts. The White House sent two Justice Department officials in an air

force jet. By then commuters were lying on the floor on the Lake Street el while passing the projects, afraid they'd get shot by snipers. The public-housing high-rises seemed a brilliant solution to the overcrowding crisis in the 1950s. Now they looked like fortifications for guerrilla warfare.

On the third day eight young nurses were murdered by a slow-witted white drifter named Richard Speck. The *Chicago Tribune* connected the dots: the riots, the murders, both were "symptomatic of a deep sickness in society." Chicago's police superintendent connected the dots, too: he said the time would soon come when "law-abiding citizens will have to live in walled communities." A Bungalow Belt dweller connected the dots, too, in a letter to Senator Douglas: "Last night there was a show of appreciation for all that has been done to help the colored people. . . . How much longer are we going to be the suckers, giving away taxpayer money and in return see what it has got us."

And at his next press conference Mayor Daley connected the dots:

"I think you can't charge it directly to Martin Luther King. But surely some of the people that came in here have been talking for the last year of violence, and showing pictures and instructing people how to conduct violence, there on his staff, and they're responsible. . . . Who makes a Molotov cocktail? Someone has to train the youngsters."

There were smaller riots in Philadelphia and Brooklyn. At the Capitol, Manny Celler, the House floor director of the president's civil rights bill, attempted a parliamentary maneuver to get it to the floor by bypassing the right-wing Rules Committee. Its chairman, Howard "Judge" Smith of Virginia, raged that Celler would have Congress "surrender further to the so-called revolution of the Negro race."

No one was surprised by that; Judge Smith was a notorious primitive. What was shocking was the response of the genial minority leader, Gerald Ford, the sort of moderate industrial-state Republican who voted for civil rights bills as a matter of course. He also charged to his feet and angrily challenged Celler's maneuver. When it came time to vote, two of Celler's opponents turned out to be liberals voted in on Lyndon Johnson's coattails in 1964.

Something, here, was changing. On July 18 Evans and Novak reported the opening of Watts's first movie theater. Governor Brown, who had arranged it, skipped the opening. "Nor, indeed, was he in any way publicly connected with the project." In his "uphill bid for a third term . . . to be publicly sympathetic to the Negroes of Watts is suicide."

That night in Cleveland a tavern owner put out a sign reading NO WATER FOR NIGGERS. Bar employees patrolled outside with shotguns, a menacing crowd gathered, cops fired shots overhead to disperse them, the mob torched a supermarket, then cut the hoses of the arriving fire trucks; cops shooting into a suspected snipers' nest killed a mother leaning her head out the window screaming at them to hold their fire so she could check for her children.

In Jacksonville, after a demonstration was broken up, "roving bands of Negroes"—a new journalistic cliché—began firebombing buildings. ("A white youth was pulled from a telephone booth and struck by Negroes," the *Washington Star* reported.) Vice President Hubert Humphrey, a happy warrior for civil rights since 1948, told the National Association of Counties that "the National Guard is no answer to the problems of the slums," and that if conditions didn't improve, there would be "open violence in every major city and county in America," and, indeed, if he lived in a slum, "I think you'd have more trouble than you have had already because I've got enough spark left in me to lead a mighty good revolt." The next day a thousand members of the Ohio National Guard were called out to Cleveland, and two thousand more Illinois Guardsmen were called out to Chicago, and Jake Javits gave a speech at the Senate Judiciary subcommittee hearings on the civil rights bill: "It really is almost impossible to understand the explosive character of what we are dealing with, except when you plunge in and see the conditions under which these people live. It is just beyond belief. Whatever else we may disagree on, upon this I do not see there can be disagreement."

He was answered by Judiciary chairman Sam Ervin of North Carolina, a segregationist of the old school who said that was a good reason why they shouldn't pass open housing: if conditions really were as bad as Javits said, "saying that the rioters and looters have the right to live in somebody else's house against their will" would hardly help, "because I do not think they are financially able to move."

Javits said, exasperated, "This is not a problem which is capable of some single unitary solution."

Ervin replied, "Yes. And yet the record shows that the more laws that are passed in this nation on the national, state, and local levels, the more rioting and looting we have."

The next day a roller-skating rink went up in flames in Cleveland and police riddled with bullets a car containing three children. The day after that, armed white vigilantes began cruising the Cleveland ghetto. Mayor Lindsay traveled to East New York, Brooklyn, where poor Italians, Negroes, and Puerto Ricans were on the brink of a race war. "We don't want you here, nigger-lover!" the Italian kids organized into a gang called SPONGE—the Society for the Prevention of Negroes Getting Everything—shouted. Lindsay pulled them into a pizza parlor for a rap session. (That was John Lindsay: possessed of a near-religious faith in the power of dialogue, reason, goodwill, and his own considerable charm to settle even the most festering grievances.) He returned to Manhattan convinced the situation was under control. Word came over the shortwave: an eleven-year-old Negro boy had been shot. Fifteen thousand officers flooded the streets, under orders from the commissioner to "keep their billies on their belts and their guns in their holsters"; bricks and tire jacks rained down on them from rooftops.

At the Sherman House Hotel in Chicago, Cook County Democratic headquarters, Martin Luther King warned in a press conference, "We are in for darker nights of social disruption," and that "the power elite seems to prefer sporadic outbreaks of violence to the rightful recognition of an organized nonviolence movement," and to whites who saw King as the riot's ringleader it sounded like a threat. He then announced he had brokered a truce among Chicago's street gangs. (The next day a gang member shot three rivals.) In an ornate reception room in New York's City Hall, fifty-nine East New York youths screamed about "our turf" and "their turf" and nearly broke into a fistfight. (Mayor Lindsay sent out his youth board director and a rabbi to convince the local godfather, Don Alberto Gallo, to broker a peace.) A nightclub in the Bohemian district of the North Side of Chicago was raided for obscenity ("Included in the skits," the papers reported, "were love-making scenes . . . and the tearing of clothing"). In Cleveland white vigilantes shot dead a twenty-nine-year-old black man; a black sniper shot out the rearview mirror of an Ohio National Guard jeep.

These bizarre outbreaks of black people burning down their own neighborhoods, what did they *mean*? Was it some kind of political blackmail, a gun pressed to the head of a Congress debating a civil rights bill? The opportunism of greedy criminals? The mania of a people losing its collective mind? The natural expression of people who were savages to begin with? A Communist plot? How was it related to bearded picketers against the Vietnam War, the orgies so vile, or singer John Lennon, who had blasphemously called his rock band "bigger than Jesus" and had to apologize that August to the pope? Was this the whirlwind a civilization reaped once the seeds of moral relativism were sown?

And, most of all: what next? When might they move out into the bourgeois utopias: the bungalow belts, the white-picket-fenced suburbs of the Midwest, the white stucco of the Southwest, your own backyard? Were there even enough peace officers in existence to respond?

The political season approached. What pundits referred to by the shorthand as "the cities" defined the battlefield.

Conservatives looked for ways to blame it all on the liberals. A 5–4 Supreme Court decision had been handed down in June requiring police to warn arrestees of their constitutional right against self-incrimination and to an attorney. Justice John Marshall Harlan pounded the table in dissent: *Miranda v. State of Arizona* meant "a gradual disappearance of confessions as a legitimate tool of law enforcement." Justice Byron White said it "will return a killer, rapist, or other criminal to the streets to repeat his crime whenever it pleased him." Even the *New York Times* found the decision "lacking either constitutional warrant or constructive effect." Truman Capote, author of the new true-crime thriller *In Cold Blood*, testified at a Senate hearing, "This is almost like *Alice in Wonderland*. . . . While many in our society today are wailing about the rights of the criminal suspect, why do they seem to totally ignore the rights of the victims and potential victims?" Robert Byrd entered an editorial into the *Congressional Record* on Martin Luther King, "whose organization is studying the Buddhist use of street gangs in Saigon demonstrations, has put the Reverend A. Sampson in charge of enlisting gang leaders in SCLC's new militant youth movement," and was preparing to "trigger a Watts-like eruption in the nation's second-largest city." Judge Smith, involuntarily retired by a liberal in a recent primary, gave a valedictory address to the House of Representatives, in which he had served since 1931: "I was distressed a few days ago to see in the press, and not refuted, the statement by the vice president of the United States that if he lived in a tenement, in the ghettos of the cities, on the second floor, he would have the spirit to 'lead a revolt.' . . . The vice president will bear a grave responsibility in blood and lives if he tries to provoke minority group members to riot for rent supplements."

Liberals steadied their grip and harnessed their reason: "The housing program is too small," ran one editorial. "The poverty program is too small. It is not the riots in the slums, but these lame and inadequate programs that are the real disgrace of the richest society on earth." The *Wall Street Journal* responded to those words in an editorial entitled "A Time for Candor": "We submit that attitudes of that sort are an unmerited rebuke to America and the millions whose hard work and hard thinking have made it the most abundant and just nation on earth. . . . Neither the society at large nor the Federal Government is responsible for the violence. Those responsible are the rioters and the teachers of casual disregard for law and order."

And Richard Nixon was off touring the world, unwilling to comment on the matter at all.

A Cuyahoga County grand jury convened to investigate the Cleveland riot, which claimed a total of four lives, on July 29—the same day when, in the town of North Amityville in the middle of Long Island, a mob of four hundred Negroes chanting "Kill those cops!" pelted police with rocks and Molotov cocktails after a meeting intended to improve community-police relations—handed down eight indictments charging "a relatively small group of trained and disciplined professionals at this business" with responsibility, "some of whom also are either members or officers in the Communist Party."

Would that it were so simple. "They didn't need any Communists to tell them they were suffering," a city official reflected after the riot. Indeed, while the Cleveland indictments led every newscast, another panel's report languished in obscurity. The U.S. Commission on Civil Rights had convened hearings on the Cleveland slums the previous spring and exposed a "law enforcement" apparatus lubricated to harass Negro innocents at every turn. A minister testified on how cops were collaborating with the pimps: "It has got to the place whereby a man's wife or daughter is not safe to walk the street." The police chief was quoted calling for capital punishment "to keep the Negroes in line." Witnesses told the story of a judge who convicted civil rights demonstrators without a trial, proclaiming, "They are all guilty because I saw it on TV," of ministers who showed up at city hall to demand an audience with the mayor after their written requests were ignored for three years and were thrown in jail, of black applicants to the police force turned down if they belonged to civil rights groups. The psychologist Robert Coles testified that black children in Cleveland were more traumatized than the ones he'd studied in Mississippi. He displayed the drawing one created when asked for a picture of his neighborhood: a series of concentric squares the young artist entitled "The Death House." A widow recounted the days she spent in jail *after* police confirmed that the car they'd insisted she'd stolen was borrowed from her sister. A bus-station porter described his arrest for sitting on the floor after a tiring shift, then the beatings that ensued over four days by cops who ordered him to bark like a dog. Cleveland police routinely kept suspects for seventy-two hours without charge and without access to a lawyer. A study was entered into the record: the average response time to a burglary in a white police district was 8.52 minutes, compared with 20.1 minutes in a black one.

The debate spread to the floor of the U.S. Senate. Frank Lausche, Ohio's senior senator, rose to "bow and express my gratitude as a citizen of Cleveland to the police, the firemen, and the National Guard who brought order to Cleveland." He said their response was flawless.

His junior colleague, the liberal Stephen Young, rose in incredulity, displaying from the August 1 issue of *Newsweek* a picture of an innocent housewife riddled with police bullets: "Surely that is evidence of irresponsible action by police." He recalled his own experience long ago in the Ohio National Guard, how poorly he had been trained, how inept the young weekend warriors were at handling their weapons. He related the story of a young guardsman during the riot who "thought he heard prowlers. Firing several rounds from a machine gun in a heavily populated neighborhood appears to me to have been the act of a trigger-happy guardsman." He concluded, "While there may have been extremist groups who grasped the opportunity to exploit the violence . . . to state that the riots were Communist or otherwise inspired appears to me to be a lame excuse to salve the consciences of those who do not want to, or refuse to, face the conditions that precipitated this disaster and similar ones in other great cities of our nation: rat-infested slums, unemployment, poverty, hopelessness, frustration, and despair."

Young's was the harder sell. Senator Lausche keynoted the annual convention of the Independent Growers Alliance at the Arie Crown Theater in Chicago: "The current campaign of the worst lawlessness in the history of

America," he told the four thousand farmers, had been "brought to the boiling point by those who are living in luxury by conducting so-called nonviolent crusades." He got a standing ovation.

The August 8 issue of *U.S. News & World Report* featured a city-by-city chart: "Five Serious Crimes Every Minute Now ... A murder every hour ... a rape every 23 minutes ... a burglary every 27 seconds ... a car stolen every minute." The magazine quoted the FBI: "Too much foolish sentimentalism on the part of judges, probation officers, and others is bringing injurious results."

The issue was on the newsstands when a twenty-five-year-old former marine sharpshooter climbed to the top of the University of Texas's ceremonial tower and started blowing away passersby at random. Texas governor John Connally—a shooting victim himself—blamed the courts: "We've reached a point in this country where we tend to coddle criminals." Initial reports were that Charles Whitman was just another "all-American boy." *U.S. News* set their readers straight. They noted the account of an Austin merchant that "Whitman attempted to sell him 'a nice supply of pornography.'"

All this moral anarchy: all of it felt linked. A chaplain of the Maryland American Legion testified to a Senate subcommittee that open housing's supporters were "the same advocates of the new morality of situation ethics, and of liberation from the moral laws governing sex and marriage," and the "whole syndrome of unpatriotic pallor and moral disintegration." The president grasped to save the remnants of his Great Society. Bumper stickers campaigned against him: JOIN THE GREAT SOCIETY—GO ON WELFARE; I FIGHT POVERTY. I WORK. He begged Senate Appropriations chair Robert Byrd not to let his meager $20 million rent-subsidy pilot program die: "All I'm trying to do is help these people get out of the rat holes and let them see a little sunlight," he pleaded. Senator Byrd just shrugged and collected proxy votes to kill it.

What would it mean in November? What would it mean for 1968?

Governor Brown's reelection was in shambles. His campaign put out an attack pamphlet, "Ronald Reagan, Extremist Collaborator—An Exposé," charging Reagan's campaign was riddled with John Birch Society members. Reagan had long ago wriggled free of the charge with quicksilver one-liners: "If anyone chooses to vote for me, they are buying my views. I am not buying theirs." Birchers no longer seemed so frightening at any rate. "The Bircher isn't identifiable," a frank Reagan strategist reflected to a reporter after the state Republican convention voted down a renunciation of the Birch Society but voted in a proclamation against open housing, "but the Negro is."

The hit piece unearthed supposedly embarrassing Reagan quotes, such as this one on juvenile delinquents: "I'd like to harness their youthful energy with a strap." Liberals in the Brown camp were oblivious that lines like this were why so many middle-class Californians were turning to Reagan in the first place.

Brown opened his general-election campaign at a Catholic trade-union breakfast on Labor Day with a stumbling attempt to chip at Reagan's strengths, proposing an antipornography law. It would, he said, "class some materials as obscene for children which are not obscene for adults." Reagan, on the other hand, was backing Proposition 16, an initiative to simply ban obscene materials, which Brown considered unconstitutional. Pat once again had the grays. Reagan snapped back in black and white: "In Paris they no longer buy French postcards. They buy California postcards."

Brown also proposed fighting juvenile delinquency by reforming the family court system to better merge "the techniques of science with law enforcement" and address "the tragic aftereffects of broken homes."

Reagan's position? Black and white: "Harness their youthful energy with a strap."

Brown spoke at the Los Angeles Fairgrounds, preaching his accomplishments: "six new state colleges, three university campuses, the greatest freeway system in the world, and only one tax increase." The amphitheater was only half-full. Sturdy proletarians now spent Labor Day at lakeside vacation cabins. At the L.A. County Fair he examined an apiary exhibit. "There's no welfare in the beehive," the beekeeper pointed out.

"What happens if the bees don't work?" the governor asked.

"They die."

Is this what voters wanted? The death penalty for indolence? According to Reagan, in his January kickoff speech, "Working men and women should not be asked to carry the additional burden of a segment of society capable of caring for itself but which prefers making welfare a way of life, freeloading at the expense of more conscientious citizens." To Brown, it made no sense. If California's welfare system was overburdened, it was because of elderly people moving into the state for its generous old-age pensions. But the elderly were sympathetic. So Reagan went after supposed abuses of Aid to Dependent Children. Freeloaders on welfare by choice? Pat Brown would never forget what he had learned canvassing the riot zone in 1965. Women told him they were desperate to work but couldn't find child care; one told him what it was like to scrounge for food to keep her baby from starving the week before her monthly relief check arrived. He remembered, too, that the chairman of his commission convened to study the riot—the conservative former CIA director John McCone—had learned it took a five-hour round-trip by bus from Watts just to file the papers to get on relief—for a stipend that hadn't been adjusted for a decade, despite the inflation Ronald Reagan was always carping about ("The $5 you saved twenty years ago will only buy you $1.85 in groceries today"). The *Los Angeles Times* did an investigation: they could only find abuses in four-tenths of 1 percent of relief cases and editorialized that for the sins of these 180 families, and $31,960 lost from the state treasury, "innocent children whose birthright was poverty" were being put at risk of starvation. "If there is a better answer, it won't come from demagogic moralizing."

Reagan was the preeminent demagogic moralizer—and the *Times* endorsed him in the general election nonetheless. In the agricultural San Joaquin Valley, speaking atop a mammoth harvesting machine, after loosening up the crowd with quips ("They say God is dead. *Wel-l-l-l,* he isn't. We just can't talk about him in a schoolroom"), he started talking about what his handlers had told him to talk about, farm policy. His audience shifted in their seats, bored. He started talking about how anyone coming to California could start drawing a welfare check within twenty-one days. That was false: only those who could prove five years of California residence in the last nine could get welfare, and *then* only after twenty-one days. It delivered him the crowd nonetheless. "Everything he says is America," a young woman told a reporter. An old lady chimed in, "Brown has practically ruined the state. He has a nice home but he lets the Negroes come right next to you."

Reagan shuttled down to L.A. to speak to assembly-line workers at Hughes Aircraft: "Able-bodied men should no longer receive a check for sitting on the front porch," he said to what columnists Evans and Novak called "an animal roar of approval." They observed how white California was "somehow frustrated in the midst of affluence," and that their rage was "encapsulated in the welfare issue."

Brown was now down six points in the polls. The Associated Press was reporting that 3 percent of GOP state chairs and national committeemen were predicting that Reagan would be their next nominee for president.

Richard Nixon passed through Los Angeles for Ronald Reagan late in June, rousing nine thousand Republican donors to their feet at the Los Angeles Sports Arena. Then came the more important conclave: with two dozen members of his informal campaign team. The meeting was captained by Maurice Stans; they combed through lists of possible contributors to raise $100,000 to get through the fall. Then Nixon took off for nine cities in seven days to reintroduce himself to the Republican faithful. The airplane problem had been taken care of when jet magnate William Lear loaned him a six-seater. Although he really needed only two seats. He traveled with a single aide, who literally held his coat. The national press paid scant attention. To sophisticated observers the notion that Nixon was positioning himself for a presidential run was still not quite credible. In the *New York Times,* items on Nixon speeches made for handy two- or three-line squibs to fill in space between the end of real articles and the department store ads.

The *Baltimore Sun*'s Jules Witcover took a chance that there was a story in Nixon's perambulations. Tagging along, he found Nixon's sheer willpower astonishing, nearly religious. In Detroit, as the cameramen set up their equipment, reporters warmed up with gag questions: "Mr. Nixon, are you going to run forever?" Their laughs turned to deferential smiles as he swept into the room. He was nice to them. The press was now a constituency to be courted. They asked their usual questions; he gave his usual answers. It suddenly struck Jules Witcover that "this man never seemed, even in a crowded room, to really *be* with anybody—and that he much preferred it that way."

Nixon was speaking at the annual convention of the Jaycees, the bright-eyed future executives of America, playing it light. The emcee, he said, in his gracious introduction, neglected to mention "that I was a dropout from the electoral college."

An old joke—new to them. Laughter. Flashbulbs popped.

"I want to make sure these people get their pictures. I've had trouble with pictures." There was a pause. Paul Keyes had apparently written timing into Nixon's jokes as well.

"I've had trouble with television, too." They roared.

"I got stoned in Caracas. I'll tell you one thing, it's a lot different from getting stoned at a Jaycees convention."

Pandemonium.

There were still pockets of innocence in America—where *getting stoned* meant just "getting drunk," and where getting drunk was a guilty pleasure. It was the week of his twenty-sixth wedding anniversary. Perhaps Pat thought of the time Dick forgot their twentieth, in 1960. They had been appearing at the Jaycees convention then, too. "Dick didn't give me a thing," she had said that year, "but the Jaycees gave me a spray of roses."

Not recognizing his own wife's anniversary on the campaign trail was a PR mistake, and he wasn't making mistakes now. In L.A. it was near to his mother's birthday, so he invited a slew of reporters to record the moment on her front porch. "Happy birthday, Mum," he said, and shook her hand.

After Detroit it was off to a fund-raiser in little Bay City for Don Riegle, a twenty-eight-year-old businessman running against one of LBJ's forty-seven coattail-freshmen. On the way out Nixon had an aide stop in a shopping center for a razor, to give himself his third shave of the day.

Another part of the routine was the intimate gathering with the big money. In Tulsa, the Republican mayor's front lawn became a parking lot for twenty luxury sedans; the women, Jules Witcover observed, sported "more and bigger diamond rings than I had seen in one place in years"; and the oilman who footed the bill made an unsubtle appeal to buy in early on Oval Office shares: "As you go in, you'll see some blank checkbooks. Just think of what you want to give and then write it right out, while you still have the chance. You might not get the chance again." Nixon spoke from atop a patio chair, noting that Tulsa had given him 63 percent of its vote in 1960 and that they would make it "seventy percent next time." When it came time to raise big money, the fiction that he wasn't running for anything went by the wayside.

Then it was to the ultramodern Tulsa Assembly Center to address the Republican hoi polloi, the great Sooner football coach and NFL commentator Bud Wilkinson beside him on the dais. The congressman who introduced him reminded the crowd of the Hiss case, that pink poltroon Helen Gahagan Douglas, the Checkers Speech: "Here was a young man with his back to the wall." (You, too, know what it feels like to have your back to the wall.) "America faces a storm, and I only regret we don't have him at the helm."

Witcover was startled at the standing ovation at the sound of Nixon's name. He was supposed to be a loser. "One would have thought he had just received the party's presidential nomination."

Then he gave the same old speech, touching up Lyndon on inflation and Vietnam.

The latter was an awkward issue to bring up in any partisan context. Each party had its hawks and doves, even each ideological wing of each party. *Atlantic Monthly* called Vietnam "the most complex of all political issues." Polls showed 38 percent wanted a negotiated settlement, 33 percent wanted to "expand the war to win, no matter what it costs," and a strong majority, encompassing both groups, doubted Vietnam affected America's national security in any event. And yet Nixon strafed LBJ on Vietnam in every speech, as if there were some obvious political upside. It certainly wasn't on principle: the line by which he strafed changed from week to week. For months he'd said only Democratic "appeasers" doubted that holding the line in Vietnam was what it took "to prevent World War III." By late June, however, he said Republicans believed "that we should not continue to commit thousands of young Americans to the bottomless pit of a land war in Asia."

Then he jetted off for a monthlong stature-enhancing trip to Europe and Asia, his family photogenically in tow.

In Chicago on July 29, Martin Luther King led what was supposed to be an all-night vigil in front of F. H. Halvorsen Realty in the Bungalow Belt neighborhood of Gage Park. The police rescued his group from an advancing mob. They returned to the same spot the next morning and were met by a hail of rocks.

Senator Paul Douglas received a raft of letters dated July 30. One was from a self-described "staunch Democrat" who "cannot help but wholeheartedly agree with Barry Goldwater. . . . I feel Mr. Johnson is much responsible for the present riot by his constant encouragement for the Negro to take any measure to assert himself & DEMAND his rights—Rights, and respect are earned!" Douglas, a beloved senator since 1954, a sage former University of Chicago economics professor, architect of many New Deal policies, a civil rights champion, was up for reelection. His opponent, a dashing, moderate-Republican CEO twenty-seven years his junior, Charles Percy, was also known as a liberal on civil rights: he funded his own private war on poverty in the Chicago slums, complete with a hotline tenants could call to report recalcitrant slumlords, and came out for the Civil Rights Act of 1966, open housing included, in June. The issue seemed to have been taken off the table, and the race would be fought over Vietnam: Douglas was a die-hard hawk and Percy was a dove who had recently proposed an "all-Asian peace conference" to settle the Vietnam War.

Then came Martin Luther King.

"As a Gage Park resident & that of my in-laws & my parents, & their families we are living as decent hard-working people, you should consider martial law to prevent a peaceful community from being harassed, that you should consider re-establishing law & order & change laws to protect the people and not criminals & people who openly voice their opinions against the majority as well as the government," an Eleanor M. Gavion wrote her senator on July 29. "I have 3 sons & I will gladly have them defend this country here." Soon, Mrs. Gavion's three sons got the chance to do just that, from their very own Gage Park front yards.

Five hundred marchers first moved out into the Bungalow Belt on Sunday, July 31, daring the mob of four thousand to attack as if it were Selma, to offer the spur to a nation's conscience that might deliver up transcendence.

A fusillade of rocks, bottles, and cherry bombs came. Priests and nuns ("*Whores!*") were singled out. A first-grade teacher, Sister Mary Angelica, was pummeled to the ground. A cheer went up: "We've got another one!"

"*White Power! White Power!*"

"*Polish Power! Polish Power!*"

"*Burn them like Jews!*"

Marchers returning to their cars found them torched, overturned, or rolled into the muddy Marquette Park lagoon. Dante's inferno, right there in the Bungalow Belt.

A neighborhood newspaper called it "the blackest day in the history of the Southwest Community," but also found the violence "understandable." The attackers, after all, had "earned their way into the community by hard work and expect others to do the same."

On Tuesday, Pat, Julie, and Tricia Nixon appeared in a photograph on the *New York Times* society page at the Paris unveiling of Pierre Cardin's fall line. A news brief noted RN's visit with the pope, part of every presidential aspirant's ethnic stations of the cross; his next stop was Tel Aviv, and he had already visited Ireland. Then he jetted off for Asia, where he'd earn notices such as these: "Former Vice President Nixon met with President Mohammed Ayub Khan in Rawalpindi today. They are old friends. Field Marshal Ayub came to power in 1958 when Mr. Nixon was vice president. Mr. Nixon, on a world tour, will leave for Bangkok, Thailand, tomorrow." While, back in

Chicago, Mayor Daley met with Bungalow Belt civic leaders, who looked forward to solidarity from one of their own.

But Daley was in a difficult spot. Arrest Martin Luther King, and Daley would become an international pariah. A committee of Chicago VIPs was shuttling back and forth from D.C. to lobby for the Democratic Party's 1968 convention. Hosting it was Mayor Daley's dream. Winning elections for the Democratic Party was the focus, the meaning, of Richard J. Daley's entire life. Here before him was the heart of his machine. Black Chicago had, meanwhile, given him 90 percent of their vote in 1963—and his margin of victory. This was perfect agony: his constituencies were at war with each other. And so he did something extraordinary: he lectured the stunned white ethnics. Told *them* not to demonstrate. And ordered the police to offer King's marchers safe passage.

August 5. Six hundred open-housing activists, ten thousand counter-demonstrators. Some wore Nazi helmets. Others waved Confederate battle flags, carried George Wallace banners, swastika placards that helpfully explained THE SYMBOL OF WHITE POWER.

Martin Luther King, Mahalia Jackson by his side, led his legions forth: "We are bound for the promised land!"

"*Kill those niggers!*"

"*We want Martin Luther Coon!*"

Police trying to keep the two sides apart were screamed at: "*Nigger-loving cops!*" "God, I hate niggers and nigger-lovers," a reporter overheard an old lady say.

Martin Luther King walked past.

"*Kill him! Kill him!*"

"*Roses are red, violets are black, King would look good with a knife in his back.*"

Instead he got a baseball-size rock above his ear. He slumped to the ground—the Gandhian moment of truth. "I think everybody in that line wanted to kill everybody that was on the other side of the line," a marcher later recalled. King got up and kept on marching. *We shall overcome.*

On the approach to Halvorsen Realty, someone *did* throw a knife at King's back. It caught some white kid in the neck instead. King had marched six weeks earlier through the Mississippi town where the civil rights workers Goodman, Chaney, and Schwerner were murdered. He had called it the most savage place he had ever seen. Now he revised his opinion: "I think the people of Mississippi ought to come to Chicago to learn how to hate."

The march concluded, marchers dispersed. White neighborhood kids started battling police, clambering away with blood streaming down their cheeks, yelling what they heard the niggers yell on the news: "Police brutality!" A yellow convertible tried to run a policeman down. Two hundred teenagers set out to storm Mayor Daley's house. As police closed in,

teenagers threw their incriminating arsenal of chains, cleavers, and clubs over
the Thirty-fifth Street overpass of the Dan Ryan Expressway (an inattentive
newspaper reader wrote to Senator Douglas and in the cognitive dissonance
at the notion of lawless Caucasians called them "a gang of Negroes").

"There must be some way of resolving questions without marches,"
Daley whined plaintively into the TV cameras, haunted now by the most
frightening chant of all:

"Don't vote for Democrats! Don't vote for Democrats!"

Richard Nixon was in Saigon, denouncing Vietnam War critics at an airport
press conference: they were "prolonging the war, encouraging the enemy,
and preventing the very negotiations the critics say they want." He was
simultaneously in *U.S. News & World Report* with a guest editorial: "If Mob
Rule Takes Hold in U.S.—A Warning from Richard Nixon."

"Who is responsible for the breakdown of law and order in this country?"
it asked. (The rhetorical question: a favorite Nixonian device. It made him
look open-minded.) He framed the answer as a new version of his oldest
political appeal. Blame the actual individuals who burned down buildings,
certainly. But "the more important collaborators and auxiliaries" were otherwise. "It is my belief that the seeds of civil anarchy would never have taken
root in this nation had they not been nurtured by scores of respected Americans: public officials, educators, clergymen, and civil rights leaders as well."
He named Hubert Humphrey, who'd declared he could "lead a mighty good
revolt"; the "junior senator from New York," who declared "there is no point
in telling Negroes to obey the law"; and generically, "the professor" who,
"objecting to de facto segregation," ends up turning youth into insurrectionists: to him "it may be crystal clear where civil disobedience may begin and
where it must end. But the boundaries have become fluid to his students."
Then, to prove "the professor" had nothing on him, he quoted Chaucer: "If
gold rust, what shall iron do?" This was the argument he'd been making since
Whittier: the Franklins were putting one over on the plain people.

Back in Washington, the long, hot summer played havoc with the Democratic coalition. Charlie "Mac" Mathias, a liberal Republican congressman
from Maryland, had spent the summer pushing a compromise amendment to
the civil rights bill exempting property covering four or fewer families—thus
excluding the nation's suburbs and the bungalow belts. Enraged civil rights
activists—at least the ones who weren't too militant to oppose legislative
solutions at all—asked how something could be a constitutional right, just
not for the 62 percent of Americans thus excluded. The president came out
against the compromise for that very reason. Dan Rostenkowski, one of the
Bungalow Belt's congressmen, begged the White House to backtrack. His
Bungalow Belt colleague Roman Pucinski told the press the president should
order civil rights activists to shut down marches altogether. These were men,

like most Northern Democrats, who answered to the label "liberal"—Great Society men. The fight over the 1966 civil rights bill was calling all that into question. The Great Society was threatening their jobs.

Once it had been simple. Civil rights supporters knew who their enemies were: special interests such as the real estate associations (who lobbied against the Mathias compromise for making something evil "palatable to the American people"). The lunatic far right (the executive director of the Liberty Lobby testified that King's movement employed "mass brainwashing" just like "in Nazi Germany, Fascist Italy, Communist Russia, and Communist China"). The old-line racist Dixie gargoyles (they kept on rehearsing for a revival of *Birth of a Nation*: Senator George Smathers wondering why "when a colored boy rapes a white girl, he gets off easier"; Representative William C. Cramer raising the specter of the "Social Security widow in my district" forced to rent to a black man—and you could almost picture the lusty young buck he had in mind). *This* opposition was predictable. The curveball was the *new* opposition: the Pucinskis and the Rostenkowskis; the Jerry Fords, moderate Republicans who used to be the backbone of every civil rights vote. Now, the Dixie gargoyles were gloating, an ancient piece of Southern political folk wisdom was receiving its vindication: that once civil rights bills started affecting North as much as South, it wouldn't just be Southerners filibustering civil rights bills.

The *Wall Street Journal* articulated an argument echoing through Congress: "It is strange, although to an extent understandable, that the more civil rights legislation is piled onto the statute books, the more Federal money poured into attempts at Negro betterment, the more help freely proferred by businesses and individuals—the more the anger rises. . . . Every legislative enactment seemed to incite more mob activity, more riots, demonstrations, and bloodshed." Sam Ervin reported that the Senate Judiciary Committee had received over 8,000 letters on Title IV. Only 125 favored enactment.

On July 25, when the bill was called up for ten hours of debate, the House floor had become a raging cauldron of incommensurate arguments over whether civil rights bills prevented riots or caused them. A conservative from Mississippi entered every news item about violent crime from that day's *Washington Post* into the *Congressional Record.* A liberal from California pleaded that the "thousands of young Negroes who are militant and on the march" that Congress should be listening to were the soldiers, sailors, airmen, and marines fighting in Vietnam, who needed open housing to enjoy the fruits of the American dream upon their return. Republican Jim Martin of Alabama—running against Lurleen Wallace for governor—said, "The FBI has positive evidence that professional Communist agitators have helped to stir up recent Negro riots" via "secret messages by code transmitted from radio stations." Cleveland Democrat Wayne Hays blamed civil rights marchers: "Are they Americans? Are they traitors? What kind of people are they?" Six of the freshman Democrats who'd replaced Republicans on Lyndon Johnson's coattails voted to strike the open-housing section altogether.

When the Mathias Amendment was put to a full House vote, an oddball coalition saw to its passage by one vote: liberals trying to save a half-loaf version of open housing so that the final bill might pass; conservatives trying to save a half-loaf version of open housing so the final bill might *fail*. Some congressmen were just confused about what they were voting on at all. The bill was sent to the Senate by a vote of 259–157 on August 9. That same day in Lansing, Michigan, five cops were injured by firebombs and rocks; in Detroit, whites started stoning cars filled with blacks; in Milwaukee, a bomb tore open the office of the NAACP. In Cleveland the grand jury turned in its verdict that the riots were the responsibility of Communists. In Brooklyn two white men were shot after a brawl over racial slurs; in Grenada, Mississippi, "while," the *New York Times* reported, "state and local law-enforcement officials stood by, laughing and chuckling," a white mob ran off six hundred desegregation marchers. ("You're going to see a show tonight," the sheriff had promised newsmen.) In Philadelphia, Pennsylvania, that week, Secretary of State Dean Rusk's twenty-five-year-old son, a leader of the National Urban League's militant faction, stepped up to the podium at the group's convention and said the civil rights movement suffered, if anything, from "too much reasonableness." He finished, to a standing ovation, "Watts came at noon. What will be our midnight?"

And in the Senate, Everett Dirksen, Paul Douglas's conservative Republican senior colleague, whose acquiescence had been instrumental to the passage of the landmark 1964 Civil Rights Act ("Stronger than all armies is an idea whose time has come," he had said then), now made the same argument Goldwater had made in 1964: "I have no doubts whatsoever as to its unconstitutionality."

Even Paul Douglas started to waver. He claimed residential segregation was merely the result of a benign "consciousness of kind," birds of a feather flocking together. The former social scientist was willfully ignoring, for instance, his own city's Dan Ryan Expressway, fourteen impregnable lanes built to separate Mayor Daley's neighborhood of Bridgeport and the black West Side. The previous year, Martin Luther King had called Douglas "the greatest of all senators." Now he was aping Daley. Without Daley's support, after all, he might just lose his job, now that he was getting letters like these:

"It is my firm belief, and of all my neighbors, that King should be taken into custody. . . . Today, the insufferable arrogance of this character places him on a pedestal as a dark-skinned Hitler."

"Is the ultimate aim the same as the Soviet Union when all property was collectivized?"

"We are writing you and requesting legislation for a repeal of the Civil Rights Act of 1964."

"If our present leaders are confused, perhaps a completely new group would be able to handle the situation better."

"IT IS TIME TO CHANGE THE LAW TO PROTECT <u>ALL</u> THE PEOPLE."

In Chicago, movement Turks like Jesse Jackson were insisting it was time to move on Cicero—the nation's largest municipality without a single black resident. The last time a black man tried to live there, in 1951, the ensuing white riot was so big it made news around the world. This very summer a teenager who crossed over the border looking for work was beaten to death. "We expect violence," Jackson said, "but it wouldn't be any more violent than the demonstrations last week." Another King deputy, James Bevel, said, "We will demonstrate in the communities until every white person out there joins the Republican Party."

At that, Daley gave in: he would negotiate with King.

An August 17 meeting with Daley and civic leaders ended with a pledge to hash things out in an all-day "summit" at the Palmer House Hotel. The next day, Daley played an ace stored up his sleeve. A machine judge issued a clearly illegal injunction against future marches. Daley presented his doughy mug on all three TV networks and offered a brilliant rationale: he claimed a 25 percent increase in crime in August so far, especially "those areas where there are the most families," because so many police were being diverted to protect marchers. (A letter to Senator Douglas the next day: "We believe sir, that unless you take action, blood will be shed on every street corner of our great city.") King played an ace of his own: if the Palmer House meeting didn't yield a satisfactory agreement, they would march on Cicero. The Cook County sheriff called that "awfully close to a suicidal act" and readied the governor to call the National Guard.

The Klan received a permit to rally in Marquette Park. The mayor was asked if that meant they were welcome in Chicago. No more or less, he said, than Martin Luther King. He went to the Palmer House meeting, advised by his City Council speaker, Tom Keane, to "fuck 'em," and negotiated an agreement Mike Royko called "an impressive document, chock full of noble vows and promises" that "wasn't worth the paper it was printed on." King's organizers signed off on it and left Chicago, not a single bungalow-block breached. Fuck 'em Daley had. He just did it in slow motion.

His white constituency was not sated. Their mayor had negotiated with a terrorist. "When greedy Mr. Hitler started taking over other countries, people at first thought 'give him a little more, then he will be satisfied,'" one wrote Senator Douglas. "Give greedy Mr. King a little more freedom then he will stop. Isn't that what we are being told today?"

Stokely Carmichael's barnstorming lectures made all the papers: "When you talk of Black Power, you talk of bringing this country to its knees . . . you talk of building a movement that will smash everything Western civilization has created"; "In Cleveland, they're building stores with no windows. I don't know what they think they'll accomplish. It just means we have to move from Molotov cocktails to dynamite." Senator Abraham Ribicoff opened hearings to "undertake a detailed, full, and in-depth appraisal of the crisis in America's cities and the role of the Federal Government in meeting it." The proceedings trailed fumes of apocalypse. The attorney general said, "There are thirty or forty cities with the same problems" as Chicago. (The *New York Times* reported that under the headline "Katzenbach Warns Senate 30 or 40 Cities Face Riots.") The *U.S. News* roundup ran under the headline "A Trillion Dollars to Save the Cities?" The liberal *Sacramento Bee* editorialized that if such sums were not spent, the "explosive ghettoes . . . are in danger of becoming the cities themselves." Joseph Alsop, perhaps the most influential columnist in the United States, wrote a series of columns making the same argument demographically: in 1961, twenty-six thousand white children attended Washington, D.C., elementary schools. Now so many whites had fled to the suburbs that the number was thirteen thousand. He predicted there would be, "one day, a President Verwoerd in the White House."

Hendrik Verwoerd was the prime minister of South Africa, the architect of apartheid. A few days later, that particular premonition of apocalypse was capped off when Verwoerd was assassinated on the floor of parliament.

Perhaps our Verwoerd would be Wallace. He gave a speech to the Fraternal Order of Police explaining what the Johnson administration knew full well but would not admit: that the summer's riots had been planned at "a conference of world guerrilla warfare chieftains in Havana, Cuba," that "bearded beatnik bureaucrats" were "contributing leadership, and in some instances, public funds to help finance the discord," and that if the "police of this country could run it for about two years—*then* it would be safe to walk in the parks!" The men in blue gave him more than a standing ovation. They stood on their chairs.

A third wave of disturbances broke out in late August: Milwaukee; Brooklyn; Benton Harbor, Michigan; Dayton, Ohio (the National Guard stayed in town to make sure things were safe enough for the president to make a scheduled Labor Day speech). After one broke out in Waukegan, Illinois, a Republican official buttonholed Charles Percy: "Chuck, do you *have* to talk so much about open housing?" Though the remarkable fact now was that it didn't matter if he talked about it or not. He was beginning to benefit from the issue by the simple fact of being a Republican. The old calculus of what kind of voters were bedrock Democrats and which were susceptible to Republican appeals was slipping away week by week.

That August was a watershed in American history. Throughout the first half of the twentieth century, the "party of Lincoln" was identified by the public as the party more favorable to the aspirations of Negroes. The

Democrats' situation was complicated: they simultaneously began winning the allegiance of black voters by dint of the New Deal and relied on Southern segregationists for their majorities. But by the early 1960s, with Goldwater conservatives in the ascendancy among Republicans, and Northern liberals in the ascendancy within the Democratic coalition, a crossover point had been passed. Decades later, two political scientists crunched the opinion poll numbers and identified 1958 as the key date at which both parties were judged equally Negro-friendly. After that, the two parties diverged. The trend had been plotted through contingent accidents of history: John F. Kennedy's decision to phone Coretta Scott King with words of support as her husband sat in jail in Atlanta on the eve of the 1960 election, sending troops to integrate the University of Mississippi in 1962, introducing a sweeping civil rights bill in response to the violence in Birmingham in 1963; and Nixon sending Barry Goldwater to campaign for him in the South in 1960, then the selection of Barry Goldwater as the next Republican nominee. The evolution was uneven: plenty of Southern Democrats were still segregationists, plenty of Republicans championed civil rights—such as John Lindsay, who as a congressman pushed for a civil rights law to the left of JFK's, then was hailed as the savior of the post-Goldwater GOP when he won New York's mayoralty in 1965. The first black since Reconstruction likely to be senator, Attorney General Ed Brooke of Massachusetts, was a Republican. George Romney won and rewon the governorship of Michigan by championing civil rights. One official party brochure pointed in 1965 to LBJ's "failure to enforce civil rights legislation" as a reason to vote Republican.

The long, hot summer of 1966 was when the national Republican Party changed its mind.

Manny Celler had been shocked by the vituperative response of Minority Leader Ford at his July motion to rush the civil rights bill to the floor. Evans and Novak reported that Ford had been coming "under heavy, concealed pressure from liberals and moderates . . . not to put the Party's stamp on an amendment to strip the housing section from the administration's civil rights bill." But in a statement on August 2, that was exactly what Ford's House Republican Policy Committee did. Ford began the press conference with a flourish toward the GOP's historical leadership in "the fight for justice and progress and human rights." He then declared, however, "Respect for law and order is basic to the achievement of common goals within our nation," and blamed the open-housing struggle for law and order's decline. "Since its inception, it has created confusion and bitterness. It has divided the country and fostered discord and animosity when calmness and a unified approach to civil rights problems are desperately needed."

And so on the first anniversary of the riots in Watts, twenty-one months after the 1964 Johnson landslide, Goldwaterism became official House Republican policy on civil rights.

The Republicans were only following the lead of the public. Millions of voters were newly equating Republicanism with preserving their homes, and voting Democratic with surrendering them. In California, people who'd voted Democrat their entire adult lives were pledging fealty to Ronald Reagan. In Chicago, John Hoellen, a George Wallace–style backlasher and one of the city's few Republican aldermen, was mounting a surprisingly strong challenge against Roman Pucinski—an unheard-of threat to the invincible Daley machine. Pucinski plunged forth to save himself by urging court-ordered restraints on civil rights marches. Hoellen did him one better by proposing that Martin Luther King be taken into immediate custody. In the *Saturday Evening Post* Stewart Alsop recorded his pleasure that two "men of genuine ability" were contending for Illinois's Senate seat, and that both "courageously maintained stands for open housing"—but had to admit that "Percy benefits from the backlash nearly as much as the backlasher Hoellen.... In a system accustomed to straight-ticket voting, many an angry white voter will simply pull the Republican lever."

As for Senator Douglas, he got more and more letters like this:

"While you sit on your butt in Washington Martin Luther King is violating everything I bought and paid for. That jackass Percy is beginning to look good to me."

And at that jackass Percy's headquarters, certain ideological adjustments were being considered.

Curiously, Richard Nixon referenced the issue only once that summer and fall, in *U.S. News & World Report.* In his speeches, he said nary a word on law and order, nor on open housing.

In his turn at the Los Angeles Sports Arena back in June, he predicted "the greatest political comeback by either party in the twentieth century"—but said nothing about the spreading panic over the supposedly imminent Independence Day riot. The night Martin Luther King was at the Sherman House in Chicago predicting "darker nights of social disruption," Nixon, speaking at the Hilton Hotel on South Michigan Avenue in the same city, promised a Republican Congress would bring "new leadership to fight Vietnam and high prices"—but nothing on how a Republican Congress would fight Carmichael and King. Nixon knew the issue was the royal road to Republican victory in November—in California, he told his protégé Robert Finch, running on Reagan's ticket for lieutenant governor against the incumbent lieutenant governor, Glenn Anderson, "I want everyone in California to believe that Glenn Anderson was responsible for Watts." Nixon just left it to others to push it.

Race had always been the best-oiled hinge in the strange contraption that was Nixon's ideology, swinging from one position to the next year to year, month to month—even, at the 1960 convention, from hour to hour. In 1963 he supported JFK's civil rights bill. Then, when the bill was debated in the House, he savaged efforts "to enforce integration in an artificial and unworkable manner." He had no problem catering to fear of Negroes if political expediency demanded it. (It was indeed what he felt in his heart. *Went through his whole thesis re: blacks and their genetic inferiority,* Bob Haldeman wrote in his diary one day of a May 1969 meeting with the boss.) Why he didn't wish to be associated with the hottest Republican issue, as he jockeyed for the Republican grass roots, was a bit of a mystery. The front-runner for the nomination, George Romney, was appealing publicly for Title IV to be kept in the civil rights bill, riots be damned. Behind closed doors, Richard Nixon was telling other Republicans to hit the riot issue as hard as they could. And he was an ex officio member of the House Policy Committee, which had come out against the open-housing title of the civil rights bill as a menace to law and order.

Every move he made was calculated for 1968. But what was the calculation behind *this*?

CHAPTER SIX

School Was in Session . . .

Richard Nixon returned from his round-the-world tour on August 20. In New York he convened a boot camp for his advance team (predict attendance for your event, then rent a too-small hall, earning the blessed press notice "standing room only"; tell reporters you were only a volunteer so Nixon could tell them he wasn't running for president because "I have no staff"). Then he made a tour of the District of Columbia, his intentions now beyond doubt: this was, Evans and Novak reported, the opening bell of "the second presidential campaign of Richard M. Nixon."

Though actually it was his third. Sometimes it was hard to keep count.

Over the previous weeks, in press conferences at airports across Asia, designating himself "a chief Republican spokesman on foreign policy issues," Nixon laid out his hardest Vietnam line yet: "We are fighting in Vietnam to prevent World War III and to keep the Pacific from becoming a Red Sea." He said that "for the first time now I am leaving Vietnam with confidence that it is not possible for us to lose this war from a military standpoint," that calls for a negotiated settlement would only "encourage the Communist leaders to prolong their resistance," that Fulbright types who claimed to be for peace were only "prolonging the war. . . . We have had the debate on the war. All sides have had the opportunity to present their views. The decision has been made. Further debate on the basic issue is not going to change anything—all it can do is to give our friends, our enemies, and our own people a continuing picture of American disunity." He said the argument must be limited to "tactics."

Then, immediately reversing his pledge, he argued strategy.

According to "some American leaders" (not Dick Nixon, mind you), the war might last twenty years if the president's course didn't change. So it was time to pour in half a million troops at least. "I don't believe the Communist Chinese have the military capacity to take on the United States," he pronounced in Tokyo. "Now that we have hit the oil supplies, we should not be inhibited by the fiction that targets in the Hanoi area should not be hit," he said in Saigon. Do this, he said, and our side could reach its "conclusion militarily" in "two or maybe three years." He added slyly, "Possibly the elections can achieve this."

That was in practically the same breath in which he said that politics had to be kept out of foreign policy.

The *New York Times* welcomed Nixon home with a mordant Sunday lead editorial: "The issue he raises is precisely the one he insists should no longer be a subject for debate: the American objective in the conflict." He said it should be "victory." But the *Times* noted Pentagon sources who said that "victory" would take five to eight years and 750,000 troops—and risked a gate-crashing by Vietnam's nuclear-armed neighbors. "President Johnson repeatedly has proclaimed more limited aims: to prevent a Communist victory and achieve a negotiated settlement.... A commitment to endless escalation in pursuit of military victory on the Asian mainland would be a commitment to disaster." Nixon's "prescription for Vietnam has less to do with the war than with the congressional battles in the United States this year and the Presidential contest of 1968," the editorial writers chided, congratulating themselves on seeing through Nixon's play.

They needed only to wait a few days before a different play emerged. Chuck Percy's idea to settle Vietnam through a conference of Asian nations was now all the rage in Republican circles. An unnamed senator, according to David Broder, approached Nixon to sign him on to the idea and was doubtful of his chances, considering Nixon had just said negotiations would only prolong the war. The senator needn't have feared. Nixon "instantly grasped the importance of the proposal to Percy's campaign for Senate," the senator told Broder. Nixon said he would support it and, the senator related, "left my office and walked into a press conference and, on the spot, constructed a better argument for the All-Asia Conference than I had ever heard before"—claiming the conference idea was "running through Asia like wildfire." North Vietnam and China should participate in such a conference, he added, arguing also that the bombing should be scaled back.

Which were things he had previously said would turn the Pacific into a Red Sea.

Then he took questions, so eager to please that when a reporter suggested that Republicans were tired of "old faces," Nixon quickly conceded the point. The only questions he wouldn't answer, he said, concerned 1968—though he did volunteer that President Johnson might have to pick Robert F. Kennedy as a running mate if his poll numbers continued to slip.

Different moments carried with them different political requirements; this week's was oleaginous demonstrations of Republican unity.

Watching Nixon go soft on Vietnam confirmed conservatives' suspicions that he wasn't *really* one of them. "Movement" conservatives, they had taken to calling themselves in the wake of the Goldwater crusade, after the example of the civil rights crusaders. They were a tribe, with their own rituals, kinship structures, origin myths, priests—foremost among them the men atop *National Review,* editor William F. Buckley and publisher William Rusher.

The same day as his Capitol Hill press conference, Nixon had scheduled a sit-down with twenty of them at the Shoreham Hotel. His rottweiler Pat Buchanan had got the ball rolling. Buchanan loved Nixon, whom he called the Old Man; Nixon loved to be called it, though he was only in his middle fifties—it was the name they'd called General Eisenhower in the White House. Buchanan was determined to make his fellow conservatives love Nixon, too. The vice president had written to William Rusher twice, and twice his letters hadn't been answered. So Buchanan wined and dined a kid named Tom Charles Huston, a slack-voiced Indianan who was president of Young Americans for Freedom, and begged him to dine with the vice president. At dinner, the Old Man won Huston over. Huston played hardball, shutting down the Young Americans for Freedom leaders who wanted nothing to do with Nixon. Then he got himself quoted in *Esquire* saying "only Nixon is generally acceptable to all kinds of Republicans." For Nixon that was quite a coup: YAF had been formed at the 1960 convention out of an ad hoc attempt to try to sabotage his nomination in favor of Barry Goldwater's. Then Huston brokered the meeting at the Shoreham Hotel.

Nixon held a weak hand with conservatives, and not only because he'd just backed away from a military solution in Vietnam. He had spent 1964 ingratiating himself with them, telling Buckley, "If Barry showed that the Republicans can't win with just the right wing, I showed in 1962 that we can't win without them." But then, back in October of '65, after *National Review* had put out an entire issue devoted to excommunicating the John Birch Society from the conservative movement, Nixon told a group of journalists "the Birchers could be handled, but that the real menace to the Republican Party came from the Buckleyites."

But Buckleyites were riding high. Buckley had just gone on the air nationwide as the host of his own public affairs program, *Firing Line.* Americans for Constitutional Action, which rated congressmen 0–100 on their conservativism, had just released its scores for the first half of 1966: the previous year, forty-four congressmen had received zeros on their zero-to-hundred scale; now there were only four, and four more solons earning hundreds. Goldwater Republicans won primary upsets in Indiana, Idaho, and upstate New York.

Segregationist Democrats did fantastically well in the South's late-summer gubernatorial primaries. A pattern repeated itself: moderates of sterling credentials became the favorite of swooning national pundits. In Arkansas it was former congressman and Johnson aide Brooks Hayes. In the border state of Maryland they were the fine liberal congressman Carlton Sickles and the outgoing governor's protégé, Attorney General Tom Finan.

In Georgia they were three: Ellis Arnall, a former governor that political scientist V. O. Key called the most effective in the century; Ernest Vandiver, reputed to have saved the Georgia educational system after segregationists threatened to shut it down after *Brown v. Board of Education;* and a dark horse, a handsome young navy man some called Kennedyesque, Jimmy Carter. The Democratic field in Georgia was so fine, some pundits thought no Republican would emerge to challenge the winner.

Then, the second part of the pattern: a far-right lunatic won the Democratic nomination. In Georgia it was high school dropout Lester Maddox, who took out regular ads for his restaurant in Atlanta papers that excoriated, for example, "the ungodly Civil Rights legislation that the politicians and the Communists and the Communist-inspired agitators are trying to pass in congress that will enslave all Americans." In Arkansas it was state supreme court justice James "Justice Jim" Johnson, best known for his 1956 ballot initiative to nullify federal civil rights laws. In Maryland, it was George Mahoney, a malcontent who picked up racial demagoguery as a political convenience after his sixth electoral loss, took as his slogan "Your Home Is Your Castle— Protect It," and gave some of his speeches in minstrel dialect. Maddox's path was smoothed by a riot during which Stokely Carmichael tooled through Atlanta telling milling throngs it was time to "tear this city up." Jim Johnson overcame a nasty rumor he was related to the president (old-timers might remember when it used to be an advantage for a governor to be able to boast of having the ear of the president). As for George Mahoney, he was so racist the state's prominent Democrats endorsed the Republican, Spiro Agnew, the undistinguished chief executive of Baltimore County. All three were now Democratic gubernatorial nominees. In Baton Rouge a twelve-term incumbent congressman who supported the Great Society was labeled the leader of the "Black Power voting block" and swamped by John Rarick, a member of the Ku Klux Klan, who went on to become Congress's spokesman for Americans who believed Communists were fluoridating the water supply. In the Senate, Everett Dirksen came just nine votes shy of passing through his perennial bill to restore prayer in public schools (only three Republicans voted against it). The Supreme Court upheld a landmark obscenity prosecution; civil libertarians noticed a sudden spike in obscenity arrests and warned of "a witch hunt the likes of which we haven't seen since the Salem trial."

"I would say the overall trend is, at the moment," allowed George Gallup in *U.S. News & World Report,* in an understatement, "towards more 'conservative' sentiment."

Seventy-five percent of the delegates to the 1968 Republican National Convention, according to one survey, would be identifying themselves as conservatives. And now their self-proclaimed leaders sat before Richard Nixon in one room: the American Conservative Union, the group formed from the old Draft Goldwater organization; the Free Society Association, the outfit established by Barry Goldwater's "Arizona Mafia" from money left over from his presidential campaign; Americans for Constitutional Action; Young Americans for Freedom; *National Review*'s publisher, William Rusher. Many were already talking about drafting Ronald Reagan for president.

Nixon played hard to his strength. When the former vice president needed to sway an intellectual into loyalty to him, he gave a dazzling geopolitical lecture. People who heard it used the same phrase to describe it: *tour de force*—like listening to St. Augustine lecture on the Bible, or Darwin on the flora and fauna of the Galápagos. "Take any political situation in the damn world, and he has war-gamed it this way and that, considering every which way it might go," one aide later recollected. "One senses that he knows the political geography of Planet Earth about as well as most Congressmen know their own districts," recalled another. It had been his method with Leonard Garment during his bizarre little slumber party the previous spring, hopping the fence to spend the night in Elmer Bobst's pool cabana, keeping Garment up half the night with descriptions of the strategic situation obtaining in every last nook and cranny of a vast and shifting globe. Garment remembered Nixon baring his soul at the conclusion. He "said he felt his life had to be dedicated to great foreign policy purposes. This man, fiercely determined to stay in the political life for which he was in many ways so ill suited, told me he felt driven to do so not by the rivalries or ideological commitments or domestic politics but by his pacifist mother's idealism and the profound importance of foreign affairs." It was the deepest thing Nixon possessed: this passion to play the game of statecraft from the only seat that mattered—the captain's. The one solid thing that lay behind all the poker player's feints, blinds, bluffs. It was why he stayed in the game.

Forty years later, one of the YAFers remembered the tour de force at the Shoreham as if it were yesterday:

"No notes. . . . He goes around the world. Rattling off names, connections, 'this is what we have to look for here . . . Russia and China . . . the Sino-Soviet split,' and he starts mentioning *names,* and names below names, and names below names below names, and 'here is what France is saying,' and de Gaulle is saying this, and whoever was the British prime minister, and the prime minister of Japan . . . I mean, he was *rattling* off all these names."

The performance was tailored to his audience. For Garment, the liberal Democrat, he pointed up his Quakerism and used the word *pacifist.* For these conservatives, he skipped his inklings that a diplomatic rapprochement with Red China and some kind of working détente with the Soviets were possible and desirable. But part of it was not a performance at all. Woodrow Wilson was the only twentieth-century U.S. president he worshipped. A permanent world accord, a benevolent American hegemony at its heart: this was his redeeming glint of idealism. "Nixon said he would do anything, make any sacrifice, to be able to use his talents and experience in making foreign policy," Garment remembered. Even, on August 23, the sacrifice of lying that the notion of an all-Asia peace conference was spreading like wild-fire, then crossing his fingers that no one in the *National Review* crowd would hammer him with it later in the day. They didn't. They were Nixon skeptics. He won them over. A participant leaked to the *Washington Post* that "lines of communication were opened that should be helpful later on." That, for now, was enough.

The Franklins were none too pleased; an umbrella of liberal GOP groups rushed out a self-pitying press release that said continued conservative influence in the Republican Party would bring costs "far greater than those incurred in 1964." The *Times* reported in their dispatch on the Shoreham meeting that Nixon's painting himself "as the Goldwater candidate of 1968" was "a tactical error of major importance." Let the sophisticates say so. Nixon knew Goldwater followers would knock on doors on Election Day until their hands bled, while "moderates" put out self-pitying press releases. The *Times*'s tactical sense would better have been served by casting its eye downtown, at the padlocked headquarters of its ancient and honorable rival the *New York Herald Tribune.* That liberal Republican citadel had just gone out of business—a symbolic casualty not merely of bad days for the news-paper business, but of the new conservative upsurge.

School was in session. A new front opened in the sixties civil war. For twelve years, Southern schools had hardly done a thing to honor *Brown v. Board of Education.* The federal government had hardly done anything to punish them. County after county maintained "dual" school districts: superior schools for whites, inferior ones for blacks. Title VI of the 1964 Civil Rights Act stipulated that no segregated institution of any sort could receive federal funding. In 1965, Lyndon Johnson signed the first federal school-funding law, the Elementary and Secondary Education Act, and a series of federal courts ruled that jurisdictions with dual school systems would have to file desegregation plans with the Department of Health, Education, and Welfare (HEW) to get federal money (which would, in some school districts, make up a quarter of the budget). In April of 1965 HEW's Office of Education announced the guidelines schools would have to meet to comply.

They were piddling: they counted a district as making good-faith efforts toward integration even if district lines stayed exactly the same, but black families were allowed to file individual requests to enroll their children in white schools. These were known as "freedom of choice" plans. They weren't worth the paper they were printed on. In real life when a black fam-ily tried to exercise freedom of choice, they were as likely as not to be visited by some insistent white man asking whether there hadn't been some mis-take, waving their home lease or car note in front of them to back up the threat. Not a single school district with a freedom of choice plan had subsequently integrated. By the end of 1965, only 6 percent of Southern pupils attended school with children of another race.

In March of 1966 HEW secretary John Gardner issued firmer guidelines; these demanded statistical proof of "significant progress."

And that led to the first shot on Fort Sumter.

There were twenty-two senators from states of the Old Confederacy. Eighteen of them signed a letter to the president calling the revised guidelines an "unfair and unrealistic abuse of bureaucratic power." George Wallace's first political act after his wife's nomination was to read a joint statement standing beside the Alabama congressional delegation that the guidelines were an "illegal" and "totalitarian" "blueprint devised by socialists." His school superintendent observed that Section 256 of the state constitution—"Separate schools shall be provided for white and colored children, and no child of either race shall be permitted to attend a school of the other race"—forbade the state from compliance. Wallace went on statewide TV to announce that HEW had "the unqualified, one hundred percent support of the Communist Party, USA, as well as all its fronts, affiliates, and publications."

On July 18, 1966, the height of riot season, HEW took steps to defund three school districts in Mississippi. Senator Lister Hill threatened mutiny from President Johnson's entire legislative program. LBJ's East Texan aide Harry McPherson made a political warning: "Undoubtedly we are going to curse the day these cuts were made." Preserving the dual-schools citadel was a question of power. It was a question of Lost Cause pride. It was a question of racialized sexual panic—*"Please wake up!"* read one of Lester Maddox's newspaper ads in 1965, after a Negro admitted to the state university married a white classmate (this blot on the escutcheon of the University of Georgia, Charlayne Hunter-Gault, would end up being one of America's most distinguished journalists).

On August 9, the twelfth day of debate in the full House on the civil rights bill, a North Carolina congressman by the apt name of Basil Whitener introduced an amendment to moot Title VI of the 1964 Civil Rights Act outright (Whitener had earlier whined of an amendment offering relief for Negroes injured or intimidated while voting, "Why cannot a person who is injured or intimidated be a white person for once?"). Georgia Republican Howard "Bo" Callaway played good cop, offering a more realistic substitute: "Nothing in this title shall be construed to authorize action by any department or agency to require the assignment of students to public schools in order to overcome racial imbalance."

Debate on the motion was called. There followed a shocking development. Back in the spring during House subcommittee hearings on the civil rights bill, northern Republicans with liberal records on race took turns offering their own states as models of the sort of biracial harmony that was possible in places where politicians didn't demagogue on civil rights. One of them was Clark MacGregor of Minneapolis, proudly noting that racial back-lash over school integration was "not a factor in my part of the country." But that had been May. This was August. Minneapolis had just suffered a riot. Word subsequently got out that in the riot's wake the mayor had implored the city's business establishment to create at least 145 new jobs for impover-ished black teenagers. Evans and Novak reported what happened next: "The mayor had never experienced such a city-wide outbreak of hostility—phone calls, telegrams, and letters by the scores—as hit him after he decided to respond to the riot with a promise of jobs and only limited police action."

And on the floor of the House, Clark MacGregor now went on a Dixie-style tear in support of his Georgia colleague: "If this amendment is defeated, we will be putting our stamp of approval on administrative action to destroy the neighborhood schools. . . . Mr. Chairman, it is not only the Southern states which have been affected."

The Speaker called the vote. The Callaway amendment passed. A new national panic had burst to the surface: that the federal government would deliver the chaos of rioting urban slums to your own quiet, bucolic neigh-borhood via yellow bus, in the guise of combating "de facto" school segre-gation.

The "busing" panic was premature. Actual federal efforts to redraw school district boundaries, or to transport children across them, were years in the future. It made no difference. A September 9 column from Evans and Novak claimed, "In the highest reaches of the Department of Health, Edu-cation and Welfare . . . planners have secretly put together an education bill" that would "make a radical departure in government policy by supplying extra federal funds to school districts that achieve an integrated racial bal-ance." What it referred to were pilot discussions to provide municipalities with carrots to enhance educational opportunities for Negroes stuck in sub-standard districts—by, for example, setting up "education parks" or "educa-tion plazas" within cities where students could be sent for language, remedial reading, science, or art-enrichment classes a couple of times a week. The same weeks the 1966 civil rights bill was filibustered to death, congressmen North and South behaved as if Washington, D.C., were about to cart schoolchil-dren off in tumbrels.

The commissioner of HEW's Office of Education, Harold Howe, the man who, at Vassar's graduation in June, had observed that the civil rights battles of the future would be fought "in quiet communities, in pleasant neighborhoods," was a vocal critic of the conservatives' claims to be merely preserving the concept of the neighborhood school, impassioned about pro-viding equal educational opportunities to kids who lived in the "world of wall-to-wall carpeting, pleasant back yards, and summer camp," and "their neighbors in the central city . . . who play in alleys and live six to a room." The House Rules Committee called him to testify and treated him like a vis-

itation from hell. "Mr. Speaker," South Carolina's Mendel Rivers pronounced, "this misfit should be fired. He is destroying the school system of
America lock, stock, and barrel. . . . He talks like a Communist. . . . That is
the reason why those of us who know call him a commissar of integration."
And playing to type, the commissar, like some parody of a rich and out-of-
touch professor, pulled on his pipe and responded in clouds of technicalities.
Mendel Rivers's side was winning the debate.

On Wednesday, September 21, Rules Committee Republicans engineered
a surprise investigation into HEW's desegregation guidelines; on Thursday
the Senate Appropriations Committee slashed HEW's enforcement budget;
on Monday, the same committee argued the guidelines were illegal under the
terms of the 1964 Civil Rights Act; on Tuesday there was a riot in the San
Francisco ghetto (the *New York Times:* "the police reported that a group of
Negroes had broken into a gun store in Daly City, just to the south, and
stolen all the guns"); and on Wednesday, September 28, Lester Maddox won
a runoff to become the Georgia Democratic gubernatorial nominee. And on
Thursday the Senate voted 55–11 in favor, more or less, of what George Wallace had decreed back in April when he resegregated Alabama's mental
wards: that segregation would be allowed in hospitals if the doctor deemed
race-mixing "detrimental to the health of a patient." Among the senators
who agreed to the amendment were, the *Times* reported, "a surprising number of Northern and Western liberal Democrats." Explained Majority
Leader Mike Mansfield, HEW was going "too fast." Indeed in May, 32 percent of Americans thought that the federal government was "pushing integration too fast." Now the number was 58 percent, with only 10 percent
saying it should move faster. Crowed Senator James Eastland of Mississippi,
"The sentiment of the entire country now stands with the Southern people."

The House took up debate on a $5.8 billion extension of the Elementary
and Secondary Education Act. Paul Fino of Queens, New York, had combed
the language and discovered—*aha!*—that it authorized funds for "pupil
transportation services." The Democratic floor leader was taken aback; the
clause, no more controversial than outlays for teachers, textbooks, or chalk,
was put there to help districts accommodate handicapped pupils.

"Maybe so," Fino shot back, "but my fear is that local administrators of
this program will force busing."

John Brademas, a liberal Democrat from Indiana, pleaded for his colleagues to pay attention to "F-A-C-T-S, not allegations." An "antibusing"
amendment was offered nonetheless, by Jim O'Hara, Democrat of Macomb
County, Michigan. Buses, not Reds, were what Washington now saw
beneath every bed. Roman Pucinski rose in support: "They have auditors
crawling through all of Chicago in the school system," he boomed. "I have
educators all over the country tell me that they have to answer piles and piles
of questionnaires and fill out mountains of reports while funds are being held

up." In an October 6 press conference, President Johnson all but apologized for the drive for school integration: "In some instance there has been some harassment, some mistakes." These were not the most hopeful times since Christ was born in Bethlehem, and once more liberals felt blindsided. It made no *sense:* the nation had made its commitment to racial equality, proudly and with eyes open. How could they be moving too fast when funds were set to be held back from only eighty-nine of seven thousand segregated hospitals and seventy-four of eighteen hundred segregated school districts? "We accept tokenism," a HEW spokesman wailed. "What more do they want?"

What did they want? In the steel-mill suburb of South Holland, Illinois, one Elizabeth Kluzyk wrote her senator:

Dear Senator Douglas:

It seems HEW is determined to take away the civil rights of the white person. . . . I'm beginning to think our nightly prayer should be this, "Dear God, please save us from the bureaucrats in Washington!"

Richard Nixon broke with his reluctance to dwell upon law and order only once, in 1966, in that *U.S. News* essay—and had seemed apologetic to be raising the matter at all, concluding, "The polls still place the war in Vietnam and the rising cost of living as the major political issues of 1966." He was lying. As far as domestic issues went, Gallup showed race far outstripped inflation as a concern. And yet, launching two months of sixteen-hour days campaigning coast to coast for other Republicans, Nixon stubbornly kept to the same script.

It served a political requirement. What Richard Nixon was campaigning for now was respectability. Yes, law and order was breaking down; the crime rate was making ordinary Americans terrified to walk the streets; "the cities" were becoming wastelands. But others were doing just fine tying these facts to Lyndon Johnson, softening him up for 1968: George Wallace, Ronald Reagan, dozens of lesser figures. There was no percentage for Nixon in adding to the pile-on. The task now was in making sure the pundits and the papers no longer considered the idea of him competing for the presidency as a joke. The key to that was raising his stature.

Another key to raising his stature was pulling in an accomplice. That accomplice was . . . Lyndon Baines Johnson. Just as in 1950, when as a backbench congressman he had pushed himself to the front ranks of a leaderless party by turning himself, on the subject of Alger Hiss, into the de facto debating partner of the president, he would acclimate the nation into thinking of him as Lyndon's 1968 opponent—because Johnson would start treating Nixon as an opponent. He would do it by drawing the president into a public fight over Vietnam.

What did Richard Nixon *really* believe then about Vietnam? The best tes-

timony comes from the memoirs of Leonard Garment, his partner in clambering over the pool-house fence belonging to financial backer Elmer Bobst.
That next morning, Garment recalled, Nixon had a long, intimate conversation with Bobst. The subject turned to Vietnam. "Bobst thought it was an
unmitigated disaster from which the United States must quickly withdraw.
Nixon, said Bobst, agreed that Vietnam could not be 'won' and that we
would eventually have to withdraw." That withdrawal, however, must take
place under the most strategically propitious circumstances—whether they
be one, five, or ten years in the future. Until that time, the public would just
have to be told what the public had to be told.

A morally enormous position, perhaps. But a rather politically advanta-
geous one. Nixon had given himself license to lie about Vietnam. The trick
was devising the most politically useful lies for any given interval. Hindsight
makes the pattern obvious. Nixon had taken just about every possible position on Vietnam short of withdrawal—we should escalate, we should negotiate, we should bomb more, we should pause the bombing, we should pour
in troops, pouring in troops would be a scandal. Liberals who paid attention
were enraged. They congratulated themselves for spotting the hustle. It
hardly bothered Nixon; their derision only helped him with the Orthogonians. He was receiving little coverage during those eventful months. It took
someone with the eye of a hawk and the obsession of a neurotic to mark all
the twists and turns.

However, one man was just that neurotic, and just that attentive: Lyndon
Johnson. And Johnson was the intended audience for every Nixon utterance.
Every Nixonian twist and turn on Vietnam fit a specific pattern: whatever he
said, whenever he said it, was always exactly 180 degrees from the current
line the president was taking. Nixon was endeavoring to drive the Texan
crazy, and to make Nixon the public focus of his rage.

"If Johnson wants to run again, he'll get the nomination. Any incumbent
president can always get renominated. Look at Truman in 1948," Nixon told
the *Times* in a Week in Review interview Labor Day weekend. "If he could
then, anyone could anytime." That dig tore deep into Lyndon Johnson's psychological skin. Harry Truman, in 1966, was seen as the personification of
political failure. And when Truman, like Johnson an accidental president,
faced the prospect of going up for reelection in 1952, he abdicated in the face
of an unpopular war.

Johnson was haunted by a sense of illegitimacy. Even at the height of his
popularity in 1964, he had considered dropping out of the presidential race.
Now, as he approached his 1,036th day in office—the last day JFK served—
his popularity was dropping week by week. It didn't take much for a man
like Nixon to probe LBJ's deepest anxieties. Many of those anxieties he
shared.

They shared a need to humiliate, but a horror of being humiliated—and that nagging sense that the worst humiliations always, *always* came at the hand of some damned Kennedy or another. Pundits spoke of a "Kennedy wing" of the Democratic Party, complete with shadow cabinet of exiled JFK aides. "If Lyndon thinks he's in trouble, if Lyndon thinks he needs Bobby on the ticket to win," Nixon said one morning on the *Today* show, "he'll sugarcoat him, swallow him, and regurgitate him later." He was reminding Johnson that his political future might just rely on his greatest political enemy. "I don't know what it means," Nixon said at a Fort Lauderdale auditorium, "but the sign outside says, 'Nixon Tonight—Wrestling Next Week.' I'd suggest coming back. It'll be Bobby versus Lyndon."

That was the sound of Dick hitting Lyndon over the head with a chair.

The shared Kennedy anxiety betokened others: over their provincial backgrounds, the hair-trigger sensitivity to those who would remind them of it, the cruel delight their Georgetown betters took at the yokels' ill-mannered missteps. One of Johnson's worst such humiliations came in 1964, when cameras caught him lifting up his beagle by the ears. So Nixon described Johnson's relationship with Congress thus: Lyndon "barks and it barks. He tells it to roll over and it rolls over. He tells it to play dead and it plays dead. He doesn't even have to pick it up by the ears."

They shared a public reputation as unprincipled, and a self-image as statesmen. After the 1963 James Garner picture *The Wheeler Dealers*, about a Texas hustler who goes East to strike it big in New York, Johnson got tagged with a hated nickname. That was the sore Nixon rubbed when he said the president was working with "a stacked deck" and that "the country hasn't won a hand since he started to deal."

And above all, they shared a bone-deep obsession with control, terror whenever the world proved uncontrollable. And what the commander in chief controlled the least was Vietnam. Nixon knew how hopeless it was in Vietnam. He knew that Johnson knew it, too, but could never say so publicly. Forced to act presidential, Johnson could only sit there and stew while Nixon rubbed his nose in it: that we had to escalate to prevent World War III; that if we escalated, we might start World War III.

Nixon was hitting Johnson with the same chair every time he mentioned inflation. Inflation was something a president could little control in the best of circumstances. Because of his need to dissemble about Vietnam, Johnson could control it less than ever. Since spring, his economists had been telling him that increased military spending, coming on top of record-breaking prosperity in the civilian economy, made an inflationary spiral almost a certainty unless he pushed through a quick tax hike. But to acknowledge he needed a tax hike was to acknowledge that the situation in Vietnam was an emergency. The notion that the nation could afford both Vietnam and the Great Society—"guns and butter"—was the central organizing principle of his presidency. Which is why Nixon hyped high prices as often as he did. He was planting a kind of rhetorical time bomb. He knew inflation would accelerate soon enough.

In the middle of August the interest rates banks paid depositors were edging toward their legal limit, 5.5 percent; banks began curtailing loans. There were whispers of a financial panic. A twenty-eight-year-old Phoenix mother, outraged at the price of bread, took out a four-line classified ad calling for a protest. Five thousand housewives responded. Her movement soon had chapters from Connecticut to California. Reminding the president of this grassroots groundswell, and pairing it in the same sentence with Vietnam, was Nixon's way of reminding LBJ how little control he had over anything at all.

Nixon harped on one more matter in every speech: that the loudest voices opposing the president on Vietnam came from the president's own party— people like Senator Fulbright, chairman of the Foreign Relations Committee, who spoke of America as a "sick society" rotted through with the "arrogance of power which has afflicted, weakened, and in some cases destroyed great nations in the past." The junior senator from New York insisted publicly that he was still with the president on Vietnam. But at every Georgetown cocktail party, conversation circled around to when Bobby would put his widening differences with the president on record.

Nixon knew how much pressure it put on a man to lie consistently. He knew that Lyndon Johnson was given to towering rages. Maybe, just maybe, he could push LBJ into displaying one in public. And then Richard Nixon would be the one who looked presidential.

CHAPTER SEVEN

Batting Average

NIXON'S GENERAL-ELECTION TOUR STEPPED OFF SEPTEMBER 13 WITH a luncheon of the Overseas Press Club in D.C. He said the president might soon "find it necessary to announce a substantial increase in our forces in Vietnam" and that he "owes it to the American people to come clean and tell them exactly what his plans are"—"now, and not after the election." A reporter asked if Nixon was calling Johnson a liar. Nixon replied with a stealthy blow to the presidential kneecap: no, but that Johnson "may not have thought this thing through" given the pressure he was under, "losing popularity because of the loss of some 'dove' support among Democrats."

Nixon hit Ohio: Columbus, Athens, and a "Republican Jamboree" in Cincinnati. Then over the border to Kentucky, where he said that unless prices stopped rising, "the major issue in 1968 could well be President Johnson's recession. . . . The leadership gap we have in Washington now in foreign policy and in dealing with inflation is because we have a one-party Congress that will go all the way with LBJ. . . . What we need now in order to restore the greatness of America is to increase the members of the Republican Party—the loyal opposition—in Congress."

(This was masterly Nixonian aural illusion: *leadership gap* sounded like *credibility gap*, *loyal opposition* raised McCarthyite red flags about Democratic *dis*loyalty.)

"Any nation that insists on trading with the enemy should have all its foreign aid cut off right now."

(Red meat to sate the conservatives, and further agita for the president: Nixon knew the nation's diplomat in chief could not and would not do any such thing.)

Thence to Denver, then Davenport, then Salt Lake City.

The ritual was always the same. A press conference beforehand. Men moved away the bulky podium, the better for his audience to see that the master spoke without notes. Introduction by a local dignitary. A dramatic entrance down a flower-strewn gauntlet laid out by the Republican lady auxiliaries, his head lowered in false modesty as the electrified thousands roared in welcome. The review of the dais ("The best group of candidates I've seen in twenty years of coming to Colorado"). The insinuating speech, hands balled over his stomach, his jaw working upward and downward—thought Garry Wills, *Esquire* magazine's mordantly brilliant political correspondent, "like Charlie McCarthy's."

Geographically, the itinerary felt random. Politically, it was anything but. He received over a thousand speaking invitations a month. The ones he chose were triangulated with scientific precision. The *New York Times*'s John Herbers reviewed the crazy-quilt itinerary and concluded Nixon was campaigning "in districts where races are close." The failure of discernment was profound. It was the opposite: he was campaigning in traditionally Republican districts where a Democratic congressman had won in 1964 on Lyndon Johnson's coattails, but was likely to be swept out in the conservative backlash.

For instance, Iowa's First District. A five-term Republican, Fred Schwengel, was running to recover the seat he'd lost to a young political-science professor from the Bronx named John Schmidhauser. One day, Representative Schmidhauser appeared at a farm bureau meeting, prepared for a grilling on the Democrats' agricultural policies. The questions, though, were all on rumors that Chicago's Negro rioters were about to engulf Iowa in waves, traveling, for some reason, "on motorcycles." The liberal political-science professor was as vulnerable as a sapling. Hence Nixon's visit to Davenport. Nixon visited Iowa as often as he could. Despite the old joke about Iowa going Democratic when hell goes Methodist, five of its seven congressional seats belonged to freshman Democrats. Now that farmers were afraid that Martin Luther King would send Negro biker gangs to rape their children, the Republican restoration was inevitable.

Come November, Richard Nixon could remind the *New York Times* that what these districts had in common was that Richard Nixon had campaigned there. He could reap credit for making water flow downhill. The *new* Nixon—the one who didn't bait liberal Democrats on law and order—would have saved his party from Armageddon. He would leapfrog the competition, the oh-so-glamorous GOP liberals that the likes of the *Times* kept puffing up, and become the presidential nominee.

In Gallup's poll of the Republican faithful at the start of 1966, Nixon was ahead by twenty-three points. Michigan governor George Romney sat fourth. But Romney was the one all the pundits were picking—or, if Romney stumbled, a Senator Chuck Percy, or Nelson Rockefeller if he wanted it, or perhaps Oregon's Republican dove Mark Hatfield or Pennsylvania's Governor Scranton or New York mayor John Lindsay. The quality they were said to have in common was "charisma"—"Kennedyesque" charisma. To the talking heads on the Sunday panel shows, it was obvious: the man who went into the showdown with Lyndon Johnson would have to be a TV star. It simply *couldn't* be Nixon. The logic of the times demanded it.

This new political science had a prophet, and his name was Marshall McLuhan—"the new spokesman of the electronic age," as the blurb to his 1964 magnum opus, *Understanding Media: The Extensions of Man,* called him. A key hinge of that book's argument that "the medium is the message" was his exegesis of the Kennedy-Nixon debates. He thought Nixon resembled the railway lawyer in westerns "who signs leases that are not in the best interests of the folks in the little town. . . . Without TV, Nixon had it made." The influence of TV had only accelerated in the eight years since. That was how, in defiance of all the doughy-faced bald men whose constituencies returned them to Congress year after year, in defiance of the presidential landslide won in 1964 by the jug-eared, poky-voiced Texan, pundits proclaimed with such confidence that 1968 would be the year of "Republican Camelot."

The politicians they lionized were antipoliticians—"mavericks" who talked straight, directly to the people, over and around the grubby old exigencies of partisan machinery. George Romney was the template: a Republican who'd won in a Democratic state, who got into politics running a nonpartisan commission to reform Michigan's antiquated constitution, a familiar face on TV from his days as CEO of American Motors deriding the Big Three's "gas guzzlers." Percy's political debut was in assembling a panel of disinterested experts to charter a new Republican agenda for 1960 beyond the partisan clichés of the past, a panel modeled on the Rockefeller Brothers Foundation's Special Studies Project of the mid-1950s. Scranton—dubbed upon his inauguration in 1963 as "the first Kennedy Republican"—got into politics pioneering public-private partnerships to refurbish the dying industrial town that bore his family's name. John Vliet Lindsay (his 1965 campaign motto, borrowed from a line from a pundit's column, was "He is fresh and everyone else is tired") was seen as the epitome of the antimachine politician—the matinee idol always on the front page of the *Times* walking the streets of Harlem, working over a pair of bongos, saving New York from social chaos by the pure force of his charisma.

All were independently wealthy ("A man needs money to address the people over and around party structure," Garry Wills sardonically observed). All shared a social network (Percy's future son-in-law was a Rockefeller; Romney's presidential advisers were borrowed from Rockefeller's staff) with the Alsops and Lippmanns and Harrimans of the world. No evidence existed for these pundits' conviction that by the intervention of virtuous and public-spirited men like themselves, politics could at last become enlightened. No evidence, that is, save the echo chamber their intimacy with one another helped produce. They were men who hardly noticed the ideological ground shifting beneath their feet.

When John Lindsay, the very liberal Republican congressman from Manhattan's "Silk Stocking" district, ran for mayor against Abraham Beame in 1965, his posters had him leading a brood of smiling black kids, handsome as a movie star—"Kennedyesque." Journalists from Italy, Peru, England, Denmark, rushed to cover him. "Where Beame symbolized a shabby yesterday, John Lindsay symbolizes a brighter tomorrow," editorialized the *World-Telegram and Sun.* The *Herald Tribune* practically made its last year of publication an adjunct of his campaign; the liberal Republicans of the Ripon Society rhapsodized that he was "the first leader his party has given our generation." One of his campaign flyers pictured him erect at a debate podium, six feet four inches tall, his two opponents flanking him in chairs, with the legend "Will the real liberal please stand up?"

The other opponent was fringe candidate William F. Buckley. At Buckley's luncheon with the *New York Times* editorial board, the magazine editor was asked, "Do you realize that as a practical matter your candidacy . . . is likely to result in a grave setback to the fortunes of New York by depriving the city of a Lindsay administration?"

Lindsay triumphed; the *Times* predicted Shangri-la: "The thorough research and thoughtfulness that went into the writing of position papers during his campaign," they editorialized, "will stand him in good stead now." New York's fortunes proved grave nonetheless. His inauguration coincided with a nearly biblical disaster: a two-week subway and bus strike. Oblivious, Lindsay went on the radio and declared New York "Fun City." It was followed by a nurses' strike. And then a new subway fare, the first since 1953. And the city's first income tax. "A Long Six Months for Lindsay," read a July 4, 1966, *New York Times* op-ed.

Part of his crusade to break apart the city's ossified bureaucracies was taking on the NYPD—largely seen by the coalition of liberal professionals, minorities, young idealists, philanthropic Establishment Republicans, and college-educated middle-class Jews that elected Lindsay as clannish, racist, and corrupt. They were seen rather differently by white ethnics in the outer boroughs, hoping against hope for a financial break that would finally let them escape to the suburbs. To them, the New York City Police Department was their only defense against a city becoming a jungle. Over the previous decade, the murder rate had doubled. Robberies and thefts nearly tripled, despite 35 percent more cops on the streets.

One of Lindsay's campaign promises on law and order was a Civilian Complaint Review Board. The police *were,* after all, corrupt; a 1964 investigation had traced gambling graft all the way up to the department's elite forty-eight-man "watchdog" group. Law-abiding ghetto residents carried receipts for every possession with them so as not to be accused of stealing them. The cops had lost the confidence of the public, Lindsay said; restoring trust between the police and the community would make it easier to fight crime together—or so he reasoned. Policemen disagreed. The idea of liberal bureaucrats second-guessing their work was, according to their commissioner, Michael Murphy, "a calculated mass libel of the police." Lindsay replaced Murphy with a commissioner loyal to him, Howard Leary. Some saw Lindsay as deliberately breaking the cops as a rival, working-class, Catholic power center. "All cops are scum," one of Lindsay's appointees was reported to have said.

In May, Leary handed down General Order No. 14, officially establishing the Civilian Complaint Review Board. Its membership was announced: the president of the New York Society for Ethical Culture, the acting director of the Puerto Rican Development Congress, the former president of the Catholic Interracial Council—the kind of panjandrums called "limousine liberals" for all the times they were seen on the news getting into limousines after some civic function or another. The president of the Patrolmen's Benevolent Association, John Cassese, snapped, "I am sick and tired of giving in to minority groups with their whims and their gripes and shouting." The New York Civil Liberties Union denounced Cassese's "thinly veiled racism."

Then during the riot in the Brooklyn neighborhood of East New York in July, cops were sent in with orders not to use their nightsticks. The PBA got 96,888 signatures to get a referendum on the November ballot to dissolve the Civilian Complaint Review Board. The law required them to get only 30,000.

Both sides opened bustling campaign offices. Cassese of the PBA opened theirs with a speech recalling how his boys had handily put down the riot in Harlem in 1964—while supposedly, Rochester and Philadelphia had burned near to the ground. "Why? Because they have review boards there. . . . Communism and Communists are mixed up in this fight. If we wind up with a review board, we'll have done Russia a great service. . . . The doctrine of the Communist Party is to knock out religion and break the spirit, as well as create confusion in the police department, cause chaos, and interrupt the public function."

The liberal coalition organized to fight to keep the review board couldn't have been more delighted with the opposition, its laziness with the facts (Rochester and Philadelphia had fared no worse than Harlem in 1964) and their Red-baiting. They called their opposition "a coalition of right-wing groups—the Conservative Party, the fascist National Renaissance Party, the John Birch Society, and the American Legion allied with the PBA against the forces of reason and civic leadership in this city." The facts were on their side, and that was enough: of the 113 cases the CCRB had investigated since June, disciplinary action had been recommended in only three of them. Trumpeted Commissioner Leary, "It has certainly strengthened the spirit of cooperation between the police and the public."

It all just made so much *sense*—just as the facts the liberals had marshaled in hearings for the 1966 civil rights bill and its open-housing title had made so much sense.

Which, the same week Commissioner Leary spoke, was resoundingly thumped in the Senate.

The pro-review-board liberals' billboards read DON'T BE A "YES" MAN

FOR BIGOTRY, VOTE "NO." Boasted their spokesman, "Before this campaign is over, people will feel ashamed to do anything but vote against this referendum." They couldn't lose.

In California, Pat Brown was trying the same strategy, isolating his opposition as an extremist fringe—just as Barry Goldwater's supporters were isolated as an extremist fringe. It worked about as well as it did for Brown in California. "The police of New York like William Buckley," the liberal journalist Dick Schaap had written after the *National Review* editor's quixotic mayoral campaign in 1965. "He lost only in the real world." Since then Schaap had cowritten a series on New York's crime epidemic: "Cab drivers rest iron bars on the front seat next to them," he reported. "The weapons were justified." The world had changed. The ground was shifting.

September 17: incredible, astonishing news from a lakeside suburb of Chicago. The Senate candidate's wife, Lorraine Percy, was awakened at 5 a.m. by the sound of breaking glass. She witnessed a man bludgeoning her beautiful twenty-one-year-old stepdaughter, Valerie, to death. The only clues were an opening cut in a pane of glass, barefoot prints on the beach, fingerprints. This was the kind of awful, brutal, monstrous crime you expected to hear about once in a generation. But this summer there had already been the Richard Speck murders and the Texas Tower shootings. Chuck Percy wouldn't appear in public again until October 5. His surrogates, however, ground on, intimating that *all* voters risked Valerie Percy's fate under Democratic rule. On September 20, Gerald Ford, the gentle man who had risen in the House because he had no enemies, spoke at the Illinois State Fair on Republican Day and said Democrats were "the party with the big riots in the streets. How long are we going to abdicate law and order—the backbone of any civilization—in favor of a soft social theory that the man who heaves a brick through your window or tosses a firebomb into your car is simply the misunderstood and underprivileged product of a broken home?"

The busing panic broke out in Congress. On September 27, a riot broke out in San Francisco. "There is no rationale for these riots," an agonized Pat Brown lamented. "We have forty thousand jobs in California unfulfilled, but these people are not equipped to handle them. They have yet to learn their ABC's, and then they have to learn how to deal with the sophisticated complexities of industry. It's going to take years." Ronald Reagan had his own rationale: San Francisco went up in flames because Brown hadn't "profited at all from the experience of Watts and has done nothing to forestall future disturbances in other trouble spots." And in New York City, Mayor Lindsay started canvassing the outer boroughs for civilian review. A typical stop was in Flatbush, Brooklyn. He was interrupted by a housewife's shriek: "Why do you always kowtow to the coloreds?"

The anti–Civilian Complaint Review Board campaign canvassed with TV commercials: "The addict, the criminal, the hoodlum: only the policeman stands between you and him." Its brochures showed pictures that looked like wartime Dresden: "This is the aftermath of a riot in a city that had a civil review board." The pro-review-board forces went hunting for prime billboard space, but it had all already been snapped up by the PBA—a white woman in a white raincoat walking in the night: "The Civilian Review Board must be stopped. Her life . . . your life . . . may depend on it." Then they won their most important endorsement: Barry Gray, America's first radio call-in host. He was famous throughout the five boroughs for saying what others were afraid to say aloud. In the 1950s it was that Joe McCarthy was a blackguard. Now it was that New York "will become an asphalt jungle" if the review board remained. Lindsay started limiting his campaigning to voter registration drives in black neighborhoods. He couldn't alight anywhere else without getting heckled.

It shocked him. It shouldn't have. When he had campaigned in some of these same neighborhoods in 1965, young white men carried SUPPORT YOUR LOCAL POLICE signs, and he was guarded by cops wearing orange BUCKLEY FOR MAYOR buttons. The resistance was never taken as evidence of a lack of popular will that might cripple the kind of reforms he had in mind. "The city is beset with extremists of a dangerous kind" was how Lindsay explained— dismissed—it, as his constituency swaddled themselves in self-righteousness. "The policeman's inner world is bound by 'us' and 'them,' the latter being all punks or potential criminals at best," the *New York Times Magazine* helpfully explained. The *World Journal Tribune* published an essay entitled "Why Cops Behave the Way They Do." It told the story of a cop who passed an art gallery in the hippie precincts of the Lower East Side "filled with paintings of what appeared to be female genitalia" and did the only thing his worldview would permit him: he went in and started arresting everyone in sight. "All a cop can swing in a milieu of marijuana smokers, interracial daters, and homosexuals is a nightstick."

Pathetic opponents, went the thinking, obviously easy to defeat.

Some liberals were beginning to come to terms with these forces by which they were being blindsided. An AP reporter opened up his notebook as the governor flew to the riot scene in San Francisco: "slowly realizing the immensity of the blow his campaign had suffered," the reporter wrote, "Brown looked out the window. . . . He was slumped in his favorite seat, toward the front of the plane, his coat off. Finally, he talked of the riots, puzzled as to why they happened in 'the most affluent nation in the world.' He also talked about how he was now disliked by Negroes as well as whites. He had met with fifty Negro leaders recently, he recalled, and 'all they would say was, "You sold us out, Gov."'"

The next day, Ronald Reagan was on the cover of *Time*, looking young and handsome.

*   *   *

Richard Nixon turned south on September 29. The name "Maddox" was on every tongue: St. Lester of the Blessed Ax Handle had just won the Georgia Democratic gubernatorial runoff. Martin Luther King responded, "I am afraid of what lies ahead of us. We could end up with a full-scale race war in this country." Atlanta's conscience-stricken liberal congressman Charles Longstreet Weltner announced that he would give up his House seat rather share a ticket with Maddox.

Nixon finessed the situation with his usual insinuating delicacy. At the New Southern Hotel in Jackson, Tennessee, he reminded his audience that he had supported *Brown v. Board of Education,* the 1964 Civil Rights Act, and the 1965 Voting Rights Act, but that he would not condone "mob rule" by "any" group—knowing that to the people in front of him "mob rule" referred to black people carrying picket signs, though up North he could claim he also meant Dixie vigilantes. Then, after baiting the president for his "complete failure" to lower the rate of black unemployment, he promised Southern Republicans would run nonracial campaigns. "In building this party of the future in the South, one of the foundation stones will be a new concept of states' rights," Nixon said in Columbia, South Carolina. "The old concept was to use states' rights as an instrument of reaction, whereas Republicans view these rights as instruments of progress." It was Democrats who fielded "racial demagogues."

The *New York Times* was impressed. "Tanned, fit, relaxed, he moves swiftly from town to town, parrying questions about his political future with his left, throwing hard rights and combination punches at the Democrats," John Herbers wrote in the Week in Review, reporting as news Nixon's declaration that the racial issue was "a dead horse," missing the point that Southern politics had always followed this good-cop/bad-cop pattern: Bubba-baiters who decried "mongrelization" with tobacco-spitting rage; and gentlemen who spoke of states' rights in sonorous tones as a crucial component of regional uplift, as Nixon just had.

Nixon kept on hounding the president on the twinned time bomb of Vietnam and inflation. LBJ had just met with governors and implored them not to make any new bond issues, so as to hold down inflation. The media reported—and the White House furiously denied—that this was because he was going to spend $10 billion more than announced in Vietnam in 1967.

Then, the president announced that he was traveling to six countries in Asia in the middle of October for a "peace offensive" that would culminate in a multilateral meeting with South Vietnam's Prime Minister Ky and other Asian leaders in Manila.

For Nixon, this development was poised between peril and opportunity. Johnson might be maneuvering to pull a peace rabbit out of his hat on the eve of the congressional elections. On the second day of the president's sojourn in Asia, as it happened, Vermont's seventy-four-year-old Republican senator,

George Aiken, wondered whether the best way to get out of the Vietnam mess wasn't just to "declare victory and go home." For years the president's friend Richard Russell had been advising him much the same. It was one of the tracks Johnson was working on in Manila. So Nixon began laying the groundwork to defuse its effect. In his syndicated column he said, "From diplomats in Tokyo to members of the President's own party in Washington"—not by Dick Nixon, mind you—"the question is being posed: Is this a quest for peace or a quest for votes?" Arriving in Greensboro, North Carolina, Nixon wielded the forgotten cudgel of "an Asian conference to solve this Asian war," the chances of which he claimed the president's trip might sabotage.

"He has put politics ahead of policy so many times that leaders of both parties on Capitol Hill are publicly asking today whether—in going to the Far East—he is even playing politics with world peace," Nixon said in Wilmington. He noted a comment by UN ambassador Arthur Goldberg that the United States was prepared to halt the bombing of North Vietnam "the moment we are assured privately or otherwise that this step will be answered promptly by a corresponding de-escalation from the other side." "If Mr. Goldberg's naive proposal—still outstanding—is accepted by Hanoi," Nixon rumbled, "we will have repeated the great blunder in the Truman administration during the Korean War. It was during the period of truce that American units sustained two-thirds of our dead and wounded during the war."

(References to Korea and 1952: always handy for gashing Johnsonian flesh.)

Then Nixon flashed the reddest meat of all, McCarthy stuff: Goldberg's speech "returns American diplomacy to the naive days of Yalta, Tehran, and Potsdam, the days of the secret agreement based solely on the Communist promise."

In Chicago on October 8, Nixon said, "I'm not going to judge the conference at this point because it must be judged by what it produces"—then he judged it: "a grandstand play for votes. . . . There have been many firsts in the Johnson administration but this is the first time a president may have figured the best way to help his party is to leave the country."

On the ninth the Orioles swept the Dodgers in the World Series in four, and so, according to ancient political lore, now that the boys at the bar wouldn't have baseball to talk about, campaign season began in earnest. Nixon went to London Mills, Illinois, home of Johnson freshman Gale Schisler, thence to Sheboygan, Wisconsin, the bailiwick of freshman John Abner Race. Then he broke from the campaign trail to spend two weeks preparing with Len Garment for a reargument before the Supreme Court in the case of *Time Inc. v. Hill*—his fall bid for the always-important Franklin vote on Wall Street and Capitol Hill.

Nixon didn't talk about law and order in Chicago, though he was campaigning for John Hoellen, the Chicago alderman who'd launched his strong bid to defeat Roman Pucinski for Congress by arguing Martin Luther King should have been thrown in jail. Nixon didn't have to mention the backlash, for an announcement had just come from RNC headquarters that it was official Republican policy. "GOP Will Press Racial Disorders as Election Issue," the *New York Times* reported, noting one of the speakers, President Eisenhower, had declaimed against "deliberate riots engendered for no purpose except to hurt the rest of us. Republicans ought to take the strongest possible position and pledge to remove this curse."

Whereas, in 1964, Eisenhower had said that if politicians "began to count on the 'white backlash,' we will have a big civil war."

Perhaps that war was coming. In Milwaukee, members of the Youth Council of the NAACP, whose office had been firebombed in August, outfitted themselves in military fatigues, christened themselves the Commandoes, and guarded their clubhouse with a shotgun. The Republican state attorney general challenger promptly sent a telegram to the incumbent: "I am shocked that the NAACP has formed a Hitler-like group that would apparently take the law into their own hands." He didn't ask for an injunction against the armed Klansman posted outside the Waukesha home of their grand dragon.

Republicans simultaneously coordinated a push on Nixon's favorite issue. The media was reporting that supermarkets had begun shortening their hours now that housewives' boycotts were cutting into their business. So Republican candidates posed for the cameras pushing grocery carts. The Republican Congressional Campaign Committee printed "Great Society Play Money" (a pair of Texas longhorns over a worried-looking LBJ: "Progress Is a Shrinking Dollar"). Paul Douglas complained in every speech that there *wasn't* an inflation problem: wages had raced ahead of inflation every year since Kennedy was inaugurated. A frank GOP official explained to a reporter why they were making the nonissue an issue nonetheless: "Barry Goldwater and Ed Brooke"—the Negro Republican running for the Senate in Massachusetts—"can speak on inflation with equal conviction."

Claims that Republicans would whip inflation mitigated the embarrassment that they were actually counting on victory by abandoning the mantle of Abraham Lincoln. Charles Percy went on CBS's *Face the Nation* and said that while he still supported the "principle" of open housing, he disagreed with Senator Douglas on one thing: including "single-family dwellings" would be "an unpassable and unenforceable" attack on property rights. "Right now, we aren't ready to force people to accept those they don't want as neighbors," he said in tones of rue. Douglas stiffened his spine: "I am for open occupancy. I believe in equal opportunity of every man and woman. I do not intend to switch or to equivocate."

Handbills started appearing in Chicago's Bungalow Belt:

> OUR SLOGAN: *"Your Home is your castle—Keep it that way by Voting STRAIGHT REPUBLICAN.*

VOTE <u>STRAIGHT REPUBLICAN</u> IF YOU ARE:
AGAINST—violence, riots, and marches in the streets;
AGAINST—disregard for law and order;
AGAINST—The 3 Rs of today—Riots, Rape & Robbery. . . .
Did Mayor Daley make a secret deal with Martin Luther King to
stop the marches until after the election? . . . This is your chance to show
where you stand on FORCED HOUSING. . . . Renters, as well as
homeowners, would be effected for the law applies everywhere, includ-
ing the suburbs. WHERE WOULD YOU GO TO BE SAFE?
The only way to stop this program is by you, your family, and neigh-
bors voting Republican on November 8th.

Vote Republican to preserve home and hearth, vote Democratic to surrender them: the understanding was now implicit. "Backlash in Jersey Is Favoring Case," the *New York Times* reported of the Garden State's incumbent
liberal senator, "simply because he is a Republican although he was singled
out for praise this week by the National Association for the Advancement
of Colored People" as a "frontier fighter for civil rights."

President Johnson spoke to the United Nations on October 7, then ducked
into his bubble-top limousine ahead of the antiwar picketers chanting a new
slogan: "Hey, hey, LBJ, how many kids did you kill today?" Then he began
a tour before the Democratic faithful. "Glad to see you," he cried from his
loudspeaker before jumping out impromptu style, just as he used to do on
the campaign trail, in 1964, to shake hands with the commuters whose right-
of-way his motorcade blocked. He was entering one of his manic phases.

Before thirty thousand screaming fans in Newark, he opened with a
favorite ritual: calling the roll of the people's champions on the dais beside him:

"The leader and the dean of your delegation, a fighter for immigration
reform—a leader in the field of human rights! My supporter—Pete Rodino!

"The sponsor of the Arts and Humanities Act . . . that *greaaaaat*
progressive—Frank Thompson!

"The energetic congressman who gave us the Vocational Rehabilitation
Act, and my supporter—Dominick Daniels!"

Johnson launched into the topic of his address: the opposing party.

"A great man once said, 'In the Democratic Party, even the old seem
young.'"

And the people before him roared, because they were Democrats.

"But in the Republican Party even the young seem old!"

The president was feeling his oats. He turned his attention to an old
adversary, "the New York lawyer," "a consistently poor political prophet,"
who once said, "This is the last time the press will ever kick me around.

"And who is kicking who or what around? . . .

"Fooling the people has become the name—of—the—game for a good many Republicans in Congress," Johnson said, craning out his neck. "They have no constructive programs to fight inflation. They have no program to ease racial tensions. They don't know what to do about crime in the streets, or how to end the war in Vietnam. But they do know that if they can scare people, they *may* win a few votes!"

Five days later he repeated the old Democratic ritual of ethnic obeisance on Columbus Day. The theme was an appeal to his audience's better angels.

At the banquet of the Italian-American Professional and Businessman's Association in downtown Brooklyn: "It hasn't been too many years since Italian-Americans have felt the raw pain of discrimination here in America.... Italians, of all people, understand and practice the cardinal American virtue: fairness to all, regardless of race." At the monument to explorer Giovanni da Verrazano on Staten Island: "We have stopped asking people these days ... 'Where were you born?' Now all we want to know is '*What—can—you—do? What—can—you—contribute?*" In Staten Island: "*Afraid! Afraid! Afraid!* Republicans are afraid of their own shadows, and they are afraid of the shadow of progress. But the only thing most Americans are afraid of are Republicans!" He was having so much fun that he ordered his advance men to go forth and firm up plans for a closing-weekend cross-country tour. Maybe he could stanch his party's projected losses yet.

But if Lyndon Johnson's triumph in 1964 was convincing the nation that he was the moderate and the Republicans were the extremists, now Republicans were winning the battle the same way. Johnson understood this and was rather desperately trying to turn the Republicans back into the scary party. In the event, he overreached. And Richard Nixon, who had been trying to bait the president into personally attacking him for months, was ready to pounce.

In Delaware the president launched into a soaring liberal litany. "In the first 174 years before I became president, eighty-eight Congresses passed only six education bills. Since November 1963 Congress has passed not six bills as the first eighty-eight Congresses did, but eighteen education bills for the benefit of your children. . . . In 1960, the last Republican administration appropriated $841 million for health; this year this Congress will spend not $841 million but $8 billion 200 million . . . ten times as much for health. Twice as much for education in all the history of government. . . . Food and recreation and income and education and nursing homes and defense and that spells out what the Democratic Party stands for: that spells *friend.*"

Then he wound up with no mean bit of fearmongering himself. A GOP vote on November 8, he said—a line not in his prepared remarks—"could cause the nation to falter and fall back and fail in Vietnam."

At that, Richard Nixon pounced.

*   *   *

Nixon released a statement the next morning from Nixon, Mudge entitled "Playing Politics with Peace." It was classic Nixon: courting sympathy for getting attacked in a fight you yourself had started.

"Yesterday, in Wilmington, Delaware, President Johnson said that a vote for the Republicans could cause the nation to 'falter and fall back and fail in Vietnam.'

"This is a vicious, unwarranted, and partisan assault upon the Republican Party that has given President Johnson the support for the war that his own party has denied him. . . . With this insensitive attack, President Johnson has gravely jeopardized the bipartisan backing he should have when he goes to Manila. . . .

"It has been the President's party that has harboured those who have counseled appeasement of Communist aggression in Vietnam.

"It has been the 25 Democratic senators and 90 Democratic congressmen whose cries for peace at any price have given heart to Hanoi and thus has been directly responsible for encouraging the enemy, prolonging the war, and lengthening the risk of American casualties. The Republican Party has not failed America. The only failure has been President Johnson's. He is the first president in history who has failed to unite his own party in a time of war."

It was clearer now, the markers Nixon had been laying down since spring. Now that he was the president's debating partner on Vietnam, his meaning in the upcoming election had been framed in terms most favorable to himself: as protector of American unity and strength in a time of war. "I predict that the President's shocking attempt during this past week to play domestic politics with international peace," Nixon concluded, "will cost him congressional seats at home and will gravely weaken his voice as the spokesman for all Americans in Manila."

The president, in Pennsylvania to consecrate a soaring Catholic shrine to Polish-Americans before crowds as far as the eye could see, told the story of Tadeusz Kościuszko's manumission of his slaves, of the first Polish immigrants arriving in Jamestown and going on a work stoppage when the English colonists disenfranchised them as "foreigners." He concluded, "When I leave tomorrow, I shall say that my purpose will not be to accomplish any miracles, but to tell the people of the countries that I visit that the best way to judge America's foreign policy is to look at our domestic policy." He had just signed seven conservation bills, and the bills to create a Department of Transportation, a Child Nutrition Act, and a higher minimum wage for the District of Columbia. Then he jetted off to Asia to try to settle up a war, as the *New York Times* headlined a big front-page package "In Tight Races Backlash Vote May Mean Victory." It quoted a "high White House source" that this was the number one issue in the campaign. Lee Hamilton, an Indiana freshman Democrat, described what it was like to defend his civil rights record at the local taverns:

"'Haven't we done enough for the Negro?' someone will ask. . . . That's where they begin calling me names."

Nixon had two weeks to lay siege to a damaged president who, in Asia unable to defend himself, would just get angrier and angrier as he learned of the attacks.

Johnson visited the six "third country" nations whose sixty thousand troops in Vietnam let Americans call their force there an "alliance." He claimed to be saving Asia from Communism, but several Asian appearances had to be cut short or canceled because of protests. In Canberra, Australia, he was stalked by a drunken mob.

At the Manila summit, Johnson said everyone at the table was an "equal among equals," united in their determination "that aggression must fail." He referred to the protesters: "I have seen their banners that say 'We want peace.' And I say, 'So do I.' I have seen their banners that say 'I hate war,' and I say, 'So do I.' But I would also like to say to those men and women, those young people carrying those signs, 'You brought the banners to the wrong person. Take your banners to Hanoi, because there is where the decision for peace hangs in the balance.'" At least that was the part of the meeting Bill Moyers related to the waiting reporters. Delicate discussions had gone on, too, though they could not have gone too well.

Then Johnson disembarked for a stunt, surprising thousands of assembled U.S. servicemen at Cam Ranh Bay in South Vietnam.

One wonders how much comfort it provided. The soldiers had flown in at the start of their tours on commercial airliners; avoiding the spectacle of fleets and fleets of troop transports was one of the ways the government disguised and sanitized the scale of the American buildup. (The landing pattern no tourist had ever experienced: a short, sharp cut downward to avoid potential VC ground fire.) They emerged into heat like a blast furnace, a smell that most remarked was disgusting, looked out at Tan Son Nhut Air Base, the second busiest airport in the world, and wondered why they had been told at boot camp that this war was just a skirmish. They got on buses covered in wire mesh to protect them from the debris thrown by the people they were supposed to be saving. The first briefing at the base: "Be alert from this moment, and don't trust nobody with slanted eyes."

Support personnel outnumbered combat troops by five or ten to one, though "you could be in the most protected space . . . and still know that your safety was provisional," Vietnam correspondent Michael Herr wrote; "you heard so many of those stories it was a wonder anyone was left alive to die in firefights and mortar rocket attacks." The hazards reserved for infantry made nightmares seem tame: humping the boonies in swamp water up to the waist on search-and-destroy missions or through elephant grass that cut like razors; catching malaria; catching diseases the army surgeon general barely had names for yet (melioidosis, which killed a fourth of its victims in days, but could lie dormant for six years, and was caught from the mud kicked up by helicopter blades). The soldiers' job was to lure the enemy, which they did once out of every twenty-one or so patrols; "then the twenty-first time, zap, zap, zap, you get hit—and Victory Charlie fades into the jungles before you can close with him." Units competed to see who could chalk up the biggest "box scores"; a lucky soldier might notch enough "confirmed kills" for a bonus five days of R&R. ("What he seeks and what he does in his five days is as various as American youth itself," *Time* wrote of the typical R&R trip to Bangkok or Singapore—though *Time* didn't mention the GI folklore about prostitutes with razor blades hidden in their pudenda or children with explosives strapped to their stomachs.)

Back at base, they lived side by side with Vietnamese who lived off scavenged waste in dwellings constructed from flattened beer cans and C-ration tins, the same stuff they also used to make into booby traps, packing them with explosives from the 5 percent of U.S. ordnance that turned out to be duds. Then it was back to the inferno, perhaps to watch a buddy catch a "bouncing betty," a particularly heinous sort of pressure-release mine that popped into the air and exploded at waist level, or to see a buddy wasted by a sniper who emerged from an underground hole, then disappeared (a seventy-five-mile tunnel system would be discovered directly beneath Twenty-fifth Infantry Division headquarters).

This was the reality Richard Nixon was playing political games with. This was the reality that Lyndon Johnson was descending upon for an election-season photo op.

"There are some who may disagree with what we are doing here, but that is not the way most of us feel and act when freedom and the nation's security are in danger," their president told the soldiers. "We know you are going to get the job done. And soon, when peace can come to the world, we will receive you back in your homeland with open arms, with great pride, and with great thanks."

He circulated through the throng, backslapping, telling the boys to "nail the coonskin to the wall." Then he flew home to an electorate itching to nail liberal hides to the wall. As for Nixon, all those incendiary words he'd been laying down since January, so carefully chosen to make the president explode—now he lit the fuse.

In late October the Republican Congressional Campaign Committee sent out a tape to GOP House candidates to use in their campaigning from a speech LBJ gave to a farm audience in Iowa in June in which he said folks "ought to vote Republican." Edited out were the words of context: that you ought to vote Republican if you thought "wages were getting too high." For once, it appeared the Republican Party was doing Richard Nixon's dirty work instead of the other way around. Or maybe not. The chair of the RCCC, Representative Bob Wilson of San Diego, was a Nixon operative.

Nixon returned to his circuit of temporarily Democratic congressional districts: Kalamazoo on October 25 (Johnson's 1967 tax increase "will trigger a recession that will wipe out all economic gains of the past ten years"); Jerry Ford's Grand Rapids (Nixon said the Asia trip was the president's attempt "to cushion the fall of Election Day"); then Oregon (where he finessed the awkward fact that he was endorsing a dove for Senate, Mark Hatfield, by noting that he had imposed a "moratorium" on mentioning Vietnam while the president was in Asia). Then he flew to Spokane in a chartered jet. You could fly there next to him, for a $150 donation.

He said that if the war was still ongoing in 1968, it would represent a "great tragedy for the United States." That a candidate might "yield to temptation" and propose "hasty solutions not serving peace." In Boise he noted that China had just announced the launching of a missile that could carry a nuclear warhead and said that made it all the more imperative for LBJ to bring "diplomatic, economic, and military" pressure to end the war by 1968," or we would be "running an immense risk of World War III." Maybe, just maybe, he concluded, Johnson's time in the Far East would help him better understand the war and persuade more Democrats to support it. Then he repaired to the Boise Hotel, where he had time to reflect on how dangerous a game he was playing. What if LBJ *did* pull off something spectacular in Manila?

As Johnson worked on diplomacy, Bill Moyers was on the horn, firming up a closing-weekend tour of competitive congressional races from one end of the country to the next, in case there was capital to reap from the trip. LBJ would be returning the next day armed with a communiqué outlining the agreements arrived at in Manila. If he could claim a dramatic breakthrough for peace, he might dash every hope Nixon had of claiming credit for a Republican sweep. Nixon tossed and turned, unable to sleep at the thought. Soon, his aides weren't sleeping either. At 4:29 a.m. Nixon woke them up so they could start game-planning their countermoves.

Thence to Albuquerque, thence to Arkansas, then to Indiana, where Nixon said the same thing he always said in Indiana: "How can you have your mother be from Indiana and not be a fighting Republican?"

He was in Lodi, New Jersey, when Bill Safire, back in Manhattan, learned the Manila Communiqué had been released. No literary critic ever read text with the attentiveness Safire studied that entente between President Johnson and Prime Minister Ky. Just as Nixon worried, it held out the boilerplate promise that peace might soon be at hand. It also contained a restatement of the "graduated pressure" doctrine under which America was fighting the war: that "as the military and subversive forces of North Vietnam are withdrawn, infiltration ceases, and the level of violence thus subsides," allied forces might be withdrawn—for continued action "must depend for its size and duration on the intensity and duration of the Communist aggression."

This was boilerplate. But as William Safire studied that language, he thought he saw an opening—something to light the fuse: if they fudged the words just right, they could spin this as a *mutual* withdrawal, a sort of surrender. He started banging out notes, arranging for Len Garment to drive him out to New Jersey, and proposed they release some sort of open letter on the Manila Communiqué. The Old Man loved the idea of a public statement; it was sure to grab the press. But Nixon knew the flack's art better than Safire did. He told him an "open letter" would be dismissed as gimmicky. This was about looking statesmanlike. He sent Safire back to the drawing board and arranged for them all to get together in two days at 20 Broad Street to go over the draft. In an aboard-plane interview with Tom Wicker, Nixon called for the formation of a war cabinet along the British models of 1917 and 1940, "representatives of both political parties to develop a strategy for victory in Vietnam within the next year" to keep it from becoming a "devastating political issue" in the presidential campaign. The American people would never "tolerate a long, endless war." So without a "light at the end of the tunnel," Republicans would be "grievously tempted" to run on a peace platform, undercutting Johnson's hard-won commitment to Vietnam.

To the president of the United States, these words were truly devious. Nixon was threatening him: make me your foreign-policy partner, or I'll blow the whole Vietnam mess sky-high. That was what Johnson learned when his plane arrived in the United States: that Richard Nixon was claiming a right to act as copresident.

On November 1, Nixon's syndicated column sought to disassociate him from the backlash once and for all. He wrote that he *used to* think the Republicans would do well in the South this year. Now, however, "my prediction in the South must be revised—downward. The reason is that the Democratic Party—in a desperate throw of the dice—has gambled upon racism, demagoguery, and backlash to win for it what the caliber of its candidates cannot. The gamble will pay off in some backwaters of the South. But the Democratic Party has made a fatal mistake. It has risked the next generation, just to win the next election."

That was brazen. The Republican National Committee had produced a film to be shown the Sunday before the voting called *What's Going on Here?*, a jagged assemblage of news clips that depicted America under Lyndon Johnson as an orgy of crime, riots, and caskets coming home from Vietnam, interspersed with clips of the president's soaring affirmations of the Great Society. Some Republicans were trying to get it canceled as a tasteless embarrassment. Conservatives were complaining it wasn't hard-hitting enough.

❋   ❋   ❋

On the Thursday morning before the election Pat Buchanan announced the imminent release of a document called "Appraisal of Manila," and the clerks at 20 Broad Street were scurrying madly to get it out by the deadline. In the afternoon, Lyndon Johnson stepped up to the podium in the White House pressroom to announce that his doctor recommended he undergo surgery in fifteen to eighteen days to fix a vocal polyp and to repair a defect at the site of his gallbladder incision from 1965 (the one whose scar a caricaturist imagined looked just like Vietnam). The White House doctor, he further noted, recommended "a reduced schedule of activity in preparation for the operation." He would be leaving the next day for Texas. There would be no final-weekend campaign tour. The stress would be bad for his surgery.

This was the confirmation: the Democrats were utterly without hope on Tuesday. Experienced observers had long ago learned to read the president's entrails like Greek oracles, seeking in his changing medical humors clues to his political fears. Whenever they were harshest, some genuinely debilitating psychosomatic illness always seemed to be popping up. On the eve of his first Senate election, when he won by the stolen votes of a single precinct, it was a kidney stone. There was another kidney stone in 1955, a heart attack later that same year. This time the procedure looked suspiciously elective. "It's not an emergency in any way," military surgeon George G. Burkley told the press after the president withdrew—just some routine maintenance of a protrusion that "has enlarged somewhat in the last three weeks," which "indicates against a weekend trip."

What also indicated against a weekend trip, of course, was the necessity of avoiding presidential association with a bloodbath of a congressional election. He was always coming down with symptoms like these when no choice was a good choice.

Meanwhile, at 20 Broad Street, they struggled to complete their "Appraisal of Manila."

"Do you think it will get any sort of play in the papers?" the Old Man asked the flack.

Not if they didn't finish it in time for the morning papers' deadlines, Safire replied.

At that, Nixon struck an idea: "Do you suppose they would run the text in the *New York Times*?"

He referred to the *Times*'s practice, as "newspaper of record," of running, in toto, papers of state, crucial public documents, and speeches of paramount importance.

"That's what I had been thinking about, too."

Get his "Appraisal" printed there, and it would make Nixon more than some carping has-been political hack. It would make him the president's equal. It would set up a public showdown, in a fight they had jerry-built to win.

Safire got to work. He was acquainted with Harrison Salisbury, the *Times*'s great foreign correspondent, now assistant managing editor. Safire wrote what happened next in his memoirs: "I sold as hard as I ever sold anything in my life." The *Times* had been neglecting Nixon, he flacked (that was absurd). It would be *partisan* not to give Nixon the space (yet more absurd). Safire appealed to Salisbury's news sense (more absurd still: if its importance was its newsworthiness, a front-page article about it would do just as well).

Finally, Safire pulled out his final argument. He appealed to the halcyon memories they shared of Moscow, in 1959, when Salisbury had been the pool reporter for the Kitchen Debate, and Safire was flacking the American exhibition.

Salisbury reminded Safire that for him to even consider the request the appraisal would have to be submitted before the afternoon deadline. If so, he promised to read and consider it.

A gaggle of reporters gathered in the Nixon, Mudge antechamber awaiting the promised document. Within unfolded a scene out of screwball comedy. Three secretaries typed up separate pages. Safire hurtled from station to station making corrections. Messenger boys hovered, awaiting instructions. Buchanan calmed the assembled scribes, promising them they'd get their copy in time for deadline. Safire snatched pages out of the secretaries' typewriters as they finished each one. Pages flew. Staplers *clomped.* Buchanan dealt forth finished pages, announcing that the appraisal had eight points.

There were only seven on the pages. Safire later wondered whether they had numbered it wrong or forgot to put in one of the paragraphs.

The lead article in the November 4 *New York Times* began, "Richard Nixon said yesterday that the recent Manila Conference achieved nothing toward achieving peace in Vietnam." It appeared right next to "President Faces Minor Surgery; Calls Off Tour."

The jump on page 18 led to Nixon's entire twenty-five-hundred-word statement. "The effect of this mutual withdrawal would be to leave the fate of South Vietnam to the Viet Cong and the South Vietnamese Army. . . . Communist victory would most certainly be the result of 'mutual withdrawal.'"

Nixon was now, for the world to see, Lyndon Johnson's equal: the shadow president of the United States, accusing the president of selling out his own policies in Vietnam. It was a lie: the words in quotation marks in Nixon's assessment, *mutual withdrawal,* did not appear in the communiqué. It *wasn't* a call for mutual withdrawal. The language negotiated in Manila in fact specified that America could keep its troops in South Vietnam *six months* after the last enemy troops withdrew. Both Lyndon Johnson and Richard Nixon kept a careful eye on the polls, and they both knew that even where the war was most unpopular, withdrawal was the most poisonous option you could mention. It made America look cowardly. The *Times* had sacralized a Nixon con job. The fuse had been lit. And now, the fireworks began.

Johnson yowled when he saw the morning's *Times:* "Don't they know it's all a lot of politics!?"

He was ready to hit back. *His* Nixon was still the Nixon of the Last Press Conference: the most vulnerable man in American politics. He *wanted* to run against Nixon—not Romney, not Rockefeller, not Percy. He couldn't lose. Nothing united Democrats like bashing Richard Nixon. So he would build Nixon up.

The president, supposedly too sickly to travel, was apparently healthy enough to stride into a 10 a.m. press conference in the East Room to take questions. Someone asked whether the strenuous trip to Asia had contributed to his ill health. The president fidgeted out a lie: "I didn't get weary." Then, the question that gave him the opportunity he was looking for: "Mr. President, in your estimation, will the outcome of the elections have any influence on the Communist willingness, or attitude, toward continuing the war in Vietnam?"

He said he didn't think so, then expanded the scope:

"There is no one that I know of that thinks there is going to be any great change in the Senate. Although my delightful friend, Senator Dirksen, optimistic as he is, feels that there may be at least a gain of seventy-five, I notice the chronic campaigners, like Vice President Nixon, have begun to hedge and pull in their horns."

Nudges. Murmurs. In the theater of Washington Kabuki, this was significant: the president had called out Nixon by name.

He returned to the subject while lashing out at a question from Chalmers Johnson of the *Post,* who had the guts to ask, "Does the cancellation of your big campaign trip mean that you do not intend to do anything to help Democratic candidates before the election, such as one little speech in Texas, or maybe a TV pep talk?"

The heavy-lidded presidential eyes fixed intently. "*First,* we don't have any plans, so when you don't have plans, you don't cancel plans." He snapped, "We get invited to most of the states. In the last six weeks we have been invited to forty-seven. . . . But we have not accepted those invitations."

Then, he weaseled. "We *do* contact the people who extend them. We do investigate in some instances going there."

He couldn't hide that Secret Service men had scouted secure routes for at least eleven sites, including a lunchtime parade in Chicago, that 125 rooms were on hold at the Great Northern Hotel in Billings, that bands had been reserved in Portland.

"The people of this country ought to know that all these canceled plans primarily involve the imagination of people who phrase sentences and write columns and have to report what they hope or what they imagine."

He was losing his cool: a Last Press Conference of his own.

He worked over Nixon some more: "It is his problem to find fault with his country and with his government during a period of October every two years. . . . He never did really recognize and realize what was going on when he had an official position in the government. You remember what President Eisenhower said, that if you would give him a week or so he would figure out what he was doing. Since then he had made a temporary stand in California, and you saw what action the people took out there. Then he crossed the country to New York. Then he went back to San Francisco, hoping that he would be in the wings, available if Goldwater stumbled. But Goldwater didn't stumble. Now he is out talking about a conference that obviously he is not well prepared on or informed about."

What was the conference about? Figuring out a way to declare victory and go home, Johnson implied. That "if the violence would cease from the standpoint of our adversary, the allies would gladly reciprocate by withdrawing their troops, and that they would withdraw them in a period of not to exceed six months. . . . We think we did that, until some of the politicians got mixed up in it and started trying not to clarify it but to confuse it. . . . Mr. Nixon doesn't serve his country well by trying to leave that kind of impression," Johnson wound up with particular vitriol, "in the hope that he can pick up a precinct or two, or a ward or two."

No wonder the president was angry. What he was accusing Richard Nixon of, and credibly, was working to make it harder to end the Vietnam War.

But to the untutored public the technicalities were cryptic. The message that was received was of a presidential rant against a political rival. "Says Republican Does Not 'Serve Country Well,'" ran the second line of the *New York Times* headline. It made the president look like a McCarthyite, three days before the election. Which was exactly as Richard Nixon intended it: the old jujitsu at work. Johnson saw himself as pouncing on a mistake of Nixon's. That meant the mark had taken the bait. Johnson presumed the media would amplify his ridicule into one more political obituary of Richard Nixon. Instead he found himself cast as Goliath to Dick Nixon's David. It went back to old Jerry Voorhis, to the "Pink Lady," Helen Gahagan Douglas: let them pounce on your "mistake," then garner pity as you wriggle free by making the enemy look unduly aggressive. Then you inspire a strange sort of protective love among voters whose wounds of resentment grow alongside your performance of being wounded. Your enemies appear to die of their own hand, never of your own. Which makes you stronger.

"He hit us! Jesus did he hit us!" Pat Buchanan yelped elatedly at the Old Man as he boarded an old rattletrap propeller plane in New York for a campaign flight to New England. "You'll never believe how he hit us!"

All that needling, all that playing to Johnson's deepest anxieties, had paid off: a providential presidential loss of control, a huge strategic blunder. "The only time to lose your temper in politics is when it is deliberate," Zen master Nixon told a friend in 1953. "The greatest error you can make in politics is to get mad." Jules Witcover wrote that this was, "in the memory of veteran reporters, the most brutal verbal bludgeoning ever administered from the White House by Johnson, or any of the Presidents for that matter, to a leader of the opposition party." That testified to Nixon's mastery, too. Now the pundits were calling him *leader of the opposition party.* The comeback could not be denied. Everyone was watching him now. He was running against the president.

Nixon wasn't finished yet. Since the tirade included a proper name, the press would be extending him the parliamentary courtesy of the right of response, as Johnson more than anyone else on earth should have known they would. Mike Wallace of CBS secured the use of a Learjet that let him beat Nixon to the airport in Manchester to record his observations as he got off the plane. Nixon piously intoned what a shame it was that Johnson had "broken the bipartisan line on Vietnam policy." He must have been "tired." Of this "shocking display of temper" on matters that must be discussed "like gentlemen," he said, "I regret that the administration chose to reduce this debate to a personal level, and I will not travel that road with them."

Then, speaking at the armory that every presidential candidate tried to book for his concluding rally for New Hampshire's first-in-the-nation primary, Nixon said, "Like every other American I trust that the president's health problems are minor [*Like every other American, I do not trust the president*], and I regret that he could not exert his energies to the fullest in behalf of his own party in this national campaign." (*Maybe it was time for the president to retire?*)

Down at the LBJ Ranch, press secretary George Christopher said, "I don't think the president showed any temper or personal attack toward Nixon. I think the president is in as good humor as he ever has been in his life. I know for a fact he rather likes Mr. Nixon personally."

That was only stepping in the, er, credibility gap a little deeper.

Nixon said, "Is every public figure who rationally questions the means to achieve goals in Vietnam to become the victim of a presidential attack to silence his dissent? More important than President Johnson or Richard Nixon are the lives of thousands of American men fighting in Vietnam. I believe that the current Johnson policies resign us to a war that could last five years and produce more American casualties than Korea."

Resign! Korea!

Nixon was really on a roll now. He concluded his latest statement by urging the nation to watch him on TV on Sunday, where he would "lay it on the line" and "tell the president and the country what I believe is wrong with the means we are using to achieve our goals in Vietnam."

Both parties had been provided a half hour of TV time on Sunday afternoon on NBC. The RNC had planned to show the scurrilous documentary *What's Going on Here?* But that never suited Nixon's purposes at all: publicizing the nationalization of the election around the issue of anti-Negro backlash was the opposite of his master plan. For over a week now his ensigns had been strategizing about how they could get Nixon on TV instead. RNC chair Bliss resisted: he didn't want to give any one 1968 contender a leg up. They even considered one of his patented telephone campaigns to create a "spontaneous," "grassroots" groundswell. Then came the Johnson blowup—and Nixon prevailed. House Republican Conference chairman Mel Laird announced that the film would be withdrawn out of respect for President Johnson's illness, and that, instead, Nixon would give a speech in the time slot. The Republicans also said they would make copies of *What's Going on Here?* available to TV stations that wished to *report* on the controversy. Which was all rather brilliant. You have to wonder how much Nixon had to do with that play—a reprise of the famous 1964 "daisy commercial" affair, whose images, so devastating to Goldwater, appeared only once as a commercial, and several more times for free on the evening news.

Sunday morning, Nixon appeared on ABC's *Issues and Answers,* where he promised, "After this election I am going to take a holiday for at least six months with no political speeches whatsoever." Then came his afternoon speech on NBC, in which he sealed his campaign to control the interpretation of the election Tuesday hence as a referendum on President Johnson's temperament as leader of a nation at war. "I respect you for the great energies you devote to your office, and my respect has not changed because of the personal attack you made on me. You see, I think I can understand," he said, looking into the camera, "how a man can be very, very tired and how his temper can be very short."

Tuesday came the deluge. "In the space of a single autumn day," announced *Newsweek,* "the 1,000 day reign of Lyndon I came to an end." Twenty-seven of Johnson's forty-eight Democratic freshmen were swept out—the class that had brought America the Voting Rights Act, Medicare, federal aid to education. The Republicans won their first gains in party identification in twenty years. Hell not being Methodist, Iowa was once again Republican. George Romney was resoundingly reelected, sweeping in a Republican senator, Robert Griffin, and five more Republican congressmen besides. Handicappers had said "Lonesome George"'s only political weakness was his lack of coattails. Not anymore.

Nine of ten new governors were Republican, twelve of thirteen Western state legislatures. Republicans now controlled statehouses representing 293 out of the 535 electoral votes. A breakthrough to make the Kennedys proud took place in Protestant Oklahoma: it elected its first Catholic governor. Only problem was that he was a conservative Republican.

To measure it by party underestimated the carnage for liberalism. By one estimate the power of the conservative coalition in Congress—including both Southern Democrats and Northern Republicans—doubled. Lurleen Wallace won by more than two to one. The Georgia gubernatorial race was so close it was thrown into the state legislature; they chose Lester Maddox. "The plague of Wallace politics did not, thank God, spread to Florida," the *Nation* had reported after the Florida Democratic primary. Actually, the plague just waited for the general election, when a handsome young Republican insurance salesman named Claude Kirk won on the slogan "A Man's Home Is His Castle." The liberal who'd knocked off Judge Smith in the primary lost the general election to a conservative Republican. Nelson Rockefeller survived, barely; but for the first time in New York history the upstart Conservative Party polled more votes than the Liberal Party. Nelson's brother Winthrop beat Justice Jim in Arkansas—on a platform of school prayer, opposition to the 1964 Civil Rights Act, and excoriation of HEW education commissioner Harold Howe II. In New York City, civilian police review was crushed by twenty-six points; even Jews, supposedly liberal, opposed it 55 percent to 40. In Colorado an anti-death-penalty initiative went down two to one.

The pundits' interpretation was myopic. The antiliberalism was downplayed. They wrote the second chapter of "White Backlash Doesn't Develop." They doted on Tennessee's forty-year-old senator-elect Howard Baker, Everett Dirksen's son-in-law, who had explicitly denounced racial code phrases; and the first Negro senator since Reconstruction, Massachusetts Republican Ed Brooke; and George H. W. Bush in Texas, who lost in 1964 running as a Goldwaterite and won in 1966 running as a moderate; and Spiro Agnew, who owed his gubernatorial victory against the racist George Mahoney to the 60 percent of Maryland Negroes who voted for him (the previous Republican got only 6 percent). Republican dove Mark Hatfield won in Oregon. A cartoon in the *Washington Star* enshrined the Establishment's thinking: an elephant leapt from his wheelchair into a creek marked "'68," singing, "Down by the old mainstream! . . ." Even though Reagan ended the distinguished public career of Pat Brown by almost a million votes, in an election that drew a stunning 79.2 percent of registered voters.

Chuck Percy was the new senator from Illinois, 55.6 percent to 44.3. Percy's celebration at the Sheraton was as jubilant as a party for the father of a murdered daughter could be—marred by violent new realities: he was detoured through the kitchen to his victory address by his full-time FBI guard. He was now, said Stewart Alsop, "a potential candidate for President of the United States." He had proved himself a statesman, Alsop said: he won without exploiting the backlash. "If he had done so, the whole issue of race relations would undoubtedly have been the key issue in the campaign."

But it was the key issue in the campaign. At Percy's victory celebration a well-dressed suburbanite yelled at two reporters blocking his view, dripping with venom, "*We* elected him after all." A reporter snapped in return, "It was hatred that elected this guy, and don't you ever forget it." Conservatives had erected a giant billboard along Chicago's Eisenhower Expressway in 1964 with Barry Goldwater's slogan: "In Your Heart, You Know He's Right." It became, after that election, "In Time, You Will Know He Was Right." Presently that billboard read, "Now You Know He Was Right."

Attempts to deny the backlash's influence were systematic. Pundits pointed to the sympathy factor. But if people voted for Percy because he was a grieving father, the ratio of the sympathetic to the callous was suspiciously high in the Bungalow Belt neighborhoods where Martin Luther King had marched. A ward analysis demonstrated that in Chicago neighborhoods threatened by racial turnover, new Percy voters were enough to account for Douglas's 80 percent decline in the city vote since 1960. He had won Cicero that year. This time he didn't even get 25 percent there. Pundits also pointed to people's unwillingness to vote for such an old man. But in the backlash wards the vote for younger Democrats declined almost as significantly. Roman Pucinski was reelected by forty-seven hundred votes where he had won by thirty-one thousand in 1964. "I've been the guy who was claiming there was no backlash," said Pucinski, "but I'm first to admit now I was dead wrong."

As it had been since Tocqueville, it took foreigners to see ourselves. White House aide Ted Van Dyk reported back to Hubert Humphrey on the visit of a group of British parliamentarians: "They believe that backlash was far more important than it might appear to be. In district after district, and city after city, they found an undercurrent of resentment concerning civil order and gains made by the Negro population."

Pat Brown never doubted it. His shell-shocked reaction was "Whether we like it or not, the people want separation of the races." He had a hard time processing it all: "Maybe they feel Lyndon Johnson has given them too much. People can only accept so much and then they regurgitate." Bakersfield punished its Negroes for rioting back in May by passing an initiative, by a margin of two to one, refusing federal poverty aid.

The pattern was there for those with eyes to see. The Republican won the governorship in Nebraska; in Omaha, where there had been a race riot, they picked up 62 percent more votes than four years earlier in the blue-collar wards. In Ohio, urban Poles decreased their support for Democrats by 45 percent. Thirty-six House incumbents with ratings from the AFL-CIO's Committee on Political Education of seventy-five or higher were defeated—especially traumatic since Republicans had filibustered labor's fondest legislative wish: a repeal of the right-to-work provision of the 1947 Taft-Hartley Act. Union members voted for politicians who weakened their unions because the Democrats supported civil rights. Some confused backlashers even voted for Edward Brooke because he had an (R) by his name. Though voters who knew he was black told reporters things like "It's nothing personal, but if he got in, there would be no holding them down; we'd have a Negro president."

The misinterpretation that this was not a backlash election suited Richard Nixon just fine. He had studied the districts that Democrats had picked up in the sweep of 1964 and found them still, essentially, Republican. There were forty-seven of them. And though the districts didn't match up exactly, *forty-seven* was the number of seats the Republicans picked up in 1966, in an election the press now retroactively framed, not as what it actually was, a referendum on the Negro revolution, but as what Nixon said it was: a referendum on Lyndon's Vietnam leadership, with Nixon's vision as the alternative. Warren Weaver of the *New York Times* obliged the Nixon interpretation by writing the next week that of the sixty-six House candidates Nixon campaigned for, forty-four had won. The victory rate of the 319 Republicans who weren't afforded a Nixon visit was 44.8 percent. RFK's record was only 39 of 76. "President Johnson probably preserved an average above .500 by canceling the coast-to-coast tour that the White House had set up for the weekend before the election." The result: "The political equivalent of the batting championship for the 1966 campaign season went to former Vice President Richard M. Nixon."

Better yet, the article added, "national political leaders do not like to waste their time campaigning for heavy favorites; if they did, their average could be much higher."

Nixon had bamboozled the *Times*. Wasting his time on candidates he thought most likely to win was exactly what he had been doing.

And on this first day of the rest of Richard Nixon's life, the reaction was orgasmic. The Old Man fielded the results at a headquarters at the Drake Hotel in Manhattan. Phone call after phone call: Rocky won, Winthrop won, Spiro won, Romney won, Chuck won, Ed Brooke won. Nixon intoned excitedly after every one, "It's a sweep."

"He's all right, Ron is—it's a sweep in California, too."

"Have you seen those numbers? We're on the move. Have another drink on the house, everyone."

Nixon had a few himself. It was 3 a.m., and he pulled a couple of his confreres who were still around in close: "This is too great a night to go home. Let's go to El Morocco and have some spaghetti." He hailed the cab himself, in the rain. "We won! We won!" he said, slapping his companions' shoulders. "We're going to kill them in '68."

He also slurred a confidence to Leonard Garment: "You'll never make it in politics, Len. You just don't know how to lie."

BOOK II

CHAPTER EIGHT

The Bombing

Presider Johnson authorized new air strikes on North Vietnam in early December. Reports circulated overseas that targets overlapped civilian neighborhoods. The Pentagon said that was absurd. Then the first accredited American correspondent to visit Hanoi in twelve years, Harrison Salisbury of the *New York Times,* wired back his eyewitness accounts. The first ran December 25 on page 1. Merry Christmas, Mr. President:

A Visitor to Hanoi Inspects Damage Laid to U.S. Raids.

President Johnson's announced policy that American targets in North Vietnam are steel and concrete rather than human lives seems to have little connection with the reality of attacks carried out by U.S. planes.

Salisbury ended up publishing twenty-two pieces on the subject that winter. He reported eighty-nine civilian deaths in one town, forty in a second, twenty-four in a third—and that, in this "brushfire war," more bombs had been dropped on Vietnam since 1966 than the entire tonnage dropped on Japan during World War II. In Nam Dinh, North Vietnam's third-largest city, he wrote of "block after block of utter desolation." He said the targeting of civilians was going on "deliberately."

The Pentagon claimed what civilian casualties there were came from the Communists' deliberate emplacement of surface-to-air missiles in populated areas. Or from the necessity of jettisoning bombs when attacked by MiGs. And that the eighty-nine deaths were evidence of "rather precise" bombing. Spokesman Arthur Sylvester—he called Salisbury's paper the "New Hanoi Times"—said if Salisbury doubted them, he should take a gander at the anti-aircraft guns up the main street of Nam Dinh, right by the railroad tracks. Salisbury, who'd been covering bombings since the London Blitz, said he'd already been there and had found only a destroyed textile factory.

Lying about Vietnam: it had become a Washington way of life. When a shipment of American helicopters arrived on an aircraft carrier in the early

169

1960s, a reporter remarked to an officer, "Look at that aircraft carrier." The officer replied, "I don't see nothing." Air force pilots signed statements that if they were shot down, the government would deny any knowledge of them. With the Gulf of Tonkin incident in August of 1964, Lyndon Johnson took the opportunity to bring American involvement out in the open with a congressional resolution. But that was a lie, too. "Some of our boys are float-ing around in the water," he told congressmen. He said later, after the deed was accomplished, "Hell, those dumb, stupid sailors were just shooting at flying fish." After the escalation, General William Westmoreland, the com-mander of U.S. forces, banned the CIA from pegging the number of enemy fighters at more than 399,000. There actually were over 600,000. That num-ber included guerrillas, and to count them would acknowledge the insur-gency had popular support. They lied, as well, to one another. When McNamara came to visit, commanders doctored maps and records to make the enemy look smaller and the ARVN, the South Vietnamese army, look bigger. They even lied to themselves. In 1965, Walter Lippmann, a Vietnam War skeptic, was shocked to discover that Mac Bundy, one of the adminis-tration's top foreign policy experts, didn't even seem aware that South Viet-nam had no independent reality prior to the Geneva convention.

By 1967, the biggest lie was that we were winning. Flying into Andrews Air Force Base after what was termed a "fact-finding" trip, Defense Secre-tary McNamara drew one of his consultants into an argument he was hav-ing with some of his mates: were things better now in Vietnam than a year previous, worse, or about the same? The consultant, whose name was Daniel Ellsberg, said about the same. McNamara turned to his interlocutors: "That proves what I'm saying! We've put more than a hundred thousand more troops in the country, and there's been no improvement! . . . That means the situation is really *worse.*"

The plane disgorged its passengers, and McNamara briefed waiting reporters: "Gentlemen, I've just come back from Vietnam, and I'm glad to be able to tell you that we're showing great progress in every dimension of our effort."

On January 31, 1967, Secretary of State Dean Rusk, flanked by eight security guards, briefed some one hundred student-government presidents and campus-newspaper editors who had signed a letter questioning the war: football players, fraternity presidents, mainstream kids, stunned into silence by the obvious lies their secretary of state expected them to believe.

A kid from Michigan State: "Mr. Secretary, what happens if we continue the policy you've outlined . . . this continued gradual escalation until the other side capitulates . . . up to and including nuclear war, and the other side doesn't capitulate?"

Rusk leaned back, hissed forth a stream of tobacco smoke, and solemnly replied, "Well, somebody's going to get hurt."

Here, before their eyes, was the maniacal air force general Buck Turgid-son from *Dr. Strangelove.* The room drew silent, their thoughts as one: *My God, the secretary of state is crazy.*

The madness was not hard to spot, if you chose to spot it. The problem was facing the wrath of all those decent Americans who didn't want to face that their government was mad. Bobby Kennedy once made the mistake of candor: he said Prime Minister Ky lacked popular support. Richard Nixon promptly started earning lusty cheers with the line that such "highly irre-sponsible" statements "only weaken the hand of the president."

In a way, the most honest messages about Vietnam available in the main-stream came from the massively popular annual NBC broadcasts of Bob Hope's Christmas shows for the troops. *Time* was the place to go each week if you wanted to read about how the American GIs "main concern in off-duty hours is aiding Vietnamese civilians." None of that bullshit from Bob; he told winking jokes about prostitutes. To connect with his audience, Hope had to earn their trust. He did it by telling home truths. At Qi Nam, he acknowledged the war's hopelessness with a joke about LBJ's proposed tax hike: "When a Texan says we need money, you know we're really in trou-ble." To a crowd at Da Nang, fifteen thousand marines bigger than the year before, he acknowledged the conflict's uncontrollable growth: "I probably look like Mickey Rooney from back there!"

Hope's show was broadcast amid raging debate about Harrison Salis-bury's articles. Twelve religious leaders excoriated the president for sanction-ing targets "in or near residential sections of Hanoi, even if many civilians die." General Eisenhower responded, "Is there any place in the world where there are not civilians?" *Time* said antiwar activists had hoodwinked Salis-bury into the "impression that the U.S. is a big powerful nation viciously bombing a small, defenseless country." *U.S. News* called it "a massive pro-paganda campaign over the accidental killing of a few hundred North Viet-namese civilians" by which "the Communists hope to hide a whole decade of deliberate murder of tens of thousands of non-military South Viet-namese." Senator Bourke Hickenlooper of Iowa said it was hardly surpris-ing that Hanoi would "let a *New York Times* reporter in but not objective reporters." House Armed Services Committee chairman Mendel Rivers said we should "flatten Hanoi and tell world opinion to go fly a kite." Senator Sam Ervin said, "We ought to bomb the North Vietnamese out of existence." In private briefings with dovish congressmen, President Johnson claimed that for every American dying now, five would die if he stopped the bomb-ing. The Pulitzer jury voted to give Salisbury its garland for international reporting. The full board vetoed their decision: they were publishers, and had to worry about insulting the commander in chief.

For some, Salisbury's reports were occasion for reflecting on how Amer-ica was drifting dangerously from its founding ideals. For others, the discussion was over whether the first group were Americans at all. By the beginning of 1967, the war in Vietnam had ended America's "consensus" for good.

This winter of LBJ's discontent began the day after the 1966 elections, when he announced he'd propose fewer programs and shrink funding for existing ones. The January issue of the liberal magazine *Commentary* published an article called "Death of a Slogan: The Great Society." The State of the Union address was its eulogy. The president quoted Lincoln: "We must ask 'where we are and whither we are tending.'" In Vietnam, "we face more cost, more loss, more agony." He proposed a 6 percent income and corporate tax surcharge because his proposed budget in 1966 had assumed the war's end by July 1967. Instead, the conservative prediction for FY '67 was that the war would cost $20 billion, twice as much as the year before.

When his closest aide, Bill Moyers, quit to become publisher of *Newsday*, it fueled speculation that Johnson wouldn't be running for reelection. A former associate, Bobby Baker, was convicted of a one-man white-collar-crime wave, after invoking LBJ's name four times during the trial. The Beltway gossip was over William Manchester's book on the Kennedy assassination, *The Death of a President*, which would soon go on sale with a six-hundred-thousand-copy first printing and was already being excerpted in *Look* magazine. It portrayed LBJ as an embarrassing hayseed, and made the "unconscious argument," Arthur Schlesinger said, that Johnson was responsible for the tragedy by dragging JFK to Texas to settle a political dispute he should have been able to settle himself. The cult of the Kennedys continued to haunt the president. "Until Robert Kennedy has made his presidential bid," pollster Sam Lubell predicted, "Kennedy-Johnson competition will operate as a major polarizing force that will affect all politicking and every important piece of legislation that comes up."

On January 25, Richard Russell told Johnson the only way he could survive in Georgia, where people thought he was "kind of backing the Stokely Carmichaels and Martin Luther Kings," was to become a conservative. Johnson replied that he got it just as bad from the liberals. On the twenty-seventh, astronauts Gus Grissom, Ed White, and Roger Chaffee roasted to death on the launching pad at Cape Canaveral. Walter Lippmann moved to New York City and was asked by the press if in the dark days of LBJ Washington was no longer a desirable place to live. "I'm not leaving because of Lyndon Johnson," he replied. "We decided on this before Johnson went off the deep end."

Some held out hope for a Vietnam negotiated settlement. From time to time Johnson would halt the bombing as an expression of American "goodwill." But the United States' nonnegotiable condition was keeping the country divided. This made no sense to Hanoi, whose nonnegotiable condition was elections to unite the country, and that negotiating under a rain of bombs, no matter how imperiously "halted," was an insult to their sovereignty. On February 8, Lyndon Johnson appealed directly in a letter to Ho Chi Minh "to seek earnestly the path to peace." Ho's public response was that the way for America to end the war was to remove its 340,000 troops and its fleets of fire-dealing behemoths and "let the Vietnamese people settle themselves their own affairs." Cold War orthodoxy considered this insolence; the carnage continued unabated—in Vietnam and in Lyndon Johnson's soul. "I'll destroy you and every one of your dove friends in six months!" he raged at Senators William Fulbright and Frank Church. He raged, because he was the one being destroyed.

The Republican jockeying began. Richard Nixon, jujitsu-style, jockeyed by not jockeying.

The front-runner, everyone knew, was glamour boy George Romney. The Harris poll reported he had a better chance of winning the White House than any Republican since Dwight D. Eisenhower.

Romney, a Republican who kept on getting elected in a Democratic state (he called America's cult of rugged individualism "nothing but a political banner to cover up greed"), was a media darling. The Mormon bishop with what Jules Witcover joked was a "full head of silvering Presidential hair" made great copy: he didn't work on Sundays. He fasted before big decisions. His granddad had fled with three wives one step ahead of the polygamy laws. A new book of personal reminiscences of JFK had just come out. "The fellow I don't want to run against is Romney," it reported him saying. In May of 1966 Rockefeller took himself out of presidential contention "completely and forever, without reservation," and endorsed a Romney-Javits ticket.

But even then, an Achilles' heel was visible. "It is clear," Scotty Reston columnized in the summer of '66, "that he has not yet had the time to polish up his arguments, particularly about Vietnam."

Hangers-on urged Romney to run in the open to build his national following and prove his grasp of the issues. His statehouse aides cringed: they knew the last thing that would help their boss was to rehearse in public. He was too damned *forthright*, too *earnest*—especially about Vietnam. He grappled with it honestly. Which would make what he said sound absurd, since everyone else was in denial or lying.

Romney announced a small tour of Western states. Nelson Rockefeller financed it with a $300,000 gift. An exploratory campaign office sprang up a few blocks from the state capitol; a reporter noticed a line of books on Vietnam on the unpainted bookshelves. Romney kicked off his six-state tour warning that he wouldn't say anything about Vietnam at all until he had a chance to study the situation more, perhaps after a second visit (his first had been in 1965, on a junket with other governors). But the longer he said nothing, the more the reporters pressured him to say *something*. He was being chased by no less than forty, each vying to see if Romney had what it took to play at this level of the game. In Anchorage, he uttered the apparently inoffensive observation that Republicans had a better chance of taking a fresh look at Vietnam because LBJ was "locked in." In Salt Lake City, he said the problem was LBJ's flip-flopping between escalation and negotiation offers. A salivating scribe pointed out the contradiction: was LBJ "locked in" or a flip-flopper? Romney issued a clarification that clarified nothing. (It was around that time Jack Germond of Gannett coined the joke about the special key he was having installed on his typewriter reading "Romney later clarified.") In Idaho, Romney fended off Vietnam questions for forty minutes. Then he mentioned Johnson's "political expedience . . . getting his country in trouble at home and abroad, including Vietnam." He had violated his moratorium not to talk about Vietnam, the vultures said, demanding a follow-up: would he give an example of LBJ's expedience?

"No, I will not."

"Why not?"

"Well, because I choose not to."

It portended disaster. His forthright honesty was his calling card, his contrast with the wheeler-dealer LBJ and the used-car salesman Nixon, what made him, along with that strong, square chin and silvering hair and popularity with Democrats, look like a contender. But honesty was a dull blade to take into a knife fight with Richard Nixon—who was simply willing to lie.

Nixon let a reporter ride along with him to the airport for a Thanksgiving vacation to Florida and spun him blind with his favored interpretation of the congressional elections. When Nixon returned, old hands started showing up on his doorstep, pledging to help him take the fight to the floundering Romney. Nixon pleaded disingenuously that he was in the middle of a political moratorium and could neither approve nor disapprove of any efforts made on his behalf. The old hands served his purposes admirably by plumping for him independently nonetheless—as he knew they would. The amateur, Romney, went on hanging himself with his own rope, while the professional, Nixon, insisted he wasn't running for anything at all, and the publisher of the *St. Louis Globe-Democrat*—crafty Buchanan's old boss— ran a full-page article arguing that Nixon's activities over the last two years "annihilated the argument that Nixon is a loser, a candidate who can't win."

Behind closed doors Nixon posted flattering missives ("I have heard a number of very favorable comments from some of the political 'pros' in the New York area with regard to your appearance on 'Issues and Answers,'" he wrote to California's governor-elect), oiled his political machine, shored up the right flank. He convened another meeting with conservative leaders, this time at the sumptuous Newport mansion of Eisenhower's former chief of protocol. Tom Charles Huston promised the YAFers they'd get jobs in a Nixon White House. Then Nixon had Buckley, Rusher, and the bestselling conservative author Victor Lasky to his town house for the patented foreign policy *tour d'horizon*.

On the first of the year Nixon, Mudge merged with another Wall Street firm, Caldwell, Trimble & Mitchell. Their lead partner, John Mitchell, was a bald, long-faced, pipe-smoking World War II PT-boat commander, a former semipro hockey player with a bloodlust proper to the sport. His legal experience was in putting together municipal-bond deals. That gave him just the right political qualifications: intimacy with officeholders around the country, right on down to the precinct level, who owed Mitchell as their conduit to Wall Street money. With blinding speed, Nixon promoted him to be his closest strategic confidant—"the heavyweight," he announced to William Safire.

At the winter Republican National Committee meeting in New Orleans, as Romney's surrogates buttered up the press to follow along on the governor's lecture tour, two Southerners shopped around a plan for Republican unity in 1967. Fred LaRue, the Mississippi national committeeman, had been a Goldwater field organizer in 1964. Peter O'Donnell, the chairman of the Texas Republican Party, had chaired Barry Goldwater's legendary nominating organization. They buttonholed Republicans and reporters, arguing that the best way to avoid the party-killing rancor their efforts had lamentably produced in 1964 was not for no one to declare his candidacy but for *everyone* to declare his candidacy. Republicans had such a wealth of talent—Romney of Michigan, Rockefeller *and* Javits of New York, John Tower of Texas, Rockefeller of Arkansas, Kirk of Florida, Percy of Illinois, Reagan of California, Shaffer of Pennsylvania, etc.—that as many as possible should declare themselves favorite-son presidential candidates, to keep their states' delegations in abeyance until the party could quietly settle on a consensus ticket.

They succeeded. Favorite-son boomlets for second-tier officeholders, who, prima donnas to a man, encouraged the attentions, spread from sea to shining sea.

In New York, Richard Nixon smiled. LaRue and O'Donnell were his secret agents. Sowing a dozen or more presidential "contenders" starved the five or six who actually *were* contenders of attention, leaving Nixon to plot behind the scenes in peace.

LaRue and O'Donnell baited a big fish in New Orleans for Nixon, Dr. Gaylord Parkinson, the California Republican chair and San Diego ob-gyn and quite an operator himself. While preaching "Thou shalt not speak ill of a fellow Republican" in 1966, he was working on a $33,000 retainer for Reagan. Romney had unsuccessfully tried to lure him to run his presidential campaign. O'Donnell and LaRue convinced Parkinson to travel to New York to dine with the boss. One *tour d'horizon* later, he agreed to head the first aboveboard Nixon for President Committee, whenever that should surface. Hiring "Parky" was brilliant: he was the best-known apostle of Republican unity, and the best person possible to influence the favorite son Nixon most wanted to keep out of the running—Ronald Wilson Reagan. Romney's people tried to leak the hiring to the press as a violation of Nixon's "moratorium." In this they floundered, too. Parkinson said he was just one more concerned private citizen trying to "convince Dick that he's got enough delegates so that he ought to run."

On January 7, 1967, Nixon met with his delegate-hunting team at the Waldorf. O'Donnell explained how they'd done it for Goldwater: "Collectin' delegates is just like washin' dirty dishes, you gotta take 'em one by one," he said, swabbing the air with a make-believe towel. Nixon told them not even to tell their closest friends about the meeting, clinching the plea with Nixonian skill: "We don't want to hurt the feelings of anybody we've left out," he said—signifying to those present they were his *true* inner circle. (Then he lied to them, saying he thought the Vietnam War would be over by 1968.) He said to pass the word that he was running, but quietly: "Don't give out any franchises, but get started contacting the power groups in each state. . . . Peter O'Donnell is the nonchairman of a nonexistent group." Someone joked that they were his brain trust, just like FDR's. The boss shot him a dagger-eyed look. "No help on the issues," he said sharply. "That's something else. Stick to politics."

In the middle of February Nixon denied he was running for president by telling the *Saturday Evening Post* that if he was, he'd "have locked it up by now." Meanwhile he locked up organizations for his five carefully selected primaries, New Hampshire on March 12, Wisconsin on April 2, Indiana on May 7, Nebraska on May 14, and Oregon on May 28. Then he left for stature-enhancing trips to Europe, South America, and Asia, which would take him through summer. In between calls on Pope Paul, Willy Brandt, and Harold Wilson, he acknowledged to the press that, yes, he had heard Gaylord Parkinson had formed some sort of committee back in Washington, but that "I have made no decision with regard to my own political activities."

It hadn't been all work that winter. At the end of December Nixon presented his youngest daughter, Julie, for her debut at the Waldorf-Astoria, escorted by David Eisenhower, the general's grandson. The debutante ball played widely on television: a blushing David Eisenhower in white tie and tails, a beaming Julie in a floor-length, white gown, the proud parents gazing down lovingly from the balcony as the band played "America the Beautiful"—a tonic for elders growing dismayingly accustomed to very different images of this generation.

Robert McNamara had visited Harvard. Students lay down before his car, forcing him to escape through a steam tunnel. On the Sunset Strip in Hollywood a teenage riot broke out when the city dared enforce its 10 p.m. curfew. "The majority of them come from good, solid families with money in the bank, plenty of food on the table, and a bright future ahead of them,"

a startled cop observed, baffled. In December thousands of Berkeley students went on strike after demonstrators were arrested while protesting the
presence of navy recruiters' tables in the student union. They shouted down
the vice chancellor; Ronald Reagan promised that upon his inauguration
they "would be treated like any other person charged with a crime."

Then, on January 14 in San Francisco's Golden Gate Park, twenty thousand gyrating young tatterdemalions spouted poetry, chanted mantras, listened to Moby Grape and the Jefferson Airplane, and ingested ten thousand
free tablets of now illegal LSD, drawn forth by Day-Glo posters that
enjoined, "Now in the evolving generation of America's young the human-
ization of the American man and woman can begin in joy and embrace without fear, dogma, suspicion, or dialectical righteousness. A new concept of
human relations being developed within the youthful underground must
emerge, become conscious, and be shared so that a revolution of form can be
filled with a Renaissance of compassion, awareness, and love in the Revelation of the unity of all mankind." The "Human Be-In" made all the news
shows, too, just like Julie's deb ball.

They were strange, these hippies, very strange. Beatniks had been flout-
ing the canons of decent civilization for a long time now, but at least they had
the decency to do it in dark, dank coffeehouses. Now kids did it out in the
open, expected you to congratulate them for it. But in some sense they were
only doing what their elders told them to. *Time*'s January 6 issue was its annual
"Man of the Year." They chose "a generation: the man—and woman—of 25
and under." The lead article was not dissimilar to ads for the Human Be-In:
"In the closing third of the 20th century, that generation looms larger than all
the exponential promises of science or technology. . . . This is not just a new
generation, but a new kind of generation. . . . He is the man who will land on
the moon, cure cancer and the common cold, lay out blight-proof, smog-free
cities, enrich the underdeveloped world, and no doubt, write *finis* to poverty
and war. . . . Today's youth appears more deeply committed to the fundamental Western ethos—decency, tolerance, brotherhood—than almost any
generation. . . . In the omphalocentric process of self-construction and discovery, he stalks love like a wary hunter, but has no time or target—not even
the mellowing Communists—for hate." *Reader's Digest* republished the article as "Here Comes the *Now* Generation." *Time* published another essay proclaiming, "most American youngsters now work harder, think deeper, love
more, and even look better than any previous generation."

It was as if someone had called to this boom of babies sired by the domes-
ticity-starved veterans of World War II, "Ye shall be as gods." And they
believed it. Because they were told it all the time.

"In the sixth decade of the twentieth century, America entered its middle
age, and discovered its youth," as two typical commentators put it. "And the
young people themselves began to develop a sense of their own identity and

with it a radically critical attitude about the society that their elders had created. They dissented, they dropped out, they said 'No'—and the reverbera-
tions of that No are still being heard."

The new generation's ethos had something to do with JFK, all agreed,
and the Bomb, and a celebration of the immediate against their parents' cult
of deferred gratification. Their favorite politician, Bobby Kennedy, was like
them addicted, Andrew Kopkind of the *New Republic* wrote, to "sudden,
spontaneous, half-understood acts of calculated risk." They reviled a society
lost "among the motorized toothbrushes, tranquilizers, and television commercials" (wrote Kennedy brother-in-law Sargent Shriver, in an article on
their signature government program, the Peace Corps). Their radical activists
were a "prophetic minority," said the *Village Voice*'s Jack Newfield—
building "a brotherly way of life even in the jaws of the Leviathan," according to historian Staughton Lynd. Their signature mood was "taking
America's promises seriously," struggling "for identity in a vast, impersonal
education and research factory run by IBM cards." For them, "the Death of
God," a minister wrote, was a "rallying cry for those who wished to confront
head-on the question of the relevance of religion to contemporary life."
"They don't merely hang out together," Tom Wolfe observed. "They establish whole little societies for themselves."

And here was the thing: they were *told* all this, explicitly and incessantly.
When they got to college—the research factories run on IBM cards—and
took freshman composition class, they might receive as their textbook a volume called *The Sense of the Sixties.* All the quotations from the paragraph
above come from this entirely typical production of its age. In a feedback
loop, young people taught about young people, assured they had more to
teach the teacher than the teacher had to teach them. "What we have gathered are of the quanta of contemporary experience," the editors of the book
explained. "You will very quickly become aware of areas of concern we have
missed." Young people took the glory as offered. "The outcry of a generation is finally being taken seriously," ran a letter responding to *Time* from a
Steve Forrer, Gettysburg College, Class of '69 (*Time* always included young
letter-writers' ages). "We are thinkers, cool guys, picketers, workers, fighters, but most of all we are the future of America—and that doesn't scare us."

Pundits spoke of the 26 million new citizens who would come of voting
age by the time the 1972 presidential election rolled around, politics' new
X-factor. In "paisley ghettos" such as Haight-Ashbury and New York's East
Village and Old Town in Chicago, teenagers chartered brave new worlds.
The manifesto of the first gathering of publishers of the new "underground"
press proclaimed as their purpose, "To warn the 'civilized world' of its
impending collapse," through "communications among aware communities
outside the establishment." (San Francisco that summer, the underground
paper *IVO* promised, would be "the Rome of a future world founded on

love.") Some in the Establishment entertained the possibility. Arnold Toynbee said hippies were "a red warning light for the American way of life."
Episcopalian bishop James Pike noticed "something about the temper and
quality of these people, a gentleness, an interest—something good." *Time*
observed in a long and respectful cover story in the summer of 1967 that their
"drug use is primarily Eucharistic in nature" and reported on pilgrimages to
"psychadelicatessens" by "shoppers who intend trying nothing stronger
than a Bloody Mary" such as Jackie Kennedy, a regular knickknack pur-
chaser in the head shops of the East Village. Though a *Time* letter-writer
expressed another proliferating opinion: "I fail to see much real altruism or
idealism in my children or their friends. I see, rather, a perverted, sentimental self-centeredness."

In fact, the more attention paid the psychadelicatessens, the more the
squares worked at chartering a youth culture of their own. In January of
1966, the names of 477,000 students from 322 colleges who supported the
war were presented by student leaders to the White House. Five hundred
gathered at a pro-war teach-in at Princeton. The next month fifteen thousand sat in the pouring rain at Atlanta Stadium for an "Affirmation: Vietnam" rally organized by Emory students. "The Ballad of the Green Berets"
hit number one that March. The far-right Orange County entrepreneur
Patrick Frawley underwrote a national "Moral Re-Armament" movement
that gathered students, statesmen, business leaders, scientists, and Olympic
champions to a conference on Mackinac Island in Michigan. A "college coed," *Reader's Digest* reported, stole the show. She stood up and cried indignantly, "I'm fed up with the image of American youth being created by
beatniks, draft-card burners, campus rioters, and protest marchers."

"The response from the audience was electric," said the *Digest*. "High-
school and college youth spoke up from all over the assembly. Said John
Everson, a track star from Iowa State University: 'The loudmouthed, pacifist minority scream about what they're against. Why don't we stage a
demonstration of what we're *for*!'

"Richard 'Rusty' Wailes, a 1956 and 1960 Olympic gold medalist in row-
ing and one of the conference's directors, inadvertently suggested the kind of
demonstration needed when he said, 'If we're going to debunk the myth of
a soft, indulgent, arrogant American and show the world that we care about
tomorrow, we've got to sing out our convictions, loud and strong!'"

It was the genesis of Up with People, a 130-performer musical extrava-
ganza that debuted at the World's Fair in 1965, emceed by Pat Boone. The
finale was the rousing "Freedom Isn't Free," which eulogized the debauched
ancient Romans, "so busy being merry ones, / That they didn't notice the
barbarians!" A 1967 *Reader's Digest* article ascribed to the show powers a
Red Chinese propaganda sheet might bestow on Chairman Mao. A former
Watts rioter saw the show, it was reported, then "went to stores I'd looted

and offered to pay for the things I'd taken." Naval Academy midshipmen submitted to the performers a "41-minute salvo of applause."

You could laugh—if you were a Franklin. But you also couldn't find a seat at one of their concerts at the Hollywood Bowl. Something was happening here. What it was wasn't exactly clear.

The antiwar movement grew more militant; Leviathan kept on showing its snarling jaws. McNamara told Congress no "bombing that I could contemplate in the future would seriously reduce the actual flow of men and matériel to the South"; the bombing continued. In 1967 an average of 150 Americans were dying a week, up 54 from 1966; in the third week of August, 211 died; in the fourth, 274.

Heavyweight champion Muhammad Ali—hostile whites and stubborn old-school Negroes still called him by his birth name, Cassius Clay—refused to be inducted, exhausted his appeals, and was ordered to report on April 11. He said he'd rather die first: "I ain't got no quarrel with them Vietcong." Carrying *Quotations from Chairman Mao* became a campus fad. In February, Catholic pacifist David Miller, twenty-four, became the first convicted under a new law criminalizing draft-card burning. The Supreme Court refused to review his conviction. The new law's threat of five-year jail sentences only brought more defiance: a way to prove one's manhood by *refusing* to go to war. On March 8, four Palo Alto militants began a national campaign to collect pledges to turn in draft cards—the "Resistance," just like the underground insurgency against the Nazis in World War II. The national council of SDS studied the draft laws and adopted a resolution explaining how members would violate each one.

At the beginning of April, David Miller had his sentencing hearing. The judge gave him a chance to repent, then another. His infant began to cry; his wife pulled back her hair and began breast-feeding. The judge pronounced sentence—two and a half years—and released him to spend time with his family before surrendering. Instead, Miller sat on the courtroom floor: "I want to show you it's against my will." "Many of our fellows on the campuses and in the community at large," an SDS flyer announced, were becoming "moved to action by a fresh instance of that repression which is becoming an increasingly important factor in American life."

Even worse for the government was a concomitant *lack* of militancy: that antiwar ranks were filling up with responsible grown-ups. "I expected to see a bunch of crazy-looking beatniks," a cop said of thirty thousand from the middle-aged, middle-class, middle-American peace organization SANE who marched down Pennsylvania Avenue, "but this is really a respectable-looking group." On Martha's Vineyard, the McNamaras played tennis only with the Bundys; the rest of the vacationers had organized a boycott. At Aspen, antiwar skiers rocked McNamara's chairlift. The same day that Rusk met with student leaders, 2,400 clergymen marched up Capitol Hill to tell their representatives about their forthcoming antiwar fast. Senator Scoop Jackson of Washington State was amazed to learn that eighty-five of his constituent divines had chartered a plane. Senator Eugene McCarthy, who worried the only Minnesotans who shared his doubts about the war were "undirected students," realized it was time to criticize it in public. Twenty-five hundred members of Women Strike for Peace stormed the Pentagon, many with children in tow, carrying blue shopping bags reading MOTHERS SAY STOP THE WAR IN VIETNAM. Refused entrance, they banged their shoes on the doors. Establishment insiders, former war supporters such as historian and former Kennedy administration special assistant Arthur Schlesinger, started joining the antiwar lists. Federal Reserve chairman Mariner Eccles and three hundred business executives took out an antiwar open letter to LBJ in the *Wall Street Journal.*

The risks in speaking out could be considerable. In Houston a professor of medicine working to organize a Christmas vigil outside the LBJ Ranch backed off when Baylor University threatened to fire him; high school teachers were refused tenure, expelled from their unions; students in L.A., Des Moines, and Prince George's County were suspended for wearing antiwar pins; in Honolulu, two citizens were arrested for waving a flag with dollar signs instead of stars. In Durham, New Hampshire, selectmen issued a parade permit to antiwar marchers with the provision that no one be allowed to participate who'd ever been arrested. Cops stood by studying rap sheets, collaring offenders as they passed.

Against the advice of fellow civil rights leaders, the *New York Times,* and the *Washington Post,* Martin Luther King began marching against the war: the two struggles felt to him one, and silence began to feel to him self-betrayal. He was convinced to take the plunge by the antiwar militant the administration feared most of all: Dr. Benjamin Spock, whose *Common Sense Book of Baby and Child Care* was one of the most influential books in the history of Western civilization, the author a secular saint. He received fan letters by the truckload; a typical one read, "I feel as if you were talking just to me." He had cut a commercial for the 1964 Johnson presidential campaign, and there had been talk that LBJ might make him secretary of health, education, and welfare.

Then Spock started speaking at antiwar demonstrations. Copies of his baby book were returned to him in shreds. He picketed in front of the White House. A teenager shouted, *"Traitor!"* and hit him with an egg (Spock's wife was just glad it wasn't a bullet). Here was a generation of mothers' security blanket. Now he was taking a security blanket away: the belief that the government was worthy of implicit trust. "We teach our boys to be men," a parent wrote him, "and now you're tearing that down." He retired from the medical school at Case Western Reserve University in 1967 to work full-time for peace before angry colleagues could push him out.

In April he led the largest antiwar march yet, the Spring Mobilization Against the War, in a three-piece suit and a sign reading CHILDREN ARE NOT BORN TO BURN, a kindergartener in tow. A contingent marched after burning their draft cards in a Maxwell House coffee can, and another who pulled down an American flag to burn, and another that flew the flag of the National Liberation Front, the South Vietnamese Communists. "Vassar girls" marched, Columbia students wore caps and gowns, twenty-four Sioux from South Dakota came and a band of Iroquois, frat boys chanted "Draft beer, not boys." Wrote Jimmy Breslin, "Most were members of nothing . . . young people in raincoats . . . out in a parade because they didn't like the war." Of the 531 who traveled by train from Cleveland, Ohio, 43 percent had never been to a demonstration before.

The right was also out in force. They chanted, "Dr. Spock smokes bananas" (smoking the fibrous insides of "mellow yellow" was the latest hippie fad), shouted the Pledge of Allegiance, shrieked "Cossacks!" and "Commies" at the cops who held them back. Former soldiers marched behind a VETERANS FOR PEACE banner, some in uniform; when they passed, counterprotesters paid them a respectful silence.

The march concluded at UN Plaza at twilight. Some said there were 125,000, others 400,000. Either way, it exploded what *Reader's Digest* subscribers were told a few months earlier: that the New Left was "surprisingly small—perhaps 5,000, with another 5,000 at its fringes." Stokely Carmichael, with whom King had once pledged to never again share a podium, spoke, calling Dean Rusk a "fool" and Lyndon Johnson a "buffoon." When King spoke, a chill wind frosted his breath:

"Let us save our national honor!—stop the bombing!

"Let us save American lives and Vietnamese lives—stop the bombing.

"Let us take a single instantaneous step to the peace table—stop the bombing.

"Let our voices ring out across the land to say the American people are not vain*glorrrrious* conquerers—stop the bombing!"

They began to think: we can end this war.

The White House's response was to drop 1.75 million leaflets on North Vietnam proclaiming that America hadn't lost her will to fight. Hubert Humphrey spoke with tears in his eyes to the League of Jewish Women in Atlanta: "America needs to tell the world of the lives it is saving." Dean Rusk went on *Meet the Press* and said that the "Communist apparatus" had organized the march.

In May the Veterans of Foreign Wars responded with a pro-war march. They predicted a turnout of 150,000. They only got 7,850. A "Support Our Boys in Vietnam" parade down Fifth Avenue two weeks later was bigger—because it was secretly organized out of the White House. "8 Hour Parade Backs GIs," headlined the faraway *Chicago Tribune,* in Dewey-Beats-

Truman-size type. Distinguished politicians were flushed out to pack the reviewing stands ("Where's the mayor?" angry marchers yelled of the absent and left-wing John Lindsay). These marchers burned a flag, too—the Russian one—and threw eggs at the French mission to the United Nations (de Gaulle had criticized the war). Children marched in army uniforms, toting plastic machine guns. A "Flower Brigade" of East Village "freaks" (the self-identification for what the dominant culture called hippies), led by Abbie Hoffman in a psychedelic cape, fell in behind a Boy Scout troop. They were attacked by the Flatbush Conservative Club; a mother passed off her baby to a friend to get in a few kicks.

The portion of Americans who thought the war had been a good idea was now below 40 percent. But between November and March the number of Americans in favor of "total military victory" went from 31 percent to 43. An argument proliferated on the right: that winning would be easy—only, *Reader's Digest* argued, "Our government has not permitted it." A woman reading that in a dentist's waiting room might sink down into the chair a confirmed hawk. But if she happened to choose *Ladies' Home Journal* instead, she might read this letter to the editor: "Before I went to Saigon, I had heard and read that napalm melts the flesh, and I thought that's nonsense, because I can put a roast in the oven and the fat will melt but the meat stays there. Well, I went and saw these children burned by napalm and it is absolutely true." That might make you a dove. "It makes you think," a janitor who witnessed the Mobe (National Mobilization Committee to End the War in Vietnam) parade on his lunch break told the *Washington Post*, "who is right?"

The unity was only in ambivalence. One result was a surfeit of ritual invocations against ambivalence. "Marine Dies Believing Viet War Is Right," ran a typical headline in the *Chicago Tribune*. *Time* featured a study by a retired newsman who pored over aerial photographs and decided reporters were doubling and tripling the attendance at peace demonstrations. George Wallace appeared on ABC's *Issues and Answers* on Mother's Day and promised, "I would drag some of these professors by their beards." Doctors King and Spock announced "Vietnam Summer," an organizing drive to train ten thousand antiwar activists across the country. The *Chicago Trib* responded, "When American soldiers are dying daily in Vietnam, demonstrations that block traffic on busy streets are very likely to lead to violence"—and that this would be the demonstrators' fault.

Ronald Reagan maneuvered to force Berkeley president Clark Kerr's resignation. Evidence suggests it may have been quid pro quo to J. Edgar Hoover. Reagan's security clearance form as governor required him to answer the question "Are you now, or have you ever been, a member of any organization which has been designated by the United States Attorney General under the provisions of Executive Order 10450?" and warned that "any false statement herein may be punished as a felony." Reagan answered no, untruthfully, but the FBI looked the other way. Hoover was like most conservatives: they tended to cut Ronald Reagan slack. Though he had just proposed the largest tax increase in California history, they were promoting him for president. He answered a need: he humiliated the liberals. He would tell young people harassing him with signs reading MAKE LOVE, NOT WAR that the problem was that they looked incapable of doing either. To him, a hippie was someone "who dresses like Tarzan, has hair like Jane, and smells like Cheetah." His national audience swooned.

CHAPTER NINE

Summer of Love

W HILE SOME AMERICANS SWOONED ABOUT REAGAN, AN ENTIRELY noncontiguous group, which included portions of the national commentariat, were swooning about something called the Summer of Love—in which, a *Washington Post* reporter sent to its epicenter in the Haight-Ashbury district of San Francisco wrote in his book *We Are the People Our Parents Warned Us Against,* "youth drew attention to itself by clustering in large numbers in most major American cities, where they broke the narcotics laws proudly, publicly, and defiantly. At the same time, they enunciated a different social philosophy and a new politics, and perhaps even mothered into life a subculture that was new to America." Legend had it that one day two freaks started interviewing each other. One was a reporter from *Newsweek,* the other a reporter from *Time.*

Love was in the eye of the beholder. At first downtown merchants welcomed the hippie district that sprang up on Plumb Street in Detroit; it was attracting people to their stores. Then they realized that the hippies liked their stores so much because they could panhandle from paying customers ("I wish we could have had the hippies without the dope," said one merchant, after the forty-three shops on Plumb Street had shrunk down to six). A love-in on Belle Isle, organized by a local narcotics enthusiast and rock musician named John Sinclair, descended into a brawl: Sinclair's "TransLove Rangers" promised they'd handle security themselves, perhaps by the power of the paper daisies they handed out; then had to call in the cops when leather-clad bikers started clubbing their way through the crowd.

John Lindsay granted a meeting to a group of white youth and Puerto Ricans seeking to clean up the East Village. A mob of six hundred landlords crashed the glass front doors of City Hall: "Lindsay sees the hippies," they said, "but he won't see the taxpayers." Paul Fino, the antibusing congressman from Queens, said Lindsay was giving "the city's punks, Vietniks, and banana-sniffers flag-burning rights in Central Park." Lindsay's parks commissioner, August Heckscher, the patrician Republican former head of the charitable foundation the Twentieth Century Fund, replied that the law-and-order types were "scared by the abundance of life."

The month of March came in like a lamb with Frank Sinatra sweeping the Grammy Awards and went out like a lion with Jimmy Hendrix in the hospital after burning himself while immolating his guitar. Carl Wilson of the Beach Boys was arrested by the FBI for refusing his military call-up; Mick Jagger was railroaded for possession of legally bought Benzedrine tablets, and his Rolling Stones band mate Keith Richards was on trial for smoking pot. Hendrix was dropped as the opening act for the Monkees after complaints from the Daughters of the American Revolution. Some suspected this last move was PR-agent cover for a commercial decision; insurrection was now the stuff of which hit records were made.

At the beginning of June an album had come out that was more than a record album: the Beatles' *Sgt. Pepper's Lonely Hearts Club Band*, a staging ground for the new kind of cultural war. Critic Kenneth Tynan called it "a decisive moment in the history of Western civilization." Paul McCartney said in an interview in *Life* of LSD: "It opened my eyes. We only use one-tenth of our brains. Just think what we'd accomplish if we could tap that hidden part. There wouldn't be any more war or poverty or famine." People were saying that LSD brought them closer to God. Then Billy Graham, jealous for his hold over his flock, rebuked that there was only one way to God and that "LSD should be shunned like the plague by young people."

But *Sgt. Pepper's* was not merely some marker in a generational war. It was also great art, staging that war within itself. Its most beautiful moment was a song called "She's Leaving Home," a haunting cry of sympathy for the Depression-generation parents who wished nothing more than to love their children, and whose alienated children's thanks was to run away—perhaps to a place like Haight-Ashbury.

All you need is love: an injunction easier to honor in the breach. Perhaps especially in the midst of a summer of love. For simultaneously, the other abiding media obsession was a hawklike watch over which city would be the first to erupt in a riot. "It would be ironic, indeed," George McGovern said on the Senate floor, "if we devoted so heavy a proportion of our resources to the pacification of Vietnam that we are unable to pacify Los Angeles, Chicago, and Harlem."

Maybe it would be Cleveland.

On May 2 the chief of the city's subversives squad testified to the Senate Internal Security Subcommittee that Cleveland Black Power organizations had merged under the leadership of a mysterious figure known as Ahmed, who preached the solar eclipse set for May 9 would be the opening of a war between Communist China and the United States and called, the officer said, "for a Negro uprising at a time when such a war will leave local cities helpless before a revolutionary movement."

Or would it be Chicago? On May 4 the sheriff of Cook County, Joseph Woods, accepting an award from the Kiwanis Club, predicted "the longest, hottest summer in history." On the twenty-first, two undercover policemen were chased from a rally to change the name of Washington Park to Malcolm X Park. "The crowd rose like a tornado," one of them reported. Sheriff Woods, the brother of Nixon secretary Rose Mary Woods, relished such incidents as opportunities. When black students acted up in the Negro suburb of Maywood, he rushed to the scene with a bullhorn, telling officers to fire upon any rioter who raised his hand above his head, and to shoot carefully because they didn't have extra men to take the wounded to the hospital. "The bystanders got my message," the sheriff proudly told a reporter.

Perhaps it would be Milwaukee, where the inner-city civil rights priest James Groppi was arrested on May 5 for interfering with an officer in the performance of his duty, so his copastor sermonized: "Dig your trenches. Shutter your windows. The harvest is near. . . . Are we so blind and stupid as not to realize that?"

Or Louisville, where the governor called out the National Guard and the mayor defiantly pronounced, "The Kentucky Derby will be run," despite threats by militants to shut it down if an open-housing law wasn't passed. Martin Luther King arrived. Heckled by a mob of whites, he had his driver pull to the curb for an impromptu sermon. "God has given us an opportunity," he began—and was interrupted with the interjection "God has put a curse on the Negroes!" then saw his car slammed with a rock.

Perhaps down South, in Jackson or Houston, where students at Negro universities exchanged gun salvos with police. Or Birmingham, where Stokely Carmichael visited in June and said when they draft a black man and "tell him to shoot his enemy, and if he don't shoot Lurleen and George and little junior, he's a fool." Or New York, where sixteen members of the Revolutionary Action Movement, including the assistant principal of P.S. 40 in Queens, were arrested and charged with plotting to kill Whitney Young and Roy Wilkins and with possession of a thousand rounds of ammunition and 275 pounds of heroin. (At the NAACP convention in Boston, one militant leader mocked the news by picketing with a sign reading KILL THE TOMS.)

Or maybe Oakland. That seemed, in fact, quite likely.

A new group had emerged there in the fall of 1966, the Black Panther Party for Self-Defense. Its founders, Huey Newton and Bobby Seale, were the sons of among the fifty thousand blacks who had migrated to Oakland during World War II. By 1960, they were a quarter of the population, but a city council election-at-large scheme kept them politically toothless, and the most ferally racist police force outside of Mississippi—from which, in fact, many of the police were recruited—worked to keep them cowed. On Friday nights officers lay in wait outside the bars that served as the ghetto's de facto banks. A factory worker would emerge, find himself arrested for drunkenness, and be robbed of his week's wages on the way to the precinct house. Such was the city in which Seale and Newton grew up.

Since Huey Newton had grown up on the streets sharing a name with Donald Duck's nephew, with a squeaky voice and light skin at that, "throwing hands," preemptively and with the biggest dude he could find became a survival reflex. In 1964 he stabbed a man at a party with a steak knife for calling him *Negro* instead of *black*—Malcolm X's preferred locution. Bobby and Huey began splitting their spare time between burglarizing houses in the Berkeley Hills and discussing Sartre, Camus, and radical African psychoanalyst Frantz Fanon. They set out to consolidate their control of the Soul Students Advisory Council at Merritt College by packing a meeting with armed street thugs. Then they retired from campus politics to form an organization of their own. The bourgeois brothers at Merritt were all talk. Their group would be men of action.

On April 1, 1967, in the adjacent, largely black town of Richmond, a child was shot dead by the cops. According to the white press, he was caught in a burglary, fled, and violently resisted; according to his neighbors, he had a hip injury that made the notion of Denzill Dowell "fleeing" a farce. The coroner's report was proved to contain fabrications. The Panthers came up from Oakland to investigate, bearing guns. The locals told them that white teachers slapped their black students. So Panthers in paramilitary uniforms formed armed ranks outside the elementary school while the parents confronted the teachers. ("The Dog Cops made no attempt to break up the meeting like they generally do when Black people get together to sound out their grievances against the white power structure," the mimeographed *Black Panther* newspaper related.) The Panthers demanded a new investigation of Denzill Dowell's death. The county sheriff's response was flippant: "You should go to the legislature." It gave them ideas.

Here was one of the things that made these young men remarkable: beneath their berets and leather jackets, behind their bandoliers, they were also naively earnest. They believed implicitly in the majesty of the law. Revolutionaries in an only-in-America kind of way, they perceived themselves as a fully functioning ghetto counterconstabulary, apparently surprised when the response of the police—whom they called an "army of occupation"—was to wish them dead.

"What are you doing with the guns?" a patrolman would ask them, a little afraid.

"What are you doing with *your* gun?" Huey Newton would shoot back, and pull out one of the law books he always carried with him as others stood by with cameras and tape recorders. Huey would step out of his car and snap a live round into his chamber: California law only outlawed the carrying of loaded weapons inside a motor vehicle. The cops would slink; the Panthers would call them "pigs"—another fruit of Newton and Seale's research: it wasn't an obscenity, so you couldn't be arrested for it. The Panthers harvested recruits from the gawking young male bystanders. It was a miracle Bay Area cops and Panthers hadn't shot one another yet. After the riots in San Francisco at the end of October, one precinct had taken to displaying a poster of Klan leader Robert Shelton with the caption "Our Hero."

The Panthers started patrolling in rich white neighborhoods: let *them* find out what it was like to have hostile forces stalking your streets with guns. Which was how they caught the attention of Don Mulford, the assemblyman who had conspired with the FBI to help Reagan get elected. He introduced a bill to ban the carrying of loaded firearms in public places. It was set for its first committee hearing on May 2.

"Gunmen Invade W. Coast Capitol," read the front-page banner in far-off Chicago:

"The Negroes, shouting they were members of the Black Panther party, forced their way into the assembly chamber while the legislators were in session, and scuffled with state highway patrolmen."

Upon their arrest Huey Newton read the Black Panther Executive Mandate No. 1, which called on "Americans and particularly Negroes to take careful note of the racist California legislature which is now considering legislation aimed at keeping the black people disarmed and powerless." For many whites this statement settled it: *Black Power* meant arming black people.

Which only made sense, if you were a Black Panther. A rumor was spreading across America's ghettos: the government was preparing concentration camps for blacks. The Panthers took it for settled fact. Which was why the Executive Mandate continued, "At the same time that the American government is waging a racist war of genocide in Vietnam, the concentration camps in which the Japanese Americans were interned during World War II are being renovated and expanded. Since America has historically reserved the most barbaric treatment for nonwhite people we are forced to conclude that the concentration camps are being prepared for black people who are determined to gain their freedom by any means necessary. . . . The Mulford Act brings the hour of doom one step closer."

In Washington that same day, a police official from Ohio told U.S. senators of Black Power militants' plans to take Cleveland by force of arms.

Two scared sides, black and white, each convinced the other was about to fire the first shot. The long, hot summer could not end well. The only question was, where would it begin?

In Newark.

The biggest city in New Jersey was a frighteningly corrupt town. Mayor Hugh Addonizio, a former member of the U.S. House of Representatives, once explained his career change this way: "There's no money in being a congressman, but you can make a million bucks as mayor of Newark." Its tenements, purchased at fire-sale prices during the Depression, were gold mines for their owners, so long as they didn't sink any money into them. So Newark had the highest percentage of substandard housing of any American city: 7,097 units had no flush toilets; 28,795, no heaters. Twenty-eight babies died in a diarrhea epidemic in 1965, eighteen of them at City Hospital, which was also infested by bats. The city's major industry was illegal gambling. Cops ran heroin rings. Food stores raised prices the day welfare checks arrived. All the same, downtown was filled with construction cranes. "Urban renewal" served Mayor Addonizio's political purpose: by continually scattering Negroes, who were 65 percent of the population, it radically reduced their power.

Wednesday, July 12, 1967, police manhandled a cabdriver during an arrest. He had bushy hair, and they might have thought that made him a Black Muslim, whose lairs they had recently been raiding. A false report got around that he had died in police custody. Angry citizens massed at the Fourth Precinct. Shortly before midnight, a Molotov cocktail burst against the wall. Police in riot helmets surrounded the protesters. The two sides yelled racial slurs. Kids started throwing rocks. The first liquor-store windows were broken. The looting began; that was always next. Cars with makeshift towlines ripped the iron grates from store windows so their contents could be stripped; junkies cleaned out drugstores; ordinary citizens by the thousands took what they liked from white businesses as fast as they could carry it. Some skipped black-owned stores with SOUL BROTHER signs marking their status like lamb's blood. Others didn't. A disgusted Urban Leaguer rued the "carnival air." Social scientists spoke of "the revolution of rising expectations" as one cause of riots: more and more Great Society abundance all around, success without squalor, beauty without barrenness — just not so much for blacks. Looters, too, took America's promises seriously.

The mayor and the director of police temporized. That made everything worse. Certain dysfunctional civic responses would become a pattern in urban riots. The only preparations Newark officials had made had been orders to street cops for restraint: maybe that would tide things over. But police who perceived they'd been "handcuffed" tended to act in a less, not more, restrained manner. (The hapless cabbie had been kicked so repeatedly in the groin that by the time he had arrived at the precinct house he couldn't walk; that was before he was assaulted with gun butts, nightsticks, and dirty water from the jailhouse toilet.) Police were ordered to avoid arrests for looting, for arrests would be an acknowledgment there was a "riot." Insurance companies didn't cover riots. Maybe it would die out before anyone went on record using the word. "The situation is normal," police director Dominick Spina announced, piles of broken glass lying at his feet.

A second wave flared, then burned itself out around midnight Thursday.

Relieved officials decided the crisis was over. Mayor Addonizio soon had to admit it wasn't. At 2:30 a.m. he called Governor Richard Hughes in a panic to call out the state police and the National Guard. Spina announced over every police radio, "If you have a gun, whether it is a shoulder weapon or whether it is a handgun, use it." The same Governor Hughes who had determinedly refused to interfere with the tenure of the Communist history professor Eugene Genovese during his reelection fight in 1965 announced, "The line between the jungle and the law might as well be drawn here as any place in America." By 4:30 a.m. the first state police had appeared. By 7 a.m. National Guard units had rolled up Springfield Avenue, the Essex County main drag that started in leafy Short Hills and ended in Newark's heart of darkness. White residents set up shotgun patrols, standing ready for Negroes "to spill over onto white ground." They shouted at the passing military trucks, "Go kill them niggers."

And that is what they did. Thus began the second Newark riot: not looting, not arson, but scared offices of the law committing officially sanctioned murder.

Three were dead by daylight Friday. One was Rose Abraham, a forty-five-year-old mother of five, out looking for one of her children. Tedlock Bell Jr., twenty-eight, a father of four, a former basketball star, had just told his companions to submit quietly to the police when he was killed. A young man named James Sanders was shotgunned in the back while running from a liquor store. The commander of the antiriot forces, Colonel Kelly of the New Jersey State Police, pronounced that the looting was under control. Another looter was shot dead in the back at the end of the day. His name was Albert Taliaferro. By then nine Newark residents had died.

A group of citizens were milling around outside the Scudder Homes housing project when three police cars turned the corner. The crowd assumed they must be firing blanks—until a .38-caliber bullet ripped through Virgil Harrison's right forearm. Men took off their undershirts to wave as white flags. The cops kept on shooting—at ground level, claiming they were hunting a sniper on the upper floors. That was how Rufus Council, thirty-five, Oscar Hill, fifty, and Virgil's father, Isaac "Uncle Daddy" Harrison, seventy-two (and perhaps Robert Lee Martin, twenty-two, and Cornelius Murray, twenty-eight), lost their lives. Oscar Hill was wearing his American Legion jacket. Murray's body was missing $126 and a ring. Robert Lee Martin's family reported that cops stripped money from his body. There indeed had been snipers in Scudder Homes. But they began shooting an hour later, in response to the cops. They killed a police detective, Fred Toto, thirty-three, a father of three.

Seventy-six residents of Beacon Street signed an eyewitness petition: "At approximately five-thirty PM on the fourteenth of July, most of the residents of Beacon Street were sitting on their porches watching their kids playing in the front. Without provocation, members of the state police approached the corner and sprayed the street from left to right. They shot James Sneade, 36, in the stomach, as he made repairs on his car out front. Karl Greene, 17, was shot in the head as he stood on his sister's porch."

At eight thirty a father driving with his family to White Castle slowed for a barricade. Guardsmen opened fire. His ten-year-old son, Eddie Moss, was mortally wounded in the head.

At around ten thirty, Leroy Boyd, thirty-seven, father of two, was shot to death. A funeral home director reported finding six .38-caliber bullets—police bullets—in his body.

A man named Albert Mersier died shortly before midnight after being shot while attempting to load a stolen vacuum cleaner into his car.

By Saturday morning, fourteen square miles were sealed off by National Guard roadblocks, pacifying the rioters—but not ending the violence. Saturday afternoon twenty-four-year-old Billy Furr got into a debate with a Black Muslim who had just told a *Life* magazine reporter that the riot would continue "until every white man's building in Newark is burned." Billy demurred, "We ain't riotin' agains' all you whites. We're riotin' against police brutality, like that cabdriver they beat up the other night. That stuff goes on all the time. When the police treat us like people 'stead of treatin' us like animals, the riots will stop." Furr and the reporter ran into each other later. Furr gave him a beer he'd looted and went back into Mack Liquors. A police car skidded to a halt as Billy Furr emerged with a six-pack. He ran and was cut down by a high-velocity double-0 shot to the head. Particles from three shells went completely through his body and sprinkled the reporter. An errant shot cut down a twelve-year-old boy, Joey Bass, who survived.

At 6 p.m. bullets ripped through the windows of Eloise Spellman, a forty-one-year-old widow, on the tenth floor of the Hayes Homes project. Her son and daughter watched her die. The shooters were guardsmen and state troopers, who reported she died from sniper fire.

Rebecca Brown, thirty, liked to sit at her second-floor window. She kept a color photo of the Star-Spangled Banner clipped from the *New York Sunday News* on the wall. An adjacent wall was pocked with twenty-six automatic-weapons bullets from street level, one of which killed Mrs. Brown.

Mrs. Hattie Gainer, also on the second floor, was cut down by the same flurry of bullets. A conscience-wracked state trooper barged in as she lay moaning in a pool of blood and cried, "We made a mistake. We shot the wrong person. We're killing innocent people." The ambulance didn't collect her for another three hours.

By Saturday evening four thousand National Guardsmen were harassing residents at random from hundreds of checkpoints set up around the city. A man described driving to the hospital to visit his injured wife: "I saw a guy get pulled from a car at Bergen and Sixteenth Avenue and the cops were beating him." Officers shot out one of the man's tires, taunting him from their jeeps, "Kennedy's not with you now"; "Let's kill all these black bastards."

A kid named Howard Edwards drove down from Staten Island to see a girlfriend, who had assured him the riot was over. Since he hadn't taken out the registration for the '57 Chevy he'd just bought, he didn't respond when the National Guard told him to "Stop, motherfucker." By some miracle he survived the hail of bullets that ended up rattling Fire House Eleven on Ninth Street and the fire-sprinkler pipes of a nearby factory. One of the fire captains who answered the resulting fire alarm, Mike Moran, a father of six with a pregnant wife, died from a ricocheting bullet. The unsuspecting Lothario whose '57 Chevy was responsible for it all spent thirty days in solitary confinement ("I'm sure it was a tommy gun," a fire captain testified) as the most dreaded suspect in the Essex County lockup, until they finally let him slink back to Staten Island a month later with a charge of violating curfew. The story of the fiendish Negro with the tommy gun who held off an entire company of National Guardsmen, then engineered the false alarm that made firemen his sitting ducks, made good PR cover for what was actually going on: state police going up and down Springfield Avenue, smashing up every not-yet-molested SOUL BROTHER store.

On Sunday afternoon James Rutledge Jr., rummaging through a shuttered bar with three other kids, was shot thirty-nine times. The cops put a knife next to him when they were done and said he tried to throw it at them.

Michael Pugh expired at 1 a.m. Monday morning. He'd been shot by a guardsman in front of his home on Fifteenth Avenue while taking out the garbage. A boy with him called the guardsmen names, and they opened fire. Michael Pugh was twelve years old.

Raymond Gilmer, the last official death, twenty years old, may or may not have been running from a stolen car. He got a bullet to the back of the head.

One more corpse wasn't included in the Newark death toll: a cop with a conscience who testified against his comrades during the grand jury investigation of the riot died of "occlusive coronary arteriosclerosis" while "visiting friends at 25 Gold Street," a newspaper said. That address was the police clubhouse.

This, too, was another riot pattern: a lack of investigative energy where police offenses were concerned. When the Newark grand jury presentment was made public the following April, it described all these killings in inculpating forensic detail: "Albert Mersier Jr. was fatally shot by a police officer as he was fleeing from the scene of a burglarized warehouse"; "Rose Abraham suffered a fatal bullet wound of the right hip . . . police were attempting to clear this area of looters." But each count ended with the identical refrain: "Due to insufficient evidence of any criminal misconduct, the jury found no cause for indictment." The bullets recovered often weren't from service revolvers. Some cops had used personal weapons, making ballistic reports uncheckable.

The press was interested in making the carnage make sense. A turkey shoot of grandparents and ten-year-olds did not fit the bill. The New York *Daily News* ran an "investigation" of the death of the Newark fire captain and called it "The Murder of Mike Moran." Twelve-year-old Joey Bass, in dirty jeans and scuffed sneakers, his blood trickling down the street, lay splayed across the cover of the July 28 *Life*. The feature inside constituted a sort of visual and verbal brief for why such accidents might have been excusable. The opening spread showed a man with a turban wrapped around his head loading a Mauser by a window, captioned, "The targets were Negro snipers, like the one above." In actual fact the photo had been staged by a blustering black nationalist, and what the copy claimed was an upper-floor vantage onto the streets was actually a first-floor room overlooking a trash-strewn backyard. "The whole time we were in Newark we never saw what you would call a violent black man," *Life* photographer Bud Lee later recalled. "The only people I saw who were violent were the police."

CBS camera crews recorded wrenching footage of Uncle Daddy's funeral. Producers decided not to run it. A sympathetic portrait of "rioters" would have been far too controversial. Concluded Governor Hughes, "I felt a thrill of pride in the way our state police and National Guard have conducted themselves."

The Detroit riot started a week and a half later, when police raided illegal saloons on a hard-partying Saturday night. Word got out that at one of them, on Twelfth Street, cops were going crazy. And that was all it took: the first bashing in of liquor-store windows; the first burning down of empty wood-frame houses; timorous officials telling cops to lay back in the hopes that the rioting would "burn itself out"—and more looting following street reports that cops were standing by and letting folks strip stores clean. City Hall, claiming there had been no disturbance, let the afternoon's doubleheader with the Yankees go on as planned. That was when rioters started torching the back offices of department stores, where they stored the debt records, taking advantage of all the cops preoccupied at Tiger Stadium. White vigilantes were already out in force. "I emptied my Luger over and over," one of them reported.

The next day broke ninety degrees. "I'm gonna shoot at anything that moves and that is black," an arriving National Guardsman declared. Looters mocked the ducklike armored cars carrying chubby accountants and farmers—"Quack! Quack!" Night fell; guardmsen shot out streetlights for cover. That took them several shots per light; troops the next street over would think they were under sniper attack, squeezing triggers until they ran out of ammo. (One victim was a fireman.) Others wandered like lost boys, crouching, darting, shooting every little thing that moved, or didn't; one cop laughed as a young guardsman took out a store's electric sign one lightbulb at a time until the barrel of his .50-caliber machine gun burned out. The city editor of the *Milwaukee Journal* came upon a hysterical woman in a stalled car holding a crying baby in one arm, waving a hospital outpatient form with another. Fifteen cops approached on foot, crouched, and took aim. "Press! Press!" he cried. A cop commanded him to back up his car and get the hell out. At which other cops, seeing a car lurch, raised their own rifles.

On TV screens, it looked to much of white America like our boys crouching in the jungle, fighting unseen Vietcong. Which was how it looked to white radicals, too. Many called themselves "revolutionaries" now. They watched *The Battle of Algiers* and cheered when the insurrectionists' bombs went off in crowded cafés, thrilled to Che Guevara's "Message to the Tricontinental" and its call for "two, three, many Vietnams." They thought of the Vietcong as surrogates in their own anti-imperial war against "Amerika." They thought of black men stealing cases of beer in Detroit in exactly the same way. "We live in a society which trains its sons to be killers and which channels its immense wealth into the business of suppressing courageous men from Vietnam to Detroit who struggle for the simple human right to control their own lives and destinies," read a statement to the press from the National Mobilization Committee to End the War in Vietnam.

Fire departments from forty Michigan towns raced to help. But what if riots broke out in Lansing, Jackson, Flint, Saginaw, Grand Rapids? In the state capital, office workers refused to drive home. In Chicago, where rumors reported carloads heading their way from Detroit, Mayor Daley went on TV to warn that lawlessness would not be tolerated and sent out a helmeted police task force on continual alert. A rural Michigan county sheriff bragged to *Esquire*'s Garry Wills, "I can deputize anyone over eighteen years of age who will carry a gun. If I had to, I would swear out a posse." Wills emerged convinced that it was only a matter of time before the nation broke out into a second civil war. The official death toll was forty-three. "We got the forty-fourth," a National Guardsman bragged to Garry Wills—a sniper, he claimed, who kept shooting after they raked his building with machine-gun fire. "So on the second night the building 'accidentally' caught fire," the guardsman owned up—though just as likely, of course, they were shooting at another guardsman. The Michigan National Guard didn't have enough field radios, so they'd been reduced to communicating via pay phones.

There followed an early skirmish in the 1968 presidential race. The two executives ultimately responsible for keeping the peace were the two parties' presumptive nominees: President Johnson and Governor Romney. Both suspected it would require the United States Army. But neither wanted to take responsibility for installing martial law in an American city—though both wanted credit should the decision prove right. A dance began. Constitutionally, the governor had to make the request by avowing that Detroit was under a state of insurrection and that the resources at his control were exhausted. Practically, it was a president's duty, honoring his pledge to defend the Constitution against enemies foreign and domestic, to volunteer the army.

Since 1964, when riots wracked Harlem, Lyndon Johnson had been agonizing about riots, how to stop them, what they meant, how to keep them from wrecking his war on poverty—and why his war on poverty wasn't *preventing* the riots. Asked at his July 18 news conference for his "views on what happened in New Jersey in the last couple of days," he launched into his standard peroration about the healing power of antipoverty programs—prefacing his remarks with the absurd claim "I don't think I have any more information on it than you have." Attorney General Ramsey Clark got his back, saying, "There are few activities that are more local" than law enforcement, so there was little the federal government could do—an unsatisfying answer to those who pointed out that the response of liberals to every other problem was to call for *federal* action. Then came the second conflagration, Detroit. Johnson could, of course, call out the army—but that would set a dangerous precedent: the nation would start looking to the White House to tamp down every riot, make each one his own responsibility, each one his *fault*. Would he find himself commander in chief of an army occupying American cities, shooting American citizens? But if he didn't call out the army, would his rivals for the presidency in 1968 tell white America he couldn't protect them?

One of those rivals had a problem of his own: he could *ask* the president for troops. But wouldn't that be to admit he couldn't keep order in his own state—and what kind of audition for commander in chief would *that* be?

Politicians fiddled. Detroit burned. Once the ninety-six hundred paratroopers from the One Hundred and First and Eighty-second Airborne finally arrived, it took only hours for them to restore order with hardly a further shot fired. And at the White House, the debate turned to whether the president should address the nation. Harry McPherson said he should stay quiet, lest he be saddled with the blame for turning a great American city into a garrison. The pollster Benjamin Wattenberg said the president had no choice: "Wallace, for sure, and probably Nixon and Reagan" would be pinning responsibility on Johnson whether he went on the air or not, so he might as well get out in front of the story. He ended up taking the advice of Wattenberg, the White House's specialist on the tender political sensitivities of angry middle-class whites, and a voice LBJ was listening to more and more. The president went on TV close to midnight, J. Edgar Hoover, Robert McNamara, and Ramsey Clark by his side, speaking in bland legalese, a bold man become timid in the face of cities out of control.

＊ ＊ ＊

The same hot week in New York, a drunken mob of two thousand smashed and looted in Harlem after cops broke up a craps game, then hundreds smashed and looted their way to Saks Fifth Avenue after a Smokey Robinson concert in Central Park. Mayor Lindsay called it "a demonstration, not a riot." The commander of New York's National Guard announced they were ready to fight back with hand grenades and bazookas.

Stokely Carmichael had abdicated the leadership of SNCC, traveled to Hanoi and Havana, and was replaced by a kid out of Baton Rouge named H. Rap Brown, who visited the racially tense town of Cambridge on Maryland's Eastern Shore. "Detroit exploded, Newark exploded, Harlem exploded! It is time for Cambridge to explode," he cried, and pointed down the street to a rickety all-black elementary school: "You should have burned it down a long time ago!" A few hours later, they did.

In Philadelphia cops got garbage cans thrown down on them from the roofs. The police chief, Frank Rizzo, bought up all his men's vacation time and had them patrol in air-conditioned buses in shifts, twenty-four hours a day. A rumor flashed that Washington would be set ablaze July 31. The thirty-first passed unscathed. Violence flared instead eight days later—on, of all places, Capitol Hill, when seventy-five demonstrators pushed their way into the House gallery chanting "Rats cause riots!" and "We want a rat bill!" and got in a brawl with police.

It was the sound of a presidency breaking.

Back in March, President Johnson had proposed $40 million in matching funds for municipal extermination programs to control rodents. "The knowledge that many children in the world's most affluent nation are attacked, maimed, and even killed by rats should fill every American with shame," he said. The proposal passed the Banking and Currency Committee in June by a margin of 22–6. Then, Newark—and on July 20, the House debate on the rat bill, when what had been uncontroversial a month earlier became a subject for hooting derision.

"Let's buy a lot of cats and turn them loose," Jim Haley of Florida howled. An Iowa Republican proposed a "high commissioner of rats." Another solon joked about proliferating "rat patronage" and "rat bureaucracies." "*Civil rats!*" someone cried. The chamber rocked with guffaws.

Then Representative Martha Griffiths of Michigan stood up to speak—trembled, in fact, with rage. Rats, she said, had killed more people "than all the generals in history." They "carry the most deadly of diseases. Do you think that's funny?"

She talked about the fancy expense-account restaurants where the congressmen took their lobbyist friends: "Rats swish their tails through sewers and brush across the food you eat." Griffiths drove the message home: "If you're going to spend seventy-nine billion dollars to kill off a few Vietcong,

I'd spend forty million dollars to kill off the most devastating enemy that man has ever had."

To no avail. The House slapped down the civil rats bill by a vote of 207–176. Only twenty-two Republicans voted in favor. The anguished cries of liberals masked the magnitude of their retreat: that their dreams of warring on poverty had once been so much grander than $40 million for rats.

Johnson had never seen the political squeeze coming. "Push ahead full tilt," he had said on one of his first days as president, when his new economic adviser told him President Kennedy had been considering a poverty initiative—a program on which President Kennedy was proceeding exceedingly cautiously, for fear of offending middle-class whites. Now, middle-class whites were indeed sorely offended by the War on Poverty.

Lyndon Johnson's poverty programs were doing, after all, what they were supposed to be doing: redistributing wealth, and thus redistributing power. When polled in 1961, 59 percent of the electorate said the federal government bore responsibility to make sure every American had an adequate job and income. Then the government started making modest steps toward that goal, and by 1969, only 31 percent still thought that. The income of non-whites had started rising faster than the income of whites, and though the gap was not nearly closed, many whites' incomes were beginning to stagnate, even, in real terms, to fall. The War on Poverty came out of their hard-earned tax dollars—draining money, some whites thought, toward ungrateful rioters. Who still demanded their welfare checks. A White House study found that three-fourths of white Bostonians thought most welfare cases were fraudulent. Backlash against the War on Poverty had always been latent. Civil rats showed that backlash to now be mature—as, in places such as Detroit, the races made ready for war.

A local black nationalist minister, Albert Cleage, observed to a reporter that the shooting ranges were packed and the city was way behind in processing gun registrations. "So, naturally, any black man who can get hold of a gun is getting hold of it." A flyer circulated in white neighborhoods: "Are YOU READY NOW to PREPARE YOURSELF for the NEXT ONE? Or will you be forced to stand helplessly by because you were UN-prepared to defend your home or neighborhood against bands of armed terrorists who will murder the men and rape the women?" An outfit called Breakthrough offered a $10,000 reward for the "arrest and conviction" of Detroit's mayor on the charge of criminal negligence and organized workshops in VFW and Knights of Columbus meeting halls with representatives of the National Rifle Association, who suggested each family stockpile two hundred rounds of ammunition.

The NRA, once a hobby club for sportsmen, was becoming a new kind of organization altogether. Its magazine, *American Rifleman*, had a new column, "The Armed Citizen," which ran glowing accounts of vigilantes. Connecticut senator Thomas Dodd, a conservative, had a bill pending to limit the sale of firearms through the mail. It had once seemed uncontroversial. Now white and black would-be vigilantes agreed the Dodd bill was a prelude to the confiscation of all firearms. *Guns & Ammo* called the bill's supporters "criminal-coddling do-gooders, borderline psychotics, as well as Communists and leftists who want to lead us into the one-world welfare state." One of those supporters was Massachusetts' junior senator, Edward Moore Kennedy—whom *American Rifleman* said was following the "Communist line" for trying to outlaw the method by which his brother's assassin had obtained the murder weapon.

The president called a cabinet meeting, demanding to know whether the Communists were behind the riots. His new attorney general, Ramsey Clark, was a Texas boy, a marine, the son of Truman's law-and-order attorney general, Tom Clark, a Supreme Court justice who had dissented from the *Miranda* decision. But this Clark said there simply wasn't evidence for blaming Communists.

"It is incredible to think you can't make a case," Treasury Secretary Henry Fowler responded.

The vice president said evidence or no, better safe than sorry: "There are fifty-two cities potentially about to explode."

The secretary of state, incredulous, said that Stokely Carmichael had personally threatened his life.

The secretary of health, education, and welfare complained that the Communists could be planning to hit the next city as they spoke.

They read their president's mind. He ordered the search for the conspiracy to continue: "I have a very deep feeling that there is more to that than we see at the moment." America had enemies. They *had* to be responsible. Subsequently, he murmured a judgment about civil-liberties-minded Ramsey Clark to White House aide Joseph Califano: "If I had ever known that he didn't measure to his daddy, I'd never have made him attorney general."

A Justice Department memo listed the summer's lesser riots alphabetically: " . . . South Bend, Indiana . . . Springfield, Massachusetts . . . Spring Valley, New York . . ." And whatever pretensions the Black Panthers had to a mere self-defense ideology dissolved with a Bobby Seale quote in the August 6 *New York Times Magazine* on what to do if you spied a cop on his coffee break: "shoot him down—boom, boom—with a 12-gauge shotgun." And by this time politicians and pundits were learning to call this inchoate, ambiguous knot—riots and street crime, flag burning and antiwar marches, children leaving home to drop acid in San Francisco, all of it, whatever the causes and whatever the complexities—by a disambiguating name: the law-and-order issue. And soon Richard Nixon, once reluctant, would move all in on the game.

CHAPTER TEN

In Which a Cruise Ship Full of Governors Inspires Considerations on the Nature of Old and New Politics

R ICHARD NIXON'S SUMMER OF LOVE WAS SPENT ABROAD.
There were triumphs: a face-to-face interview with Romanian president Nicolae Ceauşescu (who intrigued Nixon with his suggestion of serving as a go-between between Vietnam and China); brilliant toasts at diplomatic banquets; a warm reception on a crowded street in Lima, where he had once feared for his life. There were also, as ever, humiliations. The Polish government denied him a visa. The Kremlin refused his interview requests. In Tashkent, Uzbekistan, two hundred factory hands surrounded him and demanded America withdraw from Vietnam. "We, too, want peace," Nixon said, "but it takes two to make peace." "Yes," one shot back, "the two are North Vietnam and South Vietnam." Nixon was now one for two in the Soviet Debating League.

While he was on the plane from Paris to Rabat, war broke out between Israel and an Arab alliance of Egypt, Jordan, and Syria. He offered sagacities to waiting reporters on the tarmac: "I do not believe that either side has the capacity . . . of winning a quick victory." Unfortunately for his reputation as a foreign policy sage, it turned out to be a six-day war. Nixon dispatched Pat Buchanan to convince the press he'd been right anyway.

Nixon flew from India to Pakistan, two countries nearly at war. His Piper Apache was cleared to cross the border at 4 p.m. If it crossed it an hour later, it might have been shot down. He landed in Pakistan to a mob carrying the usual signs: NIXON GO HOME, DOWN WITH THE U.S. A teenager flung himself in front of the limousine. The crises made him feel alive. Diplomacy: the greatest game of all.

Ambassadors tried to get local American VIPs an audience with the visiting celebrity. These Nixon courteously avoided. He barely held any press conferences. This trip was not about running for president. This trip was preparing to *be* president.

Quietly, between trip legs, he put out political fires. Gaylord Parkinson had proven a disappointment. He had devised a jazzy logo for his Nixon for President headquarters in D.C., a lightning bolt in the shape of an *N*. In New Hampshire, "Parky" peppered granite-faced old Republicans with California pizzazz. It was the last thing Nixon needed in the stealth stage of the game: a used-car salesman. Parky's wife came down with cancer, so Nixon was able to ease him out quietly, by transoceanic phone calls, in favor of former Oklahoma governor Henry Bellmon. Then it was back to his pashas, his premiers, and the Taiwanese society doyenne and anticommunist intriguer Anna Chennault—his back-channel contact with the South Vietnamese leadership.

He also made time for something else. Before leaving each embassy residence, he met with the household help, giving each laundress and butler and cook a thoughtful word and a handshake. "They don't vote," he told a companion, "but it means a lot to them." His mother, that summer, was dying. She passed away in September.

For each trip, he brought along a single retainer; literally, each held his coat. In Europe, it was former Kansas congressman Bob Ellsworth. In South America, it was his mysterious Cuban-American friend Bebe Rebozo. In the Middle East, it was Buchanan. In Asia, it was a new member of the cast. Raymond Price had been head of the editorial page at the *New York Herald Tribune,* the house organ of liberal Republicanism. When his beloved newspaper closed down, he started working on a novel. Then he got the call to become Nixon's second speechwriter, the Franklin counterbalance to Pat Buchanan. In Asia, Price watched the Old Man size up the sultans and shahs and foreign ministers, gauging their sense of the Chinese and Soviet threats. Price learned something his aerie at the *Herald Tribune,* from whence he'd told America's Establishment how to think, had apparently not prepared him for: "Often, what the leaders told him in private was very different from what they were saying in public."

Together they drafted an article for the October issue of the prestigious quarterly *Foreign Affairs,* the review of the Council on Foreign Relations. "Asia After Viet Nam" was scholarly, sweeping, and high-minded, couched in the chessboard abstractions of strategic studies (the government massacre of hundreds of thousands of Communists, family members of Communists, ethnic Chinese, and alleged Communist sympathizers and their family members in Indonesia was referred to as its "turnaround" from "the Chinese orbit"). It argued for the diplomatic "long view" toward China, the nation that had descended into a sanguinary revolutionary madness, against which Nixon had spoken of in tones of Red-baiting demagoguery for decades: "We simply cannot afford to leave China forever outside the family of nations." The USSR had softened its hard line, the essay argued; so, with the proper "dynamic detoxification" and "creative counterpressure," might the Middle Kingdom.

The paper was an audition before the Franklins. But Nixon didn't neglect the Orthogonians. Another article, drafted by Pat Buchanan, came out simultaneously in *Reader's Digest* for the masses behind their white picket fences called "What Has Happened to America?" Now that Nixon's two '68 opponents, Johnson and Romney, were tangled up in a post-riot battle of legalistic recrimination, the strategic conditions were finally propitious: he introduced himself as a crusader for law and order.

"Just three years ago this nation seemed to be completing its greatest decade of racial progress," the article began. Now the country was "among the most lawless and violent in the history of free peoples." Racial animosity was only the "most visible" cause. The riots were "the most virulent symptoms to date of another, and in some ways graver, national disorder—the decline in respect for public authority and the rule of law in America. . . . The symptoms are everywhere manifest: in the public attitude toward police, in the mounting traffic in illicit drugs, in the volume of teenage-arrests, in campus disorders and the growth of white collar crime. . . . Far from becoming a great society, ours is becoming a lawless society."

The linkages were now familiar. What made it original was the deflection of the blame onto the Franklins.

"Our opinion-makers have gone too far in promoting the doctrine that when a law is broken, society, not the criminal, is to blame.

"Our teachers, preachers, and politicians have gone too far in advocating the idea that each individual should determine what laws are good and what laws are bad, and that he then should obey the law he likes and disobey the law he dislikes.

"Thus we find that many who oppose the war in Vietnam excuse or ignore or even applaud those who protest that war by disrupting parades, invading government offices, burning draft cards, blocking troop trains, or desecrating the American flag."

When George Wallace made similar points, he drawled, "It's gettin' nowadays that a policeman gets hit over the head and before they can get him to the hospital, the judge is orderin' that the man who hit him be turned out of the jailhouse and back on the street to hit somebody else." Nixon said it as a statesman: "Our judges have gone too far in weakening the peace forces as against the criminal forces."

But not *too* statesmanlike. In *Foreign Affairs,* for the Franklins, he wrote, "Dealing with Red China is something like trying to cope with the more explosive ghetto elements in our country . . . in each case dialogues have to be opened." There was no call for such "dialogue" in *Reader's Digest:* "This country cannot temporize or equivocate in this showdown with anarchy. . . . Immediate and decisive force must be the first response." Then Nixon introduced a refrain for his 1968 stump speeches: the "primary civil right" was "to be protected from domestic violence."

He had laid down his policy markers. It was time now to move on the presidential nomination machinery.

Time told Nixon they'd be publishing a cover story on him in August. They withdrew it on the judgment of editors that Nixon was still yesterday's news. A mole at *Time* passed Nixon the interview notes, so he was able to learn what others had planned to say about him without attribution—more useful than any cover of *Time*, like seeing the other fellows' poker cards. Colorado senator Peter Dominick, a Goldwaterite whose loyalty Nixon desperately wanted, was the "conservative Western GOP senator" who said, "He's the most qualified man, but can we win with a man who's lost twice?" A "high-ranking liberal Northeast Republican" (Senator Ed Brooke of Massachusetts) was blunter: if Nixon was the presidential candidate, "it wouldn't be a contest in '68—it would be a giveaway." The off-the-record opinions made the political lay of the land plain as day: Nixon couldn't bluff his way past the problem of the "loser image." (Former Eisenhower aide Bryce Harlow was the exception: he said that Nixon deserved to be rewarded for his party loyalty with the nomination. Nixon thus offered Harlow a job in his camp.)

Delegates to national conventions were chosen in several ways. Binding primaries—where rank-and-file voters chose delegates pledged to a certain candidate (or unpledged to any of them)—were operative in only a handful of states. Most delegates were chosen in party caucuses or conventions, or through a series of ballots so labyrinthine that the delegates may as well have been chosen in smoke-filled rooms. Mastering this painstaking, one-dish-at-a-time work was how F. Clifton White had won the nomination for Barry Goldwater. It required assembling file cabinets full of information—economic, ideological, familial, social, biographical—on the players in every precinct: To what clubs did Mr. X belong? To whom did he owe money? What letters to the editor had he written? And who in town might sell him out? This information was how delegate-hunters locked in adherents, then ensured their loyalty.

Goldwater had an ace in the hole in '64: the ideological loyalty of his supporters. Nixon couldn't hope for that—he couldn't compete with Reagan for conservative loyalties. He had to sate Republicans' hunger for a winner. Which meant that that other, minor exigency by which delegates got chosen—the primaries, often called "beauty pageants"—took on outsize importance. Goldwater had won but one major contested primary in 1964 and dominated the convention nonetheless. Nixon, those *Time* quotes made unblinkingly clear, had to crush the competition in the two big early pageants, in New Hampshire and Wisconsin, to kill any doubts that his loser image remained.

This task was delegated to agents like John Mitchell. In the 1950s, Mitchell had helped set up Wisconsin's new bond-offering agency. The Republican state senator who oversaw it, Jarris Leonard, was planning to run for Senate and needed Nixon. Mitchell directed Leonard to put together Nixon's organization. By the end of July, they had a full-time staff of forty-two in Wisconsin, plans for chairmen in all the Badger State's one hundred congressional districts, counties, and major towns, and the services of a top advertising agency. Wisconsin thus wired, Mitchell moved on to the next states. Others took care of the file-cabinet operation. Nixon began giving frank interviews with major papers about his plans for the campaign. Romney was, meanwhile, wounded by the riots. Then he all but finished himself off with a gaffe.

On September 4, a TV interviewer asked the Michigan governor about Vietnam: "Isn't your position a bit inconsistent with what it was, and what do you propose we do now?" The Mormon bishop, wearied by months of duck-and-weave, decided to lay it on the line:

"When I came back from Vietnam in 1965, I just had the greatest brainwashing that anybody can get when you go over to Vietnam. Not only the generals but also the diplomatic corps over there, and they do a very thorough job."

He was improvising, the way meticulous Nixon never would.

"And since returning from Vietnam I have gone into the history of Vietnam all the way back into World War II and before that, and as a result I have changed my mind in that particularly I no longer believe it was necessary for us to get involved in South Vietnam to stop aggression in Southeast Asia and to prevent Chinese Communist domination of Southeast Asia."

Any intelligent observer studying America's history in Vietnam since World War II might come to the same conclusion: the war was not doing, could not do, what the government said it was doing and could do. But that was too complex to hear. What people heard was the word *brainwashing*.

The term *brainwashing* had come into use after the Korean War to explain why some prisoners of war, supposedly insufficiently sturdy in their patriotism to resist, chose to stay behind in enemy territory and denounce the United States—what the ruthless did to the soft-minded. Neither side of the association appealed to the voters: the notion that the architects of the Vietnam War were ruthless, and the notion of a soft-minded president. Henry Bellmon knew better what to say. He had been on the same trip in 1965, and now piped up at an RNC press conference, "I believe we were fully and factually informed. There was no indication we were misled or brainwashed in any way."

As Romney attempted to "clarify," digging himself in deeper and deeper, the hometown *Detroit News* demanded he step aside so his financial backer Nelson Rockefeller could enter the race in his stead. The paper pointed out Romney had supported the war publicly for two years after his trip: "How long does a brainwashing linger?" In the next Harris poll, Romney dropped sixteen points. Nixon hadn't seen anything like it in twenty years in politics: "One moment he's the front-runner, the next he's down. Words are so very, very important."

A national brainwashing continued apace.

In March of 1967, U.S. commanders had reviewed the statistics and concluded there had been even more enemy attacks in the previous year than they'd realized. In April, General Westmoreland came to D.C. and begged for at least one hundred thousand more troops "as soon as possible"—better yet, two hundred thousand; that is, if the president wanted the war to end in two years instead of five. LBJ was skeptical: we would add troops, they would add troops; "Where does it all end?" He worried the Joint Chiefs of Staff still wouldn't be satisfied. They'd beg to bomb the locks, the dikes, mine the harbors, starve the peasants. They'd call for invasions of Laos and Cambodia. They'd ask for biological warfare, for nuclear weapons. He knew how the generals thought.

His thinking was also political. Meeting Westmoreland's request would mean calling up reserves and National Guard. Those units came from specific localities—places such as Tip O'Neill's Eighth District, where, the congressman wrote to the president July 18, protesters "were mainly from a solid middle class social and economic status and there was no evidence of youth agitators." Communities losing fathers and brothers in bulk would make the war immeasurably more unpopular. The fact that only 1.5 percent of reservists ever made it to Vietnam was part of what helped sell it as not really a war at all.

Vietnam was obviously stalemated to all but administration apologists. In late July, for the first time, a poll majority disapproved of the president's Vietnam performance. A *New York Times* front-page story based on a leak of the Westmoreland request reported that "American officers talk somberly about fighting here for decades." Houston's congressman, George H. W. Bush, a Republican ideological weather vane (he lost as a Goldwater conservative in '64, then won as a smiling centrist in '66), wrote his constituents, "I frankly am lukewarm on sending more American boys to Viet Nam. I want more involvement by Asians." Chuck Percy wondered why we had to spend "$66 million a day trying to 'save' the 16 million people of South Vietnam while leaving the plight of the 20 million urban poor in our own country unresolved." And Kentucky's Republican senator Thruston Morton, the former RNC chair, said the president had been "brainwashed by the military-industrial complex" into believing in the possibility of a military victory. He told a group of businessmen, "I am convinced that unless we gradually and, if necessary, unilaterally reduce the scope of our military involvement, we may well destroy the very society we sought to save." Businessmen were open to the argument. The fiscal year ended with the worst deficit since 1959, and a congressional committee said the administration had deliberately underestimated the cost of the war by $10 billion.

Defense Secretary McNamara wrote to the president that General Westmoreland's lust for cannon fodder "could lead to a major national disaster." McNamara had already commissioned a massive historical study by Pentagon staffers and consultants to come up with an explanation of the Vietnam mess. On the third anniversary of the Gulf of Tonkin resolution, the president announced the authorization of forty-seven thousand more soldiers and made William Westmoreland stand on his hind legs and tell the press that that was all he'd asked for. We'd rain more bombs instead. The public overwhelmingly approved of that.

On September 3, the South Vietnamese would go to the polls to elect a government for the first time since Ngo Dinh Diem won the fishy balloting of 1961, then was overthrown by the first of several military juntas. That an election was planned was *proactively* used to declare South Vietnamese democracy a reality. The vice-presidential candidate Nguyen Cao Ky had deployed the South Vietnamese air force to smuggle opium and gold; asked who his political heroes were, he replied, "I have only one—Hitler." He was running for vice president virtually unchallenged and won—and had fixed the constitution to give the real power to a military council run by the vice president. Meanwhile, back in America, that an election had just taken place was *retroactively* used to declare South Vietnamese democracy a reality.

For the achievement, 6,721 American soldiers had died in 1967. "Rising Doubt About the War," ran the cover of *Time* (accompanied by a spine-stiffening essay insisting that such doubts were no different from those in any war). *Reader's Digest*'s Vietnam was a nonstop procession of school reconstructions and orphanage visits by American doughboys; a typical story was about the beloved mess cook who caught a VC grenade while planning a Christmas feast for the local children. The magazine ran an editorial from the conservative *Indianapolis Star:* "Let us not forget the only thing the Communists are aiming at with their stand in Vietnam": a United States "under Communist influence and control."

Readers of the prestige press received a different view. Harrison Salisbury's *Behind the Lines: Hanoi, December 23, 1966–January 7, 1967* described a North Vietnam indifferent to submitting the United States to "Communist influence and control"—the country was just interested in defending their civilians from slaughter by American F-111s. *The Village of Ben Suc,* by a twenty-four-year-old Harvard graduate named Jonathan Schell, described what it looked like when American personnel "pacified" a once-prosperous South Vietnamese hamlet: first it was bombed and shelled; then a joint U.S.–South Vietnamese army assault killed forty-one people on its first day; then, the traces were bulldozed, then bombed, its farmers transferred to a barren "strategic hamlet" behind barbed wire. (*Time,* in its negative review, savaged him for not pointing this out as an act of charity.) Schell quoted the reassurance of an American commander: "What does it matter? They're all Vietnamese."

What was it all for? It was confusing, even for *Reader's Digest* readers. In the same issue as Nixon's "What Has Happened to America?" jeremiad, an article allowed, "Despite rosy progress reports from Washington, the fighting is not going too well." The next issue ran the memoir of a Vietcong defector who said that most of his colleagues *weren't* Communists. Support for the war fell from 72 to 61 percent. Over a quarter found the war, simply, "immoral." Lyndon Johnson invited a covey of Senate doves to the White House for a stag dinner. George McGovern subsequently wrote in his diary, "The President is a tortured and confused man—literally tortured by the mess he has gotten into in Vietnam."

In October the formation of an anti-antiwar group was announced by World War II hero General Omar Bradley and former senator Paul Douglas. "Voices of dissent have received attention far out of proportion to their actual numbers," they stated at the National Press Club in inaugurating their Citizens' Committee for Peace with Freedom in Vietnam. "Our objective is to make sure that the majority voice of America is heard—loud and clear—so that Peking and Hanoi will not mistake the strident voices of some dissenters for American discouragement and a weakening of will." Their members included Harry Truman and Dwight D. Eisenhower. They said they were speaking "for the great 'silent center' of American life." Douglas said he'd come up with the idea himself and emphasized, "We are not supporters of a president or of an administration."

He lied. The committee had been invented by a White House aide, John Roche, who promised in an "EYES ONLY" memo to the president, "I will leave no tracks." If press secretary George Christian was asked, Roche urged, he should say, "Up to now, everything the President knows about the committee he has read in the newspapers." The ruse succeeded. The media reported the group as spontaneous. Letters to the editor gushed, "The riffraff have held center stage long enough and their performances grow more sickeningly disgusting with each added publicity stunt. It is heartening indeed that some of our forthright and knowledgeable leaders have taken the initiative in speaking for the vast majority." One letter to *Time* was signed, "Yours in LSD—Let's Save Democracy." Maybe the letters had been manufactured at 1600 Pennsylvania Avenue. Roche had promised the president "letter-writing squads."

It hadn't been easy. Roche had been working on the project since May. Signing up the promised "Great Names" had proven backbreaking labor. An undersecretary of agriculture who visited Kansas State University to do some recruiting reported, "no one with whom I talked would admit that any significant element in the University community would support present policies." The wider public in the Sunflower State, he added, was "beginning to turn the same corner on this subject that intellectuals turned some months ago."

School was in session, and insurgent youth felt themselves a nation, instantly at home wherever they alighted—same dope, same struggle, same music. (Jimi Hendrix called it "electric church music, a new kind of Bible you carry in your heart . . . to create a buffer between young and old.") One bestseller at Ivy League bookstores, *Revolution in the Revolution?*, instructed how to organize urban guerrilla combat cells (for which activity its author, Régis Debray, was serving a thirty-year jail sentence in Bolivia). The White House considered ending student draft deferments, then demurred when presented an estimate that a quarter would simply refuse to serve. Even high school kids published "underground" newspapers—advocating the legalizing of marijuana, labeling football games Nazi Youth rallies, leading strikes over the expulsion of students who wore beards to school.

The semester coincided with the opening of a gangster picture, but a gangster picture of a new sort. The old Hollywood moguls were conservative men, kowtowing to the country's loud and well-organized moralists via a strict "production code." "One basic plot only has appeared daily in their fifteen thousand theaters," the greatest screenwriter of old Hollywood, Ben Hecht, wrote in his 1953 memoir—"the triumph of virtue and the overthrow of wickedness." Hecht was also the inventor of the gangster genre, and wrote of the frustrating constraints under which he was forced to work:

> *Two generations of Americans have been informed nightly that a woman who betrayed her husband (or a husband his wife) could never find happiness; that sex was no fun without a mother-in-law and a rubber plant around; that women who fornicated just for pleasure ended up as harlots or washerwomen; that any man who was sexually active in his youth later lost the one girl he truly loved; that a man who indulged in sharp practices to get ahead in the world ended in poverty and with even his own children turning on him; that any man who broke the laws, man's or God's, must always die, or go to jail, or become a monk, or restore the money he stole before wandering off into the desert; that anyone who didn't believe in God (and said so out loud) was set right by seeing either an angel or witnessing some feat of levitation by one of the characters; that an honest heart must always recover from a train wreck or a score of bullets and win the girl it loved; that the most potent and brilliant of villains are powerless before little children, parish priests or young virgins with large boobies; that injustice could cause a heap of trouble but it must always slink out of town in Reel Nine; that there are*

*no problems of labor, politics, domestic life or sexual abnormality but can
be solved happily by a simple Christian phrase or a fine American motto.*

Bonnie and Clyde sounded the death knell for all that.

The action opened with a close-up of the siren lips of Faye Dunaway as
the young Bonnie Parker, all flouncing sexuality, imprisoned in a respectable
Christian home. She stares languidly out her bedroom window, Rapunzel-
like, spies the radiant Clyde Barrow (Warren Beatty) stealing her mama's car.
Rather than save her family's property, she chooses to join him. He explains
that he has just got out of prison for armed robbery. He lets her stroke his gun.

The setting was 1932. But the scenarios were anachronistic—Faye in
makeup like Twiggy and a beret like a Black Panther, Warren (who, they said,
had been one of JFK's favorite actors) with a mop of Bobby Kennedy hair.
The police ride in riot tanks like the ones in Detroit and Newark. The abiding sin of the bad guys, cops, and ordinary townfolk—who in any previous
movie would have been the *good* guys—is their bourgeois inauthenticity.
When the Barrow Gang holes up at the farm of a young member's father, the
old man ends up selling out his son: not because he is a murderer, but because
his tattoo (a 1932 stand-in for long hair) makes him look like "trash." "Don't
shoot, the kids are in the cross fire," you hear at one point above the cacophony. The cops shoot anyway. The Barrow Gang would never put kids in the
cross fire. They *were* the kids.

They weren't bad folks, went the movie's moral logic, until an evil system forced them to extremity: robbing banks that repossessed farms, killing
only when the System began closing in all around them ("You oughtta be pro-
tectin' the rights of poor folks instead of chasin' after the likes of us," Clyde
tells a Texas ranger, that embodiment heretofore of everything upright and
true.) Bonnie and Clyde made those around them feel alive—all except the
squares who were chasing them, who were already more or less dead anyway,
with their sucker obsession with honest toil. Defiant indolence (Beatty's
Clyde Barrow walked with a limp from cutting off two of his own toes to
avoid a prison work detail) made Bonnie and Clyde honest in a world of lies.
They also were McLuhanite outlaws. They lived to get their pictures in the
paper. The first time it happened, in fact, it cured Clyde Barrow's unfortunate
impotence.

Clyde held up a grocery store. The grocer attacked this charmed youth
who pilfered the fruit of his honest sacrifice. Barrow replied incredulously,
"What does he have against *me*?"

Life and freedom versus living death and toil: this was the movie's struc-
turing antinomy—a generation-gap Rorschach. Everyone watching had to
choose a side: was this new immorality that Hollywood was offering actually a *higher* morality? Or just a new name for evil? "Not in a generation has
a single Hollywood movie had such a decisive and worldwide impact," the

Hollywood Reporter concluded of the furor that ensued—a public symposium over the meaning of the present.

The producers—Warren Beatty was one, and later claimed he preferred Bob Dylan for his role—let there be no mistake: forcing this debate was their intention. They advertised it with the slogan "They're young . . . they're in love . . . and they kill people." Clyde's proudly insouciant self-introduction— "We rob banks"—was a dream-factory counterpart to the words of the SNCC militant who complained about Urban League types around the time the picture opened: "We're trying to get jobs in a bank we ought to destroy."

Director Arthur Penn also broke the old production code's most ironclad rule: show all the shooting you like, but never show what happens on the receiving end. In *Bonnie and Clyde,* the bullets were shown from first to last—not least in the final shot, Bonnie and Clyde riddled from law enforcement tommy guns in a low-down and dirty ambush. The *New York Times*'s schoolmarmish film critic Bosley Crowther, aghast that "so callous and callow a film should represent [the] country in these critical times," led the party of the outraged with not one but three attacks in the Paper of Record. *Newsweek* called it "reprehensible." *Film in Review* tagged it "dementia praecox of the most pointless sort." Others recollected a generational primal scene. If "you want to see a real killer," Jimmy Breslin wrote in disgust, "then you should have been around to see Lee Harvey Oswald." Tom Wolfe compared its "pornoviolence" to the Zapruder film of JFK's assassination. Arthur Penn led his own defense by, more or less, agreeing. He boasted of the black man who emerged from a preview screening and said, "That's the way to go, baby. Those cats were all right." Pauline Kael published nine thousand words saying much the same thing: that "*Bonnie and Clyde* brings into the almost frighteningly public world of movies what people have been feeling and saying and writing about." Afraid of *Bonnie and Clyde*? Then you were afraid of the abundance of life.

New Left Notes, the theoretical journal of Students for a Democratic Society, devoted a quarter of an issue to the film's meaning for the struggle ("We are not potential Bonnies and Clydes, we are Bonnies and Clydes"). A college girl from Peoria wrote *Time:* "Sir: *Bonnie and Clyde* is not a film for adults, and I believe much of its degradation has come from that fact. Adults are used to being entertained in theaters—coming out smiling and humming the title song. . . . The reason it was so silent, so horribly silent in the theater at the end of the film was because we liked Bonnie Parker and Clyde Barrow, we identified with them, and their deaths made us realize that newspaper headlines are not so far removed from our quiet dorm rooms."

The insurgent youth nation, like any other nation, had its tensions, even civil wars. With more and more young militants subscribing to competing Marxist dogmatisms, clashes between New Left factions took on the apocalypticism of doomsday cultists. The National Mobilization Committee to End the War in Vietnam (the Mobe) was the umbrella group that tried to forge some kind of operational consensus out of the cacophony. Their meetings often ended up devolving into party-line screechings of dueling revolutionists.

This wasn't even to mention two entire, contrary, radical constituencies: politicized freaks and the nonwhite. The freaks, led by Abbie Hoffman, held the earnest dialecticians in hardly less contempt than they did men in gray flannel suits. They loved nothing more than to invade SDS strategy conclaves with whooping Marx Brothers–style disruptions (they agreed with Timothy Leary: the New Left were "young men with menopausal minds"). The minorities—they called themselves "internal colonists," or the "Third World" community—were worshipped by every self-respecting white radical as repositories of an authenticity they could only pretend to, who in turn condescended to white leftists as annoyances, pretenders, or marks for guilt-tripping entertainment.

The factions were supposed to come together Labor Day weekend in the most dramatic attempt so far to make of these strands something unified. The National Conference for a New Politics was held at Chicago's sumptuous Palmer House hotel (shared that week with a bridge tournament and a wedding reception in the Red Lacquer Ballroom). The aim was to influence the 1968 presidential election. The shimmering dream was for the thousands of delegates to emerge unified behind a radical presidential ticket of Martin Luther King and Dr. Spock. It wasn't quite to be. A fifty-member Black Caucus, which comprised only a portion of the blacks present, insisted on meeting separately, with goon squads at the door. They emerged pushing a thirteen-point manifesto to be adopted as the conference's official statement. One clause demanded the formation of "white civilizing committees" to confront "the beast-like character" of "all white communities"; another ordered condemnation of "the imperialistic Zionist war" in the Middle East. The Reverend William Sloane Coffin Jr., chaplain of Yale University, was among those who insisted the thirteen points be adopted without discussion as a gesture of interracial unity. Jewish delegates who considered the Six Day War a struggle for national survival walked out. People walked out practically hourly—some screaming of extremist hijacking, some screaming of Establishment sellout. The Black Caucus demanded 50 percent of the delegate vote. A white antiwar organizer from Cambridge said that was the least they could do in honor of "the ten thousand activists in Newark who were willing to die to change their way of life" back in July. Abbie Hoffman barreled in and tried to steal the floor. When Martin Luther King spoke, Black Power teenagers who'd been heckling him put out a box marked CONTRIBUTIONS FOR OUR BLACK BROTHERS IN PRISON and snickered openly when guilty white suckers deposited money. One delegate offered himself for endorsement for president of the United States and said the 1966 Italian art-house film *Blowup* was his platform. He was serious.

The first and last annual National Conference for a New Politics adjourned, having contributed, the *New Yorker* thought, "as much to serious national concern with the problems of war, racism, and poverty as a mean drunk to the workings of a fire brigade."

Revolution, clearly, wasn't nigh, whatever the skyrocketing box office receipts of *Bonnie and Clyde*. And yet, a parodox: the very angriness displayed at Palmer House, leaking from the newscasts on America's TV screens, only made the overthrow of decent civilization look closer than ever. No New Left factions existed in the dark imaginings of the other America, only a unified front of pinko hippies who dressed like Tarzan, smelled like Cheetah, and lay in wait like Bonnie and Clyde to swipe the fruit of honest toil.

This other America had its own leaders, more self-conscious month by month. They were, AFL-CIO president George Meany insisted, "the vast, silent majority in the nation." Al Capp, the cartoonist who'd invented L'il Abner and the Shmoo, now filled his Sunday strips with the adventures of Joanie Phoanie, a folksinger so disappointed when her last song triggered only three riots she composed another: "A Molotov cocktail or two / Will blow up the boys in blue." (The real-life folksinger and tax-resister Joan Baez demanded an apology, but Capp protested Joanie wasn't Joan Baez: "Joanie Phoanie is a repulsive, egomaniacal, un-American, non-taxpaying horror. I see no resemblance to Joan Baez whatsoever, but if Miss Baez wants to prove it, let her.") The other America's publications, such as *Reader's Digest*, published article after article on Communist atrocities ("On January 5, 1967, Vietcong terrorists shot to death the chief of a hamlet ten miles north of Saigon . . ."). Atrocities were what the enemy committed; when people said Americans did so, they were making things up. (An episode of CBS's *Mission: Impossible* laid out a possible scenario. Related the TV listings: "When a Communist film producer [J. D. Cannon] alters news films in order to depict U.S. soldiers in Viet Nam as murderers, the I.M. Force is sent on a search and destroy mission.")

The notion of the "Summer of Love" as some kind of untroubled idyll became impossible for the media to sustain: too many desperate flower children were addicted to hard drugs, turning tricks to survive. Joan Didion published an essay in the *Saturday Evening Post* about what she saw when she looked in on *Time* magazine's Man of the Year in Haight-Ashbury: catatonics who left toddler children alone to start electrical fires and scolded them only for ruining the hashish. She called her piece "Slouching toward Bethlehem," after a poem by Yeats: "The blood-dimmed tide is loosed, and everywhere / The ceremony of innocence is drowned." She didn't even note the charismatic outlaw in Haight-Ashbury that summer luring young girls into his orbit the way Clyde lured Bonnie: a songwriter by the name of Charles Manson.

The NYPD maintained a twenty-man undercover detail to help terrified parents find runaways. The *New York Times*'s J. Anthony Lukas won a Pulitzer Prize for his harrowing account of one such teenage girl. "I didn't even know there was an East Village," he quoted Irving Fitzpatrick, "the wealthy Greenwich spice importer whose daughter, Linda, was found murdered with a hippie friend in an East Village boiler room on October 8." The condensed version in the Christmas issue of America's most widely read magazine was billed as "probably the most nightmarish article the *Reader's Digest* has ever published."

"Red and white are Linda's favorite colors; she thinks they're gay," Mrs. Fitzpatrick told the reporter, showing off Linda's third-floor bedroom, while the reporter alternated images like that with ones from Linda's other world in italics: *"Linda told people she was a witch. . . . Her face would go expressionless; her eyes would get narrow, reptilian, with only the whites showing. Sort of an evil eye. The other girls would go hysterical."* "'Linda was never terribly boy crazy,' Mrs. Fitzpatrick said. 'She was very shy.'" *"'She had lots of men up there all the time,' said the desk clerk, 'anybody off the street—the dirtiest bearded hippies she could find.'"*

Linda had "dropped out," as the argot went. Her parents, in a way, had, too. The New Left called their ideology "participatory democracy." *Non*-participation—running away—was becoming more popular. "Don't vote. Don't politic. Don't petition. You can't do anything about America politically," recommended Timothy Leary, the LSD guru who coined the slogan "Turn on, tune in, drop out." World leaders would "banish war, poverty, and famine" if they tried LSD only once, Paul McCartney had said, before turning instead to Transcendental Meditation with the Maharishi Mahesh Yogi. When Bobby Kennedy spoke at a Catholic girls' college, he discovered that many favored carpet bombing of North Vietnam as the fastest way to end the war. "Don't you know what that means?" he shouted. "Don't you understand that what we are doing to the Vietnamese is not very different than what Hitler did to the Jews?" The youth's new slogan, he wrote in his book *To Seek a Newer World*, now seemed to be "'Escalation Without Participation,' or at any rate, 'Without Me.'"

This was something Richard Nixon, with his gift for looking below social surfaces to see and exploit the subterranean truths that roiled underneath, understood: the future belonged to the politician who could tap the ambivalence—the nameless dread, the urge to *make it all go away;* to make the world placid again, not a cacophonous mess.

On Vietnam, no cacophony protesters could make, nothing they could do, seemed to make any difference. Some dropped out in frustration. Those that remained, and the newest recruits, were tending to extremism. Rumors circulated among them: the United States was about to invade Hanoi, level the port at Haiphong, unleash nukes, round up dissenters in concentration camps. More alienation, more anger, yet more apocalyptic visions—never less: this was the direction of the antiwar movement now. SDS opposed further marches. "We are working to build a guerrilla force in an urban environment; we are actively organizing sedition," their national secretary alerted the *New York Times*. Marching only encouraged the delusion that anything less would work.

October 16 was declared the opening of "Stop the Draft" week. In Berkeley four thousand hotheads decided to try to close down the Oakland Induction Center. Across the street, in a three-story parking structure, a Praetorian guard of police and California highway patrolmen awaited the signal to move. They advanced in a flying wedge, with looks on their faces baby boomers had seen on dirty Japs rushing machine-gun nests in World War II pictures. The macing was indiscriminate; though also, at times, discriminate: reporters and photographers were attacked with intentional vehemence. The movement called it Bloody Tuesday. Ronald Reagan said it was "in the finest tradition of California's law enforcement agencies." A kid on the receiving end said it felt like being in *Bonnie and Clyde*.

College students went after recruiters for Dow Chemical, the manufacturer of napalm. Dow's president said they wouldn't feel a thing from it financially if they discontinued this product line, but patriotic principle was at stake: "As long as the U.S. is involved in Vietnam, we believe in fulfilling our responsibility to this national commitment of a democratic society." Announced the chairman of the board, "I am proud to do my duty." Students at Harvard considered it their duty to barricade the company's lab director inside a conference room for seven hours. In Madison a riot kept the interviewers off the campus. "Murderers," movement leaders were now intoning, "do not respond to reason." Reason was faltering across the spectrum. At Southwest Texas State College, President Johnson's alma mater, students sponsored a burn-in of antiwar literature.

At the end of Stop the Draft Week, the target was the Pentagon. The organizers, led by World War II draft resister David Dellinger, accommodated different levels of commitment. Speeches at the Lincoln Memorial, and a march across the Arlington Memorial Bridge behind a banner reading SUPPORT THE GI'S . . . BRING THEM HOME, for the likes of housewives and businessmen; a "direct action" march to the war machine's headquarters for the kids who wanted to go heavy. Che Guevara, Fidel Castro's enforcer, had just been assassinated at Yuro ravine. A picture circulated of him on his deathbed foreshortened like a Renaissance Christ: "One need only look at the face of comrade Che and the face of Lyndon Johnson to know who represents Life and who represents Death. Even the most reactionary person cannot resist the gentleness and the beauty in the face of comrade Che," wrote radical columnist Julius Lester. Some marchers honored Che with a moment of silence.

Militants moved out to the Pentagon parking lot. "Unarmed people in our lines were being bayoneted and kicked into unconsciousness, then dragged away," wrote the Washington, D.C., *Free Press*'s reporter. "We, like the Jews, had come nonresisting into this isolated house of death, and we sat in the dark, at the mercy of robots before the gas chambers waiting for the proverbial bar of soap." The even-more-militant broke for the building, hacking through the parking-lot fence with wire cutters.

Night fell; nonrevolutionaries went home; the cadres who remained camped out amid drift clouds of tear gas, breaking up protest signs for kindling. Draft cards and discharge papers fed the fire. Placards survived only if they packed the proper punch, like JOHNSON, PULL OUT—LIKE YOUR FATHER SHOULD HAVE.

Dawn broke; five thousand National Guard troops and MPs formed a line of battle: kids holding rifles fixed with bayonets, facing kids arrayed with bullhorns, helmets, and gas masks. A group of MPs pushed forward to tighten control near the steps at the north mall. They raised their rifles for the maneuver. The kids pushed back against their line, fighting them with picket-sign poles. As if they knew the MPs wouldn't fire. Or could it be that they didn't care?

They jerked an MP from the line, stole his helmet, and roughed him up. *"Hey! Hey! Viva Che! Hey! Hey! Viva Che!"*

Hippies in Halloween drag had chanted incantations to levitate the five-walled monster ten feet off its foundations, sprayed "Lace" at U.S. marshals (it "makes you want to take off your clothes, kiss people, and make love"), chanted "Beat Army" as if they were at a homecoming game, and wrote mash notes to Ho Chi Minh on the walls.

Kid with bullhorn: *"We've given enough speeches! Let's rush them!"*

Military voice, over loudspeaker: *"Your permit has expired. If you do not leave this area, you will be arrested. All demonstrators are requested to leave the area at once. This is a recorded announcement."* Six thousand extra troops from the Eighty-second Airborne were in town from Fort Bragg. Some guarded the National Archives: "They might go for the Constitution," a Pentagon official told *Newsweek*.

From the same window where he'd seen Norman Morrison immolate himself, Robert McNamara gazed down upon the scene. TV cameras doted on the not-inconsiderable number of young women, yielding the weapon of sex. Some teasingly opened soldiers' flies. Others placed flowers in the barrels of their guns. On the surface, a gesture of sweetness. Deeper down, for a soldier steeled for grim conflict, just doing his duty, the most unmanning thing imaginable: *you are slaves, and we are free.*

Marshals drew back their billy clubs. Some were ripped from their hands before they could bring them down. Laughter: *flowers are falling from the brim of your helmet!*

The peaceniks grew progressively more brazen. Giggling, some charged an unguarded door.

In the end, it all looked "futile and inconclusive to outsiders," Garry Wills of *Esquire* observed. He recorded a different conclusion among militants: they described "with undisguised enjoyment the massive retaliation into which our government had been prodded."

The president was once again sure Moscow was behind the demonstration (when the CIA reported back, "we see no significant evidence that would prove Communist control or direction," Dean Rusk insisted they "just hadn't looked hard enough"). McNamara reflected that if professionals had truly led the ragged insurrectionists, they could have shut the building down. He now thought Vietnam a colossal blunder. Dean Rusk, on the other hand, said abandoning the fight would put the U.S. mainland itself in "mortal danger."

Hip and square lived in separate mental worlds. Two contending sets of rumors circulated: that cleanup crews found "nothing but bras and panties. You never saw so many." And that two marchers had been dragged into the building and summarily executed. The next week at Indiana University, Dean Rusk was drowned out by hecklers crying "Murderer!" and "Fascist!" He begged for calm and got it, until a little old lady started whapping one of the bearded hecklers with her umbrella. A chant broke out from another quarter of the audience: "Hit him again harder! Hit him harder!"; radicalization was breaking out all over. The Pentagon, Abbie Hoffman promised in the pages of the hippie rag *The Realist,* was nothing: "Get ready for a big event at the Democratic National Convention in Chicago next August."

Meanwhile the nation's governors spent the third week of October on a cruise ship, dancing political dances, behaving the way politicians do, as if nothing had changed since the times of James Garfield.

The annual conference of the National Association of Governors was where pols let their hair down in exotic locales, gossiped, jockeyed, sized up who was who, put on a show for reporters, flaunted their privileges as men who ran the world. This year the setting was the S.S. *Independence,* steaming to the Virgin Islands. Reporters chucklingly mutinied for better access, signing a "Press Power" manifesto banning "honky" governors from the media lounge, demanding busing from the lower to upper decks. Lobster was on the menu every day.

One night state executives sashayed to the steel-band beat at a tropical-themed costume ball (though Lester Maddox limited himself the whole hot trip to a black suit and black tie). A reporter tapped the shoulder of the governor of Michigan mid-mambo with the wife of the governor of Washington. What did he make of this latest kerfuffle about the president?

(LBJ had posted a telegram to the ship, intended for his onboard assignee, a former Democratic Texas governor. An incompetent in the mailroom delivered it to a Republican governor's stateroom by mistake. It contained instructions on which arms to twist to win a resolution praising Johnson's Vietnam policy.)

Romney, dressed like Xavier Cugat and stepping lively on the floor (in his younger days he'd taken dancing lessons), said the ruse was typical Johnsonian "news manipulation," then deftly picked back up the beat. (No one feared the power of the president anymore; *Esquire* had recently run eight thousand words titled "The Dark Side of LBJ," exposing his every dirty trick, neurotic tic, and distasteful toilet habit.)

Nancy and Ronnie Reagan sipped crèmes de menthe through straws at dance floor's edge. The journos plied him, too. He returned noncommittal aw-shucks pleasantries and pulled upon his pastel drink.

(They said that Reagan might be the third full-fledged Republican presidential aspirant. On the most recent cover of *Time*, he was pictured alongside Nelson Rockefeller on an old-timey campaign poster, the sages who decided such things having declared Rocky-Reagan, or Reagan-Rocky, was the Republican dream ticket.)

Nelson Rockefeller downed seasickness pills and said that while it was flattering to be on the cover of *Time*, "I'm not a candidate, I'm not going to be a candidate, and I don't want to be president."

(No one quite believed him. Since his 1959 inauguration, the oil heir was always drafting himself for president, then ostentatiously withdrawing himself from consideration, then drafting himself back in at the last minute.)

Onboard, Rocky was seen everywhere huddling with Romney. Romney thought he'd received a pledge in blood from him that Rocky was out for good and had laid plans for an official candidacy announcement. But then, there were those polls: Rocky led LBJ by fourteen points while Nixon and Romney were ahead by only four. As the press corps had sung at the last Gridiron Dinner: "His mouth tells you no! no! But there's yes! yes! in his eyes."

(Maryland's new governor, Spiro Agnew, was running a one-man Rocky-for-President crusade. No one knew much about Agnew, except that he'd beaten a Democrat in November by running to his left on civil rights.)

Outside the reach of the steel band's strains, Nixon agents quietly prowled, urging governors to stay uncommitted. Another onboard Johnson proxy, John Connally, governor of Texas, was locked in his cabin with aides, trying to figure out the next move for the president. It turned out to be a duck-out: canceling the "spontaneous" presidential drop-in on the governors' final port of call. Johnson held terrible cards. An unprecedented movement was afoot on the left wing of the Democratic Party, led by an energetic young activist named Allard Lowenstein: "Dump Johnson"—just as Republicans used to launch movements in the fifties to "Dump Nixon." On bad days the president moaned to his aides he'd prefer to take them up on the offer.

The soul of Johnson's problem was that Richard Nixon, on the campaign trail in 1966, had been right: the Democratic Party was splitting down the middle over Vietnam.

At the board meeting in September for Americans for Democratic Action, the group that had set the agenda for the Democratic Party's liberal wing since 1947, an unthinkable debate broke out: whether to withdraw support for the greatest presidential champion of liberalism since Franklin Delano Roosevelt. One bloc said Vietnam betrayed everything ADA was supposed to stand for. Another bloc saw holding the line in Vietnam as honoring ADA's founding principle: liberal anticommunism.

This latter faction had a friend in high places: their cofounder, Hubert Humphrey, who as Minneapolis mayor marched into the 1948 Democratic National Convention and proclaimed that the party must break with segregation, risking his political future for liberal principle. Speaking to ADA in 1965, he had delivered the liberal-hawk case for Vietnam: "This is the clearest lesson of our time. From Munich until today we have learned that to yield to aggression brings only greater threats." He had repeated it again to the group's inner circle in April of 1967. Arthur Schlesinger had replied, "Hubert, that's shit and you know it." Hubert said he didn't remember Arthur saying that when he was working under JFK, when the commitment to Vietnam began.

This is what Vietnam was doing to the Democratic Party: people who agreed about 98 percent of everything else were throwing schoolyard taunts at one another.

At the ADA board meeting before the governors' conference, the youngest member, Allard Lowenstein, said that liberal principle demanded they join his Dump Johnson efforts. He was opposed by the old-guard labor leaders, who thought this was crazy talk. These men lived by negotiation, through give-and-take, storing power through patient institution-building. That was how they had *made* the world's first mass middle class—their glory, their legacy, a human accomplishment more awesome than all the Seven Wonders of the World. Johnson was their partner in the endeavor, the man to take it to the next step. And these *kids* were willing to piss it away, with their airy talk about idealism and revolt and Lyndon Johnson's "evil." Gus Tyler of the International Ladies' Garment Workers' Union said they were changing the whole point of liberal politics—"away from economics to ethics and aesthetics, to morality and culture"—and would thus throw America's poor "to the Republican wolves." Sure, LBJ was a son of a bitch. But he was *our* son of a bitch. And liberals had precious few son of a bitches to triflingly throw away.

Arthur Schlesinger and Kenneth Galbraith formulated a compromise that carried the meeting: ADA would advocate for an antiwar plank at the Democratic convention instead of the divisive distraction of taking on the power of the presidency. Lowenstein didn't sign on. He couldn't imagine how a movement of liberal ideals could countenance a colonial war. He couldn't understand how anyone saw a political future for the Democrats behind a war and a leader less popular by the day. He didn't understand how the Democrats could stake their fortunes on the *old* way of doing things— governors brokering presidential nominations on cruise ships—in a world where everything worthwhile was *new:* where all authenticity and truth concentrated on the side of idealism, of revolt, of the anticolonial—of *youth.*

He spoke for a new Democratic mood: the idea that the insurgencies of the 1960s had rendered the old rules of power obsolete. "One cannot speak of Black Power, or the riots or even Vietnam, in a departmentalized vacuum," Jack Newfield wrote. "They are all part of something larger. We have permitted political power in America to pass from the people to a technological elite. . . . Representational democracy has broken down."

People such as Lowenstein and Jack Newfield called their movement to harness insurgent idealism within the two-party system the New Politics. It was defined by disgust with the business-as-usual political dances of the old politicians in a time of moral enormity, and by the belief that organizing youthful and not-so-youthful idealists to kick that elite and their son-of-a-bitch handmaidens clean out of power was no less than a prerequisite for national survival. "If we have LBJ for another four years, there won't be much of a country left," another young New York writer, Pete Hamill, wrote in a letter to Bobby Kennedy. And the Democrats "will be a party that says to millions and millions of people that they don't count, that the decision of 2,000 hack pols does."

They ran the Dump Johnson movement on a shoestring out of a D.C. hotel room. They built organizations in Wisconsin, Minnesota, New York, New Jersey, Pennsylvania, California—states where Democratic reform clubs filled with earnest and bespectacled college professors and social welfare professionals had been fighting quixotic (and sometimes successful) battles against entrenched urban machines for decades. An ADA board member who ran a pizza parlor in Eau Claire, Wisconsin, declared himself sympathetic. But he said he'd be branded as unpatriotic in his small town if he signed up. He finally came around: "Why am I in politics if they're going to take my boys and send them off to a war I don't believe in, and I can't do anything about it?"

The foot soldiers were mostly students. They knocked on doors, armed with idealism and intellectual arguments: that a Democratic house built on a foundation of Southern whites in an age of the Voting Rights Act, by a labor movement defending the Cold War status quo, overseen by a malodorous class of D.C. power brokers, could not thrive in an America where the median age by 1970 would be 26.5. That the old order was built for a fearful era of scarcity, not this era of full employment and abundance. That the New Politics was the only way to save an idealistic but increasingly alienated generation from the violent snares of SDS-style nihilism. They canvassed, too, armed with McLuhanite assumptions: that, enmeshed in the new tactile media world, people would prefer the "new face" over the old one; the "authentic" over the plastic; the *happening* instead of the *happened.*

What they were not armed with, as 1968 approached, was a candidate.

The New Politics was flavored Kennedy. Everybody knew it. "He's a Happening" was the title of a 1966 profile of Bobby Kennedy by Andrew Kopkind, the *New Republic*'s most radical young writer. The article luxuriated over Kennedy's passion for "sudden, spontaneous, half-understood acts of calculated risk," his denouncing of "easy solutions" (even more, he "seems to dislike solutions in general"). Kennedy was always searching for new frontiers of meaning. "Where does he look? Among the grape-pickers on strike in central California, in Cloth Market Square in Cracow, on the Ole Miss campus. . . . Maybe the poor know; he studies the condition of the urban ghettos. Is it in Latin America? He'll go and see. Is it in South Africa? Get him a visa. Whatever the object of his quest, Kennedy is unlikely to find it. He is looking not for a thing, but for a happening—what is happening to politics, to people." Kennedy preferred speaking at schools rather than civic clubs. When the kids asked when he was running for president, he replied, "When you're old enough to vote for me." The rumor was that Bobby had sampled LSD. Wrote countercultural journalist Hunter S. Thompson, "There is a strange psychic connection between Bobby Kennedy's voice and the sound of the Rolling Stones."

The Happening released a book that fall, the kind that presidential aspirants put out before announcing their campaigns. The first chapter of *To Seek a Newer World* was entitled "Youth" and spoke of "the white power structure," "the Establishment," and Watts as a "revolt against official indifference." He complained we "send people to jail for the possession of marijuana" and do nothing about cigarettes, which "kill thousands of Americans each year," then launched into an indictment of the phoniness of the old men that Holden Caulfield couldn't beat, of "the terrible alienation of the best and bravest of our young" that existed "hand in hand with the deepest idealism and love of country."

This Bobby Kennedy was the New Politics made flesh.

But there was another Bobby Kennedy. Who was one of the son of a bitches.

This Bobby Kennedy was his brother's point man for the secret assassination attempts against Fidel Castro, was a staffer to Joe McCarthy, ran his brother's presidential campaign in a way that rendered *ruthless* a word that forevermore attached itself to him. Eldridge Cleaver, the Black Panther Party's eloquent minister of information, wrote of the time he met Bobby Kennedy: "I sat up close and got a good look at his mug. I had seen that face so many times before—hard, bitter, scurvy—all those things I had seen in his face on the bodies of nighttime burglars who had been in prison for at least ten years." This Bobby was at best a slightly left-of-usual practitioner of the malodorous old kind of politics, a man for the proverbial smoke-filled rooms, cutting smelly little deals about whom they'd let run the country while ghettos and peasant hamlets burned. This Bobby was visible in the Vietnam chapter of *To Seek a Newer World*—full of technicalities and legalistic half measures. Above all, this Bobby was a calculator: if he took on the president in 1968 as Allard Lowenstein was begging him to do, the tea leaves told him he might lose. This Bobby was greeted by placards at a Brooklyn College lecture in memory of JFK: BOBBY KENNEDY—HAWK, DOVE, OR CHICKEN?

The older RFK advisers—JFK White House people—were all caution, watching the polls: the same ones that showed him beating LBJ 52–32 in a head-to-head contest also showed that 50 percent more people "intensely disliked" him as they did LBJ. The advisers knew a presidential run wouldn't be New Politics hearts and flowers: it was war against the power of an entrenched Establishment that knew how to draw blood, even against the brothers of martyrs. The young staffers in his Senate office simply didn't accept the argument. They were sure that such risk was his *essence*. "Those New Frontier cats were out of the fifties," one of the young Turks told reporters. "Don't forget that JFK campaigned in '60 on Quemoy and Matsu and all that Cold War crap."

It was a Georgetown soap opera for the ages. In March 1967, as Ethel Kennedy gave birth to the couple's tenth child, a columnist at *Time* told LBJ that Bobby was all but "decided to get into the race"; then in April the magazine reported he'd submit sworn affidavits to keep his name off any primary ballot. Reports reverberated, too, across Washington of his tirades against the president: "How can we possibly survive five more years of Lyndon Johnson? Five more years of a crazy man?" Then in June he made a florid toast to the president at a New York fund-raiser, praising "the height of his aim, the breadth of his achievements, the record of his past, and the promise of his future."

Lowenstein searched desperately for a second option. All the best antiwar senators had reelection fights in 1968—some, like George McGovern, tough ones. Senator Fulbright, the dove chair of the Foreign Relations Committee, who spoke of how "the war in Vietnam is poisoning and brutalizing our domestic life," was a Southern senator who voted down the line against desegregation. Lowenstein wrote them all letters nonetheless, begging them to stand in the gap.

Only Eugene McCarthy, the diffident, difficult senator from Minnesota, expressed any interest, proposing a meeting later in the year. The prospect hardly inspired. McCarthy was an odd duck. The small-town Minnesota native who'd turned himself into an intellectual at a tiny Catholic college had once considered entering the priesthood, even a monastery. When Richard Nixon entered the House of Representatives, he started a club for freshmen Republicans—a congressional branch of the Orthogonians. He gave them the hail-fellow-well-met moniker the Chowder and Marching Club. When McCarthy pulled together a like-minded cadre of young Midwestern liberals, on the other hand, he called it the Democratic Study Group. McCarthy *liked* to study. He wrote poetry in his spare time, difficult, modern stuff, inspired by Wallace Stevens and William Carlos Williams. Not the sort you'd pick for a street fight with LBJ.

The tensions came out at the ADA board meeting on September 23. They came out, too, later that same night, at a council of war on Robert Kennedy's political future at his Virginia mansion. All the old Kennedy hands were there. The younger aides, the hotheads, were banished, their views represented by Allard Lowenstein and *Village Voice* writer Jack Newfield.

The junior senator from New York moderated languidly from the sofa, wearing a sweater and a necklace of the style referred to as "love beads," evaluating the debating points.

Schlesinger peddled his "peace plank" compromise. "You're a historian, Arthur. When was the last time millions of people rallied behind a *plank*?" Senator Love Beads mocked.

Lowenstein, sitting cross-legged in stocking feet, launched into his Dump Johnson spiel: national redemption versus national suicide. The president was *weak*, and Kennedy himself admitted he might well withdraw rather than risk a humiliating defeat. A lame duck, growing lamer by the day. And only he, Kennedy, could rescue America from this moral cretin—couldn't he *see* it?

The Kennedy of the cigar chompers replied how that would go down in the real world. "People would say that I was splitting the party out of ambition and envy. No one would believe that I was doing it out of how I feel about Vietnam and poor people."

He did, however, allow for a scenario in which he *might* do it: "I think Al is doing the right thing, but I think someone else will have to be the first."

The *first.* Coolly, calculatedly, Mr. Seek-a-Newer-World seemed to be proposing a sacrificial lamb to test out the Dump Johnson idea first with the power brokers—after which he could swoop in and cash in on the other man's risk. The idealist Lowenstein was livid: "The people who think that the future and honor of this country are at stake because of Vietnam don't give a shit what Mayor Daley and Governor Y and Chairman Z think!"

But here, precisely, was the thing. Governor Y and Chairman Z, twirling each other's wives around on the dance floor of the governors' conference Ship of Fools, for all their untoward *old*ness, happened to harbor expertise at discerning what voters wanted—had some sense of *how many* "people who think that the future and honor of this country are at stake because of Vietnam" there were. Which is to say they knew how to win elections—an achievement necessarily prior to seeking a newer world.

Here would be the New Politics' tragic flaw: everywhere it recognized only enthusiasms. It couldn't see, for instance, what Nixon did: that one wave of the political future was an ambivalent, reactionary rage.

Boston had a mayoral election that November of 1967. The liberal incumbent, Kevin White, faced a challenge from the antibusing hero of the Boston School Committee, Louise Day Hicks. "I have guarded your children well," she would say. "I will continue to defend the neighborhood school as long as I have a breath left in my body."

There were seventy thousand vacant desks in Boston's white neighborhoods. But for the city to bus them there, Hicks said, would create an "unfair advantage" for black children. A couple of years before, black parents, exploiting an open-enrollment loophole that let them choose their children's schools if they provided the transportation, had put up funds to run their own private bus service. Hicks nastily put up bureaucratic roadblocks to stop Operation Exodus. Boston's Cardinal Cushing told her he was considering joining the civil rights groups marching against her. "Your Eminence," she responded, "if you had done that, I hope you would have marched right upstairs to my office on the third floor so that I could have handed you my resignation in person." The cardinal expressed astonishment that she would resign from the school committee. She replied, "No, Your Eminence. I didn't mean from the school committee. I mean my resignation from the Catholic Church."

Hicks was helped when *Newsweek* featured her on the cover in an article that was supposed to hurt her. They described her supporters as "a comic strip gallery of tipplers and brawlers and their tinseled overdressed dolls . . . the men queued up to give Louise their best, unscrewing cigar butts from their chins to buss her noisily on the cheek, or pumping her arm as if it were a jack handle under a truck." Orthogonian-style, she featured the article in her advertisements. She came within a minuscule 12,249 votes of becoming the mayor of Boston.

George Wallace was running the same game nationally. The night of his wife's inauguration in January of 1967, his veteran speechwriter, Klansman Asa Carter, and Selma sheriff Jim Clark, had hosted a secret meeting at Woodley Country Club in Montgomery to start planning Wallace's third-party presidential run. When his wife left the capitol for the day, George would sit in the governor's chair and regale the press with a history lesson:

eleven American presidents had been elected without a popular majority, three without even a plurality. "Lincoln was a plurality winner, and I'll be a plurality winner. In a four-man race he didn't get a majority of the people's votes, but he had enough to get a majority of the electoral votes. Well, if I run, this will be at least a three-man race, and the same thing could happen." In spring he once more toured the North, winning over skeptics with his talk of "that left-winger in New Jersey who says he *longs* for—that's what he said, he *longs* for—a Vietcong victory. . . . If I were president, I would order the attorney general to institute action against those people who give aid to the enemy, including treason charges, and would put some of these people in the penitentiary"—acting for the "workin' folk fed up with bureaucrats in Washington, pointy-headed intellectuals, *swaydo*-intellectual morons tellin' 'em how to live their lives."

Then he left under armed guard, a sweaty savor of imminent violence hanging in the air.

In November he made a six-city tour of Ohio to stir up the 433,100 signatures he'd need to get on the ballot as the candidate of his own American Independent Party. Then it was off to California. To boost the interest of the press, he brought along his wife the governor, once again delicately recovering from a cancer operation. His haunts were the working-class suburbs where Reagan had done best. A country band warmed up for him with his campaign song, "Stand Up for America," replete with references to "rioting and looting and the cities being burned," and the "sovereign state with rights" that was "about to be destroyed" by the Great Society. He needed 66,059 signatures by January the first. He had 25,000 so far.

"How would you people like it if you were told you would have to bus your children out of your neighborhood?" he would bray, from behind what three British journalists described as "a curious bulletproof structure known as a 'lectern.'"

"You people work hard, you save your money, you teach your children to respect the law. Then when someone goes out and burns down half a city and murders someone, *swaydo*-intellectuals explain it away by sayin' the killer didn't get any watermelons to eat when he was ten years old. . . . The Supreme Court is fixing it so you can't do anything about people who set cities on fire."

(It sure made Nixon look respectable when he couched the same sentiments in four-syllable words.)

A memo from General Lewis B. Hershey, the administrator of the Selective Service system, recommended to the nation's 4,088 draft boards that they immediately induct draft-deferred protesters. The generation-gap comedy *The Graduate*, starring Dustin Hoffman, was an enormous hit. A single called "An Open Letter to My Teenage Son" was holding steady in the top ten in time for enjoyment during holiday family gatherings, behind

"Daydream Believer," "I Heard It Through the Grapevine," and "Incense and Peppermints," but ahead of "Please Love Me Forever" by Bobby Vinton. In the song, the father told his son that if he burned his draft card, he should also burn his birth certificate, for "from that moment on, I have no son."

Eugene McCarthy announced on November 30 that he would enter four primaries against Lyndon Johnson. "I am concerned that the administration seems to have set no limit to the price which it is willing to pay for a military victory," McCarthy said, and that one of the reasons he was throwing his hat in the ring was to salve a "sense of political helplessness": "there is growing evidence of a deepening moral crisis in America—discontent and frustration and a disposition to take extralegal if not illegal actions to manifest protest." *Time* magazine dug it: "McCarthy's candidacy will at last give legitimate dissenters a civilized political voice."

The other kind of dissenters had set upon Dean Rusk's limo when he visited New York, splattering red paint on one window and kicking in another. A cop yelled that his brother had died in Vietnam and challenged any protester to fight in an alley. Other cops shouted "Fairies!" and "Jew bastards!" and "Commies!" One said to another, "You pull these guys' pants off and they ain't got no pecker."

Cop militancy was spiraling, too.

General Westmoreland was in the United States, telling the National Press Club that "we have got our opponents almost on the ropes," that "the end begins to come into view," that there was "light at the end of the tunnel." *Time* argued victory was imminent:

November 17: "so wide-ranging is Allied surveillance . . . that few safe spots remain to the Communists in South Vietnam."

November 24: "slow but promisingly tangible progress. . . . Viet Cong recruitment, running last year at a rate of some 7,500 per month, has now dropped to 3,500."

December 8: "In recent weeks in South Viet Nam, Communist troops have been regularly beaten back, hurled from prepared positions, put to flight and slaughtered in huge numbers."

December 29: "Even by the Jovian standards of Operation Rolling Thunder, the code name for the air war against North Viet Nam, it was a spectacular performance: the most devastating six days of the air war."

January 5: "ARVN: Toward Fighting Trim."

January 12: "Administration officials, long convinced that there is no realistic hope of peace negotiations until after the 1968 elections—if then— were admitting last week that they may have been too pessimistic."

Time opined, too, on the "Real Black Power": Negroes getting elected to public office in Southern towns where only racists had served before; a Negro, Carl Stokes, elected mayor of Cleveland; a cover story celebrating the ceremony in which "Dean Rusk, Secretary of State of the U.S.... grandson of two Confederate soldiers, had given his only daughter's hand to a Negro." You could read that before ducking in to see the kindhearted integrationist allegory *Guess Who's Coming to Dinner* and dream, as the New Year began, along with Bob Hope closing his Christmas broadcast from Vietnam, "With God's help, this will be the end." A White House pollster exulted that now that the nation was finally coming around with the president on Vietnam, they could soon "shift gears to the domestic side": the Great Society would somehow live yet.

And you could even believe it.

CHAPTER ELEVEN

Fed-up-niks

W AY BACK IN FEBRUARY OF 1967, SO VERY LONG AGO, *TIME* MAGAZINE described the magic of Tet Nguyen Dan, the Vietnamese lunar New Year:

"When Ong Tao, the Spirit of the Hearth, returns home each year after his call on the Heavenly Jade Emperor, all Viet Nam takes a holiday from war and erupts in the festival of Tet to welcome the Lunar New Year. It is a time of dancing and dragon masks, of firecrackers rigged from snail shells and gunpowder, of feasting on roast pork and sugared apricots. It is also a time of homecoming." The piece went on to report that many Vietcong fighters were taking advantage of the four-day holiday truce to defect.

This year was different. While Americans read in *Time* about the light at the end of the tunnel, in Saigon women secreted guns, ammunition, land mines, and grenades in flower baskets and laundry bundles, and spies set up as taxi drivers and noodle sellers prepared to breach the U.S. embassy. They succeeded—as eighty-five thousand troops of the National Liberation Front and the North Vietnamese army overran thirty-nine of forty-four South Vietnamese provincial capitals. The Tet Offensive: the tidal wave dousing the light at the end of the tunnel.

The administration pushed back with public relations. The president told the nation the Communist charge had been a military failure. General Westmoreland said we had "the enemy on the run." Johnson's chief Vietnam ideologist, Walt Whitman Rostow, called it "the greatest blunder of Ho Chi Minh's career." "If this is a failure," Senator George Aiken averred, "I hope the Vietcong never have a major success."

The cruel futility of the war on both sides was revealed as never before. The Associated Press's Peter Arnett came across the charred remains of hundreds of bodies in the provincial capital of Ben Tre. A major explained, "It became necessary to destroy the town to save it." (It fulfilled a prophecy made seven months earlier by Senator George McGovern: "We seem bent on saving the Vietnamese from Ho Chi Minh even if we have to kill them and demolish their country to do it.") By the time the Vietcong were dislodged from their stronghold in the imperial city of Hue, out-of-control Communist cadres had massacred thousands of "class enemies," including Catholic priests burned alive and four hundred men killed while holed up in a cathedral. An AP photographer and an NBC camera crew captured a South Vietnamese police commander executing a man in civilian clothes with his hands tied behind his back. It was the kind of thing *Reader's Digest* reported only the savage enemy did. The photo ran on the front page for breakfast-time perusal in even staunchly pro-war papers. In the *New York Times* it stretched across four columns, beneath a headline reading, "Johnson Pledges Never to 'Yield.'"

He pledged never to yield as reporters questioned administration officials on rumors he was moving in tactical nuclear weapons to defend the besieged mountain base of Khe Sanh, where 543 marines were killed in seven days. CBS News's Walter Cronkite, the "Most Trusted Man in America," left his anchor desk and traveled to Saigon. He uttered an unprecedented editorial: "How could the Vietnamese Communists have mounted this offensive with such complete surprise? . . . After all, the cities were supposed to be secure. . . . To say that we are closer to victory today is to believe, in the face of the evidence, the optimists who have been wrong in the past. . . . It is increasingly clear to this reporter that the only rational way out then will be to negotiate, not as victors, but as honorable people who lived up to their pledge to defend democracy, and did the best they could. This is Walter Cronkite. Good night."

In Gallup's last pre-Tet poll the number of self-described "hawks" was 60 percent. "Doves" were 24 percent. Now it was 41 to 42. The president's approval rating was darting below 40 percent. Only 26 percent approved of how he was handling the war.

Robert F. Kennedy spoke in Chicago on February 8: "Our enemy, savagely striking at will across all of South Vietnam, has finally shattered the mask of official illusion. . . . We have sought to resolve by military might a conflict whose issue depends upon the will and conviction of the South Vietnamese people. It's like sending a lion to halt an epidemic of jungle rot." He called for peace talks to include the Vietcong. That cut off administration rhetoric, which didn't even acknowledge their existence as a legitimate political entity, at the knees. Old Kennedy friends further to the right lost hope in him altogether; Joseph Alsop fielded calls from them calling RFK a traitor. Which, to some of his left-wing devotees, only added to his glamour. Kennedy concluded by implying the president was a liar: "It is the truth that makes us free" — so did that mean he would be running for president himself?

Mayor Richard Daley was up on the dais. It was well-known that Daley thought the war was shaping up as a disaster for the Democratic Party. Would he let Bobby Kennedy say such things if he wasn't auditioning the idea of a Kennedy antiwar candidacy? Pete Hamill, a young journalist who'd given up his *New York Post* job to write a novel about Che Guevara, wrote Kennedy a letter from London: "I wanted to remind you that in Watts I didn't see pictures of Malcolm X or Ron Karenga on the walls. I saw pictures of JFK . . . if a 15-year-old kid is given a choice between Rap Brown and RFK, he *might* choose the way of sanity. . . . Give that same kid a choice between Rap Brown and LBJ, and he'll probably reach for his revolver." Older, wiser Kennedy staffers tried to keep stuff like this away from him: a messiah complex was not conducive to senatorial work. But a younger staffer, press secretary Frank Mankiewicz, slipped Hamill's letter to the boss. Kennedy kept it in his briefcase, read it over and over, and passed it to friends, puzzling out whether Tet had changed America enough to render this New Politics the wave of the future.

Some had no doubt. College students, housewives, celebrities, swarmed New Hampshire to volunteer for Eugene McCarthy. Capitol Hill staffers packed their bags to work for him with the words ringing in their ears that they'd never work in Washington again. The polls gave the aloof Minnesotan 11 percent, which seemed about right. "He seemed like a nice enough man," a Granite State matron who met him at a shopping center said—though she couldn't quite remember his name. McCarthy counted his lack of charisma as a virtue. He refused to mention he was Catholic, though New Hampshire was two-thirds Catholic. An odd duck, this politician who didn't care what others thought of him. But that was also one of his strengths. It's amazing how easily the average politician can be intimidated. Not Eugene McCarthy. In 1952 he went on national TV to debate that other McCarthy, the senator from Wisconsin, who huffed that liberals like Eugene were the reason we no longer "have" China. The dry-witted former professor fearlessly came back, "It is not our policy to 'have' people."

He hated being a senator, called the upper chamber "the last primitive society on earth." He would craft a brilliant amendment to an intricate tax bill to help the poor, then he wouldn't show up to vote for it, scoffing at colleagues who criticized him. He seemed to care more for the opinion of intellectuals, and published poetry that frankly insulted his colleagues: "Stubbornness and penicillin / hold the aged above me." However, he was like other senators in that he believed he could be president. In 1960 he complained, "I'm twice as liberal as Hubert Humphrey, and twice as intelligent as Stuart Symington, and twice as Catholic as Jack Kennedy"—so why was the speculation settling on *them*?

He made his national reputation that year with a nominating speech for Adlai Stevenson that celebrated the pure-hearted nobility of Adlai's defeats: "Do not turn away from this man. . . . Do not leave this man a prophet without honor in his own party!" It marked a certain structural weakness of liberalism: seeing honor as an end in itself. And in 1968, amid the dishonor of

Vietnam, that made the only man with the guts to take on the president seem all the more attractive to liberals. They bestowed upon him wild-eyed devotion—this man who saw an honorable speech as one without applause lines, usually concerning some obscure Roman emperor.

Still, the kids flocked to New Hampshire to work for him. It had been a risky strategy to encourage them. When many middle-aged Americans thought of antiwar youth, they pictured smelly hippies trying to levitate the Pentagon. The shrewd McCarthy manager who took charge of the college volunteers made them shave their beards and eschew miniskirts and segregated them by sex: "All we need is for the press to report that we are all sleeping together up here, and we will blow all the good we hope to achieve." On their own, the kids banned alcohol. Local staffers invited the press to one of their parties. The staffers back in D.C. were horrified at the prospect. It turned out to be the most brilliant move of the campaign. The clean-cut kids blew the likes of the *Washington Post*'s Mary McGrory away: "Where he has already been visibly and dramatically successful is in closing the gap between the generations and making good on his promise to civilize dissent."

The president's humiliations compounded. The first couple couldn't travel to college campuses and cultural functions. (Neither could the second couple. Hubert Humphrey addressed the National Book Awards ceremony, and the novelist Mitchell Goodman shouted, "We are burning children in Vietnam!") In January, Eartha Kitt attended a White House luncheon on juvenile delinquency hosted by the first lady. "They don't want to go to school because they're going to be snatched from their mothers to be shot in Vietnam," the nightclub singer and *Batman* villainess said. It made Lady Bird Johnson cry.

On January 23, North Korea captured an American spy ship, the *Pueblo*. The president was helpless to do anything about it. John Birch Society bumper stickers blossomed: REMEMBER THE PUEBLO. Then, on January 30, Tet. On February 13, the board of Americans for Democratic Action voted 65 to 47 to endorse McCarthy. (The presidents of the Steelworkers, the Communications Workers, and the International Ladies' Garment Workers' unions resigned in a huff. McCarthy didn't care. He called labor bureaucrats "old buffalos.") Walter Cronkite's broadcast detonated over the White House: "I've lost Mr. Middle America," said a president who was now sallow and gaunt, terrified he'd be hit with another heart attack or a stroke, the kind that had crippled the second term of Woodrow Wilson. Walter Lippmann wrote that the president's reelection "will not arrest but will force the disintegration of the party" and that Robert Kennedy ought not to wait until 1972, when the Democrats would be ruined by "four more years of distrust, division, and dissent."

The White House rushed a rearguard action to save face for the president in New Hampshire. It had seemed a little too desperate for a man who had won one of the greatest landslides in presidential history to interrupt his duties as Leader of the Free World to hie himself to the secretary of state's office in Manchester to register as a candidate. So he deployed New Hampshire's Democratic governor and senator to slap together a hasty Johnson write-in campaign to keep McCarthy to his predicted 11 percent.

Governor King began making absurdly high predictions: McCarthy would get 40 percent (and it would bring "dancing in the streets of Hanoi"). Senator McIntyre called McCarthy the candidate of "draft dodgers and deserters." As American bombers began raining savage reprisals on Buddhist temples in Hue, JFK's legendary speechwriter Richard Goodwin presented himself as a volunteer at McCarthy headquarters. "With these two typewriters," he told the McCarthy campaign's press secretary, an intense young Chicagoan named Seymour Hersh, "we're going to overthrow the government."

He did not say, significantly, "We're going to elect Gene McCarthy."

At that prospect, many Dump Johnson volunteers were indifferent, even hostile. Some thought Kennedy had set up McCarthy as a "stalking horse" — the steed who ran at the front of the pack to tire the competition while the favorite hung back staying fresh until it was time to make his move. Kennedy insisted he wouldn't run "under any conceivable circumstances." But he had also recruited a staffer to prepare a paper on primary entrance requirements, publicly disparaged McCarthy, and stepped up his attacks on the president: "If there is stealing in Beaumont, Texas," he said on the Senate floor March 7, after the president dismissed corruption in the Saigon government by saying there was stealing in Beaumont, too, "it is not bringing about the death of American boys."

A Kennedy-shaped ghost trailed McCarthy's every step. McCarthy's shrewd managers encouraged the apparition. One of their posters showed JFK and Gene side by side, asking, "What's happened to this country since 1963?" General MacArthur was pictured on one puffing on his corncob pipe: "Anybody who commits the land power of the United States on the continent of Asia ought to have his head examined." Another slogan flattered New Hampshirites' legendary flintiness: SHRINKING DOLLAR, GROWING WAR. Others appealed to their live-free-or-die vanity: "Independence: Ask for the Democratic ballot and vote for Senator McCarthy." A poster with Pope Paul VI—"We cry out in God's name—stop!"—was judged too hot for circulation; their method was the soft sell. None of them argued explicitly *for* McCarthy.

"Don't argue with anyone," the forty-five hundred volunteers who came the final weekend, almost one for every ten voters, were briefed. "Remind them that Vietnam is causing inflation." The *New York Times* had reported that Westmoreland was requesting 206,000 more soldiers. On primary Tuesday it snowed. Dump Johnson and Vietcong insurgents both knew that tricky weather favored insurgents.

The guerrillas gathered, hopeful, at the Sheraton-Wayfarer in Manchester to watch the returns. Precincts started reporting: 35 percent, 40 percent, 45 percent. The whooping was more intense than any political reporters had ever heard. McCarthy ended up with 42.4 percent of the vote—and twenty of twenty-four delegates. *Newsweek* called it an "astonishing political upset": "In the space of five days last week, a phenomenon that began as little more than a courageous exercise in political dissent was transformed into a convulsion that shook every corner of the American political landscape." Lyndon Johnson tried to pooh-pooh it: "New Hampshire is the only place where the candidate can claim twenty percent as a landslide, forty percent as a mandate, and sixty percent as unanimous." McCarthy's New Hampshire co–campaign manager told reporters not to be fooled: "For the first time, a large proportion of the country was capable of being convinced that the government had lied to them."

That, at least, was one interpretation. Later, two polling experts, Richard Scammon and Benjamin Wattenberg, looked more closely at the data and learned that 60 percent of the McCarthy vote came from people who thought LBJ wasn't escalating the Vietnam War *fast enough*. They weren't voting for McCarthy because he was "liberal." They pulled their lever for him, Scammon and Wattenberg convincingly argued in a book, *The Real Majority*, that came out two years later, because they were "Fed-up-niks." They saw McCarthy as an alternative to the status quo, and the status quo was a nation gone berserk.

Richard Nixon, as usual, understood the subterranean dynamics better. He won his victory in New Hampshire with 79 percent of the vote. But the tea-leaf readers barely paid attention. He was still their favorite joke.

Their second favorite joke was now Romney. He'd kept on leaping over New Hampshire snowdrifts like a guy who didn't know he was licked, when he wasn't in Wisconsin milking cows. His theory seemed to be that if he could shake every hand in the state, he couldn't lose. The futility was symbolized by a trip to a duckpin bowling alley. He rolled a solid nine on his first throw. He kept on firing until he picked up the spare—thirty-four shots later.

No such hyperactivity for Nixon. He officially announced his presidential campaign at the last moment possible, arriving in New Hampshire on February 2, the same day 150,000 letters announcing his run, prepared entirely in secret, arrived at 85 percent of New Hampshire households. The day went off with Prussian discipline. He arrived in Boston at midnight at a tiny, out-of-the-way hotel that wasn't informed it had a celebrity guest. He got a good night's sleep for his first Manchester press conference—in the afternoon, where campaign kickoffs had traditionally come early in the morning—where he laid down an anti-Rockefeller-and-Romney marker: only "the decisive winner of the primaries will and should be nominated."

He gave his opening speech in Concord in the evening, resting in between. In 1960, he'd nearly killed himself. This year, it was all about avoiding mistakes.

The message was tested using the latest survey-research techniques. Five hundred New Hampshire Republicans sat down for long tape-recorded interviews. At the headquarters in New York, the staff pored over the transcripts. It was not a pleasant project:

"He's a loser."

"Frankly, I don't think he stands much of a chance."

"He's always running for something but never getting there."

"Should be honest with himself and quit running."

Len Garment found a diamond in the rough. "He's proven he can take it," someone told the tape recorder. "He's been slapped down before and can come back." Garment underlined the sentences twice: "That's it!" Here was something they could work with. Like Churchill, like Abraham Lincoln— *Nixon's the man who came back.*

That was the message 150,000 New Hampshirites read February 2: "During fourteen years in Washington, I learned the awesome nature of the great decisions a President faces.... During the past eight years I have had a chance to reflect on the lessons of public office. . . . I believe I have found some answers." (They spent hours haggling over the verbs: *believe, hope,* or simply *have? Believe,* they decided, was the ticket: not too arrogant, not too diffident.) His campaign posters proclaimed, "You can't handshake your way out of the kind of problems we have today. You've got to think them through— and that takes a lifetime of getting ready." That made a virtue of the thing the jackals of the press might soon be hammering him for. For Richard Nixon would hardly be shaking any hands at all.

His Concord speech was all shining idealism: America was suffering a "crisis of the spirit." The president had lost the "soul of the nation." The nation needed leadership to provide "the lift of a driving dream." It was followed by a most un-Nixonian function: an open-bar reception for the press. The candidate circulated, ham-fistedly slapping backs and telling jokes, then leapt upon a chair for an informal speech. This campaign, he promised, would be the most open he'd ever run. The press corps, charmed, composed an impromptu ditty around the bar about this New Nixon—"the newest ever seen."

First thing next morning, the candidate slipped out before any reporters or handshake-hungry voters could spot him. For actually, this was to be the most *closed* campaign he'd ever run.

The idea had come of an appearance the previous autumn on Mike Douglas's afternoon chat show. As Nixon sat in the Douglas show's makeup chair, he chatted perfunctorily with a young producer about how silly it was that it took gimmicks like going on daytime talk shows to get elected in

America in 1968. The producer, a twenty-six-year-old named Roger Ailes, did not come back with the expected deferential chuckle. Instead he lectured him: if Nixon still thought talk shows were a gimmick, he'd never become president of the United States. Ailes then reeled off a litany of Nixon's TV mistakes in 1960, when Ailes had been in high school—and, before he knew it, had been whisked to New York and invited to work for the man in charge of the media team, Frank Shakespeare. Shakespeare had been a division president at CBS. There had been talk of him as the fair-haired boy who might one day replace William S. Paley, the network's president. A friend of William F. Buckley's, what he really wanted to do was destroy liberals. He would have done it for his first presidential choice, Ronald Reagan, if he hadn't finally decided that the actor was too untested.

His young confederate Ailes was a TV-producing prodigy, transforming Douglas from a local Philadelphia fixture into a national icon of square chic: "Each weekday more than 6,000,000 housewives in 171 cities set up their ironing boards in front of the TV set to watch their idol," said a feature story in *Time*. Ailes was perfect to execute the newest Nixon's new idea, the most brazen in the history of political TV. Ailes, Garment, Shakespeare, Ray Price, and a young lawyer from Nixon, Mudge, Tom Evans, met in a CBS screening room. Like football coaches, they reviewed game film: seven hours of Nixon TV appearances. As a stump speaker, the medium could make him look like an earnest, sweaty litigator. He did better on camera in informal settings, looking a questioner in the eye. They decided that this would be how they would make sure Nixon was seen—all through 1968.

But Richard Nixon had enemies. Genuinely impromptu encounters—the sort that were supposed to be the charm of New Hampshire campaigning—had a chance of turning nasty. Thus the innovation. They would film impromptu encounters. Only they would be staged.

Shakespeare brought on board a TV specialist from Bob Haldeman's old employer, J. Walter Thompson. Harry Treleaven was a TV-obsessed nerd who perennially bored people by rhapsodizing over the technical details of his craft. Militantly indifferent to ideology, his last triumph was rewiring the image of George Herbert Walker Bush, the new congressman from Houston who'd lost a Senate race as a Goldwater Republican in '64. Men-on-the-street in Houston had thought George Bush likable, though "there was a haziness about exactly where he stood politically," Treleaven wrote in a postmortem memo. Treleaven thought that was swell. "Most national issues today are so complicated, so difficult to understand," he said, that they "bore the average voter." Putting 85 percent of Bush's budget into advertising, almost two-thirds of that into TV, he set to work inventing George Bush as a casual kind of guy who walked around with his coat slung over his shoulder (he was actually an aristocrat from Connecticut). Since the polls had him behind, Treleaven also made him a "fighting underdog," "a man who's working his heart out to win." His ideology, whatever it was, wasn't mentioned.

Nixon gave this team carte blanche: "We're going to build this whole campaign around television. You fellows just tell me what you want me to do and I'll do it."

On February 3, he was slipped out a back door in Concord and spirited to tiny Hillsborough, where an audience of two dozen townsfolk hand-picked by the local Nixon committee sat waiting in a local courtroom. Outside were uniformed guards to keep out the men to whom Richard Nixon had just pledged his most open campaign ever. Lights, camera, action; citizens asked their questions; cameras captured their man's answers; then, Treleaven, Ailes, and Garment got to work chopping the best bits into TV spots. Garment, the neophyte, thought editing was neat. It reminded him of the creative flights of jazz improvisation.

The reporters threatened mutiny. Ailes offered them a compromise: from now on they'd be allowed to watch on monitors in a room nearby and interview the audience after the show. If they didn't like it, tough. A man who raged at what he could not control, Richard Nixon had found a way to be in control.

Romney's approach was rather different. He preferred naked honesty. His position paper "A New U.S. Foreign Policy for the 1970s" argued that letting small conflicts on the global periphery become referenda on American prestige could only end in disaster. His stump speech insisted that "there can't be adequate progress" on race and crime until the war was ended, that the "Johnson-Nixon policy of military escalation was self-defeating," that LBJ was "spinning a web of delusion over the events in Vietnam": "When you want to win the hearts and minds of people, you don't kill them and destroy their property. You don't use bombers and tanks and napalm to save them." Audiences proved nonresponsive—though they did cheer his call for the end of student draft deferments. Jules Witcover thought Romney's Vietnam address at Keene College in New Hampshire "one of the most straightforward speeches given by any candidate." That was the one where a student shouted out afterward, "Were you brainwashed *this* time?"

THE WAY TO STOP CRIME IS TO STOP MORAL DECAY, read Romney's billboards. Wags said it sounded like an ad for a dentist. Nixon's slogan was all studied Madison Avenue vagueness: NIXON'S THE ONE. His Vietnam talk was full of finely canted phrases signifying nothing. He would "end the war and win the peace." "The goal of our diplomacy should be to prevent future wars by strengthening the countries seeking freedom. But if war comes and they appeal to us for help, let's help them fight the war and not fight the war for them." ("There was always sustained applause," the *New York Times* observed.)

He got the world's attention when in the middle of a patriotic stem-winder in rural Hampton he said, "If in November this war is not over, I say that the American people will be justified in electing new leadership, and I pledge to you that new leadership will end the war and win the peace in the Pacific." Reporters raced for the phones: it sounded as if he was promising a plan to end the war. Democrats pressed him on the specifics of his "pledge," asked whether it was responsible to keep secret from the president any plan that could end the war. Nixon's response only proved how much more adept he was at backing out of the kind of corners that George Wilcken Romney backed himself into: "People ask me, 'What will you give North Vietnam?'" (That old Nixon trick, the unsourced question.) "Let me tell you why I won't tell you that. No one with this responsibility who is seeking office should give away his bargaining positions in advance. That's why I will not be tied to anything Johnson has said except the commitment. Under no circumstances should a man say what he will do in January. The military situation may change, and we may have to take an entirely new look."

People were trusting Nixon's answers. People still assumed Romney was Rockefeller's stalking horse—even when he dragged Rockefeller along to say he didn't want to be president. They didn't *trust* Romney—a situation not helped by the mysterious pamphlets that started circulating: "Supreme Court Declares Romney Not Qualified Under the Constitution." (Romney had been born while his parents were in Mexico.) He was even accosted by a man in Manchester who said Romney drank too much. Mystified, the Mormon replied, "I've never had a drink in my life."

The Michigander was mincemeat. His lieutenants told him he might get fewer votes than Rockefeller write-ins and gingerly suggested he quit. It was still a shock when he stepped up to the microphones on February 28 at a governors' conference in Washington and did just that. The pundits learned that few beyond their incestuous claque were entirely aware of who their anointed front-runner was. Immediately, the *Times* put the hometown boy on the front page: "Rockefeller Could Open a Campaign in 2 Weeks."

Nixon began campaigning in code against Rockefeller. "I take no pleasure, no gratification," he said, in Romney's retreat. "I admire men who get into the arena. Some of the others have not"—adding that primaries should decide the nominee, not the "kingmakers at Miami." That was code to play to conservative resentments: Phyllis Schlafly's 1964 argument in *A Choice, Not an Echo* was that liberals like Rockefeller always won Republican nominations when Wall Street kingmakers pulled strings behind the scenes.

Nixon also took a calculated risk. He was already projected to win big in New Hampshire. But now he needed a *blowout* to scare Rocky out of the race. Nixon had a nationwide radio address scheduled for March 7, the Thursday before the New Hampshire balloting. The domestic mood provided him his text. It was finally time to move all in on the subject upon which he'd heretofore been sedate: the crisis of law and order. It was time to blame it all on the liberals.

Liberals: like the blue-ribbon panel convened by New Jersey governor Richard Hughes, which released its report on the Newark riot on February 10 (that same day, department-store executives from around the country met in Cherry Hill, New Jersey, for training on how to evacuate their customers in a firebombing). The Hughes Commission noted "a pattern of police action for which there is no possible justification," that "the single continuously lawless element operating in the community is the police force itself," and that the ultimate cause of the violence was "official neglect." They concluded, "The question is whether we should resort to illusion or finally come to grips with reality."

The public was choosing illusion. Newark's police superintendent said his own investigation found no abuses; Chief Dominick Spina wondered where he could find the Hughes Commission's "kind words concerning the dedication, the courage, and the loyalty of the men in blue who worked inhuman tours of duty to help establish order in this troubled city." Mayor Addonizio responded to the report by naming a Negro to command the riot precinct; cops protested the move in an hour-long demonstration outside city hall in subzero weather. Politicians from miles around joined the chorus: Mayor Thomas G. Dunn of Elizabeth called the Hughes report "an open invitation to lawlessness." A white Newark knockabout named Anthony Imperiale gathered two hundred armed citizens for vigilante patrols of ghetto streets in cars they called "jungle cruisers."

The feds later recorded Mayor Dunn taking money from a Mafia associate. Tony Imperiale had a long criminal record. The white public accepted these malefactors as tribunes of law and order nonetheless. Both whites and blacks, Garry Wills wrote in *Esquire*, were "arming for Armageddon."

On February 8, in Orangeburg, South Carolina, black students had gathered to picket a segregated bowling alley. Police responded by firing into the crowd, killing three. At the International Association of Chiefs of Police convention, four different kinds of armored personnel carriers were on display. The army laid stockpiles of heavy weaponry in half a dozen depots to supply seven special brigade-size civil-disturbance task forces and offered weeklong riot-training sessions for police forces at a Fort Gordon staging area called Riotville. (The *New York Times* came to visit: "Mobs may flood an area with gasoline or oil and ignite it as troops advance into an area," an instructor lectured.) The White House seriously countenanced a rumor that black soldiers back from Vietnam would try to take over cities guerrilla-style. A book went on sale called *How to Defend Yourself, Your Family, and Your Home,* advertised as "guidance that you, your wife—yes, and your children—must have as the crime rate continues to soar in the Great Society jungle," as liberals transform America "into a happy hunting ground for the thief, the rapist, the drug addict, the pervert, the arsonist, the murderer for kicks, the looter." Imaginations, too, were running riot.

Or maybe they were just being realistic. On February 17, five thousand militants rallied at the Oakland Auditorium for the birthday of Black Panther founder Huey Newton, in jail for the shooting death of Oakland policeman John Frey. H. Rap Brown called Newton "our only living revolutionary in this country today. He has paid his dues. *He has paid his dues.* How many white folks did *you* kill today?" James Forman, now Panther "minister of foreign affairs," said that in the event of his own assassination, "I want thirty police stations blown up, one Southern governor, two mayors, and five hundred cops dead." In the event of Huey's, he said, "The sky is the limit."

An ancient concept from the common law was enjoying a resurgence: the *posse comitatus.* Sheriff Woods of Cook County announced plans to form a thousand-volunteer armed-and-helmeted, khaki-clad riot force to muster for the Democratic National Convention. (A Chicago circuit judge shut down the plan two weeks later, though not before Woods had fielded thousands of enthusiastic inquiries from men willing to work for free.) The Republican convention would take place at Miami Beach—located on an island that could be sealed off from marauding hordes by closing down the causeways.

A new movie, *Planet of the Apes,* imagined what life would be like if whites suddenly found themselves a subject population. It graced theaters as New Yorkers dodged rats and waded chest-deep through garbage from a wildcat sanitation workers' strike. Mayor Lindsay wanted to enlist National Guardsmen as garbagemen. Governor Rockefeller, horrified, had visions of trench warfare in the rubbish piles between the armed scabs and strikers. H. Rap Brown threw in with the mayor: "We want troops. We want to overthrow the government. We want to have rioting. We want to fight the soldiers." A sort of hippie street gang from the Lower East Side added their two cents. They called themselves Up Against the Wall Motherfuckers, after the command supposedly barked by Newark cops to Negroes under custody, transformed into a line of poetry by LeRoi Jones. They collected the nastiest Hefty bags from the rotting piles, marched them through the streets, boarded the IRT subway line, and deposited them on the gleaming marble steps of the Lincoln Center for the Performing Arts.

The hot story among the pundits was the kids and their New Politics. But Gallup released a poll on February 27: for the first time in American history, "crime and lawlessness" ranked as the most important domestic problem. Almost two-thirds said courts didn't deal harshly enough with crime. Half the women said "they'd be afraid to walk alone at night" in their neighborhood. The *Los Angeles Times* had reported before Christmas that George Wallace had less than a third of the 66,059 signatures he needed to get on the California ballot; the day after New Year's, he triumphantly turned in

100,000. He also received the endorsement of the National Fraternal Order of Police—having stamped the John Birch Society slogan "Support Your Local Police" on Alabama license plates.

The simple baseline condition of orderliness that middle-class Americans expected as their birthright was being cast adrift. America: she was starting to smell. And then came the Kerner Commission report.

Lyndon Johnson had convened a commission to study the riots when the Eighty-second Airborne was still bivouacked in Detroit. It released its findings February 29. By March 3, nine days before the New Hampshire primary, the *New York Times* released a paperback version. Johnson had wanted his commission to wax cautious concerning solutions—to take into account the limits posed by an unfriendly Congress and the constraints of a nation at war. He wanted them to blame outside agitators. He thought he had it wired: Chairman Otto Kerner, Illinois's governor, was a creature of the Daley machine. What Johnson didn't count on was Vice Chairman John Lindsay, who maneuvered himself as the Kerner Commission's de facto chairman and saw to it the report demanded $30 billion in new urban spending—the very amount Martin Luther King had announced as the goal for his upcoming Poor People's Campaign. Lindsay also, considering the draft report too cautious, had a young aide write an aggressive introduction and got the panel to adopt it almost verbatim. Its words were to become famous:

"This is our basic conclusion: Our nation is moving toward two societies, one black, one white—separate and unequal. . . .

"The vital needs of the nation must be met; hard choices must be made, and, if necessary, new taxes enacted.

"Segregation and poverty have created in the racial ghetto a destructive environment totally unknown to most white Americans.

"What white Americans have never understood—but what the Negro can never forget—is that white society is deeply implicated in the ghetto. White institutions created it, white institutions maintain it, and white society condones it."

"Johnson Unit Assails Whites in Negro Riots" was the headline in the *New York Times*. The next day on Capitol Hill, where a new civil rights bill had been sailing toward Senate passage with a bipartisan open-housing provision to cover 66 percent of all housing units, Everett Dirksen and his son-in-law Howard Baker coordinated crippling amendments to cut that protection by two-thirds. The bill might not have passed at all had not Strom Thurmond and Frank Lausche slapped on an "H. Rap Brown amendment" that made it a federal crime to travel from one state to another with the intent to start a riot—rammed through even though Vice President Humphrey, presiding in the Senate chamber, ruled the amendment procedurally out of order. Florida conservative Spesser Holland baited his fastidious colleagues: "Mr. President, it is simply amazing to me that some senators seem to be unwilling to cast a yea or nay vote on an amendment which deals with the subject of riots."

The president was aghast at the Kerner Commission report. It did the one thing he'd been so careful never to do when laying the political groundwork for his sweeping social and civil rights legislation: blame the majority, instead of appealing to their better angels. None wanted to be hectored as oppressors. They thought they had enough problems of their own.

Indeed, in a sense, they did. Life was not as easy for middle-class Americans as it had only recently been. Their purchasing power was leveling off, even dropping. Unemployment among white teenagers—prime age for throwing rocks at Martin Luther King—was now 12 percent. ("Come back when you have that draft thing out of the way," they heard at the factory gates, while richer kids had no problems getting out of their military obligations.) That the unemployment rate was 27 percent among young blacks did not change the alchemy of status anxiety: as the lot of blacks improved somewhat, the marginal privilege of possessing white skin proportionately weakened. This had political consequences, as one of Richard Nixon's new young advisers, Richard Whalen, wrote the boss in a memo: "The ordinary white American lacks the wherewithal to purchase what I call 'social insulation' . . . [like] the well-heeled liberals who, for example, zealously promote integration of the public schools while they send their own children to expensive private schools." The "blind demagogs" (*sic*) of the Kerner Commission, editorialized the *Chicago Tribune,* were "awash in tears for the poor oppressed rioters." At the expense of the people who couldn't afford private schools. At the expense of the people who paid all the taxes—and who, the Kerner Commission insisted, should have to pay more.

It was a boon season for white expressions of grievance. A correspondent with the *Milwaukee Journal* responded to an article about a white, female civil rights activist with his own explanation of why she stuck up for the colored man: "he has more sex than the poor overworked white man." In a fifteen-city poll only one-fifth of whites agreed that Negroes suffered "some" job discrimination; 40 percent thought they didn't suffer any at all. Black athletes were talking about boycotting the Olympics in Mexico City. "I'd give up my life if necessary to open a door or channel to reduce bigotry," said one of them, Tommie Smith, a star sprinter at San Jose State who wasn't able to rent an apartment in the city where he was a sports star. A white letter-writer to the *Saturday Evening Post* responded as if *he* were the victim: "We who have worked and played with our Negro companions seem to be forced into a situation of being either for the Negro or for America, but not for both."

Into this context stepped Richard Nixon. Garry Wills had written, alluding to the Kerner Commission, "many of those who have awakened to the concept of two countries are determined that their side must win in any conflict between the two." On the radio nationwide, on March 7, the Thursday before New Hampshire went to the polls, Richard Nixon cast himself as the white side's field marshal:

"We have been amply warned that we face the prospect of a war in the making in our own society. We have seen the gathering hate, we have heard the threats to burn and bomb and destroy. In Watts and Harlem and Detroit and Newark, we have had a foretaste of what the organizers of insurrection are planning for the summer ahead. . . .

"We must take the warnings to heart and prepare to meet force with force if necessary. . . .

"The riots shook the nation to a new awareness of how deep were Negro resentments, how explosive the grievances long suppressed. But that lesson has been learned." Further agitation "could engulf not only the cities, but all the racial progress made in these troubled years. . . .

"Our first commitment as a nation in this time of crisis and questioning must be a commitment to order."

That following Monday night, the day the Senate finally passed a civil rights bill with an open-housing provision, in Grosse Point, Michigan, a rich white enclave next to Detroit, Martin Luther King received the most terrifying heckling of his career. The next day, Richard Nixon received 79 percent of the New Hampshire Republican vote. Only 11 percent wrote in Rockefeller. The "Nixon can't win" trope was being extinguished—so much so that a billionaire found him worthy of an investment: two days later, from his penthouse atop Las Vegas's Desert Inn, Howard Hughes dispatched a lieutenant to see Nixon. "I feel there is a really valid possibility of a Republican victory this year," the recluse explained, "that could be realized under our sponsorship and supervision every inch of the way."

"The people of this country don't like absentee candidates," Nixon said of the New Hampshire results, then hied himself to Wisconsin, armed with a separate focus-grouped message for *its* voters, where the whole thing would repeat itself three Tuesdays later. Wisconsin was also set to become another showdown between the president and Gene McCarthy.

Then things got a little complicated—the most frenzied three weeks in American electoral history, ending in a tragedy.

The day after New Hampshire, followed by a cloud of reporters through a Senate corridor, Robert F. Kennedy blurted an admission: "I am now reassessing my position."

It made him sound like a creep: Gene McCarthy had jimmied the lock, but Bobby would snatch up the jewels. But Bobby thought McCarthy was a creep. "If someone could appeal to the generous spirit of Americans to heal the race question, this is what the campaign should be about," he had told a January background breakfast with reporters. "McCarthy is unable to tap this spirit"—after which the scribes had pleaded with Kennedy to make a public statement about his intentions. He replied, "I have told friends and supporters who are urging me to run that I would not oppose Lyndon Johnson under any foreseeable circumstances." It was only hours before the unforeseeable occurred: the Tet Offensive.

Also on the day after New Hampshire, Kennedy went to the Oval Office and insolently presented LBJ an ultimatum: name a commission, including Kennedy, to negotiate a Vietnam withdrawal plan with the enemy. Nothing could have enraged Johnson more. When he had faced that agonizing choice whether to fish or cut bait in Vietnam after November 22, 1963, he acted partly from fear of retaliation from an angry RFK for retreating from his brother's commitment. Now RFK claimed his brother never intended to escalate the war. A recurrent nightmare troubled the president's sleep: *"Chased on every side by a giant stampede . . . I was forced over the edge by rioting blacks, demonstrating students, marching welfare mothers, squawking professors. . . . Robert Kennedy had openly announced his intention to reclaim the throne in the memory of his brother . . . the American people, swayed by the magic of the name, were dancing in the streets."*

That same day, the new defense secretary, Clark Clifford, told Johnson the army was prepared to respond to summer riots. He was worried about the generals, though: "Their insensitivity to the civilian considerations has been quite manifest." The Ohio legislature had passed a bill providing a twenty-year penalty for damaging fire hydrants. New York voted in a bill outlawing the "encouraging" of violence. Minneapolis's police chief took delivery of a shipment of AR-15 semiautomatic rifles. Omaha recovered from a riot spurred by the opening convention of the state branch of George Wallace's American Independent Party.

Martin Luther King was shuttling in and out of Memphis in support of striking garbage workers. Or, as Governor Buford Ellington put it, "training three thousand people to start riots." Five hundred Tennessee citizens signed a complaint asking a U.S. district judge to suspend Governor Ellington's frightening plans for National Guard training exercises that would simulate riots in black neighborhoods. Ellington huffed in return, "When we say we are going to train the Guard to protect the lives of people and their property, there is a big hullabaloo about it" from "people who would like to see riots." A third of the *New York Times*'s dispatch on the controversy focused on one of the five hundred petitioners having been arrested for possession of marijuana.

The 1968 civil rights bill moved to the House. Minority leader Gerald Ford announced he would fight the open-housing provision. Southern governors, ignoring outright a 1967 decision of the Fifth Circuit articulating an "affirmative duty . . . to bring about an integrated, unitary school system in which there are no Negro schools and no white schools—just schools," were served a deadline by the dreaded Harold Howe II of the HEW education office: comply by September of 1969, or else. The California Democratic Council adopted a pro–Gene McCarthy resolution at their annual convention. The keynote speaker—Martin Luther King—refused to indicate a preference for McCarthy or RFK, but made it clear he opposed the incumbent: "Flame throwers in Vietnam fan the flames in our cities—I don't think the two matters can be separated."

The next morning, a Saturday, the president popped around to the Sheraton Park Hotel for a breakfast speech to the National Alliance of Businessmen that all but accused his critics of being against the troops:

"Earlier this week in the East Room of the White House, I awarded the Medal of Honor to two of our bravest fighting marines. . . .

"As your president, I want to say this to you today: We must meet our commitments in the world and in Vietnam. We shall and we are going to win.

"To meet the needs of these fighting men, we shall do whatever is required."

Pay any price. Bear any burden.

That afternoon, his nightmare came true. Robert F. Kennedy pronounced the precise same phrase his brother had in 1960 in the exact same spot: "I am announcing today my candidacy for the president of the United States." He continued, "My decision reflects no personal animosity or disrespect toward President Johnson. . . . It is now unmistakably clear that we can change these disastrous, divisive policies only by changing the men who are now making them. . . . At stake is not simply the leadership of our party or even our country—it is our right to moral leadership of this planet."

(But no disrespect intended.)

Allard Lowenstein was enraged: the great existential hero, who said he couldn't run because it would make him like an opportunist, had made his move months too late, at the moment of minimum risk—just like any other Old Politician. Among McCarthy supporters, metaphors proliferated: a dog stealing another's bone, a scrooge, a miner jumping a claim; Paul Newman said Kennedy was taking "a free ride on McCarthy's back."

Bobby was now the sun around which the rest of the political universe revolved. Reagan lovers fantasized that Richard Nixon would drop out rather than face a Kennedy-Nixon rematch. Wallaceites fantasized victory, thanks to Southerners who would sooner slit their throats than vote for the former attorney general who had invaded their states. Rockefellerites, hoping to position *their* man as the charismatic liberal in the fight, were crushed, and even the freaks dreaming of framing the Democratic convention in Chicago in August as a "Festival of Death" were bereft: "We expected concentration camps and we got Bobby Kennedy," Jerry Rubin lamented. As for Gene McCarthy, he hated Kennedy as much as Nixon and Johnson did: just like that Little Lord Fauntleroy, scooping up others' hard work as if it belonged to him by birthright.

Johnson, speaking that Monday to the National Farm Union in Minneapolis, called Vietnam War skeptics like the two fellows he was running against something close to traitors.

"Most of these people don't say, 'Cut and run.' They don't say, 'Pull out.' . . . They say that they want to do less than we are doing. But we are not doing enough to win. . . .

"We love nothing more than peace, but we hate nothing more than surrender. . . .

"So as we go back to our homes, let's go back dedicated to achieving peace in the world, trying to get a fair balance here at home, trying to make things easier and better for our children than we had them, but, above all, trying to preserve this American system, which is first in the world today.

"I want it to stay first, but it cannot be first if we pull out and tuck our tail and violate our commitments."

Stay in Vietnam or surrender "this American system." Robert F. Kennedy had once given friends three conditions under which he would run for president. One was that he would have to become convinced that LBJ was psychotic. Perhaps this was evidence of the final break.

Forty-four U.S. soldiers died in Vietnam the day of the New Hampshire primary. The next day, March 13, fifty-three; March 14, sixty-two. March 15: forty-one. The day of the president's breakfast speech and RFK's announcement: forty-eight, five of them shy of their nineteenth birthday.

Perhaps eager for good news to report, the *New York Times*'s front page related on March 17 an operation in Quang Ngai, the bloodiest of Vietnam's provinces, where forces of the newly formed Americal division killed a reported 128 enemy soldiers in a pincer action: "The operation is another American offensive to clear enemy pockets still threatening the cities. While the two companies of United States soldiers moved in on the enemy force from opposite sides, heavy artillery barrages and armed helicopters were called in to pound the North Vietnamese soldiers." The official brigade report on which the dispatch was based quoted one Lieutenant Colonel Frank Barker: "The combat assault went like clockwork. We had two entire companies on the ground in less than an hour."

Richard Goodwin quit the McCarthy campaign to join Kennedy's. Seymour Hersh, a fierce moralist, was almost ready to quit McCarthy in disgust at all the opportunism in Democratic politics and go back to his previous trade—investigative journalism.

Ferment on the Republican side. Liberal Republicans took out newspaper ads begging Nelson Rockefeller to announce. Pundits such as Walter Lippmann and James Reston said he was the GOP's only hope.

Rockefeller would have loved to be the man to destroy Richard Nixon. Maybe now he'd have the chance. He received a spontaneous delegation of

Oregonians at his Fifth Avenue town house begging him to campaign in their state's crucial May primary. The next day, at his mansion on Foxhall Road in Virginia, he entertained the pleadings of the powerful liberal Republican from Kentucky, Senator Thruston Morton. Maryland's Governor Agnew shuttled around the country promoting a Rockefeller candidacy, and was seen emerging with Lindsay, Rhode Island governor John Chafee, and South Dakota governor Nils Boe from Rockefeller headquarters. On March 19, the *Times* reported it outright: Rockefeller would be running.

He had a press conference scheduled for 2 p.m. the next day at the New York City Hilton. The freshman governor of Maryland invited the Annapolis press corps to watch the presidential candidacy announcement with him on his office TV, so they could record his delighted reaction to the eventuality he'd been working toward for months.

Agnew sat a yard from the set, the reporters in a half moon behind him.

In Manhattan, Rockefeller parted a festive crowd, signaled for the cheering to stop, and made straight for the kind of upbeat rhetoric fit to launch a presidential crusade.

Then, a sudden swerve:

"I have decided to reiterate unequivocally that I am not a candidate campaigning directly or indirectly for the presidency of the United States. . . . Quite frankly, I find it clear at this time that a considerable majority of the party's leaders wants the candidacy of former vice president Richard Nixon, and it appears equally clear that they are keenly concerned and anxious to avoid any such divisive challenge within the party as marked the 1964 campaign." He added, "We live in an age when the word of a political leader seems to invite instant and general suspicion. I ask to be spared any measure of such distrust. I mean I shall abide by what I say."

In New York, his audience moaned in disappointment. In Annapolis, reporters filed out confirmed in their sense of their governor as something of a buffoon. Rockefeller had never bothered to call his number one backer with advance word. Agnew, shutting down his Draft Rockefeller office, began thinking about whether Richard Nixon better suited him.

In Nashville, then Georgia and Alabama and Kansas, Bobby Kennedy launched his campaign tacking right, condemning those who "burn and loot." He also opened a vein of astonishing vituperation at the president of the United States. He spoke of his proposed commission to settle Vietnam: "I wanted Senator Mansfield, Senator Fulbright, and Senator Morse. . . . And the president, in his inimitable style, wanted to appoint General Westmoreland, John Wayne, and Martha Raye." He quoted Tacitus to describe Johnson's war: "They made a desert and called it peace."

But no disrespect intended.

This was supposed to be the heartland, where disloyalty to the commander in chief in wartime was tantamount to treason. But people were eating it up. They seemed to share with the tousle-haired charismatic a bracing sense of catharsis—finally free to release bottled-up anger at Vietnam. That they had struggled together to achieve belief in this war and could now finally acknowledge it was all a mistake. The sense of political momentum was overwhelming.

Kennedy called Mayor Daley three separate times to beg an endorsement. His younger brother Teddy, the senator from Massachusetts, called, too. They knew the mayor was heartsick about what the war was doing to the families of the Bungalow Belt, what it was doing to his beloved Democratic Party. But he replied that the president was unbeatable. The notion that Kennedy would have an easier time than McCarthy at pulling off party regulars receded. So now came this remarkable thing: a three-way fight for the Democratic Party nomination, with one of the candidates an incumbent president.

Deciding who would be the nominee was far from a simple matter. Only seventeen states even had primary elections. Some had filing dates that had already passed; others had loopholes that made them irrelevant as indicators of popularity. Usually presidential aspirants ended up doing battle on the same ballot and on the same hustings against each other in half a dozen states or less. New Hampshire and Wisconsin were often among them: they were early and had entrance requirements and a history behind them that made them difficult to duck. Wisconsin also required no party registration from primary voters, which could make a contest there a crucial indicator of a candidate's general-election crossover potential. Oregon and California were often showdown states, too: Oregon because of its unique requirement that every candidate named in the press as a presidential possibility was automatically on the ballot unless he filed a public affidavit avowing he would not accept the nomination if offered; California because of its size, because its delegate primary was winner-take-all, and because of its date, early in June.

But 75 percent of the delegates to the Democratic National Convention were chosen in state and district conventions and caucuses and backroom meetings populated by regular Democratic politicians, with bosses such as Mayor Daley and Indiana's Governor Roger Branigan and New Jersey's Richard Hughes first among equals. The theory was that the people would speak whether their states had primaries or not: politicians, responsible to electorates, would lean toward the popular choice as revealed in other states' primaries. But the theory had never been put to the test in a rodeo as wide open as this. Perhaps the race would be over only in late August, when the Democrats fought it out on the floor of their convention, like in 1924, when it took 103 ballots before John W. Davis won the required majority.

Bobby Kennedy toured California starting March 23. He had a hard time holding on to his cuff links. At the first rally, he was almost pulled out of a moving car by enthusiasts; in Griffith Park in Los Angeles, people scaled sixty-foot pylons to secure a view. Mexican-Americans serenaded him in San Jose; at Salinas, fans almost caved in the airport roof. Women held up their babies to him; teenagers tore after the motorcade; in Watts, where once they threw firebombs, they greeted Kennedy as a conquering hero. He said LBJ was "calling on the darker impulses of the human spirit," that "integrity, truth, honor, and all the rest seem like words to fill out speeches, rather than guiding principles." In a time of political darkness, people came to believe he could make all the hurt go away. Some senators began doing the unthinkable, like Abraham Ribicoff of Connecticut, who had been JFK's secretary of health, education, and welfare: coming out against their own party's sitting president. The *New York Times* pointed out that a poll of state Democratic chairmen still gave the president 400 more votes than the 1,312 needed to be nominated. Kennedy held fast to the notion that the regulars could not but listen to these screaming crowds, speaking the New Left's language of participatory democracy: "Why should a thousand politicians, using casual arithmetic, consult among themselves and make this choice?"

According to the Gallup poll published March 24, Kennedy was preferred to Johnson 44–41 in a head-to-head matchup; Johnson beat McCarthy 59–29. McCarthy had a chance to gain ground in Wisconsin, where Kennedy had missed the filing deadline to get on the ballot. His TV commercials—"McCarthy is *the best man* to unify our country"—were hitting a nerve. McCarthy kids were on their way to ringing nearly a million doorbells.

Which doorbells was a subject of some tension.

Gene McCarthy was not a favorite of Negro voters. At a disputatious conclave at headquarters, a senior staffer proposed skipping the ghetto: "We need those Polish votes to get Milwaukee"—who, if they saw Gene McCarthy in the ghetto, "will think he's soft on Negroes." These were fighting words to the caucus of militants who via McCarthy were giving representational democracy one last chance before taking to the streets. "White racists! White racists!" they shouted. The meeting broke up in disarray.

The acrimony was a product of higher stakes: the experts were talking about McCarthy winning Wisconsin and perhaps humiliating Johnson out of the race for good, making it a two-way fight between RFK and McCarthy. White House political aides tried to find their footing in this new political world: one where presidents had to fight for renomination, and college kids seemed as important as precinct captains. "Organize one of those electric guitar 'musical' groups to travel around to meetings," Johnson's white-haired, pipe-puffing press secretary, George Reedy, suggested. "It is not too difficult to get some kids with long hair and fancy clothes and give them a title such as 'The Black Beards' or 'The White Beards' and turn them loose. They don't have to be very good musically to get by as long as they have rhythm and make enough noise."

The commander in chief scrawled on the face of the memo, "This may deserve attention."

He sent his biggest gun to Wisconsin: Postmaster General Lawrence O'Brien, JFK's campaign manager in 1960 and LBJ's in 1964. But O'Brien phoned the boss from the barren LBJ headquarters in Milwaukee that things looked bad. James Rowe, an old FDR political aide, sent Johnson a brutally frank memo: to Americans he was now the "war candidate," and "hardly anyone today is interested in winning the war."

The hands that were reaching out for RFK: in 1964, they had been reaching out for Johnson.

He was going to lose a primary.

If he lost the Democratic nomination, became a lame duck *within his own party,* how in the world could he govern in the next nine months, let alone run a war?

The president began to look almost demented. At a March 25 speech to the AFL-CIO Building Trades Department, as North Vietnamese troops made their deepest penetration into the South so far, he cried:

"Now, the America we are building"—he paused and hit the words deliberately for emphasis—"*would—be—a—threatened—nation* if we let freedom and liberty die in Vietnam. . . .

"I sometimes wonder why we Americans enjoy punishing ourselves *so much* with our own *criticism.*

"This is a pretty good land. I am not saying you never had it so good. But that is a *fact,* isn't it?"

He pulled himself close to the podium and stared into the audience, his eyes as wide as saucers. Being president was becoming a living hell. And that was all before the second Wise Men meeting.

The bipartisan mandarinate known formally as the Senior Advisory Group began preparing that night at the Pentagon for their meetings with the president. Among them were advisers who'd steered the course of the Cold War before the Cold War had even been named. The last time the Wise Men had met, on November 2, 1967, they had told the president to stay the course. Now, the head of counterinsurgency briefed them that because Americans had killed eighty thousand enemy soldiers, Tet was a marvelous U.S. victory. UN ambassador and former Supreme Court justice Arthur Goldberg questioned the figures. Wasn't the usual ratio of casualties to deaths four to one?

The briefer acknowledged that was so.

Then, Goldberg replied, that meant some 320,000 Communists had been removed from the field of battle. But the general had just told them that the Communists had only 240,000 soldiers.

Another briefer was more forthright. He said progress on the ground in Vietnam would take five to seven more years. Clark Clifford asked him if the war could ever be won: "Not under present circumstances." Clifford asked him what he would do if he were president: "Stop the bombing and negotiate."

Which was exactly what President Johnson had been going around telling audiences he'd never do.

They greeted Johnson the next morning. "Mr. President, there has been a very significant shift in most of our positions since we last met," McGeorge Bundy began. He invoked Truman's legendary secretary of state: "Dean Acheson summed up the majority feeling when he said that we can no longer do the job we set out to do in the time we have left, and we must begin to take steps to disengage."

When Lyndon left, he raged to wise man George Ball, "Your whole group must have been brainwashed!" It was a last gasp. He was finally beginning to get the picture: he had to prepare the American people for the reality of eventual disengagement from Vietnam.

On March 27, Richard Nixon announced a national radio talk for three nights later, the Saturday before the Wisconsin balloting. He was still squirming out from under his implication that he had a plan to end the war; his speechwriters were agonizing over how they could formulate something that would say nothing but sound like a way to end the war. Nixon was still haunted by the same fear as in 1966: that his opponent Lyndon Johnson would pull a peace rabbit out of his hat. Nixon wouldn't put anything past any Democrat. "Of course they stole the election," he apprised a new aide about 1960, "and Johnson will do anything to win the next one, too." By the same token, he didn't put anything past the Eastern Establishment media. Look at the cover of the new *Esquire*—a composite photo of Nixon's face and a pair of hands applying hairspray, foundation, eye makeup, and lipstick. *Cocksuckers!*

No other Republicans were on the ballot in Wisconsin. But Reagan supporters dreaming of a write-in surprise had bought time for his TV special to run the final weekend. Johnson showed a flash of his old fire, lecturing at a March 27 bill signing for the House to "quit fiddling and piddling" on the pending civil rights bill. The magic of that spring day in 1965, when he held a joint session of Congress speechless quoting Martin Luther King— "And . . . We . . . Shall . . . Overcome!"—seemed so very long ago. "We have permitted the Stokely Carmichaels, the Rap Browns, the Martin Luther Kings to cloak themselves in an aura of respectability," a presidential assistant and family friend wrote Johnson, reviewing King's recent statements about "violating the law by obstructing the flow of traffic in Washington or stopping the operations of the government." He advised the president to speak of the civil rights hero as an enemy. The president's Gallup approval rating was 35 percent. And that was before the riot that accompanied Martin Luther King to Tennessee.

King had been reluctant to involve himself in the sanitation workers' labor grievances in Memphis. He was planning the crusade of his life, a "Poor People's Campaign" in Washington, D.C., and was frazzled beyond recognition. He'd first thought of the idea in the autumn after the agonizing 1966 Chicago campaign: a general strike of the poor in the nation's capital. "We ought to come in mule carts, in old trucks, any kind of transportation people can get their hands on. People ought to come to Washington, sit down if necessary in the middle of the street, and say, 'We are here; we are poor; we don't have any money; you have made us this way; you keep us down this way; and we've come to stay until you do something about it.'" What his movement's exertions had already won—the right to vote; the right to a lunch-counter hamburger—had long ago begun to feel to him a mockery. Americans still remained indifferent, perhaps even more than before, to the abject racialized privation in their midst. He said the Kerner report showed how "the lives, the incomes, the well-being, of poor people everywhere in America are plundered by our economic system." He now frankly called himself a socialist.

The plan, as it shaped up through early '68, was for the initial assault on D.C. to come on Eastertide: one hundred leaders lobbying for a government jobs or guaranteed income program. That failing, three thousand destitute Americans would "tent in" on the Mall. If that didn't get results, King imagined a "massive outpouring of hundreds of thousands of persons" the weekend of June 15. Civil disobedience had never been attempted on such a scale. To transform what he now called "a sick, neurotic nation" would require disruption "as dramatic, as dislocative, as attention-getting as the riots without destroying life or property." "The city will not function," he'd told reporters after his testimony to the Kerner Commission. He spoke of similar demonstrations nationwide: "We got to go for broke this time."

The notion that Martin Luther King was seeding violent insurrection became a conservative article of faith. And in Memphis, where garbage piled up in the streets, talk of anarchy was the city's daily bread.

The striking garbage workers were all Negro. Mayor Henry Loeb referred to them as "*my* Negroes." He spoke pridefully of his city's "plantation" race relations. During one of the garbagemen's first marches, conservative black ministers, the kind who'd been scorning Martin Luther King ever since Montgomery in 1956, were among those teargassed. Now they were ready to fight, begging Dr. King to come. He squeezed in an appearance March 18 between recruiting stops for the Poor People's Campaign. He was discouraged, tired, despairing, facing indifference and open avowals of violence everywhere he turned: his life's work, adding up to shambles. The thought of further riots terrified him: "They'll treat us like they did our Japanese brothers and sisters in World War II. They'll throw us into concentration camps." But the energy of this little movement in Memphis inspirited him. He decided to come to lead a mass march there ten days later, March 28.

He was an hour late to the point of disembarkation. The crowd was rest-less: the rumor was that the Memphis cops had killed a high school student. Everyone knew the police were eager to keep youngsters out of the march; a gang of young militants that went by the pacific name of the Invaders had been trying to seize control of the local movement.

The march stepped off, King in the lead, arm in arm with two other ministers.

The procession snaked from Beale Street onto Main. A commotion developed. Wooden pikes that held protest signs were being used to stave in Beale Street shop windows. Street people started looting. What had been rumor became a fact: police shot a sixteen-year-old boy, claiming he'd attacked them with a knife.

What happened next was the lead story in the next day's *New York Times*. "Dr. King was whisked away from the march. . . . He was reportedly taken to a motel and could not be reached immediately. His office in Atlanta also declined to comment. . . . The destruction that broke out at various points along the march is expected to raise more questions about Dr. King's projected crusade in Washington next week." This was all the proof some needed: the appearance of Dr. Martin Luther King brought forth riots. Or, at least, couldn't stop them.

He led another procession the next day. It was ringed this time by four thousand National Guardsmen. The garbagemen known locally on their rounds as "walking buzzards" marched wearing placards reading I AM A MAN. For each one, a helmeted guardsman stood planted a yard or so away, rifle pointed at the ready at his head.

King insisted, "We are fully determined to go to Washington. We feel it is an absolute necessity. . . . Riots are here. Riots are part of the ugly atmosphere. I cannot guarantee that riots will not take place this summer. I can only guar-antee that our demonstration will not be violent." Senator Byrd, chair of the D.C. subcommittee, called for a court order to stop him: "If this self-seeking rabble-rouser is allowed to go through with his plans here, Washington may well be treated to the same kind of violence, destruction, looting, and blood-shed." Edward Brooke, the Negro senator, agreed: "How do you avoid assembling that many people under the inflammable conditions that exist today where one little spark—some irresponsible kid—could set it off?"

As for the president, he wondered if he was equal to history's demands. He gave a speech to Philadelphia schoolchildren: "If our country is to sur-vive, Lincoln said, we must realize that 'there is no grievance that is a fit object of redress by mob law.'"

The next morning, a Saturday, Johnson announced that the next night, he'd give a national television address on Vietnam. Nixon's speechwriters sighed with relief: their candidate couldn't give *his* scheduled Vietnam speech Saturday if the president was speaking on the war the very next day.

Sunday morning Dr. King preached at National Cathedral: "I don't like to predict violence, but if nothing is done between now and June to raise ghetto hope, I feel that this summer will not only be as bad but worse than last year." Then he gave a press conference to send a chill down the president's spine: if he got no results in his Poor People's Campaign by August, he said, Democrats "will have a real awakening in Chicago"—where they would be holding their national convention to renominate Lyndon Baines Johnson. The *Chicago Tribune* editorialized that King claimed to be for nonviolence "while clandestinely conspiring with the most violent revolutionaries in the country." They quoted J. Edgar Hoover: King was "the most notorious liar in the country."

The president's speech Sunday evening started gravely, befitting the weeks of grave portents: "Today I want to speak to you of peace in Vietnam and Southeast Asia. No other question so preoccupies our people." His thrust was conciliatory: "we are prepared to move immediately to peace through negotiations," the "first steps to de-escalate the conflict." He proposed a partial bombing halt (though hemmed around with caveats). Boys wouldn't actually be brought home; instead, he said he was bringing in 13,500 more. There were things to please both hawks and doves, and a few things to anger both, too—if any, by the end, were paying much attention: the speech was ponderous, lugubrious, as if to slow the furious onrush of events.

On the radio, you could hear pages flap. On television, you could see him, around half an hour into the thing, glance over at something offscreen. He had looked to his wife.

He started talking, strangely, about himself: "Throughout my entire public career, I have followed the personal philosophy that I am a free man, an American, a public servant, and a member of my party, in that order, always and only."

He paraphrased Lincoln: "It *is* true that a house divided against itself, by the spirit of faction, of party, of region, of religion and race cannot stand."

Then:

"Accordingly, I shall not seek, and I will not accept, the nomination of my party for another term as your president."

That was the bombshell. One thousand days ago he was changing the world: passing federal aid to education, immigration reform, voting rights, Medicare. Now, he was announcing his retirement.

Wisconsin tramped to the polls. Reagan won 11 percent in write-ins. Then Nixon did what he always did in 1968 after a few weeks of intense campaigning: he rested, flying off to quiet, undeveloped Key Biscayne, Florida, where his friend Bebe Rebozo owned land. "That's how I keep up the tan," he explained to Jules Witcover. The tan he had never rested enough to achieve running against John F. Kennedy.

The Democratic vote in the Badger State was the punctuation at the end of LBJ's electoral life: 412,150 for McCarthy, 253,696 for the noncandidate LBJ, 46,507 write-ins for RFK. Antiwarriors danced in the streets. They had taken down an evil president. They were forcing him to wind down a war.

Once again, Scammon and Wattenberg later showed the numbers were not so simple. Madison, Wisconsin, the left-wing college town, had had a referendum on Election Day calling for a cease-fire in Vietnam. That got only 42 percent—thirty points less than McCarthy got. They voted, too, for McCarthy in Milwaukee—and gave their authoritarian mayor, who'd established martial law during a 1967 riot, praising his German city's "Teutonic" discipline, 84 percent. Mayor Henry Maier's opponent, a young civil rights activist and lawyer named David Walther, was despondent. He thought they'd run an outstanding campaign; they'd published forty position papers. Among the fed-up-niks, forty position papers were no match for Mayor Maier's twenty-four-hour curfew.

Chicago police began carrying a new item in their kit on April 1: chemical Mace. James Farmer of CORE said cities were "stockpiling war weapons instead of antiriot weapons" and aggressively warned cops that the rioters they'd be facing this summer had been trained in 'Nam—and they "will not just be throwing bottles and bricks." In Newark, Anthony Imperiale's jungle cruisers patrolled under the influence of rumors that Negroes were planning Easter Sunday knife attacks on white women and children ("If anyone does that around here, and I catch him, I will personally send his head home without his body," Imperiale said at a rally in Nutley). Richard Rovere of the *New Yorker* said he could "imagine the coming to power of an American de Gaulle, or even someone a lot more authoritarian than de Gaulle. . . . I can even imagine the imposition of a kind of American apartheid—at least in the North, where Negroes live in ghettos that are easily sealed off. If there should be the will to do it, it could be done, quite 'legally' and 'Constitutionally.' There are enough smart lawyers around to figure out how."

Fortunately this was only the start of April—months before riot season was predicted to begin.

CHAPTER TWELVE

The Sky's the Limit

For over a decade now, Martin Luther King had faced the risk of violent death every day of his life. The threats had now become so serious that the plane that bore him on his next trip to Memphis, a seething city rotting beneath fifty days of uncollected garbage, had to be guarded overnight. The takeoff had to be delayed an extra hour nonetheless, for one more search of the baggage compartment. More people bore a murderous hatred toward him than toward any other single American. After all, hadn't the governor of Tennessee just said he was "training three thousand people to start riots"? But this was the same man, simultaneously, toward whom more Americans bore such a love that they'd be willing to lay down their lives for him. Here was a symbol of how divided the nation had become.

King spoke often of his own death, more and more frequently as 1968 advanced. He never did so more eloquently than the night of April 3, 1968. It was a rainy night, biblically rainy. (Elsewhere in Tennessee, tornadoes caused five deaths.) Memphis's giant Masonic Temple held two thousand people waiting eagerly to hear him speak, to hear him stir them for a planned "redemption" march five days later, to hear his guidance about what to do about the city's attempt to enjoin it. But the last time he had spoken there, fourteen thousand had heard him, so it hardly seemed worth the candle this time. He hung back at the Lorraine Motel, where black celebrities stayed when they were in Memphis, and told his associate Ralph Abernathy to speak in his stead. But when Abernathy arrived at the hall, the disappointment of the crowd was too palpable for him to bear. These humble garbagemen were risking their lives for justice and had practically risked their lives in a calamitous thunderstorm to get to the Masonic Temple. Abernathy called Dr. King and begged him not to let them down, so King ventured forth into that awful black night and told the rapt audience of the time he had nearly been stabbed to death in 1958, and of the flight he had just taken from Atlanta to Memphis, and how the pilot had announced for the entire plane to hear that the reason for their delayed departure was a bomb threat against the most famous passenger.

"And then I got into Memphis," he said. "And some began to say the threats—or talk about the threats—that were out, what would happen to me from some of our sick white brothers."

(What threats? Well, for one, a black merchant later testified that he heard a white businessman bark into a phone, "Shoot the son of a bitch on the balcony," and mention $5,000.)

"Well, I don't *know* what will happen now. We've got some difficult days ahead. But it doesn't matter with me now.

"Because I've been to the mountaintop," he said, and the two thousand communicants clustered at the front of the cavernous hall began cheering, to the relief of King's associates, because the speech heretofore had not been up to his standards.

"And I don't mind," he said, as people started rising and shouting in waves, which upon their abeyance brought a quiet reflection.

"Like anybody, I would like to live a long life. Longevity has its place. But I'm not concerned about that now. I just want to do God's will."

And the energy in the room began once more to crescendo, as a great preacher led his flock to transcendence.

"And he's allowed me to go up to the mountain.

"And I've looked over, and I have s-e-e-e-e-n the promised land.

"And I may not get there with you, but I want you to know, tonight, that we as a people will get to the promised land! So I'm happy tonight! I'm not worried about *any*-thing! I'm not fearing *any* man! Mine eyes have seen the *glor*-y of the coming of the Lord."

King stumbled, spent, into Abernathy's embrace. This movement would make a way where there had been no way. They would march; they would win. The party repaired to the Lorraine Motel for the next day's work of planning, negotiating, exhorting, organizing, shuttling back and forth from each other's rooms. Here was a strange American thing: that the most distinguished Memphis hostelry for visiting Negroes—Count Basie; Martin Luther King—was a humble *motel.* But such were the wages of segregation, and so it was that, every time King wanted to go from one room to another, the most hunted man in America had to do so traversing the rain-slicked outdoor motel catwalks.

Across the street in a flophouse next to a fire station, a two-bit drifter and petty criminal named James Earl Ray thrust his .30-'06 Remington through a bathroom window. King emerged from his room for dinner, chatted up some of his associates, hangers-on, admirers, made the acquaintance of a member of the band that was to play for them that night. The shot rang out.

Martin Luther King had always been warning, as he put it at the Sherman House in Chicago in 1966, of "darker nights of social disruption" should his freedom movement's nonviolent aspirations be frustrated. He was again, as in the prediction of his own death, a prophet. Some three and a half hours later, the president read a statement carried live: "We can achieve nothing by

lawlessness and divisiveness among the American people. It is only by joining together and only by working together that we can move toward equality and fulfillment for all of our people." At a drugstore at Fourteenth and
U in the Washington, D.C., ghetto, patrons heard him over the radio.

"Honky!" shouted one man.

"He's a murderer himself," said another.

"This will mean a thousand Detroits," said a third.

Someone threw a trash can through a window. It was the opening shot of
a riot that left ten people dead, including a white man pulled from a car. The
flames came within two blocks of the White House, whose lawn became an
armed encampment. The riots broke out in city after city, catching authorities who'd been girding their loins for summer unprepared. In New York,
John Lindsay was catching a Broadway play. He rushed up to Harlem, insisting on walking the streets. Aides traveled alongside him, cringing. One
reflected on his boss's ostentatious paleness and height: "Jesus, this is just the
night for someone to take a shot at him." Another, fat and jowly, realized
with a start how much he resembled a Southern sheriff. Jostling broke out.
The mayor was rescued by the limo of Manhattan's Negro borough president. What followed was a riot by any normal reckoning. Lindsay insisted
afterward "no serious disorders have taken place." It helped his case that he
ordered Streets and Sanitation into the affected areas early enough to sell the
notion to the national press. The next month, he made the cover of *Life:* "The
Lindsay Style: Cool Mayor in a Pressure Cooker."

Seventy-five ghettos went up in flames by one count, 125 by another:
Baltimore, Cincinnati, Kansas City, Pittsburgh. Detroit—again. In Newark,
a voice crackled over the police radio: "Can we use shotguns?"

"Knock that off! Do *not* use any shotguns!"

"Some of the kids in the group have guns! They have guns!"

Rioters in Newark started 195 fires and left six hundred citizens homeless.

Violence broke out on military bases in Vietnam. Many black soldiers
refused to report for duty. On the campus of Cornell University, a black student turned to another: "We can't afford to have white friends anymore."
Even in this remote, bucolic college town, fires broke out, too. A rock was
thrown through the window of a newspaper office with a message wrapped
around it: "You are as much to blame as anyone."

In some cities, charismatic figures kept the peace. In Boston, it was the
soul singer James Brown. In Milwaukee, it was the radical priest Father
Groppi, leading the biggest civil rights march in the history of the city. (The
Milwaukee Journal ran a letter to the editor headlined, "Best Day for Teaching": "This was the first day in years that I didn't have to raise my voice to
demand attention and quietness. . . . Only the 'cream of the crop' students
were in attendance. The scum: Absent—marching with James Groppi. *Scum*

and *dumb* rhyme, don't they?") In Indianapolis, it was Bobby Kennedy, campaigning in the ghetto for the crucial May 7 Indiana primary. Kennedy, nervous, intense, established with aides that his audience had not yet heard the news. So he broke it to them, and reflected on the lust for revenge: "I can only say that I feel in my heart the same kind of feeling. . . . I had a member of my own family killed."

Indianapolis did not riot, and the legend of RFK as a pol with magic powers grew.

In Oakland, the patrolling of the Black Panthers saved the city from a riot. Then a group of them drove past some police officers who were not in a mood to thank them. The pattern would repeat itself many times in the years to come: Panthers met police, and no one would ever know which gang had fired first. Two of the fleeing Panthers, Eldridge Cleaver and eighteen-year-old Bobby Hutton, were pinned down in a basement. Dozens of police fired on the house for thirty-nine straight minutes. Cleaver announced his surrender, tossed out his shotgun, and, so they couldn't claim a concealed weapon, walked out naked. "Li'l Bobby" was too shy to follow suit. Gagging and retching from the tear gas, dropping his arms for balance after a stumble, he was turned into a block of Swiss cheese. Left-wing writers including Norman Mailer and Susan Sontag released a statement on his martyrdom: "We find little fundamental difference between the assassin's bullet which killed Dr. King and the police barrage which killed Bobby Hutton two days later . . . both were attacks aimed at destroying this nation's black leadership." Oakland's police chief saw things differently. His statement said, "This must be done if we are going to have peace in this city."

President Johnson declared April 9 a national day of mourning. Two hundred thousand bodies trooped through downtown Atlanta for King's funeral. Governor Maddox called him "an enemy of our country" and holed up in his office with 160 riot-helmeted state troopers for his protection, threatening to personally raise the capitol's flags up from half-mast.

Conservatives pronounced that Martin Luther King, with his doctrine of civil disobedience, was responsible for his own murder. Ronald Reagan said that this was just the sort of "great tragedy that began when we began compromising with law and order, and people started choosing which laws they'd break." Strom Thurmond wrote his constituents, "We are now witnessing the whirlwind sowed years ago when some preachers and teachers began telling people that each man could be his own judge in his own case."

Moderates found themselves newborn conservatives. In Maryland, lowly Spiro Agnew bounced back from his Rockefeller humiliation by calling one hundred black civic leaders to the State Office Building in Annapolis. He lectured them before a battery of TV cameras, his full detail of state troopers at the ready, the commander of the state National Guard standing attention in a jumpsuit and riding crop. The governor said he made little distinction between the ministers and Urban League officers before him (who had been working day and night to prevent rioting) and the "circuit-riding, Hanoi-visiting type of leader" and the "caterwauling, riot-inciting, burn-America-down type of leader."

Many stomped out in rage. To those who remained, Agnew concluded, "The fiction that Negroes lack any opportunity in this country is dispelled by the status of those of you in this room." The governor started counting telegrams: 1,250 in approval, 11 opposed.

The Oscars ceremony, delayed by two days for the funeral, was the same day as Agnew's jeremiad. *Bonnie and Clyde* won two statues. But *In the Heat of the Night* won Best Picture—one of not one, not two, but three Sidney Poitier hits in 1967 that cosseted white liberal audiences in the message that with enough reason and dialogue, any racial impasse could be overcome.

The *Chicago Tribune,* in an editorial the morning of the funeral, refused to acknowledge the existence of any racial impasse at all. "The murder of Dr. King was a crime and the sin of an individual," it said. "The man who committed the act must come to terms with his maker." The "rest of us" were "not contributory to this particular crime."

"Yes, this nation and people need a day of mourning," the *Trib* allowed. America should mourn, but not for King. They should mourn because "moral values are at the lowest level since the decadence of Rome...."

"Drug addiction among the youth is so widespread that we are treated to the spectacle at great universities of faculty-student committees solemnly decreeing that this is no longer a matter for correction...."

"At countless universities the doors of dormitories are open to mixed company, with no supervision.... Dress is immodest. Pornography floods the news stands and book stores. 'Free Speech' movements on campuses address themselves to four-letter words.... We are knee-deep in hippies, marijuana, LSD, and other hallucinogens. We do not need any of these: we are self-doped to the point where our standards are lost...."

"If you are black, so goes the contention, you are right, and you must be indulged in every wish. Why, sure, break the window and make off with the color TV set, the case of liquor, the beer, the dress, the coat, and the shoes. We won't shoot you. That would be 'police brutality.' ..."

"If you are white, you are wrong. Feel guilty about it. Assume the collective guilt of all your progenitors, even if neither you nor anyone you know is a descendant of slave owners. Yield the sidewalk to the migrants from the South who have descended on your cities. Honor their every want, because the 'liberals' tell you that it is your fault they have not educated themselves, developed responsibility, trained themselves to hold jobs, or are shiftless and dependent on your taxes."

Mourn, the *Chicago Tribune* was arguing, only because Martin Luther King had won.

That city where King had invested so much was hit by the worst rioting of all. It was the thirteenth anniversary of the first mayoral election of the boss who ran Chicago like a feudal lord, who had promised in the summer of 1966, in order to shut King up, the "elimination of slums by December 31, 1967." The slums still stood, and now the slums seemed determined to eliminate themselves.

Shortly before 4 p.m., the Chicago violence began. Mourners gathered in Garfield Park spilled over onto the main commercial drag of Madison Street and started with burning, window-smashing, looting. Daley went on TV at four twenty. The flames shooting down Madison Street were visible from downtown. "Stand up tonight and protect the city. . . . Let's show the United States and the world what the citizenry of Chicago is made of. . . . Violence in a free society leads to anarchy. . . . Be proud of the grateful city . . . which has given opportunity to all."

Daley tried to deflate the rumor that the violence was spreading citywide. Whites clogged Lake Shore Drive's outbound lanes. Five thousand cops mustered on twelve-hour shifts, three to a car, the vast majority deployed outside the riot zone, at Loop department stores, at City Hall, in office buildings in ghetto neighborhoods that were still peaceful—helping fuel the rumors that the rioting had spread citywide. A smaller number of cops were left to rein in the Wild West Side. The National Guard were unable to muster until midnight. They protected two thousand firemen logging new blazes an average of one every 144 seconds. One thousand sanitation workers were stoned and jeered as they attempted to clear away debris. Cops seethed under orders to use "minimal force."

Chicago cops were angry anyway. They had been angry for years. In 1960, after a corruption scandal, they had inherited a new police superintendent, Orlando W. Wilson, who was a college professor, one of the founders of the academic discipline of criminal justice. They saw him as an ivory-tower puritan, obsessed with showing arrests for the kind of "victimless" crimes— drinking, whoring, gambling—by which cops from time immemorial had padded their weekly pay envelopes by looking the other way. They hated his rigid new bureaucracy. And his new Internal Investigations Committee. They hated him for his policy of replacing retiring white commanders with Negroes (40 percent of new sergeants were black his first year); in one survey, two-thirds of Chicago cops *called* themselves racists. These cops hated him most especially for holding them back from busting "civil rights" troublemakers. During the riots in 1966, ten thousand officers working twelve-hour patrols felt as if they were hardly allowed to arrest anyone. Sixty-four quit that July alone, thirty-seven before they were eligible for pensions.

Wilson quit in 1967. His successor continued his policies. One of his first acts had been to shut down a Ku Klux Klan cell operating within the force, with its own arsenal of firearms and hand grenades. In February, special training sessions began for the upcoming Democratic National Convention. They were open to the press. Cops learned how to perform minimal-force "come alongs" and liberal-approved methods for dealing with hippies' taunts: "It is up to the officer, unless he is being physically assaulted, to avoid making a personal issue of the insult, to be firm, but yet use some degree of persuasion."

At that, a cop whispered dismissively to a reporter, "If the fight starts, don't expect it to last long. We'll win in the first round and there won't be a rematch."

The late L.A. police chief William Parker had called cops "the most downtrodden, oppressed, dislocated minority in America." The crime rate was going up five times faster than the population. Ramp up police tactics to match, though, and you got savaged for "police brutality." "The better we do our job, the more we are attacked," the executive director of the International Association of Chiefs of Police, Quinn Tamm, wrote. Cops were convinced they did a hell of a lot more than any civil rights agitators to make the ghettos livable. Ninety percent, Harvard's Seymour Martin Lipset reported in a paper called "Why Cops Hate Liberals," believed the Supreme Court protected criminals at their expense: the *Miranda* decision of 1966; *Escobedo v. Illinois* (1963), affording criminals the right to counsel in the accusatory stage; *Mallory v. United States* (1957), which forbade lengthy interrogations before arraignment. In Chicago, two-thirds of cops thought the local papers were too critical—this in a city dominated by sheets that were practically printed in blue ("Unsung Heroes Invade Terror Ranks" went one *Trib* article on the force's ominous "Red Squad"). Cops felt like scapegoats, damned if they fought crime and damned if they didn't—"singled out by virtually all of society's factions," Quinn Tamm complained.

Now in Chicago, they were risking their asses in the war zone, over ten thousand of them by midnight, told they could fire only as a last resort, to arrest only the most "serious" lawbreakers.

But every person seemed a serious lawbreaker.

When they tried to clear routes for ambulances and fire trucks, more rioters seethed forth from the alleys. "Arresting them doesn't seem to help because they don't care," one cop later testified, endorsing the emotional satisfaction of a swift knock on the head. "It's been my experience that they beat me out of court back onto the street." Stokely Carmichael had gone on the radio after the assassination: "White America has declared war on black people. . . . Go home and get your guns." Chicago's West Side ghetto was in rubble, and by the time the mayor inspected the wreckage at 2:30 a.m., nine people had died.

The president accepted Governor Kerner's representations that Chicago was in insurrection and sent out regular army troops. The *Trib* proactively laid the blame for future carnage at Mayor Daley's feet: he had "conceded . . .

that the city not only underreacted at the outset of the crisis but that it did not move with sufficient speed. . . . The rioters here have taken advantage of the wave of sentimentality and assumed guilt that has swept the country. . . . We hope Mayor Daley will not fall into the same category as spineless and indecisive mayors who muffed early riot control." The *Trib* also weighed in with a theory: that a King memorial set that day for Grant Park, across the street from the Michigan Avenue hotels that would serve as hosts for the conventioneers in August, would be the point of embarkation for a second, downtown riot, instigated by the same New Left radicals who were "working for Communist North Vietnam planning to disrupt the Democratic convention."

At that, Mayor Daley's heart had to skip several beats. Daley had everything staked on that convention.

Mayor Richard J. Daley, a master of public finance, had built up "the City That Works" like no mayor anywhere else: great modern towers of glass and steel on every downtown block, a mighty Civic Center by Mies van der Rohe with Pablo Picasso's only example of public sculpture out front, a new South Side campus for the University of Illinois. But the city had hosted only one major party convention since Daley's 1955 election, after hosting twenty-three of fifty-six in history, both parties' in 1952. It was a little embarrassing.

He had given the Democrats' site-selection committee the hard sell: Chicago was "the greatest convention city in the world." A Chicago convention guaranteed Illinois's twenty-six electoral votes in the general election. He even sold its "good time zone for viewing on TV." What he sold most of all was *control*—including five thousand extra cops so that "no thousands will come to our city and take over our streets, our city, our convention." "If it requires seven thousand or twenty thousand more—whatever necessary—I back your statement to the hilt," council speaker Tom Keane added.

Daley promised political control, too. When Gene McCarthy came to the January DNC meeting in Chicago, the mayor's gift to his president was to keep the Minnesotan off the speaker's rostrum. He also promised the president, sotto voce, Kennedy-control. Daley, too, thought Bobby a pissy little snot, which may have been the clincher: the Democrats chose Chicago. Daley was overjoyed. But now his dream convention was threatened by the specter of anarchy in the streets. He couldn't risk further riots, whatever the fine sensibilities of his police superintendent.

At his press conference on April 15, Daley said, "I have conferred with the superintendent of police this morning and I gave him the following instructions, which I thought were his instructions the night of the fifth that were not carried out.

"I said to him very emphatically and very definitely that an order be issued by him immediately to shoot to kill any arsonist or anyone with a

Molotov cocktail in his hand, because they're potential murderers, and shoot to maim or cripple anyone looting."

And children? someone asked.

"You wouldn't want to shoot them," Daley allowed, "but with Mace you could detain youngsters."

He wondered why he had to go into all this. "I assumed any superintendent would issue instructions to shoot arsonists on sight and to maim the looters, but I found out this morning this wasn't so and therefore gave him specific instructions." He added, "If anyone doesn't think this is a conspiracy, I can't understand."

Attorney General Clark called Daley's words "dangerous escalation" and, when he saw him face-to-face, said, "That's murder, and if you're not indicted in Cook County, we'll indict you for civil rights violations." Other people thought Daley's words were just what the doctor ordered. He got mail from all fifty states. It ran fifteen to one in his favor.

He was legally in the wrong (Illinois General Order 67–14 prohibited such "deadly force") and backed off the next day: "There was no shoot-to-kill order. That was a fabrication." But those who needed to get the message got the message.

Police were buzzing with word of what the hippies had planned for their city in August. Some kid out of New York, Abbie Hoffman, wrote in the *Village Voice,* "We can force Johnson to bring the 82nd Airborne and 100,000 more troops to Chicago next August." The FBI told the Chicago police's Red Squad, "The New Left wants publicity and will go to any length to get it. They want to discredit law enforcement and have demonstrated ability."

And wouldn't you know it, the brats had a warm-up scheduled, an April 27 "nonviolent peace march" to City Hall Plaza. The Park District announced it was their policy "to keep unpatriotic groups and race agitators" from using the plaza. Streets and Sanitation, which controlled parade permits, said it couldn't issue one because a Loyalty Day march was already scheduled. The Public Building Commission said Civic Center Plaza—later renamed Daley Plaza—was off-limits because a corner of it was being repaired.

A lawsuit forced a compromise: a rally in Grant Park, a march on the sidewalk, dispersal after circumnavigating Civic Center Plaza. It was then that a couple of protesters ducked the construction rope. Police official James Rochford, who would be commanding the field operations for convention week, ordered the marchers to disperse.

It was as if he'd issued a signal.

Five hundred riot-helmeted cops erupted forth, billy clubs flailing. Some removed their badges and nameplates. There was no route for marchers to disperse along if they wanted to. A University of Chicago junior professor, a protest veteran of these sorts of things, told his comrades to come with coats stuffed with newspaper and Vaseline on their faces to dilute the tear-gas sting. That didn't help with the blows. "I never saw so much blood in my life," he recalled. Chicago's constabulary had laid down their marker: *if the fight starts, don't expect it to last long.*

At Nixon's new headquarters in New York in the former American Bible Society building on Madison Avenue—where he had not been allowed to use the office originally prepared for him after the Secret Service found a clean rifle shot from a building across the street—they had debated what he should do about the funeral of Martin Luther King. Garment and Safire said he had to go; John Mitchell, saying it would make Nixon look like "a prisoner of the moment," gave his judgment a patina of righteousness: "There can't be any grandstanding." The boss, recalling how Kennedy had won a critical edge on campaign eve in 1960 by supporting King when he was in jail, recalling, too, his ongoing negotiations for the loyalty of the Pope of Southern Republicans, Strom Thurmond, ended up playing it down the middle: he traveled to Atlanta to pay his respects to the family, but when the funeral procession made its way down the street, he was nowhere to be seen.

The president beseeched the House to bring the civil rights bill to a vote "at the earliest possible moment." He signed the 1968 Civil Rights Act on April 11. The reason for its sudden passage was not entirely altruistic: in addition to its limited open-housing provision, it made conspiring to cause a riot a federal crime. "We've got a civil rights act!" Nixon exclaimed when he heard the news, delighted to have a contentious issue removed from the presidential campaign.

In New York, up near Harlem, radical students at Columbia University were protesting the participation of their university in defense research and its plans to build a gym that would extend the school's footprint into the surrounding black community. SDS leader Mark Rudd commandeered the microphone at an MLK memorial service to announce, "Columbia's administration is morally corrupt, unjust, and indulges in racist policies." Afterward, Rudd posted an open letter to the university president: "If we win, we will take control of your world, your corporation, your university and attempt to mold a world in which we and other people can live as human beings. Your power is directly threatened, since we will have to destroy that power before we take over. . . . And we will fight you about the type of mis-education you are trying to channel us through. We will destroy at times, even violently, in order to end your power and your system. . . .

"Up against the wall, motherfucker, this is a stick-up. Yours for freedom, Mark."

They called the students who opposed them "conservatives," and some of them were. But often they were simply short-haired strivers who resented the way the radicals arrogated to themselves the right to control the education their parents had worked so hard to obtain: "Staten Island versus Scarsdale," some described the standoff; "jocks versus pukes," to use the two sides' denigrations of the other. On April 23 the two sides met, the pukes for a demonstration to call their administrators "war criminals," the jocks to interpose themselves against a rumored student strike. The radicals fought through their cordon to take a dean hostage in his office in Hamilton Hall. ("Now we've got the Man where we want him. He can't leave unless he gives in to some of our demands.") Then they broke into the stately administration building, Low Library, with a wooden plank. Nothing this violent had ever remotely occurred in a political protest at an American university.

Militants among Columbia's eighty or so black students, and some Harlem Black Power activists, kicked out the white occupiers of Hamilton and demanded the building for themselves. By the time of the Columbia strike, the deference a white radical owed to a black radical was nearly infinite. Huey Newton was in jail. The story of him bleeding and limping into the hospital after shooting two policemen, then a patrolman torturing him in the treatment room until he blacked out from the pain, had taken on the status of radical liturgy, the photo of him splayed out like Che Guevara on his deathbed, the policeman hulking over him, a New Left pietà. Eldridge Cleaver built his legend into a cult—posing a picture of Huey sitting regally in a giant wicker chair, machine gun at his left hand, tribal spear at his right, that graced every radical's dorm-room wall. Fund-raising letters signed by Hollywood celebrities spoke of him as a jailhouse messiah: "His love for people is so strong that it is impossible not to feel it when in his presence." Radicals wore pins reading FREE HUEY and THE SKY'S THE LIMIT and talked about scheduling the revolution for the day Huey left prison to lead them. The whites were glad to give Hamilton Hall up to brave black militants, who as a bonus provided a tactical coup in their dealings with the administration: it exaggerated their operational unity with Harlem-based radicals such as Rap Brown, who could presumably call in the hordes at the snap of his dusky fingers.

Night became day. A group of visiting radicals took over Mathematics. At Low, students ransacked files, desecrated furniture, consecrated the walls with Che and Mao and Malcolm X slogans, breached Grayson Kirk's office and drank his sherry, smoked his cigars, kicked back at his desk, inspected his library. They found hidden away a book on masochism—a perfect index of the corrosive hypocrisy of the Establishment!

His masochism flattered their narcissism. A campus minister flattered their narcissism, too. He married a couple by candlelight in occupied Fayerweather Hall, pronouncing them "Children of the New Age." Though in a less idealistic moment, students burned a professor's life's work on a bonfire at the barricades.

The university stood still for days. The paralyzed administration feared a gang war between right- and left-wing students. They feared reinforcing mobs from Harlem. They also feared for their liberal self-regard. The *New York Times* grasped the nub of the dilemma: liberating Columbia from "hoodlum tactics" would take the kind of police tactics an Ivy League university was "properly reluctant" to apply.

Some militants *hoped* for repression. You started hearing a phrase in antiwar circles around the time of the Pentagon march: "Heighten the contradictions." Force Leviathan to show its "true," fascist, face. A revolutionary lectured female cadres, "And when they blow, they'll be there naked and the whole country will see the naked face, the naked ass of fascism." Thus their ranks of sympathizers would grow. "What we are dealing with is a certain kind of Irish Catholic prudery," he instructed, "with a lot of sadism thrown in. We've seen these men before. They beat up black kids and take graft, but they get their rocks off with a priest once a week. So they have this crazy sense that they're guardians of morals. They're the kind of guys who have a hard time with sex, a hard time getting hard is what I mean."

(Funny. That was what Ronald Reagan said about hippies.)

"So here's what we want to do. . . . Pick up your shirt. They won't know whether to jerk off or go blind. . . . Tell 'em their mother sucks black cocks or takes black cocks in the ass. The important thing is you got to use these words. I know that can be tough. We aren't all completely liberated. But if we use words like *suck* about their mother, these fucking cops will blow like a balloon."

Working-class cops had to stand there and watch as a young girl walked down the line of mediating professors shouting, "Shit! Shit! Shit! Shit!" and cried, "Go home and die, you old people, go home and die"—and think, how nice to be able to *have* professors. Seven busloads of tactical police sat fondling batons. They assumed the kids were stockpiling Molotov cocktails—they called themselves revolutionaries, didn't they? "If we had held them in that bus much longer, they would have hit *us*," a mayoral aide recollected. Finally the police got the signal—and stained ivy walls in a bloody mass arrest.

The last act at Columbia took place on May Day. A small number of policemen remained behind on campus to maintain order. One bent down to pick up his hat after a kid knocked it from his head. At that moment, someone leapt on his back from a second-floor window. The cop spent the next twelve weeks in the hospital.

The cops got the confrontation they wanted. The revolutionaries got the confrontation they wanted. Lo, a new crop of revolutionaries; lo, a new crop of vigilantes: *Nixonland.*

Richard Nixon added a stanza to his stump speech: Columbia was "the first major skirmish in a revolutionary struggle to seize the universities of this country and transform them into sanctuaries for radicals and vehicles for revolutionary political and social goals. . . . The eyes of every potential revolutionary or anarchist on an American campus are focused on Morningside Heights to see how the administration at Columbia deals with a naked attempt to subvert and discredit its authority and to seize its power." It was as the *Chicago Tribune* had concluded its April 9 editorial: holding the line against anarchy must "be the underpinnings of any Republican platform. This country will turn to a party and a man who resolutely stand up to the fomenters of strife and say: 'This far and no farther.'"

Richard Nixon stood up. Ramsey Clark, he lectured, said crime had risen "a little bit, but there is no wave of crime in this country." Then Nixon would hurl forth a torrent of statistics: "murder up 34 percent, assault 67 percent, narcotics violations 165 percent, and home burglaries 187 percent." A President Nixon, he promised, would choose a new attorney general "to restore order and respect for law in this country."

He released a six-thousand-word position paper, "Toward Freedom from Fear," whose title borrowed from Franklin Roosevelt's economic rhetoric: "If the present rate of new crime continues, the number of rapes and robberies and assaults and thefts in the United States will double by the end of 1972. This is a prospect America cannot accept. If we allow it to happen, the city jungle will cease to be a metaphor, it will become a barbaric reality." Poverty "played a role," he allowed. But it was "grossly exaggerated" by LBJ. On the stump, Nixon said that doubling the conviction rate would do more to eliminate crime than quadrupling the funds for any government war on poverty—and when he said it, he had the crowd in the palm of his hand.

A new paperback campaign edition of *To Seek a Newer World* had come out with a picture of Bobby Kennedy's soft-focused face cropped just so, to make the light behind him appear almost like a halo. Commentators increasingly rhapsodized about Kennedy as a youth-culture prophet—"a complete master of the style they themselves were trying to achieve . . . informal but authoritative, involved but cool." RFK posters showed up alongside Huey Newton's and Jim Morrison's on dorm-room walls; BOBBY IS GROOVY, read a sign spotted by a reporter in one ecstatic crowd. Reporters noted his friendship with peripatetic New Left radicals such as Tom Hayden. His campaign song was "This Land Is Your Land" by Bob Dylan's muse Woody Guthrie.

But in Indiana, people noticed his hair looking suspiciously shorter.

Tom Hayden had been one of the outside agitators who'd camped out in Mathematics Hall during the Columbia strike. He then wrote, "Students at Columbia discovered that barricades are only the beginning of what they call 'bringing the war home.'" Kennedy aides now spent hours puzzling over how their man's association with even a buttoned-down version of the psychedelic zeitgeist would fly with the Eastern European immigrants who worked in the steel mills outside Chicago and Dixie migrants along the Ohio River. Black people loved him ("I *knew* you'd be the first to come here," a woman told him in Washington, D.C., as he toured the ravaged ghetto streets the Sunday after the assassination, calling him her "darling"); for that very reason, white people hated him (YOU PUNK read the sign of one man who, when Kennedy reached to shake his hand, squeezed Kennedy's as if he were trying to do permanent damage).

The last straw might have been a cartoon in the *Indianapolis Star* depicting Bobby and wife Ethel as Bonnie and Clyde. The liberal who'd said after Watts, "There is no point in telling Negroes to obey the law," started criticizing "welfare handouts" and boasting of his record fighting "lawlessness and violence" as attorney general. Ronald Reagan said Bobby was "talking more and more like me." Which was slightly unfair, as a group of students found out who heard Kennedy call for greater Medicare and Social Security benefits in a speech at the Indiana University medical school.

"Where are you going to get all the money for these federally subsidized programs you're talking about?" one inquired in a put-upon tone.

"From you," the candidate shot back, and pointed out how few black faces he saw. "You are the privileged ones. . . . You sit here as white medical students, while black people carry the burden of fighting in Vietnam."

The messy Kennedy ideology mirrored a messy presidential field. By May there were two more candidates. Vice President Hubert Humphrey was not groovy. Nor was he at all cool. The keynote of his character was his exuberance—a Happy Warrior. In 1966 he had enraged the right when he said if he lived in a slum he'd "lead a mighty good revolt." That was his boyish exuberance running away with him. In 1968 he enraged liberals when he posed for a photograph beaming and embracing Lester Maddox. That was his exuberance talking, too.

His Achilles' heel came from a failure to exuberate: when challenged by his president, he cowered. Everybody knew it; Bob Hope made jokes about it—when LBJ's daughter Lynda Bird and her new groom left the White House, "LBJ threw a pair of old shoes at them. Unfortunately, Hubert was still in them." The president had toyed with Humphrey mercilessly before naming him his vice-presidential candidate in 1964. Then, before the swearing in, when Humphrey told the press that he expected to influence the administration as an education policy expert, Lyndon Johnson made it clear to him that he would have no influence at all, calling in reporters to the White House to regale them with tales of how he had Hubert's "pecker in my pocket." In February of 1965 Humphrey made some tough-minded observations about the political dangers of the "graduated pressure" doctrine in Vietnam. The president rewarded him by removing him from the foreign policy loop. "I want real loyalty," Johnson liked to say. "I want someone who will kiss my ass in Macy's window and say it smells like roses." Which was more or less what Hubert had been doing since.

And now, announcing his candidacy during the Columbia strike,

Humphrey expected to harvest his just reward. With so many delegates already committed to voting for him in Chicago out of loyalty to the administration, he wouldn't be campaigning in any primaries. He would put himself over the top via the thirty-three states where convention votes were controlled by regular Democratic organizations. He would hold his tongue concerning his doubts about Vietnam and expect his president to crack the whip for him.

What he didn't know was that he wasn't his president's favorite contender. Lyndon Johnson's preferred replacement, in fact, was the other new presidential candidate: Nelson Rockefeller.

Richard Nixon had offered William Safire an explanation for Nelson Rockefeller's baffling refusal to enter the race back in March: simple politics. He was twenty points behind in Oregon. "It's all over for him," Nixon said. "The only one who can stop us is Reagan." Then, on April 7, LBJ told the head of the 1964 Republicans for Johnson organization that he wouldn't mind if he led a Draft Rockefeller committee. Three days later, the president met with Rockefeller—after which Rockefeller announced his "availability" for such a draft. Two weeks after that, Rocky dined at the White House, where the president urged him outright to run and said he wouldn't campaign against him. Which meant he wouldn't campaign for Humphrey. ("He cries too much," he told reporters one day in the White House about his vice president. "That's it—he cries too much.") Rockefeller made his announcement April 30: he *had* to run for president, because "the dramatic and unprecedented events of the past few weeks have revealed in most serious terms the gravity of the crisis we face as a people."

By then he had already moved all in with a stupefyingly overwhelming organizational plan. That was the Rockefeller way. "Gentlemen," his press secretary joked to the press one afternoon, "my candidate will appear in two hours to address a huge crowd which is even now being expensively recruited." In New Orleans they got thousands of uproarious greeters by offering free beer in an ad in the Tulane campus newspaper.

The plan turned on polling. Polls, Rocky knew, could be self-fulfilling prophecies, shaping reality as much as they described it—especially if, like Rockefeller, you had millions to produce and publicize your own. All Nixon's hard work over the last two years was predicated on proving that "Nixon could win." Rockefeller would now endeavor to *unprove* it. The blueprint was drawn up by a top New York City advertising agency. They chose thirteen "northern tier" states plus Texas, which together made up 60 percent of the population, in order to collect auspicious numbers to trumpet. They reserved 377 full-page ads in fifty-four newspapers in forty cities, 462 television commercials a week in one hundred stations in thirty cities to do the trumpeting.

The ads featured testimonials from influential citizens testifying that in an age of riots, Rockefeller and only Rockefeller was the Republican who could speak to Negroes. His speeches retailed a sophisticated new Cold War doctrine, drafted by his national security expert, Henry Kissinger, to open negotiations with our mortal enemies: "In a subtle triangle with Communist China and the Soviet Union, we can ultimately improve our relations with each—as we test the will for peace of *both*." (Henry Kissinger also wooed potential female backers at dinners and teas, until he quit, groaning, "Don't you have any prospects under sixty and worth looking at?") Field men fanned out to beg politicians to hold off on making commitments, bearing polls showing that Rockefeller was ahead of Humphrey or McCarthy or Kennedy in their state. And that Nixon was still "the one who lost it for us in '60." Pick him, and watch it happen again.

Nixon probably had enough pledges by then to win a first-ballot nomination. But Rockefeller was horning in. In Massachusetts, the day of his announcement, the only Republican name on the presidential primary ballot was Governor John Volpe's. But Volpe got less than half the votes; 25.8 percent wrote in Nixon—and 30 percent wrote in Nelson Rockefeller.

The public knew none of the behind-the-scenes shenanigans. Even Hubert Humphrey could only vaguely suspect the treachery of his boss. To the young Americans who'd been dancing in the streets on March 31, having forced the architect of an illegal and unjust war out of politics fair and square, the sight of the "old politics" Democratic Establishment falling in behind Humphrey was like watching a salamander grow a new tail when they thought they had killed off the beast. Some who were traveling to Chicago in August to plump for Kennedy or McCarthy, and to lobby delegates to pass an antiwar resolution, wondered whether they wouldn't be better off in the streets with the revolutionaries, heightening the contradictions.

On May 7 the Democrats of Indiana voted—the first contest in which Kennedy, McCarthy, and a pro-administration favorite-son governor were on the ballot together. Robert F. Kennedy thrashed Gene McCarthy, despite the six thousand McCarthy students who knocked on doors for two straight weekends. Humphrey's stand-in, Governor Branigan, got only 31 percent.

It wasn't only Kennedy, Branigan, and McCarthy ads that filled Indiana airwaves. There was also, in small markets during the most undesirable time slots, a crude TV film for a third-party candidate. And every time "The Wallace Story" ran, the money came in torrents—dollar bills, five-dollars bills, bags of wrinkled bills. "It's a gold mine," a backer said. In presidential polls where Wallace had scored 9 percent before the King riots, he now got 14 points. "They can laugh at George Wallace, but you can bet nobody is going to whisper in his ear," a Linotype operator in rural Pennsylvania told a *Saturday Evening Post* reporter. "He is for America first."

In Michigan, Alabama's first gentleman said his wife's cancer was "improving." She was actually shrunken down to eighty pounds and finally succumbed a couple days later. Twenty-five thousand mourners waited up to five hours to pay respects at a silver casket—open, at George Wallace's insistence, despite Lurleen's dying wish that it be closed—engraved with a line from her inaugural speech: "I am proud to be an Alabaman." The pageant left the pundits goggle-eyed. It left his supporters exhilarated—countersymbol to the presidentially sponsored outpouring of grief for the criminal Martin Luther King. "I didn't see any flags in the city of Newark lowered to half-mast when Governor Lurleen Wallace died," Tony Imperiale said. "Why not, when they could do it for that Martin Luther *Coon*?"

The Wallace upsurge felt to pundits like America gone crazy. Then, the day after the Indiana primary, columnists Rowland Evans and Robert Novak reported a political miracle: "While Negro precincts were delivering around 90 percent for Kennedy, [Kennedy] was running 2 to 1 ahead in some Polish precincts"—the same ones, outside Chicago, where in the 1964 presidential primary George Wallace first scared liberals that he might someday win elections in the North. What Mark Rudd and Rap Brown had torn asunder—Franklin Delano Roosevelt's New Deal coalition—the groovy one had joined together: he united "Black Power and Backlash," Joseph Kraft, the *Washington Post* syndicated columnist, now proclaimed.

There was only one problem: it may have been a statistical fallacy. In Gary, Indiana, only 15 percent of Kennedy's votes came from whites (who gave more votes to McCarthy). In white suburbs, he lost decisively. Forty-nine percent of Hoosiers said they didn't like Kennedy; 55 percent called him "too political." Indeed the harder he campaigned—the more the images of the frenetic mobs grasping at his garments showed up on television, as if in reminder of frenetic mobs at Columbia, urban riots, hippies cavorting at "love-ins"—the more he had driven white voters *away*. In the last three weeks, Kennedy lost eight points among undecided voters. They swung to the calmer choice: Gene McCarthy.

The pundits said Kennedy was a uniter. The facts showed he was a divider. But to an Establishment hungry beyond measure for signs of consensus, the myth answered a psychic need. Moderates can be seized by ideological fever dreams as much as extremists; it has always been thus.

McCarthy prevailed in Pennsylvania and Massachusetts. RFK won in Nebraska and South Dakota. It came down to Oregon on May 28 and California on June 5: the insurgent still standing would take on the Humphrey Machine. The drama was inescapable. The tousle-haired First Brother, traveling through Oregon in JFK's old bomber jacket with his brood of photogenic children and their cocker spaniel, Freckles, scampering down the jet gangway ahead of Bobby and whatever local pol was by his side; the intense former college professor, the "man the people found" and the "Clean for

Gene" hordes that followed him, a piercing wind of idealism in a low-down and dirty age. Shirley MacLaine, Sammy Davis, Bobby Darin, Peter Lawford, Sonny and Cher, superstar Olympic decathlete Rafer Johnson, and football star Rosey Grier traveled with Kennedy. McCarthy campaigned with Elaine May, Tony Randall, Eli Wallach, and Robert Ryan—and as a reproach to Kennedy, who, McCarthy fan Mary McGrory wrote, "thinks the American youth belongs to him as the bequest of his brother," Dustin Hoffman, star of the anti-grown-up hit *The Graduate.*

Hubert Humphrey didn't travel with celebrities. He traveled to smoke-filled back rooms—where, presumably, he told delegates and the bosses who controlled them what miseries would await them if he became president and they had not played ball.

On May 17, a new antiwar faction flamed into the news: the "ultraresistance." Catholic priests and nuns burst into a Knights of Columbus hall in Catonsville, Maryland, that housed the town selective service office and ignited draft files with napalm they'd concocted from a recipe in a military handbook: "We confront the Catholic Church, other Christian bodies, and the synagogues of America with their silence and cowardice in the face of our country's crimes."

Sympathy actions erupted in a dozen cities. "Certain property has no right to exist," the ultraresistance proclaimed: "concentration camps, slums, and 1-A files." They had an ally in Richard Cardinal Cushing of Boston: "Would it be too much to suggest this Easter that we empty our jails of all the protesters—the guilty and the innocent—without judging them; call back from over the border and around the world the young men who are called 'deserters'; drop the cases that are still awaiting judgment on our college youth?"

On May 23, McCarthy won Oregon, a state that had elected an antiwar Republican governor and one of the two senators to vote in 1964 against the Gulf of Tonkin resolution. McCarthy had pointed up Kennedy's implication in the original Vietnam escalation, and muckraker Drew Pearson's scoop that Kennedy had approved FBI wiretapping of Martin Luther King. ("Senator Kennedy has never discussed individual cases and isn't going to now," his press secretary, Pierre Salinger, responded, reminding voters of his candidate's ruthless lineage.) Kennedy stepped in it himself by soliciting a testimonial from Robert McNamara—at the end of the most violent two-week period in the history of the war, double the U.S. casualty rate of the Tet period. Oregon was in no mood for wobbly antiwarriors. It was the first political loss in Kennedy family history.

California: sunshine, showbiz, freneticism, melodrama. Kennedy attended the Easter Sunday mass where César Chávez of the United Farm Workers ended a twenty-five-day fast on behalf of striking grape pickers with a Communion wafer. Then Kennedy reclaimed his status as the existential risk-taker by promising that this one would be do or die: if he lost California, he'd withdraw from the presidential race. In a statewide poll, 61 percent said Robert F. Kennedy "spends most of his time courting minority groups." So on TV he played the sheriff, assuring the nervous womenfolk he knew how to contain riots: "Cordon off the area in which the rioting or disturbances take place, move in rapidly with sufficient force to deal with it, and cut it off from the community." A print ad listed, on one-half of the page, all his proposals for "Law Enforcement and the Cities"—and left McCarthy's side of the page blank.

McCarthy won a tactical battle. Kennedy had been refusing the Minnesotan's entreaties to debate. After the Oregon setback, Kennedy relented, agreeing to appear in a joint-appearance broadcast from a San Francisco station. The discussion turned to reviving the inner cities. Kennedy laid out a highly technical plan: job training, tax incentives, reconstruction funds. McCarthy said solving the problem would require a mass transit system so that the ghetto unemployed could find their way to where the jobs were, spoke movingly of "a kind of apartheid in this country, a practical apartheid," and said that "housing has got to go out of the ghetto so there is a distribution of the races."

Now it was RFK's turn to play hardball.

"I am all in favor of moving people out of the ghettos," he began, then disingenuously questioned the practicality of McCarthy's "plan" to relocate them to the suburbs: "I mean, when you say you are going to take ten thousand black people and move them into Orange County . . ."

Kennedy's last day was marathon parades through San Francisco, San Diego, and Los Angeles. In Watts the motorcade speeded down side streets. Reporters debated whether it was because they were trying to make up lost time or avoiding giving the TV cameras too many chances to record Kennedy courting minority groups.

The win was narrower than the Kennedy people expected, but decisive enough to proclaim it to his followers before midnight in a ballroom at L.A.'s Ambassador Hotel. He piggybacked upon the myth launched by Evans and Novak that his campaign was uniting every opposite: "The vote in South Dakota—the most rural state—and in California—the most urban state—indicates we can end the division within the United States."

Then he indicated his speech was coming to a close with a sidewise jab at an old adversary:

"Mayor Yorty has just sent me a message that we have been here too long already."

Hearty, satisfied laughs, the kind warriors share after a brutal but successful battle. It wasn't terribly interesting stuff, but anything Bobby Kennedy did was newsworthy, so the ABC producer kept the camera rolling.

"So my thanks to all of you, and on to Chicago, and let's win there."

He shyly thrust his hand skyward in the two-fingered V-salute, embodying every RFK ambiguity: was this the V-for-victory salute trademarked by General Eisenhower, appropriated by Richard Nixon? Or was it the peace salute beloved of hippies and antiwar activists?

A moment of ambiguity before all ambiguity was erased.

He was led to exit through a kitchen corridor. The six shots came fast enough that they sounded like three.

"My God, he's been shot!"

"Get a doctor!"

"Get the gun! Get the gun!"

"Kill him! Kill him!"

"Kill the bastard!"

"No, don't kill this one!"

"Oh, my God, they've shot Kennedy!"

"Kneel down and pray! Kneel down and pray! Say your rosary!"

Rosey Grier and Rafer Johnson fought off the mob that lunged to tear the swarthy gunman limb from limb.

People wondered what kind of country America would become, now that enforcing political opinion at the point of a gun appeared to be becoming routine. The man who legend said could heal all wounds was dead, so how could the wounds be healed?

CHAPTER THIRTEEN

Violence

"H AS VIOLENCE BECOME AN AMERICAN WAY OF LIFE?" *NEWSWEEK*'S cover story asked. *Time*'s cover pointed a stark black handgun at the reader. "The country does not work anymore," a young columnist for the *Philadelphia Inquirer* wrote. "All that money and power have produced has been a bunch of people so filled with fear and hate that when a man tries to tell them they must do more for other men, instead of listening they shoot him in the head."

That same week, a madwoman named Valerie Solanas shot Andy Warhol. (She had a manifesto: "Life in this society being, at best, an utter bore and no aspect of society being at all relevant to women, there remains to civic-minded, responsible, thrill-seeking females only to overthrow the government, eliminate the money system, institute complete automation, and destroy the male sex.") Three days after that, with Kennedy's killer in custody—his name was Sirhan Sirhan, and he had acted out of some mysterious grievance involving Israel and Palestine—James Earl Ray was apprehended in London.

Who *were* these loners who shot great men, who always seemed to succeed despite their manifest oafishness of character? Truman Capote went on NBC's *Tonight* show and said they were patsies brainwashed by plotters determined to bring America to its knees. *Time*, which used to rush to debunk any JFK conspiracy theory, passed on Capote's thoughts without criticism, noting that "a cheap crook with Ray's dismal record of bargain-basement villainy could not have traveled so far without extensive help from experts." In a cover essay in *Life*, a psychiatrist blamed it on a surfeit of images that "arouse susceptible people to violent acts." The piece was illustrated with stills of the death throes of Bonnie and Clyde. Said William F. Buckley, "In a civilized nation it is not expected that public figures should be considered proper targets for casual gunmen. But in civilized nations of the past it has not been customary for parents to allow their children to do what they feel like; for students to seize their schools and smash their equipment; for police to be ordered to stand by while looters empty stores and arsonists burn down buildings."

The countercultural journalist Hunter S. Thompson recalled that after the abdication of Johnson, "Nobody knew what would come next, but we all understood that whatever happened would somehow be a product of the 'New Consciousness.' By May it was clear that the next President would be either Gene McCarthy or Bobby Kennedy, and the War would be over by Christmas." Now, farewell to all that.

The drama of the second Kennedy assassination obscured another kind of New Consciousness. The *Tonight* show and *Newsweek* and the rest of the national media paid little attention to it. But the Republican side of the California primary was as portentous in its way for the future of American politics as the short rise and tragic fall of the presidential ambitions of Robert F. Kennedy. Tom Kuchel of California, a liberal Republican, had only recently been presumed one of the most popular members of the Senate. But in that same California primary, he had the Republican nomination taken from him by a man further to the right than Barry Goldwater.

The grassroots right-wing army that had lost with Goldwater in 1964 had survived to fight a thousand battles more. For instance, since 1966, they'd been battling the toxic eighth-grade history textbook *Land of the Free* by John Hope Franklin, circulating a filmstrip that alternated passages from the book with readings from the *Communist Manifesto*, and putting out pamphlets by FACTS in Education—the acronym stood for Fundamental issues, Americanism, Constitutional government, Truth, and Spiritual values—tut-tutting the book's favorable mention of Martin Luther King despite his "record of 60 Communist front organizations." One parent said he'd sooner go to jail than let his daughter be in the same room with the book.

Thomas Kuchel was the Senate Republican whip. By one estimate, he voted with the president 61 percent of the time, and excoriating the excesses of the right was one of his signature issues. No one who counted took his conservative critics seriously; Kuchel hadn't lost a campaign in nine tries. His Republican challengers in 1962 had only embarrassed themselves; two years later, they embarrassed themselves again when, after Kuchel turned his back on Barry Goldwater, three men forged an affidavit claiming Kuchel had been arrested during an act of sexual perversion, and Kuchel successfully sued them within an inch of their lives. In 1966, when Kuchel endorsed Brown for governor over Reagan and became one of only three Republicans to vote against Everett Dirksen's school prayer amendment, conservatives floated the name of John Wayne as a challenger. Then they started talking about General Curtis LeMay, an inspiration for *Dr. Strangelove*. It all seemed like a bad joke. "The state gets twenty-five percent of its gross product from the federal government," an L.A. power broker pointed out when asked whether California Republicans were crazy enough to turn out a Senate whip with eighteen years of seniority. "Conservative businessmen are realists. They understand that Kuchel works well with the powers in the Senate and knows his way around the federal Establishment."

Kuchel himself knew enough to be worried. After the Goldwater crusade, his enemies now controlled the California Republican Party. In 1966 he called in Richard Nixon to broker a series of peace meetings with conservatives. It wasn't enough. Someone more formidable than John Wayne arose to challenge him: the man who led the campaign against *Land of the Free.* For saving their children from what he called the "sick sixties," California conservatives loved Max Rafferty more than Watts Negroes loved RFK.

The Louisiana native and son of an autoworker had been an obscure school administrator in 1961 when he was invited to address a school board meeting in his new district outside Pasadena. He chose not to dilate upon the topic of his dissertation, "Personnel-Pupil Ratios in Certain California Elementary School Districts"; instead he excoriated activists who "seem to spend every waking moment agitating against ROTC, booing authorized congressional committees, and parading in support of Fidel Castro. . . . This sizable minority of spineless, luxury-loving, spiritless characters came right out of our classrooms. They played in our kindergartens, went on field trips to the bakery and studied things called 'social living' and 'language arts' in our junior high schools. They were 'adjusted to their peer groups.' They were taught that competition was bad. They were told little about modern democratic capitalism. They were persuaded that the world was very shortly to become one big, happy family. They were taught to be kind and democratic and peaceful."

What they were *not* taught were the immortal words of Decatur: "our country, right or wrong!" "The results," Rafferty went on (the words were toned down when reprinted in *Reader's Digest*), "are plain for all to see: the worst of our youngsters growing up to become booted, sideburned, ducktailed, unwashed, leather-jacketed slobs, whose favorite sport is ravaging little girls and stomping polio victims to death."

Someone in the audience stood up on his chair and shouted, "You're preaching hatred!" Another leapt up and answered, "This man is a patriot, shut up and hear him!" A conservative hero had been born.

In 1962 Rafferty won statewide election for superintendent of public instruction. He turned the powerless position into a bully pulpit—a "lobbyist for the children." Certain school libraries, it arrived, were stocking the *Dictionary of American Slang.* Said slang included obscenities. Announced Rafferty, "This sort of pornography is just as dangerous to the morals and minds and souls of our children as cholera bacillus would be to their bodies." His supporters sent twenty thousand pieces of hate mail to Rafferty's most prominent critic, the liberal board of education president Tom Braden—a "Com-symp," a "homosexual," "not fit to associate with children." Rafferty became a nationally syndicated columnist, expanding his targets to include the juvenile crime rate ("so much the highest in the world that it has become an object of shuddering horror to the rest of the human race"), busing and the "survival of the neighborhood school," and Lyndon Johnson's budget (a "rathole"). He won reelection on a platform of prayer in the classroom and teaching biblical creationism alongside evolution, as competing theories. He went on to savage the student uprisings at Berkeley—where professors taught a "four-year course in sex, drugs, and treason" and "encouraged and egged on the student rebellion in order to make the regents look ridiculous."

On the Senate campaign trail in 1968, he added another count to the "sick sixties" indictment: the cowardice of young men who refused to fight in Vietnam—tying it all to progressive education, the "fraud of the century." And soon he was on his way to the Senate from the most populous state in the union, with an impressive come-from-behind victory the day of RFK's assassination. He received an astonishing seventy-three thousand financial donations, of an average of $13 each.

California, always on the cutting edge. Now that blade had two edges, and one of them was right-wing reaction to everything Eugene McCarthy and RFK represented. But few noticed.

Richard Nixon noticed. An intellectually ambitious memo by a new kid, Kevin Phillips, a former aide to the right-wing Bronx congressman Paul Fino, "Middle America and the Emerging Republican Majority," was circulating among the Nixon strategists. The language was new, but the theory was as old as the crusade against Alger Hiss: elections were won by focusing people's resentments. The New Deal coalition rose by directing people's resentment of economic elites, Phillips argued. But the new hated elite, as the likes of Rafferty and Reagan grasped, was *cultural*—the "toryhood of change," condescending and self-serving liberals "who make their money out of plans, ideas, communication, social upheaval, happenings, excitement," at the psychic expense of "the great, ordinary, Lawrence Welkish mass of Americans from Maine to Hawaii."

Nixon groped toward giving that Lawrence Welkish mass a name and a nobility of purpose in a May 16 national radio address. William Safire took special delight in poaching the keynote from a liberal. Paul Douglas once gave a speech labeling all those millions of Americans condescended to by their economic overlords the "silent center." Nixon described the "silent center" as "the millions of people in the middle of the American political spectrum who do not demonstrate, who do not picket or protest loudly." *They* were loud. *You* were quiet. *They* proclaimed their virtue. *You,* simply, lived virtuously. Thus Nixon made political capital of a certain experience of humiliation: the humiliation of having to defend values that seemed to you self-evident, then finding you had no words to defend them, precisely because they seemed so self-evident. Nixon gave you the words. "A great many quiet

Americans have become committed to answers to social problems that preserve personal freedom," he said. "As this silent center has become a part of the new alignment, it has transformed it from a minority into a majority."

This story of a "silenced" majority was also told in a new hit movie. In the opening scene, a public lecture at Fort Bragg, a Negro Special Forces officer explains Communist tactics in Vietnam: "extermination of a civilian leadership," "torture of innocent children." A woman stands up to ask, "Sergeant, I'm Gladys Cooper, a housewife. It's strange that we haven't read of this in the newspaper." A bulldog-looking officer answers the housewife, "Well, that's newspapers for you, ma'am. You can fill volumes with what you *don't* read in 'em." The movie, *The Green Berets,* produced with extensive Pentagon help, was the first studio picture about the Vietnam War. Who got to speak and who was silenced was a major theme.

Who could oppose a war against an enemy that tortured little children? The elite media, it turns out. "I'm not convinced," a reporter played by a nerdy David Janssen tells the Green Berets' commander, played by none other than John Wayne. He calls the sergeant he just heard "brainwashed." Wayne invites him to join the company as they ship out to Vietnam. There, Janssen all but demands that rat-faced VC infiltrators be read their Miranda rights, then realizes the truth only after the Communists slaughter a darling little Vietnamese girl he has taken into his care. Now he understands: *he* is the one who was brainwashed—by his fellow liberals. His only fear going forward, he says, is "if I say what I feel, I may be out of a job."

A *New York Times* film reviewer, twenty-nine-year-old Renata Adler, found *The Green Berets* "vile and insane." (Indeed, in reality, enemy atrocities were the second-most common news report out of Vietnam.) Her review was the subject of a peroration on the floor of the Senate by Nixon's friend Strom Thurmond. "I have not yet had the opportunity to see this movie," he drawled. But "I have become convinced that this must be one of the most admirable movies of our generation, after reading the review which appeared last week in the *New York Times. . . .* That set me to wondering what on earth the standards of criticism are that are current in the *New York Times* for a film which is patriotic and pro-American."

He read from another *Times* review, of a Broadway show:

What is so likable about "Hair," that tribal rock musical that Monday completed its trek from downtown, via a discotheque, and landed, positively panting with love and smelling of sweat and flowers, at the Biltmore Theatre? I think it is simply that it's so likable. So new, so fresh, and so unassuming, even in its pretensions. . . .

A great many four-letter words, such as "love," are used very frequently. At one point a number of men and women (I should have counted) are seen totally nude and full, as it were, face.

Frequent references—frequent approving references—are made to the

expanding benefits of drugs. Homosexuality is not frowned upon. . . . The
American flag is not desecrated—that would be a Federal offense, wouldn't
it?—but it is used in a manner that not everyone would call respectful. Chris-
tian ritual also comes in for a bad time. . . . So there—you have been warned.
Oh yes, they also hand out flowers.

Senator Thurmond: "We have come to the point described by Orwell in
1984, where he talks about Newspeak. In Newspeak, words are used to mean
the opposite of the commonly accepted meaning. *Love* means 'hate,' *peace*
means 'war,' and so forth. We are now at the point where depravity is fresh
and likable, whereas virtue is apparently false and insane."

In New York, *The Green Berets* was playing at a two-thousand-seat cinema on that selfsame Broadway, between Forty-seventh and Forty-eighth
streets. Outside, protesters bore Vietnam flags and placards reading UP
AGAINST THE WALL, JOHN WAYNE and GREEN BERETS—SAGA OF FASCIST TER-
ROR. The theater was guarded by armed police. Playing a block down at the
New Embassy on Forty-sixth was *Wild in the Streets*—"by far the best film
of the year so far," Adler of the *Times* said—a fantasia about a rock star who
organizes to give fourteen-year-olds the vote, becomes president of the
United States, and sentences the over-thirty to concentration camps where
they are force-fed LSD.

It was coming to this: insurgents and patriots paying good money to
watch the other side silenced and humiliated.

The two sides were not symmetrical. Only one had the power to put the
other in jail.

For years Dr. Benjamin Spock had watched mysterious men in slouch
hats take notes wherever he spoke; "one Dr. Spock is more dangerous to the
war effort than 1,000 draft-card burners," the *Nation* pointed out. In January 1968, Spock was indicted for criminal conspiracy to interfere with the
draft laws, along with four others who had signed a petition counseling draft
resistance before the Pentagon protest. The trial of the "Boston 5" began at
the same time Nixon was lecturing Orthogonians about their place in a new
majority, John Wayne was lecturing them about the media's perversion of
the noble Vietnam War, and seventy-three thousand Californians were rushing checks to Max Rafferty. The jury was told the government needn't prove
these "conspirators" were ever in the same room, or even in on the same
phone conversations—only that "a meeting of the minds" had taken place.

Hundreds had signed the same document. Why had the government chosen these five? Mitchell Goodman was the forty-four-year-old novelist who
had shouted, "We are burning children in Vietnam!" during Hubert
Humphrey's appearance at the National Book Awards. Marcus Raskin was
a thirty-three-year-old former Kennedy administration defense official. The
Reverend William Sloane Coffin was the forty-four-year-old chaplain of Yale

University, a former CIA officer. Only one, a twenty-three-year-old Harvard graduate student of no particular public reputation named Michael Ferber, resembled a typical antiwar activist. The state was on the lookout for gurus: "teachers, preachers, and politicians," as Nixon had put it in *Reader's Digest,* who led children astray. Our children were the symbol and substance of American innocence. The thought that they'd come to insurrectionist conclusions on their own was too painful for some to bear. Their Svengalis had to be punished.

Svengalis were in patriots' sights everywhere. On May 13, 112 Americans died in Vietnam, of an average age of twenty-two. An American delegation in Paris led by Ambassador-at-Large Averell Harriman began peace talks with the North Vietnamese. The next week, students overran Paris and set fire to the stock market, sparking a general strike that almost brought down the government. *"Sous les pavés, la plage"* was one of their slogans ("Underneath the paving stones, the beach"); "Marx Mao Marcuse" was another. Everyone knew who Marx and Mao were. But who was this Marcuse? Imagine the shock upon discovery that he was a teacher at the San Diego campus of the University of California.

"Marcuse Calls for Sabotage of U.S. Society," reported the *San Diego Union* after he appeared on a platform with H. Rap Brown, in a headline next to a cartoon of a rat-faced, bearded radical burrowing beneath "Our Universities and Colleges," poised to strike them with a dagger; "Marcuse Is 'Dad' of Student Revolt," trumpeted a Drew Pearson column. KCET-TV in Los Angeles ran a special, "Herbert Marcuse: Philosopher of the New Left." "How is it, Professor," a polite newsman asked the distinguished, graying gentleman as they strolled the bucolic campus, "in this country of unprecedented prosperity, that there can emerge so powerful a force of discontent?" "It *ees* precisely because of *zhis* prosperity that you have such a tremendous discontent," he replied. His theory, sketched in his key text, *One Dimensional-Man,* was that Western industrial society waged "warfare against liberation, dulling the masses by their very prosperity." Enlightened youth understood that total refusal—*sous les pavés, la plage*—was the only dialectical salvation, a rage all the greater for the massive bulk of the official repression that suppressed it.

To right-wing conspiracy theorists, the children couldn't have conceived of such things as Columbia or Paris on their own; the likes of "Marcuse—a Dangerous Guru with a Bad Seed"—as one headline called him—had to be behind it. "They had riots in Paris, when the French had to bring out the troops and the tanks. Marcoo-see was there," the San Diego American Legion commander said on TV. "When they had the riots with the students in Berlin, Marcoo-see was there. It seems to me that wherever, uh, the radicals in this New Left, this so-called New Left, appear, this Marcoo-see is somewhere in the background. We are convinced that he *has* to convey some of his ideas and thoughts *directly* to the students. And in this lies his danger to the University of California."

The commander tried to get Marcoo-see fired. That failing, the Legion tried raising $20,000 to buy out his contract. A vigilante cut the professor's telephone lines; another fired a shot at his garage. His graduate students started surrounding him in a cordon during his morning walks across campus. In July, he fled San Diego behind death threats: *72 hours more, Marcuse, and then we kill you. Ku Klux Klan.* Also: *Hey, you worthless pig. I hope you are soon eliminated from this country and I hope the world, you anarchist atheist murderer being paid by the people of California to advocate bloodshed.*

The Establishment hated the gurus. Which was why they went after a far more prominent guru with even greater fury—the guru who was first among equals. "Is Dr. Spock to Blame?" asked the cover of *Newsweek,* next to an infant wearing buttons reading UP AGAINST THE WALL, MOTHER and DON'T TRUST ANYONE OVER 3. *The Common Sense Book of Baby and Child Care* was the taproot of the new generation's insolence, said a friend of Richard Nixon's, Dr. Norman Vincent Peale: "Feed 'em whatever they want, don't let them cry, instant gratification of needs." And now Dr. Spock was fighting off jail.

It was all a little fantastic: Dr. Spock's actual prescriptions were only permissive in the context of a previous generation of baby books ("Infants should be kissed, if at all, upon the cheek or forehead, but the less of this the better" went the typical counsel). People needed scapegoats. "Liberal parenting" fit the bill. Like the parents, for example, of Mark Rudd. He was profiled on the front page of the May 19, 1968, *New York Times:* "Mrs. Jacob Rudd pointed out the picture-window of her brick ranch house to a colorful rock garden. . . . 'My revolutionary helped me plant those tulips last November, my rebel,' she said with motherly pride. . . . On Mother's Day last weekend, his parents went to the Columbia campus and brought a veal parmigiana dinner, which the family ate in their parked car on Amsterdam Avenue."

Marx, Mao, Marcuse, Mother: the rot could come from anywhere now. And such was the context, as spring became summer, within which Ronald Reagan's presidential bandwagon gathered speed.

The wealthy California businessmen who'd backed Ronald Reagan's entrance into politics had been pushing their man toward the presidency since before he was governor. Reagan himself proved diffident. "Ron honestly believes that God will arrange things for the best," a Republican told David Broder in January of 1968. "But some of the people who made him governor are willing to give God a hand in making him president, and they're not too happy with the slowdown." His backers' frustrations magnified as his cultural moment arrived.

His governorship was floundering. He proposed a budget that cut every department by 10 percent, which made as much sense as trying to lose 10 percent of one's body weight by extracting tissue from every organ; he didn't even know that much of the budget was set by statute. He never came within a mile of the goal. Then he passed the largest tax increase in the history of a U.S. state. Meanwhile a cabal of aides, including Lyn Nofziger and Edwin Meese, plotted to overthrow his chief of staff by bugging hotel rooms to try to uncover evidence of gay sex. They were so indiscreet about it that Drew Pearson reported speculation "whether the magic charm of Governor Ronald Reagan can survive the discovery that a homosexual ring has been operating in his office." Reagan was in way over his head. "Can anyone tell me what's in my legislative program?" he once plaintively asked aides in the middle of a press conference. It hardly mattered to those who wanted to see him president.

All the top Goldwater plotters from 1964 were in the Nixon camp, even William F. Buckley, even Goldwater himself—all, that is, except F. Clifton White. All the Republican candidates had approached White to work for them. Nixon did it twice, the second time offering him the party chairman-ship. "No thank you," White replied, as Nixon pitched his tumbler of Scotch forward in shock at his Fifth Avenue town house. Clif White loved Ronald Reagan, and Clif White had a plan. He had broken the Republican Establishment once. He was convinced he could do it again.

He would use Nixon's greatest strength against him. To win at a nomi-nating convention, a candidate needed a *majority* of delegate votes. Failing that, a second roll call was taken—then a third, and so on. Nixon had won first-ballot commitments from Republicans of every stripe by reminding them of the pain of the 1964 blowout. But with a range of commitments that broad, none could be very deep. A grassroots insurgency to persuade some small number of conservatives, Southerners especially, to vote their con-sciences for Reagan, just enough to deny Nixon his 50 percent plus one on the first ballot, could blow the whole thing open. Nelson Rockefeller, wav-ing around Nixon-can't-win polls he had commissioned using his bottom-less financial resources, would be attempting the same thing. Up to the taking of that first convention ballot, their interests were identical—stop Nixon. On the second ballot, White was convinced, Rocky would be overwhelmed. And Reagan would be the Republican nominee.

White explained it to Reagan at a meeting with a co-plotter in Reagan's inner circle, Tom Reed, his Sacramento appointments secretary. (This being a conservative-Republican sort of grassroots insurgency, the meeting was held at a new Greenwich, Connecticut, country club founded by Tom Reed's father, a mining magnate and $100,000 Reagan donor, where they all were charter members.) Reagan was noncommittal. He always was: God would arrange things for the best.

Reagan did agree to stay out of his supporters' way while they gave God a hand. The governor would claim ignorance of White's travels under an assumed name among the delegates, continuing to do what he always did: make barnstorming speeches in support of conservatism. Only he would now do it on the schedule Tom Reed proposed: heavy on appearances in states with wobbly Nixon delegates; light on ones with upcoming primaries where his presence might raise suspicions that he was running. In those, they scheduled a half-hour biographical film to show on TV before the primaries and secretly prayed for strong Rockefeller showings, which, combined with votes for Reagan, would make Nixon look like a loser.

By the middle of May, the Reagan bandwagon started to look to Nixon like a recurring nightmare: as in 1960, what was supposed to be his coronation was shaping up as a fight. So he went back on the road, back to the slow, soiling humiliation of firming up wobbly supporters. To Arizona to secure Barry Goldwater. To Texas to ply the conservative senator John Tower. Then, on May 31, to Atlanta, where Southern Republican chairs were meeting in the city where Dr. King had been interred six weeks earlier.

Strom Thurmond had installed his top political aide, Harry Dent, as chairman of the South Carolina Republican Party, and Dent had organized his fellow Southern chairmen in a scheme to vote as a bloc at the convention. But first they would play hard to get, making the top contenders come down South and beg for their hand. According to legend, Rockefeller—despised by them anyway as a civil rights liberal—disqualified himself by committing the mortal sin of pouring sugar on his grits. Reagan, the sentimental favorite, ruled himself out by refusing to say whether he was officially running. Now, on May 31, it was Nixon's turn to supplicate. He arrived armed with his argument that he was the only candidate who could win. His campaign manager, John Mitchell, spun the press silly: "The people here all like Ronald Reagan, but they love Dick Nixon." It wasn't so. Strom Thurmond was supposed to be for Nixon. But every time he was asked about Ronald Reagan, he said, "I love that man. He's the best we've got."

After taking the political temperature of the room, Richard Nixon was sorely nervous. He got on the phone to D.C. and begged Strom Thurmond to come down to straighten things out. Thurmond agreed. He arrived on June 1. One historian called the secret conclave that followed "probably the single most important event in the election of 1968." Another compared it to the 1877 meeting in which the end of Reconstruction was brokered in exchange for Rutherford B. Hayes's presidency. Each side had something to offer. Each side had something to threaten. Lyndon Johnson had a name for these kinds of meetings. He called it "getting down to the nut cuttin'."

A unanimous Supreme Court decision had been handed down on May 27. It concerned New Kent County, Virginia, a rural district with two schools, evenly scattered black and white populations—and twenty-one separate bus routes to keep those schools racially pure. The county also had a phony "freedom of choice" plan that not a single black family had signed up for. *Green v. New Kent County* rang with eloquent finality: "this deliberate perpetuation of the unconstitutional dual system can only have compounded the harm of such a system. Such delays are no longer tolerable." School districts would now have to "fashion steps which promise realistically to convert promptly to a system without a 'white' school and a 'Negro' school, but just schools." The NAACP Legal Defense Fund immediately asked federal district courts to revisit all desegregation plans for compliance with *New Kent County.* And how to keep on fighting federally mandated integration was now the abiding obsession of every ambitious Southern politician. That was the context for the meetings in Atlanta.

Senator Thurmond had just released a new book, *The Faith We Have Not Kept,* which blamed "crime in the streets, a free rein for Communism, riots, agitation, collectivism, and the breakdown of moral codes" on the "Supreme Court's assault on the Constitution," and argued that the cause of "the War Between the States" was the "social revolutionaries" who "refused to stop at the Constitutional barrier" of *Dred Scott v. Sandford.* That would be the 1857 decision in which Chief Justice Taney declared that free blacks had no rights that the white man was bound to respect; one of those "social revolutionaries" was the founder of Strom Thurmond's political party: Abraham Lincoln.

Thus the choice Nixon faced in Atlanta was stark: What kind of Republican Party would he propose to lead? One that was committed to the spirit of Lincoln? Or one committed to the spirit of Strom?

Thurmond unsheathed his sharpest blade: he *thought* he could preserve Nixon's first-ballot victory, he said. But it would be easier if he could come to his people with some promises. . . .

Delicately, Nixon carved out his own position. *Brown v. Board of Education* was a done deal, settled law, he said. But a "strict construction" of the Constitution unfortunately limited the federal government's ability to enforce it; and of course, he would only appoint "strict constructionists" to the bench. What was more, he would consult with the good senator on a vice-presidential candidate "acceptable to all sections of the party." He hoped that would prove to Southern Republicans' satisfaction, because it would be a shame if the party slated another conservative presidential candidate in 1968 only to chalk up another noble loss and end up with four more years of liberal tyranny. It would be a shame, too, if Southern Republicans would have to face the consequences of turning their backs on the Republican nominee should it turn out to be Nelson Rockefeller (whom, perhaps he added, Martin Luther King had thought would make a better president than Hubert Humphrey).

Perhaps Nixon added something else (the records of nut-cutting sessions tend not to be fully preserved): what a shame it would be if he ascended to the

Oval Office and had to shut out Southern Republicans for not having supported him. And sometime in 1968, Nixon also cemented the alliance by promising to protect South Carolina from cheaper textile imports from Japan.

Nixon and Thurmond strode out of their meeting and into the hotel ballroom where the state chairs were assembled. They were smiling, arm in arm—Thurmond's signal that Nixon had capitulated. Three weeks later, after some nut cutting of his own back home, Thurmond announced publicly that Richard Nixon "offers America the best hope of recovering from domestic lawlessness; a bloody, no-win war in Southeast Asia; runaway spending and rising costs of living; strategic military inferiority; loss of influence in world affairs; and a power-grasping Supreme Court"; and that the South Carolina delegation would not be giving any votes to Ronald Reagan.

Having quietly secured Strom Thurmond's loyalty, Nixon could now raise his voice against George Wallace without fear of the consequences of offending the South. "From what I've read," he said in an airport interview in New York, "Wallace's support is in the direction of the racist element. I have been in politics twenty-two years and I have never had a racist in my organization." And having quietly secured Nixon's loyalty, Strom Thurmond embarked on his next political project: scuttling Lyndon Johnson's new nominee for chief justice of the Supreme Court.

LBJ had made one last play to secure his ideological legacy no matter who was the next president. Earl Warren, seventy-seven years old, broke precedent three weeks after securing the *New Kent County* decision by offering his retirement to a lame-duck president. On June 27, Lyndon chose a crony as his successor—Associate Justice Abraham Fortas, a prosperous regulatory lawyer from Memphis who'd been his friend since they were both young New Dealers. Observed *Time,* "No one outside knows accurately how many times Abe Fortas has come through the back door of the White House, but any figure would probably be too low." And since Johnson was promoting from within the court, that opened up a second vacancy—for which he nominated another crony, former Texas congressman Homer Thornberry.

Thurmond made destroying Fortas his crusade—not merely, as he put it in a June 28 floor speech, because of "his long reputation as a fixer and his involvement with many questionable figures," but because his jurisprudence "extend[ed] the power of the federal government and invaded the rights of states." The seventeen conservative Republicans who signed a petition against Fortas were joined in their opposition, sotto voce, by Southern Democrats. It all was in the objective interest of Richard Nixon: if Abe Fortas was defeated, and Nixon was elected president, *he* would make the appointment to set the direction of the Court for a generation.

The hearings were unprecedented. Never had a sitting justice sat to answer questions before the Judiciary Committee, lest he have to answer questions about pending decisions. The Republican grilling was led by the new Michigan senator, Robert Griffin, who pressed him on his advisory role to the president; Fortas was evasive. Strom got his turn on July 18, the third day of the proceedings. He began with a list of prepared questions about his positions on the liberal decisions of Earl Warren's Supreme Court.

Fortas's first response: "As a person, as a lawyer, as a judge, I should enjoy the opportunity—I always do—of discussing a problem of this sort. But as a justice of the Supreme Court, I am under the constitutional limitation that has been referred to during these past two days and must respectfully ask to be excused from answering."

Fortas would repeat some version of that over fifty times. And in Fortas's dilemma Thurmond spied an opportunity: that he could say just about anything, and Fortas would be powerless to fight back.

Thurmond brought up a case from before Fortas's tenure, *Mallory v. United States* (1957): "A criminal, a convict, a guilty man, who committed a serious rape on a *lady* in this city . . . [s]imply because the Court said they held him a little too long before arraignment. Do you believe in that sort of justice?"

"With the greatest regret, I cannot respond to that, because of the constitutional—"

Thurmond, interrupting: "I want that word to ring in your ears! *Mallory! Mallory! Mallory! . . .* A man who *raped* a woman, *admitted* his guilt, and the Surpreme Court turned him loose on a technicality. . . . Is not that type of decision *calculated* to encourage more people to commit rapes and serious crimes? Can you as a justice of the Supreme Court condone such a decision as that? I ask you to answer that question!"

Fortas could not. He sat silently for a full minute: just like a liberal, silent in the face of evil.

On the eighth day, Thurmond moved in for the kill. A Cincinnati attorney named James J. Clancy testified on behalf of his Catholic lay group, Citizens for Decent Literature. Noting that enforcing obscenity laws "has proven essential to the development of good family living," Clancy wondered why Justice Fortas had cast the "deciding" fifth vote reversing lower-court obscenity rulings forty-nine of fifty-two times—and had thus directly caused "a release of the greatest deluge of hard-core pornography ever witnessed by any nation—and this at a time when statistics indicate a pronounced breakdown in public morals and general movement toward sexual degeneracy throughout our nation." Then he got down to cases: one rapist, for example, had been arrested after watching stag films; another was arrested with "a girlie magazine in his pocket."

Clancy did not explain how complex the legal issues under review in those fifty-two rulings were, and that there were plenty of sound technical legal reasons to reverse lower courts' acceptance of bans regardless of the materials' contents. Instead, Clancy hammered the specious claim that if the lower court had made the determination that something was obscene, and the Supreme Court had reversed the lower court, that must mean the Supremes did *not* find the material in question "obscene." He read off titles: paperbacks such as *Sex Life of a Cop, Lust School, Sin Whisper, Orgy House, Sinners Séance, Bayoo Sinner, Passion Priestess, Flesh Avenger.* He quoted a judge's descriptions in a case considering short movies designed to be displayed with coin-operated projectors in bars, so furtive they didn't even have proper names; in the one labeled O-7, for instance, "the model wears a garter belt and sheer transparent panties through which the pubic hair and external parts of genitalia are clearly visible. . . . At one time the model pulls her panties down so that the pubic hair is exposed to view . . . the focus of the camera is emphasized on the pubic and rectal region, and the model continuously uses her tongue and mouth to simulate a desire for, or enjoyment of, acts of a sexual nature." And Justice Fortas didn't find this *obscene*?

Like a traveling salesman, Clancy brought with him a sample case: a thirty-five-minute documentary reel; a complete and uncut print of the masterpiece O-7. Clancy concluded his statement by requesting "the opportunity to show both the documentary and the film to the full committee and to the press, recognizing that the film is not the type of subject matter which should be shown to the general public. We would ask the committee for permission to do this, possibly in a different room. Thank you very much."

The senior senator from South Carolina thought that a swell idea. He arranged a screening for the press that very afternoon, himself feeding the coin-operated projector.

The next morning, as Chairman Ervin tediously plied Deputy Attorney General Warren Christopher on arcane points of separation of powers, Senator Thurmond ostentatiously paged through a magazine called *Nudie-Fax*. When it came his turn to question Christopher, he repeated the information in Clancy's testimony in every particular, judge's descriptions and all.

The press, prepared, scribbled madly:

"From what Judge Hauk described about the film, O-7, you think that would be a very wholesome film for the public to see?"

"Senator, I would not comment without having seen the film. . . ."

"I want to ask what you think. You probably have a family, don't you?"

"Yes, sir."

"You would not want your wife or daughter to see a film that was described as O-7 or O-12, would you?"

"Well, I have not seen the film, Senator. The description does not make it sound like family entertainment."

The senator asked his cornered prey to repeat himself.

"The description does not make it sound like family entertainment."

Thurmond: "Yet Justice Fortas . . . held it was not obscene."

"Speaking overall, Senator Thurmond," Christopher allowed, "our view would be that Justice Fortas has taken a moderate and reasonable position in the field of obscenity."

Thurmond had what he wanted on the record: the Johnson Justice Department apparently endorsing pornography. His work done, and in time for the morning-paper deadlines, he launched into his final peroration. He had a clerk hand down to the administration official the pornography his staff had been able to procure within view of the Capitol (including one in which the content "is only males"): "Mr. Christopher, how much longer are the parents, the Christian people"—Fortas, it happened, was Jewish—"the wholesome people, the right-thinking people going to put up with this kind of thing? . . . the Supreme Court has made it commonplace. . . . And to believe this material does not find its way into the hands of young people is wishful thinking."

The surprise issue was a strategic godsend. Fortas's opponents, among them Judiciary chairman Sam Ervin, had been casting about for excuses to stretch the hearings out until after the August recess to give them time to find more damning information, hoping for enough votes to win a filibuster. Thurmond's politics were razor-sharp. Blocking a president's Supreme Court nominee was an unpopular decision and was hard to defend. Explaining the technical issues behind the "lame-duck" charge to constituents was daunting. But protecting kids from porn—that was easy. It gave Southern Democrats cover for defying their president. It gave Republicans cover to not appear partisan.

Thurmond arranged a movie screening for his colleagues, who in private forgot their horror, laughing, shouting crudities at the images projected on the wall—until they screened a print, seized during a 1967 raid on the University of Michigan campus, of the underground polysexual art film *Flaming Creatures*, which received less glowing reviews: "I was so sick, I couldn't even get aroused," one senator said—acknowledging publicly for the first time that *shocked, shocked* senators sometimes got aroused, too.

Given their learned South Carolina colleague's legendary sexual appetites, it must have been hard not to laugh. Cartoonists reviewing the spectacle had a field day. Let the sophisticates sneer. These were now known as the "Fortas films"—as in, as Senator Russell Long said, "I have seen one Fortas film— I have seen enough." Frank Lausche said he wouldn't "vote for a man who would approve the films" if it were his own brother. Columnist James J. Kilpatrick said they should be shown on the Senate floor, if that was what it took to grasp the "pattern that runs through the fabric of constitutional law as tailored by Mr. Justice Fortas. . . . Boil the issue down to this lip-licking slut, writhing carnally on a sofa, while a close-up camera dwells lasciviously on her genitals. Free speech? Free press? Is this what the Constitution means?"

Sex sells, Strom Thurmond knew that. From Southern segregationists insisting dogs had been rendered rabid by the Selma marchers' "sex smell" to Ronald Reagan's "orgies so vile" to the claims of a sea of panties left behind at the Pentagon in October of 1967, circulating sexual imagery was a right-wing stock-in-trade—even more so than for the libidinal politicians of Haight-Ashbury. The latest titillating national outrage issued from newly pacified Morningside Heights: a Columbia student was living off-campus and in sin with a Barnard student, named Linda LeClair. Wrote William F. Buckley, "In an age in which the *Playboy* philosophy is taken seriously, as a windy testimonial to the sovereign right of all human appetites, it isn't surprising that the LeClairs of this world should multiply like rabbits, whose morals they imitate."

Spectacles: that, as the presidential campaign season got ready to launch, was American politics now.

The trial of Dr. Spock had wound down in Boston. Half the defendants had been eager to use the courtroom to "put the war on trial." The others wanted simply to mount the best defense possible. They united behind the latter course; the latter course failed. "Where law and order stops, obviously anarchy begins," the judge pronounced, before giving three of the five, including Spock, two years in prison and a $5,000 fine.

It only redoubled the conviction of the activists working day and night planning their stand against the Democratic National Convention in Chicago. Amerika was becoming a prison. The only sane thing to do was to work for a jailbreak.

Two separate groups were organizing independently and at cross-purposes. The first insisted they were neither a "group" nor "organizing" at all. Its leaders, who also insisted they weren't "leaders," two gentlemen of such extraordinary will and vision they might have been famous in any era, had brainstormed their Chicago plan on New Year's Eve, puffing weed and musing as they always did on how to overthrow reality itself. Which, this era being what it was, was what Abbie Hoffman and Jerry Rubin ended up becoming famous for.

Rubin was from Cincinnati. His dad was a union activist. His favorite uncle was a former vaudeville performer. Rubin started his career in his father's footsteps, as an organizer, with the earnestness native to that profession. Later, he moved to Berkeley and decided politics was most radical when it resembled vaudeville. It was Jerry who came up with the idea to follow armament shipments in a government-gray pickup truck displaying a flashing yellow sign reading DANGER, NAPALM BOMBS AHEAD; Jerry's idea to throw WANTED FOR WAR CRIMES flyers in General Maxwell Taylor's face during a San Francisco visit; Jerry who testified in full Revolutionary War regalia when called before the House Un-American Activities Committee. Drugs completed the transformation: "I began to see that we had to create a movement that was an end in itself—not an external goal or revolution, but living revolution every day." One morning at the New York Stock Exchange, with his new best friend Abbie Hoffman—the leading levitator at the Pentagon— they dropped money from the gallery onto the trading floor below. The resulting greedy mêlée made the evening newscasts.

Which was precisely their point, precisely their theory. The "straight" left said the media was the problem—New Left journalist Robert Scheer wrote that the rot at the heart of Sirhan Sirhan came from his having "spent his whole life watching television." Abbie and Jerry's view was rather the opposite. "Those who grew up before the 1950s live today in a mental world of Nazism, concentration camps, economic depression, and communist dreams Stalinized," Rubin wrote in his book *Do It!* "A pre-1950s child who can still dream is very rare. Kids who grew up in the post 1950s live in a world of supermarkets, color TV commercials, guerrilla war, international media, psychedelics, rock and roll. . . . For us nothing is impossible. We can do anything." The world as people understood it to exist was a myth propagated through media. Abbie and Jerry believed all you would need to make the world anew was to propagate a more seductive myth. Abbie tried to explain how things worked to a reporter: "*You* need three hundred pages, you know, beginning with a capital letter, ending with a period. Young kids don't need that, they don't even want it." The reporter responded with bafflement. Richard Nixon might have understood better. That's why he hired Roger Ailes—who was four years younger than Abbie. "I fight through the jungles of TV" was Abbie's watchword. It could have been Roger Ailes's, too.

They planned rock concerts, a be-in, a *happening,* Haight-Ashbury in the streets of Chicago. They called their unorganizable organizing body the Youth International Party—a put-on like everything else: its acronym was YIPPIE! They held a press conference the day after RFK entered the presidential race: "We will create our own reality. And we will not accept the false theater of the Death Convention . . . everything we do is going to be sent out to living rooms from India to the Soviet Union to every small town in America." They borrowed language from the Kerner Report: "It's a real opportunity to make clear the two Americas. . . . At the same time we're *confronting* them, we're offering our . . . alternative way of life."

Their bravura was inspiring. Their arrogance could render them little better than punks. In New York, the Lindsay administration enlisted Abbie as a community liaison to keep the peace in the East Village. Part of the deal was that the cops weren't allowed to arrest him. So he marched into the local precinct one day and made himself increasingly obnoxious. The captain who was his police handler, refusing the bait, retreated to his office. Abbie followed him inside and smashed the precinct's prized possession, the trophy case containing the precinct's service citations, sending the cop into the hoped-for rage.

You are slaves, and we are free: "love" could be a hateful thing.

They hosted a "Yip-in" at Grand Central Station in March. Several thousand kids showed up, milling, smoking, grooving, chanting "Burn, baby, burn!" and scrawling FUCK YOU on the walls. Commuters tried to wiggle through to their trains. Police officials had to physically restrain their men. Kids unrolled an UP AGAINST THE WALL, MOTHERFUCKER banner from the top of the information booth. Someone snapped the hands off the famous clock. Cops couldn't be restrained anymore. A New York Civil Liberties Union official called it "the most extraordinary display of unprovoked police brutality I've ever seen outside of Mississippi." But cops didn't feel unprovoked. "Here's a bunch of animals who call themselves the next leaders of the country. . . . I almost had to vomit. . . . It's like dealing with any queer pervert, mother raper, or any of those other bedbugs we've got crawling around the Village. As a normal human being, you feel like knocking every one of their teeth out. It's a normal reaction."

The Yippie calls to action for the Democratic National Convention were put-ons, provocations, playful threats: "We will burn Chicago to the ground! We will fuck on the beaches! We demand the Politics of Ecstasy! Acid for all! Abandon the Creeping Meatball! YIPPIE! Chicago—August 25–30."

The other faction planning for Chicago, the National Mobilization Committee to End the War in Vietnam (the Mobe), more resembled military tacticians. One architect, Tom Hayden, had helped take a building at Columbia, then called for "two, three, many Columbias." But he also was the movement's inside man, its slickest operator, who had met with Averell Harriman and traveled to Hanoi to negotiate for the release of prisoners of war and wept publicly in St. Patrick's Cathedral over the coffin of RFK. His partner Rennie Davis, the New Left's most dogged organizer, reminded one *New York Times* reporter of "a Kansas 4-H leader" (indeed, the first time the Kansan had traveled to Chicago was to show a prize chicken at a 4-H fair). Their adviser, David Dellinger, was a pacifist who had gone to jail rather than submit to a seminarian draft deferment during World War II. He was a WASP who wore tweed and had graduated from Yale with Walt Rostow and Stewart Alsop. Abbie thought they were the Establishment's doppelgängers. "They understand each other," Abbie said. "They all wear suits and ties, they sit down, they talk rationally, they use the same kinds of words."

But the Mobe was no less interested than their Yippie brethren in spectacle. Davis brought an American fragmentation bomb from North Vietnam with him everywhere he went, a visual aid to demonstrate how America was "liberating" Vietnam. In 1967, living in Newark as a community organizer, Hayden wrote, "Riots must be viewed both as a new stage in the development of Negro protest against racism and as a logical outgrowth of the failure of the whole society to support racial equality. A riot represents people making history." The Mobe was going to Chicago to manufacture revolutionaries. The idea was to draw in hordes of people who had never demonstrated before. Rennie Davis told a reporter that he'd like to see every newspaper in the country displaying photos of the International Amphitheatre surrounded by soldiers, tanks, and barbed wire, guarding the nominee being forced down the people's throats. "It'll show the Democrats can't hold a convention without calling in the army."

The Timesman pointed out this was a dangerous game: "Wouldn't it be even more effective if the soldiers shot a little girl? Or two girls? Or twenty? Wouldn't that radicalize the McCarthy kids a lot quicker?"

Davis seemed to misunderstand. "Perhaps," he responded. "But we're not after bloodshed. A symbolic confrontation will make the point."

As if the Mobe had any control over what kind of confrontation there would be. As if Tom Hayden, when speaking in private to other activists, wasn't talking about working toward a confrontation between "a police state and a people's movement."

A third faction had considered making the trip—the "McCarthy kids," to demonstrate in the streets for an antiwar resolution on the convention floor, to pressure the cigar-chompers in the back rooms to let delegates vote their consciences. But most McCarthy kids had long ago made other plans. Their Coalition for an Open Convention dissolved, fearing violent mêlées inevitable. Which meant those finally coming to Chicago would be the most militant—many who welcomed confrontation.

The City of Chicago had its own definition of the word *open*. It had to do with her definition of other words. "No one is going to take over the city," Mayor Daley announced. "We'll permit them to act as American citizens and no other way." A *citizen* was someone who was orderly, obedient, who followed the rules. Anyone else, in this argot, was an *outsider*—whether McCarthy activists fighting the machine's nominee Humphrey, or hippies who grew up in Chicago. Daley told a Justice Department representative who urged a close working relationship with demonstration planners that he had his city under control. "Any trouble, it would come from outsiders." *Outsiders* were what threatened the convention's *openness*. Explained the city's assistant corporation counsel, Richard Elrod, "Our division is willing to do everything possible to make sure that the city is peaceful this summer, that the city is open for all." Those not with the city's program were by definition openness's despoilers.

The city had sheafs of intelligence on these outsiders. A city bureaucrat traveled to Haight-Ashbury to reconnoiter, reporting back that the outsiders stank, had VD, committed crimes, and took lots of drugs. The Red Squad had listening devices in SDS national headquarters on Sixty-third Street: the members talked of Mao- and Che-inspired revolution. These were the same forces deranging the third world, who had taken over Havana, overthrown the Cuban government on New Year's Eve, 1958.

Movement negotiators thought they knew what the game was: the same dance had happened before the Pentagon demonstration. They'd get their permits, only at the last minute, after the city was able to depress their turnout. Chicago peaceniks knew better, especially ones with working-class ties—whose brothers, cousins, school chums, were Chicago policemen. They knew how the cops were talking after their impotence during the April riots, their delight at Mayor Daley's words "shoot to kill." Which Tom Hayden might not altogether have minded. He was spinning fantasies of McCarthy kids emerging from their confrontation with "the new Nazis" as "participants in the creation of a new society in the streets."

On April 11, the city council passed a disorderly conduct ordinance making illegal "any unreasonable or offensive act, utterance, gesture, or display which . . . creates a clear and present danger of a breach of peace." Two weeks later, cops flexed their muscles at City Center Plaza. Those with press passes were systematically manhandled. They were seen by most cops as the root of the problem. The press, Quinn Tamm of the International Association of Chiefs of Police wrote in the June *Police Chief* magazine, "overpublic[ized] militants, assiduously stoking the fires of unrest." Mayor Daley agreed. He didn't anticipate any trouble convention week—"unless certain commentators and columnists cause trouble."

Yippies made yet more surreal intimations: a march of bare-breasted maidens down Michigan Avenue, "long distance conga lines," dosing the water supply with LSD. Mobe leaders made their intimations in private, as spies among them took down every word: "Make sure that if blood flows, it flows all over the city," Tom Hayden said, meaning—if the police clubs started swinging, protesters should fan out so as many Chicagoans as possible could see what was happening. What the police spies heard was—attack police.

Officials dutifully fielded an estimate of how much acid it would take to affect the water supply: five tons, of a substance sold on the streets in micrograms. They laid plans to guard the pumping stations anyway. Then they learned that a rich Chicago dowager, Lucy Montgomery, had provided money to bail out Black Power advocates after the King riots. Montgomery was also a financial angel to the Mobilization. Putting two and two together, a bizarre idée fixe took shape: the white radicals were the foot soldiers for Negro insurrectionists, with the McCarthy delegates as the conspiracy's inside team, sabotaging Hubert Humphrey as their allies made mayhem in the streets.

The Daley Machine projected its own internal cohesion onto its enemies. That helped city planners countenance ever more ruthless countermeasures. The police rank and file made a similar projection: these outsiders coming in to take over their streets were *the same people* they had not been able to deal with in the King riots, from whom they had feared for their lives.

The Chicago police's greatest fears were confirmed in Cleveland. The same night the senators watched Strom Thurmond's dirty movies, a new kind of riot erupted: a planned one. "They shot at us from every direction imaginable," a police detective said of the ambush by members of a group called the Black Nationalists of New Libya. Three cops and four militants died. One militant, Fred "Ahmed" Evans, said he was sorry his carbine had jammed so he couldn't take out more cops. This man's prediction that a lunar eclipse would touch off World War III and a national Negro uprising had riveted Senate Internal Security Subcommittee hearings the previous year. He had now finally demonstrated, said a delighted Eldridge Cleaver, "that psychologically blacks are not only prepared to die but kill."

A terror over law and order engulfed the nation's cities. Bus drivers in the nation's capital started demanding paper scrip in lieu of cash because so many were getting robbed. In New York, firemen who suspected false alarms were being pulled to lure them into attacks were arming themselves with blackjacks ("It's bewildering," a man from a Bronx engine company complained to the *New York Times*. "They're rebelling against the Establishment. . . . We're part of the Establishment all the sudden?"). An explosive placed inside a police call box in Queens forced suspension of the use of call boxes citywide.

In Chicago, the Red Squad began spying on every black leader. They reported the Black Panthers were planning "the creation of incidents in the Negro area and involvement of white policemen to initiate complaints of police brutality," and were working with Tom Hayden to employ prostitutes to solicit delegates. The U.S. Army sent seventy-five hundred men from Fort Hood in Texas to undergo riot exercises in Chicago. Forty-three black soldiers refused to go and were arrested—the "Fort Hood 43." George Wallace climbed to 20 percent in some polls. He claimed ballot status in thirty-six states. "Outside of the visible return of Jesus Christ," a Chattanooga minister proclaimed, "the only salvation of the country is the election of George Wallace."

The National Governors' Conference forwent tropical cocktails to meet in Cincinnati, adopting a resolution declaring "crime in the streets of America as a problem which demands the utmost concern and attention of all Americans" (they refused to endorse a gun control bill requested by the nation's police chiefs). Nixon delegate-hunter Richard Kleindienst met Reagan delegate-hunter F. Clifton White, and a fistfight almost broke out (John Mitchell took Kleindienst by the lapels: "Dick, how can I make you attorney general of the United States if you let that one inconsequential figure get under your skin?"). Lester Maddox bumped against something hard in the hotel lobby and alerted security, who seized a gunman. Reports were that his intended target was Ronald Reagan, whose Sacramento mansion had, two weeks earlier, been stalked by youth armed with Molotov cocktails who were driven off by a warning shot fired by a Secret Service agent.

As the two parties prepared to convene to decide who their candidates would be to govern over the madness, all the candidates were guarded by Secret Service agents now.

CHAPTER FOURTEEN

From Miami to the Siege of Chicago

THE PARTY OF LINCOLN HELD THEIR CONVENTION ON AN ISLAND SEP-
arated from the Florida mainland by two narrow causeways. The self-
insulation worked. The night of the presidential nomination, a riot broke out
in the all-black neighborhood of Liberty City. The forces of Miami's get-
tough police chief, Walter Headley—who had said in April of Daley's shoot-
to-kill order, "That could have been me talking," and "When the looting
starts, the shooting starts"—killed four rioters. The national press remained
sufficiently distracted by the funny hats and windy speeches to hardly
notice. Another big story in Miami also remained mostly hidden from view:
the slow, soiling humiliation of Richard Milhous Nixon, working day and
night to secure a victory he was already supposed to have won.

The cover of *Newsweek* was a sea of posters for the surprise Republican
nominee of 1940, Wendell Willkie, and the words "Can It Happen Again?"
The platform hearings at the rococo Fontainebleau Hotel were undramatic,
by the design of the Nixon strategists—until Ronald Reagan showed up
Wednesday, July 31, after concluding an eight-state tour.

"We must reject the idea that every time the law is broken, society is
guilty rather than the lawbreaker," he testified.

"It is time to move against these destructive dissidents; it is time to say,
'Obey the rules or get out.' . . .

"It is time to tell friend and foe alike that we are in Vietnam because it is
in our national interest to be there!"

Committee members broke into their only cheering in four days. (John
Lindsay testified—"The root cause of most crime and civil disorder is the
poverty that grips over thirty million of our citizens"—to silence.) Reagan
rode off into the sunset, insisting he was still only a favorite son. The thought
that this might not last, or that Rockefeller might be the new Willkie, was the
waking nightmare in the compound at Montauk, Long Island, where Richard
Nixon was working on his acceptance speech, making contact with the outside world only to request more yellow legal pads.

Monday morning, August 5. The news from beyond the Republican island: Malcolm Brown of the *New York Times* interviewed the young French-born theorist of Marxist urban warfare Régis Debray in prison in Bolivia: "Canonized by the New Left . . . his parents, wealthy Paris lawyers from respected families, have arranged for a restaurant two blocks away to provide him with food and wine twice a day." The morning's *Times* also claimed it was in possession of intelligence that Richard Nixon would balance his ticket with a liberal vice-presidential candidate, perhaps Rockefeller or Lindsay. And every last conservative who had offered his support to Richard Nixon wondered to whom he had sold his soul.

The conservatives were guided by the heavy hand of folklore, the legend that past conventions had been sabotaged by what Phyllis Schlafly called "a few secret kingmakers in New York." "The double cross is on"—the phrase echoed across the white-sand beaches, the turquoise swimming pools, the pink-marble foyers, the catered caucus breakfasts. You couldn't turn around without seeing a copy of the new fawning biography of Ronald Reagan by Young Americans for Freedom's Lee Edwards, distributed free to every delegate and alternate.

The gavel crashed down for the opening session. An invocation from the archbishop of Miami: "Our hearts are heavy . . . a heavy cloud of fear hangs over many of our citizens."

An "inspirational reading" followed: "It took me a long time to decide to stand up here at a political convention because I am about as political as a Bengal tiger," drawled John Wayne, the sometime John Birch Society member who had appeared in commercials for Ronald Reagan—though "I read some of the reviews that some of my left-wing friends wrote about my last efforts and there is some doubt about that." (Applause.)

Wayne went on to explain how he would be teaching his baby daughter "some of the values that an *ar-TIC-ulate* few now are saying are old-fashioned."

(Nixon's Kevin Phillips, a native New Yorker, later explained to a reporter, "Wayne might sound bad to people in New York, but he sounds great to the schmucks we're trying to reach through John Wayne. The people down there among the Yahoo Belt.")

When Nelson Rockefeller arrived, he claimed he had almost twice as many firm delegates as Reagan. The standing ovation John Wayne had just received put that notion rather in doubt.

Over and over again, delegates Ronald Reagan had visited on his recent Southern tour told him they might switch their votes to him if he were a declared candidate. At 4 p.m. Reagan returned to Miami Beach and stepped up to the press conference microphones and announced that this was what he now was.

Harry Dent, Strom Thurmond's man, said he'd never seen anything like what happened next. Reagan enthusiasts appeared out of nowhere. Reagan was queried for his reaction: "Gosh, I was surprised. It all came out of the blue." Evans and Novak reported that Rockefeller's most important backer, Ohio governor James Rhodes, said it was a "whole new ball game." Rhodes was a notorious political opportunist who'd switched from anyone-but-Goldwater to Goldwater at the height of the civil rights backlash in 1964.

Nixon's people tried to remain calm, recalling to themselves how reporters always manufactured evidence of conflict to justify their pay. The favorite sons they'd secured in New Orleans in early '67 announced for Nixon right on schedule: first Senator Tower, then Governor Agnew of Maryland, the former Rockefeller man, Governor Dewey Bartlett of Oklahoma, and Governor Louie Nunn of Kentucky.

Nixon arrived at Miami International Airport. His egress from the campaign jet had been planned for live pickup on the network newscasts. But no one planned on favorable tailwinds, which blew him onto the tarmac early. Nixon waited patiently in his seat. Then he strode down the airplane steps and . . . apologized for being late: he had just returned from the citizenship ceremony, he said, of his beloved valet, Manolo Sanchez, and his wife, refugees from Castro's Cuba.

Woodenly he said, "This marks the end of the journey, and, we think, the beginning of another that is going to lead us to a new leadership for this nation." The huge crowd, carefully advanced, cheered deliriously. Nixon forced himself to maintain a smile as intelligence was whispered into his ear by Senator Thurmond that people were mobbing him wherever he went expressing regret they ever trusted "Tricky Dick."

Nixon motorcaded to the brand-new Hilton Plaza. Security stood watch at every overpass; helicopters buzzed overhead. Another "spontaneous" crowd was at the entrance. A van door opened, releasing a flock of balloons; Nixon's face lit up as if he'd never seen such a spectacle in his life. Some expected a rifle shot to ring out any minute: if you planned an assassination, this would be the time.

At the evening session, things were deadly dull. General Eisenhower addressed the crowd by telephone ("One more thing: I am not a candidate"). Senator Brooke was presented a gavel hewn of Florida wood for his installation as master of ceremonies (a black face on TV looked good). The action was in the parking lot, where Ronald Reagan received a steady stream of Southern delegates in his trailer. The old trouper poured on the charm. Clif White explained how Reagan would win. It had to do with the Southern delegations' "unit rules," which held that if a majority of the delegation voted for a candidate, the candidate won the delegation unanimously. White claimed commitments from the chairs of the Florida, Georgia, Louisiana, and Mississippi delegations to cast the deciding vote for Reagan if he could get to one vote shy of a majority in each. Reagan asked each delegate to be the one to put him in that position. It was not going too well: lots of "We *really* want to go with you, Gov, but—" They'd all received telegrams from Strom: "Richard Nixon's position is sound on law and order, Vietnam, the Supreme Court, military superiority, fiscal sanity, and decentralization of power. He is best for unity and victory in 1968. Our country needs him, and he needs our support in Miami. See you at the convention." They had also received Strom's phone calls—which, since they left no written record, were franker: "A vote for Reagan is a vote for Rockefeller." That played straight to conservative paranoia: that if the convention was thrown to the chaos of multiple ballots, the Eastern Establishment kingmakers were capable of anything.

The Reagan trailer emptied as the evening's main attraction was introduced: "Ladies and gentlemen, I present to you a great American, a great Republican, the next senator from Arizona, my friend and colleague, the Honorable Barry Goldwater!"

The Convention Center leapt to its feet: *"We want Barry! We want Barry! We want Barry!"*

The anchormen in the broadcast booths were flabbergasted. They thought this party had come to its senses. They'd been talking up a Harris poll showing Rocky doing better against Humphrey than Nixon, that in a world gone mad the steady managerial competence of Nelson Rockefeller was looking better to people every day, how dignified and brave he'd been in 1964 standing up to the right-wing crazies who tried to shout him down on the convention floor.

But on this floor, it was 1964 all over again.

At the Hilton, the Nixon team was gobsmacked by the Reagan boom. At the convention center, the South Carolina delegation's phone rang: John Mitchell for Harry Dent. They had a meeting scheduled between their bosses for the next day. Mitchell wanted it moved up to *now*.

Dent and Thurmond arrived at the Nixon suite after ten o'clock. They were led through elaborate security mazes, not the Secret Service's, but the ones set up by the two foreboding men who had steadily risen to the top of the campaign hierarchy, Bob Haldeman and John Ehrlichman (the old Wall Street crew found themselves refused access to the suite by this new Praetorian guard and were reduced to spittle-flecked rage).

Thurmond and Dent were led into the suite (one bedroom for Dick, another for Pat).

Thurmond and Dent had been making the rounds of wobbly Southern delegations to put out fires. Dent would speak to them first, saying all the things a senator could not afford to say. Thurmond would tell old war stories and stress Nixon's commitment to passing a Thurmond pet project, the antiballistic missile system, and promise, "Nixon will not ram anything down our throats." *Tricky Dick, Tricky Dick, Tricky Dick*, was what they heard back.

Each understood the other's dilemma implicitly: Thurmond was far out on a limb, vouching for a candidate his constituency did not trust; Nixon was far out on a limb vouching for the prodigal South's place in the Republican Party of the future. Not many words were exchanged at their meeting; they looked into each other's eyes. That was why there had to be a meeting.

Thurmond extracted a promise, then pressed a slip of paper into Nixon's hand.

Tuesday morning's newspapers: "Columbia Administration Drafts a Plan for Disciplinary Reforms"; "A Vietnam mine today blew up one of the two trains that had still been operating in South Vietnam"; "Kill Arsonists in Waukegan, Mayor Orders." Reagan and Thurmond had a meeting. It lasted an hour. A new rumor circulated that if true would kill the Reagan charge: that Reagan would be Nixon's vice-presidential candidate. Reagan killed the rumor with a quip—"Even if they tied and gagged me, I would find a way to signal no by wiggling my ears"—and Dent died a little inside: he felt the slippage from Nixon minute by minute.

But Nixon was about to fulfill a promise to Thurmond that would reverse his slippage. Nixon had agreed to face every Southern delegate, answer every question they asked—groveling like the callow navy vet in 1946 who wanted to run for Congress, begging South Californian petty plutocrats, navy hat in hand; begging Southern Republicans, *again*, for what he thought he had already won: their sufferance for him as their nominee.

First he spoke to delegates from six states; then he spoke to a meeting of the other six. Only those present know what he said at the first one. At the second, the *Miami Herald* slipped in a tape recorder and published the transcript in that evening's early edition of the next day's paper.

Dent spoke first: "We have no choice, if we want to win, except to vote for Nixon. We must quit using our hearts and start using our heads. Believe me, I love Reagan, but Nixon's the one."

(The most grudging sort of compliment, like the one he'd received from Ike in 1958: "Your courage, patience, and calmness in the demonstration directed against you by radical agitators have brought you a new respect and admiration in our country.")

Nixon opened with the concern uppermost in their minds—the vice presidency: "I am not going to take, I can assure you, anybody that is going to divide this party."

The delegates applauded furiously. This was the fruit of the little slip of paper Strom Thurmond had slipped into Richard Nixon's hand the night before. It contained three columns of names: "unacceptable" (Lindsay, Rockefeller, the antiwar Oregonian Mark Hatfield); "acceptable" (George H. W. Bush, Howard Baker); "no objections" (a late addition of two Eastern governors, Spiro Agnew and John Volpe, favorite sons who had been put on the schedule to nominate and second Nixon for Wednesday night).

A North Carolina delegate asked if Nixon accepted "forced busing of schoolchildren for the sole purpose of racial integration." First Nixon said: "There is a problem in the North, too. . . . I don't believe you should use the South as the whipping boy, or the North as the whipping boy."

That showed how well he grasped the delicate psychological sensitivities of the region that still smarted from the humiliation of losing what he had learned, during his law school days at Duke, to call when occasion demanded the "War Between the States." The idea that cultural bigotry lay behind the North's calling to account of the South on civil rights was central to Southern identity.

Then, Nixon said, "I think that busing the child—a child that is two or three grades behind another child and into a strange community—I think that you destroy that child. The purpose of a school is to educate."

That showed how well he grasped Southern bad-faith rhetoric on racial questions: he played into the myth that the *only* reason students were bused was to force racial integration—though the Supreme Court's decision in *New Kent County* showed that, as often, busing was used as a tool to force *segregation.*

He rang through the rest of the usual Dixiecrat changes, with Nixonian grace notes: "I don't think there is any court in this country, any judge in this country, either local or on the Supreme Court . . . that is as qualified to . . . make the decision as your local school board." Open housing, "just like gun control, ought to be handled at the state level, rather than the federal level." A Nixon administration, he wound up, wouldn't bend to "satisfy some professional civil rights group." He left with Strom Thurmond on his arm.

Another boring session in the convention hall. An interminable train of Republican congressmen each got two minutes at the podium, after having been put through their paces by coaches with stopwatches in a trailer equipped with teleprompters and simulated lighting angles. The official proceedings record audience response for every speech. Thomas Dewey got "cheers and applause." Only a backbencher named Buz Lukens got a "standing ovation"—Buz Lukens having been one of the architects of the Draft Goldwater movement in 1963.

Wednesday was balloting day ("Israeli Forces, in Pursuit, Cross into Jordan Again"; "Top Cubans Linked to Guevara Band"; "5 Policemen Shot in Chicago Suburb"; "Youth Hit by Sniper While Watching Fire"; massacres in the breakaway Nigerian province of Biafra; Soviets warily eyeing Czechoslovakian reformer Alexander Dubček).

Rockefeller's manager, Leonard Hall, and Reagan's, Clif White, both friends, shared anti-Nixon intelligence on how to intercept Nixon's first-ballot victory—each believing he would come up with the ball once it was tipped in the air. On delegates, Rockefeller was not even close—even, White discovered when he called his regional directors to the trailer at five for one last count, if Reagan and Rockefeller delegates were added together.

"We only have one option left," White said. "We can fold the tent now. Or we can keep working and hope for a break."

The old trouper came to the rescue, Mickey Rooney and Judy Garland putting on a show in the old barn: "Well, that's what we're here for, isn't it? Let's get to work."

Then suddenly, a miracle. The *Herald* evening edition hit the beach with a story by Don Oberdorfer: "Hatfield Veep Pick."

Tricky Dick, finally caught red-handed. Clif White commandeered two thousand copies of the *Herald* and had his army of Young Americans for Freedom volunteers personally press a copy into every delegate and alternate delegate's hand: Nixon was selling them out, choosing a dove for vice president.

Opening gavel. A song by Up with People ("Freedom is a word often heard today / But if you want to keep it there's a price to pay"), a standing ovation. Interminable nominating speeches, "demonstrations," multiple seconding speeches for each nomination, most ceremonial and immediately withdrawn by the honoree.

The *Herald*'s Don Oberdorfer was wandering the convention floor hours before the roll call vote. Dent, who knew his people, had an idea for an anti-Reagan counterstrike. He cornered Oberdorfer at the intersection of the Georgia and Louisiana delegations and said something about betting him $300, though on what Oberdorfer couldn't hear over the din. Presuming it a joke, he wandered off. Dent grabbed a megaphone and said Oberdorfer had just refused to put money on the line that Hatfield would be the VP.

Word got around: Oberdorfer was just another yellow Eastern Establishment journalist whose word could not be trusted. The final anti-Nixon fire had been extinguished.

The roll call began at 1:19 a.m. Nixon sat far from anyone else in the crowded suite, keeping score to the TV on a yellow legal pad. Mrs. Nixon sat alone on the other side of the room.

Nixon got 692 votes, and the nomination for Republican candidate for president of the United States, on the first ballot, only 26 more than 50 percent and 203 less than Barry Goldwater received in 1964. Nixon was being sent into the general-election war with barely the endorsement of his party. Everyone had it in for Dick Nixon.

Rockefeller got 277 delegates. His campaign had spent $28,881 for each.

In the Reagan trailer, Clif White's fifteen-year-old daughter was disconsolate. Her father could not comfort her. Ronald Reagan, however, could. He put his arms around the tearful adolescent and said softly, "Carole, the good Lord knows what He is doing. This wasn't our turn."

Reagan traveled to the podium to move to make the count unanimous. Rockefeller still got ninety-three votes and Reagan got two: some still couldn't stomach Tricky Dick. In New York, an aged liberal rose at his breakfast table to boom out a toast: "To Richard Milhous Nixon, may the son of—"

Whereupon, as if unable to survive the thought, he had a fatal stroke.

To choose a running mate, Nixon tried something new: he poll-tested hypothetical tickets. No satisfactory name emerged. So Nixon was left to his own judgment. He already had the person in mind, but it wouldn't do to simply announce it.

The first "consultative" meeting he called, early Thursday morning, was with his inside team, people such as Haldeman and Frank Shakespeare and Maury Stans and Pat Buchanan. They tossed out their favorite names. Nixon's favorite was not among them. So he brought it up himself.

"How about Agnew?"

No one thought much of this one way or another. No one knew much about him. Agnew hadn't been on a list of eight first-tier Nixon VP possibilities published in *Time;* he hadn't been on *Time*'s twelve-name second-tier list, either. Nixon mentioned Agnew's fine nominating speech; no one remembered it as particularly fine. Nixon called in the next group, made up of politicians from key states and distinguished by the presence of the Reverend Billy Graham and the absence of any liberals. He had *them* throw out names. Nixon's favorite was not among them. So:

"How about Agnew?"

Nixon went down to the Hilton ballroom at 1 p.m. to meet the reporters who'd been smoking, waiting, smoking, playing the vice-presidential guessing game for two hours. One name no one mentioned. When Richard Nixon announced it from the platform, he was met with puzzled looks. "The face of one longtime aide, Charlie McWhorter," a reporter later wrote, "was white." Nixon strode out without taking questions. The famous political question of 1968 was born: "Sparrow who?"

Nixon had a habit of impetuously falling in love. He had not known Spiro Theodore Agnew long, but he felt a kinship with him. They came of common roots: both the sons of grocers who were strict disciplinarians, both had worked their way through college, both junior officers in World War II—strivers, grinders, resentful outsiders. Agnew (originally "Anagnostopoulos") was the son of Greek immigrants and went to law school at night. "Spiro was always neat," his half brother recalled. "He was never a noisy individual . . . he loved to read." Just like Richard Nixon, the only kid at school to wear a necktie, stealing away alone in the bell tower of the former church his father had converted into a grocery store.

When they were finally met, it came through a common wound: humiliation at the hands of Nelson Rockefeller. As a new governor in 1967, Agnew styled himself in the Rockefeller mold: fighting water pollution, eliminating the death penalty, ridding the nation of its last state board of motion-picture censors, passing open-housing legislation and ambitious programs in the fields of mental health, alcoholism, and highways. Positioning himself in front of Rocky's presidential parade seemed natural.

And then came March 21, when he called the entire Annapolis capitol press corps to watch Nelson Rockefeller's candidacy announcement on TV with him and suffered the deflating shame of Rockefeller's announcement "unequivocally that I am not a candidate."

John Mitchell took advantage of the opportunity, inviting Agnew to meet Nixon in New York. They hit it off. They shared the same resentments. They shared the same enemy. A new Orthogonian was inducted.

There was something *culturally* conservative about Agnew. His greatest crusade had been against pinball machines. His open-housing advocacy was of the most limited and risk-free sort. His explicit reason for backing that and no more was that anything else would generate "controversy and conflict." "Negroes," he explained in a message endearing to his 97 percent white constituency, "have historically been charged with running down neighborhoods." The Cambridge riot in July of '67 was a watershed; as he toured the damage brought on after H. Rap Brown incited Negroes to burn down a school, he announced, "It shall be the policy of this state to immediately arrest any person inciting a riot and not allow that person to finish his vicious speech." He started snapping randomly at black leaders, any black leader: "The violent cannot be allowed to sneak unnoticed from the war dance to the problem-solving meeting." It was as if, having once led a fight for some civil rights, he experienced demands for more as a direct affront. When black ministers complained, he would break out a tape of Rap Brown's Cambridge speech and start gesticulating: "Listen to that. Isn't that incitement?"

Spiro Agnew came to believe that whenever he gave dissenters an inch, they took a mile, and anarchy was loosed upon the land. So he would no longer give even an inch. In his first experience handling student unrest, at Towson State University, he had been measured and calm. In his second, when students at a black university, Bowie State, sat in to protest the decrepit campus, he announced a three-hour deadline by which students would "be removed from the buildings by whatever means are necessary." And so a week after his first lunch with Nixon, three weeks before the Battle of Morningside Heights, and the afternoon before the assassination of Martin Luther King, Agnew made headlines as a law-and-order vanguardist by having 227 college students arrested.

You could sum up his beliefs in a word, the "liberal" positions, the "conservative" positions, all of it: *order.* A veritable mania for order—against anyone "going too far." He boasted unblemished shirts, crisply creased pants, wrinkle-free suit jackets (his secret: "Never let your back touch the back of the chair"). One of his county employees told a journalist how, after a two-week camping trip, he was so eager to get back to work he returned straight to the office. The boss sent him home with orders not to come back until he shaved.

Agnew *hated* beards. At that, a lot of people hated beards. It explained his "liberal" gubernatorial campaign: he played to a suburban, middle-class longing for respectability. Maryland had some of the most disorderly and violent racists in the nation, and Agnew was running against them: "They are here, in Maryland," his commercials intoned. "The extremists, the robed figures. The faceless men . . . the fanatics." He asked voters to imagine their embarrassment if Mahoney won, "as you watch this man make a complete idiot of himself before the country." Spiro who? He was the tribune for those who felt visceral disgust at a society gone too far—a sound road to political stardom in gone-too-far 1968.

And now Spiro Agnew was at the podium in Miami Beach, accepting the vice-presidential nomination: "I stand here with a deep sense of the improbability of this moment. . . ."

Pat Buchanan would later write a planning memo for the 1972 convention in which he suggested all the speeches be like Nixon's 1968 acceptance speech: "orchestrated and advanced, with an audience cheering at the right times." Not many people had been watching the Republican convention every night on TV; ABC showed a mere ninety-minute wrap-up after summer reruns and killed CBS's and NBC's wall-to-wall coverage in the ratings. But Nixon's acceptance speech was the crucially important moment when people *would* be tuning in. This was when he was going to reassure them: under Nixon, everything was going to be all right. Under Nixon, America would be *quiet* again.

"A party that can unite itself will unite America," he began. Strom Thurmond sat close beside him on the platform.

"As we look at America, we see cities enveloped in smoke and flame.

"We hear sirens in the night.

"We see Americans dying on distant battlefields abroad.

"We see Americans hating each other; fighting each other; killing each other at home.

"And as we see and hear these things, millions of Americans cry out in anguish.

"Did we come all this way for this?

"Did American boys die in Normandy, and Korea, and in Valley Forge for this?

"Listen to the answer to those questions. It is the voice of the great majority of Americans, the forgotten Americans—the nonshouters; the non-demonstrators.

"They are not racist or sick; they are not guilty of the crime that plagues the land."

That word—*sick*—was used advisedly. That America was a "sick society" was a cliché of the age—a staple of gloomy conservatism (the serial killer of nurses, Richard Speck, was "symptomatic of the deep sickness in society," said the *Chicago Tribune*); the cry of black militants such as Eldridge Cleaver ("There is no end to the ghastly deeds of which this people are guilty. GUILTY"); even the cry of the pope, in his 1967 encyclical *Populorum Progresso:* "The world is sick. The poor nations remain poor while the rich ones become still richer." Three British journalists writing a book on the 1968 elections noted in America "a hysterical form of social hypochondria," a morbidly self-conscious sense of "being torn apart by the war and the cities." And here was Richard Nixon to say the *majority,* at least, weren't sick:

"They give drive to the spirit of America. They give lift to the American dream. They give steel to the backbone of America. They are good people, they are decent people; they work, and they save, and they pay their taxes, and they care."

Then he drew the contrast: government by Democrats, unequal to this forgotten majority.

"When the strongest nation in the world can be tied down for four years in a war in Vietnam with no end in sight;

"When the richest nation in the world can't manage its own economy;

"When the nation that has been known for a century for equality of opportunity is torn by unprecedented racial violence;

"And when the president of the United States cannot travel abroad or to any major city at home without fear of a hostile demonstration—then it's time for new leadership for the United States of America. . . .

"For five years hardly a day has gone by when we haven't read or heard a report of the American flag being spit on; an embassy being stoned; a library being burned; or an ambassador being insulted some place in the world. And each incident reduced respect for the United States until the ultimate insult inevitably occurred.

"And I say to you tonight that when respect for the United States of America falls so low that a fourth-rate miltiary power, like North Korea, will seize an American naval vessel on the high seas, it is time for new leadership to restore respect for the United States of America. My friends, America is a great nation. And it is time we started to act like a great nation around the world."

The longest section was on crime and poverty; that crime wasn't caused by poverty. "Tonight, it is time for some honest talk about the problem of order in the United States . . . the first civil right of every American is to be free from domestic violence." Then he personified the problem: "We are going to have a new Attorney General of the United States of America."

Making Ramsey Clark the bull's-eye, the civil-liberties-loving attorney general who the right-leaning *Washington Star* said wanted to fight crime "with speeches at twenty paces," was a brilliant move: the nation might be able to elect a new Democratic president, he was saying. But they wouldn't be electing a new *administration*. Nixon knew LBJ; knew he would never grant his vice president the charity of letting him announce preemptively that he would be making any changes in the cabinet. That tied Humphrey, through Ramsey Clark, to every rape, murder, and assault in the country, without ever having to mention Humphrey's name. It also abrogated any need for Nixon to come up with any actual *program* to cut down crime. A brilliant move, empty and effective: he'd repeat it in the upcoming months almost as often as he drew breath. It always got an enormous ovation.

It was a conservative speech—surely more conservative than he could have imagined it being, dreaming this moment in 1965, when Republican conservatism was supposed to have been dead and buried. That, however, was before 1966—and the rise of Ronald Reagan, whose ideas Nixon seemed to be cribbing: "For the past five years we have been deluged by government programs for the unemployed; programs for the cities; programs for the poor. And we have reaped from these programs an ugly harvest of frustration, violence, and failure across the land."

The speech ended with a homily:

"Tonight, I see the face of a child.

"He sleeps the sleep of childhood and he dreams the dreams of a child.

"And yet when he awakens, he awakens to a living nightmare of poverty, neglect, and despair.

"He fails in school.

"He ends up on welfare."

But for the poor, Nixon concluded, there was also a better way than welfare. For once Richard Nixon was poor.

"I see another child tonight.

"He hears the train go by at night and he dreams of faraway places where he'd like to go.

"It seems like an impossible dream.

"But he is helped on his journey through life.

"A father who had to go to work before he finished the sixth grade, sacrificed everything he had so that his sons could go to college.

"A gentle, Quaker mother, with a passionate concern for peace, quietly wept when he went to war but she understood why he had to go.

"A great teacher, a remarkable football coach, an inspirational minister, encouraged him on his way.

"A courageous wife and loyal children stood by him in victory and also defeat.

"And in his chosen profession of politics, first there were scores, then hundreds, then thousands, and finally millions worked for his success.

"And tonight he stands before you—nominated for president of the United States of America. . . . The time has come for us to leave the vale of despair and climb the mountain so that we may see the glory of the dawn— a new day for America, and a new dawn for peace and freedom in the world."

The balloons dropped, Dick arm in arm with Pat, who was arm in arm with Spiro's wife, their clean-cut kids smiling and clapping behind them.

Nixon was pleased with his performance. He told Bill Safire, "They call me 'intelligent, cool, with no sincerity'—and it kills them when I show 'em I know how people feel. I'd like to see Rocky or Romney or Lindsay do a moving thing like that 'impossible dream' part, where I changed my voice. Reagan's an actor, but I'd like to see him do that."

More sincere than Reagan, and a better actor, to boot; after all, he was the one who had *won*.

The most fateful decision for the Democrats was made the Thursday prior to their convention, not by a politician but by a federal district court judge. William Lynch, Mayor Daley's former law partner, withheld marching permits for the Mobe and sleeping permits for the Yippies. Mayor Daley's pleased reaction was recorded in a *Tribune* article headlined "Daley Blasts Suppression of the Czechs": "We don't permit our own people to sleep in the park, so why should we let anyone from outside the city sleep in the park?" (Actually they did let "their own" people sleep in the park, if they were Boy Scouts out on jamboree or National Guardsmen on weekend training.) "We don't permit our own people to march at night, so why should we let a lot of people do snake dances at night through the neighborhoods?"

"Snake dancing" was a maneuver Tokyo students had used to break through police lines and shut down the universities that summer. In Lincoln Park, several miles north of downtown, hapless Mobe "marshals" struggled to teach it to one another, but couldn't even break through their own lines. TV crew members outnumbered the snake dancers: "Wa'*shoi!* Wa'*shoi!*" they chanted every time a producer asked. Downtown in Civic Center Plaza, Abbie Hoffman and Jerry Rubin and folksinger Phil Ochs literally unleashed the Youth International Party's presidential candidate—Pigasus, a greased and ornery insult on four legs with a curly tail. Officers chased the animal around the plaza for a half hour, cameramen scurrying, cops greedily fingering their service revolvers, Abbie Hoffman crying, "Our candidate! Don't shoot our candidate!"

Thursday night at 11 p.m. in Lincoln Park, the same thing happened that had been happening at 11 p.m. all week: obediently, the drum circles broke

up, the political bull sessions ceased, guitars were returned to cases, litter
bagged and packed out. The protesters had shown goodwill against the glar-
ing stares of the blue-shirted constabulary in the expectation that the 11 p.m.
curfew would eventually be suspended, even though now they felt they'd
been double-crossed: a freak named Dean Johnson had just been shot to
death. Many feared the next cop bullet would be for them.

Contentious hearings drew to a close at the headquarters hotel, the gigantic redbrick Conrad Hilton at Michigan and Balbo. Committee members
fanned themselves furiously against the failure of the air-conditioning system
under the stress of too many bodies. At the Rules Committee, the McCarthy
insurgents introduced a motion to disallow the unit rule as the antidemocratic tool of bosses. Southern regulars said over their dead bodies—thus confirming the New Politics insurgents in their conviction that boss-ridden
Dixiecrats weren't interested in democracy in the first place. The controversy
before the Credentials Committee was over the right of Dixiecrats to be
present at all. The settlement of the Mississippi Freedom Democratic Party
controversy in 1964 in Atlantic City banned future segregated delegations.
Insurgents were fighting to get the all-white Mississippi and Georgia delegations unseated. It was a way to dramatize the illegitimacy of Hubert
Humphrey's imminent nomination: he hadn't entered a single primary. The
lion's share of his supporters were "delegates at large," officeholders automatically appointed to the convention—the kind of people who made their
decisions in between turns around the dance floor on cruise ships.

In Georgia, Governor Maddox had appointed most of the delegates.
Maddox himself hadn't been elected by the Georgia citizenry; when no candidate in 1966 won 50 percent, the Democratic legislature elevated him to the
governorship in a move of dubious constitutionality. He spent a busy week
in Chicago exploring then abandoning a presidential run, endorsing George
Wallace, and clearing up for the press that he had chased Negroes off his
property in 1964 not with "ax handles," but with "pick handles." Now in the
Hilton's muggy Imperial Ballroom, brilliant, young Ivy League–trained legal
minds delivered themselves of brilliant arguments about why his regular delegation should not be seated. The regulars—"slow, florid, insistent men,
Southern party hacks," one reporter described them, "accustomed to delivering mechanical rhetoric to courts that want nothing else"—drawled about
the way things had always been done. Chairman Richard Hughes of New
Jersey made the Solomonic choice, awarding half the seats to the regulars and
half to the insurgents, and the insurgents' leader, Julian Bond, who had gone
all the way to the Supreme Court to win the right to sit in the Georgia legislature with these men, expressed appreciation at the half loaf. "So now we
can't trust Julian Bond anymore," a New Leftist immediately responded—a
crux of the New Politics: compromises were always suspect.

At the Platform Committee—chaired by one of those florid, insistent regulars, Congressman Hale Boggs of Louisiana—debate raged over where the Democratic Party would stand on the war that Democrats had started. The Humphrey people's Vietnam War plank avowed, "We reject as unacceptable a unilateral withdrawal." It said bombing could stop only "when the action would not endanger the lives of our troops. This action should take into account the response from Hanoi." That enraged the peace forces because it framed them as quislings indifferent to the safety of American troops. Their opposing minority report called for "an unconditional end to all bombings in North Vietnam" and negotiations for "mutual withdrawal of all United States forces and all North Vietnamese troops from South Vietnam . . . over a relatively short period of time." It also encouraged "our South Vietnamese allies to negotiate a political reconciliation with the National Liberation Front"—recognizing the Vietcong as a legitimate political entity where Cold War orthodoxy saw them as puppets of North Vietnam, which in turn was a puppet of Moscow and/or Peking. This war had consumed twenty-seven thousand young American lives over four years, was costing America $82 million a day. What did that mean for America? The Democratic Party was split clean down the middle over the answer.

One of the minority's witnesses was a last-minute dark-horse entrant for the nomination. Senator George Stanley McGovern of South Dakota had punted away his first chance to enter the presidential race when approached in 1967 by Allard Lowenstein. "Do it," political associates advised him, "and kiss the Senate seat good-bye." He changed his mind as a favor for a grieving family: he would be the candidate for the delegates Robert F. Kennedy had won in tough state fights against Gene McCarthy. McGovern entered the race three days after the Republican convention in the same Senate Caucus Room where JFK and RFK had announced before him. Though the frumpy, quiet senator, who used the same tone of voice discussing corn yields with South Dakota farmers as he did haranguing his colleagues on the evils of Vietnam, was anything but Kennedyesque. The first time the glamorous Manhattan journalist Gloria Steinem arranged to interview him, she thought she had been stood up: "I was looking around for a man who looked like a senator." The assumption of the pundits was that McGovern was there to step aside for the younger brother, Senator Edward M. Kennedy, when the right moment came along.

McGovern introduced himself to the Platform Committee by pointing to his writings: the intellectual history *Agricultural Thought in the Twentieth Century;* his account of the Food for Peace program under President Kennedy, *War Against Want;* his Northwestern University doctoral dissertation on the Ludlow massacre of 1914. His proposal was radical: withdraw 300,000 troops from Vietnam in sixty days and move the remaining 250,000 into safe coastal enclaves.

John Connally, another slow, florid, insistent regular, rose to testify. He was asked, deadpan, by a South Carolina delegate, "Have you ever written a book, Governor?"

"No," the Texas governor replied, grinning, to rollicking laughter and applause. Then he gave a speech on national honor and the flag.

Michael Harrington, the newspaper columnist and old-line socialist leader, tried but failed to win similar laughs by beginning, "I'm afraid I have published a few books." In the middle of Harrington's testimony, Hale Boggs rudely got up from his seat to chat with friends in the front row.

The debate would be taken to the full convention on Wednesday afternoon, August 28. It was what Richard Nixon had been fantasizing about since 1966, when he bellowed that LBJ was "the first president in history who has failed to unite his own party in a time of war." Nixon knew the opposing party's Achilles' heel. Now they would have to display it in the open, in a televised spectacle.

The Russians invaded Czechoslovakia. Young Czech citizens stood around the tanks and soldiers and asked, "Why are you here?" By Friday, young American citizens in Lincoln Park, itching for confrontation, asked Chicago cops the same thing. "Czechago" cops answered, the protesters self-righteously thought, just like Brezhnev's jackbooted thugs: "This is my job." Ralph Yarborough, the liberal Texas congressman and John Connally's great rival, speaking for the Texas challenge delegation before the Credentials Committee, pleaded with Mayor Daley not to crush the "idealism of the young" with "political power" as the Russians crushed the Czechs with "military power." But the Soviet invasion also provided a moral template for the self-righteousness of the regulars: it showed what would happen if we didn't stand up to the enemy in Vietnam. "You people got no right to wave a Communist flag in the United States of America!" yelled one of the solid citizens who circled the park, taunting and gawking at hippies. "Because they got a right to cut you down, just like in *Doctor Zhivago*! Get out of this country!"

Saturday night, Yippies were only convinced to leave Lincoln Park at curfew time on the moral authority of Allen Ginsberg, who pied-pipered them into the adjacent Old Town neighborhood with a soothing Buddhist chant: *Ommmmmmmm.* Cops arrested and beat a few nonetheless. Sunday morning, Yippies drove a flatbed truck onto a swath of grass between the park lagoon and the Outer Drive lakeside freeway for their Festival of Life concert. Cops arrested a presumed ringleader, dragging him bodily through the crowd as an example. Kids started screaming insults. Cops waded in and started clubbing indiscriminately. Kids started wondering whether next time they should just sit and take it.

Eugene McCarthy arrived at Midway Airport. He didn't have any politicians with him as he descended the stairs. He did, however, have a poet, Robert Lowell, and a novelist, William Styron. The reporter for the countercultural *Evergreen Review* was convinced McCarthy was the only candidate in Chicago with enough charisma to get assassinated. Certainly not Hubert Humphrey; he was "a man with doldrums between his eyes." Unless Teddy Kennedy entered the race. The boom for him was peaking: Mayor Daley, presumed to be in the bag for Humphrey, had called a caucus of the Illinois delegation and announced that he wouldn't commit their votes for another forty-eight hours "to see if something develops." When Gene McCarthy emerged from the windswept, insecure tarmac unscathed, the *Evergreen Review*'s man drew a political conclusion: "the fact that McCarthy was still alive must have meant that he didn't have a chance in the convention."

Southern delegates kept alive a rumor that Lyndon Johnson might still sweep in and claim the nomination. Humphrey himself had no idea if they weren't right. Polls showed Humphrey behind George Wallace in Oklahoma, Tennessee, Kentucky, and North Carolina. The happy warrior with the mawkishly inappropriate campaign slogan—"the politics of joy"—spent the week moping. He reserved a pasted-on smile for those public moments where he had to appear as if nothing whatsoever was wrong.

Sunday morning, August 25, the nation learned, from an article by Seymour Hersh in the *New York Times Magazine,* that America maintained large stockpiles of weapons for chemical and biological warfare.

Sunday afternoon was the Festival of Life rock concert. *Time* ran a picture of a naked, goateed longhair in the middle of the crowd, a dowdy matron averting her eyes.

Sunday night, at ten forty-five, Yippies debated whether it was physical suicide to defy the cops or moral suicide not to. A floodlight swept a central sidewalk—a TV light, not a police light. A fourteen-year-old boy with the hair of an Indian brave leapt up on the shoulders of a friend and started waving the red, white, and yellow flag of the Vietnamese National Liberation Front: *"Stay in the park! Stay in the park! Parks belong to the people! Parks belong to the people!"* It was only his second demonstration. The first had been the peace march downtown in April, when the cops had beaten him up. "I'll probably never get to be twenty-one," he told a reporter.

Yippies started massing. Marshals from the Mobe cried, "This is suicide! Suicide!" They tried to pull the kid down from his friend's shoulders. It was five minutes to eleven—five minutes to midnight, for those hearing radio reports back East. Some melted onto the sidewalks, accommodating to police commands. Then the fourteen-year-old cried, *"Onto the streets!"* He ran into the intersection of LaSalle, Clark, and Eugenie with his flag. A crowd swarmed behind him. He'd refashioned retreat into a victory. A wave of righteous confidence surged through the crowd: they *owned* the streets. Nothing was going to stop them.

"The streets belong to the people! The streets belong to the people!"
"Pig! Pig! Pig! Oink! Oink! Oink!"

Some said they saw kids throwing rocks. Others said they saw nothing of the kind. A legend spread of the final insult that finally brought the cop rampage from every direction: *"Your mother sucks dirty cock!"*

They split skulls of yippies, marshals, bystanders. Some kids started charging back. Photographers swarmed to capture the images. They were set upon two by two—one cop to collar them for a beating, another to smash their camera. A radio reporter spotted Tom Hayden; he was supposed to be one of their leaders. The "leader," baffled, spoke for the record: "Man, what's going on down there?"

What was going on was pandemonium, right there in the streets of Chicago, for the delegates to read and gossip about the next evening, when the opening gavel at the Chicago Amphitheatre would ring out.

Monday morning, the Chicago police tracked down and arrested Thomas Hayden. The Mobe organized a "Free Hayden" march from Lincoln Park to police headquarters on South State Street, obediently confining themselves to only half the sidewalk. *"Fuck the marshals! Marshals are pigs!"* chanted some, aghast that they were granting legitimacy to the cops who had split their skulls the night before. (Hayden was bailed out, arrested again, and bailed out a second time by some *Village Voice* writers, who overheard some cops: "We had to fumigate after we led all those animals through"; "I'm going to kill those Yippies who lost me that good lay.") The march ended with a rally in Grant Park in front of the Hilton. Someone clambered up the equestrian statue of Union general John A. Logan, waving the Vietcong flag. A massive crowd formed to hold the hill beneath him as if it were a military objective—for the thousands of delegates and alternates to see as they lined up for the buses and taxis that transported them to the Stockyards Amphitheatre.

The way was flecked with hand-scrawled signs: GET READY FOR KENNEDY IN '68. '72 IS TOO LATE, '68 IS THE DATE—DRAFT TEDDY KENNEDY. City workers had removed every rock bigger than a pebble from a several-block radius of the amphitheater; every manhole cover was sealed shut or actively watched; the parking lot was ringed with a half mile of barbed wire. Security headquarters next to the great white-granite hall had an eight-by-twelve-foot magnetic map of the city and a hotline to the White House and the Pentagon. The *Evergreen Review,* however, recognized a gaping hole in the security: a man holding a shotgun over his head could have gotten in if he also wore on his back and front one of the ubiquitous, identical WE LOVE MAYOR DALEY signs.

The convention floor accommodated 6,511 delegates, but was designed to hold 4,850. The air hung heavy with summer sweat, cigarette smoke, the smell of the nearby stockyards. The gavel rang, Aretha Franklin belted out a rock-and-roll version of "The Star-Spangled Banner," and the first of many brawls broke out: the compromise on the Georgia delegation voted by the

Credentials Committee wouldn't go into effect until Wednesday, and liberals jumped on their seats and started shouting at Georgia, "Throw them out! Throw them out!" Senator Daniel Inouye delivered his keynote speech, addressed to the hippies infesting Chicago's parks: "What trees do they plant?" The ringers carrying WE LOVE MAYOR DALEY signs were exuberant. A Negro California delegate in African robes and a necklace fashioned of animal teeth held up his delegate credentials and tried to burn them like a draft card. Concessionaires were instructed not to put ice cubes in the drinks lest people throw them. Word arrived of that night's riot in Lincoln Park, how the Yippies built a massive barricade of picnic tables, trash baskets, and anything else they could get their hands on. In the park, a cop car stealthily glided up at 12:20 a.m., turned its lights on, and met the fate of Richard Nixon in Caracas in 1958: every window was smashed, and a kid grabbed the driver by the neck and almost pulled him out the door.

Then, the retaliation: wave after wave of tear gas, assaults with shotgun and rifle butts, a seminarian beaten nearly to death, more ambushed cop cars, dueling screams (*"Hell, no, we won't go!"; "Kill the fucking commies!"*)— running battles in the streets of Chicago. And in the parking lot, reporters watched policemen slash the tires of every car bearing a daisy-festooned Eugene McCarthy bumper sticker. The liberal *Chicago Daily News* called it "the most vicious behavior on the part of the police" in twenty-five years. The papers also reported that Abbie Hoffman had been arrested for having FUCK written across his forehead.

The California delegation was pledged to a dead man. The primary had been so nasty that many were reluctant to switch. So they had all three candidates, Humphrey, McCarthy, and McGovern, give a speech before their caucus and the cameras—the only occasion before the convention roll call when all the candidates actually competed. Hubert Humphrey said of the 1967 elections in South Vietnam, "When you look over the world scene, these elections stand up pretty well," and that we were only in Vietnam to "resist aggression." He was booed. George McGovern got the biggest ovation.

California and New York were strongest in support of the peace plank. Which is why they had to sit in the far back corner of the hall. In Lincoln Park, as word passed of the forty-three black soldiers in the stockade at Fort Hood for refusing to muster for Chicago riot duty, kids started showing up with armloads of ceramic building tile, clinking them together for rhythmic effect, eyeing the cops. A coalition of solid citizens met with the Eighteenth Police District commander to beg his forces to allow the kids to sleep in the park. The officer affected sympathy, asked for the badge numbers of the rogue officers beating kids, and described the fears they were operating under: "We even heard they are going to throw flaming spears."

At about 7 p.m. on Tuesday, by account of the federal commission later convened to study the violence, "a crowd estimated at 1,500 persons listened to Bobby Seale of the Black Panther Party and Jerry Rubin call for revolution in the United States." Police spies recorded their words. Seale, whose partner Huey Newton's murder case was wrapping up in Oakland, said, "Pick up a gun and pull that spike out from the wall. Because if you pull it on out and if you shoot well, all I'm gonna do is pat you on the back and say 'keep on shooting.' . . . If the police get in the way of our march, tangle with the blue-helmeted motherfuckers and kill them and send them to the morgue slab." He also offered tactical advice: "Large groups are wrong. Get into small groups of three, four, and five. Be armed and spread out so we can 'stuckle' pigs." Rubin promised, "We'll take the same risks the blacks take."

At eleven, a phalanx of clergymen marched around the park with a life-size cross in a vigil for calm. The cops dispersed tear gas in industrial quantities from sanitation department trucks and made their move. They didn't bother with arrests: they just waded into the crowd, leaving maimed victims behind.

At the amphitheater, the day's chaos was gaveled to a close after one last brawl on the convention floor when Mayor Daley slashed his finger across his neck, instructing House Majority Leader Carl Albert to adjourn when peace delegates tried to commandeer the microphones to register protest at the police repression in Lincoln Park. Not a single important agenda item of the convention had been completed.

The *Chicago Daily News* ran a picture of an unidentified man pointing a rifle out of his car window toward passing Yippies outside Lincoln Park. NBC News developed its film for the next morning's *Today* show, where it was narrated by correspondent Jack Perkins:

"In the darkness and confusion, policemen used their nightsticks with great zeal, clubbing and injuring about sixty people. Seventeen of them were newsmen—there trying to cover it—including a CBS cameraman . . . an NBC cameraman, and NBC News reporter John Evans.

"They beat cameramen to keep them from filming policemen beating other people, and newsmen not in spite of the fact they were newsmen but because of it.

"This suppression of the news and these beatings were in direct violation of police orders, but they happened. And none of the newsmen we talked to had ever seen anything to match it in any other city in this country."

CHAPTER FIFTEEN

Wednesday, August 28, 1968

SOMETHING EXTRAORDINARY WAS HAPPENING IN CHICAGO. BY WEDNES-day, August 28—the fifth anniversary of Martin Luther King's "I have a dream" speech—even political indifferents were watching the convention. It was the most extraordinary TV show imaginable.

Let us suppose you are one of those apathetic Americans. You flip to NBC at quarter past four Chicago time to see what all the fuss is about.

Things wouldn't have seemed interesting at first: anchors Chet Huntley and David Brinkley kibbitzing in their sonorous voices about the inevitability of the Humphrey nomination and the scuttlebutt on running-mate possibilities. Then a floor reporter related a conversation with the vanquished Gene McCarthy: McCarthy had offered to withdraw in favor of Teddy Kennedy, then was told that Kennedy's decision not to run was final; now McCarthy said Hubert Humphrey "should be stopped at almost all cost" and that his support for the ticket was dependent on Humphrey's reaction to the pro–Vietnam War plank. Dramatic stuff, if you followed this sort of thing. A boring blizzard of disconnected names if you didn't.

You might have readied to turn off the set—and then:

"At Grant Park in downtown Chicago there has been in progress for some time a sizable peace demonstration. Jack Perkins, NBC News correspondent, was there and has a report for us by way of videotape."

Cut to people milling around bleacher-style seats at a band shell, and a voice over a loudspeaker: "Sit down! Sit down! Sit down!" Then the camera view sweeps to the left, and you see a mass of men in riot helmets sweeping through the rows.

"At first the police had said they would not clear the demonstrators out of this rally, that the officers, they would protect them and let them have it here. But then the demonstrators began throwing paper, tomatoes, stones, tried to kick in one of their police cars, so the police responded with tear gas and moving back the line of demonstrators from the corner of the park. And the speaker on the platform trying to keep some degree of order—"

New camera angles: young men in flannel shirts and leather jackets and coats and ties and young women in peasant skirts eyeing the cops on their approach.

"It is fairly tense here, and one factor to consider is that whenever the police appear, they are automatically referred to as 'pigs'—is the automatic term by these demonstrators. This does not tend to ease tensions—"

A demonstrator waves a red flag, another gets blood wiped off his face.

"These demonstrators have been making their plans about what to do this afternoon. And they have decided they are going to march on the amphitheater, they will go ahead with it, despite police determination to stop them short. They will leave this park at four o'clock and try to get as far as they can. . . . Those are their plans. And the plans of the police are to stop them. Jack Perkins, NBC News, Grant Park."

And then it's back to the convention hall, and Chet Huntley explaining that they'd be showing such field reports on videotape because a telephone workers' strike had prevented them from setting up microwave equipment for live reports. John Chancellor has a report from one of the delegations on the convention floor—cut to Chancellor wearing one of those funny space-man antennas and holding a microphone and a heavy, black equipment pack:

"Those of us who have been covering political conventions for a long time have almost never seen anybody cry, weep tears, at a convention, but when it became apparent that the minority report on the Vietnam plank failed today, some people in the New York delegation began crying. This is one of those ladies—"

". . . a military cemetery, my brother is buried, was buried, over in Maas-tricht, Holland, and I don't want to see any more of this war, that's all. . . . And I was hoping that our party would be the party to put in a real antiwar plank. . . . Everyone knows that the thing that is going to stop this war is the stopping of the bombing—"

A sob, then a convulsed sniff.

"We're not going to give up, not any of us. . . . When you've been in a party as long as I have, and you love it, and you see the end of something—I'm just saying good-bye, is what I'm doing."

You notice that some of the men have white and blue paper flowers affixed to their suit jackets, the same flowers some of the kids have on their leather jackets in Grant Park—McCarthy flowers. Another reporter inter-views a "peace-plank architect" who speaks with an air of resigned futility about how the convention orchestra immediately started blaring martial music whenever a peace delegate tried to be recognized and says the votes to defeat them all came from Southern delegates who wouldn't even be voting for the Democratic nominee in November.

Then a commercial for Gulf Oil, which you sit through to see what hap-pens next.

There's another interview, with the California leader Jesse Unruh, who says that at least *their* delegation didn't have any "secret caucuses," and that "I hope by our example we have said to the young people of this country . . . learn to believe in the mainstream of our society . . . to the black people . . . have been shoved out of our society . . . to the other minorities who do not share in any measure of the affluence in our society."

They cut to the New York delegation waving curiously flimsy STOP THE WAR signs, standing on their chairs and singing "We Shall Overcome," and John Chancellor:

"This floor is a cacophony of sound! When the New York delegation, or most of it, began standing on their chairs and singing this song, the podium tried to 'get order' as it called it, and then the band, under orders from the podium, began to play—"

("We Shall Overcome" and "You're a Grand Old Flag," simultaneously.)

David Brinkley:

"A rather furious contest between the delegation and the convention orchestra—"

The string section, sawing away furiously in their tuxedos.

"The conductor keeps on asking for 'one more chorus.'"

"They're now raising in the middle of the delegation a long piece of black cloth in mourning for their hopes, which they had to smuggle into the hall."

Someone explains why the STOP THE WAR signs are so flimsy: they were printed on tissuey paper and smuggled inside within newspapers. "One New York delegate was stopped by security police here in the convention hall yesterday for bringing in a copy of the *New York Times,* which is considered by some people in the United States to be a dangerous instrument."

They throw to another reporter describing another interview with Eugene McCarthy, denying that he was about to start a third or fourth party, but that he certainly wouldn't rule it out for future elections.

"We can now count New Hampshire, Mississippi, Colorado, Oregon, Wisconsin, Nebraska, Alaska, and Vermont, who have joined New York in this extraordinary demonstration of antiwar sentiment on the convention floor along with a great part of the alternate section and the galleries—"

"John, they may realize that the orchestra may run into a union problem! I'd think an orchestra has to be given five minutes' rest every hour or something like that."

"And these people," John Chancellor says from the midst of an arm-in-arm chorus of McCarthy delegates bellowing the "Battle Hymn of the Republic," "I think they could go on forever."

The anchor announces that the chairman has managed to belt out a call for a recess until six thirty. You decide to tune in then. A war has broken out on the floor of an American major-party convention. You can't imagine anything more engrossing than this.

✳   ✳   ✳

"I'm with two adornments of the Florida delegation," says Edwin Newman, putting his microphone before two smartly dressed suburban women.

"Mrs. Heatter, you're not particularly happy with the way the convention has gone, I think."

"No, I'm a McCarthy delegate, and this is my first time at a convention, and I had the dreams from high school democracy class, that everybody voted their conscience, and everyone voted for their constituents, because they were elected delegates. And that's not how it goes. I hear people say, 'What am I supposed to vote here?' not, 'What is the issue?'"

"Who are 'they,' Mrs. Heatter?"

"I don't know, but they look like they've had a lot of experience with conventions. . . . I think we should have a new system . . . the people at home want things so badly, and the delegates-at-large and people like that don't give it to them . . . there's going to be people who say, 'It doesn't matter at all.'"

The Wisconsin chairman, reflecting on the changes in his old friend Hubert Humphrey: "His subservience to the president seems to have *changed* him." Richard Goodwin, the former JFK speechwriter, on the pro-LBJ Vietnam plank that passed 1,567 votes to 1,041: "If the vice president is nominated, I think he has the task of going to the country and saying, 'I offer you more of the same.' . . . I think it's an untenable position."

That position is countered by hangdog old Paul Douglas, the former Illinois senator beaten in 1966, the liberal hawk who had fronted for the White House's fake Citizens Committee for Peace with Freedom in Vietnam.

John Chancellor: "I assume you're pleased with the plank."

"Yes, I am, and I don't think it's a pro-war plank. It's a plank for mutual progress toward peace. . . . After the record the Communists have made in various parts of the world, that it would be putting our troops in danger if we made a series of one-sided sacrifices that were not met by any reciprocal actions on their part. . . . In the long run, people will react properly . . . the vast majority will fall in and support Humphrey."

A Connecticut McCarthy delegate complains about the galleries being empty for the dramatic peace-plank vote—something "they did to control the demonstration in the galleries."

The reporter, with agitation: "Well, then, I'm trying to find out—I've been trying to find out for the past two days, *who* are you talking about when you say *they*? It sounds like a Kafka novel."

The Connecticut delegate, who has sideburns: "It's very hard to find out. I know that earlier in the day, we were trying to bring in minority-report literature, and we were told for the first time that a delegation"—he sighs incredulously—"could not bring literature to the floor. Other literature has been coming in constantly . . . a new rule came up and we were not able to bring pertinent materials to the floor."

Chet Huntley: "Ahhh, do? What—I understand that Mayor Daley is in the hall."

The camera is now on Daley, his jowls, his scowl, men attending to him as if he were a Bourbon potentate. Brinkley jokes, "Well, he left the hall in a fleet of black limousines, spent a while, and came back in a fleet of black limousines. And so we take it for granted that he did better than hot dogs.

"Which no one else has done," Brinkley adds with some irritation, before cutting to a cartoon of Goofy and Professor von Drake toodling along in their Model T singing praises for Gulf Oil's miraculous "No-Nox" gasoline.

You flip on the set after supper. A young Colorado delegate is being interviewed: "Peter, I'm going to get a little personal. You have fairly long sideburns, and a cowlick hanging down there"—Peter smiles shyly—"but you are after all a very clean and good-looking young man. And yet we heard this morning Wayne Hays from the podium denounce those who wore long sideburns and a whole list of things."

(Ohio congressman Wayne Hays had spoken from the podium about those who "substitute sideburns for sense" and "beards for brains.")

"What kind of effect did that have on you?"

"I think it's very funny. It's an unfortunate situation where it judges its people by the length of their hair, by the clothes that they wear. I think indications of this in Chicago, with the almost garrison state that we have existing downtown in Chicago, is disgraceful in America.

"The freedom of speech, the freedom of choice in what you wear, how you look, is one of the most important things we have."

A New Jersey delegate, Mrs. Elizabeth Wenk, asked about the announcement of Boston 5 codefendant Marcus Raskin that he would be holding a meeting the Friday after the convention to form a fourth party, and whether she would be attending: "Maybe if Senator McCarthy is not nominated."

David Brinkley, going through some registration figures: Americans aged twenty-one to twenty-nine "have the poorest record of all, with forty-nine percent unregistered. So it provokes the question—is neither of the parties attracting the youngsters?"

A Gulf commercial: A couple pulls into a filling station, where they're giving out a free donkey or elephant pin with every fill-up. The husband wants the donkey. The wife wants the elephant: "I think it's very important to be strict."

The broadcast is rejoined. Huntley goes into a reflection about Humphrey: "The Southern delegations that hated him, walked out on him twenty years ago, are now among his warmest friends, and the liberals to whom he was a hero twenty years ago are now among his warmest enemies."

Paul Newman boringly reading out a boring speech: "I hope and pray

that we Democrats, win or lose, can campaign not as a crusade to extermi-
nate the opposing party, as our opponents seem to prefer, but as a great
opportunity to educate and elevate." This is from Adlai Stevenson's 1952
acceptance speech, read in tribute to Stevenson's insistence that Democrats
remain nicer than Richard Nixon.

You step to the fridge for a beer.

You hear from the kitchen the anchors giggling a little about the hassles at
the headquarters hotel, the Conrad Hilton: "Long waits for the elevator, you
cannot get clothes pressed, you can't get laundry done, you can't get room
service, and now it's filling up with tear gas!"

This is something. You return to your seat.

A correspondent in front of a Humphrey poster (SOME TALK ABOUT
CHANGE. OTHERS CAUSE IT), describing how they're giving out hundreds of
HHH signs, of the sort that were banned for McGovern and McCarthy:
"I've just learned that about fifty of the loyal Mayor Daley political aides
have been allowed to enter the convention hall. As a matter of fact they came
in through the main delegate gate carrying alternate delegate tickets for last
Monday night's session!"

John Chancellor with John Connally of Texas, who smiles with phoniness about the vice presidency: "I doubt I've ever been in the running. . . . I
made the decision last fall not to run for another term as governor and retire
to private life, and those are my very firm wishes and desires." But the person whom Vice President Humphrey *does* choose should have "a background and experience slightly more moderate than his own. . . . I'm not sure
this year is a year when a great liberal is going to get all of the support that
is needed to be elected. . . . The people are frustrated, the people are upset,
you see it at every turn, you see it at this convention. People are operating
more and more on an emotional basis. They're . . . frequently overreacting
to any given situation."

At the guest entrance, where a group of people carrying HHH WIN IN ILLI-
NOIS signs file by. The reporter: "The anti-Humphrey people are considerably unhappy about it."

The camera zooms in on a stream of beefy men lumbering down the stairs
past the California delegates at a remote corner of the hall:

"And there have been some words exchanged between them."

"And the rules on the floor, David, have undergone a sudden change."

And a Gulf filling-station clerk dashes through a pack of rabid dogs to
make it to a customer's car within ten seconds.

Then back again to Chet Huntley:

"There have been demonstrations at this early hour in downtown
Chicago's Grant Park. We heard a moment ago that tear gas has been used.

As the demonstrators are attempting to form a line of parade and march toward, or on, the amphitheater, Aline Saarinen has a report describing what is going on."

The TV images that would shake American politics like none had since Watts in 1965 began innocuously enough: on NBC, above a chyron reading TAPED, it looked like a busy New York rush hour, though some are holding handkerchiefs to their faces.

Peace marchers who started out walking south met a wall of police and turned northward into the plaza containing Buckingham Fountain, then looped around to head south again, avoiding the cops. So the hemmed-in cops threw tear-gas canisters across the street at the apex of the marchers' U-turn—which was the sidewalk in front of the building that billed itself as "the world's largest and friendliest hotel."

GRANT PARK, CHICAGO, ILLINOIS, the chyron now reads, and a woman's voice says, "The kids are still marching, it looks like a whole gathering of people with terrible colds"; and then Brinkley back in the convention hall: "Mrs. Saarinen has been gassed in the course of that report, has received medical attention, and is all right."

The next image, appropriately enough, is a commercial about the joy brought to a small Louisiana town when Gulf built a chemical plant.

"Now to Edwin Newman on the floor."
"I am with the Reverend Richard Neuhaus, the chairman of Clergy and Laymen Concerned about Vietnam. Reverend Neuhaus, you're organizing a walkout tonight because of the anticipated nomination of Vice President Humphrey. How big a walkout will it be?"
"Well, if Vice President Humphrey is nominated, it won't take much organizing. I anticipate we're going to have at least two hundred delegates walking out of the convention—not necessarily walking out of the party."
"What will the walkout mean?"
"I think the walkout will mean that they can under no circumstances support the presidential candidate. I think it will mean further that the Democratic Party has made a grievous mistake and just entirely missed, you know, the action of the past year and a half.... When, as we fear, with Vice President Humphrey as the candidate, the Democratic Party is defeated, we will be in a position to work for the renewal of the party."
Panning the hall: HHH flags, signs, balloons, banners, streamers, crowding every corner; then to a John Chancellor interview with the Reverend Channing Phillips of Washington, D.C., the first Negro to be put in nomination at a major-party presidential convention:
"Why are you wearing the black crepe paper around your arm, Reverend Phillips?"

"We put that piece of paper on after the minority plank on Vietnam lost at this convention. We think it's a sign of mourning for this country for its refusal to recognize its error in Vietnam and for continuing the policy of slaughter."

And the camera cuts to a plump woman in a tent of an orange floral dress with a HUMPHREY banner flowing down her buttocks dancing maniacally around with two HUMPHREY balloons, and an Indian in full HUMPHREY war-bonnet, and Muriel Humphrey sitting expectantly in her VIP box; and a quantity of windbaggish favorite-son nominating speeches; and vice-presidential prognostications in the aisles; and more speeches; and pans of balloons and streamers and placards, and the band plays, and the seconding speaker for North Carolina's Governor Dan Moore drones; and David Brinkley says, "We are told that Vice President Humphrey got into the tear gas down in the area of Grant Park across from the Hilton Hotel a while ago. We'll have more details as soon as we get them. In the meantime we'll have this message from Gulf."

"By late afternoon when this film was made, over ten thousand demonstrators were gathered in Grant Park. . . . The demonstrators resisted when police attempted to arrest a young man who tried to rip down an American flag.

"Police fired tear-gas canisters, demonstrators threw them back at police, and it was clear that Chicago's first real battle of the day was joined. . . . Chanting 'Kill the Pigs,' they began bombarding the police with cans, bottles, boards, firecrackers, tomatoes, and just about anything else they could find.

"Demonstration leaders, hoping to save all the energy for later tonight, used bullhorns to try to restore order."

Screams, then upward of one hundred cops, a sea of blue (if you have a color TV) shirts and blue riot helmets arrayed in a wedge like a giant bowling-pin setup, carrying their clubs across their chests, Plexiglas shields down, barreling into the crowd and beating anyone they can reach, kids tripping over the band shell's park benches in chaotic retreat, the closing image a man and woman desperately clutching each other.

"This night is far from over; demonstrators say they will still march, and if police try to stop them, they will sit down in the Chicago streets. This is Douglas Kiker."

The transition that follows immediately upon those words: men in suits with pursed lips and rage in their eyes pushing, shoving, swinging fists on the convention floor, Edwin Newman of NBC barking into a microphone but no sound issuing forth, at the borderlands between the New York and the Alabama delegations.

"Your microphone is broken, Ed! . . .

"There's a huge amount of pushing—watch it, you're going to knock that over!—the man being pushed is a delegate, how this started, we don't know."

A guttural screech in a full-on New York City accent: *"Check with our state chairman! He's an elected delegate! What are you trying to spring on us!"*

"No one's springing—"

"You are! Check with the—where are the rules that say we must show 'em every minute? Who the hell are you to—the rules! The rules!"

John Chancellor fights through with a working microphone: "Are you the delegate they're trying to throw out?"

"Yes, I am."

("Check the rules of the Democratic Party!")

"Why is that?"

"Because I objected to their behavior."

Chancellor explains that the raid began with shouts of "Secret Service! Push! Push!" although the people doing the pushing appeared only to be ushers, "and nobody is showing the usual insignia of the Secret Service."

("They keep coming all day checking our credentials! And it's time they stop! There's nothing in the rules of the Democratic Party that says they have a right to check us every ten minutes! It's been like this every day!")

Chancellor confirms that the man they're trying to kick out, Alex Rosenberg, is indeed an elected delegate, who got sick of showing his credentials. A man fights his way to Chancellor's microphone, smirking, and drawls, "Just another peaceful demonstration by New York trying to demonstrate in Alabama!"

Chancellor comments, "The issue of law and order seems to be taking place in a rather active dispute on the floor of this convention," and the Alabaman now grins like the cat who ate the canary. Chancellor passes off to Sander Vanocur interviewing Colonel John Glenn of Ohio, then they cut back to Chancellor, looking startled:

"The Chicago police are now in the aisle with billy clubs, clearing people out! . . . They're dragging people right out of the aisle. One, two, three, four, five, six—some of them wearing the blue helmets."

Photographers hoist their cameras above their heads and into the scrum: *click, click, click.*

"This is the first time in my memory of going to political conventions that the police have come in, on the floor, armed as they were, and taking out people who were disputing the checking of credentials."

"First time in the United States, John."

As Chancellor describes "some very large men who came along with security badges," a camera cuts to Chicago's implacable Buddha boss, and then the screen fills with a dozen blue helmets as an out-of-breath young man spins himself out of the scrum, looking as if he's just seen a ghost. "I started getting shoved up against a wall, the crush just started, I got carried along by the wave . . . and finally the 'Secret Service' men just *picked me up* and carried me out."

He is a reporter for United Press International, and his hair is long.

More windy nominating speeches:

"At no time has Senator McCarthy recommended unconditional withdrawal from Vietnam. At no time has he recommended any move that would deprive our fighting men of full protection."

NBC cuts to Daley, scratching distractedly, crossing his arms. But every time this show starts getting boring, something more astonishing is thrown up on the screen. You're on your fourth beer by now, wondering what country you're living in, as they cut to taped exterior shots.

It's dark. A cone of TV light emerges, and out of the murk comes an endless rush of blue helmets, darting into a crowd sitting down in an intersection. The back door of a paddy wagon opens, at the moment the first *crack* rings out. It is all flailing nightsticks, a kid pulled by the scruff of the neck. Dark again. A halo of TV lights as he's thrown into the back, then another, then another, each with a superfluous whack of a nightstick. Door closes; wagon drives off; the sound of an explosion; darkness; line after line of cops awaiting their turn; the next wave into the wagon; a chant:

"*The whole world is watching! The whole world is watching!*"

If it shames the cops, they aren't showing it. TV techs flash lights in their faces, then darkness, then bobbing seas of blue helmets, a camera flash; a kid with a mustache squirms free and a cop follows him off into the inky maw.

"*The whole world is watching! The whole world is watching!*"

The next wagon drives off, medics in white coats attend to the fallen; SUPPRESSING DISSENT IS FASCISM—scrawled on a scrap of corrugated cardboard; inky black; camera flashes; screams; more knots of blue helmets pushing into another crowd; a strobe-light effect, a dull hum of screams, it doesn't look like TV. A man wriggles free from his windbreaker. A cop pulls him down with a wrestling move.

"*Sieg Heil! Sieg Heil! Sieg Heil!*"

The next cop wave arrives in formation. Finally the sonorous voice interrupts, "We're at the Conrad Hilton, where peace demonstrators have blocked the intersection, and now a phalanx of police has come through . . . right outside the headquarters hotel of the Democratic convention . . . police swirling all around us."

One more supernova flash of light, and an immediate cut to Julian Bond, seconding the nomination of Eugene McCarthy:

"All over the world, 1968 has been a year in which people have been rising up and demanding freedom! From Biafra to Georgia! From Czechoslovakia to Chicago—"

Huge applause.

". . . *Don't* tell me we're going to win that freedom from the leaders of the past, because those leaders don't even understand what we're talking about!"

The biggest cheer of the convention so far.

"He is the *only* candidate who can win, because he is the *only* candidate the American people can believe. . . .

"Americans realize there is *one* candidate who has never spoken on the side of repression and violence—

"*One* candidate who has spoken steadily of bringing together black and white people—"

In the hall, some people are watching tiny portable TVs. And the word from the streets is out, for the next thing he says is "Fellow delegates, the whole country is watching us now. As indeed, the *whole world* is watching us. . . .

"It is not too late."

"Here is a little more on the action downtown. . . . The guardsmen have bayonets at the end of their rifles, they're wearing gas masks; part of the central hallway of the Hilton Hotel has been made into a first aid station, sort of a receiving hospital. McCarthy volunteers are now going out in the streets to find injured demonstrators. . . . There's now a report that some guests in the hotel are getting mixed up in it and are throwing glasses and other things out of hotel rooms at the police."

"Here's one more, Chet: Mrs. McCarthy, Mrs. Abigail McCarthy, is not here in the convention hall because she is staying in her hotel room under Secret Service guard. They have decided it is not safe for her to leave the hotel because of all this rough stuff outside."

"We'll be back after this message from Gulf."

("Let's take a trip into the world of Gulf chemicals! . . . Lids for your coffee, detergents for your dishes, plastic bags of all sorts, toys, luxurious carpeting . . . tires . . . fertilizers that help good things grow!")

Brinkley, sardonically, before they show the donkey/elephant pin commercial again: "We are told that the Chicago police are under orders that if they come into the hall to arrest delegates or otherwise do their duties, they are not to wear helmets. Presumably because it doesn't look very good."

Huntley, holding a headphone to his ear: "David, I think we can establish this without fear of contradiction: this is surely the first time policemen have ever entered the floor of a convention."

Brinkley, with a weary, slow shake of the head: "In—the—United—States."

* * *

Bald-headed Joseph Alioto, mayor of San Francisco, is called to the podium to nominate HHH. The band plays on: *"San Francisco, open that Golden Gate . . ."* Huntley breaks in: "Well, the news media has taken another casualty. NBC News reporter Don Oliver reports that Mike Wallace of CBS was being detained by the Chicago police in a command post trailer on the second floor of the amphitheater after a disturbance on the floor of the convention. There is a report that Wallace has been struck by a security guard."

Mayor Alioto intones, "Hubert—Horatio—Humphrey!" Mayor Daley is shown clapping and grinning like a schoolboy.

Alioto: "It isn't enough, I say, to mouth to the youngsters, that you mouth this talk about 'New Politics,' and the inflexible status quo, because here is a man who has done more in the last twenty years than any discernible man to bring America not only to a recognition of what is old and good, but what is new and good as well."

"To John Chancellor on the convention floor."

"The mayor has said he would give a little comment. Can you comment while applauding on the speech?"

The mayor acknowledges the existence of the man dangling a microphone in his general direction by turning and facing the other way.

The roll call of the states for the nomination: Arkansas passes, California already yielded, the Canal Zone passes, Colorado . . .

"Mr. Chairman, Colorado rises to a point of information. Is there any rule under which Mayor Daley can be compelled to suspend the police-state terror perpetrated this minute"—a roar of approval rises up—"on kids in front of the Conrad Hilton?"

Gavel gavel gavel.

"Hello? Hello?" you hear, but not over the convention loudspeakers, for the podium has turned off his microphone.

Just how drunk are you, you wonder, as Senator Ribicoff winds up his windbaggery for Senator McGovern:

"He is a man without guile. He is a whole man. . . .

"George McGovern is a man with peace in his soul. . . .

"George McGovern is not satisfied that ten million Americans go hungry every night. . . ."

Cut to a bored Mayor Daley.

"George McGovern blows out of the prairies of South Dakota a new wind": blah blah blah blah blah.

"The youth of America rallied to the standard of men like George McGovern, like they rallied to the standard of John F. Kennedy and Robert Kennedy": same old, same old.

"And with George McGovern as president of the United States, we wouldn't have to have gestapo tactics in the streets of Chicago!"

Quick cut to Daley, then Ribicoff, then Daley, then Ribicoff, a simpering downward turn of his mouth, then Daley, who was no longer bored.

"With George McGovern, we wouldn't have to have a national guard" — And the hall was filled with cheers and boos.

"He *looked* at Mayor Daley!" Huntley says.

"Would like to know what the mayor is saying," Brinkley responds.

(Later an expert lip-reader suggested an answer: "Fuck you, you Jew son of a bitch, you lousy motherfucker, go home.")

"How hard it is to accept the truth," says the senator, as one of the anchormen intones solemnly. "The aisles of the convention are crowded, and we don't quite know with whom. We do know that wherever our reporters go on the floor, they are followed by unidentified, faceless men, trying to listen to everything they say."

Hubert Humphrey wins the Democratic nomination. But is he leading a party, or a civil war?

CHAPTER SIXTEEN

Winning

AFTER CHICAGO, HUMPHREY CAME OUT OF THE GATE WITH A DOUBLE-digit deficit. He leapfrogged the country, East Coast to West then back again in a week, less popular after each stop. When he was met by the chants of angry antiwar activists ("We felt if we could elect Nixon, we'd get to the revolution that much sooner," one recalled), law-and-order devotees were confirmed in their presumption that wherever Democrats went, scream-ing chaos followed; doves were reminded that Humphrey was pro-war. He was hurt just as badly by those he *wasn't* met by at each stop. John Connally snubbed him in Texas. Jesse Unruh and Sam Yorty did so in California.

To college students in Philadelphia, he said, "I would think that, negoti-ations or no negotiations, we could start to remove some of the American forces in early 1969 or late 1968." The next day, LBJ made an unannounced appearance at the American Legion convention in New Orleans to undercut Humphrey: "No man can predict when that day would come." He still had Hubert's pecker in his pocket. The great exuberant Humphrey started look-ing, of all people, like Barry Goldwater—an unpopular nominee of a divided party, putting his foot in his mouth day after day. *Newsweek* ran an elec-toral-vote projection headlined "Will HHH Come in Third?"

Some New Politics supporters were considering voting for the ticket of the Berkeley-based Peace and Freedom Party, which had nominated Eldridge Cleaver, especially after a crowning insult: the Chicago police's predawn raid after the convention's close on McCarthy headquarters on the fifteenth floor of the Hilton. The cops said people on the fifteenth floor had been throwing things at them. So they roused people out of bed and beat them. (One cam-paign bureaucrat had a nightstick broken in two over his head.) Humphrey aides nine floors up heard the screams. But Humphrey's only public com-ment on the convention-week violence was, "We ought to quit pretending that Mayor Daley did something wrong." Reasoned his chief political deputy, "Nothing would bring the real peaceniks back to our side unless Hubert uri-nated on a portrait of Lyndon Johnson in Times Square before television— and then they'd say to him, 'Why didn't you do it before?'"

* * *

As for Nixon, rarely had a presidential candidate campaigned more conservatively to keep a lead. "I am not going to barricade myself into a television studio and make this an antiseptic campaign," he promised the press corps. That was only literally true. He wasn't going to barricade himself into a television studio and make this an antiseptic campaign. He had much more innovative methods on tap to make it an antiseptic campaign. He began his general election campaign with an announcement that he was observing a moratorium on discussing the Chicago convention—and also on Vietnam while sensitive negotiations were ongoing in Paris. It was part of a strategy unprecedented in modern times. Never before had a candidate devoted so much to saying so little to so many.

Bob Haldeman had it game-planned perfectly. Nixon most often held but one rally a day. The news cameras shot on celluloid. The precious cans then had to be shipped to New York for developing. So Nixon's events were near airports—timed exquisitely for insertion into the evening's newscasts. Eager to be fair, the networks would always show one clip of the Democrat and one clip of the Republican. Nixon's staff always helpfully pointed producers to the most important sound bite. Humphrey, on the other hand, had upward of a dozen events a day. The producers had plenty of chances to locate some newsworthy Humphrey gaffe, some incoherent vagueness on Vietnam, a shot of some hippie calling Humphrey a "murderer."

The rest of the time, Nixon rested, met with backers, pored over a briefing book kept updated nonstop by an army of twentysomething research assistants tasked with thinking up the nastiest questions possible. With Prussian efficiency, aides handed out position papers according to a.m. and p.m. newspaper deadlines. Even the elephant at the rallies was carefully prepped—with an enema, to foreclose any embarrassing accidents.

Nixon couldn't give the press no contact, because that would then become the story. So he gave what the press corps called "three-bump interviews": two minutes in the candidate's cabin just before the flight attendant sent everyone back to his seat for landing. Reporters didn't seem to mind. Maurice Stans was raising $24 million for Nixon. That bought a lot of bottomless cocktails and delicious food; a British reporter described the press plane as in an "astounded torpor." Humphrey's biggest financial backer, on the other hand, was the Minnesota-based frozen-food magnate Jeno Paulucci. Apparently his firm had an overstock of cocktail weenies—which were served, in lieu of cocktails, morning, noon, and night.

Nixon's notices were glowing. *Newsweek* led its first week's dispatch, "He moved easily among the cheering multitudes, a poised and confident figure, his smile radiant, his pronouncements calm and reasoned." It also noted the surging numbers of young people at every stop, "screaming, squealing, and jumping up and down—yes, jumping up and down—wherever he appeared." (So this is what it felt like to be a Kennedy.) The "kids" were supposed to be hippies. So every time kids showed up for Nixon, the press ran with the story: man bites dog.

Another arm of the juggernaut was the televised panel shows, of which New Hampshire's had merely been a primitive foretaste. Roger Ailes called it the "arena concept," after a quote from Theodore Roosevelt that Ailes had on a plaque on his office wall: "The credit belongs to the man who is actually in the arena, whose face is marred by dust and sweat and blood," not "the man who points out how the strong man stumbles, or where the doer of deeds could have done them better"—the press, in other words, who watched the show on TV monitors, as Nixon declaimed from a customized, round, blue-carpeted platform, the panel of ordinary citizens sitting around him in a semicircle, before bleachers packed with two hundred loyalists as spectators. The emcee was Bud Wilkinson, the legendary University of Oklahoma football coach and ABC color commentator.

The press secretary, Herb Klein, former editor of the *San Diego Union,* warned that the newsmen might mutiny. Frank Shakespeare said that was a risk they'd have to take; if you let them in, they'd only talk about the cameras, the lights, the warm-up man issuing the audience's instructions. ("Now, when Mr. Nixon comes in, I want you to tear the place apart. Sound like ten thousand people. I'm sure, of course, that you'll also want to stand up at that point. So what do you say we try it now?") The press should see "no more, no less, than what they would see from any living room in Illinois," Shakespeare told Klein. The audience was part of the set—"an applause machine," and for "a couple of reaction shots."

Ailes made sure Nixon didn't sweat under the hot lights by arranging for the studio air-conditioning to be pumped at full blast hours before the show. The makeup man was from the *Tonight* show. In Chicago the original set sported turquoise curtains. "Nixon wouldn't look right unless he was carrying a pocketbook," Ailes grumbled, ordering the curtains replaced with wood panels with "clean, solid, masculine lines."

The first thing the television audience saw was a canned shot of the candidate waving his arms in his patented double-V in a motorcade through local streets, the kind that customarily ended in a live rally—"a quick parading of the candidate in the flesh so that the guy they've gotten intimately acquainted with on the screen takes on a living presence," in the words of a young aide named William Gavin, a former high school English teacher who'd been recruited to the team after he wrote an unsolicited memo on how to repackage Nixon for TV. This way, viewers could enjoy the frisson of seeing a celebrity in familiar surroundings. It was especially effective in Chicago—the same streets slicked with blood at the Democratic convention, redeemed by adoring, well-starched Republican crowds.

The shows aired regionally; thus Nixon could tailor his message to suit local tastes. In Charlotte, North Carolina, a fast-growing New South metropolis where the NAACP had recently filed a school desegregation lawsuit, he boldly, boldly affirmed the Supreme Court's 1954 decision in *Brown v. Board of Education.* Then he added, undercutting that message, "To use the power of the federal treasury to withhold funds in order to carry it out— then I think we are going too far. . . . In my view that activity should be very scrupulously examined, and in many cases, I think should be rescinded."

The panel questioners were unrehearsed. But they were also an effect of stagecraft. They were like those heterogeneous World War II–picture platoons: here a Jewish physician; there the president of an immigrant advocacy group; an outnumbered newsman or two to show the man in the arena wasn't ducking them; a suburban housewife; a businessman. In Philadelphia they hit a snag when the Jewish physician turned out to be a psychiatrist. "You should have heard Len on the phone when I told him I had one on the panel," one staffer related. "If I've ever heard a guy's voice turn white, that was it." (Garment had remembered his evening with Nixon in Elmer Bobst's Florida pool house: "*anything except see a shrink.*")

Ailes hit upon an idea for a substitute: "A good, mean, Wallaceite cabdriver. Wouldn't that be great? Some guy to sit there and say, 'Awright, Mac, what about these niggers?'" Nixon then could abhor the uncivility of the words, while endorsing a "moderate" version of the opinion. Ailes walked up and down a nearby taxi stand until he found a cabbie who fit the bill.

Sometimes the questions could get tough. More often they were low-hanging fruit. Asking a hard question—let alone following it up—is a skill, one ordinary citizens could not expect to have mastered. They were also easily intimidated by the pro-Nixon audience. One problem the producers found was that sometimes the audience cheered *too* much.

A black panelist took his turn (the panels always featured one; the audience, just enough blacks so the press couldn't use the dreaded phrase *all-white*). He asked, "What does law and order mean to you?"

Nixon responded, "To me law and order must be combined with justice. Now that's what I want for America. I want the kind of law and order that deserves respect."

The panel's one journalist would ask the solitary tough question. That had another fortunate effect: it let Nixon look like a put-upon martyr, the reporter like an arrogant pedant:

"You say that the Rutgers professor 'called for' the victory of the Vietcong, but as I recall he didn't say that at all. This is what I mean about your being able, on this kind of show, to slide off the questions. Now the facts were—"

"Oh, I know the facts, Mr. McKinney. I know the facts."

"The facts were that the professor did not 'call for' the victory—"

"No, what he said, Mr. McKinney, and I believe I am quoting him *exactly,* was that he would 'welcome the impending victory of the Vietcong.'"

"Which is not the same thing."

"Well, Mr. McKinney, you can make that distinction if you wish, but what I'll do is turn it over to the television audience right now and let them decide for themselves about the semantics. About the difference between 'calling for' and 'welcoming' a victory of the Vietcong."

The producers were delighted: their man had been tested and passed, stern but cool. It fit the story they were telling: that Nixon had come through every sort of hardship and emerged only stronger and smarter. The makeup: carefully applied. The face: intense, stern, engaged—tough but compassionate. Teeth white. Hands relaxed—or relaxed enough. His dark eyes not too sunken, his deepening jowls not too saggy—for the lighting was perfect. The execution was the opposite of 1960 in every way. Nothing was being left to chance: this was the power of TV.

Once, McLuhanite thinking was invoked to support the proposition that only a glamorous new face could lead the Republican Party. The Nixon team deployed McLuhan to sell Nixon—to break the back of the public's conviction, as Roger Ailes put it, that "he's a bore, a pain in the ass." Ailes circulated excerpts from *Understanding Media:* the one where Professor McLuhan praised both Perry Como and Fidel Castro for demonstrating the power of *coolness* on TV (Castro "manages to blend political guidance and education with propaganda so skillfully that it is often difficult to tell where one begins and the other ends"); how Kennedy won the debates because "he is visually a less well-defined image"; how Nixon finally got it right in 1963 by self-effacingly showing off his modest skills on the piano on the *Jack Paar Show* ("A few timely touches like this would have quite altered the result of the Kennedy-Nixon campaign").

They had, in fact, a Paar-like moment planned for the 1968 campaign.

Television was America's most hidebound medium, the three commercial networks cowed into lowest-common-denominator uniformity by corporations obsessed with controlling the image of their national brands. There really were only two exceptions, both midseason replacements—which meant that they were accidents. *The Smothers Brothers Comedy Hour* on CBS was intended as a generic variety show, until the younger Smothers brother, Tommy, began injecting New Leftish touches into the skits, to the great consternation of network executives. *Rowan & Martin's Laugh-In* (think *sit-in, teach-in, be-in*) was a deliberate attempt to harness insurgent new cultural energies for the mainstream. It featured a giant, hairy, falsetto-voiced folksinger named Tiny Tim, a deadpan comic Nazi, a nubile go-go dancer with psychedelic slogans painted on her torso, and more sexual innuendo than you could shake a stick at.

And on Monday, September 16, 1968, it featured Richard Milhous Nixon.

One of *Laugh-In*'s writers was Nixon's old joke-man, Paul Keyes. One of their running gags enlisted random celebrities to utter the innuendo-laden non sequitur "Sock it to me."

A hippie girl, drenched by water, answered a telephone call, supposedly from Governor Nelson Rockefeller: "Oh, no, I don't think we could get Mr. Nixon to stand still for a 'Sock it to me.'"

The screen filled with the famous ski-jump-nosed, fifty-five-year-old mug, intoning in cool self-mocking bafflement, "Sock it to *me*?!"

Paul Keyes was sure to nab the tape after they got the take before Nixon's dubious aides got to it first. Their doubts disappeared after the show ran. Humphrey was supposed to be the live wire, the happy warrior, selling the politics of joy. Not going on *Laugh-In* himself was one of the things Humphrey lamented cost him the election.

Humphrey couldn't catch a break. Nixon won the hipness battle both ways: Stewart Alsop called him "the quintessential square"; his celebrity surrogates were the likes of Bud Wilkinson and the saccharine pop singer Connie Francis. Hubert Humphrey's was Frank Sinatra. But Sinatra inspired contempt from the youth culture and was too much a swinger to comfort the squares.

Nixon's TV spots were groundbreaking. The man who made them, Gene Jones, was a former marine combat photographer who'd never directed a commercial. What attracted the campaign to pay him exorbitant fees nonetheless was *A Face of War*, a visually overwhelming, unnarrated documentary that followed a marine company over ninety-seven days of combat in Vietnam. When it was screened for the Nixon media team, the only female in the audience walked out three minutes into the second reel, saying, "I can't watch that." It was the last thing anyone said for twenty minutes.

Nixon's commercials would run without narration as well. The sound would only be music and snippets from stump speeches. The images, rapid-fire collages of still photographs, told the story just as effectively with the sound off, a visual semaphore. TV specialist Harry Treleaven was so proud of their aesthetic force that he screened them for curators at the Museum of Modern Art, hoping they might be added to the collection. The aesthetes were unimpressed: "The good guys are either children, soldiers, or over fifty years old." It was a telling moment: that was why Treleaven believed they belonged in the museum. He responded, "Nixon has not only developed the use of the platitude, he's raised it to an art form"—a mirror of Americans' "delightful misconceptions of themselves and their country." (He meant it as a compliment.) Jones's assistant imagined staging the State of the Union this same way—intercut with heart-tugging stills.

To tripping, jarring music:

"It is time for an honest look at the problem of order in the United States."

(Firefighters dousing a burning apartment building; white-helmeted Chicago cops; a banner at a march: INDEPENDENT SOCIALISM.)

"Dissent is a necessary agent of change, but in a system of government that provides for peaceful change, there is no cause for a resort to violence."

(A sign, NONE DARE CALL IT TREASON: YAF DARES, which was visually clever. The biggest, most noticeable word was *treason,* that old Nixon trick: *he* wasn't calling anything "treason," just reporting what others were saying; what's more, that he sign-posted Young Americans for Freedom signaled his outreach to Reagan and Thurmond conservatives; and for those for whom the light struck from another angle, it showed that he was against "extremists on both sides." Another sign: STAMP OUT VD. Perhaps the full acronym, not visible, was VDC, standing for Berkeley's most prominent antiwar group, the Vietnam Day Committee; either way, the anxiety over sexual dissolution was tapped.)

"Let us recognize that the first civil right of every American is to be free from domestic violence."

(More burning buildings, rubble; the naked torso of a female mannequin. No black men in these pictures, just depictions of the consequences of what black men did—and in that naked white female torso, a suggestion of the most awful thing black men did of all.)

"So I pledge to you we shall have order in the United States."

Another group of American image-makers were aghast. The network news divisions and the men who ran them prided themselves as the oasis in the vast wasteland. The networks poured money into news after the quiz show scandals of the late 1950s, loss leaders to clean up their image and preserve their precious government licenses to use the public's airwaves. TV news styled itself a moral center of American civic life, independent and public-spirited. It was *their* footage of Bull Connor's fire hoses in Birmingham that catalyzed the Civil Rights Act of 1964, *their* footage at the Edmund Pettus Bridge that brought about the Voting Rights Act of 1965.

NBC, with its flagship evening news show the *Huntley-Brinkley Report,* was the most morally self-assured. They had a young producer out of Chicago named Lew Koch, whose specialty was covering the civil rights and antiwar movements. They'd turned to him the previous January when they wanted to know if there would be violence at the Democratic convention. Knowing the parties involved, he said, yes, absolutely. During convention week, Koch had led the teams that went into the streets and parks to capture the footage of that violence.

He was inordinately proud of what they'd produced—1968's version of Bull Connor's fire hoses: glorious moral theater, naked evil being visited upon innocents. He repaired to NBC headquarters at the Merchandise Mart after that first broadcast filled with self-satisfaction. A sympathizer with the antiwar movement, he thought he had advanced their cause considerably.

The assignment editor asked him to help with the phones; the switchboard was overwhelmed.

The first call: "I saw those cops beating the kids—right on for the cops!"

Another: "You fucking commies!" He was referring to NBC—as if *they* had instigated the riots.

The calls kept coming, dozens. They came to all the networks, for days upon days. Some people saw noble cops innocently defending themselves. Others accused the networks of hiring cops to beat up kids to spice up the show. Lew Koch was so shaken by the experience, he left for a soul-searching six-month leave of absence.

The media had left Chicago united in the conviction they were heroes, prophets, martyrs. "The truth was, these were our children in the streets, and the Chicago police beat them up," the *New York Times*'s Tom Wicker wrote. "In Chicago," Stewart Alsop wrote, "for the first time in my life it began to seem to me possible that some form of American fascism may really happen here." Top executives at all the networks, *New York Times* publisher Arthur Ochs Sulzberger, *Washington Post* and *Newsweek* publisher Katharine Graham, Time Inc. editor in chief Hedley Donovan, and *Los Angeles Times* publisher Otis Chandler, posted an unprecedented telegram to Mayor Daley, excoriating the way newsmen "were repeatedly singled out by policemen and deliberately beaten . . . to discourage or prevent reporting of an important confrontation between police and demonstrators which the American public as a whole has a right to know about."

Then they learned the American public thought differently.

The *Chicago Daily News* devoted an entire page on August 29 to a set of pictures documenting a circle of cops and an off-duty army paratrooper beating one of their photographers, James O. Linstead, even after he'd pulled out his press card. He was wearing a helmet; they pulled it off. They kept on going until they'd broken bones. The *News* was a liberal paper, the kind that editorialized high-mindedly that "the International Amphitheatre, dressed up and fortified, lies in the shadow of one of the worst slums in the nation," that the National Rifle Association should lose its tax exemption, that "the closer one gets to the campus scene, the less black-and-white the picture becomes." They turned their letters section over to the debate over the convention violence. Some supported the paper's position. They wrote things like "When I was with the Marines, I thought I was fighting for democracy, but now I come home to find a police state as bad as the Communists'"; and "We need to establish immediately a 'humane society' for the prevention of cruelty to our finest people, who are still human enough to protest the wholesale killing of a wonderful people in the name of patriotism by a nation of moral imbeciles."

Many more, however, converged upon another narrative.

"The major television networks have shown a completely one-sided story of what happened. . . ."

"The Yippies and McCarthy people were not just throwing beer cans and ashtrays at the police and National Guard. They were throwing plastic bags of excrement and bricks from the 15th floor. . . ."

"They insulted the police with words that can't be printed, and wrote these same words on their foreheads. The Chicago police reacted as any police force in the country would have. . . ."

"I failed to see reports of the lewd activities, the vile provocations, or violence committed by the degenerates who invaded our city. . . ."

"We are amazed and angry at the shameful lashing our city and our mayor have been subjected to because of the events of last week. Much of this undeserved criticism is the result of the distorted presentation of the events by television, newspapers, and radio. . . ."

"My neighbor is a Chicago policeman, one of those assigned to protect the Hilton Hotel from mob invasion. On Monday and Tuesday he worked sixteen hours straight. I met him coming home Thursday morning. He was covered with human excrement thrown on him by the mob."

Hard-nosed Chicago newsmen pointed out these were obviously just-so stories. A cop has to return to the station house after his shift; they let him inside covered with feces? He drives back home to his wife and children still covered with the same shit? And where, exactly, does one procure *bricks* on the fifteenth floor of the Conrad Hilton Hotel?

The narrative came from Chicago city government. Mayor Daley proclaimed on August 29 in an appearance on the *Today* show, "The television industry is part of the violence and creating it all over the country. . . . What would you do if someone was throwing human excrement in your face? Would you be the calm, collected people you think you are?" Bumper stickers proliferated nationwide: WE SUPPORT MAYOR DALEY AND HIS CHICAGO POLICE. Sixty percent of Americans polled supported the sentiment, and 90 percent of the seventy-four thousand letters City Hall received in the mail in the two weeks after the convention. It wasn't, they said pace Tom Wicker, *their* children being beaten in the streets of Chicago. And these media mandarins, they said, weren't their moral authorities.

And the public being their customers, it wasn't long before the media mandarins' interpretations changed.

Walter Cronkite had Mayor Daley on his program. "Perhaps he had been called to heel by management," a Tocqueville out of Great Britain, Godfrey Hodgson, of the *Times on Sunday*, speculated. "Perhaps he felt that he had erred and strayed from the path of strict professionalism. Whatever the reason, his manner with Daley was almost obsequious. He repeatedly addressed him as 'sir.' He introduced him with the ingratiating remark, 'Maybe this is a kiss-and-make-up session, but it's not intended that way. . . . I think we've always been friends.'"

Daley reeled off fantastic lies: "They had maps locating the hotels and routes of buses for the guidance of terrorists from out of town. . . . How is it that you never showed on television, Walter, the crowd marching down the streets to confront the police?"

Cronkite gingerly pointed out that many of the victims were members of the press.

Daley retorted, "Many of them are hippies themselves. They're part of this movement. Some of them are revolutionaries and they want these things to happen. There isn't any secret about this." Then he shared with Cronkite something "that I never said to anyone": the miscreants had been planning assassinations. "I didn't want what happened in Dallas or what happened in California to happen in Chicago."

Cronkite sat and took it. The editor of the *Chicago Daily News*, whose publisher had signed the telegram to Daley, abjectly apologized for one of his reporters who had shouted at policemen beating three women, "For God's sake, stop that!": "He acted as a human being, but less than a professional, he was there as a reporter and not to involve himself."

Chicago's American was the conservative Hearst paper, and even their tough-guy, cop-loving columnist Jack Mabley had written about how "a policeman went animal when a crippled man couldn't get away fast enough." Shortly thereafter, Mabley climbed down from his short career as a cop critic in a moment of severe self-doubt: "80 to 85 percent of the callers and letter writers cheering for Daley and the cops: You can't help that gnawing feeling—can all these people be right and I be wrong?"

Godfrey Hodgson wrote of the media about-face: "They had been united, as rarely before, by their anger at Mayor Daley. Now they learned that the great majority of Americans sided with Daley, and against them. It was not only the humiliation of discovering that they had been wrong; there was also alarm at the discovery of their new unpopularity. Bosses and cops, everyone knew, were hated; it seemed that newspapers and television were hated even more."

Nixon paid attention. The public was on *his* side in his war against the media Franklins, in a way deeper than Nixon had ever dared dream. Again, he had it both ways: for actually the media was, if anything, accommodating him. Frank Shakespeare fantasized aloud to a reporter about calling in NBC's chairman of the board and telling him, "We are going to monitor every minute of your broadcast news, and if this kind of bias continues, and if we are elected, then you just might find yourself in Washington next year answering a few questions. And you just might find yourself having a little trouble getting some of your licenses renewed." Then Nixon gave a speech on his conception of the presidency (on the radio, so not too many people would hear it): "It's time we once again had an open administration. . . . We should bring dissenters into policy discussions, not freeze them out." The Johnson administration had been one of angry division; as president, he would be the guardian of "intellectual ferment," both a "user of thought and a catalyst of thought," for "the lamps of enlightenment are lit by controversy." The punditocracy swooned. Walter Lippmann (he had called the Checkers Speech "the most demeaning experience my country has ever had to bear") wrote, "I believe that there really is a 'new Nixon,' a maturer and mellower man who is no longer clawing his way to the top, and it is, I think, fair to hope that his dominating ambition will be to become a two-term president." Kenneth Crawford, *Newsweek*'s columnist, found him ready "to steer a middle course, emulative of the Eisenhower Administration." Joseph Kraft of the *Post* said that with the "crisis in authority" brought on by the Democrats, "It makes sense to vote for Richard Nixon and the Republicans." Theodore White, who'd worn his Kennedy button on the Nixon train in 1960, would later inscribe a copy of *The Making of the President 1968* to the man he called its "hero": "My previous reporting of Richard Nixon must I know have hurt. If I feel differently now it is not that there is a new Richard Nixon or a new Teddy White but that slowly truths force their way on all of us. . . . This book tries to describe the campaign of a man with courage and conscience." Even Norman Mailer called Nixon "less phony."

A Nixon campaign commercial called "Convention":

A brass band, like the brass band that played over the McCarthy delegates standing on their chairs singing peace songs, blares "A Hot Time in the Old Town Tonight." The familiar, old-fashioned convention scenes: standards, balloons, placards, Hubert at the podium, exuberant delegates.

The music distorts electronically into a hideous pulse. With each new picture, someone's mouth is open wider. Hubert's is the punctuation mark. It looks as if he is screaming.

A new set of photographs, cutting quicker: firemen and flames; bleeding protesters running from the police; a bearded, screaming peacenik; more flames; another bearded screamer.

(No black people were seen rioting in commercials like these; that would have been labeled "racism." Instead, only the *aftereffects* of black rioting were shown: rubble and flames. Rioting white hippies in Chicago were thus a visual godsend.)

The music returns to the proper track. A picture of Hubert with his jaw clenched, waving American flags, Hubert at the podium again—cue for the music to distort again, and pictures of soldiers dying in other soldiers' arms, all olive drab. Then the brass band again, then Hubert, smiling—as the sound track starts shrieking again for a set of photos of Appalachian poverty.

(This was incredibly brazen. Fighting poverty had been Hubert Humphrey's greatest contribution to American public life. They were attacking him at his greatest *strength:* well, you said you were warring on poverty. And here was plain evidence: poverty still existed. The Johnson administration is a failure. The Democrats were failures. Hubert Humphrey is a failure.)

Brass band. Hubert. Hubert distorted in triplicate.

"This Time"

"NIXON."

More chaos in the streets. Whenever a new Black Panthers chapter was founded, violent confrontations with police soon followed. New York's new Panthers threw a Molotov cocktail at an empty police cruiser in July; patrolmen led into an ambush were wounded by a shotgun blast in August; and on September 4, after two Panthers left the Brooklyn criminal court for a preliminary hearing on an assault charge, off-duty cops in the gallery pummeled exiting spectators with the blackjacks and billy clubs they pulled out from under their jackets, crying, "Wallace! Wallace! Wallace!" Four days later J. Edgar Hoover called the Panthers "the greatest threat to the internal security of the country." On September 10, Huey Newton was convicted. The next day, Berkeley announced a new "social analysis" course with guest teacher Eldridge Cleaver. Max Rafferty, whose boon chances for California's Senate seat were the subject of a September 1 *New York Times Magazine* profile, announced he was withholding Cleaver's paycheck and ordered the Board of Regents to cancel the course. In Mexico City, already rocked by a massacre of student protesters, the Olympics reached their dramatic climax: two sprinters, Tommie Smith and John Carlos, lowered their heads and raised their fists in a Black Power salute on the medal stand rather than acknowledge the American flag.

The old distinctions and gradations on the left—freak, pacifist, New Leftist, black militant—were breaking down into an undifferentiated, and paranoid, insurrectionism. In Detroit and Ann Arbor, Michigan, a New Left hotbed, a group calling itself the White Panthers pledged "total assault on the culture by any means necessary, including rock and roll, dope, and fucking in the streets." "Get a gun, brother, learn how to use it," one of their statements proclaimed. "You'll need it, pretty soon." There followed a wave of bombings in southern Michigan, including the burning of a clandestine CIA recruitment office. It was the first serious incidence of New Left violence. The White Panthers became a target of the FBI's COINTELPRO secret counterintelligence initiative.

If anyone was keeping score, right-wing vigilantes were far worse. In July and August, a group of right-wing Cuban exiles firebombed the publisher of the diary of Che Guevara—the thirteenth anti-Castro bombing in New York since April—along with the British consulate in Los Angeles, the Mexican government's tourist office in Chicago (twice), and a British cargo ship in Miami harbor. On August 13, state troopers uncovered a half ton of dynamite, automatic weapons, tear gas, and crates of ammunition in Johnsonburg, New Jersey, belonging to the group Cuban Power. Eleven days later, in Connecticut, Minutemen invaded the pacifist farm in Voluntown in an attempt to burn it down, then shot it out with state police, blinding one of their members. ("I think all of us would rather see our place burned down than to see a Minuteman blinded," a pacifist told the *New York Times*. A local, less conciliatory, said, "I see them come to the post office. They're a cruddy bunch. They don't wash up and shave.")

But people weren't keeping score. Certain hegemonic narratives prevailed. A Harris poll offered several statements with which people could agree or disagree. The consensus: "liberals, long-hairs, and intellectuals have been running the country too long." Sixty-four percent of respondents classified as "low income whites" thought so. Eighty-one percent of the sample thought "law and order has broken down in this country," 84 percent that a "strong president can make a big difference in directly preserving law and order." Forty-two percent of Americans said blacks were "more violent than whites." But the poll didn't ask about the danger posed to law and order by right-wing Cubans, or white survivalist Minutemen.

Labor Day weekend in Atlantic City, a new kind of radical stormed a sacred citadel—parading a flock of sheep down the Atlantic City boardwalk at the Miss America pageant and crowning one, Yippie-style, "Miss America." Then they tossed "instruments of torture to women"—typing manuals, girlie magazines, *Ladies' Home Journal,* false eyelashes and high-heeled shoes, and most notoriously, bras—into a "freedom trash can" that they had hoped to light aflame. (They couldn't get a fire permit.) During the pageant ceremony, as the outgoing queen bade farewell, sixteen radical feminists unfurled a banner and shouted, "Freedom for women!"

Amid it all, George Wallace preached defiance to the same symptoms as Nixon, with precisely the opposite remedy. Nixon appealed for quiet. Wallace said, "We need some *meanness.*" It turned pundits white-knuckled: "Never again will you read about Berlin in the '30s without remembering this wild confrontation of two irrational forces," the *New Republic*'s TRB remarked after a Madison Square Garden rally that required a thousand police to keep the peace. (Wallace had tried and failed to get the city to let him have Shea Stadium.) Wallace was approaching ballot access in all fifty states, polling consistently around 20 percent. When his campaign film *The Wallace Story* aired nationwide, its appeal for funds earned five times more than Hubert Humphrey's. A North Carolina political analyst compared it to an iceberg: "There's a lot more to it than shows on the surface and what's beneath is the dangerous part."

Even some Wallace aides were frightened. "Now let's get serious a minute," the president of a Polish-American club told Wallace's right-hand man, Tom Turnipseed, arranging a rally outside Webster, Massachusetts. "When George Wallace is elected president, he's going to round up all the niggers and shoot them, isn't he?" When the aide replied, laughing, "We're just worried about some agitators. We're not going to shoot anybody," his host responded, with dead seriousness, "Well, I don't know whether I'm for him or not." Wallace's aides met some of their organizers only at night, lest decent folks see the kind of bottom-feeders they were working with. News crews started bringing extra cameras to the rallies—one aimed at the podium, another at the demonstrators pelting it with eggs, tomatoes, bottles, and sandals (a reference to Wallace's mockery of bearded sandal-wearers). Wallace would respond with the story of the demonstrator who lay down in front of President Johnson's limousine: "I tell you when November comes, the first time they lie down in front of my limousine, it'll be the last one they'll ever lay down in front of because their day is *over*!" The story got delirious ovations. As did "We don't have riots in Alabama. They start a riot down there, first one of 'em to pick up a brick gets a bullet in the brain, that's all."

He was a conquering hero in Newark, where he helped Anthony Imperiale win a city council seat. In Columbia, Illinois, an all-white town outside East St. Louis, he swept a high school mock election after the student speaking for him at the assembly said, "I have nothing against niggers. Every American should own one." The AFL-CIO held top-secret findings that one of three of its members supported Wallace. A *Chicago Sun-Times* poll taken the same week found the number at 43 percent for Chicago steelworkers.

For a New Deal romantic like Hubert Humphrey, sacrificing the working class to a reactionary demagogue was agony. However, the real harm Wallace posed was to Richard Nixon: all those union members, all those Dixiecrats breaking from the Democrats, were it not for Wallace, might be heading straight for *him*; also those Strom Thurmond Republicans Nixon coveted— Wallace's natural constituency. That was why Wallace hit Nixon hardest in his speeches—assailing him as part of the team that had sent troops to Little Rock and installed Earl Warren: "Nixon is just like the national Democrats. He's for all this federal invasion of the states' right to run their own affairs."

Warning Southerners off Wallace consumed enormous energies in the Nixon campaign. Only there was a catch. It was like with those Wallace supporters whom Wallace deputies would only visit at night. Fred LaRue of Mississippi articulated the strategy in a memo September 7: "The anti-Wallace message will be indirect—'between the lines' and 'in regional code words.'" That Nixon was working to poach Wallace's vote was something decent folks were never supposed to find out about. Harry Dent ran the operation, though he was never brought aboard the campaign payroll.

For instance, they commissioned a country music ballad:

Tell me where there's a man . . . in this fair land,
Who can get us back on the track?
Dick Nixon is a decent man
Who can bring our country back.

And since Southerners hate outsiders telling them what to do, LaRue explained, "the multi-stanza ballad will allow issues to be included or excluded as the local situation indicates. The song's technical aspects will be such that 'local talent' as well as a variety of 'stars' can render it effectively." His biggest problem was finding singers to perform the Nixon jingle. They all were backing Wallace. LaRue was skilled, though, at getting the commercials played during the right programs. "Now you take Orlando, Florida, for instance," he explained. "There is no country-and-western show in town there, so we go to wrestling instead."

A Thurmond Speaks for Nixon-Agnew Committee campaign poster blared, "SENATOR THURMOND Denied The Republican Nomination To The Liberal Gov. Rockefeller. . . . Help Strengthen STROM THURMOND'S Position In The New Republican Administration With A Rousing Endorsement Of RICHARD NIXON ON NOV. 5." And: "Help Strom Thurmond lead South Carolina back to its rightful position in the nation." A pamphlet published quotes from Nixon's "Man in the Arena" segment from Charlotte: "I wouldn't want to see a federal agency punish a local community"; "I don't believe you should use the South as the whipping boy"; "There has been too much of a tendency . . . for both our courts and our federal agencies to use the whole program of school integration for purposes which have very little to do with education." Southern editors started writing about the rise of the "Nixiecrat." And "Uncle Strom's Cabinet."

Humphrey had a Southern strategy, too. It was to appeal to Southerners' material interests: "WALLACE'S ALABAMA ranks 48th among states in per-capita annual income and is $900 below the national average. WALLACE'S ALABAMA meets only one of eight key standards for state child labor laws." Humphrey also plied their better angels. A five-minute commercial featured E. G. Marshall, star of the long-canceled courtroom series *The Defenders,* dreadfully earnest in front of a picture of Wallace: "When I see this man, I think of feelings of my own which I don't like but I have anyway. They're called prejudices. . . . He would take that prejudice and make it into national law." Gubernatorial candidates such as Ernest Vandiver, Ellis Arnall, and Jimmy Carter had tried that "better angels" stuff in 1966. It didn't work.

Elsewhere, the commercials featured Humphrey's talking head, stumbling over himself in earnest on-the-other-handedness. ("Law and Order": "When a man says that he thinks that the most important thing is to double the rate of convictions, but he doesn't believe in, and then he condemns, uh, the vice president, myself, for wanting to double the war on poverty, I think he has, uh, lost his sense of values. You're not going to make this a better America just because you build more jails. What this country needs are more decent neighborhoods, more educated people, better homes. Ah, if we need more jails we can build them, but that ought not be the highest objective of the presidency of the United States. I do not believe that repression alone can bring a better society.")

Nixon exploited his long-standing friendship with the Reverend Billy Graham. First, in 1967, he invited Graham to spend a few days with him to "help" him decide whether to run; later he told the incredible fib that Graham had been more responsible than anyone else for his decision. Graham seated him in the VIP section of his nationally televised Pittsburgh crusade in September 1968 and called Nixon one of his most cherished friends (then, in a private meeting, Nixon entrusted the preacher with a secret message for the president, that Nixon would give him the major share of the credit when the war was settled and do what he could to ensure Johnson's historical legacy). Shortly before Election Day, Graham broke his announced policy of not involving himself in partisan politics by conceding he had voted for Nixon absentee. Graham, Nixon's research showed, was the "second most revered man in the South among adult voters."

That supposed nullity, Spiro Agnew, toured the South to great effectiveness. The media were forever comparing him unfavorably to Humphrey's supersound choice, Senator Edmund Muskie of Maine. Muskie made the only speech at the Democratic convention that seemed to satisfy all factions. *Time* had maintained a schoolgirl crush on the guy since 1954: "Lawyer Edmund Sixtus Muskie, 40, in whose grey-blue eyes shines a light seen in the early days of the New Deal . . . an enthusiastic fisherman, a good skier, and a competent trackman . . . tall, ruggedly handsome . . . a stubborn political independence . . . a New England legislator's characteristic attention to detail and distaste for florid rhetoric." Late in September, Muskie made the front pages of newspapers around the country as a hero of conciliation. Humphrey's appearances were being disrupted left and right by longhairs calling him a warmonger, a murderer, an American Adolf Hitler. During a speech on the steps of the courthouse in Washington, Pennsylvania, some long-haired kids from the local college tried the routine out on Muskie, chanting, "Stop the war! Stop the war!" Muskie decided he wasn't in the mood to outshout them and offered to let them choose a spokesman to take the podium for ten minutes if they agreed to listen to him afterward. The chosen kid nervously argued, while learning what it was like to speak when the heckling was directed at him, "Wallace is no answer, Nixon is no answer, Humphrey is no answer. Sit out this election; don't vote for president."

Muskie then took the podium. He reviewed his modest upbringing. He described what the price of political apathy had been for the poor Maine region he came from: the special interests ran things and made the people poorer. But once the people became engaged and started electing Democrats, things started getting better. He concluded, "Don't misjudge the basic good-will of this American system." The students swarmed him like a hero. The Wallace partisans in the crowd were praiseful, too—mingling, for the first time, with the dirty hippies. The *Washington Post* called it "one of the spec-tacular performances of the 1968 political campaign." When Agnew made the news during the campaign, it was always for making gaffes.

Agnew called a Hawaiian reporter, in front of the other reporters, a "fat Jap." Asked why he didn't campaign among the poor, Agnew answered, "If you've seen one slum, you've seen them all." He used the word *Polack* in Polish Chicago, though the Democratic vice-presidential candidate's father's name at birth was Stephen Marciszewski. When the Nixon media team came calling to John Lindsay for an endorsement, the mayor said he was "not going to endorse anybody, goddammit, particularly Richard Nixon, unless someone strangled Agnew." One of the Humphrey team's few clever com-mercials focused in on a corner of a TV set. A man on the sound track was laughing uproariously; as the camera slowly pulled back, you saw what he saw on the screen: "Agnew for Vice President."

But the visuals were more clever than the politics. Many viewers weren't sure what they were supposed to be laughing at; just that Democrats were telling them to laugh at someone—just the thing a sanctimonious liberal would do. And if it so happened that you *liked* Spiro Agnew, that voice on the TV was laughing *at you*.

Agnew called Humphrey "soft on inflation, soft on Communism, and soft on law and order over the years," and "squishy soft" on Vietnam. That crossed the media Establishment's unwritten rule against "McCarthyism." Agnew compounded the problem by claiming he wasn't aware of the McCarthyite resonances of his phraseology. The big editorial pages all but claimed a scalp. But Nixon couldn't have been too impressed: he knew a thing or two about good-cop/bad-cop president/vice-president routines. Such rhetoric helped them in Dixie; it was a stock-in-trade for people like Strom Thurmond.

"Senator Thurmond Speaks for Nixon-Agnew" commercials started late in September, produced entirely outside Treleaven and Shakespeare's opera-tion by Dent, off the payroll, and cleared through campaign manager John Mitchell (conversely Thurmond was given the right to veto anything in a national commercial that might be offensive to the South: an image of a black soldier, for instance, in a Vietnam ad). The money was raised by the South Carolina textile magnate and Thurmond confidant Roger Milliken. The coor-dinator of Nixon's Southern organization, Bo Callaway, the former Georgia congressman who'd lost the governorship to Lester Maddox, campaigned baldly for Wallace supporters: "I think the ideas expressed by George Wal-lace are the ideas a great many Republicans espouse." Indeed the message of the Thurmond ads was not that Wallace was wrong, but that Wallace couldn't

win; that boosting the fortunes of a third-party candidate only hastened the
Yankee apocalypse. And Thurmond had matchless credibility to deliver that
message: he had invented the Southern third-party strategy himself, in 1948.
It worked: whenever Thurmond's commercials ran in a certain town, Tom
Turnipseed lamented, Wallace's numbers immediately tanked.

So it seemed, as September became October, Nixon was going to win,
Humphrey was going to lose. Wallace was going to show respectably, but
not respectably enough to matter.

Then suddenly, things started to change. Hubert Humphrey phoned Lyndon
Johnson from the campaign trail in Salt Lake City on Monday night, September 30.

"Mr. President?"

"Hi."

"How are you this evening?"

"Fine."

"Say, I'm going to be on your TV in about five minutes."

"All right, I'll turn it on."

"On NBC, and I thought I should have called you a little earlier, but they
had me taping here all day and I've been about half-dead."

"Is it taped?"

"Yeah, it's taped."

"Good. Well, I'll turn it on."

"And it points out the things that we've done here on Vietnam. . . . It says,
for example, that we've given the time for Asian nations to strengthen themselves and work together, and so we see a stronger Southeast Asia—a
stronger South Vietnam—contrasted with a few months ago when peace
negotiations were started. And there are new circumstances which will face
the new president, in light of these circumstances, and assuming no marked
changes in the present situation, how would I proceed. And let me make
clear first what I would not do. I would not undertake a unilateral withdrawal . . . I make that very clear . . ."

What the vice president was telling the president was that he had finally
inched to his master's left on Vietnam. The words were that he would "be
willing to stop the bombing of the North as an acceptable risk for peace
because I believe it could lead to success in the negotiations and a shorter
war." Johnson asked some perfunctory questions about what exactly the new
doctrine entailed. Humphrey replied, "I think I've done it carefully here
without jeopardizing what you're trying to do." The president didn't blow
up in anger. He just said, "I'll turn it on, thank you." The vice president,
clearly relieved, signed off, "God bless you. Thank you."

None of this was news to the president—who had talked on the phone
forty-five minutes earlier with Richard Nixon in a much longer and more

intimate conversation. Nixon described to him an early AP wire story on Humphrey's new position. Johnson told Nixon he thought the consequences of Humphrey's move would be disastrous: that if the bombings were stopped, the enemy "could just come day and night." Johnson quoted a telegram from Commander Creighton Abrams that a bombing halt would mean "a several-fold increase in U.S. and allied casualties." Then Johnson spelled out what his present negotiating position was in Paris—demanding far greater concessions before even considering stopping the bombing—and said the United States would only prevail in negotiations by hanging tough in the field. Nixon replied that the AP called what Humphrey was up to "a dramatic move away from the Johnson administration foreign policy"—and assured the Democratic president, "it's not my intention to move in that direction." Nixon spoke of Johnson's position as "our" position. And that "that's what I'm going to continue to say."

Nixon was calling the Democratic standard-bearer the president's betrayer. And when he finished, the president thanked him warmly. But the president didn't know that he also was being betrayed: Nixon already had it on secret authority from a source inside the Paris peace negotiations that LBJ himself planned to initiate a bombing halt sometime in October—intrigue upon intrigue upon intrigue.

Humphrey's speech was not bold; there were all kinds of conditions. But it was his first sign of defiance to the president. He even directly contradicted the president's earlier slap-down of him, that "no man can predict" when troops could be withdrawn, and said he thought some could be withdrawn starting in 1969. He also said Nixon had "taken a line on Vietnam policy which I believe could lead to a great escalation of the war." Even more important were the atmospherics. Usually Humphrey appeared with the vice-presidential seal and flag. Usually Humphrey was introduced as the vice president. Not this time. This time, he was introduced as the "Democratic candidate for president." Hubert Humphrey had reclaimed his pecker.

On October 9, he ran an ad during a network showing of *Dr. Strangelove* that took up where LBJ's "Daisy" ad of 1964 had left off: it argued against Nixon's position that the nuclear nonproliferation treaty should be delayed by showing an exploding mushroom cloud. Another ad showed Nixon speaking without any sound for twelve seconds, then a voice-over: "Mr. Nixon's silence on the issue of Vietnam has become an issue in itself." It concluded with a quote from Mark Hatfield, the Republican senator who had seconded Nixon's nomination, that deflated Nixon's very masculinity: "The Paris peace talks should not become the skirt for timid men to hide behind."

Campaigning started getting fun again. The peacenik pickets started abating or began carrying signs reading IF YOU MEAN IT, WE'RE FOR YOU. Humphrey started rising in the polls, and soon both Harris and Gallup were predicting a toss-up.

But something seemed off. The candidate brought it up to his campaign manager, Lawrence O'Brien, after a trip to West Virginia:

"Larry, I don't see any Humphrey signs, any Humphrey literature. I'm out there breaking my butt and I don't see any campaign activity to back me up."

His people hadn't wanted to worry him. Now they realized they had no choice. "We're broke, Hubert," O'Brien told him. "We don't have the money and we can't get credit. We're not going to have the materials we wanted, and the television campaign has to be cut to the bone. The money just isn't there."

Campaigning was a cash-on-the-barrelhead business: vendors had no interest in being stuck with unpaid bills by losing candidates. The Democrats raised $5 million for the presidential campaign; $3.4 million of that was loans. But the Republicans spent $6.27 million on TV alone. Nixon's well was bottomless. One friend, eccentric billionaire Chicago insurance man Clement Stone, pledged to match donations up to $1 million. Eventually, he raised that to $2 million. There were advantages to being the party of business. Most years, the Democrats could at least count on huge donations from corporations hedging their bets. But this year, the big guns ceased their commitments when the early polls showed Humphrey so far behind. The week of October 13, Humphrey ran no state or regional commercials at all.

It was stark, awfully stark. One day, Humphrey operatives Bob Strauss and Bob Short and two Humphrey backers from Minnesota, Dwayne Andreas of Archer Daniels Midland and Jeno Paulucci, the wiener king, sat down in Texas to ask a group of oilmen for a $700,000 advance. The cowboys asked whether Humphrey would maintain the oil-depletion allowance. The Humphrey men tried to hint diplomatically that this wasn't the sort of request polite millionaires made outright. "No confirmation, no seven hundred thousand dollars," their spokesman replied. Paulucci, a blunt man, asked if they insured their buildings. They replied that they did, of course. Paulucci said, "My advice to you would be, even though you are for Nixon because you think he's going to save your oil-depletion allowance, to spend that seven hundred thousand dollars on insurance. . . . If I were Hubert Humphrey and you didn't give me that money, I not only would take away your depletion allowance, I'd cut off your balls." The gambit didn't work. Paulucci found his way to a pay phone and reported, "We have to cancel next week's advertising. We don't have the money."

As for Wallace, he had shot himself in the foot—or nuked himself, as the case may be.

When the time came for the governor to think about a running mate, his people cast about for a national name. J. Edgar Hoover was suggested, or Curtis LeMay, or Kentucky Fried Chicken's Colonel Sanders. His aides liked former Kentucky governor and baseball commissioner A. B. "Happy" Chandler. Wallace was reluctant: "That fellow's a liberal," he said. His aides wore him down: "We have all the nuts in the country," one said. With Chandler, "we would get some decent people—you working one side of the street and he working the other side." Reluctantly, Wallace agreed, and the decision was leaked to reporters.

In Montgomery, the phones started ringing off the hook. John Birch Society members, a crucial component of Wallace's national organization, especially flooded the switchboards. Chandler had had a role in the hiring of Jackie Robinson by the Brooklyn Dodgers. He had protected children integrating Kentucky schools in 1955. Wallace's Kentucky chair resigned, calling Chandler an "out-and-out integrationist." Oilman Bunker Hunt, who'd donated a briefcase filled with $250,000 in hundred-dollar bills for the "rainy day fund," called in a rage: he preferred John Birch Society leader and former agriculture secretary Ezra Taft Benson. Wallace rescinded Chandler's invitation.

The Wallace team turned their consideration to General LeMay. The eccentric air force veteran was vastly proud of the savagery of his bombing runs over Tokyo, disconcertingly eager to repeat the performance when he'd been commander of America's nuclear fleet. But he also was a hero and a genius, the man who engineered the Berlin Airlift. He was frustrated and bored after his 1965 retirement and gung ho for George Wallace—the only candidate, he said, committed to "turning the Vietnam War effort over to the military." LeMay was chairman of the board of an electronics company that threatened to fire him if he ran, so a Wallace aide flew to Dallas and got Bunker Hunt to put up a million-dollar trust to reimburse the general's loss of salary. A meeting was arranged for September 27 in Chicago, where the candidate gave his potential running mate the assurances he needed. LeMay was flown to Pittsburgh, where Wallace was appearing, and in a hotel suite aides gave him a crash course in the politician's most crucial skill: deflecting troublesome questions. They were especially adamant in explaining to him—they were still at it at 4:30 a.m.—that as much as he might not like it, the American people had a phobia about nuclear warfare, and it was not worth trying to disabuse them.

Then came LeMay's debut press conference, broadcast live on all three networks.

George Wallace introduced him as a man unafraid to appreciate the "tender and the trivial."

Second question. Jack Nelson of the *Los Angeles Times* asked the man who might be a heartbeat away and so forth a question about his area of expertise: "If you found it necessary to end the war, you would use nuclear weapons, wouldn't you?"

The general started in enthusiastically: "We seem to have a phobia about nuclear weapons. . . . I think there are many times when it would be most efficient to use nuclear weapons. However, public opinion in this country and throughout the world just throw up their hands in horror when you mention nuclear weapons, because of a lot of propaganda that's been fed to them."

He went on to make his point by describing the negligible effects of the nuclear tests on Bikini atoll: "The fish are all back in the lagoons; the coconut trees are growing coconuts; the guava bushes have fruit on them; the birds are back. As a matter of fact, everything is about the same." The land crabs, he allowed, "were a little bit 'hot.'" But if it came to it, "I would use anything we could dream up, anything we could dream up—including nuclear weapons, if it was necessary."

Reporters dashed to the phones. One of them upset a chair in his rush. As it happened, within two weeks the Wallace campaign would achieve its long-standing goal: being on the ballot in all fifty states (it came when the dreaded Supreme Court ruled that Ohio's ballot-access laws were too restrictive in a case called *Socialist Labor Party v. Rhodes.* Thank you, Socialist Labor Party). There was nothing to celebrate. Bombs-Away LeMay and Wallace had begun their downward spiral to the 13.8 percent they ended up receiving on November 5.

A neck-and-neck campaign, a spoiler to break a tie: things started getting nasty in the Nixon camp. That was the Nixon way. In his last campaign, in 1962, running behind against Pat Brown, a circular was sent out from the "Committee for the Preservation of the Democratic Party in California," addressed to "Dear Fellow Democrats," alleging that Brown was under the thumb of "left-wing forces" who had adopted the "entire platform of the Communist Party." Another superimposed a picture of a bowing Pat Brown next to one of Nikita Khrushchev. Bumper stickers started appearing reading IS BROWN PINK?

Agnew started in on the dirty work, just as Nixon used to do for Ike. A heckler shouted, "Humphrey! Humphrey Humphrey!" Agnew retorted, "You can renounce your citizenship if you don't like it here," and said when Nixon was inaugurated, people like the heckler were going to "dry up and disappear." As for HHH himself, Agnew accused him of conciliating those who "condone violence and advocate overthrow of the government."

Then, Nixon joined Agnew, to the puzzlement of those who believed in a "New Nixon." He said Humphrey had a "personal attitude of indulgence and permissiveness toward the lawless" and hated the military: "I am the one who stands for a stronger United States and Mr. Humphrey who stands for a weaker one." The campaign monitored crime figures in municipalities around the country and cut last-minute radio commercials for the ones that were ticking upward. It fit the new slogan devised for those last few weeks, commanding thousands of billboards across the country: VOTE LIKE YOUR WHOLE LIFE DEPENDED ON IT. In 1964, Lyndon Johnson had campaigned telling bedtime stories: that the sixties were scary (because of nuclear weapons), Barry Goldwater was scary, and that a vote for Johnson banished the monster under the bed. The story Nixon told was identical, with the terms reversed: that if the Democrats won—apocalypse.

He was convinced of it himself. He was also convinced his plane was bugged. He was convinced the work of a lifetime might go down the drain. He was convinced he had to do anything to win—before the bad guys did it first. So he had John Ehrlichman set up a paid goon squad to rough up demonstrators at his speeches. He was also convinced the Democrats would pull the rabbit of peace out of the hat in Vietnam, timed perfectly to destroy him. After all, his contact in Ambassador-at-Large Averell Harriman's negotiating team in Paris told him so. That would be the killing blow. In an election season where the public didn't perceive many major differences between the candidates on the issues, Nixon had a strong advantage on Vietnam. Those who perceived a difference in the ability of the two parties to avoid an expanded war preferred Nixon to Humphrey two to one. The Republican, the man who'd dropped broad hints in New Hampshire of some secret plan to end the war, was the man the public trusted to make peace. He reinforced it with unsubtle digs: "Those who have had a chance for another four years and could not produce peace should not be given another chance."

But Nixon couldn't be elected to produce peace if peace had already been produced.

And in Paris, the chances of peace seemed to be receding every day. Every time the North Vietnamese appeared ready to agree to a condition, the South Vietnamese raised the bar.

The reason was that Nixon had sabotaged the negotiations. His agent was Anna Chennault, known to one and all as the Dragon Lady. She told the South Vietnamese not to agree to anything, because waiting to end the war would deliver her friend Richard Nixon the election, and he would give them a better deal.

The brazenness was breathtaking. The previous May, after the triumphant announcement by the lame-duck president that the United States would be negotiating with the North Vietnamese in Paris, Nixon said that this removed Vietnam from the table as an issue. In Evansville, Indiana, he said, "Let's not destroy the chances for peace with a mouthful of words from some irresponsible candidate for president of the United States. Put yourself in the position of the enemy. He is negotiating with Lyndon Johnson and Secretary Rusk and then he reads in the paper that, not a senator, not a congressman, not an editor, but a potential *president of the United States* will give him a better deal than President Johnson is offering him. What's he going to do? It will torpedo those deliberations, it will destroy any chance for the negotiations to bring an honorable end to the war. The enemy will wait for the next man." To the American Association of Editorial Cartoonists, when one of that hated tribe asked him sharply, "How could you stand up and ask us to vote for you when you don't want to be specific?" Nixon responded, in tones of wounded innocence, "If there is a *chance* we can get the war over before this election, it is much more important than anything I might wish to say to get you to vote for me. . . . I will not make any *statement* that might pull the rug out from under him and might destroy the possibility to bring the war to a conclusion." Which was true. He didn't make a statement. He had the Dragon Lady whisper it instead.

This head-spinning stuff would be for future generations to find out about. For now, the bottom line was this: there was no chance of getting the war ended before the election. Because Richard Nixon had made it impossible.

Labor poured unprecedented resources into the Democratic campaign going into the home stretch, registering 4.6 million voters, sending out 115 million pamphlets, establishing 638 phone banks, fielding 72,000 house-to-house canvassers and 94,000 Election Day volunteers. Humphrey nabbed fifteen last-minute points from Wallace among unionists. He also ran a lachrymose print ad: "Don't let him buy the White House," over a picture of a smiling Nixon. "No man has ever paid more trying to be President. Richard Nixon has spent more in the last month alone than Hubert Humphrey will spend in his six-month campaign. . . . If you don't do something about it, he will spend at least $5 for every $1 Mr. Humphrey spends. . . . It means we could pick a president, not on what he says, but on how much he spends to say it."

Nixon, panicking at the last minute, tried one last trick: he asked Humphrey to agree that if neither of them won the required majority in the electoral college, the winner of the popular vote would become president. Nice try, but not so fast: the Constitution's provision was an election in the House of Representatives, which was overwhelmingly Democratic. Humphrey said he would "stand by the constitutional process." Election Day.

Leonard Garment, watching Nixon preparing for this moment as far back as Lincoln Day season in 1966, had imagined that this was what a man training for an Olympic decathlon must live like—the staggeringly punishing schedules, the mastering of ten political disciplines at once, the planning, the pushing, the endurance, the *pain.* And that had been a long, long thirty months in the past. It hadn't let up since—hadn't let up, really, since Nixon's political career began in college, organizing his Orthogonians, plotting his ascendance as student body president, the dour, plodding soul who astonished contemporaries later imagined must have practiced his handshake in the mirror, "the man least likely to succeed in politics." Maybe it hadn't let up since he was but a boy, the brother surviving the loss of two brothers— "trying," as his sainted mother told a journalist inquiring into what made Nixon Nixon, "to be three sons in one, striving even harder than before to make up to his father and me for our loss."

At thirty-four years old, when his law school classmates were making partner, he was a congressman; at thirty-five, with the Hiss case, he was a household name; at thirty-eight, a senator; by the time he was forty, vice president of the United States, the proverbial heartbeat away from the presidency (and the president, an old man, had a weak heart). By the time he was forty-five, he was standing toe-to-toe with Khrushchev in Moscow, the most fearsome dictator in the world. Then the soul-incinerating loss in 1960, the closest *any* man had come to the presidency without winning. (And now, exactly eight years later, the early indications were that it would be no less close.) Then the second soul-incinerating loss but two years later, for governor of California—upon which, *Time* magazine reflected in its political eulogy, "Perhaps he had risen too far too fast."

Nothing to do after that but to strive ever harder than before. As he had told Pat Buchanan, also in 1966, "If I had to practice law and nothing else, I would be mentally dead in two years and physically dead in four." Well, then, what of it? What if he lost?

He climbed into his campaign plane bound for New York City that November Tuesday morning in 1968, decorated by some overzealous campaign worker with an AIR FORCE ONE sign that Nixon clearly found excruciating; he wasn't so confident. He drew close his family, who were shocked at his candor, and told them not to take his public confidence as anything but a show. "I want to tell you what's really going to happen," Teddy White recorded him telling them in *Making of the President*. "If people in this country are still really concerned about peace, we could win big. But if they've been reassured about peace and now they're concerned with their pocketbooks and welfare, we could lose."

The self-righteousness, the self-pity of the formulation were fulsome: *Richard Nixon* was offering the American people peace. If they rejected Richard Nixon, it would be because they were willing to accept . . . war. Their greed—"their pocketbooks and welfare"—would have gotten the better of them. Thus did he, psychically, prepare himself for a likely eventuality: that, once more, he would lose. That he would be known as a loser for the rest of his life. Something, anything, to redeem the dread: if he lost, he was telling his family, it would be because America had proven herself unworthy of his idealism.

He might lose. The previous night, on a two-hour Nixon telethon broadcast across the West Coast, a last-ditch attempt to guarantee his home state, he had made a gaffe: he swore.

Richard Nixon had been retailing his white-picket-fence piety to the voters since 1946. The only Nixon America's television audiences knew was the one who, in his third debate with Kennedy in 1960, had solemnly chided Harry Truman for a recent comment that the Republican Party could "go to hell." "One thing I have noted as I have traveled around the country are the tremendous number of children who come out to see the presidential candidates" is what square old Dick Nixon had said then. "It makes you realize that whoever is president is going to be a man that all the children of America will either look up to or will look down to, and I can only say that I am very proud that President Eisenhower restored dignity and decency and—frankly—good language to the conduct of the presidency of the United States." Americans would have to wait another six years to learn that privately, Nixon cursed like a sailor. "Cocksucker!" was a favorite plosive burst. And that was the other Nixon revealed—just a brief glint—during the wearying, waning minutes of that telethon. "Now we get down to the nut-cutting," he disarmingly uttered.

How many votes might that shift? Enough, in the next twenty-four hours, to render him Job once again? Would the same torture of retrospection that had haunted him since November 8, 1960, be renewed for the rest of his life?

The plane passed over Indiana, a toss-up state. "How can you have your mother be from Indiana and not be a fighting Republican?": his habitual line for Hoosiers. An observer recorded him still and forlorn, peering at the cornfields from the window, as "if by looking down and concentrating he could pull in more votes."

Richard Nixon's evening: that biennial torture. First glimmers from Kansas: eight points ahead of Humphrey in the popular vote, with 19 percent for the spoiler George Wallace.

Eight o'clock: Humphrey picks up a little more steam.

Ohio: too close to call.

Missouri: Humphrey ahead in the vote tally; Nixon ahead in CBS's computer projection.

Ten twenty: a slew of Eastern states have gone for the Democrat.

The stroke of midnight: Hubert Humphrey was ahead by a point in the popular vote, with four of ten returns counted. In Nixon's familiar old suite at the Waldorf, the televisions were turned off by order of the decathlete, scribbling on yellow pads, working the phones, puzzling out the nation's precincts, the labyrinth he knew better than any other man alive, as the nation's will slowly, agonizingly revealed itself.

He knew it by 3:15 a.m.

The networks weren't sure until well into the 9 a.m. hour.

Humphrey didn't concede until eleven thirty. In fact, the victory wouldn't be certified for weeks. But the old gentleman's convention of the concession sealed this strangest American apotheosis: the boy who'd spent his childhood cloistered in a tower reading, who hated to ride the school bus because he thought the other children smelled bad, the feral junior debater, this founder of fraternal societies for the decidedly unfraternal, would, come January 20, be the leader of the free world.

Not only that, he did so with something no other Republican presidential candidate, with minor exceptions, had ever had before: electoral votes from the South. Wallace took Alabama, Georgia, Mississippi, Louisiana. But Nixon got Arkansas, Tennessee, Florida, Virginia, North Carolina—and Strom Thurmond's South Carolina.

George Wallace sent a congratulatory telegram. Nixon never acknowledged it. It spoke to the agony of victory. For it was barely a victory: 301 electoral votes for Nixon and 191 for Humphrey, 46 for George Wallace—and, in the popular vote, 43.42 percent, 42.72 percent, and 13.53 percent. Only five or so points more than Barry Goldwater's humiliating share in 1964. With George Wallace claiming that symbolically the victory belonged as much to him as to Nixon: "Mr. Nixon said the same thing we said," he declared. If he hadn't, was Wallace's point, Nixon wouldn't have won. And indeed, a few thousand more votes for Wallace in North Carolina and Tennessee, a shift of 1 percent of the vote in New Jersey or Ohio from Nixon to Humphrey, and the election would have been thrown into the House of Representatives, because Nixon wouldn't have won an electoral college majority. If Nixon didn't "carry out his commitments," Wallace said—lay off desegregation guidelines and appoint "constitutionalists" to the federal bench—the Alabaman would run for president again in 1972. Nixon hadn't even been inaugurated, and his reelection was already imperiled.

Some victory: look at what happened with Congress. The Republicans gained but four seats in the House. They did a little better, percentage-wise, in the Senate. One heartbreaker: Max Rafferty's loss. At the last minute, the *Long Beach Independent* reported that he had dodged the draft during World War II, digging up the standing joke in the town where he had been teaching: "Max Rafferty celebrated V-J day by throwing his cane away." It was symbolic of a Pyrrhic-victory gloom astonished aides began noticing in the boss over the next few days. "I need Max in the Senate," Nixon had announced to California's voters. He needed him because he had dreamed not merely of victory, but *victory:* a mandate to remake the world. As he had told Len Garment in that pool-house slumber party in 1965, "He felt his life had to be dedicated to great foreign policy purposes. This man, fiercely determined to stay in the political life for which he was in many ways so ill suited, told me he felt driven to do so not by the rivalries or ideological commitments or domestic politics but by his pacifist mother's idealism and the profound importance of foreign affairs."

At the very least, that would take a lukewarm, friendly Congress. But he would be the first president since Zachary Taylor in 1849 to start his term without a majority in either chamber.

Merely holding the Oval Office? It hardly seemed half enough.

He would just have to strive harder. Someday, he would finally *win.*

BOOK III

CHAPTER SEVENTEEN

The First One Hundred Days

Aﬀter all Richard Nixon had been through, how couldn't it but rain on the biggest day of his life?

It was less than two weeks after his fifty-sixth birthday. Kennedy, eight years earlier to the day, at the age of forty-two, had received a pure white blanket of snow for his inauguration, got to stand without an overcoat in the stinging cold and show the nation he was hail, young, stalwart, brave. Nixon, bundled up behind a thick scarf, got one of those muddy, awful January rains, and a bulletproof partition ahead of his lectern—"a reminder," the *Washington Post* observed, "of the assassinations which so suddenly had altered the political fortunes of the leaders present." Rain was not salubrious for his appearance: it made his dark hair dye run, and risked showing the gray in his short sideburns. *Public speaking*—a president's first task—was also not salubrious for his appearance. "The disjointedness," as Garry Wills described it, "seemed expressed in his face as he scowled (his only expression of thoughtfulness) or grinned (his only expression of pleasure). The features do not quite work together. The famous nose looks detachable. . . . The parts all seem to be worked by wires, a doomed attempt to contrive 'illusions of grandeur.'"

The audience, too, was not salubrious. He was sworn in by Justice Black with the defeated vice president by his side, before a crowd of but 250,000—and the *Post* just had to inform the world that this was "far smaller and at times less enthusiastic than the 1.2 million" that came out for Lyndon B. Johnson on January 20, 1965.

He was, though, a man used to overcoming hardship. That was what Richard Nixon *did.* He overcame these, and delivered a brilliant inaugural address—one fit, adjudged grateful pundits, to bind up a broken nation's wounds.

The speech was solemnly intoned. It was a paean to the glory of quiet:

"To lower our voices would be a simple thing.

"In these difficult years, America has suffered from a fever of words: from inflated rhetoric that promises more than it can deliver; from angry rhetoric that fans discontents into hatreds; from bombastic rhetoric that postures instead of persuading.

"We cannot learn from one another until we stop shouting at one another—until we speak quietly enough so that our words can be heard as well as our voices.

"For its part, government will listen. We will strive to listen in new ways—to the voices of quiet anguish, the voices that speak without words, the voices of the heart—to the injured voices, the anxious voices, the voices that have despaired of being heard."

The speech included Johnsonesque stanzas on "rebuilding our cities and improving our rural areas . . . protecting our environment and enhancing the quality of life," and a call for racial transcendence—"What remains is to give life to what is in the law"—and Kennedyesque visions of reaching the moon; and Wilsonian ones of global harmony: "The greatest honor history can bestow is the title of *peacemaker*. This honor now beckons America—the chance to help lead the world at last out of the valley of turmoil and onto that high ground of peace that man has dreamed of since the dawn of civilization."

The thirty-seventh president of the United States concluded, "To the crisis of the spirit we need an answer of the spirit. And to find that answer, we need only look within ourselves. . . . We have endured a long night of the American spirit. But as our eyes catch the dimness of the first rays of dawn, let us not curse the remaining dark. *Let us gather the light.*"

Afterward, the Justice Department's Warren Christopher met with new White House counsel John Ehrlichman. Christopher handed over a packet of documents and instructed the president to keep them on hand at all times: proclamations to declare martial law, with blanks to fill in the date and the name of the city.

Just then, it could have been San Francisco, where the state university was on strike and President S. I. Hayakawa had ordered police to clear the campus: "There are no more innocent bystanders." Or East St. Louis, Illinois, where a sniper, or snipers, was picking off what the black underground-newspaper columnist Julius Lester called "known enemies of the black community." Lester praised this "move from self-defense to aggressive action," citing the example of Vietnam's National Liberation Front. "What is happening in East St. Louis points up once again the advantage of medium-sized cities, leaving Saigon, Danang, and other large cities for the last," he wrote, like a military officer filing a field report. "That is not to say that the large cities should be ignored."

Or Washington, where thousands of antiwar activists were huddled in the freezing rain for a "counterinaugural" protest. The inaugural parade stepped off; a jug of wine was thrown at the marine commandant's convertible. George Romney, the new HUD secretary, passed; a mob chanted, "Romney eats shit!" Protesters braced themselves for the passage of the presidential limousine. The problem was identifying which limousine it was. Decoys absorbed the brunt of the rocks, beer cans, and bottles, until they finally spotted the president and first lady waving through narrow slits in what one reporter described as a "hollowed-out cannonball on wheels." A phalanx of Secret Service men trotted alongside, swatting down the thrown objects. At Fifteenth Street a group almost halted the procession with a smoke bomb. Some burned tiny American flags passed out along the parade route by Boy Scouts.

"Ho, Ho, Ho Chi Minh! Ho Chi Minh is going to win!"

"Four more years of death! Four more years of death!"

But the protest was smaller than expected. To a *New Yorker* writer, "they seemed like voices from another era—disgruntled remnants out to ruin the new atmosphere of peace and conciliation." Journalists took Nixon at his word: this was a new day in Washington. They fell over themselves to take him at his word.

They used such words as "cool," "efficient," and "confident"—and, of the first press conference, "great" and "tremendous." The *New York Times* education columnist said that only the winding down of the war—first, the implication went, on Nixon's agenda—stood "in the way of a dramatic escalation by President Nixon of the urban- and egalitarian-minded Johnson policies." "The incoming Nixon men seem relaxed and almost mellow," a columnist observed; Chalmers Johnson of the *Post* wrote, "There is none of the moralistic sense of good guys replacing bad guys." Hugh Sidey, proprietor of the *Life* magazine column "The Presidency," wrote of the new executive's "remarkable ease and sense of pleasure." Lyndon Johnson's former public-opinion expert, Benjamin Wattenberg, published a column entitled "Upbeat Auguries Belie the Alarmists." He lamented, "Incessantly, during the last year we heard from Democrats, Republicans, and Independents alike that 'America faces its greatest crisis of a hundred years.'" Thank God that was over. "The ground has been prepared for an era of better feeling," wrote Joseph Kraft.

Nixon introduced his new cabinet at an unprecedented live television ceremony, modestly standing off to one side, pledging to them before the world that his door would always be open: "I don't want a cabinet of yes-men." Herb Klein, the new communications director, promised the press corps, "Truth will become the hallmark of the Nixon administration. . . . We will be able to eliminate any possibility of a credibility gap in this administration." And at the bureaucracies, the grown-ups were back in charge. Evans and Novak said Nixon would "change the whole character of the White House staff operation."

Nixon established something called the Urban Affairs Council, a domestic NSC, and named a Democrat, Daniel Patrick Moynihan of the Kennedy-Johnson Labor Department, to run it; the cup of bipartisanship, that Holy

Grail of the pundit class, runneth over. Moynihan helped prepare Nixon's
first message to Congress, a conciliatory performance that endorsed Johnson's poverty program. The Senate majority leader, Mike Mansfield, predicted a *stronger* role for the Senate than under LBJ. "He knows that if his
administration is to succeed," the *Post* observed, "he will have to have the
cooperation of the Democratic Congress." In February, Nixon took his
presidency's first overseas trip, to England, France, West Germany, and
Italy—to "listen," Nixon said. The *New Republic* found the March 4 press
conference upon his return "dazzling"; the *New York Times* called it a "tour
de force." The editorial headlines ran "A National Good Deed," "Good
Work, Mr. President," "Mission Accomplished." Franklin seals of approval
were issuing from all over. *Let us gather the light.*

The presentation of Nixon as the Great Conciliator wasn't exactly a confidence game, because Richard Nixon on some level believed it. It showed in
the personal exhortations he wrote to himself on yellow legal pads in the
hideaway office he established in the Old Executive Office Building: *Each
day a chance to do something memorable for someone. . . . Need to be good
to do good. . . . The nation must be better in spirit at the end of term. Need
for joy, serenity, confidence, inspiration.* But neither was any of it precisely
true. It would be a mistake, for example, to say Nixon cherished domestic
tranquillity. He welcomed conflict that served him politically. A briefing
paper came to the president's desk in the middle of March instructing him to
expect increased violence on college campuses that spring. "Good!" he wrote
across the face. The lies had, in fact, started with his victory speech in
November. He said, his eyes blinking quickly in the TV lights, his presidency
would be inspired by a sign he saw on the campaign trail held up by a young
girl in Ohio: BRING US TOGETHER. A reporter tracked the girl down and
learned her placard actually bore the rather more divisive words LBJ TAUGHT
US VOTE REPUBLICAN.

You could debunk the points one by one. An open door to cabinet members? Actually Nixon told his chief of staff, Bob Haldeman, "Keep them
away from me." Remarkable ease? "I want everyone fired, I mean it this
time" went a typical Nixon command, this one on the sixteenth day of his
presidency. The people he wanted fired were holdover Johnsonites from the
Office of Economic Opportunity: pace Chalmers Johnson, the Good Guys
would replace the Bad Guys.

The credibility gap was inscribed in the job title of the very man who said
there wouldn't be a credibility gap. The traditional job of the "press secretary" was to smooth things over with newsmen. Nixon didn't want that.
Herb Klein was a "communications director"—a kind of full-time public
relations agent. PR was also handled by the dashing young Bill Safire. One
of the president's first utterances at the meeting of his new Cabinet Commit-

tee on Economic Policy was that its chairman, economist Paul McCracken, should "work with Safire." Safire grasped their assignment implicitly: point up what Nixon had called on the campaign trail "the economic straitjacket fashioned by the present administration," even though in 1968 the GNP grew 7 percent and the stock market swelled. At the same meeting, Nixon showed what he meant by not being surrounded by yes-men. His agriculture secretary, Clifford Hardin, started in on the problem of hunger. "Millions of Americans," he began, then the president interrupted him: "It is not constructive to say that people here are starving."

At his first press conference, Nixon reversed a campaign promise. He had said he'd pursue "clear-cut military superiority" over the Russians—it was in the telegram Strom Thurmond sent out to wavering Republican delegates. Now he said the goal was "sufficiency." At his first political meeting, former Nixon, Mudge colleague John Sears and anti-Wallace point man Fred LaRue recommended a year-round opinion-polling operation. The president eagerly agreed. When Klein made the mistake of telling a columnist, Nixon blew up, as he always did at any suggestion that he was what he actually was: obsessed with his image. *Not concerned by Press, TV, or personal style,* went one of his legal pad musings. *Zest for job . . . Strong in-charge President. Aggressive. Anti-crime measures . . . On the ball. Honest.*

A better description was *mercurial.* Every morning, staffers would study Herb Klein's face to know how to handle the boss that day. Another was *insecure.* Hours were taken up after important meetings grilling Haldeman or his national security adviser, Henry Kissinger, about whether he did well or bragging about how well he did. After entertaining the prime minister of Canada, he asked Haldeman whether the soup course might be eliminated from state dinners: "Men don't really like soup." Actually, Haldeman learned from the presidential valet, the president had spilled soup down his vest the night before.

Every meeting was political. At his first economics gathering, he suggested cutting federal aid to education (so much for the *Times*'s "dramatic escalation") and housing construction loans. Spiro Agnew, who had made his bones as a politician placating suburban voters, shot down the second immediately: "You are thrusting against the young, white, middle-class factor." The idea was never heard from again.

Nixon hired a press secretary after all, a twenty-nine-year-old who'd worked under Haldeman at J. Walter Thompson (and before that as a tour guide on the Jungle Ride at Disneyland). Watching young Ron Ziegler flounder, some hard-nosed boys in the press decided the hiring was meant to signal the president's contempt for them. Ziegler made an immediate and indelible contribution to American political culture: the phrase *photo opportunity.* (Haldeman once ordered thousands of dollars of landscaping installed in Honolulu just to improve the pictures taken after a conference on Vietnam.)

Nixon would lie about anything: spreading word that he took no naps though he took them almost daily, marked as "staff time" on his public schedule; claiming to the Council on Urban Affairs that his management philosophy was to stick to the big picture—"John Quincy Adams and Grover Cleveland read every bill and almost killed themselves"—even though precious hours of the Leader of the Free World's time were spent worrying over details such as the spray of the presidential shower, or the precise lighting angles in his TV appearances.

A memo on his first day as president:

"To: Mrs. Nixon

"From: The President"

It wasn't a love note. "With regard to RN's room, what would be the most desirable is an end table like the one on the right side of the bed which will accommodate TWO dictaphones as well as a telephone. . . . In addition, he needs a bigger table on which he can work at night. The table which is presently in the room does not allow enough room for him to get his knees under it."

In the middle of March, Nixon ordered the bombing of the sections of the Ho Chi Minh Trail that meandered through Cambodia, the beginning of a long-term plan called Operation Menu (its component parts were "Breakfast," "Lunch," "Snack," "Dinner," "Dessert," and "Supper"). This scaled new peaks of deception: the bombings were recorded on a secret ledger, which was later destroyed. A half million tons of ordnance were eventually dropped on this neutral country, 3,875 sorties without congressional knowledge. "State is to be notified only after the point of no return," he instructed on March 15. Then he called in his secretary of state, who opposed the bombing, and secretary of defense, who favored the bombing but opposed doing it secretly, and asked them to advise him on whether to bomb. Sixty B-52s were already on their way.

To the nation, on the inaugural platform on the Capitol steps, Nixon had said he would give life to the civil rights laws. Behind closed doors, he said, "Nothing should happen in the South without checking with Dent"—White House special counsel Harry Dent, Strom Thurmond's man. Five school districts in North Carolina, South Carolina, and Mississippi were scheduled to have their federal funding pulled the week after the inauguration. Dent arranged for a sixty-day delay. Just to make sure, Nixon met with his HEW secretary, Robert Finch, and told him to personally monitor that any action on school desegregation was "inoffensive to the people of South Carolina."

Harry Robbins "Bob" Haldeman was the linchpin of the White House system. He and his partner and UCLA college buddy John Ehrlichman, they of the twin militaristic brush cuts, were known as Nixon's "Berlin Wall." Federal Reserve chairman Arthur Burns came in for an Oval Office

meeting one Wednesday. On the way out the door, he remembered something else he needed to discuss. Haldeman blocked him bodily: "Your
appointment is over, Dr. Burns. Send a memo." Boasted Haldeman to an
underling, "Even John Mitchell has to come through me now." Mitchell was
the attorney general.

Haldeman was an isolated man's conduit to the outside world. Shovelfuls
of reporting, analysis, warning, summary, advice, were delivered to the presidential desk every day. And every day, dozens of these texts floated to the
top of the pile for assault by the presidential pen—which marginalia, along
with sundry oral outbursts, it was the immediate responsibility of Haldeman
to translate into "action memos" to distribute to relevant staff.

Such as, on Day 17: "I still have not had any progress report on what procedure has been set up to continue on some kind of basis the letters to the
editor project and the calls to TV stations."

This project was a Nixon obsession. The RNC and state and local Republican parties put together lists of loyalists—the "Nixon Network"—willing
to write on their own or lend their names to ghostwritten missives on items
of presidential concern. Day 52, it was the *Smothers Brothers Comedy Hour*:
"They have a sequence in which one said to the other that he found it difficult to find anything to laugh about—Vietnam, the cities, etc., but 'Richard
Nixon's solving those problems' and 'that's really funny.'" Nixon told aides
he wanted letters to the producers, stipulating their argument: the gag was
inaccurate "in view of the great public approval of RN's handling of foreign
policy, etc., etc." The show was canceled one month later.

A press aide, Jim Keogh, a former *Time* editor, pointed out on Day 29,
"Media treatment of the President is almost uniformly excellent." The president answered, "You don't understand, they are waiting to destroy us."

The Nixon White House, a machine for manipulation: its story can only be
told by observing two separate documentary records. There was a public
transcript: the inauguration address, the photo opportunity, the bill proposal.
Then there was a private transcript, only to be revealed by historians in later
generations from the traces a presidency leaves behind, even in the lies the
president tells himself.

On the subjects of law and order, however, the public and private transcripts were not that far apart. The matter was just about the president's only
domestic focus. It was his obsession.

The first news summary the president read included a front-page editorial from the *Washington Star*, the capital's right-leaning daily, on the eighty-
one-year-old D.C. "mother of the year" who was mugged and thrown down
a flight of stairs. Nixon wrote a note to himself: "We're going to make a
major step to reduce crime in the nation—starting with D.C." He couldn't
start anywhere else: that was the only place the federal government had

street-level law-enforcement authority. His proposed District of Columbia Court Reorganization Bill allowed "no-knock" entry and sixty days "preventive detention." Senator Sam Ervin of North Carolina, a constitutional obsessive, said it would "better be titled 'A Bill to Repeal Fourth, Fifth, Sixth, and Eighth Amendments to the Constitution.'" D.C.'s police chief said he didn't want or need it. That wasn't important to the White House, for whom it was a no-lose proposition: they didn't expect it to pass, but got points for proposing "bold" action all the same.

Two days later, President Nixon made his first major domestic policy statement in conjunction with a letter sent from his HEW secretary to college presidents, calling attention to laws allowing the federal government to withdraw funds from students found guilty of crimes in connection with campus disorders: "Freedom—intellectual freedom—is in danger in America.... Violence—physical violence, physical intimidation—is seemingly on its way to becoming an accepted, or, at all events, a normal and not-to-be-avoided element in the clash of opinion within university confines.... The process is altogether familiar to those who would survey the wreckage of history: assault and counterassault, one extreme leading to the opposite extreme, the voices of reason and calm discredited." Nixon nodded in a Franklinesque direction, a moderating patina: "We have seen a depersonalization of the educational experience. Our institutions must reshape themselves lest this turn to total alienation.... There must be university reform including new experimentation in curricula such as ethnic studies, student involvement in the decision-making process, and a new emphasis in faculty teaching." Then he delivered the sound bite: "It is not too strong a statement to declare that this is the way civilizations begin to die."

On March 19 the president had a photo opportunity in the Roosevelt Room with seventeen-year-old Perry Joseph Lundy of Oxnard, California, recipient of the Boys Club Boy of the Year award. Richard Nixon read the citation ". . . in recognition of superlative service to his home, church, school, community, and Boys Club. Perry typifies juvenile decency in action." Nixon awkwardly kibbitzed about Perry's college plans: "For the boys at the top of their class with leadership abilities, this is a seller's market right now, isn't it?" The next day, the Justice Department announced a federal indictment: "Beginning on or about April 12, 1968, and continuing through on or about August 30, 1968, in the North District of Illinois, Eastern Division, and elsewhere, DAVID T. DELLINGER, RENNARD C. DAVIS, THOMAS E. HAYDEN, ABBOT H. HOFFMAN, JERRY C. RUBIN, LEE WEINER, JOHN R. FROINES, and BOBBY SEALE, defendants herein, unlawfully, willfully, and knowingly did combine, conspire, confederate, and agree together . . . to travel in interstate commerce and use the facilities of interstate commerce with the intent to incite, organize, promote, encourage, participate in, and carry on a riot." The indictment was the fruit of the antiriot amendment added to get the 1968 Civil Rights Bill passed. Just as with the Boston 5, the Chicago 8 had neither ever communicated together nor sat in the same room.

Eight Chicago cops were also indicted for their activities during convention week. But that was only for show: Chicago juries did not convict Chicago cops. After one of them was acquitted after the prosecution had clearly proved he was merely beating hippies at random, the judge was so incredulous he asked the jury if they were sure. For his part, the cop told reporters his trial had proven that "most of the public wants this kind of justice in the streets." But when another of the Chicago officers was acquitted of beating a *Chicago Daily News* photographer named James Linstead, a more conservative judge pronounced himself satisfied with the jury's verdict: "The language Linstead used was vile and degrading to the officers; language which I suggested would provoke in such a manner that any red-blooded American would flare up."

These were the sort of actions that might once have set distinguished editorialists' tongues to clucking. Not now. The *New York Times* found the White House's "how civilizations begin to die" statement dead-on—"The crisis is nationwide. It stems from the adoption of terroristic methods as a substitute for rationality"—and his course of action one of "sound restraint." The Establishment was tacking right on law and order. That was why, on this subject, the White House's public and private transcripts were so similar.

When the battleship of Washington conventional wisdom pivots, it is often following the lead of some revered mandarin. In this case it was Joseph Kraft, who had filed an existential cri de coeur the week after the Democratic convention. The Chicago police, he admitted, deserved no prizes. But "what about those of us in the press and other media? Are we merely neutral observers, seekers after truth in the public interest? Or do we, as the supporters of Mayor Daley and his Chicago police have charged, have a prejudice of our own? . . .

"The answer, I think, is that Mayor Daley and his supporters have a point. Most of us in what is called the communication field are not rooted in the great mass of ordinary Americans—in Middle America. And the results show up not merely in occasional episodes such as the Chicago violence but more importantly in the systematic bias toward young people, minority groups, and the kind of presidential candidate who appeals to them.

"To get a feel of this bias it is first necessary to understand the antagonism that divides the middle class of this country. On the one hand there are highly educated upper-income whites sure of themselves and brimming with ideas for doing things differently. On the other hand, there is Middle America, the large majority of low-income whites, traditional in their values and on the defensive against innovation."

Kraft was the syndicated columnist who had a year earlier celebrated Bobby Kennedy for uniting "Black Power and Backlash." Now he concluded, "Those of us in the media need to make a special effort to understand Middle America"—and be nicer to Richard Nixon.

His fellow pundit Stewart Alsop wrote that the American proletariat was now middle-class and would defend their property "as ferociously as the classic capitalists of Karl Marx's day." He had seen it with his own eyes when he visited a factory with Senator Ribicoff in Connecticut. Ribicoff was the one who'd accused Mayor Daley of "gestapo tactics" at the convention.

The factory worker: "We saw you on television, Senator, and it seemed like you were for those hippies. You're not getting our vote this time."

The senator: "Look, suppose your kid was beaten up by the cops, how would you feel?"

"Those hippies . . . were wearing beards, and anybody who wears a beard, he deserves to get beat up."

The next day, Ribicoff dedicated a high school in Waspy Litchfield County. There, he got a standing ovation.

Kraft and Alsop's fellow pundits had not thought much heretofore about being members of a social class. They saw themselves as guardians of the general good. They had not thought much about their identification with the "toryhood of change"—Kevin Phillips's phrase for liberals "who make their money out of plans, ideas, communication, social upheaval, happenings, excitement," whose vision of the "general good" could come at the expense of other Americans' simple desire for stability. The pundits started thinking about it now. "The blue- and white-collar people who are in revolt now do have a cause for complaint about us," a media executive was quoted in *TV Guide*. "We've ignored their point of view." Said another, "We didn't know it was *there*!"

"It" was the white American majority.

To sit, as one of those executives, in one's sumptuously appointed office on Sixth Avenue or Forty-third Street or Columbus Avenue in Manhattan must now have been a traumatic thing. Before, it had been your command center: the place where you captained the consciousness of a nation. Now it was a bunker, where you looked out on a "Middle America" that suddenly seemed hostile and strange. The executives had come up in the McCarthy years. They wondered if that had made them *fear* these great sleeping masses. They began stereotyping, and idealizing, this noble cipher. They became like the Jewish executives of early Hollywood who never, ever put Jewish heroes up on the screen, and overcompensated by inventing the "blond bombshell." They weren't kicking Dick Nixon around anymore. They started bending over backward to be accepted by him and his supporters instead.

Pete Hamill, fresh from his overseas sojourn attempting to write a novel about Che Guevara, who'd begged Robert F. Kennedy to run because he was the white man whom black militants respected, now held up a new alienated, despised, voiceless subaltern in an article called "The Revolt of the White Lower Middle Class" for the trendy weekly *New York*. He "feels trapped and, even worse, in a society that purports to be democratic, ignored. . . . The working-class white man is actually in revolt against taxes, joyless work, the double standards and short memories of professional politicians, hypocrisy and what he considers the debasement of the American dream." Richard Nixon loved Hamill's article. He passed it around the White House.

Robert Shad Northshield, the *Huntley-Brinkley Report*'s producer, had joked, on election night, how he could have got Nixon to concede just by having one of his anchors say that Humphrey had won. Now he seemed ashamed of this plenipotentiary power. During coverage of the Nixon inauguration, Northshield ordered that no protesters be shown on the air. When NBC held meetings to plan their new newsmagazine program, *First Tuesday*, someone asked what the three biggest stories in the country were that they should cover. "The war, the blacks, and the economy," someone responded. Someone else shot back, "I don't want to see a single black face on *First Tuesday*."

If liberal media had ever been overfriendly to protesters, it was hard to say they were now. A University of Chicago sociology professor named Richard Flacks, one of the early members of SDS, appeared on local TV, defending a takeover of the administration building. A man who said he was from a St. Louis newspaper called up to ask for an interview. At the appointed day and time, Professor Flacks welcomed him into his office.

The man asked, "Just what is happening on American campuses? How do you explain it?"

It was the last thing Flacks remembered. He awoke in a hospital bed, having received a beating that left a permanent dent in his skull. The "reporter," actually a right-wing vigilante, left him for dead. Flacks's right hand, on which he wore a gift from the National Liberation Front—a ring fashioned from the metal of a downed U.S. aircraft—was almost severed clear off. No one was ever arrested. The *Chicago Daily News,* which had editorialized sympathetically on the antiwar movement for a week the previous August, didn't denounce the attempted murder. The *New York Times* gave it three small paragraphs on page 26. On the president's one hundredth day in office, vigilantes in Cairo, Illinois, shot out the rectory of a civil rights priest, and the governor had to call out the National Guard to tamp down the ensuing tensions. That was relegated in the *Times* to page 30 and didn't make the *Chicago Tribune* for a week. In a May editorial, the *Times* seemed to all but license vigilante responses to campus disturbances: "Either the administrators, faculty, and responsible student majority call the would-be professional revolutionaries to order, or the community at large will do so."

Neither the Chicago nor the Cairo attacks were recorded as a subject of presidential concern. The most recent Gallup poll said 61 percent of Amer-

icans approved of the job Nixon was doing. Only 11 percent disapproved.
Still, the president ordered a full-dress PR offensive for the occasion of his
one hundredth day: "We can, of course, assume now that the opposition will
be yelping on our heels on that date."

The first foreign policy crisis of Richard Nixon's presidency hit on April 15.
North Korea shot down a navy reconnaissance plane forty-eight miles from
its shores only four months after President Johnson had negotiated for the
release of the imprisoned crew of the USS *Pueblo*. National Security Adviser
Henry Kissinger was pushing to bomb an airfield in response. That would
be risky, Secretary of State William Rogers, Secretary of Defense Melvin
Laird, and Joint Chiefs chairman Earle "Bus" Wheeler all warned. Forces
weren't in place for the operation, and even if they were, such an attack could
ignite a second Asian ground war. Haldeman and Ehrlichman pointed to politics: flyboy heroics would keep them from framing the new administration
as ready to wind down the war in Vietnam—especially after Kissinger
answered their question as to what would happen if the situation escalated:
"*Vell*, it could go nuclear."

Kissinger, who had just had his first meeting with Soviet ambassador
Anatoly Dobrynin, told the president the administration wouldn't get anywhere without a show of force—"They will think you are a weakling."

Nixon ruminated. He was in the kind of spot he hated: a situation he
couldn't control. He ended up doing nothing on Korea; he couldn't. For the
first time, the public witnessed President Nixon lose his cool. In a press conference on April 18, in answer to the question "Mr. President, now that you
have had about three months in a position of presidential responsibility, do
the chances of peace in Southeast Asia seem to come any closer at all?" he
called South Vietnam "South Korea" three times.

"They got away with it this time," he told Henry Kissinger, "but they'll
never get away with it again." The next day, he regained his sangfroid, and
the respect of his national security adviser, by green-lighting the next rain of
steel on Cambodia, Operation Lunch.

Nixon had become president to play this poker game of world diplomacy.
He and Kissinger had an entire novel vision of international order, one
defined not by Cold War categories of good versus evil, but by metaphors of
control: *balance of power, equilibrium, structure of peace*. They learned early
that control was not easy to achieve. Then they raged at what they could not
control.

Nixon had auditioned Kissinger in a suite at the Hotel Pierre on Fifth
Avenue after the election. Kissinger agreed that foreign-policy decision-
making should be centered in the White House, bypassing the old Establishment in the State Department. Nixon's choice as secretary of state, William

Rogers, was a member of that Establishment, a former colleague of Tom Dewey's, a legal adviser to the *Washington Post*. He had also been a confidant of Nixon's since the 1940s—the man Nixon had gone to for advice on how to handle the Establishment during his slow, soiling humiliations. Perhaps that was why Nixon singled out his secretary of state for systematic humiliation again and again. Kissinger was glad to oblige—once spreading the rumor that Rogers was a "fag" who kept a hot, young stud in a Georgetown town house.

No one would have predicted that they would have become close partners: Nixon, the hard-line Cold Warrior since the days of Alger Hiss; Kissinger, a former Kennedy administration official and Nelson Rockefeller's foreign-policy right-hand man. But Richard Nixon's thinking had been changing in the years he was distant from government. Freed from playing demagogue to a domestic audience, traveling, absorbing, reflecting, he started to take (a favorite phrase) "the long view"—thinking less like a Cold War evangelist and more like a European balance-of-power realist. Which was what Henry Kissinger was. Upon Nixon's return from Asia in 1967, he attended the annual late-July retreat at Bohemian Grove, where Republican power brokers did silly Boy Scout rituals before a forty-foot stone owl and listened to daily afternoon, off-the-record "Lakeside Talks." Nixon would later say his own talk was his favorite speech of any he ever gave. Communism was no longer "monolithic"; the Soviet Union was on the verge of strategic parity with the United States; the booming capitalist economies of Japan, Korea, Taiwan, Malaysia would have more to do with checking the spread of revolution in Asia than any American saber rattling; you couldn't export American democracy to the third world anyway. "Diplomatically we should have discussions with the Soviet leaders at all levels to reduce the possibility of miscalculations and to explore the areas where bilateral agreements would reduce tensions." It sounded like what Kissinger had gotten Rockefeller to say in '68—that in "a subtle triangle with Communist China and the Soviet Union, we can ultimately improve our relations with each, as we test the will for peace of both."

These were heresies of a sort, certainly to the right-wing Republicans Nixon had been courting since 1964. He delighted in the heretic's role. One role model was Charles de Gaulle—an unsentimental amoralist, a gutsy, unconventional diplomatic chess player: granting independence to Algeria, loosening ties to the United States, inching toward the accommodation with the Soviet Union he labeled "détente." De Gaulle's influence had shaped Nixon's 1967 *Foreign Affairs* article "Asia After Vietnam," with its assertion that "the role of the United States as world policeman is likely to be limited in the future"; that diplomats should encourage "a collective effort by the nations of the region to contain the threat themselves."

Nixon's press conference substitution of "sufficiency" for "superiority" seemed hardly a slip of the tongue: he wanted Leonid Brezhnev to bid farewell to Old Nixon, who'd spoken of "Dean Acheson's College of Cowardly Communist Containment." Balancing nations' interests against each other, vouchsafing stability even at the price of apparent moral inconsistency, now seemed the highest good. His belief that this was moral was signaled by his choice of Oval Office furniture: Woodrow Wilson's desk. He also rationalized it in terms of his mother's piety, and the Quaker concept of "peace in the center."

Kissinger came to similar intellectual conclusions from different roots: from the trauma of growing up Jewish in Nazi Germany. He once told an interviewer what it was like to flee with his parents in 1938 at the age of fifteen: "All the things that had seemed secure and stable collapsed, and many of the people that one had considered the steady examples suddenly were thrown into enormous turmoil themselves and into fantastic insecurities." Warding off insecurity became the highest good—a psychic inclination tailor-made for appreciation of the great European intellectual tradition of balance-of-power thought. The subject of his dissertation was the Congress of Vienna of 1815, which locked into place a system of reciprocal recognition that produced stable power alignments for almost a century. It was the kind of achievement he hoped, with Nixon, to create in the here and now.

Still, they made an unlikely pairing. Kissinger was even on the record as once opining that Richard Nixon "was not fit to be president."

But then, Kissinger was as ruthless a bastard as any Nixon had seen. Each appreciated how the other played the game. That was another place where their minds met.

After Rockefeller lost the nomination, Kissinger became an informal adviser to the Paris peace talks, indispensable because he had French contacts in Hanoi. The Johnson team trusted him implicitly. They shouldn't have. Kissinger was the double agent feeding the intelligence to Nixon that let him scotch the peace deal before the election.

Kissinger understood his boss's psyche better than anyone else. Their psyches were actually quite similar, which also brought them together: Kissinger was a fuming outsider, a Bismarckian who was also Orthogonian.

He had transferred from City College to Harvard, with pretensions of becoming a gentleman. But a Jew couldn't become a gentleman at Harvard; not in the 1940s. He was brilliant enough to be named a professor there. But he seemed to have to work twice as hard as anyone else to earn tenure. He cultivated high manners, perfect taste, social connections, savoir faire. (His great anxiety in the White House was losing cachet with his former Harvard colleagues.) He counted slights from Establishment patrons. Revering and resenting the same men brought Nixon and Kissinger together. So, too, a rage at Kennedys: Kissinger had resigned his position in McGeorge Bundy's NSC because he felt unappreciated and unwelcome.

He was a prima donna. He didn't like having a boss. He was famous for volcanic temper tantrums when Rockefeller's speechwriters fiddled with his prose: "When Nelson buys a Picasso, he doesn't hire four housepainters to improve it!" Together Nixon and Kissinger revolutionized American foreign affairs across a Shakespearean tangle of mutual manipulation, affection, and resentment.

Nixon issued National Security Decision Memo 2 during the inauguration parade. The document disbanded the group within the State Department that checked the NSC. That made Kissinger the most powerful foreign policy officer in history. It also produced a paradox. Nixon and Kissinger had given themselves more single-handed control over foreign affairs than any other two men in American history. They fetishized the secrecy of their deliberations more than any other two officers in American history as well. It promised them control—and made those things they could not control all the more enraging: the secrets that slipped their containment chambers, the negotiating miscues, the battlefield blunders, the public relations setbacks. It made them all the more susceptible to losing *emotional* control.

Blunt Helen Thomas of UPI asked the second question of the first Nixon press conference: "Mr. President, now that you are president, what is your peace plan for Vietnam?" Now, surely, there wasn't a moratorium on an answer.

His response was somehow both short and meandering, merely repeating proposals already on the table. Senator McGovern, with a former college professor's faith in the power of reason and dialogue, had gone to the White House to meet Henry Kissinger and suggest a plan: since our involvement was a disaster and a mistake, couldn't Nixon just say that his predecessors Kennedy and Johnson had committed troops in good faith, but that events had shown that commitment no longer consistent with the national interest? Kissinger allowed that the war had been a mistake. But he said America couldn't pull out because the right wing would go crazy: "We couldn't govern the country." Thus did George McGovern become one of the first in a long line of Americans to be gobsmacked by the realization that Richard Nixon's pledge back in New Hampshire—"new leadership will end the war and win the peace in the Pacific"—would not mean anything dramatic if it would mean anything at all.

Another man surprised to learn that Nixon's inauguration did not mean an early Vietnam withdrawal was Stewart Alsop. Alsop met with William Rogers and made the opposite point as Kissinger: that *without* some quick announcement of a pullout of, say, fifty thousand or one hundred thousand, and an end to the bombing, the president would find it impossible to govern—just like Lyndon Johnson. "I'd rather not comment on that," Secretary Rogers said nervously, adding that Nixon eventually intended to stop the bombing of North Vietnam. But what Nixon did or didn't intend was never something that Rogers was privy to.

On February 21 Kissinger received five scenarios from experts on how to end the war. One of them was "technical escalation" to atomic, biological, or chemical weapons. Something more proximate they were considering was mining Haiphong Harbor, the economic lifeline of North Vietnam, to "jar the North Vietnamese into being more forthcoming at the Paris talks."

The president's second press conference, on March 4, included broad hints about troop drawdowns. The talk in Washington was over the notion of effecting national reconciliation by extending amnesty to draft resisters; deep within the White House, the talk was of changing draft eligibility from seven years to a single year. At his press conference the president was asked if he thought he "could keep American public opinion in line if this war were to go on for months and even years." He replied, "Well, I trust that I am not confronted with that problem, when you speak of years." His first budget proposed a reduction of defense spending from 45 percent of the budget to 37 percent, $1.1 billion below Lyndon Johnson's; as part of the economy move, Defense Secretary Laird announced a 10 percent cut in B-52 raids. "Public pressure over the war," the *New York Times* reported, "has almost disappeared."

That was Nixon's first one hundred days. A remarkably successful public relations campaign selling the new presidency as a magnanimous respite from a cacophonous era of division. A popular set of moves to clamp down on dissent, greeted by a media Establishment newly eager to kowtow to a conservative "Middle America" as eminently responsible. Already, a secret escalation of the Vietnam War. Already, Nixon's own grand dreams that he could make the world order anew, bring new peace and stability to the globe.

And already, a refusal by a paranoid president to believe that the media's acceptance of him as a responsible leader had happened at all. Already, a palimpsest of lies.

CHAPTER EIGHTEEN

Trust

THE TRUST IN PRESIDENT NIXON MIGHT HAVE BEEN SHAKEN SOMEWHAT on Day 101, when the ranking Republican on the Senate Foreign Relations Committee repeated something he had first said in 1966: time to declare victory and go home. "Common sense should tell us that we have now accomplished our purpose as far as South Vietnam is concerned," Vermont's George Aiken proclaimed, recommending "orderly withdrawal." It might have been shaken more on May 9, when after six straight days with nothing on the front page of the *New York Times* about the war, a tiny item in the bottom right corner obscured by a feature on Governor Rockefeller's art collection revealed that bombing was taking place in Cambodia.

But the trust wasn't shaken much. In a May 14 TV speech the president announced, "The time is approaching when the South Vietnamese will be able to take over some of the fighting fronts now being manned by Americans," proposing simultaneous mutual withdrawal of U.S. and North Vietnamese forces. (He counted on short memories, having charged in 1966, "Communist victory would most certainly be the result of 'mutual withdrawal.'") Columnists vied with each other to predict the drawdown numbers: fifty thousand, one hundred thousand, even two hundred thousand. Gallup was about to announce Nixon's approval rating at 64 percent. Maybe, a nonplussed public concluded—if any had noticed the *Times*' dispatch—Cambodian bombing was what it took to bring the horses into the barn.

Henry Kissinger was not nonplussed. On the morning of the ninth, a Germanic screech rang out from the porch of the Key Biscayne Hotel:

"Outrageous! Outrageous! . . . We must crush these people! We must destroy them!"

Kissinger referred to the secretaries of defense and state, whose offices he suspected had leaked Operation Menu to the *Times*. He rang up Melvin Laird, pulling him off the golf course at Burning Tree: "You son of a bitch!" (Laird hung up.) Or maybe the leak had come from the NSC office in the basement of the White House. The thought of a runaway staff was enraging to Kissinger—not just for diplomatic reasons, but for what it suggested to the security-obsessed bulldogs around Nixon about an NSC top-heavy with Harvard grads and Kennedy vets.

The Cambodia article wasn't even damning. It was *flattering*. The subject of "Raids in Cambodia by U.S. Unprotested" was how nicely the Cambodian government was cooperating, and that "there is no Administration interest at this time in extending the ground war into Cambodia or Laos."

That wasn't the point. The point was that Kissinger and Nixon feared the White House's secrets were being betrayed.

Kissinger called J. Edgar Hoover and told him it was time to move forward on a project they had discussed: wiretaps of Laird, Laird's senior military assistant, and three NSC staffers, including Morton Halperin. Thus did the FBI learn about such things as Mrs. Halperin's concern for the surgery of a relative in New York, and the Halperin boys' favorite playmates—and that, when reporters asked Mr. Halperin to leak Kissinger statements, he steadfastly refused. The tap on Mel Laird was more productive; from it Kissinger drew a bead on the activities of a hated bureaucratic rival. What he didn't find was any leakers. So he had wiretaps extended to encompass two more NSC staffers.

A reporter was next. This time, however, it wasn't Kissinger working through the FBI. The president wanted to monitor Henry Kissinger. So John Ehrlichman called on John Caulfield, a new addition to the White House staff, a former detective on New York's version of the Red Squad who'd known Nixon since he'd protected him on the campaign trail in 1960. Caulfield called a friend, who'd worked sweeping Nixon's hotels for bugs during the 1968 campaign. Together, they cased the target's Georgetown town house and told Ehrlichman the job would be difficult. Ehrlichman insisted they try anyway, because national security was at stake. So they scrounged up some phone company credentials and shimmied up a pole to affix a bug to the reporter's phone wire. He was Joseph Kraft, the same journalist who'd lectured his fellow media professionals to stop coddling liberals. But he also was Henry's favorite journalist friend, and Nixon needed to know what his foreign-policy right-hand man was up to. Which was only fair. Kissinger was already working toward opening an entirely separate channel to glean what secrets Nixon might be keeping from him.

The rage for control was spreading as the myths of American tranquillity that rang in the administration began unraveling one by one.

Parents' weekend at Cornell University began on April 18. At 5:30 a.m. a custodian came across three Afroed students carrying wires, chains, knives, and a crude bayonet to Willard Straight Hall, the student union, where a banner reading WELCOME PARENTS was strung across the threshold. Around back other students demanded employees arriving for work relinquish their keys and leave the premises, smacking one in the face. Then they barricaded the doors and windows as a third group entered through a terrace and a fourth commandeered the campus radio station.

Parents slumbering in the guest rooms were roused by Negroes in Black Panther berets:

"Your lives are in danger; you had better get out fast!"

"The black man has risen!"

One father called security. The first question he was asked was whether the intruders "were white or black." He replied that they were black and was told, "Do as they tell you. If they'll let you out, go out. Don't argue with them."

Cornell was the Berkeley-style "multiversity" among the Ivies. Its president, James Perkins, shared much with Berkeley's Clark Kerr, including a desiccated procedural-liberalism ideology that fetishized reasoned negotiation. Which made the going tough when things got unreasonable. As in 1965, when Cornell students shouted down Averell Harriman as an "agent of imperialism." Or, in 1967, when 130 students blockaded marine recruiters, and the Undergraduate Judicial Board voted four to three not to discipline them.

Perkins was proud of his civil rights credentials. Eight Negro students had attended Cornell in 1963. By the 1968–69 school year, he had recruited 250. He had also assigned officials to negotiate with the school's Afro-American Society for the establishment of some kind of black studies program. That drew praise from the *New York Times:* "With the rise of black consciousness, many colleges are under pressure to start programs in black history and culture, but none have come so far and fast as Cornell."

It wasn't nearly far and fast enough for the Afro-American Society. In early 1968 a visiting economics professor said that in the ghetto "there are no pleasures except those satisfying lower tastes." Militants took over the economics department to demand his firing. That same day Martin Luther King was shot. At Cornell University's memorial service for the slain champion of nonviolence, AAS members lined up to out–mau-mau each other: "Maybe it's *time* we started defending our homes and families from this vicious honky," one screamed. "When this honky drives through your neighborhood like they are going to do tonight, and they start shooting at your houses, brothers and sisters, *you shoot back and you shoot to kill! . . .* Now if you honkies think you bad enough to fuck with us, just try it!"

Black militants began browbeating less militant blacks—those who roomed with whites, for example—into tears. Two factions fighting for leadership of the AAS chased each other around a university building with chains and knives. The *Times* article praising Cornell's racial progress appeared October 29, 1968; two days later, on Halloween, black students kidnapped a white liberal, took him out into the woods, and verbally abused him for his whiteness while menacing him with a knife. The administration discouraged him from pressing charges. As Tom Hayden once said of liberal college administrators, "Listening to them is like being beaten to death with a warm sponge."

The board of trustees promised a black studies program by the next school year and set aside building space. The AAS promptly commandeered the proposed building and refused to let any other university unit inside (the administration responded by granting them the building). The charter they filed for black studies banned white faculty, staff, or students and demanded student control of the board, power over degree requirements, a budget of $250,000 with $50,000 in an "emergency fund" available "at all times"; exclusive use of a student union dining room; payment of black students' tuition directly to the new entity; and "full control over the admission of black students to Cornell University and the allocation of financial aid." Thereupon Perkins stood, as he believed it, firm, insisting state law prevented him from banning whites, as much as he might be convinced that was reasonable.

Perkins thought he was negotiating. He couldn't recognize his adversaries were playing an entirely different game.

The militants had embraced a revolutionary dialectic. Escalating demands, impossible to meet, served "the objective of raising the level of awareness among blacks" to that of the vanguard, which would come to share with the vanguard "another objective, the destruction of the university—if not its complete destruction, at least its disruption." Issue unreasonable demands, and "the beast we are dealing with will use all the means at his disposal to maintain control of power." That would reveal the fascism behind the liberal facade.

Even "the average honkie can be a tool if we know how to use him," a planning document declared. The militants certainly used Perkins. "Mr. Perkins," a spokesman told him, "don't think that we think the better for you because you're chairman of the United Negro College Fund, because we know that all nigger lovers think well of the black colleges, because that's where they want us all to be." They gave him a deadline of December 10 to sign off on their demands. Instead, Perkins made a counteroffer. Laughing, militants responded by rushing the main dining room, dancing on the tables, then dumping thirty-seven hundred books at circulation desks of the campus libraries because "these books have no relevancy to me as a black student."

Perkins responded by announcing he would not restrain them so long as they were "peaceful"—though an AAS militant had already punched out a newspaper reporter. On December 17 militants met with Perkins in his office. One student put his arm around him and scowled, a knife handle sticking out of his jeans.

On February 28 President Perkins rose to introduce Allard Lowenstein at a symposium on South Africa. A student rushed the lectern and lifted Perkins by the collar. Another stood by with a two-by-four strapped to his belt. Perkins couldn't believe it. He thought the black students were his friends. In the middle of April the trustees approved the Center for Afro-American Studies, but also announced punishment for three students who'd participated in the December disruptions. Thus did the takeover begin. It was announced as retaliation for the punishment—though it began fifteen minutes *before* the judgment was announced.

Fire alarms began ringing out in the dorms. A makeshift cross was burned on the porch of the black women's cooperative. It was almost certainly an act of AAS provocateurism—cover for heightening the contradictions.

Militants had intended to hold Willard Straight Hall for a few hours, for the campus to awake in the morning to the spectacle of their exit. The administration was willing to wait things out, letting AAS supporters come and go. SDS members guarded the perimeters. (They called themselves "voluntary niggers.") The fateful escalation came when twenty-five brothers from the "jock fraternity" Delta Upsilon entered the building through an unguarded window. They, too, had their ideology, their guru: not Marx, Mao, or Marcuse, but the Orthogonian in Chief. As a DU brother later explained, "We felt we had as much right in the building as the blacks did; it's a building for Cornell University students. . . . Being athletes and competitors, which usually goes hand in hand with a law-and-order philosophy, we just couldn't let anybody get away with seizing the Straight."

What one side saw as liberation the other saw as apocalypse: and what the other saw as apocalypse, the first saw as liberation: *Nixonland.*

The black students came at the white students with pool cues and fire extinguishers, barked forth threats about "filling the whites with lead"; this was the fascist attack they had been anticipating. The whites asked to negotiate; the blacks said, "It's too late for that, because the sisters have already been harmed." Rumors shot through campus: 250 whites massing to storm Willard Straight Hall; AAS preparations to burn down the building; a time bomb ticking in a second building; another set beneath the DU house.

One rumor was even true.

Sunday morning a statement was released: "Officials of the Cornell University Division of Safety and Security have confirmed that at 10:35 last night, April 19, a rifle with a telescopic lens, two or three gun cases, and some hatchets were moved into Willard Straight Hall, the student union being held by black students." Black students had been stocking up on arms since February, convinced of the ghetto rumor that the government was preparing prison camps for militants. ·

At 1:30 a.m. a fire broke out in a fraternity with a black president. Two of the frat brothers stormed into campus police headquarters: "My fraternity is on fire! They've cut telephone wires!" It turned out to be an unrelated electrical fire. Then a reporter saw what he thought was a spotlight and a rifle in the Cornell clock tower, pointed directly at Willard Straight Hall. It turned out to be merely a janitor sweeping up. Over the campus radio station one of the militants announced, "Before this is over, James Perkins, Allan Sindler, and Clinton Rossiter are going to die in the gutter."

The administration negotiated with aggressive truculence: "We aren't sacrificing any principle if we save lives," a vice president said. Sunday afternoon the two sides struck a deal: ending the takeover in return for amnesty. James Perkins counted it a successful conclusion: mission accomplished, accommodation achieved.

The AP sent a Pulitzer Prize–winning photo over the wires: one of the AAS students strides purposefully out of the building, head and rifle held high, a massive bandolier of shell cartridges wrapped around his waist and shoulder. Two more flank him with rifles. Two white men in suits look down, a black campus police officer looks away, all as if ashamed. It ran on the front pages of newspapers around the world.

London's *New Statesman* declared, "The U.S. is on the brink of racial revolution." Alistair Cooke on the BBC said it reminded him of the civil strife he'd seen in the Congo and street-fighting students in the Weimar era. Beijing announced that "the U.S. ruling clique . . . is scared out of its wits and is plotting still more frenzied suppression of the students."

The Era of Good Feelings between press and president had not rubbed off on the students who had come back to school the previous September buzzing about Chicago. To them, that Nixon would be escalating the war was self-evident, noises to the contrary more evidence of his phoniness. *Fortune* magazine had built its first issue of 1969 entirely around a survey: "American Youth: Its Outlook Is Changing the World." The *Fortune* writers pronounced themselves "captivated by the straightforwardness and eloquence of this younger generation." But they were also worried that the future of capitalism was at stake: two-fifths of the nation's 6.7 million college students defined themselves "mainly by their lack of concern about making money." One SDS leader interviewed by *Fortune* snapped, "We know what you're trying to do. You're trying to awaken business to its social responsibilities. But it won't work." He would be one of the 12.8 percent of the country's university students who identified themselves as "revolutionary" or "radically dissident."

Students from forty schools were surveyed. The two-fifths from the most distinguished universities were labeled "forerunners." They were asked to select personalities they admired. All three presidential candidates ran behind Che Guevara. Two-thirds of the forerunner students supported civil disobedience; "10 percent say that they would support civil disobedience no matter what issues were involved." The business magazine partly blamed the economic conditions in which these baby boomers had grown up: their parents had known the Depression and war. This generation had never known scarcity—which gave them, the lead editorial said, the "Freedom to Be Idealistic."

And here was the fruit, just as Tom Hayden had hoped for: two, three, many Columbias.

Cornell heralded a new station of the academic calendar: fall term, Christmas break, Easter break, building-takeover season. Then commencement—where, this year, university presidents around the country were jeered and students accepted degrees wearing black armbands symbolizing refusal to be inducted. They used to talk about the long, hot summer. James J. Kilpatrick coined the phrase "the long, hot generation." Stanford students voted to demand an end to military research, then seized the Applied Electronics Laboratory. The faculty voted only to phase out classified research—so, on May Day, a Maoist professor (and Melville expert), H. Bruce Franklin, led his followers in a break-in of the building where university salary and personnel records were stored. At out-of-the-way Kent State University in Ohio, SDS leaders rampaged through classes chanting, "Work! Study! Get ahead! Kill!" then brawled their way past cops into the administration building. Students at mighty Harvard ejected eight deans from their offices on April 9 before four hundred policemen carted two hundred students away; then nearly the entire campus went on strike:

> *STRIKE FOR THE EIGHT*
> *DEMANDS STRIKE BE*
> *CAUSE YOU HATE COPS*
> *STRIKE BECAUSE YOUR*
> *ROOMMATE WAS CLUBBED*
> *STRIKE TO STOP EXPANSION*
> *STRIKE TO SEIZE CONTROL*
> *OF YOUR LIFE STRIKE TO*
> *BECOME MORE HUMAN STR*
> *IKE TO RETURN PAINE HALL*
> *SCHOLARSHIPS STRIKE BE*
> *CAUSE THERE'S NO POETRY*
> *IN YOUR LECTURES*
> *STRIKE BECAUSE CLASSES*
> *ARE A BORE STRIKE FOR*
> *POWER STRIKE TO SMASH THE*
> *CORPORATION STRIKE TO MAKE*
> *YOURSELF FREE STRIKE TO*
> *ABOLISH ROTC STRIKE BECAUSE*
> *THEY ARE TRYING TO SQUEEZE*
> *THE LIFE OUT OF YOU STRIKE*

On April 19 the New York Police Department distributed to its detectives a manual it said was being passed around by local radicals. The second section was headed "Supplies, Ordnance, and Logistics" and taught how to turn a cherry bomb into an antipersonnel weapon. On April 21 four hundred students at Queensborough Community College overpowered security guards to occupy the administration building. On April 23, one hundred students seized NYU's Hall of Languages after a popular English instructor was fired; City College was shuttered after black and Puerto Rican students locked themselves inside the gates of the South Campus; Fordham students sat in outside the president's office against ROTC; twelve hundred students at Yeshiva University sat in to demand school be closed for Israeli Independence Day. At Columbia, radicals reoccupied Mathematics and Fayerweather Hall. At Queens College students rampaged through the main library, emptying card catalogs, overturning bookshelves, and smashing display cases, while another group held the administration building.

Something else happened at Queens College, a familiar part of the building-takeover pattern—though news accounts tended to stick it in the last few paragraphs. "There was also a third group of demonstrators," the *New York Times* said, "a conservative group calling themselves the Students Coalition—who organized a sit-in in the registrar's office . . . protesting the college president's failure to call the police to evict the students occupying the administration building." At Kent State, athletes and fraternity brothers faced down SDS in a street fight on the university Commons. Just as at Columbia in 1968, just as at Cornell, "Staten Island versus Scarsdale" ruled: escalating confrontations between the radicals and the antiradicals who just wanted to keep their colleges open for business.

The class fissure showed up in *Fortune*'s polling: 51 percent from the "forerunner" schools agreed that America was a "sick society," but only 32 percent of all students. Was Vietnam a mistake? Sixty-seven percent of forerunners said so; only 51 percent of all students. Were the police's actions in Chicago unjustified? Sixty-one percent versus 40 percent. The University of Buffalo nearly shut down after four hundred students took over the administration building and flew the black flag of anarchy from the belfry after the conviction of the leader of the "Buffalo 9" anti-ROTC demonstrators. Then the full student body voted 1,245 to 783 to *keep* ROTC.

That majority was starting to raise its voice. "The hypnotically erotic [Jim] Morrison," as the *Miami Herald* put it in a review of a concert by the Doors, "flaunting the laws of obscenity, indecent exposure, and incitement to riot, could only stir a minor mob scene toward the end of his Saturday night performance"—after which he was arrested. Morrison's outrage inspired high school students to stage a Rally for Decency at the Orange Bowl that drew nearly three times as many kids as the original concert (the performers included Anita Bryant, Kate Smith, and comedian Jackie Mason). Miami inspired a national fad: the day of the Straight Hall takeover, ten thousand kids from Ohio, Kentucky, Indiana, Michigan, Pennsylvania, and West Virginia gathered for a Teens for Decency rally at Cincinnati Gardens. Forty thousand attended a similar show in Baltimore.

"Decency rallies" were something else relegated to *New York Times* back pages. Every trend line seemed to point to the coming hegemony of the radicals. "The freshmen are more radical than the seniors," said Father Edwin Quinn of Georgetown, "and I'm told the high school students are even more so." On April 21 alone, there were high school riots in Queens, Brooklyn, Long Island, and New Jersey. That same week Jerry Rubin visited his old high school in Cincinnati (where, as the newspaper editor, he had fervently editorialized for Student Council Clean-Up Week and "worship and reverence" for the school's World War II veterans). The kids followed him like a pied piper. By May, three of five administrators surveyed by the National Association of Secondary School Principals reported "some form of active protests in their schools." Two sympathetic teachers traveled the country collecting testimonies of "high school revolutionaries" for a Random House book. "The pigs' schools will be destroyed unless they serve the people," one student told their tape recorder. The biggest SDS chapter in the country was at Steubenville High School in Ohio, down the highway from Kent State University.

Bad enough when the people starting riots were Negroes cooped up in their ghettos; now, the people rioting were the white middle class's own children. "Che Guevara is thirteen years old," the *Berkeley Barb* gushed, "and he is not doing his homework."

Richard Nixon's favorite way of unwinding after a hard day at work was to sit down for a movie in the White House or Camp David screening room. Amid the high tide of university-building takeovers, an administration group took in *Doctor Zhivago.* Haldeman recorded it in his diary: "Strange to sit in room with leader of free world and Commander in Chief of Armed Forces and watch the pictures of the Russian revolution, Army overthrow, etc. We all had the same thought." Justice Department officials were sent out to deliver barnstorming speeches commemorating Law Day on May 1. Richard Kleindienst imagined a time when "concentration camps" might be necessary for America's "ideological criminals." William Rehnquist, speaking to a Newark Kiwanis Club, called them the "new barbarians."

McCarthy campaign veterans held a shouting match with John Ehrlichman at liberal columnist Mary McGrory's apartment after she prevailed on him to at least *meet* some antiwar leaders:

"Sir, there are thousands of us ready to be arrested because we will not serve in this war."

"You *will* go!"

"Never!"

"Then we will put you all in jail for a long time."

"There aren't enough jails to hold us all."

"Then we will build the wall of our stockades higher and higher."

A month later, Kissinger and Ehrlichman hosted seven student leaders in

the White House Situation Room. They represented 253 student government officers and student newspaper editors who had signed a pledge of draft
resistance. Ehrlichman said, "If you guys think that you can break laws just
because you don't like them, you're going to have to force us to up the ante
to the point where we have to give out death sentences for traffic violations."

On May 15 the president walked into his morning NSC/cabinet meeting to
a standing ovation for his speech to the nation on Vietnam. As it broke up,
he learned a long-term desire had come to fruition: Abe Fortas had resigned.

The saga of the lip-licking slut and the Supreme Court justice who loved
her had picked back up at the Fortas confirmation hearings in September
1968. Republicans learned that Fortas had taught a seminar at American University that had been paid for by private donations. Fortas declined to reap-
pear before the Judiciary Committee to defend himself. Strom Thurmond
called an officer from the LAPD's anti-obscenity department to testify in
Fortas's stead; he introduced two more porno films and 150 more dirty magazines into evidence. A cloture vote failed on October 1, 1968. Fortas
returned to the bench as a mere associate justice. The enemies of liberal
jurisprudence still smelled blood, however. A *Life* magazine reporter learned
that Fortas had taken an inflated consulting fee from the foundation of a convicted stock swindler; the reporter hadn't quite had enough evidence to nail
the case, so FBI director J. Edgar Hoover helped. *Life* hit the streets on May
5 with "A New Charge: Justice Fortas and the $20,000 Check" emblazoned
across the cover. And just in case Fortas still refused to quit, Hoover held
additional ammunition in reserve: the dubious claim of "an active and aggressive homosexual who has been an informant of the Washington Field Office"
and who "over the years has provided a great deal of reliable information"
that "he had 'balled' with Abe Fortas on several occasions prior to Mr. Fortas becoming a Justice of the United States Supreme Court."

Hoover didn't need to release it. Fortas announced his resignation the
morning of May 15. Then Chief Justice Warren said he would retire at the
end of the spring 1969 term. Richard Nixon would be getting to name both
an associate and a chief justice in a space of less than a year—and maybe
another associate, since Hugo Black was eighty-three years old.

That made May 15 a good day. Though, taking the long view, it was a bad
one. Events three thousand and nine thousand miles away sounded the death
knell for any remaining claim that, under Nixon, Americans were lowering
their voices. There was Berkeley. And there was Hamburger Hill.

Ronald Reagan had a theory about campus anarchy. Way back in the mists
of time, December of 1964, Berkeley chancellor Edward Strong had told the
hundreds of students occupying Sproul Hall, "Please go!" To Reagan the
guns at Cornell were the simple consequence of that single word. *Please*

hadn't worked; only 635 law enforcement officers had. Reagan's campus role models were the university presidents who didn't say *please:* S. I. Hayakawa and Notre Dame's Father Theodore M. Hesburgh, who ordered on-the-spot expulsion to "anyone or any group that substitutes force for rational persuasion, be it violent or nonviolent" once they'd been given "fifteen minutes of meditation to cease and desist."

On January 5, 1969, Reagan had said during the strike at San Francisco State, "Those who want to get an education, those who want to teach, should be protected in that at the point of bayonet if necessary." On January 15, down in San Diego, where Herbert Marcuse's contract was up for renewal, locals hung him in effigy from the city hall flagpole. In February San Diego's chancellor announced Marcuse's reappointment. Subsequently, the Santa Barbara campus announced it was hiring the Marxist sociologist Richard Flacks, who had been clubbed nearly to death in Chicago. Reagan said that hiring flacks was like hiring a pyromaniac to make fuses in a fireworks factory. Then San Diego student militants broke down the glass door of the registrar's office to demand the construction of a Lumumba-Zapata College. Professor Marcuse stepped through the threshold to begin the occupation. Berkeley's World Liberation Front manhandled students who tried to enter campus through Sather Gate during their student strike. Reagan called out the California Highway Patrol to Berkeley and told his press secretary, "I'll sleep well tonight."

That all set the stage.

In Berkeley, the university had torn down houses to build a soccer field, which had not yet materialized, leaving a nasty vacant lot in the middle of town. The *Berkeley Barb* led the call to claim and improve it in an act of Aquarian eminent domain. *What Trees Do They Plant?* was the name of the propaganda film the city of Chicago produced to defend itself after the Democratic convention. Berkeley freaks were determined to plant trees.

This place, dubbed People's Park, became a community-wide ingathering; without benefit of a feasibility study, soil tests, budget, or zoning ordinance. Rock gardens had taken shape, playground swings, as had sandboxes, monkey bars for the kids, three transplanted apple trees, and a "People's Revolutionary Corn Garden," by the time Chancellor Roger Heyns handed down a stern reminder that "the property belongs to the Regents of the University of California and will not be available to unauthorized persons," announced that a perimeter would be put up "to reestablish the convenient fact that the field is indeed the university's," and scolded People's Park's builders for failing to constitute a "responsible committee" with which the university could consult.

That was May 13. Two days later, in the middle of the night, California highway patrolmen and Berkeley police in bulletproof vests stood guard as workers began putting up a chain-link fence. Word spread. By noon the forces of private property were being taunted mercilessly. Two thousand congregated at an impromptu rally on Sproul Plaza, the university commons where they'd gathered in 1964 around that captured police car. The Reverend Richard York of the Berkeley Free Church spoke in his rainbow-colored vestments: "We are committed to stand with the poor and alienated who are trying to create a new world on the vacant lots of the old." The call to arms was issued by the president-elect of the Berkeley student body: "Let's go down and take the park!"

They were by then six thousand strong. Someone opened a fire hydrant. Police moved to shut it off. People started throwing rocks. Police released tear-gas canisters. Berkeley militants remembered the day Alameda County sheriffs beat them in 1967 at the Oakland border as Bloody Tuesday. This went down in the annals as Bloody Thursday.

Students moved out to take downtown. Sheriff's deputies moved in with shotguns. A city car was overturned and set afire. Officers started shooting into the crowd with bird shot.

Then they ran out of bird shot.

Someone started throwing bricks from above. Officers clamored roofward to hunt him down. Two blocks from the incident an officer shot a twenty-five-year-old in the back as he turned to run away. James Rector lay bleeding, a cartridge's worth of double-O buckshot as big as marbles having torn away at his stomach, spleen, pancreas, kidney, intestines, and a portion of his heart. A friend grabbed him to keep him from falling to the street below. Another begged a cop in vain to loan the downed man his gas mask. The ambulance arrived a half hour later. Rector was alive, but only barely.

At nine, Reagan activated three National Guard battalions. Tanks stood waiting at Berkeley Marina. A curfew and ban on public assembly were enforced by the California Highway Patrol and gendarmes from ten Bay Area communities. On May 19 James Rector expired in the hospital. A right-wing city council member defended his shooting: "If I had a gun and I was cornered, I'd use it." Berkeley hippies pondered taking his advice. The next day thousands gathered in a memorial vigil convened by faculty on the Sproul Hall steps. When it was over, they found their exit blocked by bayonets. A crowd made its way in the other direction, but was beaten back with tear gas and clubs. About seven hundred drifted back to the main plaza, some to vote in a university-sponsored referendum on what to do with People's Park.

Ronald Reagan had stated that building the park was "a deliberate and planned attempt at confrontation," and cops were fighting back against a "well-armed mass of people who had stockpiled all kinds of weapons and missiles."

An announcement was made over loudspeakers in Sproul Plaza at 1:58 p.m. that chemical agents were about to be dropped.

Helicopters whirred overhead.

Seven hundred students were surrounded by a tight ring of guardsmen.

The Sikorskies swooped down to two hundred feet. Shrieks of panic, bodies scattering; they realized they were trapped. White clouds billowed from helicopter bellies. Lawmen and guardsmen pitched in more gas from three sides.

(Perhaps some premeds had read the "Medical Brief" in the latest issue of the AMA magazine *Today's Health:* "The Armed Forces Institute of Pathology reports that 14 eyes were removed from 13 patients because of tear gas—five of these within two months after the injury, nine after a period of up to 15 years.")

People doubled over, spewing vomit. Winds swept the clouds over a schoolchildren's picnic. Patients and nurses at Cowell Hospital were gasping for breath.

A snatch of dialogue was heard over the patrolling helicopters:

"Just get a .22 rifle and do it."

"I'm not a violent man. I really don't believe in—you know."

"It's tempting, though."

"Well, it would take a .30-06 to do the job anyway."

A sign: THIS TIME GAS-GUNS. WHAT NEXT, BOMBS?

One hundred twenty-eight people were injured—"25 police among them," *Rolling Stone* reported with pride. For the first time, a white American neighborhood was under military occupation. (The guardsmen worried about the oranges and cookies the hippie gamines gave them: were they dosed with acid?) A young colonel became so disgusted with the duty—like most guardsmen he had joined up to stay *out* of combat—he threw down his rifle and helmet. *Rolling Stone* put him on the cover, a hero who had changed sides in a civil war.

The fifth day of the seventeen-day occupation, Reagan held a press conference. An angry, mustachioed reporter raised his voice: "Over one hundred people shot down! Over one hundred people, I'm sure the record will show. Gas, lethal gas—"

Reagan, as stern as a schoolmarm: "Once the dogs of war are unleashed, you must expect that things will happen, and people being human will make mistakes on both sides—"

The reporter: "We're here because people are being shot and killed today in Berkeley!"

Cross talk.

Reagan's voice rang out. "*Negotiate?* What is to negotiate?"

A middle-aged reporter with a beard tried to explain: "Governor Reagan, the time has passed when the university can just ride roughshod over the desires of the majority of the student body. The university is a public institution—"

Reagan interrupted him, yelling, "All of it began the first time that some of you who know better, and *are old enough to know better*, let young people think that they have the *right* to choose the laws that they can obey as long as they are doing it in the name of social protest!"

Reagan stood bolt upright, shoved photographers aside, and exited the room. That same day, May 21, Wednesday, Richard Nixon announced his choice for the Supreme Court: Warren Burger, an appeals court judge on the D.C. circuit. Nixon had read a speech of his reprinted in *U.S. News & World Report:* "Society's problem with those who will not obey the law has never loomed so large in our national life as it does today." European countries get more "swiftly, efficiently, and directly to the question of whether the accused is guilty."

Toward the end of that week the Berkeley student newspaper ran an editorial in defiance of their governor: "We will have that park. We will have it or lose the university."

There was a rearguard action in the Battle of People's Park. John Lennon and his new wife, Yoko Ono, exiled themselves to a bed at the Fairmont Hotel in Toronto and staged a publicity stunt for peace in Vietnam. Celebrities visited their hotel room to talk about the world situation as cameras clicked and boom microphones hovered. Timothy Leary poked his head out the window: "What a green trip." A gray-haired rabbi rehearsed a new song with the Lennons, "Give Peace a Chance." "The love these two have for each other extends itself to all humanity," he said. And every day, John and Yoko would broadcast live to Berkeley, to try to calm the situation.

The Bed-In for Peace's mood shifted when Al Capp came calling. The sixty-year-old creator of Li'l Abner and the Shmoo, a former proud New Dealer, was now a barnstorming right-wing lecturer, dispensing such wisdom as "Students are tearing up campuses today for the same reason a few years ago they were wetting their bed"; "Never before has it been so profitable to kiss the ass of kids"; and when asked what we should do in Vietnam answered—"Shoot back."

Capp bounded into the Lennons' hotel room with a smirk, introduced himself as the "dreadful Neanderthal fascist," and asked for something "hard" to sit on. He confronted the newlyweds: "What about during World War II? What if Hitler and Churchill had gone to bed?"

John answered, "A lot of people would be alive today," and asked the cartoonist what he was doing for peace in Berkeley.

"I'm cheering the police. That's precisely what I'm doing about it. . . . You people have a home in London. Do you permit people to smash the windows and defecate on the furniture, like they're doing in Berkeley?"

Capp started calling Yoko Ono names like "Dragon Lady." It seemed that he was trying to bait her husband into punching him. New Left radicals weren't the only people who understood the propaganda value of heightening the contradictions.

"*I* write my cartoons for money. Just as you sing your songs. And that's what this is for."

Now the Beatle looked almost ready to punch him. He asked Capp to leave. Capp's parting words: "It's not for me to forgive you, it's for your psychiatrist."

It pointed up a dynamic of Nixonland: war and the efforts to end war looked alike on TV. They all just looked like more war.

On May 15, paratroopers from the 101st Airborne Division stormed up an objective Americans called Hill 937 and Vietnamese called Ap Bia Mountain. The AP ran an evocative dispatch on May 19. "The paratroopers came down the mountain, their green shirts darkened with sweat, their weapons gone, their bandages stained brown and red—with mud and blood." It reported them cursing their commander, whose radio call was Blackjack:

"That damned Blackjack won't stop until he kills every one of us."

It became known as Hamburger Hill. The soldiers won the objective, just as Americans often won their military objectives; 633 North Vietnamese main-force soldiers were killed, fewer than 100 Americans. Then the hill was abandoned, just as Americans often abandoned objectives in Vietnam. "We are not fighting for terrain as such. We are going after the enemy," Commander Creighton Abrams explained. "Don't mean nothin'," answered the troops—a refrain that echoed all the way back home.

The first politician to spoil the president's honeymoon on Vietnam had been George McGovern, back on March 17. "There is no more time for considering 'military options,' no more time for 'improving the bargaining position,'" he orated to a crowded Senate chamber. "In the name of decency and common sense, there must be no further continuation of the present war policy, however distinguished in rhetoric or more hollow predictions of victory yet to come. . . . I believe the only acceptable objective now is an immediate end to the killing." When a senator gives a major speech, he traditionally summons friendly colleagues to the floor to compliment him for the record. But Alan Cranston of California and Harold Hughes of Iowa had not expected anything like this. They said nothing. Ted Kennedy, for his part, told reporters that McGovern's words were "precipitate."

Now, two months later, Kennedy shifted toward McGovern. The Hamburger Hill assault, he said in a May 24 speech to the New Democratic Coalition, a party reform group formed after Chicago, was "cruelty and savagery." Five days later he called it "senseless and irresponsible," "madness"— "symptomatic of a mentality and a policy that requires immediate attention."

The president paid attention to Ted Kennedy. Nixon was obsessed with everything Kennedy—had been since 1946, when JFK stole the front page of the *Los Angeles Times* from him after his first election victory ("Son of Kennedy Congress Winner"). He had had to step over the bodies of two Kennedys to become president—then watched the torch passed to this thirty-seven-year-old who had been kicked out of Harvard for cheating but had already been put on *Time*'s first cover of the year as the favorite for the 1972 Democratic nomination.

Kennedy ghosts rattled around the White House; they were whom Nixon blamed for his acts that would otherwise look venal or petty. His fifth day in office, dictating a memo to Ehrlichman, he said, "The cabinet officers should fill at least ninety percent of all the available positions with new people regardless of the competence of the old people. . . . This is exactly what Kennedy did when he came in." On the president's first trip to Europe, he dashed as quickly as possible through Berlin: it was a "Kennedy city." He was averse to "Battle Hymn of the Republic": "That's a Kennedy song."

When Gallup did its monthly poll in May, it asked, "Which one of the men listed on this card would you like to see take over the direction of the plans and policies of the Democratic Party during the next four years?" Edward M. Kennedy won by more than Muskie and Humphrey combined. "Which of these men do you admire?" asked *Fortune* in its poll of college students: Kennedy, number one; the president of the United States, number three. John Ehrlichman suggested they put a surveillance tail on Kennedy. On March 26, Nixon approved the idea. And now Edward M. Kennedy was feasting vulturelike off the misfortune of Nixon's first setback in Vietnam. That figured. It was how those Kennedys worked.

Nixon didn't like senators or congressmen at any rate. He thought of them the way he thought of the press: they had the luxury of criticism without responsibility. His own party's congressional leadership got information on his legislative strategy on a strictly need-to-know basis (Congressman Jerry Ford thought Haldeman and Ehrlichman treated them like "the chairman of the board of a large corporation regards his regional sales managers"). A new president's first-year State of the Union address was where he traditionally unveiled his legislative program; Nixon didn't even give a State of the Union. He didn't know the name of some of his congressional liaisons. A Republican from Illinois moved to commemorate the names of the thirty-three thousand dead in Vietnam in the *Congressional Record;* Nixon scrawled an order to an aide: "Harlow—Don't ask him to see me again." Nixon didn't invite a single congressman to his daughter Tricia's White House wedding in 1971. Legislators—petty, grandstanding, insolent.

The worst were the ones who read the Constitution, especially Article I, Section 8, granting them powers "to declare War . . . to raise and support Armies . . . to make Rules for the Government and Regulation of the land and naval Forces." Interference with what Nixon saw as his sovereign foreign-policy-making prerogatives drove him nearly around the bend.

One day Nixon raged to his press aides to sever all ties with the *Times* and the *St. Louis Post-Dispatch*. Next he added the *Washington Post*, after it jumped the gun in announcing his meeting with the president of South Vietnam on Midway Island June 8. (Nixon had decided he needed an excuse to be out of the country that day to get out of a scheduled address at Ohio State after the FBI told him it was one of the hottest antiwar campuses.) Three days later Hedrick Smith of the *Times* reported talk in Washington that Hamburger Hill "would undermine public support for the war and thus shorten the administration's time for successful negotiations in Paris." The reporter with the best contacts in the West Wing, the *New Republic*'s John Osborne, reported the president was enveloped in "a passing phase of extreme frustration." Nixon spent hours each day alone, brooding, or bitching to Haldeman about the staff's failure to get the press to write that he worked twenty-hour days. And that he cared nothing about public relations.

By the end of the school year, law enforcement officials counted eighty-four acts of arson and bombings or attempted bombings at colleges, twenty-seven at high schools. Almost one hundred anti-campus-violence bills passed committees in the California State Senate. West Virginia passed a law declaring anyone a "rioter" who failed to obey an order of any law enforcement officer. That included onlookers *deputized* as law enforcement officers. It also declared law enforcement officers automatically guiltless in any rioter's death.

The president embarked on a speaking tour before friendly audiences. If he couldn't speak at Ohio State, he found a campus where he could: tiny General Beadle State College. Ever alert for opportunities to take a hatchet to the weakest joints in the Democratic coalition, perhaps Nixon chose this particular institution of higher learning because it was in George McGovern's home state, South Dakota. McGovern's profile had recently risen considerably. The Democrats had just named a commission to reform their nominating procedures to heal the divisions of 1968, with McGovern as chair. The senator from the modest, conservative Great Plains state was becoming a national figure— hobnobbing with Franklins. Here was an opportunity to wound him.

"I feel at home here because I, too," the president began, "grew up in a small town. I attended a small college, about the size of this one; and when I was in law school, at a much larger university, one of the ways that I helped work my way through that law school was to work in the law library." He talked about a South Dakota mine claim his wife was left by her father: "No gold was ever discovered there." In the form of flattery toward his hosts, he stuck in a barb against his enemies: "Opportunity for all is represented here. This is a small college, not rich and famous like Yale and Harvard." It was at General Beadle State where "we still can sense the daring that converted a raw frontier into part of the vast heartland of America.

"We live in a deeply troubled and profoundly unsettled time. Drugs and crime, campus revolts, racial discord, draft resistance—on every hand we find old standards violated, old values discarded, old precepts ignored. A vocal minority of our young people are opting out of the process by which a civilization maintains its continuity: the passing on of values from one generation to the next. Old and young across the nation shout across a chasm of misunderstanding, and the louder they shout, the broader the chasm becomes.

"As a result of this, our institutions in America today are undergoing what may be the severest challenge of our history. . . . The nation has survived other attempts at insurrection. We can survive this one." If, he added, we had the will: "It has not been a lack of civil power, but the reluctance of a free people to employ it, that so often has stayed the hand of authorities faced with confrontation. . . . The student who invades an administration building, roughs up a dean, rifles the files, and issues 'nonnegotiable demands' may have some of his demands met by a permissive university administration. But the greater his 'victory,' the more he will have undermined the security of his own rights."

Nixon ended with a call to morality. "In pubic life, we have seen reputations destroyed by smears and gimmicks paraded as panaceas. We have heard shrill voices of hate shouting lies and sly voices of malice twisting facts." This he and his audience—*we*—would never do. "The values we cherish are sustained by a fabric of mutual self-restraint woven of ordinary civil decency, respect for the rights of others, respect for the laws of community, and respect for the democratic process of orderly change. The purpose of these restraints, I submit, is not to protect an 'Establishment,' but to establish the protection of liberty; not to prevent change, but to insure that change reflects the public will and respects the rights of all."

That same day the *New York Times*' Hedrick Smith broke the story of secret negotiations to return political control of Okinawa to Japan and became the seventh American citizen to be unlawfully wiretapped by the administration.

The next morning Nixon's audience was a football stadium full of graduating Air Force Academy cadets. A favorite Nixon defense program, a promise to Strom Thurmond on the campaign trail, was under congressional threat: the antiballistic missile system, traditionally considered destabilizing in arms control circles. Full-page newspaper ads appeared savaging it: "From the people who brought you Vietnam—the antiballistic missile system." The ads appeared in the same editions where Pentagon cost overruns graced the front page. Here was Nixon's response: it was all the Franklins' fault.

"It is open season on the armed forces. Military programs are ridiculed as needless, if not deliberate waste. The military profession is derided in some of the so-called 'best circles' of America. Patriotism is considered by some to be a backward fetish of the uneducated and the unsophisticated."

We knew better. *They* did not. They were ready, indeed, to disarm us.

"They believe that we can be conciliatory and accommodating only if we do not have the strength to be otherwise. They believe that America will be able to deal with the possibility of peace only when we are unable to cope with the threat of war."

Then, to the sea of crisp white caps, he delivered a good old-fashioned tribute to American power and destiny. "It would be easy, easy for a president of the United States to buy some popularity by going along with the new isolationists."

(He wasn't going to take the easy way out.)

"If America was to become a dropout" — *dropouts: hairy, smelly, insolent things* — "the rest of the world would live in terror. . . . Our adversaries have not yet learned peaceful ways to resolve their conflicting national interests."

He even promised Orthogonians the moon — and insinuated that the "sick society" yammerers, Franklins all, were ready to snatch it away from them.

"My disagreement with the skeptics and the isolationists is fundamental. They have lost the vision indispensable to great leadership. They observe the problems that confront us, they measure our resources, and then they despair.

"When the first vessels set out from Europe for the New World, these men would have weighed the risks and they would have stayed behind. When the colonists" — or that's what his prepared text said; he made a Freudian slip and used the New Left's word "colonialists" — "on the Eastern seaboard started across the Appalachians to the unknown reaches of the Ohio Valley, these men would have counted the costs and they would have stayed behind. Our current exploration of space makes the point vividly; here is testimony to man's vision and to man's courage. . . . When the first man stands on the moon next month, every American will stand taller because of what he has done, and we should be proud of this magnificent achievement. . . . Only when a nation means something to itself can it mean something to others."

The so-called best circles would have us stay right here on Earth and mean nothing to anyone.

The best circles responded obligingly: "It sounded like the old Nixon I used to know," said Senator Albert Gore, the liberal Vietnam War skeptic from Tennessee. "For my money, the president has been showing his worst side — the side that earned him the name Tricky Dicky." *Time* reported, "A few of his own staff admitted privately afterward that some of Nixon's language was unfortunate." When that quote showed up in his news summary, Nixon dashed off an action memo: "On an urgent basis I want the whole staff to be questioned on this."

The speeches ended the presidential funk. He jetted off to Midway Island and made President Thieu stand by his side as he humiliated him — announcing the withdrawal of twenty-five thousand American troops from South Vietnam. On June 9 the Senate voted to confirm Warren Burger as chief justice, 74–3 (*Time* put him on the cover: "The Supreme Court: Move Toward the Center"). At his next press conference the *New Republic*'s correspondent thought he heard a sneer in Nixon's voice when answering a question about Clark Clifford's suggestion in *Foreign Affairs* that the drawdown should be greater. During Clifford's year in the defense secretary's chair, Nixon responded, "our casualties were the highest of the whole five-year period, and as far as negotiations were concerned, all that had been accomplished, as I indicated earlier, that we had agreed on, was the shape of the table." A sneer was a sign Nixon was feeling himself again. Afterward he spent hours on the phone asking associates how he had done—something he did only when he was confident he would hear praise. The president was in the arena, and all was well with the world.

For instance, two prominent Democrats from opposing wings of the party were at each other's throats: Senator McGovern, who brought his reform commission to Chicago for regional hearings in June, and Mayor Daley, who offered his own detailed proposal there for reorganizing the nomination process. McGovern responded by suggesting that hizzoner might better help heal the Democrats by recommending dismissal of the federal indictments of the eight alleged ringleaders of the 1968 convention riots: "A lot of raw wounds were opened in the convention," McGovern pointed out from the dais of the Sherman House Hotel, Daley Machine headquarters. "One thing keeping open those wounds is the city's determination to press the indictments. I earnestly hope, with your influence, you can alleviate the situation and put the events behind us, end the anguish, and heal the wounds."

The mayor reared back angrily at the insolent guest in his home.

"Senator, you must realize that the bitterness and the attacks within our party were present long before the convention and were built up by those within our party in their attacks on President Johnson. *They* have a responsibility for what happened, not the people of Chicago. People came here to destroy President Johnson, and in doing it, they did not care if they destroyed the Democratic Party in the process."

It was one those political utterances in which a silk glove hid an iron fist. Senator McGovern had been one of "those people." Mayor Daley never did make much distinction between those politicians out to unseat President Johnson and the hippies fornicating in his streets.

"If a person violates the law," Daley barked, "he should suffer the consequences."

McGovern interrupted, "It is *very important* to try to heal all the divisions, and perhaps the mayor could exert his influence—"

Daley interrupted, "If you're asking for amnesty for anyone who violated this law, I'll have no part of it.... The people came here with the intentions of being disruptive.... It's all in the public record."

The hearing, Rowland Evans and Robert Novak reported, "weakened and embittered the party in the contest for its schizophrenic soul that is certain to intensify in the months ahead."

On domestic policy Richard Nixon's positions were not too different from those of all the best circles. Nixon didn't *care* much about domestic policy—except for the kind of stuff he hired Harry Dent to worry about: blocking school integration. The running of a welfare state he dismissed as "building outhouses in Peoria." "I've always thought the country could run itself domestically without a president," Nixon once told Theodore White. "You need a president for foreign policy." Now that it was time at long last to turn to configuring a domestic agenda, Nixon was content to let the bureaucrats and policy intellectuals take care of it, following the conventional wisdom of their trade.

That conventional wisdom, in 1969, was liberal. A growing state was seen as the natural companion to human progress—"the price of rapidly expanding national growth," President Eisenhower had said in 1958. The day before Nixon's Vietnam speech the Harvard economist and bestselling author John Kenneth Galbraith testified to a rapt joint congressional subcommittee in favor of nationalizing any company that did more than 75 percent of its business with the Pentagon.

That this mood was shifting on the ground—that the toryhood of change was outstripping the public's willingness to accept its nostrums—was something Nixon didn't pay much attention to, a lacuna in his obsession with the mood of the middle-class masses. Gallup, in its January polling, described a plan to provide every American family a guaranteed minimum income. "Would you favor or oppose such a plan?" Sixty-two percent said they would oppose it. Nixon ended up proposing something similar anyway. Such was the idea's momentum in the best circles.

The imminent end of material scarcity had been a hobbyhorse of American intellectuals since the fifties. Via "automation" and "cybernetics," the theory went, society would be able to meet its production needs with ever-diminishing human input. Social critics considered the boredom, anomie, and alienation that would follow in postscarcity's wake as the preeminent social problem of the age. It was put forward as the explanation for the generation gap, campus disorder, the new sexual libertinism, the decline of religious piety, the rise of alternative spirituality, anything. An article in *Time* in February 1967 quoted the director of research at New York's Rockland State Hospital: "Those dated objectives of adequate food, housing, and racial equality are now within sight. The sense of great purpose and broad adventure which those goals engendered have vanished." Hence "curiosity and action are directed inward," so drugs that "sever the tenuous ties with the outside world are highly prized." Timothy Leary, at a famous 1967 "Houseboat Summit" with Alan Watts, Gary Snyder, and Allen Ginsberg, said the coming postscarcity portended the evolution of two separate species: the "anthill" people who still insisted on working, and "the tribal people, who don't have to worry about leisure because when you drop out then the real playwork begins."

In that context a modest guaranteed minimum income seemed a middle-of-the-road option.

Even conservatives agreed. Milton Friedman, in the 1962 book that brought him to Barry Goldwater's attention, proposed a "negative income tax": people declaring income on their returns below a certain minimum would receive a remittance from the government to bring them up to the minimum. Richard Nixon was fond of the idea because it would eliminate the welfare bureaucracy. He asked his new favorite White House staffer, an idiosyncratic forty-year-old former Kennedy and Johnson Labor Department official, about the negative-income-tax proposal he was working up: would it get rid of social workers?

"Wipe them out," said his smiling bow-tied aide, now in his boss's best graces.

This Orthogonian named Daniel Patrick Moynihan was a hard-charging and convivial Irish-Catholic striver out of New York whose alcoholic father had abandoned his family to relative deprivation when Daniel was ten. He graduated first in his high school class, worked as a stevedore and attended City College and Tufts, and completed a Ph.D. thesis at the London School of Economics. Nixon recruited him by pleading that he was hardly the hard-hearted conservative of legend, that he was a child of the Depression and knew poverty, too. Richard Nixon always exaggerated the degree of his youthful privation, simultaneously self-pitying and self-aggrandizing. But then, so did Daniel Patrick Moynihan. He'd hint he'd grown up in Hell's Kitchen. Actually, he learned the neighborhood when his mother bought a bar there when he was in college.

Moynihan had became nearly a household name in 1965 when Evans and Novak got ahold of a Labor Department study he'd written called "The Negro Family: A Call to Action." The "Moynihan Report," as it came to be known, argued that the path to the low-income blacks' full integration into American life was blocked by flaws in its matriarchal family structure. The message that culture, not economics, was the driving force in poverty delighted conservatives and made Moynihan public enemy number one among left-wing antipoverty activists. Nixon's people had kept their eye on Moynihan ever since 1966, when he wrote a jaundiced review of the War on Poverty in the policy magazine he coedited, the *Public Interest,* which included the line "The Republicans are ready to govern." Then in a head-turning 1967 speech to his fellow members of Americans for Democratic Action, he said America must "prepare for the onset of terrorism" from minority activists. How to fight it? Not the way LBJ said. "Liberals must divest themselves of the notion that the nation—and especially the cities of this nation—can be run from agencies in Washington."

Moynihan reserved special scorn in the speech for liberals' "curious condescension which takes the form of sticking up for and explaining away anything, however outrageous, which Negroes, individually or collectively, might do." Confronting them, he told the ADA liberals, "would not be pretty." But not confronting them would be worse. "Liberals [must] see more clearly that their interest is in the stability of the social order, and that given the threats to that stability, it is necessary to make much more effective alliances with political conservatives who share that concern, and who recognize that unyielding rigidity is just as much a threat to the continuity of things as is an anarchic desire for change."

Time magazine loved it. William F. Buckley adored it. A Black Power leader called it "a statement that the time had come when white liberals and white bigots had to get together." When the liberal biweekly the *New Leader* published the speech under the title "The Politics of Stability," Len Garment sent a reverential note to the author and rushed a copy to the boss (who must especially have adored Moynihan's take on Vietnam and urban riots as the "especial problem of American liberals because more than anyone else it is they who have been in office, in power at the time of, and in large measure presided over the onset of both"). In his employment interview Moynihan bonded with the president-elect over a shared hatred of "the professional welfarists." But Moynihan also came armed with a warning: that the urge to slip the yoke of the New Deal and the Great Society was not a conservative notion. It would be wildly disruptive: "The urban ghettos would go up in flames."

Moynihan had a better idea. Nixon could play a role vis-à-vis his forebear Lyndon Johnson the way Eisenhower had with Roosevelt and Truman: as a consolidator of their reforms—though Moynihan didn't put it quite that way. Moynihan was a master of rising in politicians' esteem by dressing up their existing inclinations in intellectual finery. Moynihan loaned Nixon a book: a biography of the great nineteenth-century Tory Benjamin Disraeli—consolidator and reorganizer of his liberal forebear William Gladstone. "Tory men and Whig measures are what changed the world," Moynihan explained. Nixon, an Anglophile to boot, was a sucker for the flattery.

In July, when Nixon reorganized the executive branch, he centralized domestic-policy decision-making in the White House to shut out the old bureaucracies just as he had for foreign policy. Moynihan became the Kissinger figure, entrusted to devise the legislative program, freeing Nixon to worry over the chessboard of geopolitics. "The boss is in love again," Bill Safire observed.

In "The Politics of Stability" Moynihan said the state was "good at collecting revenues and rather bad at distributing services." (Liberals should be "ashamed of ourselves" for not recognizing the fact, he added.) Thus, the domestic program Nixon would reveal in an early-August speech began with a diagnosis: "A third of a century of centralizing power and responsibility in Washington has produced a bureaucratic monstrosity, cumbersome, unresponsive . . . a colossal failure."

Two fixes, he promised, would make the state work better. The first was scrapping Aid to Families with Dependent Children. The Nixon-Moynihan "Family Assistance Program" was cleverly devised to ameliorate its structural flaw: AFDC penalized work. Get a job, and you couldn't get welfare. Under Nixon's plan anyone earning $720 or less from outside sources would receive a federal benefit of $1,600. But the more money a family earned from work, the less the federal benefit—the benefit adjusted so that *additional* money from work would always earn a family a bigger total income. Earn $1,000 a year and the government would send you an extra $1,460, for a total family income of $2,460. Earn $2,000 and the government would send you $960, for a total income of $2,960. Any family earning less than $3,920 would get an annual government check. No American would be forced to live on under $1,600 a year, while under the current system a poor mother in Mississippi had to survive on $468. Labor Secretary George Shultz came up with a brilliant line to please the conservatives: "What the nation needs is not more welfare, but more 'workfare'" (though that was slightly artful, since a layabout who never worked a day in his life would apparently still be guaranteed an annual $1,600 from the government). For the liberals it increased federal welfare grants to the states and provided federal funding for 450,000 additional openings in new or expanded day-care centers.

The other part of the package was revenue-sharing, or what the president grandiosely announced as the "New Federalism"—a remittance of federal tax revenues, with few strings attached, to the states. Weakening Washington control was an idea beloved of conservatives. But such schemes were also a longtime favorite of liberal Republican good-government types. It all was a political masterstroke, a story to please elites of all stripes. The reviews were stellar. John Lindsay called the Family Assistance Program welfare's "most important step forward in a generation." *Time* gave the president the cover, holding up a surfboard: "Nixon Rides the Waves." The magazine delighted at the spectacle of a chief executive who transcended ossified ideological divisions.

The White House was pleasing the Franklins, and that seemed to relax the president. He even revised the chart for access to the Oval Office, from HEK—Haldeman, Ehrlichman, Kissinger—to HEHK—Haldeman, Ehrlichman, Harlow, Kissinger, slipping in the name of congressional liaison Bryce Harlow. "RN is riding high," wrote the president in a memo to Haldeman and Ehrlichman. And if it wasn't enough that men were also about to fulfill JFK's dream of walking on the moon, and on Richard Nixon's watch, a certain Kennedy brother, surfing so gracefully heretofore, had just suffered a calamitous wipeout. He was returned to the cover of *Time*—wearing a neck brace and a pained, guilty expression.

CHAPTER NINETEEN

If Gold Rust

A T 11:15 P.M. ON JULY 18, 1969, THE APOLLO 11 ASTRONAUTS WERE CIR-cling the moon and in Martha's Vineyard a '67 Oldsmobile veered from a ten-foot-wide bridge near the road to the Chappaquiddick ferry. It was found eight hours later by two boys looking for a fishing spot. Fire department scuba divers pried out a dead body inside. The police chief tracked the license number to the driver, who had escaped, then wandered to a nearby restaurant, asked friends to drive him to the inn where he was staying, then walked around "for a period of time," never mentioning he had been in an accident. He was the junior senator from Massachusetts, in town for the yacht races. The dead passenger *Time* described as "Mary Jo Kopechne, 28, a pretty, witty blonde who had worked as a secretary for Robert Kennedy."

Everyone knew what "pretty, witty" secretaries were for; every other joke on *Laugh-In* was about how fun they were to poke, prod, and goose. There had long been rumors about JFK and RFK and Marilyn Monroe, about the two lithesome White House aides nicknamed Fiddle and Faddle, about the room at the Mayflower Hotel President Kennedy kept handy for trysts. Everyone also knew, in their own lives, privileged little rich boys for whom the rules never seemed to apply. Under Massachusetts law, leaving the scene of a fatal accident where there had been "willful or wanton" conduct was manslaughter. And yet Senator Kennedy was not charged with manslaughter. He explained that he had been "exhausted and in a state of shock." The Kennedy family doctor reported he'd suffered a concussion.

An aristocracy can convey grace and nobility; it can convey dissolution and decadence. Overnight, the Kennedys learned for the first time what it was like when the former became the latter. Richard Nixon could not be more overjoyed.

Bill Safire warned him not to get too excited. By the time America learned the name Mary Jo Kopechne, astronauts would be walking on the moon, swallowing every other news story for days. The boss was more astute: "No. It'll be hard to hush this one up; too many reporters want to win a Pulitzer Prize."

Though just in case, they would send a "reporter" of their own.

The White House's on-staff private eye, Jack Caulfield, was dispatched to the Vineyard to join the ravening press throng through summer and fall to ask the most embarrassing questions. He brought with him an assistant, another former NYC police detective who traveled with an American Express card stamped "Edward T. Stanley." His real name was Anthony Ulasewicz, and they paid him his salary off the books, from a secret fund of leftover campaign cash set up by the president's personal lawyer, Herb Kalmbach. Ulasewicz and Caulfield even talked about setting up an apartment on New York's East Side with a secret photography apparatus. Some lothario from the NYPD was going to try to entrap one of Mary Jo Kopechne's companions from the fatal evening into revealing what she knew about the cover-up. "We want to be sure Kennedy doesn't get away with this," Ehrlichman instructed.

No one would ever really find what "this" was. The doubt would hang ambiguously in the air forever, shadowing the entirety of Edward M. Kennedy's career. On July 20, at 4:17 eastern standard time, Neil Armstrong landed the lunar module *Eagle* on the surface of the moon: "One small step for [a] man—one giant leap for mankind." Here was a brief, shimmering moment of patriotic transcendence, a respite from the sordid doings on Earth. But the doings on Earth were *so* sordid, the conquest of space didn't distract too many for too long. In the annals of tabloid sex scandals, after all, this one *was* the moon shot.

Time's August 1 cover story: "After the first brief inadequate statement at the station house . . . his silence allowed time for both honest questions and scurrilous gossip to swirl around his reputation and his future." *Time* was not above repeating the scurrilous gossip. ("In another version now in the gossip stage, a federal agent secretly assigned to guard Kennedy saw Mary Jo wearily leave the cottage party about 11 p.m. and curl up to sleep in the back seat. Some time later, according to this theory, Kennedy and another girl at the party, Rosemary Keough, got into the car without noticing Mary Jo asleep in back.") *Time* featured Chappaquiddick speculation in seven issues in a row. Why had the senator and the secretary left the shindig early? What was a senator doing at a party with six middle-aged men and six young women not their wives? "No one was drinking heavily," said one of the ladies present. Just how much drinking was that? Why had Ted Kennedy missed the bright reflecting arrow pointing the way to the Chappaquiddick ferry, on a road he would frequently have driven? Why didn't the two friends he met up with afterward, both lawyers, call the police? Why wasn't an autopsy performed? Why was the inquest scheduled for September 3 delayed by order of a justice of the Massachusetts Supreme Court? "Why"— this from the *Richmond News Leader,* the conservative movement's flagship daily—"do the tire tracks leading into the pond reportedly show no signs that the Senator put on the brakes?"

And so Ted Kennedy broadcast a speech on all three networks in a bid to save his political life: a Kennedy performing a Checkers Speech. It was all there: the homey set (his father's Hyannis Port living room in front of a shelf of books the stroke-ridden Joe Kennedy could not read); the simultaneous acceptance of, and self-pitying distancing from, responsibility ("I regard as indefensible the fact that I did not report the accident to the police immediately"; "My doctors informed me that I suffered a cerebral concussion and shock"). The artfully sentimentalizing, self-exculpatory language ("I was on Martha's Vineyard island participating with my nephew, Joe Kennedy, as for thirty years my family has participated in the annual Edgartown sailing regatta"—reciting that *name*, Joe Kennedy, shared by the crippled father and the heroic brother martyred in World War II; "sailing," not "yachting," a Kennedy version of the respectable Republican cloth coat).

"I made immediate and repeated efforts to save Mary Jo by diving into the strong and murky current, but succeeded only in increasing my state of utter exhaustion and alarm," he claimed; Nixon-like, one was supposed to construe the suspect as victim. Mary Jo Kopechne was cast in the part of the cocker spaniel; Kennedy said he was going to keep defending her honor, regardless of what they said. "Mary Jo was one of the most devoted members of the staff of Robert Kennedy. . . . She worked for him for four years, was broken up over his death. For this reason, and because she was such a gentle, kind, and idealistic person, all of us tried to help her feel that she still had a home with the Kennedy family. . . . I know of nothing in Mary Jo's conduct on that or any other occasion, and the same is true of the other girls at that party, that would lend any substance to such ugly speculation about their character."

And how dare you even *think* such a thing.

Kennedy concluded, Checkers-like, by throwing the question to the voters of Massachusetts, who were "entitled to representation . . . by men who inspire their utmost confidence. For this reason I would understand full well why some might think it right for me to resign. For me this would be a difficult decision to make. I seek your advice and opinion in making it."

The public was rather forgiving—58 percent said, "He has suffered and been punished and should be given the benefit of the doubt"—even though by 44 to 36 percent they thought he had failed to "tell the real truth" and a majority thought "there still has been no adequate explanation of what he was doing at the party or with the girl who was killed," and 77 percent said he was wrong not to report the accident immediately. Only 16 percent disapproved of his Senate performance. But that was not the question at hand. Ted Kennedy was a presidential prospect. The question was, even giving him the most gracious benefit of the doubt, whether a man who under some combination of impairment and pressure wasn't able to act decisively was the kind of man you wanted to have his finger on the nuclear button.

The worst-case scenario was that he *had* acted decisively. The conservative *Manchester Union Leader* reported that Kennedy had charged five long-distance phone calls in the forty-five minutes after the accident to family retainers such as Theodore Sorenson and Burke Marshall. "The phone calls, if indeed made, would be damaging evidence, that far from being a dazed accident victim, Kennedy was a lucid politician trying to avoid a scandal," *Time* helpfully explained. And the Establishment, having coronated a 1972 presidential nominee, showed buyers' remorse. The *Times*'s Scotty Reston said the real question "is not whether the voters of Massachusetts can live with the Senator's account of the tragedy, but whether he can." *Time* suddenly realized it had never much trusted him anyway: "The youngest, handsomest, and most spoiled of the Kennedy brothers had often seemed shallow and irresponsible." Two liberals, Tom Braden and Frank Mankiewicz, in their new syndicated column, called Chappaquiddick "the end of the Kennedy era." Mankiewicz had been Bobby Kennedy's press secretary.

After Kennedy announced that, yes, he would be running for reelection in 1970, Al Capp, at the bidding of the White House, switched his registration to run against him. Middle America—or at least a Mrs. Keith H. Johnson and an Eleanor M. Wilson—spoke in letters to the *Chicago Tribune*: "Edward Kennedy may be the chosen son of Massachusetts, but we in the Midwest cannot accept that 'outing' as normal family procedure"; "We read daily of men who perform magnificently under the utmost stress in Vietnam. There are others whom stress does not seem to affect in the same way."

The liberal inhabitants of the best circles: they weren't like you and me.

On August 8, in the middle of the darkest Chappaquiddick speculations, four more mysterious deaths captured headlines: a stunning actress, eight months pregnant, Sharon Tate; a male hairstylist to the Hollywood stars; a coffee heiress; her rich young Polish émigré boyfriend—all brutally murdered in a beautiful house high in the Hollywood hills.

A young *New York Times* reporter, Steven V. Roberts, filed dispatches from California, not on the investigation, which was going nowhere, but on what he termed the murder victims' "life-styles." Tate and her husband, the filmmaker Roman Polanski, "had been near the center of a loose group of filmmakers who were described with all the current clichés: mod, hip, swinging, trendy." Polanski had just directed a very hip film, *Rosemary's Baby,* starring the hippie gamine Mia Farrow who had just left her square, old husband, Frank Sinatra. "Most of their friends lived in apartments and hotels, restaurants and shooting locations, airplanes and steamships. . . . They talked about three-star restaurants in Paris and discotheques in New York with equal facility"—people such as Warren Beatty, Paul Newman, John Phillips of the Mamas and the Papas. They were "young, handsome, and free." They were, also, liberal: when Gibby Folger wasn't off jet-setting, she campaigned for Robert Kennedy and cared for children in Watts. "She realized she didn't have to conform to that Protestant ethic," a friend recalled. "I remember once asking her how she was and she laughed, 'Well, I'm not my old constipated self anymore.'"

The members of the "Tate-Polanski Circle," Roberts concluded, "were more European than American in many ways, especially in regard to sex, which was always plentiful and, actually, important." One of their young actor friends was quoted: "We are living in the midst of a sexual revolution."

No one knew why they were murdered, or by whom. But this "lifestyle," went the clear implication—the one shared by Kennedys and what Nixon called privately their "their superswinging jet set"—must have had something to do with it.

The liberal inhabitants of the best circles: they weren't like you and me.

And yet the cultural moment was confusing. *Time* also had another obsession that summer of Chappaquiddick. The great newsweekly was the American middle class's arbiter of normalcy. As if self-consciously, its editorial policies had always served an integrative function in a fast-changing American culture. Whenever something new and shocking emerged in society, the magazine tended to patiently explain that it was actually continuous with our most ancient and honorable ways: the Vietnam War was like World War II; the Negroes that Negroes *really* admired were quiet and industrious; and religion remained as vital and relevant as ever—as evidenced, indeed, by those supposedly frightening hippies themselves, for whom, the magazine observed in a long and respectful cover story in the summer of 1967, "drug use is primarily Eucharistic in nature." And what *Time* seemed especially eager to domesticate now was something called "Woodstock"—a rock concert. Or, as the enterprising young men who'd conceived the business proposition promoted it, a "gathering of the tribes," an "Aquarian Exposition."

They had at first talked about drawing fifty thousand people if they were lucky. They signed a contract for a site in Wallkill, New York. One hundred and fifty citizens packed the town's usually sleepy board meeting, where they railed about what had happened the last time thousands of young Americans had gathered together—the Democratic convention. The site's landlord started getting threatening phone calls. People started saying they'd shoot the first hippie that crossed the town line. On July 15, the zoning board beat back the demons about to set upon them by declaring public toilets illegal. The kids would have to find another place to stage their show. They'd raised over $2 million from backers. They pulled in all the best acts by promising twice as much money as they'd ever made before. Though they weren't anywhere close to the famous artist-colony town of Woodstock, they stuck with the original name because it was perfect: Bob Dylan had a house in Woodstock. They sold the movie rights to Warner Bros., pitching it as a crapshoot: "Spend one hundred thousand dollars and you might make millions. If it turns out to be a riot, then you'll have one of the best documentaries ever made." They found a Sullivan County alfalfa field whose proprietor, Max Yasgur, was sympathetic, and eager for the $75,000 fee. They advertised their more-than-a-rock-concert on FM radio and in the underground press. By the time the music started Friday, August 15, so many people were there they couldn't continue to collect tickets. (Abbie Hoffman did his part from a Yippie tent outside the gates, telling people to refuse to pay.) The New York State Thruway was rendered a parking lot. Abandoned cars scattered along the roadside like jackstraws. It started raining. A menacing wind threatened the monstrous speaker towers. Things started getting chaotic. The *New York Times* complained that 99 percent of the crowd was smoking dope, passing their editorial judgment: "What kind of culture is it that can produce so colossal a mess?"

Time, on the other hand, claimed to see what the kids saw. And this was a watershed. It meant that Middle America was supposed to be embracing Woodstock, too.

The cover of the August 29 issue featured Defense Secretary Melvin Laird. Page 33 featured a full-color photograph from Woodstock captioned, "Boys and girls related in a nearby river"; none of the relating boys and girls wore clothes. The accompanying essay, "The Message of History's Biggest Happening," noted that though *Time* usually recognized "battles won, treaties signed, rulers elected or deposed," Woodstock should be counted among them "as one of the significant political and sociological events of the age." It was "the moment when the special culture of U.S. youth of the '60s openly displayed its strength, appeal, and power." The magazine called the attendees "pilgrims" and cited the scholar Theodore Roszak, author of the celebratory new book *The Making of a Counter Culture*—"these rock revolutionaries bear a certain resemblance to the early Christians"—and snubbed "the oversimplification that all narcotics are dangerous and thus should be outlawed" as something as "absurd and hypocritical as Prohibition." *Time* also complimented the *New York Times* for finally coming around—in a second editorial that redubbed Woodstock "essentially a phenomenon of innocence."

There were, *Time* admitted, some things to deplore at Woodstock: three deaths, one from an overdose; "hundreds of youths . . . freaked out on bad trips." (The magazine explained that away in the voice of *Consumer Reports:* the fault lay with manufacturers of "low-grade LSD.") The bottom line, however, was "the agape-like sharing of food and shelter by total strangers; the lack of overt hostilities despite conditions that were ripe for fear and panic. . . . In spite of the grownup suspicions and fears about the event, Bethel produced a feeling of friendship, camaraderie, and—an overused phrase—a sense of love among those present." *Time* quoted two of the young stars, both twenty-five, in support of the conclusion that it could not but have epochal if mysterious consequences for politics: "We don't need a leader," Janis Joplin said. "We have each other. All we need to do is keep our heads straight and in ten years this country may be a decent place to live in." Jimi Hendrix, who closed the festival with a blistering performance of "The Star-Spangled Banner," told *Time,* "From here they will start to build and change things. The whole world needs a big scrub down." *Time*'s sister publication, *Life,* went even further. Their special edition entirely given over to Woodstock was only the third in its thirty-six-year history.

The hosannas were remarkable. They were also understandable. The new school year was soon to arrive. Tom Charles Huston, the former Young Americans for Freedom leader and army intelligence officer who was now a White House assistant, wrote a long memo for the president's desk: "I am willing to state unequivocally that we will witness student disorder in the fall which will surpass anything we have seen before. Student militancy will sweep major campuses and flow into the streets of our major cities as competing factions of SDS strive to prove that each is more 'revolutionary' than the other." J. Edgar Hoover released a public letter on how this school year violent militants would be seeking to "lure students into their activities" with the argument that school was "irrelevant." Max Ascoli, the editor of the liberal magazine the *Reporter,* said that Nixon faced a task harder than Lincoln's: "He must save the Union not from a civil but a guerilla war." As such *Time*'s argument was tinged with yearning: if what these uprisings added up to was caring and sharing beneath pacifying clouds of marijuana smoke, there was nothing much to worry about at all.

But many of *Time*'s readers were not embracing Woodstock. Some, in fact, wondered whether their arbiter of normalcy had gone out of its mind.

A letter-writer from North Carolina: "So 'the whole world needs a big wash, a big scrub-down.' Granted—and why don't we start with the loonies who wallowed for days in Bethel's 'beautiful' mud, litter, and garbage? Your whitewash of this youth culture may well precipitate the flood that will inundate us all." From North Dakota: "The message is that of all the different kinds of love in the world, there is no love to compare to the love of one bum for another. The other message is that they will, as usual, all end up in the gutter." *Time* was still running letters two weeks later: "a superb job of furthering the moral decay of this nation"; "They're gonna build, no matter how they destroy. They're gonna teach love, no matter who they hurt. They're gonna be useful by being useless. . . . They want to be nonproductive on someone's production. Now I understand why I don't understand."

The letters had a put-upon tone: why, from all sides, were they being asked to swallow this nonsense? Wasn't this "Age of Aquarius," this "sexual revolution," something decent people should obviously condemn? Not, some parts of the Establishment seemed to be saying, if you wanted to be "with it." The irruption of the radical into the mainstream had been an uneven and uncertain process. But by 1969, it was unmistakable. *Time* meant to be making peace. Some spied in their olive branch a declaration of cultural war.

In that August 29 *Time* was an extraordinary advertisement. On the inside cover, in an artist's-model pose, sat a beautiful young nude. The facing page was headlined, "Conglomerate, like naked, is not a dirty word." The text continued:

"The Signal Companies has been called a 'conglomerate.'

"If 'conglomerate' implies a profit-making monster who gobbles up unsuspecting companies by means of underhanded tender offers, we do not qualify.

"The main trouble with the word 'conglomerate' is that it has been used to infer something ominous and evil.

"We suggest that in 'conglomerates,' as in nudity, the evil often exists only in the eyes of the beholder."

Multibillion-dollar corporations do not undertake multimillion-dollar ad campaigns designed to spruce up their public image without long and hard reflection. This corporation had concluded that the average *Time* readers would knowingly nod at the absurdity of the hypocrisy and irrationality of the prejudices surrounding the display of naked flesh in American culture—and perhaps, by a chain of mental equivalences, toss overboard their prejudices concerning multibillion-dollar corporations.

But domesticating what the pundits were calling the New Morality wasn't so simple. By the end of the summer of 1969, basic assumptions about the line between common decency and archaic prejudice were up for grabs. *Newsweek* tried to grasp the conundrum in its own dispatch on the New Morality: "Sheer numbers tell the tale. There are more explicitly erotic films, more blunt-spoken novels, more nudity on stage." They concluded, conservatively enough, "More than ever we need direction from mature leaders." They offered their direction by heralding the piece on the cover with a graphic of a stark naked couple.

Sophisticated Establishment opinion endorsed a key tenet of the New Morality: sexual pleasure was good and proper, shame and denial unhealthy. It was seen as a mark of education to recognize the casual cruelties behind the old regime of sexual hypocrisy—which divided girls into the categories of "those who did" and "those you married" but reserved no stigma for tomcatting boys; which let Kiwanis Clubs, American Legion halls, and college fraternities screen sex films at "stag nights" put on by promoters in a traveling circuit (conservative state legislatures in Illinois and North Carolina exempted them from state obscenity laws) but put the producers of these movies in jail. In November of 1966 the *Atlantic* ran a dossier of pro-divorce articles (including a short story by Philip Roth—who, two years later, received almost a million dollars for his bestselling novel, *Portnoy's Complaint,* in which the protagonist masturbated into a chunk of liver). The January 1967 *Atlantic* ran a piece celebrating "Pornography and the New Expression." Even *Reader's Digest* reported "A Victory Over the Smut Peddlers" in the same issue in which it excerpted an article from the women's magazine *McCall's* by the "sex therapists" William Masters and Virginia Johnson advising, "Today's methods of 'sex education' are failing to produce warm, responsible human beings. . . . Perhaps if we ourselves honor and respect sexuality, the children will sense its promise." Another 1967 *Digest* was warm in praise of "An Experiment in Sex Education" at a school where seventeen girls had become pregnant the year before. Such sex education programs were sweeping the country, and who could object? "Silence is criminal," *Time* quoted an expert on the subject—an expert speaking in 1914. Luckily popular opinion was catching up to him, as *Look* magazine noted enthusiastically: "Backwardness is succumbing as surely as snow to spring."

A similar attitude obtained on abortion. In 1962, the host of a popular children's show in Arizona, Sherri Finkbine, pregnant with her fifth child, accidentally took a tranquilizer containing thalidomide, which caused babies to be born without limbs. Her doctor recommended an abortion—forbidden in Arizona as everywhere else in the United States. Finkbine took her case to court. The judge turned her down. She traveled to Stockholm for the procedure. The story was covered widely; Finkbine's plight helped catalyze a nationwide movement to liberalize abortion laws. *Time* grew especially sympathetic. In June of 1967 they lamented that only ten thousand abortions had been allowed in 1966 under the available therapeutic grounds while a million to a million and a half were performed illegally—"with a high rate of resulting infections and hundreds of deaths." They took ending this as uncontroversial: as progress. The previous month they had put "The Pill" on the cover in an evangelical dispatch on its potential in "eliminating hunger, want, and ignorance." They buried a glancing discussion of the moral objections of "Roman Catholics and . . . the smaller number of Orthodox Jews" in the twenty-first paragraph.

The results were the same as with Woodstock: the revelation, on the letters page, of one more front in the Franklin-Orthogonian war. "Could it be possible that *Time* condones her desire for abortion?" a reader wrote about Sherri Finkbine, incredulous. Another: "Abortion is murder. . . . Is it not doubletalk to deny they are human lives?" Then, on the other side, the dueling moral absolutism—liberals and feminists asserting the choice as a right: "The very idea that abortion should present a dilemma infuriates me. The morality of satisfied, waistcoated male legislators complacently discussing the academics of ending a prenatal life while terrified women are desperately inserting pointed objects into their wombs is, to my mind, infinitely more questionable than the subject of abortion itself."

The Harris organization released a poll on the New Morality two months before Woodstock. Two-thirds of the entire sample thought morality had declined over the last ten years. Only 11 percent said it had risen. Franklin and Orthogonian agreed society was becoming decrepit. They just disagreed over whether Vietnam or venereal disease was the leading indicator. And the opinions seemed to divide along class lines: 29 percent thought "unjust laws may be ignored"; the figure rose to 38 percent among "professional people." Thirty-one percent of the full sample thought that "the use of four-letter words" didn't make sex "dirty"—as compared to 45 percent among college-educated, 41 percent of those earning over $10,000 per year, and 46 percent of professionals. *Time*'s own interpretation was patronizing: there was "a huge gulf between the old verities and life as it is actually lived by the American people today"—as if the lesser-educated, less well-off, and nonprofessional lived in simple denial of social reality. As if their objections were not really moral ones at all.

There was condescension, in 1967, in New York mayor John Lindsay's parks commissioner August Heckscher's insisting to those complaining of filthy doings in the parks that they were "scared by the abundance of life." Condescension was in a new president at the University of Wisconsin campus in rural Stevens Point starting the 1967–68 school year boasting to students that his initials were LSD and proposing, "We're going on a trip together." It was, that Christmas, in the posters for *The Graduate* on New York buses and in subway stations depicting Anne Bancroft and Dustin Hoffman in bed. It was, in 1968, in how *Newsweek* answered the question on its cover "Is Dr. Spock to Blame?" with a resounding no, that the new laxity in child-rearing practices was based on simple scientific progress and that objecting to it was like objecting to the invention of the automobile. It was in the *Nation* noting the emerging position that abortion was a woman's right was "prevalent among the educated." *Pleasure* was a new front in the Franklin-Orthogonian war, a new vein of anger rumbling beneath the social surface. And Richard Nixon got out his miner's lamp and shovel.

Pat Buchanan, the president's most culturally conservative top adviser, prepared Nixon's daily news summary. He made sure every story on the encroachment of moral decadence was prominently featured: *Newsweek*'s cover on the New Morality; the decency rally in Miami; the Swedish erotic film *I Am Curious (Yellow)*, which had been seized at the border, then released after a landmark court decision, becoming a hit at the fashionable 57 Rendezvous Theater in Manhattan (of special interest to Nixon, the *Times* reported that the former Mrs. John F. Kennedy attended with her new husband, the playboy Greek shipping magnate Aristotle Onassis). "Pornography and filth are gut issues with millions of decent people," Buchanan wrote in a memo to the president, who agreed. "P had me in quite a while before NSC, mainly on wanting to take stronger action on obscenity," Haldeman recorded in his diary March 28, 1969. "Even decided he'd go to a play in New York where they take off clothes, and get up and walk out, to dramatize his feeling." Nixon delivered a special message on obscene and pornographic materials, prepared with the help of a bright young associate deputy attorney general, John W. Dean III, at the height of the spring insurrections on the campuses: "The courts have not left society defenseless against the smut peddler; they have not ruled out reasonable government action"; Congress had to strengthen laws letting the citizen "protect his home from any intrusion of sex-oriented advertising."

Nixon concluded, "The ultimate answer lies not with the government but with the people. What is required is a citizens' crusade against the obscene." Americans answered the call. And the subject of their crusade was the movement over which *Look* magazine had gushed that backwardness was succumbing as surely as snow to spring: "sexual education" in the schools.

Two weeks after Woodstock a conference opened at the infamous Hilton in Chicago, where across the street a rally was commemorating the countercultural victims of the 1968 Democratic convention. The conference opened with a prayer for the Lord's blessing in the struggle against "the humanistic, godless effort to destroy the sanctity of the home and the well-being of America." That was followed by the Pledge of Allegiance and the national anthem. Then the chairwoman, a Mrs. Albert Flemming, asked the cameramen in the back to turn down the TV lights. When the cameramen didn't respond, someone shouted, "Who the hell wants the news media anyway?" The National Convention on the Crisis in Education had come to order.

Delegates came from twenty-two states, groups with such names as Mothers for Moral Stability (MOMS) and Parents Opposed to Sex and Sensitivity Education (POSSE). The hallways burbled with talk of the recent "so-called protest music festival," Woodstock, the "unshaven faces and their tumbling blankets"; of the gym class in which students supposedly went into a closet in pairs to explore what made boys different from girls; of the boy and girl who said they were performing a "scientific experiment" based on what they'd learned in class when found coupling in a toolshed; the kindergartens where copulation was taught; the alleged move to coed bathrooms without partitions separating the toilets. The teacher in Minneapolis—or Wichita, Texas, or wicked New York City, or in Flint or Lansing, Michigan—who fornicated in front of a rapt classroom in the interests of pedagogy. The seventeen boys who raped a sex education teacher after being aroused by her lecture. The classes that taught about copulation between people and livestock. The moral dissolution society was falling to as surely as snow to spring. And the villain responsible for it all: a woman named Mary Calderone.

The former medical director of Planned Parenthood, Calderone had come up with the idea for her organization, the Sex Information and Educa-

tion Council of the United States, at a 1961 conference of the National Association of Churches. By the 1964–65 school year SIECUS's "Guidelines for
Sexuality Education: Kindergarten through 12th Grade" had been requested
by over a thousand school districts. A typical exercise for kindergarten was
watching eggs hatch in an incubator. Her supporters saw themselves as the
opposite of subversives. "The churches have to take the lead," Dr. Calderone,
herself a Quaker, would say, "home, school, church, and community all
working cooperatively." The American Medical Association, the National
Education Association, and the American Association of School Administrators all published resolutions in support of the vision. Her theory was that
citizens would be more sexually responsible if they learned the facts of life
frankly and in the open, otherwise the vacuum would be filled by the kind
of talk that children picked up in the streets. An Illinois school district argued
that her program would fight "'situation ethics' and an emerging, but not yet
widely accepted standard of premarital sex." Even Billy Graham's magazine,
Christianity Today, gave the movement a cautious seal of approval.

They didn't see it as "liberal." But it *was* liberal. The SIECUS curriculum
encouraged children to ask questions. In her speeches Calderone said her
favorite four-letter word ended with a *k: T-A-L-K.* She advised ministers to
tell congregants who asked them about premarital sex, "Nobody can judge
that but yourself, but here are the facts about it." She taught that people "are
being moral when they are being true to themselves," that "it's the highest
morality to live up to the best in yourself, whether you call it God or whatever." Which, simply, was a subversive message to those who believed such
judgments *came* from God—or at least from parental authority. The anti-
sex-education movement was also intimately related to a crusade against
"sensitivity training": children talking about their feelings, about their home
lives, another pollution of prerogatives that properly belonged to family and
church. "SOCIALISTS USE SEX WEDGE in Public School to Separate
Children from Parental Authority," one of their pamphlets put it. Maybe not
socialists, but at the very least *someone* was separating children from parental
authority. More and more, it looked like the Establishment.

And, given that the explosion issued from liberals obliviously blundering
into the most explosive questions of where moral authority came from,
thinking themselves advancing an unquestionable moral good, it is appropriate that the powder keg came in one of America's most conservative suburbs:
Anaheim, the home of Disneyland, in Orange County, California, where
officials had, ironically enough, established a pioneering flagship sex education program four years earlier.

During the consultation period in 1965, 92 percent of parents approved.
It was expanded to full scale—an ungraded four-and-a-half-week unit for
seventh to twelfth graders—in 1967–68. The Family Life and Sex Education
program announced as its goal preparing students to build "a family with

strong bonds of affection, loyalty, and cooperation . . . whose members are happy and enjoy living together." By 1968–69 such programs existed in forty states. And the public was reconsidering its approval.

A science consultant to the Racine United School District opened a letter: "Dear Dick, I know you don't realize you're being used by Communists, but . . ." He picked up his phone: "You're nothing but a dirty Communist traitor." (In fact he was a Republican.) The district suspended the program "until misinformation and misunderstanding are corrected." Fifty miles to the north, in the rural town of Cedarburg, Wisconsin, the farm wife whose chickens supplied the incubator cried, "If I'd known what the school was up to, they never would have gotten their hands in my eggs." In Park Forest, Illinois, an eighth grader served a week's suspension for boycotting the science unit on plant and animal reproduction at the bidding of his parents; in Springfield, Ohio, school administrators got death threats. That was four towns within a 140-mile radius. Reported the *National Observer*, "Put a finger almost anywhere on the map and chances are it will land on a town where the radio talk shows and letters to the editor are stoking the controversy over sex education in the schools."

It wasn't entirely spontaneous. The vanguard cadre included people like the radio preacher Billy James Hargis (whose pamphlet *Is the Schoolhouse the Proper Place to Teach Raw Sex?* labeled Calderone "the SIECUS SEXPOT") and a John Birch Society front group called Movement to Restore Decency and far-right congressmen such as Orange County's James Utt, who gave speeches on the House floor linking sex ed, "the Beatles and their mimicking rock and rollers," and Communists using "Pavlovian techniques to produce artificial neuroses in our young people." Much was made of the Communist-front connections of one of Calderone's uncles, the poet Carl Sandburg.

All this, to be sure, was rather comical—and often easily debunked. One of the urban legends was that a twelve-year-old boy had copulated with his four-year-old sister, just as he'd learned about in school. *Parade* magazine got to the bottom of that one; it originated with a fundamentalist Protestant minister who heard it from a parishioner, who heard it from another woman who was not particularly noted for her emotional stability. Liberals steadied their grip and harnessed their reason: "The venereal disease and divorce rates keep rising and these people refuse to understand," the administrator from Racine told the *New York Times*. "It's as if they were saying, 'There's an epidemic of polio, but we're not going to let you do anything about it.'" What liberals did not understand was that the hysterical anti-sex-ed crusaders were not without reason. Said one parent, "I know teachers I wouldn't want teaching math to my kids, let alone sex education." Sex, people were realizing once they had suddenly been given the opportunity to give it thought as a public policy issue, was *intimate*. Complained one parent, "My wife and I have never discussed sex in seventeen years of marriage."

In Anaheim, a receptionist for the Quick-Set Lock Company named Eleanor Howe related how she had walked into her son's classroom and found the names of sexual acts chalked on the board, including "69." Perhaps it was all a misunderstanding. Perhaps the teacher had just chalked up what year it was. Either way: spark, powder keg, war—for which the conditions had been gathering for years.

Activists commandeered Anaheim school board meetings and recited the "findings" of anti-sex-ed pamphleteers ("Sex education is just one of the many deadly weapons in the armory of the Communist-Humanist Complex"). The superintendent had to reassure citizens that "film strips showing human or animals engaged in sexual intercourse" and instruction in the "techniques of sex" were not part of the curriculum. Sex education became the only issue in the spring 1969 school board election. The crusaders won two of three contested seats. By Woodstock, the California legislature passed a law banning attendance at sex-ed classes without written parental permission. Mrs. Howe started barnstorming the nation, an anti-sex-ed celebrity. Her visual aide was *Life*'s special issue on Woodstock. A September issue of *Look* reported that Anaheim was now famous "as a community where, it is alleged, venereal disease and illegitimacy run rampant because of a pioneering curriculum in Family Life and Sex Education."

The new school year arrived. The Friday after Labor Day the California Supreme Court ruled that the state's Reagan-signed abortion law, the nation's most liberal, wasn't nearly liberal enough: the California constitution, they ruled, gave women an absolute right "to choose whether to bear children." Orange County's first antiabortion group was founded. Billy Graham's 20th Anniversary Crusade sold out Anaheim Stadium ten days running. An anti-sex-ed leader used a TV interview to announce, "In order to protect the children . . . all people with any affiliation to this program [should] be investigated concerning their private and public lives and be given tests by a psychiatrist to see if they are considered sexually normal. These results should then be made public." The head school nurse and codirector of Anaheim's Family Life and Sex Education program reported of the phone calls she'd been getting in the middle of the night, "People have the dirtiest minds. It's astonishing." The superintendent told the media, "People in the community have stopped talking to each other." The September 14 *New York Times* reported that a score of state legislatures now had anti-sex-education legislation pending. In Netcong, New Jersey, the school board ordered daily readings of the same prayers recited by chaplains in the U.S. Congress and tried to get around the Supreme Court by calling them "inspirational remarks." Outside Chicago, a federal judge said schools could kick a kid out for long hair: "Teachers have rights, too. They have better things to do than follow him around to make sure his grooming doesn't cause any problems in the school."

And so, in downtown Chicago at the Hilton, speaker after speaker raged on against the humanistic, godless effort to destroy the sanctity of the home and the well-being of America.

"A couple of girls from our community went down to Kalamazoo Teachers College and in one year they were completely changed. What do they *do* to our girls?"

"We know our enemy is promoting revolution in this country by every means possible: sex education, drugs, music."

"You'll be robbed as I was of the privilege of telling your child in your own way of the beauty of creation."

"Behavioral scientists, they don't know what people are like. You and I are in a bad state of mental health."

The same *Time* magazine that celebrated abortion and Woodstock and called drug-taking "Eucharistic" didn't judge any of this backlash much of a happening (indeed the most reliable way to get an ovation at the conference was to denounce a bright pink volume entitled *How Babies Are Made*—published by Time-Life Books). But the war that *Time* wasn't reporting on was helping realign American politics. One angry Anaheim anti-sex-ed housewife told a reporter, "I'm still a registered Democrat and I thought I was liberal, but I really don't understand the meaning of the word." Another told a long-haired graduate student interviewing participants at the Chicago conference, "Boy, if you think you all are fighting the Establishment, you oughtta try fighting the NEA!"

But Richard Nixon didn't miss this new cultural war. As he prepared for his next big Vietnam speech, set for November, he made ready to turn the divide between "normal" Americans and the immoral Establishment that pretended to speak for them into his next political advance.

The liberal inhabitants of the best circles: they weren't like you and me.

CHAPTER TWENTY

The Presidential Offensive

Ronald Reagan's administration prepared for the 1969–70 school year by asking the FBI to help in its "psychological warfare campaign" against campus radicals. J. Edgar Hoover responded enthusiastically—"this has been done in the past and has worked quite successfully"—and dispatched his number two man, Clyde Tolson, to help. A Reagan aide said they wanted to shut down radical bookstores for building code violations and hoped the Justice Department would charge "those elements which disrupted the peaceful pursuit of studies by right-thinking students" with civil rights violations. He said he'd heard people in the Pentagon could help with intelligence. Tolson assured him, "We are well aware of such potentials."

The federal government was developing many such "potentials." Senator Sam Ervin, the North Carolina conservative and civil libertarian, learned that Treasury Department officials checked library lists to see what books certain suspicious Americans read, that HEW kept a blacklist of antiwar scientists, that the Secret Service was asking government employees to report anyone with an interest in "embarrassing" the president.

Ervin had only glimpsed the tip of the iceberg. Since 1966 army intelligence had been keeping an eye on protesters who might specifically represent a threat to the army. The Nixon administration tapped an attorney in the Justice Department, William Rehnquist, to write a memo justifying expanding the program to spy on any antiwar activity. Soon, one thousand undercover agents in three hundred offices nationwide were compiling dossiers on such groups as the NAACP, ACLU, Southern Christian Leadership Conference, and Clergy and Laymen Concerned about Vietnam.

On May 14, the attorney general had met with the director of central intelligence for a briefing on the apparatus the CIA had set up in 1967—Operation CHAOS—to determine which protesters were getting support from America's enemies abroad. Four separate reports to LBJ had assured him that none were. The Nixon White House now learned the same thing. Nonetheless, Mitchell arranged for CHAOS to expand—and to no longer bother with honoring the CIA's charter to spy only on non-Americans. In

October, it began infiltrating the antiwar movement. "Our insider information has caused SDS to get more conspiratorial in a lot of places," an agent remarked. It "makes it harder for them to draw the kinds of crowds they used to get at their rallies."

The Nixon administration set up an apparatus to haunt dissidents via their tax returns. When Nixon learned that the IRS had audited John Wayne and Billy Graham—as Nixon himself had been audited in 1961 and '62—he growled, "Get the word out, down to the IRS, that I want them to conduct field audits of those who are our opponents if they're going to do our friends." He suggested the IRS start with the new Democratic National Committee chairman, Larry O'Brien, who, like Nixon's brother, had possibly shady dealings with the Howard Hughes organization. The IRS's Activist Organizations Committee went online in July—then they changed the name to the Special Services Staff, the better to keep its purpose secret. Their target list included over a thousand groups and four thousand individuals—stored in a locked, soundproof room in the IRS basement. "What we cannot do in a courtroom via criminal prosecutions to curtail the activities of some of these groups," a White House memo explained, "IRS could do by administrative action."

Meanwhile the Justice Department worked to do things in the courtroom—especially the one belonging to Judge Julius J. Hoffman in Chicago, who was to preside over the trial of Abbie Hoffman, Tom Hayden, Bobby Seale, and the rest of the alleged "Chicago 8" convention conspirators. The government possessed wiretaps on five of them. The Supreme Court had ruled heretofore that wiretap logs must be submitted to the defense. Then, in July, three months after the indictment and two months before the trial was set to begin, Attorney General Mitchell made an extraordinary announcement: since the executive branch had the power "to gather intelligence information concerning those organizations which are committed to the use of illegal methods to bring about changes in our form of government and which may be seeking to foment violent disorders," it would violate the national interest for the defense to review the logs. Lawyers howled that the chief law enforcement officer of the United States had just violated his oath of office. The chief law enforcement officer thought precisely the opposite: if ever he was upholding his duty to "preserve and defend the Constitution against all enemies foreign and domestic," this was it. The FBI had been saying it since March of 1968: the Chicago organizers were "a substantial threat to national security."

They believed they were doing their duty: protecting the national security. And perhaps they were.

Students for a Democratic Society held the last national convention of its institutional life in June in the shabby and underlit Chicago Coliseum. One faction, the Progressive Labor Party, a severe, crew-cutted Maoist cell that banned the use of drugs, had stealthily taken over the SDS bureaucracy. Another faction—for Byzantine reasons of factional history, they called themselves Revolutionary Youth Movement II—joined in tactical alliance with a group that called themselves Weathermen to try to win the organization back. They labeled Progressive Labor false Maoists and ersatz revolutionaries and had attempted to prove their revolutionary superiority by recruiting angry white working-class high school students, who were supposed to serve as foot soldiers under the vanguard leadership of the Black Panther Party. The Weathermen were, meanwhile, working to harden themselves as urban guerrilla warriors and had brought black and Latino street toughs into the meeting as ringers. When an entirely separate faction, the Women's Liberation Caucus, offered a motion against male chauvinism, the street toughs roared back in mockery, chanting, "Pussy power! Pussy power!" The floor disintegrated into a cacophony of contending chants: "Fight male chauvinism! Fight male chauvinism!" "Read Mao! Read Mao! Read Mao!" The Weathermen and Revolutionary Youth Movement II withdrew to reconstitute the meeting, expelling Progressive Labor from SDS as "objectively anticommunist" and "counterrevolutionary." Upon which, declaring victory, a Revolutionary Youth Movement II leader called a press conference to read the telegram he had just sent to Mao Tse-tung describing their "great victory" over the false Maoists of the Progressive Labor Party.

Such was the burlesque that New Left politics had become. The Weathermen withdrew, put out a clotted manifesto studded with quotes from Lin Biao's *Long Live the Victory of People's War!,* and undertook frightening rituals to temper themselves against their "bourgeois" disinclination to violence. In August some met with representatives of the National Liberation Front in Cuba, who advised them to "stop the airplanes." So they traveled to California air bases and haplessly attempted some sabotage.

They were hardly one big happy family. But what united them vindicated Attorney General Mitchell. All, after their different fashions, wished to see the existing society gone. That any two given New Leftists were more likely to break into fisticuffs than join in any effective conspiracy did nothing to dissuade the forces of law and order that they must be destroyed.

The Chicago conspiracy trial opened September 24. A cabdriver shared his take with a visiting journalist: "Those anarchists will be in jail by Christmas." Things weren't quite so efficient. Bobby Seale, also under indictment in Connecticut for conspiracy to murder another Black Panther, had been driven out from California in chains by U.S. marshals. Since his lawyer, Charles Garry, had obtained a court order to keep him in California that the marshals had ignored, Seale claimed he'd been kidnapped. Garry was undergoing surgery in California, so Seale rose at the opening gavel on the third day to request a six-week continuance. The judge refused.

Seale shouted, "If I am consistently denied this right of legal counsel of my choice . . . then I can only see the judge as a blatant racist of the United States court."

Judge Hoffman was an excruciatingly proud man. One of the things he was most proud of was having presided over the North's first school integration case. "Just a minute! Just a minute!" he barked, asking the clerk to read the words back. He turned to Seale: "Watch what you say, sir." They bickered on and on, then the jury finally entered. Defendant Tom Hayden raised his fist in salute. Prosecutor Richard Schultz angrily asked the judge to send out the jury. The judge chewed out Hayden for "shaking his fist." Hayden replied, "It is my customary greeting, Your Honor."

Prosecutor Schultz began his opening statement. He mentioned Abbie Hoffman, who rose with a flourish and blew a kiss at the jury.

The judge, sternly: "The jury is directed to disregard the kiss from Mr. Hoffman."

The long-haired defense lawyer Leonard Weinglass started *his* opening statement, reminding the jury that according to the common law, they were the courtroom's "highest authority."

Judge dismissed jury again and warned Weinglass against further "contumacious conduct."

Every morning, a miniature trial-within-a-trial between Seale and Judge Hoffman unspooled; every afternoon, a generational civil war between defendants and judge. The second week of the trial began with two women on the jury getting letters at home reading, "You are being watched—the Black Panthers." One said she could no longer be impartial and was dismissed. The word flashed through the underground media covering the trial as the opening round of the government's conspiracy to jail all youthful dissenters: since these were the only jurors in their twenties, the prosecution had sent the letters to rid the jury of potential defense sympathizers.

The trial would not be over by Christmas.

Perhaps it would not be over by Easter.

On October 3, the Chicago police riddled Black Panther headquarters on the West Side with bullets (somehow no one died). Three days later, out in California, Angela Davis, a young professor at UCLA and disciple of Herbert Marcuse and an admitted Community Party member, completed the first lecture of Philosophy 99 (Recurring Philosophical Themes in Black Literature) to a standing ovation. The Reagan-dominated majority on the Board of Regents had already voted to fire her. So two thousand students showed up to take her class.

Two days after that, on October 8, the Weathermen tried to jump-start the revolution.

Their analysis led them to the conclusion that thousands of young people would gather in Chicago in solidarity with the conspiracy defendants to

tear down Pig City. One of their major organizing efforts had been among
the toughs in working-class high schools, alienated proletarians who, their
dialectic concluded, would *flock* to radicals who didn't just talk. The revolution would finally have been made concrete. The war would be brought
home. Youth would "feel the Vietnamese *in ourselves*" — and the third world,
witnessing their sacrifice, would rise up in revolutionary solidarity.

After dark, around a bonfire in Lincoln Park, the "Days of Rage" began
with a commemoration of the martyrdom of Che Guevara. The warriors cast
nervous glances: there were only three hundred of them, and two thousand
waiting police. They had already blown up a statue memorializing the policemen who died in the 1886 Haymarket riot. An officer told the *Trib*, "We now
feel it is kill or be killed."

Tom Hayden, through a bullhorn, pledged the solidarity of the defendants (actually, the defendants were divided on the question).

An NBC producer felt something like a knife pressed up against his
giblets: "Pig newsman, just make sure to tell the story straight."

A ringleader shouted, "I am Marion Delgado!" — the signal. Delgado was
a five-year-old boy who had, in 1947, derailed a passenger train with a chunk
of concrete. This was whom the Weathermen had chosen for a folk hero.

The warriors shrieked down the streets of the Gold Coast armed with
clubs, chains, pipes, and bats, smashing windows of apartment buildings and
cars. They charged police lines; the police shot six of them, and suffered
twenty-eight injuries themselves.

Out-of-towners not arrested slept in the basements of Movement-
friendly churches and seminaries. The next night a "women's militia" of seventy gathered in Grant Park to raid a draft board, but were overpowered
before they could hit the streets (the *Trib:* "5 Cops and City Aide Beaten and
Bitten by Women Rioters"). The next day's scheduled "jailbreak" of area
high schools was called off when Governor Ogilvie announced he was calling out twenty-five hundred National Guardsmen. Meanwhile the city's
assistant corporation counsel Richard Elrod leapt to tackle a Weatherman,
slammed into a concrete wall, and ended up paralyzed for life. Brian Flana-
gan was charged with attempted murder. The Weatherman's mother told the
press, "I don't blame the Chicago police. They should have knocked the
heads off every one of them."

The Weathermen declared dialectical victory. As one pointed out, "We're
not trying to end wars. We're starting to fight war." Defendant Jerry Rubin
told reporters in the federal courthouse cloakroom, "They brought the
movement a qualitative step forward." His Yippie colleague Stewart Albert
elaborated, "What if you picked up a history book and read that in 1938 a
thousand University of Berlin students ran through the streets on behalf of
the Jews in the camps, breaking car windows, knocking over fat, old German
ladies, and beating up the Gestapo? . . . On a moral level, they're perfect."

Nixon, Mitchell, Reagan, and J. Edgar Hoover could declare dialectical victory as well: their theory was confirmed that these antiwarriors, from the street fighters on down to the fellow travelers who sheltered them in their churches, were essentially about ending our constitutional republic.

The self-fulfilling polarization of presidents and the revolutionaries intensified, even as, by the ninth month of Richard Nixon's presidency, antiwar conviction was more mainstream than ever. In June, 47 percent of America backed Nixon's handling of the war and 45 percent opposed it. By September, 35 percent backed it and 57 percent opposed it. It seemed to many that Nixon's secret plan to end the war was to escalate it. And an astounding number of people, even those who had voted for him, were willing to fight to stop it.

In March the ministers, priests, and rabbis of Clergy and Laymen Concerned about Vietnam (CALCAV) sent out sixty thousand posters listing the number of Americans and Vietnamese killed in the war. Pastors led Eastertide marches: thirty thousand people in the rain in Chicago, forty thousand in San Francisco, one hundred thousand in New York. Quakers read out the names of the thirty thousand American war dead in front of draft boards, then on the Capitol steps—then, after they were threatened with arrest, arm in arm with congressmen. When CALCAV held its convention in Michigan, the president of Dow Chemical, Gil Doan, a devoted Episcopalian, invited them to his home. In 1967, in response to student riots over napalm, which was manufactured by Dow, Doan had responded, "As long as the U.S. is involved in Vietnam, we believe in fulfilling our responsibility to this national commitment of a democratic society." Now he told the divines that if they could demonstrate that napalm was primarily affecting civilians, he would try to get the company out of the contract. Soon after, Dow reportedly intentionally overbid for the Department of Defense napalm procurement contract and stopped producing the weapon because it was hurting their recruitment efforts among students.

The news from Southeast Asia helped spread the alienation. In late August the army announced that eight Green Berets, including the commander of Special Forces in Vietnam, Colonel Robert B. Rheault—the "Nha Trang 8"—would be charged with the murder of a Vietnamese civilian. The victim was a suspected enemy agent. Shadow upon shadow upon shadow: somehow, the trial got canceled. One of the men's lawyers pronounced darkly, "People in high places made a mistake and are refusing to admit it." (He was right: the high place that had fixed the trial was the Oval Office.)

In its June 27 issue, *Life* ran the portraits of the men who'd died in Vietnam the week after Memorial Day. They looked like children. The next week the Senate passed the first small reassertion of a congressional role in warmaking since the Gulf of Tonkin resolution. Women Strike for Peace picketed

the White House in black veils. A book called *Truth Is the First Casualty,* by
Washington correspondent Joseph C. Goulden, came out in August; it
revealed that the Gulf of Tonkin pretext LBJ used to secure congressional permission to escalate had been a fraud. One of its blurbs was from the former
commandant of the Marine Corps, General David M. Shoup. Another retired
marine and former high officer in Vietnam, William Corson, published a book
called *The Betrayal.* His epiphany, he explained, had come when a jarhead
died in his arms, asking him "why someone didn't tell them the truth about
the war." Corson rose at 5 a.m. every morning during his last tour of duty to
write it. When the top brass found out about the project, they convened a task
force to consider a court-martial, then decided against it when they realized
this book needed as little publicity as possible. It argued that most South Vietnamese considered the government in Saigon worse than the Communists.

The week after the Days of Rage, all these mainstream voices would have
occasion to sound together. It was the idea of a Boston envelope manufacturer,
the kind of figure Richard Nixon was used to approaching for political contributions: a one-day nationwide general strike against the war. Most antiwar
leaders were skeptical. One who wasn't, who knew something about quixotic
successes, was Sam Brown, the organizer of the McCarthy "Children's Crusade" in 1968. The usual spots where dissidents gathered, he realized—New
York, San Francisco, Washington—were foreign territory to most Americans.
This action would be determinedly *local.* Get pictures on the AP wire of antiwar butchers, bakers, and candlestick makers in Schenectady, Cincinnati, and
Bakersfield, and a new antiwar narrative might emerge. Since *strike* sounded
like something bomb-throwers did, they adopted, instead, a Nixon word:
moratorium. A moratorium from everyday life, smack-dab in the middle of
the week.

The first press release went out: "On October 15, 1969, this nation will
cease 'business as usual' to protest the war in Vietnam and for the Nixon
administration to bring the troops home." (Nixon issued a dictate to John
Ehrlichman on June 24, using a favorite football metaphor: come up with an
anti-Moratorium game plan by July. What was significant about that order
was that the protest was not publicly announced for another week.) The
Vietnam Moratorium Committee organized on a scale never attempted
before. The core was the 253 student-government officers and student-
newspaper editors who had signed an antidraft pledge in the spring. The
spring clashes on campuses actually worked to the organizers' advantage.
People wanted desperately to talk to these clean-cut kids knocking on their
doors—to grasp the baffling events just past. That was the conversation
starter, the opening to points like "Isn't twenty-five thousand a rather token
amount of troops for Nixon to withdraw, given that there are over five hundred thousand American boys in Vietnam? Doesn't that rate of withdrawal
mean we would still be in Vietnam in nine years?"

To Nixon and Kissinger, it was the most cataclysmic development imaginable. The only things worse than loud antiwar demonstrations were *quiet* antiwar demonstrations. A mass movement of ordinary citizens resisting the war screwed up what they had in mind to win it: a haymaker, the knockout blow.

"I call it the madman theory, Bob," the Republican presidential nominee had told his closest aide, walking on the beach one day in 1968. "I want the North Vietnamese to believe I've reached the point where I might do *anything* to stop the war. We'll just slip the word to them that 'For God's sake, you know Nixon is obsessed about Communism. We can't restrain him when he's angry—and he has his hand on the nuclear button.' And Ho Chi Minh himself will be in Paris in two days begging for peace."

The strategy hewed to a Nixon maxim: *the only time to lose your temper in politics is when it is deliberate.* What it did not hew to was anything he had said on the campaign trail. Candidate Nixon—and President Nixon, in his public pronouncements—was a *de*-escalator.

Privately, since 1966, he had said Vietnam was unwinnable in any proper sense, and that the job for the president was to end the war on acceptable terms. The madman theory was his idea as to how: scare them to the negotiating table to give you those terms, on threatened pain of total incineration.

A madman's credibility must be vouchsafed by signs of his madness. That was one reason for the massive bombing of Cambodia; also one reason why it was so secret. It was intended for a select audience: the enemy. If the public thought their president was war-mad, they would do exactly what they threatened to do now: turn against Nixon in such numbers as to make warmaking, in a democracy, impossible. Which was why the Moratorium horrified him so. To convince Hanoi he could savage them unmercifully, Hanoi had to believe him a popular president. Which meant, paradoxically, that publicly he had to be seen as winding down the war.

Hanoi responded to his May 14 public offer of mutual withdrawal as per usual: America was the aggressor and must withdraw—unilaterally. In July, via secret channels, Nixon released a frightening hint: unless significant progress was made in peace talks by November 1, he would unleash "measures of great consequence and force." Publicly, he announced the Nixon Doctrine, that he would "avoid the kind of policy that will make countries in Asia so dependent on us that we are dragged into conflicts such as the one we have in Vietnam," thus earning headlines such as "Nixon Plans Cut in Military Role for U.S. in Asia."

Ho Chi Minh, on his deathbed, rebuffed Nixon's negotiating terms. In September the NSC began planning for a four-day holocaust if the November deadline passed: intensive bombing of military targets, population centers, and rail lines to China; mining Haiphong Harbor, Hanoi's lifeline port;

destruction of the major passes of the Ho Chi Minh Trail, possibly via low-yield nuclear weapons; perhaps a land invasion of North Vietnam. And another, even more frightening possibility: bombing the dikes. North Vietnam's dikes protected the country's agricultural lowlands from flooding. If enough were breached, by one estimate quoted to Nixon, a million people would be drowned. The planning was code-named Duck Hook, after the most nasty kind of errant golf shot: a duck-hooked ball seemed somehow to accelerate faster the farther it careened out of bounds. "I can't believe," Henry Kissinger said, "that a fourth-rate power like North Vietnam doesn't have a breaking point."

Some of the tough talk was bluff, some in earnest; only Kissinger and Nixon knew for sure (Defense Secretary Laird didn't even know about the planning studies). Some possibilities Nixon shared with friendly senators, hoping they would leak it to the press to throw Hanoi off-balance. But this was a dangerous game they were playing; if too much leaked, the demonstrations on October 15 might rage out of control.

And so another part of the military planning was the attempt to turn off the antiwar movement, through any means, fair or foul.

Ehrlichman named as the anti-Moratorium game plan's quarterback Nixon's favorite football coach, Bud Wilkinson, late of the University of Oklahoma. What Wilkinson proposed, since "no one likes to be used," was that he jawbone the kids into realizing the Moratorium was "an attempt to exploit students for the organizers' own purposes." "It's easy to manipulate kids," Haldeman agreed, "because they love to get excited. You can foment them up for a panty raid, or in the old days, goldfish swallowing." But six weeks after Bud Wilkinson started meeting with student leaders to shame them into the realization that they were cat's-paws, he apologetically reported back that kids were laughing in his face. "The problem of dealing with the Vietnam Moratorium Committee," Wilkinson noted, with understatement, "is difficult."

Some Establishment leaders surveying the antiwar disruptions began concluding that the best way to end them was to end the war. Notre Dame's Father Hesburgh earned an Oval Office audience for his get-tough policies against student protesters and took the opportunity to beg the president to reform the draft and end the war "as soon as possible." The president of the most violence-racked campus in the country, the University of Michigan, practically thundered against the war in an opening convocation. Word came down about him from the president: "not to be included in any White House conferences."

Simultaneously, the White House launched an anti-Moratorium Plan B: leaking word that they *were* responding to demonstrations. The *New York Times* printed the testimony of an anonymous "critic" within the administration that there would soon be "a temporary suspension of the draft for an unspecified time," and that when conscription resumed, men would only be eligible for a year after their nineteenth birthday, and only professional soldiers and draftees who volunteered would be sent to Vietnam.

These moves were part of a sorely needed White House public relations campaign that summer and fall they called the Presidential Offensive. The president's approval rating was now a perilous 52 percent. A Yale professor read a paper at the convention of the American Political Science Association (which avoided, but only barely, the brawls over antiwar resolutions that broke out at the conclaves of the sociologists and the psychologists) arguing that the president "was a dangerous man with wild, but predictable, mood swings." The *New York Times* and *Time* both ran articles on the study; the newsmagazine concluded Nixon might "commit himself irrevocably to some disastrous course of action." A humiliating book, *The Selling of the President,* which revealed the backstage secrets behind Richard Nixon's television campaign in 1968, would soon be a number one bestseller. The *New York Times* heralded it with an article on how Nixon continued to keep Roger Ailes on standby to advise the president on makeup, lighting, and camera angles. "But he said he didn't have to teach the President much," the paper observed.

The president found succor in Dixie. The Fifth Circuit had ordered thirty-three Mississippi school districts integrated before the opening of the school year. The districts filed the court-mandated plans; HEW approved them. Then Nixon ordered HEW secretary Finch to send the judge a letter with language dictated by Mississippi senator John Stennis: the September deadline would bring "chaos, confusion, and catastrophic educational setback" for children "black and white alike." The judge moved back the deadline to December; whence it would, perhaps, be moved back some more. The NAACP Legal Defense Fund took out a full-page ad in the *New York Times:* "*On August 25, 1969, the United States Government broke its promise to the children of Mississippi.* The promise was made in 1954. By the highest court in the land." Roy Wilkins accused the administration of actively helping the South prolong segregation and said that if Nixon was serious about civil rights, he'd fire John Mitchell. HEW's civil rights chief, Leon Panetta, a thirty-one-year-old former aide to Thomas Kuchel, did what he thought was his job: he piped up that Nixon *was* serious about civil rights, just as he'd said at his inauguration.

Panetta immediately got a call from Ehrlichman: "Cool it, Leon!"

Silly Leon. HEW general counsel Robert Mardian, a top operative in Barry Goldwater's presidential campaign, marveled, "Doesn't he understand Nixon promised the Southern delegates he would stop enforcing the Civil Rights and Voting Rights acts?"

Nixon announced his replacement for Abe Fortas: Clement Furman Haynsworth Jr., a fifth-generation South Carolinian. On September 8, flying back from a sojourn at the Western White House in San Clemente, Cal-

ifornia, Nixon touched down in Gulfport, Mississippi, for what was planned
as a ten-minute stopover. He was met at the airport by his most delirious
reception since he'd returned from South America in 1958, seventy-five
thousand patriots who'd waited hours for his arrival in furnacelike heat. A
sign read NOT MANY REPUBLICANS HERE, BUT LOTS OF NIXONCRATS.

Everywhere else it was open season.

In San Francisco, slogans from six thousand protesters drifted humiliatingly from Union Square into the ballroom where he hosted a state dinner
for President Park Chung Hee of South Korea—the first trip where his handlers had been unable to keep demonstrators from the president's sight lines.
Back in Washington, he read a column by Kissinger's friend Joe Kraft listing
all the the national security experts quitting the administration because they
could not get past the "former adman" Haldeman—"an ultraloyalist with little feel for substantive problems." *Newsweek* was preparing a "Nixon in
Trouble!" cover. *Time* led its "National Affairs" dispatch with "Nixon's Worst
Week." *U.S. News* reported "Nixon's Staff in Disarray." David Broder would
soon file a column that came to Nixon's aid. "A Risky New American Sport:
'The Breaking of the President'" argued, "It is becoming more and more obvious with every passing day that the men and the movement that broke Lyndon B. Johnson's authority in 1968 are out to break Richard M. Nixon in
1969." He begged his colleagues to effect a cease-fire: for "when you have broken the President, you have broken the one man who can negotiate the peace."

The president dictated eight memos outlining a public relations push-
back. It was part of the foreign policy game. De-escalation was contingent
on the enemy believing Nixon would escalate; which was contingent upon
keeping presidential approval ratings high; which was contingent on the
appearance of de-escalation. As one of the big syndicated columnists, Roscoe
Drummond, observed, only grasping one-tenth of the complexity, unless
Vietnam looked to be winding down, "popular opinion will roll over him as
it did LBJ." At which Nixon thundered upon his printed news summary,
"E&K—Tell him that RN is less affected by press criticism and opinion than
any Pres in recent memory." Because he was the president *most* affected by
press criticism and opinion of any president in recent memory. Which if
known would make him look weak. And any escalatory bluff would be
impossible. Which would keep him from credibility as a de-escalator; which
would block his credibility as an escalator; which would stymie his ability to
de-escalate; and then he couldn't "win" in Vietnam—which in his heart he
didn't believe was possible anyway.

Through the looking glass with Richard Nixon: this stuff was better than
LSD.

The public relations didn't work. Senator Birch Bayh (D-Ind.) dug up
financial conflicts of interests on Judge Haynsworth that made Abe Fortas
smell like a rose. On Saturday, September 20, Nixon initiated the next phase

of his anti-Moratorium agitating: he met with 225 student council presidents, accompanied by university presidents and deans, none from schools to which any of the best circles would send their children, for a conference called Evolution Not Revolution: A Time for Constructive Action. But even this carefully sanitized group berated administration officials. "It was a mistake to even invite them," Nixon fumed, and went off to golf at Burning Tree with Bob Hope.

The frustrations were enough to drive a president crazy, just like the political science professor said. Nixon started making mistakes—losing his temper, and not deliberately. On September 26 he held his first press conference since June. Aides urged him not to sneer at something so obviously broad-based as the new antiwar surge. Asked first about the proposal of Charles Goodell, the Republican senator Nelson Rockefeller had appointed to fill out the late Bobby Kennedy's term, to cut off funding for the war after December 1, 1970, he responded like something out of *1984:* "That inevitably leads to perpetuating and continuing the war." The third question was a softball: "What is your view, sir, concerning the student moratorium and other campus demonstrations being planned for this fall against the Vietnam War?" He replied, with monarchical bluntness, "Under no circumstances will I be affected whatever by it."

Mistake.

The remark was the next day's lead story. VMC leaders put on a press conference timed for the Sunday papers. Dozens of reporters showed up instead of the usual five or six. The VMC had done what Nixon had done in 1948 with Truman, and 1966 with Johnson: massively inflated their stature by making themselves debating partners of a president. They also played skillfully into the emerging media narrative: that the stresses of the job were getting to Nixon. They said what distressed them about his statement "is the degree of isolation which it reflects. It is the kind of rigid stance which contributed so much to the bitterness of debate during the last days of the Johnson administration."

The VMC was speaking the Establishment's language, and the Establishment suddenly started showing respect. *Newsweek* reported, "Originally, October 15 was to have been a campus-oriented protest. But it has quickly spread beyond the campus. And, if everything goes according to the evolving plans, the combination of scheduled events could well turn into the broadest and most spectacular antiwar protest in American history."

Everything was going better than planned. As Weathermen tore up Chicago, the *New York Times* reported on a letter from six of the top Vietnam experts from the Rand Corporation, the top defense think tank. America should withdraw, they said, unilaterally and immediately—not "conditioned upon agreement or performance by Hanoi or Saigon." They went on, "Short of destroying the entire country and its people, we cannot eliminate the enemy force in Vietnam by military means." Even further, if every enemy soldier or sympathizer *was* somehow magically eliminated, the other side would still not make "the kinds of concessions currently demanded"—a divided Vietnam with the South overseen by a government that the people there thought fundamentally illegitimate. "'Military victory' is no longer the U.S. objective," despite what the American government told the American people, and that wasn't even the worst of the lies: "The importance to U.S. national interests of the future political complexion of South Vietnam has been greatly exaggerated, as has the negative impact of the unilateral U.S. withdrawal"—whose risks "will not be less after another year or more of American involvement." The *Times* called them "men of considerable expertise who normally shun publicity" and said that one, "Daniel Ellsberg, spent two years working for the State Department in Saigon before joining Rand." The *New Yorker*, in the issue that hit newsstands three days before the Moratorium, ran a report called "Casualties of War" about a five-man reconnaissance squad who kidnapped and gang-raped a South Vietnamese girl, then murdered her. The anti-antiwar side fought back with a national newspaper ad headlined, "Everyone who wants peace in Vietnam should: TELL IT TO HANOI." It listed in the left-hand column seven steps "the President of the United States has done to end the war in Vietnam." The right-hand column named Hanoi's contribution: "Nothing." It printed a coupon to clip out and send to Citizens for Peace with Security, promising, "We'll see to it that the evidence of your support for the President without dishonor for the United States is transmitted to the enemy in Hanoi. The time has come for the 'silent Americans' to speak out."

Two precisely incommensurate propositions: that either patience or impatience with the war was the road to national dishonor. On the fifteenth, the American people could vote on that referendum with their feet.

Richard Nixon lost. *Life* called it "the largest expression of public dissent ever seen in this country." Two million Americans protested—most for the first time in their lives.

Everywhere, black armbands; everywhere, flags at half-staff; church services, film showings, teach-ins, neighbor-to-neighbor canvasses. In North Newton, Kansas, a bell tolled every four seconds, each *clang* memorializing a fallen soldier; in Columbia, Maryland, an electronic sign counted the day's war deaths. Milwaukee staged a downtown noontime funeral procession. Hastings College, an 850-student Presbyterian school in Nebraska, suspended operations. Madison, Ann Arbor, and New Haven were only a few of the college towns to draw out a quarter of their populations or more (New Haven's Vietnam Moratorium Committee had called up every name in the city phone book). The nation's biggest college town brought out one hundred thousand souls in Boston Common. A young Rhodes Scholar out of

Arkansas, Bill Clinton, got up a demonstration of one thousand people in front of the U.S. embassy in London. *Newsday* publisher and former LBJ right-hand man Bill Moyers, Paris peace talks chief negotiator Averell Harriman, the mayor of Detroit, even the Connecticut state chairman of Citizens for Nixon-Agnew, participated in protests. The *Washington Post* drew a man-bites-dog conclusion: "Anti-Vietnam Views Unite Generations."

George McGovern spoke in Boston and Bangor, Maine—backyard of the new front-runner for the '72 Democratic nomination, Edmund Muskie—where the Great Plains backbencher was announced as "the next president of the United States." Conservative Houston was one of the cities where the names of the war dead were read out in public squares. (A reader stumbled and stopped; he had come upon the name of a friend.) The Duke student newspaper editorialized, "We believe a careful study of history shows that the war in Vietnam is an imperialist conflict. And we support the struggle of the Vietnamese people for their liberation." At the University of North Carolina, the *Village Voice*'s Jack Newfield won an ovation from twenty-five hundred children of the Dixie elite for arguing that the United States had already lost "because we fought on the wrong side."

Another public square was Wall Street, where some twenty thousand businessmen gathered for a procession to Trinity Church, where the ceremony reminded communicants of Martin Luther King's March on Washington. In midtown Manhattan, one hundred thousand marched to Bryant Park to hear Tony Randall, Lauren Bacall, Woody Allen, Shirley MacLaine, both Republican New York senators, and Mayor Lindsay, who draped City Hall with black crepe and ordered all city flags flown at half-staff. The lowly New York Mets were up two games to one against the mighty Baltimore Orioles going into the fourth game of the World Series at Shea Stadium—where the flag was also flying half-staff. People darted in and out of taverns to check the score. At Columbia, Jimmy Breslin reported what the day's starting pitcher, Tom Seaver, had told him, "If the Mets can get to the World Series, the U.S. can get out of Vietnam."

And then there was Washington, D.C. On the evening of the fourteenth, twenty-three congressmen began an intended all-night session on Vietnam on the House floor. Gerald Ford managed to shut them down after four hours. It was the longest time Congress had ever talked Vietnam at a stretch. The next day, congressmen vigiled on the Capitol steps. At lunchtime, bureaucrats at the Department of Health, Education, and Welfare could choose from twelve different antiwar discussions. Or they could simply play hooky, joining the fifty thousand who gathered at the base of the Washington Monument listening to Coretta Scott King say that this war was "destroying the very fabric and fiber of our society."

Then, in ranks of ten, they moved out to the White House.

There wasn't a single Vietcong flag in evidence. There were hardly any

signs at all. There were candles, shimmering in an unbroken line all the way
back to the Washington Monument. (Charleston, West Virginia's police chief
described his city's pro-war counterdemonstration: "We won't creep around
in the dark with candles like those traitors do. . . . We'll march at high noon
on Monday and let free people fall right in line.") An NSC staffer took a
break from working on the president's November 3 speech on Vietnam to
witness the flickering encirclement of the White House. He looked up with
a start: it included his wife and children. The president affected to have
noticed nothing: "I haven't seen a single demonstrator—and I've been out."

Another public square was the nation's high schools. At over a thousand,
students boycotted classes. In Blackwood, New Jersey, Craig Badiali, president of the drama society, and his girlfriend, Joan Fox, a cheerleader, chose
Moratorium day to borrow the Badiali family sedan and to turn it into a carbon monoxide chamber: "Why—because we / love our fellow /man enough
to / sacrifice our lives / so that they will. Try to find the ecstasy in just being
alive."

The MIT student newspaper eulogized, "Two more of the domestic casualties of our war policy and the jungle which is called society. How many
more will there be?"

The conspiracy to sabotage it all had consumed the West Wing. One black
op consisted of sending a letter to every congressional office on simulated
Moratorium letterhead announcing that the vigil had been moved to Union
Station. Yet more ads from the supposedly independent Citizens for Peace
with Security—a White House front—enjoined Americans to blame Hanoi
for the continued warfare. (The man listed in the ads as the group's chairman, William J. Casey, was a former intelligence officer who had lost a 1960
campaign for Congress as a Nixon Republican, then cemented his
Orthogonian bona fides by having his membership application rejected by
the Council on Foreign Relations; in 1971 Nixon nominated him for Securities and Exchange Commission chairman.) Conservative congressmen
were recruited to assail antiwar colleagues for advocating a "bugout" that
would bring "the slaughter of untold millions to Vietnam." Americans
who'd been held hostage by the Communists in Vietnam were wheeled out
as political props. Two POWs had been released by the North Vietnamese
in August. In September, the Pentagon sent them around the country to
describe their "ordeal of horror." And surely their confinements had been
horrible. But journalists noticed their stories became more extravagant and
inconsistent as time went on. The secretary of defense announced of their
captivity: "There is clear evidence that North Vietnam has violated even the
most fundamental standards of human decency." But two years later, when
Seymour Hersh investigated, he discovered a letter from the Pentagon in
which Laird reassured the prisoners' families he was exaggerating: "We are

certain that you will not become unduly concerned over the briefing if you keep in mind the purpose for which it was tailored."

For the first time, the president sent out Spiro Agnew to do what Nixon used to do for Ike: call the administration's critics traitors. On the eve of the protest North Vietnamese prime minister Pham Van Dong broadcast an open letter on Radio Hanoi praising the Moratorium's efforts "to save the honor of the United States and to avoid for their boys a useless death in Vietnam." The vice president demanded the Moratorium's leaders "repudiate the support of a totalitarian government which has on its hands the blood of forty thousand Americans" and said pro-Moratorium congressmen were "chargeable with the knowledge of this letter." The legalistic insinuation— *chargeable*—nicely recalled the master, in 1952, calling President Truman and Secretary Acheson "traitors to the high principles in which many of the nation's Democrats believe."

Jack Caulfield was sent out to investigate the Red hand in the planning. He claimed the Communist Party "has maintained a background identity," with the Socialist Workers Party making "the heaviest outlays of funds." The Kennedys were in on it, too—in order, he said, to keep the media focus away from Chappaquiddick. Two new White House aides who shared a taste for blood, Governor Reagan's former press secretary Lyn Nofziger and an eager former cosmetics company junior executive named Jeb Stuart Magruder, who had run the congressional campaign of Donald Rumsfeld in Illinois in 1962, cranked up the Nixon network to send angry letters to congressmen who supported the Moratorium. It can't be known whether this letter in *Time* was their handiwork—"How tragic, too, Kennedy's professed concern with the loss of lives in Vietnam when he was so negligent about saving the one young life over which he had direct control at Chappaquiddick"—for the president specifically instructed Haldeman to discuss matters concerning Kennedy "only orally."

As the conspiracy to blunt the antiwar upsurge unfolded, Senate minority whip Robert Griffin, a loyal Nixonite, warned the president to withdraw the Haynsworth nomination as yet more shady business deals were revealed. Griffin thought it was friendly advice; the president didn't take it that way. He pledged to "destroy Griffin as whip." A White House that was already ruthless was becoming more so by the day. The hatred of the press became more obsessive. The political wisdom of press-baiting was buttressed by the first major new poll on the subject since the Democratic National Convention: 40 percent trusted local news sources "very much," but only one in four trusted national news. Asked to name a syndicated columnist they paid attention to, only 16 percent of those polled could come up with one (the plurality were advice and humor columnists). The newsmagazine most trusted by its readers was conservative *U.S. News.* David Brinkley summarized the findings: they "want me to shut up."

On October 10 the White House attempted a distraction from the upcoming Moratorium, set for five days later. They announced a major policy address on Vietnam for November 3—which announcement, if tradition held, would lead to columnists' predictions that Nixon was about to announce a major disengagement. That same day the president announced the retirement of the hated General Lewis Hershey as head of the Selective Service Administration. On October 13 White House couriers pulled a kid out of class at Georgetown for a photo opportunity. Randy Dicks had written to the president about his September 26 press conference, "It has been my impression that it is not unwise for the President of the United States to make note of the will of the people." Dicks was selected from thousands of letter-writers to hear back from the president, to show that he cared.

An NSC aide drafted Nixon's response. Kissinger kept on tossing them back: "Make it more manly."

The president ended up saying, "Whatever the issue, to allow the government policy to be made in the streets would destroy the democratic process."

The press corps asked Randy Dicks what he thought of that. Not much, he said, before launching into a peroration about his indifference to "the democratic process": monarchy, he said, "was the superior form of government."

The aides had carefully selected one undergrad. They had carelessly neglected to learn that he was president of something called the Student Monarchist Society.

On Moratorium Day, the aides recruited parachutists to touch down on the Mall and in Central Park, bearing American flags: perhaps the crowd would seize them, maybe burn them, and that would become the story. Instead, the crowds just laughed.

One reason for the enormous Oval Office stress was that November 1 would be coming and going without any swift, savage blow to North Vietnam. The president had shut down Duck Hook, partly for military reasons—fear that the promised knockout blow would be greeted by the enemy as just another love tap—but also partly for political reasons: fear that any new escalation would increase the number of Americans willing to march in the street by an order of magnitude. They would need at least six more months, Kissinger said after the moment passed, to build up the credibility a true escalation would take.

That left the problem of conveying madness some other way.

At an air base off the Atlantic City airport, MPs wondered why they were on twenty-four-hour alert. A team of soldiers stood guard around two B-52s. Their pilots sat in the ready room carrying guns. An MP madly scanned the newspaper in vain for some international crisis. He knew what it meant when B-52 copilots started carrying sidearms. It was for one copilot to shoot the other if he was too chicken to follow orders and drop the big one.

The nuclear alert to convince the Soviet Union that ending the Vietnam War was in their best interests was ordered October 6. It swung into action on October 13, eighteen planes flying eighteen-hour loops over the northern polar ice cap just shy of the USSR. The flights kept up through the end of the month, until Nixon was sure Moscow knew exactly what was taking place—but not a moment longer than that, for then someone else, say China, might notice, too. American bombers and refueling tankers danced so closely that the Strategic Air Command, which had no clue of the purpose of the exercise, worried it might cause an unthinkable accident.

Another antiwar happening was planned for Saturday, November 15. This one might be a little different. White House intelligence had sniffed out a civil war within the antiwar forces. These organizers, the New Mobilization Committee to End the War in Vietnam, were an edgier crowd. The Weathermen were carving out a role for themselves. So was the Revolutionary Contingent in Solidarity with the Vietnamese People, and a faction calling themselves "the Crazies." The "New Mobe" was, for its part, recruiting thousands of marshals whose job it would be to make sure there wasn't violence.

The Moratorium, the Mobe, these congressmen and senators mucking with the prerogatives of the commander in chief: to the White House, they were all tentacles of the same beast. The trick was to convince the country of that, too—"to seize the day and break the back of the sell-out movement in this country," as one White House assistant put it.

Haldeman's desk was the clearinghouse. White House assistant Bill Gavin called for a full-scale "campaign of counterrevolution," an "unrelenting propaganda drive" to convince the media "that they've been *had* by the radicals for the past few years." Dwight Chapin proposed, "In New York the networks should be visited by groups of our supporters—the highest level—and cold turkey should be talked"; then the following Monday morning they should put on a Justice Department press conference to reveal the interlocking revolutionary directorate common to both demonstrations, softening the ground for a weeklong showing of "the appearance of pro-administration sentiment": "thousands of wires, letters, and petitions to the networks"; letters to congressmen; "everyone wearing a flag lapel pin." Another aide suggested patriotic Americans "spontaneously" run their headlights all day November 15 (National Guard officers could order it of their troops). The New Mobe protest was set for a Saturday; perhaps, Chapin suggested, the president could attend a college football game, with a tribute to the commander in chief at halftime.

Tom Charles Huston's memo was the most extravagant. "Secretly, of course, but nevertheless decisively," the White House could set up a phalanx of front groups to rally "in carefully selected sites where it is possible to turn substantial numbers out." Huston even suggested the slogan: "Support the

President and End the War in Vietnam." (The adman Haldeman's response: "Need to work on wording—there's no sex in *Support the P.*")

A warning came forth from Pat Moynihan: some of these war skeptics had supported the president or might do so in the future. Nixon perished the very thought: "No, RN $ and votes came from West and South," he wrote across the memo. It was a strange observation for him to make, considering that he'd won New Jersey, New Hampshire, and Vermont and raised plenty of money from Wall Street; and that the "West and the South" had protested the war on October 15, too. It made sense as a spiritual geography. Pat Buchanan, its most dedicated cartographer, wrote to the president October 17, "Americans are confused and uncertain and beginning to believe they may be wrong and beginning to feel themselves the moral inferiors of the candle carrying peaceniks who want to get out now." The "want to get out now" constituency, in other words, whatever their numerical or geographical distribution, no matter that they included the *Sports Illustrated* "Sportsman of the Year" Tom Seaver (who now recorded a TV commercial: "If the Mets can *win* the World Series, the United States can get out of Vietnam"), were strangers to the group Buchanan labeled "Americans."

The theory was further developed by Richard Nixon's new bulldog, the vice president of the United States.

Agnew was scheduled to speak October 19 at a party fund-raiser in New Orleans. He was still sufficiently low on the White House totem pole that his speeches tended to fixate on the tiny policy portfolio they'd given him (maritime affairs, urban renewal, Native Americans), or to repeat what the president had said the week before. His public appearances ran to affairs like the ribbon-cutting for the Spiro T. Agnew Mental Health Center in Maryland. For New Orleans, his speechwriter drafted him seven dry pages of facts for the party faithful on the administration's accomplishments and goals, thirty-nine methodical bullet points from "casualties for the first nine months of this year are down by two-thirds" to "the Soviets have already deployed 64 ABMs."

Agnew was of a mind to go further. On October 8 and 11, in Texas and Vermont, he'd delivered rip-roaring speeches on the nation's moral crisis. The president, though few others, noticed: three days later he invited Agnew in for a one-on-one meeting and gave him the assignment of answering Pham Van Dong's congratulatory telegram to the peaceniks. Feeling his oats, Agnew decided to pen his own one-page introduction for the New Orleans speech. He turned to his favorite subject: *order.*

"Sometimes it appears that we are reaching a period when our sense and our minds will no longer respond to moderate stimulation. We seem to be approaching an age of the gross. . . .

"The young, and by this I don't mean all the young, but I'm talking about those who claim to speak for the young, at the zenith of physical power and sensitivity, overwhelm themselves with drugs and artificial stimulants. Subtlety is lost, and fine distinctions based on acute reasoning are carelessly ignored in a headlong jump to predetermined conclusion. . . .

"Education is being redefined at the demand of the uneducated to suit the ideas of the uneducated. The student now goes to college to proclaim rather than to learn. The lessons of the past are ignored and obliterated in a contemporary antagonism known as the generation gap.

"A spirit of national *masochism* prevails, encouraged by an effete corps of impudent snobs who *characterize* themselves as intellectuals."

The Moratorium was "a reflection of the confusion that exists in America today," the product of a generation "conditioned since childhood to respond to great emotional appeals . . . an emotional purgative for those who felt the need to cleanse themselves of their lack of ability to offer a constructive solution to the problem. Unfortunately, we have not seen the end. The hard-core dissidents and the professional anarchists within the so-called 'peace movement' will continue to exacerbate the situation. November 15 is already planned—wilder, more violent, and equally barren of constructive result." *Time*'s 1966 Man and Woman of the Year were just children after all. And not innocent ones at that.

Louisiana Republicans took it in with delight. That one unforgettable phrase—"effete corps of impudent snobs"—made front pages all over the country. The next night he spoke in Jackson. Bill Safire and Pat Buchanan helped with the speech. It folded in a bow to the Southern Strategy ("For too long, the South has been the punching bag for those who *characterize* themselves as intellectuals"), then hit even harder: "These arrogant ones and their admirers in the Congress, who reach almost for equal arrogance at times, are bringing this nation to the most important decision it will ever have to make. They are asking us to repudiate principles that have made this country great."

Complaints from Republican Franklins flooded the RNC. Chairman Rogers Morton didn't need to be prodded: he thought this war was too controversial to start using gutter language on its critics. The House and Senate minority leaders, Jerry Ford and Hugh Scott, met with John Mitchell and Harry Dent at the White House and said the word from Republicans up on the Hill was that this was counterproductive, that Agnew should be shut up. They reminded the president of how he had rung in his administration: "*Bring us together . . .*"

Let them howl. "Now have to take the offensive," Haldeman had written in his diary. "Tag those involved with left-wing—and take the heat." For his own part, as if to top Agnew, Ronald Reagan charged antiwar demonstrators with manslaughter: "Some Americans will die tonight because of the activity in our streets." The left wing was scary, getting scarier. The Chicago conspiracy trial had become a spectacle consumed each night on the evening news through courtroom sketches and reporters' incredulous narrations. "I admonish you, sir," the judge would say to Bobby Seale, "that you have a lot of contemptuous conduct against you." "I admonish you," the Black Panther would return, "you are in contempt of people's constitutional rights." Their exchange of insults came to a head October 29, when the judge had Seale handcuffed, gagged, and bound to a metal chair like a slave.

There had, up to then, been a joke about Spiro Agnew: Bob Hope said he'd seen Mickey Mouse wearing a Spiro Agnew watch; that is, Spiro was Mickey Mouse even to Mickey Mouse. But after Agnew delivered his next speech, at a Republican dinner in Harrisburg, Pennsylvania, the day following Bobby Seale's confinement, a new national Agnew was born.

"A little over a week ago," went Spiro's opening witticism, "I took a rather unusual step for a vice president. I said something."

Laughter.

"Particularly, I said something that was predictably unpopular with the people who would like to run the country without running for public office. I said I did not like some of the things I saw happening in this country. I criticized those who encouraged government by street carnival. . . . It appears that by slaughtering a sacred cow I triggered a holy war. I have no regrets. . . . What I said before, I will say again. It is time for the preponderant majority, responsible citizens of this country, to assert *their* rights."

There were no more jokes from then on out. It was the night before Halloween, and this was a scary speech.

The antiwar leaders, he said, were "political hustlers . . . who would tell us our values are lies." They claimed to be for the people. But they "disdain to mingle with the masses who work for a living." They claimed to be leading our youth. But "America cannot afford to write off a whole generation for the decadent thinking of a few," who "prey upon the good intentions of gullible men everywhere," and "pervert honest concern into something sick and rancid. . . .

"They are vultures who sit in trees and watch lions battle, knowing that win, lose, or draw, they will be fed."

They were "ideological eunuchs."

They were "parasites of passion."

"Their interest is personal, not moral."

But they claimed to be your moral betters.

This wasn't "bring us together" anymore; now the administration was up to something else: the bad people, Spiro regretted to have to say, had to be challenged. And "if in challenging we polarize the American people, I say it is time for a *positive polarization*. . . . It is time to rip away the rhetoric and divide on authentic lines."

It was as if he'd been reading the New Left's own theorists—the ones who spoke of "heightening the contradictions." Agnew closed by quoting what one revolutionary, Eldridge Cleaver, whose book *Soul on Ice* had received warm reviews in all the best circles, had said from his "Moscow hotel room": "Many complacent regimes thought that they would be in power eternally—and awoke one morning to find themselves up against the wall. I expect that to happen in the United States in our lifetimes."

Liberals, Agnew said, coddled these outright insurrectionists—people hoping, praying, and *working* for the collapse of American civilization. "Right now," he put it to the Harrisburg Republicans, "we must decide whether we will take the trouble to stave off a totalitarian state. . . . Will citizens refuse to be led by a series of Judas goats down tortuous paths to delusion and self-destruction?"

The bad cop had spoken. Then, on November 3, a Monday, the president filled TV screens from sea to shining sea.

The tone was gentle, grandfatherly, as if he were emulating Ike. He acknowledged the nation's confusion and anger: "I believe that one of the reasons for the deep division about Vietnam is that many Americans have lost confidence in what their government has told them about our policy. The American people cannot and should not be asked to support a policy which involves the overriding issues of war and peace unless they know the truth about that policy. . . . Tonight, therefore, I would like to answer some of the questions that I know are on the minds of many of you listening to me."

There was an acceptance of responsibility (though a selective one: pulling out to "avoid allowing Johnson's war to become Nixon's war . . . would have been a popular and easy course to follow," but he refused to take the easy way out).

There was a history lesson (though selective, too: "Why and how did the United States become involved in Vietnam in the first place?" Because North Vietnam invaded South Vietnam, and we came to their aid "in response to the[ir] request").

There was a gesture of reconciliation: "Let us all understand that the question before us is not whether *some* Americans are for peace, and *some* Americans are against peace. . . . The great question is, How can we win *America's* peace? . . .

"For the future of peace, precipitate withdrawal would thus be a disaster of immense magnitude . . . eventually even in the Western Hemisphere. Ultimately, this would cost more lives. It would not bring peace; it would bring more war. . . . Now that we are in the war," his aim was "the best way to end it."

For Americans disposed to trust their president—the vast majority of Americans—it was a convincing performance. It was, so far, a *boring* speech, intentionally so. It gained its trust by its quiet.

Then he introduced a jarring note:

"For the first defeat in our nation's history would result—"

The first defeat in our nation's history.

Lyndon Johnson had talked of being the first president to lose a war—but only in private. Nixon took the anxiety public. He spoke of the potential of "our defeat and humiliation in South Vietnam. . . . Let us be united for peace. Let us also be united against defeat."

He promised he had come up with a method to end the war: "Vietnamization"—slowly scaling back the American commitment by stepping up the military training of the South Vietnamese army. He assured 70 million Americans that it had already began, that it was already working: 20 percent of American troops would be home by the middle of December, air operations were down 20 percent. He couldn't publicly announce a timetable the way some congressmen wanted—the "enemy would simply wait until our forces had withdrawn and then move in"—but, trust him, he had a timetable in mind, and if anything, the withdrawal was ahead of schedule.

"Honest and patriotic Americans have reached different conclusions as to how peace should be achieved," he allowed.

But there were two ways to end a war. One had been suggested to him in San Francisco.

"In *San Francisco,*" he intoned, gaining intensity, "a few weeks ago, I saw demonstrators carrying signs reading '*Lose* in Vietnam'"—that one word, *lose,* was practically shouted—"'bring the boys home.'

"Well, one of the strengths of our free society is that any American has the right to reach that conclusion. . . .

"But as president of the United States, I would be untrue to my oath of office to be dictated by a minority who hold that view and who try to impose it on the nation by mounting demonstrations in the street."

Quieter than Agnew, Nixon repeated Agnew's argument—about, implicitly, the violent spring offensive on the nation's college campuses; about, implicitly, Woodstock; about the Black Panthers; and about the cultural elite that seemed to gladly countenance it all: "For almost two hundred years, the policy of this nation has been made under our Constitution by those leaders in the Congress and the White House elected by all the people. If a vocal minority, however fervent its cause, prevails over reason and the will of the majority, this nation has no future as a free society."

The conclusion was drenched in bathos.

"It might not be fashionable to speak of patriotism or national destiny these days. But I feel it is appropriate to do so on this occasion." ("Nixon," Jack Newfield wrote in the *Voice,* "you are giving plastic a bad name.")

"Two hundred years ago this nation was weak and poor. But even then, America was the hope of millions in the world. . . . Let historians not record that when America was the most powerful nation in the world, we passed on the other side of the road and allowed the last hopes for peace and freedom of millions of people to be suffocated by the forces of totalitarians."

He then turned the phrase for which the speech became known.

"So tonight, to you, the great—silent—majority of my fellow Americans"—he sounded pleased with himself—"I ask for your support."

He'd spoken since 1967 of "quiet Americans," a "new majority," "forgotten American," "the forgotten majority," "the backbone of America," "the nonshouters, the nondemonstrators." Now he finally found the formulation he'd been grasping for: the *sex* Haldeman sought when he looked for better words than "Support the president and end the war in Vietnam." The *silent majority:* the speech made that case brilliantly—that if you were a *normal* American and angry at the war, President Nixon was the peacenik for you. "Let us be united for peace," he concluded. "Let us also be united against *defeat.* Because let us understand: North Vietnam cannot defeat or humiliate the United States. Only Americans can do that."

Some people wanted peace because they didn't want America to be humiliated. Some people wanted peace because they preferred America's humiliation. Now the president invited Orthogonians to join him in defining themselves by this split—in a wager that the majority on his side would grow for it. Forever more, he would point his speechwriters to "the November 3 speech" as what they should be aiming for. He had declared the United States of Nixonland, and planted Old Glory on her surface.

Nixon's Silent Majority speech came, not coincidentally, the day before state and municipal elections. The results, as the White House expected, provided Nixon a way to illustrate his point. Virginia elected its first Republican governor since Reconstruction. In New Jersey, a Republican won the statehouse for the first time in sixteen years, having campaigned against pornography and for government aid to parochial schools, and did best in areas of strong Wallace support. On the same day, New Jersey also voted down a referendum to lower the voting age to eighteen.

In the cities mayoral candidates succeeded by "making Alabama speeches with a Los Angeles, Minneapolis, and New York accent"—George Wallace said that. In Minneapolis a burglary squad detective named Charlie Stenvin won the mayoralty without the support of either party, against a Republican endorsed by Gene McCarthy and on a platform to "protect law-abiding citizens from hoodlums." (He was asked who his top adviser would be. "God," he replied. "God first of all.") In Los Angeles, a black former cop named Tom Bradley had been predicted to unseat Sam Yorty. Then Yorty said Bradley was the "antipolice" candidate of "black militants and left-wing extremists" and scored a come-from-behind victory. In New York John Lindsay barely won reelection—after losing the Republican primary to a man who called his declaration of the Moratorium on October 15 as a citywide day of mourning "a dagger in the back of American servicemen in Vietnam," and facing a third candidate, conservative Democratic Mario Procaccino, who labeled Lindsay a "limousine liberal" whose supporters "live in penthouses and who send their children to private schools and have doormen and who don't ride the subways." Without that split conservative vote—and without a torrent of focus-group-driven commercials in which Lindsay admitted his mistakes, called his "the second toughest job in the America," and had actor Jack Klugman suggest New Yorkers take a day trip to Newark: "We haven't had a Newark under Lindsay"—his career would have been over. Three out of five New Yorkers voted against him.

Jack Newfield, writing in *Life*, trilled that Lindsay's victory proved a left-wing presidential candidate could defeat Nixon—that "Lindsay has invented, in cynical, fragmented New York, the scale model for a national New Politics campaign in 1972." Nixon trumpeted the municipal election results as clear proof that the nation was behind him, that the Silent Majority was real and the New Politics a chimera. The White House had the better of the argument. Fifty thousand telegrams and thirty thousand letters flooded in praising the Silent Majority speech—far too many to have merely been a Nixon Network setup. The president displayed bales of them, put his feet up among them on his desk, as if they were part of the Oval Office furniture. In an instant poll, 77 percent said they supported his handling of Vietnam (it had been 58 percent before the speech). Only 6 percent opposed it outright. His flash approval rating was 68 percent. Three hundred House members signed a resolution of support.

But the media still controlled the microphones. They were, Nixon was convinced, out to get him.

Before his speech pundits had noted that dovish senators had been letting up on their Vietnam criticism and surmised Nixon had perhaps promised them troop withdrawals, a cease-fire, a bombing halt. One betting line was that he would pledge a pullout of two hundred thousand soldiers over the next twelve months.

So when the network experts went on the air immediately afterward, "no new proposals" seemed to them the news. On ABC, hosted by Howard K. Smith, Averell Harriman held forth: "I'm sure it would be presumptuous to give a complete analysis of a very carefully thought-out speech by the president of the United States." He noted, "I'm sure he wants to end this war and no one wishes him well any more than I do," and that as former chief negotiator in Paris, he was "utterly opposed to these people that are talking about cutting and running." Then, he offered criticisms: Nixon had made out his speech to be a bold departure, but he was still following the advice of "many people who advised President Johnson." Nixon made out the North Vietnamese to be pushing for a military takeover of the South; but "I don't think from the talks we've had that the North Vietnamese, or their colleagues, the VC—NLF—*want* to have a military takeover." Harriman especially scorned Nixon's peroration that those who disagreed with him were a minority: support for Senator Goodell's idea to pull out under a fixed timetable, he pointed out, was 57 percent.

CBS put on Eric Sevareid (Nixon *hated* Eric Sevareid). He called Nixon's position self-contradictory: "If this war and our presence there was of this cosmic and universal importance, then the war should be won, but he has said that it is not to be—a military victory is not to be sought." That cut rather nastily to the quick.

It wasn't all unflattering to Nixon. NBC was generous: they pointed out that after the Moratorium, support for his Vietnam policies had *increased.* Many network commentators noted that if Nixon's preferred candidates did well at the polls the next day—which in fact they did—Nixon would have accomplished something impressive with his Silent Majority bet. These were the proverbial mixed reviews—the kind of thing a president approaching the end of his first year in office with middling approval ratings could reasonably expect.

Unless you were a president who considered these men not experts but enemies. He had spent weeks of twelve-hour days brooding over every comma of twelve drafts of that speech. Now the networks opened their microphones to Averell Harriman, who'd said at a 1950 cocktail party, "I will not break bread with that man," and Howard K. Smith, who'd emceed the 1962 TV special *The Political Obituary of Richard Nixon,* so that they could do nothing but mock him. They had to be destroyed.

The White House was "shotgunning" their enemies in the press, Jeb Magruder argued, spraying instead of focusing their countermeasures. He pointed to two particularly high-powered and precise rifles at their disposal: the Federal Communications Commission, which handed out broadcast licenses, and the Justice Department, whose antitrust division regulated media outlets that owned other media outlets—such as the *Washington Post,* which owned several TV stations. Magruder pointed out they had a new FCC commissioner coming in, one of Barry Goldwater's campaign managers from 1964, Dean Burch.

When Richard Nixon had a dirty job to get done, he often dispatched it to a Goldwater conservative. "Healthy right-wing exuberants" were more likely to understand that civilization was at stake in defeating the enemy, and that the end thus justified the means.

Dean Burch beforehand asked for transcripts of the network commentators' remarks. Herb Klein went down a list of local TV stations and asked if they, too, would be making editorial comment, to chill them before they began.

Then they pulled out the howitzer. Buchanan came up with the idea: "Let Agnew go after these guys!"

The idea came together quickly. The president had a booking at the Midwestern Regional Republican Conference in Des Moines for November 13. The White House sent the president's regrets and said the vice president would speak instead. Buchanan drafted the text, Nixon edited it, and Dean Burch respectfully asked the three networks to air it live. Agnew, acting his part admirably, claimed to be surprised at the presence of the network cameras. Then he said the whole speech had been his idea.

"Monday night, a week ago," it began, "President Nixon delivered the most important address of his administration, one of the most important of the decade. . . . For thirty-two minutes, he reasoned with a nation that has suffered almost a third of a million casualties in the longest war in its history.

"When the president completed his address—an address that he spent weeks in preparing—his words and policies were subjected to instant analysis and querulous criticism. The audience of seventy million Americans— gathered to hear the president of the United States—was inherited by a small band of network commentators and self-appointed analysts, the *majority* of whom expressed, in one way or another, their hostility to what he had to say. . . .

"It was obvious that their minds were made up in advance. . . . One network trotted out Averell Harriman for the occasion. Throughout the president's address he waited in the wings. When the president concluded, Mr. Harriman recited perfectly. . . .

"Every American has a right to disagree with the president of the United States, and to express publicly that disagreement. But the president of the United States has a right to communicate directly with the people who elected him, and the people of the country have the right to make up their own minds and form their own opinions about a presidential address without having the president's words and thoughts characterized through the prejudices of hostile critics before they can even be digested" by "this little group of men who not only enjoy a right of instant rebuttal to every presidential address, but more importantly, wield a free hand in selecting, presenting, and interpreting the great issues of our nation." They became, "in effect, the presiding judge in a national trial by jury."

In actual fact that was how the founders, brave men, intended it. Indeed, they reveled in it. A querulous American press—far more opinionated, nasty, and partisan than anything Nixon would have to suffer—predated American government. Thomas Jefferson used to lay out the most scabrous articles about him in the White House antechamber where emissaries of foreign potentates waited to be received by him. They would stride forth, waving the pages: *Mr. President, are you aware of the things they're writing about you?* Jefferson found nothing so delightful. Yes, he would reply, and they're welcome to say it, and there's nothing I can do about it. This is what America means. But Agnew argued these gentlemen of the media were a usurping cabal.

"A raised eyebrow, an inflection of the voice, a caustic remark dropped in the middle of a broadcast, can raise doubts in a million minds about the veracity of a public official or the wisdom of a government policy. . . . What do Americans know of the men who wield this power? . . . Little, other than that they reflect an urbane and assured presence, *seemingly* well-informed on every important matter. . . . To a man, these commentators and producers live and work in the geographical and intellectual confines of Washington, D.C., or New York City. . . . Both communities bask in their own provincialism, their own parochialism. . . . They talk constantly to one another, thereby providing artificial reinforcement to their shared viewpoint." That viewpoint, what was more, did "*not* represent the view of America. That is why such a great gulf existed between how the nation received the president's address—and how the networks reviewed it.

"The American people would rightly not tolerate this kind of concentration of power in government. Is it not fair and relevant to question its concentration in the hands of a tiny and closed fraternity of privileged men, elected by no one, and enjoying a monopoly sanctioned and licensed by government?"

Howitzering the messenger that controlled the means of interpretation: This. Just. Wasn't. Done. It was another Nixon administration dare that proved brilliant.

Americans took in an increasingly unpleasant world through their TV screens. Agnew told them the fault was not in the world, but in our networks. It was they who "made 'hunger' and 'black lung' disease national issues overnight," who "have done what no other medium could have done in terms of dramatizing the horror of war," who were even responsible for the outrages of the Chicago convention: "Film of provocations of police that was available never saw the light of day, while the film of the police response which the protesters provoked was shown to millions."

Agnew said he wasn't calling for "censorship." But Walter Cronkite called it "an implied threat to freedom of speech." His boss, Frank Stanton, called it "an unprecedented attempt by the vice president of the United States to intimidate a news medium which depends for its existence upon government license." Julian Goodman of NBC said it was an attempt to "deny to TV freedom of the press." David Brinkley, urbane and assured, launched a snooty riposte: "If I went on the air tomorrow night and said Spiro Agnew was the greatest American statesman since Washington, Jefferson, Madison, Adams, and Hamilton . . . the audience might think I was biased. But he wouldn't." Syndicated columnists Braden and Mankiewicz heard Nazism in the speech—the "theme that America's press and television is controlled by a small group of Jews in New York and Washington." Ambassador Harriman himself said it "smacked of totalitarianism."

* * *

Be that as it may, it worked. "Everyone is scared about licenses," a network executive explained to the *Los Angeles Times.* "You can't have a television station without a government license, and you can't have a network without stations." Two days later, the peaceniks gathered in Washington, D.C., for the New Mobilization's "march against death." Conspicuously absent were live network cameras.

They missed a radiant spectacle. At four thirty in the afternoon, in front of the White House, forty thousand pilgrims took turns reciting the names of dead Americans and destroyed hamlets, one after another, until eight thirty the next morning. Each placed a card with the name of one dead in a coffin. The coffins were borne in procession to the Washington Monument to a rolling drum cadence. Three hundred thousand souls took in the subsequent rally. Arlo Guthrie, the folksinging star of *Alice's Restaurant,* spoke last, and most briefly: "I don't need to say anything. It's all been said before." He said it as nine thousand troops were stationed to guard the city, and marines manned a machine-gun nest on the Capitol steps.

"We love America enough to call her away from the folly of war," proclaimed Senator McGovern, who had stuck with the protest after Senators Kennedy and Muskie dropped out when officials warned of plans for "serious violence." McGovern said the cause was too desperate to abandon: "We meet here today because we cherish our flag."

Not everyone did. A small group of street fighters chanting, "War, war, one more war! Revolution now!" had tried and failed to break through the line of marshals to rush the White House—ringed by a barricade of empty city buses, just in case. The morning before the vigil began, crazies had marched down Constitution Avenue forty abreast chanting, "One, two, three, four, we don't want your fucking war!" and carrying signs such as STOP THE TRIAL and BEAT NIXON INTO PLOUGHSHARES, then stoned the Justice Department and bashed in the windows with red flags. Helmeted demonstrators pulled down Old Glory and replaced it with the Vietcong banner. The rioting was subdued with tear gas—leading Congressmen Edwin W. Edwards of Louisiana to complain to Washington's police chief that "gunfire was not only justified but required." Three days earlier, in the middle of the night, a New York collective had bombed the Manhattan Criminal Courts Building. The day before that—Veterans Day—they bombed the empty offices of Chase Manhattan Bank, Standard Oil, and General Motors. "Corporations have made us into insane consumers," their manifesto pronounced. "Spiro Agnew may be a household word but it is the rarely seen men like David Rockefeller of Chase Manhattan, James Roche of General Motors, and Michael Haider of Standard Oil who run the system behind the scenes."

It advanced Richard Nixon's preferred story line admirably: that the peopled who vigiled and the people who rioted were working hand in glove.

*   *   *

A series of newspaper articles that began running November 15 lent credibility to a counternarrative of the radicals: that the Vietnam War was turning the United States into something akin to Nazi Germany. The article headlined "Lieutenant Accused of Murdering 109 Civilians" appeared, not in the *New York Times* or *Washington Post,* but in several midtier papers that subscribed to a small outfit called the Dispatch News Service. The author, Seymour Hersh, couldn't interest the big papers in what he had found.

He reported that in the awful, bloody wake of the Tet Offensive, on March 17, 1968, the leader of a platoon that had suffered heavy casualties, one William L. "Rusty" Calley, twenty-six years old, received orders to retaliate at a hamlet called My Lai. "The orders were to shoot anything that moved," Hersh reported. That would be Calley's court-martial defense: he was only following orders, that he was told the village was an enemy stronghold. "None of the men interviewed about the incident denied that women and children were shot. . . . The area was a free fire zone from which all non–Viet Cong residents had been urged, by leaflet, to flee. Such zones are common throughout Vietnam." A second article recorded the recollections of an eyewitness who had refused to participate: "It was point-blank murder and I was standing there watching it. . . . I don't remember seeing one military-age male in the entire place, dead or alive." A second installment ran November 20. It noted death toll estimates from 170 to 700 and that 90 percent of the company had participated, and that the army only began investigating a year later after receiving a whistle-blowing letter by a former GI. One paper, the *Cleveland Plain-Dealer,* got hold of army photographs of the massacre, and ran them with that second article.

That night, Spiro Agnew gave a speech in Montgomery, Alabama, at the state Chamber of Commerce dinner: "When three hundred Congressmen and fifty-nine senators signed a letter endorsing the president's policy in Vietnam, it was news. . . . Yet the next morning the *New York Times,* which considers itself America's paper of record, did not carry a word. Why?" (He lied; actually the *Times* ran three articles on the resolution in three days.) The papers were "grinding out the same editorial line"—as if they were *Pravda.* "The day when the network commentators and even the gentlemen of the *New York Times* enjoyed a diplomatic immunity from comment and criticism about what they say is over!" Agnew got several standing ovations.

The next Hersh article, on November 25, featured an interview with one of the participants, a twenty-two-year-old coal miner's son from Indiana named Paul David Meadlo: "There must have been about 40 or 45 civilians standing in one big circle in the middle of the village," said Meadlo (who had his right foot blown off by a mine the day after the massacre). "So we stood about 10 or 15 feet away from them. . . . Then he told me to start shooting them. . . . They didn't put up a fight or anything. The women huddled against their children and took it. They brought their kids real close to their stomachs and hugged them, and put their bodies against their children and took it." That night, Meadlo told the same story in an interview on the CBS News. Hersh started getting more and more phone calls from GI's describing atrocities they'd witnessed themselves, going back to 1965.

Senator Ernest "Fritz" Hollings stood up on the Senate floor and asked whether all GIs guilty of "a mistake of judgment" in combat were "going to be tried as common criminals, as murderers"; that Meadlo was "obviously sick"; that a sick man "ought not to be exposed to the entire public."

The senator was contradicted by another interview, on CBS, with a member of the squad who said he had fired 320 bullets at civilians, and that he had been following orders, too.

It was the last Wednesday in November—in time to ruin a million family Thanksgiving dinners. "During World War II, Calley would have been a hero," a father in northern California growled. "Yeah, if you were a Nazi," snapped his teenage son.

The *New York Times* reported from Meadlo's hometown of New Goshen, Indiana: "How can you newspaper people blame Paul David?" "Things like that happen in war. They always have and they always will. But only just recently have people starting telling the press about it." He was "a very nice boy." The idea that massacring innocents was something only the enemy did was built into the rhetorical architecture of the war effort. People struggled to make sense of it all. Spiro Agnew suggested a way: blame the press. A bumper sticker began appearing: SPIRO IS MY HERO.

The next week the My Lai pictures ran in color in *Life:* a boy with a stump where his leg should be; a pile of adult and infant corpses lying on a dusty road like broken toys; a woman splayed in rape position—did she have a head? *Time*'s essay began with an epigram from the president's speech, "North Vietnam cannot defeat or humiliate the United States. Only Americans can do that," and said these "Everymen, decent in their daily lives . . . called in question the U.S. mission in Viet Nam in a way that all the anti-war protesters could never have done." *National Review,* reflecting upon that, cited the atrocities of Sherman's march to the sea: "Does *Time* conclude that the Union, therefore, should have been permitted to disintegrate?" Ronald Reagan and George Wallace were among the right-wingers who said the press was profiteering off the story, and that the photographs were "unverified."

Man-on-the-street interviews began appearing. My Lai "was good," an elevator operator in Boston said. "What do they give soldiers bullets for—to put in their pockets?" A Los Angeles salesman: "The story was planted by Vietcong sympathizers and people inside this country who are trying to get us out of Vietnam sooner." A woman in Cleveland: "It sounds terrible to say we ought to kill kids, but many of our boys being killed over there are just kids, too." Cleveland was where the photos had first run in a paper. The *Plain-Dealer* fielded calls like "Your paper is rotten and anti-American." In a poll by the Minneapolis paper, half the respondents were certain the reports were faked.

On December 8 Richard Nixon faced the press for the first time in months. He said America's Vietnam "record of generosity, of decency, must not be allowed to be smeared and slurred because of this kind of incident. That is why I am going to do everything I possibly can to see that all of the facts of this incident are brought to light and that those who are charged, if they are found guilty, are punished."

Clement Haynsworth had just been turned back by the Senate 55–45 under a cloud of corruption allegations—the first rejection of a Supreme Court nomination in forty years—but the press was kindly in not even asking Nixon about it. The next day, he traveled to New York to be honored by the National Football Foundation for his ability to "confront our problems with steadfastness." Read the plaque, "Courage in the true tradition of our sport has marked your career." Responded Nixon, "The competitive spirit, the ability to lose and come back, to try again . . . the character and drive of our youth is an essential characteristic."

Nixon's motorcade had been forced to detour through a slum to avoid an assassination threat. At his hotel, Nixon harangued Haldeman about how much he hated big cities, as outside the Waldorf-Astoria, five thousand youth showed their character and drive by chanting, "Ho, Ho, Ho Chi Minh, Ho Chi Minh will surely win," dodging counterprotesters with signs reading I LIKE SPIRO and PEACE WITH HONOR, THE SILENT MAJORITY and cops who chased them in and out of a glistening row of Park Avenue Christmas trees.

Another massive rock festival made the papers; at this one, on a sun-parched drag strip outside Altamont, California, Hells Angels beat hippies to death with pool cues. In Chicago, on December 4, seven Black Panthers "staged a wild gun battle with police"—according to the *Chicago Tribune*—in a West Side apartment. "We were met with a shotgun volley" while serving a warrant, the police sergeant said; "our men had no choice but to return fire." On December 9 the prosecution rested in the Chicago conspiracy trial.

Also that week indictments were handed down in the mysterious summer shootings in the Hollywood Hills. It turned out not to be the bloody fallout of some sort of jet-set love triangle after all. The murderers, allegedly, were a "nomadic band of hippies," the *New York Times* reported, led by a thirty-four-year-old guru, Charles Manson, who had picked them up cruising Haight-Ashbury during that 1967 Summer of Love. Four other members of the "Manson Family" were implicated in three other murders. "He played the guitar, he sang," an outsider to the group observed. "He preached love and peace and all that." A female member of the cult—he called them his "slaves"; they referred to him as "God" and "Satan"—explained his appeal: "You're brought up to believe that you can't have sex unless you're married. Here girls could do whatever they wanted." The *Times*'s California correspondent Steve Roberts now reported the victims had been preyed upon by a hippie gang who "lived a life of indolence, free sex, midnight motorcycle races, and apparently blind obedience to a mysterious guru," and recast the Tate-Polanskis as almost just another affluent suburban couple. The December 19 *Life*, above a picture of a wild-eyed Manson, called it "The Love and Terror Cult." "Could Your Daughter Kill?" asked *Los Angeles* magazine.

The Silent Majority had Richard Nixon to protect them. He would bring the My Lai renegades to justice—if indeed that massacre had even happened. He would keep our daughters from killing us. CBS News ran a poll after his December 8 press conference: Nixon's approval rating was 81 percent—up thirty points in two months. In the South, it was 86. Fifty-eight percent now said they wished America had never gotten involved in Vietnam. But then, Richard Nixon said he wished that, too. Sixty-nine percent, in a third poll, agreed that antiwar protesters were "harmful to public life." Nixon was the peacenik they could trust.

CHAPTER TWENTY-ONE

The Polarization

Six of the eleven top-rated TV shows in 1969 were Bob Hope specials. But Bob's annual Christmas special from Vietnam took on a harder edge this year. During their round at Burning Tree Country Club, the president had lined up the comedian as a soldier for positive polarization, and just before the New Mobe protest, Hope sent out a letter to every senator:

"How about a big cheer for the great USA?

"A committee has been formed to salute a work of national unity and I am proud to serve as their national chairman. There are millions of Americans, of all ages, who make up the Silent Majority and we are urging them to participate in activities from coast to coast to display unity in America.

"I certainly hope you will accept my invitation to serve as a co-chairman. Please wire your confirmation to me at Hollywood, California, so that we may unite in this program together.

"Warmest regards,

"Bob 'FOR A WEEK OF NATIONAL UNITY' Hope."

Unity was in the eye of the beholder. Bob's specials had always flown the standard of patriotic reassurance. ("Bob wasn't born—he was woven by Betsy Ross," a friend told *Time* in a 1967 cover feature.) Now the hunger for reassurance was desperate. That was what gave Hope, who started his tour for the first time with a command performance at the White House, his new right-wing edge.

Bantering with Romy Schneider, the German ingenue who costarred in Woody Allen's *What's New, Pussycat?* Hope called Allen "the little spider monkey with the falsetto voice." He called *Laugh-In* "fruitcake galore." He dipped into drug humor to reach his live audience; "GI's in Vietnam High on Hope's Marijuana Jokes," the *New York Times* reported from Vietnam December 23. But none of those jokes made it into the broadcast when it ran in January. That would have soured the story they were telling—that the old, good, pure Betsy Ross America that only talked about sex with a wink and nudge was still going as strong as ever.

But jingoism was a difficult sell these days. At First Division Headquarters, the camera panned over the crowd, the traditional mocking banners (WELCOME, BING CROSBY!)—but many weren't wearing shirts; most had shaggy hair; some wore mustaches and necklaces with garish medallions. Tom Sawyer–faced Neil Armstrong, the first man to step on the moon, an icon of the new square chic—he brought his fraternity pin along on Apollo 11—did a question-and-answer session. The NBC cameras trained upon a blond nurse in hippie sunglasses asking him in all earnestness "when you're going to take the first woman to the moon." Armstrong answered with leering innuendo. Bob chimed in with a joke about diet-conscious ladies: "I'm sure they'll all go when they find they can go up there and be weightless." Meanwhile, the camera found a banner out in the crowd: a peace symbol and the circle-and-cross emblem of women's liberation.

The show ended, as always, with a sentimental Bob Hope exhortation. This year it folded in clumsy damage control for My Lai: "The numbers of them who devote their free time, energies, and money to aiding Vietnamese families and caring for orphans would surprise you. Or maybe it wouldn't. I guess you know what kind of guys your brothers and the kids next door are. . . . They need our full support. . . . They deserve our backing to a man, and our prayers. It's the least you can do. Good night."

Betsy Ross was taking on a partisan edge, too. Eighteen million *Reader's Digest* subscribers received detachable flag decals inside the special February 1969 "America in Transition" issue. Thirty-one million more wrote in to request one. The left-wing folksinger John Prine responded, in song, upon "digesting *Reader's Digest* in the back of a dirty book store," that waving flags didn't "get you into heaven anymore—they're already too crowded from your dirty little war." Five years after Lyndon Johnson was elected on a platform of consensus, every conceivable cultural expression fell to one or another side of the American ideological divide.

Smart businessmen figured out ways to sell to both sides. The Christmas season's most brilliant entrepreneur was surely the guy who invented the Spiro Agnew wristwatch. Hipsters bought it as a kitschy screw-you to his admirers. The Silent Majority bought it as a screw-you to his detractors. Soon TV producer Norman Lear would have a new hit show, *All in the Family.* The sympathetic character was supposedly the long-haired, liberal son-in-law. The racist, know-nothing father was the butt of the jokes. Lear never dreamed what would happen next: Archie Bunker was embraced as a hero by the very people the show was meant to lampoon.

To be taken seriously as a voice of cultural authority you had to somehow straddle the cultural canyon. The nation's flagship Panglossian weekly, *Time,* had chosen as its 1966 Man of the Year "not just a new generation, but a new kind of generation." In 1969 they excused that generation's LSD-taking as a near-religious sacrament. The editors had placed a *Time* sort of bet: that they could frictionlessly ease new sensibilities into the mainstream, the better to shore up consensus. This year they made a different bet by naming as "Men and Women of the Year" the "Middle Americans"—"a state of mind, a morality, a construct of values and prejudices and a complex of fears."

Middle Americans were those whom "pornography, dissent, and drugs seemed to wash over . . . in waves, bearing some of their children away." They loved the moon shot—"a victory purely accomplished." "'This,' they will say with an air of embarrassment that such a truth needed be stated at all, 'is the greatest country in the world. Why are people trying to tear it down?'" And though *Time* couldn't bring itself to admire all their enthusiasms (Middle Americans liked Spiro Agnew, the editors claimed, only "to some extent"), it celebrated Richard Nixon for reflecting, "like many Middle Americans," a "contradictory mixture of liberal and conservative impulses." He was "pursuing not so much a 'Southern strategy' as a Middle American strategy." "His draft reforms, instituting selection by lottery, brought a new equity to the Selective Service system." He'd ended U.S. production of biological weapons, begun the Strategic Arms Limitation Talks (SALT) with the Soviet Union. He was "allowing some Southern school districts more time to formulate their desegregation plans," but chose as his chief justice Warren Burger, whose Supreme Court "unanimously rejected the delays": perfect equipoise.

Some of the Middle Americans *Time* profiled were bitter. Richard W. Paul, forty-three, a white-collar worker at GE in Pittsfield, Massachusetts, said, "I'm angry because I keep getting kicked around. I'm getting squeezed by the Urban Coalition, these bankers, everybody who thinks they are doing these poor people a favor by moving them into somebody else's backyard—as long as it isn't their backyard." But the package ended with a feature on nine former high school football stars in a small Arizona town who joined the marines together on Independence Day, 1966. "Only three of Morenci's nine Marines made it back alive. . . . Yet none of the three is really angry about the war."

Perfect equipoise: a perfect fantasy. A more realistic American tableau was unfolding in Chicago, where the conspiracy trial was at its entropic height.

During jury selection, the questions the defense wanted the pool to be asked included "Do you know who Janis Joplin and Jimi Hendrix are?" and "If your children are female, do they wear brassieres all the time?" In a pretrial hearing Judge Hoffman described the "intent" standard by which the defendants were to be judged: "The substance of the crime was a state of mind." (That was just the way *Time* had defined Middle America: a state of mind.) To that standard, the defense was glad to accede. When the twelve jurors turned out to be middle-class and middle-aged, except for two girls in their early twenties, Leonard Weinglass, the lead defense attorney, moved for a mistrial, claiming his clients weren't being judged by a jury of their peers—which would have to be chosen also from people *not* drawn from the voter rolls, because blacks, the young, dropouts, and misfits were not well-enough represented on them.

The government had selectively indicted to display a cross-section of the monstrous personages rending the good order of American civilization: the older guru (David Dellinger); two long-haired freaks (Abbie Hoffman and Jerry Rubin); the by-any-means-necessary Negro (Bobby Seale); two SDS militants (Tom Hayden, Rennie Davis); two radical young faculty members (a chemistry professor, John Froines, and a sociology professor, Lee Weiner, who were supposed to have planned a bombing). The prosecutors warned on TV that the defendants might walk into court the first day naked.

That didn't happen, though when court adjourned on New Year's Eve defendant Froines and his girlfriend did pass out autographed nude posters of themselves.

The jury was sequestered every minute they were outside the Federal Building: if states of minds were on trial, even the cultural air was prejudicial (some stories they missed: the Mobilization, the Silent Majority speech, the Moratorium, the rise of Spiro Agnew, the second moon shot, the My Lai massacre). They received a respite from cabin fever the day after Christmas when they were treated to a *Disney on Parade* show. But even that was prejudicial: the monkeys in the *Jungle Book* number were go-go girls. *Alice in Wonderland* was done up in psychedelic patterns.

Jerry Rubin called his indictment "the Academy Award for protest." Judge Julius Hoffman seemed to relish the notion. "Tell me something," he asked *New York Times* reporter Tony Lukas, who had called up to ask for press credentials. "Do you think this is going to be the trial of the century?"

Outside, trial marshals confiscated spoons, books, compacts, nail clippers, attaché cases—and two pistols. Defense sympathizers waited half the night in line for a spot in the gallery; the judge gave seats instead to Chicago socialites (one hippie who survived the gauntlet leapt up in the spectators' gallery during a defense argument to cry "Right on!" and was swarmed so badly a witness thought marshals might have broken some bones). When Bobby Seale's family managed to get seats, Judge Julius Hoffman summoned a marshal and had these strange people with bushy Afros removed. The jury wouldn't be able to watch his child's and wife's reactions when Seale was bound and gagged like a slave. They weren't there on November 5, 1969, either, when Judge Hoffman sentenced Seale to an unprecedented four years in prison for sixteen counts of contempt of court and severed his case from the rest, turning the Chicago 8 into the Chicago 7. Reporters made a mad dash for the phones. The courtroom marshals unpinned their badges, put them into their pockets, and scoured the jammed courtroom for anything else sharp, fearing an outbreak of hand-to-hand combat.

The next day a defense lawyer argued the four-year sentence was illegal and asked the judge to explain himself. Judge Hoffman replied, "I have known literally thousands of what we used to call Negro people and who are now referred to as black people, and I have never heard that kind of language emanate from the lips of any of them." That was the day Bob Hope sent out his letter to senators "FOR A WEEK OF NATIONAL UNITY."

Judge Julius J. Hoffman was a strutting, little bantam cock of a man. On the first day of jury selection he read out the indictment to the jury pool like a nineteenth-century thespian. Defense lawyer William Kunstler objected. Judge Hoffman boomed, *"Motion denied!"* and said he'd never apologize for "the vocal facilities the Lord hath given me." When one of his young law clerks was told to prepare a denial of the defendants' motion to see the wiretap logs and replied, "But, Judge, that's not fair," citing the plain letter of the law, the old man flew into a rage that awed his clerk—who was told not to return to work after his vacation.

Federal judge selection was supposed to be random. But in Chicago, the fix was always in. In big mob cases, the state always angled to argue before Judge Hoffman: he always decided against the defendant and made the prosecuting attorneys look like heroes. He "is the bane of do-gooders who would give every bum a second chance, and a third and a fourth and a fifth," *Chicago's American* said. He was also a self-hating Jew who took willful pleasure in mispronouncing his fellow Jews' names (Weinglass: "Fineglass," "Weintraub," "Weinruss," "Weinrob") and wouldn't let one witness wear a yarmulke in court ("Take off your hat, sir"). He popped a vein when Abbie Hoffman called himself his "illegitimate son," but hated David Dellinger ("Derringer," "Dillinger") most of all: he was a WASP who'd surrendered privileges the judge so dearly wished to possess. Hoffman was especially taken aback when one of the defendants informed him that the plaque for the Northwestern Law School classroom named after him had been ripped from the wall.

"The *plaque*?"

"Apparently while the board of trustees feels affection for you, the student body does not."

The defense was determined to put the war on trial and the defendants' lifestyle on proud display (the Boston 5 had "sat like good little boys called into the principal's office," Dr. Spock had pointed out, and were railroaded nonetheless). The Chicago defendants were determined to show why their state of mind was morally *superior.* The seventy-four-year-old they called Mr. Magoo was a hanging judge, hired to grease the rails for a conviction that would only be overturned on appeal. It was a show trial. So why not put on a show?

The prosecution presented its case first. Their witnesses were undercover infiltrators. Once, when a witness was called just as one of the defendants exited a side door, the rest of the Chicago 7 braced themselves: was one of *their own* a police spy? (Actually, he was just going to the bathroom.)

One prosecution witness was simultaneously a member of the executive committee of Veterans for Peace, the Chicago Peace Council, the New Mobilization Committee to End the War—and the Chicago Police Department Red Squad. The people most useful in the movement, radicals often learned too late, were the ones later revealed to be spies; being paid for their time by the government, they were the most avid "volunteers." Another had enrolled in the Northeastern Illinois State College SDS and had led a group that pushed Northeastern's president off a speaker's platform. (The most militant activists, radicals also discovered too late, were often police-agent provocateurs.) He testified that Rennie Davis said their plan to recruit for Chicago was to "lure them here with music and sex"; at the meeting where he claimed he heard that, he himself had suggested disabling army jeeps with grappling hooks. A third prosecution witness was a college newspaper reporter hired as a spy by the *Chicago's American* columnist Jack Mabley. A fourth had worked as Abbie Hoffman and Jerry Rubin's dirtbag motorcycle-gang "bodyguard." A fifth was a policewoman who'd dressed for her work in Lincoln Park every day in white hippie bell-bottoms carrying a .38 Colt in her bag.

This witness, Officer Barbara Callender, testified blushingly, "Every other word was that F-word."

Cross-examination: "Haven't you ever heard that word in the station house?"

The government objected to the line of questioning. The objection was sustained. Part of the prosecution's strategy was to establish that the defendants were obscene. Ten days later, when another Red Squad member testified, he said he'd told a newsman "to turn the *censored* cameras around because of that civilian brutality." His side believed it was obscenity to say [censored] without blushing; the other believed it was obscenity during an evil war to save your shame for mere words: the war was the obscenity. (A joke going around the New Left: a policeman tells a protester to come back after she has removed the obscenity from her FUCK THE WAR placard and she returns with one reading FUCK THE _____.)

The prosecutors, U.S. Attorneys Richard Schultz and Thomas Aquinas Foran, were perfectly cast. Schultz was so ploddingly literal-minded he could call the most obvious Yippie put-ons devious incitements to riot. Foran was a Democrat who said he had been a closer friend of the late Bobby Kennedy's than Tom Hayden had been. In his summation he spoke of his empathy for the kids, who "feel that the lights have gone out in Camelot." But "these guys take advantage of them. They take advantage of it personally, intentionally, evilly, and to corrupt those kids, they use them, and they use them for their purposes and for their intents. And you know what are their purposes and intents? . . . This is in their own words: to 'disrupt.' To 'pin delegates in the Convention hall.' To 'clog streets.' To force the use of troops. To have actions so militant the Guard will have to be used. . . . 'Tear this city apart.' 'Fuck up this convention.' . . . 'We'll lure the McCarthy kids and other young people with music and sex and try to hold the park.'"

The prosecution's aim was to reduce a complex stew of motives, interests, approaches, and personalities to a concentrated, unified plot. They said David Dellinger, the Gandhian who had little direct role in Chicago, was only pretending to be a pacifist and was really the rioting's "chief architect" ("Oh, bullshit. That is a complete lie," Dellinger shouted. "Did you get that, Miss Reporter?" Judge Hoffman replied, and revoked Dellinger's bail). Prosecutors said the ham-handed self-defense training in Lincoln Park was combat training. Patrolman Frapolly described a meeting in which he claimed he heard plans to throw burning flares at the cops.

Mr. Foran: "Were any of the defendants present?"

The Witness: "Yes. Weiner and Froines were at this meeting. So was Abbie Hoffman."

Mr. Foran: "Do you see Mr. Hoffman here in the courtroom?"

The Witness: "Yes, I do."

Mr. Foran: "Would you step down and point him out, please."

The Witness: "Mr. Hoffman is sitting with the leather vest on, the shirt— he just shot me with his finger. His hair is very unkempt."

The hippies' hippie-ness was on trial; style was a battleground. Abbie Hoffman, asked why they lured innocent youth to Chicago with sex and rock bands, replied, "Rock musicians are the real leaders of the revolution." Posture was a battleground. When Judge Hoffman admonished William Kunstler not to slouch on the lectern designed by the Federal Building's distinguished architect Mies van der Rohe, Abbie replied, "Mies van der Rohe was a Kraut." He added that the courtroom was a "neon oven"—thus deploying his Madison Avenue brilliance in the service of the defendants' pet theory that America was becoming Nazi Germany. Pencils, even, became a battleground: "primly squared off and neatly sharpened beside a few neatly stacked memos on the prosecution table," the *Evergreen Review*'s John Schultz wrote; "askew and gnawed and maybe encrusted with a sliver of earwax," a proud part of the "unholy clutter," on the defense table. (When Abbie Hoffman, a very hard worker, took the stand, he said, "*Work* is a dirty word instead of *fuck* is a dirty word.")

Humor was a battleground most of all.

The judge fancied himself a rapier wit. But when the defense table laughed *at* him, or *with* the defense—as when Abbie and Jerry showed up in judicial robes—he made sure the court reporter got it in the record, for in the courtroom laughter wasn't appropriate. Which jurymen laughed when was how both sides kept score.

Based on that calculus, when the prosecution rested on December 9, the day after the Nixon press conference that earned him a snap 81 percent approval rating, movement sympathizers predicted a hung jury. That prediction led to a debate in the defense camp. Tom Hayden said that, since they weren't going to be convicted, they could best get on with the revolution if they rested their case without mounting a defense, ending the affair in a mistrial. Others—Abbie, Jerry—said the trial *was* the revolution. The Yippies won: they would use their defense to introduce "Woodstock Nation"—the title of Abbie's new book—to America. They would fight through the jungles of TV.

They spoke at colleges, women's clubs, and churches to raise money for their defense, to warm receptions. At a tony synagogue in suburban Highland Park, Illinois, fourteen hundred turned out to hear them. At universities they were treated like the Beatles. At a University of Chicago rally, Rennie Davis announced he would continue fighting the way he was fighting even if they put a pistol to his head: "How can you be a young person and have any other position?"

Thomas Aquinas Foran would have said the same thing, if asked about his own position.

It seemed an auspicious week to indict an Establishment gone mad. As Wednesday night, December 3, 1969, became Thursday morning, December 4, what the *Chicago Tribune* had called the "wild gun battle" at Black Panther headquarters in a West Side apartment building left two Panthers, twenty-one-year-old leader Fred Hampton and lieutenant Mark Clark, twenty-two, dead. Lewis Koch, the young New Left producer for the local NBC affiliate, smelled a rat in the cops' claim they were met with "a shotgun volley." He'd seen film of the cops leaving the building: smiling, embracing, exulting as if they'd won a football game—not the behavior of men who had just survived an ambush. He put Panther Bobby Rush on the afternoon news the next day, who called it cold-blooded murder and invited viewers to the apartment to see for themselves. The *Chicago Daily News* columnist Mike Royko took him up on his offer. The morning that the conspiracy-trial prosecution rested its case, Royko published a column called "The Hampton Bullet Holes." According to the police account, Royko wrote, "miracles occurred. The Panthers' bullets must have dissolved in the air before they hit anybody or anything. Either that or the Panthers were shooting in the wrong direction—namely, at themselves." Royko had examined the building with a ballistics expert, who identified at least seventy-six bullets coming in, including twenty-four in the wall near Hampton's bed—and not a single one coming out.

Chicago cops failed to secure the crime scene. People lined up around the block to tour the open-and-shut evidence. Years later it came out that the

FBI COINTELPRO had provided Chicago cops with the floor plans of the apartment, and an FBI infiltrator had slipped secobarbital in Fred Hampton's drink the previous evening to make it easier to murder him in his bed. Such revelations would only have confirmed what the Chicago 7 defense already knew: the "justice system" wasn't a system of justice, "law and order" was a cover for state-sponsored crime.

Those same days the last cop indicted for crimes during convention week was on trial. The jury absolved him of beating a twenty-year-old hitchhiker after only an hour of deliberation. The prosecution was so convincing, the defense so obviously false, the shocked judge implored of the foreman, "Are you certain, not guilty?"

The Silent Majority was practicing jury nullification, just as the Chicago 7 opened their defense.

The first defense witness was a supervisor at a candy factory. He displayed slides he had taken of police chopping their way through a crowd, kicking kids when they were down—without provocation, he said. The next day he was fired from his job. And any pretense to a straight defense was abandoned. The prosecution said the Chicago 7 had lured lambs to slaughter with music and sex. So the Chicago 7's defense would be . . . music and sex.

Jacques Levy, director of *Oh! Calcutta!* (the off-Broadway play where the cast took off their clothes), Timothy Leary, Allen Ginsberg, Country Joe McDonald were all called to the stand. ("Dr. Leary, what is your present occupation?" "I am the Democratic candidate for governor in California." "Doctor, can you explain what a psychedelic drug is?") Judy Collins broke out into a chorus of "Where have all the flowers gone?" (Judge Hoffman: "We don't allow singing in this court.") William Kunstler presented folksinger Phil Ochs with exhibit D-147, the guitar he'd used to perform "I Ain't Marching Any More" at the Festival of Life. He, too, tried and failed to sing.

The following colloquy ensued: Abbie Hoffman had "led the crowd in a chant of 'Fuck LBJ,' didn't he?"

"Yes, I think he did. . . ."

"Now, in your plans for Chicago, did you plan for public fornication in the park?"

Allen Ginsberg had been in Chicago helping calm things with his Buddhist chants. Judge Hoffman had once been an ally of Ginsberg's. He'd ruled in 1960 that the avant-garde Chicago literary magazine *Big Table* wasn't obscene, noting that William S. Burroughs's *Naked Lunch* was intended "to shock the contemporary society in order perhaps to better point out its flaws and weaknesses," quoting the *Ulysses* decision on the subversive necessity of art. But that was a different age, when such nuances were possible. Now everyone had to choose a side.

One day a clerk at Barbara's Bookstore in Old Town saw a middle-aged man pacing around. A member of the prosecution team, he asked, "Do you have any of Allen Ginsberg's books?" She went to hunt some down. He said, "Could you hurry up? The future of the country may depend on this."

Later that day, on the stand, Ginsberg explained, "I was chanting a mantra called the Mala Mantra, the great mantra of preservation of that aspect of the Indian religion called Vishnu the Preserver."

Thomas Aquinas Foran leafed through one of his newfound literary treasures.

Mr. Foran: "In *The Empty Mirror,* there is a poem called 'The Night Apple'?"

The Witness: "Yes."

Mr. Foran: "Would you recite it for the jury?"

The Witness:

THE NIGHT APPLE

Last night I dreamed
of one I loved
for seven long years,
but I saw no face,
only the familiar
presence of the body;
sweat skin eyes
feces urine sperm
saliva all one
odor and mortal taste.

Foran, sarcastically: "Could you explain to the jury what the *religious* significance of that poem is?"

Ginsberg, earnestly: "If you could take a wet dream as a religious experience, I could. It is a description of a wet dream, sir."

Defense witness Linda Hager Morse was a pretty Quaker girl from Philadelphia who had won the Kiwanis Decency Award and first marched for peace on New York's Fifth Avenue in 1965. She was now a revolutionary. The defense wanted her to talk about why it was necessary to overthrow capitalism. The judge ruled that out of order. The prosecution, however, was glad to pick up the thread in cross-examination, and the judge was glad to let them. What Morse said encapsulated the strangeness of the last four years of American history. One part sounded quite like Lyndon Johnson's Great Society speech: "My ultimate goal is to create a society where everyone is fed, where everyone is educated, where everyone has a job, where everyone has a chance to express himself artistically or politically, or spiritually, or religiously" (Johnson: "*a society of success without squalor, beauty without bar-*

renness, works of genius without the wretchedness of poverty"). The other part couldn't have been further afield from Johnson's consensus bromides. Assistant DA Schultz posed the question: "You practice shooting an M1 yourself, don't you?"

The Witness: "Yes, I do."

Mr. Schultz: "You also practice karate, don't you?"

The Witness: "Yes, I do."

Mr. Schultz: "That is for the revolution, isn't it?"

The Witness: "After Chicago I changed from being a pacifist to the realization that we had to defend ourselves. A nonviolent revolution was impossible. I desperately wish it was possible."

Rennie Davis thought this was the defense's most effective witness with the jury. He asked a reporter what *he* had thought of Morse's testimony. The reporter's answer spoke to the polarization: "It certainly was a disaster for you. Now you've really had it."

Could your daughter kill?

The defendants had intended to win the sympathy of the big jury out there, the general public. Their message was seen through a glass darkly. "What *did* go on in Judge Julius Hoffman's courtroom?" asked the back cover of one of the many paperback books that appeared later reproducing court transcripts. With no cameras to record it, it was hard to know. Afterward a friend asked Tony Lukas of the *Times* which of the defendants had defecated in the aisle of the courtroom.

Most newspaper coverage came from secondhand wire reports, built from a written record that the judge made sure reflected every defense outrage and whitewashed every prosecution one. The *Times*'s Lukas paid careful attention to such unfairness, but his editors pruned him ruthlessly: Abbie Hoffman always "shouted"; Judge Hoffman always "said" (even if it was really the other way around). To much of the public, the presumption was that the defecation was nonstop.

William Kunstler offered his summation to the jury on February 13, 1970: "I think if this case does nothing else, perhaps it will bring into focus that again we are in a moment of history when a courtroom becomes the proving ground of whether we do live free or whether we do die free. . . . Perhaps if you do what is right, perhaps Allen Ginsberg will never have to write again as he did in 'Howl,' 'I saw the best minds of my generation destroyed by madness,' perhaps Judy Collins will never have to stand in any courtroom again and say, as she did, 'When will they ever learn?'"

Thomas Foran offered his summation: "At the beginning of this case they were calling them all by diminutive names, Rennie and Abbie and Jerry, trying to pretend they were young kids. They are not kids. . . . They are highly sophisticated, educated men, and they are evil men."

The jury returned their verdict after five days. All seven were acquitted on the conspiracy count. Froines and Weiner were acquitted of the charge they'd constructed an incendiary device. But Dellinger, Davis, Hayden, Hoffman, and Rubin were found guilty on the indictment's counts two through six, which cited Title 18, United States Code, Section 201—the provision of the Civil Rights Act of 1968, passed to honor the martyr Martin Luther King, outlawing the "travel in interstate commerce . . . with intent to incite, organize, promote, and encourage a riot" and to "speak to assemblages of persons for the purposes of inciting, organizing, promoting, and encouraging a riot."

The liberal editorialists praised the jury's ruling as judicious and well considered, a complex split decision: the system worked. Spiro Agnew called it an "American verdict." It was indeed an American verdict: almost as soon as the trial began, the jury had split into polarized camps. One believed the defendants were not guilty on all accounts. The other believed they were guilty on all counts. Only three jurors actually agreed with the decision as rendered.

They had socialized apart, eaten apart—and, when together, spent most of their time in the jury room debating child-rearing philosophy. One of the convict-on-all-accounts jurors talked about the time she took her willful daughter to see a shrink who said she just needed "love and patience"—and how she stalked out saying of her daughter that she needed to have something "shoved down her throat." They voiced their fears that their children would end up hippies, said things like "They are evil" and "This is like Nazi Germany—hippies want to take over the country" and "They had no right to come into your living room." The liberal jurors argued that slovenliness wasn't a crime, the prosecution was corrupt, and that for the first time they were afraid the government might be spying on *them*. They wondered whether the antiriot statute was constitutional. At that, the conservative side wondered, if the law didn't protect decent people from *this*, then what did it protect them from?

A journalist later observed the sociology that divided the two groups. "The convict-on-all-counts jurors tended to be people who had moved recently from the city of Chicago itself to the suburbs. They were the hardline we-worked-hard-and-won-our-way-according-to-the-standard-rules-of-social-mobility-people. . . . The acquittal jurors tended to be those who had been longer situated in the suburbs or outlying parts of the city, and were easier in their attitudes about raising children."

Franklins and Orthogonians: they hated each other too much to agree on anything. They sent out notes to the judge that they were a hung jury. The judge refused to accept them: "Keep deliberating!" A juror finally brokered the split-verdict compromise. Judge Hoffman still was not satisfied. So he exercised his discretionary power. Over two long days, he called each defendant and each defense lawyer before the bench and delivered contempt specifications for each act of schoolboy naughtiness, sometimes reading out long stretches from the record: *"Specification 1:* On September 26, during the opening statement by the Government, defendant Hoffman rose and blew a kiss to the jurors. Official Transcript, Page 9."

Abbie Hoffman got a day in jail for that. He got six days for calling the judge, in Yiddish, *shanda für di goyim.* (The judge read the phrase, which meant "a Jew who shames Jews in front of the gentiles," from the transcript haltingly and pronounced, "I can't understand the following words.") David Dellinger had insisted, on Moratorium Day, on reading a list of the war dead. For that, he got six months.

The law had spoken. John Lindsay responded, "The blunt, hard fact is that we in this nation appear headed for a new period of repression—more dangerous than at any time in years." Foran, at a booster club rally at a parochial high school, said, "We've lost our kids to the freaking fag revolution." Rennie Davis said that when he got out of jail, "I intend to move next door to Tom Foran and bring his sons and daughters into the revolution" and "turn the sons and daughters of the ruling class into Vietcong." Jerry Rubin signed his new book—*Do It!*—to "Judge Hoffman, top Yippie, who radicalized more young Americans than we ever could." And Tom Hayden said, "*Our* jury now is being heard from."

In Ann Arbor, five thousand students and hangers-on marched to city hall busting windows and wrecking cars. The FBI put a "White Panther" on the ten most wanted list, who wrote from exile in the Michigan woods, "I don't want to make it sound like all you got to do is kill people, kill pigs, to bring about revolution," but "it is up to us to educate the people to the fact that it is war, and a righteous revolutionary war." In Madison a student stole an Air Force ROTC training plane and tried to bomb an army ammunition plant (just as a student radical stole a plane in the newly released *Zabriskie Point*).

The preliminaries in the trial of the "Manson Family" were all over the news: Manson had hoped, it turned out, to foment a race war. Weatherman Bernardine Dohrn said of the murders, "Dig it, first they killed the pigs, then they ate dinner in the same room with them, then they even shoved a fork into a victim's stomach! Wild!" On February 17, what appeared to be a copy-cat crime emerged, a hideous attack on a military family: a Green Beret captain, Jeffrey MacDonald, reported regaining consciousness from a knife attack to find his wife and two children, Kristen and Kimberly, dead. He remembered what one of the intruders, a woman wearing a "floppy hat" and carrying a burning taper, chanted: "Acid is groovy, kill the pigs."

In St. Louis, at 2 a.m. on February 23, the Quonset hut housing Washington University's Army ROTC program was burned to the ground. In frigid Buffalo, on February 24, the president of the State University of New York campus summoned cops to control the threatened disruption of a basketball game. The next night, forty students stormed his office. A police squad chased them into the student union. Eight hundred students attacked the police. At the precinct house, amid the Jewish-looking haul, one arrestee heard a cop say that America "should have let Hitler win, he'd have known how to take care of these fuckers."

That same day, William Kunstler, facing two years in jail for contempt of Judge Hoffman's court, gave a speech at the UC–Santa Barbara stadium. Ten years earlier he had dropped out of the executive-training program at R. H. Macy's; how things had changed. "I have never thought that [the] breaking of windows and sporadic, picayune violence is a good tactic," he now said. "But on the other hand, I cannot bring myself to become bitter and condemn young people who engage in it." Students whistled and cheered. Hundreds strolled to a rally in the adjacent town of Isla Vista. One of them idly swung around a bottle of wine. The cops, thinking it a Molotov cocktail, arrested him. Violence broke out. Kids burned down a Bank of America branch. Ronald Reagan ordered his attorney general to look into charging Kunstler with crossing state lines to incite a riot.

On March 6 a mysterious explosion collapsed an entire town house in Greenwich Village. Cops searching through the rubble pulled out three dead bodies and enough live-wired dynamite bombs to blow up the entire block if detonated at once. The house had been a bomb factory, and one of the bombs was intended to slaughter attendees at an upcoming dance at Fort Dix. One decapitated body was identified by a print taken from the severed little finger of the right hand: Diana Oughton, a Weatherman. Another was a leader of the 1968 Columbia University strike. The third was a Weatherman based at Kent State University, in Ohio.

On March 11 a bomb gashed a chunk out of the corner of the Dorchester County Courthouse in Maryland, site of pretrial hearings for H. Rap Brown for inciting the burning of the schoolhouse in Cambridge in 1967.

The next night, in Buffalo, hundreds of students fought a running battle with police, throwing Molotov cocktails at the faculty peace monitors trying to keep the two sides apart.

Three days later Judge Hoffman received an enthusiastic clap on the shoulder from Richard Nixon. He was a special guest at the president's weekly Christian service in the East Room, where the Reverend Billy Graham preached that America's "differences could melt in the heat of a religious revival."

In New York City one day in March, fifteen thousand people were evacuated from office buildings from three hundred separate bomb threats. On April 4, Governor Reagan, in a reelection campaign speech to the Council of California Growers, said of government's dilemma of beating back the mounting violence, "If there is to be a bloodbath, let it be now." That America was in the middle of a civil war had once been but a metaphor. How soon before it became real?

CHAPTER TWENTY-TWO

Tourniquet

I N THE NIXON ADMINISTRATION, A BUREAUCRATIC MUTINY TOOK SHAPE.
    On January 19, 1970, President Nixon announced his next Supreme
Court nominee, G. Harrold Carswell, a good ol' boy from South Georgia.
An ad that Carswell had taken out advertising his run for state legislature in
1948 was discovered: "I Am A Southerner By Ancestry, Birth, Training,
Inclination, Belief, And Practices. I Believe That Segregation Of The Races
Is The Proper And The ONLY Practical And Correct Way Of Life In Our
States." Staffers in the civil rights division of the Department of Health, Edu-
cation, and Welfare took in the situation with disgust and watched their boss
for a response.

Nixon made it at a press conference on January 30 when asked if he
would still have nominated Carswell if he'd known. "Yes, I would," the president responded. "I am not concerned about what Judge Carswell said
twenty-two years ago when he was a candidate for state legislature. I am very
much concerned about his record . . . as a federal district judge."

The *Post* reported on that record the next day: an embarrassing two-
thirds of his decisions had been overturned by higher courts. Then it came
out that in 1956 Carswell had schemed to make a public golf course private
to keep blacks out. Two weeks later Leon Panetta picked up the *Washington Daily News* and read an article about himself: "Nixon Seeks to Fire
HEW's Rights Chief for Liberal Views." He dutifully submitted his resignation that Tuesday. Then he delivered a speech to the National Education
Association: "The cause of justice is being destroyed not by direct challenge but by indirection, by confusion, by disunity, and by a lack of leadership and commitment to a truly equal society." Six of Panetta's
subordinates resigned in solidarity.

On March 1, the *New York Times* published a leaked memo from Daniel
Patrick Moynihan. The White House was putting "as much or more time
and effort from this administration than any in history" on civil rights, he
reassured the boss. But the administration wasn't getting the credit because
the discourse was controlled by "hysterics, paranoids, and boodlers on all

sides. . . . The time may have come when the issue of race could benefit from a period of benign neglect. The subject has been too much talked about."

Over two hundred civil servants at Health, Education, and Welfare petitioned Secretary Finch: "We are gravely concerned about the future leadership role of HEW in civil rights." The day of the town-house bombing Nixon grumbled that what they "can't understand is that the confusion is deliberate."

Then he turned to a more important subject. Larry O'Brien had just taken over again as Democratic National Committee chairman, to Nixon a clear signal that Ted Kennedy was reasserting control of the party. (Coincident with O'Brien's reascendency, the Democrats played neatly into the emerging right-wing charge that they were no longer the party of the people but instead the party of chic elites. The DNC moved to the swankiest address in Washington, two floors below the Federal Reserve Board: "Watergate, Where Republicans Gather," the *Post* headlined a February 25, 1969, spread on the $70 million complex where it cost an unheard of $3,500 a year for a space in the underground garage, and where Rose Mary Woods, the White House protocol chief, and four Nixon cabinet secretaries now lived. "Why, we could have a cabinet meeting here" was the favorite line of exuberant real estate agents showing off the $250,000 penthouses.) The president told Haldeman to have Murray Chotiner, Nixon's old dirty trickster from the forties he had brought in to help with the 1970 campaign, investigate O'Brien. And if for some reason Chotiner wouldn't play ball, Nixon had already had J. Edgar Hoover get the goods on his old friend.

This was the Nixon who once shared in a moment of introspection to an aide, "It's a piece of cake until you get to the top. You find you can't stop playing the game the way you've always played it because it is part of you and you need it as much as an arm or leg. . . . You continue to walk on the edge of the precipice because over the years you have become fascinated by how close to the edge you can walk without losing your balance."

Nixon had rung in the year with flights of Kennedyesque rhetoric. His New Year's message to the nation marked the signing of the National Environmental Policy Act of 1969: "The 1970s absolutely must be the years when America pays its debts to the past by reclaiming the purity of its air, its water, and our living environment. It is literally now or never." He didn't care much about this stuff one way or another—"I think interest in this will recede," he wrote on a memo three months later—but it presented a political opportunity. According to polls, environmental concern had tripled since 1965. Since the publication of the perennial bestseller *Silent Spring* in 1962 (its title referred to the imminent day when birds stopped singing: "Can anyone believe it is possible to lay down such a barrage of poisons on the surface of the earth without making it unfit for all life?"), environmentalism had sometimes seemed a sort of transideological apocalypticism. Ehrlichman considered himself an environmentalist. So did General Curtis LeMay, an overpopulation obsessive. Edmund Muskie and Scoop Jackson, both likely 1972 presidential contenders, were strong for the issue. Wisconsin's Democratic senator Gaylord Nelson was planning something called Earth Day, for April. Best of all, the radicals were obsessed with it. Linda Morse, she of the M1 rifle, spoke in her testimony at the Chicago 7 trial of "companies just pouring waste into lakes and into rivers and just destroying them." Allen Ginsberg said "overpopulation, pollution, ecological destruction brought about by our own greed" was "a planetary crisis not recognized by any government of the world."

Well, now Richard Nixon recognized it. The latest edition of *Silent Spring* put Nixon's "literally now or never" quote on the back cover.

He cleared his schedule for thirteen days to write his January 22 State of the Union address. (Though he took time out to write a memo to Haldeman: "Will you give me a recent report sometime this week on what we are doing to sanitize the White House staff. You will recall my concern with regard to one of the offices where big pictures of Kennedy were in the office in a rather sensitive area where some form letters are prepared to send out.")

The address began, "The seventies will be a time of new beginnings, a time of exploring both on earth and in the heavens, a time of discovery. But the time has also come for emphasis on developing better ways of managing what we have and of completing what man's genius has begun but left unfinished. . . . Ours is, and should be, a society of large expectations."

He wound up with this soaring peroration: "I see an America in which we have abolished hunger, provided the means for every family in the nation to obtain a minimum income, made enormous progress in providing better housing, faster transportation, improved health, and superior education. I see an America in which we have checked inflation and waged a winning war on crime."

He had sounded all the Kennedyesque notes. The *New York Times*'s headline was a four-column haiku: "Nixon, Stressing Quality of Life / Asks in State of the Union Message / For Battle to Save Environment." Pundits spoke hopefully of the end of the "positive polarization" strategy.

Nixon delivered his most precious baby on February 18, his 160-page "First Annual Report to the Congress on Foreign Policy for 1970," what he called a "State of the World" message. "The postwar period in international relations has ended," it began, then gave full expression to what a new "Framework for a Durable Peace" would look like. In-depth discussion of Vietnam only began around page 70. He concluded by printing the toast he'd given to the president of India, a paean to Mahatma Gandhi: "A peace responsive to the human spirit, respectful of the divinely inspired dignity of man, one that lifts the eyes of all to what man in brotherhood can accomplish and that now, as man crosses the threshold of the heavens, is more necessary than ever."

The *New York Times* printed all 37,425 words in a stand-alone supplement.

Thus, the Nixon public transcript, circa early 1970.

As the danker corners of his mind got busy with things the public needn't know.

Nixon had a favorite young dirty trickster, former Young Americans for Freedom president Tom Charles Huston. In his 1965 YAF inaugural address Huston had excoriated conservatives "who abuse the truth, who resort to violence and engage in slander," and "who seek victory at any price without regard for the broken lives . . . incurred by those who stand in the way." In the White House he sometimes signed his memos "Cato the Younger," after the statesman of the late Roman Republic famous for his stubborn incorruptibility.

He embodied a certain paradox of the right: to those who believed civilization unraveling at the hands of barbarians, it was principled to be unprincipled. Mark Felt of the FBI described Huston as the White House "*gauletier*"—a French word for the chief official of a district under Nazi control. By the sixth month of the new administration, Nixon was assigning the twenty-eight-year-old former army intelligence officer delicate security requests like setting up the IRS antiradical unit, or developing evidence of Red China ties to antiwar activists (". . . or if not Huston, someone with his toughness and brains"). He put Huston to work in February putting together an internal-security apparatus to run out of the White House; Nixon though John Mitchell and the Justice Department too soft for the job. On February 9, the president's aggressive new special counsel, Charles W. Colson, recommended another healthy right-wing exuberant to help: E. Howard Hunt, a former CIA agent who'd helped run the Guatemala coup in 1954 and the Bay of Pigs in 1961. He had just quit the company because he thought it "infested with Democrats."

The Justice Department stumbled along in the internal-security business as best it could. Its latest tack was subpoenaing unedited footage from network documentaries on the Black Panthers and notes and unused magazine photographs of the Weathermen. As more and more embarrassing evidence of G. Harrold Carswell's persistent segregationist loyalties emerged, unflattering information somehow came forth about the leaders of the fight against him: George McGovern and Hubert Humphrey owned real estate with racially restrictive covenants; Senator Birch Bayh had failed the bar exam.

Another secret bombing campaign began on February 16, over the Ho Chi Minh Trail in Laos. But bombs were loud, and it was reported in the newspapers. Antiwar senators asked why they shouldn't suspect there were also

American ground troops in Laos. The Pentagon promised there were none. That proved too easy to check. The *Los Angeles Times* discovered the death of a Captain Joseph Bush in a firefight on February 10, 1969; NBC interviewed an American CIA pilot who reported fifty or sixty U.S. military installations in Laos; *Newsweek* reported the existence of a 150-plane secret CIA air force, Air America, whose pilots flew wearing thick gold bracelets to barter for supplies when they landed in the bush. "To say that a credibility gap is developing with regard to Administration statements on U.S. involvement in Laos," the *Philadelphia Inquirer* editorialized, "is to understate the case."

The White House then admitted at least twenty-seven Americans had died fighting in Laos. The president's approval rating was back down to 53 percent. Again, Nixon felt his loss of popularity as a loss of control. He thrashed about in rage to free himself and made the situation worse.

March 2 and 3 were busy days; Nixon received his plaque from the NFL in New York, held a state dinner with the French president, worked on his next televised Vietnam speech (and conferred with the vice president over another matter of state: the piano duet they were to perform at the Gridiron Dinner). He also dispatched a blizzard of memos. To Haldeman, he said a cabinet post for the former Democratic governor of Texas should be looked into; John Connally "has the subtlety and the toughness and the intelligence to do a good job." He told Haldeman to "get the names of 20 men in the country who can give $100,000 or more. We should concentrate on them. Have them in for a small dinner, let them know that they are RN's personal backers." Nixon also noted with pleasure something he had heard from Billy Graham: that a right-wing consortium from Texas and Arizona was considering a bid to buy a controlling interest in CBS.

A memo to Pat Buchanan directed him to game-plan a fight against "the institutionalized power of the left concentrated in the foundations that succor the Democratic Party." Buchanan took to the charge with relish, suggesting not only defense but offense: a new right-wing "talent bank" working at the secret bidding of the White House, with a figurehead board of directors. "Some of the essential objectives of the Institute would have to be blurred, even buried, in all sorts of other activity that would be the bulk of its work, that would employ many people, and that would provide the cover for the more important efforts." The plan would require "a strong fellow running the Internal Revenue Division. . . . We would be striking at the heart of the Establishment."

The president also commanded Ehrlichman to cut the share of the federal budget sent to Missouri, New York, Indiana, Nevada, Wisconsin, and Minnesota—the homes of Republican congressional enemies, especially senators balking at the nomination of G. Harrold Carswell.

* * *

This last was an abiding obsession. He needed the South to achieve a Republican majority. But for over a century Southern patriots had grown up learning to spit when they heard the name of the party of the Yankee interlopers. That started breaking down in the 1950s, when Eisenhower campaigned in the South's urban areas, and in the early 1960s, when the RNC launched Operation Dixie, sending fresh-faced young organizers door-to-door to show Southerners Republicans didn't have horns—and, especially, in 1964, when 87 percent of Mississippi voted for the presidential candidate who had voted against the Civil Rights Act. Every year, a few more state legislators joined Strom Thurmond in switching parties. But that lingering distrust remained.

The coming congressional elections were a stand-or-fall moment. The GOP had a chance to take a majority of the five Southern Senate seats up in 1970. Harry Byrd of Virginia was considering switching parties. Statehouses looked to be in play in Tennessee, Florida, South Carolina, and Georgia.

The Southern Strategy was the media's label for the White House's project. The White House denied any such thing existed. But it had been chartered during the first hundred days, as Southern Republican chairmen demanded their price for having backed Nixon for the nomination and presidency: the heads of four liberal bureaucrats at the HEW regional office in Atlanta. Slowly, sedulously, maneuvering around civil service protections, the Nixon administration got to work.

In June, John Mitchell had gone up to Capitol Hill to testify to a House judiciary subcommittee on the 1965 Voting Rights Act, set to expire in August of 1970. The legislation was so important it should apply uniformly nationwide, he said. Civil rights activists saw through that straightaway. It was an old segregationist debating trick, like Strom Thurmond going to New York in 1948 and declaring, "If you people in New York want no segregation, then abolish it and do away with your Harlem." The subcommittee's ranking Republican, liberal Bill McCulloch of Ohio, accused Mitchell of doing the bidding of unreconstructed Mississippi racists. A week later the Justice Department officially affirmed that the administration was "unequivocally committed to the goal of finally ending racial discrimination in schools, steadily and speedily, in accordance with the law"—but that "a policy requiring all school districts, regardless of the difficulties they face, to complete desegregation by the same terminal date is too rigid to be either workable or equitable." The next day was the NAACP's July 4 national convention. There, HUD secretary George Romney said every American was "entitled to full and equal citizenship." Roy Wilkins responded that the administration's double-dealing was "almost enough to make you vomit."

It was hard to play both sides sedulously, the higher the stakes got.

"Complete desegregation by the same terminal date"—the start of the 1969–70 school year—was exactly what the federal Fifth Circuit Court of Appeals had demanded of Mississippi on August 11, 1969. Two weeks later,

HEW gave them an extra sixty days. The NAACP, correctly suspecting White House interference, appealed to the Supreme Court. The president was asked about press reports that John Stennis of Mississippi, the chairman of the Senate Armed Services Committee, was threatening to block the administration's defense authorization bill if more desegregation went through. Nixon replied, "Anybody who knows Senator Stennis and anybody who knows me would know that he would be the last person to say, 'Look, if you don't do what I want in Mississippi, I am not going to do what is best for this country.' He did not say that, and under no circumstances, of course, would I have acceded to it."

Nixon lied. Stennis had sent him a four-page, single-spaced letter on August 11: "As chairman of the Armed Services Committee I have major responsibilities here in connection with legislation dealing with our national security, but I will not hesitate to leave my duties here at any time to go to Mississippi to do whatever else must be done to protect the people of Mississippi and to preserve our public school system. While I have not yet spoken to Senator Symington, I am sure that as the ranking member . . . he will be glad to assume those committee responsibilities if I am called away."

Senator Stuart Symington of Missouri was against Nixon's pet proposal in his defense authorization bill: the antiballistic missile system. The threat was rather transparent.

In September, the Atlanta HEW regional director was kicked upstairs to Washington. The man who replaced him, a friend of Harry Dent's, gave an interview in which he claimed, "There is no more segregation."

The Fifth Circuit's stay for Mississippi went to the Supreme Court. For the first time since *Brown v. Board of Education,* the federal government argued on the side *against* school desegregation. It lost. On October 30, 1969, in the middle of Nixon's preparations for the Silent Majority speech, the Supreme Court handed down *Alexander v. Holmes County Board of Education,* ruling Southern "dual" school districts and "freedom of choice" plans illegal. Of course, it had ruled similarly in 1968 in *New Kent County.* Only this time, the South was aided in its intransigence by the president of the United States.

The Supreme Court nomination of Haynsworth of South Carolina was killed on November 21, 1969. "Find a good federal judge further South and further to the right!" Nixon told Dent. The president's otherwise noble State of the Union soliloquy included not a word on civil rights. Carswell was announced; his Judiciary Committee hearings began early February. One former NAACP lawyer explained what kind of racist Carswell was by sharing how the lawyer used to prepare his black subordinates for what they could expect before Carswell's bench by screaming at them as they delivered their arguments. Another lawyer told of a time Carswell released illegally arrested voter-registration volunteers from jail so they could be rearrested "properly" the moment they left the courthouse. The dean of the Yale Law

School said Carswell had "more slender credentials than any nominee for the Supreme Court put forth in this century." Deans of several other schools, and two hundred former Supreme Court clerks, signed an open letter charging Nixon with degrading the court.

The administration responded with a full-court press. Bill Rehnquist of the Justice Department wrote speeches for Judiciary Committee conservatives such as Nebraska senator Roman Hruska, who said, "There are a lot of mediocre judges and people and lawyers. They are entitled to a little representation, aren't they, and a little chance?" Perhaps that line had not been scripted by Rehnquist, as well as the anti-Semitic fillip that followed: "We can't have all Brandeises and Cardozos and Frankfurters and all stuff like that there."

Rehnquist promised that there was "nothing else in Carswell's record to worry about." But more revelations of racism as late as 1966 kept coming. Carswell managed to pass the Judiciary Committee on February 17; then the American Bar Association withdrew its approval after an affidavit he swore out to help an all-white booster club at the University of Florida stay segregated was produced. Senators started peeling off. Southern folk started feeling put-upon. No Southern leaders, of a certain age, were free of such blemishes in their past. Did that mean Southerners were banned from the nation's highest councils?

Nixon knew just how to placate them. He pointed out that in 1940 a hero among Southern liberals, Ralph McGill, the editor of the *Atlanta Constitution,* "wrote a column in which he came out unalterably against integration of education of Southern schools. He changed his mind later." Wasn't Judge Carswell *also* allowed to change his mind?

The precincts of the West Wing devoted to Southern Strategizing grew frenetic. Georgia governors weren't allowed to succeed themselves, and Lester Maddox was considering a 1970 run for lieutenant governor. A rich Georgia Republican offered him $500,000 for the right to use his name on a chain of fried-chicken outlets. Not long after, Maddox traveled to Washington for meetings. (He took with him his usual travel companion: a crate of autographed pick handles to distribute to fans.) Whatever transpired in those particular nut-cutting sessions went unrecorded. Apparently, it wasn't enough. "The Democratic Party brought a little better way of life to our people," he announced upon his return. "I shall remain in the Democratic Party and carry it to victory in the election of 1970." He was disappointed, he said, that Republicans "came to my office and to the mansion to talk about switching, then afterward, trying to deny it. But I've grown accustomed to expecting this kind of thing from politicians."

Moynihan's "benign neglect" quote that came out March 6 was benign compared to the next memos to leak. On March 15 the *Washington Post* reported that a few days after Harry Dent became the top White House political liaison, the chairman of the Georgia Republican Party told him he had "been given assurance by some very wealthy individuals" that "there will be little financial worry for the Republican Party in Georgia if the school situation in Washington can be worked out." Another memo, from Dent to Finch on White House stationery marked CONFIDENTIAL, asked Finch to drop a desegregation case in Strom Thurmond's Columbia, South Carolina. A third indicated that Dent had intervened with a judge.

Winning the South for the Republicans was starting to resemble a criminal enterprise. On the first day of April at 11:45 a.m. a tall, dour man with an expensive briefcase sat in the tiny lobby of the Sherry Netherlands Hotel in a New York City made nervous by New Left bomb scares.

A man with a Southern drawl approached him. "Are you Mr. Jensen of Baltimore?"

The first man responded, "No, I'm Mr. Jensen of Detroit."

That was the signal to exchange briefcases.

"Where's your briefcase?" Mr. Jensen of Detroit asked.

"I didn't bring one," the other man said, suddenly panicking. "I figured that you would give me that one."

Mr. Jensen was actually Mr. Herb Kalmbach, the president of the United States's personal attorney. He glared and said, "I'm not about to give you my briefcase." Instead he started stuffing a manila envelope with one thousand $100 bills. They came from a safe-deposit box at Chase Manhattan Bank, accessible only by Kalmbach, a brother-in-law of Bob Haldeman, and one of the partners at Nixon's old law firm. It was one of the slush funds left over from the 1968 campaign, the one that also paid the salary of their private investigator Tony Ulasewicz. The recipient—so nervous he was almost run down by a taxi while holding $100,000 of the president of the United States's illicit cash—worked for Alabama's governor, Albert Brewer. George Wallace was running against Brewer to regain the governor's chair. Richard Nixon was working to make sure Wallace lost, to end his political career before the 1972 presidential election season. For the runoff election on June 1, Kalmbach passed to Brewer another $300,000.

There was no longer any doubt about Wallace's continued presidential aspirations. "The so-called Southern Strategy has been all talk," he had said at the beginning of the year. "The administration has done more to destroy the public school system in one year than the last administration did in four." Then he hustled to the Fort Benning stockade for an audience with Lieutenant Calley. He said he didn't think there'd been any My Lai massacre. But if there was, it was the Communists' fault—"a direct result of the North invading South Vietnam." Wallace met with Calley for an hour, then said, "I'm sorry to see the man tried. They ought to spend the time trying folks who are trying to destroy this country instead of trying those who are serving their country."

"Blount—$100 G for Brewer. Move on this," Nixon had scrawled to Haldeman soon after. Winton "Red" Blount was a wealthy contractor from Alabama and Nixon's postmaster general—the cabinet officer traditionally responsible for distributing administration patronage. Blount got to work arranging the drop. Nixon also had another White House staffer dig up dirt on Gerald Wallace, his brother George's purported bagman. Murray Chotiner passed what he found to muckraker Jack Anderson, whose column ran in over three hundred papers.

During the New York City bomb scare, the mail stopped circulating. On March 17, 1970, letter carriers voted 1,555 to 1,055 to go on strike, against the wishes of their leadership. The walkout spread to sorters, clerks, and drivers throughout the region—then across the country. Without warning, by March 21, the first national strike by federal employees in U.S. history was in full effect.

All of it was illegal. The government issued an injunction. Strikers ignored it. The government issued a second injunction. They ignored that, too. Labor Secretary George Shultz personally negotiated with the leader of the National Association of Letter Carriers, which, since the carriers thought their leadership quislings, only spread the walkout further.

Nixon went on TV on March 23 to announce he was sending in 2,500 army and air force National Guardsmen, and 15,500 navy and marine reservists, into the nation's largest city to deliver the mail. "If the postmaster general deems it necessary to act in other affected major cities, I will not hesitate to act," Nixon said. "What is at issue . . . is the survival of a government based on the rule of law."

Mailmen started returning to work, though in New York, some still stayed out. It was "well worth going to jail for," one told *Newsweek*. You didn't have to be a Yippie, it turned out, to judge law and order a tool of the oppressor.

One reason was economic. In 1969, the average factory worker earned 82 cents less a week in real terms than he did in 1965. Nixon was right in 1966: stagnation in the standard of living *was* imminent. Only now it was his problem. In New York, some letter carriers were eligible for welfare. Across the economy, long-term labor contracts that had failed to keep pace with prices were expiring. Workers started demanding and getting generous pay increases. Where union leaders weren't able to settle to their restive membership's' satisfaction, a price was being exacted: the "wildcat" strike—the working class's way of giving the middle finger to its own Establishment. In New York alone, longshoremen, taxi drivers, building-service workers, even employees of the Metropolitan Opera, struck. Tugboat deckhands shut down harbors for two months and won a 50 percent raise over three years. Some 450,000 Teamsters struck and increased their pay by 27.5 percent just as the letter carriers were returning to work—under a settlement that gave them amnesty for breaking the law. Postal workers, for their part, got a 14 percent increase, the first 6 percent retroactive to the end of 1969, which would also be applied to every one of 5.6 million federal employees.

Richard Nixon judged the inflation risk acceptable. Economics was one more aspect of domestic policy that he tended to ignore. But he did harbor one core economic conviction. In the traditional trade-off between recession and inflation, he would always choose inflation. As Haldeman wrote in his diary, "P made point that he never heard of losing an election because of inflation." But a recession, he was sure, had lost him his first try at the presidency: Eisenhower had taken his dour former treasury secretary George Humphrey's fiscally conservative advice instead of his labor secretary Jim Mitchell's fiscally liberal advice, allowing a slowdown in 1960. Nixon's was the first Republican presidency in eight years, he pointed out to his economic policy committee in April of 1969—and those eight years had seen no further such slowdowns. "We can't allow—wham!—a recession. We will never get in again."

At first Nixon left the details up to his economic team, a humble and pragmatic bunch who proposed a policy of cooling the economy gradually. No one saw any reason why the old ways of doing things should no longer hold.

But creeping price hikes were shaking that confidence. Dour old financiers were once more warning a president to cool the economy—the same ones who, worried about the value of their bond portfolios, had lost him the 1960 election when General Eisenhower took their advice. The Federal Reserve chairman Nixon inherited, William McChesney Martin—he had three names; how much could you trust a guy like *that*?—waxed gloomily in a June 1969 speech to an audience of bankers: with federal expenditures growing 60 percent in three years and revenues and productivity not keeping pace, the U.S. economy was a "house of cards." The time had come to cool it down: "We're going to have a good deal of pain and suffering before we can solve these things."

This economic counsel the president was not ready to accept. "I remember 1958," he grumbled to his economic advisers. "We cooled off the economy and cooled off fifteen senators and sixty congressmen at the same time." Conservative talk about silent majorities was one thing. He wasn't about to become a *fiscal* conservative—not in an election year.

In September of 1969, he called on Congress to fatten Social Security checks by 10 percent and index them to inflation. Nobody shoots Santa Claus, as liberal Democrats liked to say. If that didn't help keep the economy humming, Nixon told his economic team ten days after the Silent Majority speech, "let's build some dams."

But Fed chair Martin, statutorily independent of White House pressure and counsel, would not cooperate. Martin said prices would rise beyond reason unless the people felt some economic pain—pain the Federal Reserve had the power to bring about by raising interest rates.

Bill Martin's term expired in January. In October, the president announced he would not reappoint him. He offered instead for Senate confirmation Republican economist Arthur Burns. Burns had worked with him for twenty years. This man would, he hoped, be tractable. "You see to it," Nixon told Burns in a private meeting on October 23. "No recession."

Burns was appointed as signs of an economic slowdown took hold. But the one thing that was supposed to accompany every economic slowdown was not occurring: decreased inflation. By the January 22, 1970, State of the Union address it was 6.1 percent, the highest in ten years. The system was short-circuiting. Inflated labor settlements were partly to blame. So was the Vietnam War. Richard Nixon had ruthlessly exploited the intertwined conundrums of the economy and the war to tighten the psychic tourniquet against Lyndon Johnson. Now, in 1970, he was the one being squeezed.

At the presidential press conference on January 30, the AP correspondent read out the latest economic headlines—"Balance of Trade Makes Slight Progress in 1969"; "Big Firms' 1969 Profits Down"; "Dow Average Hits New Low for 3 Years"; "GNP Rise Halted"; "U.S. Steel Will Raise Sheet Prices February 1"—and asked if America "may be in for perhaps the worst sort of economic conditions—inflation *and* recession." The next afternoon associate Supreme Court justice William J. Brennan swore in Arthur F. Burns as the tenth chairman of the Federal Reserve Board in the White House East Room. The president said, "I have never heard so much applause in this room for some time. This is an historic occasion." (The president loved to call events in his White House historic occasions.) He said the applause was "a standing vote of appreciation in advance for lower interest rates and more money."

This was the setup to a joke; everyone knew the Fed chair was supposed to be independent. This was the punch line: "I hope that *independently* he will conclude that my views are the ones that should be followed."

To the president's considerable chagrin, Burns did not. Burns had already effected an act of fiscal blackmail. In the State of the Union address the president said his first economic priority was "controlling inflation." He lied. If that was his first priority, he wouldn't be preparing a liberal $212 billion budget to send to Congress in February for FY 1971. Burns said it wouldn't be a credible act to try to cool the economy through monetary policy if the president wasn't showing a commitment to cooling it through fiscal policy— and that unless Nixon cut that down to under $200 billion, Burns wouldn't be able to lower interest rates. Nixon's budget director, Robert Mayo, got it down to $203.7 billion. Burns said that still wasn't enough. Mayo didn't see anywhere else he could squeeze and proposed tax increases instead. Burns said no dice. The Fed chair finally acceded to increasing the money supply when Nixon lowered his budget request to $200.3 billion—by postponing a scheduled pay raise for federal employees by six months. That was what had led to the postal strike in March.

Nixon had blamed Burns, and regressed in his rage to childhood: the sensitive son absorbing the anger of a hard-pressed, helpless, small-town independent grocer of particularly bitter disposition. It was meat prices driving inflation, Nixon decided, big supermarkets who refused to pass lower cattle prices on to consumers. "Kick the chain stores," he said in early February ("kicking" was always the favorite Nixon metaphor when expressing violent moods; a psychobiographer once wondered whether Frank Nixon had kicked Richard as a child). "I think you will find that chain stores who generally control these prices nationwide are primarily dominated by Jewish interests. These boys, of course, have every right to make all the money they want, but they have a notorious reputation in the trade for conspiracy."

Nixon said that on March 16, the day after the Harry Dent segregation memos leaked, the day before the postal strike vote, as Manhattan banks and corporate headquarters were being evacuated under bomb threats. A new issue of *U.S. News,* the most Nixon-friendly magazine, came out March 17. Its *Washington Whispers* gossip column reported he had lost thirty-five senators' votes and counting on the Carswell nomination. When was the last time a president had *two* Supreme Court nominees rejected in a row? That was the kind of historic first Nixon preferred not to remark upon.

He was choking with a sense of impotence. He petulantly banned Kissinger from the Oval Office after the NSC muffed the Laos public relations (the NSC told the press, "No American stationed in Laos has ever been killed in ground combat operations," two days before the *Los Angeles Times* reported the death of an American stationed in Laos). Kissinger was, meanwhile, flying back and forth to Paris for a secret back-channel set of negotiations with Le Duc Tho of the North Vietnamese politburo (unbeknownst to Secretary of State Rogers or Secretary of Defense Laird). Amid it all, the leader of Cambodia traveled to France for cancer treatment. Prince Norodom Sihanouk tilted toward China and the Soviet Union and tolerated North Vietnamese military sanctuaries in his kingdom. His prime minister, Lon Nol, in the prince's absence, staged a coup. That was March 18. Lon Nol was a CIA asset. But here he was freelancing. Le Duc Tho pitched fits with Henry Kissinger in Paris over what looked like a breach of faith. This sudden, surprising geostrategic opportunity—a newly friendly Cambodian government eager to kick out Communists—became yet one more headache for the president. The fog of war was not salubrious to delicate negotiations.

Now Nixon was raging at the drop of a hat. He said John Mitchell was "not a nut-cutter." Republican senators refusing to back Harrold Carswell were to be banned from the White House. Nixon penned a letter to William Saxbe of Ohio, who was on the fence: "What is centrally at issue in this nomination is the Constitutional responsibility of the President to appoint members of the Court—and whether this responsibility can be frustrated by those who wish to substitute their own philosophy or their own subjective judgment for that of the one person entrusted by the Constitution with the power of appointment. . . . The question arises whether I, as President of the United States, shall be accorded the same right of choice in naming Supreme Court justices which has been freely accorded my predecessors of both parties."

But presidents had the right to *nominate* judges, not *name* them, and senators did not appreciate being lectured to with constitutional solecisms. Saxbe released the letter on April 1 to the newspapers. Thereby Nixon lost yet more senators.

Worse, the Democrats started attacking his economic jugular. The Dow was down 29 percent since the end of 1968 to under 700 and counting, unemployment was up 1.5 points to 4.8, 78 percent of business executives blamed Nixon, and Edmund Muskie, the talk of the pundits for '72, was quoted in the *Wall Street Journal* on April 3: "In the 1920s it took Republicans eight years to go from prosperity to unemployment and now they've learned to do it in one year." Paul Samuelson, the MIT economist, in his *Newsweek* column, really hit Nixon where it hurt: "If Mr. Nixon were to announce defeat in Vietnam and cutting of our losses, the market would jump 50 points."

April 3 and 4 were movie nights. On Friday, at Camp David, Nixon took in Laurence Olivier in *Hamlet.* The next night, at the White House, alongside Pat, Julie, and son-in-law David Eisenhower, an increasingly impotent president enjoyed the exploits of a more decisive hero.

The three-hour epic *Patton* had come out in February. It shared with the Spiro Agnew wristwatch the power to appeal to both sides of the cultural divide. The film began with George C. Scott as General George S. Patton in front of a gargantuan American flag, giving a speech to the troops so bombastic the left experienced it as a satire of militarism gone mad ("We're not just going to shoot the bastards, we're going to cut out their living guts and use them to grease the treads of our tanks"). The next scene opened with Arab children picking battlefield corpses clean; its profane stylishness recalled *Bonnie and Clyde.*

To those who'd seen comrades thrown in jail in Chicago for using "obscenity" in the courtroom, Patton's response to the visiting chaplain who asks the general if he had time to read the Bible ("every goddamned day") was *funny.* So, in a sick-humor sort of way, was the scene in which Patton read a prayer he'd commissioned for good weather for a more efficient slaughter, over scenes of infantrymen roasting the enemy with flamethrowers. Throughout, "Old Blood and Guts" was depicted heedlessly sacrificing boys for no other reason than his vainglorious rivalry with Field Marshal Montgomery—justifying it via bathetic abstractions about God and country: *Dr. Strangelove* stuff.

In the penultimate scene, the war over, Patton is interviewed while sitting atop a Napoleonic white horse, complaining that the politicians always "stop short and leave us with another fight," and that it was time to press forward and take out the Bolsheviks. In the next, he is sitting for a Napoleonic portrait, plotting: "In ten days I'll have us at war with these sons of bitches and I'll make it look like they're at fault."

For conservatives, lines like that were what made Patton a hero.

Richard Nixon couldn't stop talking about *Patton*. This dandy with ivory-handled revolvers was a kindred soul. (Nixon was in love with pomp and finery, too: for a time, he dressed the White House police in uniforms that resembled monarchical livery, until the press started making fun of him.) The movie action was constantly being interrupted so Patton could deliver blunt apothegms, and you can imagine the president of the United States hearing the great general speaking directly to *him:*

"All this stuff you hear about America not wanting to fight, wanting to stay out of the war, is a lot of horse dung."

"Americans traditionally love to fight. All real Americans love the sting of battle."

(Nixon certainly did. During his turn at Oval Office generalship during the postal strike, Haldeman found him "cool, tough, firm, and totally in command; fully aware of it, and loving it.")

"Americans love a winner and will not tolerate a loser."

(Nixon could have said it himself.)

"That's why America has never lost and will never lose a war."

Patton even excoriated the nancy-pants liberals of the press, "bilious bastards" who "don't know anything more about real battle than they know about fornicating!" After he slaps a shell-shocked soldier taking up a bed in a field hospital, his aide-de-camp shows him a political cartoon lacerating him as a Nazi. Richard Nixon must especially have appreciated that: since he slept with a Patton biography by his bedside, he surely knew that in real life the journalist who publicized the slapping incident was Drew Pearson, a longtime Nixon bête noire. And always, Patton was punished for being too tough, too dogged, too distasteful, too foul—but not too foul to be deployed when the hoity-toity *need* a son of a bitch. Then, afterward, they benched him, emasculated, using the stench of the task they had just delegated him as their excuse.

The offscreen presence trifling with Patton's destiny was the exact same man who did it to Nixon: *Eisenhower.* "Sometimes," Patton sneered, "I wonder if he isn't a limey at heart." This Patton is a *victim,* put upon by those who claim to be his betters, victimized for being too tough. The *people,* however, know better: Patton's aide shows him his overwhelming fan mail, his very own silent majority. *The enemy* knows better: Patton is the only general Hitler fears. When Patton is finally given the chance to lead, unencumbered, he proves himself the most daring and valiant hero of the war, liberating twelve thousand cities and towns. Not that Eisenhower appreciates it: at the end, Patton is once more relieved of a command.

Patton even spoke to Nixon's feelings for the upper chamber of the U.S. legislature—uncannily so. In one scene, Patton's men pin a new insignia to his collar, three stars, because he's just been promoted. Karl Malden, as the *press's* favorite general, Omar Bradley, affects a whimpering look.

"What's the matter, Brad? I've been nominated by the president."

"But it doesn't become official until it's approved by the Senate."

"I know. But they have their schedule, and I have mine."

The following Tuesday Nixon ordered Haldeman to see *Patton,* and decided he would give another televised speech on Vietnam in a week and a half. Then the Senate turned back the nomination of G. Harrold Carswell. Nixon made a spur-of-the-moment TV speech. Some thought he sounded angrier than at his 1962 Last Press Conference:

"I have reluctantly concluded—with the Senate as presently constituted—I cannot successfully nominate to the Supreme Court any federal appellate judge from the South who believes as I do in the strict construction of the Constitution. Judges Carswell and Haynsworth have endured with admirable dignity assaults on their intelligence, their honesty, and their character. . . .

"But when all the hypocrisy is stripped away, the real issue was their philosophy of strict construction of the Constitution, and the fact that they had the misfortune of being born in the South. . . . I chose them because they were both men of the South. . . . I understand the bitter feelings of millions of Americans who live in the South about the act of regional discrimination that took place in the Senate yesterday. They have my assurance that the day will come when men like Judge Carswell and Haynsworth can and will sit on the high court."

Suddenly, Nixon was on the cover of *Time* for an article on the "most serious setback of his young presidency." (Turn the page, and the article was "Acid by Accident," on the latest turn in the drug culture, "dosing": "These days, if an American escapes being hijacked in an airplane, mugged in the street or sniped at by a man gone berserk, he apparently still runs the risk of getting accidentally zonked by the hors d'oeuvres at a friendly neighborhood cocktail party.") Suddenly three astronauts who were supposed to be landing on the moon were hurtling through outer space, hanging between life and death, their spacecraft practically out of control after an oxygen tank exploded.

Nixon announced his next Supreme Court nominee, Harry Blackmun. A "Harvard man from the suburbs," the *New York Times* called him, a relative moderate whose few influential decisions included a judgment against physical abuse of prisoners as cruel and unusual punishment. It looked like a retreat.

But that was only true if you knew solely the public transcript. William O. Douglas, the most liberal Warren Court justice left, had a weakness for taking outside fees, and Nixon convinced Jerry Ford to form a House committee to look into his impeachment. Ford cosponsored the resolution with the Dixiecrat Joe Waggonner of Louisiana and said he'd decided to press forward after seeing an article on youth culture by Justice Douglas in *Evergreen Review,* the countercultural magazine whose advertisements for sex books and erotic photographs Ford said he found "shocking." It was the thinnest of gruel, and the attempt to pull off a duplicate Fortas coup fizzled out speedily. But Nixon was following Old Blood and Guts's one standing order: "Always take the offensive, never dig in."

Jerry Rubin was on a speaking tour. On April 10, 1970, he said, "The first part of the Yippie program is to kill your parents. And I mean that quite literally, because until you're prepared to kill your parents, you're not ready to change this country. Our parents are our first oppressors." His audience was fifteen hundred students at the relatively quiet campus of Kent State University in Ohio.

On April 18 Nixon traveled to Houston to present the presidential Medal of Freedom to the Apollo 13 astronauts, who had miraculously survived their spacecraft malfunction while orbiting the moon, a classic White House photo op, though one that did not satisfy Nixon's occasional image adviser Roger Ailes. Richard Nixon had a wife. She mostly seemed to exist for these photo opportunities—as did the two Nixon daughters, and Julie's fiancé, Edward Cox, who seemed to be mustered for every last White House family photo. But this wife was a cipher to the press and the nation, and perhaps to her husband, too. Complained Ailes in his notes to Haldeman on the Houston pageant, "I think it is important for the President to show a little more concern for Mrs. Nixon as he moves through the crowd. At one point he walked off in a different direction. Mrs. Nixon wasn't looking and had to run to catch up. From time to time he should talk to her and smile at her. Women voters are particularly sensitive to how a man treats his wife in public."

On April 20 Nixon went on TV from San Clemente to talk about Vietnam, cool and undramatic (Ailes's note: "Someone said they thought perhaps he had a yellow cast to his makeup"). "I have requested this television and radio time tonight to give you a progress report on our plan to bring a just peace to Vietnam," the commander in chief began, and noted the progress was excellent. Training the South Vietnamese army "has substantially exceeded our original expectations"; significant advances had been made in pacification; thousands of Communist soldiers were indeed stationed in neutral Laos and Cambodia, but "despite this new enemy activity, there has been an overall decline in enemy force levels in South Vietnam since December." There were fewer dead Americans in the first three months of 1970 than in any first quarter since 1965. One hundred fifteen thousand five hundred troop withdrawals had been completed so far: this at last truly seemed like light at the end of the tunnel. The only problem Nixon dwelled upon was on the negotiating front, where the enemy was demanding conditions "that would mean humiliation and defeat for the United States. This we cannot and will not accept."

But, otherwise, everything was going swell. "I am, therefore, tonight announcing plans for the withdrawal of an additional 150,000 American troops to be completed during the spring of next year. This will bring a total reduction of 265,500 men in our armed forces in Vietnam below the level that existed when we took office fifteen months ago."

This was exceedingly clever. The White House had leaked word that the withdrawal would be some forty thousand to fifty thousand. For once Nixon looked more optimistic than the pundits.

He continued, "If I conclude that increased enemy action jeopardizes our remaining forces in Vietnam, I shall not hesitate to take strong and effective measures to deal with the situation." But the safe return of the brave men of Apollo 13 had reminded us all that "the death of a single man in war, whether he is an American, a South Vietnamese, a Vietcong, or a North Vietnamese, is a human tragedy."

It had an air of finality: "The decision I have announced tonight means that we finally have in sight the just peace we are seeking."

In the movie *Patton,* near the last reel, Patton gave a similar speech: the end was just around the corner. One of his aides-de-camp responded, "You know something, General? Sometimes they can't tell when you're acting or when you're not." Patton responded, "It isn't important for them to know. It's only important for me to know."

The president, on Air Force One, on the flight back to Washington, suggested something similar: "Cut the crap out of my schedule. I'm taking over here." He was planning a new invasion. "Troop withdrawal was a boy's job. Cambodia is a man's job."

Mayday

AFTER RICHARD NIXON TURNED OFF OPERATION DUCK HOOK IN November 1969, Kissinger had explained that it would take six months to rebuild enough credibility to try anything like it again. Six months now had passed. Nixon went back on TV on the last day of April and noted a loophole in his last speech:

"Ten days ago, in my report to the nation on Vietnam, I announced a decision to withdraw an additional 150,000 Americans from Vietnam over the next year. I said then that I was making that decision despite our concern over increased enemy activity in Laos, in Cambodia, and in South Vietnam.

"At that time, I warned that if I concluded that increased enemy activity in any of these areas endangered the lives of Americans remaining in Vietnam, I would not hesitate to take strong and effective measures to deal with that situation.

"Despite that warning, North Vietnam has increased its military aggression in all these areas, and particularly in Cambodia. . . . To protect our men who are in Vietnam and to guarantee the continued success of our withdrawal and Vietnamization programs, I have concluded the time has come for action."

He took out a pointer, made indications on a great big map, and said, "In cooperation with the armed forces of South Vietnam, attacks are being launched this week to clean out major enemy sanctuaries on the Cambodian-Vietnamese border."

A week and a half ago he'd said Vietnamization was going so well we could pull 150,000 troops out of Southeast Asia. Now he was saying it was so vulnerable he had to invade *another* country?

The maximalists of the Joint Chiefs of Staff had wanted a president to invade the enemy's sanctuaries in Cambodia since 1964. In their more expansive moments they imagined such an operation could end the war for good—just knock out the floating master command center the Communists hid out in the jungle. Now, thanks to Lon Nol's freelancing, a friendly government was in place to let them try. In a closed session of a House appropriations subcommittee on April 23, Secretary Rogers assured the congressmen, "We recognize that if we escalate and we get involved in Cambodia with our ground troops that our whole [Vietnamization] program is defeated. . . . I think one lesson that the war in Vietnam has taught us is that if you are going to fight a war of this kind satisfactorily, you need public support and congressional support." Then, on TV on April 30, Nixon said ground troops in Cambodia were what were *required* for Vietnamization.

He had decided it long ago. On April 24, Laird was briefed on the planning. He suggested consulting with Congress. Kissinger told Laird not to worry his pretty little head about it. Nixon *did* tell one senator—trusty John Stennis of Mississippi. Then Nixon watched *Patton* again. And drank a lot of whiskey.

"*All real Americans love the sting of battle.*"

"*Remember what Frederick the Great said:* 'L'audace, l'audace, toujours l'audace.'"

"*All my life I've wanted to lead a lot of men into a desperate battle. Now I'm going to do it.*"

"*Dammit, I don't want these men to love me, I want them to fight for me.*"

Maybe, just maybe, Nixon could actually *win* in Vietnam—not just merely not lose. April 25 he went over the battle plans, cruised on the presidential yacht, watched *Patton* again. The young Harvards at the NSC tasked with pulling the invasion together started talking about resignation. The secretary of state, finally in on the operation, said he wouldn't lie if asked about it, and asked the president if he had factored in the inevitable campus uprisings. "If I decide to do it," the commander in chief responded, "it will be because I have decided to pay the price."

He had gone above the heads of the Establishment before, on November 3, spoken straight to his Silent Majority; heightening the contradictions had worked. Surely he could do it again. He dictated a memo to Rose Mary Woods: "Return no calls whatever to any *Post* reporter." He told Henry Kissinger, "This is what I've been waiting for."

The speech began ploddingly, déjà vu if you'd listened to presidents talk about Vietnam since 1965: the enemy's unquenchable aggression, the unceasing and unanswered American initiatives for peace, the one final blow it would take to knock them out once and for all ("Tonight, American and South Vietnamese units will attack the headquarters for the entire Communist military operation in South Vietnam"), the last turn of the corner before the light at the end of the tunnel. He spoke of enemy "sanctuaries," right there on the South Vietnamese border. To eggheads it might have sounded logical, until they realized the North Vietnamese already had a sanctuary along the border of South Vietnam. It was called North Vietnam.

It made more sense to the Silent Majority. The speech was really for them.

"My fellow Americans, we live in an age of anarchy, both abroad and at home. . . . We see mindless attacks on all the great institutions which have been created by free civilizations in the last five hundred years. Even here in the States, great universities are being systematically destroyed. Small nations all over the world find themselves under attack from within and without."

(The campuses, Cambodia: it was all the same fight.)

"If, when the chips are down, the world's most powerful nation, the United States of America, acts like a pitiful, helpless giant, the forces of total-itarianism and anarchy will threaten free nations and free institutions throughout the world. . . .

"In this room Woodrow Wilson made the great decisions which led to victory in World War I. Franklin Roosevelt made the decisions which led to our victory in World War II. . . . John F. Kennedy, in his finest hour, made the great decision which removed Soviet nuclear missiles from Cuba and the Western Hemisphere."

That was a windup for a gibe at the press. They had been *nice* to Wilson, Roosevelt, Kennedy.

"I do not contend that it is in the same magnitude of these decisions that I just mentioned. But between those decisions and this decision there is a dif-ference that is very fundamental. In those decisions, the American people were not assailed by counsels of doubt and defeat from some of the most widely known opinion leaders of the nation."

Then he spoke to the American manhood these opinion leaders were imperiling.

"It is not our power but our will and character that is being tested tonight. The question all Americans must ask and answer tonight is this: does the richest and strongest nation in the world have the character to meet a direct challenge by a group which rejects every effort to win a just peace, ignores our warning, tramples on solemn agreements, violates the neutrality of an unarmed people, and uses our prisoners as hostages?

"If we fail to meet this challenge, all other nations will be on notice that despite its overwhelming power the United States, when a real crisis comes, will be found wanting. . . . I would rather be a one-term president and do what I believe is right than to be a two-term president at the cost of seeing America become a second-rate power and to see this nation accept the first defeat in its proud 190-year history."

Two hundred State Department employees immediately signed a petition of protest. Nixon responded by calling an undersecretary in the middle of the night: "Fire them all!"

Friday, the next morning, was not quite a typical spring day on the campus of the second-biggest public university in Ohio. It was Derby Day. Every May 1, Kent State frat brothers wore silly hats, and sorority sisters chased them down to plant kisses. This year the squealing "coeds" gave chase near the field where black students were staging a rally—angry young Mau Maus in dashikis with a bullhorn threatening to shut down the school they called Kenya unless five thousand black students were added to the student body "with no complaint that black high school students aren't prepared for college work."

Kent was a nervous campus, on pins and needles over a yearlong movement to get rid of ROTC. All over town, walls and sidewalks were covered with graffiti: FREE BOBBY. FREE HUEY. U.S. OUT OF CAMBODIA. However, the townies in the Ohio college towns of Columbus, Athens, and Oxford were jealous of Kent. Their schools were even less peaceful. At Ohio State, the National Guard was patrolling the campus.

At noon the Victory Bell on the commons was tolled by a group of history graduate students for a ritual interment of the Constitution: "It is now our task to see that it is resurrected in its original form." One attendee was a Bronze Star–winning infantryman. He announced, "I'm so disgusted with the behavior of my country in invading Cambodia that I'm going to burn my discharge papers." About three hundred students witnessed the ceremony.

In broader perspective it was a blip; the eyes of the nation's protest watchers were focused on New Haven. A Black Panther trial was set to begin in June, and Yale's patrician president, Kingman Brewster, had told a faculty assembly, "I am appalled and ashamed that things should have come to a pass that I am skeptical of the ability of black revolutionaries to achieve a fair trial anywhere in the United States." Black Panthers had organized three days of fund-raising and rallying for early in May on the New Haven Green. Brewster volunteered Yale's resources for food, shelter, day care, and first aid. Attorney General Mitchell had the Pentagon station four thousand troops nearby; National Guardsmen positioned themselves in a cordon in front of the Hall of Records; carpenters covered downtown windows with plywood panels (militants tore them down); a hotel cleared its lobby of furniture; city fathers arranged for the sixty-foot flagpole above the World War I memorial to be slathered with grease (the flag in front of Center Church had already been replaced by a Yippie banner). Fifteen thousand gathered. A former government security consultant explained why he was there: "I guess you could say that a couple of weeks ago I crossed over. The Post Office strike, the Teamster strike, all that had the general prerequisites of a revolutionary situation." A student who came out from Denver said it showed how "young people could drop out of America and become part of the new nation. . . . New Haven wasn't a weekend thing. Yale is still wide-open."

Student militancy had only recently seemed to be winding down; the Vietnam Moratorium shut its doors on April 20, with the explanation that demonstrations were having less and less effect on the administration but attracting more and more violent lunatics. Now things seemed to be stirring again. Cambodia and the Panthers were catalysts. So was Seymour Hersh's new book *My Lai 4: A Report on the Massacre and Its Aftermath*. It was excerpted in the May issue of *Harper's*. A *New York Times* editorial on April 15 featured quotes:

"Then somebody said, 'What do we do with them?'"

"A G.I. answered, 'Waste them.'"

"Suddenly there was a burst of automatic fire from many guns. Only a small child survived. Somebody then carefully shot him, too."

Hersh's newspaper articles had only been a rough sketch. He had traveled fifty thousand miles to complete the book. It described Robert McNamara's Project 100,000, an initiative whereby almost a million men who'd scored poorly on the Selective Service qualifying test were drafted anyway, purportedly for the noble purpose of giving them a better chance in life, actually populating the army with imbeciles. Led by imbeciles, too—such as Lieutenant William L. Calley Jr., twenty-four, who'd flunked out of Palm Beach Junior College but was given command of a platoon anyway, even though he couldn't properly read a map. In March of 1968, just as they were eager to avenge one of their men just booby-trapped off the face of the earth, the platoon was dropped beside a hamlet and told one of the strongest enemy battalions was dug in there. Methodically, Hersh narrated what happened next: three hours straight spent slaughtering women, children, and old men; then a break for lunch; then a second platoon joining in, helicopters cutting down those that fled. "You could see the bones flying into the air chip by chip," one eyewitness recounted. "When she fell, she dropped the baby," recounted another; then one of his buddies "opened up on the baby with his M16. . . . You can tell when someone enjoys their work." Hersh also explained that high-ranking officers had observed the action from helicopters, and he related the cover-up that kept the massacre secret for over a year—and described, with an authority and detail no journalist had accomplished before, how the dehumanizing routines of the Vietnam conflict ("free-fire zones," where soldiers were authorized to shoot anything that moved; the rule that if a hut had an air-raid bunker it could be burned to the ground, its occupants listed as enemy kills) had rendered a massacre like this possible, even likely.

Were villages like My Lai, you could wonder, the kind of "enemy sanctuaries" the president was talking about in his speech?

Nixon's May Day began with a briefing to Ron Ziegler on the day's line to the press: "Cold steel, no give, nothing about negotiation. . . . Stay strong, whole emphasis on 'back the boys,' sell courage of the President." Then he went to the Pentagon for a briefing. The top brass meticulously took him through the order of battle: this was where they suspected sanctuaries were; these were the ones we were targeting; these were the ones beyond reach.

The president, impatient, replied, "Could we take out *all* those sanctuaries?"

They didn't really know what to say.

"I want to take out *all* those sanctuaries. Knock them all out!"

Someone launched into a technical explanation about why that was literally impossible.

The president cut him off: "You have to electrify people with bold decisions. Bold decisions make history. . . . Let's go blow the hell out of them!"

"It scared the shit out of me," Laird's public affairs officer later recalled.

Pentagon staffers mobbed the president near the briefing room. His speech, one said, "made me proud to be an American."

"Oh, how nice of you," Nixon responded, as reporters transcribed his remarks. "I wrote the speech. I finished it five o'clock in the morning the night before. I had been writing for a little while. I had a lot of help from my staff, including people over here. Well, we could not do it without the backing of all of you, you know. . . .

"You finally think of all those kids out there. I say *kids.* I've seen them. They're the greatest. You know, you see these bums, you know, blowing up the campuses. Listen, the boys that are on college campuses today are the luckiest people in the world, going to the greatest universities, and here they are, burning up the books."

The sons of Franklins, spitting on America.

Nixon took another cruise on the presidential yacht. Then he settled in at Camp David and watched *Patton* one more time.

That night, on the strip of taverns on Water Street in Kent, Ohio, a bar owner nabbed a spray-painting vandal. She called him a "capitalist pig" and squirmed loose. Someone started a bonfire in the middle of the street; someone threw a bottle. A mob rocked an old man's car; he sped off under a hail of beer bottles. A group of girls chanted, "Pigs off the street! We won't go to Cambodia!" Motorcycle gangs arrived. The cops read the riot act and released tear gas. Some students retreated to campus. A voice from a bullhorn drifted across rolling hills: "The revolution has begun! Join us! We're going to burn the ROTC!" One kid picked up a brick and made to throw it through the window of the rickety old wooden ROTC structure. A policeman arrested him before he could; Kent State had been pacified.

"Revolution": not really. Just the same kind of arrant bonfires and restless vandals that had been an annoyance of town-gown relations as long as there had been universities and sunny spring days. A bunch of jocks had taken to the streets and smashed windows, too; they were mad at the cops for clearing their favorite bar during the Knicks-Lakers game.

* * *

On Saturday, May 2, the *New York Times* reported the first escalation in the pace of bombing in North Vietnam since the halt before the 1968 election. (Secretary of Defense Laird admitted he learned about the new policy from the article.) South Vietnamese and American army units drove twenty miles inside Cambodia. Bob Hope, the featured attraction at a carnival in Barberton, Ohio, near Akron, interrupted the jokes to solemnly note the window-breaking in Kent the night before, but said he still had faith in the younger generation.

At that very moment, radicals were circling the Kent State ROTC building, passing out handbills to the gathering crowd as if programs for a show about to begin.

"There's no need to condone violence," a faculty marshal told one of the onlookers.

"The point of discussion is passed," the student returned. "The time for action is here. . . . I don't want to hear anything a fucking pig like you has to say." Then he spat on the professor.

A chant went up: "Down with ROTC! Down with ROTC!" Two thousand more students straggled toward the site from the high-rise dorms to the east, acting together in ways they'd never act alone, throwing rocks at the rickety wooden building. A teaching fellow, seeing one of her brightest students rushing across the common with an empty oil drum, said, "Stop that!"

"We've just got to do this. The building has got to go. . . . Six years of peaceful protest got us nowhere. They'll listen only when they see flames, and tonight they're going to see flames."

The oil drum became a battering ram. Its wielders missed a door, bounced off a wall, and tumbled backward in a heap. Lit railroad flares rebounded off the building and spluttered out, except for one, which set off a pair of curtains. The mob cheered, then groaned as the flame smothered. Another group took torches to a wall, but only singed the paint. Ohio boys and girls were proving themselves poor arsonists.

An American flag burned much more effectively, illuminating the evening sky. A football player pulled out a camera to capture the scene by its light. The communards did to him what cops did to photographers in Chicago '68: tackled him and kicked him in the stomach when he was down.

By 8:30 p.m. the building was finally afire. National Guard battalions moved out from Akron. The fire department arrived, hooked up a hose to a hydrant, then students ran away with the nozzle. A second hose was attached. Students hacked at it with knives. Three kids dipped rags into motorcycle gas tanks, lit them, threw them, and battered firemen who tried to stop them with sticks, as coeds remade themselves as Ulysses' sirens: "Leave that hose alone and come on up in the dorm. We'll make it worth your while."

At 9:55 a group moved out to try to torch the library. At 10:10 a thou-

sand rounds of .22 ammunition went up in the north end of the ROTC building. Someone heaved a chunk of concrete from a construction site at a retreating policeman that put a bloody cut in his head through his dented helmet.

The first companies of guardsmen convoyed into town by the light of the
orange glow. They arrived to a hail of rocks and the chants of thousands of
students: "Burn, baby, burn! Burn, baby, burn!"

That was what the mobs had chanted in Watts in August of 1965. The
long, hot summer had spread to the manicured groves of academe.

National Guardsmen were the Orthogonians of the warrior class. The Ohio
Guard's put-upon sense of resentment was the subject of their unofficial ballad, "Billy Buckeye":

> We aren't no cheap tin soldiers, no, nor we aren't no loafers too,
> But Buckeye boys from Buckeye schools remarkable like you.
> And if we're sometimes careless-like and just a bit too gay,
> We're steady down to business when the band begins to play.

Perhaps 80 percent were "draft-motivated"—they joined to avoid Vietnam. Most resented kids who had the means and wherewithal to get out of
the draft via the far more pleasant route of the student deferment. Others
had done tours in Vietnam—and saw these marauding students as rearguard
allies of the same enemy that had scattered their buddies' body parts. Commanders tried to keep these guys off the Kent front lines. They didn't want
berserk Vietnam vets with live weapons anywhere near protesters.

The units were a little like the troops of Charlie Company in Quang Ngai
province: battle weary after being hunted by a shadowy enemy. Truckers
were on a wildcat strike in eastern Ohio. Scabs were getting their tires shot
out on the Ohio Turnpike. Ohio governor James Rhodes called out jeeps full
of soldiers to keep the freight moving. Strikers called out harassment raids
on scab trucks over CB radios; guardsmen came under sniper fire.

Such was the lot of a National Guardsman in the 1960s. Terrified guardsmen shooting up ten-year-olds in Newark. Untrained guardsmen burning
out machine-gun barrels shooting out electric signs in Detroit. "In North or
South Carolina, I forget which," an former Interpol bureaucrat told a *New
Yorker* correspondent who wrote a subsequent devastating article on the
entire weekend-warrior system, "guardsmen were clearing a school, and they
went through the doorway too close and started bayoneting each other."
They had learned to fear other Americans; in Ohio, especially—where in
1968, the race-war vanguardist Fred "Ahmed" Evans and his Black Nationalists of New Libya set up their ambush of Cleveland police.

Guardsmen sent home for a respite after the trucking strike were called
back for Kent State. Kent citizens were thrilled to see the tanks and jeeps rum-

ble through town. Rumors poured into City Hall: "I saw an Illinois car loaded with six Weathermen armed with shotguns!" The units established a perimeter around the ROTC building. Students greeted them with obscenities and rocks. The guardsmen sent out their first volley of tear gas, which blew back due to a miscalculation of the wind. Daring students got in the troops' faces and screamed. A sergeant moved in on a jeep to try to arrest ringleaders. "A very pretty girl stuck her hand right under my nose, gave me the finger, and uttered four words I've never used myself," he recalled. "I'm not sure I want my daughter to go to college if that's how they teach her to talk."

Such psychic considerations were not trivial, not to men who sang songs to guard against the humiliation of being called tin soldiers. "You have enough girls throwing wisecracks at young soldiers," an observer reflected, "it does something to them."

The students were subdued with minimal force. The shabby old ROTC building, which was built to be carted to the South Pacific as a temporary World War II field hospital, burned itself out by 10:30 p.m. Commanders corrected their wind bearings and cleared out the mob with tear gas. The boldest protesters kept on harassing them, which didn't take that much courage: after the disasters of the sixties urban riots, it had widely been reported that National Guard commanders only let their men carry rifles loaded with blanks. Before midnight, the adjutant called staff headquarters: "The situation at Kent is under control." Every riot had a moment like that: anxious authorities announcing the all-clear, the calm before the storm.

Sunday morning the rolling campus hills had the feel of a carnival. Children climbed around the tanks and helicopters; coeds struck up innocent flirtations with guardsmen; a private joked with a freshman, "Hang around, buddy. There's a rumor that the state is going to cut our pay from $25 a day to $12.80. If they try that, Governor Rhodes will be calling you characters out to subdue us." The two kids struck up such a friendship that the student went off and bought him some oranges. The soldier said he couldn't accept them. "Didn't you hear what the girls did to us at Berkeley? Injected the damned fruit with acid, and you had guys all over the place going off on trips."

Governor Rhodes flew into town at 9 a.m. on a helicopter—there to look tough because the Republican primary was on Tuesday. He was running for Senate. His opponent, Robert Taft III, was running as a New Politics liberal calling for "irreversible" withdrawal from Vietnam. And Taft was ahead in the polls.

The governor met in Fire House No. 1 with the mayor, the National Guard commander, the federal district attorney, the district prosecutor, and the commander of the State Highway Patrol. Rhodes banned university officials from the meeting. He didn't want any liberal administrators whimpering *please.*

Gruff, dough-faced Rhodes laid out the goal: keep the university open without any further demonstrations so as not to hand a victory to the "dissident element."

Someone knocked on the door: "The press is outside."

The governor invited them in. Then, he put on a show. Perhaps he recalled what a similar situation had done for the political career of Spiro Agnew in 1968.

"We have seen here in the City of Kent, especially, probably the most vicious form of campus-oriented violence yet perpetrated by dissident groups and their allies in the state of Ohio. They make *definite* plans of burning! destroying! and throwing! rocks! at police! and at the National Guard! and the Highway! Patrol!"

He ground his fist into the table at each exclamation point.

"This is when we're going to use every part of the law enforcement agency of Ohio to drive them out of Kent. We are going to *eradicate* the problem."

Pound.

"We're not going to treat the symptoms. And these people just move from one campus to the other and *terrorize* the community.

"They're worse than the brownshirts and the Communist element and also the night riders and the vigilantes. They're the worst type of people that we harbor in America. And I want to say this: they're not going to take over a campus."

Radio stations broadcast and rebroadcast the tape. The goodwill drained from campus. A soft-spoken girl told an interviewer, "If the president thinks I'm a bum and the governor thinks I'm a Nazi, what does it matter how I act?" Rumors circulated amid mustering town vigilantes about which buildings were set to go up next. A National Guard colonel added his two cents: "We have men that are well trained. But they're not trained to receive bricks. They won't take it. The next phase that we have encountered elsewhere is where they start sniping. They can expect us to return fire."

Some guardsmen started removing their name patches because kids were looking up their numbers in the Akron phone book and harassing their wives: "Hey, you beautiful chick, who are you fucking now that your pig husband is here on the Kent campus?"

Night fell. Students gathered at the Victory Bell, though rallies were supposed to have been banned:

"One, two, three, four! We don't want your fucking war!"

"Fuck *you*! Ag-*new*!"

A jeep, a bullhorn: "You are breaking the law. You must disperse. If you continue to demonstrate, you will be arrested."

"Fuck you, pig!"

Shortly before 8 p.m. a guardsman found two bottles of gasoline and a wick in the bushes by university police headquarters. Fifteen minutes after that, five gallons of gasoline were found on the roof of the administration building. After nine, radicals marched to the president's house, surging past the dormitories: "Join us! Join us!" They were turned back by tear gas, and two hundred detached themselves to take Main Street. They were met by an armored personnel carrier. When it rumbled onto a side street, they cheered a tactical victory. They sat in the middle of a busy intersection. Helicopters flashed antiriot lights over rooftops, searching out snipers. At the street corner the cops handed over a car's PA system to a student who seemed responsible. He turned out not to be so responsible. He claimed the police had told him they wouldn't be arrested and that the National Guard was leaving campus. At eleven, the hour of a hastily called curfew, police started making arrests. The man with the microphone was delighted: "They've lied to us. We've been betrayed!" He had heightened the contradictions. Newly radicalized students rained down a barrage of rocks. Two students were gored by bayonets.

An Akron reporter asked a guardsman what would happen tomorrow. He replied, "There will not be any demonstrations on campus. Those are our orders."

Tomorrow: Monday. A school day.

President Nixon received an urgent open letter from thirty-seven college presidents warning of a new wave of campus demonstrations unless his efforts to end the war became credible. Nixon refused to meet with them.

On the Kent State campus there were bomb threats at fifteen-to-thirty-minute intervals. Eleven a.m. classes were cut short; the commotion outside was too great. The university radio station and intercoms announced, "All outdoor demonstrations and gatherings are banned by order of the governor. The National Guard has the power of arrest." But when a class session let out on a major university campus, it looked all the world like a "gathering." Only a fraction of students had heard the radio and intercom announcements anyway. University administrators could have told law enforcement that. But the governor had banned university administrators—quislings—from the operation's planning.

Fifteen minutes to noon. Students made their way toward whatever it was they did on an ordinary Monday. A general saw what looked to him like a mob. Three minutes later, someone rang the Victory Bell and started rousing rabble for a noon rally. A minute after that, a campus police officer shouted the riot act into a bullhorn. He was standing by the ROTC rubble; now the military's staging area, its ashes a constant reminder of what these students were capable of. Hardly anyone could hear the announcement.

A jeep made its way across the common: another hail of rocks.

At 11:55 guardsmen were ordered to load and lock their weapons and prepare to disperse gas. Two columns of troops moved out in a V, one directly

east, another northeasterly. The eastbound company had to summit a steep hill
south of Taylor Hall, a major campus building—the kind of slope, on college
campuses, useful for wintertime sledding on cafeteria trays. As they trudged,
they dispensed tear gas from their M79 canister guns. The boldest demonstrators picked up the hot metal cans and threw them back. Under suffocat-
ing gas masks, their visibility limited, the guardsmen pressed forward,
determined to push the students into retreat. The militants hustled beside Taylor Hall for cover. The soldiers were unaware that they had only about a hundred yards to go before they would run into a fence. The fence curled around
to keep them from moving east or north; a gymnasium kept them from moving south. They were trapped, with nothing to do but turn around—a retreat
under fire, the most dangerous of military maneuvers. Sixty or seventy soldiers, trapped. What was it President Nixon had said about the "pitiful, helpless giant," faced with "the forces of totalitarianism and anarchy"?

Lots of roofs: from which one would the sniping begin?

They were afraid they were out of tear gas. Radicals who thought their
adversaries only armed with blanks shrieked insults, threw rocks, waved
strange flags. *Pigs off campus! Pigs off campus! Pigs off campus!*" The
guardsmen couldn't tell, but felt like they must have been surrounded.

They looped around for their humiliating return journey.

Then, at 12:24 p.m., several guardsmen stopped, turned almost completely around, dropped to one knee, and took aim at a cluster of students
far away in a parking lot beyond the fence.

Sixty-seven shots in thirteen seconds.

Thirteen students down, mostly bystanders.

One was paralyzed. Four were killed: Allison Krause, William Schroeder,
Jeff Miller, and Sandra Lee Scheuer, ages nineteen, nineteen, twenty, and
twenty. The Associated Press's dispatch went out. The Dow dropped 3 percent in two hours—the most dramatic dip since John F. Kennedy's assassination.

Two Students, Two Guardsmen Dead, the local paper reported. Those two
students had it coming, much of Kent decided.

A respected lawyer told an Akron paper, "Frankly, if I'd been faced with
the same situation and had a submachine gun . . . there probably would have
been 140 of them dead." People expressed disappointment that the rabble-
rousing professors—the gurus—had escaped: "The only mistake they made
was not to shoot all the students and then start in on the faculty."

When it was established that none of the four victims were guardsmen,
citizens greeted each other by flashing four fingers in the air ("The score is
four / And next time more"). The Kent paper printed pages of letters for
weeks, a community purgation: "Hurray! I shout for God and Country,
recourse to justice under law, fifes, drums, marshal music, parades, ice cream

cones—America—support it or leave it." "Why do they allow these so-called educated punks, who apparently know only how to spell four-lettered words, to run loose on our campuses tearing down and destroying that which good men spent years building up? . . . Signed by one who was taught that 'to educate a man in mind and not in morals is to educate a menace to society.'" "I extend appreciation and whole-hearted support of the Guard of every state for their fine efforts in protecting citizens like me and our property." "When is the long-suffering silent majority going to rise up?"

It was the advance guard of a national mood. A Gallup poll found 58 percent blamed the Kent students for their own deaths. Only 11 percent blamed the National Guard.

A rumor spread in Kent that Jeff Miller, whose head was blown off, was such a dirty hippie that they had to keep the ambulance door open on the way to the hospital for the smell. Another rumor was that five hundred Black Panthers were on their way from elsewhere in Ohio to lead a *real* riot; and that Allison Krause was "the campus whore" and found with hand grenades on her.

Many recalled the State of Ohio's original intention for the land upon which Kent State was built: a lunatic asylum. President White was flooded with letters saying it was his fault for letting Jerry Rubin speak on campus. Students started talking about the "*Easy Rider* syndrome," after the Dennis Hopper and Peter Fonda movie about hippies murdered by vigilantes. Townspeople picketed memorial services. "The Kent State Four!" they chanted. "Should have studied more!"

"Anyone who appears on the streets of a city like Kent with long hair, dirty clothes, or barefooted deserves to be shot," a Kent resident told a researcher.

"Have I your permission to quote that?"

"You sure do. It would have been better if the Guard had shot the whole lot of them that morning."

"But you had three sons there."

"If they didn't do what the Guards told them, they should have been mowed down."

A letter to *Life* later that summer read, "It was a valuable object lesson to homegrown advocates of anarchy and revolution, regardless of age."

Time had called the Silent Majority "not so much shrill as perplexed," possessed of "a civics-book sense of decency." Pity poor *Time,* whose America was but a memory.

If much of nonstudent America decided the students had it coming, much of student America decided they might be next. At one school, students put up five grave markers: one for each Kent State corpse, one for the next student to fall.

Jane Fonda, the actress, had separated from her husband and was taking a *Wanderjahr* around the United States. She had been agonizing about the war in Vietnam since 1967. Now she started speaking up. Prominent on her itinerary were college dorms and cafeterias and the new GI coffeehouses popping up near military bases, where she would informally rap. On Monday, May 4, when she showed up at the University of New Mexico, students convinced her to give her first formal speech. She was a bit baffled why so many students crowded the hall to hear her. Then she learned what had happened. The word *Strike* was chalked on the blackboard behind her. She urged the students to defy the administration by keeping their protests peaceful and to support the growing GI antiwar movement. She shared with them what she had learned from GIs: that this was not the first incursion by American troops over the Cambodian border. The students who marched to the president's house named their group They Shoot Students, Don't They? after Fonda's recent movie.

Within the week, in front of the burbling fountain on Revelle Plaza at UC–San Diego, George Winnie Jr., twenty-three, held up a cardboard sign reading IN GOD'S NAME, END THIS WAR, struck a match, and went up in a burst of flame. That didn't make the *New York Times, Washington Post, Wall Street Journal,* or *Chicago Tribune;* a nationwide student tsunami had broken, too much drama to keep track of it all. By that time guardsmen were posted on 21 campuses in sixteen states, 488 universities and colleges were closed (three-quarters of the schools in Nevada, Massachusetts, and Maryland), the entire public high school system in New York City was shut by order of the board of education, and Boston University informed Ted Kennedy not to show up to give the commencement speech because, in honor of the slain students, there wouldn't be any commencement.

To take three representative campuses, one of the New York City schools that struck was Finch College, Tricia Nixon's alma mater. So did Whittier College. And at Duke Law, President Nixon's portrait was removed from the wall of the moot courtroom.

"The splintered left on the campuses has been suddenly reunited," the *Wall Street Journal* concluded, quoting an electrician who worked at Case Western Reserve: "They figure they might just as well die here for something they believe in as to die in Vietnam." Case was one of the schools where students burned down an ROTC building. So were Kentucky, the University of Cincinnati, Ohio State, Ohio University, Miami of Ohio, Tulane, Washington University in St. Louis (their second) and St. Louis University. At Colorado State they torched Old Main, the original campus structure, erected in 1878. In farm-belt Carbondale, home of Southern Illinois, a center of military research, martial law was declared. At Syracuse nearly every window was smashed; UCLA students forced the entire Los Angeles police force onto tactical alert, and Governor Reagan subsequently shut down all twenty-seven state university campuses. Austin students were teargassed after charging the state capitol. They followed with the biggest march in Texas history (they chanted, "More pay for police!" to keep the cops at bay). At Macalester College in St. Paul, students barricaded the office of a new political science professor and demanded his resignation. But the professor, Hubert Humphrey, was away in Israel.

A National Strike Information Center at Brandeis claimed to be coordinating things, and that the strikes were united around three demands: immediate withdrawal from Southeast Asia, an immediate end to defense research and ROTC, and, like point nine of the Black Panthers' program, release of "all political prisoners." But most of the center's work was fielding CB radio reports from the field, just trying to keeping up with developments.

A report from Madison, Wisconsin, noon, May 5: "Wide-scale rioting, burning, trashing, tear gas everywhere."

The next day: "One hundred arrested, school shut, National Guard, fires in street every night, fifty or sixty hurt, tear gas, 'open warfare.'"

A new tactic developed, blocking traffic: on highways, at expressway on-ramps, at busy intersections, even on U.S. 1 outside Washington, D.C. A National Economic Boycott Committee decided to boycott Coca-Cola and Philip Morris for "their dependency on the youth market for a large part of their sales." Quinnipiac College in Connecticut did them one better, urging "colleges and universities across the country to join with them in a boycott of ALL consumer goods (except necessary foods) the week of May 25–31." Five thousand students at Northwestern did *them* one better by voting unanimously to secede from the United States. NYU students demanded $100,000 in protection money not to smash an Atomic Energy Commission supercomputer so they could bail out a jailed Black Panther. The National Republican Governors' Conference was canceled.

But once more mass protest brought forth a paradox: the *real* radicalness was the extent to which demonstrations were mundane and mainstream. On only one out of twenty campuses was there any violence; at Grinnell students accidentally broke a window and collected $14.30 to pay for it. Faculty participated en masse; university presidents made accommodations for students to preserve their grades. At Oberlin, university facilities were turned over to antiwar activity for the rest of the year. Princeton announced it would shut down for several weeks before the fall elections so students could volunteer for the political candidates of their choice. In New Jersey, even a draft board went on strike.

That only redoubled some people's rage. Emory's president wired President Nixon, "On behalf of these deeply concerned students, I beg that you consider the prompt withdrawal of all U.S. troops from Vietnam and Cambodia." The regents thereafter received a letter from one Wade Murrah, Rt. 2, Blairsville, Georgia, cc'ed to Governor Maddox: "I am sorry to see Emory apparently joining this anarchistic parade of university destroyers."

Other university bureaucrats learned what it was like to give an inch and be taken for a mile. The administration at the University of Denver called an all-university assembly and signed off on the strike vote. Students promptly assembled a rambling, anarchic outdoor commune on campus, "Woodstock West." Vigilantes phoned in threats to administrators: "If you don't do anything to clean out that nest of radicals, then we will—with shotguns." The chancellor decided that such martyrdom was just what the students desired— so he preemptively called in the National Guard to raze Woodstock West and said some students deserved the electric chair, borrowing President Nixon's language about Cambodia: campuses "are being used as protected sanctuaries" by people "who would like to see the free world destroyed."

At the U.S. Merchant Marine Academy, seventy-three cadets signed a petition pledging not to participate in the Armed Forces Day parade; the petition's drafters found themselves bound and gagged by a mob of hooded cadets. At the University of Washington, a band of vigilantes calling themselves HELP (Help Eliminate Lawless Protest) ran around clubbing strikers. In Buffalo, police broke up a rally with bird shot. At Hobart College in the Finger Lakes region of upstate New York, American Legion members organized a disruption of commencement. The police weren't much help; they were in on the organizing. (Julie Nixon's graduation from Smith was peaceful; the president arranged the previous fall to be out of the country rather than attend.)

At his May 8 press conference the president was asked if he agreed with those who argued America was heading for a revolution. A staffer for the federal commission set up to study the turbulence wrote a memo: "Several small schools in New York City are not going to open this year because their backers are no longer interested in backing education." He reported that the last six college presidents he'd spoken to had received death threats (three had taken bodyguards). Al Capp added a new line to his speeches: "The real Kent State martyrs were the kids in uniforms. . . . The president showed angelic restraint when he called the students 'bums.'" The rock musician Neil Young saw the pietà-like picture of a young girl leaning in anguish over the body of Jeff Miller. He hastily composed a song:

> Tin soldiers and Nixon's coming.
> We're finally on our own.
> This summer I hear the drumming.
> Four dead in Ohio.

The song was banned from Ohio playlists at the urging of Governor Rhodes. That helped send it shooting up the hit parade: one more scene in the new American civil war.

The battleground was often Betsy Ross's flag, as counterdemonstrators put their bodies on the line to keep it from being lowered to half-staff. In Silver Spring, Maryland, at the high school Allison Krause had attended, left-wing students commandeered the PA system and demanded the flag be lowered. An argument broke out: "People talking about this chick who was killed at Kent. Two GIs from this school have been killed in Vietnam. Why didn't we lower the flag for them?" The school had two flagpoles, so the principal devised a compromise: one flag was raised all the way, the other halfway. Compromise didn't work. Right-wing students pulled down the flag memorializing Allison and burned it in a trash can. At Northwestern, students carried a flag upside down, the symbol for distress. "A hefty man in work clothes," according to *Time,* tried to grab it, saying, "That's my flag! I fought for it! You have no right to it!" The kids started arguing. "There are millions of people like me," the man responded. "We're fed up with your movement. You're forcing us into it. We'll have to kill you. All I can see is a lot of kids blowing a chance I never had."

In Albuquerque—where Jane Fonda found herself on a blacklist that kept her from getting a hotel room—students approached the standard outside the University of New Mexico's Union Hall. National Guardsmen approached with bayonets fixed as students fussed with the flag. The soldiers advanced, impaling seven, one in a cast and on crutches. A newsman came to his aid. The guardsmen stabbed him, too.

That flag: during the Vietnam Moratorium, New York's Mayor Lindsay ordered it flown at half-staff as a memorial to the war dead. An enraged city council member from Queens tramped up to the City Hall roof and pulled the banner back up himself. "Meanwhile," the *Washington Post* reported on October 16, 1969, "officials of the Patrolmen's Benevolent and Uniformed Firefighters Association claimed almost total success in their campaign to keep firehouse and precinct station flags at full staff."

After Kent State, Lindsay ordered city flags lowered again. At noon on Friday, May 8, in a cold Manhattan drizzle, students from across the city gathered at George Washington's statue in front of Federal Hall on Wall Street, where representatives of the thirteen colonies first met to petition King George. "You brought down one president," a fifty-six-year-old lawyer told them with delight, "and you'll bring down another!" The mood was joyous.

Suddenly, from all directions, two hundred construction workers marched in to the cadences of "All the way! USA!" and "We're number one!" and "Love it or leave it!" In their identical brown overalls, carrying American flags of the sort that topped off construction sites, they looked like some sort of storm trooper battalion.

They started arguing with the police: Why weren't flags flying in front of Federal Hall like at all the Wall Street banks? Had the hippies stolen them? (The flags, actually, per federal regulations, were not flying due to inclement weather.)

The police report: *They argued that this was a government owned building, that it was owned by all the people, and that they had a right to an equal portion of the steps to express their view in support of the American flag and the foreign policy of the United States; that everyone had an equal right to freely express their views.*

Some students tried to shout the workers down. Others, nervous, tried to melt into the lunchtime crowd.

The construction workers, reinforced by the rear by some thousand vocal supporters from the Wall Street area, suddenly burst through the easterly terminus of the police line.

Demonstrators observed that the police were not particularly enthusiastic about stopping them.

Once atop the steps, the construction workers implanted a number of American flags on the pillars and on the statue of George Washington.

An insurance underwriter, in admiration: "Wow, it was just like John Wayne taking Iwo Jima."

The unusual lunch hour crowd which had, by now, inundated the area completely from building line to building line, loudly applauded the construction workers and their singing of the National Anthem; many onlookers joined in, openly displaying much fervor.

At this juncture a neatly groomed conservatively dressed middle aged man suddenly took a position in the pedestal in front of the statue of George Washington where he thumbed his nose at the construction worker group, shouted obscenities, and ultimately committed an act of desecration upon one of the American flags implanted there by them. He was variously reported as blowing his nose in the flag, tearing the flag with his teeth, and eating the flag.

The riot began. Workers singled out for beating boys with the longest hair. The weapons of choice were their orange and yellow hard hats.

A construction worker recalled, "The whole group started singing 'God Bless America' and it damn near put a lump in your throat. . . . I could never say I was sorry I was there. You just had a very proud feeling. If I live to be one hundred, I don't think I'll ever live to see anything quite like that again."

A student recalled, "When I was on the ground, I rolled myself into a ball just as four or five pairs of construction boots started kicking me."

The proletarians marched on City Hall, now joined by hundreds more workers from the city's biggest construction site, the twin-towered "World Trade Center." They were joined, in solidarity, by the capitalists; the New York Stock Exchange ended up having its lowest-volume day in months.

"Lindsay's a Red! Lindsay's a Red!"

"Lindsay must go!"

"Raise our flag! Raise our flag!"

A mail carrier scrambled onto the roof to hoist Old Glory. A mayoral aide followed and relowered it. Construction workers furiously rushed City Hall, crying, "Get Lindsay!"—almost breaching the building. A deputy mayor raised the flag back up to appease the mob. Workers launched another chorus of "The Star-Spangled Banner"; good patriots, the cops removed their hats and stood at attention instead of attending to the gleeful ongoing beatings.

A municipal secretary: "I saw one construction worker arm himself with a pair of iron clippers and head toward a student already being pummeled by three workers. . . . He yelled at me, 'Let go of my jacket, bitch'; and then he said, 'If you want to be treated like an equal, we'll treat you like one.' Three of them began to punch me in the body. My glasses were broken. I had trouble breathing, and I thought my ribs were cracked.'"

The *Wall Street Journal:* "'These hippies are getting what they deserve,' said John Halloran, one of the construction workers, while the mêlée was still going on. As he talked a coworker standing with him yelled, 'Damn straight,' and punched a young man in a business suit who said he disagreed."

The mob moved on to nearby Pace University, setting fire to a banner reading VIETNAM, LAOS, CAMBODIA, KENT. The glass doors to the building were chained shut from the inside against attack. Hard hats crashed through them and chased down unkempt students, joined by conservative students angry at strikers interfering with their education. Some longhairs were beaten with lead pipes wrapped in American flags. Trinity Church became a makeshift field hospital (the mob ripped down the Red Cross banner). The *New York Times* ran a picture the next day of a construction worker and a man in a tie charging down a cobblestone street to beat someone with an American flag. Pete Hamill, who had only the previous year offered his solidarity to "The Revolt of the White Lower Middle Class," now withdrew his endorsement in horror: "The police collaborated with the construction workers in the same way that Southern sheriffs used to collaborate with the rednecks when the rednecks were beating up freedom riders."

Police made only six arrests. Perhaps they agreed with the construction worker who told the *Wall Street Journal,* "I'm doing this because my brother got wounded in Vietnam, and I think this will help our boys over there by pulling this country together."

The action shifted to Washington, D.C., for a weekend outbreak of civics. A bipartisan group of senators had mapped out a three-phase strategy to use the congressional power of the purse to end the Vietnam War. John Sherman Cooper (R-Ky.) and Frank Church (D-Idaho) would introduce an amendment banning funds for ground forces in Cambodia or Laos. The Gulf of Tonkin Resolution would be put up for a revote. And George McGovern (D-S.Dak.) and Mark Hatfield (R-Ore.) would introduce a new amendment to the military procurement authorization bill to provide that without a congressional declaration of war all American troops must withdraw from Vietnam by June 30, 1971. Sixteen senators and eighteen House members founded a Congressional Committee to End the War with McGovern as chair. And from hundreds of colleges and universities across the land, students congregated to lobby more congressmen to the cause. Haverford College moved lock, stock, and barrel to D.C.: 575 of 640 students, 40 of 70 faculty, 10 of 12 administrators. Birch Bayh addressed the assembled student-citizen army on Capitol Hill: "We can make this system responsible from within instead of trying to destroy it from without." He got a standing ovation. George McGovern, the former college professor, announced, "Let us get twenty million signatures and let us call or write every congressman and senator, and we will pass this amendment."

A federal court waived a fifteen-day prior-notice requirement and allowed a Saturday rally at the Ellipse. One of Ehrlichman's young aides, Bud Krogh, showed off the prized basement command post the White House had set up to John Dean, a young Justice Department staffer they were thinking about hiring. The bunker had shelves and shelves of supplies, beds, a presidential desk flanked by flags, a conference room with three TV monitors, direct phone lines to the police chief, mayor, National Guard, FBI, and Pentagon. In the basements of government buildings around the federal city, five thousand soldiers waited at the ready. After all, organizers from the New National Mobilizing Committee to End the War claimed twenty thousand of the one hundred thousand expected to show up would be willing to commit civil disobedience.

Either as fears or boasts, the predictions of disorder proved unfounded. *"All we are saying is give peace a chance"*: the press could hear the refrain wafting from outside the White House gates as the president, visibly weary and nervous, stepped to the podium for a televised press conference the evening before the rally. Flyers were everywhere: "NIXON WOULD LIKE *YOU* TO USE VIOLENCE IN THIS DEMONSTRATION TO DISCREDIT THE STUDENT PEACE MOVEMENT. DO THE HARD THING . . . *AVOID VIOLENCE.*" Jane Fonda, in a T-shirt and braless, welcomed the crowd: "Greetings, fellow bums!" She gestured to the men in uniform patrolling the perimeter: "Those men may well have seen combat in Vietnam. They know better than any of us what this war is like. Don't assume they are against us for opposing war." A booming cheer went up. A GI flashed a conspicuous peace sign. A massed contingent marched into sight behind a banner reading FEDERAL BUMS AGAINST THE WAR. The crowd went wild. Thousands bathed in the Reflecting Pool. A black man strapped himself to a giant crucifix. Shirley MacLaine, Coretta Scott King, Dr. Spock, David Dellinger delivered soaring perorations. *Time* reported with pleasure how some government officials, even John Mitchell, circulated through the crowd, inviting students back to their offices for raps. The father of one of the slain Kent State students, a Pittsburgh steelworker, announced, "My child was not a bum."

Senator Muskie, the Democratic presidential front-runner, modified his position. He had earlier proposed a timid nonbinding antiwar "sense of the Senate" resolution. Now, he announced himself as McGovern-Hatfield's nineteenth cosponsor. The congressional antiwar committee scheduled a half-hour broadcast on NBC for May 13 in support of the amendment; to raise money for airtime, students circulated a petition on campuses and asked signers to contribute fifty cents each. They collected $30,000 in two days.

Even Nixon backtracked a little. His initial undiplomatic two-sentence response to the Kent State shootings read by Ron Ziegler began, "This should remind us all once again that when dissent turns to violence, it invites tragedy." Now he met for an hour with Kent State students. And in the middle of the night the morning before the rally, he embarked on the strangest perambulations in the history of the presidency. "After a nearly sleepless night in an empty and barricaded White House, President Nixon emerged early yesterday morning to talk to student demonstrators about 'the war thing' and other topics," according to the *Washington Post*. "'Sure, you came here to demonstrate and shout your slogans on the Ellipse. That is all right. Just keep it peaceful,' Mr. Nixon told the students on the steps of the Lincoln Memorial as dawn was breaking over the city."

Then this visitation from another planet took his valet, Manolo Sanchez, for a tour of the Capitol.

"I hope it was because he was tired," a Syracuse student reported. "But most of what he was saying was absurd. Here we had come from a university that's completely uptight, on strike, and when he told him where we were from, he talked about the football team. And when someone said he was from California, he talked about surfing."

Nixon was becoming a discombobulated president, politically on the run. His interior secretary, Walter Hickel, posted a letter to the president that leaked to the *Washington Star:* "Youth in its protest must be heard." Thomas Jefferson, James Madison, and James Monroe were young people in their day, Hickel argued; their "protests fell on deaf ears and finally led to war." (The president's response was to bulldoze the White House tennis court, beloved of Hickel.) Paul Harvey, the sentimental radio announcer *Esquire* had called in a recent profile the "voice of the Silent Majority," said, "America's six percent section of the planet's mothers cannot bear enough boy babies to police Asia—and the nation can't bleed to death trying."

Nixon had tried to talk to the student demonstrators. He concluded he preferred the hard hats. "Thinks now the college demonstrators have overplayed their hands," Haldeman wrote in his diary, "evidence is the blue collar group rising against them, and P can mobilize them."

New York construction workers now took every lunch hour for boisterous patriotic demonstrations. So did hard hats in San Diego, Buffalo, and

Pittsburgh. Some of the rallies were not entirely spontaneous: "Obviously more of these will be occurring throughout the nation," White House staffer Stephen Bull wrote in a memo to Chuck Colson, "perhaps partially as a result of your clandestine activity." Peter Brennan, the combative head of the Building Trades Council of Greater New York, accused of organizing the "hard hat riot," defiantly denied it—then showed what he *could* do as an organizer: one hundred thousand marchers on May 20, complete with a cement mixer draped with a LINDSAY FOR MAYOR OF HANOI banner. Signs read GOD BLESS THE ESTABLISHMENT and WE SUPPORT NIXON AND AGNEW. *Time* called it "a kind of workers' Woodstock."

"Thank God for the hard hats!" Nixon cried. He had been so delighted by the liberal Pete Hamill's exposé of the political alienation of the white working class in *New York* magazine in 1969 that he ordered a Labor Department study on the question. Assistant Secretary Jerome S. Rosow had just delivered his report "The Problem of the Blue Collar Worker." It described a population "on a treadmill, chasing the illusion of higher living standards," fighting via the only apparent weapon at their disposal: "continued pressure for high wages." Their only champions "seem to be the union leaders spearheading the demand." But to reduce the problem to economics, Rosow suggested, was to miss more than half the story. The more profound distress was cultural—a problem of recognition. Negroes at least had a clamoring lobby—Daniel Moynihan's "hysterics, paranoids and boodlers"—making noise on their behalf. Blue-collar whites "feel like 'forgotten people'—those for whom the government and society have limited, if any direct concern and little visible action."

Here was the germ of a revolution in the Republican's message. Unless they took workers' votes from the Democrats—as Ronald Reagan had in California in 1966—Nixon would never be able to achieve the New Majority he dreamed of. But to do so with ongoing economic concessions—previously the only way politicians imagined working-class voters might be wooed—offended a more foundational Republican constituency: business. And contributed to the inflation that was driving the stock market into the low 600s.

But to extend to blue-collar workers the hand of *cultural* recognition—that was a different ball game altogether. It's not that right-leaning politicians hadn't tried it before—Nixon had done something like it in the Checkers Speech, when he styled the people accusing him of corruption as hopeless snobs, and himself as an ordinary striver just trying to make an honest living. But the hard-hat ascendency set into motion a qualitative shift: the first concerted effort to turn the white working class, via its aesthetic disgusts, against a Democratic Party now joining itself objectively, with their Cooper-Church and McGovern-Hatfield amendments, to the agenda of the smelly longhairs who burned down buildings.

The Democratic Party: enemy of the working man. It was the political version of that *New York Times* photograph of the stockbroker and the pie fitter joined in solidarity in the act of clobbering a hippie—their common weapon the American flag. That white men in ties and white men in hard hats were radically opposed to one another was a foundational left-wing idea. But as a Republican state senator from Orange County observed, "Every time they burn another building, Republican registration goes up."

Nixon told his team to get to work putting the Rosow Report's insights, "even if only symbolic," into action. Peter Brennan, and Thomas Gleason of the International Longshoremen's Association, vice president of the AFL-CIO executive committee, were summoned to the White House on May 26—the day the Dow reached a new yearly low, nine days after the Cooper-Church amendment passed a Senate committee. Brennan presented the president with an honorary hard hat reading COMMANDER IN CHIEF and left a four-star hard hat to present to General Creighton Abrams, the American commander in Vietnam, and promised continued patriotic marches: "The hard hat will stand as a symbol along with our great flag, for freedom and patriotism and our beloved country." Nixon eventually made Brennan secretary of labor. One member of the delegation said, "If someone would have had the courage to go into Cambodia, they might have captured the bullet that took my son's life." The president choked up. Sweet triumph: who could be more Democratic than union leaders?

The Republican business class, small-town America, backyard-pool suburbanites, Dixiecrats, calloused union members: now it was as if the White House had discovered the magic incantation to join them as one. Nixonites imagined no limit to the power of this New Majority: "Patriotic themes to counter economic depression will get response from unemployed," Haldeman wrote in a note to himself. *Then no one would be a Democrat anymore.*

Tuesday, November 3, 1970, Nixon decided, would be the day of his apotheosis. Of the thirty-five seats at play in the Senate, twenty-five were held by Democrats. And just as Nixon had figured out that most Democratic congressmen swept in on Lyndon Johnson's coattails in 1964 could be swept out in 1966, the new Democratic senators elected in 1964 were vulnerable in exactly the same way. Add in the Senate election in New York, where the Rockefeller appointee Charles Goodell was up for election for the first time: the New York Conservative Party was going to run a candidate against him—William F. Buckley's brother James—and Clif White would be running his campaign. Conservative Harry Flood Byrd would be running as an independent in Virginia. A net shift of seven seats in these races would produce a pro-Nixon majority—for a conservative Supreme Court nominee, against the quislings who wanted to sabotage him in Vietnam.

He would finally get to be *president.*

CHAPTER TWENTY-FOUR

Purity

RICHARD NIXON RANG UP THE CURTAIN ON THE 1970 ELECTION ON May 28, two days after entertaining the hard hats in the White House, in the stadium where the University of Tennessee's Volunteers played football. Billy Graham was holding one of his ten-day crusades and had "invited" the president to speak on Youth Day. It all was an exceedingly ingenious political contrivance. There was a student uprising, so Nixon would listen to students—on a playing field he controlled, where if they booed him, they'd be booing America's Pastor.

First, the Nixon people got Graham invited to a campus—one big enough to make an impact, but pacific enough to forestall embarrassment. The University of Tennessee in Knoxville, in the heavily Dixified eastern corner of the state, was perfect: a rah-rah wonderland, "Big Orange Country," where stores that sold *Playboy* were raided, and students sat segregated by fraternity at football games.

And Billy Graham's crusade, you see, just happened to coincide with the day UT's chancellor had invited President Nixon to speak for the university's 175th anniversary.

All concerned had to explain their way past the murmurs of protest that the Crusade, and the university, were being politicized. Dick Gregory and Adam Clayton Powell Jr. had been banned as campus speakers; the administration said they were too political. Back then, students received a court order demanding an open speaker policy—and now the chancellor used the court order as reason why he couldn't exclude Nixon, as Graham assured all and sundry there "will not be anything political, I hope, in his visit." (Every Beltway insider knew that Billy Graham was the most politically sophisticated preacher since William Jennings Bryan.) Then there were those who were opposed to a public educational institution and a president facilitating so massive a call to Jesus. The conservative *Knoxville Journal* dispatched that objection by explaining that Nixon's intention was not religious but "to get closer to today's college students." The university, compounding the bamboozlement, said Graham was merely a customer renting the stadium—

though the university president had signed a petition inviting him and led the "offertory prayer" soliciting funds, and the Knoxville mayor sang in the choir and issued a proclamation to all city employees to renew their commitment to God. For liberals who doted on procedural niceties, the whole thing was an affront—"the rape of this university," said one. That was a win-win situation from a political perspective: let the liberals bicker against patriotism and piety at a moment of moral crisis. That set the table for the rally perfectly—for putting such conflicts on display was more than half the point of this exercise.

The day arrived. There were fewer than a hundred protesters, which was perfect; the drama wouldn't have worked unless there was *some* dissidence. They were but a drop in the ocean of one hundred thousand Silent Majority communicants, many in white dress shirts and ties. In the stadium-cum-Baptist-church, the tatterdemalion outcasts became as the early Christians.

A pacifist professor planned a pageant of nonviolent protest: dissidents would join the march down the field at the invitation to receive Christ, then kneel and hold up the two-fingered peace sign at the altar. They marched to the stadium in a mock funeral procession, carrying biblical injunctions on their signs. These were confiscated at the gate as potential weapons. Police circulated Tennessee statute TCA 39–1205—prohibiting disruption of a religious service—and photographed the picketers.

A student tried to bring in a loudspeaker. Cops ostentatiously escorted him out of the stadium across the length of the football field, to roars. ("Outside slime!" one lady screeched.) A congregant wearing a crucifix pin was offered an antiwar pamphlet. He retorted, "Stick it up your ass." A cop rubbed his service revolver; it reminded a liberal Eastern reporter of masturbation. The protesters' resolve for a silent vigil began to break down.

Nixon's motorcade arrived. The Fellowship of Christian Athletes guarded the stage at the twenty-yard line; thereupon sat an array of Republican officeholders and candidates, including thirty-eight-year-old Knoxville congressman William Brock III, whom Nixon had personally recruited to run against Senator Albert Gore, who had voted against the ABM, for the anti-Vietnam amendments, against Haynsworth and Carswell—and had conspicuously not been invited. His absence softened him up for Brock's general election strategy: to zero in on the votes the devoutly Baptist Gore had dared to tender against the late Senator Dirksen's school-prayer constitutional amendment.

President and Mrs. Nixon strode down the field with the Reverend and Mrs. Graham. A two-minute ovation drowned out the protesters' "One, two, three, four, we don't want Nixon's fucking war." A black minister offered the opening invocation, a prayer for "our beloved president." Graham took the pulpit and could have ignored the barely audible jeers. But that wasn't the point. Instead, he addressed the jeerers. "I'm for change—but the

Bible teaches us to obey authority. . . . In this day of student unrest on the campus, here on one of the largest universities in America tens of thousands have been demonstrating their faith in the God of our fathers!"

The protesters started chanting, *"Politics! Politics! Politics! Politics!"*

Graham continued, "All Americans may not agree with the decisions a president makes, but he is our president."

A Baptist ministry student leapt up: "Get out of Vietnam!" An usher ran to subdue him but tripped; a woman whapped the protester with an umbrella.

The president began his remarks: "As one who warmed the bench for four years, it's finally good to get out on the football field here at Neyland Stadium. And even if we're on the twenty-yard line, we're going over that goal line before we're through."

The demonstrators responded with the old football cheer: "Push'm back, push'm back, wa-a-aaay back!" Massed together, they were easy to spot: they were the ones not wearing white dress shirts and ties.

Nixon made the interruption the text for his sermon: "Billy Graham, when he invited me to come here, said that this was to be Youth Night. He told me that there would be youth from the university, from other parts of the state, representing different points of view. I am just glad that there seems to be a rather solid majority on one side rather than the other side tonight."

The congregants roared their delight. The president talked about all the young people who worked for him—"the largest proportion of staff members in responsible positions below the age of thirty of any White House staff in history"—because young people "have something to say and I want them in the high councils of the government of this country."

He said he was for all those noble reforms young people were for.

"But I can tell you, my friends, that while government can bring peace, that while government can clean up the air, that while government can clean up the streets, and while government can clean up the water and bring better education and better health, there is one thing that government cannot do. . . .

"America would not be what it is today, the greatest nation in the world, if this were not a nation which had made progress—under—*Godddd*"—he drew out his words like a preacher. "If we are going to bring people together as we must bring them together, if we are going to have peace in the world, if our young people are going to have a fulfillment beyond simply those material things, they must turn to those great spiritual sources that have made America the great country that it is."

"Bullshit! Bullshit! Bullshit!" cried the heretics, once more drowned out by the pious.

Billy Graham took to the pulpit and introduced the Negro singer Ethel Waters. She called Nixon "my blessed child." She, too, chose to address the protesters: "Now, you children over there, listen to me! If I was over there close enough, I would smack you, but I love you and I'd give you a big hug and kiss!" A piano tinkling behind her, she referred to the president as if he were Christ: "He belongs to everyone who wants to receive and accept him."

The Reverend Billy Graham began his altar call with a warning: "If you come for any other reason, you are in danger of blasphemy, and that's one sin that cannot be pardoned." Some damned themselves to hell nonetheless: they displayed the peace symbol. Many more raised their index finger to the sky—Christ, the one way to peace.

The flock streamed for the exits; the cops stood by and arrested eight of the protesters for disturbing public worship. The local newspaper critiqued the "unspeakable nastiness of a handful of undisciplined brats" and gave over the letters page to public outrage over them for days. The student newspaper editorialized, "There was no need for the demonstrators to try to interfere with the prayers or hymns at the service. Their purpose was to communicate their feelings to Nixon, not to alienate Billy Graham or those who were there to participate in the crusade."

That made the student editors either exquisitely naive or gifted Republican publicists: the protesters *couldn't* make their feelings known to the president without also alienating the participants in the crusade. That was the whole point.

And the drama had come off like a charm. *Time* called it "one of the most effective speeches he has yet delivered." *Newsweek* termed it "a suitably evangelistic ending for a Presidential week that started out seemingly beyond redemption." By the time the crusade was broadcast nationwide, the political juice from disruption having been squeezed suitably dry, the protests were edited out, leaving just the president looking presidential, addressing his fellow Americans, uniting the youth and Silent Majority in reconciliation. The Tuesday following, the first day of exams, Knoxville police squads cruised campus armed with photographs and fifty-seven arrests warrants, snatching protesters from street corners. One teaching assistant was contacted by a dean's office to get his address to "update department files"; the cops arrested him at home. Leonard Garment turned off the bad public relations with a wire requesting they wait to complete the arrests until the semester was over. Billy Graham released a statement: "Certainly a President of the United States should be allowed to attend a ball game, entertainment, or a religious service without it being interpreted as political."

And thus the curtain was raised on the most active White House campaign for an off-year election since 1938.

The sharp point of the spear was the vice president. Spiro Agnew began the year with a stature-enhancing state visit to Asia. In Manila for the second inaugural of President Ferdinand Marcos of the Philippines, Agnew experienced a rite of passage: his limousine was attacked by leftist students, just like Nixon's in South America. Then Agnew made a frenetic tour of Lincoln Day dinners, just as Nixon used to do. "The liberal media have been calling on me to lower my voice and to seek accord and unity among all Americans," he would say. "Nothing would please me more to see all voices lowered . . . to see an end to the vilification, the obscenities, the vandalism, and the violence that have become the standard tactics of the dissidents who claim to act in the interests of freedom. But I want you to know that I will not make a unilateral withdrawal and thereby abridge the confidence of the Silent Majority, the everyday law-abiding American who believes his country needs a strong voice to articulate his dissatisfaction with those who seek to destroy our heritage of liberty and our system of justice.

"To penetrate the cacophony of seditious drivel emanating from the best-publicized clowns in our society and their fans in the fourth estate, yes, my friends, to penetrate that drivel, we need a cry of alarm, not a whisper."

Agnew carried the torch through the South after the scuttling of Haynsworth and Carswell via "the most nebulous set of trumped-up charges ever contrived by the labor and civil rights lobbies and their allies in the news profession." In Columbia, Strom Thurmond said of 1966's civil rights candidate for governor of Maryland, "South Carolina will favor Spiro Agnew for president in 1976."

Listeners especially enjoyed his savage "humor"—the story of how he had argued with the president when Nixon decided to convert the White House swimming pool into a pressroom: "I resisted his insistence that the water be drained out"; his worry that, playing golf with George McGovern and William Fulbright, "I just might accidentally tag one of them with a golf ball. And then he might respond the way they usually do to aggressive and brutal treatment. And I hate to be kissed on a public golf course." Bumper stickers reading SPIRO OF '76 were added to a growing shelf of Spiro kitsch pro and con: record albums of Agnew speeches; the "Spiro T. Agnew U.S. History Challenge" board game; Spiro "mouthwash" that was actually a bar of soap. His face, so sloping and planar, was something of a caricaturist's dream—one more similarity to his mentor Nixon. Some people thought he looked like a ferret. Some people thought he looked like a Roman emperor.

In April he recalled how the *New York Times*'s Tom Wicker "made a lugubrious lament that those were 'our children' in the streets of Chicago giving the Bronx cheer to the Conrad Hilton. To a degree Wicker is right—and the fact that we raised some of the crowd that was out there in Grant Park is one of the valid indictments of my generation. But precisely whose children are they? They are, for the most part, the children of affluent, permissive, upper-middle-class parents who learned their Dr. Spock and threw discipline out the window—when they should have done the opposite. They are the children dropped off by their parents at Sunday school to hear the 'modern' gospel from a 'progressive' preacher more interested in fighting pollution than fighting evil—one of those pleasant clergymen who ... has cast morality and theology aside as not 'relevant' and set as its goal on earth the recognition of Red China and the preservation of the Florida alligator."

He referred to "the score of students at Cornell who, wielding pipes and tire chains, beat a dormitory president into unconsciousness." (The new president of that beleaguered institution released an angry statement: "No such incident even remotely fitting this statement has ever occurred at Cornell University." The vice president's office was pleased to issue a correction: "The beating of a dormitory president by students wielding tire irons and chains occurred this month at the University of Connecticut rather than Cornell. It was at Cornell University this month that the African Studies and Research Center was destroyed by fire, probably arson ... by SDS and the Black Liberation Front with no action taken against them.") And that "the next time a mob of students, waving their nonnegotiable demands, start pitching bricks and rocks at the student union, just imagine they are wearing brown shirts or white sheets—and act accordingly."

Three days later Agnew appeared on the cover of *Life* magazine: "Spiro Knows Best: Stern voice of the silent majority."

Three days after that, the Kent State killings happened.

Agnew had a speech scheduled for that night to the American Retail Federation. He changed nothing, lustily reading his swipes at liberal elites "all too willing to believe that the criminal who throws a bomb at a bank is a hero and the policeman who gets killed while trying to stop him is a pig" exactly as written.

A week after the Kent State killings, the adjutant general of the Ohio National Guard backed off from any claim that his men had been fired at by a sniper; the FBI said that guardsmen had been in no imminent danger; a new photo surfaced confirming beyond a shadow of a doubt that the closest students were so far away from the guardsmen that Willie Mays couldn't have thrown rocks at them. The order-loving son of Greek immigrants was earning a reputation as part of the problem. A columnist for the conservative *Washington Star* wrote, "Vice President Spiro T. Agnew, at his unmuzzled worst, is a danger to the country, not because of his own rhetorical excesses or crudity of thought, but because of the response which his aggressiveness produces." Four hundred faculty members in Massachusetts voted to invite Agnew to speak at their campuses so that he could be indicted for crossing state lines to incite a riot. And when, by the middle of May, weeks passed without a public appearance, the press reported that the president had applied the muzzle. Then, six days before the president's Billy Graham speech, at a $500-a-plater in Houston, Agnew said, "Lately, you have been exposed to a great deal of public comment about vice-presidential rhetoric and how I should 'cool it.' ... Nowhere is the complaint louder than in the columns and editorials of the liberal news media of this country, those really illiberal, self-appointed guardians of our destiny who would like to run the country without ever submitting to the elective process as we in public office might do."

The venom in the address he went on to deliver so stunned expectations that the *New York Times* republished it in full.

He excoriated the "wild, hot rhetoric" that "pours out of the television set and the radio in a daily torrent," from the *Washington Post, Life,* and the *New York Times,* working together to "tear our country apart." He quoted Jerry Rubin on the Kent State campus "one month prior to the confrontation that brought the student deaths there": "Until you people are prepared to kill your parents, you aren't ready for revolution." And even so, he thundered, James Reston, in his May 10 column, "saw fit to equate *me* with Jerry Rubin as an extremist. . . . And yet they ask *us* to cool our rhetoric and lower our voices!"

Houston Republicans screamed their acclaim.

His claim about Reston, whose May 10 column mentioned neither the vice president nor Jerry Rubin, was a brazen lie. Reston had focused the piece, instead, on his delight that more and more students were rejecting protest and working within the political system. The lie made political sense; Reston's column was about the electoral consequences of a surge of students working for Democratic congressional candidates, and Princeton's decision to cancel classes for a few weeks in the fall so students could work on campaigns. Agnew's job, on behalf of his president, was to shove such developments onto the "anarchy" side of the polarization ledger.

Hubert Humphrey said of his successor as vice president, "I personally doubt that our country has seen in twenty years"—i.e., since Joseph McCarthy—"such a calculated appeal to our nastier interests." John Ehrlichman responded in textbook tones of wounded innocence: "I don't think it is illegitimate for someone in his situation to help bring a balance into communications. It seems to me a sort of desperation defense to say the vice president is polarizing people when he says the press is unfair."

Ehrlichman added that, after all, "politics is the art of polarization."

And Agnew would keep on practicing the art: there was a lot more polarization to accomplish before November.

The Democrats were gaining traction by hammering on the economy. Nixon *could* make things easier for ordinary Americans, they hectored, with wage-and-price guideposts like President Kennedy's. But Nixon had ruled that out in his first presidential press conference—"I do not go along with the suggestion that inflation can be effectively controlled by exhorting labor and management and industry to follow certain guidelines"—because, Democrats said, he was a greedy Republican.

He was also a wily Republican, with congressional elections to win. And on June 17, he went on TV and promised that the Council of Economic Advisers would issue "inflation alerts"—wage-and-price guideposts by another name.

So frustrating for Democrats, running against a party led by a man with principles like that—though many Democrats were convinced this was their ace in the hole. The president's men were the greasiest of the greasy Old Pols. The way to defeat them was to contrast them with the *idealism* of the New Politics coalition that seemed to be surging all around.

Save the party, save the nation, save your soul: it had been the New Politics message ever since the 1968 Dump Johnson movement. The ideals were rooted in the founding slogan of Students for a Democratic Society: *participatory democracy.* New Politics theorists saw it as an increasingly postparty age, one in which people made up their minds via media that delivered experience directly into their homes. And that, in a society where the average age was falling every year and more and more young people were going to college, conservatism could only but yield diminishing returns.

Kent State seemed logically to hasten the tide. The Voting Rights Act reauthorization vote was set for June; in March, Southerners desperate to see Harrold Carswell nominated had quietly put aside filibuster plans. Ted Kennedy and Senate majority leader Mike Mansfield spied an opportunity to lower the voting age to eighteen, an idea floating around in liberal circles since the 1940s. General Eisenhower had come out for it in 1966, reasoning that if you were old enough to die for your country, you were old enough to choose the leaders who sent you to do it. In 1968 *Time* underwrote a straw primary in which over a million college students voted (Eugene McCarthy got 285,998 votes, HHH 18,535). That June, LBJ suggested introducing the eighteen-year-old vote by constitutional amendment.

There hadn't been much movement since. Kennedy and Mansfield decided to force the issue by attaching a rider to the Voting Rights Act extension to give eighteen-year-olds the vote in federal, state, and local elections, effective January 1, 1971. Since the Constitution was silent on setting a voting age, critics argued the Tenth Amendment reserved that power for the states (four had already lowered theirs), and that lowering it by statute would be struck down by the courts. Critics preferred the slower, safer course: a constitutional amendment.

Mansfield and Kennedy insisted the foul deed in Ohio made the situation too urgent for that.

On May 10 Mansfield warned he'd filibuster Voting Rights unless the Senate voted in his rider; the full Senate skipped committee hearings to do so. The House Rules Committee reported a similar bill out June 4; it passed the House with a veto-proof majority on June 17. When Speaker McCormack announced the vote, the teenagers packing the galleries exploded. The eighty-year-old McCormack, so feeble he rarely appeared on the floor, would ordinarily have gaveled down such noise. But the spirit was electric. He let the hubbub stand. And Al Capp tried out a new one-liner: "The opinions of eighteen-year-olds are valuable on things they know something about, such as puberty and hubcaps, but nothing else."

This was New Politics nirvana: a tide of 11 million newly eligible eighteen- to twenty-one-year-olds to ban the smoke-filled rooms forever, end the war, pass every ecology bill, *change the world*. The story was allegorized in the 1968 youth exploitation picture *Wild in the Streets*, in which a rock star led a crusade to lower the voting age to fourteen: "We got more cats than little ol' Mahatma Gandhi had." Then Max Frost became president after cops shot kids in a riot, and the kids remade America in their own image: "You know, if we didn't have a foreign policy, we wouldn't even have small wars . . . and at home, everybody's rich, and if they're not, they can sleep on the beaches and live like they're rich anyway."

In the real world, New Politics theorists were hardly less exuberant. Fred Dutton, the LBJ White House aide, Pat Brown gubernatorial campaign manager, and University of California regent, had moved steadily leftward ever since watching Sirhan Sirhan assassinate his hero. He published a book in 1971, *Changing Sources of Power*, outlining a New Politics Democratic presidential strategy. "The increased share of the eligible electorate gained by the 18- to 34-year-old group during the 1970s alone will be about as large as the additional slice attained by senior citizens during the last third of a century." He quoted a voice of this group, a young Harvard instructor named Martin Peretz: "These are times of moral enormity, when cool reasonableness is a more pathological and unrealistic state than hysteria." Dutton spun out the political implications: "While the prevailing personal goal of Americans in recent decades has been *security,* the objective may gradually shift not back to the older cry for *opportunity* but to *fulfillment.* While there have been pretensions recently of striving for the . . . law and order society, the growing want among young people is simply a *humane society.* While there has long been a preoccupation with *national* purpose, the rising concern is again with *individual* purpose. And not even *purpose* so much as *being.* . . . The balance is unmistakably shifting toward a concern with *process, variety, and spontaneity.* . . . There will be an increasing insistence on *now.*"

Unmistakably. It was already happening. As Max Frost sang in *Wild in the Streets,* in a song that made it to number twenty-two on the charts (in the real, not movie, world, and right before the 1968 presidential election): "Nothing Can Change the Shape of Things to Come."

The president had a difficult decision to make. He said he favored the eighteen-year-old vote, but that its unconstitutional implementation would sabotage its arrival. New Politics liberals assumed he was bluffing—surely Nixon knew the youth vote would keep him from ever being reelected. They were wrong. Nixon *did* favor the measure. It would help him wedge the Democrats.

The people most terrified of the eighteen-year-old vote were Old Politics Democrats afraid of New Politics primary challenges. Passing it would harden the split in time for when the party would have to attempt to unite around a candidate for 1972. Nixon signed the Voting Rights bill—he was afraid of urban riots if he didn't—and released a signing statement indicating that he worried the eighteen-year-old-vote rider would be ruled unconstitutional, urging the attorney general to get the inevitable constitutional challenge over and done with, and imploring Congress to get to work on a constitutional amendment.

As usual Nixon saw subterranean fissures rumbling beneath the surface, understood the enemy better than they understood themselves. George McGovern's commission was succeeding beyond its wildest hopes in reforming the Democratic Party's nominating procedures after the disaster of 1968. Nixon recognized the power of this development to slice the Democratic Party clean in half.

It is a lesson of the sixties: liberals get in the biggest political trouble—whether instituting open housing, civilian complaint review boards, or sex education programs—when they presume that a reform is an inevitable concomitant of progress. It is then that they are most likely to establish their reforms by top-down bureacratic means. A blindsiding backlash often ensues.

The effort to reinvent how the Democratic Party nominated presidential candidates was one of those stories. It began at the Connecticut State Democratic Convention in June of 1968. The Nutmeg State Democratic Party was run by a classic Old Politics machine: delegates to the national convention were effectively chosen by party officials. Only nine of the forty-four had been for McCarthy in Chicago, in a state where most rank-and-file Democrats were against the war. It wasn't fair, Connecticut McCarthyites thought. But then, procedures across the country for choosing delegates to the national conventions weren't fair. In Hawaii, "proxy votes" were cast on behalf of vacant lots. In Missouri, where caucuses took place unannounced in private homes, one official cast 492 proxies on behalf of a municipality with a third that number of Democrats. In Pennsylvania, McCarthy won 78.5 percent of the votes in the state primary and less than 20 percent of the state's delegates for his trouble. In New York, state law *prohibited* delegate candidates from telling voters which presidential candidates they preferred. Eleven states had chosen delegates before calendar year 1968, sometimes over a year earlier—before the Newark and Detroit riots, before the Tet Offensive, before President Johnson's withdrawal, before the Kennedy and King assassinations, *before the world changed.* Ten states had no written rules about delegate selection, ten had rules that were all but inaccessible. Hubert

Humphrey was about to exploit the messiness of the whole unpleasant back-room system to clinch the nomination. The reformers wanted to make their stand at the Rules Committee hearings in Chicago so that by 1972 no Old Politics hack could do that again. "Do you know what it's like to work six-teen to eighteen hours a day and sleep on couches and win the election and get no delegates?" one of them asked. The bosses "were subverting every-thing I was raised to believe. They were corrupting democracy."

The reformers recruited Iowa governor Harold Hughes, a prominent member of their ranks, to chair a Commission on the Democratic Selection of Presidential Nominees to study the problem, and placed their eight-page report on the chair of every Rules Committee member in Chicago. It con-cluded, "State systems for selecting delegates to the National Convention display considerably less fidelity to basic democratic principles than a nation which claims to govern itself can safely tolerate." It argued, "This conven-tion is on trial. . . . Recent developments have put the future of the two-party system itself into serious jeopardy. . . . Racial minorities, the poor, the young, members of the upper-middle class, and much of the lower-middle and working classes as well—are seriously considering transferring their alle-giance away from either of the two major parties."

The Humphrey people rushed out a counterdocument: "An unofficial, largely self-appointed group under the chairmanship of Governor Hughes of Iowa, composed principally of McCarthy supporters, has prepared a lengthy document embodying a long series of quite radical changes in the convention rules" that "would seem designed expressly to *alter the outcome* of the con-vention by disenfranchising large numbers of duly elected delegates."

The documents became the basis for the committee's minority and majority reports. The full convention voted on the reports on Tuesday, August 27, 1968. It was late at night in the fetid, brawling Stockyards Amphitheatre, and word was trickling in about the violence in the streets. Representative Carl Albert had the one-page minority report read out inaudibly over the din for a vote. It passed by a large margin. Humphrey del-egates had voted under instructions to throw the left a bone, though the con-vention was such chaos by then that many hardly knew what they were voting for. Thus did the 1968 Democratic National Convention call for the formation of a commission to "study the delegation selection processes in effect in the various states" and "recommend to the Democratic National Committee such improvements as can assure even broader citizen participa-tion in the delegate selection process" for 1972. The newspapers hardly reported it at all, what with all the heads being cracked on TV.

In 1969 the DNC chair Fred Harris named the delegate-selection reform commission and chose as its chair a compromise figure: George McGovern, a dove who was friendly with Humphrey. The commission's twenty-eight members, Theodore H. White wrote in *The Making of the President 1972*, were "spread nicely among regulars, Southerners, and insurgents, with scattered places for such traditional allies as labor and academics (two members each)." But openness feels like closedness to those previously overrepresented, and that was the beginning of the trouble. Labor's old buffalos were used to *running* the Democratic Party. They saw the reformers as wreckers whose only accomplishment was to hand the presidency to the Republicans. Steelworkers president I. W. Abel withdrew from the commission on the instructions of AFL-CIO chief George Meany. Absent the Old Politics counterweight, the vague and contradictory convention minority-report injunction simultaneously to "recommend ... improvements" and "mandate ... all feasible efforts" was interpreted in every instance in favor of mandates. At the first meeting, in March of 1969, the only person who spoke up for the old ways was a former Texas Democratic chairman, Will Davis. "There are plenty of conservative Democrats who are in control of the legislatures in several Southern states, for example, and they are not going to line up like sheep to pass reform legislation." Immediately, two other commissioners, David Mixner of the Vietnam Moratorium Committee and Fred Dutton, responded that if anything, reform wasn't being pushed aggressively enough.

The word for it might have been *revenge,* but reformers didn't use words like that. They tended to couch things in terms of principle. The McCarthy and Kennedy campaigners of 1968 had placed their faith in the system. They believed they had won in a fair fight, then that the game had been fixed against them—Humphrey hadn't entered, let alone won, a single primary! The bosses, on the other hand, believed that they would never have become bosses unless they had demonstrated a proven sensitivity to the will of the electorate—a will these radicals knew nothing about. "The so-called 'political bosses' were smart enough to pick candidates who could win," the AFL-CIO's political director, Al Barkan, thundered. "These 'bosses' gave us a Truman, a Stevenson, a Kennedy, a Humphrey."

To the reformers the flaw in that reasoning was obvious. Stevenson was a two-time *loser.* Humphrey had been nominated—and *lost.* The Old Politics had failed in what it claimed it was best at—giving the public what it wanted. Surely *that* was a mandate for change—as was the charnel house in Vietnam. They insisted it was *reformers* who knew what the public wanted now.

The reformers could betray a certain callowness. They suffered a certain sociological narrowness. You might call them the liberal 1960s version of the kind of people Richard Nixon organized his Orthogonians against at Whittier College: graceful, well-rounded, fluid talkers—the toryhood of change. They were people like the spokesman of the Harvard Vietnam Moratorium Committee, who said after Richard Nixon's November 3, 1969, Vietnam speech—the one where he scored a 68 percent overnight approval rating—"What Nixon has tried to show is that there is a silent majority behind him. We know better."

And now they were in the driver's seat of the Democratic Party, anti-bossists who sometimes appeared to behave like bosses—who in their self-righteous arrogance had a hard time seeing how anyone could accuse *them* of making power plays. The McGovern Commission met only four times. The small staff, along with a squad of college interns, did all of the drafting. The research director, Ken Bode, was an assistant professor of political science who had been George McGovern's floor manager at the '68 convention. The chief counsel, Eli Segal, was a twenty-five-year-old McCarthy organizer. Both shared a semiconspiratorial view of how the party regulars kept their power. Both burned with an idealistic flame. Bode had considered exiling himself from America after the RFK assassination; Segal was so distrustful of power he wanted to ban elected officeholders from convention delegations altogether. They based their recommendations on regional hearings stacked with reform constituencies. They couldn't imagine that the old buffaloes in their back rooms might bear any wisdom worth preserving. They never seemed to ponder whether the kind of candidate that could win majorities in open Democratic primaries, where activists were overrepresented, would always be the best ones to win over the full electorate—or to arrest the exile of working-class and Southern voters to a Nixonian Republican Party. They viewed "openess" and "participation" as ends in themselves, and presumed victory would follow.

And when the full commission met to sign off on their draft reforms, the staff bore a certain psychological advantage: it was hard to come out openly against openness. Especially when the old, unreformed ways had brought the nation to an inferno. Here was the kind of thing Senators Mansfield and Kennedy exploited when they arranged it so you could not vote against the eighteen-year-old vote without voting against an extension of the Voting Rights Act, telling anyone who would slow the deliberative process down that the crisis was too great to ignore—*kids were burning down buildings!*

The conclusion of the final McGovern Commission report, *Mandate for Change,* released in a well-covered press conference at the Capitol two days before Nixon's Cambodia speech, was apocalyptic: "If we are not an open party, if we do not represent the demands of change, then the danger is not that people will go to the Republican Party; it is that there will no longer be a way for people committed to orderly change to fulfill their needs and desires within our traditional political system. . . . The only alternative to broader citizen participation in politics was the anti-politics of the street." It claimed that the 1968 "minority report of the Rules Committee, subsequently passed by the delegates assembled in Chicago, carried an unquestionably stern mandate for procedural reform." Which wasn't precisely true. In an unguarded moment, Segal admitted to an interviewer, "There were only maybe half a dozen people . . . who knew what they were actually doing, who understood what the votes meant in political terms. . . . I must admit I was amazed at the way they let us run things."

With the best of intentions, the reformers conflated what savage cops did in the streets with the backroom deal-making that wired the convention for Hubert Humphrey—just as Mayor Daley's police tarred peaceful McCarthy campaign bureaucrats with the rampages of the revolutionary left. The reformers were heir, too, to the spirit of Eugene McCarthy's 1960 nominating speech for Adlai Stevenson, which celebrated his pure-hearted nobility: "Do not turn away from this man. . . . Do not leave this man a prophet without honor in his own party!" They used a curious word in describing their intentions: "to *purify* . . . the power exercised by future Democratic conventions."

But some would say that purity and power don't mix.

The last full meeting of the McGovern Commission, the week after the New Mobilization protest brought three hundred thousand to Washington in November of 1969, saw the process's only contentious debate. The first section of the guidelines draft, A-1, demanded "State Parties overcome the effects of past discrimination by affirmative steps to encourage minority group participation." It was an attempt to honor the spirit of the Mississippi Freedom Democrats disenfranchised at the 1964 convention—and the fact that in 1968 the number of black delegates, at 5.5 percent, was a fraction of their representation in the Democratic Party as a whole (Mississippi and Georgia's regular delegations didn't include a single one). The second section, A-2, required state parties to extend the same representational consideration to people between the ages of eighteen and thirty, and women.

Austin Ranney, a political science professor at Wisconsin, suggested the guidelines "at the very least urge" states to choose minority delegates commensurate with their representation in the state population. Chairman McGovern reminded him that at their September meeting they had unanimously decided "that it was not feasible to go on record for a quota system." Senator Bayh suggested adding "two or three words to sort of give guidelines saying that to meet this requirement there should be some reasonable relationship between the representation of delegates and the representation of the minority group in the population of the state in question."

The motion was put to a vote. It passed ten to nine.

Fred Dutton said the same language should apply to women and youth in section A-2. Sam Beer of Harvard objected, "It's not for us to say to the voters of a state you've got to elect fifty percent women. If the voters want seventy-five percent women or seventy-five percent men, it's up to them. . . . I think it would be a great mistake and would make us look really ridiculous."

Dutton returned with a political argument: "I can't think of anything more attractive or a better way to get votes with media politics than to have half of that convention floor in 1972 made up of women." It would be a symbol that would "activate young people." Professor Beer complained, "Our charge is to clean up this process. . . . Our charge is not to decide what the outcome is supposed to be." George Mitchell, the national committeeman from Maine, Edmund Muskie's representative, said it would be interpreted as "some sort of quota." Professor Ranney said he feared he'd opened a "Pandora's box." Will Davis of Texas said the South would never stand for it. The vote was called; what would later come to be called "affirmative action" won 13–7. However, *Mandate for Change* included a footnote: "It is the understanding of the Commission that this is not to be accomplished by the mandatory imposition of quotas."

The *New York Times* gave the release of the McGovern Commission's report on April 28, 1970, a big spread. They led with the commission's apocalyptic claim that "the only alternative to broader citizen participation in politics was the anti-politics of the street." Chairman McGovern was quoted acknowledging that "Certainly party leaders in some states have been critical." But they were "a tiny minority. I expect that we will get a broad compliance."

The AFL-CIO's Al Barkan swore, on the other hand, "We aren't going to let these Harvard-Berkeley Camelots take over our party."

Reformers were confident by the time the 1970 election season rolled around: about the failure of Nixon's economy, the overwhelming passage of the eighteen-year-old vote, the nearly one thousand college campuses that had protested against Cambodia in May. Garry Wills, in his *Esquire* article on Nixon's Billy Graham appearance, profiled a former fraternity brother who led the protests. Once he had been "rah rahiest of rah-boys." His conversion was a leading indicator, thought Wills, that "tips the balance for Nixon to defeat. It heralds the end of the hard-hat war on long hair."

That summer the McGovern-Hatfield amendment to end the war by July of 1971 generated the greatest flood of supportive mail in Senate history. One letter came from a twenty-three-year-old marine set to go to Southeast Asia. It pointed out that the war "hasn't been declared, can't be fought, and can't be won." The marine was the son of Senator William Saxbe of Ohio, a Nixon Republican elected in 1968 on a promise to rein in dissent. The father was especially haunted by his son's paraphrase of General Patton: "Old soldiers don't die, young ones do." Saxbe let his California colleague Alan Cranston—who was receiving some eight thousand antiwar letters a day—enter it into the *Congressional Record*.

In July, *Life* published photographs of the "tiger cages" in which our Saigon allies confined ninety-six hundred prisoners on the island of Con Son, some for merely advocating peace: four-by-nine-foot concrete pits, each holding three to five prisoners, chained together. A U.S. spokesman replied that Con Son was "like a Boy Scout recreation camp"; Illinois Republican Phil Crane said the cages were "cleaner than the average Vietnamese home." (Later, *Time* magazine described what prisoners looked like after they were released: "grotesque sculptures of scarred flesh and gnarled limbs . . . skittering across the floor on buttocks and palms.") Four heartland senators, Harris of Oklahoma, McGovern of South Dakota, Hughes of Iowa, and Bayh of Indiana were positioning themselves for "reform Democratic" presidential runs. Possibly Ramsey Clark, too. McGovern sent a young Denver lawyer, Gary Hart, to Washington to open McGovern for President headquarters.

But reformers seemed not to notice how poorly antiwar challengers did in June congressional primaries. They seemed not to notice the overwhelming defeat in Oregon of a change in state law to lower the voting age to nineteen. They seemed not to notice new data out of the University of Michigan's Survey Research Center that twice as many voters under thirty-five had voted for George Wallace in 1968 than had voted for Barry Goldwater in 1964. Youth's vanguard might be left-wing, the professors wrote. "At the polls," though, "the game shifts to 'one man, one vote,' and this vanguard is unmercifully swamped within its own generation."

States got to work dissolving caucus and convention and committee systems falling afoul of *Mandate for Change*. Delegates would now have to be selected via "procedures open to public participation within the calendar year of the National Convention." *Open* was a magic word for reform Democrats. They were convinced the banning of the back rooms was what it would take to win in 1972. Richard Nixon understood things differently. His political operation was all back rooms.

Reformers such as Fred Dutton saw the Democrats' moves toward what would later be called affirmative action as an imperative to save the Democratic Party. When Richard Nixon had made his own steps toward affirmative action, he saw it as a tool to destroy the Democrats. Building trades unions controlled apprenticeship opportunities that often passed from father to son, making construction sites among the most segregated workplaces in the nation. Labor Secretary George Shultz, hoping to reform them, came up with the idea of voluntary goals for integrating government building projects. In Philadelphia, the plan's original target, he suggested a goal of increasing black employment from less than 5 percent to over 25 percent in the next four years. Nixon spied a thrilling political opportunity. "With our constituency, we gained little on the play," he noted. But it drove a wedge through the *Democratic* coalition at its most vulnerable joint: between blacks and hard hats. The president told Shultz to go full steam ahead with the "Philadelphia Plan."

Another longtime dream of reformers was to do away with the antiquated and antidemocratic electoral college. The House had passed a bill for direct popular election of presidents in September of 1969 by vote of 338 to

70. But as Senator Strom Thurmond knew better than anyone else, the South's major political trump card was the threat of a renegade third-party presidential candidate using his electoral votes to keep either of the major parties from an electoral college majority. Thurmond had Senate Judiciary chair James Eastland of Mississippi bottle the bill up in committee. Birch Bayh threatened to block consideration of Harrold Carswell unless the debate came to the floor. When it did, in the summer of 1970, Thurmond, Eastland, and Sam Ervin filibustered. Nixon tried to use the presidential bully pulpit to force a vote. Stirringly he intoned, "Our ability to change this system in time for the 1972 elections is a touchstone of the impulse to reform in America today. It will be the measure of our ability to avert calamity by anticipating it." Like the Philadelphia Plan, it made him look noble.

His motives, though, were not noble. Getting rid of the electoral college would crush George Wallace's power as a presidential candidate. Unfortunately for Nixon, cloture failed, and the electoral college survived its greatest threat in two hundred years. Alabama's once and future governor, who had won the Alabama Democratic gubernatorial primary decisively, was asked if he was going to run for president. "If Nixon don't give us back our schools," he said—and Wallace was back in business.

Enemies were everywhere, even in Nixon's own house. *U.S. News & World Report* noted "a confidential survey of political leanings of career government workers in Washington" that showed 73 percent favoring the policies of the Democrats. It quoted a high administration official: "The president is aware that, among the people who worked to elect him, there is a rising tide of resentment against any officials who look as if they are out to embarrass Mr. Nixon, or to try to dictate their own pet policies to him." Nixon proposed a comprehensive reorganization of the executive branch, his second in two years. That, too, was less noble than it looked.

The advisory council worked in secret, incinerating their trash in "burn bags" every night. Their plan revived the spirit of National Security Decision Memo 2: draining power from independent bureaucracies; concentrating it in the White House. The Interstate Commerce Commission, the Civil Aeronautics Board, the Federal Maritime Commission, the Securities and Exchange Commission, and the FCC were slated for merger, fragmentation, reduction, or abolition. Bipartisan governing boards with fixed statutory terms would be replaced by chairmen serving at the pleasure of the president. A new Office of Management and Budget, a Domestic Policy Council, their duties deliberately unspecified, were proposed, to which Nixon planned to appoint his smartest loyalists—seizing power from ornery cabinet departments, forging a weapon to exact political retribution against recalcitrant legislators via the federal power of the purse. Their personnel would be vetted not by senatorial advice and consent, but by his favorite "internal security" bulldog, the right-wing exuberant Tom Charles Huston.

Nixon quietly submitted the plan to Congress, obscuring its implications. Congress took no action within sixty days—which the president then announced allowed it to take effect unilaterally. Then, by executive order, he created a new Environmental Protection Agency—more nobility the less noble the closer you looked: its 5,650 employees all came from existing agencies, its $1.4 billion budget taken from existing programs, the only difference being that these previously scattered centers of authority were now directly controlled from the White House.

The sales job was successful. In a boon for governmental transparency, the *New York Times* editorialized approvingly, Nixon was placing "the making of policy in highly visible executives."

The reviews would not have been so kind had the press had access to the arm of the reorganization presided over by Tom Charles Huston.

The FBI and the CIA and the NSA and Defense Intelligence Agency had been carrying on uninterrupted the business of spying on and harassing antiwar activists. Teams of FBI informants, for instance, combed Jane Fonda's speeches for violations of the 1917 Espionage Act, which criminalized incitement to "insubordination, disloyalty, mutiny, or refusal of duty in the military," and "disloyal, profane, scurrilous, or abusive language about the form of government of the United States." Fonda proved a disappointment. She never incited, and abusive language wasn't her style. The president, however, was obsessed with her case ("What Brezhnev and Jane Fonda said got about the same treatment," one aide later recalled), and in fall the powers that be arranged for her to be stopped at customs at the Cleveland airport. When she pushed aside agents who refused her access to the bathroom (she was having her period), she was arrested for assaulting an officer. In her possession were pills marked, mysteriously, *B, L,* and *D;* for possessing vitamins to be taken with breakfast, lunch, and dinner, she was also charged with narcotics smuggling. Her daughter was followed to kindergarten. (America needed to know, FBI files later revealed: did her school teach "an anti–law enforcement attitude"?) Her bank accounts were investigated; a friendly FBI asset, Jesse Helms, the editorialist at WRAL-TV in Raleigh, North Carolina, invented a line he attributed to her praising Communism during a speech at Duke. A death threat was sent to her father with a demand for $50,000. (The sender, attentive to presidential rhetoric, signed it "The Silent Ones.") The FBI's special agent in charge in Detroit prepared a 107-page report on the White Panthers, "potentially the largest and most dangerous of revolutionary organizations in the United States." John Mitchell installed wiretaps at their Ann Arbor commune without a judge's say-so. (Two years later the Supreme Court reviewed the case and ruled such domestic wiretaps were foreign to the American Constitution.)

Tom Charles Huston wasn't satisfied any of this went far enough. He prepared talking points for the president's meeting with the heads of the CIA and the Defense Intelligence Agency arguing, "We are now confronted with a new and grave crisis in our country—one which we know too little about. Certainly hundreds, perhaps thousands, of Americans—mostly under 30— are determined to destroy our society." The president told the intelligence chiefs to prepare a more aggressive plan to contain them—and to report to twenty-nine-year-old Tom Charles Huston.

Huston prepared a forty-three-page outline of what the plan should include: opening mail, tapping phones without warrants, infiltrating student movements, purging those not loyal to the White House from the IRS. ("We won't be in control of the government and in a position of effective leverage until such time as we have complete and total control of the top three slots," he wrote.) He also proposed "black bag" jobs—breaking into homes and offices: "clearly illegal," he allowed, and "could result in great embarrassment if exposed," but these were desperate times. "If we reach the point where we really want to start playing the game tough, you might wish to consider my suggestion of some months ago that we consider going into Brookings after classified material they have stashed over there. There are a number of ways we could handle this. There are risks in all of them, of course; but there are also risks in allowing a government-in-exile to grow increasingly arrogant and powerful as each day goes by." "Brookings" meant the Brookings Institution, the capital's most distinguished think tank, professional home to many former Kennedy administration figures.

The president found the document splendid. Haldeman directed Huston to prepare a formal decision memo outlining it as a mandate to the heads of the intelligence agencies. Though President Nixon did want one revision: skip the carefully delineated procedures for getting the agencies' approval. "He would prefer that the thing simply be put into motion on the basis of this approval," Haldeman said.

Another unusual function had already been placed directly under Oval Office supervision: congressional campaign fund-raising, to keep turncoats such as Saxbe and Charles Goodell from getting their hands on Republican money. Nixon's lawyer Herb Kalmbach forwarded to him a list in June 1970 of sixty-four "angels" that might be willing to contribute to slush funds, no questions asked: old standbys such as Elmer Bobst and Clement Stone; newer names such as Richard Mellon Scaife and William J. Casey; Thomas J. Pappas, a Greek-American businessman who in 1968 conveyed a $549,000 donation to Nixon from the Greek military dictator's intelligence service. A political fund-raiser, Jack Gleason, was attached to Secretary of Commerce Maurice Stans's staff to establish a secret office in a Georgetown town-house basement. Republican candidates were instructed to appoint a figurehead finance chair and invent names for up to a dozen "committees." Rich men started getting calls: "The president is very interested in such and such campaign and they need such and such amount of money right away." They were told to sign over a check to one of the "committees," sent "care of Jack Gleason" at the D.C. town house. It was, the White House thought, practically legal, since campaign fund-raising disclosure requirements apparently didn't apply to donations "in" the District.

A team was formed to carry out sensitive political tasks. It included Colson, Jeb Stuart Magruder, Murray Chotiner, Lyn Nofziger, and the new hire John Dean (who was surprised in his first meeting with the president that he had "a rather weak handshake," fidgeted constantly, and was utterly awkward in conversation). The pace grew hectic toward the end of July. On the twenty-third Nixon met with John Swearingen of the American Enterprise Institute about the Kennedys' "government in exile" at Brookings, then assigned Chuck Colson to work funneling donations for a countervailing conservative "ammunition factory," either to the preexisting AEI, or perhaps a new "Silent Majority Institute" or "Institute for an Informed America" (the Scaife-Mellon Foundation and Pew Family Trust each kicked in a million dollars). The next day Nixon raged to Haldeman about protesters, "We have to find out who controls them. Get our guys to rough them up at demonstrations." ("Get a goon squad to start roughing up demos," Haldeman added to his to-do list.) The next day Nixon savaged Chet Huntley's "almost totally negative approach to everything the administration does." It was, he said to his chief of staff, "important to destroy him for [the] effect on all other commentators."

Nixon acted not despite the Silent Majority he described as so pure and decent, but in a sense on their behalf, and even at their request. His paranoia and dread were their own. Across the state of mind known as Middle America, a subterranean viciousness was bubbling ever closer to the surface.

Jane Fonda saw it in a jailhouse in Cleveland. "What are you in for?" she was asked. She replied, "You might call me a political prisoner."

"Well, they ought to throw you in jail. We don't want no commies running around loose."

She asked what *he* was in for. "Murder," he replied.

It reminded one of a new movie. In *Joe*, Peter Boyle played a tool-and-die maker from Queens, what the *New York Times* described as an "ape-like, dese-dem-and-dose type," who strikes up a conversation with a businessman in an East Village bar. "Forty-two percent of liberals are queer and that's a fact," Joe says. "The George Wallace people took a poll." He said he'd like to kill "just one"—just like, in real life, the Chicago ad salesman quoted in the May 18, 1970, *Time*: "I'm getting to feel like I'd actually enjoy going out and shooting some of these people. I'm just so goddamned mad. They're trying to destroy everything I've worked for—for myself, my wife, and my children."

In *Joe* the businessman, played by Dennis Patrick, murmurs, "I just did"—murder his missing teenage daughter's hippie boyfriend, he said.

Joe likes this man very much. Together, they search his daughter out. When they happen upon a hippie commune, their anger turns to lust, and they enjoy the favors of two of the gamines. Thus sated, they go on their shooting spree. But one of the people they shoot, in the back, is the business-man's own daughter.

The filmmakers' thesis resembled a book by the radical sociologist Philip Slater, *The Pursuit of Loneliness: American Culture at the Breaking Point*, which came out around the same time. It argued that people loathed and feared the hippies because deep down they knew the hippies, whose freedom they envied, were right: "We fear having our secret doubts about the viabil-ity of our social system voiced aloud." *Joe* made Slater's argument celluloid—an attempt to shock viewers into the recognition that the terminal point of all this hating what you desire was death.

The movie's fans did not receive that message. In real life, Peter Boyle, a *Life* reporter in tow, visited a butcher shop in his Manhattan neighborhood. An excited little old lady approached and said, "I agree with *everything* you said, young man. Someone should have said it a long time ago." Kids didn't take its message as peaceful, either. They yelled at the screen, "I'm going to shoot back, Joe!" On the street, Boyle was afraid they would shoot him.

New rages dissolved old rules of decorum. The rioting hard hat who threatened the New York City Hall secretary—"*Let go of my jacket, bitch. If you want to be treated like an equal, we'll treat you like one*"—evinced one of the changes. The spring and summer of 1970 were the months when "women's liberation" erupted beyond mimeographed newsletters and beauty-pageant guerrilla theater to the nation's kitchen-table debates. Congress-woman Patsy Mink called Harrold Carswell's nomination "an affront to the women of America" for his role in upholding the legality of firing women for having pre-school-aged children. Five thousand demonstrated in New York for a liberal abortion law (it passed July 1, in spite of stacked hearings that called fourteen male witnesses and one female—a nun). Two hundred feminists took over the offices of *Ladies' Home Journal* until the editors, good liberals all, agreed to let them produce an eight-page insert for the August issue. ("Joan Kennedy Today"; "The Midi—and How to Wear It"; "'Women's Liberation' and You: Special Feminist Section Everyone's Been Talking About." It included a Housewives' Bill of Rights: "Unionization, 6-day work week, paid maternity leave, health insurance, better working conditions, free 24-hour child care centers.") *Time* put leader Kate Millett on the cover, in honor of Women's Strike Day for the Equal Rights Amendment, August 31, a feature that introduced many Americans to the epithet *male chauvinist*.

To some it seemed natural, inevitable. "I became a feminist as an alterna-tive to becoming a masochist," writer Sally Kempton wrote in the July *Esquire*. The Equal Rights Amendment, buried in House Judiciary Committee limbo since 1947, was a staple of both parties' presidential platforms. And yet for many Middle Americans it was the most horrifying development imaginable—the one thread that, once pulled, might unweave the fabric of civilization itself.

The lead letter in response to the Kate Millett cover in *Time* read, "Sir: Women's Lib [August 26]—phooey! They are only leading us to Orwell's 1984, when men and women are such equals that life is sterile and children are reared by the state in nurseries away from their parents. Brrr." Another: "Who is supposed to run these round-the-clock child-care centers—robots? Men?" The Women's Board of the West Virginia GOP was outraged that the National Federation of Republican Women was calling for a discharge petition for the ERA; equal rights for women were part of the "Communist conspiracy."

Jane Fonda arrived at the set one day for her new movie, *Klute,* and found a huge American flag draped above the door of her character's room. The hostile act from the working-class crew was intended not merely for her anti-war stand, but for her defiance of feminine convention: she had stopped wearing makeup. Wrote William F. Buckley, "She must never even look into the mirror anymore." Each new outrage interlaced the others.

Also in August, black radicals—the "Soledad Brothers"—raided the courthouse where Black Panther George Jackson was on trial for allegedly throwing a Soledad Prison guard over a third-tier railing. His comrades stormed the courtroom, tied up the judge and three other hostages with piano wire, murdered three of them, then died themselves in a blaze of gunfire. Angela Davis, the UCLA philosophy professor recently fired by Ronald Reagan, was named an accomplice, disappeared, and made the cover of *Newsweek* and the FBI's ten most wanted list (actually, at Nixon's instigation, now a sixteen most wanted list, nine of the slots occupied by radicals). Philadelphia police raided Black Panther headquarters and strip-searched those detained in the street. Chief Frank Rizzo, mulling a 1971 run for mayor, said they "should be strung up." He added, "I mean, within the law."

Rizzo was Nixon's sort of Democrat. Chatting with the press in Denver during a meeting of the Law Enforcement Assistance Administration in August, the president reflected, "I don't see too many movies, but I try to see them on weekends when I am at the Western White House or in Florida" (he lied; he saw about ten movies a month in screening rooms at the White House and at Camp David), and had caught the new western *Chisum.* The commander in chief reflected upon why John Wayne kept attracting audiences: "The good guys come out ahead in the westerns; the bad guys lose." He dilated on the "attitudes that are created among our younger people . . . which tend to glorify and to make heroes out of those who engage in criminal activities . . . for example, the coverage of the Charles Manson case when I was in Los Angeles, front page every day in the papers. It usually got a couple of minutes in the evening news. Here is a man who was guilty, directly or indirectly, of eight murders without reason."

The liberal editorialists pointed out that the president of the United States had just prejudged the guilt of a criminal defendant. Let the fastidious quibble: the voters weren't about to take Nixon to the woodshed for beating up on Charlie Manson.

School was in session. The Popular Front for the Liberation of Palestine hijacked four planes simultaneously, culminating in a standoff that almost ended with the emptied jets blown up in the middle of the Jordanian desert. *Time* reported that the *Berkeley Tribe* editorialized, "Maybe soon, planes carrying very prominent international pigs . . . will be hijacked from the U.S. to parts unknown. By, say, freaks." In Madison, radicals bombed a building in the middle of campus, destroying the entire physics department. They had mimicked the Weathermen's standard procedure of bombing after hours and with a warning. That hadn't kept an after-hours researcher, Robert Fassnacht, from being blown to bits. In November, on the other side of the ideological ledger, Rabbi Meir Kahane's Jewish Defense League—a vigilante group modeled on the Black Panthers—firebombed the New York offices of the Soviet airline Aeroflot.

Harris reported that 76 percent of college students favored "basic changes in the system" and that half of high school students were "disaffected." The *New York Times* revealed between five hundred and a thousand underground newspapers were published in the nation's high schools. The University of Tennessee's new president promised a reporter there would be no interruptions in the coming school year: "When the faculty comes to me with complaints, I threaten them—well, I don't openly threaten them, I kind of subtly threaten them—by mentioning all the letters I got from the community during our three-day strike this year. . . . And I can tell you this: we have an academic calendar announced for next year, and we will stick to it."

On September 1 Senator McGovern gave the concluding speech in the debate over his amendment to end the Vietnam War. Opposing senators had spoken of the necessity of resolve in the face of adversity, of national honor, of staying the course, of glory, of courage. McGovern responded:

"Every senator in this chamber is partly responsible for sending fifty thousand young Americans to an early grave. This chamber reeks of blood."

Senators averted their eyes or stared at their desks or drew their faces taut with fury; this was not senatorial decorum.

"Every senator here is partly responsible for that human wreckage at Walter Reed and Bethesda Naval and all across our land—young men without legs, or arms, or genitals, or faces, or hopes. . . .

"Do not talk about bugging out, or national honor, or courage.

"It does not take any courage at all for a congressman, or senator, or a president to wrap himself in the flag and say we are staying in Vietnam, because it is not our blood that is being shed. But we are responsible for those young men and their lives and hopes."

The presiding officer rapped down the gavel: "The senator's time has expired . . ."

From the Republican side, men rose from their seats: "Regular order! Regular order!"

The former history professor kept pushing on over the din: "So before we vote, let us ponder the admonition of Edmund Burke, the great parliamentarian of an earlier day: 'A conscientious man would be cautious how he dealt in blood.'"

Richard Nixon was not without resources in the fight. In private meetings with senators he warned that if Congress voted against Vietnam appropriations, it "must assume responsibility" for all the subsequent deaths of American troops and would be held accountable "for an ignominious American defeat if it succeeds in tying the president's hands." The president won. McGovern-Hatfield went down 55–39.

Shortly afterward, the presidential commission studying Kent State, chaired by former Pennsylvania governor William Warren Scranton, pronounced the killings "unnecessary and unwarranted." But the grand jury in Ohio had already handed down twenty-five indictments, most against students, none against guardsmen. They spoke for the Silent Majority, which had itself spoken in angry letters to the Scranton Commission: "What these young radicals need is a good beating. And I will be the first to break the back of one of these little bitches or bastards."

It was this sentiment to which Nixon made ready to supplicate, now that Election Day, November 3, 1970, was fast approaching.

CHAPTER TWENTY-FIVE

Agnew's Election

Spiro Agnew was sent off on another stature-enhancing Asian trip. He came back and promised, "I will be urging the election of a more responsible Congress that will help—rather than frustrate—President Nixon's efforts to do what he promised the people in 1968 he would do." Agnew set off on an RNC-chartered 727 (equipped with the latest in airport technology, X-rays to peer into luggage; "Pirates in the Sky," read the cover of *Time,* alongside a now-iconic image of Arab militants alighting from a jumbo jet). The vice president landed first in Springfield, Illinois, where at high noon on the steps of the state capitol he announced "a contest between the remnants of the discredited elite that dominated national policy for forty years and a new national majority, forged and led by the president of the United States."

Illinois was the perfect place to launch the crusade. Agnew spoke on behalf of the lightweight incumbent senator, Ralph T. Smith, whose opponent, Illinois's state treasurer, was Adlai Stevenson III—son of the egghead who had been making Orthogonians feel inferior for decades.

"There was a time when the liberalism of the old elite was a venturesome and fighting philosophy—the vanguard political dogma of a Franklin Roosevelt, a Harry Truman, a John Kennedy. But the old firehorses are long gone. Today's breed of radical-liberal posturing about the Senate is about as closely related to a Harry Truman as a Chihuahua is to a timber wolf."

Buchanan and Safire had worked hard devising that particular rhetorical bomb. It wouldn't do to vilify *Democrats;* most voters called themselves Democrats. Calling them *radicals* posed a problem, for no senators called themselves radicals. *Radical-liberals* won out over *radillectuals.* Agnew also excoriated *ultraliberalism*—which, the man some now called Nixon's Nixon pronounced to four thousand Illinoisans, "translates into a whimpering foreign policy, a mulish obstructionism in domestic policy, and a pusillanimous pussyfooting on the critical issue of law and order. . . . The troglodytic leftists who dominate Congress . . . work themselves into a lather over an alleged shortage of nutriments in a child's box of Wheaties." They "cannot get exercised over that same child's constant exposure to a flood of hard-core pornography that could warp his moral outlook for a lifetime."

"Nutriments," "troglodytic," "pusillanimous": Bill Safire loved writing lines like these; Ted Agnew loved delivering them; Orthogonian audiences loved hearing them. Ten-dollar words, in Agnew's cool, uninflected voice, salved the wound delivered whenever fashionable opinion-mongers told you that if you were *really* smart, you would be for the kids.

Stevenson himself was not running as a liberal. He had done so, once, in 1966, when Mayor Daley had blocked him from running for the Senate because he refused to pledge loyalty to LBJ's war. After the 1968 convention Stevenson called Daley's cops "storm troopers" and blamed the violence on the city's "denying parks for peaceful protest." He had changed his tune severely since then—campaigning with Chicago 7 prosecutor Thomas Aquinas Foran by his side, an American flag pin on his lapel. Agnew wasn't about to let Adlai get away with it. Castrating would-be Democratic sheriffs was precisely the point of Agnew's tour:

"Any public official, especially from the state of Illinois, who still believes the riots at the Chicago convention were the result of 'denying parks for peaceful protest' has no business in the United States Senate. Any individual who, in these times, will slander the men of the Chicago police force by calling them 'storm troopers in blue' ought to be retired from public life."

AFL-CIO president George Meany, enraged at the usurpations of the McGovern Commission, had recently been wooed to a White House dinner of seventy-four labor leaders followed by a torchlight parade on the South Lawn—the most lavish White House Labor Day observance in history. Afterward, Meany told the press that the Democrats had been taken over by "extremists." Haldeman shuffled the Supreme Council of the Sons of Italy into the Oval Office for a photo opportunity. Their "supreme venerable" told the press Nixon was "our terrestrial god." At a Stevenson rally, DNC chair Larry O'Brien offered a postreform olive branch to the regulars—lacerating unspecified "extreme and irresponsible statements" by "so-called Democrats on the far left." This was the kind of Democratic division Nixon fed on. He had Agnew, in Casper, Wyoming, tell his listeners not to "let this stampede to the center fool you." Democrats were pulling "the fastest switcheroo in America politics": they were under the thumb of what he soon shortened to *radiclibs.* (He made the argument with a straight face, though the incumbent Democrat in Wyoming was one of the most hawkish senators.)

At the California Republican convention in San Diego, Agnew mentioned how Democratic candidate John Tunney had started riding in police cars before the cameras—"Tunney-come-lately." (After Ted Kennedy told students at Boston University that violent protest was immoral and futile, Agnew labeled him "Teddy-come-lately.") Then Agnew loosed Safire's most triumphant linguistic confection: "In the United States today, we have more than our share of the nattering nabobs of negativism. They have formed their own 4-H club—the hopeless, hysterical hypochondriacs of history."

Agnew knew the scribes would write about it, if only to mock him. That was good: let the elites mock patriotism! Next, it was Las Vegas for Republican Senate challenger William Raggio, where Agnew read out the lyrics to shocking rock songs: "I get *high* with a little help from my friends. . . . One pill makes you larger and one pill makes you small. . . . Eight miles *high.* . . ." The press made fun of that, too—observing that after being met at the airport by a thousand bused-in schoolchildren, Agnew waved from his limousine to revelers at Sin City vice dens with marquees reading WELCOME VICE PRESIDENT AGNEW—KENO—POKER and FOLIES-BERGÈRE—WELCOME VICE PRESIDENT. Let them mock decency! The Franklins were falling right into their hands.

Nixon reinforced Agnew's message in a televised lecture at Kansas State: worse than violence was "the passive acquiescence or even fawning approval that in some fashionable circles has become the mark of being 'with it.'" Then, the good-cop statesman, he was off for the third European trip of his presidency. *Life* put Spiro Agnew on the cover for the second time—alongside features on *Joe* and the deaths of the two rock stars, both twenty-seven, both from drug overdoses, who had been quoted on the nobility of their generation in the 1969 *Time* panegyric to Woodstock: Jimi Hendrix and Janis Joplin.

The Nixon campaign team refined their technique from 1968: they didn't just hold the rallies near airports to facilitate the dispatch of news footage; they held them in airport hangars. Agnew alighted in Saginaw. The footage was great. Central Michigan's longhairs assembled beneath a banner: IMPUDENT SNOBS UNITE HERE. Agnew's introduction by the Republican Senate candidate, who was also Michigan's former first lady, Lenore Romney, running against incumbent Philip Hart, one of the Senate's great liberals (his wife was a tax resister who'd been arrested in an antiwar protest at the Pentagon), was swallowed up by obscene chanting. Agnew leaned close to the microphone: "That's exactly what we're running against in this country today. . . . You people out there preach a lot about dissent. But you're afraid to tolerate dissent. . . . you're not intellectual; you're intellectually stagnant."

In response: "Agnew is a social disease! Agnew is a social disease!"

Agnew soldiered on. A vote for Mrs. Romney, he said, could "help rescue the Democratic party from radical-liberals so that America can stand safe and secure in this dangerous world."

Time had once feted Nixon for surfing the waves of moderation. The president made a different bet this fall. John Mitchell, drunk at a party, was quoted by a reporter: "There is no such thing as the New Left. This country is going so far to the right you are not even going to recognize it." Reflected Nixon, "If the vice president were slightly roughed up by those thugs, nothing better could happen for our cause. If anybody so much as brushes against Mrs. Agnew, tell her to fall down."

Agnew turned to the South to finish off Albert Gore of Tennessee. Gore, who had never had to spend more than $50,000 winning his previous races, had been bloodied in a primary challenge from the conservative Democratic governor, Buford Ellington, who had said in 1968 that Martin Luther King was "training three thousand people to start riots." Ellington eviscerated Gore as an outsider from Washington, D.C. Gore fought back with a commercial by the Kennedy family's media guru Charlie Guggenheim. As Gore rode horseback with his son, also named Albert, the voice-over intoned, "The people of Tennessee have learned to take the measure of Albert Gore by the battles he has fought for them along the way, for TVA, tax reform, Medicare, interstate highways, Social Security, and education. 'I may have run ahead of the pack sometimes, but I'm usually headed in the right direction.'"

Ellington accused him of bringing the horse out from Hollywood. Gore, as true a son of the Volunteer State as anyone—even if he found the Vietnam War a moral abomination—nicely countered, "I just want you fellows to know that I bought him off my neighbor for two hundred dollars, and he was a darned good buy."

Nixon had made Gore's opponent, William Brock, the Southern Strategy's poster boy, sending out a top organizer to put together Brock's campaign almost a year earlier. Liberal senators took defending the incumbent as their sacred duty. After Gore squeaked past the primary, the entire Democratic establishment flocked to an unprecedented fund-raiser at Ted Kennedy's house in Virginia.

Gore hopped on a tree stump: "I *denounce* the Southern Strategy, of which I'm victim number one. . . . I will say to the people of Tennessee that this is a *slur* upon them."

"*Amen, brother!*" some High Church Episcopalian bellowed back.

"It's based on the concept that people will have enough prejudice, provincialism, intolerance, and ignorance that if the national leadership will make an appeal to it, it will win." Politics, he said, "should uplift the people, not downgrade them."

On September 22 Spiro Agnew landed in Memphis. Crafty Gore one-upped an absent Brock by meeting Agnew on the tarmac and telling the press that "in earlier and less hospitable days," the "governor of a Union state located on the Eastern seaboard . . . might have been referred to as a 'carpetbagger' by our more section-minded folk." Agnew called him "a fellow who rides a white horse on TV commercials down here and who suffers a paranoid fear of being the number one political target of the Silent Majority," but was really the "Southern regional chairman of the Eastern liberal establishment," who "found his obligations to the citizens of Tennessee secondary to his liberal community credentials" and was "sincere in his mistaken belief that Tennessee is located somewhere between *New York Times* and the Greenwich *Village Voice.*"

In Indianapolis, Agnew said that Senator Vance Hartke, a presidential hopeful, "represents some people in Berkeley, California, some people in Madison, Wisconsin, and some people at Columbia University in New York." In Salt Lake City—a sign read SMASH RACIST AGNEW IN HIS RACIST MOUTH—Democratic senator Frank Moss was "the Western regional champion of the Eastern liberal establishment," a friend of "the Spock-marked generation." In Minot, North Dakota, plumping for the Senate challenge of Congressman Thomas Kleppe, Agnew reveled in the presence of an un-Spock-marked cadre near the front waving placards reading MOTHERHOOD, APPLE PIE, AND SPIRO; SPIRO IS SEXY; and GROOVE ON SPIRO!

President Nixon was in Europe doing what he enjoyed most. Three weeks after the Middle Eastern hijacking, Syrian tanks painted in the colors of the Palestinian national movement rumbled into Jordan. Jordan counterattacked; a Middle East war seemed in the offing. The president was handling the crisis, Haldeman wrote in his diary, "strong & cool," game-planning what it would or wouldn't mean in their ongoing efforts to negotiate to good advantage with the Russians even as Nixon slipped a story to the *Chicago Sun-Times* about CIA photographs that suggested the Soviets were building a submarine base in Cuba (it turned out to be a soccer field). Nixon did an interview with *Time* on the long view in foreign policy: "If there is anything I want to do before I die, it is to go to China. If I don't, I want my children to." In Rome he met American hostages released by the Palestinians thanks to the State Department's secret diplomacy; he toasted with Tito in Yugoslavia; in between stops he huddled with Kissinger to scheme how to undo the Chilean election won by Marxist Salvador Allende and to juggle the consequences of Gamal Nasser's death on September 28 and to word the "cease-fire in place" they would be offering to the North Vietnamese in Paris. Nixon was living the global chess game, his face on another fawning *Time* cover: "Facing the Middle East: When to Use and When Not to Use Power."

But he was restless to do what he enjoyed second most: campaigning. He had started his European trip in the Vatican, visiting the pope, and made his last stop Ireland—an old-school play to the Catholic swing vote. The Catholic voters he had his eye on most of all were the constituency of presidential enemy number one, New York senator Charles Goodell. When Governor Rockefeller appointed Goodell to fill Bobby Kennedy's seat, he seemed a moderate-to-conservative choice. Goodell turned out to be a reliable White House vote on domestic issues—and a thorn in Nixon's side on Vietnam. President Nixon used to excoriate President Johnson as "the first president in history who has failed to unite his own party in a time of war."

That made President Nixon the second. Goodell was the first senator to propose legislation cutting off congressional funding for the war. It was Goodell, in June of 1970, that Jane Fonda and Mark Lane and Donald Duncan of Vietnam Veterans Against the War approached to set up a clearinghouse to hear allegations of American misconduct in Vietnam.

Conservative Republicans were beside themselves. So, in fact, was Nelson Rockefeller. He didn't disagree with Mitchell's drunken prediction that the country was hurtling right; he had begun remolding himself for the shift, declaring war on drugs and crime, cutting state spending across the board—and quietly dropping his support for Goodell and asking Spiro Agnew to campaign for his gubernatorial reelection. When the president heard that—Rocky had specifically asked Nixon *not* to campaign for him back in '66 and '58—he exulted, "Isn't that something! They're really reading the tea leaves, aren't they?"

James Buckley—William F.'s quieter younger brother—had been reading the tea leaves, too. He had been one of the Catholic conservatives outraged by the passage of New York's abortion bill in April. (Not as outraged, however, as Buckley family friend Brent Bozell. When his group Los Hijos de Tormenta—Sons of Thunder, after the Spanish fascist group—learned that George Washington University hospital was performing abortions, they marched there in khaki uniforms and red berets, carrying papal flags and rosaries: "America . . . you are daggering to death your unborn tomorrow," a priest intoned. "The very cleanliness of your sterilized murder factories gives off the stench of death." They smashed a plate-glass window in the ensuing scuffle with security guards.) Jim Buckley asked *National Review* publisher Bill Rusher if he had a chance of winning a three-way Senate race on the Conservative Party line. Rusher told him yes. Clif White spent $10,000 on a poll confirming it. The hard-hat riot was further, if anecdotal, evidence.

In June, Jim Buckley traveled to Vietnam, said America was winning, and that "I would strongly urge President Nixon to announce that after the completion of the scheduled withdrawal of 150,000 troops, no draftee will be required to engage in combat in this conflict against his will." This statement had likely been coordinated with the White House, which was privately already circulating that as their intention. At a July 22 White House meeting, Haldeman, Finch, Harlow, Dent, Chotiner, and a nut-cutter named Donald Rumsfeld discussed how to distribute the secret town-house funds. "We are dropping Goodell over the side," the president announced. The administration couldn't campaign directly against a Republican; that was beyond the pale. Agnew, scheduled to appear in Rochester Wednesday, September 30, was instead instructed to ask New Yorkers to vote for a senator who would "support the president"—meaning the non-Republican Buckley.

That Wednesday started as a bad day for the White House. A commission on pornography convened by President Johnson had earlier completed its report, finding "no evidence" linking dirty pictures to delinquency, and recommending a massive sex education campaign. Charles Keating of Citizens for Decent Literature, a Nixon appointee to the commission, successfully sued to enjoin its publication. The injunction was reversed, and the morning of Agnew's New York visit, America learned that the President's Commission on Pornography didn't have a problem with pornography. Agnew blasted the report the next day in Salt Lake City, blaming the heresies on its Democratic origins, pledging, "As long as Richard Nixon is president, Main Street is not going to turn into smut alley."

In Rochester, Agnew trotted out that classic Nixonian rhetorical trope, the unsourced, invented rhetorical question: "Earlier today, I was asked if I would support a member of the radical-liberal clique who is running in New York as a Republican. I made clear that I will not support a radical liberal no matter what party he belongs to." Goodell hit back by accusing Agnew of "sophisticated McCarthyism." Agnew proved him a piker six days later by invoking the name of the former soldier who'd become a celebrity in the 1950s by turning himself surgically into a woman. Goodell was the "Christine Jorgensen of the Republican Party"—a man who had surrendered his manhood. ("Miss Jorgensen Asks Agnew for Apology," the *New York Times* headlined demurely.)

That was a little too much for Nelson Rockefeller, who rescinded his invitation for Agnew to campaign for him. But it didn't faze the man who had won in 1950 by calling his opponent "pink right down to her underpants." Nixon was chomping at the bit to enter the fray. He took up the cudgels October 12, motorcading to Hartford, Connecticut, for a quick word on behalf of Congressman Lowell Weicker's Senate bid.

Vietcong flags were amid the crowd. This was handy. Nixon made sure to point them out to reporters.

The next leg was the airport in Westchester County. No speech, only a quick wave—and a carefully advanced maneuver in which a knot of Young Americans for Freedom clustered by his side carrying NIXON & BUCKLEY posters, the wordless endorsement worth a thousand words.

On Wednesday, October 14, Nixon made a statement against the menace of hijacking and spoke at a White House conference on drug abuse. On Tuesday he had signed the Organized Crime Control Act of 1970—mentioning three more New Left bombings, praising the FBI's apprehension of Angela Davis, and, tying the American radicals to the Palestinian plane hijacking, announcing his determination to "see to it that those who engage in such terroristic acts are brought to justice." Then he headed out to give an unmemorable speech in Vermont for Senator Winston Prouty. A concrete chip or three issued from the crowd, landing seventy-five feet from Air Force One. Chuck Colson said to a reporter, "Those rocks will mean ten thousand votes for Prouty." The president was struck only by inspiration. In Green Bay, Wisconsin, as a small contingent chanted, "One, two, three, four! We don't want your fucking war!" Air Force One taxied into place. A police sergeant gave orders to two of his patrolmen: when the president strode down the steps, White House advance men wanted them to turn the banks of portable floodlights not on the leader of the free world, but on the shrieking hippies. The officers stared, incredulous; the sergeant barked, "That's what they want us to do—*now do it.*"

Nixon recited his script: ". . . I will also note, my friends, as we look out at this crowd, that we have a few here that indicate that they have other views with regard to my visit. Let me say that I respect their right to be heard even if they do not respect my right to be heard. And let me also say, ladies and gentlemen, I can assure them that they are a very loud minority in this country, but they are a minority, and it's time for the majority to stand up and be counted."

He wound up Tuesday in Kansas—where he visited a policeman hospitalized by a radical's bomb. He seemed to be enjoying himself enormously. "Vermont, they threw a few rocks. Several other places, they tried to shout me down. In other places, they shouted the usual four-letter words. . . . If you were to simply read the newspaper and look at the television, the amount of space that those who engage in that kind of protest are concerned, as distinguished from peaceful protest, the amount of space they get gives you the impression that that kind of young American is either a majority of young Americans or will be the leaders of the future.

"Well, I have got news for you. They aren't the majority of young Americans today and they aren't going to be the leaders of America tomorrow."

Campaigning against the hippies seemed a can't-miss strategy. They had made reading the typical newspaper a kind of torment. Take the *Rockford Star,* which served a hard-hat town in north-central Illinois. The picture on the front page on October 20 was of the ruins of a sumptuous modern mansion with a kidney-shaped pool. The caption read, "Scene of five slayings." A wealthy optometrist from Santa Cruz, Dr. Victor Ohta, his wife, two sons, and secretary had been bound with silk scarves, shot execution style, and thrown into the swimming pool. "Ohta's home stood on a rise 100 miles south of San Francisco in a scenic area dotted with the homes of the rich and middle class, but also with hippie communes and wandering young people, whom the Ohtas had reportedly 'chased off' their property more than once."

It was joined on the *Star*'s front page by "Army Ends Testimony on My Lai" ("They appeared to be mostly women and children. . . . Some appeared to be dead, but some were definitely alive. I remember they looked at me and followed me with their eyes as I crossed the ditch") and an installment in a five-part series reporting from a commune on Madison's Mifflin Street that led by quoting the reading material lying around: "We must lead an armed revolution to overcome hypocrisy and oppression in a government that can only be defeated through revolutionary violence."

That was page one. A small item, "Guitar Sparks Triple Slaying in California," was relegated to page two, next to the weather map.

Two days later the *Star* reported on the Santa Cruz murder note, "signed with symbols used on gypsy fortune telling cards" of the sort hippies favored: "Today World War 3 will begin as brought to you by the people of the Free universe. From this day forward anyone and any company of persons who misuses the natural environment or destroys same will suffer the penalty of death by the people of the free universe . . . materialism must die or mankind will." Next to that, a UPI story datelined from Central America: "The Costa Rican government agreed Wednesday night to prevent the execution of four U.S. citizens aboard a Costa Rican airliner hijacked in Cuba." Next to that: "Guevara Hero to Miffland's Anarchists" and a Quebec labor minister kidnapped and strangled by separatist terrorists. Second page: a dynamite theft that preceded five bombings in Rochester; and the sudden appearance of Weatherman Bernardine Dohrn at Eldridge Cleaver's exile lair in Algiers beside Timothy Leary, whom the Weathermen had recently sprung from jail.

The next day: twenty Rockford youths arrested in a park with a suitcase full of hashish; "SAN FRANCISCO (UPI)—A time bomb exploded outside a church Thursday as mourners gathered for the funeral of a policeman killed in a bank holdup"; the arrest of a mild-mannered auto mechanic in the Ohta case; "ALGIERS—Eldridge Cleaver declared that he intends to extend his party into an international operation dedicated to overthrowing the U.S. government"—and way back on page 11, the terror wracking the campus of Northern Illinois University after a coed's body had been discovered in a field shortly after the institution of new open-dorm hours.

The day after that: "Berserk Pilot Crash Dives into Church" in Texas; "Raped Co-ed's Cry for Aid Unheeded" in Chicago; "Ohta Murder Suspect Captured, Charged" in Santa Cruz.

The Sunday paper, October 25: from Algiers, "Cleaver: Asylum Granted Leary"; from Detroit, "Black Panther Shootout—15 Charged in Police Shooting"; "William A. Campbell, Democratic candidate for sheriff, claimed Sunday morning that in the past year, 17 Rockford teenagers had died as a result of the misuse of drugs"—and finally, "Bomb Blasts Post Office in Washington," the post office blocks from the Capitol.

These newspaper readers faced a choice the Tuesday after next: voting for a Republican or a Democrat for Senate. On Thursday, October 29—along with citizens in Minnesota, Nebraska, and California—they would be graced with a visit from their president to help them make up their minds.

On Tuesday the twenty-seventh Nixon signed the Comprehensive Drug

Abuse Prevention and Control Act of 1970 for the cameras in front of a table of confiscated pills, weeds, powders, and cash. On the twenty-eighth he made four stops in Florida, where Congressman William Cramer was fighting Lawton Chiles for the Senate, and three in Texas for Senate aspirant George H. W. Bush—another Southern Strategy hopeful. Bush's opponent was the conservative Democrat Lloyd Bentsen, a protégé of John Connally's, who, in the primary, had knocked off Texas's legendary liberal senator Ralph Yarborough thanks in part to an ad with a picture of the liberal incumbent and the legend NO rubber-stamped over the word *prayer*. Bush promised that the only way Bentsen could outflank him to the right was to "drop off the face of the earth." One ploy to burnish Bush, who suffered from a fey Yankee air, was a press release to the *Houston Chronicle* and the *Houston Post* from the Texas Air National Guard concerning his son: "George Walker Bush is one member of the younger generation who doesn't get his kicks from pot or hashish or speed. Oh, he gets high, all right, but not from narcotics. After his solo, a milestone in the career of any fighter pilot, Lt. Bush couldn't find enough words to adequately express the feeling of solo flight. 'It was really neat. It was fun, and very exciting,' he said."

In Rockford some found it curious that the president spoke in an airplane hangar despite the brilliant sunshine outside. (Sunshine wasn't a reliable way to light a set.) A heckler obligingly shouted obscenities as Nixon walked down the Air Force One steps; Senator Ralph Smith delivered his only speaking part: "Ladies and gentlemen, the president of the United States." Nixon raised both arms in twin V-salutes, the trademark gesture he mimicked from the first time he'd seen General Eisenhower, at the New York City V-E day parade in 1945. Nixon greeted Smith, Illinois congressman John Anderson, a visiting Wisconsin congressman, and congressional aspirant Phyllis Schlafly. He won cheap applause feigning familiarity with the locale: "Any rally that will bring East Rockford and West Rockford together has to be quite a rally." Then, the standard peroration:

"The president of the United States cannot do the job unless he has a Congress that will work with him, not against him . . . men who will have the courage to vote against spending that will raise prices for all the people. . . . They are not a majority and they're not going to be the leaders of America. . . . As we talk about what's wrong, let's stand up and speak about what's right in this country. . . . I pledge our goal will be to end this war to bring us a generation of peace."

Outside the hangar an overflow crowd of thousands listened on loudspeakers. A man ripped a protest sign from a girl. He said she was "abusing my right to hear the president speak." Fists flew; plainclothesmen broke it up. The next morning the *Star* ran an AP report out of Chicago that federal agents were investigating a possible presidential assassination plot. Next to that, a quarry thirteen miles to the east had reported six hundred pounds of dynamite missing. Next to that, "Illinois crime investigator accuses FBI fugitive and other members of Students for a Democratic Society of plotting anarchy."

In *Life,* Hugh Sidey reported that the president's campaign speeches were not the only thing the White House scripted: "Nixon's advance men this fall have carefully arranged with local police to allow enough dissenters into the staging areas so the President will have his theme well illustrated as he warms to his job." Thursday night in San Jose, just over the hills from the Ohta hippie murders, the president spoke for Senator George Murphy in an auditorium. At least a thousand demonstrators unsuccessfully tried to storm the doors. Bob Haldeman, disappointed that there were no hecklers inside, was thrilled at the news. He arranged for an interval between the speech and the motorcade so the protesters would have time to mass themselves. Nixon leapt up on the hood of his bulletproof limousine, made the two-handed V-salute, and jutted out his chin. He told his handlers, "That's what they hate to see!"

He was answered with a hail of rocks, flags, and candles from the candlelight vigil: Caracas in California.

Press secretary Ron Ziegler was later asked why the leader of the free world had placed his person in such danger. He responded that Nixon had spotted a "friendly face" in the crowd. Haldeman put it differently in his diary: "Made a huge incident and we worked hard to crank it up, should make a really major story and might be effective." Ziegler released a statement: "The stoning at San Jose is an example of the viciousness of the lawless elements in our society."

It proved the setup for his subsequent speech, from a hangar at Sky Harbor International Airport in Phoenix, taped for election-eve broadcast on all three networks:

"Let's recognize them for what they are: not romantic revolutionaries but the same thugs and hoodlums that have always plagued a good people. . . . For too long we have appeased aggression here at home, and, as with all appeasement"—*appeasement,* that word that worked so well in the 1950s—"the result has been more aggression and more violence.

"Let us understand that this is not a partisan issue. . . .

"The new approach in violence requires men in Congress who will work for and fight for laws that will put the terrorists where they belong—not roaming around civil society, but behind bars." The acolytes of the old approach "are sincere Americans; they have every right to their point of view. But . . . for a decade their approach dominated America and it has obviously failed."

On TV, the final voice-over: "Support men who will vote for the president, not against him. Bring an end to the wave of violence in America."

The Silent Majority tramped to the polls Tuesday to the tune of one more White House statement: "It should be further said that reporters from various news organizations inspected the Presidential limousine and noted chips in the roof glass." In Rockford the morning paper sent voters on their way with yet more horrifying images: "DENVER (UPI)—National Guard officials have ordered a buildup of security forces in the Denver area as a response to threats of coordinated bombings around the country"; "Homeowners and policemen in suburban Annandale, Va., were on guard Saturday night for a Halloween appearance of a mysterious 'bunny Man' who wears a furry rabbit costume with two long ears and carries an ax"; "Girl, 2, Has Trip on Loaded Candy"; and from a town nearby, "Rochelle police chief Jerry Bratcher displays sticks of dynamite, wiring, and a battery which had been rigged in bomblike fashion inside a suitcase discovered Saturday in a Rochelle motel."

Then Rockford joined an Illinois electoral majority in voting in . . . Adlai Stevenson.

In California, Democrat John Tunney unseated George Murphy.

In Texas, George Bush lost his second Senate race in a row. Two other of the White House's handpicked hopefuls, William Cramer in Florida and Nelson Gross in New Jersey, wouldn't be going to the Senate either. In Nevada, North Dakota, Utah, the Republicans lost, too. Mrs. Romney lost in Michigan. Democrat Vance Hartke from Indiana kept his seat, as did Bill Proxmire from Wisconsin. In Minnesota, Hubert Humphrey won back a spot in the Senate. Save for James Buckley in New York—who was helped by a commercial cut by John Wayne saying that if he lived in New York he'd sure vote for him—mighty Spiro had struck out. The only other gain for the White House was Bill Brock in Tennessee, campaigning viciously with ads like "On school prayer, Tennesseans said Yes, but Albert Gore said No," and "On busing of schoolchildren, Tennesseans say No, but Albert Gore said Yes." But what it took for a Republican to win a Senate seat now bid fair to cost them another. Forty-six-year-old Senator William Saxbe of Ohio said he was now thinking about not running for reelection: "I am not ready to abandon the Republican Party and turn it over to a bunch of unreconstructed rebels from the South. You know who they are."

Publicly the president claimed victory—a "working majority of four" in the Senate, including conservative Democrats such as Lloyd Bentsen, to enhance his negotiating hand abroad and "enormously strengthen our hand at home."

Privately, he raged. Ehrlichman reminded him they'd have to schedule more time with Congress. Nixon bit his head off: "Don't keep saying that, John. I know I have to—I'll work twenty-two hours a day instead of twenty." A Senate full of liberal harassers and obstructionists, some from his own party: it wasn't supposed to end like this.

Richard Nixon had forgotten his own lesson of his 1968 victory: the political power of *quiet*. He was right: Americans were tired of shouters. But now
Nixon and Agnew were shouting loudest of all.

It came out in that election-eve broadcast. The Republicans bought a half
hour on all the networks. Then DNC chair Larry O'Brien challenged the
purchase under the FCC's fairness doctrine, asking the networks to split the
time in half. They acceded (rejecting the other request of the Democrats, who
were $9 million in debt, to make the airtime free; the $100,000 to pay for the
time was raised by Averell Harriman)—a Solomonic result that forced the
Republicans to hack a carefully crafted half-hour speech in half. It jerked
around mercilessly; the sound levels shifted abruptly; a background hum, and
the enthusiastic Goldwaterite audience in the echoey jumbo-jet hangar,
obscured the words. The thing was an unholy mess. The president's supporters thought the way their president thought: they flooded network switchboards with calls charging Democratic sabotage. But the Western White
House admitted that the flaws were present in the tape provided by the RNC.

Then came the Democrats' response from Edmund Muskie, a man best
known by the American public as an advocate for the uniting issue of ecology and as the only conciliatory voice from the 1968 Democratic National
Convention. The media reported their two broadcasts as a preview of the
presidential race. If so, it was Muskie by a mile.

He sat, relaxed, in an armchair in his summer home. "I am speaking from
Cape Elizabeth, Maine," he began, "to discuss with you the election campaign which is coming to a close. In the heat of our campaigns, we have all
become accustomed to a little anger and exaggeration."

Calmly, he said the charge Democrats appeased thugs was "a lie, and the
American people know it is a lie"—a lie about the party "which led us out
of depression and to victory over international barbarism; the party of John
Kennedy, who was slain in the service of the country he inspired; the party
of Lyndon Johnson, who withstood the fury of countless demonstrations in
order to pursue a course he believed in; the party of Robert Kennedy, murdered on the eve of his greatest triumph. How *dare* they tell us that this party
is less devoted or less courageous in maintaining American principles and
values than they are themselves?"

His voice rose slightly; some passion was called for.

Occasionally the camera closed in on his chiseled face. The word *Lincoln-
esque* appeared in the press reports. His tone turned rueful: "This attack is
not simply the overzealousness of a few local leaders. It has been led,
inspired, and guided from the highest offices in the land. . . .

"Let me try to bring some clarity to this deliberate confusion," he said.
Democrats wanted security against lawlessness, too, but Democrats also
thought you deserved *economic* security. The Republicans? "They oppose

your interests" and "really believe that if they can make you afraid enough or angry enough, you can be tricked into *voting against yourself*. It is all part of the same contempt, and tomorrow you can show them the mistake they have made." The debate wasn't between left or right, but between "the politics of fear and the politics of trust. One says: you are encircled by monstrous dangers. Give us power over your freedom so we may protect you. The other says: the world is a baffling and hazardous place, but it can be shaped to the will of men. . . . In voting for the Democratic Party tomorrow, you cast your vote for trust, not just in leaders or policies, but trusting your fellow citizens, in the ancient tradition of this home for freedom and, most of all, for trust in yourself."

Maybe it was these marvelous sentiments that stopped the Agnewite tide. Maybe it just was the economy: 1970 was the first year in over a decade to post a decline in the production of real goods and services. The United States now accounted for 18 percent of the trade with the top industrial nations compared with 30 percent twenty years earlier. On October 21 the Labor Department released September consumer price index numbers showing inflation on essentials had risen by half a percentage point. On October 27 the headlines were that eighteen metropolitan areas, from Los Angeles to nearly all of New Jersey, were on a Substantial Unemployment List, up from six listings at the end of 1969.

The Democrats' success showed the brilliance of a Democratic Congress's political maneuver. In August, Congress had handed the president new powers to impose wage and price controls—because they knew a business Republican such as Nixon would never use them. Republicans, boxed in, lamely called Democrats economic pessimists. Democrats returned that they had given the president authority to *do something* about people's economic misery—but instead he sat on his hands. Muskie had spoken of a previous generation of working men's "assurance of a constantly rising standard of life which was his only a few years ago and which has been cruelly snatched away"—which the president knew only to fight "by withdrawing money" from "the workingman, the consumer, the middle-class American." The *New York Times* found a typical blue-collar swing voter to quote in Akron, Teamster Mike Mangione. He said the National Guardsmen were "one hundred percent right in Kent State." But his wife was taking a job for the first time because he had lost his overtime and they wanted to keep three kids in Catholic school. He was voting Democratic. "This summer only ten out of forty guys were working because of the slowdown in the construction industry."

The president learned the lesson. In a meeting on his reelection campaign, he told Haldeman, "I really want the economy to boom beginning in July '72." He didn't really care how it was accomplished. On November 7 in Key Biscayne, he listed seven priorities for the coming year. The first was sprucing up his hermit image. The second was the economy—"greater changes than the President has been willing to consider." (The sixth: "The Vice President . . . must be toned down.")

He began seeing 1972 in apocalyptic terms: if he lost the presidency, America might end. Any imaginable Democratic nominee was "irresponsible domestically" and "extremely dangerous internationally." He had come to understand something profound in his two years as president, in all those lonely afternoons brooding alone in his hideaway office in the Executive Office Building—the kind of profundity too deep to share with the mere public: "America has only two more years as the number one power." America had either to "make the best deals we can between now and 1975 *or* increase our conventional strength. No Democrat can sell this to the country."

So it was that the Old and New Nixon, serpent and sage, collided in a single astonishing insight: in order to responsibly steward the American people through the coming crisis, he first had to bluff America into believing in its own invincibility.

Indeed, to keep from losing another election, he was willing to consider just about anything. This time around he would leave *nothing, nothing, nothing* to chance.

BOOK IV

CHAPTER TWENTY-SIX

How to Survive the Debacle

O BVIOUSLY, THE WORLD WAS ENDING: BY 1971, THE CONCLUSION WAS unmistakable. Steve Roberts of the *New York Times* wrote about the enveloping apocalypticism in California, where every trend began: "Prophets of doom are as common as girls in bikinis (there are even a few prophets of doom in bikinis). Some predict the whole state will break off and sink into the Pacific—probably this month." At the Timeless Occult shop on Sunset Boulevard, the young proprietor listed his bestselling items: astrological charts, magic candles, books by the psychic Edgar Cayce. "Some people just wander in and want to know how far they should drive inland. I tell them not to worry. This one won't be so bad. Utter devastation won't come until 1972."

The proximate anxiety was earthquakes. But when it came to existential terrors, Americans could choose from a banquet. In February, forty-eight students at the University of Louisville undertook a fifty-four-hour weekend hunger strike to dramatize what the overpopulated earth would be like in the year 2000. Twelve quit before the end; they were said to have not "survived." "We've found people can adapt to stressful conditions," an organizer told the media. "We know that we will be able to keep living—miserably."

Apocalypse, up and down the culture: there were get-rich-quick versions (*How You Can Profit from the Coming Devaluation* offered "a plan that shows how to survive the debacle . . . and even make money out of it!") and religious ones (the cover of *The Late Great Planet Earth* by Hal Lindsey of Campus Crusade for Christ announced, "The rebirth of Israel, an increase in natural catastrophes, the threat of war with Egypt and the revival of interest in Satanism and witchcraft . . . were foreseen by prophets from Moses to Jesus as being the key signals for the coming of an Antichrist. And a war which will bring man to the brink of destruction.") and biological (Paul Ehrlich's *The Population Bomb* went into a new paperback printing every couple of weeks: "While you are reading these words four people will have died from starvation. Most of them children," the cover read). *The Andromeda Strain*, a hit in the new "disaster movie" genre, was about an apocalyptic virus brought down to earth by a fallen satellite. Dr. B. F. Skinner's new bestseller, *Beyond Freedom & Dignity*—seven paperback printings in one year—asked, "If all of modern science and technology cannot significantly change man's environment, can mankind be saved?" His solution: "We can no longer afford freedom." *Future Shock*, by Alvin Toffler—seven printings in four months—said Americans were suffering a collective nervous breakdown: "In the neural system as now constituted there are, in all likelihood, inherent limits to the amount and speed of image processing that the individual can accomplish." The public appetite for counsels of doom was bottomless.

But the bestselling paperback of all—seven printings in *two* months—proposed an antidote. *The Greening of America*, by Yale law professor Charles A. Reich, was introduced to the public as a thirty-nine-thousand-word article in the September 26, 1970, *New Yorker*. Its thesis was printed on the paperback's front cover: "There is a revolution coming. It will not be like revolutions of the past. It will originate with the individual and with culture, and it will change the political structure only as its final act. It will not require violence to succeed, and it cannot be successfully resisted by violence. . . . This is the revolution of the new generation."

Reich called it Consciousness III and said it was born of the baby boomers: "Their protest and rebellion, their culture, clothes, music, drugs, and liberated life-style. . . . And it promises a life that is more liberated and more beautiful than any man has known, if man has the courage and the imagination to seize that life. . . . The process of that creation, which has already been started by our youth in this moment of utmost sterility, darkest night, and extremest peril, is what we have undertaken to describe in this book."

They did it simply by choosing what Reich called their "life-style." Their marijuana: "a maker of revolution, a truth serum"—"what happens when a person with fuzzy vision puts on glasses." Their bell-bottom pants: they "have to be worn to be understood. They express the body. . . . They give the ankles a special freedom as if to invite dancing right on the street. . . . The new clothes demonstrate a significant new relationship between man and technology." An entire new civilization had "sprouted up, astonishingly and miraculously, out of the stony soil of the American Corporate State." And as its avatars aged into adulthood, their revolution would become general. "It is both necessary and inevitable, and in time it will include not only youth, but all people in America."

Reich, as all the most ecstatic hymners of the new consciousness seemed to be, from Fred Dutton down to Herbert Marcuse, was middle-aged. So were his most enthusiastic readers. One of them was *New Yorker* editor William Shawn. Another was that plain-speaking product of the soil of South Dakota, Senator George McGovern, who distributed it to his staff. He found *Greening* "one of the most gripping, penetrating, and revealing analyses of American society I have yet seen." Supreme Court justice William O. Douglas found it "a first-rate piece of creative thinking." Such testimonials covered three paperback pages. Mrs. Aldred Cosmann of Great Neck: "For the first time I began to understand the reason behind some of my 18-year-old son's views which had heretofore perplexed and worried me." Mrs. Edward M. Post of Louisville: "I write this letter less for your gratification than my own—a piece of evidence that at thirty-six, five kids, two dogs, *things* all around, it is possible to begin."

Mr. Reich answered a need. His New Jerusalem would just sort of *happen.* Automatically. No more riots, no more cataclysm, no more protests, no left, no right—no *politics.* A comforting thought—now, as a skeptical young reviewer of *Greening* wrote, "that the daily editorial page reads like the Revelation of St. John the Divine." These *were* the most hopeful times since Christ was born in Bethlehem. For announcing this miracle, fifteen thousand copies of Reich's tract rolled off the presses every week.

For Americans of a thousand different descriptions, finding a path of retreat from the daily editorial page was the new way of life. Hippies were, of course, living on their communes, exploring "inner space." But middle-class suburbanites, heeding *How You Can Profit from the Coming Devaluation*'s warning of "an increasingly likely runaway inflation similar to the one in pre-Nazi Germany," were taking its advice to sock away their assets in gold, silver, and Swiss francs. Many more citizens were "dropping out" by retreating from politics altogether. Turnouts for elections were growing so anemic that when geostrategist Edward Luttwak published an article in *Esquire* on "A Scenario for a Military Coup d'État in the United States," he said necessary and sufficient conditions were already in place. "Phase One" of his timetable was labeled "The Growth of Indifference . . . 1970–1976."

The one growth area of mass political participation was the antibusing movement, which fit into the same pattern. Since 1965, the riots on TV had been white people's window onto a world on the verge of chaos. Now it was coming to you. More and more Americans were manning the barricades—fighting the judges and the politicians who ordered black students from decrepit and overcrowded schools shifted to uncrowded and pristine ones in the suburbs. Protecting yourself, keeping a scary outside world at bay: by 1971, for many Americans, left and right, that was what politics was *for.*

Richard Nixon understood.

Nixon began the year as he usually did, with flights of statesmanlike rhetoric. At the University of Nebraska, he spoke of "the problems of overpopulation, the problems brought about by technology, the problems of achieving full and equal opportunity for all our people, of health, the problems of prosperity itself, of poverty in the land of plenty," and called for "an alliance of the generations" to solve them. The greening of Richard Nixon: "As we put our hands together, your generation and mine, in the alliance we forge we can discover a new understanding, a community of wisdom." The State of the Union was another Kennedyesque ode: "We have gone through a long, dark night of the American spirit. But now that night is ending. Now we must let our spirits soar again. Now we are ready for the lift of a driving dream." He renewed the call for passage of his guaranteed-income Family Assistance Plan and his program for sharing federal tax revenues with the states, which he dubbed the "New American Revolution—a peaceful revolution in which power was turned back to the people, in which government at all levels was refreshed and renewed and made truly responsive." He proposed $100 million to cure cancer, a universal health-insurance program, quoted T. S. Eliot—"Clean the air! Clean the sky! Wash the wind!"—in proposing a program "to end the plunder of America's natural heritage."

That, at least, was the public transcript. He put it a little differently to two Ford executives in the Oval Office: Ralph Nader and the environmentalists, he said, would rather "go back and live like a bunch of damned animals. . . . What they're interested in is destroying the system." In a strategy meeting for the '72 election, he proposed either sabotaging passage of the welfare plan—or passing it and letting the actual implementation die after passage, getting credit for caring, without doing anything at all.

In public, Nixon no longer spoke about "thugs and hoodlums" or the wayward senators who enabled them, his obsessions on the 1970 campaign trail. In private it was all the president could think about. The November losses, the anticipation of November 1972, made of his imagination a dungeon, rotted through with paranoia and dread.

Jetting to Nebraska to utter his fine phrases on the alliance of generations, he plotted how to screw DNC chair Larry O'Brien. He decided to pass off the portfolio to John Dean, who had suffered a dark night of the soul back in August the first time he had been tasked with such "intelligence" duties, harassing a new left-wing magazine, *Scanlon's Monthly,* that published an Abbie Hoffman–style prank purporting to be a memo linking Agnew to a plot to cancel the presidential election. Dean was baffled by the assignment; to him the piece seemed obviously a put-on. He caviled to Murray Chotiner, Nixon's dirty trickster since 1946, who told him not to ask questions: "If the president wants you to turn the IRS loose, then you turn the IRS loose. . . . Do you think for a second that Lyndon Johnson was above using the IRS to harass those guys who were giving him a hard time on the war?"

John Dean followed orders. He found his stature increased in the event— if not as much as Chuck Colson's, who enjoyed a staff of twenty-three to carry out such malodorous tasks. As the president's approval rating approached a new low—near 50 percent—and the Muskie-Nixon presidential matchup was a statistical dead heat, willingness to play dirty tricks was the currency of White House success.

Murray Chotiner fielded intelligence from an agent within the Muskie presidential exploratory team. Colson collated a private detective's photos of Edward M. Kennedy dancing with an Italian princess. An ongoing project was the drafting of a White House "Opponents List": "I refer not simply to press and TV," ran Nixon's action memo, "but the University community, religious organizations, finance, Eastern Establishment, the major Senate/House/Gubernatorial/Party leaders on the other side, and the special interest groups like Labor and Minorities." The first tally included journalists Hugh Sidey, Evans and Novak, Joseph Kraft, and David Broder. The third, drafted by Tom Charles Huston, included actress Carol Channing. The most venturesome came from Colson. It listed as White House "enemies" the AFL-CIO, NAACP, and the Brookings Institution.

On January 31, 1971, the *New York Times* front page wondered why cargo flights to Saigon were being preempted by "higher priority traffic," as American bombers targeted the Laotian border. State and Defense Department officials refused comment and threatened to kick out Saigon correspondents who reported anything was going on in Laos. Explained Ron Ziegler helpfully, "The president is aware of what is going on in Southeast Asia. That is not to say there is something going on in Southeast Asia."

What was going on was that U.S. airpower was softening up the border for an attack by the South Vietnamese army. It was thought that a single big push into Laos could sever the Ho Chi Minh Trail for good, and the Communist insurgency in South Vietnam would wither away—or at least America casualties could be held down for the 1972 presidential campaign season.

Laos couldn't be hit with American troops: the Cooper-Church amendment's December passage had seen to that. That was a tactical opportunity for Nixon: the chance to prove that Vietnamization was working. The Pentagon defended its news embargo as necessary to ensure the operation's security. Why the safety of South Vietnamese troops might be enhanced by keeping secret from *Americans* the news of the B-52s, F-111s, and F-4 Phantoms whistling ostentatiously above Communist positions was left unexplained. The intimidation effort, though, worked: film of the operation called (in Vietnamese) Lam Son 719 and (in English) Operation Dewey Canyon II stayed off TV for the time being, and a repeat of the Cambodian invasion backlash was avoided.

The president plotted political plots. On February 4, in between Laos updates, accepting the annual Humanitarian Award from the America College of Cardiology, and delivering a high-minded speech on the Constitution, he huddled for two hours with Mitchell and Haldeman. One subject was J. Edgar Hoover. The FBI chief of forty-seven years was proving an unexpected nuisance. When he had received Tom Charles Huston's July memo advising break-ins, harassment, and surveillance against domestic critics under a White House directorate, Hoover, perhaps fearing an assault on his turf, called in Huston (ostentatiously forgetting his name) and told him his plans were "too dangerous." Nixon, Mitchell, and Haldeman puzzled out ways to institute the Huston Plan by other means, and schemed to put Hoover out to pasture for good. Then the subject turned to Governor Wallace, who, Haldeman confided to his diary, appeared "interested in making a deal of some kind that will make it unnecessary for him to run for P." They kicked around ideas on neutralizing Mayor Daley; maybe they could convince him to sit on his hands in 1972 in exchange for Clement Stone not contributing to the Republican candidate for Illinois governor in 1974.

On February 8, T. S. Eliot's words on cleaning the air and washing the wind rang from Richard Nixon's lips, and twenty thousand troops of the Army of Vietnam poured over Laos's border. For a good ten days they marched without real Communist resistance, a splendid romp: confirmation of the wisdom of Vietnamization, *Time* reported, noting the prowess of the ARVN's "crack" First Division.

Then the tide turned.

Forty thousand Communist troops counterattacked in waves—made easier because South Vietnam's President Thieu hoped to have as few ARVN casualties as possible so the army could protect him against coups. Two Communist divisions hammered the South Vietnamese mercilessly. Nixon, panicking, demanded, "We must claim victory regardless of the outcome." The military objective was to be the Laotian town of Tchepone, the "hub of the Ho Chi Minh Trail." Nixon came up with a plan: "It would be a great public relations coup if the ARVN actually reached Tchepone."

So they scripted a military dumb show: two thousand bedraggled South Vietnamese soldiers were airlifted to the town, whose once fearsome antiaircraft batteries—and every building besides—had already been pounded into rubble by U.S. ordnance. William Rogers and President Thieu both announced a triumph. "Major Victory by South Viets," dutifully rhapsodized the always gung ho *Chicago Tribune;* "Viets Overrun Key Laos Base," reported the usually skeptical *Chicago Daily News.*

In fact ARVN radio frequencies had been commandeered by the North Vietnamese, who used them to call in American salvos against ARVN positions, and the "crack" ARVN units hugged the skids of the helicopters that had inserted them into battle rather than fight—images that soon made the U.S. evening news.

The president was once more politically on the ropes. When he traveled to the Midwest on March 3 to sell the New American Revolution, a White House special assistant described "construction workers and farmers among the ranks of obscenity-shouting antiwar forces." A week after that Nixon did an extended interview with C. L. Sulzberger of the *New York Times:* "I rate myself as a deeply committed pacifist, perhaps because of my Quaker heritage from my mother." The 291-year-old Philadelphia Yearly Meeting responded in an open letter: "This is not our understanding of the Quaker peace testimony."

CBS earned a privileged place on the White House enemies list with the documentary *The Selling of the Pentagon,* which exposed a Pentagon public affairs budget that deployed generals for political sales jobs in plain violation of army regulations, enlisting trusted anchors such as Walter Cronkite as unwitting dupes. TV critic Jack Gould called the program "a whale of a constructive blow for unfettered TV journalism free from Washington manipulation." President Ahab reacted predictably. Vice President Agnew called it "a subtle but vicious broadside against the nation's defense establishment" and accused its producers of ethical lapses in 1966 and 1968, one for a show that never aired, and one in a complaint the FCC dismissed. Then he charged the interviews had been edited out of order, one obtained for a separate program; "the matter of the network's own record in the field of documentary making," he concluded, "can no longer be brushed under the rug of national media indifference."

It inspired a renewed bout of morbid self-examination in media executive suites: were they, as Joe Kraft had argued in 1968, "biased" toward liberal causes? The *Washington Post* took Agnew's side: "It seems a great pity and a waste to let a documentary on such an important subject . . . be undermined in terms of credibility and public confidence by these editing techniques." The House Armed Services Committee subpoenaed CBS's files. CBS refused to turn them over. For months the constitutional debate flared, as Nixon did some Pentagon-selling of his own. He told Howard K. Smith that the Laos operation had been a success. Unconvinced, one group of Republican senators met with Defense Secretary Laird at Jake Javits's home and pleaded for an end to the war—even as another senator, party chair Bob Dole of Kansas, Nixon's favorite congressional hatchet man, called Democrats who said the same thing publicly "the new Chamberlains in what they hope will be another era of appeasement." He singled out George McGovern, who had made the earliest major presidential candidacy announcement in history, on January 18, as coming "as close as anyone has yet come to urging outright surrender."

Dole's salvo didn't work. Pat Buchanan, in a March 24 memo recommending a "Muskie Watch" based in the White House, warned that Vietnam was no longer a handy wedge with which to slice the opposition: "Less and less is this an issue dividing Democrats; more and more is it a unifying issue as conservative Democrats begin to adopt a 'let's get the hell out' stand." "Another Stormy Spring Foreseen for Nixon," Max Frankel of the *Times* reported two days later. The White House reviewed novel political options. They loved what cartoonist Al Capp was up to, especially his speech to the annual convention of the National Association of Broadcasters excoriating Tom Wicker of the *New York Times* and the three networks for bias against

Nixon. Chuck Colson spied a new potential recruit on the horizon: Frank Sinatra. "Sinatra has the makings of another Al Capp; he is thoroughly disenchanted with liberals, as evidenced by his support of Reagan and his current friendship with the Vice President. Most of our Hollywood friends believe that Sinatra is the most influential celebrity in the country because if he goes, so go many other prominent figures, particularly new young stars."

The renewed public relations push was driven by paranoia—a consuming rage for control. The White House was starting to smell from it, and some were noticing the stench.

Senator Sam Ervin was on the case. He didn't understand, when he first started looking into abuses of army intelligence begun under Lyndon Johnson, why he couldn't interest the Nixon administration in following up on the Democrats' sins. His suspicions were pricked when he learned in February of 1970 from the army's general counsel that certain army domestic intelligence activities were being transferred to the Justice Department. During debate on the D.C. crime bill that July, the attorney general announced his intention to spy on political activists, citing "the inherent powers of the federal government to protect the internal security of the nation." Ervin shot back in a speech on the Senate floor, citing a recent *Washington Monthly* exposé, that army domestic spying programs "appear to be part of a vast network of intelligence-oriented systems which are being developed willy-nilly throughout the land" and represented "a potential for political control and intimidation which is alien to a society of free men."

One month after the 1971 State of the Union address, Ervin convened hearings titled "Federal Data Banks, Computers, and the Bill of Rights." With a folksy, aw-shucks manner, he opened by hefting a fat book:

"This particular family Bible weighs eleven pounds."

He displayed a tiny spool of film.

"Contrast it to this piece of microfilm, which contains on it 1,245 pages of a Bible, with all 773,346 words of it. This means a reproduction of 62,500 to one."

He paused.

"Someone remarked that this meant the Constitution could be reduced to the size of a pinhead. I said I thought maybe that was what they had done with it in the executive branch because some of those officials could not see it with their naked eyes." An appreciative audience laughed.

TV viewers learned the army had infiltrated a church youth group in Colorado Springs, that army agents compiled lists of "potential troublemakers" in Kansas City high schools, that Martin Luther King, Julian Bond, folksinger Arlo Guthrie, Adlai Stevenson III, Governor Otto Kerner, and Congressman Abner Mikva had been profiled in army intelligence data banks. Senator Roman Hruska of Nebraska countered that the army's surveillance program was a military necessity. He had a good trump card for his argument: the latest Weather Underground bomb had just gone off—in a restroom in the Capitol, near the spot where George Washington had laid the building's original cornerstone in the fall of 1793.

Hruska cited the bombing in his opening remarks when the surveillance hearings reopened in March: "The people must receive every protection possible against those elements who consider even the United States Capitol Building as a legitimate object of their violence." Ervin countered that moments of national peril were exactly when we needed civil liberties protections the most: "When people fear surveillance, whether it exists or not, they grow afraid to speak their minds and hearts freely to their government or to anyone else." Assistant Attorney General Rehnquist answered for the administration: "self-discipline on the part of the executive branch," he promised, would "provide an answer to virtually all of the legitimate complaints against excesses of information gathering."

Though it most certainly would not.

Tuesday morning, March 23, 1971, the president of the United States and his new secretary of the treasury met with representatives of the dairy industry. Nixon began by assuring them the meeting was off-the-record. He bade for their trust with a joke playing off his Tricky Dick reputation: "Matter of fact the room is not taped. Forgot to do that!"

As a matter of fact, it was one of the first meetings picked up by Richard Nixon's brand-new Oval Office taping system.

While Ervin's hearings were unfolding at the Capitol, Secret Service agents had been installing voice-activated microphones in the Oval Office, Cabinet Room, and Executive Office Building. Reel-to-reel tape recorders in the White House basement would produce a record of every word uttered when the president was in one of those rooms. Back in 1954, when Eisenhower was saying one thing in private about Joe McCarthy and another thing in public, Nixon said he'd love to have a hidden recording gadget to "capture some of those warm, offhand, great-hearted things the man says, play 'em back, then get them press-released." Now his dream had come true.

Eventually, the White House tapes would become public. A follow-up meeting on March 23 with advisers to prepare him for his next consultation with the dairymen was later transcribed as Exhibit 1 in the case *United States v. John Connally,* in which Nixon's treasury secretary was charged, among other things, with two counts of arranging bribes.

The Department of Agriculture had just lowered agricultural price supports for milk, a decision with which the president had concurred. Connally reminded him in a preparatory meeting that the economic reasoning behind the decision was sound, but, "looking to 1972, it, uh, appears very clear to me that you're going to have to move, uh, strong in the Midwest. . . . These dairymen are organized; they're adamant; they're militant. . . . And they,

they're amassing enormous amounts of money that they're going to put into political activities, very frankly." Economics take the hindmost; these people required a political payoff.

Connally briefed the president on what they would be asking for: a price peg for milk at $5.05 a hundredweight instead of $4.92. Nixon could wait to give it to them next year, closer to the election, but that would look like extortion. If he did it now, "they think you've done it because they got a good case and because you're their friend."

Nixon weighed countervailing political considerations: that Congress might get credit from the dairymen instead of him; that he would get blamed for higher prices by supermarket shoppers. The ranking minority member of the House Agricultural Committee suggested how to play it. The price supports were going to be raised by Congress anyway, and Nixon would have to sign it. When it came to that, he'd be able to blame the liberals for raising the price of babies' milk, while in the upcoming meeting with milk producers he could feign reluctance, then let them make a hard case, then adjourn. Later, the White House could "pass the word" to the dairymen that it had decided they were right and would lean on Congress to pass the increase. The appreciative milkmen would flood his reelection coffers with cash.

"Heh, heh," an unidentified voice kicked in. A Department of Agriculture undersecretary added, "If you give them cookies, they, they'll love it." John Ehrlichman suggested making it only a two-year deal—then they could do the same thing for the 1974 elections. They went back and forth about how to correct the $35 to $100 million trade imbalance that would ensue from the payoff they were about to give the dairymen. They decided they could sock it to the meat producers: "Fortunately, beef prices have held up very well." Ehrlichman ended the meeting with a joke: "Better go get a glass of milk."

The assemblage roared.

"Better get it while it's cheap."

"Milk is a sedative," the commander in chief awkwardly contributed, before his team dispersed to get to work on the intricate task at hand. Lawyer Kalmbach, the master of inventing front groups, put together the details: groups with names like Americans Dedicated to Better Public Administration, Volunteers Against Citizen Apathy, Supporters of the American Dream, and Americans United for Objective Reporting became the conduits for the laundering of $250,000 in milk money to a secret campaign committee linked to the group Richard Nixon set up to run his campaign without interference from anyone else in the Republican Party, his new Committee to Re-Elect the President, down the street from the White House.

CHAPTER TWENTY-SEVEN

Cruelest Month

T HE LAOS OFFENSIVE DID NOT RESULT IN WIDESPREAD PROTEST: THE bombing of the Capitol privy, an occupation of the Stanford computer building led by the Maoist Melville scholar H. Bruce Franklin, some fires at the new University of California campus at Santa Cruz, little else. The really dangerous antiwar uprisings were all in Southeast Asia, among GIs.

On March 20, alongside Route 9 by the Laos border, a captain ordered two platoons to wade into heavy enemy fire. They refused to budge: why fight for these cowards who refused to fight for themselves? A lieutenant colonel pleaded, then ordered; fifty-three still refused. They also refused to give their names. No disciplinary action was taken. The brass feared that the mutiny would spread brigade-wide.

The American army was collapsing in the field. "I just work hard at surviving so I can go home and protest the killing," explained one GI. At Fort Bliss, soldiers were calling commanding officers by their first name, who in turn passed anyone through basic training who promised he wouldn't go absent without leave (AWOLs went up fivefold between 1966 and 1971). MPs used to arrest soldiers who attended off-base protest rallies. But if MPs did that now, they would do little else. In Vietnam soldiers wrote semi-seditious slogans on their helmet headliners ("The unwilling, led by the unqualified, doing the unnecessary, for the ungrateful"; "Eat the apple, fuck the Corps") and, caught in infractions, responded, "What are you going to do about it, send me to 'Nam?"

Life had first reported on the GI protests in May of 1969: the off-base antiwar coffeehouses; the underground newspapers; the terror it struck in the brass. The Student Mobilization Committee started mailing bundles of antiwar newsletters to a list of three hundred active-duty supporters, with articles laying out legal options for soldiers who'd like to resist. *New York Times* columnist Scotty Reston wrote on August 27, 1969, that Nixon "has been worried about the revolt of the voters over Vietnam against the war . . . but now he also has to consider the possibility of a revolt of the men if he risks their lives in a war he has decided to bring to a close." Reston was paraphrasing a common soldier's lament: which of them would be the last to die for a war even the president seemed to admit was a mistake?

A sergeant wrote on behalf of his infantry company that "the Moratorium had wide support. It was, in fact, very much a morale builder. The men are intelligent enough to realize that the peace demonstrations are on their behalf. . . . While many wore black arm bands for the October 15 Moratorium, they are for the large part prevented from demonstrating their feelings on the war." *Life* interviewed one hundred soldiers across Vietnam and reported that protests "are not demoralizing troops in the field," that "many soldiers regard the organized antiwar campaign in the U.S. with open and outspoken sympathy." In the words of one private, "I think the protesters may be the only ones who really give a damn about what's happening."

Monkey-wrenching was epidemic. Vietnamese-speaking psy-ops officers rewrote propaganda leaflets to condemn the *Saigon* government. Aircraft carrier crews grounded planes. Government-issued amphetamines—"speed"—meant to keep soldiers alert on patrols were taken recreationally. So was marijuana, which traded for tobacco cigarettes at an exact one-to-one rate. The army started cracking down. So, just as in Haight-Ashbury, soldiers moved on to heroin, which when smoked mixed into cigarettes was odorless: "I can salute an officer with one hand," a soldier explained, "and take a drag of heroin with the other."

The GI movement at home entered a new phase the week before the Route 9 mutiny: the debut outside Fort Bragg of an anti–Bob Hope variety show called *FTA*. The organizers, which included Jane Fonda and her *Klute* costar Donald Sutherland, said the name originated from an army recruiting poster that promised "Fun, Travel, Adventure" and signified "Free the Army"—though when the troupe sang the show's theme song, they left a long pause where the word *free* should be. The soldiers who made it off base to attend—which the brass strongly discouraged—responded with "more than a cheer," the *Washington Post* said, "a roar, a visceral reflex that burst from five hundred throats in the same instant."

In one vaudeville-style routine, Sutherland drawled Gomer Pyle–ishly, "I think I'm gonna get me a watchdog."

"What do you need a watchdog for, Sarge? You're surrounded by 250,000 armed men."

"That's why I'm gonna get me a watchdog!"

He referred to something called "fragging": soldier-murder of hated officers (the word was short for "fragmentation bomb"—they scattered pellets so indiscriminately it looked like an accident). In 1970, there were at least 109 cases. One officer walked around with a $10,000 bounty on his head.

The *Post* quoted an audience member: "Man, if I had it to do over, I would have gone to Canada." He was a returnee from Vietnam. There were more returnees from Vietnam every day; Nixon's Vietnamization policy assured that. They were the fastest-growing segment of the antiwar movement.

That part of the movement came of age in 1970. In public hearings, Vietnam Veterans Against the War members testified about the My Lai–like crimes they had themselves seen or taken part in. They marched eighty-six miles from Morristown, New Jersey, to Valley Forge, just like George Washington's army in 1777. (In small town squares along the way they staged guerrilla theater simulating search-and-destroy missions, announcing their arrival with firecrackers, rushing a crowd from all directions, "forcing" prearranged allies down on their knees for "capture," "killing" those who resisted, as leaflets circulated explaining that this was how America "pacified" Vietnamese villages.) Entering Valley Forge July 4, they were met by the World War II–vintage members of the town's Veterans of Foreign Wars chapter:

"Why don't you go to Hanoi?"

"We won our war, they didn't, and from the looks of them, they couldn't."

A Vietnam vet hobbled by on crutches. One of the old men wondered whether he had been "shot with marijuana or shot in battle."

In January 1971, 105 ex-soldiers testified at "Winter Soldier" hearings in Detroit. The rest of the world didn't notice—despite the presence of Jane Fonda, who had moved full-time to Detroit to help the organizing. Media outlets refused to believe the men were veterans. The *New York Times* buried the story in a skinny little column on page 17. The *Post* didn't cover it at all. A *Times* dispatch on a subsequent hearing in Albany, New York, read, in full, "A small group of legislators sat impassively today as, one by one, a half dozen young veterans of the Vietnam war quietly told of their 'war crimes.' The former soldiers, members of Vietnam Veterans Against the War, told their stories in an alcove of the Capitol in an effort to 'bring the horror of the war closer,' one of them said."

Hugh Hefner donated VVAW a full-page ad in the February 1971 *Playboy*. It brought in over ten thousand new members. Their next step, in April, was to be spectacular: a five-day encampment on the Mall in Washington, D.C. Their public face was a handsome, charismatic twenty-seven-year-old Yalie who had volunteered to command a "swift boat," the most dangerous naval duty in Vietnam. John Kerry led off the press conference on March 16 with his Purple Hearts and Silver Star flashing in the TV lights. He said enlistees were but offered "a chance to die for the biggest nothing in history." A statement was read from retired brigadier general Hugh B. Hester; he charged Nixon with prosecuting "a genocidal war," whose napalm, white phosphorous, and cluster bombs were "as evil as Hitler's crematories."

Camera savvy, the VVAW put wounded veterans up front. Their press release was devastating, too—a parody of the Pentagon's Newspeak: "Operation Dewey Canyon III [is] a limited incursion into the District of Colum-

bia [that] will penetrate into the country of Congress for the limited purpose
of severing supply lines currently being utilized by the illegal mercenary
forces of the Executive Branch . . . to ensure the safe withdrawal of our limited forces of Winter Soldiers from the countries of the District of Columbia."

White House tapes registered hours upon hours of strategizing to neu-
tralize the political threat of the "alleged veterans"—the phrase White House
spokesmen always used. Antiwarriors who had been warriors cut off the
Silent Majority argument at the knees. These were not spoiled brats: they
were the people who weren't able to get college deferments, who couldn't
work the system to get documentation to excuse them from service (in Los
Angeles, at least ten dentists would fit kids for service-disqualifying orthodontics for $1,000 to $2,000), who re-upped because their families needed
the reenlistment bonus. They were unglamorous, empirical witnesses. They
were also former officers, trained to *fight,* who had seen a lot worse in their
previous job than anything any pale bureaucrat could throw at them.

They had to be destroyed.

The president was glad for a politically useful distraction. On March 29, after
the longest court-martial in history, Lieutenant William "Rusty" Calley,
commander at the My Lai massacre, was convicted of murder by a jury of
his military peers.

When Calley had first been called to Washington in June of 1969, he
thought it was to receive a medal. He was shocked to learn it was for a court-
martial: "It seemed like the silliest thing I had ever heard of. Murder." It
betokened a national confusion. His defense lawyer argued, "This boy's a
product of a system, a system that dug him up by the roots, took him out of
his home community, put him in the army, taught him to kill, sent him overseas to kill, gave him mechanical weapons to kill, got him over there and
ordered him to kill." The lawyer said the decision to scapegoat Calley went
all the way up the chain of command—better to indict a fall-guy lieutenant
than the entire "pacification" and "free-fire zone" atrocity-manufacturing
system. The lawyer tried to call Defense Secretary Laird as a witness. The
judge overruled him.

The argument was lent support by the fate of the commanding officer of
Calley's division, Major General Samuel Koster, who had witnessed the massacre from an observation helicopter, complaining only that they weren't
recovering enough enemy weapons. He signed off on an army report that
said noncombatants were "inadvertently killed . . . in the cross fires of U.S.
and V.C. forces." He suffered a mere reduction of a grade in rank. Everyone
else involved ended up acquitted or had his charges dropped.

At his sentencing—life at hard labor—Calley mewled in a breaking voice
about his victimhood: "Yesterday, you stripped me of all my honor. Please,
by your actions that you take here today, don't strip future soldiers of their

honor." But you didn't have to construe Calley a put-upon innocent to conclude that something stank. "Calley Verdict: Who Else Is Guilty?" read
Newsweek's cover line. "Who Shares the Guilt?" asked *Time.*

John Kerry had an answer: "We are all of us in this country guilty for
having allowed the war to go on. We only want this country to realize that
it cannot try a Calley for something which generals and presidents and our
way of life encouraged him to do. And if you try him, then at the same time
you must try all those generals and presidents and soldiers who have part of
the responsibility. You must in fact try this country." It was a common conclusion of liberals. For that reason, Calley became conservatives' hero.

The VFW's national commander led the way: "There have been My Lais
in every war. Now for the first time we have tried a soldier for performing
his duty." A little Mormon boy in Utah wrote his senator begging him to
intervene: "I'm only eight years old, but I know that Lieut. Calley was defending our freedoms against Communism." His mother—many mothers—had
explained that the villagers of My Lai must have done something to deserve
it. So did Joseph Alsop. He complained in his second column after the verdict about the way his first one was edited, that "By no fault of this reporter,
the persons Lt. Calley was convicted of killing were miscalled 'civilians.' . . .
These victims from My Lai in fact came from a 'combat hamlet' of a 'combat
village.' From about the age of four on up, all persons in a 'combat village,' of
both sexes, are trained to kill. By the iron rules of the Viet Cong, if they do not
follow their training, they are killed themselves after one of the VC kangaroo-
trials."

The American Legion post in Columbus, Georgia, home of Calley's Fort
Benning jail cell, promised they would raise $100,000 to help fund his appeal
"or die trying": "The real murderers are the demonstrators in Washington
who disrupt traffic, tear up public property, who deface the American flag.
Lieut. Calley is a hero. . . . We should elevate him to saint." At a revival at
Columbus's football stadium, the Reverend Michael Lord pronounced,
"There was a crucifixion two thousand years ago of a man named Jesus Christ.
I don't think we need another crucifixion of a man named Rusty Calley."

FREE CALLEY stickers blossomed on car bumpers like toadstools after a
spring rain. A Nashville record producer slapped a solemn recitation as if in
William Calley's voice over a backing track of "The Battle Hymn of the
Republic" and moved two hundred thousand 45 rpm records in a day.
"While we were fighting in the jungles they were marching in the street," it
pronounced. "While we're facing V.C. bullets they were sounding a retreat."
The narrator also claimed, of that village of women and children and not a
single weapon captured, to have "responded to their rifle fire with every-
thing we had."

Radio stations played the song in nonstop rotation, interrupted only by
calls for donations to Calley's defense fund. Respectable editorialists were

aghast; the *Wall Street Journal* pointed out, "This is a young man duly convicted of taking unarmed prisoners entirely at his mercy, throwing them in a ditch, and shooting them. Is this nation really to condone such an act, as a strange coalition of super-patriots seems to urge?" The *Washington Star* said, "The day this country goes on record as saying that unarmed civilian men, women, and children of any race are fair game for wanton murder, that will be the day that the United States forfeits all claims to any moral leadership of this world." Scotty Reston wondered whether "somebody were going to propose giving Lieutenant Calley the Congressional Medal of Honor."

And, above all the commotion, Nixon spied a commonality. Superpatriots and peaceniks both thought Calley a martyr. The White House had done its polling: 78 percent disagreed with Calley's sentence; 51 percent wanted him exonerated outright. Within twenty-four hours the White House got one hundred thousand telegrams, calls, and letters, 100 to 1 for Calley's release. Meanwhile approval of the president's handling of Vietnam was heading into Lyndon Johnson territory: 41 percent. The White House alerted the media that on April 7 the president would go on TV to announce more troop cuts. Then the staff got to work exploiting Calley.

Nixon delegated the legal questions to John Dean's office, which concluded the conviction was by the book, the president was extremely limited in his power to intervene, and any White House interference could have a domino effect weakening the good order of the entire military justice system.

Military justice be damned. Nixon complained that the "lawyers provide no political gain for us on the argument." Chuck Colson came up with a solution: the president could immediately order Calley released from the stockade until his appeal was decided. On April 1 Nixon made the call to Admiral Thomas Moorer of the Joint Chiefs of Staff ("That's the one place where they say, 'Yes, sir,' instead of 'Yes, but'"). The House of Representatives broke out in spontaneous applause at the news. And a man convicted by fellow army officers of slaughtering twenty-two civilians was released on his own recognizance to the splendiferous bachelor pad he had rented with the proceeds of his defense fund, as featured in the November 1970 *Esquire,* complete with padded bar, groovy paintings, and comely girlfriend, who along with a personal secretary and a mechanical letter-opener helped him answer some two thousand fan letters a day.

At his April 3 briefing Ron Ziegler said before any sentence was carried out, the president would "personally review the case and finally decide it." Ehrlichman took the podium: this "extralegal ingredient" was appropriate in a case that had "captured the interest of the American people" and that required "more than simply the technical, legal review which the Code of Military Justice provides."

The political reviews were stellar. Senator Margaret Chase Smith of Maine, the "Conscience of the Senate," released a statement: "I think the

President performed a very wise and useful service to his nation. . . . It was impressively evident that the President caused many Americans to pause in their judgement, to gain perspective, and to replace emotion with reason." Senator Robert Taft (whom Nixon called in other contexts a "son of a bitch . . . peacenik") said Nixon had restored the morale of the military. The White House's private polling showed his actions found favor with 75 percent of the American people. Only 17 percent disapproved.

The legal reviews were not so salubrious. Privately, Secretary Laird complained, "Intervention in the Calley case repudiates the military justice system." The case's prosecutor, Captain Aubrey Daniel, wrote the president, arguing in a four-page, single-spaced letter—made available by presidential candidate George McGovern's office—"The greatest tragedy of all will be if political expedience dictates the compromise of such a fundamental moral principle as the inherent unlawfulness of the murder of innocent persons." William Greider, who had covered the trial in the *Washington Post,* wondered, "Should it open the doors at Fort Leavenworth, Kansas, and release all the other soldiers convicted of the same offense as Calley?"

John Dean once more proved his usefulness to the president by crafting the White House's subsequent talking point: that in such ongoing legal cases "it would be improper and inappropriate for White House staff members to make any comments or statements." Secretary Laird, Captain Daniel, the *Washington Post,* and all the rest would just have to howl in the wilderness.

Luckily for the president the papers weren't howling as loudly as they might. On April 5 Senator Hatfield read Winter Soldier testimony into the *Congressional Record:* that GIs were trained to believe the Vietnamese "subhuman"; that atrocities were caused by "policies adopted by our military commanders"; that crowded fishing boats were used for target practice. One witness told the story of a woman stabbed in both breasts when she asked for water, then raped with an entrenching tool. "And then they took that out and they used a tree limb, and then she was shot." A POW interrogator described as "normal" "utilizing a knife that was extremely sharp, and sort of filleting them like a fish. You know, trying to check out how much bacon he could make of a Vietnamese body to get information." The *Times* and *Post* didn't report on Hatfield's speech. The *Times* did, however, run a sentimental story on Nixon's April 7 address: "SALUTE RETURNED TO A BOY BY NIXON / President Recalls Son of a Hero in Ending Speech."

Nixon went on TV after reading a handwritten pick-me-up from Henry Kissinger: *Before you go on tonight I want you to have this note to tell you that—no matter what the result—free people everywhere will be forever in your debt. Your serenity during crisis, your steadfastness under pressure have been all that has prevented the triumph of mass hysteria. It has been an inspiration to serve.*

The speech was the usual: it announced new troop withdrawals, gave an optimistic assessment for the future ("Tonight I can announce Vietnamization has succeeded"), affirmed the pure-heartedness of the American effort ("never in history have men fought for less selfish motives—not for conquest, not for glory, but only for the right of a people far away to choose the kind of government they want"), included a mournful lament that the only roadblock to progress was the recalcitrance of the enemy negotiators in the face of generous American offers, and excoriated the wild-eyed insanity of setting a date for withdrawal ("Shall we leave Vietnam in a way that—by our own actions—consciously turns the country over to the Communists?"). Then, after a cheap shot at those who disagreed ("I know there are those who honestly believe that I should move to end this war without regard to what happens in South Vietnam"), he moved in for the sentimental climax, a masterpiece:

"While we hear and read much of isolated acts of cruelty, we do not hear enough of the tens of thousands of individual American soldiers . . . building schools, roads, hospitals, clinics, who, through countless acts of generosity and kindness, have tried to help the people of South Vietnam. We can and we should be very proud of these men. They deserve not our scorn, but they deserve our admiration and our deepest appreciation. . . ."

His voice took on a honeyed Norman Rockwell tone.

"Every time I talk to a brave wife of an American POW, every time I write a letter to the mother of a boy who has been killed in Vietnam, I become more deeply committed to end this war, and to end it in a way that we can build lasting peace."

(*You* care about peace because you care about those brave Americans left behind in the Hanoi Hilton. *They*, on the other hand, do not.)

"I think the hardest thing that a president has to do is present posthumously the nation's highest honor, the Medal of Honor, to mothers or fathers or widows of men who have lost their lives"—he was nearly whispering—"but in the process have saved the lives of others. . . .

"We had an award ceremony in the East Room of the White House just a few weeks ago. And at that ceremony I remember one of the recipients, Mrs. Karl Taylor." Her husband had "charged an enemy machine gun single-handed and knocked it out. He lost his life. But in the process the lives of several wounded marines in the range of that machine gun were saved.

"After I presented her the medal, I shook hands with their two children, Karl junior—he was eight years old—and Kevin, who was four. As I was about to move to the next recipient, Kevin suddenly stood at attention and saluted."

Pause.

"I found it rather difficult to get my thoughts together."

His voice deepened.

"My fellow Americans, I want to end this war in a way that is worthy of the sacrifice of Karl Taylor."

He was speaking very slowly.

"And I think he would want me to end it in a way that would increase the chances that Kevin and Karl, and all those children like them here and around the world, could grow up in a world where none of them would have to die in a war; that would increase the chance of America to have what it has not had in this century—a full generation of peace."

The after-action review: "We've thrown the best punch we could, Henry. . . . That little conclusion we stuck on there," the president said, "that's what made it for Mr. Average Joe."

"Absolutely. Oh, yes."

"Don't you think? They couldn't help but be moved by that."

"They couldn't very well go up there afterwards and start nit-picking you. . . . Haig had tears in his eyes, I had tears in my eyes—even though I had heard it before! I talked to a friend on the right who usually thinks you aren't tough enough, and she said, gosh, she was so proud of you, and she says your whole bearing was in command, and it was the best she'd ever seen you. . . . Even the parts you didn't write you put into your idiom. . . . And I talked to a young man at Harvard who's one of my few remaining friends there—I have no intention of going back there . . . I would under no circumstances go back to Harvard—but this man who also says of course the war must be ended very quickly was tremendously moved, says it was a very tremendous speech."

Nixon picked up the thread when Kissinger ran out of steam: "Any person knows deep down I'm right, he knows goddamned well I'm right!"

Nixon changed the subject, rambling, like someone on a high. Senator Bayh had thundered that "President Nixon is playing political football with a very sensitive issue," noting that the fifty-nine servicemen convicted for murder of Vietnamese civilians could now demand similar presidential intervention. Nixon scorned Bayh's political opportunism. "I know what it is. The doves are really, really, you're right, deeply worried about Calley. They're worried because—they realize that what it is, is an animal instinct in this country coming up, and most of the people don't give a shit whether he killed them or not!"

"*Zhat's* right"—Kissinger's amen; then the president: "I don't—I don't—I don't impugn military justice at all! I uphold it!"

That was one of the things the president liked to do in these conversations: probe novel ways to salve his guilty conscience.

Kissinger, perhaps moved beyond the bounds of what sycophancy would allow, changed the subject, relating the story of a Republican he had spoken with in Georgia. "He said how moved and proud he was by the president, and he said, of course, your major problem, your basic problem is—and I think it's right—he said the basic problem is 'the American people want to win this war. It drives them crazy to be in a war they can't win.' But he said, 'We recognize at least the president wants to win. Maybe those bastards won't *let* him win.'"

This was useful political intelligence. It meant the falsehood Nixon had been selling since 1966 was taking root: that we *could* "win."

"We aren't going to 'win,'" Nixon growled. "You realize that if we get out the way we want, we win! If the Communists don't win, we win! . . . We'll say it at the right time. We can't say it now because every goddamned dove will go off the wall."

Nixon warmed now to his least favorite subject, the press: "I don't give the bastards an inch!" He complained that his staff, "goddamn it, they're people who, they're in Washington, the Establishment's brainwashing them, they're reading the *Washington Post,* the weekly newsmagazines. . . . The Congress beats their goddamned brains out."

His voice crescendoed as smoothly as it had softened on TV the night before.

"And they get sort of discouraged and so forth, they don't realize that *that* is the time to get tough, to kick the guys"—he shouted at the top of his lungs—*"in the BALLS!"*

(It overdrove the room's microphones.)

"That's what they won't do. *That's* what I always do. They won't do it. . . . Some do. Colson does, but he's not in the top group." (Colson had "the balls of a brass monkey," Nixon elsewhere observed. Replied Haldeman, "He's going to get caught at some of these things, but he's got a lot done he hasn't been caught at.")

Haldeman came in to discuss the overnight polls. The president who rated himself a deeply committed pacifist had something else he wanted to discuss first. "I don't have any use for weak men, Bob, I have no use for 'em. I don't want to have 'em around. I'd rather have a bunch of right-wing fascists around me than weak men. I really mean that. I feel very strongly about it."

Haldeman said that those who had seen the speech gave it the highest "very favorable" rating Nixon had ever gotten. At that Nixon wondered what Birch Bayh could possibly be up to: "He's going against the vote." The presidential approval rating was up to 54 percent from 51. (Leak it, Nixon ordered, and say it was taken before the speech.) Then Haldeman presented his boss with a treat: the *New York Times's* "SALUTE RETURNED TO A BOY BY NIXON." Halderman said, "It's a great story. . . . Got some great quotes from her about her husband . . . 'and he believed in what he was doing and he thought he had to do it for the sake of his children.' . . . If we'd staged it, we couldn't have thought it up better. . . .

"A dream story," Haldeman concluded with a sigh. "I tell you, if they had called her up and she'd said, 'I'm sick of this goddamned war' . . ."

The pair was heartily relieved. Everyone was sick of this goddamned war.

On Sunday, April 18, Vietnam Veterans Against the War's John Kerry appeared on *Meet the Press*. Their Washington pageant began the next morning, the anniversary of the "shot heard 'round the world" in 1775. Eleven hundred veterans, most in wrinkled fatigues, medals pinned to hippie headbands, marched to Arlington National Cemetery, five Gold Star mothers in the lead; two vets carrying the VVAW banner; then a contingent in wheelchairs and crutches, blind men walking with canes. Two mothers and two veterans approached the Tomb of the Unknowns with a wreath. The great iron gates shut in their faces. One of the marchers threw his toy M16 against the iron; the plastic shards scattered. TV cameramen crowded around a screaming mother. "My boy was killed in Vietnam," she sobbed. "I didn't speak out then. It's my fault." She gestured toward the rest of the marchers: "They're all my boys now."

(Haldeman called Daniel Patrick Moynihan, now teaching at Harvard, who observed, "One of them looked like she couldn't have been over forty. . . . I felt like going up there and saying, 'Honey, if you're a Gold Star mother, you sure started early.'")

They marched in formation to the Capitol. Congressman Pete McCloskey, who'd led a marine platoon in Korea, joined them. He'd just returned from Laos, where he'd toured refugee camps filled to bursting by Operation Dewey Canyon II. (Haldeman: "Someone has to demolish McCloskey. He staged a phony operation over there to try to discredit the American effort.")

A bus full of air force recruits passed the procession. The men inside cheered them and flashed the V-sign.

They passed Constitution Hall, where President Nixon would address the Daughters of the American Revolution that night; the ladies turned up their noses. They passed the Justice Department, where lawyers were working out a plan to keep the veterans from camping on government property. A young staffer went out on the balcony and flashed them a V-sign.

At the Capitol they fanned out to lobby. Hawks spurned them outright. Some antiwar liberals seemed to find them unclean. On the underground congressional tramway, a group cornered Strom Thurmond and tried to prevail upon a fellow soldier's sense of honor (Thurmond had parachuted behind enemy lines before D-day). He answered them with a lecture on duty to country. So they pulled out their toy M16s and staged a guerrilla theater raid.

"Goddamn gook VC!"

"Commie asshole pink bastards, get a job!" came the spittle-flecked response.

VVAW spokesmen convened a "Five o'Clock Follies" briefing on the day's activities—named after the comically upbeat afternoon briefings Pentagon spokesmen gave in Saigon. They retired to bars to watch the news. Walter Cronkite gave them respectful attention.

Colson told the president in his hideaway office that one of his secret agents was having "quite a job keeping his people from, uh, raising hell with some of the demonstrators."

Nixon: "Why doesn't he let them do it?"

Haldeman: "All the hard hats could go in and bust 'em up."

The president was convinced most weren't even veterans. He suggested they get "our reporter"—a White House secret agent within the press corps—to, as an agent provocateur, suggest reporters investigate the protesters' credentials. It was a good thing for Nixon the reporters didn't: the demonstrators had taken to carrying their discharge papers and medal citations everywhere they went.

The D.C. Court of Appeals lifted the government's injunction that Winter Soldiers couldn't camp outdoors. They bedded down behind the Lincoln Memorial; scores of young men in civilian clothes and brush cuts—soldiers from Fort Belvoir and Fort Meade—mixed easily among the crowd, joining arguments about whether their movement should be violent or nonviolent; whether their medals should be returned to Congress or tossed on the White House lawn or, as the angriest vets preferred, dropped into "shit cans filled with blood."

The next day, at the Old Executive Office Building, Haldeman was delighted to see "a nice, decent American lady from Texas" on TV requesting the microphone from the veterans, then accusing them of being welfare cheats: "I'm a taxpayer. I pay tremendous amounts of money to support you people. Now get out of here and go to work and earn a living." A Winter Soldier contingent ducked inside the ropes at the Capitol Rotunda, draped an American flag over a "dead" comrade, and staged a military funeral. Itchy Capitol police moved to arrest them. Tourists angrily shouted the cops down.

The vets ducked in to watch hearings before Senator Fulbright's Foreign Relations Committee on the six bills pending to end the war, frustrated they hadn't been able to get any senators to put them on the schedule. That night Senator Phil Hart hosted a party for the vets at his home. John Kerry was given the floor. Fulbright was so impressed he decided to let Kerry testify the next day. Meanwhile the Justice Department submitted an emergency petition to Chief Justice Warren Burger to reverse the vets' license to sleep on the Mall. As the party was breaking up, in what some called the speediest decision on record, Justice Burger announced he was reinstating the camping ban "in full force and effect," giving the vets until four thirty Wednesday afternoon to vacate government property.

WHITE BACKLASH DOESN'T DEVELOP

Vote in Suburbs in North Is Strong for President

By ANTHONY LEWIS

Rich and poor, Protestant and Roman Catholic and Jew, farmer and city-dweller and suburbanite all showed marked shifts toward President Johnson in yesterday's extraordinary election.

Only in the Deep South did Senator Barry Goldwater score any significant gains for the Republican ticket over four years ago. Riding the crest of the racial issue there, he swung Mississippi, Alabama, Georgia, South Carolina and Louisiana to his party.

The white backlash, on which Mr. Goldwater had counted so strongly, failed to materialize in most parts of the North. Only among voters of Polish and other East European origins were there signs of this resentment toward Negroes, and even this phenomenon was scattered.

Continued on Page 26, Column 1

The New York Times

Yoichi Okamoto

Left: After Republican presidential nominee Barry Goldwater's landslide defeat in 1964, pundits declared a permanent American liberal consensus. On Christmas, President Lyndon B. Johnson declared, "These are the most hopeful times since Christ was born in Bethlehem."

Above: On August 6, 1965, under the Capitol dome, he signed the Voting Rights Act, and observers declared, "There is no more civil rights movement. President Johnson signed it out of existence."

Five nights later, the Watts district of Los Angeles broke out into the first major 1960s race riot. The White House drafted a document in case the army had to invade: *"Section 2. In furtherance of the authority and direction contained in section 1 hereof, the Secretary of Defense is authorized to use such of the armed forces of the United States as he may deem necessary."* Riots became an annual nightmare. After twenty-six died in Newark in 1967 (*below*), a white vigilante army mustered: "If anyone does that around here, and I catch him, I will personally send his head home without his body," their leader declared.

Al Lowe

The inheritor of this new political era would be Richard Nixon, an insecure man who longed for order and stability. He called his mother "a saint"—but she told tall tales about him constantly, teaching her son the lesson that a lie unexposed does no harm. His father was demanding and cruel. "Do you like water? Have some more of it!" he cried while dunking one of his sons for swimming in a forbidden irrigation ditch. This awkward, unpolished striver was the least likely of political heroes. "I had the impression he would even practice his inflection when he said 'hello,'" someone observed.

Nixon rose by speaking to his fellow unpolished strivers of the white middle class as if they were society's oppressed—to the disgust of sophisticated liberals. Walter Lippmann called his famous 1952 televised speech to stay on the vice-presidential ticket, featuring his family's cocker spaniel, Checkers, "the most demeaning experience my country has ever had to bear." Revering or reviling Richard Nixon became a key seam of the American divide.

In 1966, Martin Luther King marched in Chicago for open housing. He was greeted with thrown rocks, knives, and swastika placards that helpfully explained, "The Symbol of White Power."

The student antiwar insurgency exploded (*above,* Berkeley sit-in); Stokely Carmichael proclaimed the era of "Black Power"; Ronald Reagan exploited both disorders to seize the governorship of California with lines such as "I'd like to harness their youthful energy with a strap." Nixon, disgraced in his failed run for president in 1960 and for California governor in 1962, established a beachhead for his 1968 presidential race as a statesman, without associating himself with the angry backlash.

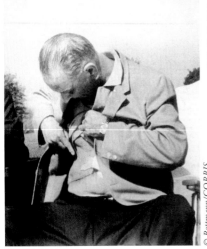

Left: No one trusted Lyndon B. Johnson. When he had gallbladder surgery, the press accused him of covering up heart surgery. So he lifted his shirt to show off the scar. The cartoonist for the *New York Review of Books* drew it in the shape of Vietnam, dramatizing the president's "credibility gap."

Right: In October of 1967, militants marched on the Pentagon, sporting signs like JOHNSON, PULL OUT—LIKE YOUR FATHER SHOULD HAVE. A rumor spread among protesters: two of their number had been dragged into the building and summarily executed. The next week, Secretary of State Dean Rusk was drowned out at Indiana University by chants of "murderer" and "fascist"; an old lady started whapping one of the hecklers with her umbrella, and another chant arose: "Hit him harder!" In New York, protesters kicked in the window of Rusk's limousine. Cops pulled protesters into an alley to fight, as other cops shouted, "Fairies!" "Jew-bastards!" "Commies!" and "You pull these guys' pants off and they ain't got no pecker."

Left: Some antiwar figures wore suits. George Romney, seen here (*center*) with fellow Republican presidential prospects Reagan and Nelson Rockefeller, pronounced that same fall that he had been "brainwashed" against realizing Vietnam was a disaster. Formerly the frontrunner by far, his campaign collapsed. At the beginning of 1968, a bipartisan clerisy of foreign policy "Wise Men" told LBJ that Romney was right—Vietnam was beyond redemption. He cried back, "Your whole group must have been brainwashed!"

Nineteen sixty-eight opened with police forces stockpiling machine guns and riot tanks. In New York, Mayor John Lindsay wanted to call out the National Guard to break a garbage strike, to the delight of Black Power leader H. Rap Brown: "We want troops. We want to overthrow the government. We want to have rioting. We want to fight the soldiers."

Lyndon Johnson abdicated his reelection campaign; Robert F. Kennedy and Eugene McCarthy (*below*) ran for the nomination as candidates of reconciliation. Robert F. Kennedy was assassinated after clinching the California primary. "The country does not work anymore," one columnist wrote.

How had America gone off the rails? Millions blamed spoiled rotten kids. *Time* had announced as its 1966 Man of the Year "not just a new generation, but a new kind of generation." A letter-writer to *Time* responded: "I fail to see much real altruism or idealism in my children or their friends. I see, rather, a perverted, sentimental self-centeredness." "Human Be-In" in San Francisco's Golden Gate Park, January 1967 (*above, left*); advertising poster (*above, right*).

In May of 1968 the kids took over Columbia University — "Up against the wall, motherfucker, this is a stickup," strike leader Mark Rudd (*below*) wrote the university president. Richard Nixon, gliding toward the Republican nomination, found a new campaign issue: the "revolutionary struggle to seize the universities of this country and transform them into sanctuaries for radicals . . ."

Left: August 1968 saw violent clashes between protesters and police at the Democratic convention, and between antiwar convention delegates and cops who raided the convention floor with clubs flailing. "The whole world is watching," protesters chanted—though most Americans agreed with a new bumper sticker: WE SUPPORT MAYOR DALEY AND HIS CHICAGO POLICE.

Hubert H. Humphrey won the Democratic nomination without entering a single primary, his ascent brokered by machine politicians like Mayor Richard J. Daley (*below*).

Hubert Humphrey's nomination victory was pyrrhic. Nixon won the November election by proclaiming that "the first civil right of every American is to be free from domestic violence." At his inauguration, Nixon implored the nation to "lower our voices."

Nixon's Justice Department would soon indict eight antiwar insurgents, including Jerry Rubin (*above*), who proclaimed upon his conviction, "The first part of the Yippie program is to kill your parents."

As protesters burned little Boy Scout flags at Nixon's inauguration parade, the teen singing troop Up with People exorcized the demons with patriotic songs. The clean-cut Orange County duo the Carpenters (*above,* with Nixon) were derided by sophisticates as "Nixon music." But more and more Americans were embracing "squareness" with avidity. Six of the eleven top-rated TV shows in 1969 were Bob Hope specials. His 1969 Vietnam show followed reports that American soldiers had massacred hundreds of women and children at My Lai. Hope exhorted, "The numbers of them who devote their free time, energies, and money to aiding Vietnamese families and caring for orphans would surprise you. Or maybe it wouldn't. I guess you know what kind of guys your brothers and the kids next door are."

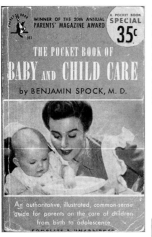

THE POCKET BOOK OF

BABY AND CHILD CARE

by BENJAMIN SPOCK, M. D.

An authoritative, illustrated, common-sense guide for parents on the care of children from birth to adolescence.

Nixon culture was shot through with rage. After Dr. Benjamin Spock began marching against the war, women returned copies of his best seller *Common Sense Book of Baby and Child Care* in shreds. "We teach our boys to be men," a mother wrote him, "and now you're tearing that down."

© Ted Streshinsky/CORBIS

HAIR PEACE.

BED PEACE.

Violence spread to bucolic college campuses (*above*, the Berkeley "People's Park" riot, in May 1969, is put down by the National Guard). Cartoonist Al Capp made a second career as an angry anti-hippie lecturer: "The opinions of eighteen-year-olds are valuable on things they know something about, such as puberty and hubcaps. . . ." At John Lennon's "Bed-In for Peace" during the Berkeley uprising, Capp tried to goad the Beatle into a fistfight by calling his wife the Dragon Lady. The White House tried to run Capp for Senate against Ted Kennedy and to deport John Lennon.

© Bettmann/CORBIS

A feature of every campus uprising was generally relegated to the newspaper back pages: the angry reaction of conservatives (here, at Harvard), who saw the disruptions as a usurpation of their rights.

The antiwar movement took an enormous leap toward the mainstream on October 15, 1969. Two million Americans of every description, including Mets World Series ace Tom Seaver, participated in a national moratorium against the war.

Nixon regained political momentum on November 3 with a brilliant speech calling Americans who did not protest the "Silent Majority" and announcing Vietnam troop withdrawals—reaping thousands of grateful telegrams (with Bob Haldeman, *below*) as the peacenik Americans could trust.

On March 6, 1970, Weathermen bomb makers accidentally collapsed an entire Greenwich Village town house, killing three. They were planning to bomb a servicemen's dance. When National Guardsmen cut down four students at Kent State University in Ohio on May 4 after the burning of an ROTC building, almost a thousand universities suspended operations in solidarity.

That same week, hundreds of Manhattan construction workers beat demonstrators with their hard hats. One bludgeoner recalled, "The whole group started singing 'God Bless America' and it damn near put a lump in your throat." The New York construction trade unions then held a one-hundred-thousand-man, celebratory, pro-war march, and a grateful President Nixon accepted an honorary hard hat from their leaders at the White House.

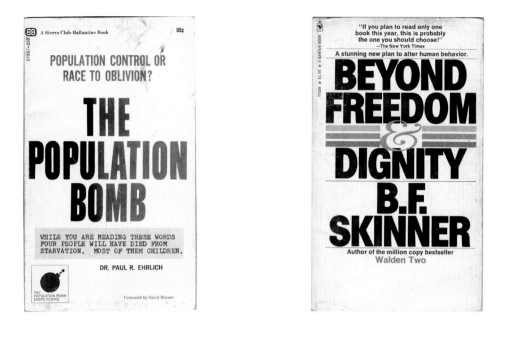

By 1971, apocalyptic books topped the bestseller list: Paul Ehrlich's *The Population Bomb* ("While you are reading these words four people will have died from starvation. Most of them children"), B. F. Skinner's *Beyond Freedom & Dignity* ("If all of modern science and technology cannot significantly change man's environment, can mankind be saved?"), Hal Lindsey's *The Late Great Planet Earth* ("Is the earth rushing toward catastrophe?").

But the best-selling paperback of all—seven printings in two months—proposed an antidote to the gloom: that the youth counterculture that has "sprouted up, astonishingly and miraculously, out of the stony soil of the American Corporate State" would redeem America. Charles Reich's *Greening of America* had this to say about bell-bottoms: they "have to be worn to be understood. . . . The new clothes demonstrate a significant new relationship between man and technology."

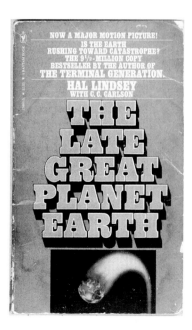

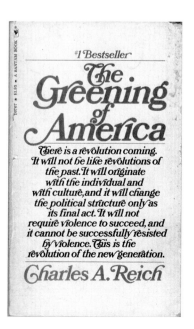

Richard Nixon entered the presidential election year of 1972 battered and bruised, with two Republicans and as many as a dozen serious Democratic challengers. The front-runner by far was Edmund Muskie— because Ted Kennedy (*left*), scarred by a 1969 car accident that killed a young woman at Martha's Vineyard, did not run. "How tragic," one *Time* letter-writer wrote, "Kennedy's professed concern with the loss of lives in Vietnam when he was so negligent about saving the one young life over which he had direct control at Chappaquiddick." The letter may have emerged from the White House.

In 1971, the twenty-sixth Amendment to the Constitution gave
some ten million new eighteen- to
twenty-one-year-olds (seen here
voting in Wisconsin) the vote.
"New Politics" reformers put forward antiwar senator George
McGovern as their presidential
candidate, presuming that youth—
"the growing edge of the present,"
McGovern aide Fred Dutton
proclaimed, the rising "coalition
of conscience and decency"—
would move the center sharply to
the left.

One reason McGovern won the nomination was because Richard Nixon's "ratfuckers" sabotaged
the campaigns of those they thought would be harder to beat. They were helped in the general
election of 1972 by the visual impact of the wide-open Democratic Convention (*below*, Jesse Jackson, co-leader of Illinois's delegation, which unseated Mayor Daley). "I'm the first, man!" one delegate effused on the floor of the convention to Abbie Hoffman, whose endorsement McGovern
proudly accepted.
    "The first what?"
    "The first fucker ever to cast a vote on acid."

Howard Park

In July 1972 McGovern cut loose his running mate Tom Eagleton after it was revealed that Eagleton had received electroshock therapy, destroying McGovern's reputation as a straight shooter—even as Nixon directed a criminal cover-up of the Watergate break-in from the Oval Office.

Nixon won the 1972 presidential election in a historic landslide. He responded like a defeated man. His congressional coattails were short; "That's how they'll piss on the whole thing," he said of his nemeses in the press. Twenty months after his landslide victory, he would no longer be the leader of anything.

The Gallup Poll

Nixon More Believable, 59% to 20%

PRINCETON, N.J. — Although McGovern's party strategists have sought to make political capital by ascribing a credibility gap to Mr. Nixon, the President is seen as "more sincere and believable" than McGovern by a 6-to-2 margin with the nation's voters.

Even among McGovern's own party members, many see Mr. Nixon as the more "sincere and believable" of the two candidates.

In the case of young voters, 18-29 years, on whom McGovern has pinned high hopes, Mr. Nixon wins by a sizable margin on this issue.

Following is the question asked and the results:

Which candidate — Mr. Nixon or McGovern — do you think is more sincere, believable?

	Nixon	McGov.	No Opin.
National	59%	20%	21%
Whites	62	17	21
Non-whites	24	52	24
Under 30	57	28	15
30-49 Years	61	16	23
50 and over	57	19	24
Republicans	85	5	10
Democrats	38	37	25
Nixon backers	85	3	12
McGovern backers	6	65	29

As the above table indicates, non-whites are the only major population group which credits McGovern with being more sincere or believable than Mr. Nixon; they give McGovern a 2-to-1 edge over Mr. Nixon on this question.

A total of 1,534 adults, 18 and older, were interviewed in person in this survey, which was conducted in more than 30 scientifically selected localities across the nation during the period of Aug. 24-27.

Findings, up to this point in the 1972 race, indicate that President Nixon's personal popularity has remained fairly constant in the three presidential races in which he has engaged. In tests to date, McGovern does appreciably better than Barry Goldwater in 1964, but slightly less well than Hubert Humphrey in 1968.

The personal popularity of candidates in elections since 1952 is reported below. The figures represent the percentage of those interviewed who give the candidate the highest positive rating.

1972 Nixon 39.8%—McGovern 23.4%
1968 Nixon 37.5%—Humphrey 28.5%
1964 Johnson 48.6%—Goldwater 16.2%
1960 Kennedy 41.6%—Nixon 39.7%
1956 Eisenhower 56.7%—Stevenson 33.8%
1952 Eisenhower 47.2%—Stevenson 37.0%

©1972. Field Enterprises

The Washington Post

Wednesday's papers were sympathetic to the campers. Nixon was livid: "The press is so, so desperately trying to show only the good-looking ones, aren't they?" He had first noticed it Tuesday afternoon, after his customary lunch of cottage cheese with a pineapple ring on top: "Those veterans down there looked pretty scrubby on TV." Haldeman chimed in, "It's great . . . the *Washington Star* last night had a great story about how they're, they got girls all in their sleeping, in their sleeping bags with 'em, and they're all smoking pot and drinking beer on the Mall." And yet, they noted, George McGovern had been quoted saying, "I've never been as proud of a group of Americans as I am of this group."

"They *could've* really done some harm if those guys had put on their neat uniforms, worn their ties, and done themselves up," Haldeman noted. "Yeah, to look like Calley," Nixon responded. Nixon decided to call off the Justice Department's plan for mass arrests. *Not* arresting them would be more effective. Film of police hauling off amputees—"That'll kill us," Nixon told Henry Kissinger. Clouds, fortuitously, were gathering. "Let those bastards stay there throughout. It'll start raining one of these days. It'll rain good."

What's more, it was hard to say how they'd be *able* to do it—and how many of these combat veterans were hair-trigger crazies ready to snap. They had visions of the "bonus marchers" in 1932—when General MacArthur's troops had shot down aged World War I vets in cold blood. Or maybe not, this time, in cold blood. Maybe those crazies would be armed.

Ron Ziegler told the press that the president "was taking no part in handling the situation." In fact he did little else. "Leave the sons of bitches there," he directed, "and I want them up there at the Capitol. I'd like a few scruffy people up there grabbing congressmen when they come through, screwing their secretaries." John Mitchell visited the president's command post to spell out how they'd be handling the arrests. Nixon stopped him: "Leave 'em there."

Mitchell: "Well, uh, we, we can't get a court order and then ignore it—"

The law-and-order president commanded, "John, ignore it as much as you can." (To Haldeman later in the day: "Mitchell was arguing strenuously about the *law* this morning. I said, 'Goddamn it, forget the law!'")

The only problem was that Ramsey Clark, arguing for the veterans, filed for a poll of the full Supreme Court on Burger's ruling. And the Supremes unanimously joined Burger. The Justice Department now said they'd allow them to *stay* overnight, but not to sleep. After spirited debate the entire encampment voted 480–400 for defiance: to stay *and* to sleep.

Twilight fell; a Vietnam-like tension descended. Another group of protesters, the People's Coalition for Peace and Justice, a Weatherman-like formation led by Chicago 7 defendant Rennie Davis, was planning to bring seventy thousand to camp out in Rock Creek Park in May and shut down Washington, D.C. Would these Vietnam veterans serve as the revolutionaries' shock troops? The Eighty-second Airborne was put on standby. Some marines, and four hundred of five hundred military guards from Arlington, refused orders to participate.

The Winter Soldiers posted a perimeter guard, just as if they were deep in the boonies. Haldeman's last lame hope was to pray for rain: "That'll fix the veterans: their sleeping bags'll leak and their girls'll get damp."

It started drizzling. Some thought the clusters of bedraggled warriors in their rubber ponchos looked like men in body bags. With each passing hour more Americans were perceiving them as martyrs to a heartless president. Congressmen started to arrive, Shirley Chisholm of Brooklyn, Bella Abzug of Manhattan, Senator Kennedy.

The next day John Kerry testified, proud in his rumpled fatigues. He related the findings of their Winter Soldier panels—the first time most Americans had heard of them. He explained where the name had come from—the "words of Thomas Paine in 1776 when he spoke of the sunshine patriots and summertime soldiers who deserted at Valley Forge because the going was rough. We who have come here to Washington have come here because we feel we have to be winter soldiers now." Point by point, he debunked the war's "thousands of rationalizations."

Then he cut to the quick.

"We are asking Americans to think about that, because how do you ask a man to be the last man to die in Vietnam? How do you ask a man to be the last man to die for a mistake?"

This "Kennedy-type guy," Haldeman called him, wasn't balling chicks in his sleeping bag. He was putting a president on trial: "This administration has done us the ultimate dishonor. They have attempted to disown us and the sacrifice we made for this country. In their blindness and fear they have tried to deny that we are veterans or that we served in 'Nam."

The next day, solemn and respectful, eight hundred veterans lined up in front of the wood-and-wire fence erected in front of the Capitol to protect Congress. Each presented his discharge papers, then got a turn at the microphone. The first man said his medals were "a symbol of dishonor, shame, and inhumanity." He threw them over the fence as an offering to the Vietnamese people, "whose hearts were broken, not won." Some cast off their medals in memory of fallen comrades; others were too choked up to speak at all; one said, "I am prouder today of the service I have given my country than at any time when I was in uniform." A Gold Star mother took the microphone: "I am here to join these men. In each one of them I see my son." Others, though, were less dignified. One called his medals "merit badges for murder." Another intoned, "Death to the fascist pigs." Still another, throwing away a Purple Heart, said, "I hope I get another one fighting these fuckers."

* * *

If that blood-lusting soldier stuck around Washington, he might just get the chance. Two more protests were left that spring, the first designed to be a peaceful mass rally, the second—the May Day Tribes—designed to be anything but. The organizers of the second, Haldeman briefed the president, "want a riot."

The rally on Saturday, April 24, was by now a routine affair: the speeches, the singing, the chanting, the banners. But it was organized from behind the scenes, Rowland Evans and Robert Novak had pointed out in a column, by the Socialist Workers Party, the disciplined Trotskyist masters of turning out massive and photogenic rallies for the consumption of what they called among themselves the "bourgeois press." "We had a great break in Evans and Novak this morning," Haldeman had told the boss, reading "Muskie and the Trotskyites" aloud: "*That Senator Edmund Muskie of Maine endorsed Saturday's anti-war demonstration here without even considering its domination by Trotskyist Communists typifies the cloak of respectability inadvertently provided for the far left by liberals.*'"

"Inadvertently, huh?" the president responded. "Circulate that to every member of the House and Senate. . . . The word is, Evans and Novak, from these *liberal* columnists."

Though the column wasn't entirely a good break. Evans and Novak went on to note that "Muskie as president would continue—for a time, at least—aiding the Saigon regime." They wrote, in other words, as if a Muskie presidency was likely—which, given current polling, it was. Destroying him was another White House obsession. "There's a separate organization called May Day that's pretty much the Weathermen," Haldeman had briefed the president on April 12. "Their whole thing is that they're the ones that want to bring the government to a halt."

"Good," the president pronounced. "Let's get Muskie on that one, too."

The May Day Tribes' goal was keeping federal workers from getting to their jobs: blocking bridges with barricades, sitting in the middle of busy intersections, vandalizing cars—"If the government won't stop the war, we'll stop the government." Haldeman read the president an intelligence report: ". . . knocking out the telephone system, having Hanoi radio announce a state of martial law and insurrection in Washington and the cutting of all power sources in capital. They've decided to take over Rock Creek Park as a campsite for the demo and have stated that federal troops will be required." Haldeman advised mass arrests.

"That's the one we bust," Nixon agreed. "If they start blocking bridges, we'll throw them right off the culverts."

These protesters began hit-and-run attacks Monday the twenty-sixth. Some 224 were arrested by Wednesday; on Friday, 224 more. They started moving on the key arteries in the middle of the night Monday, May 3. Cops incarcerated seven thousand in pens in the RFK Stadium parking lot, sans toilets or food. (They made buttons: I WAS AN AMERICAN POW. CAMP NIXON, MAY '71.)

On Tuesday insurgents surrounded the Justice Department and 2,680 more were taken into custody. Processing them for court dates proved a problem. So the Justice Department told the D.C. police to doctor the forms. Assistant Attorney General Rehnquist provided the legal cover: "qualified martial law." When the polls arrived, 75 percent approved of the mass detentions. Meanwhile the May Day Tribes tarred the antiwar veterans, of whom only 32 percent now said they approved. "Tying them all together" had been Haldeman's strategy all along.

That part was working. The problem, however, was that polls also showed two-thirds of the country thought they weren't being told the truth about what was going on in Vietnam.

As the White House started gearing up in earnest for the November 1972 presidential election, it seemed an inauspicious time to be building its new majority. Conservative icons were falling—heroes the White House had relied on as surrogates.

Papers ran a mind-blowing AP dispatch on May 8:

> EAU CLAIRE, Wis. (AP)—District Attorney Lawrence W. Dunning said today that a warrant charging Al Capp, the cartoonist, with a morals offense against a 20-year-old Eau Claire State University coed had been issued by County Judge Thomas H. Barland....
>
> The District Attorney said Mr. Capp had been charged with sodomy, attempted adultery, and indecent exposure, following an investigation by his office and Eau Claire city policemen....
>
> The complainant, who is married, told the authorities that the alleged offense took place April 1 in Mr. Capp's motel suite, where she had gone to report to him on the liberal point of view on the Eau Claire campus. Mr. Capp, a conservative, had requested the information, and the woman had been assigned to brief him on opinions and viewpoints, she said.

Other women started coming forward. The cartoonist came out with a statement: "The allegations are entirely untrue. I have been warned for some time now that the revolutionary left would try to stop me by any means from speaking out on campuses. My home has been vandalized and I have been physically threatened. This is also part of their campaign to stop me. Those who have faith in me know that I will not be stopped."

The president of the United States seemed to have faith in him. Or perhaps Nixon just feared embarrassment if his ties to a sex criminal were exposed. Either way, Chuck Colson sent an operative to pressure the Eau Claire DA to drop the case. (He refused, then won a conviction against Capp the following February, shortly after Capp filed a column averring, "The shock is not that there's so much anti-Americanism in America, but there is still so much anti-anti-Americanism left.")

The most popular box office attraction of 1971 had also attenuated his political usefulness to the White House in an interview in the May issue of *Playboy*. "I believe in white supremacy until blacks are educated to a point of responsibility," John Wayne said. And: "I don't feel we did wrong in taking this great country away from the Indians. There were great numbers of people who needed new land, and the Indians were selfishly trying to keep it for themselves."

An article in the new issue of *Armed Forces Journal* by retired Marine Corps colonel Robert D. Heinl argued that "morale, discipline, and battleworthiness" were "lower and worse than at any time in this century and possibly in the history of the United States." On May 24 at Travis Air Force Base in California, the primary point of embarkation for flights to Indochina, the bachelor officers' quarters were burned down by rioting airmen.

The president scheduled a televised press conference for June 1 that was supposed to show off his foreign policy advances: a breakthrough in the stalemated Strategic Arms Limitation talks with the Soviets, his unexpected advances toward opening relations with China, possible Soviet troop reductions in Europe. Instead, it was an inquisition.

"Mr. President, what are you going to do about the tens of thousands of American soldiers who are coming back with an addiction to heroin?"

"How do you respond to the suggestions that the bombing constitutes immoral, criminal conduct?"

"Mr. President, women make up more than 50 percent of the population. . . . Out of the top ten thousand federal supervisory posts, only one hundred and fifty are filled by women, and in two years you have appointed only two hundred women to federal jobs, sixty-two of them to one single arts commission."

"Mr. President, a Republican congressman who is a Marine Corps veteran from your own state, Pete McCloskey, has been going around the country talking against your Vietnam policies and has plans to run against you in the primaries next year. Do you welcome this as a challenge . . . ?"

Then Herb Kaplow of NBC asked whether it was an admission of impropriety that charges against two thousand protesters arrested on May 3 had been dropped. The president responded, "That kind of activity which is not demonstration, but vandalism, lawbreaking, is not going to be tolerated in this capital."

Then, two questions later: "Mr. President, regarding the mass arrests, I wonder—you seem to have thought that . . . keeping [government] running . . . was so important that some methods such as suspending constitutional rights was justified. Was it that important?"

A follow-up: ". . . if that is true, then why are the courts releasing so many of the people that have been arrested?"

Because, Nixon said, their guilt wasn't proven.

Another follow-up: "But they are not being released on the grounds that guilt hasn't been proved. They are being released on the grounds they weren't properly arrested."

Visibly shaken, the president turned to a conservative reporter, a favorite lobber of softballs. She asked him what would happen to all the surplus goods like trucks and telephone poles after he'd wound up involvement in Vietnam. Reporters saw the tension release from his face.

The next week's Gallup poll revealed that in a trial heat for the 1972 presidential election, Nixon ran two points behind Edmund Muskie. Two days later Gallup reported a record 61 percent of Americans saying sending troops to Vietnam had been a mistake. Nixon didn't submit himself for another prime-time TV grilling for over a year and in 1972 held a historical low of seven press conferences. "What we assumed, and it seems sort of dumb in retrospect," David Broder later reflected, "was that just because the press conference had grown up from Wilson on and seven or eight presidents had adhered to it, it had somehow become institutionalized. It's not institutionalized at all. In fact, you could effectively say that Richard Nixon has abolished the presidential press conference as an institution."

CHAPTER TWENTY-EIGHT

Ping-Pong

STAKES WERE HIGH FOR THE PRESIDENT TO REHABILITATE HIS IMAGE. Negotiations for his new global structure of peace were entering a critical stage.

Nixon had told his patron Elmer Bobst in 1966 that his profoundest dream was "to bring China into the world." It was a radical notion. Americans counted the Soviet Union as an enemy. But they spoke of China as an unmitigated horror. Madmen ruled it. Nixon's diplomatic mentor John Foster Dulles caused an international incident by rebuffing rather than shaking Premier Chou En-lai's hand at the 1954 Geneva conference. President Kennedy's people had talked about letting China have a seat in the United Nations. Richard Nixon said that would "irreparably weaken" the rest of Asia, and Eisenhower warned that if any rapprochement began—say, if Kennedy recognized Outer Mongolia, a territory claimed by Taiwan—he would come out of retirement to beat it down.

China's alleged expansionism was why they said we were in Vietnam. Secretary of State Rusk menacingly warned, "Within the next decade or two there will be a billion Chinese on the mainland, armed with nuclear weapons, with no certainty about their attitude toward the rest of Asia." *Time,* whose founder Henry Luce's parents had been missionaries in China, claimed China provided 80 percent of the Vietcong's weapons. A 1966 Harris poll found 58 percent of Americans would vote against a candidate who advocated giving mainland China the UN seat; a right-wing publicist claimed to have collected over a million petition signatures protesting the very notion. *China* was the word Nixon used when he wanted to scare an audience—as on October 28, 1966, in Boise, Idaho, after the most recent Chinese nuclear tests, saying that if Lyndon Johnson didn't win Vietnam, "We are then running an immense risk of World War Three."

Any notion that *Nixon* would change his mind seemed perfectly absurd. "Our leader has taken leave of reality," Henry Kissinger told his staff in February of 1969. "He thinks this is the moment to establish normal relations with Communist China. He has just ordered me to make this flight of fancy come true . . . China!"

And yet Kissinger dutifully went to work: such an achievement would redound to his greater glory as well. That first summer, Kissinger met with potential go-betweens: General Yahya Khan, the military dictator of Pakistan; Nicolae Ceauşescu of Romania, Nixon's favorite Communist. That August the president met privately in San Francisco with South Korean president Park Chung Hee and explained a strategic rationale: "I do not want to give the impression to the eight hundred million people of Communist China that they have no choice but to cooperate with the Soviet Union." A crucial piece of the rationale was the Vietnam War: that China and Russia, as rivals, might someday compete for America's favor by directing North Vietnam to reach a negotiated settlement.

When Ceauşescu visited America in the fall of 1970, the president toasted him as the man who "heads a government which is one of the few in the world which has good relations with the United States, good relations with the Soviet Union, and good relations with the People's Republic of China." Nixon had sounded a dog whistle that only connoisseurs of diplomatic code could hear: previously, American presidents had only referred to the government domiciled in Peking as "mainland China" or "Communist China."

That November, Pakistan's Yahya met with Chou En-lai, who told him, for American ears, "A special envoy of President Nixon's will be most welcome in Peking." The Pakistan channel was secret. The general had won a bloody concession in return for his favor to Richard Nixon. In December 1970, "East Pakistan," the Muslim province controlled by Pakistan and later known as Bangladesh, had its first free election in a decade. The wrong man won, General Khan kept the new government from convening, and at the end of March, he sent troops through India to put down what he called an insurrection. Ten thousand civilians were slaughtered the first three days. America said nothing.

On April 6, 1971, the American consulate in East Pakistan sent a horrified wire: "Our government has failed to denounce atrocities. . . . The overworked term *genocide* is applicable." Nixon did nothing. The very next day, the American team competing in the World Table Tennis Championships in Nagoya, Japan, convened a news conference: they had been invited to play exhibition matches that weekend in China—the first American group of any size to visit Red China since John Foster Dulles turned his back on Chou En-lai's outstretched hand at the Geneva Convention in 1954. China had just come through the Cultural Revolution, as ruthless a disruption of any civilization in history. Its society was so closed that the American media reported on it—when they could get inside the country—as if on another planet. *Time* managed to get an Australian reporter to Canton in October of 1967. He saw mobs "surround and beat an old man who dared look at an anti-Mao poster." Then they surrounded the reporter: "What are you doing here, white devil?" He observed, "Practically no one smiles."

Now, in 1971, team member Tim Boggan reported back in the *New York Times* of a China in which everyone smiled: "sumptuous" nine-course meals, "lush green paddy fields framed by pine-clad hills," an arena "grander than Madison Square Garden," "a large playground where perhaps 200 children of all ages were playing soccer, basketball, and other sports" (a twelve-year-old handed him his hat at a Ping-Pong table with a net made of bricks). The hospitality was so overwhelming, Boggan wrote, that one team member's wife started crying. He quoted his hippie teammate Glenn Cowan of Santa Monica, California, "whose casual, outgoing manner has made him a favorite with photographers and reporters on the other side of the border": "I really believe life is simple. It's all the other people that make things complicated."

This was what Nixon had been dreaming of. "You know, young people really like 'people to people,' they really do," he pronounced with satisfaction to Ehrlichman. "Sure. Their ideal is to think everybody's good, pure. . . . That's why the China thing is so *really* discombobulating to these god-damned liberals—really kills 'em! The China thing—must just kill 'em. For me to do it. Don't you think?"

Kissinger: "Sure."

"Because it's *their* bag."

"Sure."

"Not supposed to be *my* bag."

"But *you* went at it in a way that made it possible to do."

Editorialized the *New York Times*, "A ping pong ball has cracked the bamboo curtain," not making altogether too much out of it. The most Scotty Reston could imagine coming of it was that Americans would be able to enjoy a visit from the Peking Opera. The vice president had no idea of the astonishments to come; to reporters at a Republican Governors' Conference, the man who fulminated in Lincoln Day speeches against progressive preachers who set as their "goal on earth the recognition of Red China and the preservation of the Florida alligator" said "Ping-Pong diplomacy" had handed Mao a propaganda victory.

At the end of April, as the senior signatory of the cable about genocide in Bangladesh was relieved of his duties, the latest breakthrough came in via the Pakistani ambassador: "The Chinese government reaffirms its willingness to receive publicly in Peking a special envoy of the President of the United States (for instance Mr. Kissinger) or the U.S. Secretary of State or even the President himself." Kissinger relayed a message of thanks to the butcher of Bangladesh for his "delicacy and tact."

China was only one of the diplomatic balls Nixon was juggling. Three weeks later, on May 18, as Nixon conferred with Haldeman and Colson about how they would get Edmund Muskie and Teddy Kennedy more closely tailed, Kissinger exploded into the room. "The thing is okay!" he cried. Colson, puzzled, was ushered out; it was hard to communicate super-secret diplomatic breakthroughs in the presence of unauthorized individu-als. "The thing" was a back-channel agreement for a framework on antiballistic missiles—heralding, as the public statement put it (only hours after Secretary of State Rogers and the head of the Arms Control and Disar-mament Agency learned about the existence of the secret talks), "more favor-able conditions for further negotiations to limit all strategic arms."

On May 31 Kissinger got word from the Pakistani ambassador that "a very encouraging and positive response to the last message" had come from China: "Level of meeting will be as proposed by you." In other words, Nixon was going to China—and hardly a soul in the world knew it.

The next night was that 1971 Last Press Conference, when Nixon had expected fascination with his breakthroughs, but the gnats swarmed over him instead for the dodgy arrests of the May demonstrators in the capital. Well, he had had enough of the gnats. He didn't need them anymore.

He'd attended the White House Correspondents' Association Dinner in May: "Every one of the recipients was receiving an award for a vicious attack on the administration," he moaned. "They are truly a third house support-ing the Democratic candidates." He told Kissinger and Colson during a Potomac River cruise celebrating the SALT breakthrough, "We'll get them on the ground where we want them. And we'll stick our heels in, step on them hard and twist . . . no mercy." Colson met with the president of NBC on June 8 for a nut-cutting session: the White House, like a Mafia outfit, "suggested" they run a special on Tricia Nixon's June 12 wedding, even though all three networks would be covering it live. "They couldn't oblige us fast enough," Colson reported. "Julian Goodman jumped out of his chair."

Nixon had a theory about the media: the only thing they respected was force. Let them twist in the wind until he needed them—when it came time to announce the China trip.

This "triangular diplomacy" was a paradoxical thing, a product of that com-plex transit between the raging, mercurial Nixon and the coolly rational Nixon, the riverboat gambler and the chess player, Nixons old and new. He was getting out of Vietnam in the most unhinged possible way: dribbling out American troops while stepping up the bombing for fear of showing Amer-ica "a pitiful, helpless giant" (according to one estimate, 350,000 civilians died in Laos from the bombing for Operation Dewey Canyon II and 600,000 in Cambodia for Operation Menu). But his backstage maneuvering was based in a pragmatic understanding few others were wise enough to reach: that America was no longer the world's eight-hundred-pound gorilla.

He had read the economic tea leaves: America's exports had grown by two-thirds over the past decade but Western Europe's had more than doubled. Japan's had more than quadrupled, and doubled with the United States from 1965 to 1967 alone. The world trading system agreed to at the Bretton Woods Conference in 1944 set a gold standard: $35 of U.S. currency could always be exchanged for an ounce of gold. That was swell when the United States was the free world's unquestioned economic superpower. But this novelty—a trade deficit—was making it more worthwhile for a foreign country to exchange dollars for gold than to buy any U.S. goods, the ounce being worth more in real terms than the thirty-five bucks. America was becoming weaker vis-à-vis the rest of the world.

Nixon outlined all this in a strange and apocalyptic July 6, 1971, *tour de horizon* to a gathering of media executives at a Holiday Inn in Kansas City. The High Cold War was over, he explained; the last third of the twentieth century would be "an era of negotiation rather than confrontation." The real arms race was over trade and markets. "Economic power will be the key to other kinds of power." Thus the global chessboard became not a chessboard at all. The game was multipolar: "When we think in economic terms and economic potentialities, there are five great power centers in the world today," the United States, Western Europe, Japan, the Soviet Union, and China— with Japan and Western Europe the real potential rivals.

Had they known where this was headed, the execs' media outlets might have given Nixon's speech more notice. But his diplomacy was so secret, it was hard to see why the speech was significant: that the tilt away from Europe and Japan would be balanced by a lean toward Russia and China. The significance of Kansas City's Holiday Inn in the annals of world diplomacy was only recognized years after the fact. For all his listeners knew, when Henry Kissinger disappeared from the diplomatic press corps' radar the next day on an official visit to Pakistan, it was just as his handlers claimed: that he was indisposed with a stomachache. He had actually ducked inside the People's Republic of China to close the deal for a presidential visit.

The stakes for keeping secrets had never been higher. And yet it happened as the White House suffered one of the most dramatic leaks in the history of the republic—one that saw Richard Nixon revert to his most irrational self.

Thus, in the summer of '71, the doors were opened to Watergate.

The June 13 Sunday *New York Times* front page had one feature to delight the president: a picture of him arm in arm with his daughter, walking her down the aisle in her billowing white dress on her wedding day.

The bad news was two columns to the right.

The headline read, "Vietnam Archive: Pentagon Study Traces 3 Decades of U.S. Involvement." The lead paragraph began, "A massive study of how the United States went to war in Indochina, conducted by the Pentagon three years ago, demonstrates that four administrations progressively developed a sense of commitment to a non-Communist Vietnam, a readiness to fight the North to protect the South, and an ultimate frustration with this effort—to a much greater extent than their public statements acknowledged at the time."

It was a polite way of saying Americans had been lied to for twenty-five years.

The lies went back to Harry Truman, the article explained. Military aid to France had "directly involved" the United States in preserving a European colony; the Eisenhower administration played "a direct role in the ultimate breakdown in the Geneva settlement" and the cancellation of free elections scheduled for 1956. (President Nixon always said honoring Geneva was the reason we had to continue the war.) Kennedy—this in the Pentagon study's words—transformed the "limited-risk gamble" he inherited into a "broad commitment." Lyndon Johnson laid plans for full-fledged war as early as the spring of 1964—campaigning against Barry Goldwater with the line "We seek no wider war."

What became known as the Pentagon Papers—three thousand pages of historical narrative and four thousand pages of government documents— was shocking to all but the most hardened antiwar cynics. The expansion into genuine warfare began, the *Times* summarized, "despite the judgment of the government's intelligence community that the measures would not cause Hanoi to cease its support of the Viet Cong insurgency in the South. . . . The bombing was deemed militarily ineffective within a few months." To catalog the number of times Lyndon Johnson and Richard Nixon looked the American people squarely in the eye and said the exact opposite would require another book.

Astonishments popped from every column of six inside pages. The new Saigon government, Secretary McNamara had written December 21, 1963— sold to the American people as the first light at the end of the tunnel—was "indecisive and drifting," and "Viet Cong progress has been great during the period since the coup." The Joint Chiefs of Staff had recommended extending military operations to Laos and Cambodia at a time when, officially, they hadn't even started in Vietnam. Then there was the stunning revelation of 1964's "OP PLAN 34-A": American frogmen demolishing bridges and piers, Special Forces kidnapping prisoners, planes bombing railroad tracks, "cross-border penetration" into Laos, "general harassing activities against Pathet Lao military installations," "Strikes on targets of opportunity," a "Corridor interdiction program." This was what had inspired the North Vietnamese to harass our ships at the Gulf of Tonkin in August of 1964—a response sold to Congress as unprovoked.

The next day's *Times* revealed the White House's "general consensus" to bomb North Vietnam began the same day as LBJ's presidential campaign, and the paper quoted a memo on the "need to design whatever actions were taken so as to achieve maximum public and Congressional support"—to lie, in other words. The third day revealed the smokingest gun of all—a memo from Assistant Secretary of Defense for International Security Affairs John McNaughton breaking down, in Robert McNamara's preferred statistical terms, why we were persisting in Vietnam:

> 70%—*To avoid a humiliating U.S. defeat.* . . .
> 20%—*To keep SVN (and the adjacent) territory from Chinese hands.*
> 10%—*To permit the people of SVN to enjoy a better, freer way of life.*
> ALSO—*To emerge from the crisis without unacceptable taint from methods used.*
> NOT—*To "help a friend."*

That was written two weeks before the nationally televised address in which President Johnson explained "the principles for which our sons fight tonight in the jungles of Vietnam"—that they were the same "for which our ancestors fought in the valleys of Pennsylvania." Thus it was that June of 1971 marked the deadline beyond which any morally aware American could believe anything the government told them about Vietnam.

On June 15 the *Times* headlined, "Mitchell Seeks to Halt Series on Vietnam but *Times* Refuses." There was no installment the next day nonetheless. In its customary spot was an article on the Justice Department's investigation into the identity of the leaker, and the ruling of U.S. district judge Murray Gurfein temporarily enjoining further publication while he reviewed "espionage charges against the *Times* and persons unknown."

Then the *Washington Post* started running the Pentagon Papers. Reported the *Post*, "There are 15 'legitimate' copies of the controversial Pentagon report on Vietnam, the administration disclosed yesterday, and a massive hunt is on to identify the one in which the *New York Times*"—and now, they didn't add, the *Washington Post*—"was given access."

The president was at first indifferent to the whodunit game. He had his suspects—Leslie Gelb, deputy director of the Defense Department's Office of Policy Planning under Johnson, now a fellow at the Brookings Institution; or another one of those "fucking Jews"—but he wasn't disposed to worry about a document completed before he was inaugurated and covering events only through 1968. "Make sure we call them the Kennedy-Johnson papers," he had told Haldeman at first, prepared to let the chips fall where they may.

Historians would debate the reasons for the president's subsequent change of heart. They agree Kissinger was crucial in changing his boss's mind. Some suspect Kissinger was terrified the study might tarnish him—Gelb had been Kissinger's student at Harvard; or perhaps the leaker was one of Kissinger's former staffers who'd quit after the Cambodian invasion. Others suspected that Nixon and Kissinger worried that another suspect had high-level access to the Single Integrated Operational Plan—the nation's nuclear secrets—and might be enough of a wild man to make releasing them his next act of bureaucratic terror.

But the reasons for panic weren't really that complicated. Nixon-Kissinger diplomacy made credibly guaranteeing discretion to negotiating partners the first, even sacred, priority. Nixon was reminded of this by Kissinger (pretending to be on vacation, but really firming up plans for a scouting trip to China): "It could destroy our ability to conduct foreign policy. If other powers feel we cannot control internal leaks, they will not agree to secret negotiations." Of course he also uttered a colorful Kissingerism that his boss never failed to find persuasive: "It shows you're a weakling, Mr. President." And so the panic burst forth.

Nixon had ten minutes scheduled on June 16 with a twenty-five-year-old former naval officer named John O'Neill, the spokesman for the front group Chuck Colson had set up to combat John Kerry, Veterans for a Just Peace, they called it. O'Neill had earned his time with the president with an appearance on CBS's *Face the Nation* that sent Colson over the moon—"I don't think he said 'we support the president' more than eighteen times," he gushed, adding, "O'Neill is a very attractive, dedicated young man—short hair, very square, very patriotic, very articulate."

The president ended up spending half an hour with O'Neill and didn't want the meeting to end. O'Neill left pledging he would spend every waking moment campaigning for Richard Nixon—a welcome respite for the president, for whom every other meeting was ending in tirades about who was out to destroy him via the Pentagon Papers leaks.

By the next day, they had only one suspect—the one man who knew too much. His name was obscure to the public. It had only appeared in the *New York Times* five times. Once was for his 1950 wedding to a general's daughter: "Mr. Ellsberg . . . is attending Harvard College, where he is president of the Harvard Advocate, a member of the editorial board of the *Harvard Crimson,* and a member of Signet Society." The announcement of his second marriage in 1970 (to, Nixon noted, a millionaire's daughter) added more ornaments to his résumé: "The bridegroom was graduated summa cum laude from Harvard College, where he was a member of the Society of Fellows and where he received a doctorate in economics. He served as a lieutenant in the Marine Corps and worked as a strategic analyst with the Rand Corporation in Santa Monica, Calif." In between, the *Times* mentioned his argument in a 1969 anthology of essays on Vietnam that the war was so unmitigatedly horrifying because "to paraphrase H. Rap Brown, bombing is as American as cherry pie." Then, on October 9, 1969, the *Times* ran "Six Rand Experts Support Pullout;

Back Unilateral Steps Within One Year in Vietnam"; he was one of the experts—and the lead signatory of a November 1970 letter to the editor of the *Times* from MIT faculty accusing Nixon of "vastly expanding this immoral, illegal, and unconstitutional war . . . and the moral degradation of our country."

Thus was limned an evolving identity: one of the defense Establishment's best and brightest had by turns become its most dedicated critic.

Dan Ellsberg had been an obvious choice for Robert McNamara as lead author when he commissioned the Pentagon Papers in June of 1967. Ellsberg's combination of book smarts, policy experience, and time spent on the ground in the jungle was unique: he had volunteered for Vietnam in 1965, serving two years with General Edward Lansdale, one of the war's architects, and as a combat officer his commander called "the best platoon leader I had." McNamara had recruited the anonymous authors for their expertise, whatever their feelings about the war. And by then Ellsberg was a Vietnam critic, if a quiet one. After General Westmoreland came to the United States to preach to Congress about the "light at the end of the tunnel," Ellsberg lectured the *Times*'s Vietnam correspondent, Neil Sheehan, and its Washington bureau chief, Tom Wicker, "You guys have been conned." Westmoreland's presentation, Ellsberg said, had been pure propaganda, though propaganda softened up at the last minute. "You should have seen what they *wanted* to tell you"—lies so exaggerated Westmoreland would have been laughed off the House floor.

The lying: it burned Daniel Ellsberg to the core. But there was nothing he could do about it: the cables proving it were top secret.

It was only natural that Henry Kissinger had called Ellsberg, one of his most brilliant students at Harvard, to Nixon transition headquarters at the Hotel Pierre in New York City to consult on policy options in Vietnam. But by that time, December 1968, Ellsberg was neck deep in primary documents demonstrating that the wisest American policymakers had understood from the beginning that South Vietnam could never survive on its own as a viable political entity, that it would take upward of a million troops or even atomic bombs to sustain it, that the reason the war was kept going was domestic politics. One of the options Ellsberg presented Kissinger at the Pierre was unilateral and total withdrawal. That didn't make it into Kissinger's report to the president-elect. Ellsberg realized then and there that the Nixon administration would be willing to sustain massive carnage to end Vietnam the way it preferred.

Ellsberg had lectured Henry Kissinger in that hotel room, lectured him about the narcotic effect of secrets: "It will become very hard for you to learn from anybody who doesn't have clearances. Because you're thinking as you listen to them: 'What would this man be telling me if he knew what I know?'. . . . You'll become something like a moron . . . incapable of learning from most people in the world, no matter how much experience they may have." Lyndon Johnson, after all, did it: "I'm just not in a position to know how much information each critic of my policy in Vietnam happens to have," he'd say. "It makes me wish that all this information was available to everybody who is assuming responsibilities in this matter." American Legion counterprotesters would say, "All of the sudden, you guys on the streets, you know more than the secretary of state."

Well, Daniel Ellsberg *did* know more than the secretary of state. And by the time the Pentagon Papers were done at the beginning of 1969, it was driving him nearly insane. William Rogers and Melvin Laird had access to the Papers. But it hadn't seemed to affect any of their recommendations.

Ellsberg had been given one of only fifteen existing copies to hold in his safe. He was lying in bed in September of 1969 when he read the army was dropping the charges against Green Berets alleged to have murdered a Vietnamese civilian, and that according to the White House press secretary, "The president had not involved himself either in the original decision to prosecute the men or in the decision to drop the charges against them." It was easy for Ellsberg to spot a Vietnam lie by then. This one was the straw that broke the camel's back. He called a colleague, Anthony Russo: "Tony, can you get ahold of a Xerox machine?"

Ellsberg had seven thousand pages of photocopying to do.

He spent over a year trying to convince someone to take them public. But neither Senators Fulbright, McGovern, nor Goodell were willing. McGovern told him it wasn't the place of a lawmaker to break the law, but that the First Amendment made it altogether appropriate to make the documents available to a newspaper. Neil Sheehan of the *New York Times* proved ready to take on the risk. Thus, the *Times* on June 13, 1971: "Vietnam Archive: Pentagon Study Traces 3 Decades of U.S. Involvement." Now every Vietnam lie was public.

Kissinger figured out by the seventeenth that Ellsberg was the culprit. Destroying him became a White House crusade. Something snapped in Richard Nixon. He seemed to think it was 1948. "Go back and read the chapter on the Hiss case in *Six Crises* and you'll see how it was done," he would say. "This takes eighteen hours a day. It takes devotion and dedication, a loyalty and diligence such as you've never seen, Bob. I've never worked as hard in my life and I'll never work as hard again because I don't have the energy. But this thing is a hell of a great opportunity." The theory was that, once upon a time, another Harvard-educated traitor, Alger Hiss, had been taken down at what appeared to be his moment of maximum vindication—not only establishing Congressman Nixon's career, but retarding half a generation of progress for the Democrats as they tore each other's eyeballs out debating Hiss's guilt or innocence.

Chuck Colson—who had defiantly turned down a full scholarship to

Harvard because it was too liberal, and to snub the administrators who told him, "No one has ever turned down a full scholarship at Harvard"—was so eager to please his boss that he read the Hiss chapter fourteen times. Ellsberg, he told Haldeman he now understood, was "a natural villain to the extent that he can be painted evil. We can very effectively make the point of why we [had] to do what we did with the *New York Times*"—to take down a conspiracy as vast and perfidious as the one Alger Hiss had joined. Some in the White House even believed it; the Justice Department's Robert Mardian, tapped by Nixon to run the federal prosecution of Ellsberg, claimed that days before the Pentagon Papers were delivered to the *Washington Post*, they passed through the Soviet embassy.

"We have the Democrats on a marvelous hook because thus far most of them have defended the release of the documents," Colson said. Take down Ellsberg and you took down those Democrats, too—perhaps took down the opposition party itself. "I have not yet thought through all the subtle ways in which we can keep the Democratic Party in a constant state of civil warfare," Colson summed, "but I am convinced that with some imagination and creative thought it can be done."

Such talk got Richard Nixon's creative juices flowing. Provide top-secret documents to an infiltrator in one of the peace groups, which could then get caught "peddling them around," he suggested on Monday the twenty-third. (Haldeman assured him they were already working on it.) The next day Nixon proposed that an "Ellsberg who's on our side" could dig up pre–World War II documents to declassify—Richard Nixon's own pumpkin papers—to prove that FDR knew about the Japanese attack on Pearl Harbor in advance. The Democratic Party would be "gone without a trace if we do this correctly," Nixon pronounced lustily. Haldeman thought that a fine idea, too, but suggested they start with documents from the Cuban missile crisis or Bay of Pigs instead: "Those are the ones that are likely to get lost the fastest." The president, who salved his basest guilts by presuming everyone else as venal as himself, caught his drift right off: Democrats all over town were by then "probably burning stuff and hiding stuff as fast as they can."

The work proceeded amid smoldering political frustration. Senate majority leader Mike Mansfield had an amendment to the Selective Service reorganization bill—Nixon's crucial bid to turn down antiwar sentiment by removing young people's fear of getting drafted—that would require withdrawal of all troops once Hanoi released all prisoners of war. Mansfield's amendment passed the Senate by a vote of 57–42. Nixon called the majority leader to the White House for breakfast and threats: if the Paris peace talks and the strategic arms negotiations collapsed by the end of the month, he would go on television and blame Mansfield personally—and escalate the bombing to boot. Then he warned Speaker Carl Albert that if the House passed a similar resolution, he would scuttle the Paris talks himself, saying Congress had given him no other choice.

But the bluffs were not working. Given the ongoing Pentagon Papers revelations, the antiwarriors held all the cards.

Then Nixon hit on the idea of finding evidence that the Kennedys ordered the 1963 assassination of South Vietnam president Ngo Dinh Diem, CIA complicity in Diem's pre-assassination overthrow having been one of the Pentagon Papers' most explosive revelations. Said Haldeman, "Huston swears to God there's a file on it at Brookings"—the Brookings Institution think tank, their imagined Kennedy government-in-exile.

Nixon, straightening bolt upright: "Now, if you remember Huston's plan. I want it implemented. Goddammit it, get in there and get those files. Go in and get those files."

Nixon repeated the order every day, frustrated that no one was carrying it out: "I want Brookings. I want them to just break in and take it out. . . . *Do you understand?*"

Haldeman pointed out a delicacy that might hold them up: "You have to find somebody to do it."

Where, in other words, do you find a figure of the cunning and criminal skill, with *omertà*-like loyalty to a Republican president, who still had no lingering loyalties to the meddlesome bureaucrats of the CIA or FBI?

That became the next obsession. Edgar Hoover was too squeamish. (Robert Mardian was busy on a project to blackmail him into retiring by exposing the illegal wiretap transcripts Hoover had helped them obtain in 1969.) They batted around Caulfield and Ulasewicz, the former New York cops. (They weren't up to the magnitude of the task.) Richard V. Allen, the Kissinger staffer? (He might not be trustworthy enough.) Pat Buchanan? (He was offered the job and turned it down because he thought the project's "dividends" didn't "justify the magnitude of the investment recommended.") Huston? (He was too toxic to the intelligence Establishment and didn't have the public relations skills to "move it to the papers.") Ehrlichman? (More of a lawyer than a dirty trickster.) John Dean? (Too much the "little old lady.") Colson? (Plate too full: infiltrating the Muskie campaign; trying to catch Ted Kennedy en flagrante with a hooker; lining up antitrust threats against ABC, NBC, CBS; preparing John O'Neill for a debate with now-congressional candidate John Kerry on the *Dick Cavett Show*.)

Colson suggested E. Howard Hunt, the former CIA agent, a friend of the Buckley family: "He's a brilliant writer. He's written forty books on espionage."

Hunt's name had floated around the White House for various projects since 1970. Nixon worried if the fifty-three-year-old had the energy for the eighteen-hour days. But Nixon liked that Hunt had run the Bay of Pigs for the CIA: "He told me a long time ago," Colson said, "that if the truth were ever known, Kennedy would be destroyed."

Nixon asked Colson and Haldeman if they had any compunctions about the avenues they were exploring. Colson: "Oh, hell no." Haldeman: "We've got to be repressive." The president contributed his own two cents: "They did that to me. . . . I want to go in and crack that safe."

And yet for a time they vacillated, approaching the abyss, then hanging back—until the possibility of keeping the Pentagon Papers from the public was foreclosed, on June 30, when the Supreme Court, after a labyrinthine court battle, ruled 6–3 that they could be published freely. Justice Brennan's decision argued that press reports that embarrass the government were precisely the reason the First Amendment was invented. Justice Black concurred: "Every moment's continuance of the injunctions against these newspapers amounts to a flagrant, indefensible, and continuing violation of the First Amendment. . . . [F]or the first time in the 182 years since the founding of the Republic, the Federal courts are asked to hold that the First Amendment does not mean what it says." Just in case the court ruled the other way, the previous evening Mike Gravel, the forty-one-year-old senator from Alaska, had called an extraordinary two-man night "hearing" of his Subcommittee on Buildings and Grounds. He began reading aloud from a four-thousand-page typescript—the historical narrative portion of the Pentagon Papers, provided to him by an anonymous source.

He started at 9:45 p.m. "The story is a terrible one," Gravel warned. "It is replete with duplicity, connivance against the public. People, human beings, are being killed as I speak to you. Arms are being severed; metal is crashing through human bodies." Then, he began to weep.

Word of mouth spread; aides and reporters working late started filtering into the hearing room. Gravel read for three hours and then recessed, noting to reporters he might be risking expulsion from the Senate. He stopped at 1:12 a.m., promising to continue the next day. By then, he had broken out in sobs once more.

Gravel kept his Senate seat and was able to introduce the entire document into the *Congressional Record.* That turned it into public property. Congressmen have extraordinary privileges.

Which was why, the next day, Nixon discussed as his next move recruiting "another Senator McCarthy"—some right-wing exuberant to crush the conspiracy as only someone with congressional immunity against libel and slander could do. They brought up John Ashbrook, the former Draft Goldwater leader; Illinois's Phil Crane, a former leader of Young Americans for Freedom; the John Birch Society members in Congress, John G. Schmitz and John Rousselot. ("Mean, tough, ruthless," Nixon praised Rousselot, a protégé. "He'll lie, do anything.") They regretted that Senator Dole of Kansas was already preoccupied as RNC chief. (He did the best he could for the team, telling reporters the Pentagon Papers' disclosure had left heads of state around the world "at the mercy of sensation-seeking newspapers.")

The Twenty-sixth Amendment to the Constitution passed that same day. No one had expected it that fast: the Supreme Court had only struck down Ted Kennedy and Mike Mansfield's gambit to lower the voting age by congressional statute the previous December; the *Times* had predicted a constitutional amendment would "almost certainly not be effective in a presidential election before 1976." Now eighteen-year-olds would be able to vote in time for 1972. Samuel Lubell, the prescient electoral analyst, wrote in *Look:* "As of now, the nation's newest voters would defeat Nixon. . . . Crammed into my interview notebooks are angry outbursts from business-oriented youths who say, 'The Republicans are better for my career,' but vow, 'I'll vote for almost any Democrat to end the war.'" Some spoke to him of their gratefulness that younger friends would be turned from a revolutionary path by their ability to vote. The early reports out of California were that despite predictions of widespread youth apathy, or that kids would mimic their parents, 90 percent of eligible high school students were registering, mostly as Democrats.

The White House seemed to question its earlier easy assumption that Republicans wouldn't be hurt by the eighteen-year-old vote. Haldeman started worrying about strange things, such as the obscure new art-house documentary on Nixon's career by Emile de Antonio, *Millhouse: A White Comedy.* John Caulfield was tasked with studying de Antonio's FBI file for leakable information, lest his film turn the kids off from Nixon.

Meanwhile, on the Ellsberg front, trusty Chuck Colson arrived at a new idea: firebomb Brookings, then get G-men posing as firemen to rush in and retrieve the Diem file from Leslie Gelb's safe.

If they only knew Leslie Gelb didn't have a safe and kept his office door unlocked, Jack Caulfield wouldn't have had to burst into John Dean's office, face flushed, in a panic:

"Jesus Christ, John! You've got to help me! This guy Colson is crazy! He wants me to firebomb a goddamn building, and I can't do it!"

On Thursday night, July 15, the president went on TV for three minutes: "I have requested this television time tonight to announce a major development in our efforts to build a lasting peace in the world"—he would be traveling to China to seek normalization of the relations between the two countries.

No one stormed the White House; there wasn't even much protest from the right (whom Nixon, planning the announcement, had referred to as "the animals"). It was experienced like a healing spring rain, as if suddenly enemies were a thing of the past. All those decades of tension: Nixon made this one announcement, and there it was—gone. Love: just as the hippies said.

Peace: just as the hippies said. *"I really believe life is simple. It's all the other people that make things complicated."*

Meanwhile the White House operationalized its longtime goal of expanding its internal secret-policing capacity. They called it ODESSA, or the Special Investigations Unit, or the Room 16 Project, for its suite number in the White House basement. It contained the kind of "sterile" telephones used by the CIA (a Secret Service agent used an IBM card to enter the access code every morning) and a safe that required three combinations to open. A doddering elderly relative of the coleader of the operation was proud to learn her boy was working on "leaks": "Your grandfather," she said, "was a plumber." In jest, he put up a sign on his office door: MR. YOUNG—PLUMBER. The Plumbers was the name by which the group became known.

Mr. Young—David Young—had been Kissinger's personal assistant. His superior in the enterprise, Egil "Bud" Krogh, thirty-two, grew up with John Ehrlichman and saw him as a father figure. Both, like Haldeman, were Christian Scientists. An acquaintance described Krogh as "a brisk, polite, dynamic young executive. . . . Never mussed, never damp, absolutely spick-and-span." Though some in the White House had taken to calling him "Evil" Krogh. This healthy right-wing exuberant was so proud watching his president rap with student demonstrators on the Mall in 1970 that he decided he was willing to take a bullet for him.

On July 19 they hired on another staffer, a former FBI agent, assistant district attorney, and failed congressional candidate from Dutchess County, New York. As an FBI agent, G. Gordon Liddy had been pushed out because he was, in the words of a superior, "a wild man" and a "superklutz." As assistant DA he had fired a pistol at the ceiling while summing up a case before a jury. When he lost a Republican congressional primary in 1968 (slogan: "Gordon Liddy doesn't bail them out—he puts them in") but won the Conservative Party's line, he was rewarded for throwing the race with a job at the Treasury Department—which he lost, in 1971, for speaking against the administration's gun-control bill at an NRA convention. He liked to show off his toughness by putting his hand in a candle flame. He also liked to demonstrate the best way to assassinate a man with office supplies: a puncture to the neck with a freshly sharpened pencil, directly above the Adam's apple. He confessed an admiration for Adolf Hitler and wrote in his memoirs about the Pledge of Allegiance, "I *enjoyed* the mass salute and performed it well, unexcelled in speed of thrust and an iron-shaft steadiness throughout the remainder of the pledge. That habit became so deeply ingrained that even today, at assemblies where the pledge is made or the national anthem played, I must suppress the urge to snap out my right arm."

Such was the caliber of the men now called to work in the Executive Mansion.

Colson had wanted Howard Hunt to lead the Plumbers, but Ehrlichman

had other plans for him. Furnished with a red wig, a CIA-issue voice modi-
fier, and "pocket litter" in the name of Edward J. Warren, he was assigned to
the Ted Kennedy floozy watch. Meanwhile, from newspaper clippings and
interviews with Ellsberg's first wife and a restaurant owner whose mistress
Ellsberg had apparently hit on, Hunt was amassing "all available overt,
covert, and derogatory information." He was also poring over the Pentagon
Papers to find a portal to tie the Kennedy brothers to Diem's assassination,
and ghostwriting purple prose for use by a friendly *Detroit News* writer
about Ellsberg's defense attorney: "The art of espionage, of course, is seldom
conducted in the open. . . . Nevertheless, it has been said with some certainty
that over the years Leonard Boudin"—a prominent left-wing lawyer—"has
been a contact of both the Czech and Soviet espionage agencies, the latter
best known by its initials, KGB."

By the end of July the distinction between Hunt's projects and the
Plumbers' dissolved. Each new scheme spun off others; best not to duplicate
efforts, especially since Hunt and Liddy got along famously. The Ellsberg
witch hunt had reached a snag. From FBI reports Hunt knew Ellsberg saw
a shrink, Dr. Lewis J. Fielding. Perhaps they could do to Ellsberg what had
been done to Barry Goldwater in 1964: discredit him as a madman. Perhaps
they could figure out this mysterious figure's mysterious motives: money,
fame, ideological loyalty to the Soviet Union? Some vicious blackness deep
within his soul?

(Some angles they didn't consider: conscience, patriotism.)

FBI agents visited Dr. Fielding July 20. The doctor wouldn't hand over
his records. The CIA did a psychological profile based on publicly available
information. Its utility proved limited. It was time, the Plumbers decided, to
plan a black-bag job. Ehrlichman brought the proposal to the president.
"Krogh should, of course, do whatever he considered necessary to get to the
bottom of the matter," the president replied, "to learn what Ellsberg's
motives and potential further harmful action might be." His only complaint
was that the plan wasn't aggressive enough.

Young and Krogh filed the action memo, with the customary boxes for
"approve" and "disapprove." Ehrlichman scrawled his initials in the former
and added, "if done under your assurance that it is not traceable."

Hunt approached a Cuban friend, Bernard Barker, whom he'd worked
with at the Bay of Pigs. There was "a matter of national security" to carry
out, Hunt apprised him, for an organization "above both the FBI and CIA,"
against "a traitor to this country who had given information to a foreign
embassy."

The team Barker recruited moved out to California in late August, casing a shrink's office in Beverly Hills in the service of their president, reporting back to David Young, "I think we have a perfect situation here for
clandestine entry."

CHAPTER TWENTY-NINE

The Coven

Apulp thriller of relevance to the White House situation came out in 1971. It was called *The Coven*. The author was David St. John, and his hero was a Washington, D.C., private investigator named Jonathan P. Gault (kind of like the protagonist of Ayn Rand's *Atlas Shrugged*), who lived in a Georgetown that had become a warren of head shops and strung-out fourteen-year-old junkies: "The Aquarians had taken over." So had venal union bosses ripping off honest workingmen, and the kind of young defense lawyer who charges "police brutality" at the drop of a handkerchief and "affects a storefront desk in the ghetto and lunches at the Metropolitan Club where he feels more comfortable."

The detective's favorite old-time jazz joint was now polluted with the stylings of a sort of Afro-voodoo songstress named Andree Lescaut. The old Bojangles-like hoofer she's put out of work winds up murdered in the alley out back, then the temptress Lescaut herself. Suspicion falls on two hippies, Stud and Hugehead. The gumshoe cases their commune: "Peeling pink paint, sagging steps that suggested active termites . . . fingerpaintings, Day-Glo posters and scrawls instructing passers-by to undertake unnatural connection with the President, and murder a pig a day. About average for the humanistic lifestyle within."

He questions one of the denizens: "He shrugged elaborately, scratched at the beaded headband, and wiped more dribble from his mouth. . . . 'What's his problem?' 'Hash. He has no mind left.'"

It arrives that the mastermind behind the crime is Senator Newborn Vane, who resembled a certain libertine solon from Massachusetts, and his glamorous wife. Mrs. Vane "gets her jollies from the artists, writers, and beach boy types Vane gets public grants for," and procures prostitutes for her husband, and tosses down cocktails after toasting in Russian. The senator flies his own plane "to save time getting between here and the grass—the grass roots."

A clue—a pack of tarot cards, the same kind the real-life hippie murderer of Dr. Victor Ohta in Santa Cruz in 1970 left at the scene of the crime—leads

Gault to a bizarre ritualistic scene staged out of a government-funded "Community Involvement Center." Black men and women "naked except for a loincloth" dance maniacally before Lescaut's coffin. A priestess shrieks, "In the name of Belial, Sasa, Behemoth, Asmodeus, Obayifo, Lilith, Nahemah, Set, Thoth, and the Black Goat, we beseech thee, Master, to sanctify this sacrifice." Then, the heroic gumshoe surreptitiously looking on, the senator's wife "dipped into the throat and drew a bloody line across her pelvis, then tossed the dead pullet under the bier and stood with arms lifted and outstretched, displaying the inverted cross painted against her flesh."

Gault lays it all out before the skeptical cop: "Suppose I told you Newbold Vane was a devil-worshipper?"

So much for the senator's presidential ambitions.

"David St. John" was E. Howard Hunt, writing, like a good spook, under a pseudonym. He had started writing novels out of boredom from being put on ice at the CIA. He was quite successful at it, too.

The Coven provided a window into the mind of a Plumber. Everette Howard Hunt believed, as many in the White House believed, that behind the earnest humanitarian face of liberalism lay irredeemable evil. George Gordon Battle Liddy suspected Daniel Ellsberg was a KGB agent, or that the *Times* had acquired the Pentagon Papers through a black-bag job. In their minds, every evil was linked. Liddy gave over twelve pages in his memoirs to an account of his involvement in a raid on the home of Timothy Leary — "one more problem of the sick '60s." When he moved to Washington in 1970, Liddy noted his neighbors as "career Democrat-liberal bureaucrats who hated Richard Nixon and had a laissez-faire attitude toward the raising of their children" — so he threatened one of these children with "a restraining hold I had learned before in the FBI." For, "To permit the thought, spirit, life-style, and ideas of the '60s movement to achieve power and become the official way of life of the United States was a thought as offensive to me as was the thought of surrender to a career Japanese soldier in 1945."

And when he considered the 1972 presidential election — "in view of the thousands of bombings, burnings, riots, and lootings of the '60s, to say nothing of the murders of police just because they were police, the killing of judges, and the general disintegration of the social order" — he realized that for Nixon to fight according to the normal procedures of democratic politics would have been just such a surrender. It was like one of the agents in a novel by Howard Hunt said: "We become lawless in a struggle for the rule of law — semi-outlaws who risk their lives to put down the savagery of others."

These men were not aliens. They were Americans — in a time when millions of Americans agreed with *Joe* and resonated enough with E. Howard Hunt's dank anxieties to turn him into a bestselling author.

Some scenes from sea to shining sea:

The International Association of Chiefs of Police reported that ninety-one cops were killed in the line of duty during the first nine months of 1971. In Philadelphia, former police chief Frank Rizzo campaigned for mayor as "the toughest cop in America." The iconic photograph of Chief Rizzo showed a nightstick poking out of his cummerbund at a black-tie banquet, the iconic act his club-swinging raid on what he was sure was a drug den (his evidence was the poetry, beards, and homosexuals). He won the 1971 Democratic nomination against two liberals who split the vote. In November he won the general election defending the police department practice of "turf drops": instead of charging black kids, they were left to fend for themselves in the toughest white neighborhoods. "He should build jails, not schools," one of his cabdriver supporters told a reporter. "Ninety percent of the kids are no good."

In New York vigilantes shouting "Never again!"—the slogan of the Jewish Defense League—firebombed the office of a talent booker who handled Soviet acts. (One secretary died.) A cabdriver in Queens rammed fifty welfare rights picketers calling for affordable day care: "I have a wife and four kids to support!" he cried before revving the accelerator. Down the Jersey Turnpike, an investigative journalist, Ron Porambo, came out with a book on the Newark riots, *No Cause for Indictment,* which documented, in numbing and irrefutable detail, the cold-blooded killing of innocents and the systematic trashing of black-owned businesses by police and guardsmen. Two attempts on his life followed; in their wake, the Newark police accused him of shooting himself. In that same city the Newark Boys Chorus School, 80 percent of whose students were black, moved into a three-story Georgian mansion in an upper-middle-class neighborhood. A homemade firebomb was tossed though a side window in September, doing no damage; a second attempt, over Thanksgiving, took out the entire top floor; in January, vandals torched the integrated school's buses. No one reported the fire to authorities.

Defiling school buses was a nationwide trend. Michigan was the vanguard after Judge Damon J. Keith, the federal district's only black jurist, rent de facto segregation's most sacrosanct taboo, the line between city and suburb, by ordering the white town of Pontiac to accept black students from Detroit. "What burns me to the bottom of my bones is that I paid an excessive amount of money so that my son could walk to school," one working-class resident told the *New York Times.* "I'm not going to pay big high school taxes and pay more for a home so that somebody can ship my son thirty miles away to get an inferior education." Then one hot evening just before the start of the school year, two terrorists slipped inside a depot and lit dynamite atop the fuel tanks of six school buses. Thousands of townspeople rallied to the terrorists' support, just as they used to do down South after lynchings. "Pontiac is the new South," a state legislator said. "I'm frankly ashamed to say right now that I am a citizen of this city."

In Washington, D.C., feminist Ti-Grace Atkinson, speaking at Catholic University, speculated over whether the Blessed Virgin Mary had been "knocked up." Enraged, William F. Buckley's sister Patricia raced onto the stage and started assaulting her. In Mountain Home, Idaho, residents decided they'd had enough of the GI coffeehouse in their midst and burned it to the ground. In New Mexico, in the rugged town of Ruidoso, the set the previous year for the John Wayne picture *Chisum,* barefoot Nancy Crowe Tapper and bearded Paul Edward Green, both of surburban Wheaton, Maryland, were a young couple living together without benefit of clergy. The town was well sick of hippies; Paul was arrested for falling afoul of Ruidoso's rarely enforced 125-year-old "lewd cohabitation" law. The statutory punishment for a first offense was supposed to be a verbal warning. The judge— who displayed a sign on his office door reading JUDGE PRITCHETT: THE LAW WEST OF THE RIO RUIDOSO—gave him thirty days instead. Paul didn't take his confinement particularly seriously; when given a chance to call a lawyer, he allegedly ambled away from the jailhouse. The second of two "warning shots" caught him in the back of the head. They said the hippie was running, yet Green had recently been injured and could barely walk. Charges were never pressed against the officer. This was only the latest in an epidemic of hippie lynchings in New Mexico: the nineteen-year-old heroin addict shot while handcuffed behind the back (ruled justifiable homicide) in Santa Fe; the sixteen-year-old girl who passed a bad check shot by a storekeeper in the parking lot (no charges filed) in Albuquerque; communes razed, vans dynamited—young people, the *Washington Post* reported on January 16, 1972, "beaten, raped, and killed."

The federal commissioner of public services reported 771 bomb threats in federal buildings in 1971 and 35 explosions. In January, police in New York, San Francisco, and Chicago defused bombs set in eight banks sent by a group calling itself the Movement for Amerika. A manhunt was under way for the alleged perpetrator—a former army radio operator who went AWOL, then reenlisted in the summer of 1971 under an assumed name— just as Stanford announced that Professor H. Bruce Franklin, who kept on taking over buildings, might become the first professor to lose tenure there in seventy years. On January 17, his supporters set fires around campus and a black-powder bomb was found taped to a circuit breaker. The next day, in Miami, antipollution activists shut down a Pepsi bottling plant by cementing over a drainage pipe. That same day, Mayor Daley held a press conference announcing the arrest of two college students, nineteen and eighteen years old, for conspiracy to poison Chicago's drinking water with a typhoid microorganism found in their house. Their plan had been to inoculate members of their group, which they called Rise, in order to survive and form a master race.

*   *   *

The berserk was breaking out on every side. Sometimes it was hard to *tell* the sides. The Plumbers and their patron harbored no such doubts. The left were the aggressors. Everyone else was just playing defense.

The aggressors worked, for instance, by defiling religion. The president endured a receiving line at a White House dinner honoring voluntarism; "Typical of the group," he complained to Haldeman, "was a fellow who came through the line from California who said he was a Quaker. He was an obvious, roaring fag." The aggressors poisoned the airwaves. When the president flipped through the channels after a ball game he wanted to watch was rained out, he came across an episode of CBS's *All in the Family* in which an old buddy of Archie's came out of the closet. "The show was a total glorification of homosex. . . . Is this common on TV?—destruction of civilization to build homos. Made the homos the most attractive type." He added a fillip on classical civilization: "You know what happened to the Greeks! Homosexuality destroyed them."

The aggressors poisoned the minds of the innocent young. Two University of Michigan English professors published a textbook with Random House composed entirely of articles from insurgent underground newspapers, "a logical culmination of the trend toward 'relevant' readers for composition courses," the preface read. *Black Viewpoints,* a Signet paperback for high schoolers, included Eldridge Cleaver's "Revolution in the White Mother Country," and H. Rap Brown's "Die Nigger Die" ("Discussion and Study Questions . . . 3. How does Brown's idea of 'neo-colonialism' fit into the scheme of colonized peoples as clarified by Cleaver, Forman, Jones, and others?"). Gynecological clinics opened up at universities; Michigan's booked nine hundred appointments in September alone; Boston University's was booked months in advance, though it hadn't been publicized in the student paper for fear of reaction from conservative regents. At Princeton a coed told a newspaper, "There's a general feeling that the examination is cursory and the doctors don't really care. They're just there to dispense contraceptives."

Black Panther George Jackson's prison letters were reviewed in the *New York Times* by Julius Lester: "after reading this book, whites will long for the good old days when all they had to think about was Stokely Carmichael and H. Rap Brown." On August 21, Jackson was shot to death at San Quentin in an armed rescue attempt (mourners were asked to contribute guns in lieu of flowers to his funeral). A black crime wave broke out in Wilmington, North Carolina, and a vigilante group called Rights of White People sprang up that local law enforcement warned was more dangerous than the Ku Klux Klan. In Baton Rouge, Louisiana, a group of circuit-riding black militants were arrested after a gun battle the *Los Angeles Times* reported was part of a plan "to take over towns across the United States and give them 'back to the black people.'" In upstate New York the police chief in Syracuse complained he was powerless to stop the black teenagers who'd begun "guerrilla-type warfare—hit and run" against his officers.

And, 109 miles to the west of Syracuse as the crow flies, the Labor Day revels of the good townsfolk of the village of Attica, New York, were disturbed by terrifying reports that the prison where the town's husbands and brothers and fathers worked was about to erupt.

The uprising started after inmate leaders who'd signed a July petition in protest of "brutal, dehumanized" conditions met, inconclusively, with the New York State commissioner of correctional services. The next week a routine scuffle broke out in D Block. Before long, a riot was raging. Prisoners started fracturing guards' skulls with pilfered lengths of pipe, pieces of chain, broomsticks, hammers, and baseball bats. They captured the exercise yard and burned the schoolhouse and chapel, stripped correctional officers naked and forced them through a club-swinging gauntlet.

It was chaos—until some Black Power acolytes got ideas.

They started taking hostages—thirty-eight prison guards. Two leaders from each cellblock formed a negotiating team. They demanded that a facility designed for 1,600 not hold 2,250, that they deserved more than one shower a week, that Muslim worship not be forbidden by the rule against "inmates congregating in large groups." They grew bolder: they asked for amnesty, for "reconstruction of ATTICA PRISON to be done by inmates and/or inmate supervision," for their "speedy and safe transportation out of confinement to a non-imperialist country."

The TV cameras arrived. "We have composed this declaration to the people of America to let them know exactly how we feel and what it is they must do," a twenty-one-year-old spokesman announced, cool and confident. "The entire incident that has erupted here at Attica is not a result of the dastardly bushwhacking of two prisoners September eighth of 1971 but of the unmitigated oppression wrought by the racist administrative network of this prison throughout the year.

"We are *men*! We are not beasts and we do not intend to be beaten and driven as such. . . .

"We will not compromise on any terms except those terms agreeable to us. We call upon all the conscientious citizens of America to assist us in putting an end to this situation that threatens the lives of not only us, but each and every one of you as well.

"We have set forth demands . . ."

And what kind of upside-down world was it where prisoners presented "demands"?

They were, in part, successful—arranging for Bobby Seale, Tom Wicker, Congressman Herman Badillo from the Bronx, William Kunstler, Minister Louis Farrakhan, and others to be brought in as their advocates. The state prison commissioner was confident that the local team on the ground could defuse the situation without violence, that to otherwise regain control would require a "furious hand-to-hand battle" that would end up with hostages dead. Negotiators, observers, and prison officials pleaded for Governor Rockefeller to come, but he chose to stay behind. The talks grew more complicated; the standoff continued; Tom Wicker, the liberal *New York Times* columnist, addressed townspeople in the rainy parking lot about the state of play. He announced he had spoken to five of the hostages. They were being well treated, he said; and what's more, they supported the inmates' demands for amnesty.

"I want to add my further testimony to the unity that's shown in the yard. To the unanimous testimony of these men that regard themselves as being aggrieved by the treatment that they say that they have received in the prison in past years. And they appear to be unwilling to give up the hostages—give up their situation in the prison—for anything short of complete amnesty."

A townsperson, shivering in the evening drizzle, shouted, "Is there complete amnesty for murder?"

"Why don't you talk about the unity of the guards, you double-crossing bastards!"

A wild-eyed man in prison-guard clothes, the father of one of the hostages, seething beyond control: "Nigger lover! We have to go in and bring those people out. Wet-nursing those convicts won't do it. We have to get our sons back or just bomb the hell out of the place!"

"Brutality? I don't give a good goddamn!"

"I'd like to show them a little brutality!"

"Rapers, murderers. Do you want 'em on the street? They're in there because they belong in there."

"Brutal? My husband brutal?"

"What kind of white man are you? Standing on a platform with a nigger . . . helping niggers against your own."

Nelson Rockefeller said by phone he had no constitutional authority to act. Until, that is, he decided he'd had enough and signed off on a rescue attempt, the details of which he left up to the commanders on the scene.

Monday morning, September 13. State police snipers and strike teams secreted themselves out of sight of the prison yard below.

Inmates who believed negotiations still ongoing made a bluff to strengthen their hand: they displayed eight of the hostages on an open walkway, bound and blindfolded, with blades pressed to their throats. Revenge-minded officers fired indiscriminately. Troopers in their vision-obstructing gas masks shot hostages. When the choking, blinding fog of CS gas cleared, scores of bodies littered the ground, writhing or motionless. Nine hostages and twenty-six inmates died immediately, four more of wounds in the days to come.

Pacification accomplished, false rumors spread among the officers: that one of the hostages had been castrated. That all of the hostages had died with their throats gashed. It spurred corrections officers to subsequent rounds of torture, as they took turns beating naked inmates.

The *Chicago Tribune* ran man-on-the-street reactions. A man with long hair and a beard said "it was a disaster. Uncivilized. Inhuman." A couple of women said the authorities overreacted. The consensus, however, was represented by the man who said, "There has to be law and order. That's all. . . . They did what they had to do."

Politicians struggled to make sense of it. Liberals such as John Lindsay, who'd dealt with his own prison riot at the Tombs in 1970, spoke to the imperative of prison reform; Vice President Agnew said Lindsay had fallen "right into line" with "the utopian leftists" and "on the side of the criminals." Nelson Rockefeller shocked his liberal fans with Reagan-style pronouncements: the blame must be placed on those who "exploit legitimate grievances not because they want to correct them, but because they try to use them for the overthrow of society." Edmund Muskie said, "The Attica tragedy is more stark proof that something is terribly wrong with America. We have reached the point where men would rather die than live another day in America."

Which was pretty nihilistic for a presidential front-runner. But it matched the nihilistic national mood—such as Richard Nixon, reflecting that summer in a speech to media executives upon the columns of the National Archives Building: "Sometimes when I see those columns, I think of seeing them in Greece and Rome. And I think of what happened to Greece and Rome, and you see only what is left of great civilizations of the past—as they have become wealthy, as they lost their will to live, to improve, they became subject to the decadence that destroys the civilization. The United States is reaching that period."

He said that on July 6, even as Chuck Colson was putting together his White House–based secret police. Seven weeks later, as Attica readied to blow, the Plumbers prepared for their first black-bag job.

Bud Krogh, nervous, showed late for the rendezvous in Room 16 with G. Gordon Liddy to hand over a fat envelope containing $5,000 in cash laundered from the Associated Milk Producers by Joseph Baroody, the son of the president of the American Enterprise Institute. Krogh, a Christian Scientist, didn't exactly have ice water in his veins: "Here it is. Now, for God's sake, don't get caught."

Hunt and Liddy flew out to Los Angeles. The entry team traveled separately the same day. Their leader, Bernard Barker—code-named Macho—had been Hunt's number two at the Bay of Pigs; they had renewed their acquaintance, like old college buddies, at the tenth anniversary reunion in Miami. The Cubans Barker had recruited were active, along with Barker, in the CIA's Miami station, which had continued running propaganda and sabotage operations against Castro in Cuba—and, against the CIA's charter, within the United States. They hadn't been hard to convince. "E. Howard Hunt, under the name Eduardo," Barker explained to them, "represents to the Cuban people their liberation."

The base camp was the Beverly Hills Hilton; it had sight lines to Dr. Fielding's office. At 9 p.m. on September 3, two Cubans in the guise of Air Express couriers delivered a trunk to that office containing camera equipment and cheap RadioShack transceivers. Upon their exit, they made sure the rear door to the building was unlocked.

From base camp Liddy placed a call to ensure the doctor was safely at home. Green light: at midnight the Cubans arrived, Liddy standing sentry in the parking lot in a rented car. But they discovered that the rear door was no longer unlocked. They located a relatively well-concealed window to break. They realized an adjacent loud air conditioner would keep them from hearing an enemy approach. So Liddy, who was supposed to remain in his car lest the operation be traced back to the White House, broke operational protocol, pulled out his retractable Browning hunting knife, and guarded the crime scene until they achieved entry.

Tinkling glass; Liddy returned to his car.

Howard Hunt pulled up, agitated: Dr. Fielding was no longer at home. Liddy broke radio silence to see how near the Cubans were to being finished.

No response. They had forgotten to turn up the volume on their radios.

Just then the Cubans providentially rustled into view, and the group reconvened at the hotel, where Hunt was chilling champagne in anticipation of a successful mission.

The Cubans reported that they had had to pry open the file cabinets with a crowbar, leaving behind physical evidence of their presence. Hunt asked what they'd found.

"Nothing, Eduardo. There's no file with his name on it."

"Are you *sure*?" Hunt asked, worriedly.

The Cubans pulled out photographs of the jimmied cabinets, explained how they'd pawed through every one, then strewn pills around to make it look as if a junkie had forced the window. A proud enough Liddy wrote in his memoirs, "At least the operation had been 'clean': in and out without detection. We decided to celebrate that, at least, with the champagne." He called Krogh, who green-lighted a recon mission for a possible future hit on Fielding's apartment.

Back in Washington, in the White House basement, Krogh inspected Liddy's knife incredulously: "Would you really have used it—I mean, kill somebody?"

Of course, Liddy replied.

Krogh instructed him to keep it sharp and recommended him for a salary increase.

The Plumbers sketched out possible future projects. Dosing Ellsberg with LSD before he spoke at a fund-raiser, during the soup course? ("A warm liquid is ideal for the rapid absorption and wide dispersal of a drug.") Revisiting the Brookings firebombing plan? (Maybe they could acquire a fake D.C. fire engine, suit up their Cubans like firemen, and time the bomb to go off after hours, just as the Weathermen did—though the idea was shot down because a fire engine cost too much.)

On September 8 the president grilled Ehrlichman on the Plumbers' progress: "We had one little operation," he responded. "It's been aborted out in Los Angeles, which, I think, is better that you don't know about. But we've got some dirty tricks under way. It may pay off." Ehrlichman brought up their attempts to hang alleged John F. Kennedy misdeeds around the Democratic Party's neck. "Some of this stuff is going to start surfacing," he promised, though he warned that the CIA had not been as forthcoming with classified diplomatic cables as they would like.

Hearing of his lack of control of any lever of government always sent Richard Nixon into flights of rage. He started ranting about the IRS.

"*We have the power* but are we using it? To investigate contributors to Hubert Humphrey, contributors to Muskie, the Jews, you know, that are stealing everybody . . ." He trailed off. "You know, they really tried to crucify Ho Lewis"—Hobart Lewis, *Reader's Digest*'s president and executive editor, who had been audited. "Are we looking into Muskie's return? . . . Hubert? Hubert's been in lots of funny deals. . . . Teddy? Who knows about the Kennedys? Shouldn't they be investigated?" (Like old hens, they started gossiping about Teddy's marriage.)

The next week the president took it up with Haldeman: "Bob, *please* get me the names of the Jews, you know, the big Jewish contributors of the Democrats. . . . Could we please investigate some of these cocksuckers?"

The Plumbers were part of Nixon's reelection master plan. It was the same strategy he'd chartered in 1966: set Democrats at each other's throat. The motive behind implicating JFK in the murder of Ngo Dinh Diem was to tarnish the Kennedy name among both antiwar Democrats and Catholics (Diem was Catholic). Edmund Muskie was *also* Catholic, and his foreign policy adviser—the dreaded W. Averell Harriman—could also with some creativity be implicated in the deed.

The problem resided only in the historical facts. In truth, the responsible American officer in the overthrow and murder of Diem was a Republican—Nixon's 1960 running mate, Henry Cabot Lodge, then serving as ambassador to South Vietnam. In conspiracy with the CIA, Lodge had *deceived* President Kennedy into giving an ill-advised green light for a coup that Kennedy himself had naively been shocked to see end in an execution. These truths were why Howard Hunt was hard at work cobbling together new "facts."

At a September 16 press conference, reporters started in on Nixon about South Vietnam's upcoming one-man election for president, and the suggestion of Washington senator Henry "Scoop" Jackson—a presidential hopeful—that the United States exert leverage to demand genuine democracy.

The president's response was bizarre. Indeed, none of his briefers knew what the hell he was talking about.

"If what the senator is suggesting is that the United States should use its leverage now to overthrow Thieu, I would remind all concerned that the way we got into Vietnam was through overthrowing Diem and the complicity in the murder of Diem; and the way to get out of Vietnam, in my opinion, is not to overthrow Thieu with the inevitable consequence or the greatly increased danger, in my opinion, of that being followed by coup after coup and the dreary road to a Communist takeover."

The non sequitur served a purpose. They called it, in Washington, "getting it out there"—the sleazy business of slipping in narratives to embarrass the opposition among a barrage of otherwise irrelevant information. In this case, the apposite chunk was "complicity in the murder of Diem." It was supposed to stick out like a sore thumb, as a cue to some intrepid reporter to start digging into the question of whether Kennedy had ordered Americans to stand down as Diem was murdered. That reporter could then be leaked a cable dated two days before Diem's murder that read: AT THE HIGHEST LEVEL MEETING TODAY, DECISION RELUCTANTLY MADE THAT NEITHER YOU NOR HARKIN SHOULD INTERVENE IN BEHALF OF DIEM OR NHU IN THE EVENT THEY SEEK ASYLUM. Howard Hunt had forged it from chunks of real cables using scissors, glue, and a Xerox machine.

It happened not to work: the president's words proved too oblique. But that was only one front in the battle. Another was to exploit Eugene McCarthy's festering bitterness toward the Democrats by steering him to run as a "fourth party" candidate for president. ("Five million might finance McCarthy," the president reflected one September day.) Another was to secretly push a black candidate for the Democratic nomination. Harry Dent and Delaware businessman John Rollins were the point men for this one: they could run an "independent" newspaper ad imploring a grassroots draft of Jesse Jackson, Haldeman explained, then barrage Jackson's Chicago office with thousands of "old $1 bills" from various parts of the country that look "like people have been saving their whole lives. . . . You do that two or three times and Jackson will start thinking people really want him to be president. . . . And after his ego is going, then you can't turn him off." Circumstantial evidence suggest the two schemes fused: by January, McCarthy announced he was scouting sites across the causeway from Miami Beach, site of the '72 Democratic convention, for angry delegates to form a rump convention to nominate McCarthy if the main event turned out to be "a mere rerun of 1968," perhaps with a Shirley Chisholm as his vice-presidential nominee; also in January, Colson engineered a walkout of the black delegates at a convention of the National Youth Caucus.

Meanwhile there were the broadcast networks to flay—four of them, now that PBS, which unlike the others was relatively free of the need to placate corporate sponsors, had matured into a fearless news powerhouse. The White House's Office of Telecommunications Policy was crafting a public-broadcasting funding bill. OTP general counsel Antonin Scalia had drafted a series of memos on how the Corporation for Public Broadcasting might be made a more pliant vassal of the White House. "The best possibility for White House influence is through the Presidential appointees to the Board of Directors," he wrote; the best way to shed the influence of "the liberal Establishment of the Northeast" would be to strengthen local stations at the expense of the national organization. Such subtleties were all well and good until Richard Nixon read in his news summary that Sander Vanocur, late of NBC, who'd been a Nixon bête noire since the 1960 presidential debates, was slated to coanchor a new PBS newsmagazine. Nixon issued a blunt dictate: "all funds for Public Broadcasting be cut immediately."

As that order was kicked down to staff for the difficult political problem of implementation, the Oval Office's malign attentions turned to the broader media problem. The president asked Chuck Colson if he'd read the new book *The News Twisters* by Edith Efron, an employee of one of his biggest backers, publisher Walter Annenberg. Colson replied that he had and found it a waste of time.

Wrong answer.

The News Twisters purported to be an objective study proving the networks followed "the elitist-liberal-left line in all controversies," "actively slanting" against the "white middle-class majority"—80 percent to 20, Efron concluded. To make the case, she videotaped hundreds of hours of broadcasts about the 1968 presidential election, marking each utterance for the side she took it to favor. Her judgments proved rather idiosyncratic. In heads-I-win-tails-you-lose fashion, footage of Humphrey being heckled by antiwar protesters was scored as "supports demonstrators"; footage depicting Humphrey excoriating H. Rap Brown and Stokely Carmichael and "extremists of the left and the right" was scored as "anti-conservative." A CBS report that Nixon was "warning his staff against overconfidence, but he himself hardly looks worried," was scored as suggesting Nixon "is a liar."

This, the president concluded, was *literature*. Nixon ordered Colson to get it on the bestseller list. Availing himself of $8,000 from the same funds that bought their gear for the Fielding break-in, Colson bought out bookstores' stock. Cartons of *The News Twisters* piled up in Howard Hunt's office—as it appeared on the bestseller lists beside LBJ's memoirs, B. F. Skinner's *Beyond Freedom & Dignity*, *The Last Whole Earth Catalog*, and the sex manual *Any Woman Can!*

Why not? The Kennedys were worse. Joe Kennedy had gotten his kid Jack's college thesis cleaned up and published as a book and schemed to get his ghostwritten *Profiles in Courage* a Pulitzer. "They're using any means," Nixon told Colson and Haldeman. "We are going to use any means. Is that clear?"

How would the American people have reacted if they knew about this kind of stuff? A relevant question for the future. The *New Yorker* ran a cartoon when these crimes were finally investigated of two men at a bar: "Look, Nixon's no dope. If the people really wanted moral leadership, he'd give them moral leadership." Part of Richard Nixon dreamed of world peace. Part of him gave the public something it wanted as much or more: an outlet for their hatreds. At a time when pulp readers thrilled to the notion of a dashing liberal senator as a practitioner of human sacrifice, what Richard Nixon saw as fighting evil and what much of the public saw as fighting evil overlapped. They *identified* with Richard Nixon—not despite the anxieties and dreads that drove him, but because of them.

Liberals had always had a hard time grasping how anyone could identify with Nixon. At the 1968 Republican National Convention a Rockefeller retainer came across a friendly matron from Pennsylvania wearing a Nixon button. "I thought your delegation was supposed to be in our corner," he teased.

"Oh," she said, beaming, "but *I* like Nixon."

"You mean you support Nixon. You admire and respect Nixon."

"That, too. But I like Dick Nixon."

By 1971, more and more Americans were professing to love Dick Nixon—not despite the fear and dread that produced the Plumbers, but in some sense because of it.

They loved him, too, for his squareness. A clean-cut brother-sister pop act from Orange County cooed their way into prominence in 1971. "The Carpenters are hardly what you'd call political," the *Chicago Tribune*'s music critic wrote in August, "but friends of mine on the West Coast tell me their music is known in some circles out there as 'Nixon music.'"

Part of it was nostalgia. "Boy, the way Glenn Miller play*edddd*!" Edith and Archie Bunker bleated out each week, a prelude to Archie's weekly rants against the spics and hebes and hippies and pinkos. The "Rat Pack"—the merry band led by Frank Sinatra who'd sold themselves as cutting-edge hedonists in the 1950s and early '60s but proudly identified as Nixon fans now that hedonism had become democratized—were enjoying a resurgence coincident with their rightward turn; Sinatra himself, whose simultaneous lusting after and loathing for the new culture resembled the movie *Joe* (in a 1966 *Esquire* profile, he was depicted slapping around a hippie; that same year, in Mia Farrow, he married one), had said in 1968, "I'll do anything to defeat that bum Nixon." Now he made Spiro Agnew a regular golf partner. Sammy Davis Jr. was America's most prominent black Republican.

Dean Martin hosted a nostalgic variety show on TV, then a spin-off, *The Golddiggers,* in which wholesome girls did 1930s-style production numbers in between vaudeville-style comedians. Mantovani (the king of elevator music) and Ray Conniff (the king of supermarket music) churned out hit LPs. Lawrence Welk was a hit in TV syndication. Another syndicated hit was the corny Nashville revue *Hee Haw.* Merle Haggard, a former burglar and resident of San Quentin, scored not merely a hit but a phenomenon with "Okie from Muskogee" ("We don't smoke marijuana in Muskogee / We don't take our trips on LSD"). The first time he sang it, at Fort Bragg, the soldiers rushed the stage to embrace him and made him perform it again. It spawned a slew of imitations. When Johnny Cash, awkward in white tie and tails, sang at the White House, he politely turned down a request from the president to sing one of them: Guy Drake's "Welfare Cadillac."

No TV show was more popular than *Bonanza*—steely cowboys keeping decent townfolk safe from desperadoes, just as Nixon said after watching John Wayne's *Chisum:* "the good guys come out ahead in the westerns; the bad guys lose." As Lorne Greene as *Bonanza* patriarch Ben Cartwright liked to say, "A man's never wrong doing what he thinks is right." Orthogonian culture, a tangle of rage and piety: its circumference was expanding.

But a vague sense that good-dad Nixon would take care of the bad-son hippies wasn't enough for a majority; the Republican defeats in 1970 showed that plainly enough. His unfavorable poll showings that summer against Kennedy and Muskie and Humphrey showed it, too. How much was the tacit endorsement of dulcet-voiced Karen Carpenter worth that summer when 73 percent of Americans disapproved of the president's handling of the economy? Fifty percent wanted him to do something he'd pledged since his first week as president never to do: take the Democrats' advice and institute a freeze on wages and prices. He had excoriated controls as recently as August 4, 1971: they would "stifle the American economy, its dynamism, its productivity, and would be, I think, a mortal blow to the United States as a first-class economic power."

That dynamism was in a sorry condition. Copper, railroad, dock, and telecommunications workers had gone on strike for inflationary wage settlements. Steel narrowly avoided a strike by giving workers a 15 percent wage increase. Nixon had spent July pressuring Arthur Burns for lower interest rates; when the Federal Reserve chair denied him, Colson leaked a story that Burns was begging for a salary increase for himself (actually he was asking for a salary increase for the Fed chair to follow him). On speculation of open warfare between the Oval Office and the Fed, the Dow Jones fell 3 percent in a week.

That drop happened the same day, July 20, that Nixon called in the Republican congressional leadership for a meeting: expecting huzzahs for his China breakthrough, instead they grilled him on what he was going to do about the economy. Steel announced an 8 percent price hike on August 3 — two days before the Bureau of Labor Statistics announced the biggest monthly increase in the wholesale price index since 1965 ("That little Jew cocksucker is the same guy who screwed us in the Eisenhower administration," Nixon noted of the commissioner of labor statistics, ordering White House personnel chief Fred Malek to tally up how many Jews worked for the BLS so they could be purged for conspiring against Nixon). By August 10, the Dow was down 111 points from a spring high of 950.80; the next day Great Britain announced a wager against the future of the U.S. economy by stepping up to the U.S. Federal Reserve Bank's metaphorical "gold window" and requesting an exchange of $3 billion in U.S. currency for forty thousand tons of bullion from Fort Knox.

At that, Treasury Secretary John Connally told his president it was time to put into effect the plan they had discussed.

Connally had been on the job since February 1971. Nixon had previously brought the retired conservative Democratic Texas governor into the White House as a bit player, appointing him to his Advisory Council on Executive Reorganization. When that advisory committee had presented to him their conclusions two weeks after the agonizing 1970 congressional election results, they had nearly put him to sleep with their technocratic recommendations — all except Connally, who held the president spellbound with a forceful presentation on how executive reorganization could increase his *political* base. That had been November 19, 1970, a particularly difficult day: Nixon had just tried and failed to get his original treasury secretary, David Kennedy, a stolid nullity, to volunteer his resignation (like many apparently bold politicians, Nixon hated firing people). Nixon apportioned blame to Kennedy and the rest of his economic team for the political losses Nixon had just suffered. They were "gradualists," content with responsible tinkering around the edges of monetary and fiscal policy. "They just don't get in and fight," Nixon complained to Haldeman.

Nixon had by then become convinced that one of the reasons he had to serve a full eight years was because he grasped what was true in the intimations of the apocalypticists on the bestseller lists: the imminence of America's decline as the world's number one power. He believed Nixon, and only Nixon, in a second term, safely removed from the requirement of ever winning another election, could cushion the blow by teaching Americans to live within limits. The conclusion he drew from this was paradoxical and astonishing: he would have to win the election by doing whatever he had to do to make the economy *appear* to boom in the run-up to the 1972 elections, no matter the longer-term consequences of the techniques it took to do it. The problem was cautious, fiscally conservative economic advisers such as Kennedy, who refused to make fiscal decisions for political reasons—just like Dwight D. Eisenhower's in 1958, who had cooled off the economy and cost him, Richard Nixon was convinced, the 1960 presidential election.

Then, that mid-November day in 1970, along came John Connally, making utterly mercenary political arguments about executive organization. Nixon fell in love. He asked Connally the next morning if he would like a job in the administration. There were only two jobs worth having, the Texan responded: secretary of state and secretary of the treasury.

Balls of a brass monkey!

Two weeks later Nixon closed his ears to the howls of George Bush, who had just been beaten by a Connally protégé for Senate, and offered Connally the treasury job. On Air Force One, Nixon instructed Haldeman on how to beg him to accept: "Say that 'I hope and pray you won't turn him down.' . . . 'You're the best man in the country that he could have as his adviser in national and international affairs. He feels you're the only man in the Democratic Party that could be president.'"

One of the things that delighted Nixon was that Connally had no fixed ideology. In fact, he boasted that he had no fixed convictions about anything: "I can play it round or I can play it flat, just tell me how to play it" was one of his nostrums—paraphrasing the apocryphal applicant for a job as a rural science teacher, asked about his convictions on the shape of the earth. Nixon's other economic advisers had only mocked the Democratic Congress's 1970 grandstand play in granting the president power to install wage-and-price controls. Richard Nixon instituting controls was unimaginable, his informal adviser Milton Friedman wrote in a *Newsweek* column in July of 1971, because he was a leader of "vision and courage"—not an economic demagogue. Connally had a different view: "If the legislature wants to give you a new power—you take it. Put it in the corner like an old shotgun. You never know when you might need it."

Nixon could have tamped down inflation in other ways in the summer of 1971: under the Taft-Hartley act, enjoin inflationary strikes as a threat to national security; or short of that, spend political capital jawboning less inflationary settlements. But that conflicted with another of his schemes to build a New Majority: seducing union members into the Republican Party. He had decided July 21 in a meeting with Chuck Colson, the point man for the "blue-collar strategy," that labor might be "shortsighted, partisan," and "hate Nixon personally," but in the wars to come, he needed them inside the tent pissing out. "When you have to call on the nation to be strong—on such things as drugs, crime, defense, and our basic national position—the educated people and the leader class no longer have any character, and you can't count on them." Colson explained the bottom line in a subsequent memo: "The President, regardless of what the business community urges, what the polls show, or what the Republican orthodoxy would indicate, is not going to do anything that undermines the working man's economic status."

Instead he would do what Connally had been urging him: he would play it flat and institute wage-and-price controls.

The deal was cemented in one of the most extraordinary conclaves in presidential history. Friday, Saturday, and Sunday, August 13, 14, and 15, Nixon met around a table with his fifteen top economic advisers at the president's retreat, Camp David. He brought along Bill Safire, too, who until that weekend didn't know what a "gold window" was, but was needed for the weekend's most important priority: the speech the president would give Sunday night explaining to the nation what they had just done. Herb Stein of the Council of Economic Advisers said he felt as if they'd been hired as scriptwriters for a TV special; the "image of action" was the important thing, the president explained at one of the meetings, which were quarter-backed by Connally. In two days, with all the relevant technical experts back in Washington, they instituted the biggest blow to the doctrine of laissez-faire since the days of Franklin Delano Roosevelt: a ninety-day freeze on wages and prices. A 10 percent border tax on imports. A package of tax relief for businesses and individuals (repealing the 7 percent excise tax on new cars: nothing was more American than buying a new car). And something else that was astonishing: unilaterally, without warning, Nixon scrapped the foundation of the planet's monetary system: the convertibility of dollars into gold.

"The problem of a freeze," George Shultz complained at one of the meetings, was "how do you stop it when you start?" Whenever the president ended it, prices would immediately balloon. Nixon ordered them to sweep that problem under the rug. The important thing was the sales job. He had an election to win. "This'll put the Democrats in a hell of a spot, this whole speech," he gloated to Haldeman the second morning of his economic summit, then went into the day's meetings, where Arthur Burns said closing the gold window was nuts: "*Pravda* would write that this was a sign of the collapse of capitalism." Nixon ignored his advice. "Nobody asked," a historian observed, "what kind of monetary system he envisioned to replace the one now being interred, and nobody knew." Neither, whether Japan and Europe would interpret it as a declaration of economic war.

That night, a hot one, the president sat in front of a roaring fire in his lodge, giddy with an almost narcotic glow: *control.* "Let America never accept being second best," he told Haldeman, Ehrlichman, and Caspar Weinberger of the Office of Management and Budget, forgetting in the thrill of the moment that the ultimate purpose of the exercise was winning an election so he could teach Americans to accept exactly that. His only worry seemed to be preempting *Bonanza.* But then he was providing an ample substitute, casting himself as the white-hatted TV cowboy, rescuing the good townspeople from desperadoes—the strangers from without that he successfully claimed were responsible for all their woes.

The speech began with a boast: "I have addressed the nation a number of times over the past years on the problems of ending a war. Because of the progress we have made toward achieving that goal, this Sunday evening is an appropriate time for us to turn our attention to the challenge of peace."

He continued, considering his belief that America only had two solid years of economic dominance left in her, with a lie: "America today has the best opportunity to achieve two of its greatest ideals: to bring about a full generation of peace, and to create a new prosperity without war."

He then explained how what he was about to announce—Executive Order No. 11615, "Providing for Stabilizing of Prices, Rents, Wages, and Salaries"—was an act of heroism for himself as well as for his listeners: "This not only requires bold leadership ready to take bold action—it calls forth the greatness in a great people."

He then named the desperado they would slay together, with a hint of anti-Semitic code: "We must protect the dollar from the attacks of international money speculators . . . waging an all-out war on the American dollar. The strength of a nation's currency is based on the strength of that nation's economy—and the American economy is by far the strongest in the world."

(*He* knew the run on the dollar was actually a sign of the American economy's weakening vis-à-vis the rest of the world; *they* didn't have to know that, could be made to understand instead that it was all because of insolent overseas Franklins, taking advantage of American innocence—and that the sheriff was back in town.)

"Accordingly I have directed the secretary of the treasury to take the action necessary to defend the dollar against the speculators. I have directed Secretary Connally to suspend temporarily the convertibility of the dollar into gold or other reserve assets, except in amounts and conditions determined to be . . . in the best interests of the United States."

He lied again, salving fears that a newly devalued currency would take money out of ordinary Americans' pockets: it would only, he assured them, hurt globe-trotting Franklins. "If you want to buy a foreign car or take a trip abroad, market conditions may cause your dollar to buy slightly less. But if you are among the overwhelming majority of Americans who buy American-made products in America, your dollar will be worth just as much tomorrow as it is today."

It was the Richard Nixon of the Checkers Speech, whose wife wore a respectable Republican cloth coat. It was Richard Nixon the jujitsu master, attacking by positioning America as the attacked—America had self-sacrificingly rescued Japan and Europe from economic ruin after World War II, but "now that other nations are economically strong, the time has come for them to bear their share of the burden of defending freedom around the world." He concluded by the telling the story of the time "a man wrote in his diary: 'Many thinking people believe America has seen its best days.' That was written in 1775 . . . the dawn of the most exciting era in the history of man." It was the Richard Nixon who asked *if gold rust, what shall iron do?:* "And today we hear echoes of those voices, preaching a gospel of gloom and defeat, saying the same thing: 'We have seen our best days.'"

It was Richard Nixon, king of the squares, his wife knitting an American flag. "I say let Americans reply, 'Our best days lie ahead.'"

It worked. "Nixon Stuns Democrats," a *Washington Post* headline read. The last White House poll before the speech showed only 27 percent of Americans hoped Nixon would be reelected. The next found 75 percent favored his new economic proposals: "In all the years I've been doing this business," the poll-taker said, "I've never seen anything this unanimous, unless it was Pearl Harbor." The stock market joined the unanimity: the Dow posted its biggest one-day point gain to date, 32.9 points—even as overseas markets tanked. *Time* once more rhapsodized about their favorite wave-surfer: "For the second time in two months, President Richard Nixon reversed his own and his party's policies with a swiftness and style that is virtually unmatched in modern American politics. . . . A firm show of leadership was clearly needed in order to get the U.S. industrial machine running smoothly once more." Now Nixon was up six points over Muskie, a development *Variety* didn't miss: "New Score Is Dow 32, Nixon 72."

One of his only critics was the AFL-CIO's George Meany, who pointed out that the freeze could have been extended to dividends, interest, and profits as well, but was not: "Robin Hood in reverse, robbing the poor to pay for the rich." The only national politician with the backbone to join Meany was Senator George McGovern.

Nixon would attend to Meany by the by. Right now, he was busy raiding Meany's constituency. On August 17 he became the first president to address the Knights of Columbus's annual States Dinner, with a true-blue Silent Majority speech. Alongside his law-and-order attorney general and his Catholic transportation secretary, he declaimed, "The time has come for us to speak up for America. . . . When we talk about the character of a nation, we must never forget that the character depends upon the individual character of two hundred million Americans . . . it comes from the home; it comes from the churches; it comes from the great schools of this nation."

He sang hosannas to the great Catholic football heroes Vince Lombardi and Bronko Nagurski, and to Rose Mary Woods, who never missed mass during their travels in seventy nations: "She is a very fine secretary, but she also has very great character. She grew up in a family of modest income, a large family. She went to a Catholic school, a Catholic grammar school, a Catholic high school. Just looking at my secretary, and I think John Mitchell and John Volpe will bear me out, if that is what Catholic education does, I am for more of it." Nixon got a two-minute standing ovation. It was code, brilliant code, designed to hack apart New York Democrats, just then debating the issue of government aid to parochial schools: "clearly this divides the Democrats who run the *New York Times*," the Catholic Pat Buchanan advised, "from the Democrats who run for office in Queens and the North Bronx."

Another bold move Nixon considered, then vetoed. In April the Supreme Court, 9–0, had issued its latest absolutely final ruling that the South's dual school systems were illegal, despite his solicitor general's arguments to the contrary, and Nixon had to choose his next move.

More than ever, it wasn't just a Southern issue. By the standards set by HEW, 18 percent of Southern blacks went to integrated schools in the 1968–69 school year and over 40 percent by 1971–72. But only 28 percent of black students in the *rest* of the country attended integrated schools. Nashville, Charlotte, Tampa—and Pontiac—were busing under court order. Almost a dozen cities in Pennsylvania were proceeding under tense voluntary agreements. The response was always the same, North, South, East, and West: panicked flight to the suburbs, private and parochial schools, and in the South, newly opened "Christian academies." Joe Kraft hoped the Ninety-second Congress would "hold the line against the anti-busing fanatics." But the "fanatics" spoke for 76 percent of the country—including 47 percent of blacks. Nixon ordered Ehrlichman and Haldeman to work up some kind antibusing law or executive order or constitutional amendment.

Then, he changed his mind.

He had breathed a sigh of relief when the 1968 Civil Rights Act had passed; it released him from having to take a position on open housing. Now he realized judges had granted him the same favor. He could ruefully observe, *I have consistently opposed the busing of our nation's schoolchildren to achieve a racial balance, but there is nothing I can do about it because the Supreme Court has tied my hands.* Busing would give something to the Democrats to scratch each other's eyeballs out over during the primaries. And provide all the more reason, if you hated it, to vote for Richard Nixon: he would nominate more conservative judges.

He soon had the chance. The day after that press conference where he tried to frame the thirty-fifth president of the United States for murder, as Americans absorbed the Attica massacre, he received the resignation of eighty-five-year-old Supreme Court justice Hugo Black. Almost simultaneously, Justice John Marshall Harlan announced that he, too, would retire.

John Mitchell proposed Richard Poff of Virginia, the ranking Republican on the House Judiciary Committee, who had offered an amendment to strip from the 1966 civil rights bill the power to sue for civil rights violations. Poff decided he didn't welcome the confirmation fight, so Nixon cast his eye over

Democrat Robert Byrd: another thing for the Dems to scratch each other's eyeballs out over. "He's a real reactionary. The Democrats just made him their whip. And he was in the Ku Klux Klan when he was young. Send them a message." (That was George Wallace's slogan.) A list of six candidates leaked to the American Bar Association revealed the political opportunism: Byrd, who'd never been admitted to the bar or practiced law; three undistinguished women, a nod to the ERA ferment (one was a segregationist leader); an appeals court judge who'd built his reputation defending Mississippi governor Ross Barnett against contempt charges when he'd refused to let James Meredith attend Ole Miss. Chief Justice Burger said he'd resign if any of them were appointed. "Fuck him," Nixon responded. "Fuck the ABA." Which somehow made it into the *New Republic.* Which received a prompt letter from John Ehrlichman: "The simple fact is that in the many hours I have spent with the President I have never heard him use the word attributed to him in Mr. Osborne's piece."

Nixon was deferential enough to the ABA to change course: one of the eventual nominees was a former ABA president, the Virginian Lewis Powell. The other was the Justice Department's William Rehnquist. Both were received well by the experts. The White House heaved a sigh of relief: two conservatives had passed the smell test. Powell was the author of a memo to the Chamber of Commerce arguing that "the American economic system is under broad attack . . . from the college campus, the pulpit, the media, the intellectuals and literary journals, the arts and sciences, and from politicians." He proposed a multipoint plan ("a long road and not one for the fainthearted") to ideologically monitor universities and the media, push for more aggressive pro-business intervention into the courts, and politically organize corporations. Rehnquist had reportedly called for law and order in times of domestic insurrection "at whatever cost in individual liberties and rights."

"Rehnquist is pretty far right, isn't he?" Kissinger asked Haldeman.

"Oh, Christ," Haldeman replied. "He's way to the right of Buchanan."

Perhaps that was what restored Patrick Buchanan's faith in the president. In January 1971 he had written an angry seven-page memo about the White House's erratic ideological course. "Conservatives," he complained, "are the niggers of the Nixon administration." (Nixon answered, "You overlook RN's consistent hard line on foreign policy," dissembling on the fact that he was about to sell out the "niggers" on China.)

Buchanan had turned down a chance to lead the Plumbers, but was downright lustful in strategizing for the 1972 election. He had been refining his ideas on the subject since March, when he wrote, proposing a "Muskie Watch," that the campaign goal should be to "focus on those issues that divide the Democrats, not those that unite Republicans." That, he said in July, must be their "guiding political principle."

He knew the Old Man's heart. Nixon had been working that angle since 1948.

Buchanan filed his masterpiece on the subject in October. "Top level consideration should be given to ways and means to promote, assist, and fund a Fourth Party candidacy of the Left Democrats and/or the Black Democrats," he wrote. "There is nothing that can so advance the President's chances for reelection—not a trip to China, not four and a half percent unemployment." Though they should also hedge their bets, and "continue to champion the cause of the blacks within the Democratic Party"—promoting the message that "the Power Elite within the Party is denying them effective participation." Keep a flow of letters full of damaging information on Democrats to journalists; fake a poll showing Humphrey ahead (he was third); keep the president out of everything—"the President and the Presidency" were "quintessential political assets"—cut welfare, even though the president had already increased food stamps and food assistance by 500 percent—it would "force a division within the Democratic Party." Continue the "positive polarization" formulation of Agnew in 1970—for if the presidential election "cut the Democratic Party and country in half," they would end up with "far the bigger half."

Sound political thinking, if a little bit coarse, and also out-of-date. One of Buchanan's headings, "Republican Praise for Any Democratic Support on Vietnam"—because it would go "far toward making them 'Establishment' and driving a wedge between them and the ideological hard core of their party"—was mooted by the fact that there hardly *was* any Democratic support on Vietnam anymore. Even the most conservative among the dozen or so politicians jockeying for the 1972 Democratic nomination, Henry "Scoop" Jackson, was for setting a date for withdrawal from Vietnam.

Fewer and fewer Republicans supported the president either. "Vietnamization" was beginning to sound too refined. "The sooner we get the hell out of there, the better" was how Nixon's minority leader in the Senate, Hugh Scott, now stated it. "Period."

Nineteen seventy-two would tell.

CHAPTER THIRTY

The Party of Jefferson, Jackson, and George Wallace

T HE CONVENTIONAL WISDOM HELD THAT THE PRESIDENTIAL ELECTION might be won with only 40 percent of the popular vote. There might be five serious parties on the ballot in November, Tom Wicker wrote on January 2: "the two majors, Mr. Wallace's American Independents, another independent party deriving from the middle and the left headed by someone like Eugene McCarthy, and the even farther left group currently headed by Dr. Benjamin Spock." Wicker's more sober colleague Scotty Reston estimated five days later that there would only be four, and that, given the political exhaustion sweeping the land, "barely over one in four adult Americans will have voted for the winner in 1972. . . . The consequences of that kind of a minority Presidency are hard to foretell." In 1960, 6 million voters claimed no allegiance to either of the two major political parties. Now the number was over four times that. Flux was the keynote of politics now.

The president's approval rating was 49 percent. The January 17 Harris poll showed him running only a point ahead of Edmund Muskie (Wallace pulled 11 percent). The day after the Harris poll, a Broadway musical version of *The Selling of the President,* Joe McGinniss's account of how smoke, mirrors, and Pan-Cake makeup swept Nixon to the White House in 1968, was announced. When the president sat down in the Oval Office for a live interview with Dan Rather the day after New Year's, the *Times* did a humiliating behind-the-scenes report emphasizing his familiarity with "7-N" ("a light pancake especially concocted for swarthy types like Mr. Nixon") and the recommendation of a television consultant "who still has Soupy Sales, the comic, among his clients" to refrigerate the set to thirty-five degrees; and the way Nixon angrily clenched his fist beneath his desk when asked if his diplomatic moves were timed for political effect. The "Anderson papers" were lighting up the news: muckraker Jack Anderson had discovered evidence of the National Security Council's aid and comfort to General Agha Mohammad Yahya Khan in suppressing Bangladeshi independence. The *New York Times* editorialized, "As the head of a minority party who has jettisoned much of the platform on which he once campaigned, he could solidly establish his leadership only by winning public confidence on a broad scale. . . . Despite the initiatives and accomplishments of the last year, it cannot be said that President Nixon has gained that necessary public confidence."

The public was not much confident in anything. The new movies told stories of crumbling institutions: *The Hospital,* starring George C. Scott as an suicidal doctor in a big-city hospital where patients died from bureaucratic dysfunction; Pasolini's *Decameron,* where the Catholic Church was swallowed up in lusty amorality; *Slaughterhouse-Five,* which revealed the Army Air Corps of the "Good War" as slaughterers of innocents in Dresden. *The Last Picture Show* unmasked the teenagers of 1950s Middle America, and *Harold and Maude* old ladies as no more sexually continent than the Woodstock generation. In *The French Connection* the forces of law and order proved powerless in keeping heroin from flooding New York. In *Dirty Harry,* San Francisco police were no more effectual in stopping a maniacal hippie sniper (in real life, during its run, three family pets were found mutilated and hung from a tree on January 13 in the exclusive Forest Hills district of San Francisco, then a fourth with a note reading, "I am not going to kill animals anymore. Just people").

In the entertainment pages of every big-city daily moviegoers searching out the playing times of Disney's *Fantasia* were also apprised of the latest X-rated movies: *The Stewardesses* ("Presented in the most realistic film process ever developed"), *Glass Houses* ("The Story of the Sensuous Family!"), *Boys in the Sand* ("All male cast"); *Together,* the notorious European orgy movie ("See what your children can show you about love"), showing on twenty screens in all five boroughs of New York. Rex Reed called the new western *Straw Dogs* a "blood bath for sadists." Clayton Riley of the *New York Times* called another unprecedentedly violent feature, *Clockwork Orange,* a "criminally irresponsible horror show." But that was just one man's opinion; the *Times* also ran a review by Vincent Canby that called it "a disorienting but humane comedy."

The presidential election unfolded as a referendum on the meaning of the 1960s and its toll on institutions. No institution was more up for grabs than the party of Jefferson and Jackson: Chisholm, McGovern, Lindsay, McCarthy, Hartke, Harris, Hughes, and Mink on the left to Humphrey, Muskie and Jackson in center field; and in right, Sam Yorty and the dreaded George Corley Wallace; so many Democrats intended to take on a weakened Richard Nixon that Topps came out with a set of collectible trading cards. At least Wallace *said* he would run as a Democrat. Democrats hoped he would not: when the DNC held their lottery for hotel assignments for the convention in July in Miami Beach, he was deliberately snubbed.

Back in 1968, Humphrey could win the nomination without entering a single primary. But thanks to the McGovern Commission guidelines 60 percent of the delegates in 1972 would be selected in open primaries. The rest would be chosen in party caucuses that outlawed all the old, unreformed stratagems: unannounced meetings, boss-appointed delegates, automatic berths for elected officials, "unit rules" by which a candidate favored by a mere majority of a delegation was automatically "delivered" all the delegation's votes.

No one was sure what it would take to win; nor, most of all, what kind of monkey wrench the 10 million newly eligible voters between the ages of eighteen and twenty-one would introduce. Only one thing was certain: the chances for a Democrat standing on the inauguration stand on January 20, 1973, were not just favorable, Senator Edward M. Kennedy said at a much anticipated address before the Washington Press Club on January 17, but "extremely favorable."

Ted Kennedy wasn't running, or was; it would become a quadrennial tradition, this Kennedy tea-leaf reading. California Democrats announced on January 11 he would be headlining their rally at the L.A. Convention Center, and surely that meant *something*—then the next day Kennedy filed an affidavit affirming that he wouldn't be running in the second primary of the season, in Florida, a contest being watched more closely than New Hampshire (a shoo-in for Muskie from neighboring Maine). On the seventeenth, a forest of TV cameras at the Washington Press Club recorded another Kennedy disavowal—but also set off another round of Kennedyology: if he *really* wouldn't run, why did he invoke JFK, asking America to embrace a leader "who asks not what our country can do for us, but what we can do for our country"?

The speech was featured in a major spread on the front page of the next day's *Washington Post*. Next to the jump was an ad for the February issue of *Esquire* with Teddy's face on the cover: "Is This Man the 38th President of the United States?" Five days later his friend Mike Mansfield announced he would advocate for Secret Service protection for Kennedy—even though he was "personally convinced that Senator Kennedy means it when he says he is not a candidate."

But then, they were handing out Secret Service protection like candy. Patsy Mink of Hawaii got to welcome burly men with police radios into her life for filing in a couple of primaries, though not the thirty-two-year-old poverty worker Edward T. Coll, who filed in New Hampshire even though he was too young to be inaugurated. Coll did get a spot on the podium for a televised debate. He exploited his fifteen minutes of fame by dangling a rubber rodent before the cameras and crying, "We can't do anything in this country until we do something about the rat!" Sam Yorty, the Los Angeles mayor, tooled around New Hampshire in a "Yortymobile" with the sponsorship of the right-wing publisher of the *Manchester Union Leader*, William

Loeb, who called the front-runner "Moscow Muskie." Wilbur Mills, the powerful chairman of the House Ways and Means Committee, was running even though a poll gave the pear-shaped solon 1 percent support; the rumor was that he had been put up as stalking horse for Teddy. Senator Vance Hartke made a last-minute entrance, the other Indiana senator, Birch Bayh, having already dipped his toe in the water and withdrawn, as had Wisconsin's William Proxmire.

There were even two Republicans. The former marine Pete McCloskey ("leadership as tough as the problems") said he'd gladly withdraw when Nixon withdrew from Vietnam. The other Republican, Ohio congressman John Ashbrook, spoke for conservatives disillusioned by the China opening, Nixon's supposed soft approach to Vietnam, and the heretical economic program Milton Friedman said in his *Newsweek* column would "end as all previous attempts to freeze prices and wages have ended, from the time of the Roman emperors to the present, in utter failure and the emergence into the open of the suppressed inflation." Ashbrook's slogan was "No Left Turns." Nixon moved to buy off Ashbrook's supporters by making right turns—scuttling amendments to the Economic Opportunity Act of 1964 to extend aid for child care and create a national legal services corporation as "truly a long leap into the dark for the United States government and the American people"; and appointing a forgotten right-wing martyr, Otto Otepka, a former State Department officer cashiered by President Kennedy as a McCarthyite, to the Subversive Activities Control Board. It worked: *National Review* endorsed Nixon. However, Herb Klein wasn't exactly raising expectations: he predicted a 70 percent showing in New Hampshire on March 7—eight points fewer than the president had received in 1968.

Some thought one of the Democratic aspirants resembled a Republican. Senator Henry "Scoop" Jackson of Washington called himself a "bread-and-butter shoe-leather" Democrat and proposed adding half a million new jobs to the public-sector payroll, but his standard stump speech emphasized the peril of the USSR's missile buildup, and President Nixon had twice invited Jackson to join his cabinet. The *New York Times* reported, "He hopes for major financial support from defense contractors and other businessmen." Jackson enjoyed a vogue among the chattering classes: "He stands where the majority of the voters presumably stand," Richard Whalen, a onetime Nixon staffer, wrote in a profile of Jackson in the *New York Times Magazine*, "somewhat to the right on social issues, to the left on economic issues and, withal, astride the commanding center of American politics." His campaign manager said his future would be determined by his showing in Florida. His itinerary there was in Dixiefied north Florida; his refrain, "People on welfare should be put to work," and, "I'm opposed to this business of busing people all over the place."

Another Democratic aspirant had recently *been* a Republican: John Lindsay. He was still a media darling, a regular on Johnny Carson's *Tonight Show*; dazzled by his charisma (and his opening campaign event at the Radio City Music Hall premiere of the Robert Redford movie *The Hot Rock*), the media seemed not to be noticing that his New York was becoming the symbol for everything wearying and gross about the United States. He switched parties for a presidential run late in 1971—even as a *New York Times* op-ed described Central Park under his tenure as "a combination of decadence and barbarism; a cut-rate *Fellini Satyricon*"; even though the welfare population had doubled since his first election; even though the Knapp Commission, and its star witness, Frank Serpico, revealed that much of the New York City police force operated something like the mob. The month of Lindsay's presidential announcement was a typical one in Gotham. A survey by the Addicts Rehabilitation Center found that one out of six Harlem residents was hooked on heroin. ("One of the most demoralizing experiences I have ever had in Harlem was being panhandled by a 12-year-old junkie," Congressman Charlie Rangel wrote in an op-ed.) "City Restrooms May Be Razed," one headline announced (too convenient for those junkies); "1,625 Slayings Here in '71 as Rate Continues to Rise"; and—the story would later inspire a movie called *Dog Day Afternoon*—"42d Street Crowd Helps Robber Flee." The headline below that was "Widow, 69, Is Slain in Queens Project." As if to keep the city sane, the *Daily News* ran a regular feature called "What's Good About New York."

Meanwhile the city had realized it needed more low-income "scatter site" public housing to conform to HUD guidelines. Lindsay chose to put some of it in Forest Hills, in Queens, where Brooklyn and Lower East Side Jews had moved from crowded tenements after World War II in their first step on the upward-mobility ladder. Jews, Lindsay thought, wouldn't protest the arrival of poor blacks; they were liberal. But Jews who had mortgaged everything they had to *leave* crime-ridden poor neighborhoods, it arrived, did not prove so obliging.

Lindsay had ignored the existing racial tensions in Forest Hills schools. The meetings to explain how most of the new public housing residents would be senior citizens, how families would be carefully screened, that the development would bring a slew of new social service amenities, were scheduled on Friday nights, when elderly refugees from Hitler's Germany—the most scared and vulnerable members of the community—attended synagogue. Jack Newfield tagged along at a damage-control session at the Forest Hills Jewish Community Center and heard them "call Lindsay redneck names under the shadow of the Torah." His *Village Voice* colleague Paul Cowan heard one anti-Lindsay picketer boast, "If Lindsay ever gets to be president, I'll kill him. I'll do just what Oswald did to John Kennedy." His companion replied, "You won't get the chance. Lindsay is going to get shot right here in New York."

Lindsay's presidential strategy was to pour all his energy into a massive canvassing effort among Miami's huge population of liberal erstwhile New York Jews, pledging them "an undying fight against the kind of right-wing extremism that always eventually settled on Jews as its object." He pledged a "new national effort to rescue our cities." But South Florida Jews had fled those cities for the same reason their less well-off landsmen had left the Lower East Side for Forest Hills. "That bum," one *bubbe* huffed at a shopping center. "He can't run New York and now he wants to run the country."

Old warhorse Humphrey was also pushing hard in the Sunshine State. He hoped to carry the black vote. But he was also courting backlash hero Frank Rizzo, who had been sworn in as the 120th mayor of the City of Brotherly Love on January 3 before an audience of three thousand pledging, "I will not tolerate gang rule or anarchy in the street." Humphrey promised to kick off his general election campaign in Philadelphia if Rizzo would endorse him—ignoring that the U.S. Commission on Civil Rights was begging the city to stop stonewalling an investigation into abuses in his police department. But Rizzo was already committed to another candidate. The mayor was one of only three politicians—the others were Ronald Reagan and Nelson Rockefeller—on a regular calling schedule with top White House aides. Nixon received Rizzo in the Oval Office on January 24, the day before a big Vietnam speech—despite, or possibly because of, an aide's advice that "in dealing with Mayor Rizzo of Philadelphia, representatives of the Administration should be particularly conscious of the strong anti-black overtones which characterized his campaign." The leader of the "Rizzocrats" promised the president to do anything in his power to help assure his reelection.

Nixon and Humphrey's simultaneous courting of Rizzo, Lindsay's stand against imminent anti-Jewish pogroms, Scoop Jackson's traipsing across the rural precincts where George Smathers once beat Claude Pepper for a Senate seat by calling him a "sexagenarian": it all paid silent tribute to the strangest Democratic aspirant of all.

Tom Turnipseed had been busy organizing to get George Wallace on the ballot of all fifty states as a third-party candidate when his boss casually drawled, "I'm tired of those kooks in the third-party business. It's crazy. I'm thinking about going back into the Democratic Party." Wallace traveled to Tallahassee in January to announce he was entering primaries. Soon, he was ahead in the Florida polls, where he had adjusted his rhetoric for upwardly mobile professionals who'd moved from city to suburb for a better and safer life for their children; he wasn't just for rednecks anymore. A beautiful new, young wife by his side, he explained that blacks had the same right to pull themselves up by their own bootstraps as anyone else, buy a nice home, a car or two in the garage, send their kids to nice suburban schools. The problem was *forced* desegregation, which let folks jump the queue: "Now, on this busing, I said many years ago, if we don't stop the federal takeover of the schools, there'd be chaos. Well, what've we got? Chaos." Apparently, upward of 40 percent of Florida Democratic voters agreed. The "serious" contenders stopped scheduling big outdoor rallies. It only embarrassed them when they could only pull in a quarter of Wallace's crowds.

The final group of contenders, meanwhile, believed Americans had never been more ready for an appeal to their better angels.

Shirley Chisholm, the first black woman to win a seat in Congress, gave her candidacy announcement at Concord Baptist Church in Brooklyn:

"I am not the candidate of black America, although I am *black* and *proud*.

"I am not a candidate of the women's movement of this country, although I am a *woman,* and equally proud of that.

"I am the candidate of the *people* of America. . . . Americans all over are demanding a new sensibility, a new philosophy of government in Washington. Our will can create a *new* America in 1972, one where there's freedom from violence and war at home and abroad, where there's freedom from poverty and discrimination . . . ensuring for everyone medical care, employment, and decent housing. Those of you who can vote for the first time, those of you who believe that the institutions of government belong to all the people who inhabit it, those of you who have been neglected, left out, ignored, forgotten, or shunted aside for any reason, *give me your help* at this hour."

And even if Shirley Chisholm was the longest of the long shots, a slew of New Politics candidates were telling the exact same story—that, as no less than Teddy Kennedy said at the Washington Press Club, America's problems stem "not so much from the fact that people mistrust their government as from the fact that the government so obviously mistrusts the people."

The New Politics Democrats' logic came down to a chain of antinomies. Americans were turning against Nixon in the polls, angry at his embrace of secrecy; so the candidate who could beat Nixon in November would be the one to most credibly embrace openness. Nixon dripped cynicism from every pore; so the candidate to beat Nixon would have to exude idealism. Nixon was all insincerity; the anti-Nixon had to be genuine, an antipolitician. Nixon attracted the alienated old. The anti-Nixon would have to be a magnet for the authenticity-seeking young. Nixon was a creature of the system. His vanquisher would have to come from the grass roots. Nixon was unprincipled and unpopular; the Democratic nominee would have to be principled to be popular. Nixon asked citizens to be spectators; a politics to oppose him would have to be based on *participatory democracy.*

Most of all, Richard Nixon was dragging out an evil, awful, unpopular war. The candidate to beat him would be the one who pledged to end it the fastest. Such as George McGovern, who said in an August 1971 interview, "I would announce on Inauguration Day that we were simply leaving on such and such a date—lock, stock, and barrel. Perhaps I'd take a couple of days to notify the interested governments, but no longer." He called My Lai "just a tiny pimple on the surface of a raging boil. The whole war is a massacre of innocent people and we all share in the guilt for it. Probably one million innocent people have been slaughtered or maimed by American bombs and artillery. Another four or five million have been systematically driven out of their homes and herded into miserable refugee centers."

Theorists such as Fred Dutton, in *Changing Sources of Power,* argued that the people who resonated to this message were America's ascendant political coalition: newly enfranchised students, highly educated professionals, dispossessed minorities, women coming into feminist consciousness. Even the Wallace surge fit into the theory: his followers were a subspecies of the *alienated American,* angry because they were shut out from the Establishment. Dutton insisted that "some of the younger voters who were for Wallace in '68 were concerned less with his racial connotations than his stance as a fighter and his role as the most anti-establishment candidate available that year." Speaking to those yearning for reform was not just a matter of right. The new path to power for the ambitious politician, Dutton argued, "the growing edge of the present," was the rising "coalition of conscience and decency."

Scotty Reston was one of Dutton's appreciative readers, giving his strategy an entire column. "The spreading estrangement of millions of Americans from the two traditional political parties makes increasingly relevant the possibility of a new national political base developing—not just a passing protest vote, but an important mainstream development," Dutton told Reston, "humanistic, critical of big business, big labor, and big government—probably 'Nader populist' at heart." The Timesman found it "hard to deny" and compared the message's vote-getting power favorably to Spiro Agnew's. Corporate America, after all, took New Politics arguments seriously. One index was the continued hot sales of *The Greening of America.* Another came when the huge new media conglomerate Warner Communications put out the first issue of a new feminist magazine, *Ms.,* edited by Gloria Steinem, as an insert in the year-end issue of *New York.* It brought in an immediate eighty-five thousand subscriber cards; the first stand-alone issue, which came out as the Equal Rights Amendment was about to pass the Senate, sold out in eight days.

New Politics presidential hopefuls were legion: Lindsay, Chisholm, McCarthy, Senators Harold Hughes of Iowa and Fred Harris of Oklahoma. Hughes and Harris dropped out, though, in the face of the fellow prairie populist who had concertedly been organizing for a presidential run since the summer of 1970. All he had to show for it was 3 percent in the year-opening Gallup poll. He was, however, drawing the attention of the president. George McGovern had made direct contact with the Communist enemy, and that placed him at the center of Richard Nixon's concerns.

McGovern was an idealist, confident in the power of goodwill to change the world. In graduate school at Northwestern, during a late-night bull session, another student asked him, "George, what makes you tick?" The South Dakotan thought of his father, a rural fundamentalist minister, and uttered a favorite quotation from the Gospel of St. Matthew: "Whoever shall save his life shall lose it, and whosoever shall lose his life for my sake shall find it."

He kept that verse on his Senate office wall. Others, too, though they were too small for visitors to notice:

"What doth the Lord require of thee, but to do justly, and to love mercy, and to walk kindly with thy God."

"Inasmuch as you have done it unto the least of my brethren, ye have done it unto me."

"He who is without sin among you, let him cast the first stone."

"And as you would that men should do to you, do ye also to them likewise."

A promising schoolboy debater, he had found joy in picking out the logical fallacies in his opponents' arguments. But his coach tried in vain to teach him to attack them at their other points of vulnerability, or to enliven his presentation with histrionics and hand gestures. "George's colorfulness," he recalled, "was his colorlessness."

In World War II, McGovern became a heroic bomber pilot. One time he completed a mission after taking a hit that blew out *The Dakota Queen*'s brakes and hydraulics. Still another time, he lost his number two engine, landing miraculously on a too short runway under harrowing fire, calm the whole time: "Resume your stations," he called out to his crew. "We're bringing her home."

But he was a war hero who'd come away with a sense of war's madness seared deeply onto his conscience, a Cold War skeptic who thought the people ravening for another go at Russia were nuts. He cranked the Dakota Wesleyan history department's mimeograph machine for Henry Wallace's 1948 third-party, left-wing presidential bid, fought the bill Richard Nixon cosponsored with McGovern's home-state senator Karl Mundt to require Communists to register with the federal government, then fell in love with Adlai Stevenson and nearly single-handedly built the South Dakota Democratic Party. When it came time to run for office himself, to win the loyalties of the conservative farmers and farm wives of South Dakota, he mastered a difficult straddle. "I can present liberal values in a conservative, restrained way," he explained. "I see myself as a politician of reconciliation." The young professor won a congressional seat in 1956 despite the suspicious American Legion members who sat in on his classes, taking notes. In his first roll call he was one of only sixty-one congressmen to vote against the "Eisenhower Doctrine," a kind of 1957 Gulf of Tonkin resolution for the Middle East.

His sincerity and charm weren't enough, in 1960, to bump him up to the

Senate against Karl Mundt. President Kennedy felt guilty for his lack of coattails and tapped the now unemployed McGovern to set up the Food for
Peace program, a scheme to strengthen Cold War alliances by distributing
America's agricultural surplus. It suited his idealistic faith in the power of
government to do good. He had learned about hunger in the Depression,
witnessing the dust bowl firsthand; it was "the first day I knew that big men
cried." He won the Senate seat he coveted in 1962, then in 1963 became the
first member to speak against the gathering U.S. involvement in Vietnam.
Bobby Kennedy called him "the most decent man in the Senate," adding:
"As a matter of fact, he's the only one." He also, when he looked in the mirror, saw a presidential prospect staring back. By the middle of 1971, he was
nearly alone in the opinion. "Is George McGovern Serious?" ran a typical
headline. Jimmy the Greek, the Vegas oddsmaker, gave him a 50–1 shot to get
the nomination (Muskie was 2–5).

McGovern had faced his first test in August of 1970, a fund-raising dinner at
the home of actress Shirley MacLaine. She was a good friend for McGovern
to have; she had been part, alongside her brother, Warren Beatty, of JFK's
Hollywood circle. The rich and famous guests saw him in his creased blue-
and-white-striped suit that made him look as if he'd never dressed for a
crowd outside of Pierre, South Dakota, heard him speak in what Norman
Mailer would later describe as that "damnable gentle singsong prairie voice"
(it had a hint of a lisp) and passed judgment: "This guy's better than Seconal,"
one said—the prescription tranquilizer. When McGovern had announced his
candidacy at the beginning of '71, so few people had heard of him that
George Gallup refused to poll him in matchups with Nixon.

McGovern gave an interview in *Playboy* for those thumbing their way
toward Miss August. "It may sound old-fashioned to say that I love this
country," he said, "but I do and I'm deeply distressed over the mistaken
direction we're pursuing." And: "I think a sense of decency—not prudish-
ness nor sanctimonious self-righteousness but old-fashioned concern and
love for others—will be essential in the next president." And: "My principal
assets I have as a candidate are my reputation and my record of being
myself," and "steady dependable temperament, as well as a sense of history
and some degree of imagination."

By fall, people started waking up. In September sweet, sappy George
McGovern took a brave risk for peace. It was pro forma in every Nixon
speech on Vietnam that the insolent Communists refused to entertain reasonable terms upon which to settle the war—and that no matter what the
United States did, they would refuse to release American prisoners of war.
McGovern decided to test the proposition for himself. He flew to Paris and
asked the North Vietnamese negotiators whether the establishment of a date
certain for withdrawal of American troops would get the prisoners released,

even if the United States continued to support President Thieu's government in Saigon. They responded that it was only the presence of American troops in South Vietnam that kept Thieu in power and hinted that if Thieu faced a fair election, not one in which he was the only candidate, the Communists' conditions for releasing the prisoners would have been met. The war could be ended without further bloodshed, on terms the United States had always claimed it wanted: self-determination for South Vietnam.

On September 12, McGovern announced that what he had learned in Paris was 180 degrees from the official wisdom: the roadblock to a negotiated settlement was not North Vietnam but the United States of America. Then he flew to Saigon. Nguyen Van Thieu, dependent on American sufferance for his job and terrified Vietnamization would mean his death sentence, apparently didn't appreciate this American stranger hastening that day of reckoning. In Saigon, McGovern and his party met with the non-Communist opposition to Thieu at a church with broad glass windows and a lovely courtyard. McGovern's executive assistant Gordon Weil noticed a flash of light over his shoulder: a firebomb attack. Rocks started crashing through the window. One missed McGovern's head by inches. The Saigon fire department arrived and poured water on the blaze—and, once it was out, retreated and let the rock throwing continue.

The Saigon police chief who had left the party to their fate, claiming they were meeting with Communists, was the fiancé of President Thieu's daughter. These were the thugs American boys were fighting and dying for. George McGovern redoubled his resolve.

Nixon had held a November press conference announcing a pullback of forty-five thousand more troops by the beginning of the year. Then, on Christmas Day, 350 American planes began the most punishing bombing raids since November of 1968—conducted, the White House said, "to protect the safety and security of our remaining American forces in South Vietnam."

After that, Nixon made another announcement: he was withdrawing seventy thousand more troops over the next three months. "This means that our troop ceiling by May first will be down to sixty-nine thousand.... There will be another announcement that will be made before May first with regard to a further withdrawal."

This pattern—fewer troops, more violence—gave Vietnamization a certain Lewis Carroll–like flavor: the closer the war came to ending, the more Vietnamese were massacred. It was, at least, an effective strategy for tamping down domestic dissent: fewer Americans on the ground meant fewer American deaths. The only real antiwar action after the "Christmas bombings," in fact, came from Vietnam Veterans Against the War, who commandeered the Statue of Liberty and hung an American flag upside down from her crown. They had a hard time getting anyone to pay attention. On New Year's Eve in Times Square (where the armed forces recruiting station was boarded up), antiwar demonstrators were overshadowed by the new Christian hippie movement, the Jesus People.

The president had arrived at another stratagem to neuter antiwar voices. His every utterance on what America was trying to accomplish was now framed in terms of bringing home the prisoners of war. Since America was no longer fighting for anything palpable—let alone to contain China—the new rationale was circular: we were fighting the war by air to bring home those POWs that fighting the air war had created. On their hit TV variety show, Sonny and Cher began wearing copper bracelets inscribed with a prisoner's name. Citizens, especially children, started wearing two, three, a half dozen on each arm. A new bumper sticker proliferated—a frowny face, and the legend POWS NEVER HAVE A NICE DAY. Military public relations men began touring returned prisoners around the country. "Following the President's lead," Jonathan Schell of the *New Yorker* observed, "people began to speak as though the North Vietnamese had kidnapped 400 Americans and the United States had gone to war to retrieve them." Dan Rather asked the president on January 2, 1972, about Americans who'd left the country to avoid military service: "Is there *no* amount of alternative service under which you could foresee granting amnesty?" Nixon responded, "As long as there are any POWs held by the North Vietnamese, there will be no amnesty for those who have deserted their country." After all, he said, a deal to withdraw all American forces in exchange for the release of American prisoners had been "under discussion at various times," but was "totally rejected" by the enemy.

In other words, you could protest the president's conduct of the war, but not without betraying the residents of the Hanoi Hilton.

What Nixon was telling the nation was exactly the opposite of what the Provisional Army of Vietnam's negotiators had told George McGovern in Paris. So McGovern made a move.

At a press conference on January 8 he called the president a liar: "It is simply not true, and the president knows it's not true, that our negotiators in Paris never discussed with the North Vietnamese the question of total American withdrawal from Indochina in conjunction with the release of our prisoners." If the goal *really* was getting prisoners released, why didn't Nixon announce that all troops would be withdrawn within six months of an agreement, which the enemy had said would be a satisfactory condition for releasing the prisoners? "There was nothing to lose," the idealist implored, "and, God willing, much to gain." What the North Vietnamese had told him led McGovern to believe that Nixon wasn't negotiating particularly intensely to end the war at all. Instead the president was cruelly *using* the prisoners in a rhetorical game to justify continued bombing and "propping up the corrupt Thieu regime."

A sucker's game, to try to play Vietnam politics with Richard Nixon, where honesty was always the worst policy. "They're out on a limb there," the commander in chief told Haldeman, with no small glee. He was about to saw that limb clear through.

The president stepped up to the TV cameras on January 25. He was sometimes asked, Nixon explained, if there was anything having to do with the negotiations in Paris that he wasn't sharing with the American people. He said his usual response was merely to say that "we were pursuing every possible channel in our search for peace."

Now he was ready to explain to the American people a little white lie.

"Early in this administration, after ten months of no progress in the public Paris talks, I became convinced that it was necessary to explore the possibility of negotiating in private channels, to see whether it would be possible to end the deadlock." So he sent Henry Kissinger to Paris twelve times on secret missions. "Privately," he explained earnestly, "both sides can be more flexible in offering new approaches, and also private discussions allow both sides to talk frankly, to take positions free from the pressure of public debate."

And wouldn't you know it, *quelle coïncidence:* the exact moment at which one of his Democratic opponents had seized the public's imagination with the revelation that the enemy was ready to end the war on exactly the terms Richard Nixon claimed they had rejected, he was now able to reveal what secret negotiations had yielded, "a plan to end the war now. It includes an offer to withdraw all American forces within six months of an agreement; its acceptance would mean the speedy return of all the prisoners of war to their homes."

He didn't mention George S. McGovern—just "some Americans who believed what the North Vietnamese led them to believe . . . that the United States has not pursued negotiations intensively." Nixon didn't say the timing of his speech had anything to do with this particular domestic political diversion—just that "nothing is served by silence when it enables the other side to imply possible solutions publicly that it has already flatly rejected privately." Instead, he implied that a certain meddling Democrat, who would have you trust the word of Communists over the word of the president of the United States, had almost queered the whole deal with his meddling.

"We are being asked publicly to respond to proposals that we answered, and in some respects accepted, months ago in private.

"We are being asked publicly to set a terminal date for our withdrawals when we already offered one in private."

He ended his speech in tones of rue: rue that a certain unnamed Democratic senator had let himself be used for the enemy's purposes.

"The truth is that we *did* respond to the enemy's plan, in the manner they wanted us to respond—secretly. In full possession of our complete response, the North Vietnamese publicly denounced us for not having responded at all. They induced many Americans in the press and the Congress into echoing their propaganda—Americans who could not know they were being falsely used by the enemy to stir up divisiveness in this country."

All this was only possible, he implied, because certain Americans did not behave like Americans at all. They had the temerity to believe the president would lie.

"Some of our citizens have become accustomed to thinking that whatever our government says must be false, and whatever our enemies say must be true, as far as this war is concerned. Well, the record I have revealed tonight proves the contrary. We can now demonstrate publicly what we have long been demonstrating privately—that America has taken the initiative not only to end our participation in this war, but to end the war itself for all concerned.

"This has been the longest, the most difficult war in American history.

"Honest and patriotic Americans have disagreed as to whether we should have become involved at all nine years ago."

(Remember who was president nine years ago.)

"And there has been disagreement on the conduct of the war. The proposal I have made tonight is one on which we all can agree."

("To lower our voices would be a simple thing.")

"Let us unite now, unite in our search for peace—a peace that is fair to both sides—a peace that can last.

"Thank you and good night."

A *New York Times* editorial revealed just how efficiently the olive branch McGovern had been sitting on was sawed off: "By agreeing to set a fixed date for the withdrawal of American forces from South Vietnam in exchange for the return of prisoners of war, the President has moved dramatically in the direction long advocated by many members of Congress." The tabloid *Daily News,* "New York's Picture Paper," ran a colossal front-page blare unaccompanied by a picture: "NIXON'S PEACE OFFER/Total U.S. Pullout in 6 Mos"—a wild exaggeration that revealed the skill of Nixon's bluff. "After really listening to what President Nixon had to say about Vietnam," said a letter-writer who used to be a Nixon skeptic, "I came to the conclusion that he's not as bad as I thought. He is concerned about his country, and we Americans must give him credit for doing his job as he sees it." Another skeptic—Senator Hugh Scott of Ohio, he of the "sooner we get the hell out of there, the better"—praised Nixon's "superhuman efforts" to end the war: "Last night's speech is an answer to responsible people with reasonable doubts. Of course, there could never be an answer to those who want total surrender." Said Mrs. Sybil Stockdale, whose admiral husband was a prisoner in North Vietnam, "The president has done everything he can do. We'd like to know what Senator McGovern's solution is if the Communists will simply hold on to the prisoners."

The feint did not impress everyone. Two nights later a gathering of distinguished Orthogonians in formal dress were to enjoy a dinner in the White House East Room. On the bill were the Ray Conniff Singers, two dozen well-scrubbed kids who cushioned the popular easy-listening vocalist with dulcet, wordless syllables in imitation of a string orchestra. They were adjusting their microphones when one of their number, Carol Feraci, pulled a silk banner from her décolletage reading STOP THE KILLING. She shouted, "Mr. President, stop the bombing of human beings, animals, and vegetation. You go to church on Sunday and pray to Jesus Christ. If Jesus Christ were in this room tonight, you would not dare to drop another bomb. Bless the Berrigans and Daniel Ellsberg."

Mr. Conniff broke the tension by leading the ensemble into its first number. He then apologized and started them in on the second—before a shout issued from the audience: "You ought to throw her out!" Martha Mitchell, the attorney general's wife, known to be partial to cocktails at public occasions, contributed her opinion: "She should be torn limb from limb." Mr. Conniff told Miss Feraci it would be better if she left, and the program continued to its purpose: bestowing Mr. and Mrs. DeWitt and Lila Wallace with the nation's top civilian honor, the Medal of Freedom, for their service to the nation in founding the *Reader's Digest*.

In the war at home, the Party of the New Politics was ceding momentum to the Party of *Reader's Digest*. The rogue Ray Conniff singer had mentioned the Berrigans—Fathers Daniel and Philip, Catholic priests who'd founded the "ultra-resistance" in 1967 by destroying Selective Service records in blood and fire. (The *Digest* had responded by running a poll that claimed of 3,077 Catholic priests surveyed, 2,557 thought America should mine Haiphong Harbor.) Daniel Berrigan went underground rather than submit to prison; his brother Philip was incarcerated at Lewisburg Federal Penitentiary. On January 17, 1972, Philip went back into the dock. A federal grand jury charged that before his 1970 surrender, Father Phil and another priest had cased out underground steam tunnels in Washington, D.C., to blow them up—and that subsequently, in prison, he had plotted with his lover, a nun named Elizabeth McAlister, to kidnap Henry Kissinger. The conspiracy indictment added four other nuns and former nuns, priests and former priests; and a political science professor from Chicago.

To the left it felt like a setup worse than the one in Chicago in 1969. Especially when it was announced where they were to be tried. Most of the incidents listed in the indictment took place in New York, Washington, and Baltimore. But the proceedings would be held in the "Middle District" of Pennsylvania, one of the country's most conservative areas. Early in 1968, in fact, the *Saturday Evening Post* profiled a town forty-five miles down the Susquehanna from where the "Harrisburg 7" would be tried. There, explained the article's author, hippies "are regarded the way witches once were." A factory worker said every antiwar demonstrator should be locked up. The reporter asked, "But what are you going to do when you have fifty thousand of them trespassing on the Pentagon? Shoot them?" "Maybe we'd be better off if we did," he replied.

The Middle District was also, the *Village Voice*'s correspondent explained, a bastion of anti-Catholicism and the Ku Klux Klan. Nineteen days of jury selection began after a defense motion to move the trial to less hostile territory was dismissed. Almost half the pool were excused because they said they couldn't return an impartial verdict. (One said, "You can look at them and see they are guilty"; another said that he might accept the testimony of hippie-type witnesses as long as they were "not downright dirty.") One of the alleged conspirators, Eqbal Ahmad, the political science professor, was a Pakistani refugee; a prospective juror said Ahmad was in the United States "to bring America down to Pakistan's level."

The defense retained a Columbia University sociologist to figure out how to sneak nonreactionaries onto the jury. The best he could suggest was to push to empanel jurors from among the disconcerting number who were hardly aware of the war in Vietnam—for instance the woman who, asked if she ever heard My Lai discussed in the bar she owned, had never heard of My Lai; the steelworker who said, "I don't discuss Vietnam with anybody. It doesn't involve us"; the housewife who said, "I read the obituary column, the weddings, things that interest women—not the front page." The twelve jurors ended up being all white in a city that was 37 percent black. They included three women who admitted the defendants' opposition to the war might impede their being impartial.

The "Christian left" was becoming mainstream: that same January the National Council of Churches called a four-day conference of ecumenical witness in which ministers, rabbis, priests, and even bishops resolved to denounce Vietnamization as a stealth slaughter of Asians. A "Sanctuary Caucus" of houses of worship in eight California cities announced their congregations as safe havens for military deserters. The National Conference of Catholic Charities, the nation's largest private social welfare agency, announced it would inaugurate an unprecedented program of "social activism" to "try to effect substantial changes in such areas as housing and welfare rights." The more mainstream the opposition got, the more it seemed to be repressed by the state. Daniel Ellsberg's indictment—the government's second try; the first was torn up because it was so flimsy—was but one example. The White House investigation of the financial records of the Unitarian Universalist Association, the noble faith of John and John Quincy Adams, because its book arm, Beacon Press, published a four-volume "Gravel Edition" of the Pentagon Papers, was another. The fix was in, the left decided; the Harrisburg 7 indictment was only the latest instance.

Daniel Berrigan had once written a poem: "Don't touch—make war / Don't touch—be abstract about God and death and love / Don't touch—make war at a distance / Don't touch your enemy, except to destroy him." The poem had been inspired by an incident in which a marshal had shouted "Don't touch!" after a nun had reached out to a handcuffed Father Phil in solidarity. Pete Hamill quoted that poem in the *New York Post* the day of Nixon's speech revealing Kissinger's secret talks in Paris: "Naturally, if you write like that, you end up in jail." Paul Cowan, a mere *Village Voice* reporter, was "convinced that, if the government won conspiracy cases like the trial of the Harrisburg Seven, I might some day wind up underground or in jail." After all, Bob Haldeman had just gone on the *Today* show and told Barbara Walters that Democrats still opposing the president were "consciously aiding and abetting the enemy of the U.S." Haldeman insisted he was speaking only for himself. Then, two days later, February 9, his historic China trip looming, Nixon said Democratic criticism of his Vietnam moves "might give the enemy an incentive to prolong the war until after the election."

The historic China trip would begin in two weeks, and the image of a heroic Henry Kissinger hopping from Paris to Pakistan to Moscow, setting up summits and settling wars, squiring beautiful blondes all the while, became an unlikely popular-culture fixture. The first Democratic presidential contest, the Iowa caucuses, proved inconclusive: the biggest showing, with 35.8 percent, was "uncommitted." The surprising news, though, was McGovern's second-place finish with 22.6 percent—he had scored only three points in the most recent national Gallup poll—and the weakness of Ed Muskie's first-place showing. Just about every prominent Democratic politician and power broker was backing him for the nomination, but "Endorsement Ed" barely managed a third of the vote. "The Muskie bandwagon," NBC News concluded, "slid off an icy road in Iowa last night."

The Man from Maine kept on running into bad luck. Opponents seemed to know what the campaign had planned before some staff did. A stink bomb went off in one of his offices; a mysterious press release went out in Florida that the Muskie campaign was illegally using government-owned typewriters. Ten black picketers paced back and forth on the sidewalk in front of his hotel in Tampa calling him a racist for a comment, back in September, that a Democratic ticket with a black running mate would have a hard time getting elected. An ad appeared in the February 8 issue of a Miami Beach Jewish newspaper: "Muskie, Why Won't You Consider a Jew as a Vice President?" (Muskie hadn't said a word on the subject.) Flyers referring to Muskie's Polish heritage began appearing in Jewish neighborhoods: "Remember the Warsaw Ghetto . . . Vote Right on March 14." A memo by his pollster recommending he hold hearings on property taxes in Los Angeles to "take advantage of free TV time" before announcing for the California primary somehow made it to Evans and Novak.

The aggravations put Muskie's people on edge. They knew their man had a petulant side, despite the image they were selling of him as a rock. The other campaigns were on edge, too: they were getting blamed for these dirty tricks, but every staffer swore he was innocent. The Florida primary was getting downright tawdry; one morning Scoop Jackson's staffers opened their Tampa headquarters and found it plastered floor to ceiling with Muskie stickers. A thousand cards circulated through a Wallace rally reading, "If you like Hitler, you'll just love Wallace." (The other side read, "A vote for Wallace is a wasted vote, on March 14 cast your ballot for Senator Edmund Muskie.") A press release on Muskie campaign stationery said Hubert Humphrey was anti-Israel.

It was surpassingly strange. Democratic campaigns usually weren't like this. In the watering holes where rival campaign staffers met to unwind, to gently chide each other, strike up flirtations, exchange war stories, imbibe with reporters—a veil of hostility descended between camps.

Though the press wasn't paying much attention, since the story of the century was now afoot.

On February 17, after a departure ceremony that earned him a standing ovation from even confirmed political enemies, Marine One ferried the president to Andrews Air Force Base, where he boarded the presidential 727, renamed for the occasion with a subtle reelection message: *Spirit of '76.* He took three days in Guam to acclimate himself to Peking time, then landed in China at 11:30 a.m. local time—9:30 p.m. eastern standard time, his favorite hour for televised speeches. On the flight to Peking, he called in Haldeman to go over the choreography for his egress from the plane one last time—"the key picture of the whole trip." A general's sensitivity to commanding time and space, a theater director's obsession with the pageantry: he wouldn't allow anything but perfection for the most important entrance in his life. Another detail of timing: he chose February 17 to drop the largest one-day tonnage on South Vietnam since June of 1968, to send a message that whatever his gestures toward peace, he was still a man to be feared.

The first day, February 21: so different from six short years ago, when his overseas retinue was one retainer carrying his suitcase. The press plane landed first—eighty-seven reporters. That was so they could be in place to capture the scene: the five-hundred-soldier honor guard, in blue and olive green marching into position, and stretching from one end of the horizon to the other (singing the same ballad that inspirited the Red Army during the yearlong 4,960-mile "Long March" of 1934 by which Mao's forces survived to recoup and humiliate America by defeating Chiang Kai-shek's Nationalist forces); the vivid splashes of red from the gigantic propaganda banners (LONG LIVE THE CHINESE COMMUNIST PARTY; LONG LIVE THE GREAT SOCIETY OF ALL THE WORLD'S PEOPLE)—pictures to rival a Cecil B. DeMille biblical epic, or a moon shot. Pat's coat was bright red, too. The whole world saw it live in color. It was the coming-of-age for a ten-year-old invention, the Telstar satellite, which let these historic images be broadcast around the globe.

Yesterday's imperialist running dog strode regally down the red-carpeted stairs where Chou En-lai, the Chinese premier, stood waiting in his long blue coat. Nixon boldly thrust his hand forward first—reversing the seventeen-year-old insult when John Foster Dulles had turned his back on Chou in Geneva. Everyone was smiling broadly.

The president didn't even know then whether he'd get to meet the ailing chairman. After lunch, he was informed of the good news: Mao would receive him in his private study. Chinese cameras provided the photography: Chou, the female interpreter Tang Wensheng, Mao, Nixon, Kissinger, relaxing in a semicircle of easy chairs, the chairman's stacks and stacks of books forming the background of the shot, like the living room of some affable old college don (and, cropped out of the picture at Nixon and Kissinger's request, State Department ally Winston Lord).

The pictures evidenced a truth—and not just that State was being cut out of the negotiations for the trip's final joint communiqué. Chairman Mao, whom Nixon flattered as an intellectual and not a butcher, whose "writings moved a nation and have changed the world," and President Nixon, whom Mao shrewdly gave credit for also having written a "good book," had a nifty rapport. The chairman joshed about "secret agent" Henry Kissinger's reputation with the ladies, discoursed about his preference for dealing with right-wingers; Nixon chimed in his theory about how it took a right-winger to make the kind of peace moves that left-wingers—easier for political opponents to tar as treasonous—could only talk about. Chou graciously cleared up an international mystery: the whereabouts of unreliable left-wingers within their own regime, led by Lin Biao, who had opposed Nixon's visit, and whom the world had not seen or heard from in months. The Chinese leaders clearly now believed themselves among friends. Mao explained that they had died in a plane crash. Chou hinted that it had not been an accident. Nixon winked his solidarity. "The chairman can be sure," he said, "that whatever we discuss, nothing goes beyond this room."

The potentates disappeared into their plenary sessions in the Great Hall of the People; barred entrance, the reporters followed Pat as she bore witness via Telstar to the China where everyone smiled: while slopping the pigs at Evergreen People's Commune, at the 727-acre Summer Palace of the great Chinese emperors, at Peking Children's Hospital, where the patients cheered

Pat in her white lab coat, in the kitchen of the Peking Hotel, where one of the 150 chefs transformed a turnip into a chrysanthemum and a green pepper into a praying mantis for her delight. At the Peking Zoo she admired the pandas. At one of the sumptuous banquets she reached for a cylindrical container of cigarettes, admiring the two cuddly bears on the label. "Aren't they cute? I love them," she burbled.

"I'll give you some," Chou En-lai replied.

"Cigarettes?"

"No. Pandas."

And just like that, the National Zoo ended up with two precious and extraordinarily rare Chinese pandas.

The gift foregrounded one of the ways that what could have been a horror to the Silent Majority—*appeasing the enemy*—was domesticated into its opposite. Pat Nixon was not incidental to the project. The ERA was on the verge of passage. Republican politicians who had once lined up to support it without a thought ("Let there be freedom of choice!" Richard Nixon had responded to Dan Rather on January 2 when asked what he thought of the new coinage *Ms.*) were now learning that the notion of this simple little constitutional amendment, just twenty-four words—"Equality of rights under the law shall not be denied or abridged by the United States or by any State on account of sex"—was not going down smoothly in Middle America. The *New York Times* reported from Hope, Indiana: "last summer, a woman described as a 'radical school teacher' . . . came to speak about women's liberation to members of the all-male Lions club. . . . 'She told them that people shouldn't be judged by what's between their legs, and ever since, people around here just haven't been too serious about women's lib,'" one self-described "wife, mother, and homemaker, in that order," explained. One firebrand anticommunist organizer since the 1950s had turned her *Phyllis Schlafly Report* over to fulminating that what the ERA would bring America was more horrifying even than anything the Chinese could have in store for us: "This Amendment will absolutely and positively make women subject to the draft," her subscribers learned. It would license a man to "demand that his wife go to work to help pay for family expenses. . . . The women's libbers are radicals who are waging a total assault on the family, on marriage, and on children." Then she described the inaugural issue of Gloria Steinem's new magazine—"The principal purpose of *Ms.*'s shrill tirade is to sow seeds of discontent among happy, married women so that *all* women can be unhappy in some new sisterhood of frustrated togetherness"—and another new publication called *Women:* "68 pages of such proposals as 'The BITCH Manifesto,' which promotes the line that 'Bitch is Beautiful.' . . . Another article promotes an organization called W.I.T.C.H. (Women's International Terrorist Conspiracy from Hell), 'an action arm of Women's Liberation.' . . . Tell your Senators NOW that you want them to vote NO on the Equal Rights

Amendment. Tell your television and radio stations that you want equal time to present the case FOR marriage and motherhood."

Thus the context within which the newspaper *Chicago Today* editorialized that Pat Nixon's pageant of dutiful wifeliness expressed the true meaning of the historic trip: "Mrs. Nixon's presence in Peking and her unfailingly warm, gracious conduct are accomplishing something that official discussions, important as they are, cannot do. She is establishing direct and friendly contact with the Chinese people on a normal human level; the level where children and families and food and service and health are the most important things. As, indeed, they are."

Meanwhile the men did their work. Richard Nixon had prepared for the trip by reading the *Anti-Memoirs* of the French intellectual and statesman André Malraux, who had met with Chou and Mao during the period of the Long March (the message of Malraux's book was one America had studiously ignored: that China was fundamentally isolationist and had no particular inclination to either spur or dissuade Hanoi from war). The Chinese had prepared by watching *Patton*. During the opening banquet, which all three networks covered live for four hours, the Red Army band played "America the Beautiful," and the *Times* reviewed the occasion as "a reunion of old friends rather than the first social meeting of the leaders of two nations that have been bitterly hostile for more than two decades."

Then came the famous trip to the Great Wall. ("As we look at this wall, what is most important is that we have an open world.") Next, the unveiling of the "Shanghai Communiqué," which included a joint Sino-American card played as a warning to the Soviet Union ("Neither of the two countries should seek hegemony in the Asia-Pacific region and each is opposed to efforts by any other country or group of countries to establish such hegemony"); and a brilliantly delicate fudging of the Taiwan issue ("The United States acknowledges that all Chinese on either side of the Taiwan Strait maintain there is but one China and that Taiwan is part of China").

The public was polled: 84 percent approved. William F. Buckley, invited along to placate conservatives, thought the whole thing felt like the Nuremberg prosecutors embracing the Nazis. But other conservatives figured out ways to absolve the president of anti-anticommunist heresies. Ronald Reagan explained to a Philadelphia housewife with whom he'd been a pen pal since the 1940s, "I think the Red Chinese are a bunch of murdering bums, but in the big chess game going on, where Russia is still head man on the other side, we need a little elbow room." The next Gallup poll affirmed 83 percent of Republicans still favored Nixon's renomination—far, far better than LBJ was doing in February of 1968. Richard Nixon was euphoric. "This was the week that changed the world," he boomed in his toast on the final day, at the Shanghai Exhibition Hall.

*   *   *

The political situation back home was never far from Nixon's thoughts. The third evening, as he sat in the stands at a sports exhibition, while Bob Haldeman was admiring the advance work—one section for soldiers in green uniforms, another for soldiers in blue uniforms, one for athletes in red sweat suits, another for athletes in blue sweats, all cheering on cue for the television cameras—Chou En-lai was quietly presented a folderful of papers. He leafed through them, looked up, nodded. Henry Kissinger asked an interpreter what had just transpired. Kissinger was told that Chou had just approved the layout of the next day's *People's Daily*. Nixon replied, "I'd like to rearrange a front page now and then." And at breakfast the day before his return, Haldeman briefed Nixon on a bit of news from back home that gave him yet more reason for joy.

Reporters had begun circling Muskie like buzzards, just as they had Romney in 1967: everyone wanted to be the first guy to claim the scalp of a frontrunner. Agnew, not unconvincingly, called him "Malleable Ed": he had been "a principal defender of the Johnson administration war policies" and now was "an exponent of the 'out now at any cost' position." And on Muskie's stature-building trip to the Middle East, Russia, and Europe, the press discovered a Romney-like weakness: he responded irritably when pressed for details on his Vietnam shifts. "His caution and prudence control a very quick temper," Jules Witcover wrote his editors back home. "I think we'll see more and more of the man's caution together with increasing pressure from the press for more directness on issues and positions. If it reaches the point where it triggers his short fuse, it could be his Achilles heel." R. W. Apple of the *New York Times* hit on another weakness in a piece headlined "Muskie Campaign Still Lacks Spark": "In the long-run, many politicians across the country believe that because of the lack of deep-rooted enthusiasm for Muskie's candidacy . . . if he starts slipping, he will slip rapidly."

The polling in New Hampshire was projecting two-thirds of the vote for Muskie. But cracks in his composure started showing in the face of questions like "Senator, if you get only sixty percent of the vote in New Hampshire, will you consider that a defeat?" He lost more composure in the face of sabotage: false scheduling information kept getting out to the public. Then William Loeb of the *Manchester Union Leader,* always eager to destroy a liberal, reproduced on his February 24 front page a handwritten, semiliterate letter from someone named Paul Morrison, who said he had met Muskie in Florida and asked how he could understand the problems of black people given the few minorities in Maine. A Muskie aide, the letter related, responded that they *did* have minorities in Maine: "Not blacks, but we have Canucks"—at which Muskie was reported to have laughed appreciatively.

Canucks, also prevalent in New Hampshire, were French Canadians. Muskie thought of them, evidently, as New England's niggers.

The next day a lacerating front-page editorial in the *Union Leader* relayed a *Newsweek* gossip item that feisty Jane Muskie had challenged the press bus to a round of dirty jokes, and preferred not one but two cocktails before dinner.

Muskie had had enough. He arranged for a flatbed truck to serve as his stage for a speech in front of the *Union Leader*'s redbrick headquarters. At breakfast in their guesthouse in China, Haldeman related to the president what happened next. Snow was streaming down and Muskie was bundled in an overcoat as he picked up a handheld microphone, cameras rolling, determined to prove who was tough:

"By attacking me, and by attacking my wife, he's proven himself a gutless coward. It's fortunate for him that he's not on this platform beside me . . ."

He paused, looked down; he seemed choked up. Perhaps it was a snowflake lodged in his eye, but Dan Rather on CBS, for one, reported he "began to weep." David Broder put it in his lead that he said it with "[t]ears streaming down his cheeks." It became a major news story.

Muskie, forced back on his heels, reluctantly agreed to join a full-dress television debate between all the Democratic candidates (even the "rat" candidate, Edward T. Coll). Richard Nixon showed more than a casual interest in the news. It was evidence his campaign plan to get the Democrats to scratching each other's eyeballs out was bearing fruit.

A White House staffer, not "Paul Morrison," had written the "Canuck" letter. A man on the White House payroll had hired and supervised the black picketers who greeted Muskie at his Florida hotel. His name was Donald Segretti, and he had also secured a spy to get hired as a Muskie campaign driver—which was how Evans and Novak got the secret memo on Muskie's California property-tax hearings. The director of the Youth for Nixon unit of the Committee to Re-Elect the President, Kenneth Rietz, received stolen Muskie documents on Washington street corners from a contact known as "Fat Jack." Jeb Magruder, the deputy director of the Committee to Re-Elect the President, ran another, entirely separate dirty tricks team. Thus all the fake leaflets, stink bombs, stickers, and press releases claiming unlawful use of government typewriters that were driving the Democratic campaigns insane.

Richard Nixon wasn't exactly their architect. He was more their inspiration and goad. Segretti had been recruited by the man in closest physical proximity to the president, Dwight L. Chapin—his personal aide, or "body man." A former junior executive at Haldeman's old advertising firm, he got together with another Haldeman protégé, Gordon Strachan, to effectuate the demands Nixon was always grunting to sabotage Democrats. ("Now, get a massive mailing in Florida that's he's against J. Edgar Hoover, a massive mailing that he's for busing"; "Put this down: I would say, a postcard mailing to all Democrats in New Hampshire . . . Write in Ted Kennedy.") They called such false-flag black operations "ratfucks"—the term of art of right-wing student politics at USC, of which both Chapin and Strachan were alumni— and they hit on Don Segretti, whose campaign for student senate they had worked on, as the man for the job. Chapin arranged for Segretti to meet with Herbert Kalmbach, who finalized a $16,000 salary for him from one of his slush funds.

Segretti started off on the wrong foot. A former army lawyer, he began reaching out to fellow attorneys he'd known in the Judge Advocate General's Corps to staff his team. He wanted lawyers, he would tell them, because he didn't want to *exactly* break the law. He'd asked his friend Captain Thomas Wallace, a military judge from Mississippi, if he wanted to infiltrate the George Wallace campaign. Captain Wallace, alas, wasn't interested—and neither were any of the other JAG veterans.

Segretti turned to more willing recruits: fellow veterans of conservative campus politics. Political dirty tricks were the bread and meat of the young conservative movement that organized in the early sixties around *National Review* and the Goldwater for President crusade. Young Americans for Freedom, Tom Charles Huston's old outfit, for instance, set up camp in a hotel for the 1961 conference of the National Student Association with a mimeograph machine, walkie-talkies, and a bevy of secret operatives who pretended to be strangers but identified themselves to one another by wearing suspenders—all funded with the help of Bill Rusher, *National Review*'s publisher and another former army intelligence officer—and took over the resolutions committee via a phony "middle-of-the-road caucus." The Young Republican National Federation was shot through with so much chicanery that its 1963 convention turned into a chair-throwing brawl. College Republicans put on elections more rank than banana republics: here was where young operatives learned the black art of setting up "rotten boroughs"—fake chapters—in order to control the national conventions.

Then they brought their skills to the grown-ups' game. One especially nasty operator was loaned by the College Republicans to the campaign to defeat the Democratic candidate for state treasurer in Illinois in 1970, Al Dixon. Dixon was having a formal reception to open his Chicago headquarters. This kid assumed an alias, volunteered for the campaign, stole the candidate's stationery, and distributed a thousand fake invitations—they promised "free beer, free food, girls and a good time for nothing"—at communes, rock concerts, and street corners where Chicago's drunken hoboes congregated. The kid's name was Karl Rove. The RNC soon hired him at $9,200 a year to give seminars on his techniques.

Segretti, Chapin, or Strachan would get a name of some potential recruit. Segretti would call under his alias, Donald Simmons. They would meet at an airport or motel lounge. In Tampa, Segretti hooked up with the former chairman of the Young Republican Club of Hillsborough County, Robert Benz.

Segretti explained they were looking for veteran tricksters to "screw up" the Democratic campaigns in the Florida primary for fun and profit. Benz in turn recruited a girl named Peg Griffin. She infiltrated the Muskie office. Another got herself ensconced inside the Scoop Jackson campaign. The memos they stole made their way to the White House.

Jeb Magruder's team's chief operative, Herbert Porter, was the White House scheduling director. One of Porter's masterpieces was hiring a young aide, Roger Stone, to contribute $200 to Pete McCloskey in the name of the militant homosexual group the Gay Liberation Front and forward the receipt to William Loeb (though Stone, ashamed of any imprecations against his masculinity, chickened out and made the contribution from the Young Socialist Alliance instead).

Muskie ducked in on Oregon and California, scene of early June primaries. Ratfuckers slipped his pilot a bogus schedule; he landed in the wrong city; Muskie's entire day was shot. A letter over the forged signature of a McCarthy aide, meanwhile, urged his backers to fall in behind Hubert Humphrey.

The president took in news of these exploits enthusiastically, ravening for more: "Haldeman's fellows have certainly got a source in the Muskie office," he would gloat. "I'm sending you down a copy of a memo they stole." Here was a major component of his grand strategy for 1972—beyond, that is, acting presidential at overseas summits: divide the opposition. All Republicans still bore scars from 1964. They had seen how their candidate's general election campaign was sunk by the infighting of the rival Republican factions from the primary season. That same eyeball-scratching disarray was what they had to engineer in the Democrats. The survival of civilization depended on it.

The most important caper sprang from the president: getting George Wallace to run as a Democrat.

"I don't want him in," he had told Mitchell and Haldeman in February of 1971. "We should work this out." What he didn't want was Wallace in the *general* election. If Nixon had won all the antiliberal votes that went to Wallace in 1968, he would have won a punishing landslide instead of a squeaker. He wanted Wallace in the *primaries*—to divide the Democrats.

It's hard to reconstruct exactly the steps that led George Wallace to his January announcement in Tallahassee that he was running for the Democratic nomination. He had been on a flight with several other Southern governors and the president from Key Biscayne to Alabama in the summer of 1971; Wallace and Richard Nixon looked suspiciously buddy-buddy after the plane touched down. A few days later Wallace drawled casually to his chief field operator Tom Turnipseed, to Turnipseed's surprise, "I'm tired of those kooks in the third-party business. I'm thinking of going back into the

Democratic Party." Three months later, Evans and Novak noticed, the grand jury investigating tax-fraud charges against Wallace's brother Gerald was mysteriously dissolved. Then in November 1971 the Justice Department's civil rights division announced, suddenly and improbably, that Alabama's civil rights enforcement plan "is a much better plan than many states'."

On January 2, 1972, when Dan Rather asked the president whether George Wallace's apparent preparations for another presidential campaign were "a threat to holding this country together," Nixon responded with a hint of a grin that Wallace "is not our problem"—he was the Democrats'. That was a gaffe; George Wallace had not yet announced he was running as a Democrat. The press, fortuitously, didn't notice this—nor another phase of the operation unfolding out in California. John Mitchell funneled $10,000 to a disillusioned Wallace supporter, working under a cover group called the Committee Against Forced Busing, who deployed American Nazi Party members to canvass members of Wallace's old American Independent Party to convince them to change their registration to Democrat, ostensibly so they could vote for Wallace in the California Democratic primary—but actually to make sure the AIP voter rolls fell below the number that would allow them to run Wallace on the general election ballot.

Wallace would screw the Democrats, Nixon hoped. But he wouldn't be in the race long enough to screw him.

And so in the middle of March 1972, the Nixon team reaped what they had sown: the Democratic Party's pristine new candidate-selection process, the result of the McGovern Commission's recommendations in *Mandate for Change,* which was supposed to deliver whomever the people in their unsullied wisdom should choose as their nominee, was badly distorted by Nixonian sabotage.

New Hampshire was March 7; as Election Day approached, people started complaining about getting calls in the middle of the night from a "Harlem for Muskie Committee." (Muskie's enraged campaign manager, Berl Bernhard, called McGovern's political director, Frank Mankiewicz, and demanded that they stop; Mankiewicz, enraged, asked Bernhard what the hell he was talking about.) Muskie, the man who'd weeks before been the most popular Democrat in America—outside the noncandidate Ted Kennedy—ended up with 46 percent in New Hampshire instead of the predicted 65.

The beneficiary turned out to be George McGovern, whose strategists had risked a campaign in New Hampshire on the outside hope that the same country charm that won over South Dakota farmers would work on the flinty New Englanders. He got 37 percent. Partisans of the New Politics claimed it only proved their point about what the public wanted: it was McGovern's "straight, decent, honorable answers" that won him a chunk of

New Hampshire's heart. What they didn't know was that the White House had provided them an assist: McGovern's was the only viable campaign they didn't sabotage, because they thought he'd be easiest to beat in November.

No one knew what Florida Democrats wanted; the appeals there were a confused mess. John Lindsay ran commercials starring Carroll O'Connor imploring Floridians "to vote your hopes, not your fears." Then, sticking a cigar in his mouth, he added in Archie Bunker's voice, "Ya know what I mean, stick with me as part of the Lindsay contingency." (What the point was supposed to be, no one was sure.) Hubert Humphrey's radio ads announced that "the people's Democrat . . . will stop the flow of your tax dollars to lazy welfare chiselers. He will put your tax dollars to work here at home before giving handouts around the world." Muskie whistle-stopped in a red, white, and blue train alongside "Muskie Girls" in bunny-style suits and buttons reading TRUST MUSKIE and BELIEVE MUSKIE and MUSKIE TALKS STRAIGHT. Rosey Grier, the former L.A. Rams star—famous for tackling Sirhan Sirhan after he shot Robert F. Kennedy—was there to add a Kennedyesque touch, or something. When the train pulled in, Grier sang the campaign theme song, "Let the Sun Shine In," from the up-with-hippies musical *Hair.* Muskie's publicity man told a magazine reporter he wished he were working for Ted Kennedy and speculated whether Lindsay wasn't now the Kennedy surrogate.

Florida was also a shrieking nest of mutual recrimination. On "Citizens for Muskie" letterhead, the Nixon operatives sent out letters addressed to "Dear Fellow Democrats" (the same salutation Nixon's campaign used in 1962 when it apprised potential voters that Pat Brown was under the thumb of a left-wing organization that had adopted the "entire platform of the Communist Party"). The Florida letter read, "We on Senator Ed Muskie's staff sincerely hope you have decided upon Senator Muskie as your choice. . . . However, if you have not made your decision, you should be aware of several facts." These included that Henry Jackson had sired an illegitimate daughter in high school and had twice been arrested for homosexual activity in Washington, D.C., and that Hubert Humphrey had been arrested for drunk driving in the company of a "known call girl" generously provided him by a lumber lobbyist.

Another letter on McCarthy stationery asked his supporters to ignore his name on the ballot and cast their votes for Humphrey. Actual rats scuttled through a Muskie press conference; ribbons tied to their tails read, "Muskie is a rat fink." On telephone poles, Segretti's elves posted giant signs, attributed to a "Mothers Backing Muskie Committee," reading HELP MUSKIE SUPPORT BUSING MORE CHILDREN NOW. A Miami newspaper ad implied Muskie was a big fan of Castro's. Democratic millionaires got a letter on Muskie stationery asking them *not* to donate: Muskie wanted small donors, not "the usual fat cats."

All was confusion, all was hate—just as Nixon wanted it. The Florida returns told the story of a Democratic Party about as united as the American republic in 1863. George Wallace got 42 percent, giving him three-quarters of Florida's eighty-one convention delegates. Humphrey got 18.5 percent, Jackson 12.5. Poor Muskie, the rat-fink child-buser, got 9.

As for John Lindsay, he had practically moved there—going so far as to don a scuba suit to plumb Biscayne Bay to show his concern about pollution. "As Gene McCarthy made America face the war in 1968, Lindsay now details the battles destroying its cities" ran a timely *Saturday Review* cover profile, "The Sun-Kissed Lindsay." "The switch is on to Lindsay" was his campaign slogan. It wasn't. He pulled in 7 percent, only three points more than his fellow New Yorker Shirley Chisholm. George McGovern didn't campaign in Florida and got 6. Three-quarters of Florida voted for the anti-busing referendum despite a massive campaign against it by Florida's Democratic governor, Reubin Askew.

It was hard to say these days what being "Democratic" even meant, now that the leading presidential contender was a governor who had made his political fortune forcing presidents to send out soldiers to get him to follow civil rights laws other Democrats claimed as the party's proudest legacy. Richard Nixon, whose fear of any further irritation from intraparty challenges was vitiated by his 87 percent of the primary vote among Florida Republicans, immediately revised his previous judgment about deferring to the courts on school integration. He spoke to the nation—on St. Patrick's Day—proposing a statutory moratorium on court-ordered busing. Wallace, thrilled, took it as a gauntlet, sending Nixon an open letter: "You have taken a stand against forced busing, but a position against busing is not enough. You can put an end to forced busing by an executive order without undue delay. Your stated opposition to forced busing has fallen on deaf ears in the Departments of Justice and Health, Education and Welfare."

Once more, some New Politics strategists—such as McGovern hotshot Pat Caddell, who ran his own polling firm out of Cambridge, where he was a senior at Harvard—read the Wallace results as vindication. The strong showing for the Alabaman who campaigned against the "pointy-headed bureaucrats in Washington" was taken as a sign of an embittered, cynical, and resentful electorate ready to back any candidate who could credibly pledge to tear down the ossified old Establishment. It would prove a questionable judgment.

CHAPTER THIRTY-ONE

The Spring Offensive

DONALD SEGRETTI AND JEB STUART MAGRUDER ORDERED THEIR legions forth into the next battles: Wisconsin, on April 4; Pennsylvania, April 25; Indiana, May 2; Oregon, May 23; California, June 6. In Milwaukee, where every serious candidate was pushing hard in the state where David had felled Goliath in 1968, Muskie supporters stopped showing up for campaign events: too often, the candidate arrived late or not at all. Deliverymen and limousines kept on arriving at the senator's hotel claiming to have been summoned by "George Mitchell"—one of Muskie's close advisers. The staff would then waste precious time arguing with some poor schlub that they hadn't *ordered* several dozen flowers, fifty pizzas, or two limousines at the last minute. Then they'd waste more time arguing over which campaign was working to sabotage them. By then, the whole day would be shot. (The Humphrey campaign had been able to undo a ratfuck at the last minute by getting a notice into the Saturday *Milwaukee Sentinel* saying there would be no free lunch that afternoon with the candidate and Lorne Greene of *Bonanza*, as advertised in a flyer circulated in the ghetto.)

Ratfucking took money—and drained money away from throwing a proper national party convention. The 1972 Republican meeting was to take place in San Diego: a nice, quiet, conservative Southern California city, nearby to the president's San Clemente retreat. But the city fathers had not cooperated, and the business community wasn't ponying up.

So the White House approached an angel.

The multinational conglomerate International Telephone & Telegraph had acquired three companies in 1969 in a deal bureaucrats in the Justice Department worried fell afoul of antitrust laws. Thus it was that in the middle of 1971 an ITT lobbyist named Dita Beard convened a lollapalooza negotiating session whose principals included John Mitchell, Maurice Stans, John Ehrlichman, Chuck Colson, Bud Krogh, and Vice President Agnew. The upshot: ITT promised $400,000 in donations to help stage the San Diego convention. Mitchell would protect the merger.

The deal created more problems than it solved. As the Florida campaigning entered the home stretch, columnist Jack Anderson published a 1971 memo in which Dita Beard exclaimed to her boss that their "noble commitment has gone a long way." The memo also included the observation, "Certainly the President has told Mitchell to see that things are worked out fairly." Its famous last words: "Please destroy this, huh?" Beard's boss didn't.

The reference to the president and attorney general of the United States—now Richard Nixon's campaign manager—as direct parties to a bribe was more than a little embarrassing. So Howard Hunt was sent to cajole Beard into claiming she'd never written such a memo.

"Who exactly do you represent?" Dita Beard's daughter asked of the red-headed stranger who appeared on her doorstep.

"High Washington levels who are interested in your mother's welfare," he replied.

Beard's public recantation clamped the lid on what Nixon feared was the biggest threat to his reelection so far. Convention plans were shifted to the island city of Miami Beach: same palm trees and ocean vistas, with the added advantage of placating the networks, which would be able to keep their equipment in place from the Democrats' convention in July.

Still and all, through spring, the ITT lid threatened to blow.

Which was why G. Gordon Liddy and Howard Hunt brainstormed their own solution to the problem. Liddy no longer worked in the White House. Like Mitchell, and also former commerce secretary Maurice Stans and former White House assistant Jeb Stuart Magruder, Liddy had been promoted to a more important job, with the Committee to Re-Elect the President, John Mitchell, chairman. (Harry Dent had wanted Magruder's job but Bob Haldeman thought him "too much of a boy scout": he refused dirty-tricks assignments.) Magruder was the committee's deputy director; Stans its treasurer; Liddy "general counsel." And what the general counsel suggested, at a meeting with Hunt and a physician who once specialized in nondetectable "accidents" for the CIA, was that Jack Anderson be assassinated—a car crash, perhaps, or a drugging; or, Liddy suggested, Anderson could "just become a fatal victim of the notorious Washington street-crime rate." Their consultation completed, Liddy pulled out a $100 bill from Committee to Re-Elect the President funds to pay the good doctor for his time.

Liddy carried $100 bills everywhere for such purposes; he was something of a sink for campaign cash. When Mitchell was still running the Justice Department, Liddy met with Magruder and John Dean in the attorney general's office. He came loaded down with easels and flip-charts, like an advertising account executive pitching a campaign for a new national brand, and presented his plan to keep the Democrats out of the White House.

It was called GEMSTONE, he explained. Operation DIAMOND would field a *Nacht und Nebel* sabotage team ("night and fog," Liddy said, translating from the German; the men would have Mafia experience, he explained, warning, "Like top professionals everywhere, they don't come cheap"). RUBY would tail the Democratic contenders. COAL would push Shirley Chisholm for the nomination, EMERALD would eavesdrop on the Democrats' campaign planes and buses, QUARTZ intercept telephone traffic, CRYSTAL float a barge off Miami Beach that would serve a double purpose: as electronic surveillance headquarters and a bordello to lure Democratic luminaries for blackmailable sex. GARNET was a plan for dirty hippies to stink up Democratic banquets. There were also Operations OPAL I, OPAL II, OPAL III, OPAL IV, and TOPAZ.

He saved Operation TURQUOISE—Cuban commando teams slipping by night into the Miami Convention Center during the Democratic convention to sabotage the air conditioners, engulfing the hall in 110-degree heat—for last. John Mitchell smiled at that one. What he did not do was order the man who had just marched into the office of the attorney general of the United States to outline a massive criminal conspiracy arrested on the spot. When Mitchell heard Liddy's proposed budget—a million dollars—he just asked him to come back with a cheaper plan.

"And, Gordon? Burn those charts. Do it personally."

Liddy got it down to a bare-bones $250,000, which would require untraceable cash. The campaign itself, the traditional part, would cost hardly anything: it would consist mostly of the president acting presidential. But the Republicans still had to pay for their convention. They still had to set up campaign committees and local organizations, pay for their ad buys and literature. Magruder and Segretti's ratfucking operations soaked up a budget of $100,000. Running a campaign plane and a press plane for Agnew would cost $171,088 a month for rental, $35,000 for modifications, $683 per liftoff, $325 per hour in the air, six cents a mile per passenger for insurance, plus the 8 percent transportation tax.

Saving civilization from the Democrats would be expensive.

And you couldn't exactly, in the wake of ITT, do it by approaching respectable Republican businessmen and asking them to cough up checks to finance ratfucks and prostitutes.

Which was where the man who had learned about business at a sausage-casings factory in Chicago in the 1930s came in: Maurice Stans. "Ethics in the sausage casings business were not very high," he would later write in his memoirs. Neither were they at the Committee to Re-Elect the President.

Shakedowns had previously been Herbert Kalmbach's job. In October of 1971, for example, the president's personal lawyer approached the chairman of American Airlines at a dinner and asked him to kick in $100,000. The chairman said he might be able to come up with $75,000. Kalmbach told him he couldn't be sure of the consequences with the Federal Aviation Administration should the full $100,000 not be forthcoming. And so it was. Such corporate contributions were illegal. Companies maintained slush funds to wash the money.

But by the time Stans came on board the old schemes were set to become obsolete. On January 19, the House voted final passage of the Federal Elections Campaign Act, 334–19. It required the amounts of political contributions of more than $100 to be reported; previously only the contributor had to be listed. Nixon signed it with a flourish: "By giving the American public full access to the facts of political financing, this legislation will guard against campaign abuses and will work to build public confidence in the integrity of the electoral process." He intended to follow its letter, and pound its spirit into bloody submission.

The law would go in effect on April 7. A shakedown frenzy preceded that deadline. It worked, for instance, like this. Gulf Chemical sent $100,000 to the corporate account of a Mexican subsidiary, made out as a "legal fee." A Mexican attorney then converted the money into four checks, payable to himself. He cashed them at a bank, then packed the bills into suitcases. It was flown in a plane belonging to Pennzoil and delivered to the office of Hugh Sloan, the Committee to Re-Elect the President's accountant.

A half dozen "pickup men" wandered the nation over those two months; the take was an estimated $20 million. During one two-day period $6 million passed through Hugh Sloan's hands. Hints of the backroom orgy seeped out to reporters. "Mr. President," one reporter asked at a March 24 afternoon press conference, "will you give us your views on the general proposition of large political contributions either by corporations or individuals in terms of possibly getting something back for it?"

"Nobody gets anything back," Richard Nixon replied. "As a matter of fact, I think some of our major complaints have been that many of our businesspeople have not received the consideration that perhaps they thought that an administration that was supposed to be business-oriented would provide for it."

Two reporters wondered in print why this obscure L.A. lawyer Herb Kalmbach had suddenly drawn so many of the nation's largest corporations to his once-modest client list. The insolence sent the president over the edge: "They are out to *defeat* us," he rambled to Haldeman and Ziegler. "Both have spoken in the most vicious and derogatory terms of RN in the place where you really find out what these people think—the Georgetown cocktail parties. The evidence on this is absolutely conclusive. You do not need to ask me where I got it."

The Godfather opened in April: another of those allegories infiltrating movie houses about the rot that hid behind supposedly honorable institutions. It was a gangster movie of a new sort: one that proposed that successful gangsters had loving families; and that loving families, if they were successful enough, acted like gangsters. Francis Ford Coppola's masterpiece encapsulated the sort of false-front creepiness—"I believe in America" were the picture's first words—liberals had noticed in Richard Nixon since the 1950s. A button started appearing: NIXON . . . GODFATHER IN THE WHITE HOUSE.

Sweet, gentle George McGovern made himself a vanguardist for campaign finance reform: his political director, Frank Mankiewicz, announced they would get their contributions on record five weeks before the deadline and called on all other candidates to pledge the same. As Wisconsin heated up, McGovern pointed out that only Nixon, Jackson, and Lindsay hadn't done so. "Muskie has been working on getting endorsements from the top down," McGovern said. "I have been getting them from the bottom up." Of John Lindsay, he said, "A handful of corporate leaders were bankrolling his campaign." Explained a campaign aide, "It's the populism of the prairies against the populism of Park Avenue." McGovern's ability to raise clean money was to be one of his drawing cards, the thousands of small donations he was getting proof of his appeal at the "grass roots," his long-shot bid's fetish phrase.

His grassroots financing was, indeed, impressive. A young civil rights lawyer and son of an Alabama dirt farmer named Morris Dees had fallen in love with McGovern after hearing him speak in 1970. Dees was a millionaire in the relatively new business of "direct mail." He'd been an innovator in the field since college, when he began a business to deliver cakes to kids on their birthdays, exploiting a list he had procured of University of Alabama parents as his secret weapon. "The lists" were everything in the direct-mail business. He saw no reason political fund-raising should be different. George McGovern didn't need convincing. In his 1968 Senate race he had tried and failed to hire the king of political direct mail: conservative Richard Viguerie. Dees's first letter for McGovern, early in 1971, got an astonishing 15 percent response rate. Next he signed up three thousand members for a McGovern "Presidential Club," each of whom pledged monthly contributions; the default rate was a mere 7 percent.

"Gut mail," a staffer called their appeals. Nothing canned—that was what George McGovern was selling. It was why he announced his candidacy in the first month of 1971, and in Sioux Falls instead of Washington: leave it to the old pols to make their ritualistic disavowals of candidacy until the most strategically opportune moment. Muskie had been losing in part because he was so mumble-mouthed. McGovern would win by being forthright. His conviction that an untapped majority existed for plain-speaking ideological honesty started reminding observers of Barry Goldwater. "I will not change my beliefs to win votes," the conservative had said in announcing his own candidacy in 1964—in Phoenix instead of in Washington. "I will offer a choice, not an echo." McGovern said much the same.

That wasn't the only thing that reminded people of Goldwater: like him, McGovern didn't behave like a candidate who wanted to win. Others avoided the thorny issue of amnesty for draft dodgers; McGovern sallied forth at Keene State College in New Hampshire and said the evils of the war itself had already vindicated them. (Eleanor McGovern, pointing out that only 20 percent of the country agreed, pleaded with her husband to make amnesty contingent on performing alternative service. He stuck to his guns. Sticking to his guns was what he was running on.) In Florida he came out for busing as "one of the prices we are paying for a century of segregation in housing patterns"—and against the space shuttle program, Central Florida's great hope for economic recovery. He toured Chicago without the blessing of Mayor Daley, an unheard of slight—and then, at the state capitol in Springfield, announced that his delegate slates for the March 21 Illinois primary had to be scrapped and re-formed because they didn't meet the McGovern Commission's guidelines for gender balance. He was too good for his own good.

But then maybe this was what it would take for Democrats to win in 1972. The Godfather was in the White House. The old ways no longer seemed to hold purchase. In January, DNC chair O'Brien had put on a good old-fashioned $500-a-plate fund-raising banquet to try to retire the party's debt from 1968. It felt like an old song for which everyone had forgotten the words. Humphrey didn't stay for dinner. McCarthy refused a chance at the podium. Ted Kennedy shifted in his seat, as if he had wound up in the wrong room.

Fred Dutton signed on with the McGovern campaign, along with his fellow RFK compatriot Frank Mankiewicz. Maybe what Dutton told Scotty Reston was right; maybe the emerging Democratic majority really was "'Nader populist' at heart." Front-runner Muskie was sounding more and more like McGovern, promising that Vietnam "will remain an issue for me as long as a single human being dies, not for a cause but for a mistake."

In March, after McGovern's second-place shocker in New Hampshire, two surprising developments in the heart of the Heartland helped convince prairie populists they were right.

The first was in Lordstown, Ohio. A new General Motors plant had opened in the economically suffering region. To staff it, GM followed the new industry trend of hiring younger workers: they got sick less and used up fewer benefits, an important cost hedge against onrushing Japanese competition. Meanwhile GM's new Assembly Division was radically reorganizing the production process for greater efficiency. The two developments collided in 1971, when Lordstown changed over models to Chevy's new import-style subcompact, the Vega. The line's old rate was sixty cars per hour. For Vegas, the rate was to be doubled.

The old way was to compensate for such hardships with fatter wages and benefits. Steady work, and pride in producing excellent machines, had always been blandishment enough to compensate the Vega workers' Depression-scarred parents for the monotony and alienation of factory work. But GM had not counted on the consequences of plunking a car factory full of kids down the street from Kent State.

Working-class youth were starting to think like New Leftists: identifying the meaning of life with the struggle for authenticity. Ford's labor relations chief described a "new breed of union member—a younger, more impatient, less homogeneous, more racially assertive, and less manipulable member." Absenteeism and disciplinary citations doubled. Turnover almost tripled. "Problem employees," the Ford expert said, "almost habitually violate our plant rules." He worried about "a general lowering of employees' frustration tolerance." The New Left had a word for that. They called it *alienation.*

The old-line UAW leadership pushed GM for more wages and benefits. The workers responded, in defiance of their union, by passing cars down the assembly line with parts missing. "Every day I come out of there I feel ripped off," one young worker told a radical labor union researcher. "I don't even feel useful now. . . . They could always find somebody stupider than me to do the job." The plant's various cultural factions—hillbillies, blacks, Puerto Ricans, "hippies"—united in February against a new "get-tough" policy against worker absenteeism: 97 percent voted to stop work. The *Wall Street Journal* monitored this unprecedented new "quality of life" strike obsessively, in almost the same terms as radicals. "The generation just entering the workforce," the *Journal* worried in a March 15 editorial, "The Soul Must Panic," were lashing out at "the monster of monotony." Politicians monitored the strike closely, too: here was a new kind of political demand.

The Lordstown strikers lost; the March 23 settlement answered none of their anti-monotony demands. The heralds of the New Politics took the message nonetheless: that *Greening of America* values and the emerging coalition Dutton described ("humanistic, critical of big business, big labor, and big government") were taking root in the heart of the Heartland, amid the Old Politics' supposedly sturdy labor base.

The second boost for prairie populist confidence unfolded in Pennsylvania's Susquehanna Valley. It had seemed obvious to radicals and New Politics liberals what Richard Nixon's Justice Department was up to in the trial of the Harrisburg 7. The proliferating gaggles of activists thrown in front of juries as "conspirators"—from the Harlem 4 to the Ford Hood 43—were evidence of conspiracy itself: an organized campaign of repression against anyone who dared threaten the powers that be. "The people of this country will be watching this trial," a defense statement for the Harrisburg 7 roared, "to see if men and women who have cried out to the government, 'Thou shalt not kill' will be put in jail for that."

The conspiracy attitude was easy to mock. (Did you hear the one about the Indianapolis 500? "They're innocent!" the hippie replied. "Every last one of them!"), but this prosecution was obviously Kafkaesque. A nun who taught art history at a college in upstate New York and a pacifist priest were supposed to have plotted with fellow nuns and priests and a college professor to blow up Washington and to kidnap Henry Kissinger unless their demand for an end to the war was met. "Overt Act No. 23" in the indictment was that one of the nuns moved from Baltimore to Washington.

Soon, the protest community was convinced, they would all be in prison. The *Village Voice*'s reporter in Harrisburg, Paul Cowan, had already bought a house in Canada in preparation for the final crackdown. What he saw of the jury selection convinced him it would come soon enough. Mary McGrory of the *Washington Post* columnized that the defendants had already been condemned: "They have fetched up in a locality where moral passion is considered a social error, among citizens who have either decided they are guilty or who smugly declare they were too busy to read about the whole affair." The Justice Department agreed with the radicals: it would be a piece of cake to get a jury of terrified Silent Majoritarians to sentence riffraff like this to an eternity underneath the jail, whatever the weakness of the case.

The proceedings took shape in February as doppelgänger to Judge Hoffman's in Chicago: the hulking glass federal building and sterilely modernist federal courtroom, the obsessively sequestered jury (this time they boarded up the windows of the jury bus), some of the same radical lawyers, the same sort of tough-as-nails Roman Catholic prosecution team (the lead attorney had been plucked from the Mafia beat). The defense once more welcomed the opportunity "to conduct a political trial and get the issues before the American people." A hanging judge boasted of his contempt for the Fourth Amendment: "Speak for yourself. I have nothing to hide," he answered a defense lawyer who said government surveillance "hurts all of us."

Once again, the star witness was a police spy. Boyd Douglas was a fellow inmate of Philip Berrigan's at Lewisburg Penitentiary. He had been allowed into a study-release program at nearby Bucknell University, which was how he helped Father Phil smuggle uncensored letters to Sister Elizabeth—from which they discovered Father Phil's reveries about whether the progress in ending the war would be hurt or hastened by kidnapping government officials as radicals had in Quebec. But before Douglas could take the stand, his credibility as a witness was in tatters. The prosecution accidentally released to the defense a letter he'd written to the FBI thanking them for money to buy a new car and shaking them down for some more: "Considering what I will go through before and after the trial or trials, I request a minimum reward of $50,000 tax-free." He also asked for a faked honorable discharge from the army. It didn't do much for the prosecution's claim that their star witness was a "strict Catholic" and conscience-stricken former New Leftist. Editorials compared Boyd Douglas's $50,000 request to the Nixon White House's shakedown of ITT.

Then Douglas took the witness stand. The letters he'd written to coeds were read into the record. ("I have given my life to the struggle" went one. "If I lose freedom and life to the Movement, that's the way it has to be. . . . I got warm vibrations from you." Then he invited her for a tryst.) He had to admit, too, to lying to his handlers, holding back material that might further incriminate the priest to bargain for more money. On March 15, the jury learned that an early FBI evaluation of Douglas judged him as having "many of the attributes of a confidence man."

It got worse. That same day the key informant in the Camden 28 conspiracy case filed a pretrial affidavit telling the story about how he had innocently approached the FBI in the hopes of foiling a draft board raid some of his friends were planning—and was then recruited by the FBI, trained in breaking-and-entering techniques, and instructed that under no circumstances was the raid to be suspended, because "higher-ups, someone at the Little White House in California," he was told, "wanted it to actually happen."

The next week, in Harrisburg, two weeks before the New Hampshire balloting, Boyd Douglas's FBI handler testified he had never known Douglas had been classified by a U.S. attorney as a "menace to society." The government's case was unraveling. But the government's case against the Chicago 7 had been a shambles, too. And what difference had that made in preventing conviction? This defense decided to rest without dignifying the charges with a response. The seven defendants voted on that 4–3. "It demonstrates," one of them told the press, "we can never possibly be conspirators because we can never agree"—which hadn't mattered in Chicago, either.

The jury withdrew to deliberate; the defendants steeled themselves for another Silent Majority jury nullification. An article appeared in the *Chicago Sun-Times* describing a defendant as an "ex-rapist" instead of an "ex-priest." The mortified editor sent a letter of apology—acknowledging that one of the working-class printers in the pressroom might have introduced the error as an editorial comment.

The jury deliberated a fifth day, then a sixth. One of the twelve kept pounding the table, invoking God's will, telling the story of another jury he had served on in which he had acceded to a not-guilty verdict; then God struck down the defendant with a heart attack a few days later. He demanded this bunch be jailed unanimously and immediately.

On the seventh day the jury returned a mistrial verdict. Paul Cowan of the *Village Voice* wrote of his shock: "At first, I attributed the verdict to the moral rectitude of the defendants; to the skills of their famous lawyers . . . to the sociologists' expertise. In other words, I believed that the specter of Main

Street had been neutralized by the special skills of the urban elite." But later Cowan did something remarkable. He interviewed the jurors. They said things like "How stupid did those people in Washington think they were?" They weren't, this "radical" realized, so different from him. They bore "frustration and rage" that "sat in their guts like rocks. They wished they had been able to retain the faith in the government they brought to the trial"—just as Cowan had earlier in the 1960s. "Talking to them," he concluded, "I realized that, for many Americans, democracy is a religion." He began to feel a bit of that old-time religion himself. "Sometimes it is possible to unify Americans," he realized, "in situations that call for generosity or fairness instead of dividing them into battles over physical or psychological turf."

The alienated radical sounded like the preacher's son McGovern. The lessons of Lordstown and Harrisburg seemed to suggest more and more Americans were uniting behind a New Politics message. Central Pennsylvania and central Ohio were just the kind of places McGovern was determined he could reach. He seemed to be proving it was possible: that Main Street would vote for an antiwar liberal.

The AFL-CIO revealed a poll it had taken in Wisconsin: McGovern was in the lead. It seemed the vindication not only of the new populism, but also of a year and a half's work.

The McGovern campaign had begun just after the 1970 election. Gary Hart, McGovern's campaign manager, recruited a twenty-four-year-old named Gene Pokorny off a feed-grain farm who'd been a legendary McCarthy organizer in Nebraska. By then he was contemptuous of McCarthy—for not having McGovern's hunger to win. Hart sent Pokorny to Wisconsin to make their stand in the state that had driven Lyndon Johnson from office, the home to 1920s progressive hero Fighting Bob La Follette and Tailgunner Joe McCarthy—two very different politicians whose commonality was a grassroots following contemptuous of the Washington Establishment.

Pokorny was met, seventeen months before the primary, with no little bafflement. But the jump-start was key to Hart's national strategy. By locking up the left-wing activist base early, McGovern denied it to the other New Politics aspirants. (The sentimental candidate himself, in a memo to strategists, was excited for the early start for another reason: "to have an opportunity to educate an entire nation and to learn from an entire nation over the period of the next two years. That is its own reward.") McGovern wrote ingratiating letters to anonymous activists in 1971 as assiduously as Richard Nixon had written to newspaper publishers and J. Edgar Hoover in 1965. Flattered, they gladly advanced his visits, of which McGovern kept up a wall-to-wall schedule. (The campaign always announced its events as "receptions," not "rallies," in case only a dozen showed up.) While Nixon operatives were taking meetings with ITT lobbyists and hitting up executives for $100,000 checks, Hart had field men organizing rummage sales, petition drives, and workshops on how to canvass and set up storefronts. At McGovern's Washington headquarters—it was next to the liquor store, in a neighborhood so dangerous cabbies wouldn't drive there—supporters worked through the night. Just like Nixon's Plumbers, McGovern's students were convinced they were fighting to save civilization.

Winning Wisconsin was key. They would never be able to afford to organize so thoroughly again. At Pokorny's insistence, McGovern had spent seventy-two hours in the Badger State at least once every three months, beginning early in '71. Many towns had never before seen a presidential candidate. And even on the radio, they'd rarely heard one who could speak so authoritatively and sympathetically on agriculture. ("The fact is that over the past twenty years livestock prices have remained the same while the meat marketing margins have doubled," the editor of the scholarly volume *Agricultural Thought in the 20th Century* would say; "the farmer's share of the consumer's food dollar has fallen from forty-seven cents in 1952 to thirty-eight cents today.")

A squad of professionals arrived two weeks before the balloting, bivouacking in an out-of-the-way motor lodge in Milwaukee, inheriting volunteer organizations in every one of the state's seventy-two counties, ten thousand volunteers in Milwaukee alone. In the Fourth District—the South Side of Milwaukee, where the voters were Polish just as Edmund Muskie was Polish and had beaten civil rights marchers nearly to death in 1967 and had gone for Wallace in '68 and '64—McGovern volunteers from twenty states, as young as thirteen years old, slept on the linoleum floor of a toy warehouse. Headquarters wouldn't waste bumper stickers on such inhospitable soil. The volunteers canvassed past dark all the same, in a Milwaukee "spring" when the average daytime high was thirty-four degrees. Teddy White compared them to the forces of North Vietnam's General Giap, "living off the land, tapping veins of frustration everywhere; raising money locally as they rolled . . . stirring to action hearts hitherto unstirred by politics." Timothy Crouse in *Rolling Stone* invoked "the guys who were in the hills with Castro."

It wouldn't have worked if the peasantry and proletariat weren't willing to be stirred. McGovern held a press conference in the home of a Polish family squeezed by property taxes that was featured in the *New York Times.* "You get more money but it just don't do nothing," Richard Wysocki, a car mechanic, said, gesturing thankfully to his South Dakotan protector. McGovern started dropping in on bowling alleys on league nights. "Word spread like wildfire," his earnest young traveling aide, Gordon Weil, recalled. It "turned into a triumphal tour." McGovern's favor among blue-collar voters became the key to his campaign's strategy.

George Wallace called a press conference the day after the Florida primary to announce he was coming to Milwaukee. He was armed with a poll showing he had just won 50 percent of the Democrats who had voted for Nixon in 1968 and one-third of Florida's new under-twenty-one votes: "What has happened here in Florida just makes it more clear to me—and ought to make it clear to anybody with good sense—that I am a serious candidate for the nomination." McGovern welcomed the test. He called Wallace's Florida showing "an angry cry from the guts of ordinary Americans against a system which doesn't give a damn about what's really bothering the people of this country today." Busing, he said, was merely a "symbol of all these grievances rolled into one." Wallace, Nixon, Jackson, and Humphrey were using it "to take people's minds off the problems which really concern them."

The Wednesday before the election the kind of late-season blizzard fell on southern Wisconsin that people printed up T-shirts to commemorate. Muskie was speaking, gutsily, in Kimberly, Wisconsin, a company town, for his proposal to ban the nation's biggest two hundred companies from further expansion in size (Kimberly-Clark was No. 141) and was stranded. Jackson—shifting his appeal from busing to hitting Nixon for his "elaborate machinery on wage controls, but virtually nothing on price controls," defending himself from charges his campaign was being financed illegally by Boeing executives' traveler's checks—got stuck in the sparsely inhabited north. Humphrey and Lindsay were socked in, too, and it seemed as if a sign: only McGovern plowed through to his next event. A POW's wife standing loyally by the candidate's side, he cried that "the truth is that only by ending the war can we get our prisoners of war released," that Richard Nixon's continued bombing "insures that American prisoners will remain in their cells."

The issue would become more pressing within days. South Vietnam had dodged a Tet-season attack by keeping ARVN troops in their barracks until the end of the holiday. Strategists presumed the Communists would save their final offensive for 1973, by which time many more U.S. troops would have been withdrawn. Instead, they staged a 1972 spring offensive. Some 120,000 North Vietnamese regular troops poured over the seventeenth parallel accompanied by the Communists' most intense rocket and artillery bombardment of the war. By the first day of April the entire South Vietnamese Third Division was in retreat. The next day one of its regiments stripped off their military insignia and joined the civilian refugees streaming south. The day after that another regiment bartered for their lives by turning over their artillery cannons—another spectacular failure for Vietnamization, exactly one month before American forces were scheduled to draw down to sixty-nine thousand troops.

Richard Nixon half-welcomed the news. It was, in a way, his Gulf of Tonkin incident, his excuse to move all in with the hellfire knockout punch he'd been dreaming about since planning Operation Duck Hook.

The Spring Offensive   647

The mission was christened Operation Freedom Train. The president ordered a fleet of B-52s to carpet bomb the demilitarized zone. But in Quang Tri, as in Wisconsin, foul weather clouded the skies. Air force brass told their men not to fly. So Kissinger brought in a new air force general, named him air commander, and gave him a fourth star, bypassing Admiral Moorer. Nixon delivered a Pattonesque speech to Bob Haldeman, and started bombing with savage intensity.

The bombs started falling on primary day, which the *Today* show observed with a half hour live from Milwaukee. Jackson, Wallace, and Humphrey massed in anyone-but-McGovern chorus in favor of the bombing—the government "should take whatever action is necessary to protect the remaining residual troops." Since Muskie didn't mention the matter in his segment, the president told Haldeman to get to work attacking him for showing "no concern for the POWs or the protection for the seventy thousand GIs."

Bad weather favors insurgents. At 9:40 Frank Mankiewicz announced McGovern had taken seven of Milwaukee's nine congressional districts—including the Fourth, where the residents had beaten the civil rights marchers in 1967, and the Fifth, which an organizer described as "Archie Bunker's street drawn out to infinity." McGovern called his victory a "vote of protest and hope." Reporters, having missed the story of McGovern's awesome organization, began typing phrases such as "stunning victory," and noting that the third-place finisher, Humphrey, who had the full endorsement of the state AFL-CIO and was supposed to be so beloved in the Badger State that they called him "Wisconsin's third senator," edged out Muskie, but that Muskie was edged out in turn by George Wallace. "Senator Muskie, are you finished?" a reporter asked. More or less, he was.

Senator Henry "Scoop" Jackson tied for the booby prize with the matinee-idol mayor of New York. Lindsay's press secretary lost $102, having bet his man would pull 10 percent. Lindsay only ended up with 7, and quit. George Wallace held strong in second place.

The next day McGovern people started laughing at the Establishment that had been laughing at them. His janissaries made calls to incredulous reporters claiming that despite his being in fourth place in national polls, despite his having earned only 95 of the 1,508 delegates required to win, McGovern had just about sewn it up, thanks to his strength among activists in caucus states. *Time* started planning a McGovern cover; Evans and Novak noted the emergence of an "Anybody But McGovern" movement.

Then, the day that Wisconsin helped clarify the confusing Democratic picture, the White House got to work on re-clouding it. "The P wanted to be sure that we get people to follow up on the line, that Kennedy is now the obvious Democratic candidate," Haldeman wrote in his diary. "He liked my idea of waiting a few days and then having Connally give Teddy Secret Service protection"—the Secret Service were under Connally's Department of the Treasury—"on the basis that there's general agreement that he's going to be the candidate."

On April 6, B-52 strikes pushed sixty miles farther north, accompanied by headlines like "A Big New Phase of War Is Opening." McGovern was now being called the stalking horse for Kennedy, as the Massachusetts senator gave his most lacerating antiwar speech to date: "The simple truth is that this test of Vietnamization, with or without American support, is a wholly immoral and unjustifiable test, because it is a test that is being carried out with the lives of men, women, and children. Those dead and dying bodies stretched out beside the road across our television screens last night are the bodies of human beings. We do not have the right—no one has the right—to demand a test like that."

Ten-dollar, twenty-dollar, fifty-dollar checks, with angry notes attached about ending the slaughter, started flooding McGovern headquarters. Nixon campaign headquarters, a block from the White House, was even more the maelstrom. The Federal Elections Campaign Act went into effect the next day, and the suitcases full of cash and negotiable securities were flying in in a frenzy. Rose Mary Woods scribbled out a makeshift list of all the money they were scrambling to process, to keep track of their chits. (Later that list was entered into evidence in a congressional investigation, and earned the nickname "Rose Mary's Baby.")

The next big day for the Democrats was April 25, with primaries in Massachusetts and Pennsylvania. On April 10, the president sent the B-52s another ninety miles north. He also made a carefully coded diplomatic utterance at a signing ceremony for the Biological Weapons Convention: "Every great power must follow the principle that it should not encourage directly or indirectly any other nation to use forms of armed aggression against one of its neighbors." Henry Kissinger was due in Moscow in nine days to cement the details for a presidential visit, scheduled for the last week in May—for final talks, and perhaps the signing, of a Strategic Arms Limitation Treaty, under negotiation since November of 1969. Decoded, Nixon's message meant: We've noticed that the North Vietnamese are fighting with better weapons, provided by you. *Desist,* or lose your summit, your treaty, and your chance to increase your influence with the United States to balance out your rival China's influence with the United States; *desist,* or the South Vietnamese government might fall before the U.S. presidential elections, whenceforth Richard Nixon would be very, very angry. But Russia hardly wanted to seem a pushover on the eve of a summit. The diplomatic task was complex.

Domestic politics, too, were difficult to juggle. On April 12, Nixon and Kissinger explained to the Republican congressional leadership why they were sending them into an election season while increasing the number of active B-52 bombers in the Vietnam theater from 45 to 130, ships from 22 to

40, and fighter-bombers from 150 to 275. "What the enemy seeks," said their president, "is to inflict such a defeat on the ARVN" that the government of South Vietnam would collapse and "create so much turmoil in *this* country that we will collapse. Then they will go into negotiations." The enemy attacked now, the president said, because they couldn't hold out for another year. Decoded, that meant: I am about to finish the job, and those who object will have stabbed their country in the back.

On April 16, five behemoth B-52s pounded Hanoi and North Vietnam's lifeline port, Haiphong Harbor. Fighters strafed down below. Among the casualties were four Russian ships. Nonetheless, three days later, Kissinger proceeded to Moscow without Politburo objection. The summit was on; Richard Nixon had won the diplomatic battle.

He still had a political test ahead: keeping his credibility with the public. He embarked on a series of photo ops: flying up to Ottawa, signing a Great Lakes Water Quality Agreement with Canada to mark the third annual observance of Earth Day; meeting the table tennis team from the People's Republic of China; commending the District of Columbia police for a decline in the crime rate; signing an executive order for a National Center for Housing Management. Then, the night of April 26, he went on TV to make his latest Vietnam pitch:

"Our draft calls now average fewer than five thousand men per month . . . we have offered the most generous peace terms. . . . The South Vietnamese are fighting courageously and well in their self-defense." Twenty thousand more American troops would come home by July 1. We would return to Paris to negotiate, thanks to the effectiveness of the air and naval strikes. "We are not trying to conquer North Vietnam or any other territory in the world. . . .

"That is why I say to you tonight, let us bring our men home from Vietnam; let us end the war in Vietnam. But let us end it in such a way that the younger brothers and the sons of the brave men who have fought in Vietnam will not have to fight again in some other Vietnam at some time in the future. . . .

"My fellow Americans, let us therefore unite as a nation in a firm and wise policy of real peace—not the peace of surrender, but peace with honor, not just peace in our time, but peace for generations to come. Thank you and good night."

It marked a profound chasm between the public and private transcripts. The previous day Henry Kissinger had outlined their next options: hitting power plants, docks, mining Haiphong Harbor, bombing civilians.

"I still think we ought to take the dikes out now," Nixon offered. "I think—will that drown people?"

"*Zhat* will drown about two hundred thousand people."

"Oh, well, no, no. I'd rather use a nuclear bomb. Have you got that ready?"

"*Zhat,* I think, would be too much. Too much."

"The nuclear bomb. Does that bother you? I just want you to think *big,* Henry, for Christ's sakes!"

Kissinger paused, taken aback. He collected himself, eventually responding with the one thing he knew would talk the president down from his flight of fantasy: "I think we're going to make it." Until Election Day, he probably meant; Saigon would hold on at least until then.

Democrats voted in Pennsylvania and Massachusetts. It was a split decision: the New Politics took the Bay State. The Old Politics took the Keystone State.

Massachusetts was more or less preordained: Massachusetts's plentiful antiwar Democrats had held a January caucus in which they agreed to unite behind a candidate who got more than 60 percent. McGovern, in the first public flexing of his organization's depth, did so comfortably. That he couldn't afford a campaign plane during the days of the New Hampshire primary had also helped. He would instead take commercial flights from Boston—campaigning there before boarding his campaign bus for Manchester, while Endorsement Ed soared overhead at thirty thousand feet. The tortoise won Massachusetts virtually unopposed. The next day the hare, New England's own Edmund Muskie, finally dropped out of the presidential race.

Pennsylvania was more interesting. Muskie, Wallace, and McGovern tied for second at about 21 percent. McGovern did reasonably well. The plurality, however, went to Hubert Horatio Humphrey. A story lay behind that. The Keystone State was where old-line labor, whose former commanding influence in brokering Democratic presidential nominations had been eviscerated by the reformed nominating process, staged its revenge. The AFL-CIO's president, George Meany, was a dyed-in-the-wool war supporter: "If we don't fight them there, we'll have to fight them in San Francisco," he'd said in 1965, before engineering a 2,000–6 vote against an antiwar resolution at a labor convention. Having surrendered their kingmaking role to ordinary primary voters, who were proving to be alarmingly amenable to the candidate of the antiwar hippies, old-line labor now made its move to take McGovern out. Its vehicle was old reliable Hubert Humphrey.

It had first been tried in Wisconsin. Badger State labor leaders told their memberships not to vote for McGovern because he hadn't voted to end a right-wing filibuster against an antilabor right-to-work law in 1966. This was nasty politics: actually McGovern's labor voting record was just about flawless, better than John F. Kennedy's in 1960—so good, in fact, that he feared for his reelection in 1968 in a conservative state like South Dakota. Upon which George Meany, like some labor pope, had granted McGovern an absolution to vote against right-to-work in 1966. In 1971, Meany had explicitly signed off on McGovern as an acceptable Democratic nominee. Now, in

1972, the pope ordered his Wisconsin bishops to use that vote to call McGovern a traitor to labor, and turn out their machine for Humphrey. They had been no match for McGovern's Badger State army. But McGovern had no army in Pennsylvania: he had spent all his forces in Wisconsin. But Big Labor always had an army at the ready.

Pennsylvania was Humphrey's first primary win in three presidential campaigns. Muskie and Jackson had been rebuked by the voters. Evans and Novak were reporting that any chances Ted Kennedy would enter the race were done for good. That left anybody-but-McGovern with a name and a face. A smiling, exuberant face. Which was the soul of the divided Democrats' misfortune in the spring of 1972: Hubert Humphrey personified, for New Politics voters, the forces who'd stood by when kids were beat up in the streets of Chicago in 1968. At the University of Pennsylvania he was heckled as "America's number two war criminal." As he strolled down Chestnut Street in Philadelphia, a long-haired youth screamed in his face, "I don't see how you can smile when all these bombs are dropping on innocent civilians in Vietnam! You have *no right* to smile!" The nomination had come down to this: the purest possible "Old Politics versus New Politics" show-down. A Democratic civil war.

The neatness of the Democrats' divisions was almost . . . suspicious. "The only logical explanation of the Democratic Presidential campaign so far," Scotty Reston wrote in his *New York Times* column at the end of April, "is that it must have been planned by the Republicans." Little did he know his joke was literally true. The White House was delighted at George McGovern's ascendancy; he was the one serious contender they never rat-fucked. They loved the combustion between the kind of people who loved Humphrey and the kind of people who liked McGovern; they themselves had helped set the fuse.

"The sudden surge in Senator Hubert Humphrey's prospects for another bout with Richard M. Nixon," Evans and Novak wrote in their April 27 column, the day after the Massachusetts and Pennsylvania primaries, "is more the product of Senator George McGovern's spectacular landslide in Massachusetts." Despite his apparent success in the bowling alleys of Beer Town, he'd only won 10 percent of the blue-collar wards in the Bay State. "McGovern is now being taken with infinitely more seriousness," the columnizing duo wrote. "Since Wisconsin, his eager and talented volunteers have flooded precinct conventions in such non-primary states as Kansas, Missouri, Vermont, and Idaho to ambush the regulars." And now those regulars "fear McGovern as the Democratic Party's Barry Goldwater."

They were ready now to fight back—for instance, by wielding not-for-attribution quotes like daggers in Evans and Novak columns.

One "liberal senator, whose voting record differs little from McGovern's,"

they wrote, "feels McGovern's surging popularity depends on public ignorance of his acknowledged public positions. 'The people don't know
McGovern is for amnesty, abortion, and legalization of pot,' he told us. 'Once
Middle America—Catholic Middle America, in particular—finds this out,
he's dead.'"

The phraseology was repeated almost identically by Scotty Reston three
days later: "George McGovern has run an intelligent and determined campaign and has now got to the top of the greasy pole, but with a heavy load of
promises: to slash the defense budget steeply, legalize pot and abortion, and
grant amnesty to the Vietnam expatriates. Selling this to George Meany and
the labor organization, which is about the only effective political organization the Democrats have, will not be easy, and it will not be very popular
with many other Democratic candidates who think pot, abortion, and
amnesty are explosively dangerous issues."

The formulation was about one-half libel. Some prominent figures in
American public life did indeed favor "legalization of pot"; they included
William F. Buckley. But that wasn't McGovern's position. His agreed with
the recommendation of the President's National Commission on Marijuana
and Drug Abuse: "decriminalization," or lessening penalties, because
statutes that defined at least 20 million Americans as criminals created "a
crushing burden for law enforcement agencies." He favored prioritizing in
its place $1.5 billion for treatment of addiction to drugs such as heroin—not
far off from a program the Nixon administration actually initiated (Nixon
hoped it would help them announce reduced crime rates in time for the presidential election). "Legalize abortion"? McGovern was actively hostile to it,
to his feminist supporters' chagrin: "You can't just let anybody walk in and
request an abortion," he told *Time*. Pat Nixon, in one of her rare press conferences, noted, "I really am not for abortion . . . on demand—wholesale,"
adding that this was a question "for the individual states, not as a national
issue." Which was precisely McGovern's position.

But the invention that McGovern was pushing abortion and drug legalization took hold. The story contained a certain poetic truth: not about the
policy issues specifically, but about the nation's polarization. The Chicago 7
trial had been a microcosm of that polarization, and McGovern had pleaded
with Mayor Daley to dismiss the case. It was something hardheaded
observers grasped better than either McGovern strategists in their twenties
or the middle-aged men that worshipped "youth": that success built by locking up the left-wing youth-activist base might bear seeds of future defeat.
McGovernites had discounted the signs.

Like the man on the South Side of Milwaukee who, asked by the young
canvasser what he thought of McGovern, said, "I'd vote for him if he'd turn
Christian." Or the Milwaukeean who answered the same question, long
before Evans and Novak's prompt (perhaps he'd heard it from his union),

"McGovern? He's for dope." He wasn't. But his canvassers were. Four years earlier young Eugene McCarthy workers bunked segregated by sex and voluntarily banned alcohol. That wouldn't fly now. "Jesus, we won the fucking city of Fond du Lac with thirty high school kids, three-fourths of whom are drug freaks," a Dartmouth grad proudly told *Rolling Stone*—whose political reporter, Hunter S. Thompson, was a proud drug freak, too.

On April 23, "in a spontaneous act of love for his honesty and Vietnam stand," the Yippies endorsed George McGovern. Once they became convinced that Abbie Hoffman and Jerry Rubin weren't out to sabotage McGovern and elect Humphrey in order to heighten the revolutionary contradictions, the McGovern team welcomed their help to register new under-twenty-one voters. A twenty-eight-year-old McGovern strategist set up a meeting with Abbie and Jerry in Washington. It fit their campaign theme: "McGovern can unite the country from a steelworker in Gary, Indiana, to a Yippie in Boston."

The campaign team was hoping to channel the anti-Establishment energy they believed was driving voters to Wallace. They turned a blind eye to the Wallaceites who identified McGovernites with the Establishment they were insurging against. They ignored the extent to which Evans and Novak were *right*—that if these voters got to know McGovern better, they might like him less. Like the fellow who eagerly shook the hand of George McGovern at the U.S. Envelope factory in Massachusetts. He explained to a reporter, "We feel the colored element is just getting way too much welfare, and McGovern might just be tough enough to crack down."

Instead McGovernites pointed to Nixon's escalation of the bombing in the face of an obviously war-weary public. But Evans and Novak reported something else in that April 27 column: that according to White House pollster Albert Sindlinger, the number who wanted to "go all out to win" the war rose from 23.3 percent to 29.7 percent after the Communists began their latest offensive, then another two points after Nixon started bombing. Those willing to "admit defeat and give up" hung steady at about 20 percent. Those agreeing "President Nixon is doing all he can to settle the war"—at a low of 46.8 percent after Cambodia—was now at 63.3 percent.

"Is this Wallace Country?" the emcee cried in a field house in Indiana, which had its primary the first Tuesday in May, along with Tennessee and Ohio.

"Yes!!!"

"I can't hear you. Is this Wallace Country?"

"*YES!!!!*"

The emcee introduced Billy Grammer and the Travel On Boys of the Grand Ole Opry. George Wallace's eleven-year-old daughter was introduced; then his thirty-year-old second wife. Then the man himself stepped behind his special bulletproof podium, covered in red, white, and blue bunting.

He sported more fashionable suits than in 1968, and more fashionable rhetoric: nothing about shooting rioters through the head or running down protesters with limousines. The racism was only between the lines—such as in his proposals to make child abandonment a crime to decrease the welfare rolls, and to reconfirm Supreme Court justices every six or eight years. His main appeal was "tax relief to stimulate consumer spending and bring more employment," and "a twelve-hundred-dollar tax credit for every working person and dependent." He said he was a populist, working for an America where "the average men are the kings and the average women are the queens." He said he had been all along—"and now they are taking the same stand. What does that make them? It makes them copycats."

Across the border the chief copycat was Scoop Jackson, campaigning full-time in Ohio for one final desperate last stand. He didn't have a single elected delegate. The *Washington Post* featured him on May 1 as a curiosity who threw parties where no one showed up. He called himself a "progressive Democrat"—and hit every burg with a military base, saying it would become a ghost town if George McGovern became president, scowlingly pointing out that the South Dakotan was supported by Jerry Rubin and Abbie Hoffman. His aides, who'd thought of him as a conciliatory figure, cringed in embarrassment. He defended himself to the *Post:* "I'm not trying to get into a McCarthy-type thing"; but in 1948, "why, [McGovern] practically supported the Communist Party." He hammered the South Dakotan so hard, in fact, and with such futility for his own political fortunes, people wondered if Hubert Humphrey had put him up to it. The man who'd been offered two cabinet posts by Richard Nixon explicitly denied the charge. Then, the day before the Ohio primary, Jackson withdrew, renewing suspicions.

In Vietnam the ARVN was floundering. Back home, an annoyance cleared up for Richard Nixon. J. Edgar Hoover, the man who wished to claim all power of intimidation in Washington for his very own, who began compiling his files on five hundred thousand "subversives" during the 1919 Red Scare, the director of the Federal Bureau of Investigation since its founding, who kept columnist Joseph Alsop on a string by retaining photographs of him in flagrante delicto with male KGB agents in Moscow, was dead.

"Jesus Christ! That old cocksucker!" was the president's private response.

Publicly, Nixon arranged for Hoover's half-ton, lead-lined coffin to lie in state in the Capitol Rotunda as if he'd been a president and said at his funeral, "The good J. Edgar Hoover has done will not die. The profound principles associated with his name will not fade away. Rather, I would predict that in the time ahead those principles of respect for law, order, and justice will come to govern our nation more completely than ever before. Because the trend of permissiveness in this country, a trend which Edgar Hoover fought against all his life, a trend which was dangerously eroding our national heritage as a law-abiding people, is now being reversed."

And, as if on cue, the president's men amped up their lawlessness.

A squad of Cuban operatives, led by Bernard Barker, huddled near the Capitol steps where Daniel Ellsberg was among a group reading the names of dead servicemen. "Hippies, traitors, and Communists," Barker told his men, planned to "perpetrate an outrage on Hoover." He pointed out Ellsberg: "Our mission is to hit him, to call him a traitor, and punch him in the nose. Hit him and run." (It was, like the Fielding burglary, a botched effort: his men started punching hippies at random and were chased off by police.)

The Committee to Re-Elect the President's head of security, a former FBI and CIA operative named James McCord, made a long-term reservation at a Howard Johnson's out past George Washington University, by the Kennedy Center, a mile away from the Committee's 1701 Pennsylvania Avenue office.

The big story from the Tuesday primaries was Ohio: they were still counting votes. Humphrey edged out a win; McGovernites charged election fraud in the black precincts of Cleveland. "McGovern and Humphrey Running Even," the *Times* headlined; in the *Post* David Broder pointed out that with George Wallace's wins in Tennessee and Indiana, Democratic sources said the Alabaman was on his way to enough delegates—perhaps 10 percent—to deny Humphrey or McGovern the nomination "unless one of them agrees to bargain on Wallace's terms."

The next contest was in South Dakota's neighbor Nebraska, where Humphrey hadn't been bothering to campaign in the face of an expected McGovern romp. Three thousand McGovern volunteers were eager to confirm what seemed to them obvious: that McGovern appealed to conservative farm states.

But then, all of a sudden, it was as if Scoop Jackson were speaking from beyond the political grave.

McGovern rolled across the heavily Catholic Cornhusker State for a whistle-stop tour, following the same route as RFK in 1968. But everywhere he went, everyone just suddenly seemed to *know* that their neighbor George McGovern was a fan of "abortion on demand." A group called Citizens Concerned for the Preservation of Life had taken out a half-page ad in *The True Voice*, the paper of the Omaha diocese, quoting from Evans and Novak: "The people don't know McGovern is for amnesty, abortion, and legalization of pot."

The panicked campaign distributed flyers at parish churches after Sunday mass: "The McGovern Record," on one side, rebutted the claim; a photo of the candidate with one of RFK's daughters and newspaper headlines such as "Ethel Kennedy Plans Picnic for McGovern" were on the other. The campaign pulled in a big gun: Charlie Guggenheim, the Kennedy family's favorite documentarian, who sat the senator down in front of eight ordinary

Nebraskans, including a nun, Roger Ailes–style. McGovern told them and the cameras he deplored "the last-minute smear campaign," favored no federal law on abortion, hit "the scarecrows that have been trotted out in the closing days of this campaign by a political opposition that is cowardly and does not want to address the real issues," and assured Nebraska TV viewers he wouldn't legalize pot, though it "ought to be treated as a misdemeanor . . . punishable by fines rather than jail sentences."

It was the same answer Humphrey gave on pot when asked. Humphrey's position on abortion was identical to McGovern's, too. His position on amnesty was only slightly different: Humphrey favored it coupled with national service. The *Washington Post* patiently explained all this in a long article about the controversy. But the *Washington Post* wasn't much read in Nebraska, and it wasn't Humphrey who'd been placed on the defensive. There is a saying in politics: if you're explaining, you're losing. The Republican National Committee's monthly magazine *First Monday* catapulted the propaganda: "While South Dakota Sen. George McGovern may give the impression of being a mild-mannered milquetoast . . . he is in reality a dedicated radical extremist who as President would unilaterally disarm the United States of America and open the White House to riotous street mobs."

On May 8, amid this latest flurry of Democratic disarray, the president went on TV to sell another escalation in the air campaign. Connally urged him, "Don't worry about killing civilians. Go ahead and kill 'em. People think you are now. So go ahead and give 'em some."

"That's right," concurred the president.

"There's pictures on the news of dead bodies every night," chimed in Haldeman. "A dead body is a dead body. Nobody knows whose bodies they are or who killed them."

They code-named it Operation Linebacker; the president did love his football. Its centerpiece was mining Haiphong Harbor, which was filled with Soviet ships; not since 1962 had two nuclear powers seemed to have tangled so dangerously. Some feared it might end in mushroom clouds.

Mining the port of Haiphong was the sort of gamble the Joint Chiefs of Staff were always proposing and Lyndon Johnson was refusing, and not just for the nuclear risk. Johnson also refused the idea for its cruelty: weapons arrived there, but also food, infrastructure needs, medical supplies. Ron Ziegler observed in Nixon that ruddy glow; doing what Johnson refused to do made Nixon giddy. Still high from his speech, in the middle of the night he dictated a memo to Kissinger: "I cannot emphasize too strongly that I have determined that we should go for broke. . . . Now that I have made this tough watershed decision I intend to stop at nothing to bring the enemy to his knees. . . . if the target is important enough, I will approve a plan that goes after it even if there is a risk of some civilian casualties. We have the power.

The only question is whether we have the will to use that power. What distinguishes me from Johnson is that I have the will in spades."

He had confidence in the politics. George Wallace's line on Vietnam elucidated why it worked: "Get it over with, and if you can't get it over with, get out now." Wallace followed that utterance by placing the blame other than with the commander in chief and the people who voted for him. "We face a Vietnam Dunkirk," Wallace would say, "because these *liberals* listen to a bunch of people who jumped around in the street while you folks are working hard, paying taxes." It was one of his best applause lines. Americans hated the war. They hated the antiwarriors more.

Nixon announced the harbor mining as a "decisive military action to end the war." (It wasn't decisive enough for the general counsel of the Committee to Re-Elect the President. When General Alexander Haig of the NSC traveled to 1701 Pennsylvania Avenue to brief the campaign staff on the operation, G. Gordon Liddy responded, "General, why haven't we bombed the Red River dikes? If we did that, we'd drown half the country and starve the other half.") On May 9 the Senate Democratic caucus condemned the move 29–14, endorsed a cutoff of funding for the Vietnam War 35–8, voting 44–0 against postponing a Senate floor vote on the subject until Nixon returned from his planned trip to Moscow late in the month. The caucus was now speaking with George McGovern's voice. Two Democratic war supporters, Senators Sam Ervin and Gale McGee of Wyoming, argued manfully to give the president the chance, as McGee put it, to "luck out." Republican conservatives gave similar arguments. But David Broder spoke to a Republican campaign consultant who said his clients were "in shock" from Nixon's speech and "not much enthused about crawling out on a limb with him." Broder also cited an unnamed "labor politician" who agreed with the president's message "and counseled Democrats to be cautious in condemning" it. The *New York Times,* for its part, now endorsed a cutoff in funding "to save the President from himself." Chuck Colson spent $4,400 from his slush funds for an ad signed by ten "independent citizens" rebuking the *Times* for usurping the popular will.

The campuses once more exploded, as Richard Nixon knew they would. Police, sheriff's deputies, and highway patrolmen staged an assault on five thousand violent University of Florida demonstrators. The student union in Madison was closed by trash fires and battles with club-wielding police. In College Park, Maryland, students tried to burn down an armory. The University of Minnesota suffered its worst violence in history. Spiro Agnew's limousine's rear window was smashed in Hawaii. Another hippie was shot in Albuquerque. Four hundred protesters were arrested sitting in at Westover Air Force Base in Massachusetts (the president of Amherst announced he would join them). Dozens more staged a lie-in in front of the White House. ("This is to advise you that I am planning tomorrow night to drive my Pontiac Station Wagon up onto the curb of Pennsylvania Avenue," Colson wrote to Haldeman, "and run over all of the hippies who are lying there.")

Nebraska Democrats voted. McGovern barely edged out Humphrey. Wallace was winning huge crowds in the states hosting primaries May 16: Michigan, where they liked to burn school buses; Maryland, where half the state thought like the South. The question every political analyst was now asking was whether labor boss George Meany would sit on his hands if George McGovern became the nominee.

Meany was hardly friends with Dick Nixon; in fact, they were in the middle of a simmering feud. In the fall of 1971 Nixon announced "Phase II" of his wage-and-price controls. The details—plenty of wage controls; few price controls—enraged Meany; when the president spoke at the AFL-CIO convention on November 19, the labor chieftain forbade the band from playing "Hail to the Chief." Nixon had played to his audience's cultural grievances, reminiscing about May 1970 and Cambodia, when they had battled the hippies together. ("Some wrote in those days that the president stood alone. I was not alone. One hundred and fifty thousand workers walked down Wall Street.") Then he turned to a brief discussion of Phase II, and the workers laughed in his face. The January convention pronounced defeating him labor's "primary goal" for 1972. In March, Meany resigned defiantly from the White House commission advising Phase II's wage policies, taking three labor chiefs with him. On April 20 he testified before Congress that the price controls were "a fraud": "Food prices are going up. So the GNP is going up. Goody, goody. But what does that do for my people?"

Then, along came McGovern—Meany's lone political ally, remember, in the battle against Nixon's economic policies in 1971. But McGovern was also the living symbol of reform's usurpation of labor's leverage within the Democratic Party. The timing of the Haiphong mining forced the issue. Everyone knew where George McGovern stood. Everyone knew where Nixon stood. Where, though, would George Meany stand?

The answer was: with Nixon. Meany said all Americans should close ranks behind the president's brave stand to end the war in Vietnam. Meany had his deputies give blind quotes to a *Washington Post* reporter for a May 14 article, "Leaders of Organized Labor Remain Largely Hostile to McGovern": "A number of labor leaders declared they were 'turned off' by some of the young staff people surrounding Senator McGovern, describing them as 'elitist' and 'zealots.' . . . Mr. Meany and other leaders were reported as virtually 'climbing the walls with rage' after reading an interview in which Mr. McGovern was quoted as saying that just as he had conceded he had made a mistake on the 14(b) vote, so Mr. Meany should acknowledge that he had made a mistake in supporting the Vietnam War. . . . Mr. McGovern, they say, is 'cold' and 'preachy.'"

Mr. McGovern, Big Labor was saying, was just not a *regular guy.* And that this might be enough to earn Big Labor's veto.

The guy who used to get elected by shaking every wheat farmer's hand in South Dakota was spending a lot more time with fancy liberals of questionable patriotism. You could see it, some noticed, in his clothes. One of his canvassers back in Wisconsin had remarked upon it with satisfaction: at last "he knew how to tie his tie right. Gloria Steinem showed him how to tie it. You should have seen how he tied it before that."

CHAPTER THIRTY-TWO

Celebrities

ARTHUR BREMER WANTED TO BE FAMOUS. IN THIS, HE WAS NOT ALONE. It was one the by-products of the 1960s: the currency of celebrity appreciated considerably. "In the future," Andy Warhol said in 1968, "everyone will be world-famous for fifteen minutes." The aspiration, at least, seemed universal.

Bremer was a twenty-year-old Milwaukeean who followed politics closely. Which meant, in 1972, that he also followed celebrities closely. They were everywhere during the Wisconsin primary: the hillbilly singers for Wallace; Lorne Greene for Humphrey; Muskie's Rosey Grier—and the "Mighty McGovern Art Players," as the South Dakotan's staff began calling the ever-expanding entourage: Leonard Nimoy, Marlo Thomas, John Kenneth Galbraith, a half dozen athletes—and first and second among equals, Shirley MacLaine and her luminous brother, Warren Beatty. The star of *Bonnie and Clyde* was organizing five celebrity rock-concert fund-raisers for McGovern. He was so close to the campaign's inner circle that Gary Hart started wearing his hair and clothes like him.

Bremer was an unemployed busboy whose only extended conversation with another friendly human in months was with a girl in a massage parlor whom he was disappointed to learn wasn't a prostitute. He had a plan, however, to get noticed: he would shoot the president of the United States and go out in a blaze of glory. He wrote it all down in a diary, comparing himself to Melville's Ishmael and Solzhenitsyn's Ivan Denisovich: *This will be one of the most closely read pages since the scrolls in those caves.*

But everything was going awry. He started his hunt in New York. You had to be twenty-five to rent a car there, so he wouldn't be able to tail the president. On his way back to Milwaukee he left the suitcase with his guns on the plane (he was impressed with himself to hear his name called over the airport loudspeaker). His '67 Rambler Rebel was decrepit, which at least provided him a rusted cavity beneath the floor mat in which to hide a .38. But then he pushed it too deeply into the floorboards and lost access to the gun.

Bremer headed toward Canada to meet Nixon on his pre–Earth Day trip to Ottawa. Then he worried he wouldn't be able to cross the border without his car registration—so he called U.S. customs and asked. Then, at his motel on the way, he accidentally discharged his Browning 9mm.

He got rid of his excess ammunition (except for one bullet he later found in his pocket) and threw his gun cases into a pond (and thereupon discovered they floated). He'd cut his hair to look respectable for the border guard. Then he worried he would look like an army deserter (his diary recorded almost as much semiconscious desire to fail as fantasies about succeeding). He could only find a hotel fifty-eight miles outside of Ottawa, didn't know Nixon's schedule, blamed antiwar demonstrators for the "beefed up" security that kept him from getting close enough to the motorcade, disguised in his $70 suit and VOTE REPUBLICAN! button. *(Let security slacken & I'll show you something really effective. Tons of leaflets have been handed out all over the world for years & what did they get done.)*

The next blown chance he chalked up to fastidiousness: he was busy grooming himself when the president's party egressed. *I will give very little if ANY thought to these things on any future attempts. After all, does the world remember if Sirhan's tie was on straight?* Then he heard Richard Nixon would be attending a formal concert and changed his mind: *To wear white tie & tails & get Nixon-boy, WOW! If I killed him while wearing a sweatty tee-shirt, some of the fun and Glamore would defionently be worn off.* It occurred to him his bullets might not be able to penetrate the limousine's bulletproof glass. He considered downgrading his ambitions: *killing 5 or 6 secret Service agents would get me in the papers SOMETHING to show for my effort.*

By the end of April he was enraged with himself: *I was sopposed to be dead a week & a day ago. Or at least infamous. FUCKING tens-of-1,000s of people & tens-of-millions of $. I'd just like to take some of them with me & Nixy.* Back in Milwaukee he visited the zoo, walked by the lakefront, took in *Clockwork Orange,* meditated upon an easier target. The prospect, however, worried him. *Shit! I won't even rate a T.V. enteroption in Russia or Europe when the news breaks—they never heard of Wallace. . . . I don't expect anybody to get a big throbbing erection from the news.*

Or maybe everybody would. Wallace's campaign was exploding. In March, Pontiac housewife Irene McCabe led antibusing activists in a forty-four-day march to Washington. "Our cause is to retain freedom, just like George Washington," she said, as one thousand supporters rallied her arrival on the steps of the U.S. Capitol, met by Senator Griffin and House minority leader Ford. Back in Michigan, citizens expressed their antibusing solidarity by flocking to Wallace's banner. He drew over six thousand in Dearborn; Arthur Bremer was there. He became a fixture around the campaign. He even offered to be a volunteer.

The problem was that Michigan didn't have the death penalty. *It bothers*

me that there are about 30 guys in prison now who threatened the Pres & we
never heard a thing about them. Except that they're in prison. He bought
another plane ticket: why not Maryland? They had a primary on the sixteenth, too.

George Wallace gave his rap in Wheaton, Maryland, on Monday, May 15:
"It's a sad day in our country when you go to Washington, D.C., and can't
go one hundred feet from your hotel. It's not even safe in the shadow of the
White House." He was heckled and pelted with tomatoes. His response was
calmer than in 1968. He just said, "Your vocabulary is mighty limited if that's
all you can say is nasty words like that."

On to the next stop. As usual, his caravan of admirers followed. By their
bumper stickers, you could know them: I FIGHT POVERTY. I WORK; GOD BLESS
AMERICA; POW'S NEVER HAVE A NICE DAY; REGISTER COMMUNISTS, NOT
FIREARMS. His people were relieved to find a friendly crowd. Laurel was an
overwhelmingly white town halfway between Washington and Baltimore in
mixed-race Prince George's County—a perfect spot for a Wallace appeal.
Five nights earlier, busing dominated the Fourth District congressional primary debates—and not one of the fifteen candidates was pro-busing.

The setting was one of those identical U-shaped shopping centers built
in profusion around the country in the 1950s and '60s. The Secret Service
said it was too open for a rally. The owners of the Sunoco station at the
mouth of the parking lot were afraid, too: they were from Africa and feared
they'd be attacked.

Billy Grammer's band played "Dixie." Buckets circulated in the crowd
for contributions. Their size was variously estimated at one thousand, twelve
hundred, and two thousand.

Wallace spoke for almost an hour, until about four o'clock. "You can give
'em a case of St. Vitus' dance and you know how to do it," he wound up to
the usual roars. "Vote for George Wallace tomorrow!"

Blew kisses, snapped off a smart salute. Came down from the platform
to shake hands. The sun broke from behind a cloud bank.

The kid from Milwaukee in the Wallace button pushed through the
crowd, slipped past the seventy-five police officers and knot of Secret Service men: "Hey, George! Hey, George!" He was dressed "in red, white, and
blue," the *Post* reported the next morning; and that he was "a loner with a
penchant for pornography."

Eighteen inches away, he took five shots to the beat of Billy Grammer's
band.

"I thought it was firecrackers": a familiar phrase from the sixties.

Secret Service, bystanders, police, wrestled Arthur Bremer to the ground.
Wallace was shot in the lower-right chest. A Secret Service agent, a bystander,
and Wallace's personal Alabama trooper bodyguard ("Take care of the gov-

ernor, take care of the governor first!") caught bullets, too. A black teenager pushed through the crowd to try to congratulate the assassin. The Laurel rescue squad transported the casualties twenty-five miles away to Holy Cross Hospital in Silver Spring. Wallace supporters crowded the entrance. "They'll keep shooting us down until our innocent blood runs red," one said.

The governor was conscious the whole time. The reports were that he was paralyzed. Several hundred showed up at his scheduled event in Annapolis. "I asked them to pray for three things," his Maryland campaign chairman said. "Quick recovery, the soul of the fellow who did such a thing, and a tremendous victory tomorrow."

A *Washington Post* article turned unexpectedly pensive: "The 1972 political year began with hopes that it would be unlike the bitter, divisive past. . . . But in less than a week all that has passed. The shooting of George Wallace of Alabama came exactly a week after President Nixon somberly announced the mining of North Vietnamese ports and increased bombing raids which raised the specter of a direct confrontation with the Soviet Union."

Wallace's shocked opponents suspended their campaigns. "Say a prayer for our own country," said George McGovern. A story that might any other day have made the front pages—a Republican congressman's district office in Royal Oak, Michigan, was destroyed by a firebomb—was relegated in the *Post* to a tiny item on page 11. Newspapers and newsmagazines had begun every year since 1968 with earnest, hopeful predictions that this might be the year all the bitterness and division finally passed. They hadn't been right once.

Richard Nixon's reaction to the attempted assassination was different from that of his gentle-hearted competitor. Bob Haldeman waited an hour before interrupting an important meeting—the CEO of Pepsi, Don Kendall, was reporting on his progress in recruiting executives from every state for a business branch of the Committee to Re-Elect the President—to tell the president Wallace had been shot but was alive. Nixon's immediate response was panic. He must have had the fleeting thought it could be someone tied to him: they had a lot of loose cannons in the field. A vision of November 22, 1963, flashed before him—when the immediate presumption out of Dallas was that the shooter must have been a right-winger, and Barry Goldwater's decent chance to win the presidency disappeared.

Nixon uttered his political assessment: the issue was not "the legalities or specifics. Don't worry about doing it all by the book, the problem is who wins the public opinion. . . .

"What matters for the next twenty-four to forty-eight hours is trying to get the right posture set before the press immediately leaps on exactly the wrong thing and starts making a big point of how the guy is a right-wing radical."

The big news story the morning of the shooting was the exceedingly delicate question of whether the Kremlin, as mines floated in Haiphong Harbor, would cancel the late-May summit. The Wallace shooting now spiraled the political situation similarly beyond control, and Nixon was stricken with a rage to control. He called for Chuck Colson: "He'll do anything." The president smiled. "I mean, anything!"

Colson was ordered to contact the FBI's number two man, Mark Felt, to draw a bead on the state of the investigation. Felt told him Secret Service agents had entered the suspect's apartment in Milwaukee and confiscated political paraphernalia of every description, but that the FBI was waiting for a warrant to search it further. Colson relayed that report in the Oval Office, and together he and Nixon waited for the FBI to call back.

The president, sucking down cocktails, started woolgathering: "left-wing propaganda" was what he hoped they'd find. "Too bad we couldn't get somebody down there to plant it." At which Colson realized that there was no reason they couldn't.

The next time he spoke to the FBI, it was with Nixon listening in. Colson told Felt they had heard rumors that Bremer was a left-winger. Colson wasn't reporting intelligence but inventing it, the better to cover his tracks for what he was about to do. Then Colson excused himself: certain operations it was better the president didn't know about.

When he came back, the president asked him, "Is he a left-winger, right-winger?"

"Well, he's going to be a left-winger by the time we get through, I think."

"Good. Keep at that, keep at that."

"Yeah. I just wish that, God, I'd thought sooner about planting literature out there," Colson said. The president laughed, as Colson, perhaps a bit too boastfully, noted, "It may be a little late, although I've got one source that maybe—"

"Good."

Colson grew vague, drawing back into passive voice: "I mean, if they found it near his apartment, that would be helpful."

What he was simultaneously revealing and obscuring was that Howard Hunt was on his way to Milwaukee. While the FBI waited fastidiously for their search warrant, he was going to try to sneak McGovern and Kennedy literature into Arthur Bremer's quarantined apartment. It looked, however, that he wouldn't be able to do it. Thus Colson's frustration that he hadn't thought of it earlier.

Another mission that night fared better. Nixon met with his secretary of the treasury, who was scheduled the next day to resign—like all Nixon's most trusted confidants, to take on a job in his campaign, in this case heading Democrats for Nixon. At Nixon's instigation, one of Connally's last official acts was to officially bestow Secret Service protection on two more Democrats whose status as presidential contenders Nixon wanted to boost:

Ted Kennedy and Shirley Chisholm. *Life* happened to have a photographer and reporter with Kennedy—one more will-he-or-won't-he? feature—when his detail arrived. They ran a story on what it was like to be a Kennedy when an assassination occurred, how the "harmless, disturbed" hangers-on Senate staffers called "our regulars" suddenly took on a more menacing aspect; how Kennedy had to explain to his children—and later that night, Robert Kennedy's children—what they were seeing on TV.

From then on, hungover newsmen made the extra effort to get to the morning events for the candidates they were covering. None wanted to miss the one where he got shot.

Within a week the world learned that George Wallace, having won sympathy landslides in Maryland and Michigan, would be confined to a wheelchair for the rest of his life. Humphrey had to win California in June to hope to stop the South Dakotan on the first ballot; yet McGovern, underdog no more, was spending four times as much money there as Humphrey and looked likely to pull out a landslide. That raised the awkward possibility that the labor chieftains, Dixie courthouse bosses, and Mayor Daleys would read the writing on the wall and fall in behind McGovern, holding their noses against the radical's stench—uniting the Democrats, much to the president's chagrin.

Nixon flew halfway across the world for his triumphant summit in Russia as an article ran in the *Post* with George Gallup's byline: "McGovern and HHH Abreast vs. Nixon." The point was not merely that Nixon's lead—estimated to be between eight and twelve points, depending on whether Wallace was included—was too close for comfort. It was that Humphrey and McGovern each did approximately *the same* against him. That meant the theory behind his dirty-tricks strategy—McGovern was the least electable candidate—wasn't being borne out by the facts.

But who would he face in November? Democratic county chairmen predicted Humphrey would be the nominee. But McGovern appeared to be far ahead on delegates. With the Wallace shooting, the situation became yet more confused. What would happen at the Democratic convention, opening July 10, with Wallace's delegates? If he was incapacitated, would they still be allowed to vote for him? If not, how would they be disposed of? What kind of deals would Wallace be able or prepared to make: on the nomination, on delegate credentials, on the traveling platform hearings set to get under way in eleven cities at the end of May? If things didn't work out to his satisfaction, could he still threaten a third-party bid?

A behind-the-scenes figure was now thrust to the forefront: DNC chair Larry O'Brien, who would be responsible for these delicate and unprecedented decisions. Would he decide in the interests of Humphrey, a longtime close associate? Or McGovern, who won nearly four times as many votes as

Humphrey in the May 23 Oregon primary? Or kowtow to the Wallace constituency in the face of the vociferous antibusing sentiment?

Nixon could formulate no coherent strategic plan for the general election until he knew *which* Democratic Party he might be running against. Hopefully, he would soon have the intelligence he needed. The same team that had broken into the office of Daniel Ellsberg's shrink had established a beachhead at the Howard Johnson's across from DNC chair O'Brien's office at the Watergate complex, ready to effectuate the revised CRYSTAL phase of Gordon Liddy's Operation GEMSTONE.

There had already, on May 16, been a mysterious break-in at the offices of a Washington law firm close to Humphrey. On May 22, as the president toasted the chairman of the presidium of the Supreme Soviet in Moscow, Bernard Barker's Cubans flew to D.C. A sixth-floor Howard Johnson's room had been transformed into a listening post, manned by a former FBI agent named Al Baldwin. D-day for cracking Larry O'Brien's office was May 26, the Friday of Memorial Day weekend. But already things were awry. They were smoother criminals than Arthur Bremer, but not by much.

Six Cubans checked into the Watergate's hotel Friday afternoon. But since the Committee to Re-Elect's security chief James McCord arrived with only four walkie-talkies, two men had to be struck from the team. They were supposed to refer to each other by aliases. But McCord got flustered and used real names.

Hunt and the Cubans were disguised as businessmen attending a banquet in the Watergate's Continental Room, which Hunt had booked for its convenient access to a service corridor. Apparently they decided neither inebriation nor torpor would hinder their mission: the epicurean Hunt catered an extravagant meal and libations (nursing a bleeding ulcer, he took his whiskey mixed with milk).

He chased off the waiter with a large tip and ran a movie to muffle the sound of their final consultation. Then, at ten thirty, a security guard poked his head in to tell them their rental time was up. So they turned off the lights and hid in a closet until midnight. But the team's locksmith—proprietor of the Missing Link Key Shop in Miami—couldn't open the door to the service corridor.

A second group, led by Liddy, simultaneously cased McGovern campaign headquarters across town, the first of several abortive break-in attempts there. The problem: damned idealistic McGovern volunteers never left the office, even in the middle of the night.

The Cubans tried the Watergate again the next night. This time their only cover was signing the registry that they were visiting the Federal Reserve Board offices on the eighth floor—and this time, the door to the DNC office wouldn't fall to the locksmith. "He says he doesn't have the right tools,"

Barker reported to Hunt and Liddy's listening post. Though thanks to Maurice Stans, they had the means to fly the locksmith all the way back to Miami, to return the next day with his full set of picks and pries.

Liddy's team moved out for another, more predawn run at the McGovern offices. Liddy positioned himself in the back alley. In front, they stationed an operative who worked undercover in the McGovern campaign to tell them the lay of the office. A policeman spotted him loitering nervously on this crime-ridden street and ordered him to move along. The men John Mitchell paid for "security" had just barely avoided getting the chief counsel of the president of the United States's campaign staff caught casing a burglary.

It was Sunday, May 28. The locksmith, early in the evening, pried open a door on the B-2 level of the Watergate parking garage. Alongside a Hunt-Liddy operative named Frank Sturgis—he was born Frank Angelo Fiorini, but used a cover name from one of Howard Hunt's novels—he taped the latch open. They continued picking and taping locks all the way up to the threshold. The strike team would enter later, removing the tape and locking the doors behind them.

It worked. Cubans rifled DNC files, removing documents to photograph. James McCord installed taps on two phones. He tested them with a small pocket receiver and decided they worked to his satisfaction. Across the street Hunt and Liddy spied the darting flashlight beams across the way and embraced: "The horse is in the house."

As G. Gordon Liddy wrote in his memoirs, "The experience of the past ten years left no doubt in my mind that the United States was at war internally as well as externally." Finally, the good guys had a leg up. His boss was, indeed, harvesting another triumph. In Moscow, Nixon and Brezhnev had signed their historic Strategic Arms Limitation Treaty two days earlier. On the twenty-eighth, the president made a historic radio and television address to the people of the Soviet Union—"a message of friendship from all the people of the United States and to share with you some of my thoughts about the relations between two countries and about the way to peace and progress in the world. . . . As great powers, we shall sometimes be competitors, but we need never be enemies."

To a nation well sick of Cold War tensions and the rotten jungle war it had brought, this proved catnip. In the next Gallup Poll Nixon's approval rating, 49 percent at the beginning of the year, was now 61 percent. The last six months had been his most successful as president. Inflation was down from 4.4 percent to 3.2 percent. It all threw into disarray the best-laid plans of the Democratic presidential contenders, whose assumption as they had planned their campaigns had been that the primary would be where all the action was, because beating this snore of an unpopular president would be easy.

* * *

In California two Democratic senators, next-door neighbors in Washington, once close friends, whose children left their handprints together in the wet cement of the Humphreys' patio, were scratching each other's eyeballs out. Or rather Hubert Humphrey was scratching out George McGovern's. The candidate of reform and openness simply sighed his dismay. "Dirty politics," Hunter S. Thompson wrote, "confused him."

The burbling happy warrior from Minnesota had been carrying out his third presidential campaign as a classic glad-handing, backslapping, ward-heeling, something-for-everyone Democrat; young McGovernites were convinced he was on uppers. Now, Humphrey shifted to dirty pool. His adviser the old Kennedy hand Kenny O'Donnell lied to the press that Humphrey didn't even need California to win the nomination. Actually, if he lost California, he was through. Every little constituency counted. Pamphlets circulated signed by Lorne Greene (né Lorne Hyman Greene): "Senator McGovern, now you claim to support the state of Israel, but why, before this primary campaign, have you acted and voted against her?" In actuality on the crucial litmus tests—the sale of F-4 Phantom jets and moving America's embassy to Jerusalem—their supports were pretty much identical, the same as Scoop Jackson's. But the Field poll showed McGovern 20 points ahead, and Humphrey was desperate.

The May 26 morning papers handed Humphrey an assist. *Amnesty, abortion, and the legalization of pot* simply didn't scan, but tart-tongued Senator Hugh Scott (R-Pa.) came to the rescue by declaring McGovern "the acid, abortion, and amnesty—the triple-A—candidate." McGovern responded that Scott himself was one of "these entrenched Establishment figures at the top of both political parties" who were "afraid" of his war against political privilege. Then he prepared to debate his opponent, glad for a change to fight this thing out on the issues, honestly and in the open.

ABC's *Issues and Answers* had asked McGovern earlier if he would join Humphrey in a one-hour joint appearance on national TV. Way ahead, McGovern should have turned down the debate—especially since Humphrey was $700,000 in debt and couldn't air TV commercials. Instead McGovern jumped at the chance. NBC and CBS extended the same invitation. McGovern eagerly accepted those, too.

The CBS show came first, on Sunday, May 28. The opening question was to Humphrey: George Herman asked if California was do-or-die for him. Humphrey gave a brief denial before borrowing a trick from Jack Kennedy in 1960: he changed the subject, in order to attack. Humphrey said, "We were both wrong on Vietnam," because both had voted for the Gulf of Tonkin resolution. McGovern always distinguished himself from the competition on Vietnam with the slogan "right from the start." Here, Humphrey was calling him a flip-flopper—and added, "In taxation, he is contradictory and inconsistent."

Humphrey then spoke to a Nixonite anxiety: that America would become weak. "On defense cuts . . . I believe they cut into the muscle to the very fiber of our national security." McGovern would turn America "into a second-class power."

When it came time for McGovern to speak, he spluttered, "I find it almost impossible to believe that the senator from Minnesota would attack my record on Vietnam."

He was truly taken aback that his old friend would insult the intelligence of knowledgeable voters with the claim that somehow their Vietnam records were equivalent. But most voters, of course, are not knowledgeable. A show like this might be their first introduction to the candidates. McGovern, calling his opponent "the senator from Minnesota," was following a strategy of courtesy in the hopes of mending fences with Humphrey forces for the general election. But thrown on the defensive, *he* looked like the mean-spirited one—testily recalling October of 1967, when "Senator Humphrey was saying Vietnam is 'our greatest adventure and a wonderful one it is.'"

Humphrey got dirtier. One of the panelists asked a Vietnam question. Humphrey, close-lipped, somehow changed the subject to . . . welfare: "When it comes to other aspects, such as in welfare legislation he calls a horrible mess, let me say that a seventy-two-billion-dollar welfare proposal that Senator McGovern makes today is not only a horrible mess, it would be an unbelievable burden upon the taxpayer."

When Humphrey finished, it was McGovern's turn to answer the question about Vietnam. So he answered the question about Vietnam. Then the show went on commercial break, leaving Humphrey's welfare smear hanging.

What had just happened? Basically, McGovern had become attracted, late in 1971, to a "demogrant" proposal to counter the Nixon administration's stalemated Family Assistance Program legislation. It differed from Nixon's not in kind but in detail and degree. Like FAP, the more money a family earned, the less the federal benefit—the benefit adjusted so that additional money earned would give a family a bigger total income. At least theoretically, the program as it had been presented to McGovern would be paid for by reducing income-tax loopholes for the rich. Humphrey's "$72 billion"—the defense budget was then about $80 billion—was the cost of an unrelated proposal from the National Welfare Rights Organization for a $6,500 guaranteed income for every American. The actual figure McGovern used as a concrete example when discussing his own welfare-and-taxation proposal was $1,000 per family member.

CBS came back from commercial, Humphrey's underhanded blow hanging in the air. The moderator, responsibly enough, asked Humphrey where he got the $72 billion figure; he said from a Senate Finance Committee bill McGovern had submitted. McGovern angrily shot back that he had indeed submitted the NWRO's bill as a courtesy but that he did not support it.

Responsibly enough, the moderator followed up: how much *would* his own proposal cost?

"I honestly don't know. I don't have the figures," he responded.

"Oh, God," McGovern staffers moaned. "There it goes."

McGovern wanted to campaign on issues. But he was bored by their details. Richard Nixon was bored by them, too. But Richard Nixon was willing to bullshit. Nixon's introduced the FAP on TV in 1969 by noting, "What the nation needs is not more welfare, but more 'workfare'"—fudging the fact that he was proposing a minimum income for even those who didn't work. That was what people remembered. What people remembered from this debate was Humphrey's scowling line "Senator McGovern has concocted a fantastic welfare scheme which will give everyone, even Nelson Rockefeller, $1,000, and it will cost the taxpayers sixty or seventy billion dollars," and Humphrey's claim that to pay for it "a secretary working in San Francisco, making $8,000 . . . would have an increase in his or her taxes under Senator McGovern's welfare proposal of $567."

The helpless splutter of the prairie populist, unwilling to bullshit in return: "That simply is not true."

"Well, it is true, and a family that has $12,000 a year, a family of four, would have a $409 increase."

"And that's not true."

"Now the senator can say it's not true; he doesn't even *know* what the price tag to his bill is."

The McGovern dynamo started crumbling. Humphrey got a $300,000 cash infusion from a mysterious Texas billionaire. The debate on NBC became a chance for Robert Novak, now a confirmed enemy of the doyen of "the Democratic Party's left fringe," to confront McGovern with the Humphrey campaign's claim that his spending proposals would cost $100 to $160 billion. ABC's debate was memorable for the inclusion of the clownish Sam Yorty ("I'm the only one here wearing a POW bracelet"), the novelty Shirley Chisholm, and, to cap off the irrelevance, a surrogate for George Wallace.

Another factor that may well have influenced voters was the conclusion of the last great conspiracy trial of the era. Once more a jury of ordinary Americans had decided a prosecution was trying to make them complicit in a politically motivated witch hunt: right before the election, a judge in San Jose announced the acquittal of Angela Davis, the celebrity black militant, for allegedly providing the rifles with which the "Soledad Brothers" raided the Marin County Courthouse in August of 1970 in their attempt to free Black Panther George Jackson by kidnapping, then killing, the judge.

Witnesses' accounts of the gruesome courtroom slaughter from two years earlier became a staple on the evening news. One deputy district attorney testified from a wheelchair, the Soledad Brothers having shot away portions of his spinal cord. "I saw Judge Haley's face alive—and an instant later I saw the right side of his face slowly pull away from his skull," he said. "It was as if in slow motion—the outward appearance of his face moving away from his head." Angela Davis had had nothing to do with that. But she also, representing herself, constantly pronounced her solidarity with the Soledad Brothers. She was acquitted on Election Day—news rather unhelpful to any presidential candidate associated with the left.

McGovern's predicted twenty-point landslide in California ended up a win of approximately five points. His spokesmen lied Wednesday morning that McGovern's victory had been "very convincing," "absolutely decisive," making the candidate of reform sound just like another Washington snake-oil salesman.

The California primary was decisive in the respect that mattered most: unique among the states, it was "winner take all"—the candidate receiving a plurality of the primary votes got all 271 of California's delegates. The tradition gave the Golden State awesome power in attracting the pandering attentions of presidential candidates. It also, however, seemed to fall afoul of the stipulation of the McGovern Commission's *Mandate for Change* section B-6, providing for "Adequate Representation of Minority Views on Presidential Candidates at Each Stage in the Delegate Selection Process." California's tradition had survived thanks to the single-minded efforts of the McGovern Commission's most prominent Californian, Fred Dutton. He cleverly argued that winner-take-all primaries, precisely because they forced such high stakes, were harmonious with the spirit of reform because they increased popular participation, attracted serious campaigners, reduced the pull of power brokers, and forced candidates to field demographically balanced delegate slates.

Now California had apparently clinched George McGovern a first-ballot nomination. A week before the primary, Hubert Humphrey had been asked by Walter Cronkite, "So even if you lose out here—if you lose all 271 delegates—you wouldn't challenge the winner-take-all rule?" He answered, "Oh, my goodness, no. That would make me sort of a spoilsport, wouldn't it? . . . I don't believe in that kind of politics."

That sealed it: the candidate the Nixon ratfuckers had concertedly avoided touching up all spring was the Democrats' heir apparent. That made it time, Nixon decided, to make it impossible for the regulars to fall in behind McGovern. "One of the factors that brought Goldwater down to such a shattering defeat in 1964 was the success of the media in tying him to ultra-right-wing supporters like H. L. Hunt, the John Birch Society, etc.," Nixon wrote his campaign manager, John Mitchell. "The fact that Abbie Hoffman, Jerry Rubin, Angela Davis, among others, support McGovern, should be widely publicized and used at every point. Keep calling on him to repudiate them daily."

The strategy paid immediate dividends. The McGovern camp celebrated the good news that Edmund Muskie's former campaign manager, Berl Bernhard, had promised Muskie would endorse McGovern in a speech at the National Press Club in exchange for McGovern's absorbing some of Muskie's campaign debts.

Hours later, Berl Bernard called back: Muskie was getting heavy pressure not to endorse and had not yet made a "final" decision.

The Maine senator decided to back away from McGovern as if he were gangrenous. Armed with his 176 delegates, Muskie announced he was still an "inactive" candidate. The old salts of the press saw what was happening: the regulars would be working behind the scenes to pool Muskie, Humphrey, and George Wallace delegates in a "stop McGovern" bloc being organized by Southern governors such as Jimmy Carter of Georgia. It didn't seem possible—McGovern's 271 delegates from California ensured that. The consequences would, it seemed, be in the general election: the Democrats would leave Miami Beach divided.

Muskie said he would only release his delegates if McGovern would "reexamine and refine his own position with respect to critical issues." It happened as Hubert Humphrey announced he would campaign for the New York primary June 20, whose outcome wasn't supposed to matter, and where he hadn't even filed a slate of delegate candidates. "I'm not dropping out," he burbled exuberantly. "I'm about to take off." The Lorne Greene flyer about McGovern's supposed sins against Israel started reappearing in Brooklyn Jewish neighborhoods; McGovern forces printed 3 million of their own pamphlets in response. McGovern confronted his old friend personally about the scurrilous literature that in California Humphrey had said he had nothing to do with. This time, Humphrey responded: "If you think it was rough in California, wait until Nixon comes at you."

The *New York Times* and Daniel Yankelovich came out with poll numbers showing that 40 percent of Humphrey's voters in California would, if McGovern was nominated, either vote for Nixon or stay home. On June 14 Ted Kennedy announced to reporters, "I am not a candidate for president nor would I accept a draft, nor am I a candidate for vice president, nor would I accept a draft." That same day Edmund Muskie announced a tour via chartered jet of ten states with uncommitted and not-yet-selected delegates. He was banking on an eventuality that had seemed fantastical nine days earlier: a convention deadlocked between McGovern and Humphrey, Muskie as the compromise choice between politics Old and New—backing it up by traveling with Harold Hughes, the initiator of McGovernite party reform in 1968. "A viable alternative," Endorsement Ed now called himself.

McGovern battled back with Warren Beatty in the vanguard. The fifth of his celebrity fund-raising concerts sold out Madison Square Garden on

June 14. A cordon of "celebrity ushers" showed people to the most expensive seats: Gene Hackman, Jon Voight, Candice Bergen, James Earl Jones, Jack Nicholson, Marlo Thomas, Goldie Hawn, Ryan O'Neal (star of the blockbuster *Love Story*, whose good-old-fashioned virtues Nixon adored). Paul Newman came surrounded by six policemen to protect him from screaming admirers. The theme was "together with McGovern": he can "bring us together again," the outlaw star of *Bonnie and Clyde* pronounced—"in those tight blue pants, and the brown curls that spill over his neck, and those movie star teeth, all even and strong-looking and white as a row of brand-new refrigerators," a weak-kneed female feature writer for the *New York Times* wrote. McGovern would lead the nation, the program promised, with "the assurance that we care very deeply about each other."

The unity theme was vouchsafed by reuniting acts riven by breakups. Peter, Paul, and Mary opened the show; Mary Travers invited the crowd to "take your place on the great mandala" and offered a Peter, Paul, and Mary lesson in geopolitics: "Nixon keeps saying the war will end when the prisoners are released by North Vietnam, which is insane. You never get the prisoners back before the war is over. Nixon has his own rules. What kind of crazy war is that?" Elaine May and Mike Nichols hadn't spoken to one another for twelve years, but still had chemistry. May's caricature of absurd liberal moral one-upmanship slayed them: "I've *always* wanted to get out of Vietnam—even before we got in!"

"I just *love* his economic program," she told Nichols, who parodied a McGovern economics expert who had recently become infamous for trying and failing to explain the "demogrant." "But what is it?"

Titters.

"Well, in broad outline—"

"No, I know it in broad outline. What is it specifically?"

"I can only give it to you in broad outline."

Roars.

The headliners, Simon and Garfunkel, gestured to the balcony: tie-dyed T-shirts, raggedy army jackets, wild hair, scraggly beards, curious aromas.

"These people paid eight dollars!" Paul Simon cried.

Raucous cheers from the nosebleed seats.

He gestured to the front: Pucci and Gucci; Brooks Brothers and the latest leisure suits; Hermès scarfs. "These people paid one hundred dollars!"

Resounding boos.

"I think we should do something for the eight-dollar people," Paul Simon said, breaking into "Bridge Over Troubled Water," craning his neck to the sky.

The candidate and his wife, Eleanor, took the stage. Eighteen thousand rose to their feet. "A few months ago," McGovern said, "you would have represented my entire national constituency!" Then it was off to the Four

Seasons, partying until the wee hours with three hundred of Manhattan's most glamorous.

Future generations of political observers, better attuned to the rhythms of right-wing populism, might wonder if this was the most effective use of the candidate's time. He had traveled so far, invested so much, since January of 1971. But he still had an enormous wall to surmount. Millions of people didn't see him as a uniter, or as a prairie populist. They saw him as a man who'd chosen to come down on the wrong side of the polarization—a hippie-coddling Franklin, not a hard-work-honoring Orthogonian. The hobnobbing with celebrities didn't help. But the way the McGovern people saw it, as Warren Beatty put it, was that "a great deal of the leadership of this generation comes from music and film people, whether people like that fact or not."

It was partially a Camelot thing, this notion that having liberal Hollywood celebrities ever at his elbow helped a candidate. The 1960 Democratic convention, the first held in Los Angeles, was a riot of celebrities, from Marlon Brando to Harry Belafonte to Frank Sinatra. Beatty and his sister, Shirley MacLaine, had been at the outskirts of that circle then. Now they were at its center—and the circle kept expanding. Celebrities hungered for meaning in their lives. "Why does McCarthy need you?" someone heckled Paul Newman in New Hampshire in 1968. "He doesn't need me," Cool Hand Luke replied. "I need him."

Celebrities filled politicians' hunger, too. Even modest McGovern was bitten by the bug; it showed in how he tied his tie. It also seemed to solve a political problem. Everyone had a story about the first time they entered a room George McGovern occupied without realizing they were in the presence of a senator (Hunter S. Thompson's version of the story took place in a lavatory). For a politician who blended into the woodwork, a little glamour seemed only a plus. The proximity to stars, after all, had never hurt Jack Kennedy.

But things had changed since 1960. It was the age, for one thing, of Nixon. The resentments Orthogonians harbored for Franklins were much closer to the surface; stars weren't the simple objects of aspiration they used to be. They were also what they were for Arthur Bremer: objects of resentment. For some in the Silent Majority they were the Loudest Minority: preachy, condescending, out of touch—enemies of people like you and me.

Shirley MacLaine's alienation from her audiences was never plainer than when she addressed a black women's luncheon and fashion show in Pittsburgh during the Pennsylvania primary. She spoke extemporaneously, as she always did, and said underprivileged women like them understood, as she and McGovern understood, that material things didn't matter, that too many Americans cared about the wrong things. The response was stony silence. The wealthy movie star was baffled. A young black man had to explain it to her: "You can't tell those women that stuff. You can't tell them they don't have much. They're proud people." They "*want* the things—those very things—you think are useless." Her brother Warren was politically undisciplined enough to tell a reporter that he favored the legalization of pot. Perhaps that's how people got the idea that was his candidate's position.

Chris Mitchum, the liberal son of Robert, plumped for McGovern on a talk show. His *Chisum* costar John Wayne showed up and asked Mitchum for a thousand dollars. When the young man asked him why, the Duke drawled, "McGovern promised everybody in the United States a thousand dollars, and I want mine." Republicans had their superstars, too, but they sold themselves as ordinary people.

The moment would have been a good time for McGovern aides to imitate the advice of a cynical but wise campaign manager who told his Senate candidate that summer, after he won the primary, "You're just reaching the people who agree with you already. Now we have to go for the rest."

Unfortunately, the consultant was fictional. In *The Candidate*, Robert Redford played a tireless and idealistic public-interest lawyer, Bill McKay, the son of a retired Old Politics governor played by Melvyn Douglas. The casting announced the movie's themes: Douglas was husband to Helen Gahagan Douglas, the idealistic liberal that Richard Nixon rolled over on his way to a California Senate seat in 1950. And there really was, of course, a disillusioned Old Politics former governor of California, Pat Brown, who also had an idealistic public-interest lawyer son. The movie also featured a Reagan doppelgänger: the incumbent Crocker Jarmo (a crock, and charming), a master of looking right into the camera and making whatever bromide he pronounced sound straight from the shoulder. The campaign manager, played by Peter Boyle, spots Robert Redford as a promising piece of political horseflesh and recruits him to run for Senate by telling him he has no chance, so he can say whatever he likes. The McGovern resonances were unmistakable. "What about busing?" a reporter asks. "What about it?" "What's your stand on it?" "I'm for it." "That's a first," the hack says under his breath, incredulous. Abortion? "Every woman has a right to an abortion." (His aides suggest he change his position to "I'm studying it.")

The moral was complex. Redford trims his hair and trims his sails. At the big candidate debate, asked about abortion, he responds, "It certainly deserves a lot more study than it's been given." But he also drives his handlers around the bend by veering off script with a closing peroration about his frustration that the problems of poverty and alienation, "fear, hatred, and violence," were never discussed. His settles into a stock campaign speech that, while sometimes cliché, is also sincere and inspiring. As he delivers it, the cinematography bathes him in a halo of light that makes him look like Robert F. Kennedy on the cover of *To Seek a Newer World*. He pulls off an endorsement from a corrupt old labor boss even after insulting him to his face. He wins the race. Because he sold out? Because he maintained a saving margin of integrity? Because of his Kennedyesque charisma? Because the people finally saw through Crocker Jarmon? The movie's answers were ambiguous, like real life.

The people around McGovern had a harder time allowing for this complexity. In place of cynics, McGovern had Fred Dutton, who had just filed a memo for the general election, "The Determining Margin of Difference," arguing that the royal road to victory was registering three-quarters of the 25 million voters newly eligible in 1972. McGovern's appeal to insurgent youth, Dutton wrote, "indicates very tangibly how much more he can do for the party than any of the other candidates—or than it can really do for him. . . . The input of these young people makes clear how the real center is moving, and can be moved even more. McGovern will maximize this input by standing firm on his (and most of these young people's) convictions, not moving to where the center has been in the past."

The easy confidence, the disdain for any effort to study the mysterious persistence of Nixon's appeal, was redoubled by political director Frank Mankiewicz, who told the *Times* in an article June 20 that his man would win because he was "the only alternative to the supreme politician, Richard Nixon." Mankiewicz said, "If this were England, the government would've fallen by now"—though Nixon's Gallup approval rating was then 60 percent, the highest in two years.

While McGovern's men were figuratively measuring the Oval Office for draperies, one of Nixon's was literally measuring the DNC office. The first break-in had been a failure. So Al Baldwin cased it for another go by asking for a tour of the office, posing as a nephew of a former DNC chair.

The need for a second burglary was revealed when McCord, at the Howard Johnson's, tried to monitor the two phone taps. Just as in the operation at Dr. Fielding's office, the volume had been turned down too low. One bug, on the phone of Larry O'Brien's secretary, yielded nothing. The other, on the phone of Spencer Oliver, the executive director of the Association of State Democratic Chairman—the best place to gather intelligence on convention delegations—worked, and Al Baldwin started producing transcripts of the conversations, typed up by Liddy's secretary on stationery headed GEMSTONE, mined for relevant data by Jeb Magruder at the campaign headquarters and Gordon Strachan in the White House.

They discovered the same thing the FBI had in 1969, tapping NSC staffers on Kissinger's behalf: you found out most about the target's personal life. Spencer Oliver, it turned out, was quite the ladies' man: he spent a lot of time on the phone lining up cross-country trysts. Oliver's phone, in the most secluded part of the DNC offices, was also used by secretaries to call their boyfriends. John Mitchell called Liddy into his office: "This stuff isn't worth the paper it's printed on." Liddy defended himself: "One of the bugs isn't working. And they put one of them on O'Brien's second phone instead of O'Brien's phone. But I'll get everything straightened out right away."

Baldwin took special note of the location of O'Brien's office. He almost blew his own cover when his tour guide turned out to be the secretary most explicit with her boyfriend in their conversations over Mr. Oliver's phone.

Hunt and Liddy rushed plans for one more bugging job—this time with a room microphone soldered inside a smoke detector. It was Saturday, June 16, and about to be Saturday, June 17. Once more torpor was no object: the Cubans tucked into a lobster dinner at the Terrace Restaurant overlooking the Potomac (Bernard Barker ate until he felt sick). McCord simply strode into the Watergate not long after business hours, took the elevator up, and started taping locks all the way down to the subbasement garage. Only he taped them horizontally instead of vertically.

One of those damned tireless idealists was working in the DNC office past midnight. The burglars had to wait for 12:45 a.m. for the lights to go out. By the time they forced the DNC's front door—the lock was rusty so, ever discreet, they removed the door from its hinges—the night watchman was on his rounds. He noticed the horizontally taped latches and called the police. The first squad car the police dispatcher radioed was too lazy to respond. At 1:52 a.m. the dispatcher put out an APB. An undercover car answered. Al Baldwin, looking out from the Howard Johnson's balcony, spotted three men, one in a raggedy army jacket—the kind of garb undercover cops affected to blend in with drug dealers.

Baldwin radioed Hunt in his car, "Are our people dressed casually or are they in suits?"

"What?" Hunt cried, astonished.

"Are our people dressed casually, or are they in suits?"

"Our people are dressed in suits."

"Well, we've got a problem."

Later, Howard Hunt decided McCord must have got caught on purpose, a double agent for the Democrats. The president said much the same thing four days later to Colson: "It doesn't sound like a skillful job. If we didn't know better, we would have thought it was deliberately botched."

Sunday morning Richard Nixon learned that his new secretary of the treasury, George Shultz, had learned from George Meany on the golf course that under no circumstances could he support George McGovern. Meany also said that he was working on a plan to deliver the nomination to Humphrey. This was, indeed, delightful news: Americans who didn't pay attention to politics would be introduced to the Democratic message for 1972 via a convention that resembled a train wreck.

The bad news was the appearance in the papers of the first stories on the five guys caught burglarizing the Democratic National Committee. It was in the *New York Times* way back on page 30, and without any hint of Nixonite involvement: "Two of the men, born in Cuba, were said to have claimed past ties with the Central Intelligence Agency. A third was described as an adventurer who once tried to sell his services to an anti-Castro organization called Alpha 66." James McCord was identified as a retired CIA employee. Haldeman and Ehrlichman took immediate evasive action. They prepared a statement for John Mitchell to release as soon as the truth came out—which it did that same day—that McCord was on the payroll of the Committee to Re-Elect the President.

Haldeman prepared for the worst: the possibility that the press would learn of the mastermind role of Liddy and Hunt—the first a top staffer of the Committee to Re-Elect, with an office right by Mitchell's, the second a recent occupant of an office in the White House. Fortunately Haldeman had only good news to write in his diary for Monday. The president had enjoyed a long talk with his old friend Billy Graham. The reverend was working on a political errand: keeping George Wallace out of the general election. He had a line to the governor through Mrs. Wallace, who had just become a born-again Christian. "We talked to Mitchell about who's going to talk to Wallace," Haldeman recorded, "and how we're going to handle what his price is."

The opening Watergate public relations gambit was working. McCord, Mitchell's statement announced, was "the proprietor of a private security agency who was employed by our committee months ago to assist with the installation of our security system. He has, as we understand it, a number of business clients and interests and we have no knowledge of those relationships." (*He installed our security system:* it was a nasty business, politics, and Republicans needed burglar alarms just as badly as Democrats.) "We want to emphasize that this man and the other people involved were not operating either on our behalf or with our consent," Mitchell's press release continued. "I am surprised and dismayed at these reports."

And then, the old Nixonian jujitsu. "We have our own security problems," Mitchell said, hinting darkly, positioning Nixon as the one attacked, the victim of false and hasty charges.

Larry O'Brien played right into their hands: making more apparently hasty charges. "Continuing disclosures in the wake of Saturday's bugging incident at the DNC raise the ugliest questions about the integrity of the political process that I have encountered in a quarter century of political activity," his press release read. "No mere statement of innocence by Mr. Nixon's campaign manager, John Mitchell, former attorney general, will dispel these questions, especially as the individual allegedly involved remains on the payroll of the Nixon organization. . . . Only the most searching professional investigation can determine to what extent, if any, the Committee for the Re-Election of the President is involved in this attempt to spy on Democratic headquarters."

Now that it was an issue of dueling partisan countercharges, political reporters yawned. That morning's *Washington Post* story, under the byline of two police reporters, was the exception. It led, "One of the five men arrested early Saturday . . . is the salaried security coordinator for President Nixon's reelection committee." More responsible reports, such as the *New York Times*'s, focused on the burglars' ties to the Bay of Pigs: the same kind of crazy Cubans who had been bombing the offices of left-wingers in New York for years; the same kind who, when Abbie Hoffman had recently spoken at the University of Miami, stormed the stage hurling sacks of flour and garbage.

None outside the Beltway, and not too many inside it, were paying attention to this burglary. The *Chicago Tribune* didn't run an article on the DNC break-in on the front page until the end of August.

The men directly party to the crime did the things criminals who don't want to get convicted do. McCord buried and burned his equipment. Hunt hid his wiretapping gear in his safe at the Executive Office Building, removing $10,000 in emergency cash to hire attorneys. The Central Intelligence Agency dispatched an agent who either destroyed or watched McCord's wife destroy incriminating CIA property at McCord's house. Liddy ran a shredder at Committee to Re-Elect headquarters, mulching documents and $100 bills. (The burglars had been caught with two C-notes each; they were to be used in case bribery became advisable.) Jeb Magruder burned the GEM-STONE files, including the sexy wiretap transcripts, in his fireplace.

Among the top-drawer journalists, Georgetown hostesses, lobbyists, lawyers, pols, and factotums who comprised the muscle and sinew of the Washington gossip corps, rumors started circulating. The mischievous wondered what the gruff and enigmatic pipe-smoking former attorney general might have to do with the burglary, or the CIA or FBI; more responsible voices, such as American Bar Association president Leon Jaworski, pooh-poohed the very notion that men of such stature would be involved. Maybe it was a Jack Anderson operation, was the scuttlebutt around Republican congressional offices: he was always going too far, and how *did* he always manage to get all those secret memos, anway? Other Republicans wondered if it was some ill-advised investigation of Democratic bugging of the Nixon campaign.

The most popular theory was the most plausible. From the army of Cuban exiles who had trained in Guatemalan jungles in the early sixties to overthrow Fidel Castro, to the dozens of firebombings nationwide against leftist publishers and consulates in 1968, right-wing Cuban nationalists seemed capable of any madness. The Scripps Howard newspaper chain soon quoted unnamed sources in Miami that the five men acted out of fear that a President McGovern would forge an alliance with Castro.

The Cubans had been coached to say that by White House operatives. And Haldeman reported to the president, "we've started moving on the Hill, letting it come from there, which is that this whole thing is a Jack Anderson thing, that Jack Anderson did it." The D.C. gossip corps proved easy to sucker.

The White House was doing things criminal *bosses* who don't want to get convicted do: fouling the chain of evidence, putting detectives off the scent, lying, inventing alibis—*obstructing justice*. Their first alibi was the burglary's incompetence: "I'm not going to comment from the White House on a third-rate burglary attempt," Ron Ziegler said from the pressroom in Key Biscayne on Monday. (In that he had the cooperation of Washington police officials, who, according to the *Times* Wednesday morning, said the consensus was that "the break-in was not a well-financed operation planned from 'up high,' because it was 'bungled too badly to have been the case.'")

Ziegler practiced the old jujitsu: "This is something that should not fall into the political process," he whined about O'Brien's ongoing accusations. And Haldeman and the president took charge of the obstruction. "Hunt disappeared or is in the process of disappearing," Haldeman assured the president. "He can un-disappear if we want him to. He can disappear to a Latin American country." They found that if Liddy's overexuberance had helped get them into this mess, he was a comically eager coconspirator to get them out of it. "If you want to put me before the firing squad and shoot me, that's fine," he said. "I'd kind of like to be like Nathan Hale."

That was the plan—not a firing squad, but for the burglars to take the fall. These crazy Cubans and their right-wing confreres could throw themselves on the mercy of the D.C. criminal courts, apologizing for their excess of patriotism and partisanship, insisting they'd acted on their own. Haldeman suggested a script: "We went in there to get this because we were scared to death that this crazy man was going to become President and sell the U.S. out to the Communists." As "first offenders," he supposed—thank God for liberal justice—they might end up with only a fine and a suspended sentence. That might, in turn, get rid of another headache: the million-dollar lawsuit the DNC had filed against the Committee to Re-Elect the President, the burglars, James McCord's private security firm, John Doe, and "other conspirators whose names are now unknown." Mitchell labeled that "another example of sheer demagoguery on the part of Mr. O'Brien." Mitchell knew it was anything but. In a civil suit, Democratic lawyers would get to take depositions. These, Haldeman pointed out, might expose "all kinds of other involvements." Convince the criminal judge that this was just right-wing wackos going off half-cocked, and the judge in the civil suit might give the defendants summary judgment. Howard Hunt wouldn't have to risk perjuring himself in a deposition—if, say, some Democratic lawyer took a wild-swinging guess and asked him if he had anything to do with Dita Beard's recanting the memo she wrote about the ITT bribe; or if he'd ever met this Chuck Colson character. "Jesus Christ, it's a rough deal on Colson, isn't it?" the president rued. Colson was the conduit through whom nearly every dirty trick ran.

The problem was the Federal Bureau of Investigation: they were working too hard. The man the president had appointed as acting FBI director
upon the passing of Edgar Hoover owed his career to Nixon. L. Patrick Gray
had worked for Nixon's presidential campaigns in 1960 and 1968. Then he
worked his way up to deputy attorney general. A former submarine commander, a military man through and through—he wore a brush cut even
shorter than Haldeman's—he revered the commander in chief: as acting FBI
director he went on the road about once a week to sing his praises. Gray saw
no reason not to impress his boss with a conscientious investigation that got
to the bottom of the rogue burglary so unfairly embarrassing the White
House; had no inkling that if he kept on following the scent, it would *lead*
to the White House.

His agents' first score was tracing $4,500 in $100 bills stashed in the burglars' hotel rooms back to an unsuspecting donor to the Nixon reelection
campaign. Their first frustration was the disappearance of the man, Howard
Hunt, who appeared in two of the burglars' address books. They interviewed
Hunt's boss, Robert Bennett, the son of Utah senator Wallace F. Bennett, at
the old-line Washington public relations firm the Robert R. Mullen Company, where Hunt had gone to work as a "writer" after his short career as a
White House consultant. What the FBI did not know was that the Mullen
Company was both a CIA front and, independently, a supplier of all manner of black-op services to the Committee to Re-Elect the President—among
them providing a cover job for Nixon spook E. Howard Hunt.

Thanks to the FBI's diligence the idea of directing the burglars to throw
themselves on the mercy of the D.C. criminal courts had to be discarded, and
a much more portentous obstruction of justice was devised. Haldeman and
Ehrlichman doped out the plan. "Both of us having been trying to think with
one step away from it," Haldeman explained Wednesday morning, June 21,
"see whether there's something that we can do other than just sitting here and
watch it drop on us bit by bit as it goes along. . . . The problem there is, that's
why it's important to get to the FBI. As of now, there's nothing that puts Hunt
into the case except his name in their notebooks with a lot of other things."

Thursday morning, the *Post,* back on page 9, ran a story by one of their
intrepid police reporters, Carl Bernstein, headlined, "Employer of 2 Tied to
Bugging Raised Money for Nixon." The two were Hunt and Douglas
Caddy, the cofounder of Young Americans for Freedom, whom Hunt had
called to represent the burglars as their criminal lawyer, and who handled the
Mullen Company's account with General Foods. Their boss, Robert Bennett, the article explained, was tied to the Nixon reelection campaign as chairman of some of its seventy-five dummy "committees" (such as "Supporters
of the American Dream") through which organizations such as the Associated Milk Producers had donated $325,000, which, Bernstein reported, "led
to a suit filed by Ralph Nader's Public Citizens, Inc., which charged that the

Nixon administration raise[d] government milk support prices as a pay-off for the donations."

That afternoon the president held his twenty-fourth news conference. It had been postponed from Monday so it wouldn't look as if he was responding to the break-in. But the first question was on what some were calling "Watergate": "Mr. O'Brien has said that the people who bugged his headquarters had a direct link to the White House. Have you had any sort of investigation made to determine whether this is true?" Nixon wriggled free by referring to Ziegler's statements, that the FBI and D.C. police were investigating, and that he couldn't comment on a case where "possible criminal charges were involved." Meanwhile Robert Mardian, the healthy right-wing exuberant in the Justice Department who'd been the point man in efforts to get rid of Hoover, cried to John Dean with alarm, "For God's sake, John, somebody's got to slow Pat Gray down. He's going like a crazy man."

The flames were licking closer. Luckily the eureka moment was nigh.

Nixon had a loyalist in J. Edgar Hoover's old chair. It was time to make him pay dividends. Right after the president's press conference, diligent Pat Gray called Richard Helms, the director of the CIA, to point out how many of the figures they were investigating had Agency ties, and to ask him if this was a CIA black op. Helms denied it—just the sort of thing the CIA *would* deny—and Gray briefed John Mitchell on the theories they were pursuing: "That the episode was either a CIA covert operation of some sort . . . or a CIA money chain, or a political money chain, or a pure political operation, or a Cuban right-wing operation, or a combination of any of these."

And there it was: the trick to shut the FBI down. Mitchell came up with it that night, chatting with the eager-beaver White House counsel, John Dean, who'd been brought in to help with the scheming. They could simply tell the FBI that, yes, this whole break-in *was* part of a CIA operation. A secret CIA operation *that the FBI had no business looking into.*

Haldeman explained the plot to the boss the next morning. Telling a government agency to cease and desist an operation that might blow CIA cover was "not an unusual development," he noted—blowing CIA cover could mean the death of agents in the field. "Mitchell's recommendation that the only way to solve this, and we're set up beautifully to do it," would be for the CIA's deputy director Vernon Walters to do the dirty deed—"have Walters call Pat Gray and just say, 'Stay the hell out of this . . . this is, ah, business here we don't want you to go any further on.'"

The president loved the idea. He even helped embroider the script. What was the CIA mission whose operational secrets were still most relevant? The 1961 attempt to overthrow Castro—the CIA operation that *Howard Hunt* had led. "Say, 'Look, the problem is that this will open the whole, the whole Bay of Pigs thing.'"

Nixon riffed it out, thinking aloud: "Just say this is a comedy of errors, without getting into it: 'The president believes that it's going to open the whole Bay of Pigs things again.'"

They could keep it vague, hinting at some ongoing operation to over-throw Castro—that was always plausible, given the principals involved—or that Larry O'Brien, the old Kennedy hand, possessed in his files information on just how embarrassing that 1961 operation was (no need to unduly embarrass fellow bureaucrats).

Bottom line: "Call the FBI . . . 'don't go any further into this case period!' "

Another problem, as formidable in its way as the Federal Bureau of Investigation, was John Mitchell's wife.

On Watergate weekend the top officers of the Committee to Re-Elect the President were out in California for a fund-raiser with Nixon's slate of Hollywood celebrities, including John Wayne, Zsa Zsa Gabor, Jack Benny, and Charlton Heston. Gathered poolside at a favorite Nixon Orange County beach resort, the officers were preparing to fly en masse back to Washington to help put out Watergate fires when Robert Mardian brought them the morning's papers.

Every copy he could find of the morning's papers.

They contained pictures of James McCord, and John Mitchell's statement that McCord was merely "the proprietor of a private security agency who was employed by our committee months ago." Mrs. John Mitchell, the woman who had yelled at a white-tie White House reception to tear the mis-creant Ray Conniff singer "limb from limb," was known to be a loose can-non, fond of dialing her friend Helen Thomas of United Press International with embarrassing tidbits about the Nixon circle. She knew James McCord wasn't just a guy who installed burglar alarms. She knew he was one of the top guys. A drunk, a harridan, a shrew, a troublesome woman, this Martha Mitchell. Mardian was making sure she didn't see a newspaper that morning. Then they locked her in the proverbial attic.

Mr. Mitchell told Mrs. Mitchell he had to head back to Washington to attend "a very important meeting." He pointed out, "You're tired. Stay out here for a few days, get some sun and swim."

The campaign officials jetted off on a Gulf Oil corporate jet, leaving behind Mrs. Mitchell to sulk in a bungalow amid the swaying palms, her bodyguard armed with instructions to, for God's sake, keep her away from newspapers and telephones. He failed at both. Feigning sleep, Martha Mitchell snuck the phone under the covers and got Helen Thomas on the line. She poured out her misery: she hated the turn her family's life had taken and was suspicious about all these furtive huddles and whispers about the Watergate that broke up whenever she came near. "I've given John an ulti-matum. I'm going to leave him unless he gets out of the campaign. I'm sick and tired of politics. Politics is a dirty business—"

Thomas heard a muffled shriek: *"You just get—get away!"*

In Washington the phone went dead. Mrs. Mitchell's bodyguard had ripped it out of the bungalow wall, like a scene in some Barbara Stanwyck noir.

"She's great," John Mitchell told UPI's Helen Thomas when she called asking for comment. "That little sweetheart. I love her so much. She gets a little upset about politics, but she loves me and I love her and that's what counts."

This was a nice bit of quick thinking. It fit into a favorite emerging narrative of the Georgetown chattering classes: the frightful pressure politics put on Washington marriages. (RNC chair Bob Dole had recently been divorced from his wife of twenty-four years; on the prowl, he had started sporting chocolate brown bell-bottom suits and, a Chicago reporter observed, "one of those all-year tans that celebrities manage.") Billy Graham called the president and offered to help counsel John and Martha Mitchell through their difficult patch. Another successful public relations score.

The *Post* kept on coming up with annoying little scoops: on the twenty-fifth, under Bernstein's byline, that a Miami architect said Bernard Barker had approached him the previous year asking for a blueprint of the Miami Beach convention hall's air-conditioning system. Bob Dole said what the White House told him to say, "For the last week, the Republican Party has been the victim of a barrage of unfounded and unsubstantiated allegations by George McGovern and his partner-in-mudslinging, the *Washington Post*. . . . McGovern appears to have turned over the franchise for his media attack campaign to the editors . . . who have shown themselves every bit as sure-footed along the low road . . . as McGovern." That skillfully played into another emerging popular narrative—the *Godfather* narrative. "They think that political parties do this all the time," Colson pointed out. "They think that companies do this. You know, there have been marvelous stories written about industrial espionage. How Ford agents go into General Motors to get the designs. People sort of expect this."

The president: "Governments do it. We all know that."

Bob Haldeman: "Sure."

The president: "Companies do it. Political parties do it. The point is that we—as I said, the main concern is to keep the White House out of it."

In that they were succeeding famously. A typical Watergate story, by June 29, was Nick Thimmesch's column lamenting that the Republicans, understandably paranoid about security, had gone overboard by hiring a spook like McCord in the first place to do their burglar alarms: "The Watergate break-in looks more and more like a job performed for a right-wing anti-Castro group. . . . Naturally, O'Brien grabs on to this astonishing episode for political gain, and makes all sorts of outlandish charges such as the one that there is 'a developing clear line to the White House' in the case. Humor is blessed relief in a messy episode like this one."

No one even asked about the story that afternoon at the president's first televised press conference in thirteen months. Instead, the most awkward moment was when Dan Rather of CBS, a Texas bulldog, asked about reports from Agence France-Presse and the Swedish ambassador in Hanoi that eyewitnesses had seen American planes hit the dikes in North Vietnam. That was easily flicked away: "Mr. Rather, we have checked out those reporters. They have proved to be inaccurate. . . . We have had orders out not to hit dikes because the result in terms of civilian casualties would be extraordinary."

The hot story, in the wake of McGovern's final victory in New York, was not the break-in at the Democrats' headquarters but the Democrats' disarray. Reported David Broder, "With the clinching votes that would assure him the Democratic presidential nomination still narrowly beyond his reach, Sen. George McGovern's forces yesterday set the stage for convention floor fights to obtain a platform reflecting his views on busing and other controversial issues." Evans and Novak reported Humphrey was planning to challenge the legality of California's winner-take-all primary as a violation of "the spirit of one-man, one-vote reform. . . . The challenge will likely be rejected by the McGovern-controlled Credentials Committee, setting up a showdown on the convention floor. With McGovern's own count now 100 delegates short of the 1,509 needed for nomination, he would seemingly be able to beat back the California challenge."

But that, then, would make him a hypocrite and an enemy of the spirit of reform, wouldn't it?

"Therefore, Humphrey might maneuver a convention vote splitting the California delegation if he could combine all non-McGovern delegates. In that credentials test, he probably will have the aid of Gov. George Wallace's delegates. Humphrey's campaign believes it also has backing from Rep. Shirley Chisholm. Several uncommitted leaders, such as Gov. Jimmy Carter, support the challenge."

Evans and Novak summarized, "That, in turn, could conceivably stop McGovern, and herein lies the internal anguish. Much as they fear McGovern's nomination would bring catastrophe in November, many thoughtful party regulars dread even more the holocaust if they deny him the nomination at this point." Warren Weaver of the *New York Times* quoted an anonymous Democratic leader: "In Chicago in 1968, the riots were outside the convention hall. In Miami in 1972, they're going to be inside, and the reformers are responsible for the change of scene."

Anguish, holocaust, riot inside the convention hall: words for Richard Nixon to savor. Harris was out with a new poll. Nixon ran 45 percent to 33 against McGovern with Wallace in the race and 54–38 without Wallace; he did no worse against Humphrey. "Mainstream" Democrat, "extremist" Democrat, it didn't matter: all fared poorly against Nixon.

In Which Playboy Bunnies, and Barbarella, and Tanya Inspire Theoretical Considerations upon the Nature of Democracy

Democrats started straggling into Miami Beach the second week in July 1972. One of them was Robert Redford, arriving by train, promoting *The Candidate* in a mock whistle-stop tour. Abbie Hoffman and Jerry Rubin set up housekeeping at the run-down Albion Hotel, where Rita Hayworth and Orson Welles once honeymooned. Everywhere Hoffman and Rubin were mobbed by cops hoping to make it into the documentary rumor had it that Warner's had paid them millions to shoot. They wouldn't be doing much in the way of protesting, they promised, so long as the nomination wasn't stolen from McGovern. "McGovern Backer No Longer Thinks Sons, Daughters, Should Kill Parents," the RNC magazine *First Monday* headlined an interview with Rubin. Only tiny left-wing splinter groups considered McGovern the enemy.

Yippies met with Miami Beach's glad-handing liberal police chief, who laid out the ground rules: "Fellas, I don't believe in trying to enforce laws that can't be enforced. If you guys smoke a little pot, I'm not going to send my men in after you." They got the same welcome from Mayor Charles Hall. "Call me Chuck," he said, before showing off his print of John and Yoko's wedding day—"It's the original, you know"—and offering them the city's golf courses as campsites. When the Yippies staged their first march to the convention center, "Chuck" arrived to try to lead it. Abbie and Jerry were celebrities. Celebrity was power in 1972. Abbie and Jerry were all about the new youth vote. Youth was power, too.

At McGovern headquarters at the famous Doral resort, the usual haunt of golfing Shriners, hordes of kids awaited their hero's arrival "wearing," Norman Mailer wrote, "copper bangles and spaced-out heavy eyes." He imagined the reaction of the Democratic regulars: "Where were the bourbon and broads of yesteryear?"

Not at the Doral's rooftop restaurant-bar; it was one of the few rooms left in town that still required a suit and tie. That meant this week it was empty. Prostitutes were lonely, too. The New Politics, this movement of acid and abortion for all, had a Calvinist work ethic. Many McGovern delegates had won their spots by outlasting the flabby old regulars in caucuses, just as they'd outlasted rival left *factionistas* at endless antiwar meetings. They were not in Miami to party. Germaine Greer, the women's liberationist, complained she "couldn't find anyone to ball."

Presidential candidates arrived at Miami International Airport, one by one: Wilbur Mills, still rumored to be fronting a Ted Kennedy draft; George Wallace, who touched down in a plane provided him by the White House and was honored by the DNC with a brass band; Hubert Humphrey, who responded when asked if he thought he could win, "I didn't come down for a vacation." John Lindsay landed to rumors that he was so unpopular that the New York caucus would be avoiding him. The front-runner touched down one hour late due to a tropical storm, after an airport press conference from George Meany in which the labor boss intoned, "We've made it quite plain we don't like McGovern."

But could he *stop* McGovern? That was the question. Any kind of chaos seemed possible. Meany called it "the craziest convention I've seen." And he'd seen a few.

The grand lobby of the Fontainebleau was legendary: eight-tiered crystal chandeliers, pillars trimmed with gold glass, bosomy marble nymphs, a panoramic mural of Rome. Sunday morning it started to stink. It wasn't from hippies. The air-conditioning had given out. Sunday night at the Playboy Club the stink was of cigars as lumpy old fat cats arrived for a $1,000-a-ticket Humphrey reception. This time hippies *were* the problem: a faction arrived to heckle, harass, and barricade the entrance. Then, fire engines clanged their way up the driveway, answering a fire alarm in the Playboy bunnies' dressing room. It had been set ablaze by commando feminists.

The Playboy party dispersed before the guest of honor arrived: Hubert Humphrey, droopy and fatigued, having just lost his best chance at victory in a backroom decision. The man who had told Walter Cronkite he wouldn't be a spoilsport—"goodness, no"—had decided he would challenge California's winner-take-all primary after all. McGovern said he saw "hate and vehemence in Hubert's eyes" when he announced it. Before the Credentials Committee late in June, Humphrey's people argued that the spirit of the newly reformed rules demanded they change the rules—that Humphrey deserved "Adequate Representation of Minority Views on Presidential Candidates at Each Stage in the Delegate Selection Process." The committee agreed and awarded California's convention votes in proportion to its primary vote. Thus a winner-take-all result in California was transformed by a winner-take-all vote of the Credentials Committee into a proportional result, to decide an inherently winner-take-all proposition: who would get to be the Democratic presidential nominee. The McGovern people took the decision to court—arguing that the spirit of the McGovern reforms was an abhorrence of regulars changing a democratic result after the fact to hold on to power, that the letter of the reforms preserved the winner-take-all primary, and that only a judge, deciding undemocratically, could make sure democracy prevailed.

The reformed Democratic Party was in chaos, the determination of its legitimate representatives seemingly as complex as probate hearings for a billionaire who died intestate. Forty percent of the delegates chosen to go to Miami Beach were under some sort of challenge or another.

The first judge ruled for Humphrey. The second reversed for McGovern. Humphrey appealed to the Supreme Court—which ruled on July 7 that the Democrats would have to sort out credentials challenges themselves. Which might have seemed to have thrown the victory back to the anyone-but-McGovern forces—if the Democratic Party didn't *also* have a rule that it only took the votes of 10 percent of the Credentials Committee members to bring the issue to the floor for a full debate and the vote of the entire convention.

That debate was set for the opening convention session Monday. But a crucial procedural matter had to be decided first. If the 151 delegates under dispute were *included* in the tally of the "entire convention," the McGovern side would win the vote. If they were *excluded* from voting on their own challenge, McGovern would be denied the nomination on the first ballot and the convention would be thrown up for grabs. The candidate of openness required a decision for a de facto closed convention to win.

Any political scientist could have told you that creating fair and legitimate representative institutions can be monstrously complex and paradoxical. It took the Founding Fathers twelve years to sort the problem out. This decision fell upon the shoulders of a single man: Lawrence O'Brien. He had only a couple of days to decide who would get to vote on the California challenge, a bevy of reporters breathing down his neck asking, "Will there be another Chicago?"

The Happy Warrior gave a press conference Sunday morning at his headquarters hotel, where the sign outside read WELCOME FUTURE PRESIDENT HUMPHREY. He cast McGovern as the Mayor Daley of Miami Beach, a usurping political boss. McGovern, pious as ever, said he'd never thought California's winner-take-all primary was fair in the first place. Frank Mankiewicz cast *Humphrey* as Mayor Daley: "If we lose California, half the delegates will think something was stolen. We're not sure Larry understands the fury that the situation might unleash."

O'Brien ruled for McGovern just as Humphrey was dressing for the Playboy party. Was it fair? What was fair? Whatever the case, mighty Hubert had struck out. The message in front of Humphrey's hotel was replaced by one advertising a girlie show.

Then there was the matter of the actual Mayor Daley, whose Chicago machine would be facing their own floor fight the next evening. It wasn't like the old days, recalled Chicago congressman Dan Rostenkowski. "Daley used to call us together and say, 'Well, look, we've got one hundred slots to fill. Let's get some labor people, some blacks . . . say, four for the newspapers'—usually it would be their wives who wanted to go." Now, Mayor Daley was hiding away at his vacation cottage in Michigan, negotiating for a chance to serve as a delegate at all.

This melodrama had been building since 1969, when the McGovern Commission came to Chicago, Daley offered his own reform plan, and McGovern responded that Daley's most useful contribution would be to dismiss the Chicago 8 indictments. The mayor had proposed that every delegate in the nation be decided in primary elections, which sounded democratic. It actually was a machine-lubricating hustle. If there was one skill bosses like Daley possessed, it was fixing low-turnout elections.

The Illinois primary had been on March 21. Daley ran a slate of fifty-nine delegates from Cook County uncommitted to any presidential candidate. Forty were Daley's township and ward committeemen. This all fell afoul of reform. But to the Cook County Regular Democratic Organization, there was no personage so monstrous as a reformer.

Ward healers and precinct captains had gone door-to-door with sample ballots, making clear as usual that the elaborate latticework of patronage and municipal services relied on neighborhoods voting "right." A former officer of the Chicago League of Women Voters testified about her own encounter with one of these door-knockers: she said the sample ballot violated the democratic reform guidelines; the mook responded he'd never heard of these "guidelines" of which she spoke; she replied that they demanded slates balanced by sex; he responded, "Women don't belong in politics."

Daley's delegates swept the March primary. A reform alderman later testified to the Credentials Committee that it took so much money to challenge a machine candidate that few ever bothered. One who was naive enough to try was a twenty-four-year-old from the South Side of Chicago, Maureen Bremer, who had been trampled in 1968 on Michigan Avenue. Her friends got the six hundred signatures required to get her on the ballot, outhustled the machine with volunteers, and won—only to find her victory legally overturned. Daley controlled the judges, too.

But the machine was no longer almighty. That same primary, Daley's candidate for governor lost to reformer Daniel Walker, who had chaired the federal commission on the '68 convention that accused the mayor of fomenting a "police riot." In 1971, *Chicago Sun Times* columnist Mike Royko had come out with a scathing exposé of Richard J. Daley, entitled *Boss*. Two hundred Chicago bookstores were pressured into not stocking it, but the demand proved too great and *Boss* was returned to the shelves; Eleanor "Sis" Daley, the mayor's wife, was spotted vandalizing copies. Then, also in 1971, a reform attorney named Michael Shakman began tying up the machine in court with a case charging the patronage system violated the Fourteenth Amendment. That same year Daley promoted one of his "Silent Six" Negro aldermen, Ralph Metcalfe, star of the 1936 Olympics, to Congress; Metcalfe turned on the machine with the zeal of the convert, proclaiming, "It's never too late to be black." Daley's state's attorney Ed Hanrahan was under indictment for obstruction of justice in the cold-blooded murder of Black Panther Fred Hampton. Daley was losing his grip on the ghetto. He was losing his grip on patronage. He began, simply, losing his grip, making bizarre outbursts at city council meetings.

At least he could still comfort himself that he commanded Svengali-like leverage over the Democratic presidential selection process.

Then he started losing that, too.

A white reformer, Alderman William Singer, and a black minister and civil rights leader, Jesse Jackson, filed a formal challenge of the March 21 primary results. In June the Democratic Credentials Committee sent a hearings officer to Chicago to take evidence. (McGovern, pious as ever, announced he neither favored nor opposed the challenge.) The regulars tried to sabotage the challengers, accusing the reformers of a conspiracy "to weaken the Democratic Party and enhance their ability to take it over." The reformers presented a methodical statistical case for how the machine had been subverting grassroots democracy for generations. The hearings officer returned to Washington with thousands of pages of testimony. Then, at the Illinois State Democratic convention in the middle of June, the machine whooped through a motion to increase the size of the delegation, diluting the power of the challengers should they win. The regulars insisted it was only fair. "What are we, for God's sake—lepers in the colony?" Congressman Dan Rostenkowski pleaded. "We're the ones who do the work, day in, day out."

At the end of June, the reformers held meetings in all eight of Cook County's congressional districts to choose the fifty-nine people who would travel to Miami Beach as the Jackson-Singer delegation. That was the final straw. The machine did what machines do.

At St. Thomas Lutheran Church busloads of machine musclemen arrived, wrestled the chairman to the floor, and scattered his records as Alderman Ed Vrdolyak cheered them on through a megaphone. At the downtown YWCA the session chairman was manhandled and announced the meeting would reconvene elsewhere, then a mob of several hundred

Daley supporters blocked the elevators, roughing up anyone who tried to leave. In the Third District at Hometown Christian Church, one of the mob leaders wore a sheriff's department patch; in the Ninth the mob included the machine candidate for governor; in the Fifth, in a Catholic parish church, the mob was led by the mayor's son Richard Daley Jr. Two days later, Daley Jr. orchestrated the disruption of the election of the Jackson-Singer delegation's at-large delegates, then convened a press conference to say, "They would seek to disenfranchise the nine hundred thousand voters who went to the polls and cast their votes for the delegates of their choice. . . . This could hardly take place in a dictatorship." At the mayor's next city hall press conference he denied having anything to do with it. Then he denied there had been any disruptions: just good Chicago Democrats battling the "Singer machine." "What divine authority do these people think they have? What about all their agitation in the streets and in the City Council?"

Daley traveled to Washington to try to win over the Credentials Committee. His pretext for the trip was testimony to a congressional panel on a pet subject, gun control. "Take the guns away from every private citizen," he pleaded, and found time to tell reporters he still hoped Ted Kennedy would win the nomination. ("Every mother wants her boy to be president, and every boy wants to be president," he blathered, oblivious that Rose Kennedy, having seen two sons murdered for that ambition, might be the exception.) Daley also denounced the continued mining of Haiphong Harbor. The ideological ironies were plentiful in the battle between the regulars and the reformers.

The Credentials Committee ruled for the reformers. The mayor issued threats through channels to throw Illinois to Nixon. The next day Supreme Court justice William Rehnquist granted Daley the right to take his case to Cook County circuit court. The day after that, a federal district court judge refused what Daley asked for: an injunction barring the reformers from being seated in Miami. Daley appealed. Mediators cast about for compromises. Both sides hardened their positions. "This is like Soviet Russia," a Daley delegate said of the reformers. Jesse Jackson said of the regulars, "The mayor has to understand that this is a new day." The full U.S. Supreme Court mooted the judicial wrangling with its July 7 decision that Democrats would have to iron out their difficulties among themselves. In Chicago, circuit court judge Daniel A. Covelli issued an injunction barring the Jackson-Singer challengers from taking their seats in Miami. The power play was naked. Covelli was a machine judge famous for jailing anyone who defied him. Reporters asked him if he would do it this time. "I take the position," he answered, "that if people are permitted to violate injunctions issued by the court, we should close up shop and let everyone carry a six-shooter." One reform alderman said she would gladly go to jail to keep her seat. It was, she said, like facing down a Southern sheriff: "By running to Covelli Mayor Daley has informed the world that he, Mayor Daley, is higher than the Supreme Court."

Mayor Daley's cigar-chompers arrived at George McGovern's convention not knowing whether they'd get to be delegates or not. They had a hard time enjoying themselves at Playboy Plaza Sunday night, and that was even before they were set upon by torch-bearing women's libbers. They visited the hospitality suite at the Doral that the McGovern team had set up to woo "uncommitted" delegates such as themselves; there were twelve different kinds of whiskey and Scotch. And a twenty-three-year-old host, wearing sandals and a psychedelic tie.

Jesse Jackson suggested a compromise. White reformers called him a sellout. McGovern suggested a compromise. The cochair of the reformers responded, "If he needs Mayor Daley's support more than he needs us, we don't need him."

There were to be no compromises. This was the New Politics.

Monday, the convention's opening day, the two sides scurried from hotel to hotel, lobbying delegations, each stressing the justice of its cause, each threatening dire consequences in November should its side lose. Some reformers were able to show off the scars Mayor Daley's police had given them in 1968. A New Mexico delegate recalled the teargassing he had received: "I hate Daley's guts!" Meanwhile, Daley's most fierce hometown scourge—columnist Mike Royko—spoke of the metaphorical scars of the people Daley represented. "I just don't see where your delegation is representative of Chicago's Democrats," he wrote in a column addressed personally to Singer. "As I looked over the names of your delegates, I saw something peculiar. . . . There's only one Italian there. Are you saying that only one out of every 59 Democratic votes cast in a Chicago election is cast by an Italian? And only three of your 59 have Polish names. . . . Your reforms have disenfranchised Chicago's white ethnic Democrats, which is a strange reform."

The convention's first evening would also see challenges to delegations from Alabama, Rhode Island, South Carolina, Kentucky, Georgia, Washington, Virginia, Hawaii, Michigan, Texas, Connecticut, and Oklahoma. Each side was supposed to get twenty minutes, but the rules said the convention could vote additional time. Then there would be roll-call votes. The convention secretary reported that she believed she could call the names of the 3,016 voting delegates in approximately fifty-two minutes. All of it would play out on television.

As the convention made ready to convene, a shouting match broke out in the Illinois section. Jesse Jackson showed a ticket that entitled him to a seat behind the delegation chairman. A congressman from a rural district had arrogated the spot for himself: "When you've been elected to Congress for eighteen years," he bellowed, "*then* I'll respect you." The reverend was wearing a dashiki, the flowing African-style robe favored by black nationalists, as the TV cameras recorded, and as history recalled. The cameras did not record, nor did history recall, the reverend's ambivalent feelings about his victory over Daley—"What kind of pleasure can you get by throwing a man that old out of something that's so important to him?"—nor his tireless and risky efforts to effect a last-minute compromise between the reformers and the regulars. Instead he became a visual symbol of the reformers' theft of "regular" Democrats' birthright, and a great political party's civil war.

Somewhere, Richard Nixon was smiling.

It had to be close to midnight Monday when the hippie from Arizona grabbed Abbie Hoffman around the waist and hollered, "I'm the first, man!"

"The first what?"

"The first fucker ever to cast a vote on acid." ("There goes the Polish vote," Abbie thought.)

That was during the roll call on California, the second vote of the evening. Other insurgents weren't so happy. The first roll call had been on a challenge to the regular South Carolina delegation. And thanks to a parliamentary calculation so fantastically complex and paradoxical it resembled subatomic physics, the McGovern side had decided they had to lose it on purpose to show their strength.

The people they were selling out were feminists. The South Carolina challenge was the culmination of almost a year's labor by a new organization, the National Women's Political Caucus, which had formed in the summer of 1971 to pressure the parties for 40 percent representation of women at their conventions. At one time such a demand would not have seemed particularly controversial—only a few months earlier, in fact, the Equal Rights Amendment had passed both houses of Congress with overwhelming bipartisan support. One of the NWPC's most aggressive activists was George Romney's wife, Lenore; indeed, since time immemorial, both Democratic and Republican national committees had required membership balance by gender. The NWPC had no trouble, late in 1971, convincing Democratic officials to count a paucity of women in a delegation as prima facie evidence of violation of the McGovern Commission's requirement of "affirmative steps" toward "reasonable representation." The resentment came later, as the "women's libbers" came to be considered and came to consider themselves vanguardists in pushing the boundaries of liberal consciousness.

Abortion politics was one catalyst; women were beginning to claim "abortion on demand" as a right. Gay rights was another cutting-edge issue. Some feminists still considered both outrageous; Betty Friedan labeled the lesbians organizing within the National Organization for Women the "lavender menace." It came to a head at Democratic platform committee meetings in March. Shirley MacLaine confronted Gloria Steinem at the elevators: "If you people had your way, you'd have George support everyone's right to fuck goats."

Here was another development to warm the cockles of Richard Nixon's heart: wedge issues within the New Politics coalition itself.

The National Women's Political Caucus came to Miami wearing defiant buttons: WE'RE HERE TO MAKE POLICY, NOT COFFEE. Their intention was to unseat the overwhelmingly male South Carolina delegation as an opening show of strength. They had the votes to do it, and just as important, George McGovern's "unequivocal" endorsement. Then suddenly, during the first roll call of the 1972 Democratic National Convention, their sure votes started going the other way. Larry O'Brien's decision about who would get to vote on the California challenge couldn't be shown to be the McGovern coalition's determining margin of victory—or else the anyone-but-McGovern forces would appeal O'Brien's decision to the full convention. So McGovern deputies were racing up and down the aisles begging McGovern delegates to vote against the feminists. "*Unequivocal* does not mean at the expense of the nomination," one of them said. The feminists, and their cigar-chomping strange bedfellows, lost the vote: the next roll call, on California, moved forward without objection. California's winner-take-all rule prevailed. The word shot across the convention hall that McGovern had clinched the nomination—and also that he had done it by selling out reform.

Openness was proving a damned slow way to run a convention. It was close to 3 a.m. when the roll-call vote on the Illinois challenge was finally called. It was close to dawn when the reformers finally won. They started screaming, jumping on their seats, singing "We Shall Overcome," taking pictures, incredulous they really owned the seats of the old men they despised.

"The streets of '68 are the aisles of '72!"

"The aisles belong to the people! The aisles belong to the people!"

The losers repaired with their cigars to watch the rest of the show on TV, insisting a Democrat obviously couldn't become president without the Cook County machine. Wrote the *Chicago Daily News*'s youth columnist Bob Greene, on the other hand, "This is America, and someday Richard Daley may be able to earn a place inside the Convention Hall, just like Jerry Rubin. If the Mayor is willing to be patient and to work within the system."

The next day the business was voting on platform resolutions. McGovern operatives begged the women's and gay liberationists to drop their demand for floor votes on their planks to moderate the Democrats' image for TV. These operatives ruefully discovered that political purists could also act like ward bosses, extracting their own pounds of political flesh. The gays reminded them of how McGovern would not have won the coveted spot at the top of the California primary ballot if it weren't for a last-minute signature drive in the gay bars of the Castro by the Alice B. Toklas Memorial Democratic Club. "We do not come to you pleading for your understanding or pleading for your tolerance," San Francisco delegate Jim Foster pronounced during his ten minutes. "We come to you affirming our pride in our lifestyle, affirming validity to seek and maintain meaningful emotional relationships and affirming our right to participate in the life of this country on an equal basis with every citizen."

The TV lights made his light-colored linen jacket with its patchwork of thick lines look particularly garish. Then delegate Kathleen Wilch of Ohio went to the podium on behalf of McGovern. She asked delegates to vote against the gay rights plank: it would "commit the Democratic Party to seek repeal of all laws involving the protection of children from sexual approaches by adults" and force "repeal of all laws relating to prostitution, pandering, pimping"—and "commit this party to repeal many laws designed to protect the young, the innocent, and the weak."

McGovern's convention rejected gay rights in a landslide. Be that as it may, one week later, George Meany officially announced the AFL-CIO wouldn't be endorsing a presidential candidate that year. At a Steelworkers' convention in September, he explained why: the "Democratic Party has been taken over by people named Jack who look like Jills and smell like johns."

Then, the acrimonious battle over the abortion plank: "In matters relating to human reproduction each person's right to privacy, freedom of choice, and individual conscience should be fully respected, consistent with relevant Supreme Court decisions."

A "pro-choice" woman took the podium: "The freedom of all people to control their own fertility must be an essential human health right. . . . For the first time fifty-seven percent of all Americans believe abortion should be a decision between a woman and her physician."

Then a "right-to-life" man spoke on "the slaughter of the most innocent whose right to live is not mentioned in the minority report."

Then Shirley MacLaine spoke her piece in favor of her candidate's position: equivocation. The subject should be "kept out of the political process," she said, though delegates should "vote their conscience." Some 250 McGovern floor whips raced once more up and down the aisles to defeat the plank, insisting Humphrey and Wallace supporters were conspiring to saddle McGovern with the "extremism" label to deny him the nomination. The plank lost by 472 votes. "SISTERS VS. SISTERS," headlined the *Washington Post* the next morning: "Gloria Steinem's usually controlled monotone quivered as she wept in rage, verbally attacked Gary Hart, and called McGovern strategists 'bastards.'" The paper also quoted a pro-choice Humphrey supporter: "I resent the McGovern people who say he is so pure. One of the reasons so many women supported him six months ago was because they thought he was liberal on abortion."

The New Politics reformers had fantasized a pure politics, a politics of unyielding principle—an *anti*politics. But in the real world politics without equivocation or compromise is impossible. Thus an unintended consequence for the would-be antipolitician. Announcing one's inflexibility sabotages him in advance. Every time he makes a political decision, he looks like a sellout. The reformers fantasized an *open* politics, in which all points of view had time to be heard. That meant that the Tuesday session adjourned eleven hours after it began, at 6:15 a.m.—a fortunate thing, cool-headed Democratic strategists decided, terrified over what this all looked like on TV.

On nomination day Humphrey officially announced his withdrawal. George McGovern, whose campaign had once been such a long shot the network camera crews called his campaign bus the "morgue patrol," would be the Democrats' nominee for president.

His day didn't begin happily. McGovern was quoted in the morning papers saying that, though he would order an immediate cease-fire on inauguration day, he would keep up America's "military capability in Thailand and on the high seas" until all prisoners of war were returned. He had made this promise in person to the POW wives who had traveled at their own expense to Miami. That didn't satisfy several hundred militants who refused to leave the Doral lobby, to the terror of Secret Service and police, until McGovern explained why he had just chosen to become a "puppet of the bosses," "warmonger," and "lying pig."

He came down from his suite, looked them in the eye, and said, "I'm not shifting my position on any of the fundamental stands I've taken in this campaign." He reminded them that he was against imprisoning marijuana smokers but not for its legalization, and that he believed in "amnesty for all young men who stood up against the war." His directness quieted their rebellion. Then it was back to his suite to work on his acceptance speech; then off to the convention center to learn how Pyrrhus felt.

Just as in 1968, McGovern was nominated by Connecticut senator Abe Ribicoff. During lulls in the roll call the band played the theme from the rock opera *Jesus Christ Superstar*. He was put over the top by one of Dick Daley's friends, who even announced that his delegation was endorsing the latest liberal crusade: boycotting lettuce in solidarity with Cesar Chavez and the United Farm Workers. McGovern's tally was 1,564.95 to slightly over 1,000 for everyone else combined. The regulars fell into line. That was what regulars did. "There are two reasons that we are going to win this election," boomed Oklahoma's Carl Albert, the man who had done Mayor Daley's bidding at the podium in 1968 in Chicago. "One is—*George McGovern!* The other is—*Richard Nixon!*"

The contenders dutifully stood hands raised together as the balloons dropped: Muskie, Chisholm, Scoop Jackson, Humphrey, who was flashing peace signs. But the 250 McGovern floor managers weren't able to whip up the traditional resolution to make the nomination unanimous—something even Barry Goldwater had been able to manage. Too much water under the bridge for that. One hippie's sign during the celebratory demonstration read simply MCGOVERN SUCKS! Another, a black man's, said DON'T VOTE '72!

George McGovern was learning what a mess of pottage a presidential nomination could be when your defining trait was supposed to be your purity.

He would now learn how difficult it could be, too, to deliberate on important decisions during a convention in which sensitive debates wasted eleven hours straight.

He received a midnight call of congratulations from Ted Kennedy—still America's favorite Democrat. McGovern asked him to be his running mate. Kennedy refused, citing "very personal reasons." McGovern called Abraham Ribicoff. Ribicoff turned him down. The campaign had to come up with someone by 4 p.m. Thursday, the deadline for putting names in nomination. They started assembling a hasty list, which they hadn't had time to do what with all the credentials fights and platform fights and assuaging meetings.

Leonard Woodcock, president of the United Auto Workers—a Catholic labor leader to earn back some white ethnics? (Then someone found out he hadn't been to mass in twenty years.)

Patrick Lucey, governor of Wisconsin, also Catholic? (His wife, some people feared, was another Martha Mitchell.)

The names of senators and governors started flying: DNC chiefs, network anchormen, feminists, blacks, Father Hesburgh, president of Notre Dame (surely he still went to mass?).

They settled on Kevin White, mayor of Boston. Someone thought to clear the idea with Ted Kennedy. Kennedy called back two and a half hours before the deadline and said he wasn't a fan. Kevin White was out.

A call went out to Senator Gaylord Nelson of Wisconsin, a hero of the ecologists. Senator Nelson answered with a spousal veto and suggested Missouri's young senator Thomas Eagleton, a Catholic with Kennedy looks and charm who came out of the Democrats' blue-collar, urban-boss milieu. He was a friend of labor; maybe George Meany would take a shine to him.

Though no one knew much else about him.

Thomas Eagleton's name had appeared in the *New York Times* and the *Washington Post* but sixty-seven times since he'd become a senator in 1969. (Gaylord Nelson showed up six hundred times in the same span; Kennedy, almost four thousand.) But then there was the old saying: a running mate can't help you, only hurt you. Maybe the obscurity was a plus. Someone heard he'd had an alcohol problem. They checked it out, and the reports were found lacking. McGovern personally placed the call; Eagleton said yes—before, he later quipped, McGovern had time to change his mind. When word got out just how desperate McGovern had been to make the deadline to nominate a vice president, Defense Secretary Laird insinuated that McGovern got Eagleton to take the job in exchange for agreeing to continue production on the F-15 fighter, built in a plant in Eagleton's hometown.

Another old ritual had gone by the wayside in the reformed Democratic Party: the idea that the convention rubber-stamps the nominee's choice for running mate. Endicott "Chub" Peabody, the former governor of Massachusetts, had traveled to thirty-seven states since January campaigning for the vice presidency. Feminists put Frances "Sissy" Farenthold, who had almost won the Democratic gubernatorial primary in Texas, into nomination. Senator Mike Gravel had his own name put in—then seconded himself. Hodding Carter, the liberal Mississippi newspaper editor, Congressman Peter Rodino, and a New York adman named Stanley Arnold were nominated, too. The Wallace people nominated their black delegate, a Dallas disc jockey. There were drawn-out nominating and seconding speeches for everyone. *This* would show America: the Democrats were the party of openness. Then, in a three-hour roll call, Senator Eagleton got but 58 percent, and seventy-nine other "candidates" had votes recorded for them—including Jerry Rubin, Martha Mitchell, Mao Tse-tung, and Archie Bunker.

The 1972 Democratic National Convention concluded with what some thought was the greatest speech of George McGovern's career. Unfortunately, it was delivered at 2:45 a.m. Only 3 million people saw it. Twenty million would watch Nixon's acceptance speech in prime time a month and a half later. Plenty more had been watching hours earlier during the vice-presidential roll call, when two men wearing purple shirts reading GAY POWER kissed in the aisles. Television cameramen have an eye for the peculiar. Though the vast majority of conventioneers looked utterly conventional, they dwelled on the likes of Beth Ann Labson, an eighteen-year-old California delegate, walking around without shoes. ("By 1976," wrote Abbie and Jerry, "the convention will be held in a meadow.") Larry O'Brien delivered a speech at the podium while, twenty feet below, Allen Ginsberg sat cross-legged, chanting mantras. Denim and tie-dyed T-shirts and peasant dresses; men carrying babies in papoose boards—and, the *Post* recorded in its article on the abortion floor debate, "girls in patched jeans and no bras." A black man and a white woman kissing on camera. Interracial marriage had been illegal in some Southern states until a Supreme Court decision only five years earlier.

Where were the sweaty, fat, bald men in suits and ties of yesteryear? The congressmen's wives in evening gowns? The plump matrons in floral dresses dancing with banners and balloons? The broads in cheerleader outfits, Humphreyettes, Johnsonettes, Kennedyettes, Stevensonettes, Trumanettes— where were *they*? The only men dressed in Native American dress were . . . Native Americans.

These people were . . . *the wrong kind of exuberant.* They were dressed . . . *the wrong kind of crazy.* The colors were . . . *the wrong kind of riotous.* The women were . . . *the wrong kind of sexy.*

Gus Tyler, old-line leader of the International Ladies' Garment Workers'

Union, watched it back home on TV. Tyler was a socialist. He knew something about radical. He also knew something about people's longing for security and stability. That was what had made him a socialist. He also thought he knew something about politics: there was no politics without accommodation. That was what made him a *Democrat.* He wondered what this all must look like to the farmer in Iowa, a housewife in Bensonhurst, "somebody out there," he later reflected to an interviewer, "in Peoria."

All of these people had given the Democrats a landslide in 1964. They had trusted the Democratic Party.

In the interim they had seen America plunged into chaos.

And then they looked at this convention and thought, *"Here are the people who are responsible for this chaos."*

McGovern retreated to South Dakota for a much needed vacation, press corps in tow: "I made Harry Reasoner's bed this morning," a maid at the Hi-Ho Motel in Custer told a newspaper columnist. "It was not a big deal. It was like any bed."

The press studied the latest Gallup finding: McGovern had only gained two points from Miami Beach—and even Goldwater had gained 20 points from his convention. The McGovern camp maintained its customary confidence, exchanging stories like the one about the North Dakota mayor who came to Miami complaining, "There are more hippies than mayors as delegates," but left proudly sporting a McGovern pin, having discovered these hippies decent people worthy of his respect. It didn't *feel* like Richard Nixon's America. Even in this little town in the middle of nowhere the kids looked as if they'd stepped out of Greenwich Village. Nineteen-year-old hotel maids—voting age!—talked about how they were thinking about moving into communes. A special ran on TV featuring Joe Cocker and Richie Havens—the bill from Woodstock, delivered straight into the living rooms of Custer, South Dakota.

Although choosing Custer as the billet for his vacation was not a good omen for someone entering the battle of a lifetime.

The reporters were bored and listless, thinking of packing it in. The candidate arrived late to a noon press conference Monday in a pine-paneled auditorium at a serene lakeside resort, uttered platitudes about what a pleasure it would be to work closely with them over the next three months. Thomas Eagleton took his turn at the podium—the boys weren't even bothering to take notes—and told one of those silly loosening-up politician's jokes. *He looks a little like Jack Lemmon,* some distractedly thought.

Then Eagleton switched to a quieter voice: "In political campaigning it is part and parcel of that campaigning that there will be rumors about candidates. Rumors have followed me during my political career, dating back when I first ran for office in 1956. . . ."

The press boys fumbled for their notebooks.

"On three occasions in my life I have voluntarily gone into hospitals as a result of nervous exhaustion and fatigue."

The Knight newspaper chain had been working on that scoop. It hadn't taken them much effort to track down what the McGovern staff had not been able to in the headlong rush of Miami Beach. A reporter acting on a tip (from a loyal Democrat wishing to help the ticket, it turned out) had shown up at a hospital in St. Louis, and the staff protested that they couldn't violate the confidence of one of their patients by revealing his mental maladies.

The news conference was an attempt to head off the story. Eagleton's statement tried to make of his "nervous exhaustion" a virtue: "A few in this room know me well . . . and they know me to be an intense and hard-fighting person. . . . I pushed myself, terribly hard, long hours, day and night. . . . And, for a month in 1960, four days in 1964, three weeks in 1966, being an intense and hard-fighting person put me in the hospital."

He had learned from the experience, Eagleton said. "I pace myself a great deal better than I did in the earlier years."

Gingerly, the press corps asked questions. "I don't mean to be indelicate . . ."; "I hate to persist on this subject . . ."; no one knew the protocol for this sort of thing.

Was McGovern *informed* about any of this?

"No, he was not. He was made aware of it on the weekend or the Monday after the convention."

And how did he react?

McGovern fielded that one: "When I talked to Senator Eagleton about my decision to ask him to go as my running mate, I asked if he had any problems in his past that were significant or worth discussing with me. He said no and I agree with that."

What kind of amateur hour were they running here?

"During these periods, did you receive any psychiatric help?" someone had the presence of mind to ask.

"Yes, I did . . ."

"Can you tell us what kind of psychiatric treatment you received?"

Barbara Eagleton, the loyal political wife, tried to hide her discomfort.

"Counseling from a psychiatrist, including electric shock."

Well. That seemed a little . . . intense. Especially since George Stanley McGovern had just pronounced, "I am fully satisfied on the basis of everything I've learned about these brief hospital visits" —*a month for nervous exhaustion was brief?*—"that what is manifested in Senator Eagleton's part was the good judgment to seek out medical care when he was exhausted." *Not telling McGovern he'd had electroshock therapy? What kind of judgment was that?* "As far as I am concerned, there is no member of that Senate who is any sounder in mind, body, and spirit than Tom Eagleton. I am fully satisfied and if I had known every detail that he discussed this morning . . . he still would have been my choice for vice president."

If he had it to do over again, someone asked Eagleton, would he do it differently?

"Senator McGovern's staff was aware, I believe, the night before my name was put in nomination, of the rumors . . . that were circulating on the floor of the convention and they were satisfied as to my health."

Telegrams to McGovern flooded in.

"AFTER MONTHS OF PRECINCT WORK FOR YOUR NOMINATION WE BITTERLY RESENT THAT YOU JEOPARDIZE OUR HOPE WITH EAGLETON. DEMAND HE RESIGN."

"WHILE WE UNDERSTAND YOUR COMPASSION, WE STRONGLY URGE YOU TO ACCEPT HIS IMMEDIATE RESIGNATION."

"DO YOU WANT NUT FOR VICE PRESIDENT. DROP EAGLETON."

The problem being that the resort's only working wire machine was in the pressroom. The reporters saw his supporters' reaction before McGovern did. This did not make for effective strategizing.

The reporters pressed the McGovern flacks for answers. They replied with briefings about what the McGovern family had had for dinner. McGovern himself told an AP reporter he would have to "wait and see" for the public's reaction before making a decision. That mealymouthed quote was on the wires the next morning. The flacks put out a statement claiming McGovern had been misunderstood, that he was "one thousand percent for Tom Eagleton."

Richard Nixon, or Lyndon Johnson for that matter, would have known better; they wouldn't go on the record as being more than 98 percent certain the sun would rise in the east the next morning.

Richard Nixon knew Americans didn't want to know their politicians had psychological problems like anyone else. That was why, back in the 1950s, after Walter Winchell raised suspicions about the number of visits Nixon was making to a certain Dr. Hutschnecker on Park Avenue, Nixon started seeing a military doctor in Washington instead.

That evening at a buffalo-meat barbecue the reporters tried out Tom Eagleton jokes on one another. (The week's funniest came from Julian Bond, riffing on reports that Nixon had several times come close to dumping Spiro Agnew: "At least we know ours had treatment.") For two more surreal days in South Dakota, McGovern flacks pretended nothing was wrong. Then, Friday afternoon, McGovern pulled in Jules Witcover of the *Los Angeles Times* for a ninety-minute not-for-attribution interview. That night at dinner McGovern hopped from table to table, just to make sure every reporter got the message: he himself was still confident Eagleton could serve flawlessly as vice president, and, of course, God forbid, president. He said *the people* wanted him to get rid of Eagleton, but he hoped he wouldn't have to come

to him making such a decision: he hoped Eagleton would voluntarily withdraw for the sake of the party. They could quote him, he said, as "sources
close to McGovern."

It was all a bit clumsier than when the Franklins around Dwight D.
Eisenhower attempted to ditch Richard Nixon in 1952; then, they had isolated the affable antipolitician Eisenhower from any association with the
crime. Here McGovern was spreading the dirt himself. It would prove a poor
decision, especially since McGovern's target, like Nixon, refused to go quietly. Eagleton showed up for scheduled appearances in California and
Hawaii looking for all the world like a confident man. Then Jack Anderson,
on his syndicated radio show, said, "We have now located photostats of half
a dozen arrests for drunken driving." Eagleton called it a "damnable lie"—
and when Anderson wasn't able to produce the documents, Eagleton exercised a bit of the old Nixonian jujitsu: he reaped status as a victim. Accepting
an endorsement for the ticket at the convention of the Retail Clerks International Association convention in Honolulu, he compared himself to another
Missouri senator who ran for vice president: Harry Truman. "I hope I have
some measure of the guts he possessed."

"Give 'em hell, Tom!" the unionists shouted in response.

He continued, "The people have understanding and compassion in their
hearts. I'm a stronger, better person than I was seventy-two hours ago. You
have to come under a little adversity to find out who your friends are."

Poor George McGovern. He was still getting messages out in the press
that his vice-presidential candidate should quit and save face, just as the
Eisenhower people had in 1952. But just like Nixon, Eagleton bluffed the
boss—though with a liberal's sort of bluff: *Go ahead and fire me. Show the
world you have no compassion.*

Reporters noticed Checkers Speech parallels. One asked Eagleton if he
would go on television to defend himself. He replied, "I won't put my family on television," adding, "We have a dog, too, called Pumpkin." He
appeared on CBS's *Face the Nation* on Sunday, said he'd be meeting with
McGovern the next night, and that as far as he was concerned "I'm going to
stay on the ticket. That's my firm, irrevocable intent."

The next morning the new issues of *Time* and *Newsweek* came out,
Eagleton on the covers, looking moist-eyed, unshaven—and sympathetic
("McGovern's First Crisis" displaced *Time*'s Olympic preview: "Munich:
Where the Good Times Are"). McGovern didn't help his own case. "If we
took a poll and ninety-nine percent of the people thought he should stay on
the ticket, that other one percent could still be crucial," he was quoted telling
Time—some antipolitician. The liberal *St. Louis Post-Dispatch* called him
"spineless."

Adding insult to injury, *Time* reported its own survey: 76.7 percent said
Eagleton's medical record wouldn't affect their vote. *Time* also noted, "An

almost Mafia-like atmosphere developed amid the rustic charms of McGovern's retreat." They reported that, according to Eagleton, McGovern had told him that though he "had been under pressure" to fire him, "he's one thousand percent behind me." And that McGovern, like some Tammany hack filling out a "balanced ticket," was only considering Roman Catholics. (They didn't report what happened the previous week at McGovern headquarters in Los Angeles: all thirty phone lines were cut by vandals.)

The wheels were off the bus. The Democratic pros who'd been telling him since the press conference to cut Eagleton loose now said he had no choice: donors had stopped sending checks. McGovern performed the execution at close range, standing next to the martyr at a press conference, now at the height of his sympathy with the public. Then McGovern requested time on all three networks the next night to explain himself. All three networks refused.

George McGovern also owned a dog. His name was Atticus—as in Atticus Finch, the saintly lawyer in *To Kill a Mockingbird.* But we live in a fallen world. The saintly don't survive in politics. "In the Democratic primaries, Senator McGovern managed to convey the impression that he was somehow not a politician in the customary sense," James Naughton wrote in the *New York Times.* "His reaction to Mr. Eagleton's disclosure may have seriously impaired that image."

Richard Nixon received a blow the next morning from the *Washington Post:* "Bug Suspect Got Campaign Funds," ran a small article by Carl Bernstein and his colleague Bob Woodward. Though the story was hardly noticeable among the thirteen pieces, heralded by a banner across all eight columns, on the Eagleton resignation.

Perhaps because it was such a heavy news day, the only mention of the return of Jane Fonda to the United States after a tour of North Vietnam was relegated to a brief item in the gossip column. Vietnam was becoming a forgotten war. Jane Fonda was one of the few who insisted people remember. She had once been an apple-cheeked sex symbol, a girl next door, so conventional that in 1959 she accepted the ceremonial title of "Miss Army Recruiter." She had been trying to visit North Vietnam for over a year. Finally granted a visa, she arrived during the Democratic National Convention. Upon her return, she announced she was quitting acting to work fulltime for Richard Nixon's defeat.

She wanted to help prisoners of war. It would later become easy to forget: helping prisoners of war was a strong issue for the left. (It was one of the reasons Nixon was so eager to co-opt it for himself.) Years earlier, after the Pentagon started sneaking contraband like radio parts into care packages, and Hanoi insisted all POW mail be routed through Moscow to be X-rayed, Washington decided to halt the mail deliveries altogether. Radicals traveling to "the other side" were thus the only conduit for letters. Even as the president stepped up his political exploitation of their captivity, the government's actual indifference to POWs could be chilling. In one case parents only learned their son was alive in 1971 upon his release by the NLF. He had managed to get out a letter to his family in 1969, but the Pentagon had warehoused it, claiming to be studying it that entire time for "propaganda" content.

Some POW families joined the antiwar movement. Valerie Kushner, wife of an imprisoned major, received an extraordinary letter from the president's military assistant: "Frankly, I saw no purpose in replying to your December letter to the President since his policies with regard to prisoners and missing have been made public and you and the others who wrote the letter obviously do not agree with them." She began traveling with McGovern, and seconded his presidential nomination.

By the time Fonda got her visa, she had another motive besides delivering a satchel of letters: those reports that American planes were bombing the dikes. Sweden's ambassador had inspected the damage and said it looked like a "methodic" attempt to flood North Vietnam's rice paddies, and that, with all the mines floating so menacingly in Haiphong Harbor, no other food could be imported, and the population would starve en masse.

For the hearty few still agitating full-time to stop the war, the reports were simultaneously vindicating and agonizing. Hellfire from American aircraft had surpassed anything previously imaginable in the history of warfare: 176,000 tons of bombs on Cambodia, more than fell on Japan during the entirety of World War II; over five times that on Laos. Hawks who claimed America was pulling her punches used to blare that all it would take to beat the Communists was to turn North Vietnam into a parking lot. More or less, that had already happened. In 1968 the outgoing army chief of staff, General Harold K. Johnson, calculated that U.S. planes had covered the country with enough steel to pave it over to the depth of one-eight of an inch. By 1970 he added another quarter inch to the estimate. That was *before* Richard Nixon really got started. And it excluded the bombs on *South* Vietnam, where periodic "bombing halts" didn't apply. That country we were seeking to liberate was hit with as much tonnage as all the others combined.

But as a political strategy, bombing worked. American troop strength was now below seventy thousand, few enough for the public to ignore. Vietnamization, "removed the war from our minds while it is being inflicted on the bodies of others," said Fonda. "Will the American people say 'right on,' our hands are clean because our men aren't being killed?"

Fonda arrived in Hanoi alone, a woman armed with only cameras, hobbling on a fractured foot. The day before, Jean Thorval of Agence France-Presse had been standing on one of the earthen dikes when bombs struck another nearby. It seemed, he reported in *Le Monde,* "the attack was aimed at a whole system of dikes." Fonda gave a speech over Radio Hanoi, hoping it would reach the pilots, describing, in case they didn't know, how the antipersonnel bombs beneath their wings functioned:

"They cannot destroy bridges or factories. They cannot pierce steel or cement. Their only target is unprotected human flesh." They "now contain rough-edged plastic pellets, and your bosses, whose minds think in terms of statistics, not human lives, are proud of this new perfection. The plastic pellets don't show up on X-rays and cannot be removed. The hospitals here are filled with babies and women and old people who will live for the rest of their lives in agony with these pellets embedded in them. . . . Tonight, when you are alone, ask yourselves: What are you doing? Accept no ready answers fed to you by rote from basic training on up, but as men, as human beings. Can you justify what you are doing?"

The tragic, otherworldly naiveté of Hollywood celebrities in politics: as if the world were a Henry Fonda movie, in which the pure-hearted idealist always won the day. It was quite a thing to ask active-duty servicemen: search your heart, and don't follow orders—though she never asked that of them explicitly—because those orders might be illegal.

While Fonda was in Vietnam, the *New York Times* reported that the rules of engagement for "fixed wing air operations" since May of 1971—no incendiary ammunitions were to be used in inhabited areas—included a B-52–sized loophole: unless "necessary for the accomplishment of the commander's mission." The paper reported estimates by U.S. officials of twenty-five thousand civilian deaths in South Vietnam by both sides since the start of the spring offensive. This, as Fonda inspected damage to a dike that held back the confluence of six rivers. The bombs had entered at a slant—more difficult to repair and invisible from aerial photographs, her hosts explained. Bomb craters ten meters across and eight meters deep (and two meters below sea level) flanked the wall. Rice paddies stretched to the horizon—no military targets in sight.

Fonda recorded her amazement at the men and women riding bicycles across narrow, muddy paths carrying huge baskets of earth balanced at the ends of bamboo poles in ovenlike heat to repair the dikes. All visitors to North Vietnam were struck by the same thing: as Richard Nixon might put it, they had *will in spades*. "It is impossible for this visitor to detect any atmosphere of fear," Anthony Lewis had recently reported in the *Times* after visiting hospitals that had been bombed despite red crosses painted on their roofs. ("Nixon's flying," a peasant would tell Fonda when they heard rumblings in the distance and the ground shook. "No give damn," someone would defiantly add.) Ramsey Clark, former attorney general under Lyndon Johnson, arrived in North Vietnam just after Fonda left. He noted, "The people of this country believe their cause is just. Every person I have seen has shown by his acts and his words his total commitment." American intelligence agents had been offering similar reports for years.

It could inspire a dewy-eyed romanticism among Americans of a certain temper, as if these North Vietnamese were some higher species of being. Fonda's last full day in the country, she was taken to see an antiaircraft installation. To her hosts these sites were like the Alamo: the seat of a noble, patriotic resistance. Soldiers sang a hymn to North Vietnamese independence (*"All men are created equal / They are given certain rights . . ."*). Fonda, smiling dumbly, felt warm with agape. An air-raid helmet was perched upon her head. Before she knew what was happening, she said in her memoirs, she was led to sit down on the seat of an antiaircraft gun.

The cameras clicked; they weren't some higher, nobler species of human. They were warriors, in the middle of a war, and they had a priceless propaganda shot—a smiling American celebrity, appearing to be doing what Vietnamese patriots did: shooting down American planes. The North Vietnamese news agency also misrepresented her radio broadcasts to claim, as the caption of the photo of Fonda on the antiaircraft gun that went out over the AP wires read, "Miss Fonda made a speech last week from Hanoi urging American soldiers to defect."

Fonda arrived in Paris and called a press conference. She brought film of the bombed dikes. "I believe in my heart, profoundly, that the dikes are being bombed on purpose," she said, "hydraulic systems, sluice gates, pumping stations, and dams as well." She pointed out that a Nazi commander had once been executed by the Allies for bombing dikes in the Netherlands.

The Pentagon claimed the Communists placed key roads, antiaircraft emplacements, and military installations astride the dikes. She answered by pointing to the screen: "You see fields and fields of paddy and then just at that one strategic point you see the bomb crater."

She pointed to the screen again: two healthy-looking American POWs. "Without exception," she said, "they expressed shame at what they had done." She said they asked her to tell their families to work for McGovern: "They fear if Nixon stays in office, they will be prisoners forever."

The same day, the State Department promised they would disprove Fonda's assertions with photographic evidence. Assistants carted easels into the pressroom at Foggy Bottom. Then, suddenly, the briefing was canceled. "The administration realized," the *New York Times* reported sardonically, "that Hanoi also could produce photographs." Ron Ziegler spoke from the White House pressroom: "North Vietnam is having some success with their campaign to get the world to believe that American planes were bombing dikes." State's spokesman contradicted that the next day: yes, American planes were bombing dikes, but as "a result of legitimate attacks on military installations such as antiaircraft sites." Then the State Department released an intelligence report on the dike system: it admitted damage to twelve locations, all accidental. Which unfortunately cut across the State Department's other habitual assurance: that America's laser-guided bombing systems were the most accurate in the history of warfare.

The sci-fi sex kitten from *Barbarella* had the White House sweating bullets.

Then the sex kitten was joined by the secretary-general of the United Nations: "I cannot tell you whether the bombing is accidental or not," Kurt Waldheim said. The results were the same; the problem was the war. "The United Nations can no longer remain a mute spectator of the horror of the war and of the peril which it increasingly poses to international peace."

Of a sudden, on July 27, the president invited the White House press corps for a rare Oval Office briefing, where he offered a denial in the form of a boast: "If it were the policy of the United States to bomb the dikes, we could take them out, the significant part of them, in a week." Then he confused the matter further by dilating on the moral question. Some were listening to "well-intentioned and naive people," but as Eisenhower had said about the firebombing of Dresden (in which the intentional incineration of civilians was undeniable): "The height of immorality would be to allow Hitler to rule Europe."

Then Nixon sent his UN ambassador, the failed Senate candidate George Herbert Walker Bush, to advise Kurt Waldheim to stop repeating propagandistic falsehoods. The meeting, however, was brief. Bush, a fighter pilot in World War II, emerged looking shell-shocked, suddenly unwilling to press his assigned case that the dikes had been spared. He told reporters, "I think that the best thing I can do on the subject is shut up."

The *Washington Post* never reported George Bush's climbdown. They did report that "Fonda, wearing Vietnamese peasant garb, called President Nixon a 'serious traitor'"; and a joke of Mark Russell's, the political humorist, that "if McGovern wins, he'll replace Henry Kissinger with Jane Fonda"; and Senator Hugh Scott on the debate to defund the war: "The right to negotiate the peace should not be taken away from the president and put in the hands of Jane Fonda." The *Post* also reported the attempts of the Georgia congressman fighting a Senate primary to put Fonda on trial ("Declared war or undeclared war, this is treason"), and the chairman of the Manhattan Republican Party's call to boycott her movies. Also, the paper printed a letter to the editor from an M. J. Smith of Washington: "It is no wonder that peace has not been established in Vietnam when the Communists can obtain the help of American citizens to help destroy the morale of our men."

The actress's trip marked the emergence of a new narrative about Vietnam: that people like Lyndon Johnson and Richard Nixon weren't responsible for the disaster, but people like Fonda, stabbing America's soldiers and South Vietnamese allies in the back, were. It was the most convenient possible development for Richard Nixon—who was, exactly then, planning to stab America's soldiers and South Vietnamese allies in the back.

The ostensible aim of the war was to preserve an anticommunist government in Saigon absent the United States propping it up. Nixon had privately
been maintaining since 1966 that this was impossible, and that the only question was the garb in which America would eventually cloak its withdrawal.
Sometimes he imagined a politically satisfactory denouement might come of
a knockout blow—as in his scuttled plans for Operation Duck Hook in
1969, or Operation Linebacker that spring. Other times he counted on his
"madman" theory, with its threat of nuclear annihilation. Either way the
point was to scare the enemy to sufficient concessions at the bargaining table
that it would look as if *the enemy* had capitulated. Secret and intentional
bombing of North Vietnamese dams and earthworks, if it was happening—
and the president's "madman" signal on July 27 that if he wanted to deci-
mate North Vietnamese agriculture he could do it in a week—was consistent
with this logic. Massive bombing, enough to keep the Communists from
overrunning Saigon until after his reelection, was the only way to preserve
what he had started calling, stealing a phrase from the Democratic platform
of 1952, "peace with honor."

But what he was working on now was neither honorable nor peace. His
main concern was political timing. As the president put it to Kissinger on
August 3, as the battered and bruised McGovern cast about desperately for
a new running mate, "I look at the tide of history out there, South Vietnam
probably can never even survive anyway. I'm just being perfectly candid."
The problem, he went on, was the presidential election: "It's terribly important this year."

Kissinger put two and two together. He and Nixon had been reading each
other's mind for some time now. Kissinger noted, "If a year or two years
from now North Vietnam gobbles up South Vietnam, we can have a viable
foreign policy if it looks as if it's the result of South Vietnamese incompetence." They could come up with peace agreement language—could "sell it
in such a way," some transcribed Kissinger's words; others rendered it, just
as pregnantly, "sell *out* in such a way"—that convinced South Vietnamese
president Nguyen Van Thieu that America would stick with him until the
end and get it agreed to in time for November. After which they could
regrettably let "South Vietnam" evaporate and move on to other foreign policy problems.

For now they had to keep up military pressure, mining harbors, intimating wholesale dike-bombing, whatever it took to hold back the deluge during what diplomatic historians would later call a "decent interval": to "find
some formula that holds the thing together a year or two, after which—after
a year, Mr. President—Vietnam will be a backwater." Then they could
announce peace with honor. Only they would know they'd just stabbed
South Vietnam in the back. "If we settle it, say, this October, by January '74
no one will give a damn."

But they couldn't settle it *before* October. They needed the war to keep going through the election. That way they could blame the continuation of war on the Democrats: their line could be, Haldeman wrote in a memo, that the sustained fighting proved the Communists were "absolutely at the end of their rope," their only chance of victory "to stagger through to November hoping that President Nixon will lose and they can get a good deal from the next administration."

Back in February, Nixon had said antiwar Democrats "might give the enemy an incentive to prolong the war until after the election." Actually, that was what *he* was doing, just as he had in 1968. Twenty years later, a superannuated Richard Nixon met with a group of young reporters just before the 1992 New Hampshire primary and copped to it. He explained that the incumbent Republican president would have been able to guarantee his reelection, but that it was too late: he ended the Iraq war when he should have kept it going at least until the election. "We had a lot of success with that in 1972," he told the assembled scribes.

But it was George S. McGovern's campaign that was "Mafia-like." *Time* magazine had said so.

McGovern returned to his hometown of Mitchell, South Dakota, home of the world-famous Corn Palace auditorium, nattering about how he used to see all his favorites perform there: Paul Whiteman, Tommy Dorsey, Guy Lombardo, Lawrence Welk (and they called *Richard Nixon* the square one). In between stops he worked the phones, ringing up vice-presidential possibilities: Kennedy declined (again); Ribicoff wasn't "available"; Muskie didn't merely decline, he subsequently humiliated his party's nominee by announcing McGovern's call and his rebuff in a press conference. McGovern then called Humphrey, breaking a pledge to Shirley MacLaine that he'd never stoop to such a thing; Humphrey, too, wasn't "available." Even Ralph Nader, the consumer advocate, turned him down. Nixon now had a 60 percent approval rating. Nobody wanted to be tagged for the rest of his career as a loser.

The candidate of last resort turned out to be Sargent Shriver, the former Peace Corps director, husband of JFK's sister Eunice—a counterfeit Kennedy. They unveiled him at the DNC meeting in Washington, a slick prime-time fake convention, balloons and bands and all; since their first TV show in Miami had been such as bust, they tried it again. The day before, on August 7, McGovern denied rumors his newly hired campaign manager, Larry O'Brien, had already quit. "Come January," the glad-handing emcee announced at the South Dakota Democratic convention, "I'm going to stop calling this man George and start calling him Mr. President." A *New York Times* reporter murmured under his breath, "If you do, people are sure gonna look at you funny."

In other news, Arthur Bremer's lawyers introduced his diary as evidence for his insanity plea, and Americans learned that the new-model madman wasn't a crazed Communist or Palestinian militant; like everyone else, he just wanted to be famous. Bremer was convicted; his father gave a statement to the press through clenched teeth: "Probably if he was a black or some other Communist agitator he'd be free." In New York, police were thwarted by a judge in their attempt to raid a theater showing the slapstick hard-core pornographic film that had become a surprise hit among the fashionable; even Jackie O. had seen *Deep Throat*. In Paris, the Vietnam peace talks—revived for maximum political effect during the Democratic convention—bogged down in accusations and denials about dikes; in the White House residence, Pat Nixon staged a rare availability with the ladies' press. She said Jane Fonda should have been in Hanoi on "bended knee"—Pat could barely control her anger—"asking them to stop their aggression," and that her husband's performance in a cataclysmic moment in the nation's history was like Abraham Lincoln's: he is a "steady, steady person." A reporter asked: had her husband ever had psychiatric counseling? "No, no, no," the first lady replied. She offered her read on the economy: "healthy and alive—employment is up, there's more take-home pay and a bigger gross national product. We're really making progress." More or less, that was true, thanks to certain strategic short-term interventions: such as the two-year supply of toilet paper bought in one shot by the Defense Department—part of a White House–directed 11 percent increase in federal discretionary spending for the election year.

The *Los Angeles Times* reported receiving letters to the editor calling for donations to "the Jane Fonda, Ramsey Clark assassination fund"; the *Arizona Republic* editorialized the job should be handled by a treason indictment; and the *Manchester Union Leader* said, "She should be shot if a verdict of guilty comes in."

Two policemen watched her on the news in a bar in Miami Beach: "Bombing the dikes! Ha! The only dike getting bombed is Fonda!"

"Did you see her last picture? The one where she played the hooker? Yeah, that's no acting job."

Thirteen candidates in primary elections in Michigan's Eighteenth and Nineteenth congressional districts each charged their opponents had come out too little and too late against busing. And on his first full day as the presidential nominee of the American Independent Party, founded in 1968 by George Wallace, Orange County congressman and John Birch Society leader John G. Schmitz blathered that the nomination of George McGovern had been "set up" by President Nixon, conspiring to run against an unelectable extremist.

On August 15 the House Internal Security Committee, successor to HUAC, said that if Jane Fonda's Hanoi broadcasts did not violate existing treason or sedition laws, then the Justice Department should recommend new laws. Larry O'Brien made the incredible claim that his offices had already been bugged at the time of the infamous June 17 break-in, citing "undisclosed recent evidence." O'Brien sounded as paranoid as Martha Mitchell when she said she had been made a "political prisoner" to keep her from exposing vague, unspecified Nixonian crimes. Would McGovern become the *second* presidential candidate, after John G. Schmitz, to campaign on anti-Nixon conspiracy theories?

McGovern spoke at the headquarters of Local 1112 of the United Automobile Workers Union in Lordstown, Ohio: "We don't want workers treated like robots or machines," he told the long-haired young men who assembled Vegas (*"Right on!"* they shouted back). The UAW's regional director interrupted McGovern to roar that their polls showed 84 percent in their national rank and file planned to vote for him. McGovern said he'd refuse a briefing on Vietnam from Henry Kissinger, joking that he could learn more from the newspapers.

The decorated World War II bomber pilot was asked about the recent photograph published in *Life* magazine of a shrieking naked Vietnamese girl, who'd torn off her flaming clothes fleeing a napalm attack on her school. He responded by noting the recent Pentagon statement that the incident had obviously been accidental because the school was in *South* Vietnam: "Is there anything braver or more noble about burning up children who live north of the seventeenth parallel or who live in Cambodia or Laos? They all feel pain. They're all children of the same God. Those it seems to me are the kind of conditions we have to recover if we're going to save the soul of this nation." The hall drew quiet. It was McGovern at his most inspiring.

He also said Nixon had to be "at least indirectly responsible" for the break-in at Democratic headquarters—"the kind of thing that you expect under a person like Hitler." Former Minnesota Republican congressman Clark MacGregor was quoted in every paper howling in outrage: "McGovern by his own words stands convicted of character assassination." MacGregor was the new chairman of the Committee to Re-Elect the President. John Mitchell had resigned to "meet the obligation which must come first": "the happiness and welfare of my wife and daughter."

Surely Mitchell's resignation had nothing whatsoever to do with the kind of interviews then unfolding in the Oval Office. Haldeman reported of the seven defendants in the imminent criminal trial of the Watergate burglars, "Everybody's satisfied. . . . Hunt's happy."

"At considerable cost, I guess?" Nixon asked.

"Yes."

"It's worth it. That's what the money"—all those campaign slush funds— "is for. . . . They have to be paid. That's all there is to that. They have to be paid."

Then Nixon changed the subject. "What are we doing about the financial
contributors? . . . Are we running their income tax returns? Is the Justice
Department checking to see whether or not there are any antitrust suits? . . .
We have all this power and we aren't using it. Now, what the Christ is the
matter?"

Then it was off to Camp David to prepare for the Republican convention.

Here's a riddle: Which is more "undemocratic"? A $1,000-per-person
Democratic reception at a social club that de facto excludes any woman
offended by vixens in bunny costumes? Or the sabotage of that reception by
radicals in the name of those thereby excluded?

Here's another: Which is more "undemocratic"? A primary where hundreds of thousands of Chicagoans go to the polls like robots to vote in a slate
of machine-approved Democratic convention delegates? Or the reformers
choosing their delegation after claiming the regulars' election was inherently
fixed, in meetings in which the only people who could vote were the losing
reform candidates from the primary?

The answer is: all of them and none. Each side in each of these conflicts
believed with equal sincerity that its way got closer to the will of "the people"; each side was neither fully right nor fully wrong. The Democrats
opened quite a can of worms, once they hastily plunged themselves into an
open fight over what truly represents "representation." On the other hand,
Richard Nixon's take on the question—that his own person, clothed in the
the garment of the presidency, *embodied* the will of the people—was, at least,
less messy. It surely made for a smoother TV show.

His convention opened, also in Miami Beach, Monday, August 21. Sometime during the proceedings, a messenger accidentally dropped off the script
in the BBC's in-box. It specified the exact timing for spontaneous applause
and "impromptu" remarks, even the gestures speakers were supposed to
make. A former football quarterback, for example, was directed to "nod" at
the young people congregated in the bleachers.

There were three thousand such Young Voters for the President in
Miami Beach, divided into three units, each issued different-colored
badges. These three battalions were divided, in turn, into one-hundred-
person units identified by letter, like a combat company. "If the president
calls and says, 'I need five hundred kids at a press conference,'" boasted the
staff director of Young Voters for the President, "we can get them there in
twenty minutes."

There had been hearings on the Republican platform—about as authentic as Moscow show trials. Don Riegle, an antiwar GOP congressman from
Michigan—one of Nixon's candidates in 1966—complained during his testimony to Subcommittee II on Human Rights and Responsibilities (scheduled
too late for coverage on the evening news), "As you know, certain Republi-

cans have been banned from appearing before the full platform committee. . . . When I raised this issue with platform committee chairman John
Rhodes, he said to me, 'You're crazy if you think anyone is going to appear
before the full platform committee that would embarrass the president.'"
Riegle gave a stirring speech about how Richard Nixon, "with the silent
acquiescence of the Congress," had dropped two hundred pounds of bombs
for every man, woman, and child in North and South Vietnam. A subcommittee member, a Mrs. Sullivan of Alabama, stood up and announced that
she was kin to the Fighting Sullivans, the five famous Iowa brothers all killed
when their ship went down during World War II. She demanded to know,
did Donald Riegle consider *those* boys murderers, too?

Billboards were everywhere: PRESIDENT NIXON—NOW MORE THAN EVER.
(They afforded quite the contrast to Miami Beach under the Democrats,
when Don Segretti had arranged for a plane trailing a banner: PEACE POT
PROMISCUITY—VOTE MCGOVERN.) The spectacle on the screens told the story.
Richard Nixon had brought us together. But not, you know, *too* together.
He had given Americans something to be exuberant about. But not, you
know, the *wrong kind* of exuberant. They shouted their lungs out against the
shouters and convinced the nation they were the party of quiet.

There were more protesters than there had been four years earlier in
Chicago, but they hardly got any attention. That had been another matter
upon which the Nixon team left absolutely nothing to chance. When antiwar activists had begun planning convention-week demonstrations, there
had been talk of anchoring it with a massive outdoor concert. "Lennon, formerly with the group known as the Beatles," as the FBI reports called him,
was to be the emcee, the culmination of a national anti-Nixon rock tour.
Nixon had been horrified at the prospect. "The source felt that if Lennon's
visa is terminated it would be a strategic counter-measure," an FBI memo
summarized; the source was Strom Thurmond. "The source also noted the
caution which must be taken with regard to the possible alienation of the so-
called 18-year-old-vote if Lennon is expelled from the country." J. Edgar
Hoover had personally classified the problem as a "Security Matter," the des-
ignation reserved for those considered potentially violently dangerous to the
U.S. government. ("ALL EXTREMISTS SHOULD BE CONSIDERED
DANGEROUS" read a special agent's memo on John Lennon, Jerry Rubin,
and Yoko Ono's appearance on *Eyewitness News* in New York to encourage
young people to register to vote.) CIA agents got to work proving Lennon's
strings were being pulled by Moscow paymasters. ("There are only limited
indications thus far of foreign efforts," ran a report filed on February 23, the
morning after Lennon, Ono, and Rubin appeared on the Mike Douglas
show.) Presidential assistant Bill Timmons wrote in a "Dear Strom" letter
that the singer had been served notice to leave the country by March 15. He
was still around on March 16, however, when this FBI communication came

forth: "Lennon appears to be radically oriented however he does not give the impression he is a true revolutionist since he is constantly under the influence of narcotics." By summer Lennon was too busy trying to stay in the country to either tour against Nixon or make it to the Republican convention. The threat to national security had been neutralized.

The Nixon team went after other charismatic protesters. In June the Justice Department announced an investigation of Vietnam Veterans Against the War, subpoenaing twenty-three of its members from six states who were in Florida planning a national convoy to Miami Beach. Then the FBI started arresting them without charges. They were indicted in July for conspiring to attack the Republican National Convention with "lead weights, 'fried' marbles, ball bearings, cherry bombs, and smoke bombs . . . wrist rockets, slingshots, and cross bows," and to "organize numerous 'fire teams' to attack with automatic weapons fire and incendiary devices police stations, police cars, and stores." The charges came of tape recordings made by a disturbed but entrepreneurial agent provocateur who had received a psychological discharge from the army.

What VVAW was actually planning was more dangerous: a peaceful march to the convention hall to demand an audience with the president. The VVAW members were each held on $25,000 bail in an attempt to keep them from trying. "My crime is expressing my revulsion concerning the war in Vietnam," one testified upon surrendering to authorites. On August 11 the VVAW announced a lawsuit against Attorney General Kleindienst, Defense Secretary Laird, and the FBI for tapping their phones—newly affirmed as illegal in a recent Supreme Court decision handed down two days after the Watergate break-in. Then, on August 19, VVAW's two hundred vehicles pulled up thirteen miles shy of Miami Beach. Once more they advanced in stately procession, in ragged fatigues, some clacking along on crutches, others pushed forth in wheelchairs, the rest clomping cadence in combat boots. They called it the Last Patrol.

The veterans lent a badly needed dignity to an antiwar movement that had descended into self-parody. The delegates slipped into tuxedos and evening dress for a convention-eve gala at the Fontainebleau. Their way was strewn with eggs and sixteen-year-olds using their limousine hoods as trampolines. Even Abbie Hoffman and Jerry Rubin were embarrassed. They fancied their Yippie spectacles as *creative*—such as the "puke-in" they attempted on the sidewalk outside the reception. ("The problem being," they lamented, "that a group of individuals cannot puke in unison, whatever medicine they might take.") Joe McGinniss—working on a book on the death of "the hero" in American culture—turned to a friend: "This is crazy. Nixon couldn't have hired people to make him look any better." (Unfortunately for Nixon, the TV producer present for the puke-in turned away in disgust, ordering his cameraman not to film it.)

Abbie and Jerry made their way to a welcoming reception for Pat Nixon. Three years earlier they had been indicted for conspiracy to destroy a convention. But now, they were *celebrities.* People had seen them on TV. So they had no trouble getting inside. "I want to fuck Pat Nixon," Jerry told a reporter. "I want to get close enough so that I can slip it in her. I really want to fuck that woman." Another faction—the "Zippies"—considered Yippies sellouts for embracing voting at all. Neither were radical enough for the Attica Brigade, who went around Flamingo Park chanting, "Attica means fight back! Attica means fight back!" A Women's Anti-Rape Squad (W.A.R.S.) patrolled the park with their own chant: "Sisterhood means fight back! Sisterhood means fight back!" "Zippie Free Women" cavorted topless as a gesture against sexism; which perhaps had something to do with all the hippie men—some members of a new "Pot People's Party"—asking hippie women, "Do ya wanna screw?" and if refused, retorting, "Don't you like men?"

The factions spent much of their time fighting each other over the microphone—at least those who weren't too stoned on wine and quaaludes to talk. Until, that is, an armada of crew-cutted Nazis snuck onto the stage and blessed all factions with a newfound unity as beating victims. The Vietnam veterans, joined by Jewish retirees, came to the rescue, carrying the Nazis fireman-style out of the park. The vets also discovered a protester with a cache of Molotov cocktails, lead-weighted arrows, and sharpened bolts. They turned him over to police and destroyed the weapons with sledgehammers. They tried to ask John Wayne questions during an "open" press conference at Nixon headquarters. Security wouldn't let them in. So a former West Point instructor ambushed the Duke while he was waiting for a cab and invited him to their encampment: "They just want to shoot the bull. You know, maybe talk about the war—"

Wayne's fellow western star, Glenn Ford, snapped, "What war?"

"The one in Vietnam. These guys all fought over there. A lot of them are crippled."

The war-movie hero who'd avoided fighting in a war scanned the horizon nervously: no cabs. "So they just want to talk, eh?" Wayne said in that so-famous drawl.

"Why not? It won't take long."

"Bullshit. If they got somethin' to say to me, tell 'em to put it in writing," he said, as a cab finally arrived. "Playboy Plaza," he barked at the hack. "Jesus, I need a *drink.*"

On Monday as the conventioneers massed for the opening session, a shrieking mob lay down in front of a city bus, then ripped open the gas tank, gushing fuel down the main drag, Collins Avenue. A kid tried to light a rag. Old ladies on the bus started keening and weeping. The mob started vandalizing limousines: "Cars don't bleed!" "You kill Vietnamese people!" A sixty-year-old food vendor who had the misfortune of wearing a convention tag tried to dash to the safety of the hall. Before he could, he collapsed of a heart attack. A North Carolina delegate observed, "I think next time they should issue every delegate and alternate a submachine gun."

Inside, a train of keynoters, declaiming from an ivory-colored stucco battlement that made the Democrats' twenty-foot-high podium look puny, made as if George McGovern himself had thrown the rocks.

Ronald Reagan, resplendent in an ice cream–colored suit, emceed:

"At *this* convention elected delegates are allowed inside the hall. You can even eat a lettuce salad here without losing your credentials. We'll even select our vice-presidential candidate before we go home."

"You could imagine the high drama of that moment of decision in Hyannis Port—surrounded by their families, two men watching the flip of a coin. Sargent Shriver lost."

"A man of the common people, Shriver understands their language. He learned it from talking to his butler."

"Their tactics were the old politics of bossism and the smoke-filled rooms—although in some of the rooms it was reported the smoke smelled a little funny."

"A few days ago McGovern announced that his economists would be presenting a program very shortly to which he would be committed. Now, if that means he'll stand behind it one thousand percent, we will have at least a week to look over it before he dumps it."

Barry Goldwater spoke: "I would like to call attention to what happened last month when the shattered remnants of a once great party met in this city and what I listened to and saw on my television made me question whether I was sitting in the United States or someplace else. I was reminded of the coyotes who live on my hill with me in the desert of Arizona. . . . They just wait, like the coyote, until they can tear something down or destroy part of America." Goldwater had to stop every once in a while to wait for cheers to die down.

(A motor whirred the platform into position for the next speaker; it was adjusted so no speaker would be taller than the president.)

Richard Lugar, mayor of Indianapolis: "A small group of radicals and extremists has assumed control of the Democratic Party, taking its name but repudiating its principles. The sudden storm of McGovern has devastated the house of Jackson, Wilson, Roosevelt, and Kennedy, and millions of Democrats now stand homeless in its wake. . . . We say to you millions of Democrats deserted by McGovern and his extremists, 'We are the party of the open door! That door is open to everyone!'"

Lustily, the delegates cheered: 84 percent of them were public officeholders (the sort who had once lined up municipal-bond deals with John Mitchell), many in matching blazers. In Texas, only one wasn't white, a Mexican-American; only one was under thirty.

On Tuesday evening, when conventioneers traversed the stretch of Collins Avenue from the big hotels to the convention hall, young women in Vietnamese folk costume moaned funeral chants over disemboweled dolls. A "Tower of Shame" float on a borrowed Orange Bowl chassis displayed posters of napalmed children and torsos shredded by plastic-pellet bombs, and was festooned with RE-ELECT THE PRESIDENT graphics, a satanic papier-mâché Nixon, and a complement of death masques. A borrowed elephant pulled a black-shrouded coffin. "The media," Abbie and Jerry lamented, "paid it scant attention." They were "attuned only to explosions and violence." There were, however, thrown eggs, and as Bob Greene of the *Chicago Daily News* observed, "To a Republican lady, one egg on the dress can mop up the guilt of five hundred bombs."

On Wednesday, as delegates arrived, militants pulled the engine wires to disable the buses of the Mississippi and South Carolina delegations. Lunatics lay in front of the Illinois bus, spray-painting its windshield black, slashing its tires, torching an American flag and trying to throw it into the engine. Then came the big VVAW march down Collins Avenue. It was silent but for the drill marshals' commands and the *tramp, tramp, tramp* of combat boots. They massed in vigil: silence, for ten minutes. Hunter S. Thompson said he'd never seen so powerful a scene. Then, one of the leaders took up a bullhorn: "We want to come inside!" Thompson said he'd never seen cops so intimidated, wrote that an "almost visible shudder ran through the crowd." A man next to him muttered, "Oh my God." Thompson forthwith took off his watch. "The first thing to go in a street fight is always your watch, and once you've lost a few, you develop a certain instinct."

An angry right-wing girl vigilante tried to slash through the protesters on her motorcycle. Two army helicopters *swof-swof-swoff*ed overhead, Vietnam-like, thickening the tension. Pete McCloskey, the Republican presidential-primary candidate who wasn't going to be allowed to be nominated lest an antiwar speech make it on TV took his revenge: he talked security guards into letting three of the vets inside. Ron Kovic, a veteran confined to a wheelchair, used a press pass to try to get close to the podium. He intended to approach the president to shake his hand—then refuse to let go until Nixon answered his questions.

A security guard gripped his chair tightly.

"What's the matter? Can't a disabled veteran who fought for his country sit up front?"

"I'm afraid not. You're not allowed up front with the delegates. You'll have to go back to the back of the convention hall, son. Let's go."

Kovic swung around to face three guards: "I'm a Vietnam veteran and I fought in the war! Did you fight in the war?"

One of them looked away.

"Yeah, that's what I thought."

Kovic started confronting delegates with tales of decrepit veterans' hospitals, of lying "in my own shit for hours waiting for an aide." Once again his hearers looked away. "Is it too real for you to look at? Is this wheelchair too much for you to take? The man who will accept this nomination tonight is a liar."

Kovic searched for the president. But the president was circling in Air Force One for his theatrical entrance. Three thousand Young Voters waited in the rain at the airport to meet him, crowding the perky actor who played Chip on *My Three Sons* for autographs. Police had parked city buses bumper to bumper around the convention-center perimeter in preparation of the president's motorcade later that evening; they sprayed so much Mace around the convention center it got sucked into the air-conditioning ducts, and they had to shut down the cooling system. A sweating Jimmy Stewart introduced a biographical film about Pat Nixon. Spiro Agnew gave an acceptance speech on the need to come together as "one America." John Wayne introduced the president's biopic.

A train of nominators and seconders pledged their undying devotion to Nixon. Some had once been famously anti-Nixon: Nelson Rockefeller, who had said in 1960 that the thought of Richard Nixon as president made him ill; former interior secretary Walter Hickel, forced out for criticizing Nixon for calling protesters "bums." Others were not Republicans: Senator Buckley of the Conservative Party; the president of a UAW local; an Alabama housewife and former Wallace activist; Mrs. Henry Maier, wife of Milwaukee's Democratic mayor. A token black person. A token young person. And for Vietnam Veterans Against the War, the greatest humiliation of all: the young navy vet John O'Neill, whom the White House had put on TV to sandbag John Kerry in 1971.

During the nomination roll call—"Florida casts its votes for the greatest American president since Abraham Lincoln!"—the candidate was driven to a youth rally at Marine Stadium, ten miles from the hall. The roll call went over the top. Gerald Ford read his line with feeling: "Will the delegates come to order!" That, according to the script, was at 10:33—"followed by a ten-minute spontaneous demonstration with balloons."

Across town, a communications truck gave the cue. Richard Nixon entered Marine Stadium like a Roman emperor as the scoreboard started flashing with glee NIXON IS NOMINATED! NIXON IS NOMINATED!

Nixon's face, well-practiced, lit up, as if he'd never seen such a spectacle in all his life.

He hugged the master of ceremonies, Sammy Davis Jr.

He gave a speech to the assembled "good young kids," piped in to the delegates in the convention hall.

He arrived for his acceptance speech. The hall reverberated with Republican jubilation. Some wore buttons or carried signs reading NIXON IS LOVE and NIXON CARES and HAPPINESS IS NIXON. Others held on to their gold pennies with Nixon's face instead of Lincoln's, and souvenir "McGovern boxes" with a phony $1,000 bill and a white flag of surrender inside.

Then, to 30 million Americans, Richard Nixon, the peacenik they could trust, introduced the Checkers of 1972: little Tanya, a young Russian girl.

"Speaking on behalf of the American people, I was proud to be able to say in my television address to the Russian people in May, 'We covet no one else's territory. We seek no dominion over any other nation. We seek peace not only for ourselves, but for all the people of the world.' . . .

"On your television screen last night, you saw the cemetery in Leningrad I visited on my trip to the Soviet Union—where three hundred thousand people died in the siege of that city during World War II."

(You want civilian casualties? I'll tell you about real civilian casualties.)

"At the cemetery I saw the picture of a twelve-year-old girl. She was a beautiful child.

"Her name"—his voice broke—"was Tanya.

"I read her diary. It tells the terrible story of war. In the simple words of a child she wrote of the deaths of the members of her family. 'Zhenya in December. Grannie in January. Then Leka. Then Uncle Vasya. Then Uncle Lyosha. Then Mama in May.' And finally—these are the last words in her diary: 'All are dead. Only Tanya is left.'"

Pause.

"Let us think of Tanya and the other Tanyas and their brothers and sisters *everywhere*"—Nixon's voice caught—"in Russia, in China, in America, as we proudly meet our responsibilities for leadership in the world in a way worthy of a great people.

"I ask you, my fellow Americans, to join our new majority not just in the cause of winning an election, but in achieving a hope that mankind has had since the beginning of civilization. Let us *builllld* a peace that our children— and *all* the children of the world!—can enjoy for generations to come."

At 1 a.m. police stood in formation, rhythmically beating their riot clubs. Their liberal chief finally unleashed them to make arrests. With brutal dispatch, they collared two hundred miscreants, cheered on by martini-sipping yachtsmen moored at the marina. Though one was disappointed. He had heard Yippies were going to firebomb boats and was hoping for the insurance money.

CHAPTER THIRTY-FOUR

Not Half Enough

Nixon was twenty-six points ahead in the Gallup poll before the convention. He was thirty-four points up in the first poll afterward—with only 6 percent undecided. George McGovern's boosters had spoken of harvesting the "alienated" voter. But on September 1, Harris dusted off their "alienation index," a scale concocted in 1966 based on responses to five questions: "The rich get richer and the poor get poorer"; "What you think doesn't count very much"; "The people running the country don't really care what happens to you"; "People who have the power are out to take advantage of you"; "Left out of the things around you." Nixon was ahead even among the alienated—46–43 percent.

George McGovern started out in New England and the Hudson River Valley. He rested in Woodstock, New York. That was what the sign read on the side of his conveyance: MCGOVERN WOODSTOCK BUS. "Just what McGovern needs to straighten up his image with Middle America," a reporter wrote sardonically. His standing wasn't so solid with the Woodstock generation either. On September 10, George Gallup reported "a shift to President Nixon among voters under thirty." Nixon used to trail among them 48–41. Now he was ahead, 61–36. According to Fred Dutton's *Changing Sources of Power*, politicians said the new young voters were "far and away the most fiercely independent, perceptive, and self-motivated, they have ever seen. . . . Even before coming to maturity, its vanguard members helped set the pace for the two predominant controversies of the last decade: the civil rights struggle and the Vietnam War protests. These young people have also forced the most searching reappraisals of higher education in the U.S. since the borrowing from the German universities in the last quarter of the last century. . . . Most of the present young people are considerably more likely than their elders to develop a conscious relationship with other cultures and societies."

And, what, they were flocking to . . . *Richard Nixon?*

The people moving history, apparently to the left, were so *young:* Stokely Carmichael stole the civil rights movement from Martin Luther King in 1966, the month of his twenty-fifth birthday. Janis Joplin and Jimi Hendrix were twenty-seven when they died (Jim Morrison made it to twenty-eight). Fred Hampton was twenty-one when he died. McGovern's campaign manager was a lordly thirty-four years old; his acceptance speech was written by a twenty-eight-year-old; he had top staffers as young as twenty-two—and many had got their start organizing four years earlier with Eugene McCarthy.

But there were always other voices of this generation. When hired by Nixon, Pat Buchanan was twenty-eight, Roger Ailes, twenty-six; Ron Ziegler and Tom Charles Huston, twenty-five. There had always been an active movement of young conservatives in the 1960s, a self-conscious leadership vanguard for millions of young Americans who preferred their campuses free of disruption. Richard Nixon, himself only thirty-three when first elected congressman, had always placed young people in positions of extraordinary responsibility—such as the twenty-six-year-old Bob Haldeman, who had stood a fan's vigil outside the studio where Nixon made the Checkers Speech in 1952 and was his chief advance man by 1956. "Youth Against McGovern" dogged the Democrat at every stop. The fashionable looked down their noses at them (only a dozen reporters showed up for their opening press conference at the National Press Club).

But then, Richard Nixon was good at speaking to people who felt looked down upon.

On September 5, 1972, in Munich, Israeli athletes sleeping soundly in the Olympic Village were set upon by eight Palestinian militants with guns and grenades. The terrorists killed two in the ensuing struggle and took nine hostages. Threatening athletes at gunpoint live on international TV, they demanded the release not just of comrades in Israeli jails but of two Marxist terrorists in Germany. They negotiated a 727 to take them to Egypt, and safe passage to the airport. There, a rescue attempt led to a shoot-out. Four Israelis died in a helicopter explosion; five Israelis and a German policeman were machine-gunned to death. Mark Spitz, the swimmer who won a record seven gold medals, each with a new world record, had to leave before the closing ceremonies for his own safety—he was Jewish. The world's flags flew at half-staff at Olympic Stadium—all except for ten Arab nations who refused to pay the dead the tribute.

McGovern started tromping through Northern industrial cities. The legendary downtown restaurants where families had been flocking for generations, the magnificent movie palaces, the landmarks a presidential candidate might once have visited—no one was flocking to them anymore. In Youngstown, Ohio, the camera shots of the podium included the marquee of the Uptown Adult Book Store; in Philadelphia, the once-elegant hotel where the campaign party stayed was crawling with street people.

Ted Kennedy was traveling at the candidate's side, saying the same kind of things George McGovern did, but getting three times the ovations. In

Detroit a voice cried out plaintively: "Save us! Save us, Mr. Kennedy!" A young black woman started a chant: "Kennedy in '76! Kennedy in '76!" McGovern's biggest applause came when he called out the names of dead Kennedys. In Chicago the mayor magnanimously scheduled a good-old-fashioned Democratic parade down State Street. Then again, Daley hosted a parade for the first lady in October, lest anyone doubt his conflicted loyalties. One of his more indiscreet ward bosses was quoted by ABC News: McGovern was "gonna lose because we're gonna make sure he's gonna lose."

Sargent Shriver, a Chicagoan and Daley ally, was supposed to be the point man in the bid to win back the regulars. The Democratic leaders of Essex County, New Jersey, gave him a loyal welcome at a picnic: "Some like to think there are two groups, the regulars and the McGovernites," a county clerk pronounced. "But today there is one group, the Democratic group." Off to the side, ward leaders gave blind quotes to reporters: "The Democrats are in trouble. The ethnics aren't going to vote for the national ticket. The average American is completely turned off by Bella Abzug, Betty Friedan, the gay liberation, and they identify McGovern with them. . . . Maybe we can save the local candidates at best."

That was September 17. It showed the negligible impact of two straight days of Woodward and Bernstein pieces on the *Post* front page. On the sixteenth, under the unassuming subhead "Jury Bares New Details of Break-in," beside a photograph of the Cuban Bernard Barker, the *Post* reported a grand jury indictment against the burglars and Liddy and Hunt. But the details seemed technical, the amounts penny-ante ("The only money known to be involved in the conspiracy is $1,600 that Liddy gave to suspect James W. McCord Jr."). What might have seemed the most dramatic revelation—"According to the National Archives, the indictment of Liddy and Hunt marks the first time in history that a person who has served as a White House aide has been indicted"—was buried near the bottom, where other, more dramatic stories beckoned: "Rape, Robbery, and Abduction: Gunmen Terrorize 9 Women"; "Audit Raises Tallies on Crime"; "Croats Hijack Jet, Demand 7 Be Freed"; "Israel Strikes into Lebanon." The next morning's story—"Spy Funds Linked to GOP Aides"—didn't bury the lead: "Funds for the Watergate espionage operation were controlled by several principal assistants of John N. Mitchell . . . and were kept in a special account at the Committee for the Re-Election of the President." But the story was bumped from the top of the page by a flattering profile of Maurice Stans and how the "transparently political" attacks on Nixon's fund-raising successes were causing him to enjoy his job less.

McGovern started using the word *Watergate* on the campaign trail, and the number $300,000, the amount the *Post* reported the president's reelection campaign had earmarked "for sensitive political projects." The language was always received boomingly by Nixon-hating Democratic crowds. That was as far as the enthusiasm went. For every newspaper article about the investigation, there seemed to be an equally prominent piece casting aspersions on the Democrats' probity. The Government Accounting Office was supposed to be releasing an audit of Nixon's donations. On the day of Nixon's nomination, the bureau postponed its release. Larry O'Brien, reported a two-paragraph item on page 39 of the *Times,* charged the White House was using "every ounce of political muscle" to block it. The report found eleven "apparent and possible violations of the Federal Election Campaign Act." Nixon responded that both parties may have committed some "technical violations," and Stans said "the strong and persistent pressures placed on the GAO by the Democratic members of Congress" and "McGovern campaign operatives" were responsible for "inaccuracies in the report." Stans asked for an audit of the Democrats. McGovern said he'd welcome it.

There followed a cavalcade of page 1 headlines: "G.A.O. Is Auditing McGovern's Books"; "Dole Charges 7 Violations of Election Act"; "Inquiry by GAO: Democratic Funds Probe Finds Technical Violations." One article, "McGovern Mail Lottery Charge Being Studied," followed up the charges of "apparent illegality" after McGovern announced he would pick 250 names at random from his hundreds of thousands of small contributors for an Andrew Jackson–style "People's Dinner Party" in the White House. A Republican congressman called that "a clear-cut case of dangling special favors and privileges in return for a political campaign contribution . . . a desperate, shabby inducement and the lowest insult yet to the American voter."

Both sides were bad; which was worse? *"They think that political parties do this all the time."*

Walter Cronkite got wind of a possible White House scandal and went after it hard. In July, as a fruit of Nixon's Moscow trip, the United States announced a deal to sell the USSR $750 million in grain on favorable terms over three years, and insiders had allegedly traded on early information. Cronkite's team found evidence implicating an assistant secretary of agriculture, who had taken a position at Continental Grain *after* negotiating the deal, but *before* the deal went public; Continental then closed a sketchy $150 million grain sale three days before the deal was announced. The evidentiary chain was complex. But when Cronkite went on the air September 27, his presentation was a miracle of clarity: he got up from his desk to, of all things, a schoolroom blackboard and illustrated the movement of men and money with stick figures. It took two segments on the *Evening News* to explain, the first an unprecedented eleven minutes long. It came too late to affect the Gallup poll released the next day: "Which candidate— Mr. Nixon or McGovern—do you think is more sincere, believable?" Nixon won, 59–20.

Even among self-admitted Democrats, it was Nixon 38–37; among those under thirty, 57–28. The New Politics was right about one thing: voters, especially young ones, were turning away from a politician they saw as untrustworthy. Only that politician was George McGovern. On September 30, the *Post*'s Woodward and Bernstein reported that when John Mitchell had been Nixon's campaign manager, he had personally controlled the $300,000 "secret fund." Three days later, the same paper ran a poll analysis headlined MCGOVERN LOST CREDIBILITY ASSET.

McGovern was incredulous. He decided to turn up the heat. At a speech to a conference of UPI editors in Washington, the first words out his mouth were "Yesterday on *Meet the Press,* my wife said that the current administration was the most corrupt administration in recent history. I agree with that—with one modification. I would leave out the word *recent.*"

"The Nixon mess in Washington," he said, appropriating Ike's 1952 campaign promise to clean up the mess in Washington, "includes the corruption of our ideals in an unjust war as well as the corruption of the Justice Department in the ITT case. . . . It includes the corruption of the Constitution by assaults on freedom of the press as well as the corruption of our tax code by loopholes for the wealthy few."

McGovern looked the editors in the eye: "And every one of you in this room knows it."

Then he launched into a long assault on Nixon for ducking a discussion of the issues. "I suspect the true reason Richard Nixon will not debate is that he is afraid—not of me, but of the people. He must realize that if he is forced to tell them what he really has in store, there will be little doubt of his defeat in November."

There wasn't much response. Delivered in McGovern's flat Midwestern voice, the words sounded less dramatic than they read. "What kind of lead do you put on this speech story?" one of the reporters asked on the press plane. "Something like: 'Unlike the rest of the American people, George McGovern has a low opinion of Richard Nixon'?"

Of course Nixon wasn't going to debate. He wasn't even campaigning. Persistently, Jules Witcover would ask Ron Ziegler, "Ron, what did the president do today as a candidate for reelection?" Ziegler would respond as if asked when the president had stopped beating his wife: he was the *president,* for God's sake; he was busy settling a war and had no time for the low, dirty business of *politics.*

The first bout of recognizable campaign activity began on September 26. The president dropped from the sky in a Chinook helicopter onto Liberty Island in New York Harbor, where several thousand schoolchildren had been shipped to listen to him dedicate the American Museum of Immigration. Most chanted "Four more years!" on cue; one knot of disobedient children shouted, "Stop bombing the dikes!" A small contingent of Vietnam Veterans Against the War, who had somehow made it through the awesome gauntlet of security, cried out from the crowd, "Stop the bombing! Stop the war!"

The president paused.

"I have a message for the television screens," he said, looking straight into the cameras. "Let's show, besides the six over here"—he pointed—"the *thousands* over here." In the shadow of the Statue of Liberty, the protesters were hauled off by cops. It turned out, mysteriously, that they had all received personal invitations to the event in the mail.

Then it was off to a $1,000-a-plater at the Americana Hotel, one of twenty-eight "Victory '72" dinners. It was Student Government Day across the country. Nixon gestured to the evening's special guests, student council presidents and treasurers and secretaries: "It is significant right here in this room, that at this great dinner, where it costs, I understand, a great deal to sit down and eat, that the young people were able to come in and at least enjoy the speeches." They enjoyed them more than the traveling press, who watched on closed-circuit monitors in a room two hundred feet away, eating dry turkey sandwiches.

The next day was San Francisco. The press was lectured on their plane by John Ehrlichman that McGovern should "repudiate" upcoming demonstrations that police intelligence told them were "political rather than of an anti-war nature." The president got a tour of the spiffy control center for the new Bay Area Rapid Transit system. It was walled in by glass. The reporters watched from the other side, like gawkers at an aquarium. Then it was off to Los Angeles. Bob Hope warmed up the $1,000-a-plate crowd ("McGovern's running out of money. Yesterday he mugged an Avon lady!"). The president told of the time he had invited a group of young musicians from Los Angeles to the White House. One of the kids told him, "You know, it's a long way from Watts to the White House." The president relayed how he'd responded: "Yes, I know, and it's a long way from Whittier to the White House."

His voice softened. "A boy, born in Yorba Linda, growing up in Whittier, and going to the White House . . ."

The reporters, watching on closed-circuit TV, groaned. An outsider to the "boys on the bus," Timothy Crouse of *Rolling Stone,* told a veteran he thought the whole point of having a campaign press corps was to *cover* these events: question the crowds, perhaps even the candidate, *serve the public*—not let themselves be handmaidens to a passive spectacle: "Why not mutiny?" The old salt responded that thanks to years of Agnewism "the White House people managed successfully to put the press in the ambivalent position of being an entity separate from the public interest or the public." Nixon had rendered the press one more special-interest group: "The public doesn't give a damn about our problems."

Then it was off to the Biltmore and the National Cancer Conference, where the reporters listened to a speech that sounded spontaneous, though they'd been handed it twenty-four hours before.

Jules Witcover, after McGovern's UPI speech, wrote an analysis piece for the *L.A. Times* about how since the president was claiming traditional campaign travel was too much of a security threat, he could instead schedule regular press conferences in which he entertained political questions. But no one ever saw Witcover's argument. His editors killed it for being too "opinionated."

The president did say he would entertain political questions at his October 5 press conference. The first, predictably, was on McGovern's charges. Speaking in the passive voice—lest McGovern be granted status as a debating partner with the president—he did what he'd been doing since Checkers: positioned the attacks on him as attacks on good God-fearing patriots—as attacks on *you*. "The president of the United States has been compared in his policies with Adolf Hitler," he rumbled indignantly. "The policies of the U.S. government to prevent a Communist takeover by force in South Vietnam have been called the worst crime since the Nazi extermination of the Jews in Germany." The elisions were fast and furious. McGovern hadn't compared Nixon's "policies" with Adolf Hitler's. McGovern had been speaking of a political break-in of an opposing party's headquarters. He would not, Nixon said, dignify such charges with a response: "In view of the fact that one of the very few members of Congress who is publicly and actively supporting the opposition ticket in this campaign has very vigorously, yesterday, criticized this kind of tactics, it seems to me it makes it not necessary for me to respond." In later speeches he would name this most useful of straw congressmen— Jerome Waldie of California—who was obscure enough that whatever he had said about McGovern, it hadn't been reported in any major papers.

As his high school debating coach had said, Dick could always "slide around an argument instead of meeting it head-on." He had got the important point out there: if McGovern was so noble, why was his own party abandoning him? On October 8, Republican congressional leaders filed a complaint with the Fair Campaign Practices Committee that the McGovern campaign's language—for instance, Frank Mankiewicz's claim that "Richard Nixon is a shifty politician and has always been"—was "an affront to every American and a disgrace to the political process." McGovern just wasn't playing fair.

October 10, a scoop from Bernstein and Woodward:

"FBI agents have established that the Watergate bugging incident stemmed from a massive campaign of political spying and sabotage on behalf of President Nixon's reelection and directed by officials of the White House and the Committee for the Re-Election of the President.

"The activities, according to information in FBI and Department of Justice files, were aimed at all the major Democratic presidential contenders and—since 1971—represented a basic strategy of the Nixon re-election effort."

The story featured a 1963 photo of Donald H. Segretti, identified as head recruiter for the "offensive security" operations, and of Kenneth W. Clawson, the White House aide who had admitted he had written the "Canuck letter" printed in the *Manchester Union Leader* that "in part triggered Muskie's politically damaging 'crying speech' in front of the newspaper's office." A reporter pointed out to Ron Ziegler that day that the president had said he'd assigned John Dean to get to the bottom of Watergate. Had that investigation turned up any evidence of political sabotage by anyone on Nixon's staff?

"You state as a fact a story that was written, but later denied by the reelection committee," Ziegler said.

The reporter re-torqued the question: whether the *Post*'s story was factual or not, had the investigation the president said he had ordered come up with any facts?

"He has made several points in the past regarding the Dean investigation. I have nothing more to add to that."

Someone asked it again: did John Dean's investigation turn up any of the same material as the October 10 *Post* article?

"I don't have any further comment on the subject," Ziegler said, adding that the reporters should address further questions to the reelection committee.

But, someone pointed out, "We are talking about a man who works for the president in the Executive Office Building."

Ziegler: "He has already issued a statement on that, and I have nothing to add to it."

It went on for thirteen more questions. It was like talking to . . . a stone wall.

The *Post* reported yet more fishiness: a call to McGovern financiers from someone impersonating a campaign staffer asking for information on a donor; a request from someone claiming to be a Taiwanese diplomat for McGovern's travel schedule; a call to Walter Cronkite from someone impersonating Frank Mankiewicz. The *Post* reported that this Donald Segretti had a liaison in the White House (someone named Dwight Chapin). On October 16 the paper said that one of the five people authorized to approve payments from the "secret fund" was the president's personal attorney. A *New Republic* reporter bugged Ziegler about it the next day: "This Mr. Kalmbach of Newport Beach. Is it a fact that he is Mr. Nixon's personal attorney? And two, has Mr. Nixon been in touch with him in the last two months?"

Ziegler replied that the president hadn't spoken with Kalmbach in months, leaving the first part of the question—whether Kalmbach was

Nixon's lawyer—unanswered. Political observers would later call this a "nondenial denial." Ziegler then pulled out another trick: changing the subject to Henry Kissinger—the kind of shiny distraction upon which reporters loved to pounce.

Ziegler was a new kind of flack—a *career* flack, not a former reporter vaguely ashamed of quitting reporting. Indeed, he held reporters in contempt. He pressed his advantages. Advantages such as: all these names were only recently unfamiliar to reporters (it was almost impossible to get ahold of a White House directory), so how unfamiliar must they sound to the general public? Bernstein and Woodward didn't attend these briefings. They were not White House correspondents. They were police reporters—the Orthogonians of the newsroom. Woodward had just been divorced; Bernstein's career had been going nowhere fast after he was discovered napping on the job. They had stumbled into the assignment covering the Watergate burglars' arraignment, the kind of job parceled out to low men on the totem pole. They started working twelve-to-eighteen-hour days on the Watergate story, staking out the porches of low-level Nixon campaign staffers, poring through obscure clues, at a time when the Franklins of the White House pressroom were distracted by the "hot" stories.

The *New York Times* filled in a tiny piece of the puzzle on October 18: proof that Segretti had been in phone contact with Chapin. *Time* had added a data point two days earlier, that Gordon Strachan had helped hire Segretti. But no one was doing much—since the *Post* "owned" the story, and no editor wanted to advertise another paper's scoops. To most reporters, not to mention readers, the story's blizzard of proliferating details remained obscure: fraternity-style pranks on the campaign trail. Right-wing Cubans breaking into the Democrats' offices. This person "had access to the secret fund," that person "had access to the secret fund"; Strachan hired Segretti; Chapin was Segretti's contact—why did it matter, and who the hell were Strachan, Segretti, and Chapin? No one ever read about them in Alsop's columns. Woodward and Bernstein didn't have time to explain how the accumulating threads fit together. So no one put the threads together.

McGovern later put out a campaign commercial panning over the most damning Watergate headlines, trying desperately to get the public to make the connection to the White House. But if the White House was implicated, why were so many of these stories at the bottom of the page?

The *Post*'s monopoly provided the White House an opportunity: they could isolate the story as some weird obsession of a single "liberal" newspaper, pursuing some inexplicable vendetta against the president of the United States. They rolled out the triple-barreled attack three Tuesdays before the election.

Ziegler at his morning briefing: "I will not dignify with comment stories based on hearsay, character assassination, or guilt by association"—this last being the sin liberals associated with Joe McCarthy.

Bob Dole in a speech to black Republicans: "In the final days of this campaign, like the desperate politicians whose fortunes they seek to save, the *Washington Post* is conducting itself by journalistic standards that would cause mass resignations on principle from the *Quicksilver Times*"—the drug-addled D.C. "freak" newspaper. "Given the present straits in which the McGovern campaign finds itself, Mr. McGovern appears to have turned over the franchise on his media attack campaign to the editors of the *Washington Post.*"

Campaign manager Clark MacGregor stepped up to the microphone at 5 p.m., reporters having been gathered on the promise MacGregor would answer questions—then they were told MacGregor would read a statement and wouldn't take any questions.

One of the most distinguished press veterans, Clark Mollenhoff of the *Des Moines Register,* a bluff Midwesterner who had given up a promising professional football career to be a journalist, who had out of a deep-dyed sense of patriotic duty taken a job in 1969 as the Nixon White House ombudsman and left within a year in disgust, whom Jimmy Hoffa spat on as he was led off to prison, wasn't about to let MacGregor get away with it. Earlier, Mollenhoff had demanded of Ziegler where *he* thought the money for the Watergate burglary had come from. Perhaps intimidated by the man who once, when President Eisenhower told him to sit down at a press conference, defiantly kept standing, Ziegler forgot to stonewall: "Why, I don't think there was any question but that the money came from the committee." Mollenhoff put that on the front page of the *Register* October 6. Ziegler promptly got his wits about him and released a statement accusing a towering figure in the pressroom of "misinterpretation."

Now the bluff old buzzard had Nixon's campaign manager in his sights. He shouted at him, "What credibility do you have? What documents have you seen? Because if you can't tell us, you have no right to stand there."

MacGregor didn't blink. "That is a matter you will have to determine in consultation with your editors," he blandly pronounced, then fed the reporters his statement:

"Frustrated, twenty-six points behind in the polls, with three weeks to go, George McGovern—and his confederates—are now engaging in the 'politics of desperation.'

"We are witnessing some of the dirtiest tactics and hearing some of the most offensive language to appear in an American campaign. . . .

"And the *Washington Post's* credibility has today sunk lower than that of George McGovern.

"Using innuendo, third-person hearsay, unsubstantiated charges, anonymous sources, and huge scare headlines, the *Post* has maliciously sought to give the appearance of a direct connection between the White House and the Watergate—a charge the *Post* knows—and a half dozen investigations have found—to be false."

The paper gave Watergate innuendo "huge scare headlines while proven facts of opposition-incited disruptions of the president's campaign are buried deep inside the paper." The *Post* ignored "the Molotov cocktail discovered on October eighth at the door of the Newhall, California, headquarters," arson at Nixon offices in Hollywood and Phoenix, broken windows in New York, Massachusetts, and Los Angeles. MacGregor mentioned the *Post*'s complicity in Daniel Ellsberg's crime, "for which he faces a possible 115 years in a federal penitentiary." He thundered, "While each crime is reprehensible, which is more serious? Stealing top-secret documents of the government of the United States; or allegedly stealing Larry O'Brien's political papers?" He concluded, "The purpose of the *Post* campaign is clear: to divert public and national attention away from the real issues of this campaign—peace, jobs, foreign policy, welfare, taxes, defense, and national priorities—and onto phony issues manufactured on L Street and in McGovern headquarters."

From L Street, *Post* editor Ben Bradlee released his response: "Time will judge between Clark MacGregor's press releases and the *Washington Post*'s reporting. . . . The facts are on the record, unchallenged by contrary evidence." The media gave both charge and defense equal space; even the *Post* twinned their coverage of the MacGregor press conference with a sober-sided analysis piece of MacGregor's baseless claims of McGovern ties to the violence against Nixon campaign offices. An astonishing watershed in American political history had passed: a major journalistic institution was willfully and cynically discredited by a president as if it were a rival political candidate—the *Washington Post* as Jerry Voorhis, or Helen Gahagan Douglas. And the president had no trouble getting away with it.

Every Watergate story was balanced by an imprecation against McGovern. The *New York Times* reported, "MCGOVERN DISCLOSES LARGE NEW LOANS," about two heirs to the Eli Lilly fortune who channeled $500,000 to McGovern. Far down, after the jump, the story noted that Richard Mellon Scaife, of the Pittsburgh banking family, had given a million dollars' worth of $3,000 checks to 330 Nixon committees to avoid the gift tax. The Lilly brothers' contribution was a loan the McGovern campaign paid back through thousands of small donations; Scaife's was a straight-up payout. But you had to read down to the end of the story whose headline only mentioned McGovern to learn that.

For McGovern, the media's gospel of "balance" was proving deadly. His campaign *was* overwhelmingly being funded by donors he labeled the "skinny cats." They attended "people's fund-raisers" where admission was five bucks ("John Connally and his oil-company friends have a president,"

McGovern said at one in Des Moines. "Isn't it time *we* had a president?"). They responded to direct mail with some thirty thousand envelopes a day. The letters said things like "I'm on Social Security and I don't get enough to live on, but I wanted you to have this"; and "I've got two good reasons for sending $25 to George McGovern"—enclosing a photograph of a Vietnam vet with both legs amputated. After a televised speech on Vietnam ("Mr. Nixon has described the Vietnam War as our finest hour. I regard it as the saddest chapter in our nation's history") the one-day haul was $852,248. Gary Hart himself had to work the mail table to help with the backlog. You wouldn't know it from reading the headlines in McGovernophobic organs such as the *Chicago Tribune* and the *Wall Street Journal:* "$2 Million Loaned to McGovern by Unions, Rich Contributors"; "$4.5 Million in Loans; McGovern Forces Ask Wealthy for Financing"; "Secrecy Preferred by Some McGovern Moneymen."

He wasn't mugging Avon ladies. Apparently, he was mugging heirs and heiresses instead.

His campaign, though, was all disarray. Reporters got so used to snafus that they half-expected that when the appointed hour came for McGovern's first televised fund-raising appeal, the screen would be blank. The campaign relied for their support on an increasingly balkanized left; in July, McGovern's first full-time Mexican-American regional coordinator resigned after complaining that the campaign was not attending to Spanish-speaking voters. The campaign relied, too, on a generation of activists who counted the ordinary wink-wink, nudge-nudge understanding of backroom politics the rankest betrayal. One day Vermont's popular gubernatorial candidate, a party regular, met with the leaders of McGovern's state campaign to work out the details of a mutual endorsement. In marched the entire volunteer staff, enraged at the "backroom deal" being cut in their midst.

The notion was that McGovern was the perfect Democratic candidate to run against Nixon because his shimmering idealism, his incorruptibility, his utter *straightfowardness*—not to mention his early and morally uncompromising antiwar stance—could draw brand-new strands into the Democratic coalition, perhaps for good: newly enfranchised under-twenty-ones; the activists of the new social movements; the conscience-stricken idealists of a nation suffering under an epidemic of alienation. The process was supposed to be additive. That, after all, was how the Democratic coalition had *always* worked: new groups braided into the whole, which bodies forth ever stronger in the future. But the Democratic regulars proved unwelcoming, the old magic from the days when McGovern successfully reached out to blue-collar voters in Milwaukee bowling alleys hard to recapture. One year earlier, George Meany and Richard Nixon were locked in mortal political combat. Now, Meany spoke of his president like a brother. A high school dropout at fourteen, Meany talked about the McGovern coalition as if they were aliens. "Thirty-nine percent of the delegates at that convention held postgraduate degrees. . . . During the preconvention period and during the convention itself, those people running the show repeatedly indicated their contempt, and I mean this, their contempt for the trade union movement and for the people we represent." Labor's chieftain had become one of the Orthogonians.

McGovern returned to Chicago late in October. The Cook County sheriff had just arrested eight men alleged to be responsible for a string of murders in the Chicago suburbs—members of a gang called De Mau Mau, black veterans of army intelligence in Vietnam become domestic terrorists. One witness told the *Tribune* there were branches on every military base in the United States and Asia that had a sizable black population. Police started investigating De Mau Mau links to the murder of a retired army intelligence officer in Nebraska and his family. The Midwest was falling into racial panic. The chances that Bungalow Belt white ethnics would vote for anyone but a law-and-order candidate were not helped.

Nixon's outreach to regular Democrats was more successful. He made a "nonpolitical" visit to Philadelphia as a guest of Mayor Rizzo—who told his political machine, Haldeman recorded in his diary, "either the President wins in their areas or they're to look for another job." Nixon signed his long-in-the-making revenue-sharing bill at Independence Hall. Here was the apotheosis of the blue-collar turn to cultural populism at the expense of economic populism: the bill was Nixon's deliberate retreat from the legacy of the New Deal and the Great Society and would likely do real damage to the balance sheets of cities like Philadelphia.

The ceremony was reserved for those with engraved invitations. The rest of the park was lined by cops at barricades. Forty protesters were arrested for picketing—some of them unionists demanding wage-price reforms, which used to be George Meany's crusade—despite a judge's order licensing their presence. A reporter asked to see the Liberty Bell. The irony-impaired cop's stern response: "No one sees the Liberty Bell when the president is here."

Vice President Agnew emceed: "Too much power has been flowing away from the people."

The president: "The Constitution of the United States begins with the words 'We, the people,' and the bill I shall sign is a demonstration of a principle that we have faith in the people."

Upon his retreat, the shouts of protesters were drowned out by a *My Fair Lady* medley. The president had been in the City of Brotherly Love a total of ninety minutes. Mayor Rizzo rode along in the limousine to Camp David ("We have a lot of secrets," he bragged to the press. "It was some private things we discussed"), where Nixon delivered a noontime radio address. (To his opponents "the will of the people is 'the prejudice of the masses.' . . . It is time that good, decent people stop letting themselves be bulldozed by anybody who presumes to be the self-righteous moral judge of our society.") Then he watched the seventh game of the World Series, while reading newspaper endorsements. The score: 213 for him, 12 for McGovern.

Then he left for a campaign motorcade through the Westchester County suburbs in New York State. He was already guaranteed a victory there. But this was Nelson Rockefeller's home county. Winning Westchester in November would be quite a fuck-you to his rival for the presidency since 1960.

Republicans announced a ludicrous crowd estimate of 425,000 (they had claimed 700,000 at his only other real campaign motorcade, in Atlanta, within a space that could physically contain only 75,000). Westchester was not as friendly. Leaving the airport, he passed a full-color poster of the My Lai victims. Along the route, the signs said things like CORRUPT and WHY ARE YOU AFRAID TO DEBATE? and WHAT ABOUT WATERGATE? The pool reporter piped audio commentary into the press bus: "I'm told to pass on to you that seasoned observers say these crowds are . . . unusually enthusiastic." One scribe hollered back, "Yeah. The kids are shouting 'Fuck Nixon' with uncommon fervor." Nixon finished up with a rally at the Nassau Coliseum. Entrance was by invitation only. But several dozen or so demonstrators managed to place themselves in the bleachers behind Nixon nonetheless. *"Stop the war! Stop the war!"* they heckled. Security guards, cops, and ordinary spectators set upon them in a hail of fists and feet. Police dragged them across the cement. *"Kill 'em!"* one reporter recorded hearing. Young Voters for the President started chanting, *"Four more years!"* "The Long Island campaign swing by the President was climaxed by an evening reminiscent of disruptions that once followed Gov. George Wallace," a reporter wrote. A younger reporter phoned in to his editors that it reminded him of the Third Reich, but his story was killed.

The president had responded by improvising a line on law and order: "On my part, I will say to you that any appointments I have the opportunity to make to the courts of this land or to the law enforcement officials of this land, as has been the case in the last four years, you can be sure that the age of permissiveness is gone." He also suggested "an Eleventh Commandment: No one who is able to work shall find it more profitable to go on welfare than go to work." Apparently he had forgotten the details of his own Family Assistance Program.

That wasn't improvised. A similar line showed up in one of his commercials.

It began with the piercing blast of a shift whistle. A weary hard hat perches on a beam high above New York and removes his modest sandwich from a brown paper bag (for hardworking Americans like these, it's dangerous even to eat lunch). The voice-over, as he pensively chews:

"Senator McGovern recently submitted a welfare bill to the Congress."
The camera pans in on the worker's silent face.

"According to an analysis by the Senate Finance Committee, the McGovern bill would make forty-seven percent of the people in the United States eligible for welfare."

Slowly, angrily: "*Forty-seven* percent. Almost every other person in the country would be on welfare."

The camera moves on the bustling, blaring street below—the 53 percent.

"The Finance Committee estimated the cost of this incredible proposal as *64 billion dollars* in the first year. That's six times what we're spending now. Who's going to pay for all this?"

"Well, if you're not the one out of two people on welfare—you do."

The camera fixes on the worker's bedraggled, incredulous face, and a legend appears on the screen: PAID FOR BY DEMOCRATS FOR NIXON, JOHN CONNALLY, CHAIRMAN.

Like the "Dear Fellow Democrats" attack mailers from 1962 calling Pat Brown the vassal of "left-wing forces" who had adopted the "entire platform of the Communist Party," the claims were fanciful. The figures were based on the National Welfare Rights Organization's $6,500-per-family-per-year bill that Humphrey had deceptively pinned to McGovern in California; in fact, McGovern's Democratic convention had overwhelmingly voted down a resolution for a $6,500 guaranteed income. No matter; the smear was out there. It ran over and over—once every twenty minutes in some cities. Officially, the organization Democrats for Nixon was entirely autonomous. Actually, of course, the Committee to Re-Elect the President made the spots and "loaned" the "group" the money to place them.

McGovern came back with his own, considerably less effective, ad, explaining his radically scaled-back welfare plan, cinema-verité-style, captured during one of his factory tours. An angry, haggard hard hat addressed him:

"They're payin' people who are on welfare today doin' nothin'! They're laughin' at our society! And we're all hardworkin' people, and we're gettin' laughed at for workin' every day! Why not have them people go to work cleaning up the dirty streets in our towns for their money?"

McGovern: "Well, I agree. Richard Nixon goes around talking as if I'm some sort of radical because I believe in guaranteed *jobs* for people he's throwing out of work. He said he was going to cut the welfare roles, he put four million more people on welfare. That's not my idea of delivering on a campaign pledge! Now I'm telling you, and I mean it, we're going to do whatever necessary to provide a job for every able-bodied man and woman who wants to work, and those who don't want to work shouldn't be paid anything in the way of public support." (The voice-over then gave his campaign slogan: "McGovern. Democrat. For the People.") The only problem was that the nation already "knew" that McGovern was for handing out money to people who didn't work. All the commercial did was to make him look willing to change his views to get elected—a message reinforced by another Democrats for Nixon production: McGovern's shifting positions were recited while a McGovern photo spun round like a weather vane (Nixon, one was supposed to draw the contrast, never changed ideological course).

It gave Chuck Colson an idea: a White House agent provocateur could infiltrate the welfare rights picketers in front of one of the Committee to Re-Elect the President storefront offices and throw a brick through a window that had a poster version of the weather-vane ad within frame for the TV cameras.

The in-house ad agency shot that down, saying they couldn't produce a poster in time. They wondered where this absurd idea came from. The answer might have been: the president, who found the soft-sell approach frustrating and was always honking to Colson that the campaign wasn't aggressive enough. "They don't realize how rough I can play. I've been such a nice guy around a lot of times. . . . But when I start, I will kill them. There's no question about it."

McGovern's defense-spending ad was filmed in the same factory as his welfare ad. A black man: "And whenever the war is over, we'll have more lay-offs. . . ." McGovern: "If we have to depend on war, we're in sad shape in this country. You know, that's really the argument the Communists make." (How flattering: accusing a voter you're trying to persuade that he thinks like a Communist.) "They say our society won't work unless our society has a war. Now frankly, I don't believe that. At the end of World War II, which is the war I participated in, we had full employment after that war. And the reason is that we set about doing the things that we couldn't do with the war on. Now, those problems are still here. We need new housing, new environmental protection, and if we stop the waste that's going on in this war, we can give a job to every man and woman who wants to work. And I'm pledged to do that."

The camera panned wide, showing the crowd listening in—distracted, turning their heads from him as if skeptical, looking elsewhere, perhaps at the crew—and as McGovern pronounced his last word, the commercial showed him being *interrupted* by the questioner, then the sound abruptly cut off. It was another botched job.

McGovern's commercials looked cold and defensive, reiterating critics' charges without effectively refuting them. A four-minute spot recounting the Democratic convention reveled in what many found off-putting about the event: "It was almost dawn in Miami when the final moment came," the narrator intoned, "the gift of the most open political process in all of our political history"; "The first night went ten hours." The ad included a bizarre endorsement. A woman told the story of how her seventeen-year-old McGovernite son drove her to the polls and told her that if she didn't "vote correctly" she'd have to walk home. This made the reformers sound like what the regulars said they were—the same old-style political machine, only with hippies in place of bosses.

In his law-and-order ad, from the same factory (had he only been to one?), McGovern said, "You're never gonna get on top of crime in the United States until you get on top of drugs." You could see that the people listening weren't buying it—not from the candidate of "acid, amnesty, and abortion."

George McGovern argued against charges he was disarming America in a speech to an unimpressed VFW convention, pointing out that the military's desertion rates in 1970 were so high that enough men left to fill four infantry divisions; that the introduction into combat of defective M16 rifles left men "as good as disarmed in the heat of battle," while the manufacturer said it was the soldiers' fault; that Nixon's Indochina policy was based upon "what is best for a dictator in Saigon"; that the Government Accounting Office had recently tallied up $35 billion in Pentagon cost overruns. ("There is an army vehicle known as the Goat. It is supposed to cost five thousand dollars per copy and float. Instead it costs fifteen thousand dollars per copy and sinks.") These things, he said, weakened America far more than the reasonable Pentagon budget cuts he was proposing.

Democrats for Nixon's argument was more effective. It began by panning over platoons of toy soldiers, over the *rat-tat-tat* of a snare-drum cadence:

"The McGovern defense plan: he would cut the marines by one-third" (a hand from above swept one-third of the olive-drab toys from the stark white background).

"The air force by one-third" (black toy planes: *sweep!*).

"He'd cut navy personnel by one-fourth" (little men in white sailor suits: *sweep!*)

"He would cut interceptor planes by one-half" (toy planes: *sweep!*)

"The navy fleet by one-half" (*sweep!*)

"And carriers from sixteen to six" (the man, clad in a senatorial blue suit, reaches out with both arms—*sweeeeeeeep!*—leaving behind distressing heaps of men and matériel).

The announcer intoned the punch line: "Hubert Humphrey had this to say about the McGovern proposal: 'It isn't just cutting into the fat, it isn't just cutting into manpower, it's cutting into the very security of this country.'" "Hail to the Chief" emerged out of the drum cadence and footage of the commander in chief reviewing the fleet: "President Nixon doesn't believe we should play games with our national security. He believes in a strong America—to negotiate for peace . . . through strength."

Nixon radio ads in regions with defense plants and military installations were so misleading they were almost surreal. They cited a "congressional study" (a later researcher could never find any such study) showing how many jobs McGovern's Pentagon cuts "could" cost that particular area. The one that ran in Rhode Island, for example, said thirty thousand civilians jobs. That figure was arrived at by calculating how many jobs McGovern's total cuts nationally would cost Rhode Island if *all* the cuts were applied *solely* to facilities in Rhode Island.

Most of the Nixon ads made claims neither false nor true. They made no claims at all. Two Republican consultants' research had discovered that "television news and documentaries and other specials were by far the most important media influences on the split-ticket voter." So they made spots that looked like television news and documentaries: the president being president. A four-minute one showed clips of him playing "Happy Birthday" on the piano for Duke Ellington, working out domestic policy with John Ehrlichman in the Oval Office ("What's the matter with these clowns? The whole purpose of this matter is to get property taxes down!"), dancing with his wife at Tricia's wedding, sharing a laugh with his interpreter in China. Then the voice-over: "Richard Nixon: a man of compassion, courage, and conscience. A man America *needs*. Now more than ever."

In another ad, he was once more at his desk lecturing Ehrlichman: "Massive busing produces inferior education, and education is *the name of the game*. . . . When we take kindergarten kids on a bus for an hour and a half, when they've got a school they can walk to ten minutes away, that's *wrong*. . . . It will have the effect of creating *hatreds*."

The most compelling ad was a guided tour of his weathered passport, visa by visa stamp: "In India he laid out the Nixon doctrine. In Yugoslavia he met with Marshal Tito. In Mexico he signed an agreement to combat drug traffic. In Canada he signed the Great Lakes Environmental agreement. In China he talked peace with Mao Tse-tung. In the Soviet Union the nuclear arms agreement became a reality. President Nixon's foreign policy for the United States—a policy that calls for the self-reliance of our allies, and peaceful negotiations for our enemies, all for a single purpose: world peace." Then the ad opened onto the passport's final, blank pages: "But there still are places to go. And friends to be won. That's why we still need President Nixon. Now, more than ever."

The most important Nixon broadcast was not a commercial. It did not feature the president. It featured the man he didn't generally allow out in front of the cameras because of his thick German accent—and, perhaps, out of jealousy. Henry Kissinger was the media darling now, a wizard, the man who beat swords into plowshares via "shuttle diplomacy." That he'd never given a televised press conference was also a useful alert: something huge was going on.

"We have now heard from both Vietnams," he began, "and it is obvious that a war that has been raging for ten years is drawing to a conclusion. . . .

"We believe peace is at hand."

The world would learn how cynically premature this announcement was at Christmas, after the election, when the president—hoping against hope once more for a knockout blow—ordered the most massive bombardment of the war (sixty-six airmen were killed or captured). When asked how this deal differed from any the administration could have struck in 1969, Kissinger answered that the other side had always previously insisted "we had to pre-determine the future of South Vietnam in negotiations with North Vietnam." Sophisticated peaceniks could spot the lies too easily by now—the enemy had long insisted on a temporary coalition government as a prelude to genuinely open elections in South Vietnam. *America* had insisted on predetermining the outcome. McGovern called the announcement "a cruel political deception." But most Americans were prepared to believe—including the editors of *Newsweek.* They put the words "Good-Bye Vietnam" on their cover and headlined the story "How Kissinger Did It." Nixon took a campaign turn through Ohio. The signs in the crowd said things like MY DADDY WILL BE HOME FOR CHRISTMAS; NIXON IS MY HERO; NIXON, THE MAN FOR NO MORE NAM; PEACE TIME IS NIXON TIME.

Another important broadcast that wasn't a commercial was hosted by Walter Cronkite. Its subject was Watergate.

Woodward and Bernstein were too busy to write any kind of synthesizing narrative to coherently put the Watergate pieces together; they weren't close to understanding it all themselves. After his success explaining the grain deal with his stick figures, Walter Cronkite decided to try to explain Watergate himself. The first segment aired October 27, eleven days before the election. Cronkite stood in front of a projection of both the Watergate and Committee to Re-Elect the President headquarters—and the White House. His lead: "Watergate has escalated into charges of a high-level campaign of political sabotage and espionage apparently unparalleled in American history."

The report lasted fifteen minutes, diagrams and photographs alternating with filmed segments featuring Dan Rather and Daniel Schorr—a compelling, suspenseful narrative, with three-dimensional characters. Every White House denial was given a full airing. The difference was that for the first time, the *story* was as coherent as the *denials.* It even ended with a cliff-hanger: "Next time: the money behind the Watergate affair." Which was what promised to lay the whole thing on the threshold of the Oval Office.

But there would be no next time—at least not in its intended form.

Chuck Colson was put on the problem the next morning. He bragged in a memo to Haldeman, "Paley was pleading." CBS's chairman "sounded like a whipped dog and was almost on the verge of tears. My voice was steely cold. . . . Chalk up one for our new task of destroying the old establishment."

The follow-up report was also supposed to last fifteen minutes. Cronkite was ordered to cut it down to six. The slow, patient narration became a cubist-like incoherence. Shortly after the broadcast, McGovern received one more public relations blow: in Battle Creek, Michigan, he told a "Four more years" heckler to "Kiss my ass." Consternation whipped across the nation. America couldn't have a president who swore. "Where it hurts," Chuck Colson told the president, "is that people feel he doesn't have the, he doesn't have *command* of himself. In other words, that's a loss of control, that's—"

Nixon: "Yeah, because basically, that's the thing Agnew is gaining on, that his dignity, and sense of humor, and the rest—"

Colson brought up the latest Harris poll, which had yet to be released. It had been one of Colson's coups: he had "brought Harris around," intimidating him into writing poll language the White House preferred and leaking the administration the results early. "What's it say about Watergate?" the president asked.

"He's not getting anything," Colson replied. "He now completely buys the theory, Mr. President, that Vietnam has completely knocked that right out of people's minds. His theory is that people are only thinking about one thing at a time right now, they're thinking about the end of the war, and that's helped the confidence in your leadership, and that's stopped the erosion, and it's stopped them thinking about saboteurs, and spies, and—"

"And even though they know the thing isn't over yet, they have more confidence in me than in McGovern."

Indeed, even before "peace is at hand," Gallup had shown that by 58–26 percent, the public trusted Nixon over McGovern to end the war.

Why? McGovern's Eagleton fiasco, saying he was "one thousand percent behind him," then cutting him loose, had begun setting the chain reaction in motion: the antipolitician was a normal politician after all. His rhetorical approach didn't endear him to majorities: it made people dislike him. More and more, he wasn't merely arguing against the president. He was hectoring the American people, crying out about *their* failings, trying to shock them out of their moral lethargy.

At one appearance at the University of Minnesota, he stopped speaking and played a tape recording instead:

"I am a Vietnam veteran, and I don't think the people really, really understand war and what's going on. We went into villages after they dropped napalm, and the human beings were fused together like pieces of metal that had been soldered. Sometimes you couldn't tell if they were people or animals."

The tape stopped; the gape-mouthed crowd was silent. "In a recent month," McGovern intoned in a radio ad, "a quarter of the wounded civilians in South Vietnam were children under twelve. As we vote November seventh, let us think of Tanya and all the other defenseless children of the world." The candidate was howling, howling into the wilderness. If he was going to lose, he would lose his way.

But then again, maybe the original assumption was right—maybe this moral nakedness was how he could *win*. Reporters had been marveling how McGovern seemed to be in the grip of some strange serene confidence. It wasn't bitterness that moved McGovern to yell back at hecklers, but a kind of freeing insouciance. Many of the people around him, and at the grass roots, thought he couldn't lose. The America they loved wouldn't allow it. It *couldn't* reward Nixon's evil. The world had changed too much for that.

By the end of October, his crowds *were* becoming massive. The tide seemed to be starting to turn. "I've come here with some good news tonight," he would start out, followed by his devotees' roars. "It's not news I read in the Gallup Poll or any of the newspaper columns. But it's news that I've read in the faces of thousands of people just like you, all across America. And the news is that the experts are wrong and we're going to win in November!"

Halfway through, he'd scan over the assemblage:

"We don't have John Connally with us." (*"Booooo!"*)

"He's with his rich oil-baron friends. But we don't need John Connally and the oil barons. We'd rather have the oil workers."

His final peroration: "Twenty-seven years ago, during World War Two, I served in the armed forces. I happened to be a bomber pilot. During one of our missions we were hit badly by enemy fire, and it looked as if we might not make it. Many of the crew were ready to bail out. As commander of the plane, I surveyed the damage and determined we could make it. And what I said to the crew was, 'Everyone resume your stations. We're going to bring this plane home.'

"And that's how I feel tonight. So I say to you, 'Everyone resume your stations. We're going to bring America home.'"

The ovations were as deafening as victory.

A strange little book appeared at newsstands: *How McGovern Won the Presidency and Why the Polls Were Wrong*. It argued that Americans would see through Nixon's phony "peace settlement"; would remember how, four years earlier, Americans had been bamboozled with hints of some secret plan to end the war: *Those who have had a chance for another four years and could not produce peace should not be given another chance.* The people could not be so bamboozled again. The book conjured up images of Election Day: storefronts jammed with new McGovern volunteers, all saying, "I'm disgusted with Nixon keeping the war going until just before Election Day—what can I do to help McGovern?"

The people would see McGovern's courage—and turn away from the smears. *The people* would see that he *listened*—while the president hid in the Oval Office. They would see that it was *McGovern* who brought us together—Nixon only stirred up hate. Hadn't Mayor Daley said, at one of those Chicago parades, "George McGovern awakens the best in us"?

The people would finally connect the dots, from the ITT bribe to the grain deal to the Watergate burglary, the ratfucking squads and the secret fund that paid them, the millions pouring in from corporations with business before the government. The people would put two and two together, just as McGovern said in a televised address on corruption: "Mr. Nixon is not out just to *defeat* the Democratic Party . . . he is out to *destroy* the Democratic Party." Even Republicans would not stand for that. The shallow attachment voters had with the president would be overwhelmed by the passion of McGovernites. The reports on the souring of youth support would turn out to be wrong. The polls didn't know how to adequately sample these new, young first-time voters. They wouldn't reflect the millions of Americans too poor to have phone service. They didn't factor in the love for an honest man. Maybe people wouldn't *say* they were for McGovern, but that was only testament to the president's success turning the name *McGovern* into something you were supposed to be ashamed of. America still had a secret ballot. In their hearts, they would know who was right. Pat Caddell reported that when they gave homes they were polling *sealed* ballots, McGovern did 9 percent better.

The Gallup poll showed it 59–36 for the president. One of the people who didn't believe it was one of the nation's most respected political columnists, Scotty Reston of the *New York Times,* the Sunday before Election Day. Nixon would win, "but the thought that the American people are going to give Mr. Nixon and his policies and anonymous hucksters and twisters in the White House a landslide popular victory . . . is a little hard to imagine." To believe that Gallup was right, "you must also believe that the American people regret corruption but have accepted it as an unavoidable part of American life and really don't care about all those millions of dollars given to the Republican party by a few rich men and women, all the secret funds, and the bugging and burglary of the Democratic party and the fake letters and political sabotage and the guerilla warfare used in this campaign . . . that it's all right for the President to seek four more years in the White House without defining his program for the next four years, without debating the opposition candidate, or answering questions from the press . . . that the American people don't mind or haven't noticed that Presidential power is now unbalancing the whole American system." (Though Reston added, for the sake of balance, that McGovern's claim "We now have the most corrupt Administration in the history of the Republic . . . is obvious and wicked nonsense.")

Anne Wexler, one of McGovern's whiz-kid staffers, said Reston was wrong: they *would* win. Their voter registration drive had signed up 5.5 million people in seven big states that contained almost enough electoral votes to prevail—1.5 million in Texas alone: "They're all our people. If we can get

them out, there's no way we can lose Texas." In Ohio, a microcosm of
the nation, an aide to liberal Democratic governor John Gilligan, who'd
replaced the man who had called the National Guard to Kent State, said,
"I'm not ready to predict we'll carry Ohio, but I may be in another week."
McGovern people talked about a letter that had surfaced from Nixon's campaign chairman in Michigan, warning, "President Nixon's lead in Michigan
has been slipping for the last two months. Furthermore, the commitment by
many of those who still tell pollsters they favor the President is not strong."

It would end like a Henry Fonda movie—something like *Twelve Angry
Men*, where only the jury's prejudices had blinded them from seeing that
they were about to condemn an innocent man, and where the liberal's gentle, persistent force of reason had compelled the brutish conservative, by the
last reel, to realize the error of his ways.

But America wasn't described by such liberal narcissism. It was a place
where the real Henry Fonda, in 1970, turned over to the FBI office in Los
Angeles a death threat that arrived at his home—"YOUR DUAGHTER
[*sic*] HAS BEEN TRIED FOR TREASON FOR BEING A TRAITOR.
HER DATE OF EXECUTION WILL BE DEC 1970 TO PROTET [*sic*]
HER & SAVE HER PAY 50,000 CASH"—but where FBI files reveal nothing was done to find the identity of the sender. The father had submitted the
ransom note to the same FBI office that was running a harassment campaign
against his daughter.

It was also the America where the real Henry Fonda, when his daughter
told him she opposed firing Angela Davis because she was a Communist,
said, "If I ever find out you're a Communist, Jane, I'll be the first person to
turn you in."

From the library of the White House ("This room, like all the rooms in this
great house, is rich in history"), Nixon gave his final televised speech before
the voting: "The leaders in Hanoi will be watching," he said. "They will be
watching for the answer of the American people—for your answer—to this
question: shall we have peace with honor or peace with surrender?"

The Sunday before the election, McGovern said, "I'm going to give you
one more warning. If Mr. Nixon is elected on Tuesday, we may well have
four more years of the war in Southeast Asia. . . . He's going to stay there.
He's going to keep our troops there. He's going to keep the bombers flying.
He's going to confine prisoners to their cells in Hanoi for whatever time it
takes for him to keep his friend General Thieu in office." The next morning
Newsweek came out with its campaign wrap-up. They criticized McGovern
for "the harshest rhetoric of any campaign in history."

McGovern gave his final televised speech: "Mr. Nixon will not end the
war." Nixon "has always supported the war." Nixon campaign aides were
delighted. "The more the McGovern side tried to say that the president was

in *favor* of the war, the more it worked to our advantage," Nixon's advertising chief said. McGovern's constant invocations of war's savageries were doubly antithetical to his fortunes: they heightened the people's relief that Nixon was ending the war and tainted George McGovern with the savor of someone who believed America was dishonorable, who wanted to make Americans feel ashamed.

Nixon's aides were confident. Their boss, however, was not. Election eve, and the president gathered his retainers around him, warning them to expect one final "dirty attack": these Democrats were capable of anything.

How did it end? After Lyndon Johnson's landslide 1964 victory and the declaration by the pundits of permanent liberal victory; after the Watts riot and the first long, hot summer, and then the second; after the consuming fires of Vietnam and the war at home to try to stop it, and the war against those who tried to stop it; the wars against school-integrating bureaucrats and the war on school buses and sex ed; the conspiracy trials; civil rights, civil rats; radicals bombing buildings, vigilantes shooting and beating radicals; *Bonnie and Clyde* and *The Green Berets;* the assassinations, the New Politics, the drugs, the dropouts, the Soaring Sixties—how did it all end?

After this strange, stiff man from Whittier who scaled pool-house walls rather than be photographed in a time and place not precisely of his choosing, who practiced McCarthyism before McCarthy had thought of the idea, who bravely faced down the snobs who wanted to kick him off General Eisenhower's ticket in a speech that forever divided Americans; who braved the rocks of mobs in South America and the televised onslaught of a bronzed Adonis named Kennedy; who inspired the protective love of millions of white middle-class Americans in their daily battles with existential humiliation at the hands of the media, the liberals, the know-it-alls, the slovenly, the loud, the *them*—who proved that he could *take it,* like Lincoln, like Churchill, and *come back;* the cross-bearing embodiment of a Silent Majority's humiliations, humiliating their shared tormentors in return; the bomber of dikes and the builder of miraculous new alliances with former enemies—

How did it all end?

Election Day. The president dropped his ballot by accident, then bent down to pick it up. Ron Ziegler shouted at the press corps, "Stop that! Stop that! No pictures!" You would think they would be more relaxed. The only thing in doubt was whether Nixon would win forty-eight, forty-nine, or possibly all fifty states.

And yet Richard Nixon didn't sound as if he was having much fun that night, taking in the election returns, working the phones, the sound track to *Victory at Sea* blaring in the background.

He called George Allen, the coach of the Redskins: "How do the Giants look next week?"

Coach Allen wound up his answer by saying, "You never can take for granted—"

Nixon: "No! No! No!"

It wasn't clear whether the president thought they were still talking about his favorite football team or his chances for reelection. Sixteen minutes later, Colson relayed the early reports: Nixon was at 77 percent in Georgia ("overwhelming in the South," Colson gloated); and Kevin Philips, doing analysis for NBC, was predicting that Nixon would win 60 percent of the popular vote. "What are you thinking if we don't win the House or the Senate?" Nixon grumbled back. "That's how they'll piss on the whole thing."

An hour and a half later, Colson broke the astonishing news that Nixon would probably take the city of Chicago. The boss, nonplussed, was still haunted: "It's amazing, the coattail thing just isn't working." Republican congressional candidates were faring poorly. Colson, who'd been quoted saying he'd run over his own grandmother to reelect Richard Nixon, tried out a theory to comfort him: all those Silent Majoritarian former Democrats who'd fallen in love with him were merely casting "penance votes" for Democratic congressional candidates out of guilt for their apostasy.

Nixon accepted only four congratulatory phone calls—from Frank Rizzo, Henry Kissinger, and two career-long rivals. "Mr. President, you've done the impossible!" barked Nelson Rockefeller, telling Nixon he might even get a majority in New York City. The president managed to pivot into gloominess and self-pity nonetheless. He savaged his opponent—"Wasn't that fellow unbelievably irresponsible with his charges in the last two days?"—then congratulated himself for the unwarranted magnanimity of his victory speech: "You've got to be generous, don't you think so?"

Henry Kissinger oozed oleaginous sycophancies. The president replied by bitching that his liberal-leaning speechwriter, Ray Price, had suggested he send McGovern a wire reading, "I look forward to working with you and your supporters." Nixon reported himself snarling back at the very idea. "This fellow to the last was a prick," he said. "Ray just doesn't have the right sense of this sort of thing."

Then, in an astonishing conversation with Hubert Humphrey, Nixon thanked the man he had shivved on election eve in 1968 by conspiring to sabotage talks to end the Vietnam War for being "a statesmanlike man" by not criticizing Nixon's Vietnam moves now. "Speaking as friends," the president said, "people ask very privately to compare this with '68, and I said the difference is that when Senator Humphrey and I were campaigning, and we had this terrible issue of Vietnam, we both put the country first. And this time, I said, we had a problem where one fella said any goddamned thing that came into his head." Nixon then granted Humphrey absolution for campaigning for the Democratic nominee nonetheless: "You had to fight for your man."

Humphrey's voice turned conspiratorial: "Well, I'll have a talk with you sometime. . . . I did what I had to do. If not, Mr. President, this whole defeat would have been blamed on me and some of my associates." Humphrey seemed to be admitting he had wanted McGovern to lose, and that he had tried to keep him from winning. They shared a hearty laugh, Nixon waxing effusive, telling Humphrey that Churchill had returned to the prime minister's chair at age sixty-eight—"and what the hell, you're still in your sixties!"

It recalled the Chicago ward boss who said that McGovern wouldn't win because they wouldn't let him win. And the "iron law of institutions," the truism that people care more about maintaining their power within institutions than the power of the institution itself.

Politically speaking, Nixon was right to thank Hubert Humphrey—for helping sustain the Democratic civil war between the New Politics reformers and the regulars, a civil war Nixon wished nothing more than to see continue raging. And so it would continue. Though even as election night drowned McGovern, McGovernism itself wasn't necessarily faring poorly at all. Senators and congressmen who had supported legislation to set a strict date for withdrawal from Vietnam had scored comfortable reelection victories. One night in April of 1971, after one of Nixon's Vietnam speeches, every major Democratic presidential contender had taken turns stepping before the cameras and begging Nixon to set a date certain to end the war. Even the furthest-right candidate, Scoop Jackson, had joined them (his only caveat was that Nixon should not publicly announce the date). And all through the 1972 campaign season, conservative Republicans had mightily strove to associate this position with the notion that the Democrats were all but stabbing American servicemen in the back. And yet, on Election Day, voters were not reluctant to vote for Democrats. The Republicans lost two seats in the Senate, increasing the Democratic margin to 57–43. The Republicans gained only a dozen seats in the House, putting but a negligible dent in the Democrats' majority, which was now 243–192.

Voters just wouldn't vote for McGovern—who ended up winning only one state, Massachusetts, and the District of Columbia. Nixon won nearly 61 percent of the popular vote, the third-greatest percentage in the history of the republic. He swept the South—79 percent of the vote in Mississippi. He became the first Republican presidential candidate to win the majority of Catholics. He even won a record number of Jews. Most remarkably, he won 35 percent of self-identified Democrats. He had given them a chance to vote to end the war *and* stick it to loudmouthed, smelly antiwar anarchists; to millions of Americans, this was the most tantalizing prospect of all.

But *third* place in history's popular vote, and still facing a liberal Congress? That was enough to make of his victory an agony.

On election night he had kept bugging Chuck Colson for news from Massachusetts, still 50–50, desperate to pull out an electoral college sweep.

Harry Dent comforted him the next morning, "Massachusetts deserved to be on the wrong side." Presently, Nixon snarled at Dent about the third-party candidate of the far right: "Of course, if we hadn't had that *goddamned* Schmitz in there, we would have got sixty-three!" Nixon lashed out at the Republican Party that had failed him: "Isn't it really the necessity, isn't it necessary to build a third party?" he asked. In days to come he lashed out at the eighty of eighty-nine members of the White House press corps whom he claimed to have learned had voted for the Democrat: "Freeze them!" Then, in an interview with the *Washington Star,* he lashed out at the electorate that had just given him his thumping second-term mandate: "The average American is just like the child in the family. You give him some responsibility and he is going to amount to something. . . . Pamper him and cater to him too much, you are going to make him soft, spoiled, and eventually a very weak individual."

And, on that day after the election, he joylessly annotated Pat Buchanan's news summary:

"The opposition line will be:

"1. McGovern's mistakes lost it and not his views and not RN's strength.

"2. The low vote proves no one liked either candidate.

"3. RN let down his party."

He felt dejected. Soon he would fire his entire cabinet. He needed more *control.* The landslide, a successful criminal cover-up: it wasn't half enough. In this, his gloominess was warranted. The following spring, the *final* slow, soiling humiliation of his political career began, as Congress started investigating Watergate. Twenty months after his landslide victory, he would no longer be the leader of anything. He would become the only American president to resign, disgraced.

That was how it ended for Richard M. Nixon.

But how did it end for us?

In this book I have written of the rise of two American identities, two groups of Americans, staring at each other from behind a common divide, each equally convinced of its own righteousness, each equally convinced the other group was defined by its evil. I have written of the moments where, at the extreme, members of these groups killed one another or tried to kill one another, most often in cold blood. Klansmen killing civil rights marchers in Selma; and two pacifists shot through the back of the head in Richmond, Virginia, and left in a ditch; a hippie shot in the back of the head in New Mexico. A teenager shooting a rabbi dead during a service in Louisville, crying, in the New Left's language, about the congregation's "phoniness and hypocrisy." Weathermen preparing bombs for a massacre at a servicemen's dance at Fort Dix. Vigilante Cubans setting fires and bombs at the offices of Soviet attachés and talent agents handling Soviet artists. State police carrying out extrajudicial killings following the pacification of the riot in Newark; black nationalists ambushing cops in Cleveland. I have dedicated this book to the memory of these Americans killed by other Americans, for reasons of ideology.

I have written of the rise, between the years 1965 and 1972, of a nation that had believed itself to be at consensus instead becoming one of incommensurate visions of apocalypse: two loosely defined congeries of Americans, each convinced that should the other triumph, everything decent and true and worth preserving would *end*.

That was the 1960s.

We Americans are not killing or trying to kill one another anymore for reasons of ideology, or at least for now. Remember this: this war has ratcheted down considerably. But it still simmers on.

I have written of liberals' rage at the rise of Richard Nixon, the Nixon of the Checkers Speech, who so brilliantly co-opted the liberals' populism, channeling it into a white middle-class rage at the sophisticates, the well-born, the "best circles"—all those who looked down their noses at "you and me" (a favorite phrase of Ronald Reagan's, who was both a student and a teacher of Richard Nixon's), whose aggravating moral one-upmanship seemed so often to Nixon's people to license moral relativism; a "toryhood of change" that sneered imperiously at the simple faiths of ordinary folk, their simple patriotism, their simple pleasures. I have written of these liberals' simple faiths, too, compared them to the drama staged by the Henry Fonda character in *Twelve Angry Men*: the belief that if only Nixon's people could truly see *reason*, grasp "the responsible literature in the field," their prejudices would melt away, their true interests would be recognized—and they would end up liberals, too.

I have written of a cult of "American consensus" that rose up among the punditocracy and reached its apogee with the landslide defeat of Barry Goldwater—their fervent imagining, alongside Lyndon Johnson's, that "these are the most hopeful times since Christ was born in Bethlehem," that America was united and at peace and would forever be, if only "extremists" stopped stirring up the pot. And I have written about the kind of intellectual self-repression it took to believe this: that the demonic furies of race and war were gathering even as the words were written, that America has always been divided and will always be. It is not too much to suggest that the rages that accompanied the crumbling of this myth of consensus, as the furies of the 1960s advanced, would not have been so rageful—would not have been so literally murderous—had the false rhetoric of American unity not been so glibly enforced in the years that preceded it: that some of the 1960s anger and violence was a return of what America had repressed.

I have written of how, as these furies advanced, this man Nixon was able to be so stubbornly successful in answering Americans' yearning for *quiet;*

but that, even so, in a complex admixture, Nixon also rose by stoking and exploiting anger and resentment, rooted in the anger and resentments at the center of his character. For what was his injunction to join his Silent Majority if not also an invitation to see one's neighbors as aliens, and to believe that what was alien would destroy us? I have even suggested that the demons that consumed him, the demons that led to Watergate, were part of a sincere desire to combat what he believed was truly *evil*—a battle with which many of the public in some sense identified, who embraced Nixon not despite the anxieties and dreads that drove him, but because of them. And that the vindictiveness that came of those anxieties and dreads was not separate from the fronts of pious normalcy he and his followers presented to the world, but bound up with them as well.

Richard Nixon died in 1994. At his funeral, Senator Bob Dole prophesied that "the second half of the twentieth century will be known as the age of Nixon." In a sense he surely did not intend, I think Bob Dole was correct. What Richard Nixon left behind was the very terms of our national self-image: a notion that there are two kinds of Americans. On the one side, that "Silent Majority." The "nonshouters." The middle-class, middle American, suburban, exurban, and rural coalition who call themselves, now, "Values voters," "people of faith," "patriots," or even, simply, "Republicans"—and who feel themselves condescended to by snobby opinion-making elites, and who rage about un-Americans, anti-Christians, amoralists, *aliens.* On the other side are the "liberals," the "cosmopolitans," the "intellectuals," the "professionals"—"Democrats." Who say they see shouting in opposition to injustice as a higher form of patriotism. Or say "live and let live." Who believe that to have "values" has more to do with a willingness to extend aid to the downtrodden than where, or if, you happen to worship—but who look down on the first category as unwitting dupes of feckless elites who exploit sentimental pieties to aggrandize their wealth, start wars, ruin lives. Both populations—to speak in ideal types—are equally, essentially, tragically American. And both have learned to consider the other not quite American at all. The argument over Richard Nixon, pro and con, gave us the language for this war.

Do Americans not hate each other enough to fantasize about killing one another, in cold blood, over political and cultural disagreements? It would be hard to argue they do not.

How did Nixonland end? It has not ended yet.

NOTES

ABOUT THE NOTES

Notes like these serve a threefold purpose: transparency, accountability, and as a resource for readers' own further explorations. All three functions have greatly been enhanced by the exponential expansion of material available on the Internet since my research began in 2001.

Historians have produced outstanding Web sites devoted to individual events; see, for example, "The Hard Hat Riots: An Online History Project," from George Mason University's Center for History and New Media, which cross-references documents and news accounts for a minute-by-minute reconstruction of that 1970 event. You can find out what was on the TV news every night via the abstracts at the Vanderbilt University Television News Archive (openweb.tvnews.vanderbilt.edu). Interested citizens have scanned crucial documents onto their own Web sites—such as the good soul who reproduced *Rolling Stone*'s coverage of the Berkeley People's Park riots of 1969. And, of course, classic TV moments referenced herein such as the Checkers Speech of 1952 and the Kennedy-Nixon debates of 1960 can be viewed, in whole or in part, on YouTube and other video sites. The American Museum of the Moving Image's "Living Room Candidate" site makes available every presidential campaign commercial described in the text.

Time put its entire archive online so that any passage from the magazine quoted herein can be Googled, leading the reader to the original article. (Just as this book was going to press, *Atlantic Monthly* did the same.) Readers interested in the relationship between Ronald Reagan and the University of California can review the documents reporter Seth Rosenfeld requisitioned via the Freedom of Information Act for his extraordinary "Campus Files" series, available at the *San Francisco Chronicle* Web site. Every presidential utterance recorded in the *Public Papers of the President* series has been digitized, sometimes with audio and video, by John Woolley and Gerhard Peters of the University of California—Santa Barbara. In the notes, PPP followed by a document number and date makes it easy for the reader to find Johnson and Nixon speeches at presidency.ucsb.edu.

The State Department has put online the Vietnam volumes of the *Foreign Relations of the United States* collection of documents, which includes full texts of every major high-level memo on Vietnam decision-making, and even transcripts of some telephone conversations. The Pentagon Papers have been digitized by the Mount Holyoke University International Relations Program. The Miller Center for Public Affairs at the University of Virginia adds digitized audio of Nixon White House tapes at regular intervals, and an important newly released tape—number 33, in which you can listen to the president reacting in real time to the returns on Election Day, 1972—is online at the National Archives' Nixon Project. David Leip's Atlas of U.S. Presidential Elections and Larry Kestenbaum's Political Graveyard sites are exceptionally useful as well.

Readers with online access to university libraries, or physical access to larger public libraries, may be able to download PDF files of newspapers including the *New York Times, Chicago Tribune, Wall Street Journal, Washington Post,* and *Los Angeles Times* articles cited below (these are the files subscribed to by the library I use, at the University of Chicago; others may vary) through ProQuest Historical Newspapers, with content fully searchable, and also download the full pages in which the articles appeared.

These are just some examples; there will be more with each passing month. A continually updated hypertext version of these notes will be available at my Web site, rickperlstein.org, so that readers, wherever possible, can explore *Nixonland*'s source materials on their own.

Here is how the notes below work: Phrases in italics are passages taken from the text. Paragraphing of the source citations follows the paragraphing in the text. Each page number preceding a paragraph in the notes corresponds to the page where the paragraph begins in the text.

ABBREVIATIONS

BPP: Berrigan Brothers Papers, Cornell University Special Collections, Ithaca, New York
CDN: *Chicago Daily News*
CT: *Chicago Tribune*
LAT: *Los Angeles Times*
LBJCR: "Civil Rights During the Johnson Administration, 1963–1969: A collection from the holdings of the Lyndon Baines Johnson Library, Austin, Texas" (microfilm)
MIP: Files on the events of 1970 collected by Maurice Isserman, in possession of author
MTR: Museum of Television and Radio, New York City
NLT: Nixon Library Tapes transcribed by author, National Archives, College Park, Maryland
NYDN: *New York Daily News*
NYT: *New York Times*
NYTM: *New York Times Magazine*
PDP: Paul Douglas Papers, Chicago History Museum
PDP722: Douglas Papers, Part I, Box 722, 1966 folder
PPP: *Public Papers of the Presidents.* All public utterances of the presidents are available online, listed by month and year, at http://www.presidency.ucsb.edu/ws/
RNLB: Richard Nixon Library and Birthplace, Yorba Linda, California
USNWR: *U.S. News & World Report*
WP: *Washington Post*
WSJ: *Wall Street Journal*

PREFACE

xi *In 1964, the Democratic presidential:* All election tabulations from http://www.uselectionatlas.org.
xi *Five years later, a pretty young:* Anthony Lukas, *The Barnyard Epithet and Other Obscenities: Notes on the Chicago Trial* (New York: HarperCollins, 1970), 9.
xi *"I'm getting to feel like":* "At War with War," *Time,* May 18, 1970.

CHAPTER ONE: HELL IN THE CITY OF ANGELS

3 *You might say the story starts:* KTLA, "Hell in the City of Angels," MTR.
3 KTLA's *live coverage of Watts:* Interview with Terry Anzur, "Ron Fineman's on the Record," http://www.ronfineman.com/010928.html; author interview with Terry Anzur.
4 *"Let this session of Congress be known":* PPP 91, January 8, 1964. *"Our Constitution, the foundation of our republic, forbids it":* PPP 446, July 2, 1964.
5 *Johnson's approval rating even among Republicans:* Rick Perlstein, *Before the Storm: Barry Goldwater and the Unmaking of the American Consensus* (New York: Hill & Wang, 2001), 307. *So, even, did conservative businessmen:* Ibid., 309. *"I'm sick of all the people":* Bill McKibben, "Reversal of Fortune," *Mother Jones,* March–April 2007. Great Society speech: PPP 357, May 22, 1964.
5 *"crazy figures," William F. Buckley:* John Judis, *William F. Buckley, Jr.: Patron Saint of the Conservatives* (New York: Touchstone, 1990), 207.
5 Clark Kerr quote: Milton Viorst, *Fire in the Streets: America in the 1960s* (New York: Simon & Schuster, 1979), 277.
6 *"I know that very often":* CT, letter to the editor, January 1, 1964.
6 *"Iowa would go Democrat":* Philip A. Klinkner, *The Losing Parties: Out-Party National Committees, 1956–1993* (New Haven: Yale University Press, 1995), 75.
6 *"I doubt that there has ever been":* Rowland Evans and Robert Novak, *Lyndon B. Johnson: The Exercise of Power* (New York: New American Library, 1966), 483.

6 *"These are the most hopeful times":* PPP 810, December 18, 1964.

6 *"We have achieved a unity of interest":* PPP 2, January 4, 1965.

7 *Johnson "is almost universally liked":* Editorial, *Nation,* January 11, 1965. Melvin Laird quote: John Kessel, *The Goldwater Coalition: Republican Strategies in 1964* (Indianapolis: Bobbs-Merrill, 1968), 308. *A poll that month found:* F. Clifton White and William Gill, *Suite 3505: The Story of the Draft Goldwater Movement* (New Rochelle, NY: Arlington House, 1968), 417. *Should that two-thirds dominate their party's:* Lee Edwards, *Goldwater: The Man Who Made a Revolution* (Washington, DC: Regnery, 1995), 344.

7 *One staffer, Frank Kovak:* Klinkner, *Losing Parties,* 78.

8 Martin Luther King in Selma: Taylor Branch, *Pillar of Fire: America in the King Years, 1963–1965* (New York: Simon & Schuster, 1998), 575–600; James T. Patterson, *Grand Expectations: The United States, 1945–1965* (New York: Oxford University Press, 1995), 579–84.

8 For *Judgment at Nuremberg* see J. Hoberman, *The Dream Life: Movies, Media, and the Mythology of the Sixties* (New York: New Press, 2003), 122. *Lyndon Johnson was a man given to towering rages:* Godfrey Hodgson, *America in Our Time: From World War II to Nixon—What Happened and Why* (New York: Doubleday, 1976), 219. LBJ, JUST YOU WAIT: Lyndon Baines Johnson, *The Vantage Point: Perspectives of the Presidency, 1963–1969* (New York: Holt, Rinehart and Winston, 1971), 162.

9 *"It is wrong—deadly wrong":* PPP 107, March 15, 1965. Reaction to voting-rights speech: Hodgson, *America in Our Time,* 220.

9 *"Today, we strike away the last major shackle":* PPP 409, August 6, 1965.

9 James Reston column: "Washington: The Quiet Revolution," NYT, August 6, 1965.

9 Background on Watts riot: Matthew Dallek, *The Right Moment: Ronald Reagan's First Victory and the Decisive Turning Point in American Politics* (New York: Free Press, 2000), 129–38.

11 *"White Backlash Doesn't Develop":* NYT, November 5, 1964.

11 *A prominent liberal Southern:* Sam Ragan, "Dixie Looked Away," *American Scholar* 34 (1965).

11 *"How is it possible":* Robert Dallek, *Flawed Giant: Lyndon Johnson and His Times, 1961–1973* (New York: Oxford University Press, 1999), 223. *Los Angeles radio station KNX fired:* "A Few Prized Minutes with Michael Jackson," LAT, August 24, 2004.

11 *the latest in a series of South Vietnamese:* Hodgson, *America in Our Time,* 228; Schulzinger, *A Time for War: The United States and Vietnam, 1941–1975* (New York: Oxford University Press, 1997), 170.

12 Bob Hope Christmas special: *Bob Hope: The Vietnam Years, 1964–1966, Vol. 1* (Hope Enterprises, 2004). *thirty-six hundred Rolling Thunder sorties:* Schulzinger, *Time for War,* 172.

12 *"one of the few Communist-free":* Interview with Daniel Ellsberg. *"Few Americans will quarrel":* "This Is Really War," NYT, July 29, 1965.

12 Early Vietnam protests: Tom Wells, *The War Within: America's Battle over Vietnam* (Berkeley: University of California Press, 1994), 21–27. *SDS discussed a "Kamikaze Plan":* Ibid., 44–45.

13 *"Holiday from Exams":* Todd Gitlin, *The Whole World Is Watching: Mass Media in the Making and Unmaking of the New Left* (Berkeley: University of California Press, 1981), 49. *According to one poll:* Wells, *War Within,* 63.

13 *The Republican National Committee could hardly raise:* Klinkner, *Losing Parties,* 79. *"attempted gigantic political kidnapping":* WP, "Can 26 Million Be Wrong," November 25, 1964.

13 Morley Safer report: A. J. Langguth, *Our Vietnam: The War, 1954–1975* (New York: Touchstone, 2000), 385; Daniel C. Hallin, *The "Uncensored" War: The Media and Vietnam* (Berkeley: University of California Press, 1989), 132.

13 *"Assembly of Unrepresented Peoples":* Wells, *War Within,* 51. *Vietnam Day Committee:* Ibid., 56–57. *J. Edgar Hoover called them:* David Farber, *Chicago '68* (Chicago: University of Chicago Press, 1988), 65.

14 Athens Park, Watts, meeting: KTLA, "Hell in the City of Angels"; Dallek, *Right Moment,* 129. Watts statistics: KTLA, "Hell in the City of Angels."

15 *The terror was compounded:* Dallek, *Right Moment,* 130.

15 *Situation reports, minute by minute:* LBJCR, Reel 6.

16 Chicago riot: Mike Royko, *Boss: Richard J. Daley of Chicago* (New York: New American Library, 1971), 145. Time *quoted Senator Robert F. Kennedy:* "The Far Country," *Time,* September 24, 1965.

17 *Lyndon Johnson, petrified:* Dallek, *Flawed Giant,* 223, 299. *"People are saying that the Irish":* Interview with Representative Frank M. Clark, August 15, 1965, LBJCR, Reel 6. *"What a difference between these":* Bill Boyarsky, *The Rise of Ronald Reagan* (New York: Random House, 1968), 116.

17 *The president pulled in his legislative reins:* Dallek, *Flawed Giant,* 299. Lyndon Johnson's scar: *New York Review of Books,* May 12, 1966.

18 Nixon and Leonard Garment in Florida: Leonard Garment, *Crazy Rhythm: From Brooklyn and Jazz to Nixon's White House, Watergate, and Beyond* (New York: Crown, 1997), 84.

CHAPTER TWO: THE ORTHOGONIAN

20 For Richard Nixon's early life see Leonard Lurie, *The Running of Richard Nixon* (New York: Coward, McCann, and Geoghegan, 1972), 1–41; Renée K. Schulte, ed., *The Young Nixon: An Oral Inquiry* (Fullerton: California State University, Fullerton, Oral History Program, 1978), passim; Fawn Brodie, *Richard Nixon: The Shaping of His Character* (New York: W. W. Norton, 1981), 30–170.

20 *One of Richard Nixon's biographers:* Brodie, *Richard Nixon,* 40.

21 *"I won't buy fertilizer":* Lurie, *Running of Richard Nixon,* 29.

21 Letter to mother: Ibid., 19; Brodie, *Richard Nixon,* 76; David Greenberg, *Nixon's Shadow: The History of an Image* (New York: Norton, 2004), 247. *"Please consider me for the position":* Ibid., 77.

22 *The coach bemoaned his "ability":* Brodie, *Richard Nixon,* 81.

22 *"I had the impression he would even practice":* Chris Matthews, *Kennedy and Nixon: The Rivalry That Shaped Postwar America* (New York: Free Press, 1997), 59. The Orthogonians: Ibid., 24–25; Brodie, *Richard Nixon,* 113–15. I am indebted to Matthews's book especially for the notion of the Franklin/Orthogonian rivalry as a theme of Nixon's career.

23 *"a rather quiet chap about campus":* Lurie, *Running of Richard Nixon,* 26. *"the man least likely to succeed in politics":* Brodie, *Richard Nixon,* 130.

23 Iron Butt: Ibid., 122–25; Lurie, *Running of Richard Nixon,* 32. *"List the names of any relatives":* FBI application on display, RNLB.

23 *"remnants of the old violent New Deal":* Brodie, *Richard Nixon,* 165.

24 Nick's, Nixon and poker: Ibid., 94, 167, 390; Lurie, *Running of Richard Nixon,* 40. James McManus, *Positively Fifth Street: Murderers, Cheetahs, and Bionion's World Series of Poker* (New York: Farrar, Straus & Giroux, 2003), 118.

25 Hannah Nixon's "repressed anger": Brodie, *Richard Nixon,* 55.

25 *Hannah once told* Ladies' Home Journal: Lurie, *Running of Richard Nixon,* 22.

25 Hannah Nixon's exaggerations: Brodie, *Richard Nixon,* 35.

26 1946 Voorhis campaign: Lurie, *Running of Richard Nixon,* 44–49; Greenberg, *Nixon's Shadow,* 11–31, 71; Brodie, *Richard Nixon,* 171–79; Tom Wicker, *Richard Nixon and the American Dream* (New York: Random House, 1971), 35–45; Mark Feeney, *Nixon at the Movies: A Book about Belief* (Chicago: University of Chicago Press, 2004), 66; Matthews, *Kennedy and Nixon,* 27–42.

26 Whittier College dancing ban: Lurie, *Running of Richard Nixon,* 30.

29 Alger Hiss and Whittaker Chambers: Sam Tanenhaus, *Whittaker Chambers: A Biography* (New York: Random House, 1997); Brodie, *Richard Nixon,* 127–231; Richard Nixon, *Six Crises* (New York: Doubleday, 1962), 1–71; Whittaker Chambers, *Witness* (New York: Random House, 1962).

29 HUAC background: Walter Goodman, *The Committee: The Extraordinary Career of the House Committee on Un-American Activities* (New York: Farrar, Straus & Giroux, 1968).

33 *"I have been advised":* Lurie, *Running of Richard Nixon,* 95; Russell Baker, "Chotiner Advises G.O.P. How to Win," NYT, May 13, 1956.

33 *"are everywhere—in factories, offices, butcher shops":* Lurie, *Running of Richard Nixon,* 95.

34 1950 Helen Gahagan Douglas campaign: Brodie, *Richard Nixon,* 232–45; Lurie, *Run-*

ning of Richard Nixon, 91–98; Greg Mitchell, *Tricky Dick and the Pink Lady: Richard Nixon vs. Helen Gahagan Douglas—Sexual Politics and the Red Scare, 1950* (New York: Random House, 1950).

35 *"I will not break bread with that man!":* Brodie, *Richard Nixon*, 244.

35 Vice-presidential run and Checkers Speech: Greenberg, *Nixon's Shadow*, 31–35; David Broder and Stephen Hess, *The Republican Establishment: The Present and Future of the GOP* (New York: Harper & Row, 1967), 152; Stanley Kutler, *The Wars of Watergate: The Last Crisis of Richard Nixon* (New York: W. W. Norton, 1992), 34; Wicker, *One of Us*, 80–110; Brodie, *Richard Nixon*, 271–89.

41 My account of 1950s liberals' ideological crisis and Nixon's role in it is heavily influenced by chapter 2 of Greenberg's *Nixon's Shadow*.

42 *"Electric clocks, Silex coffeemakers":* Lurie, *Running of Richard Nixon*, 98. *carnival barker:* Ibid., 21. *"This is salable merchandise!":* Brodie, *Richard Nixon*, 170. Pepsi bottle: Brodie, *Richard Nixon*, 385.

43 *He now turned to assailing:* Greenberg, *Nixon's Shadow*, 109, 120.

CHAPTER THREE: THE STENCH

44 *President Eisenhower sent Nixon:* Fawn Brodie, *Richard Nixon: The Shaping of His Character* (New York: W. W. Norton, 1981), 316–20.

44 Nixon and Joe McCarthy: David Greenberg, *Nixon's Shadow: The History of an Image* (New York: W. W. Norton, 2004), 121–23.

45 1954 campaign: Brodie, *Richard Nixon*, 313–15, 329; Greenberg, *Nixon's Shadow*, 122.

45 Eisenhower's heart attack: Richard Nixon, *Six Crises* (New York: Doubleday, 1962), 131–81; Brodie, *Richard Nixon*, 349.

45 "Dump Nixon" movement: Ibid., 247, 330, 350–53.

46 Nixon, Stevenson, Galbraith, and 1956 campaign: Ibid., 312, 327, 356–58; Greenberg, *Nixon's Shadow*, 26, 124–36; John Judis, *Grand Illusions: Critics and Champions of the American Century* (New York: Farrar, Straus & Giroux, 1992), 198.

46 *"What does concern me":* "The Speech," *Time*, August 4, 1952.

47 *"Please! Not while I'm eating":* Greenberg, *Nixon's Shadow*, 96. *"The world is so much more dangerous":* Brodie, *Richard Nixon*, 328.

48 America's history with Latin America: Lars Schoultz, *Beneath the United States: A History of U.S. Policy Toward Latin America* (Cambridge: Harvard University Press, 1998), esp. chapter 17. Nixon in South America: Richard Nixon, *Six Crises* (New York: Doubleday, 1962), 183–243; Brodie, *Richard Nixon*, 362–63, 371–73. Earl Mazo, *Richard Nixon: A Political and Personal Portrait* (New York: Harper & Brothers, 1959), 203–46.

49 *"The nomination of Slippery Dick":* George W. Johnson, *New Republic*, May 26, 1958.

49 Right-to-work and 1958 election: Brodie, *Richard Nixon*, 374, 414; Charles Baird, "Right to Work Before and After 14(b)," http://www.sbe.csuhayward.edu/~sbesc/14bb.html.

49 *And it was Richard Nixon:* "Democrats Gain 6 Senate Seats," NYT, November 5, 1958.

50 For Nixon's enduring bitterness see, for example, the wire to a Bob Hope testimonial dinner in New York on March 31, 1961, on display at RNLB: "You can't get much lower on the celebrity scale than a retired vice-president, but let me raise a humble voice in behalf of aspiring lawyers, golfing duffers, and at least 49.9 percent of Bob Hope fans everywhere (except Cook County and certain parts of Texas): we salute you Bob for the recognition so richly deserved . . ."

50 *Memories of Eisenhower:* Chris Matthews, *Kennedy and Nixon: The Rivalry That Shaped Postwar America* (New York: Free Press, 1997), 137.

50 *Memories of his mother:* Claire and John Whitcomb, *Real Life at the White House: 200 Years of Daily Life at America's Most Famous Residence* (New York: Routledge, 2000), 385.

50 *Memories of Walter Cronkite:* Mark Feeney, *Nixon at the Movies: A Book about Belief* (Chicago: University of Chicago Press, 2004), 47.

50 *Memories of Henry Luce:* William Martin, *With God on Our Side: The Rise of the Religious Right in America* (New York: Broadway Books, 1996), 54.

50 *John F. Kennedy's good fortune:* Matthews, *Kennedy and Nixon*, 28–33; Thomas P. O'Neill, *Man of the House: The Life and Political Memoirs of Tip O'Neill* (New York: Random House, 1989), 83.

51 *They weren't unfriendly:* Matthews, *Kennedy and Nixon*, 90–102.

52 Promise to campaign in fifty states: Brodie, *Richard Nixon*, 356, 424–25. Staph infection and travels: Theodore H. White, *Making of the President 1960* (New York: Atheneum, 1961), 272–78.

52 *"Television is not as effective":* Matthews, *Kennedy and Nixon*, 144.

52 Kennedy debate preparations: Museum of Broadcast Communications panel discussion with Howard K. Smith, Sander Vanocur, Don Hewitt, Ted Sorenson, and Herb Klein, September 26, 2000.

52 Day of debate: Ibid.; White, *Making of the President*, 283–90; Matthews, *Kennedy and Nixon*, 144–56. Viewed at Museum of Television and Radio, Chicago.

54 *He would recite the number of meetings:* Brodie, *Richard Nixon*, 421.

57 *The January issue of* Esquire: "The New Mood in Politics," *Esquire*, January 1960, reprinted in Carol Polsgrove, ed., *It Wasn't Pretty, Folks, but Didn't We Have Fun?: Esquire in the Sixties* (New York: W. W. Norton, 1995).

57 *John Steinbeck said that month:* John Steinbeck, *America and Americans and Selected Nonfiction* (New York: Penguin Classics, 2003), 108. *That same January, the* Los Angeles Times: "*Times* to Carry Column by Sen. Barry Goldwater," LAT, January 16, 1960.

58 Nixon's "Last Press Conference": Jules Witcover, *The Resurrection of Richard Nixon* (New York: G. P. Putnam's Sons, 1970), 13–23.

58 Theodore White and KENNEDY FOR PRESIDENT button: John C. Lundgren, *Healing Richard Nixon: A Doctor's Memoir* (Lexington: University Press of Kentucky, 2003), 65. *"One could listen to such a speech":* White, *Making of the President*, 335.

59 *Write a book, Jack Kennedy once advised:* Nixon, *Six Crises*, preface. Joseph Kennedy fixing Pulitzer: Thomas C. Reeves, *A Question of Character: A Life of John F. Kennedy* (New York: Free Press, 1991), 142. *"For the next twelve years":* Ibid., 82.

59 *"relaxed and quick with a wisecrack":* David Broder and Stephen Hess, *The Republican Establishment: The Present and Future of the GOP* (New York: Harper & Row, 1967), 152.

59 Decision to run for governor: Matthews, *Kennedy and Nixon*, 194, 203–6; USNWR, August 7, 1961; CT, September 24, 1961; Matthew Dallek, *The Right Moment: Ronald Reagan's First Victory and the Decisive Turning Point in American Politics* (New York: Free Press, 2000), 21; Kurt Schuparra, *Triumph of the Right: The Rise of the California Conservative Movement, 1945–1966* (Armonk, NY: M. E. Sharpe, 1998), 61; Richard Nixon, *RN: The Memoirs of Richard Nixon* (New York: Grosset & Dunlap, 1978), 293–97.

59 Joe Shell and California far right: Rick Perlstein, *Before the Storm: Barry Goldwater and the Unmaking of the American Consensus* (New York: Hill & Wang, 2001), 165–67.

60 *Brown accused Nixon:* Nixon, *RN*, 297. *"Would you buy a used car from this man?":* Joseph Lewis, *What Makes Reagan Run?: A Political Profile* (New York: McGraw-Hill, 1968), 64.

61 *"Barring a miracle":* "California: Career's End," *Time*, November 16, 1962.

61 The Political Obituary of Richard Nixon: Stanley Kutler, *The Wars of Watergate: The Last Crisis of Richard Nixon* (New York: W. W. Norton, 1992), 55.

61 *Nixon stood out in the cold:* Nixon, *RN*, 227.

61 Nixon and 1964 election: Perlstein, *Before the Storm*, 198–99, 253, 261, 286–98, 310–11, 318, 325, 331–32, 337, 353, 358–59.

65 *Then he played peacemaker:* Philip A. Klinkner, *The Losing Parties: Out-Party National Committees, 1956–1993* (New Haven, CT: Yale University Press, 1995), 73–74; Witcover, *Resurrection of Richard Nixon*, 105–8.

65 *The media was so starved for someone:* Tamar Jacoby, *Someone Else's House: America's Unfinished Struggle for Integration* (New York: Free Press, 1998), 74.

65 *Nixon's ambiguous stature was sanctified:* "Over-Nominated, Under-Elected, Still a Promising Candidate," NYTM, April 25, 1965.

66 *His job itself had roots in a chit:* Brodie, *Richard Nixon*, 385. For Nixon office kitsch see Nixon Room at the Bonnie Bell Wardman Library at Whittier College.

66 Rose Mary Woods: Leonard Garment, *Crazy Rhythm: From Brooklyn and Jazz to Nixon's White House, Watergate, and Beyond* (New York: Crown, 1997), 101; Kutler, *Wars of Watergate*, 82; "Nixon's Real Enforcer," NYTM, December 25, 2005. *she typed up ingratiating notes:* RNLB, PPS 32-.103.332K; PPS 501.1.4; PPS 320.103.332H; PPS 324.243f; PPS 324.244A; PPS 238.59.35.

67 *"For the United States to negotiate":* Andrew L. Johns, "A Voice from the Wilderness: Richard Nixon and the Vietnam War, 1964–1966," *Presidential Studies Quarterly* 29 (1999). *A trip to Finland:* Witcover, *Resurrection of Richard Nixon,* 111–12.

67 *His domestic politics now:* "Over-Nominated, Under-Elected." *A PR flack named Bill Safire:* Maurice Stans, *The Terrors of Justice: The Untold Story of Watergate* (Washington: Brassey's, 1995), 127.

67 Eugene Genovese affair: James Surowiecki, "Genovese's March," *Lingua Franca,* November/December 1996; Garment, *Crazy Rhythm,* 111–12; Witcover, *Resurrection of Richard Nixon,* 116–19; *Nation,* November 15, 1965.

CHAPTER FOUR: RONALD REAGAN

70 *"Now and then the police cars":* "Watts: Is the Next Time Now?" WP, May 29, 1966.

70 *"I threw the firebomb":* "CBS Reports: Watts: Riots or Revolt?" November 1965, MTR, T77–0395. *A group of Berkeley radicals:* "Students with Causes Set Up Shop at Berkeley," WP, September 30, 1965. *Liberal technocrats reasoned:* Charles Abrams, "The Housing Problem and the Negro," in Talcott Parsons and Kenneth B. Clark, eds., *The Negro American* (Boston: Beacon, 1965), 523. *Fortune magazine, speaking:* Charles Silberman in *Fortune,* November 1965, in LBJCR, Reel 2.

70 Chief Parker quotes: "CBS Reports: Watts: Riots or Revolt?"; Governor's Commission on the Los Angeles Riots, *Violence in the City—an End or a Beginning?* (Los Angeles: State of California, 1965); Johnnie Cochran, *Journey to Justice* (New York: Ballantine, 1996), 73–78.

71 *In March, there almost was another:* "Two Slain in New Watts Riot," LAT, March 16, 1966; "New Riot in Watts Kills 2, Injures 25," NYT, March 16, 1966; "Shooting Incident Blamed by Police Officials for New Riot," LAT, March 17, 1966; "Watts Is Tense but Quiet," NYT, March 17, 1966. Brown legislative package: "Watts Riot Stirs Political Battle," NYT, March 18, 1966. White House conference cancellation: LBJCR, Reel 5. *The Los Angeles Times columnist Paul Coates:* "Prayers and Work," LAT, March 17, 1966.

71 *At his announcement:* "Reagan Enters Gubernatorial Race in California," NYT, January 5, 1966. California governor's race: "Watts Riot Stirs Political Battle," NYT, March 18, 1966.

71 *He was the primary front-runner:* "Christopher Matches Reagan Before Coast G.O.P. Committee," NYT, February 28, 1966. *"You know, a tree is a tree":* Gerald J. De Groot, "Ronald Reagan and Student Unrest in California, 1966–1970," *Pacific Historical Review* 65, no. 1 (1996).

72 *More or less, Brown was doing:* "Reagan Called Brown Choice for Nomination," LAT, January 4, 1966. *"'Bring him on'":* Bill Boyarsky, *The Rise of Ronald Reagan* (New York: Random House, 1968), 113. *A young assistant was sent:* Ibid., 112.

72 *Pat was not the most inspiring:* Lou Cannon, *Governor Reagan: His Rise to Power*; Jack Langguth, "Political Fun and Games in California," NYTM, October 16, 1966.

72 *Reagan punditry fixated:* David Broder and Stephen Hess, *The Republican Establishment: The Present and Future of the GOP* (New York: Harper & Row, 1967), 246. *An editorial cartoon depicted Goldwater:* Ibid., 276. Elizabeth Taylor, Borax Boy: Ibid., 246. Lassie, Liberace: "Ronald Reagan to the Rescue!" *Esquire,* February, 1966.

73 LSD: David Farber, "The Intoxicated State/Illegal Nation: Drugs in the Sixties Counterculture," in Peter Braunstein and Michael Doyle, eds., *Imagine Nation: The American Counterculture of the 1960s and '70s* (New York: Routledge, 2001), 17–40; Jay Stevens, *Storming Heaven: LSD and the American Dream* (New York: Grove Press, 1998), 272–78; Martin A. Lee and Bruce Shlain, *Acid Dreams: The Complete Social History of LSD* (New York: Grove Press, 1994), 150–51; "LSD Parley Called Here to Stem Increase in Use," NYT, April 13, 1966; "LSD: The Exploding Threat of the Mind Drug That Got out of Control," *Life,* March 25, 1966.

73 *A group called the California League:* "California's Dirty Book Caper," *Nation,* April 18, 1966. *Other activists went to war on a textbook:* "Schools on Coast Embattled Anew," NYT, May 15, 1966; "The California Textbook Fight," *Atlantic Monthly,* November 1967. *The L.A. County Board of Supervisors:* "Art Show to Open with Heavy Guard," LAT, May 30, 1966.

73 *The head of the nation's leading association:* "Student Morals Worry Educators," NYT, March 3, 1966. *A psychiatry professor, for instance:* Raleigh Observer, May 1, 1966 (AP

dispatch). *A writer in the* Nation *asserted:* Review of *The Dignity of Youth and Other Atavisms, Nation,* March 28, 1966.

74 *In San Diego, a terrorist tossed:* LAT, March 8, 1966. *In Pacific Palisades:* "50 Longhairs Protest Clipping Order," LAT, March 8, 1966. *"This congregation is a travesty":* "Detroit Rabbi Shot Before 1,000 in Synagogue," NYT, February 13, 1966.

74 W.E.B. Du Bois Club: "U.S. Asks to Have Du Bois Clubs Registered as Communist Front," NYT, March 5, 1966; "Du Bois Members Beaten by Crowd," NYT, March 6, 1966; "Explosion Wrecks Du Bois Headquarters in San Francisco," NYT, March 7, 1966; "Du Bois 'Duplicity' Decried by Nixon," NYT, March 9, 1966.

74 *"Time's story is biased":* Letters, *Time,* April 29, 1966. *An Oklahoma minister:* Chicago *Sun-Times,* May 28, 1966.

74 *"All the most vociferous":* Champaign-Urbana Courier, in PDP, Box 1118/A (Youth: Stud. Protest).

75 Reagan and Brown in Norwalk: Boyarsky, *Rise of Ronald Reagan,* 132–34.

75 *In 1956, Eleanor Roosevelt:* Mike Royko, *Boss: Richard J. Daley of Chicago* (New York: New American Library, 1971), 134. *"I'd like to be an Alabama trooper":* "Confrontation in Chicago: Mayor Daley Meets the Movement," *Nation,* August 30, 1965.

75 *King had once believed impoverished: Saturday Review,* November 13, 1965. King moves to Lawndale: Adam Cohen and Elizabeth Taylor, *American Pharaoh: Mayor Richard J. Daley: His Battle for Chicago and the Nation* (Boston: Little, Brown, 2000), 360. *He simply announced, "All of us":* Roger Biles, *Richard J. Daley: Politics, Race, and the Governing of Chicago* (De Kalb: Northern Illinois University Press, 1995), 119; Rowland Evans and Robert Novak, "King's Chicago Pillow," WP, August 29, 1966. *Forthwith, the commissioner was fired:* Nicholas Lemann, *The Promised Land: The Great Black Migration and How It Changed America* (New York: Vintage, 1992), 196.

76 *"The principle that a man's home":* "White Castles," WSJ, June 22, 1966. *The eighty-three-thousand-member National:* "Realty Board Is Leading Drive Against Housing Ban," NYT, May 24, 1966.

76 *And if a man leaves his castle:* Clark MacGregor, House debate, August 3, 1966, *Congressional Record* 112, pt. 14, 18,915. *"Employment often depends":* Emanuel Celler, May 4, 1966, opening speech, United States Congress, *Civil Rights, 1966: Hearings Before Subcommittee No. 5, Eighty-ninth Congress, Second Session* (Washington, DC: U.S. Government Printing Office, 1966), 1. Chairman of Time Inc.: "Statement of Andrew Heiskell," Ibid., 1538. Whitney Young: Ibid., 1429. Social science: Nicholas Katzenbach testimony, Ibid., exhibits 1–8. President Eisenhower's Civil Rights Commission: James L. Sunquist, *Politics and Policy: The Eisenhower, Kennedy, and Johnson Years* (Washington, DC: Brookings Institution Press, 1968), 275. *Real estate tycoon James W. Rouse:* Civil Rights, 1966, May 24 testimony. *Attorney General Katzenbach thundered:* Ibid., 1049–75; "Katzenbach Asks Housing Bias Ban," NYT, May 5, 1966.

77 *"as long as they have breath":* Raleigh Observer, May 1, 1966.

77 *Aggrieved constituents began flooding:* PDP722, James F. Nelson to Douglas, June 16, 1966; unsigned, March 11, 1966.

77 *"the only thing that counts":* Dan T. Carter, *The Politics of Rage: George Wallace, the Origin of the New Conservatism, and the Transformation of American Politics* (Baton Rouge: Louisiana State University Press, 1996), 339. *One sweltering day late in April:* "Wallace Orders New Segregation," NYT, April 28, 1966.

78 *"If every politician is an actor":* Norman Mailer, *St. George and the Godfather* (New York: New American Library, 1972), 15. *"I'm gonna draw the water":* Carter, *Politics of Rage,* 273. *Behind the scenes, an acquaintance:* Ibid.

78 *Civil rights groups flooded the state:* Ibid., 252. *"There is no more civil rights":* Charles Silberman in *Fortune,* November 1965, in LBJCR, Reel 2. *Alabama's primary, under Justice Department:* Jason J. Battle, "Racial Politics and the 1966 Alabama Gubernatorial Election, *Alabama Review* 49:2 (1996). *Carl Elliot, the favorite of the Yankee:* Carter, *Politics of Rage,* 285. Richmond Flowers and Confederate flag: Battle, "Racial Politics."

78 Wallace campaign scenes: Carter, *Politics of Rage,* 281–84; Stephen Lesher, *George Wallace: American Populist* (New York: Addison-Wesley, 1994), 260–64.

79 *"An Alabaman would make as good":* Ibid., 263. *The pundits' darling, Carl Elliot:* Carter, *Politics of Rage,* 285. Carl Elliot billboards: Battle, "Racial Politics." *Richmond Flowers ran his campaign into a ditch:* Carter, *Politics of Rage,* 286. *"It was at Selma":* Ibid., 287.

80 *"God forbid," his liberal Republican:* "Conservative G.O.P. '68 Seen by Goldwater," NYT, May 16, 1966.

80 *In October 1965, one hundred thousand citizens:* David Farber, *Chicago '68* (Chicago: University of Chicago Press, 1988), 65. *The theologian Reinhold Niebuhr:* Gary Dorrien, *Imperial Designs: Neoconservatism and the New Pax Americana* (New York: Routledge, 2004), 21. *In February, Senator William J. Fulbright:* Tom Wells, *The War Within: America's Battle over Vietnam* (Berkeley: University of California Press, 1994), 68–69; A. J. Langguth, *Our Vietnam: The War, 1954–1975* (New York: Touchstone, 2000), 703; Paul Cowan, *The Making of an Un-American* (New York: Viking, 1970), 116.

80 *"The Whole Thing Was a Lie!":* Peter B. Levy, ed., *America in the Sixties—Left, Right, and Center: A Documentary History* (Westport, CT: Praeger, 1998), 143. *"in the direction of treason":* Wells, *War Within,* 57.

80 Draft and class rank: Christian Appy, *Working Class War: American Combat Soldiers and Vietnam* (Chapel Hill: University of North Carolina Press, 1993), 35. *At the Universities of Wisconsin and Chicago:* "Chicago U. Protesters Apologize to Office Staff," NYT, May 15, 1966; *Chicago Sun-Times,* May 18 and 19, 1966. SDS alternative draft exam: Wells, *War Within,* 82–84; Jesse Lemisch interview.

81 *When New York suffered a huge blackout:* A. M. Rosenthal, ed., *The Night the Lights Went Out* (New York: New American Library, 1965), 14.

81 *The first antiwar teach-in:* Wells, *War Within,* 25. *In Berkeley in October 1965:* Ibid., 57. *"The Ballad of the Green Berets":* J. Hoberman, *The Dream Life: Movies, Media, and the Mythology of the Sixties* (New York: New Press, 2003), 147. Bill to outlaw antiwar demonstrations: Jack Newfield, *The Prophetic Minority* (New York: Dutton, 1966).

81 *A week later, in Richmond: Richmond News Leader,* May 21, 22, 23, 27, 1966. *March 26: marchers:* Jerry Lembcke, *The Spitting Image: Myth, Memory, and the Legacy of Vietnam* (New York: NYU Press, 1998), 32–33. *April: the headquarters:* "4 Fire Bombs Flung at Leftists' Office," NYT, September 30, 1966. *On the afternoon of May 16:* "One Slain, 2 Wounded in Detroit at Socialist Workers Party Office," NYT, May 17, 1966.

81 *The barn of a pacifist communal farm:* "Pacifists' Barn Burns; Arson Evidence Sought," NYT, October 16, 1966. *A Unitarian church in Denver:* Editorial, *Nation,* October 17, 1966. *At Boston College, forty-five hundred students:* "Boston Students Chide Humphrey," NYT, October 14, 1966. *"You are in the sights":* Paul Buhle, "Radical Madison," *Baffler* 13. *In Queens, the DA seized:* "20 Minutemen, Arsenal Seized in Plot," WP, October 31, 1966.

82 *Sargent Shriver, the Office of Economic Opportunity:* "$40 Billion Could End Poverty, Shriver Says," LAT, July 4, 1966. *intellectuals preached a cybernetic:* Wilbert Ellis Moore and Robert M. Cook, eds., *Readings on Social Change* (New York: Prentice-Hall, 1967), 143; *Acid gurus:* Farber, "Intoxicated State." *"Our problems are many":* "Reagan Enters Gubernatorial Race in California," NYT, January 5, 1966.

82 *A social studies:* Marc Pilisuk and Robert Perrucci, eds., *The Triple Revolution: Social Problems in Depth* (Boston: Little, Brown, 1968).

82 *The hottest novel:* Thomas Pynchon, *The Crying of Lot 49* (New York: Harper & Row, 1966). *A new book:* Edward J. Epstein, *Inquest: The Warren Commission and the Establishment of Truth* (New York: Viking, 1966). *Another, Mark Lane's:* Mark Lane, *Rush to Judgment: A Critique of the Warren Commission's Inquiry into the Murders of President John F. Kennedy, Officer J. D. Tippit, and Lee Harvey Oswald* (New York: Holt, Rinehart & Winston, 1966).

82 *"alienation index":* For questions see "Nixon Given Edge in Alienation Vote," WP, September 1, 1972; for 1966 origins see http://www.harrisinteractive.com/harris_poll /index.asp?PID=136. *"We suddenly found ourselves seriously":* Lewis Chester, Bruce Page, and Godfrey Hodgson, *American Melodrama: The Presidential Campaign of 1968* (New York: Viking, 1969), 52.

83 *"'Great Society' or Nation in Crisis":* See *Nation,* March 14, 1966, and July 25, 1966.

83 *Ronald Reagan put on a rally:* "Reagan Demands Inquiry," NYT, May 14, 1966; "Hand Inquires Why UC Report Went to Reagan," LAT, May 13, 1966; *San Francisco Chronicle,* June 9, 2002.

83 *Governor Pat Brown spent the evening:* "Brown Labels Yorty Rightist Fright Peddler," LAT, May 13, 1966.

84 *"Pat had the grays":* De Groot, "Ronald Reagan and Student Unrest in California."

The next day, Yorty: "Yorty Charge Hit," LAT, May 14, 1966. *The state's most reliable poll:* Totton J. Anderson and Eugene C. Lee, "The 1966 Election in California," *Western Political Quarterly* 20 (June 1967).

84 Nixon and Pat Buchanan: Jules Witcover, *The Resurrection of Richard Nixon* (New York: G. P. Putnam's Sons, 1970), 122; Pat Buchanan, *Right from the Beginning* (Boston: Little, Brown, 1988), 320–22.

84 Safire's plaid coats: Leonard Garment, *Crazy Rhythm: From Brooklyn and Jazz to Nixon's White House, Watergate, and Beyond* (New York: Crown, 1997), 106. Early Nixon organization: Ibid., 99–105; Witcover, *Resurrection of Richard Nixon,* 113. *Nixon even hired Paul Keyes:* Broder and Hess, *Republican Establishment,* 153.

85 *Thus the most important member:* Maurice Stans, *One of the President's Men: Twenty Years with Eisenhower and Nixon* (Washington: Brassey's, 1995), 127–30; Witcover, *Resurrection of Richard Nixon,* 121.

85 Donors: Ibid., 123.

85 *"Dear (Insert Name Here)":* RNLB, PPS 501/18, July 22, 1966. *He hit up the Republican National Committee:* Stephen Ambrose, *Nixon, Vol. 2: The Triumph of a Politician, 1962–1972* (New York: Simon & Schuster, 1989), 83.

85 *The crusade began in January:* "Nixon Rips Johnson, Sees G.O.P. Victory," NYT, January 30, 1966. *"I will not go and talk":* Fawn Brodie, *Richard Nixon: The Shaping of His Character* (New York: W. W. Norton, 1981), 235. *The next day, he appeared:* "Nixon Says 'Appeasement Line' Will Be G.O.P. Target in Vote," NYT, January 31, 1966.

86 *His usual round of Lincoln's-birthday:* David Broder, "Nixon Campaigns at Tiring Pace for Republican Candidates," NYT, February 10, 1966; Witcover, *Resurrection of Richard Nixon,* 124; Broder and Hess, *Republican Establishment,* 148.

86 *"Day after day," he wrote:* Garment, *Crazy Rhythm,* 100.

86 *In Seattle, the local paper:* Seattle Post-Intelligencer, February 13, 1966. *Then he sat for a televised Q&A:* Seattle Times, February 9, 1966.

86 *In his memoir, Leonard Garment:* Garment, *Crazy Rhythm,* 86.

87 *inflation, Evans and Novak:* "What Inflation?" WP, March 16, 1966. *As Nixon noted in an oral history:* Brodie, *Richard Nixon,* 320, 540.

87 *The* New Yorker's *"Talk of the Town":* "Notes and Comment," *New Yorker,* March 19, 1966. *Garment thought the boss had just:* Garment, *Crazy Rhythm,* 112. *In the Gallup Poll:* D. Duane Angel, *Romney: A Political Biography* (New York: Exposition Press, 1967), 22.

87 *On April 10 a Boston University:* Wells, *War Within,* 72. *On April 15, five thousand antiwar:* Ibid., 71. *The next day Nixon spoke at Tulane:* "Nixon Backs War Drive," NYT, April 17, 1966.

87 *"We feel segregation of the races":* United States Commission on Human Rights, *Political Participation* (Washington, DC: U.S. Government Printing Office, 1968), 146. *"trying to take the remnants":* "Romney Relaxes Pace in Contest with Nixon for '68 Nomination," NYT, February 14, 1966.

88 *"I will go to any state":* "Nixon in the South, Bids GOP Drop Race Issue," NYT, May 7, 1966.

88 *At a party dinner that night:* "Nixon Building Solid Southern Base of Support for President Nomination Bid in '68," NYT, May 8, 1966.

89 *He learned that the beloved Dent:* Witcover, *Resurrection of Richard Nixon,* 310.

89 *"Strom is no racist":* Carter, *Politics of Rage,* 328.

89 *"If I had to practice law":* Witcover, *Resurrection of Richard Nixon,* 127.

89 Deadwyler case: Johnnie Cochran, *A Lawyer's Life* (New York: Thomas Dunne Books, 2002), 24–28; Terry Anzur interview; David Moberg interview; NYT, May 18, 19, 20, 21, 22, 26, 27, 28, 29, 31, 1966; UPI ticker, May 31, 1966, LBJCR, Reel 6; Califano to LBJ, May 18, 1966, LBJCR, Reel 6; Marvin Watson to LBJ, May 31, 1966, LBJCR, Reel 6.

90 *In Bakersfield, two thousand Negroes:* "Negroes on Coast Stone School Bus and Fire a Shack," NYT, May 24, 1966.

90 *On Memorial Day weekend:* "Reagan Shuns Image of Goldwater in Coast Race," NYT, June 1, 1966; Boyarsky, *Rise of Ronald Reagan,* 136.

91 Milk conviction controversy: Cannon, *Governor Reagan,* 146; "Scurrillous Attacks Sent Through Mail, Christopher Claims," LAT, June 2, 1966; "Reagan Nominated in California," NYT, June 8, 1966; "Brown Tells Christopher of Regret for Pearson's Attack," LAT, June 30, 1966. "Wanted" poster: Anderson and Lee, "1966 Election in California."

91 *Christopher fought back with theatrics:* "Christopher Puts 7 Queries to Reagan," NYT, June 3, 1966.

91 *"Thou shalt not speak ill":* Cannon, *Governor Reagan*, 145–47.

92 *At a rally in San Francisco's:* "Brown Ends Northern Drive, Likens Reagan to Goldwater," LAT, June 3, 1966. LSD ban: *Richmond News Leader,* May 30, 1966.

92 *In the California Poll:* Anderson and Lee, "1966 Election in California." *He used phrases like "basic":* NYT, May 15, June 1, July 3, 1966. *He called "the one overriding":* "Another Opinion; Reagan States His Case," NYT, October 30, 1966.

92 *The leftists of the California Democratic Council: CQ Political Notes,* October 1, 1965; Anderson and Lee, "1966 Election in California"; Boyarsky, *Rise of Ronald Reagan,* 125. *One of the president's favorite congressmen:* Wells, *War Within,* 81; "'New Left' Parley on Coast Denounces Brown and Backs Black Power," NYT, October 3, 1966. *Johnson's poverty czar:* Maurice Isserman and Michael Kazin, *America Divided: The Civil War of the 1960s* (New York: Oxford University Press, 1999), 194.

92 Watts hospital bond issue: "Watts Area County Hospital Approved; Supervisors OK Bond Issue on June 7 Ballot," LAT, March 9, 1966; "Reagan Victory Aids GOP Right," NYT, June 9, 1969; *Nation,* June 26, 1966.

92 *"against all counsels of common sense":* "California Primaries," NYT, June 9, 1966.

93 *Nixon briefed Senator George Murphy:* "RMN Call Sandy Quinn," June 16, 1966, RNLB, 501.1.

93 *Reagan dashed off a note:* Reagan to Nixon, June 14, RNLB, 501.1. Eisenhower and Scaife meetings: "Eisenhower Meets Reagan and Backs Him for Governor," NYT, June 16, 1966.

93 Reagan Washington trip: Broder and Hess, *Republican Establishment,* 243–44; "Reagan Attacks the Great Society," NYT, June 17, 1966; Sandy Quinn to Rose Mary Woods, RNLB, 501.1–10.

94 Nixon Rochester controversy: "Rochester Degree for Nixon Opposed," NYT, April 15, 1966; "Nixon Offers View on Degree Protest," April 16, 1966. *"If we are to defend academic":* William Safire, *Before the Fall: An Inside View of the Pre-Watergate White House* (New York: Ballantine, 1977), 24–25.

94 Harold Howe II speech: USNWR, July 4, 1966.

94 Louise Day Hicks speech: Charles Sumner Brown, "Negro Protest and White Power Structure: The Boston School Controversy, 1963–1966" (Boston University theology Ph.D. dissertation, 1973).

94 Sargent Shriver speech: "Shriver in Plea for Rights," NYT, June 6, 1966.

94 Arthur Schlesinger speech: "McCarthyism Is Feared," NYT, June 6, 1966.

94 *John Steinbeck pronounced himself:* "What's Happening to America," *Saturday Evening Post,* July 2, 1966. *Horrified also was the advertising agency:* NYT, June 28, 1966, 92.

CHAPTER FIVE: LONG, HOT SUMMER

96 *Early in the year a young:* John Lewis, *Walking with the Wind: A Memoir of the Movement* (New York: Simon & Schuster, 1998), 373–74.

96 *It was an old argument:* Sally Avery Bermanzohn, "Violence, Nonviolence, and the U.S. Civil Rights Movement," in Kenton Worcester, Sally Avery Bermanzohn and Mark Ungar, eds., *Violence and Politics: Globalization's Paradox* (New York: Routledge, 2001). *"If we can't sit at the table":* Charles Silberman in *Fortune,* November 1965, in LBJCR, Reel 2.

96 Stokely Carmichael biography: James Haskins, *Profiles in Black Power* (New York: Doubleday, 1971), 185–202. *"This proves," he cried:* E. J. Dionne, *Why Americans Hate Politics* (New York: Simon & Schuster, 1991), 82.

97 *"The murder of Samuel Younge":* Lewis, *Walking with the Wind,* 375.

97 *Julian Bond, a SNCC activist:* Ibid., 377.

97 *"You don't imitate white politics":* Haskins, *Profiles in Black Power,* 190. *"We need someone who":* Lewis, *Walking with the Wind,* 383. *The brackets were the* New York Times's: "Rights Unit Quits Parley in Capital," NYT, May 24, 1966.

97 *The previous Sunday, James Meredith:* "Meredith Begins Mississippi Walk to Combat Fear," NYT, June 6, 1966; Dan T. Carter, *The Politics of Rage: George Wallace, the Origin of the New Conservatism, and the Transformation of American Politics* (Baton Rouge: Louisiana State University Press, 1996), 303. *Early, inaccurate, reports:* Paul

Cowan, *The Making of an Un-American* (New York: Viking, 1970), 171. *"Meredith Regrets He Was Not Armed"*: NYT, June 8, 1966, 1.

97   Meredith sympathy march in general: David J. Garrow, *Bearing the Cross: Martin Luther King and the Southern Christian Leadership Conference* (New York: Harper Perennial, 1999), 473–90; Lewis, *Walking with the Wind*, 387–89; NYT, June 6–28, 1966; USNWR, July 11, 1966; CBS News, "The March in Mississippi," MTR (with video of "Black Power" speech).

98   *"Meredith's sacrifice might spur"*: "Freedom March," WP, June 8, 1966.

99   *"a reverse Hitler"*: *Nation*, August 8, 1966. Closing rally: CBS, "March in Mississippi"; "The 'Color' Line Closes on King," LAT, July 3, 1966.

99   Vietnam fuel depot bombings: Tom Wells, *The War Within: America's Battle over Vietnam* (Berkeley: University of California Press, 1994), 94, 99. *The next week, at the LBJ Ranch*: PPP 320, July 5, 1966.

99   *What he did not mention*: Wells, *War Within*, 98. *"Your daddy may go down"*: Ibid., 94.

100   For early history of the Vietnam War I rely on A. J. Langguth, *Our Vietnam: The War, 1954–1975* (New York: Touchstone, 2000). For combat tactics I rely on Christian Appy, *Working-Class War: American Combat Soldiers and Vietnam* (Chapel Hill: University of North Carolina Press, 1993).

100   Ho Chi Minh telegrams to Truman: Tom Bissell, "Was Uncle a Stalinist?" *Old Town Review*, December 2004, http://www.fluxfactory.org/otr/bissellhcm.htm. *Richard Nixon, after a visit*: Langguth, *Our Vietnam*, 77; Fawn Brodie, *Richard Nixon: The Shaping of His Character* (New York: W. W. Norton, 1981), 322–23. *Falter in Vietnam, Lyndon Johnson claimed*: Michael Beschloss, *Taking Charge: The Johnson White House Tapes, 1963–1964* (New York: Simon & Schuster, 1998), 370.

101   216,400 U.S. and 13,100 North Vietnamese troops: Appy, *Working-Class War*, 210.

101   *To warn VC, combat battalions*: Ibid., 265. Marching at gunpoint to refugee camps: Langguth, *Our Vietnam*, 175.

101   *It was "the wrong war"*: James T. Patterson, *Grand Expectations: The United States, 1945–1965* (New York: Oxford University Press, 1995), 231–32. *"Within five years"*: Langguth, *Our Vietnam*, 152. *the actual number of troops*: Appy, *Working-Class War*, 168.

102   *The 1964 Special National Intelligence*: Langguth, *Our Vietnam*, 318.

102   LBJ Johns Hopkins University speech: PPP 172, April 7, 1965. *But according to a memo*: Langguth, *Our Vietnam*, 350.

102   *"Fort Hood Three"*: Mary Hershberger, *Jane Fonda's War: A Political Biography of an Antiwar Icon* (New York: New Press, 2005), 19–20; Wells, *War Within*, 99; Jerry Lembcke, *The Spitting Image: Myth, Memory, and the Legacy of Vietnam* (New York: NYU Press, 1998), 35.

102   Los Angeles Times *columnist Paul Coates*: "A Long Hot Weekend?" LAT, July 3, 1966.

103   *Chief Parker was in Sacramento*: "Yorty and Parker Urge Riot Laws," June 29, 1966.

103   *Riots broke out in places like*: USNWR, July 18, 1966; "Policemen Stoned by Mob in Des Moines," LAT, July 6, 1966. *In New York City*: Tamar Jacoby, *Someone Else's House: America's Unfinished Struggle for Integration* (New York: Free Press, 1998), 94–95. *In Miami, two factions*: NYT, July 5, 1966.

103   *In Baltimore, the Congress for Racial Equality*: USNWR, July 25, 1966; Adam Cohen and Elizabeth Taylor, *American Pharaoh: Mayor Richard J. Daley: His Battle for Chicago and the Nation* (Boston: Little, Brown, 2000), 380; LAT, July 3 and 5, 1966; "CORE Will Insist on Black Power," NYT, July 5, 1966. *The next week the worst prison*: "1,000 Prison Inmates Riot in Baltimore," LAT, July 9, 1966. *The NAACP met*: "NAACP President Condemns Moves for 'Black Power,'" LAT, July 6, 1966.

103   *The* New York Times *had predicted*: "Brown and Reagan Both Seek Votes from the Other's Party," NYT, July 3, 1966. *A thousand antiwar picketers*: Bill Boyarsky, *The Rise of Ronald Reagan* (New York: Random House, 1968), 125.

103   *Nebraska's Democratic governor*: USNWR, July 18, 1966. *Then he toured Omaha's*: "Gov. Morrison of Nebraska Flies to Omaha from Coast Parley to Seek to Stem Racial Unrest," July 6, 1966.

104   RFK and LBJ poll numbers: "Johnson, Kennedy Preferred over Three GOP Candidates," LAT, July 7, 1966.

104   *"Mr. President, regarding racial"*: PPP 320, July 5, 1966.

104   *"When we view the masses"*: "Black Power Prophet; Stokely Carmichael," NYT,

August 5, 1966. Niggerhead Mountain: "Vermont Mountain to Retain Its Name," NYT, July 6, 1966.

104 *"Shots from one or two cars":* "Two Sacramento Negroes Shot Dead," July 6, 1966. *Page one was monopolized:* "Antiriot Bill; Assembly Approves Measure," LAT, July 6, 1966; see also *L.A. Sentinel,* June 30, 1966, in which Mayor Yorty warns of "urban guerilla warfare this summer."

105 *The Fort Hood Three were abducted:* Lembcke, *Spitting Image,* 35. *U.S combat deaths:* "U.S. Combat Deaths in Vietnam Hit 4,129," LAT, July 8, 1966. *"We're going to have to take":* Robert Dallek, *Flawed Giant: Lyndon Johnson and His Times, 1961–1973* (New York: Oxford University Press, 1999), 312.

105 *So married black couples:* Cohen and Taylor, *American Pharaoh,* 392.

105 For history of race and Chicago housing see Arnold R. Hirsch, *Making the Second Ghetto: Race and Housing in Chicago, 1940–1960* (Chicago: University of Chicago Press, 1998), and Dominic A. Pacyga, ed., *The Chicago Bungalow* (Chicago: Arcadia Publishing, 2003).

107 Letters to Paul Douglas: From James F. Nelson, June 16, 1966, and G. Dapuhnais, June 1966, in PDP722.

107 *On July 10, Martin Luther King:* Allen J. Matusow, *The Unraveling of America: A History of Liberalism in the 1960s* (New York: HarperCollins, 1984), 203; Cohen and Taylor, *American Pharaoh,* 382; Roger Biles, *Richard J. Daley: Politics, Race, and the Governing of Chicago* (De Kalb: Northern Illinois University Press, 1995), 123. *"They have no programs":* Mike Royko, *Boss: Richard J. Daley of Chicago* (New York: New American Library, 1971), 153.

107 Chicago riot generally: Nicholas Lemann, *The Promised Land: The Great Black Migration and How It Changed America* (New York: Vintage, 1992), 238; "City Takes Steps to Avert Rioting," NYT, July 15, 1966; USNWR, July 25, 1966; Cohen and Taylor, *American Pharaoh,* 387; Garrow, *Bearing the Cross,* 493 (for Mahalia Jackson story).

107 *"Youths crashed through":* "900 Policemen Sent into Trouble Area of Chicago," WP, July 14, 1966. *"Hundreds of persons were hurling":* Washington Star, July 15, 1966. *"A policeman, Donald Ingraham":* "Chicago Negro Snipers, Police Trade Gunfire," WP, July 15, 1966.

108 *The* Chicago Tribune *connected:* "Murder in Multiple," WP, July 15, 1966. *"Last night there was a show":* M. R. Rosen to Douglas, PDP722.

108 *"I think you can't charge it":* Royko, *Boss,* 153.

108 *There were smaller riots:* USNWR, July 25, 1966. *Its chairman, Howard:* USNWR, August 8, 1966; *Congressional Record* 112, pt. 13, 16,834 and 16,837.

108 *He also charged to his feet:* Ibid.

108 *On July 18 Evans and Novak:* "Inside Report: Watts in Cement," WP, July 18, 1966.

108 *That night, in Cleveland:* Walter Johnson, "The Night They Burned Old Hough," Cleveland Neighborhoods on the Web, http://www.nhlink.net/ClevelandNeighborhoods/hough/Eyewitness2.htm. *In Jacksonville, after a demonstration:* "Riots Flare in 3 Cities, One Dead in Cleveland," *Washington Star,* July 19, 1966. Humphrey speech: James L. Sunquist, *Politics and Policy: The Eisenhower, Kennedy, and Johnson Years* (Washington, DC: Brookings Institution Press, 1968), 285. *The next day, a thousand members:* "1000 Ohio Guardsmen Ordered to Cleveland," WP, July 20, 1966. *two thousand more Illinois Guardsmen:* Cohen and Taylor, *American Pharaoh,* 391. *"It really is almost impossible":* United States Congress, *Civil Rights: Hearings before a Subcommittee of the Judiciary, United States Senate, Second Session, on S. 329* (Washington, DC: U.S. Government Printing Office, 1966), July 19 testimony.

109 *The next day a roller-skating:* "Negro Boy, 11, Shot to Death in Brooklyn," CT, July 22, 1966. *Mayor Lindsay traveled to East New York:* USNWR, August 1, 1966; Jacoby, *Someone Else's House,* 96; Vincent J. Cannato, *The Ungovernable City: John Lindsay and the Battle to Save New York* (New York: Basic Books, 2003), 120–25.

110 *At the Sherman House Hotel:* Chicago's American, July 22, 1966. *In an ornate reception room:* Cannato, *Ungovernable City,* 124–25. *A nightclub in the Bohemian:* Chicago's American, July 23, 1966. *In Cleveland, white vigilantes:* "Rioting in Cleveland Follows Watts Script," LAT, July 31, 1966.

110 *Miranda v. State of Arizona dissents:* Patterson, *Grand Expectations,* 631. Truman Capote testimony: Chicago Sun-Times, July 22, 1966. *"I was distressed a few days ago":* USNWR, August 8, 1966.

111 *"The housing program is too small":* "A Time for Candor," WSJ, July 27, 1966.
111 *A Cuyahoga County grand jury:* USNWR, August 22, 1966. North Amityville mob: "Police Attacked in Suburban L.I.," NYT, July 29, 1966.
111 *"They didn't need any Communists":* "Cleveland Study of Riot Deplored," NYT, August 11, 1966. U.S. Commission on Civil Rights hearings: United States Commission on Civil Rights, *Hearings Before the United States Commission on Civil Rights: Hearing Held in Cleveland, Ohio, April 1–7, 1966* (Washington, DC: The Commission, 1966).
112 Frank Lausche–Stephen Young debate: *Congressional Record* 112, pt. 13, 17,410–11.
112 *Senator Lausche keynoted:* "Racial Riots Planned, Lausche Says; Fears Harm to Negro Rights Movement," CT, July 28, 1966.
113 *"We've reached a point":* USNWR, August 15, 1966. U.S. News *set their readers:* USNWR, August 22, 1966.
113 *A chaplain of the Maryland:* Senate Judiciary Subcommittee on Constitutional Rights, *Civil Rights: Hearings Before a Subcommittee on the Judiciary, United States Senate, Eighty-ninth Congress, Second Session, on S. 3296,* July 20 testimony. *He begged Senate Appropriations chair:* "Inside Report: LBJ and the Cities," WP, August 10, 1966.
113 *"Ronald Reagan, Extremist Collaborator":* Totton J. Anderson and Eugene C. Lee, "The 1966 Election in California," *Western Political Quarterly* 20 (June 1967); Joseph Lewis, *What Makes Reagan Run?: A Political Profile* (New York: McGraw-Hill, 1968), 129. *Reagan had long ago:* See, for example, "Reagan Enters Gubernatorial Race in California," NYT, January 5, 1966. *"The Bircher isn't identifiable":* Lewis, *What Makes Reagan Run?,* 132.
114 *Brown opened his general-election:* Boyarsky, *Rise of Ronald Reagan,* 124; "Brown Tells Goals as He Opens Drive," LAT, September 6, 1966. *"In Paris they no longer":* "Reagan Wooing the Farm Voters," NYT, September 16, 1966.
114 *Brown spoke at the Los Angeles:* "Inside Report: The Anti-Welfare State," WP, September 22, 1966.
114 *"Working men and women":* Boyarsky, *Rise of Ronald Reagan,* 139. *If California's welfare system:* James Q. Wilson, "A Guide to Reagan Country: The Political Culture of Southern California," *Commentary,* May 1967. *Women told him they:* "Atlantic Report: California," *Atlantic Monthly,* August 1966. *He remembered, too:* Ibid. *"The $5 you saved":* "Reagan Handles His Role as a Political Amateur like an Old Pro," NYT, October 2, 1966. *The* Los Angeles Times *did an investigation:* "Realism Needed in Welfare Criticism," LAT, March 7, 1966.
115 *In the agricultural San Joaquin:* "Reagan Wooing the Farm Voters," NYT.
115 *"Able-bodied men":* "Inside Report: The Anti-Welfare State," WP.
115 *The Associated Press was reporting:* "GOP Leaders Give Nixon an Edge for 1968," NYT, September 16, 1966.
115 *Richard Nixon passed through Los Angeles:* "Nixon Sees Big G.O.P. Victory," LAT, June 24, 1966. *Then came the more important:* Stephen Ambrose, *Nixon, Vol. 2: The Triumph of a Politician, 1962–1972* (New York: Simon & Schuster, 1989), 83; Maurice Stans, *The Terrors of Justice: The Untold Side of Watergate* (Washington: Brassey's, 1995), 130. *The airplane problem had been:* Ibid.
115 *The* Baltimore Sun's *Jules Witcover: Reporter,* August 11, 1966. Detroit: Ibid., 134–38. *"this man never seemed":* Jules Witcover, *The Resurrection of Richard Nixon* (New York: G. P. Putnam's Sons, 1970), 132.
116 *Perhaps Pat thought of the time:* Brodie, *Richard Nixon,* 420.
116 *"Happy birthday, Mum":* Mark Shields column, June 15, 2002.
116 *Don Riegle:* Witcover, *Resurrection of Richard Nixon,* 141–42.
116 *Tulsa:* Ibid., 143–44; USNWR, October 3, 1966.
117 Atlantic Monthly *called Vietnam: Atlantic Monthly,* September 1966. *Polls showed 38 percent:* CWA poll, PDP, Box 1116/Misc Correspondence. *For months, he'd said:* "Nixon Says 'Appeasement Line' Will Be G.O.P. Target in Vote," NYT, January 31, 1966; "Nixon Says G.O.P. Has Good Chance of Winning in '68," NYT, May 27, 1966. *By late June, however:* "Nixon Sees Big G.O.P. Issue," LAT, June 24, 1966.
117 *In Chicago, on July 29:* David Garrow, *Chicago 1966: Open Housing Marches, Summit Negotiations, and Operation Breadbasket* (Brooklyn: Carlson, 1989); Cohen and Taylor, *American Pharaoh,* 392; interview with Don Rose.
117 *Senator Paul Douglas received:* PDP722.

118 *Five hundred marchers:* Lemann, *Promised Land,* 238; Cohen and Taylor, *American Pharaoh,* 393–94.

118 *A neighborhood newspaper: Southwest News-Herald,* August 4, 1966, PDP722.

118 *On Tuesday, Pat, Julie:* "Chanel and Cardin Share Spotlight in Paris," NYT, July 30, 1966. *A news brief noted:* "Nixon to See Pope Today," NYT, August 1, 1966. *"Former Vice President Nixon met":* "Nixon Sees Pakistani Chief," NYT, August 4, 1966. Daley meeting with Bungalow Belt leaders: Royko, *Boss,* 155; Cohen and Taylor, *American Pharaoh,* 393–94.

119 *August 5. Six hundred:* Ibid., 395–96; Lemann, *Promised Land,* 238.

119 *White neighborhood kids started battling police:* Clipping from *Chicago's American,* August 6, 1966, in PDP722. *an inattentive newspaper reader:* letter from 7136 S. Francisco, August 8, 1966, PDP722.

120 *"There must be some way":* Royko, *Boss,* 157.

120 "Don't vote for Democrats!": Ibid.; Biles, *Richard J. Daley,* 128.

120 *Richard Nixon was in Saigon:* "Nixon, in Saigon, Bids U.S. Bare Goals," NYT, August 6, 1966. *"If Mob Rule Takes Hold":* USNWR, August 15, 1966.

120 Mathias compromise: "Congress May Ease Housing Bias Curb to Pass Rights Bill," NYT, June 9, 1966. *Dan Rostenkowski, one of the:* Jake to LBJ, August 10, 1966, 8 p.m., LBJCR, Reel 3. *His Bungalow Belt colleague:* USNWR, August 22, 1966.

121 *special interests such as the real estate:* "Realtors' Lobby Calls for Fight on Open Housing," NYT, July 29, 1966. *"mass brainwashing" just like "in Nazi":* United States Congress, *Civil Rights, 1966: Hearings Before Subcommittee No. 5, Eighty-ninth Congress, Second Session* (Washington, DC: U.S. Government Printing Office, 1966), statement from W. B. Hicks, May 24 testimony. *"when a colored boy rapes":* Senate Judiciary Subcommittee on Constitutional Rights, *Civil Rights: Hearings Before a Subcommittee on the Judiciary, United States Senate, Eighty-ninth Congress, Second Session, on S. 3296,* June 9 testimony. *"Social Security widow in my district":* House, *Civil Rights, 1966,* May 10 testimony.

121 *"It is strange, although":* "The Wages of Hatred," WSJ, July 18, 1966. *Sam Ervin reported:* Senate, *Hearings Before a Subcommittee,* July 13 testimony.

121 *On July 25: Congressional Records* 112, pt. 13, July 25 House proceedings.

122 *When the Mathias Amendment:* "Exemption of 60% in Open Housing Voting by House," NYT, August 4, 1966. *The bill was sent to the Senate:* "Civil Rights Bill Passed by House in Vote of 259–157," NYT, August 10, 1966. Detroit, Lansing violence: USNWR, August 22, 1966. *In Cleveland, the grand jury:* "Cleveland Riots Linked to Reds," NYT, August 10, 1966. *in Grenada, Mississippi:* "White Mob Routs Grenada Negroes," NYT, August 10, 1966. *In Philadelphia that week:* USNWR, August 15.

122 *And in the Senate:* "Civil Rights Bill Will Pass: Dirksen; Open Housing Clause May Be Missing," CT, August 8, 1966.

122 *Even Paul Douglas started:* Speech in PDP, Box 1108, "Civil Rights Protection Act 1966" folder. *The previous year, Martin Luther King:* PDP, Box 1007, "Proposed Brochure—Civil Rights."

122 *"It is my firm belief":* From 4476 S. Mozart, August 9, 1966, PDP722.

122 *"Is the ultimate aim":* From Rudolph R. Kostelny, August 5, 1966, PDP722.

123 *"If our present leaders":* From Mrs. E. C. Zeltmann, August 5, 1966, PDP722.

123 *"IT IS TIME TO CHANGE":* From 7134 S. Avers, August 5, 1966, PDP722.

123 *In Chicago, movement Turks:* Cohen and Taylor, *American Pharaoh,* 397. *This very summer:* Ibid., 398. *Another King deputy:* Ibid., 414.

123 *An August 17 meeting:* Ibid., 401–12; Biles, *Mayor Richard J. Daley,* 130; Royko, *Boss,* 157. *Daley presented his doughy mug:* Cohen and Taylor, *American Pharaoh,* 414. *"We believe sir, that unless":* From Edward J. Pasciak family, PDP722. *The Cook County sheriff:* Cohen and Taylor, *American Pharaoh,* 416.

123 *The Klan received a permit:* Ibid. *He went to the Palmer House:* Royko, *Boss,* 158.

123 *"When greedy Mr. Hitler":* From Jeannine L. Bartell, August 31, 1966, PDP722.

123 *"When you talk of Black Power":* USNWR, August 22, 1966. *"In Cleveland, they're building":* USNWR, September 12, 1966 (quoting Associated Press reports). *Senator Abraham Ribicoff opened:* "Urban 'Crisis' Will Be Studied at Hearings Called by Ribicoff," LAT, August 2, 1966; Frederick G. Dutton, *Changing Sources of Power: American Politics in the 1970s* (New York: McGraw-Hill, 1971), 128. *"Katzenbach Warns Senate 30 or 40":* NYT, August 18, 1966. *The U.S. News roundup ran:* USNWR, Octo-

ber 3, 1966. *The liberal* Sacramento Bee: "Opinion at Home and Abroad," NYT, Week in Review, August 7, 1966. *Joseph Alsop:* "A Modest Proposal I," "A Modest Proposal II," "A Modest Proposal III," WP, August 1, 3, 5, 1966.

124 *He gave a speech to the Fraternal:* Carter, *Politics of Rage,* 305.

124 *After one broke out in Waukegan:* "Inside Report: Dirksen vs. the Moderates," WP, September 16, 1966.

124 *That August was a watershed:* This paragraph is drawn from the argument of Edward G. Carmine and James A. Stimson, *Issue Evolution: Race and the Transformation of American Politics* (Princeton, NJ: Princeton University Press, 1990). *One official party brochure:* CQ *Political Notes,* June 11, 1965.

125 *Evans and Novak reported:* "Inside Report: Ford's Lemming Instinct," WP, August 12, 1966. *Ford began the press conference: Congressional Record* 112, pt. 13, 17,767.

126 *In Chicago, John Hoellen:* "Inside Report: Dirksen vs. the Moderates." *In the* Saturday Evening Post: "Percy vs. Douglas," *Saturday Evening Post,* November 5, 1966.

126 *"While you sit on your butt":* No date, answered October 31, 1966, PDP722.

126 *In his turn at the Los Angeles:* "Nixon Sees Big G.O.P. Victory," LAT, June 24, 1966. *Nixon, speaking at the Hilton:* "Nixon Says Voters Will Turn to GOP," CT, July 22, 1966. *"I want everyone in California":* "Politicos Look at Race Issue," LAT, July 5, 1966.

126 *Then, when the bill was debated:* "Nixon Deplores Extremism in Civil Rights," LAT, February 13, 1964. Went through his whole thesis: Richard Reeves, *President Nixon: Alone in the White House* (New York: Simon & Schuster, 2001), 110. *And he was an ex officio member:* "Nixon Says 'Appeasement Line' Will Be G.O.P. Target in Vote," NYT, January 31, 1966.

CHAPTER SIX: SCHOOL WAS IN SESSION ...

128 *"I have no staff":* "Nixon Presses Victory Theme at GOP Dinner," LAT, September 17, 1966. *this was, Evans and Novak reported:* "Special Report: Nixon's Presidential Campaign," WP, August 9, 1966.

128 *Over the previous weeks:* "Nixon Advocates Use of More GI's," NYT, August 8, 1966; Andrew L. Johns, "A Voice from the Wilderness: Richard Nixon and the Vietnam War, 1964–1966," *Presidential Studies Quarterly* 29 (1999). *He said that "for the first":* "Nixon, in Saigon, Bids U.S. Bare Goals," NYT, August 6, 1966; Johns, "Voice From the Wilderness"; Jules Witcover, *The Resurrection of Richard Nixon* (New York: G. P. Putnam's Sons, 1970), 155; Stephen Ambrose, *Nixon, Vol. 2: The Triumph of a Politician, 1962–1972* (New York: Simon & Schuster, 1989), 85; "Nixon Urges GOP Support War Aims," LAT, August 7, 1966.

128 *According to "some American leaders":* "Nixon Advocates Use of More GI's." *"I don't believe the Communist":* "Nixon Says Vietnam Could End in Two Years," NYT, August 12, 1966. *"Now that we have hit":* "Nixon Advocates More GI's."

129 *The* New York Times *welcomed:* "Vietnam and the Elections," NYT, August 14, 1966.

129 *An unnamed senator:* David Broder and Stephen Hess, *The Republican Establishment: The Present and Future of the GOP* (New York: Harper & Row, 1967), 157. *"running through Asia like wildfire":* Mary McGrory in *America* magazine, September 17, 1966; *National Review,* September 20, 1966.

130 Shoreham Hotel meeting: "GOP Leaders in Congress Back All-Asian Talk," NYT, August 26, 1966; "GOP Liberals Fear Rightists Will Control 1968 Convention," NYT, August 31, 1966; "Inside Report: Nixon's Shoreham Meeting," WP, September 7, 1966; Witcover, *Resurrection of Richard Nixon,* 154–55; interview with Lee Edwards. *Buchanan loved Nixon, whom:* Pat Buchanan, *Right from the Beginning* (Boston: Little, Brown, 1988), 4.

130 *"If Barry showed that":* Garry Wills, *Reagan's America: Innocents at Home* (New York: Doubleday, 1987), 290. *"the Birchers could be handled":* E. J. Dionne, *Why Americans Hate Politics* (New York: Simon & Schuster, 1991), 191; "Inside Report: Fifty Bucks from Buckley," WP, October 15, 1965; *National Review,* March 8, 1966.

130 *Americans for Constitutional Action:* USNWR, September 12, 1966. *Goldwater Republicans won primary:* USNWR, August 22, 1966.

130 Arkansas gubernatorial primary: USNWR, August 8, 1966; *Reporter,* October 20, 1966. Maryland gubernatorial primary: USNWR, September 26, 1966; "Repudiation of

Mahoney Urged by a Key Maryland Democrat," NYT, September 17, 1966; Alan Draper, "Labor and the 1966 Elections," *Labor History* 30 (1989): 76–92; Jules Witcover, *White Knight: The Rise of Spiro Agnew* (New York: Random House, 1972), 116–49. Georgia gubernatorial primary: Bradley R. Rice, "The 1966 Gubernatorial Elections in Georgia" (Ph.D. diss., University of Southern Mississippi, 1982); Randy Sangers, "The Sad Duty of Politics: Jimmy Carter and the Issue of Race in His 1970 Gubernatorial Campaign," *Georgia Historical Quarterly* 76 (1992).

131 *Maddox's path was smoothed:* USNWR, September 25, 1966; "Allen of Atlanta Collides with Black Power and White Racism," NYTM, October 16, 1966; *New Republic,* October 22, 1966; "Expert on Extremism Exasperates Extremes," WP, October 17, 1966. *In Baton Rouge, a twelve-term:* "Critic of Johnson Wins in Louisiana," NYT, September 25, 1966. *In the Senate, Everett Dirksen:* "Amendment on School Prayer Falls," WP, September 22, 1966. *The Supreme Court upheld a landmark:* "'Witch Hunt' Feared on Obscenity Issue," NYT, October 12, 1966.

131 *"I would say the overall":* USNWR, September 16, 1966.

131 *Seventy-five percent of the delegates:* "GOP Liberals Fear Rightists Will Control 1968 Convention," NYT, August 31, 1966. *Many were already talking about drafting:* Broder and Hess, *Republican Establishment,* 276, quoting Lee Edwards in *Human Events.*

132 *"Take any political situation":* Garry Wills, *Nixon Agonistes: The Crisis of the Self-Made Man* (Boston: Houghton Mifflin, 1970), 11. *"One senses that he knows":* Richard Reeves, *President Nixon: Alone in the White House* (New York: Simon & Schuster, 2001), 375. *He "said he felt his life":* Leonard Garment, *Crazy Rhythm: From Brooklyn and Jazz to Nixon's White House, Watergate, and Beyond* (New York: Crown, 1997), 85.

132 *Forty years later, one of the YAFers:* Lee Edwards interview.

132 *Woodrow Wilson was the only:* Reeves, *President Nixon,* 26. *A participant leaked:* Witcover, *Resurrection of Richard Nixon,* 155.

133 *"far greater than those incurred":* "GOP Liberals Fear Rightists Will Control 1968 Convention." *The* Times *reported in their dispatch:* "GOP Leaders in Congress Back All-Asian Talk."

133 HEW guidelines background: Allen J. Matusow, *The Unraveling of America; A History of Liberalism in the 1960s* (New York: HarperCollins, 1984), 188–91; and the following documents in LBJCR, Reel 8: United States Commission on Civil Rights, "Title VI . . . One Year Later"; Keppel, "Education and the Civil Rights Act"; Howe to Cater, January 19, 1966; Libassi to Cater, January 21, 1966; and Cater to Watson, February 22, 1966.

133 *In real life, when a black family:* McPherson to LBJ, May 12, 1966, LBJCR, Reel 12.

134 *Eighteen of them signed a letter:* May 2, 1966, LBJCR, Reel 8. *George Wallace's first political act:* Stephen Lesher, *George Wallace: American Populist* (New York: Addison-Wesley, 1994), 366. *His school superintendent observed:* A. R. Meadows to H. D. Nelson, May 24 and 26, 1966, LBJCR, Reel 6; http://www.legislature.state.al.us/code ofalabama/constitution/1901/CA-245806.htm.

134 *On July 18, 1966:* Libassi to Califano, July 18, 1966, LBJCR, Reel 8. *"Undoubtedly we are going to curse":* McPherson to Cater, July 22, 1966, LBJCR, Reel 8. *"Please wake up!":* January 2, 1965, *Atlanta Journal,* quoted in Rice, "1966 Gubernatorial Elections in Georgia."

134 *On August 9: Congressional Record* 112, pt. 13 (July 21, 1966), 18,701. *Whitener had earlier:* Ibid., 17,841. *"Nothing in this title":* Ibid., 18,717–18.

134 *One of them was Clark MacGregor:* United States Congress, *Civil Rights, 1966: Hearings Before Subcommittee No. 5, Eighty-ninth Congress, Second Session* (Washington, DC: U.S. Government Printing Office, 1966), 1245. *"The mayor had never experienced":* "Inside Report: Risk on Plymouth Street," WP, August 19, 1966.

135 *"If this amendment is defeated": Congressional Record* 112, pt. 13 (July 21, 1966).

135 *A September 9 column:* "Inside Report: Education Bombshell," WP, September 9, 1966. *What it referred to:* See, for example, Cater to Gardner, cc Howe, May 21, 1966; Cater to McPherson, August 5, 1966, LBJCR, Reel 8; USNWR, September 5, 1966.

135 *"world of wall-to-wall carpeting":* USNWR, October 10, 1966. *"Mr. Speaker," South Carolina's:* "Howe Attacked in House on Integration of Schools," NYT, October 1, 1966; *Nation,* October 7, 1966.

136 *On Wednesday, September 21:* "Southern Governors Unit Scores School Guidelines Enforcement," NYT, September 22, 1966. *on Thursday:* Matusow, *Unraveling of America,* 191. *on Monday: Congressional Record* 112, pt. 18, 23, 835–48. *on Tuesday:* "Racial Violence Breaks Out Again in San Francisco," NYT, September 29, 1996; Bill Boyarsky, *The Rise of Ronald Reagan* (New York: Random House, 1968), 127. *and on Wednesday:* Dan T. Carter, *The Politics of Rage: George Wallace, the Origin of the New Conservatism, and the Transformation of American Politics* (Baton Rouge: Louisiana State University Press, 1996), 306. *And on Thursday, the Senate: Congressional Record* 112, pt. 18, 23,913; "Senate Restricts Rights Guideline; Would Allow Segregation of Patients in Certain Cases," NYT, September 28, 1966. *Explained Majority Leader:* "Mansfield Asks Slowdown on School Desegregation," NYT, September 29, 1966. *Indeed, in May, 32 percent:* USNWR, October 10, 1966. *Crowed Senator James Eastland:* Carter, *Politics of Rage,* 307. See also *Reporter* magazine, October 20, 1966.

136 *The House took up debate:* "House Takes Up School Aid Bill," NYT, October 7, 1966.

136 *John Brademas, a liberal Democrat: Congressional Record* 112, pt. 19, 25,538. *"They have auditors crawling":* Ibid., 25,576. *In an October 6 press conference:* "Johnson Concedes Errors on Rights," NYT, October 7, 1966; PPP 501, October 6, 1966. *"We accept tokenism":* "Mansfield Asks Slowdown on School Desegregation."

137 *It seems HEW is determined:* Elizabeth Kulcyzk to Douglas, September 30, 1966, PDP722.

137 *He was lying:* September 11, 1966, Gallup poll in LBJCR, Reel 3.

137 *"Bobst thought it was":* Garment, *Crazy Rhythm,* 86.

138 *"If Johnson wants to":* "Nixon on Nixon and Other Issues," NYT, September 4, 1966.

138 *Pundits spoke of a "Kennedy wing":* "LBJ Still Haunted After 1,000 Days," WP, Outlook section, September 18, 1966. *"If Lyndon thinks he's":* "Nixon on Nixon and Other Issues." *"I don't know what it means":* "Nixon on the Stump—an Old Timer at 53," NYT, Week in Review, October 2, 1966.

139 *Lyndon "barks and it barks":* Stanley Kutler, *The Wars of Watergate: The Last Crisis of Richard Nixon* (New York: W. W. Norton, 1992), 58.

139 *That was the sore Nixon:* Witcover, *Resurrection of Richard Nixon,* 156.

139 *Since spring, his economists:* Matusow, *Unraveling of America,* 156–60; PPP 155, October 31, 1966; *Richmond News Leader,* May 20, 1966, quoting Michael Janeway; LAT, March 17, 1966, 1; "Vietnam: The Home Front," April 1, 1966, NBC broadcast, MTR, T81:0844; "Why All This Inflation," *Reader's Digest,* July 1966; "The Risk of Runaway Inflation," *Reader's Digest,* August 1966; "White House Sees Steel Price Rises as Inflationary," NYT, August 5, 1966; "Washington Whispers," USNWR, August 8, 1966.

140 *In the middle of August:* Matusow, *Unraveling of America,* 156. *A twenty-eight-year-old Phoenix mother: Nation,* October 10, 1966.

140 *Fulbright "arrogance of power" speech:* "The Power Akin to Freedom," *Time,* April 29, 1966; James William Fulbright, *The Arrogance of Power* (New York: Random House, 1967). *The junior senator from New York:* Jeff Shesol, *Mutual Contempt: Robert Kennedy, Lyndon Johnson, and the Feud That Defined a Decade* (New York: W. W. Norton, 1998), 299.

CHAPTER SEVEN: BATTING AVERAGE

141 *He said the president might:* "Nixon Forecasts Vietnam Buildup," NYT, September 14, 1966.

141 *Nixon hit Ohio:* "Nixon Warns of Peril to Two-Party System," NYT, September 15, 1966; *Cincinnati Inquirer,* September 15, 1966.

141 *Denver, Davenport, Salt Lake City:* USNWR, September 16, 1966; *Rocky Mountain News,* September 16, 1966; "Nixon in Iowa," NYT, September 16, 1966; "Nixon Would Curb Shipping to Hanoi," NYT, September 17, 1966.

141 *thought Garry Wills:* Garry Wills, *Nixon Agonistes: The Crisis of the Self-Made Man* (Boston: Houghton Mifflin, 1970), 13.

142 *He received over a thousand:* USNWR, July 4, 1996. *The New York Times's John Herbers:* "Nixon Asks G.O.P. to Unite in South," NYT, September 30, 1966.

142 *For instance, Iowa's:* Interview with John Schmidhauser.

142 *In Gallup's poll;* D. Duane Angel, *Romney: A Political Biography* (New York: Exposition Press, 1967), 220. *To the talking heads:* See, for example, "GOP Governors Seen Trying for Moderate in '68," LAT, July 5, 1966.

143 *This new political science:* Marshall McLuhan, *Understanding Media: The Extensions of Man* (New York: Signet, 1964); Nixon citation from 2001 Routledge edition, 360. *"Republican Camelot":* See the chapter by that name in Wills, *Nixon Agonistes,* 219.

143 George Romney: "The Dinosaur Hunter," *Time,* April 6, 1959; "The Citizen's Candidate," *Time,* November 16, 1962. Charles Percy: "A Delicate Business," *Time,* March 31, 1967; "The Temper of the Times," *Time,* April 14, 1967; Rick Perlstein, *Before the Storm: Barry Goldwater and the Unmaking of the American Consensus* (New York: Hill & Wang, 2001), 56, 79. *"the first Kennedy Republican":* George D. Wolfe, *William Warren Scranton: Pennsylvania Statesman* (State College: Pennsylvania State University Press, 1981), 65. *"He is fresh":* Vincent J. Cannato, *The Ungovernable City: John Lindsay and the Battle to Save New York* (New York: Basic Books, 2003), 43.

143 *"A man needs money":* Wills, *Nixon Agonistes,* 219–20.

143 *"Where Beame symbolized":* Cannato, *Ungovernable City,* 64. *"the first leader his party":* CQ *Political Report,* November 12, 1965. *"Will the real liberal":* Cannato, *Ungovernable City,* 64.

144 *"Do you realize that":* Ibid., 63.

144 *"The thorough research":* Ibid., 73. *"A Long Six Months":* NYT, July 4, 1966, 14.

144 New York Civilian Complaint Review Board campaign: Cannato, *Ungovernable City,* 45, 155–83; "25,000 Police Against the Review Board," NYTM, October 16, 1966; "Cassese Asserts Reds Back Board," NYT, September 20, 1966; Tamar Jacoby, *Someone Else's House: America's Unfinished Struggle for Integration* (New York: Free Press, 1998), 98–100; Nick Salvatore interview; Ryan Hayes interview. See also Peter Maas, *Serpico* (New York: Viking, 1973).

146 *On September 20, Gerald Ford:* "Right Backers Fear Backlash," NYT, September 21, 1966.

147 *"Brown looked out the window":* Bill Boyarsky, *The Rise of Ronald Reagan* (New York: Random House, 1968), 127.

147 *The next day, Ronald Reagan:* "Ronald for Real," *Time,* October 7, 1966.

148 *"I am afraid of what lies":* David J. Garrow, *Bearing the Cross: Martin Luther King and the Southern Christian Leadership Conference* (New York: Harper Perennial, 1999), 532. *Atlanta's conscience-stricken: Reporter* magazine, October 22, 1966; "A Candidate of Conscience" and "A Rebellious Southerner," NYT, October 4, 1966; "Charles L. Weltner, 64, Chief Justice of Georgia," NYT, September 2, 1992.

148 *At the New Southern Hotel:* "Nixon Asks GOP to Unite in South," NYT, September 30, 1966. *"In building this party":* "Nixon on the Stump—an Old-Timer at 53," NYT, October 2, 1966.

148 *The* New York Times *was impressed:* Ibid.

148 *The media reported:* "LBJ Rapped by Romney on Inflation," WP, September 30, 1966.

148 *"declare victory and go home":* "Aiken Suggests U.S. Say It Has Won War," NYT, October 20, 1966. *"From diplomats in Tokyo":* Jules Witcover, *The Resurrection of Richard Nixon* (New York: G. P. Putnam's Sons, 1970), 157. *Arriving in Greensboro:* "Nixon Criticizes U.S. Peace Steps," NYT, September 29, 1966.

149 *"He has put politics":* "Nixon Scores Johnson for 'Politics' on Peace," NYT, October 2, 1966. *"If Mr. Goldberg's naive":* NYT, September 29, 1966; Nixon to Eisenhower, October 4, 1966, RNLB, PPS 324.*246.5.

149 *In Chicago, on October 8:* "Draft Charter of Free Asia, Nixon Urges," NYT, October 9, 1966.

149 *Then he broke:* Leonard Garment, *Crazy Rhythm: From Brooklyn and Jazz to Nixon's White House, Watergate, and Beyond* (New York: Crown, 1997), 90.

149 *"GOP Will Press Racial Disorders":* NYT, October 4, 1966, 1.

150 *Whereas, in 1964:* David A. Nichols, *A Matter of Justice: Eisenhower and the Beginning of the Civil Rights Revolution* (New York: Simon & Schuster, 2007), 269.

150 *In Milwaukee, members:* "Rights Unit Gets Own Commandos," NYT, October 9, 1966. *He didn't ask for an injunction:* "Shotgun Blast Hits Home of Wisconsin Klan Chief," NYT, October 9, 1966.

150 *So Republican candidates posed:* "GOP Dramatizes Inflation as Key Issue," NYT, October 5, 1966. *Paul Douglas complained: The New Republic,* October 22, 1966; "Sen-

ator Douglas Takes the Gloves Off," NYT, October 20, 1966; see also, for instance, Rantoul, Illinois, speech, March 18, 1966, PDP, Box 1108, Campaign Correspondence. *A frank GOP official explained:* "GOP Dramatizes Inflation as Key Issue."

150 *Charles Percy went on CBS's:* "Percy Finds Rival Hurt by Backlash," NYT, October 17, 1966; *Saturday Evening Post,* November 5, 1966. *"I am for open":* "Senator Douglas Takes the Gloves Off."

150 *Handbills started appearing:* PDP, Box 1117, Percy Materials. See also brochure for John Lanigan for state senate with bungalow on the cover—"when our peaceful parks and streets"—opening onto shooting flames—"are turned over to a 'non-violent' marching group."

151 *"Backlash in Jersey Is Favoring Case":* NYT, October 30, 1966, 72.

151 *President Johnson spoke:* "President Scores GOP in Congress at Newark Rally," NYT, October 8, 1966.

151 *"The leader and the dean":* PPP 504, October 7, 1966.

152 *"It hasn't been too many":* PPP 513, October 12, 1966. *At the monument:* PPP 510, October 12, 1966.

152 *In Delaware the president:* PPP 515, October 13, 1966; Stephen Ambrose, *Nixon, Vol. 2: The Triumph of a Politician, 1962–1972* (New York: Simon & Schuster, 1989), 93.

153 *Nixon released a statement:* "Nixon Bids Johnson Apologize to GOP For 'Vicious' Attack," NYT, October 15, 1966.

153 *The president, in Pennsylvania:* PPP 528, October 16, 1966. *He had just signed:* PPP 508, 522, 523, 527, October 11–16, 1966. *"In Tight Races Backlash Vote":* NYT, October 17, 1966, 1.

154 *Nixon had two weeks:* Andrew L. Johns, "A Voice from the Wilderness: Richard Nixon and the Vietnam War, 1964–1966," *Presidential Studies Quarterly* 29 (1999).

154 *"third country" nations:* Christian Appy, *Working-Class War: American Combat Soldiers and Vietnam* (Chapel Hill: University of North Carolina Press, 1993), 16. *In Canberra, Australia:* Tom Wells, *The War Within: America's Battle over Vietnam* (Berkeley: University of California Press, 1994), 100.

154 *At the Manila summit, Johnson:* PPP 548, October 24, 1966; Bill Moyers interview.

154 *Then Johnson disembarked:* "President Visits G.I.'s in Surprise Trip," NYT, October 27, 1966.

154 *My account of servicemen's lives in Vietnam is drawn from Appy, Working-Class War,* 121–46, 163, 295.

154 *On melioidosis:* "Vietnam's Time Bomb," *Time,* February 10, 1967. *"What he seeks":* "Five Day Bonanza," *Time,* December 22, 1967.

155 *"bouncing betty":* Appy, *Working-Class War,* 333. *a seventy-five-mile tunnel system:* Ibid., 171; http://news.bbc.co.uk/1/hi/world/asia-pacific/720577.stm.

155 *"There are some who may":* PPP 552, October 26, 1966; Stanley Karnow, *Vietnam: A History* (New York: Viking, 1983), 501.

155 *In late October, the Republican:* WP, October 26, 1966. *The chair of the RCCC:* Witcover, *Resurrection of Richard Nixon,* 123.

156 Kalamazoo: "Nixon Says Tax Increase in '67 Would Touch Off a Recession," NYT, October 26, 1966. Grand Rapids: Witcover, *Resurrection of Richard Nixon,* 160. Oregon and Spokane: Ibid.; *Seattle Times,* October 28, 1966; "Nixon Says 'Johnson Blitz' Threatens 'Great Republican Tide,'" NYT, October 28, 1966.

156 *In Boise, he noted:* "Nixon Fears War as Issue in 1968," NYT, October 29, 1966.

156 *Bill Moyers was on the horn:* Witcover, *Resurrection of Richard Nixon,* 159. *At 4:29 a.m., Nixon woke them:* Ibid.

156 *"How can you have your mother":* "Inside Report: Doubts in Nixon Country," WP, November 3, 1966.

156 *No literary critic ever read:* William Safire, *Before the Fall: An Inside View of the Pre-Watergate White House* (New York: Ballantine, 1977), 36. *Just as Nixon worried:* PPP 549, October 25, 1966.

157 *He started banging out notes:* Garment, *Crazy Rhythm,* 113. *In an aboard-plane interview:* "Nixon Bids 2 Parties Meet Johnson War," NYT, November 1, 1966.

157 *On November 1, Nixon's:* Jules Witcover, *White Knight: The Rise of Spiro Agnew* (New York: Random House, 1972), 128.

157 *The Republican National Committee had produced:* "GOP Gives Party Film Mixed Reviews," WP, November 2, 1966.

158 *On the Thursday morning:* Safire, *Before the Fall,* 36. *In the afternoon, Lyndon Johnson:* PPP 575, November 3, 1966.

158 *Experienced observers had long ago:* Bill Moyers interview. Kidney stone: Robert Caro: *Master of the Senate: The Years of Lyndon Johnson* (New York: Knopf, 2002), 618–19. Heart attack: Ibid., 622–26. *"It's not an emergency":* PPP 575.

158 *"Do you think it will get":* Safire, *Before the Fall,* 37.

159 *"I sold as hard":* Ibid., 38.

159 *A gaggle of reporters:* Ibid., 36–37.

159 *The lead article:* "Nixon Criticizes Manila Results," NYT, November 4, 1966.

159 *The jump on page 18:* "The Text of Nixon's Appraisal of Results of Manila Conference on the Vietnam War," NYT, November 4, 1966.

160 *Johnson yowled:* Safire, *Before the Fall,* 38.

160 *"I didn't get weary":* PPP 575, November 3, 1966.

160 *Nudges. Murmurs:* Jules Witcover describes the press conference scene in *Resurrection of Richard Nixon,* 162–65.

160 *He couldn't hide that:* Ibid., 163.

161 *"Says Republican Does Not":* "Johnson Derides Nixon's Criticism of Manila Stand," NYT, November 5, 1966.

161 *"He hit us!":* Safire, *Before the Fall,* 39.

161 *"The only time to lose":* Fawn Brodie, *Richard Nixon: The Shaping of His Character* (New York: W. W. Norton, 1981), 48. *Jules Witcover wrote that:* Witcover, *Resurrection of Richard Nixon,* 165.

162 *Mike Wallace of CBS:* Ibid.; Garment, *Crazy Rhythm,* 114.

162 *Then, speaking at the armory:* "Nixon Sees Break in Bipartisan Line," NYT, November 5, 1966.

162 *Down at the LBJ Ranch:* Witcover, *Resurrection of Richard Nixon,* 167.

162 *Nixon said, "Is every":* "Nixon Defended by Eisenhower After Criticism by the President," NYT, November 6, 1966.

162 *Both parties had been provided:* Witcover, *Resurrection of Richard Nixon,* 167. *The RNC had planned:* "Nixon May Share TV with Disputed Film," WP, November 4, 1966. *But that never suited:* Safire, *Before the Fall,* 34. *They even considered:* Witcover, *Resurrection of Richard Nixon,* 168. *The Republicans also:* "Bailey Guilty of 'Smear,' Laird Says," WP, November 6, 1966.

163 *Sunday morning, Nixon:* Ralph de Toledano, *One Man Alone: Richard Nixon* (New York: Funk & Wagnalls, 1969), 332. *"I respect you for the great":* David Broder and Stephen Hess, *The Republican Establishment: The Present and Future of the GOP* (New York: Harper & Row, 1967), 197.

163 *"In the space of a single":* Andrew E. Busch, *Horses in Midstream: U.S. Midterm Elections and Their Consequences* (Pittsburgh: University of Pittsburgh Press, 1999), 101. *Handicappers had said:* Ryan Hayes interview.

163 *Republicans now controlled statehouses:* "The Temper of the Times," *Time,* April 14, 1967.

164 *By one estimate:* Busch, *Horses in Midstream,* 102. *Lurleen Wallace won:* Dan T. Carter, *The Politics of Rage: George Wallace, the Origin of the New Conservatism, and the Transformation of American Politics* (Baton Rouge: Louisiana State University Press, 1996), 292. *The Georgia gubernatorial race:* Bradley R. Rice, "The 1966 Gubernatorial Elections in Georgia" (Ph.D. diss., University of Southern Mississippi, 1982). *"The plague of Wallace politics":* Nation, June 6, 1966. *Actually, the plague just waited:* USNWR, November 21, 1966. NBC's voter analysis showed only 38 percent of whites voted Democratic in Florida compared to 54 percent previously. *The liberal who'd knocked off Judge Smith:* Bruce J. Dierenfield, "Conservative Outrage: The Defeat in 1966 of Rep. Howard W. Smith of Virginia," *Virginia Magazine of History and Biography* 89 (1981): 181–205. *Nelson Rockefeller survived: CQ Political Notes,* December 12, 1966. *Nelson's brother Winthrop: Reporter,* October 20, 1966. *In New York City, civilian police review:* Cannato, *Ungovernable City,* 183. *In Colorado:* "Proposition Vote May Doom 5 Men," NYT, November 10, 1966.

164 *They wrote the second chapter:* See "Hypotheses Unbound," *Time,* February 3, 1967. *A cartoon in the* Washington Star: Broder and Hess, *Republican Establishment,* 3. 79.2 percent turnout in California: Totton J. Anderson and Eugene C. Lee, "The 1966 Election in California," *Western Political Quarterly* 20 (June 1967).

164 Illinois results: Robert E. Hartley, *Charles H. Percy: A Political Perspective* (New York: Rand McNally, 1975), 82. *he was detoured through the kitchen:* Martha Cleveland, *Charles Percy: Strong New Voice from Illinois* (Jacksonville, IL: Harris-Wolfe, 1968), 194–97. *He was now, said Stewart Alsop: Saturday Evening Post,* November 5, 1966.

164 *"It was hatred that elected":* David Murray, *Charles Percy of Illinois* (New York: Harper & Row, 1968), 193. *Conservatives had erected:* Lee Edwards, *Goldwater: The Man Who Made a Revolution* (Washington, DC: Regnery, 1995), 364.

165 *A ward analysis demonstrated:* Richard C. Wade, "Backlash in the Percy Campaign," *Reporter,* January 12, 1967; Thomas Byrne Edsall and Mary Edsall, *Chain Reaction: The Impact of Race, Rights, and Taxes on American Politics* (New York: W. W. Norton, 1991), 60. See also Robert Evans and Rowland Novak, "Inside Report: The Permanent Backlash," WP, October 24, 1966. *Roman Pucinski was reelected:* Adam Cohen and Elizabeth Taylor, *American Pharaoh: Mayor Richard J. Daley: His Battle for Chicago and the Nation* (Boston: Little, Brown, 2000), 427.

165 *"They believe that backlash":* Herbert Parmet, *Richard Nixon and His America* (New York: Little, Brown, 1989), 487.

165 *"Whether we like it or not":* "Brown Assesses Backlash," NYT, December 29, 1966. *"Maybe they feel Lyndon Johnson":* Busch, *Horses in Midstream,* 101. *Bakersfield punished its Negroes:* "Bakersfield, Cali, Rejects Role in Antipoverty Program," NYT, November 10, 1966.

165 Statistics on Omaha, Ohio urban Poles, and AFL-CIO: Alan Draper, "Labor and the 1966 Elections," *Labor History* 30 (1989): 76–92. *"It's nothing personal":* "Backlash Enters Bay State Race; Brooke's Lead Is Said to Be Dwindling over Issue," NYT, October 23, 1966.

166 *Warren Weaver of the* New York Times: "Nixon 'Bats' .686 for 1966 Season; Leads Political Averages in Stumping for Winners," NYT, November 13, 1966.

166 *Wasting his time on candidates:* Parmet, *Richard Nixon and His America,* 491.

166 Nixon's election night: Witcover, *Resurrection of Richard Nixon,* 169–70.

166 *He also slurred a confidence:* Garment, *Crazy Rhythm,* 115.

CHAPTER EIGHT: THE BOMBING

169 Harrison Salisbury reports on Vietnam bombing: Robert Dallek, *Flawed Giant: Lyndon Johnson and His Times, 1961–1973* (New York: Oxford University Press, 1999), 449; Tom Wells, *The War Within: America's Battle over Vietnam* (Berkeley: University of California Press, 1994), 114; "Flak from Hanoi," *Time,* January 6, 1967.

169 *"Look at that aircraft carrier":* A. J. Langguth, *Our Vietnam: The War, 1954–1975* (New York: Touchstone, 2000), 162. *"Some of our boys are floating":* Ibid., 303. Westmoreland on number of enemy fighters: Christian Appy, *Working-Class War: American Combat Soldiers and Vietnam* (Chapel Hill: University of North Carolina Press, 1993), 165. McNamara and doctored maps: Langguth, *Our Vietnam,* 173–74. Lippmann and Bundy: Ibid., 354.

170 *"That proves what I'm saying!":* Daniel Ellsberg, *Secrets: A Memoir of Vietnam and the Pentagon Papers* (New York: Viking, 2002), 141.

170 Student leaders meeting with Rusk: Wells, *War Within,* 118–19.

171 Bobby Kennedy criticized by Nixon: Jules Witcover, *The Resurrection of Richard Nixon* (New York: G. P. Putnam's Sons, 1970), 158.

171 Time *was the place to go each week:* "The Inheritor," *Time,* January 6, 1967. Bob Hope quotations: *Bob Hope: The Vietnam Years, 1964–1966,* vol. 1 (R2 Entertainment, 2004).

171 Religious leaders, General Eisenhower, Hickenlooper, Mendel Rivers, Sam Ervin: "Flak from Hanoi." *"massive propaganda campaign":* USNWR, January 9, 1967. Pulitzer Prize: Langguth, *Our Vietnam,* 437.

172 State of the Union: PPP, January 10, 1967. Vietnam and budget: Stephen C. Shadegg, *Winning's a Lot More Fun* (New York: Macmillan, 1969), 83; Maurice Isserman and Michael Kazin, *America Divided: The Civil War of the 1960s* (New York: Oxford University Press, 1999), 189.

172 *When his closest aide, Bill Moyers:* Shadegg, *Winning's a Lot More Fun,* 60. Bobby Baker: "Dead Men Tell No Tales," *Time,* January 27, 1967. William Manchester: "Battle of a Book," *Time,* December 23, 1966; "Chapter II — or Finis?" *Time,* December 30, 1966; "Spreading Controversy," *Time,* January 6, 1967; "Start the Presses," *Time,* Jan-

uary 20, 1967; "The Manchester Book," *Time,* April 7, 1967. Schlesinger and "unconscious argument": Letter to the editor, *New York Review of Books,* April 20, 1967. *"Until Robert Kennedy has made":* USNWR, November 14, 1966.

172 *"kind of backing the Stokely Carmichaels":* Michael Flamm, *Law and Order: Street Crime, Civil Unrest, and the Crisis of Liberalism in the 1960s* (New York: Columbia University Press, 2005), 211. *On the twenty-seventh, astronauts Gus Grissom:* Shadegg, *Winning's a Lot More Fun,* 79. *"I'm not leaving because of Lyndon Johnson":* "Farewell to Washington," *Time,* January 6, 1967.

172 *On February 8, Lyndon Johnson appealed directly: Department of State Bulletin* 56, no. 1450 (April 10, 1967), 595–97. *"I'll destroy you and every one":* Dallek, *Flawed Giant,* 447.

173 Romney and Harris poll: D. Duane Angel, *Romney: A Political Biography* (New York: Exposition Press, 1967), 221.

173 *"nothing but a political banner":* T. George Harris, *Romney's Way: A Man and an Idea* (Englewood Cliffs, NJ: Prentice-Hall, 1968), 19. *"silvering Presidential hair":* Witcover, *Resurrection of Richard Nixon,* 179. *A new book of personal reminiscences:* Paul B. Fay Jr., *The Pleasure of His Company* (New York: Harper & Row, 1966), 259. *In May of 1966:* Week in Review, NYT, May 29, 1966.

173 *"It is clear," Scotty Reston:* NYT, June 12, 1966.

173 *Nelson Rockefeller financed it:* Witcover, *Resurrection of Richard Nixon,* 179–80. *An exploratory campaign office:* "Hypothesis Unbound," *Time,* February 3, 1967. Six-state tour: Ibid., 182, 186–89.

174 *Nixon let a reporter ride along:* Witcover, *Resurrection of Richard Nixon,* 174. St. Louis *Globe-Democrat:* Ibid., 178; Andrew L. Johns, "A Voice from the Wilderness: Richard Nixon and the Vietnam War, 1964–1966," *Presidential Studies Quarterly* 29 (1999).

174 *"I have heard a number of very favorable":* Nixon to Reagan, November 28, 1966, RNLB, PPS 501.1.17. Meeting with conservative leaders: Interview with Lee Edwards. *Then Nixon had Buckley:* E. J. Dionne, *Why Americans Hate Politics* (New York: Simon & Schuster, 1991), 191.

175 Hiring John Mitchell: Witcover, *Resurrection of Richard Nixon,* 178; William Safire, *Before the Fall: An Inside View of the Pre-Watergate White House* (New York: Ballantine, 1977), 263–71.

175 New Orleans RNC meeting: "Hypothesis Unbound"; Shadegg, *Winning's a Lot More Fun,* 67–69; Witcover, *Resurrection of Richard Nixon,* 182–84.

175 Gaylord Parkinson: Shadegg, *Winning's a Lot More Fun,* 70–72; Witcover, *Resurrection of Richard Nixon,* 184–85, 192. The revelation that Parkinson was on Reagan's payroll in 1966 is in Joseph Lewis, *What Makes Reagan Run?: A Political Profile* (New York: McGraw-Hill, 1968), 113.

176 Waldorf meeting: Safire, *Before the Fall,* 42–44.

176 *In the middle of February Nixon denied:* "In Business," *Time,* February 24, 1967. *"I have made no decision":* "On the Rim," *Time,* March 24, 1967.

176 Julie's debut: Stephen Ambrose, *Nixon, Vol. 2: The Triumph of a Politician, 1962–1972* (New York: Simon & Schuster, 1989), 191.

176 McNamara at Harvard: Wells, *War Within,* 101. Sunset Strip riot: Renata Adler, *Toward a Radical Middle: Fourteen Pieces of Reporting and Criticism* (New York: Random House, 1969), 39–59. Berkeley strike: USNWR, December 12, 1966.

177 Human Be-In: Peter Braunstein and Michael William Doyle, eds., *Imagine Nation: The American Counterculture of the 1960s and '70s* (New York: Routledge, 2001), 250.

177 Man of the Year issue: "The Inheritor," *Time,* January 6, 1967. *"Here Comes the Now Generation": Reader's Digest,* April 1967. *"most American youngsters":* "On Being an American Parent," *Time,* December 15, 1967.

177 *"In the sixth decade":* Edward Quinn and Paul J. Doyle, eds., *The Sense of the Sixties* (New York: Free Press, 1968).

178 *"The outcry of a generation is finally":* Letters, *Time,* January 20, 1967.

178 *"To warn the 'civilized world'":* Sidney Peck, *Uncovering the Sixties: The Life and Times of the Underground Press* (New York: Pantheon, 1985), 45–46. *Arnold Toynbee said hippies:* "Tourist with a Long View," *Time,* October 20, 1967. *Time* cover story: "The Hippies," July 7, 1967. *"I fail to see much real altruism":* Letters, *Time,* January 20, 1967.

179 *In January of 1966, the names:* "477,000 Students Listed as Favoring Policy on Vietnam," NYT, January 7, 1967, 1. *"Affirmation: Vietnam" rally: Atlanta Journal Consti-*

tution, February 12, 1966. *"The Ballad of the Green Berets":* "Vietnam: The Home Front," April 1, 1966, NBC broadcast, MTR, T81:0844. "Moral Re-Armament" movement and "Up with People": *Reader's Digest,* May 1967.

180 Vietnam deaths: "Gathering Intensity," *Time,* March 31, 1967.

180 *Carrying* Quotations from Chairman Mao: "The Follies That Come with Spring," *Time,* March 24, 1967. *In February, Catholic pacifist David Miller:* Wells, *War Within,* 57. The "Resistance" and SDS: Ibid., 124.

180 *"I want to show you it's against my will":* "The Show Goes On," *Time,* April 14, 1967. *"Many of our fellows on the campuses":* Wells, *War Within,* 126.

180 *"I expected to see a bunch":* Thomas Maier, *Dr. Spock: An American Life* (New York: Basic Books, 2003), 249. Martha's Vineyard, Aspen, clergymen: Wells, *War Within,* 106, 108, 119; Lewis Chester, Bruce Page, and Godfrey Hodgson, *American Melodrama: The Presidential Campaign of 1968* (New York: Viking, 1969), 84; Paul Hendrickson, *The Living and the Dead: Robert McNamara and Five Lives of a Lost War* (New York: Vintage, 1997). *Senator Eugene McCarthy:* Ibid., 121. MOTHERS SAY STOP THE WAR: Ibid., 123. *Establishment insiders, former war supporters:* Ibid., 135.

181 Repression against antiwar activists: *Nation,* August 22, 1966.

181 Martin Luther King and Dr. Spock: Maier, *Dr. Spock,* 117, 272, 280.

181 *A teenager shouted,* "Traitor!": Ibid., 290.

182 Spring Mobilization Against the War march: Ibid., 280–82; Wells, *War Within,* 129–35; interview with Dr. Jay Larkey; "The Dilemma of Dissent," *Time,* April 21, 1967; Vincent J. Cannato, *The Ungovernable City: John Lindsay and the Battle to Save New York* (New York: Basic Books, 2003), 147; WP, April 16, 1967.

182 *The White House's response:* Maier, *Dr. Spock,* 275. *"America needs to tell the world":* "The Dilemma of Dissent," *Time,* April 21, 1967. *Dean Rusk went on* Meet the Press: Maier, *Dr. Spock,* 290.

182 *In May, the Veterans of Foreign Wars:* Wells, *War Within,* 144. *"Support Our Boys in Vietnam" parade:* Ibid.; CT, May 13, 1967; Cannato, *Ungovernable City,* 147.

183 Vietnam War public opinion: Dallek, *Flawed Giant,* 452; Wells, *War Within,* 123. *"Our government has not permitted":* Francis Vivian Drake, "Let's Fight to Win in Vietnam," *Reader's Digest,* May 1967. Letter to *Ladies' Home Journal:* Wells, *War Within,* 84. *"It makes you think":* WP, April 16, 1967.

183 *"Marine Dies Believing Viet War Is Right":* CT, May 13, 1967. Time *featured a study:* "The Perils of Crowd Counting," *Time,* April 7, 1967. *"I would drag some of these professors":* "Wallace Hints He Would Have Woman for VP," CT, May 15, 1967. Vietnam Summer: Wells, *War Within,* 138. *The* Chicago Trib *responded:* CT, May 9, 1967.

183 Kerr, Reagan, and FBI: http://www.sfgate.com/news/special/pages/2002/campus-files/. Reagan tax increase: "In the Black, with Crust," *Time,* March 17, 1967. *He would tell young people harassing him:* Charles Taylor, "The Gipper's Dark Side," Salon.com, June 8, 2004. *To him, a hippie was someone:* Braunstein and Doyle, eds., *Imagine Nation,* 6.

CHAPTER NINE: SUMMER OF LOVE

185 *"youth drew attention to itself":* Nicholas Von Hoffman, *We Are the People Our Parents Warned Us Against* (New York: Quadrangle Books, 1968), 1.

185 Hippies in Detroit: Jeff A. Hale, "The White Panthers' 'Total Assault on the Culture,'" in Peter Braunstein and Michael William Doyle, eds., *Imagine Nation: The American Counterculture of the 1960s and '70s* (New York: Routledge, 2001), 124–56.

185 *"Lindsay sees the hippies":* Vincent J. Cannato, *The Ungovernable City: John Lindsay and the Battle to Save New York* (New York: Basic Books, 2003), 144. August Heckscher: Ibid., 146.

186 Sinatra, Hendrix, Carl Wilson, Mick Jagger: John Tobler, *This Day in Rock: Day by Day Record of Rock's Biggest News Stories* (New York: Carroll & Graf, 1993).

186 Kenneth Tynan: Jon Wiener, "A Day in the Life: Sgt. Pepper Turns 40," March 31, 2007, http://www.thenation.com/doc/20070618/wiener. *Paul McCartney said in an interview: Life,* June 9, 1967; "Beatle McCartney Admits Taking LSD," WP, June 18, 1967. *"LSD should be shunned":* Thomas Schultheiss, *A Day in the Life; The Beatles Day-By-Day, 1960–1970* (Ann Arbor, MI: Pierian Press, 1980), 183.

186 *"It would be ironic, indeed":* Robert Sam Anson, *McGovern: A Biography* (New York: Holt, Rinehart, and Winston, 1972), 164.

186 *"On May 2, the chief of the city's":* "Eclipse May Trigger Riot, Probers Told," CT, May 3, 1967.

187 *On May 4 the sheriff of Cook County:* CT, May 5, 1967. *"The crowd rose like a tornado":* CT, May 22, 1967. *"The bystanders got my message":* Garry Wills, *The Second Civil War: Arming for Armageddon* (New York: New American Library, 1968), 91.

187 *"Dig your trenches":* CT, May 8, 1967.

187 *"The Kentucky Derby will be run":* "National Guard Promised for Derby," CT, May 3, 1967.

187 *Or Birmingham, where Stokely Carmichael:* Dan T. Carter, *The Politics of Rage: George Wallace, the Origin of the New Conservatism, and the Transformation of American Politics* (Baton Rouge: Louisiana State University Press, 1996), 306. *Or New York, where sixteen members:* Cannato, *Ungovernable City,* 131. *At the NAACP convention in Boston: Milwaukee Sentinel,* July 14, 1967.

187 Black Panther origins: Michael Newton, *Bitter Grain: Huey Newton and the Black Panther Party* (Los Angeles: Holloway House, 1980); Hugh Pearson, *Shadow of a Panther: Huey Newton and the Price of Black Power in America* (New York: Addison-Wesley, 1994).

188 *"The Dog Cops made no attempt":* Phillip Foner, ed., *The Black Panthers Speak* (New York: Da Capo Press, 1995), 9–12. *"You should go to the legislature":* Newton, *Bitter Grain,* 25.

188 *"What are you doing with the guns?":* Ibid., 18.; Pearson, *Shadow of a Panther,* 114.

188 *After the riots in San Francisco:* Newton, *Bitter Grain,* 17. See also William J. Bopp, ed., *The Police Rebellion: A Quest for Blue Power* (Springfield, IL: Charles H. Thomas, 1971), San Francisco chapter.

189 *"Gunmen Invade W. Coast Capitol":* CT, May 3, 1967; Newton, *Bitter Grain,* 30; Pearson, *Shadow of a Panther,* 129–33.

189 My account of the Newark riot comes from Ron Porambo, *No Cause for Indictment: An Autopsy of Newark* (New York: Holt, 1971; republished in 2007 by Melville House); Michael Flamm, *Law and Order: Street Crime, Civil Unrest, and the Crisis of Liberalism in the 1960s* (New York: Columbia University Press, 2005), 85–88; *Milwaukee Star,* July 22, 1967; Wills, *Second Civil War,* 58. See Bud Lee's photograph of Joey Bass at http://www.budleepicturemaker.com/race/racepicts_02.htm.

194 My account of the Detroit riot comes from Flamm, *Law and Order,* 88–93; oral history with Cyrus Vance at http://www.lbjlib.utexas.edu/johnson/archives.hom/oralhistory.hom/Vance-C/DetroitReport.asp; Wills, *Second Civil War*; Frank A. Aukofer, *City with a Chance* (Milwaukee: Bruce Publishing Co., 1968), 2; and Cyrus Vance's report for the president, at http://www.lbjlib.utexas.edu/johnson/archives.hom/oralhistory.hom/Vance-C/DetroitReport.asp.

195 *There followed an early skirmish:* Flamm, *Law and Order,* 91–93.

196 *Asked at his July 18 news conference:* PPP, July 18, 1967.

196 Ben Wattenberg: Flamm, *Law and Order,* 9.

197 *The same hot week in New York:* Cannato, *Ungovernable City,* 135–46.

197 H. Rap Brown speech: Peter B. Levy, ed., *America in the Sixties—Left, Right, and Center: A Documentary History* (Westport, CT: Praeger, 1998), 92–95; Pearson, *Shadow of a Panther,* 139; Wills, *Second Civil War,* 26–34.

197 *In Philadelphia cops got garbage cans:* Ibid., 40, 88. *A rumor flashed that Washington:* Ibid., 42.

197 *"Civil rats!":* Robert Hendrickson, *More Cunning Than Man: A Complete History of the Rat and Its Role in Human Civilization* (New York: Stein and Day, 1983), 119; NYT, June 23, 1967; July 19, 21, 25, 28, 1967; August 1, 6, 8, 9, 11, 1967.

198 *"Push ahead full tilt":* Taylor Branch, *Pillar of Fire: America in the King Years, 1963–1965* (New York: Simon & Schuster, 1998), 175.

198 *When polled in 1961:* Kenneth Baer, *Reinventing Democrats: The Politics of Liberalism from Reagan to Clinton* (Lawrence: University Press of Kansas, 2000), 17. *A White House study found:* Herbert Parmet, *Richard Nixon and His America* (New York: Little, Brown, 1989), 487.

198 Albert Cleage: Wills, *Second Civil War,* 132. *"Are YOU READY NOW":* Ibid.

198 NRA and Dodd Bill: "Glory of Guns," *Time,* August 25, 1967.

199   Cabinet meeting on riots: Flamm, *Law and Order,* 94–95.
199   *A Justice Department memo:* Clark to Vinson, August 18, 1967, LBJCR, Reel 4. *"shoot him down—boom":* Saul Stern, "The Call of the Panthers," NYTM, August 6, 1967.

CHAPTER TEN: IN WHICH A CRUISE SHIP FULL OF GOVERNORS INSPIRES CONSIDERATIONS ON THE NATURE OF OLD AND NEW POLITICS

200   Nixon's travels: Raymond Price, *With Nixon* (New York: Viking, 1977), 20–28; Jules Witcover, *The Resurrection of Richard Nixon* (New York: G. P. Putnam's Sons, 1970), 192–94.
201   *Gaylord Parkinson had proven a disappointment:* Ibid., 207; Stephen C. Shadegg, *Winning's a Lot More Fun* (New York: Macmillan, 1969), 106–7.
201   *"They don't vote":* Price, *With Nixon,* 25.
201   *"Often, what the leaders told him":* Ibid., 24.
201   *"Asia After Viet Nam":* Ibid., 37; Witcover, *Resurrection of Richard Nixon,* 195, 217; *Foreign Affairs* 46, no. 1 (October 1967).
202   *"What Has Happened to America?":* *Reader's Digest,* October 1967; Witcover, *Resurrection of Richard Nixon,* 218. Available at http://www.wadsworth.com/history_d/special_features/ext/ap/chapter29/29.4.nixon.a.html.
202   *"It's gettin' nowadays that a policeman":* Witcover, *Resurrection of Richard Nixon,* 218.
203   Canceled *Time* story: William Safire, *Before the Fall: An Inside View of the Pre-Watergate White House* (New York: Ballantine, 1977), 46.
203   Nixon strategy for winning delegates: Shadegg, *Winning's a Lot More Fun,* 106–7.
203   John Mitchell and Jarris Leonard: Witcover, *Resurrection of Richard Nixon,* 209.
204   George Romney and "brainwashing": Shadegg, *Winning's a Lot More Fun,* 100; Witcover, *Resurrection of Richard Nixon,* 213.
204   *"One moment he's the front-runner":* Richard Whalen, *Catch the Falling Flag: A Republican's Challenge to His Party* (Boston: Houghton Mifflin, 1972), 24.
205   Westmoreland's troop increase request: Robert Dallek, *Flawed Giant: Lyndon Johnson and His Times, 1961–1973* (New York: Oxford University Press, 1999), 223; Tom Wells, *The War Within: America's Battle over Vietnam* (Berkeley: University of California Press, 1994), 150, 294; Christian Appy, *Working-Class War: American Combat Soldiers and Vietnam* (Chapel Hill: University of North Carolina Press, 1993), 36; A. J. Langguth, *Our Vietnam: The War, 1954–1975* (New York: Touchstone, 2000), 444–47.
205   Tip O'Neill to the president: Steven M. Gillon, *Politics and Vision: The ADA and American Liberalism, 1947–1985* (New York: Oxford University Press, 1987), 299. *The fact that only 1.5 percent of reservists:* Appy, *Working-Class War,* 36.
205   *In late July, for the first time:* Dallek, *Flawed Giant,* 474. *"American officers talk somberly":* Ibid. *"I frankly am lukewarm":* Mary Hershberger, *Jane Fonda's War: A Political Biography of an Antiwar Icon* (New York: New Press, 2005), 7. *Chuck Percy wondered why:* Michael Flamm, *Law and Order: Street Crime, Civil Unrest, and the Crisis of Liberalism in the 1960s* (New York: Columbia University Press, 2005), 114. *And Kentucky's Republican senator:* Whalen, *Catch the Falling Flag,* 31. *The fiscal year ended with the worst deficit:* Shadegg, *Winning's a Lot More Fun,* 83.
206   *Defense Secretary McNamara wrote to the president:* "Draft Memorandum from Secretary of Defense McNamara to President Johnson," May 19, 1967, http://www.state.gov/r/pa/ho/frus/johnsonlb/v/13148.htm. *forty-seven thousand more soldiers:* Langguth, *Our Vietnam,* 447.
206   South Vietnamese election: Ibid., 455; "U.S. Encouraged by Vietnam Vote," NYT, September 4, 1967; "A Stake Worth Fighting For," *Time,* November 10, 1967. *"I have only one—Hitler":* "Premier Ky, in Saigon, Denies That He Called Hitler His Hero," NYT, July 16, 1965.
206   *6,721 American soldiers had died:* "Cost of Commitment," *Time,* September 27, 1967. *a typical story was about the beloved mess cook:* "No Ordinary Man," *Reader's Digest,* July 1967. *Indianapolis Star* editorial in same issue.
206   *Readers of the prestige press:* Harrison Salisbury, *Behind the Lines: Hanoi, December 23, 1966–January 7, 1967* (New York: HarperCollins, 1967); Jonathan Schell, *The Village of Ben Suc* (New York: Knopf, 1967); "Vietnam in Print," *Time,* November 17, 1967.

207 *It was confusing:* "The Sobering Truth About the War," *Reader's Digest,* October 1967.
Over a quarter found the war: Dallek, *Flawed Giant,* 462. *George McGovern subse-quently wrote:* Robert Sam Anson, *McGovern: A Biography* (New York: Holt, Rine-hart, and Winston, 1972), 165.

207 *Citizens' Committee for Peace with Freedom in Vietnam:* Wells, *War Within,* 148–49; "Voice from the Silent Center," *Time,* November 3, 1967; Whalen, *Catch the Falling Flag,* 33.

207 Letters to the editor: *Time,* November 17 and 24, 1967.

207 *An undersecretary of agriculture who visited Kansas:* Wells, *War Within,* 147.

208 *Jimi Hendrix called it:* Charles Shaar Murray, *Crosstown Traffic: Jimi Hendrix and the Post-War Rock'n'Roll Revolution* (New York: St. Martin's, 1991), 161. *One bestseller at Ivy League bookstores:* Wills, *Second Civil War,* 7. *The White House considered end-ing:* Wells, *War Within,* 144–45. High school underground newspapers: "Freedom Underground," *Time,* March 31, 1967.

208 *"One basic plot only has appeared daily":* Ben Hecht, *Child of the Century,* 469.

209 *Bonnie and Clyde:* J. Hoberman, *The Dream Life: Movies, Media, and the Mythology of the Sixties* (New York: New Press, 2003), 157–58, 168, 172, 422; "The New Cinema: Violence . . . Sex . . . Art," *Time,* December 8, 1967. See the impassioned letters pro and con in *Time,* December 15, 1967, and December 22, 1967.

210 *National Mobilization Committee to End the War:* David Farber, *Chicago '68* (Chicago: University of Chicago Press, 1988), 60–68.

211 *"young men with menopausal minds":* Peter Braunstein and Michael William Doyle, eds., *Imagine Nation: The American Counterculture of the 1960s and '70s* (New York: Routledge, 2001), 69.

211 *National Conference for a New Politics:* Renata Adler, *Toward a Radical Middle: Four-teen Pieces of Reporting and Criticism* (New York: Random House, 1969), 239–59.

212 George Meany on "silent majority": Jeremy Varon, *Bringing the War Home: The Weather Underground, the Red Army Faction, and Revolutionary Violence in the Six-ties and Seventies* (Berkeley: University of California Press, 2004), 147. Al Capp on "Joanie Phoanie": "Which One Is the Phoanie?" *Time,* January 20, 1967. *"On January 5, 1967, Vietcong terrorists":* "Who Speaks for the Civilian Dead in South Vietnam?" USNWR, January 16, 1967. *Mission: Impossible:* TV listings, *Time,* March 4, 1967.

212 *Joan Didion published an essay:* Joan Didion, *Slouching Toward Bethlehem* (New York: Farrar, Straus & Giroux, 1968).

212 *The NYPD maintained a twenty-man:* William McGowan, "Dan Ran the Hippie Squad," WSJ, June 17, 2005. *The* New York Times's *J. Anthony Lukas:* "The Two Worlds of Linda Fitzpatrick," NYT, October 16, 1967; J. Anthony Lukas, *Don't Shoot, We Are Your Children* (New York: Random House, 1971), 158–89.

213 *"Don't vote. Don't politic":* Braunstein and Doyle, eds., *Imagine Nation,* 50. *World leaders would "banish war":* Life, June 9, 1967. *When Bobby Kennedy spoke:* Arthur Schlesinger, *Robert Kennedy and His Times* (Boston: Houghton Mifflin, 1978), 824; Robert F. Kennedy, *To Seek a Newer World,* 4.

213 Antiwar movement rumors: Wells, *War Within,* 155. *"We are working to build a guer-rilla":* "The New Left Turns to Mood of Violence in Place of Protest," NYT, May 7, 1967.

214 Oakland Induction Center: Hugh Pearson, *Shadow of a Panther: Huey Newton and the Price of Black Power in America* (New York: Addison-Wesley, 1994), 144; Hober-man, *Dream Life,* 179; Wells, *War Within,* 125.

214 Dow protests: "Ire Against Fire," *Time,* November 3, 1967. *"Murderers," movement leaders were now intoning:* Wells, *War Within,* 126. *At Southwest Texas State College:* Richmond *News Leader,* October 20, 1967.

214 Pentagon march: Wills, *Second Civil War,* 138, 195–201; Langguth, *Our Vietnam,* 459; Hoberman, *Dream Life,* 179–80; Abbie Hoffman, *Revolution for the Hell of It* (New York: Pocket Books, 1970), 42; "Protest! Protest! Protest!" *Time,* October 27, 1967; Thomas Maier, *Dr. Spock: An American Life* (New York: Basic Books, 2003), 293; Julius Lester, *Revolutionary Notes* (New York: Grove Press, 1970), 31–33; Norman Mailer, *Armies of the Night: History as a Novel, the Novel as History* (New York: Signet, 1968).

216 *The president was once again sure Moscow:* Dallek, *Flawed Giant,* 489. *He now thought Vietnam a colossal blunder:* Langguth, *Our Vietnam,* 461. *Dean Rusk, on the other hand:* "Counterattack," *Time,* October 20, 1967.

216 Contending rumors: "The Morning After," *Time*, November 3, 1967. *The next week, at Indiana University, Dean Rusk:* Ibid. *"Get ready for a big event":* Hoffman, *Revolution for the Hell of It*, 46.

216 Governors' conference: Witcover, *Resurrection of Richard Nixon*, 218–21; Shadegg, *Winning's a Lot More Fun*, 101; "Anchors Away," *Time*, October 20, 1967; "In Unpath'd Waters," *Time*, October 27, 1967.

217 *"His mouth tells you no!":* "The Temper of the Times," *Time*, April 14, 1967.

218 Americans for Democratic Action board meeting: Gillon, *Politics and Vision*, 195; Lewis Chester, Bruce Page, and Godfrey Hodgson, *American Melodrama: The Presidential Campaign of 1968* (New York: Viking, 1969), 64.

219 *"One cannot speak of Black Power":* Gillon, *Politics and Vision*, 199–200.

219 *"If we have LBJ for another four years":* Chester, Page, and Hodgson, *American Melodrama*, 115; Jeff Shesol, *Mutual Contempt: Robert Kennedy, Lyndon Johnson, and the Feud That Defined a Decade* (New York: W. W. Norton, 1998), 415.

219 *They ran the Dump Johnson movement:* Chester, Page, and Hodgson, *American Melodrama*, 62–67; Gillon, *Politics and Vision*, 201. *"Why am I in politics":* Theodore H. White, *The Making of the President 1972* (New York: Atheneum, 1973), xiv.

219 Median age of voters by 1970: *CQ Political Notes*, October 14, 1966.

220 *"He's a Happening": New Republic*, April 2, 1966. *"There is a strange psychic connection":* Hunter S. Thompson, *Fear and Loathing on the Campaign Trail '72* (New York: Popular Library, 1973), 140.

220 *Eldridge Cleaver, the Black Panther Party's:* Don A. Schanche, *The Panther Paradox: A Liberal's Dilemma* (New York: D. McKay Co., 1970), 27. BOBBY KENNEDY — HAWK, DOVE, OR CHICKEN?: Shesol, *Mutual Contempt*, 403; Chester, Page, and Hodgson, *American Melodrama*, 116.

221 *beating LBJ 52– 32:* WP, October 1, 1967; Arthur Schlesinger, *Robert Kennedy and His Times* (Boston: Houghton Mifflin, 1978), 822. "Intensely disliked" poll: Shesol, *Mutual Contempt*, 467. *"Those New Frontier cats":* Chester, Page, and Hodgson, *American Melodrama*, 111.

221 *In March 1967, as Ethel Kennedy:* Dallek, *Flawed Giant*, 454. *sworn affidavits:* "The Temper of the Times," *Time*, April 14, 1967. *"How can we possibly survive":* Shesol, *Mutual Contempt*, 297. *Then, in June, he made a florid:* Ibid., 297, 415.

221 *"the war in Vietnam is poisoning":* Margot A. Henriksen, *Dr. Strangelove's America: Society and Culture in the Atomic Age* (Berkeley: University of California Press, 1997), 364.

221 *Only Eugene McCarthy:* Chester, Page, and Hodgson, *American Melodrama*, 67. McCarthy generally: Stanley Kutler, *The Wars of Watergate: The Last Crisis of Richard Nixon* (New York: W. W. Norton, 1992), 28; Shadegg, *Winning's a Lot More Fun*, 127; Chester, Page, and Hodgson, *American Melodrama*, 68–70, 73, 78, 183; Michael Barone, *Our Country: The Shaping of America from Roosevelt to Reagan* (New York: Free Press, 1990), 429.

222 Meeting at Kennedy mansion: Chester, Page, and Hodgson, *American Melodrama*, 64, 89–91; Shesol, *Mutual Contempt*, 400.

223 *"I have guarded your children well":* "Louise Day Hicks Dies at 87," NYT, October 23, 2003.

223 On Hicks, Operation Exodus, confrontation with Cardinal Cushing, and *Newsweek*, see Charles Sumner Brown, "Negro Protest and White Power Structure: The Boston School Controversy, 1963–1966" (Ph.D. diss., Boston University, 1973).

223 George Wallace Woodley Country Club meeting: Dan T. Carter, *The Politics of Rage: George Wallace, the Origin of the New Conservatism, and the Transformation of American Politics* (Baton Rouge: Louisiana State University Press, 1996), 294; Witcover, *Resurrection of Richard Nixon*, 184. Wallace in governor's chair: Ibid., 198. *In spring he once more toured:* CT, May 15, 1967.

224 *In November he made a six-city tour:* "Into the Silks," November 14, 1967. California tour: Carter, *Politics of Rage*, 313–14.

224 *A memo from General Lewis B. Hershey: Time*, December 15, 1967, December 29, 1967. *A single called "An Open Letter":* Cash Box Top 100 Singles, December 9, 1967, http://members.aol.com/_ht_a/randypny2/cashbox/19671209.html.

225 *Eugene McCarthy announced:* "A Voice for Dissent," *Time*, December 8, 1967.

225 Rusk protest: Hoffman, *Revolution for the Hell of It*, 49.

225 Westmoreland in United States: Langguth, *Our Vietnam*, 467. Time *argued victory was*

imminent: "Border Troubles," November 17, 1967; "Progress," November 24, 1967; "Suicidal Intensity," December 8, 1967; "ARVN: Toward Fighting Trim," January 5, 1967; "Future Indicative," January 12, 1968.

225 Time *opined, too:* "The Real Black Power," *Time,* November 17, 1967; "A Marriage of Enlightenment," *Time,* September 29, 1967. *"With God's help, this will be the end": Bob Hope: The Vietnam Years, 1967–1969,* vol. 2 (Hope Enterprises, 2004). *A White House pollster exulted:* Flamm, *Law and Order,* 103.

CHAPTER ELEVEN: FED-UP-NIKS

227 *"When Ong Tao, the Spirit":* "Charlie, Come Home!" *Time,* February 10, 1967.
227 Tet Offensive: Langguth, *Our Vietnam,* 368–479; Dan T. Carter, *The Politics of Rage: George Wallace, the Origin of the New Conservatism, and the Transformation of American Politics* (Baton Rouge: Louisiana State University Press, 1996), 326; Stanley Kutler, *The Wars of Watergate: The Last Crisis of Richard Nixon* (New York: W. W. Norton, 1992), 27–28; Peter B. Levy, ed., *America in the Sixties — Left, Right, and Center: A Documentary History* (Westport, CT: Praeger, 1998), 162.
228 *Robert F. Kennedy spoke in Chicago:* Lewis Chester, Bruce Page, and Godfrey Hodgson, *American Melodrama: The Presidential Campaign of 1968* (New York: Viking, 1969), 117; Jeff Shesol, *Mutual Contempt: Robert Kennedy, Lyndon Johnson, and the Feud That Defined a Decade* (New York: W. W. Norton, 1998), 414.
228 *Pete Hamill, a young journalist:* Ibid., 415; Chester, Page, and Hodgson, *American Melodrama,* 115.
229 McCarthy New Hampshire campaign generally: David C. Hoeh, *1968, McCarthy, New Hampshire: I Hear America Singing* (Rochester, MN: Lone Oak Press, 1994). *"He seemed like a nice enough":* Chester, Page, and Hodgson, *American Melodrama,* 86. *"It is not our policy to 'have'":* Michael Barone, *Our Country: The Shaping of America from Roosevelt to Reagan* (New York: Free Press, 1990), 429.
229 *"last primitive society on earth":* Chester, Page, and Hodgson, *American Melodrama,* 68. *"Stubbornness and penicillin":* Ibid., 70. *"I'm twice as liberal as Hubert":* Barone, *Our Country,* 429.
229 *"Do not turn away":* Ibid.
230 McCarthy student volunteers: Chester, Page, and Hodgson, *American Melodrama,* 78–79, 96–99; Langguth, *Our Vietnam,* 483.
230 *Hubert Humphrey addressed the National Book Awards:* "Doctor's Dilemma," *Time,* January 12, 1968. Eartha Kitt: "An Activist First Lady Who Succeeded on Her Own Terms," LAT, July 12, 2007.
230 REMEMBER THE PUEBLO: Steven V. Roberts, *Eureka* (New York: Quadrangle/New York Times Books, 1974), 20. Americans for Democratic Action endorsement: NYT, February 13, 1968. *Lippmann wrote that the president's reelection:* Robert Shogan, *Bad News: Where the Press Goes Wrong in the Making of the President* (Chicago: Ivan R. Dee, 2001), 27.
231 *Governor King began making absurdly high:* Jules Witcover, *The Resurrection of Richard Nixon* (New York: G. P. Putnam's Sons, 1970), 265. Richard Goodwin and Seymour Hersh: Chester, Page, and Hodgson, *American Melodrama,* 93.
231 *"under any conceivable circumstances":* Barone, *Our Country,* 433. *primary entrance requirements:* Chester, Page, and Hodgson, *American Melodrama,* 117. *"If there is stealing in Beaumont":* Shesol, *Mutual Contempt,* 415.
231 *A Kennedy-shaped ghost:* Stephen C. Shadegg, *Winning's a Lot More Fun* (New York: Macmillan, 1969), 127. Campaign posters: Hoeh, *1968,* photo insert.
231 *"Don't argue with anyone":* Shadegg, *Winning's a Lot More Fun,* 127. *"Remind them that Vietnam":* Richard Scammon and Ben Wattenberg, *The Real Majority: An Extraordinary Examination of the American Electorate* (New York: Coward McCann, 1980), 105. *The* New York Times *had reported:* Langguth, *Our Vietnam,* 483.
232 New Hampshire Election Day: Scammon and Wattenberg, *Real Majority,* 105; Shadegg, *Winning's a Lot More Fun,* 126, 134; Shogan, *Bad News,* 31; Kutler, *Wars of Watergate,* 30; Langguth, *Our Vietnam,* 484; Barone, *Our Country,* 432.
232 *Later, two polling experts:* Scammon and Wattenberg, *Real Majority,* 27–28, 90–91.
232 Nixon New Hampshire victory: Shadegg, *Winning's a Lot More Fun,* 134; Witcover, *Resurrection of Richard Nixon,* 259.

232 Romney in New Hampshire and Wisconsin: Garry Wills, *Nixon Agonistes: The Crisis of the Self-Made Man* (Boston: Houghton Mifflin, 1970), 2; Shadegg, *Winning's a Lot More Fun*, 123, 131, 134; Chester, Page, and Hodgson, *American Melodrama*, 100; Witcover, *Resurrection of Richard Nixon*, 228, 246, 251.

232 Nixon's New Hampshire campaign opening: Ibid., 232, 245; Shadegg, *Winning's a Lot More Fun*, 131.

233 Nixon market research: Leonard Garment, *Crazy Rhythm: From Brooklyn and Jazz to Nixon's White House, Watergate, and Beyond* (New York: Crown, 1997), 57–58.

233 *"During fourteen years in Washington"*: Witcover, *Resurrection of Richard Nixon*, 232. *They spent hours haggling*: Richard J. Whalen, *Catch the Falling Flag: A Republican's Challenge to His Party* (Boston: Houghton Mifflin, 1972), 77. *"You can't handshake your way"*: Witcover, *Resurrection of Richard Nixon*, 232.

233 *His Concord speech:* Whalen, *Catch the Falling Flag*, 78. *This campaign, he promised:* Witcover, *Resurrection of Richard Nixon*, 245.

233 Mike Douglas and Roger Ailes: Garment, *Crazy Rhythm*, 128–32; Joe McGinniss, *The Selling of the President* (New York: Penguin, 1970), 59–60; "Mommy's Boy," *Time*, October 6, 1967.

234 Harry Treleaven: McGinniss, *Selling of the President*, 134–37; Garment, *Crazy Rhythm*, 131–33. George H. W. Bush memo: McGinniss, 39–40.

235 *"We're going to build this whole campaign":* Ibid., 81.

235 Romney and Vietnam: "Romney Terms War in Vietnam His Key Issue in New Hampshire," NYT, February 16, 1968; "Romney Grabbing the Peace Issue," NYT, February 22, 1968. *Jules Witcover thought:* Witcover, *Resurrection of Richard Nixon*, 228.

235 *NIXON'S THE ONE:* Chester, Page, and Hodgson, *American Melodrama*, 81. Nixon Vietnam speeches: "Nixon Cheered After First '68 Swing," NYT, February 11, 1968; "Nixon Developing a Vietnam Stand," NYT, February 14, 1968.

236 *He got the world's attention:* Witcover, *Resurrection of Richard Nixon*, 257.

236 Dirty tricks against Romney: "A Troublesome Day," NYT, February 17, 1968; Ryan Hayes interview.

236 Romney withdrawal: Shadegg, *Winning's a Lot More Fun*, 132; Witcover, *Resurrection of Richard Nixon*, 246. *"Rockefeller Could Open a Campaign":* NYT, February 29, 1968.

236 *"I take no pleasure, no gratification":* "Rockefeller Is Urged by Nixon to Make Race in the Primaries," NYT, March 1, 1968.

237 Hughes Commission and responses: Ron Porambo, *No Cause for Indictment: An Autopsy of Newark* (New York: Holt, 1971; republished in 2007 by Melville House), 27; NYT, February 11, 1968. Hughes Commission responses: NYT, February 14, 1968. Anthony Imperiale: *Bergen County Record*, February 15, 1968; Porambo, *No Cause for Indictment*, 201.

237 Dunn corruption: Ibid., 30.

237 Orangeburg massacre: NYT, February 16, 1968. *International Association of Chiefs of Police convention:* Garry Wills, *The Second Civil War: Arming for Armageddon* (New York: New American Library, 1968), 17. *The army laid stockpiles:* NYT, February 17, 1968. *Riotville:* Michael Flamm, *Law and Order: Street Crime, Civil Unrest, and the Crisis of Liberalism in the 1960s* (New York: Columbia University Press, 2005), 118; NYT, March 22, 1968. *The White House seriously countenanced:* Flamm, *Law and Order*, 120. *A book went on sale:* Ibid., 101, 228.

238 *On February 17, five thousand militants:* Hugh Pearson, *Shadow of a Panther: Huey Newton and the Price of Black Power in America* (New York: Addison-Wesley, 1994), 152.

238 *An ancient concept from the common law:* Bob Greene, *Running* (Chicago: Regnery, 1973), 73; David Farber, *Chicago '68* (Chicago: University of Chicago Press, 1988), 134; NYT, February 14, 17, 1968; March 1, 1968.

238 New York garbage strike: Vincent J. Cannato, *The Ungovernable City: John Lindsay and the Battle to Save New York* (New York: Basic Books, 2003), 196–201. *A sort of hippie street gang:* Osha Neumann, "Motherfuckers Then and Now: My Sixties Problem," in Marcy Darnovsky, Barbara Epstein, and Richard Flacks, eds., *Cultural Politics and Social Movements* (Philadelphia: Temple University Press, 1995), 55–73.

238 *But Gallup released a poll:* Scammon and Wattenberg, *Real Majority*, 37. Wallace petition signatures: Chester, Page, and Hodgson, *American Melodrama*, 287. Fraternal Order of Police endorsement: Farber, *Chicago '68*, 130.

239 Kerner Commission: Cannato, *Ungovernable City,* 204–7; Flamm, *Law and Order,* 104–7.

239 *"H. Rap Brown amendment":* Anthony Lukas, *The Barnyard Epithet and Other Obscenities: Notes on the Chicago Trial* (New York: HarperCollins, 1970), 4; Farber, *Chicago '68,* 147; NYT, March 1, 2, 6, 7, 9, 15, 24, 28, 30, 1968; *Congressional Record* 114, pt. 4 (March 5, 1968).

240 *The president was aghast:* Flamm, *Law and Order,* 109–10.

240 Economic status of whites: Carter, *Politics of Rage,* 348; Christian Appy, *Working-Class War: American Combat Soldiers and Vietnam* (Chapel Hill: University of North Carolina Press, 1993), 45. *"Come back when you have":* Ibid. *"The ordinary white American":* Whalen, *Catch the Falling Flag,* 46. The *"blind demagogs":* Farber, *Chicago '68,* 138.

240 *A correspondent with the* Milwaukee Journal: Helen Weber, *Summer Mockery: Civil Arrest Study 336* (Milwaukee, WI: Aestas Press, 1986), 46. *In a fifteen-city poll:* Chester, Page, and Hodgson, *American Melodrama,* 36. *"I'd give up my life if necessary":* Barry Edwards, "Why Negroes Should Boycott Whitey's Olympics," *Saturday Evening Post,* March 9, 1968. *A white letter-writer: Saturday Evening Post,* April 20, 1968.

240 *Garry Wills had written:* Wills, *Second Civil War,* 22.

241 *"We have been amply warned":* "Nixon Would Use Force in the Cities," NYT, March 8, 1968.

241 Howard Hughes endorsement: Howard Kohn, "Strange Bedfellows," *Rolling Stone,* May 20, 1976.

241 *"The people of this country don't like":* Witcover, *Resurrection of Richard Nixon,* 259.

241 *"I am now reassessing":* Ibid., 262.

241 RFK breakfast with reporters: NYT, January 31, 1968; Shesol, *Mutual Contempt,* 412.

242 *Also on the day after New Hampshire:* Shadegg, *Winning's a Lot More Fun,* 137–38. LBJ's nightmare: Dallek, *Flawed Giant,* 528.

242 *"Their insensitivity to the civilian":* Flamm, *Law and Order,* 116. Ohio, New York, Minneapolis, Omaha: NYT, March 15, 1968.

242 *Or, as Governor Buford Ellington put it:* "Guard Riot Test Stirs Tennessee," NYT, March 7, 1968. *Five hundred Tennessee citizens:* NYT, March 8, 1968.

242 *Minority leader Gerald Ford announced:* NYT, March 15, 1968. *Southern governors, ignoring outright:* Allen J. Matusow, *The Unraveling of America: A History of Liberalism in the 1960s* (New York: HarperCollins, 1984), 191. *The California Democratic Council:* Shadegg, *Winning's a Lot More Fun,* 147. King speech: Flamm, *Law and Order,* 114.

243 *"Earlier this week in the East Room":* PPP 141, March 16, 1968.

243 RFK presidential announcement: Shesol, *Mutual Contempt,* 422; Shadegg, *Winning's a Lot More Fun,* 137; Chester, Page, and Hodgson, *American Melodrama,* 125–26.

243 *Allard Lowenstein was enraged:* Ibid., 129. *Among McCarthy supporters, metaphors:* Ibid., 93; Shadegg, *Winning's a Lot More Fun,* 137.

243 *"We expected concentration camps":* Farber, *Chicago '68,* 39. McCarthy and Lord Fauntleroy: *Time,* March 22, 1968.

244 LBJ to National Farm Union: PPP 142, March 18, 1968; Shesol, *Mutual Contempt,* 427.

244 For day-by-day listing of Vietnam deaths, see http://www.viethero.us/Wall/panel.htm.

244 *Perhaps eager for good news:* Seymour Hersh, *My Lai 4: A Report on the Massacre and Its Aftermath* (New York: Random House, 1970), 79. *The official brigade report:* Ibid., 92–102.

244 Richard Goodwin and Seymour Hersh: Shadegg, *Winning's a Lot More Fun,* 143.

244 Nelson Rockefeller after RFK entrance: Ibid., 140; Chester, Page, and Hodgson, *American Melodrama,* 221.

245 *He had a press conference scheduled:* Jules Witcover, *White Knight: The Rise of Spiro Agnew* (New York: Random House, 1972), 3, 198; Chester, Page, and Hodgson, *American Melodrama,* 221.

245 RFK in Nashville, Georgia, Alabama, Kansas: Ibid., 126; Shadegg, *Winning's a Lot More Fun,* 146; Shesol, *Mutual Contempt,* 424–25; Witcover, *Resurrection of Richard Nixon,* 269.

246 For delegate selection process, see Andrew Busch, *Outsiders and Openness in the Presidential Nominating System* (Pittsburgh, University of Pittsburgh Press, 1977), chapter 4.

246 *Bobby Kennedy toured California:* Shadegg, *Winning's a Lot More Fun,* 147–48; Chester, Page, and Hodgson, *American Melodrama,* 129–30, 314; Shesol, *Mutual Contempt,* 425.

247 *According to the Gallup poll:* Ibid., 147–48. McCarthy TV commercials: Chester, Page, and Hodgson, *American Melodrama,* 137. *McCarthy kids were on their way:* Busch, *Outsiders and Openness in the Presidential Nominating System,* 83.

247 *"We need those Polish votes":* Chester, Page, and Hodgson, *American Melodrama,* 135.

247 *"Organize one of those electric guitar":* Shesol, *Mutual Contempt,* 429.

248 *He sent his biggest gun:* Chester, Page, and Hodgson, *American Melodrama,* 8, 137; Barone, *Our Country,* 433.

248 *The president began to look almost demented:* PPP 154, March 25, 1968. LBJ is shown delivering this speech in the Brian De Palma film *Greetings* (1968).

248 Wise Men meeting: Langguth, *Our Vietnam,* 487–92; Shesol, *Mutual Contempt,* 433.

249 Nixon Vietnam radio address discomfort: Witcover, *Resurrection of Richard Nixon,* 274; Kutler, *Wars of Watergate,* 69; Garment, *Crazy Rhythm,* 125; Whalen, *Catch the Falling Flag,* 12, 27. *"Of course they stole the election":* Ibid., 12.

249 *But Reagan supporters dreaming:* Witcover, *Resurrection of Richard Nixon,* 241; Whalen, *Catch the Falling Flag,* 16. *Johnson showed a flash:* PPP 158, March 27, 1968. *"We have permitted the Stokely Carmichaels":* David J. Garrow, *Bearing the Cross: Martin Luther King and the Southern Christian Leadership Conference* (New York: Harper Perennial, 1999), 597. *The president's Gallup approval:* George Gallup, "Johnson's War and Job Ratings Sink," WP, March 31, 1968.

250 Poor People's March and Martin Luther King in Memphis: Garrow, *Bearing the Cross,* 594–619; "A Negro Is Killed in Memphis March," NYT, March 29, 1968; "Dr. King to March in Memphis Again," NYT, March 30, 1968; April 1, 1968; Chester, Page, and Hodgson, *American Melodrama,* 11, 32; Farber, *Chicago '68,* 138.

252 *The president's speech Sunday evening:* PPP 170, March 31, 1968; Dallek, *Flawed Giant,* 510–13; Shadegg, *Winning's a Lot More Fun,* 152; Chester, Page, and Hodgson, *American Melodrama,* 4–7; Shesol, *Mutual Contempt,* 435; Barone, *Our Country,* 434.

252 Key Biscayne: Raymond Price, *With Nixon* (New York: Viking, 1977), 28; Witcover, *Resurrection of Richard Nixon,* 302.

253 Wisconsin Democratic results: Scammon and Wattenberg, *Real Majority,* 93, 108.

253 Milwaukee mayoral race: Interview with David Walther.

253 *Chicago police began carrying:* NYT, March 10, 1968. *James Farmer of CORE:* "CORE Chief Scores Police on Preparations for 'War,'" NYT, March 31, 1968. *In Newark, Anthony Imperiale's: Bergen County Record,* February 15, 1968. *Richard Rovere of the New Yorker:* Wills, *Second Civil War,* 165.

CHAPTER TWELVE: THE SKY'S THE LIMIT

254 King assassination: Taylor Branch, *At Canaan's Edge: America in the King Years, 1965–1968* (New York: Simon & Schuster, 2006), 755–66.

255 *Martin Luther King had always been warning: Chicago's America,* July 22, 1966; *Chicago Sun-Times,* July 22, 1966. *"We can achieve nothing":* PPP 179, April 4, 1968.

256 Washington riots: Lewis Chester, Bruce Page, and Godfrey Hodgson, *American Melodrama: The Presidential Campaign of 1968* (New York: Viking, 1969), 15–16; J. Hoberman, *The Dream Life: Movies, Media, and the Mythology of the Sixties* (New York: New Press, 2003), 196; Michael Flamm, *Law and Order: Street Crime, Civil Unrest, and the Crisis of Liberalism in the 1960s* (New York: Columbia University Press, 2005), 146.

256 *In New York, John Lindsay:* Vincent J. Cannato, *The Ungovernable City: John Lindsay and the Battle to Save New York* (New York: Basic Books, 2003), 210. *"The Lindsay Style": Life,* May 24, 1968.

256 *In Newark, a voice crackled:* Ron Porambo, *No Cause for Indictment: An Autopsy of Newark* (New York: Holt, 1971), 191.

256 Vietnam: Hoberman, *Dream Life,* 196. *On the campus of Cornell:* Donald Alexander Downs, *Cornell '69: Liberalism and the Crisis of the University* (Ithaca: Cornell University Press, 1969), 79.

256 *In Boston, it was the soul singer:* Anthony Lukas, *Common Ground: A Turbulent Decade in the Lives of Three Families* (New York: Random House, 1985), 32–34. *In*

Milwaukee, it was the radical priest: Frank A. Aukofer, *City with a Chance* (Milwaukee: Bruce Publishing Co., 1968), 142; *Milwaukee Journal,* April 15, 1968. *In Indianapolis:* Peter B. Levy, ed., *America in the Sixties—Left, Right, and Center: A Documentary History* (Westport, CT: Praeger, 1998), 230–31.

257 *In Oakland, the patrolling of:* Hugh Pearson, *Shadow of a Panther: Huey Newton and the Price of Black Power in America* (New York: Addison-Wesley, 1994), 154–56.

257 *President Johnson declared April 9:* PPP 180, April 5, 1968. King's funeral and Maddox: Hal Jacobs, "Lester!: The Strange but True Tale of Georgia's Unlikeliest Governor," *Creative Loafing,* March 20, 1999, http://www.southerncurrents.com/misc/maddox.htm.

257 *Ronald Reagan said:* Chester, Page, and Hodgson, *American Melodrama,* 17. Strom Thurmond wrote: Flamm, *Law and Order,* 145.

257 *In Maryland, lowly Spiro Agnew:* Levy, *America in the Sixties,* 97; Dan T. Carter, *The Politics of Rage: George Wallace, the Origin of the New Conservatism, and the Transformation of American Politics* (Baton Rouge: Louisiana State University Press, 1996), 331; Jules Witcover, *White Knight: The Rise of Spiro Agnew* (New York: Random House, 1972), 169–74.

258 *The Oscars ceremony:* Hoberman, *Dream Life,* 196.

258 *The* Chicago Tribune, *in an editorial:* "Day of Mourning," CT, April 9, 1968.

259 Chicago riots: Mike Royko, *Boss: Richard J. Daley of Chicago* (New York: New American Library, 1971), 169; David Farber, *Chicago '68* (Chicago: University of Chicago Press, 1988), 136–45.

259 *Chicago cops were angry:* Ibid., 126–30; Garry Wills, *The Second Civil War: Arming for Armageddon* (New York: New American Library, 1968), 91; William W. Turner, *The Police Establishment* (New York: G. P. Putnam's Sons, 1968), 107–42. *Sixty-four quit that July:* USNWR, October 17, 1966.

259 *In February, special training sessions:* Farber, *Chicago '68,* 134.

260 *The late L.A. police chief:* Ibid., 128. *The crime rate was going up:* Farber, *Chicago '68,* 128. *"The better we do our job":* Ibid. *"police brutality":* Cannato, *Ungovernable City,* 170; "Behind Those 'Police Brutality' Charges," *Reader's Digest,* July 1966 ("the Communists want general public acceptance of the 'police brutality' slogan so they can achieve police disarmament"); *Reader's Digest,* October 1966; Harry Byrd editorial, *Des Moines Register,* July 24, 1966; Wills, *Second Civil War.* Harvard's Seymour Martin Lipset: "Why Cops Hate Liberals—and Vice Versa," in William J. Bopp, ed., *The Police Rebellion: A Quest for Blue Power* (Springfield, IL: Charles H. Thomas, 1971). *In Chicago, two-thirds of cops thought:* Farber, *Chicago '68,* 159. *"Unsung Heroes Invade Terror Ranks":* CT, April 10, 1968.

260 *"Arresting them doesn't":* Ibid., 141. *"White America has declared":* Ibid., 234.

260 *The president accepted Governor Kerner's:* http://www.rfpolice.com/policehistory.htm. *The* Trib *proactively:* "Law and Order First," CT, April 7, 1968.

261 *But the city had hosted:* Farber, *Chicago '68,* 278.

261 *What he sold most of all:* Ibid., 122; Wills, *Second Civil War,* 94.

261 *When Gene McCarthy came:* Farber, *Chicago '68,* 136.

261 Daley "shoot to kill" order and backlash: Farber, *Chicago '68,* 145.

262 *Some kid out of New York:* Michael William Doyle and Peter Braunstein, eds., *Imagine Nation: The American Counterculture of the 1960s and '70s* (New York: Routledge, 2001), 97. *The FBI told the Chicago police's:* Farber, *Chicago '68,* 149.

262 *April 27 "nonviolent peace march":* Ibid., 151.

262 *A University of Chicago junior professor:* Jesse Lemisch interview.

263 *At Nixon's new headquarters:* William Safire, *Before the Fall: An Inside View of the Pre-Watergate White House* (New York: Ballantine, 1977), 38, 49.

263 *The president beseeched the House:* PPP 118, April 5, 1968. *"We've got a civil rights act!":* Safire, *Before the Fall,* 48.

263 Columbia uprising: "56 Columbia Rebels Seized Among 117 at Sit-In Here," NYT, May 19, 1968; Cannato, *Ungovernable City,* 238–58; Joan Morrison and Robert K. Morrison, eds., *From Camelot to Kent State: The Sixties Experience in the Words of Those Who Lived It* (New York: Oxford University Press, 2001), 267–69; Mark Kuranski, *1968: The Year That Rocked the World* (New York: Random House, 2005), 372; Levy, *America in the Sixties,* 213; Hoberman, *Dream Life,* 199.

265 *Richard Nixon added a stanza:* "Nixon Bids Columbia Oust 'Anarchic Students,'" NYT, May 16, 1968.

266 *Ramsey Clark, he lectured:* Stanley Kutler, *The Wars of Watergate: The Last Crisis of Richard Nixon* (New York: W. W. Norton, 1992), 69.

266 *He released a six-thousand-word position paper:* "Nixon Decries 'Lawless Society' and Urges Limited Wiretapping," NYT, May 9, 1968.

266 *A new paperback campaign edition:* Robert F. Kennedy, *To Seek a Newer World* (New York: Bantam, 1968). *Commentators increasingly rhapsodized:* Richard Scammon and Ben Wattenberg, *The Real Majority: An Extraordinary Examination of the American Electorate* (New York: Coward McCann, 1980), 19; Chester, Page, and Hodgson, *American Melodrama,* 138–39; White, *Making of the President 1968,* 216. BOBBY IS GROOVY: Hoberman, *Dream Life,* 195.

266 *Tom Hayden had been one of the:* Cannato, *Ungovernable City,* 238. *Kennedy aides now spent hours:* Chester, Page, and Hodgson, *American Melodrama,* 138–39. *"I knew you'd be the first":* Jules Witcover, *The Making of an Ink-Stained Wretch: Half a Century Pounding the Political Beat* (Baltimore: Johns Hopkins University Press, 2005), 109. YOU PUNK: Ibid.

267 *The last straw might have been:* Hoberman, *Dream Life,* 200. *The liberal who'd said after Watts:* Hoberman, *Dream Life,* 201. *Ronald Reagan said:* Garry Wills, "Waiting for Bobby," *New York Review of Books,* February 10, 2000.

267 *"Where are you going to get all the money":* Witcover, *Making of an Ink-Stained Wretch,* 110.

267 *In 1966 he had enraged the Right:* "Humphrey Warns of Slum Revolts," NYT, July 19, 1966; *Congressional Record* 112, pt. 13 (July 21, 1966), 16,669, Paul Fino speech. *Humphrey photographed with Maddox:* Michael Barone, *Our Country: The Shaping of America from Roosevelt to Reagan* (New York: Free Press, 1990), 439.

267 *"LBJ threw a pair of old shoes":* "The Comedian as Hero," *Time,* December 22, 1967. *"pecker in my pocket":* Joseph Lelyveld, "The Adventures of Arthur," *New York Review of Books,* November 8, 2007.

268 *Richard Nixon had offered William Safire:* Safire, *Before the Fall,* 49. *Then, on April 7:* Robert Dallek, *Flawed Giant: Lyndon Johnson and His Times, 1961–1973* (New York: Oxford University Press, 1999), 545. *"He cries too much":* Michael Drosnin, *Citizen Hughes* (New York: Holt, Rinehart & Winston, 1985), 241. *Rockefeller made his announcement:* NYT, May 1, 1968.

268 *"Gentlemen," his press secretary joked:* Robert Shogan, *Bad News: Where the Press Goes Wrong in the Making of the President* (Chicago: Ivan R. Dee, 2001), 40. *In New Orleans, they got thousands:* F. Clifton White and William J. Gill, *Why Reagan Won* (Washington: Regnery Gateway, 1981), 113.

268 *Rockefeller poll and publicity strategy:* Jules Witcover, *The Resurrection of Richard Nixon* (New York: G. P. Putnam's Sons, 1970), 307.

268 *"In a subtle triangle with Communist China":* John Judis, *Grand Illusions: Critics and Champions of the American Century* (New York: Farrar, Straus & Giroux, 1992), 205. *Henry Kissinger also wooed potential female:* Joseph Persico, *The Imperial Rockefeller: A Biography of Nelson A. Rockefeller* (New York: Simon & Schuster, 1982), 173. *And that Nixon was still:* Witcover, *Resurrection of Richard Nixon,* 319.

269 John Volpe: Shadegg, *Winning's a Lot More Fun,* 167.

269 Indiana results: Barone, *Our Country,* 438; Frederick G. Dutton, *Changing Sources of Power: American Politics in the 1970s* (New York: McGraw-Hill, 1971), 202.

269 *And every time "The Wallace Story":* Carter, *Politics of Rage,* 354. *"They can laugh":* *Saturday Evening Post,* April 20, 1968.

269 *In Michigan, Alabama's first gentleman:* Carter, *Politics of Rage,* 319–20. *"I didn't see any flags":* Porambo, *No Cause for Indictment,* 175.

270 *"While Negro precincts were delivering":* Wills, "Waiting for Bobby." *"Black Power and Backlash":* Flamm, *Law and Order,* 149.

270 *In Gary, Indiana, only 15 percent:* Ibid. *Forty-nine percent of Hoosiers:* Wills, "Waiting for Bobby."

270 Celebrity campaigners: "The Stars Leap into Politics," *Life,* May 10, 1968. *"thinks the American youth belongs to him":* Shadegg, *Winning's a Lot More Fun,* 137.

271 *On May 17, a new antiwar faction:* Tom Wells, *The War Within: America's Battle over Vietnam* (Berkeley: University of California Press, 1994), 263; *Harrisburg Patriot News,* January 2, 1972; "Philip Berrigan, Former Priest and Peace Advocate in the Vietnam War Era, Dies at 79," NYT, December 8, 2002.

271 *"Certain property has no right":* Jeremy Varon, *Bringing the War Home: The Weather Underground, the Red Army Faction, and Revolutionary Violence in the Sixties and Seventies* (Berkeley: University of California Press, 2004), 133. *They had an ally in Richard Cardinal Cushing:* Clayton Fritchey column, *New York Post,* January 24, 1972.

271 *"Senator Kennedy has never discussed individual cases":* Shadegg, *Winning's a Lot More Fun,* 172. *the most violent:* Hoberman, *Dream Life,* 202.

271 *Kennedy attended the Easter Sunday mass:* Barone, *Our Country,* 438. *In a statewide poll, 61 percent:* Wills, "Waiting for Bobby." *"Cordon off the area":* Flamm, *Law and Order,* 150.

272 RFK/McCarthy California debate: Witcover, *Resurrection of Richard Nixon,* 314; Shadegg, *Winning's a Lot More Fun,* 175, 183; Wills, "Waiting for Bobby."

272 *Kennedy's last day was marathon parades:* Witcover, *Making of an Ink-Stained Wretch,* 114.

272 Ambassador Hotel scene: Ibid., 115; Shogan, *Bad News,* 33; Shadegg, *Winning's a Lot More Fun,* 185; Barone, *Our Country,* 440.

CHAPTER THIRTEEN: VIOLENCE

274 *"Has violence become":* Newsweek, June 24, 1968; *Time,* June 21, 1968. *"The country does not work":* J. Hoberman, *The Dream Life: Movies, Media, and the Mythology of the Sixties* (New York: New Press, 2003), 353.

274 *"Life in this society being":* Valerie Solanas, *The SCUM Manifesto* (New York: Verso, 2004).

274 *Truman Capote went on NBC's:* "Ray's Odd Odyssey," *Time,* June 21, 1968. *In a cover essay in* Life: Hoberman, *Dream Life. Said William F. Buckley:* Michael Flamm, *Law and Order: Street Crime, Civil Unrest, and the Crisis of Liberalism in the 1960s* (New York: Columbia University Press, 2005), 153.

275 *The countercultural journalist:* Hunter S. Thompson, *Fear and Loathing on the Campaign Trail '72* (New York: Popular Library, 1973), 140.

275 Thomas Kuchel versus Max Rafferty: USNWR, November 28, 1967; "The California Textbook Fight," *Atlantic Monthly,* November 1967; "Max Rafferty: Gadfly on the Rump of Education," *Atlantic Monthly,* December 1967; John Hope Franklin, *Mirror to America: The Autobiography of John Hope Franklin* (New York: Farrar, Straus & Giroux, 2005), 230; "Max Rafferty Is Not a Mad Messiah of the Right—He Is More Disturbing Than That," NYTM, September 1, 1968; obituary of David Shaw, LAT, August 2, 2005; Leon Panetta interview; Nixon to Reagan, June 14, 1966, and "RMN call Sandy Quinn," June 16, 1966, RNLB, 501.1; Sandy Quinn to Rose Mary Woods, RNLB, 501.1.1–10; "Suggested for Senator Kuchel" and accompanying documents, October 1966, RNLB 501.1.8; Evans and Novak column, WP, June 11, 1966.

277 *An intellectually ambitious memo:* Robert Mason, *Richard Nixon and the Quest for a New Majority* (Chapel Hill: University of North Carolina Press, 2004), 48.

277 *Nixon groped toward giving:* William Safire, *Before the Fall: An Inside View of the Pre-Watergate White House* (New York: Ballantine, 1977), 49.

278 *This story of a "silenced" majority: The Green Berets* (Ray Kelly and John Wayne, dir., 1968); Hoberman, *Dream Life,* 145, 207–9.

278 Enemy atrocities in news reports": Daniel C. Hallen, *The "Uncensored" War: The Media and the Vietnam War* (New York: Oxford University Press, 1986), 155. *Her review was the subject of a peroration:* Peter B. Levy, ed., *America in the Sixties—Left, Right, and Center: A Documentary History* (Westport, CT: Praeger, 1998), 193.

279 *"one Dr. Spock is more dangerous":* Thomas Maier, *Dr. Spock: An American Life* (New York: Basic Books, 2003), 294. Boston 5 trial: Tom Wells, *The War Within: America's Battle over Vietnam* (Berkeley: University of California Press, 1994), 233–34, 269, 308.

280 *On May 13, 112 Americans died:* http://www.viethero.us/Wall/panel.htm. *An American delegation in Paris:* Hoberman, *Dream Life,* 202. *The next week, students overran Paris:* Ibid.; Jane Fonda, *My Life So Far* (New York: Random House, 2005), 200.

280 Marcuse: *Herbert's Hippopotamus* (dir. Paul Alexander Juutilainen, 1996), http://www.marcuse.org/herbert/soundvideo/herbhippo.htm.

281 *"Is Dr. Spock to Blame?":* Newsweek, September 23, 1968.

281 *Like the parents, for example:* Steven V. Roberts, "Leader of S.D.S. Unit: From New Jersey Suburb to the Picket Lines," NYT, May 19, 1968.

281 *"Ron honestly believes":* Lou Cannon, *Governor Reagan: His Rise to Power* (New York: Public Affairs, 2005), 259.

281 *His governorship was floundering:* Ibid., 179–200. *Meanwhile a cabal of aides:* Ibid., 238–51. *"Can anyone tell me":* Ibid., 228.

282 *Nixon did it twice:* F. Clifton White and William J. Gill, *Why Reagan Won* (Washington: Regnery Gateway, 1981), 85.

282 *White explained it to Reagan:* F. Clifton White, *Politics as a Noble Calling: The Memoirs of F. Clifton White* (Ottawa, IL: Jameson Books, 1994).

283 *So he went back on the road:* Jules Witcover, *The Resurrection of Richard Nixon* (New York: G. P. Putnam's Sons, 1970), 306.

283 Nixon in Atlanta: Jack Bass and Marilyn Thompson, *Ol' Strom: An Unauthorized Biography of Strom Thurmond* (Atlanta: Longstreet Press, 1998), 224; Arjen Westerhoff, "Politics of Protest: Strom Thurmond and the Development of the Republican Southern Strategy, 1948–1972" (M.A. thesis, American Studies Program, Smith College, 1991); White and Gill, *Why Reagan Won,* 108; Harry Dent, *The Prodigal South Returns to Power* (New York: Wiley, 1978); Witcover, *Resurrection of Richard Nixon,* 309; Stanley Kutler, *The Wars of Watergate: The Last Crisis of Richard Nixon* (New York: W. W. Norton, 1992), 64.

283 *A unanimous Supreme Court decision: Green v. County School Board of New Kent County,* 391 U.S.430.

284 *Senator Thurmond had just released:* Bass and Thompson, *Ol' Strom,* 210.

285 *"From what I've read":* Witcover, *Resurrection of Richard Nixon,* 320.

285 Abe Fortas confirmation hearings: Laura Kalman, *Abe Fortas: A Biography* (New Haven: Yale University Press, 1990), 338–54.

288 *"In an age in which the* Playboy *philosophy":* Levy, ed., *America in the Sixties;* Beth Bailey, "Sexual Revolution(s)," in David Farber, ed., *The Sixties: From Memory to History* (Chapel Hill: University of North Carolina Press, 1994), 235–62.

289 *"Where law and order stops":* Maier, *Dr. Spock,* 315.

289 *The first insisted they were neither:* David Farber, *Chicago '68* (Chicago: University of Chicago Press, 1988), 1–6.

289 *Rubin was from Cincinnati:* Anthony Lukas, *Don't Shoot—We Are Your Children!* (New York: Random House, 1971), 322–69.

290 *Which was precisely their point:* Michael William Doyle, "Staging the Revolution: Guerrilla Theater as a Countercultural Practice, 1965–68," in Peter Braunstein and Doyle, eds., *Imagine Nation: The American Counterculture of the 1960s and '70s* (New York: Routledge, 2001), 71–97. *New Left journalist Robert Scheer:* Hoberman, *Dream Life,* 205–6. *"Those who grew up before the 1950s":* Farber, *Chicago '68,* 220. *"You need three hundred pages":* Ibid., 215–16.

290 *"We will create our own reality":* Ibid., 17.

290 *In New York, the Lindsay administration:* Vincent J. Cannato, *The Ungovernable City: John Lindsay and the Battle to Save New York* (New York: Basic Books, 2003), 221.

291 *They hosted a "Yip-in":* Farber, *Chicago '68,* 30–32.

291 *The other faction:* Farber, *Chicago '68,* 71–101.

292 *A third faction:* Ibid., 101–10.

292 *The City of Chicago:* Ibid., 122, 157, 146.

293 Cleveland ambush: "The Overshadowing Issue," *Time,* August 2, 1968; "This One Was Planned," Ibid.

294 New York firemen: Connato, *Ungovernable City,* 138.

294 *"Outside of the visible return":* Carter, *Politics of Rage,* 334.

294 *The National Governors' Conference: Time,* "The Overshadowing Issue." *Dick, How can I:* Shadegg, *Winning's a Lot More Fun,* 196. *Lester Maddox bumped:* Witcover, *Resurrection of Richard Nixon,* 323.

CHAPTER FOURTEEN:
FROM MIAMI TO THE SIEGE OF CHICAGO

295 Miami riots: http://digital.library.miami.edu/gov/MiamiReport.html. *"That could have been me talking": Miami Herald,* April 18, 1968.

295 *"Can It Happen Again?": Newsweek,* July 22, 1968.

295 *"We must reject the idea":* F. Clifton White and William J. Gill, *Why Reagan Won*

(Washington: Regnery Gateway, 1981), 118; Jules Witcover, *The Resurrection of Richard Nixon* (New York: G. P. Putnam's Sons, 1970), 338.

295 *John Lindsay testified:* Ibid., 326–27. Nixon in Montauk: Ibid., 327.

295 *Monday morning, August 5:* "Debray: A Jail Interview," NYT, August 5, 1968; "Nixon Said to Want Rockefeller, Lindsay, or Percy for 2d Place," NYT, August 5, 1968.

296 *"a few secret kingmakers in New York":* Phyllis Schlafly, *A Choice, Not an Echo* (Alton, IL: Pere Marquette Press, 1964). *"The double cross is on":* Jack Bass and Marilyn Thompson, *Ol' Strom: An Unauthorized Biography of Strom Thurmond* (Atlanta: Longstreet Press, 1998), 226. *You couldn't turn around without:* Lee Edwards interview.

296 Archbishop of Miami: Republican National Committee, *Official Proceedings of the Republican National Convention.*

296 John Wayne: Ibid.

296 *Nixon's Kevin Phillips:* Joe McGinniss, *The Selling of the President* (New York: Penguin, 1970), 123.

296 *At 4 p.m., Reagan returned:* White and Gill, *Why Reagan Won*, 117.

296 Reaction to Reagan announcement: Bass and Thompson, *Ol' Strom*, 226; Stephen C. Shadegg, *Winning's a Lot More Fun* (New York: Macmillan, 1969), 200.

297 *The favorite sons:* Witcover, *Resurrection of Richard Nixon*, 342.

297 *Nixon arrived at Miami International:* Ibid., 339.

297 *Nixon forced himself to maintain a smile:* Bass and Thompson, *Ol' Strom*, 225.

297 *Nixon motorcaded:* Witcover, *Resurrection of Richard Nixon*, 340.

297 *At the evening session:* RNC, *Official Proceedings. The action was in the parking lot:* White and Gill, *Why Reagan Won*, 119.

298 *"Ladies and gentlemen, I present to you":* RNC, *Official Proceedings.*

298 *The anchormen in the broadcast booths:* Shadegg, *Winning's a Lot More Fun*, 202.

298 Mitchell, Dent, and Thurmond meeting: Bass and Thompson, *Ol' Strom*, 227.

298 Nixon suite: Witcover, *Resurrection of Richard Nixon*, 341.

298 *the old Wall Street crew found themselves:* Leonard Garment, *Crazy Rhythm: From Brooklyn and Jazz to Nixon's White House, Watergate, and Beyond* (New York: Crown, 1997), 126.

298 *Dent would speak to them first:* Ibid., 344.

299 *Thurmond extracted a promise:* Arjen Westerhoff, "Politics of Protest: Strom Thurmond and the Development of the Republican Southern Strategy, 1948–1972" (M.A. thesis, American Studies Program, Smith College, 1991); Bass and Thompson, *Ol' Strom*, 228.

299 *Tuesday morning's newspapers:* NYT, August 6, 1968; CT, August 6, 1968. *Reagan and Thurmond had a meeting:* White and Gill, *Why Reagan Won*, 123; Bass and Thompson, *Ol' Strom*, 230.

299 *At the second, the* Miami Herald: Witcover, *Resurrection of Richard Nixon*, 342–44.

300 *"War Between the States":* Fawn Brodie, *Richard Nixon: The Shaping of His Character* (New York: W. W Norton, 1981), 256.

300 *An interminable train of Republican congressmen:* "Experts Tutor 7 for TV Speeches," CT, August 7, 1968.

300 *Rockefeller's manager, Leonard Hall:* White and Gill, *Why Reagan Won*, 112.

301 *"We only have one option left":* Ibid., 125.

301 *"Hatfield Veep Pick":* Bass and Thompson, *Ol' Strom*, 230.

301 *The* Herald's *Don Oberdorfer was wandering:* Ibid., 230; White and Gill, *Why Reagan Won*, 126; Don Oberdorfer interview.

301 *Nixon sat far from anyone else:* Witcover, *Resurrection of Richard Nixon*, 347.

301 Delegate totals: RNC, *Official Proceedings.*

301 *In the Reagan trailer, Clif White's:* White and Gill, *Why Reagan Won*, 128.

302 *In New York, an aged liberal:* Robert H. Barnes, *Harry Elmer Barnes as I Knew Him* (Worland, WY: High Plains Publishing Company, 1994), 116.

302 *To choose a running mate:* Jules Witcover, *No Way to Pick a President* (New York: Farrar, Straus & Giroux, 1999), 204.

302 *The first "consultative" meeting:* Witcover, *Resurrection of Richard Nixon*, 352.

302 *Nixon called in the next group:* Ibid., 353.

302 *Nixon went down to the Hilton ballroom:* Ibid., 355.

302 Spiro Agnew biography: Jules Witcover, *White Knight: The Rise of Spiro Agnew* (New York: Random House, 1972); "The Athenian Touch," *Time*, April 7, 1967.

304 *"I stand here":* RNC, *Official Proceedings.*

304 *Pat Buchanan would later write:* Jonathan Schell, *The Time of Illusion* (New York: Alfred A. Knopf, 1975), 279. *Not many people had been watching:* "TV: Politics Fails to Lure Viewers from Adventure," NYT, August 7, 1968.

304 Nixon acceptance speech: PPP (no document number), August 8, 1968.

305 *the serial killer of nurses, Richard Speck:* USNWR, July 25, 1966. *"There is no end to the ghastly":* Ramparts, July 1966. *"The world is sick":* Time, April 7, 1967. See also William Fulbright, "The Price of Empire," esp. section 2, "A Sick Society," http://web.utk.edu/~mfitzge1/docs/374/POE1967.pdf; and "The Great Society Is a Sick Society," NYTM, August 20, 1967. *Three British journalists:* Lewis Chester, Bruce Page, and Godfrey Hodgson, *American Melodrama: The Presidential Campaign of 1968* (New York: Viking, 1969), 286.

306 *Washington Star* on Ramsey Clark: *Reader's Digest,* October 1967.

307 *He told Bill Safire:* Fawn Brodie, *Richard Nixon: The Shaping of His Character* (New York: W. W. Norton, 1981), 117, 457.

307 *William Lynch, Mayor Daley's:* John Schultz, *No One Was Killed: Convention Week, Chicago—August 1968* (Chicago: Big Table Publishing Co., 1989), 4; Adam Cohen and Elizabeth Taylor, *American Pharaoh: Mayor Richard J. Daley: His Battle for Chicago and the Nation* (Boston: Little, Brown, 2000), 75, 469–70. *Mayor Daley's pleased reaction:* "Daley Blasts Supression of Czechs," CT, August 23, 1968; David Farber, *Chicago '68* (Chicago: University of Chicago Press, 1988), 248–49.

307 *"Snake dancing" was a maneuver:* Schultz, *No One Was Killed,* 78; see also the film *Medium Cool* (Haskell Wexler, dir., 1969). *Downtown in Civic Center Plaza:* Lewis Z. Koch interview; Schultz, *No One Was Killed,* 49.

307 *Thursday night at 11 p.m.:* Ibid., 49, 79.

308 *Contentious hearings drew:* Ibid., 32; Theodore H. White, *Making of the President 1968* (New York: Atheneum, 1969), 321.

308 Lester Maddox: Bradley R. Rice, "The 1966 Gubernatorial Elections in Georgia" (Ph.D. diss., University of Southern Mississippi, 1982); Dan T. Carter, *The Politics of Rage: George Wallace, the Origin of the New Conservatism, and the Transformation of American Politics* (Baton Rouge: Louisiana State University Press, 1996), 306; Ryan Hayes interview; CQ *Political Notes,* December 12, 1966. *not with "ax handles," but with "pick handles":* CDN, August 28, 1968. *The regulars—"slow, florid":* Schultz, *No One Was Killed,* 41. *"So now we can't trust":* Ibid., 45.

308 *"We reject as unacceptable":* White, *Making of the President 1968,* 323. *This war had consumed:* Kathleen Hall Jamieson, *Packaging the Presidency: A History and Criticism of Presidential Campaign Advertising,* 3rd ed. (New York: Oxford University Press, 1996), 221.

309 McGovern 1968 presidential run: Robert Sam Anson, *McGovern: A Biography* (New York: Holt, Rinehart, and Winston, 1972), 186–212. *"I was looking around":* Steinem interviewed in documentary *One Bright Shining Moment* (Stephen Vittoria, dir., 2005).

309 *His proposal was radical:* Anson, *McGovern,* 166.

309 *"Have you ever written a book":* Schultz, *No One Was Killed.*

310 *It was what Richard Nixon:* "Nixon Bids Johnson Apologize to GOP for 'Vicious' Attack," NYT, October 15, 1966.

310 *"Why are you here?":* Schultz, *No One Was Killed,* 68. *Ralph Yarborough, the liberal Texas:* Ibid.

310 *Saturday night, Yippies:* Ibid., 79. *Yippies drove a flatbed truck:* Ibid., 81.

310 *Eugene McCarthy arrived:* Ibid., 71; White, *Making of the President 1968,* 71.

311 *Southern delegates kept alive:* Ibid., 327; Farber, *Chicago '68,* 136. *Polls showed Humphrey:* White, *Making of the President 1968,* 326.

311 *Sunday morning:* Seymour Hersh, "The Secret Arsenal," NYTM, August 25, 1968.

311 Time *ran a picture:* "Daley City Under Siege," Time, August 30, 1968.

311 *Sunday night, at ten forty-five:* Schultz, *No One Was Killed.*

312 *Monday morning, the Chicago police:* Ibid., 76, 94, 131.

312 *The way was flecked:* White, *Making of the President 1968,* 328. *City workers had removed:* Farber, *Chicago '68,* 159. *The* Evergreen Review: Schultz, *No One Was Killed.*

312 *The convention floor accommodated:* White, *Making of the President 1968,* 318. *Aretha Franklin belted out:* Ibid., 323. *"Throw them out!":* Ibid., 329; Schultz, *No One Was Killed,* 126. *Concessionaires were instructed:* Theodore H. White, *The Making of the*

President 1972 (New York: Atheneum, 1973), 19. *In the park, a cop car:* Schultz, *No One Was Killed,* 111.

313 *Then, the retaliation:* Ibid., 120–21, 140. *The liberal* Chicago Daily News: Ibid., 123.

313 *The California delegation was pledged:* Anson, *McGovern,* 205.

313 *California and New York were strongest:* White, *Making of the President 1968,* 318; White, *Making of the President 1972,* 19. *In Lincoln Park, as word passed:* Schultz, *No One Was Killed,* 139. *"We even heard":* Ibid., 136.

313 *At about 7 p.m. on Tuesday:* Daniel Walker et al., *Rights in Conflict: The Violent Confrontation of Demonstrators and Police in the Parks and Streets of Chicago During the Week of the Democratic National Convention of 1968* (New York: Bantam Books, 1968), 186–87. *Police spies recorded:* Anthony Lukas, *The Barnyard Epithet and Other Obscenities: Notes on the Chicago Trial* (New York: HarperCollins, 1970), 23.

314 *At eleven, a phalanx of clergymen:* Schultz, *No One Was Killed,* 143.

314 *At the amphitheater, the day's chaos:* White, *Making of the President 1968,* 333.

314 *The* Chicago Daily News *ran a picture:* CDN, August 28, 1968.

314 *"In the darkness and confusion":* NBC coverage, viewed at Museum of Broadcast Communications, Chicago, Illinois.

CHAPTER FIFTEEN: WEDNESDAY, AUGUST 28, 1968

315 This chapter is drawn from viewing videotapes of NBC's full coverage of the Democratic National Convention, August 28, 1968, in the offices of the Museum of Television and Radio, Chicago, Illinois.

CHAPTER SIXTEEN: WINNING

328 *After Chicago, Humphrey:* "Will HHH Come in Third?" *Newsweek,* September 23, 1968.

328 Chicago police raid on McCarthy headquarters: David Farber, *Chicago '68* (Chicago: University of Chicago Press, 1988), 201. *"We ought to quit pretending":* Letters, *Newsweek,* September 9, 1968. *"Nothing would bring the real peaceniks":* Theodore H. White, *Making of the President 1968* (New York: Atheneum, 1969), 317.

329 *"I am not going to barricade myself":* Joe McGinniss, *The Selling of the President* (New York: Penguin, 1970), 62. *He began his general election: Newsweek,* September 23, 1968.

329 *Bob Haldeman had it game-planned:* Jules Witcover and Jack Germond, *Whose Broad Stripes and Bright Stars?: The Trivial Pursuit of the Presidency, 1988* (New York: Warner Books, 1989), 55; Jules Witcover, *No Way to Pick a President* (New York: Farrar, Straus & Giroux, 1999), 55; Robert Shogan, *Bad News: Where the Press Goes Wrong in the Making of the President* (Chicago: Ivan R. Dee, 2001), 40.

329 Nixon's briefing book: Jeffrey Bell, "The Candidate and the Briefing Book," *Weekly Standard,* February 5, 2001. *With Prussian efficiency:* Dan T. Carter, *The Politics of Rage: George Wallace, the Origin of the New Conservatism, and the Transformation of American Politics* (Baton Rouge: Louisiana State University Press, 1996), 333. *Even the elephant:* Shogan, *Bad News,* 55.

329 *"three-bump interviews":* Stanley Kutler, *The Wars of Watergate: The Last Crisis of Richard Nixon* (New York: W. W. Norton, 1992), 70. *"astounded torpor":* Lewis Chester, Bruce Page, and Godfrey Hodgson, *American Melodrama: The Presidential Campaign of 1968* (New York: Viking, 1969), 689. *Humphrey's biggest financial backer:* Interview with Molly Ivins.

329 *"He moved easily": Newsweek,* September 23, 1968.

330 Nixon TV panel shows: McGinniss, *Selling of the President,* 58–73.

330 *In Charlotte, North Carolina:* Kathleen Hall Jamieson, *Dirty Politics: Deception, Distraction, and Democracy* (New York: Oxford University Press, 1993), 214.

332 *"he's a bore, a pain in the ass":* McGinniss, *Selling of the President,* 103–4. McLuhan excerpts: Ibid., 90–96.

333 *"Sock it to me?!":* Elizabeth Kolbert, "Stooping to Conquer," *New Yorker,* April 19, 2004.

333 *Nixon's TV spots were groundbreaking:* McGinniss, *Selling of the President,* 81–121. See Nixon's 1968 commercials at http://livingroomcandidate.movingimage.us/.

334 *NBC, with its flagship evening news show:* Farber, *Chicago '68,* 251; McGinniss, *Selling of the President,* 50; Lewis Z. Koch interview.

335 *"The truth was, these were our children":* "In the Nation: The Question at Chicago," NYT, September 1, 1968. *"In Chicago," Stewart Alsop wrote:* Godfrey Hodgson, *America in Our Time: From World War II to Nixon—What Happened and Why* (Garden City, NY: Doubleday, 1976), 372. *telegram to Mayor Daley:* Ibid.

335 Editorial on the International Amphitheatre: CDN, August 23, 1968. *National Rifle Association:* CDN, August 29, 1968. *"the closer one gets to the campus scene":* CDN, August 28, 1968. *They turned their letters section over:* CDN, September 4, 1968.

336 *Hard-nosed Chicago newsmen:* Lewis Z. Koch interview.

336 *Mayor Daley proclaimed:* Farber, *Chicago '68,* 252. WE SUPPORT MAYOR DALEY: Hodgson, *America in Our Time,* 373. Letters to City Hall: CDN, September 6, 1968.

336 *"Perhaps he had been called":* Hodgson, *America in Our Time,* 273.

337 *The editor of the* Chicago Daily News: Ibid.

337 Jack Mabley: Chester, Page, and Hodgson, *American Melodrama,* 594.

337 *"They had been united":* Hodgson, *America in Our Time,* 273.

337 *Frank Shakespeare fantasized aloud:* McGinniss, *Selling of the President,* 59–60. *Nixon gave a speech on his conception:* Kutler, *Wars of Watergate,* 131. Walter Lippmann, Kenneth Crawford, Joseph Kraft: Jonathan Schell, *The Time of Illusion* (New York: Alfred A. Knopf, 1975), 20. Theodore White: Richard Reeves, *President Nixon: Alone in the White House* (New York: Simon & Schuster, 2001), 21. Norman Mailer: Kutler, *Wars of Watergate,* 67.

338 *A Nixon campaign commercial:* http://livingroomcandidate.movingimage.us/.

339 *New York's new Panthers:* Michael Newton, *Bitter Grain: Huey Newton and the Black Panther Party* (Los Angeles: Holloway House, 1980), 173–77. *Four days later J. Edgar Hoover:* Ward Churchill and Jim Vander Wall, eds., *The Cointelpro Papers: Documents from the FBI's Secret War Against Dissent* (Boston: South End Press, 2002), 123. *On September 10, Huey Newton:* Hugh Pearson, *Shadow of a Panther: Huey Newton and the Price of Black Power in America* (New York: Addison-Wesley, 1994), 168. *The next day, Berkeley:* Ibid., 169.

339 *In Detroit and Ann Arbor, Michigan:* Jeff A. Hale, "The White Panthers' 'Total Assault on the Culture,'" in Peter Braunstein and Michael William Doyle, eds., *Imagine Nation: The American Counterculture of the 1960s and '70s* (New York: Routledge, 2001), 124–56.

339 *In July and August, a group of right-wing:* "Japanese Agency in City Is Bombed," NYT, July 8, 1968; "Police Unit Hunts Bomb Suppliers; Acts After 8th Blast Rocks Midtown Foreign Offices," NYT, July 11, 1968; "4 Travel Agencies and Shell Offices Bombed on Coast," NYT, July 20, 1968; "Bookshop Bombed in Union Square," NYT, July 22, 1968; "Bomb Explodes at Grove Press," NYT, July 27, 1968; "3 Cubans Hunted in Coast Bombing," NYT, August 1, 1968; "Japanese Bank in Waldorf Bombed," NYT, August 4, 1968. *On August 13, state troopers:* "Arms Linked to Anti-Castroites Found on a North Jersey Farm," NYT, August 14, 1968. *Eleven days later, in Connecticut:* "Pacifists at Connecticut Farm Consider Leaving After Minutemen's Attack," NYT, August 26, 1968.

340 *A Harris poll:* Frederick G. Dutton, *Changing Sources of Power: American Politics in the 1970s* (New York: McGraw-Hill, 1971), 22; Richard Scammon and Ben Wattenberg, *The Real Majority: An Extraordinary Examination of the American Electorate* (New York: Coward McCann, 1980), 96.

340 *Labor Day weekend in Atlantic City:* Alice Echols, *Daring to Be Bad: Radical Feminism in America, 1967–1975* (Minneapolis: University of Minnesota Press, 1989), 93.

340 *"We need some meanness":* Dutton, *Changing Sources of Power,* 96. *"Never again will you read":* Carter, *Politics of Rage,* 365–66. *A North Carolina political analyst:* Newsweek, September 23, 1968.

341 *"Now let's get serious a minute":* Carter, *Politics of Rage,* 362. *Wallace's aides met some of their organizers:* Ibid., 342. *News crews started bringing:* Ibid., 362.

341 Wallace in Newark: Ron Porambo, *No Cause for Indictment: An Autopsy of Newark* (New York: Holt, 1971), 272. *In Columbia, Illinois:* Interview with David Roediger. The AFL-CIO and Chicago steelworker polls: Carter, *Politics of Rage,* 352.

341 *"Nixon is just like the national Democrats":* Ibid., 334.

341 *Warning Southerners off Wallace consumed:* McGinniss, *Selling of the President,* chapter 10.

342 Thurmond Speaks for Nixon-Agnew Committee: Jack Bass and Marilyn Thompson,

Ol' Strom: An Unauthorized Biography of Strom Thurmond (Atlanta: Longstreet Press, 1998), 232; Arjen Westerhoff, "Politics of Protest: Strom Thurmond and the Development of the Republican Southern Strategy, 1948–1972" (M.A. thesis, American Studies Program, Smith College, 1991).

342 *Humphrey had a Southern strategy:* Kathleen Hall Jamieson, *Packaging the Presidency: A History and Criticism of Presidential Campaign Advertising,* 3rd ed. (New York: Oxford University Press, 1996), 232.

342 *Elsewhere, the commercials:* http://livingroomcandidate.movingimage.us.

343 *First, in 1967:* William Martin, *Prophet with Honor: The Bill Graham Story* (New York: Harper Perennial, 1992), 354. *Graham seated him in the VIP:* Kutler, *Wars of Watergate,* 72. *Shortly before Election Day:* Martin, *Prophet with Honor,* 354. *Graham, Nixon's research showed:* McGinniss, *Selling of the President,* 124.

343 *That supposed nullity, Spiro Agnew:* Carter, *Politics of Rage,* 332. *Time* on Muskie: "Remember Maine," September 24, 1954; "Humphrey's Polish Yankee," September 6, 1968. *Late in September, Muskie:* Carter, *Politics of Rage,* 351.

343 *The* Washington Post *called it:* "Muskie—from Jeers to Cheers," WP, September 26, 1968.

344 *Agnew's gaffes:* Jules Witcover, *White Knight: The Rise of Spiro Agnew* (New York: Random House, 1972), 3, 198; Chester, Page, and Hodgson, *American Melodrama,* 718. Lindsay on Agnew: McGinniss, *Selling of the President,* 55. Humphrey Agnew commercial: Jamieson, *Packaging the Presidency,* 237.

344 *Agnew called Humphrey "soft":* "Will HHH Come in Third?" *Newsweek,* September 23, 1968.

344 *"Senator Thurmond Speaks for Nixon-Agnew" commercials:* Carter, *Politics of Rage,* 363; Reg Weaver and Hal Gulliver, *The Southern Strategy* (New York: Scribner, 1971), 1; Bass and Thompson, *Ol' Strom,* 232.

345 *Hubert Humphrey phoned Lyndon Johnson:* United States Department of State, *Foreign Relations, 1964–1968, Volume VII, Vietnam, September 1968–January 1969,* Document 39, http://www.state.gov/r/pa/ho/frus/johnsonlb/vii/21591.htm.

345 Johnson conversation with Nixon: Ibid., Document 38.

346 *Nixon already had it on secret authority:* Christopher Hitchens, *The Trial of Henry Kissinger* (New York: Verso, 2001), 6–18.

346 *Even more important were the atmospherics:* Jamieson, *Packaging the Presidency,* 239.

346 *On October 9, he ran an ad:* Ibid., 252. *Another ad showed Nixon:* Ibid., 242.

346 IF YOU MEAN IT: Ibid., 240. *Humphrey started rising in the polls:* Stephen C. Shadegg, *Winning's a Lot More Fun* (New York: Macmillan, 1969), 3.

347 Humphrey campaign funding crisis: Jamieson, *Packaging the Presidency,* 234.

347 Wallace running-mate deliberations: Carter, *Politics of Rage,* 355.

348 Bunker Hunt and "rainy day" fund: Ibid., 336.

348 LeMay press conference: Ibid., 357–60.

349 *on the ballot in all fifty states:* Michael Barone, *Our Country: The Shaping of America from Roosevelt to Reagan* (New York: Free Press, 1990), 734. *Socialist Labor Party v. Rhodes:* http://supreme.justia.com/us/393/23/case.html.

349 *In his last campaign, in 1962:* Fawn Brodie, *Richard Nixon: The Shaping of His Character* (New York: W. W. Norton, 1981), 457–58; Frank S. Jonas, *Political Dynamiting* (Salt Lake City: University of Utah Press, 1970), 233.

349 *A heckler shouted, "Humphrey!":* Schell, *Time of Illusion,* 21. *As for HHH himself:* Ibid.

349 *Then, Nixon joined Agnew:* Ibid. *The campaign monitored crime figures:* McGinniss, *Selling of the President,* 11; Jamieson, *Packaging the Presidency,* 11. VOTE LIKE YOUR WHOLE LIFE DEPENDED ON IT: Ibid., 275; Shadegg, *Winning's a Lot More Fun,* 3; McGinniss, *Selling of the President,* 49.

351 *Election Day:* White, *Making of the President 1968.*

354 *Max Rafferty's loss:* David Shaw obituary, LAT, August 2, 2005.

CHAPTER SEVENTEEN: THE FIRST ONE HUNDRED DAYS

357 Inauguration scene: WP, January 21, 1969. *"The disjointedness":* Garry Wills, *Nixon Agonistes: The Crisis of the Self-Made Man* (Boston: Houghton Mifflin, 1970), 13.

357 Inauguration speech: PPP 1, January 20, 1969.

358 *Afterward, the Justice Department's:* Richard Reeves, *President Nixon: Alone in the White House* (New York: Simon & Schuster, 2001), 14.

358 *"There are no more innocent bystanders":* "Police Drive Back 400 Demonstrators at a Coast College," NYT, December 6, 1969. *Or East St. Louis:* Julius Lester, *Revolutionary Notes* (New York: Grove Press, 1970), 195.

358 *"counterinaugural":* Jonathan Schell, *The Time of Illusion* (New York: Alfred A. Knopf, 1975), 25; Hunter S. Thompson, *The Great Shark Hunt: Strange Tales from a Strange Time* (New York: Popular Library, 1977); Hunter S. Thompson, *Fear and Loathing on the Campaign Trail '72* (New York: Popular Library, 1973), 86.

359 Praise from columnists: Schell, *Time of Illusion,* 27; "Dr. Allen Goes to Washington," NYT, February 9, 1969; Joseph Kraft, "Winding Down; Lowering of Sights and Easier Tempers Mark Onset of New Administration," WP, January 19, 1969.

359 *Nixon introduced his new cabinet:* Schell, *Time of Illusion,* 23. *"Truth will become the hallmark":* Ibid., 24. *Evans and Novak said:* Ibid.

359 *Urban Affairs Council:* Reeves, *President Nixon,* 31. *"He knows that if his administration":* "New Bipartisan Era?" WP, November 16, 1969. Overseas trip and press conference: Schell, *Time of Illusion,* 31; Reeves, *President Nixon,* 55.

360 Each day a chance: Ibid., 124. *A briefing paper came:* Ibid., 57. BRING US TOGETHER: Stanley Kutler, *The Wars of Watergate: The Last Crisis of Richard Nixon* (New York: W. W. Norton, 1992), 73.

360 *"Keep them away":* Reeves, *President Nixon,* 71. *"I want everyone fired":* Ibid, 36.

360 Press secretary/communications director: Kutler, *Wars of Watergate,* 162. First Committee on Economic Policy meeting: Reeves, *President Nixon,* 32–33.

361 First press conference and year-round polling: Ibid., 34. Not concerned by Press: Ibid., 36.

361 *"Men don't really like soup":* Ibid., 61.

361 *At his first economics gathering:* Ibid., 78–79.

361 Ron Ziegler: Thompson, *Fear and Loathing,* 400; Kutler, *Wars of Watergate,* 162; "Ronald L. Ziegler, Press Secretary to President Nixon, Is Dead at 63," NYT, February 12, 2003. Honolulu landscaping: Reeves, *President Nixon,* 192.

362 Naps: Reeves, *President Nixon,* 30. *"John Quincy Adams and Grover Cleveland":* Ibid., 31.

362 *"To: Mrs. Nixon":* Ibid., 28.

362 *Operation Menu:* Ibid., 58–59; Schell, *Time of Illusion,* 32.

362 *"Nothing should happen in the South":* Reeves, *President Nixon,* 117.

362 *"Berlin Wall":* Kutler, *Wars of Watergate,* 81; *"Your appointment is over":* Ibid., 71.

363 *"I still have not had any progress report":* Reeves, *President Nixon,* 37.

363 *"Nixon Network":* Tom Wells, *The War Within: America's Battle over Vietnam* (Berkeley: University of California Press, 1994), 632; "Nixon Hoped Antitrust Threat Would Sway Network Coverage," WP, December 1, 1997; *Smothered: The Censorship Struggles of the Smothers Brothers Comedy Hour* (dir. Maureen Muldaur, 2002).

363 *A press aide, Jim Keogh:* Reeves, *President Nixon,* 40.

363 *The first news summary:* Ibid., 28. *District of Columbia Court Reorganization Bill:* Schell, *Time of Illusion,* 44.

364 *"Freedom—intellectual freedom":* PPP 122, March 22, 1969.

364 *"For the boys at the top of their class":* PPP 117, March 19, 1969. *"Beginning on or about April 12, 1968":* http://www.law.umkc.edu/faculty/projects/ftrials/Chicago7/indictment.html.

365 *Eight Chicago cops were also indicted:* CT, March 23, June 12, June 14, December 4, December 5, December 6, December 19, 1969.

365 *"The crisis is nationwide":* "Who Defends the University," NYT, March 12, 1969.

365 Joseph Kraft column: Godfrey Hodgson, *America in Our Time: From World War II to Nixon—What Happened and Why* (Garden City, NY: Doubleday, 1976), 371–73; Joseph Kraft, "Daley and Police Have a Point in Claiming Press Is Biased," WP, September 3, 1968.

366 Stewart Alsop and Senator Ribicoff: Robert W. Merry, *Taking on the World: Joseph and Stewart Alsop—Guardians of the American Century* (New York: Viking, 1996), 473–74.

366 *"The blue- and white-collar people":* Barbara Ehrenreich, *Fear of Falling: The Inner Life of the Middle Class* (New York: HarperPerennial, 1990), 99–100.

366 *"The Revolt of the White Lower Middle Class":* Jefferson Cowie, "Nixon's Class Strug-

gle: Romancing the New-Right Worker, 1969–1973," *Labor History* 43 (Summer 2002): 257–83.

367 *Robert Shad Northshield:* Mark R. Rasmuson, "Huntley and Brinkley Boss: Reporting Chicago or Abusing It?" *Harvard Crimson*, December 10, 1968, http://www.the crimson.com/article.aspx?ref=105240.

367 *A University of Chicago sociology professor:* Interview with Richard Flacks; *Chicago Daily News*, May 6, 1969; "An SDS Founder Beaten in Chicago," NYT, May 7, 1969.

367 *On the president's one hundredth day:* "Guard Is Ordered to Town in Illinois to Quell Disorders," NYT, April 30, 1969. *"Either the administrators":* "Revolutionary Adventurism," NYT, May 8, 1969.

367 *"We can, of course":* Bruce Oudes, ed., *From: The President: Richard Nixon's Secret Files* (New York: HarperCollins, 1989), 23.

368 *The first foreign policy crisis:* Reeves, *President Nixon*, 68–70; PPP 156, April 18, 1969.

368 My account of Nixon and Kissinger's relationship is drawn from, and deeply indebted to, the chapter on the subject in John Judis, *Grand Illusions: Critics and Champions of the American Century* (New York: Farrar, Straus & Giroux, 1992), 190–224.

368 *Kissinger was glad to oblige:* Wells, *War Within*, 289.

370 *Kissinger was even on the record:* Anthony Lukas, *Nightmare: The Underside of the Nixon Years* (New York: Viking, 1976), 46.

371 *"When Nelson buys a Picasso":* Joseph Persico, *The Imperial Rockefeller: A Biography of Nelson A. Rockefeller* (New York: Simon & Schuster, 1982), 72.

371 *National Security Decision Memo 2:* Reeves, *President Nixon*, 26.

371 *Blunt Helen Thomas:* PPP 10, January 27, 1969.

371 Senator McGovern and Kissinger: Robert Brent Toplin, ed., *Oliver Stone's USA: Film, History, and Controversy* (Lawrence: University Press of Kansas, 2000), 209.

371 *"I'd rather not comment on that":* Merry, *Taking on the World*, 475–76.

372 *On February 21, Kissinger:* Nina Tannewald, "Nuclear Weapons and the Vietnam War," *Journal of Strategic Studies* 29 (August 2006).

372 *The president's second press conference:* PPP 98, March 4, 1969. *"Public pressure over the war":* "Vietnam Dilemma," NYT, March 8, 1969.

CHAPTER EIGHTEEN: TRUST

373 *"Common sense should tell us":* "Vietnam Pullout Urged as Senators Resume Debate," NYT, May 2, 1969, 1. Bombing in Cambodia: "Raids in Cambodia by U.S. Unprotested," NYT, May 9, 1969, 1.

373 *"The time is approaching":* PPP 195, May 14, 1969. Nixon on "mutual withdrawal" in 1966: Jules Witcover, *The Resurrection of Richard Nixon* (New York: G. P. Putnam's Sons, 1970), 195; Herbert S. Parmet, *Richard Nixon and His America* (New York: Little, Brown, 1969), 491. *Columnists vied with each other:* Robert W. Merry, *Taking on the World: Joseph and Stewart Alsop—Guardians of the American Century* (New York: Penguin, 1996), 482. *Gallup was about to announce:* "Nixon Approved by 64% in Survey," NYT, May 18, 1969.

373 *"Outrageous! Outrageous!":* Richard Reeves, *President Nixon: Alone in the White House* (New York: Simon & Schuster, 2001), 75.

373 On the roots of Kissinger's rage and origins of phone taps: Ibid., 44–47.

374 On Caulfield: Ibid., 13; Reeves, *President Nixon*, 67, 75–76. On Kraft bugging see Lukas, *Nightmare*, 64–65.

374 Cornell uprising: Donald Alexander Downs, *Cornell '69: Liberalism and the Crisis of the University* (Ithaca: Cornell University Press, 1969).

378 *New Statesman*, Alistair Cooke, Beijing: Reeves, *President Nixon*, 73. See also "Yale Has Been Spared Campus Strife, but Some Administrators Are Nervous," NYT, April 20, 1969, p. 74.

378 Fortune *magazine had built: Fortune,* January, 1969.

379 *James J. Kilpatrick coined the phrase:* Frederick G. Dutton, *Changing Sources of Power: American Politics in the 1970s* (New York: McGraw-Hill, 1971), 80. Stanford protests: W. Glenn Campbell, *The Competition of Ideas: How My Colleagues and I Built the Hoover Institution* (Ottawa: Jameson Books, 2001), 139–46; "Student Protest Ends at Stanford," NYT, May 2, 1969. Kent State: James Michener, *Kent State: What Happened and Why* (New York: Random House, 1971), 104. Harvard: Winifred Breines and

Alexander Bloom, eds., *Taking It to the Streets: A Sixties Reader* (New York: Oxford University Press, 1995), 75; "Harvard Ponders Students' Strike," NYT, April 20, 1969, 75.

379	*On April 19 the New York Police:* "A How-to Guide for Protesters Covers Fighting of Policemen," NYT, April 20, 1969, 76. *On April 21 four hundred students:* "Seizure of Building by 400 at Queensborough College Precedes Protest Move," NYT, April 22, 1969, 1. *On April 23, one hundred students:* "Student Unrest in Brief," NYT, April 24, 1969, 1; "Some Faculty Members Join a Sit-in at Fordham," NYT, April 24, 1969, 35. *twelve hundred students:* "Yeshiva U. Cancels Classes as Students Mark Israeli Day," NYT, April 24, 1969, 35. *At Columbia:* "Columbia Rebels Leave," NYT, May 2, 1969, 1.

380	*Something else happened at Queens College:* "Vandals Roam at Queens," NYT, May 2, 1969, 1.

380	*The University of Buffalo nearly shut down:* "Yale Has Been Spared Campus Strife," NYT, April 20, 1969, 74; see also article republished from 1977 issue of the *Catalyst,* http://www.buffalonian.com/history/articles/1951-now/1960santiwar/powellbuff1965 to1976.html.

380	*"The hypnotically erotic":* March 3, 1969, *Miami Herald* review quoted at http://www .doors.com/miami/one.html. Cincinnati decency rally: "Ohio Rally Draws 10,000," NYT, April 21, 1969, 34. Baltimore decency rally: "Youth Decency Rally Turns into Melee," NYT, April 21, 1969, 34.

381	*"The freshmen are more radical":* Reeves, *President Nixon,* 72. Radical high schools in NYC and New Jersey: "Schools in City Shut by Protests," NYT, April 22, 1969, 38. Jerry Rubin in Cincinnati: Anthony Lukas, *Don't Shoot—We Are Your Children!* (New York: Random House, 1971), 322–25. *By May, three of five administrators:* Godfrey Hodgson, *America in Our Time: From World War II to Nixon—What Happened and Why* (New York: Doubleday, 1976), 364. *Two sympathetic teachers:* Mark Libarle and Tom Seligman, eds., *The High School Revolutionaries* (New York: Random House, 1970).

381	*"Che Guevara is thirteen years old":* Jack Newfield, *Bread and Roses, Too* (New York: Dutton, 1971), 130.

381	*Doctor Zhivago:* H. R. Haldeman, *The Haldeman Diaries: Inside the Nixon White House* (New York: G. P. Putnam's Sons, 1994), 52. *Richard Kleindienst imagined a time:* Newfield, *Bread and Roses, Too,* 139. *William Rehnquist . . . called them the "new barbarians":* http://www-stu.calvin.edu/chimes/2001.05.04/perspectives/story05.shtml.

381	*McCarthy campaign veterans:* David Mixner, *Stranger Among Friends* (New York: Bantam, 1996), 74–76.

381	*A month later, Kissinger and Ehrlichman:* Tom Wells, *The War Within: America's Battle over Vietnam* (Berkeley: University of California Press, 1994), 294.

382	*On May 15 the president:* Reeves, *President Nixon,* 82; Stanley Kutler, *The Wars of Watergate: The Last Crisis of Richard Nixon* (New York: W. W. Norton, 1992), 142. Endgame of the Fortas nomination: Laura Kalman, *Abe Fortas: A Biography* (New Haven: Yale University Press, 1990), 345–55; Marc Stein, "Did the FBI Try to Blackmail Supreme Court Justice Abe Fortas?" History News Network, July 18, 2005, hnn.us/articles/13170.html.

383	Theodore Hesburgh: "Notre Dame Gives Warning; Hesburgh Threatens Ousters," NYT, February 18, 1969, 1.

383	*On January 5, 1969, Reagan:* Lou Cannon, *Governor Reagan: His Rise to Power* (New York: Public Affairs, 2005), 291. *On January 15, down in San Diego: Herbert's Hippopotamus,* (dir. Paul Alexander Juutilainen, 1996). *the Santa Barbara campus announced:* Author interview with Richard Flacks. *Then San Diego student: Herbert's Hippopotamus.* *"I'll sleep well tonight":* Cannon, *Governor Reagan,* 291.

383	*In Berkeley, the university had:* Main source for Berkeley riot is "The Battle of People's Park," *Rolling Stone,* June 14, 1969, online at http://www.beauty-reality.com/travel/ travel/sanFran/peoplespark3.html.

385	*Perhaps some premeds had read: Today's Health,* May 1969.

385	*The fifth day of the seventeen-day: Herbert's Hippopotamus.*

386	Warren Burger speech: Kutler, *Wars of Watergate,* 143; USNWR, June 29, 1969.

386	The John Lennon/Al Capp encounter is captured in the documentary *John and Yoko's Year of Peace* (Canadian Broadcast Corporation, 2000).

387	Hamburger Hill: Colonel Harry G. Summers Jr., "Battle for Hamburger Hill During the Vietnam War," *Vietnam* magazine, http://www.historynet.com/magazines/vietnam /3031001.html.

387 *"There is no more time for considering"*: Robert Sam Anson, *McGovern: A Biography* (New York: Holt, Rinehart, and Winston, 1972), 168–69.

387 Kennedy reaction: Summers, "Battle for Hamburger Hill."

387 *"Son of Kennedy Congress Winner"*: Chris Matthews, *Kennedy and Nixon: The Rivalry That Shaped Postwar America* (New York: Free Press, 1997), 41.

388 *"The cabinet officers should fill"*: Reeves, *President Nixon*, 33. Berlin and "Battle Hymn of the Republic": Ibid., 33, 51.

388 *When Gallup did its monthly poll:* George Gallup, *The Gallup Poll*, Vol. 3 (Wilmington, DE: Scholarly Resources), 2194. *On March 26, Nixon approved:* Reeves, *President Nixon*, 67.

388 *Congressman Jerry Ford thought Haldeman:* Yanek Mieczkowski, *Gerald Ford and the Challenges of the 1970s* (Lexington: University of Kentucky Press, 1006), 57. *Nixon scrawled an order:* Reeves, *President Nixon*, 57.

389 *One day Nixon raged:* Ibid., 84. *Three days later Hedrick Smith:* "U.S. Battle Losses Stir Nixon Aides," NYT, May 23, 1969, 1. *The reporter with the best:* Reeves, *President Nixon*, 90.

389 *By the end of the school year:* Wells, *War Within*, 297–99. *West Virginia passed a law:* "The Legislatures React," *Time*, June 13, 1969.

389 *"I feel at home here"*: PPP 224, June 3, 1969.

390 Tap on Hedrick Smith: Reeves, *President Nixon*, 86.

390 *"From the people who brought you Vietnam"*: "Muting the Message: Advertising Is Subject to Stricter Censorship than Editorial," WSJ, May 21, 1969, 1.

390 *"It is open season on the armed forces"*: PPP 225, June 4, 1969.

391 *"It sounded like the old Nixon"*: Max Frankel, "Nixon and Critics," NYT, June 8, 1969, E1. Time *reported, "A few of his own staff"*: "Defending the Defenders," *Time*, June 13, 1969. *"On an urgent basis"*: Reeves, *President Nixon*, 87.

391 *He jetted off to Midway Island:* Ibid.; Wells, *War Within*, 326; Jonathan Schell, *The Time of Illusion* (New York: Alfred A. Knopf, 1975), 50; William Burr and Jeffrey Kimball, "Nixon's Nuclear Ploy," *Bulletin of the Atomic Scientists* 59, no. 1 (January/February 2003). Time *put him on the cover: Time,* May 30, 1969. *At his next press conference:* Reeves, *President Nixon*, 91; PPP 248, June 19, 1969.

392 McGovern reform commission in Chicago: "Plea for 'Soft-Stand' by McGovern Is Refused by Daley," CT, June 8, 1969; "McGovern and Daley Open Old Wounds," WP, June 8, 1969.

392 Evans and Novak: "McGovern-Daley Clash Spotlights Civil War Raging Among Democrats," WP, June 11, 1969, A27.

393 *"building outhouses in Peoria"*: Reeves, *President Nixon*, 33. *"I've always thought the country could run itself"*: Ibid., 43.

393 *A growing state was seen:* Rick Perlstein, *Before the Storm: Barry Goldwater and the Unmaking of the American Consensus* (New York: Hill & Wang, 2001), 5. Galbraith: "Nationalize Arms Contractors, Galbraith Tells Congressmen," CT, June 4, 1969.

393 *Gallup, in its January polling:* Gallup, *Gallup Poll*, 2177.

393 *An article in* Time *in February 1967:* "Beyond LSD," *Time*, February 10, 1969. *"Houseboat Summit"*: Peter B. Levy, ed., *America in the Sixties—Left, Right, and Center: A Documentary History* (Westport, CT: Praeger, 1998), 179–82. See, for instance, Robert Theobold, ed., *The Guaranteed Income: Next Step in Economic Evolution?* (Garden City, NJ: Doubleday, 1966); Marc Pilisuk and Robert Perrucci, eds., *The Triple Revolution: Social Problems in Depth* (Boston: Little, Brown, 1968).

394 *Milton Friedman, in the 1962 book:* Milton Friedman, *Capitalism and Freedom* (Chicago: University of Chicago Press, 1962).

394 *"Wipe them out"*: Reeves, *President Nixon*, 100.

394 Moynihan profile: Adam Clymer, "Daniel Patrick Moynihan Is Dead; Senator from Academia Was 76," NYT, March 27, 2003, 1; Allen J. Matusow, *The Unraveling of America: A History of Liberalism in the 1960s* (New York: HarperCollins, 1984), 194–98; Reeves, *President Nixon*, 44–46; Kutler, *Wars of Watergate*, 91; Thomas Byrne Edsall and Mary Edsall, *Chain Reaction: The Impact of Race, Rights, and Taxes on American Politics* (New York: W. W. Norton, 1991), 53–55; interview with Kevin Phillips.

394 *Then in a head-turning 1967 speech:* "The Politics of Stability," *New Leader*, October 9, 1967; Leonard Garment, *Crazy Rhythm: From Brooklyn and Jazz to Nixon's White*

House, Watergate, and Beyond (New York: Crown, 1997), 123–24; Richard J. Whalen, *Catch the Falling Flag: A Republican's Challenge to His Party* (Boston: Houghton Mifflin, 1972), 38–45; "Darts to the Heart," *Time*, October 6, 1967.

395 *In his employment interview:* Reeves, *President Nixon*, 45.

396 *"A third of a century of centralizing power":* PPP 324, "Address to the Nation on Domestic Programs," August 8, 1969.

396 For analysis of the Family Assistance Program see "Toward a Working Welfare System," *Time*, August 15, 1969.

396 Lindsay quote: Ibid. Time *gave the president:* "Moving Ahead, Nixon Style," *Time*, August 15, 1969.

396 *He even revised the chart:* Reeves, *President Nixon*, 124. *"RN is riding high":* Ibid., 108.

CHAPTER NINETEEN: IF GOLD RUST

397 Chappaquiddick: *Time*, July 25, August 1, 8, 15, 22, 29, September 5, 1969, October 31, 1969; *Richmond News Leader*, July 21, 24, 25, 26, 1969; CT, August 1, 1969.

397 *Bill Safire warned him:* Richard Reeves, *President Nixon: Alone in the White House* (New York: Simon & Schuster, 2001), 101.

398 *The White House's on-staff private eye:* Anthony Lukas, *Nightmare: The Underside of the Nixon Years* (New York: Viking, 1976), 15–16; Stanley Kutler, *The Wars of Watergate: The Last Crisis of Richard Nixon* (New York: W. W. Norton, 1992), 103.

399 Network speech: "Kennedy's Television Statement to the People of Massachusetts," NYT, July 26, 1969.

400 Al Capp running for Senate: *Esquire*, November 1970. *Middle America—or at least:* CT, August 1, 1969.

400 Steven V. Roberts on Tate-Polanski circle: Steven V. Roberts, *Eureka* (New York: Quadrangle/New York Times Books, 1974), 223–27.

401 Woodstock origins: http://www.yasgurroad.com/howwoodstock1.html.

401 *And what* Time *seemed especially eager:* "The Message of History's Biggest Happening," *Time*, August 29, 1969.

402 Yippie tent at Woodstock: Jeremy Varon, *Bringing the War Home: The Weather Underground, the Red Army Faction, and Revolutionary Violence in the Sixties and Seventies* (Berkeley: University of California Press, 2004), 131.

403 Time's *sister publication*, Life: September 6, 1969.

403 *"I am willing to state unequivocally":* Reeves, *President Nixon*, 120. *J. Edgar Hoover released a public letter:* Regularly broadcast on Technicolor Web of Sound Web radio station, http://www.techwebsound.com. *Max Ascoli:* Reeves, *President Nixon*, 72.

403 Letters to *Time:* September 12, 19, 1969.

404 Newsweek *tried to grasp:* Reeves, *President Nixon*, 62; "Sex and the Arts," *Newsweek*, April 14, 1969.

404 "Stag nights" and sexual hypocrisy: Eric Schlosser, *Reefer Madness: Sex, Drugs, and Cheap Labor in the American Black Market* (Boston: Houghton Mifflin, 2003), 126–31. *Even* Reader's Digest *reported: Reader's Digest*, February 1967. *Another 1967* Digest: *Reader's Digest*, November 1967. *"Silence is criminal":* "On Teaching Children About Sex," *Time*, June 9, 1967. *"Backwardness is succumbing":* Janice M. Irvine, *Talk About Sex: The Battles over Sex Education in the United States* (Berkeley: University of California Press, 2002), 35.

405 Sherri Finkbine: "Abortion and the Law," *Time*, August 3, 1962; "The Thalidomide Disaster," *Time*, August 10, 1962; "People," *Time*, August 24, 1962; "Thalidomide and Abortion," *Time*, December 21, 1962; "Milestones," *Time*, February 12, 1965; "More Abortions: The Reasons Why," *Time*, September 17, 1965. *In June of 1967 they lamented:* "New Grounds for Abortion," May 5, 1967. *The previous month:* "Freedom from Fear," *Time*, April 7, 1967.

405 *"Could it be possible that* Time": Letters, *Time*, August 17, 1962. *"Abortion is murder":* Letters, *Time*, February 24, 1967. *"The very idea that abortion":* Letters, *Time*, October 20, 1967.

406 Harris poll: "Changing Morality: The Two Americas," *Time*, June 6, 1969.

406 *"scared by the abundance of life":* Vincent J. Cannato, *The Ungovernable City: John Lindsay and the Battle to Save New York* (New York: Basic Books, 2003), 146. *"We're going on a trip together":* Garry Wills, *Nixon Agonistes: The Crisis of the Self-Made*

Man (Boston: Houghton Mifflin, 1970), 8. *"Is Dr. Spock to Blame?":* Newsweek, September 23, 1968. *"prevalent among the educated":* Nation, October 17, 1966.

406 *He made sure every story:* Reeves, *President Nixon,* 62. Onassis and *I Am Curious (Yellow):* "Photographer Says Mrs. Onassis Used Judo on Him," NYT, October 6, 1969. *"P had me in quite a while":* H. R. Haldeman, *The Haldeman Diaries: Inside the Nixon White House* (New York: G. P. Putnam's Sons, 1994), 43. *"The courts have not left society defenseless":* PPP 181, May 2, 1969.

407 My sources for the sexual education controversy and Chicago conference are Irvine, *Talk About Sex,* and Mary Breasted, *Oh! Sex Education!* (New York: Praeger, 1969).

409 *"Dear Dick, I know you don't realize":* "Sex Education Battles Splitting Many Communities Across U.S.," NYT, September 14, 1969.

410 *A September issue of* Look: *Look,* September 9, 1969.

410 California Supreme Court: *People v. Belous,* 458 P.2d 194 (Cal. 1969). *In Netcong, New Jersey:* "Man and Woman of the Year: The Middle Americans," *Time,* January 5, 1970.

CHAPTER TWENTY: THE PRESIDENTIAL OFFENSIVE

412 *Ronald Reagan's administration prepared:* Tolson to DeLoach, July 17, 1969, http://sfgate.com/news/special/pages/2002/campusfiles/documents/6b1.shtml.

412 *Senator Sam Ervin, the North Carolina:* Karl E. Campbell, "Senator Sam Ervin and the Army Spy Scandal of 1970–1971: Balancing National Security and Civil Liberties in a Free Society," Charlotte-Mecklenburg Historic Landmarks Commission, http://www.cmhpf.org/senator%20sam%20ervin.htm.

412 *The Nixon administration tapped:* Stanley Kutler, *The Wars of Watergate: The Last Crisis of Richard Nixon* (New York: W. W. Norton, 1992), 121. *Soon, one thousand undercover:* Christopher H. Pyle, "CONUS Intelligence: The Army Watches Civilian Politics," *Washington Monthly,* January 1970.

412 *On May 14, the attorney general:* Jonathan Schell, *The Time of Illusion* (New York: Alfred A. Knopf, 1975), 59.

413 *"Our insider information":* Tom Wells, *The War Within: America's Battle over Vietnam* (Berkeley: University of California Press, 1994), 311.

413 *When Nixon learned that the IRS:* Stanley Kutler, *Wars of Watergate,* 105, 107. *The IRS's Activist Organizations Committee:* Ibid., 325; Anthony Lukas, *Nightmare: The Underside of the Nixon Years* (New York: Viking, 1976), 22.

413 *The government possessed wiretaps:* Kutler, *Wars of Watergate,* 123. *Lawyers howled that the chief:* Schell, *Time of Illusion,* 38. *The FBI had been saying it since:* David Farber, *Chicago '68* (Chicago: University of Chicago Press, 1988), 110.

413 *Students for a Democratic Society held:* Wells, *War Within,* 303–5. *The Weathermen withdrew:* Peter B. Levy, ed., *America in the Sixties—Left, Right, and Center: A Documentary History* (Westport, CT: Praeger, 1998), 233–38. *In August some met:* Jeremy Varon, *Bringing the War Home: The Weather Underground, the Red Army Faction, and Revolutionary Violence in the Sixties and Seventies* (Berkeley: University of California Press, 2004), 151.

414 *"Those anarchists will be in jail":* Anthony Lukas, *The Barnyard Epithet and Other Obscenities: Notes on the Chicago Trial* (New York: HarperCollins, 1970), 2. Bobby Seale and Charles Garry: *Contempt: Transcript of the Contempt Citations, Sentences, and Responses of the Chicago Conspiracy 10* (Chicago: Swallow Press, 1970), 1–37.

415 *Prosecutor Schlutz began his opening:* John Schultz, *The Chicago Conspiracy Trial* (New York: De Capo Press, 1993), 115.

415 *On October 3, the Chicago police:* "2 Cops Hurt in Disorder," CT, October 4, 1969. *Three days later, out in California:* "The Case of Angela the Red," *Time,* October 17, 1969.

415 *"Days of Rage":* Varon, *Bringing the War Home,* 61–62, 74–83; Lewis Z. Koch interview.

416 *"5 Cops and City Aide Beaten and Bitten by Women Rioters":* CT, October 10, 1969. *"I don't blame the Chicago police":* Varon, *Bringing the War Home,* 83.

416 *"We're not trying to end wars":* Ibid., 108. Other left-wing reactions: Ibid., 85–86.

417 *In June, 47 percent:* Reeves, *President Nixon,* 135.

417 *Clergy and Laymen Concerned About Vietnam:* Wells, *War Within,* 294. *In 1967, in response to student riots:* "Ire Against Fire," *Time,* November 3, 1967. *Now he told the divines:* Wells, *War Within,* 295.

417 *In late August the army announced:* Reeves, *President Nixon,* 127.

417 *In its June 27 issue:* "The Faces of the American Dead in Vietnam: One Week's Toll," *Life,* June 27, 1969. *The next week the Senate:* Kutler, *Wars of Watergate,* 156. *Women Strike for Peace picketed:* Wells, *War Within,* 294. *A book called* Truth Is the First Casualty: *Publishers Weekly,* September 1, 1969, 5. *Another retired marine:* "William Corson, Marine, Author," obituary, LAT, July 24, 2000.

418 *It was the idea of a Boston envelope:* Wells, *War Within,* 328.

418 *The first press release:* David Mixner, *Stranger Among Friends* (New York: Bantam, 1996), 81. *Nixon issued a dictate:* Wells, *War Within,* 349. *That was the conversation starter:* Ibid., 330.

419 *"I call it the madman theory":* Ibid., 290.

419 *"the only time to lose your temper":* Fawn Brodie, *Richard Nixon: The Shaping of His Character* (New York: W. W. Norton, 1981), 48.

419 *Privately, since 1966:* Leonard Garment, *Crazy Rhythm: From Brooklyn and Jazz to Nixon's White House, Watergate, and Beyond* (New York: Crown, 1997), 86.

419 *Hanoi responded to his May 14:* Reeves, *President Nixon,* 80. *In July, via secret channels:* Ibid., 106; Wells, *War Within,* 355. *Publicly, he announced the Nixon Doctrine:* Reeves, *President Nixon,* 104.

419 *Ho Chi Minh, on his deathbed:* William Burr and Jeffrey Kimball, "Nixon's Nuclear Ploy," *Bulletin of the Atomic Scientists,* January/February 2003. *In September the NSC began planning:* Wells, *War Within,* 357. *North Vietnam's dikes protected:* A. J. Langguth, *Our Vietnam: The War, 1954–1975* (New York: Touchstone, 2000), 440, 446; "A Nation Coming into Its Own," *Time,* April 25, 2005. *"I can't believe,"* Henry Kissinger said": Reeves, *Richard Nixon,* 134.

420 *Defense Secretary Laird didn't even know:* Burr and Kimball, "Nixon's Nuclear Ploy." *Some possibilities Nixon shared* : Reeves, *President Nixon,* 135.

420 *Bud Wilkinson:* Wells, *War Within,* 349.

420 *Notre Dame and Michigan presidents:* Ibid., 301, 339.

420 *The* New York Times *printed the testimony:* "Nixon Said to Plan Pullout of 35,000 and Draft Shift," NYT, September 14, 1969.

421 *Presidential Offensive:* Schell, *Time of Illusion,* 67. *The president's approval rating:* Reeves, *President Nixon,* 145. *A Yale professor read a paper:* Reeves, *President Nixon,* 122. Brawls at sociologists' and psychologists' conventions: "Radicals Chide 'Uptight' Sociologists on the Coast," NYT, September 5, 1969; "Radicals Disrupt Psychologists' Parley," NYT, September 2, 1969. *A humiliating book,* The Selling of the President: See *Time* bestseller lists, December 12 and 19, 1969. *The* New York Times *heralded it:* "Nixon TV Adviser on Standby Call," NYT, September 21, 1969.

421 *Then Nixon ordered HEW:* Reeves, *President Nixon,* 119. NAACP ad: "The Blacks: Nixon Doesn't Pierce the Barrier," NYT, September 21, 1969.

421 *"Cool it, Leon!":* Reeves, *President Nixon,* 118.

421 *"Doesn't he understand Nixon promised":* Pete McClosky op-ed, *San Francisco Chronicle,* December 19, 2002.

421 *Nixon announced his replacement:* Reeves, *President Nixon,* 120. *On September 8, flying back:* Ibid., 124.

422 *In San Francisco, slogans:* Ibid. 121. *Back in Washington, he read:* "Kissinger Staff Resignations Show Flaw in Nixon Method," WP, September 16, 1969. *Newsweek, Time,* USNWR: Reeves, *President Nixon,* 134. *David Broder would soon file a column:* "A Risky New American Sport," WP, October 7, 1969.

422 *The president dictated eight memos:* Schell, *Time of Illusion,* 64. *As one of the big syndicated columnists:* Reeves, *President Nixon,* 103.

422 *Senator Birch Bayh (D-Ind.) dug:* Kutler, *Wars of Watergate,* 146. *On Saturday, September 20, Nixon:* Reeves, *President Nixon,* 128–29; Wells, *War Within,* 318, 321, 342.

423 *On September 26 he held his first:* "Nixon Asks U.S. Unity for Peace," WP, September 27, 1969; Reeves, *President Nixon,* 130.

423 *The remark was the next day's:* Wells, *War Within,* 352.

423 Newsweek *reported, "Originally":* Mixner, *Stranger Among Friends,* 91.

423 *America should withdraw, they said:* "Six Rand Experts Support Pullout," NYT, October 9, 1969.

424 *The* New Yorker, *in the issue:* Christian Appy, *Working Class War: American Combat Soldiers and Vietnam* (Chapel Hill: University of North Carolina Press, 1993), 271. *The*

anti-antiwar side fought back: See October 15, 1969, ads in NYT, 28, WP, 23, and LAT, 18.

424　Life *called it "the largest expression":* Jerry Lembcke, *The Spitting Image: Myth, Memory, and the Legacy of Vietnam* (New York: NYU Press, 1998), 45.

424　Moratorium description: Wells, *War Within*, 371–75; Bill Moyers interview; "Anti-Vietnam Views Unite Generations," WP, October 16, 1969; Jack Newfield, *Bread and Roses, Too* (New York: Dutton, 1971), 153; Schell, *Time of Illusion*, 53; Kutler, *Wars of Watergate*, 79.

426　*Charleston, West Virginia's police chief:* Lembcke, *Spitting Image*, 54.

426　*In Blackwood, New Jersey, Craig Badiali:* Eliot Asinof, *Craig and Joan: Two Lives for Peace* (New York: Viking, 1971).

426　*The MIT student newspaper: MIT Tech*, October 21, 1969, http://wwwtech.mit.edu/archives/VOL_089/TECH_V089_S0384_P004.pdf.

426　*The conspiracy to sabotage it:* Wells, *War Within*, 310–13, 350–53, 375. Casey, Nixon, and Council on Foreign Relations: Joseph E. Persico, *Casey: The Lives and Secrets of William J. Casey: From the OSS to the CIA* (New York: Penguin, 1991), 115–25, 126–32. *In September, the Pentagon sent them:* Mary Hershberger, *Jane Fonda's War: A Political Biography of an Antiwar Icon* (New York: New Press, 2005); *Chicago Sun-Times*, February 13–18, 1971.

427　*The vice president demanded the Moratorium's leaders:* Wells, *War Within*, 366.

427　*Jack Caulfield was sent out:* Reeves, *President Nixon*, 134. *Two new White House aides:* Wells, *War Within*, 350. *"How tragic, too, Kennedy's professed":* Letters, *Time*, October 10, 1969. *"only orally":* Bruce Oudes, ed., *From: The President: Richard Nixon's Secret Files* (New York: HarperCollins, 1989), 44–45.

427　*He pledged to "destroy Griffin":* John Anthony Maltese, *The Selling of Supreme Court Nominees* (Baltimore: Johns Hopkins University Press, 1998), 74. *The political wisdom of press-baiting:* "The Fourth Estate: A *Time*–Louis Harris Poll," *Time*, September 5, 1969.

428　*That same day the president:* "Nixon Relieving Hershey as Chief of Draft System," NYT, October 11, 1969. *Randy Dicks had written:* Reeves, *President Nixon*, 137; Wells, *War Within*, 353–54.

428　*On Moratorium Day, the aides recruited:* Ibid., 375.

428　Canceling Duck Hook and nuclear alert: Ibid., 357; Burr and Kimball, "Nixon's Nuclear Ploy."

429　White House "New Mobe" planning: Wells, *War Within*, 379–83.

430　*"Americans are confused and uncertain":* Reeves, *President Nixon*, 138.

430　*He was still sufficiently low:* See, for instance, speeches in John R. Coyne, ed., *The Impudent Snobs: Agnew vs. the Intellectual Establishment* (New Rochelle, NY: Arlington House, 1972), 184–247. *For New Orleans, his speechwriter:* Jules Witcover, *White Knight: The Rise of Spiro Agnew* (New York: Random House, 1972), 304–5.

430　*On October 8 and 11:* Ibid., 302–3.

430　*"Sometimes it appears":* Coyne, ed., *Impudent Snobs*, 248.

431　*Chairman Rogers Morton:* Witcover, *White Knight*, 307.

431　*"Now we have to take the offensive":* Wells, *War Within*, 366.

431　*"Some Americans will die tonight":* "Reagan Endorses Holton, Chides Vietnam Protestors," WP, October 24, 1969.

432　*"I admonish you, sir":* John Schultz, *The Chicago Conspiracy Trial* (New York: De Capo Press, 1993), 60.

432　*Bob Hope said he'd seen Mickey Mouse:* "Agnew: He's Beginning to Emerge as a Figure in His Own Right," NYT, July 13, 1969.

432　*"A little over a week ago":* Witcover, *White Knight*, 308; Coyne, ed., *Impudent Snobs*, 257–61.

433　*The tone was gentle, grandfatherly:* PPP 425, November 3, 1969.

435　*Virginia elected its first Republican:* "Holton, the Brand New Governor," WP, November 5, 1969. *In New Jersey, a Republican:* Jack Newfield, *Bread and Roses, Too* (New York: Dutton, 1971), 187; Robert Mason, *Richard Nixon and the Quest for a New Majority* (Chapel Hill: University of North Carolina Press, 2004), 67.

435　*In the cities mayoral candidates:* Ibid., 68; Richard Scammon and Ben Wattenberg, *The Real Majority: An Extraordinary Examination of the American Electorate* (New York: Coward McCann, 1980), 230. *In New York John Lindsay:* Ibid., 113, 224, 254; Vincent J.

Cannato, *The Ungovernable City: John Lindsay and the Battle to Save New York* (New York: Basic Books, 2003), 389–441; "The Battle for New York," *Time*, October 3, 1969.

436 *Jack Newfield, writing in* Life: Scammon and Wattenberg, *Real Majority*, 244. *Fifty thousand telegrams and thirty thousand letters:* Reeves, *President Nixon*, 145. *In an instant poll:* Ibid., 144.

436 *One betting line:* Newfield, *Bread and Roses*, 156.

436 *Transcripts of network analysts:* James Keogh, *President Nixon and the Press* (New York: Funk & Wagnalls, 1972), 171–91.

437 *The White House was "shotgunning":* Kutler, *Wars of Watergate*, 176; Schell, *Time of Illusion*, 55, 109.

437 *Dean Burch beforehand asked for transcripts:* Reeves, *President Nixon*, 145.

437 *"Let Agnew go after":* Reeves, *President Nixon*, 146.

438 *The idea came together quickly:* Ibid., 147–48; Schell, *Time of Illusion*, 67–68; Barry Goldwater, *Conscience of a Majority* (New York: Prentice Hall, 1970), 170.

438 *"Monday night, a week ago":* Coyne, ed., *Impudent Snobs*, 265–70.

438 *Thomas Jefferson used to lay out:* John Nichols, keynote speech at "Constru(ct)ing the Current: Theorizing Media in a New Millennium" (conference, University of Chicago, May 14, 2004).

439 Cronkite, Stanton, Goodman, Braden, and Mankiewicz responses: Goldwater, *Conscience of a Majority*, 172; Coyne, ed., *Impudent Snobs*, 7–8. *Ambassador Harriman himself said:* "Humphrey Scores Agnew," NYT, November 18, 1969.

440 *Conspicuously absent were:* Reeves, *President Nixon*, 149.

440 New Mobe description: Richard Kleindienst, *Justice: The Memoirs of Attorney General Richard Kleindienst* (Ottawa, IL: Jameson Books, 1985); Wells, *War Within*, 392–95; Varon, *Bringing the War Home*, 116–34.

440 *"gunfire was not only justified":* Editorial, *Washington Star*, June 11, 1970. *Three days earlier:* Varon, *Bringing the War Home*, 117. *"Corporations have made us into insane":* "Letter to *Times* on Bombings Here," NYT, November 12, 1969.

441 *A series of newspaper articles:* James Stuart Olson and Randy Roberts, eds., *My Lai: A Brief History with Documents* (New York: Bedford/St. Martin's, 1998), 413–27; Michal R. Belknap, *The Vietnam War on Trial: The My Lai Massacre and Court-Martial of Lieutenant Calley* (Lawrence: University Press of Kansas, 2002), 117–20.

441 *That night, Spiro Agnew:* Coyne, ed., *Impudent Snobs*, 270–74. *He lied; actually the Times:* "House Leaders Push for Vote Next Week on Pro-Nixon Vietnam Resolution," NYT, November 6, 1969; "House Unit Backs Nixon on Vietnam," NYT, November 7, 1969; "Senators Back Cease-Fire Plea," November 8, 1969; see also "Nixon, in a Visit, Thanks Congress for War Support," NYT, November 14, 1969.

441 *The next Hersh article: Reporting Vietnam: American Journalism 1959–1975* (New York: Library of America, 2000), 413–27.

442 *Senator Ernest "Fritz" Hollings:* Olson and Roberts, eds., *My Lai*, 167.

442 *The senator was contradicted:* Ibid.

442 *"During World War II, Calley":* Interview with Heather Parton.

442 *The New York Times reported:* Olson and Roberts, eds., *My Lai*, 179–81. *A bumper sticker began appearing:* "G.O.P., Aided by Agnew, Surges in South," NYT, December 7, 1969.

442 *The next week the My Lai pictures:* "The Massacre at Mylai [sic]," *Life*, December 5, 1969. *Time's essay began:* "My Lai: An American Tragedy," *Time*, December 5, 1969.

442 *Man-on-the-street interviews began:* Seymour Hersh, *My Lai 4: A Report on the Massacre and Its Aftermath* (New York: Random House, 1970), 150–51.

443 *On December 8 Richard Nixon:* PPP 481, December 8, 1969.

443 *The next day he traveled:* CDN, December 10, 1969; PPP 482, December 9, 1969; "63 Arrsted, 8 Policemen Hurt as 3,000 Protest Nixon's Visit," NYT, December 10, 1969. *"unverified":* Reeves, *President Nixon*, 154.

443 *In Chicago, on December 4:* "Attempted Murder Charge Eyed in Panthers Gun Fight," CT, December 5, 1969.

443 *The murderers, allegedly:* "2 Held, One Sought in Tate Murders," NYT, December 2, 1969; "Grand Jury Votes to Hear Evidence in Tate Slaying," NYT, December 3, 1969. *The Times's California correspondent":* "Suspects in Tate Case Tied to Guru and 'Family,'" NYT, December 3, 1969; "Charlie Manson, Nomadic Guru, Flirted with Crime in a Turbulent Childhood," NYT, December 7, 1969. *The December 19 Life:* "The Love

and Terror Cult," *Life,* December 19, 1969; "Could Your Daughter Kill?" *Los Angeles* magazine, February 1970, cited in *Bust* magazine, fall 2003.

444 *CBS News ran a poll:* Reeves, *President Nixon,* 154. *Fifty-eight percent now said:* Varon, *Bringing the War Home,* 147. *Sixty-nine percent, in a third poll:* Ibid., 150.

CHAPTER TWENTY-ONE: THE POLARIZATION

445 *Six of the eleven top-rated:* "Hope and Glory," *People,* July 31, 2003.

445 *"How about a big cheer":* Nicholas von Hoffman, WP, November 16, 1969.

445 *"Bob wasn't born":* "The Comedian as Hero," *Time,* December 22, 1967.

445 *Bantering with Romy Schneider: Bob Hope: The Vietnam Years, 1967–1969,* vol. 2 (Hope Enterprises, 2004). *"GI's in Vietnam High on Hope's":* NYT, December 23, 1969.

446 *Eighteen million Reader's Digest:* Richard Reeves, *President Nixon: Alone in the White House* (New York: Simon & Schuster, 2001), 160; see ad in January 28, 1969, NYT. *The left-wing folk singer:* http://70.84.59.228/~thepoorm/Flag_Decal.mp3.

446 *The Christmas season's most brilliant:* "Agnew Watches Selling Well, but . . . ," NYT, July 8, 1970. *TV producer Norman Lear would have a new:* Peter N. Carroll, *It Seemed Like Nothing Happened: America in the 1970s* (New Brunswick, NJ: Rutgers University Press, 1990), 61.

447 *This year they made a different:* "Men and Women of the Year: The Middle Americans," *Time,* January 5, 1970.

447 My reconstruction of the Chicago trial is drawn from Anthony Lukas, *The Barnyard Epithet and Other Obscenities: Notes on the Chicago Trial* (New York: HarperCollins, 1970), and John Schultz, *The Chicago Conspiracy Trial* (New York: De Capo Press, 1993), and the transcripts, audio clips, and documents at http://www.law.umkc.edu/faculty/projects/ftrials/Chicago7/chicago7.html.

450 *FUCK THE ———:* Garry Wills, *Under God: Religion and American Politics* (New York: Simon & Schuster, 1991), 291.

452 *It seemed an auspicious:* Lewis Z. Koch interview; Royko Column, *Chicago Sun-Times,* December 9, 1969.

455 *"What did go on in Judge Julius Hoffman's":* Contempt: *Transcript of the Contempt Citations, Sentences, and Responses of the Chicago Conspiracy 10* (Chicago: Swallow Press, 1970), back cover.

456 *The liberal editorialists:* "The Chicago Decision," NYT, February 20, 1970; "And Then There Were Five," WP, February 20, 1970. *Spiro Agnew called it:* Jack Newfield, *Bread and Roses, Too* (New York: Dutton, 1971), 261.

456 My account of the jury deliberations comes from John Schultz's remarkable interviews with jurors in *The Chicago Conspiracy Trial* section entitled "The Struggle for the Soul of the Nation," 263–341.

457 Contempt citations: *Contempt.*

457 *"The blunt, hard fact":* Newfield, *Bread and Roses,* 261. *"We've lost our kids":* Lukas, *Barnyard Epithet,* 32, 85; Schultz, *Chicago Conspiracy Trail,* 135. Rubin and Hayden reactions: *Contempt.*

457 *In Ann Arbor, five thousand students:* Kenneth J. Heineman, *Put Your Bodies Upon the Wheels: Student Revolt in the 1960s* (Chicago: Ivan R. Dee, 2002), 171. *The FBI put a "White Panther":* Jeff A. Hale, "The White Panthers' 'Total Assault on the Culture,'" in Peter Braunstein and Michael William Doyle, eds., *Imagine Nation: The American Counterculture of the 1960s and '70s* (New York: Routledge, 2001), 124–56. *In Madison a student stole:* Reeves, *President Nixon,* 175.

457 *Weatherman Bernardine Dohrn said:* James Michener, *Kent State: What Happened and Why* (New York: Random House, 1971), 91. *On February 17, what appeared to be a copycat crime:* Joe McGinniss, *Fatal Vision* (New York: Random House, 1985). MacDonald himself was convicted for the murder, having made up the "acid is groovy" cover story to conceal his guilt.

457 *In St. Louis, at 2 a.m.:* Washington University summary memo, MIP. *In frigid Buffalo:* Heineman, *Put Your Bodies Upon the Wheels,* 171.

458 *That same day, William Kunstler:* Daniel Haier, "Burning Down the Isla Vista Bank of America," *Daily Nexus,* February 25, 2005.

458 *On March 6 a mysterious explosion: Village Voice,* March 12, 1970; "2d Victim in Blast Is Identified Here," NYT, March 18, 1970.

458 *On March 11 a bomb gashed:* "Maryland Hunts Woman in Blast," NYT, March 12, 1970.
458 *The next night, in Buffalo:* Heineman, *Put Your Bodies Upon the Wheels,* 171.
458 *Three days later Judge Hoffman:* "Judges Hear Graham," WP, March 16, 1970.
458 *In New York City one day:* Reeves, *President Nixon,* 175. *On April 4:* "Reagan 'Blood-bath' Remark Criticized," LAT, April 9, 1970.

CHAPTER TWENTY-TWO: TOURNIQUET

459 Carswell nomination: Richard Reeves, *President Nixon: Alone in the White House* (New York: Simon & Schuster, 2001), 160–63; Jonathan Schell, *The Time of Illusion* (New York: Alfred A. Knopf, 1975), 81.
459 *"Yes, I would":* PPP 20, January 30, 1970.
459 *The Post reported:* "U.S. Lawyer to Testify on Carswell," WP, January 31, 1970. *"Nixon Seeks to Fire":* Reeves, *President Nixon,* 167. *Then he delivered:* "'Deep and Basic' Reversal on Rights," NYT, February 22, 1970.
459 *"Benign neglect" memo:* "'Benign Neglect' on Race Is Proposed by Moynihan," NYT, March 1, 1970.
460 *"We are gravely concerned":* Reeves, *President Nixon,* 171–72.
460 *"Watergate, Where Republicans Gather":* WP, February 25, 1969; "Party Workers Shift to HHH," WP, May 2, 1968. *The president told Haldeman:* Reeves, *President Nixon,* 174.
460 *This was the Nixon who once:* Fawn Brodie, *Richard Nixon: The Shaping of His Character* (New York: W. W. Norton, 1981), 25.
460 *His New Year's message to the nation:* PPP 1, January 1, 1970; Schell, *Time of Illusion,* 78. *He didn't care much:* Reeves, *President Nixon,* 172. *According to polls, environmental:* Ibid., 162. *Since the publication:* Rachel Carson, *Silent Spring* (Boston: Houghton Mifflin, 1962). *Ehrlichman considered himself:* Reeves, *President Nixon,* 160. *So did General Curtis LeMay:* Dan T. Carter, *The Politics of Rage: George Wallace, the Origin of the New Conservatism, and the Transformation of American Politics* (Baton Rouge: Louisiana State University Press, 1996), 376. *Linda Morse, she of the M1:* Anthony Lukas, *The Barnyard Epithet and Other Obscenities: Notes on the Chicago Trial* (New York: HarperCollins, 1970), 83. *Allen Ginsberg said:* Ibid., 30.
461 *The latest edition:* New York: Fawcett Crest, 1970.
461 *He cleared his schedule:* Reeves, *President Nixon,* 160. *"Will you give me a recent report":* Bruce Oudes, ed., *From: The President: Richard Nixon's Secret Files* (New York: HarperCollins, 1989), 86.
461 *"The seventies will be a time":* PPP 9, January 22, 1970.
461 *The New York Times's headline:* NYT, January 23, 1970. *Pundits spoke hopefully:* Schell, *Time of Illusion,* 78.
461 *"The postwar period in international":* PPP 45, February 18, 1970.
462 *The New York Times printed:* Reeves, *President Nixon,* 168.
462 *In his 1965 YAF inaugural address:* In possession of author, from the collection of Jameson Campaign. *In the White House he sometimes:* Stanley Kutler, *The Wars of Watergate: The Last Crisis of Richard Nixon* (New York: W. W. Norton, 1992), 97.
462 *Mark Felt of the FBI:* Bob Woodward, "How Mark Felt Become 'Deep Throat,'" WP, June 2, 2005. *By the sixth month:* Tom Wells, *The War Within: America's Battle over Vietnam* (Berkeley: University of California Press, 1994), 312, 319, 325. *On February 9, the president's:* Oudes, ed., *From: The President,* 96. *He had just quit the company:* "Scavenger Hunt," *Slate,* October 6, 2004, http://www.slate.com/id/2107718/.
462 *Its latest tack was subpoenaing:* Schell, *Time of Illusion,* 79. *As more and more embarrassing evidence:* Yanek Mieczkowski, *Gerald Ford and the Challenges of the 1970s* (Lexington: University Press of Kentucky, 2005), 20.
462 *Another secret bombing campaign:* Reeves, *President Nixon,* 176–77.
463 *March 2 and 3 were busy:* Ibid., 170; Schell, *Time of Illusion,* 84; Kutler, *Wars of Watergate,* 174.
464 *The GOP had a chance:* Reg Weaver and Hal Gulliver, *The Southern Strategy* (New York: Scribner, 1971), 13.
464 *But it had been chartered during:* Ibid., 21–40.
464 *In June, John Mitchell:* Peter N. Carroll, *It Seemed Like Nothing Happened: America in the 1970s* (New Brunswick, NJ: Rutgers University Press, 1990), 45. *"If you people in New York":* Rick Perlstein, *Before the Storm: Barry Goldwater and the Unmaking*

of the American Consensus (New York: Hill & Wang, 2001), 319. *A week later the Justice Department:* Schell, *Time of Illusion*, 39. *The next day was the NAACP's:* Ibid., 41; Reeves, *President Nixon*, 118.

464 Fifth Circuit order and John Stennis: Ibid., 118–19.

465 *The man who replaced him:* Weaver and Gulliver, *Southern Strategy*, 49.

465 *On October 30, 1969, in the middle:* Reeves, *President Nixon*, 141–42; *Alexander v. Holmes County Board of Education*, 396 U.S. 19 (1969).

465 *"Find a good federal judge":* Reeves, *President Nixon*, 160. Carswell nomination fight: Weaver and Gulliver, *Southern Strategy*, 131–50; Reeves, *President Nixon*, 161, 164, 186–87; Kutler, *Wars of Watergate*, 147; USNWR, April 20, 1970.

466 *He pointed out that in 1940:* Weaver and Guliver, *Southern Strategy*, 138.

466 Maddox: Ibid., "The Governor and the Ax Handles," WP, March 3, 1970.

466 *On March 15:* "Nixon Political Aide Intervened on Schools," WP, March 15, 1970.

467 Wallace payoff: Carter, *Politics of Rage*, 388–89.

468 Postal strike: Reeves, *President Nixon*, 181–82.

471 *Nixon penned a letter to William Saxbe:* Schell, *Time of Illusion*, 82; Rowland Evans and Robert Novak, *Nixon in the White House: The Frustration of Power* (New York: Random House, 1971), 166.

472 Economics: Allen J. Matusow, *Nixon's Economy: Booms, Busts, Dollars, and Votes* (Lawrence: University Press of Kansas, 1998), 55–68; Reeves, *President Nixon*, 186, 214.

472 *April 3 and 4 were movie nights:* Mark Feeney, *Nixon at the Movies: A Book About Belief* (Chicago: University of Chicago Press, 2004), 186, 341.

473 *Nixon was in love with pomp:* Oudes, ed., *From: The President*, 94.

473 *During his turn at Oval Office generalship:* H. R. Haldeman, *The Haldeman Diaries: Inside the Nixon White House* (New York: G. P. Putnam's Sons, 1994), 142; Reeves, *President Nixon*, 181.

473 Drew Pearson and Patton: Feeney, *Nixon at the Movies*, 67.

474 *The following Tuesday Nixon ordered:* Reeves, *President Nixon*, 186. *Nixon made a spur-of-the-moment:* Kutler, *Wars of Watergate*, 138; PPP 108, April 9, 1970.

474 *Suddenly, Nixon was on the cover:* "The Carswell Defeat—Nixon's Embattled White House," *Time*, April 20, 1970. *Suddenly three astronauts:* Reeves, *President Nixon*, 188.

474 *A "Harvard man from the suburbs":* "The Burger/Blackmun Court," NYT, December 6, 1970.

475 Justice Douglas impeachment attempt: Laura Kalman, *Abe Fortas: A Biography* (New Haven: Yale University Press, 1990), 374; J. F. terHorst, "Ford Leads Effort to Oust Nixon Supreme Court Picks," *Detroit News*, January 27, 2006.

475 *"The first part of the Yippie program":* James Michener, *Kent State: What Happened and Why* (New York: Random House, 1971), 179.

475 *Complained Ailes in his notes:* Roger E. Ailes to H. R. Haldeman, May 4, 1970, http://www.nixonlibrary.gov/virtuallibrary/documents/donated/050470_ailes.pdf.

475 *Ailes's note: "Someone said":* Ibid. *"I have requested":* PPP 126, April 20, 1970; see also Schell, *Time of Illusion*, 89, and Carroll, *It Seemed Like Nothing Happened*, 11.

476 *The White House had leaked word:* Reeves, *President Nixon*, 193.

476 *"Cut the crap out of my schedule":* Ibid.

CHAPTER TWENTY-THREE: MAYDAY

477 *"Ten days ago, in my report":* PPP 139, April 30, 1970; Jonathan Schell, *The Time of Illusion* (New York: Alfred A. Knopf, 1975), 88.

478 *"We recognize that if we escalate":* "At War with War," *Time*, May 18, 1970.

478 *On April 24, Laird:* Richard Reeves, *President Nixon: Alone in the White House* (New York: Simon & Schuster, 2001), 198–99.

478 *April 25:* Ibid., 200. *"If I decide to do it":* Ibid., 201.

479 *"Fire them all!":* Ibid., 216.

479 May 1 at Kent State: James Michener, *Kent State: What Happened and Why* (New York: Random House, 1971), 12–22.

480 May 1 at Yale: NYT, May 2, 1970. *"New Haven wasn't a weekend thing":* University of Denver Clarion, May 6, 1970, MIP.

481 *A* New York Times *editorial:* "Waste Them," NYT, April 15, 1970, 42.

481 *He had traveled fifty thousand miles:* Seymour Hersh, *My Lai 4: A Report on the Massacre and Its Aftermath* (New York: Random House, 1970).

481 *Nixon's May Day began:* Reeves, *President Nixon,* 209.

482 *The president, impatient, replied:* Ibid.; Tom Wells, *The War Within: America's Battle over Vietnam* (Berkeley: University of California Press, 1994), 422.

482 *Pentagon staffers mobbed the president:* Ibid.; Reeves, *President Nixon,* 208; Wells, *War Within,* 422. Full accounts of the exchange, with extensive quotes, were reported in newspapers including the *New York Times, Washington Post, Los Angeles Times,* and *Chicago Tribune.*

482 *Nixon took another cruise:* Reeves, *President Nixon,* 209–10.

482 *That night, on the strip of taverns:* Michener, *Kent State.*

483 *On Saturday, May 2:* "Allies Drive Ahead in Cambodia," NYT, May 2, 1970. *Secretary of Defense Laird:* Reeves, *President Nixon,* 211. *Bob Hope, the featured attraction:* Michener, *Kent State.*

483 *At that very moment, radicals:* Ibid., 190–98.

484 *"We aren't no cheap tin soldiers":* Ibid., 227.

484 *Perhaps 80 percent:* Christian Appy, *Working Class War: American Combat Soldiers and Vietnam* (Chapel Hill: University of North Carolina Press, 1993), 36.

484 Trucking strike: Ibid., 127–30.

484 *"In North or South Carolina":* Renata Adler, *Canaries in the Mineshaft: Essays on Politics and Media* (New York: St. Martin's Press, 2001), 230.

485 *"I saw an Illinois car":* Michener, *Kent State,* 215. *"A very pretty girl":* Ibid., 350.

485 *"You have enough girls":* Ibid., 253.

485 *"The situation at Kent":* Ibid., 199.

485 Sunday morning at Kent State: Ibid., 254–66.

486 Audio of Governor Rhodes to press online at http://www.democracynow.org/article .pl?sid=05/05/04/1342257 from the documentary *Kent State: The Day the War Came Home,* directed by Chris Triffo.

487 *President Nixon received an urgent:* "At War with War," *Time,* May 18, 1970.

487 Sunday, eleven a.m. until shooting: Michener, *Kent State,* 254–66.

488 *The Dow dropped 3 percent:* Reeves, *President Nixon,* 215.

488 Two Students, Two Guardsmen: Michener, *Kent State,* 429, 435–46.

488 Townspeople's reactions: Ibid., 446–65.

489 *A Gallup poll found:* Reeves, *President Nixon,* 226.

489 *A rumor spread in Kent:* Michener, *Kent State,* 462.

489 *A letter to* Life: Reeves, *President Nixon,* 225.

489 Time *had called the Silent Majority:* "Hitting Close to Home," *Time,* June 5, 1970.

490 *Jane Fonda, the actress:* Jane Fonda, *My Life So Far* (New York: Random House, 2005), 241–42; Mary Hershberger, *Jane Fonda's War: A Political Biography of an Antiwar Icon* (New York: New Press, 2005), 12–13.

490 UC-San Diego self-immolation: *Herbert's Hippopotamus* (dir. Paul Alexander Juuti-lainen, 1996).

490 Student strike statistics: Reeves, *President Nixon,* 214. Boston University: Ibid., 214.

490 Finch, Whittier, and Duke: "At War with War," *Time.*

490 *"The splintered left on the campuses":* "Campus Crisis," WSJ, May 6, 1970, 1. Burnings at Kentucky, Case Western Reserve, Ohio State, Ohio University, Tulane, closing of twenty-seven California campuses: "Student Strike Continues; 441 Schools Shut," *Pace Press,* http://chnm.gmu.edu/hardhats/studentstrike.html. Kentucky, University of Indiana, University of Cincinnati: "College Index" survey and "Urban Research" report, MIP. Miami of Ohio, Carbondale: Strike newsletter, May 12, 1970, MIP. *At Colorado State they torched: CSU Collegian,* May 11, 1970, MIP. Washington University and University in St. Louis: *St. Louis Post-Dispatch,* May 5, 9, 29, 1970; Washington University summary memo, MIP, *University of Denver Clarion,* May 6, 1970. UCLA: Ibid. Syracuse, Macalester College: *University of Denver Clarion,* May 7, 1970. *Austin students were teargassed:* May 8, 1970, Isserman notes, MIP.

491 *A National Strike Information Center at Brandeis:* Strike newsletters, MIP.

491 *A report from Madison, Wisconsin:* Handwritten notes, May 5, 6, 1970, MIP.

491 *A new tactic developed, blocking traffic: University of Denver Clarion,* May 6, 1970; strike newsletter #7. *A National Economic Boycott Committee:* Newsletter #5, MIP. *Quinnipiac College:* Yale strike newspaper, May 13, 1970, MIP. *Northwestern:* Strike

newsletter #7. *NYU demanded $100,000:* NYT, May 8, 1970. *Governors' conference:* Strike newsletter #7, MIP.

491 *On only one out of twenty:* "College Index" survey, MIP. *Grinnell:* "At War with War," *Time.* *Oberlin:* "Student Strike Continues," *Pace Press.* *Princeton:* James Reston, "Never Complain, Never Explain, Never Apologize!" NYT, May 10, 1970. *In New Jersey, even a draft board:* Newsletter #7, MIP.

491 *Emory's president wired:* Sanford S. Atwood to Nixon, Wade Murrah to regents, n.d., Scranton files, Series 12, Box 58, Emory folder, MIP.

492 Woodstock West controversy: *University of Denver Clarion,* May 4, 6, etc., MIP.

492 U.S. Merchant Marine Academy, University of Washington: "Urban Research" report, MIP. University of Buffalo: Strike newsletter #7, MIP. Hobart College: Memo on "Tommy the Traveler," MIP. *Julie Nixon's graduation from Smith:* Wells, *War Within,* 406.

492 *At his May 8 press conference:* PPP 144, May 8, 1970. *"Several small schools in New York":* O'Toole to Loch, staff memo, Series 12, Box 57, Scranton papers, MIP. *Al Capp added a new line:* "Cappital Punishment," *Esquire,* November 1970.

492 *In Silver Spring, Maryland:* Michener, *Kent State,* 479. *"A hefty man in work clothes":* "At War with War," *Time.*

493 *In Albuquerque:* Ibid.; Hershberger, *Jane Fonda's War,* 14; strike newsletter #7, MIP.

493 The account of the hard-hat riots is drawn from George Mason University's Center for History and New Media's extraordinary Web site http://chnm.gmu.edu/hardhats /homepage.html, which allows for a minute-by-minute reconstruction of the event.

495 *Pete Hamill, who had only the previous:* "Hard Hats and Cops," NYP, May 12, 1970.

495 *"I'm doing this because my brother":* "After 'Bloody Friday,' New York Wonders If Wall Street Is Becoming a Battleground," WSJ, May 11, 1970.

495 *A bipartisan group of senators:* "Bipartisan Senate Group Maps a 3-Pronged Antiwar Strategy," NYT, May 9, 1970.

496 *Haverford College moved:* "An Entire College Prepares to Journey to Washington," WSJ, May 6, 1970. *"We can make this system":* "At War with War," *Time.* *"Let us get twenty million signatures":* SANE full-page ad, NYT, May 17, 1970.

496 *One of Ehrlichman's young aides:* John W. Dean, *Blind Ambition: The White House Years* (New York: Simon & Schuster, 1976), 29. *In the basements of government:* Jeremy Varon, *Bringing the War Home: The Weather Underground, the Red Army Faction, and Revolutionary Violence in the Sixties and Seventies* (Berkeley: University of California Press, 2004), 131.

496 *"All we are saying":* "At War with War," *Time.* *"NIXON WOULD LIKE YOU":* Christopher Russell Reaske, ed., *Student Voices on Political Action Culture and the University* (New York: Random House, 1971), 94. *"Hello, bums!":* Hershberger, *Jane Fonda's War,* 14–15. *She gestured to the men:* Fonda, *My Life So Far,* 244. *"My child was not a bum":* Reeves, *President Nixon,* 212; Michener, *Kent State,* 433.

497 *Senator Muskie, the Democratic presidential:* "They Hope Calm Will Help Cause," NYT, May 10, 1970. *"After a nearly sleepless night":* "Dawn at Memorial," WP, May 10, 1970.

497 *His interior secretary, Walter Hickel:* Reeves, *President Nixon,* 215; Schell, *Time of Illusion,* 99. *Paul Harvey, the sentimental radio:* "If the Silent Majority Could Talk What Would It Say," *Esquire,* May 1970; Reeves, *President Nixon,* 216.

497 *"Thinks now the college demonstrators":* H. R. Haldeman, *The Haldeman Diaries: Inside the Nixon White House* (New York: G. P. Putnam's Sons, 1994), 164.

497 Hard hats in New York, San Diego, Buffalo, Pittsburgh: Jefferson Cowie, "Nixon's Class Struggle: Romancing the New-Right Worker, 1969–1973," *Labor History* 43 (Summer 2002): 257–83.

498 *"Obviously more of these":* Ibid. *one hundred thousand marchers on May 20:* "Workers' Woodstock," *Time,* June 1, 1970.

498 Rosow report: Cowie, "Nixon's Class Struggle."

499 *"Every time they burn another":* Robert Mason, *Richard Nixon and the Quest for a New Majority* (Chapel Hill: University of North Carolina Press, 2004), 70.

499 *Peter Brennan, and Thomas Gleason:* Cowie, "Nixon's Class Struggle."

499 *"Patriotic themes":* Ibid.

CHAPTER TWENTY-FOUR: PURITY

500 Nixon and Billy Graham crusade: Garry Wills, "How Nixon Used the Media, Billy Graham, and the Good Lord to Rap with Students at Tennessee University," *Esquire*, September 1970.

503 *Spiro Agnew began the year:* Jules Witcover, *White Knight: The Rise of Spiro Agnew* (New York: Random House, 1972).

504 *"The liberal media have been":* John R. Coyne, ed., *The Impudent Snobs: Agnew vs. the Intellectual Establishment* (New Rochelle, NY: Arlington House, 1972), 284–96; Peter N. Carroll, *It Seemed Like Nothing Happened: America in the 1970s* (New Brunswick, NJ: Rutgers University Press, 1990), 7–8.

504 Agnew kitsch: Barry Goldwater, *Conscience of a Majority* (New York: Prentice Hall, 1970), 165; http://tinyurl.com/22oqa5.

504 *In April he recalled:* Coyne, ed., *Impudent Snobs*, 315–22.

505 *He referred to "the score of students":* Coyne, ed., *Impudent Snobs*, 315–22.

505 *"Spiro Knows Best": Life,* May 8, 1970.

505 *He changed nothing:* Witcover, *White Knight,* 335–40.

505 *A week after the Kent State killings:* "Kent State: Martyrdom That Shook the Country," *Time,* May 18, 1970. *"Vice President Spiro T. Agnew, at his unmuzzled":* Crosby S. Noyes column, *Washington Star,* June 6, 1970. *Four hundred faculty members in Massachusetts:* "Kent State: Martyrdom That Shook the Country." *"Lately, you have been exposed":* Coyne, ed., *Impudent Snobs,* 332–36.

506 *The venom in the address:* "Text of Agnew's Speech Scoring Press," NYT, May 23, 1970.

506 *His claim about Reston:* James Reston, "Never Complain, Never Explain, Never Apologize!" NYT, May 10, 1970.

506 *Hubert Humphrey said of his successor:* Goldwater, *Conscience of a Majority,* 58. *John Ehrlichman responded:* Ibid.

506 *"I do not go along":* Allen J. Matusow, *Nixon's Economy: Booms, Busts, Dollars, and Votes* (Lawrence: University Press of Kansas, 1998), 63; PPP 10, January 27, 1969.

507 *"inflation alerts":* Richard Reeves, *President Nixon: Alone in the White House* (New York: Simon & Schuster, 2001), 265; PPP 192, June 17, 1970.

507 *And that, in a society:* Hunter S. Thompson, *Fear and Loathing on the Campaign Trail '72* (New York: Popular Library, 1973), 39–40, 48; Frederick G. Dutton, *Changing Sources of Power: American Politics in the 1970s* (New York: McGraw-Hill, 1971), 15–16, passim; Republican National Committee, "The 1964 Elections," October 1965 (in author's possession, courtesy of Phil Klinkner).

507 *an idea floating around in liberal circles:* Thomas J. Noer, *Soapy: A Biography of G. Mennen Williams* (Ann Arbor: University of Michigan Press, 2005), 137; "Governor Favors Voting Age of 18," NYT, March 3, 1966. *General Eisenhower had come out:* Eisenhower interview, *Saturday Review,* September 9, 1966. *In 1968* Time *underwrote:* Letters from editor, *Time,* December 15, 1967, May 10, 1968. *That June, LBJ suggested:* Attorney general to Speaker of the House, June 28, 1966, LBJCR, Reel 9.

507 *Kennedy and Mansfield decided to force:* Reeves, *President Nixon,* 225; NYT, May 11, June 5, 18, 20, 21, 22, 23, 1970.

508 *And Al Capp tried:* "Cappital Punishment," *Esquire,* November 1970.

508 *11 million newly eligible voters:* Week in Review, NYT, June 21, 1970. *"We got more cats":* Wild in the Streets (American International Pictures, 1968).

508 *"The increased share of the eligible":* Dutton, *Changing Sources of Power,* 15–16, passim. Martin Peretz: Ibid., 61. Dutton also quoted R. D. Laing: "The texture of the fabric of these socially shared hallucinations is what we call reality, and our collusive madness is what we call sanity."

508 *He said he favored:* Reeves, *President Nixon,* 225.

509 Signing statement: PPP 196, June 22, 1970.

509 Democratic reform process: Byron E. Shafer, *Quiet Revolution: The Struggle for the Democratic Party and the Shaping of Post-Reform Politics* (New York: Russell Sage Foundation, 1983), passim; James I. Lengle, "Democratic Party Reforms: The Past as Prologue to the 1988 Campaign," *Journal of Law and Politics* 4 (Fall 1987): 233–73; Andrew Busch, *Outsiders and Openness in the Presidential Nominating System* (Pittsburgh: University of Pittsburgh Press, 1997), 34–39; David Plotke, "Party Reform as

Failed Democratic Renewal in the United States, 1968–1972," *Studies in American Political Development* 10 (Fall 1996): 223–88.

510 *"Do you know what it's like":* Mark Stricherz, *Why the Democrats Are Blue: Secular Liberalism and the Decline of the People's Party* (New York: Encounter Books, 2007), 88.

513 *"Do not turn away from":* Michael Barone, *Our Country: The Shaping of America from Roosevelt to Reagan* (New York: Free Press, 1990), 429.

513 Debate over guidelines A-1 and A-2: Theodore H. White, *Making of the President 1972* (New York: Atheneum, 1973), 18–26, 38, 374.

514 *The* New York Times *gave the release:* "Democrats Press for Party Reform," NYT, April 30, 1970, 1.

514 *"We aren't going to let these Harvard":* White, *Making of the President 1972,* 38.

514 *Garry Wills, in his* Esquire: "How Nixon Used the Media, Billy Graham, and the Good Lord to Rap with Students at Tennessee University," *Esquire,* September 1970.

514 *One letter came from a twenty-three-year-old marine:* "A Marine Writes His Senator," WP, July 8, 1970. Cranston getting eight thousand letters: Jane Fonda, *My Life So Far* (New York: Random House, 2005), 246.

514 *In July,* Life *published photographs: Life,* July 17, 1970; Mary Hershberger, *Jane Fonda's War: A Political Biography of an Antiwar Icon* (New York: New Press, 2005), 139–44; Carol Burke, *Camp All-America, Hanoi Jane, and the High and Tight: Gender, Folklore, and Changing Military Culture* (Boston: Beacon Press, 2004), 166–67; Don Luce, "We've Been Here Before: The Tiger Cages of Vietnam," April 4, 2005, History News Network, http://hnn.us/articles/11001.html; Don Luce interview.

515 *"grotesque sculptures of scarred flesh":* "The Other Prisoners," *Time,* March 19, 1973.

515 Failed antiwar candidacies and voting-age referendum: *Washington Star,* June 8, 1970. Michigan survey on young voters and Wallace: Reg Weaver and Hal Gulliver, *The Southern Strategy* (New York: Scribner, 1971), 105.

515 *Delegates would now have to be:* Shafer, *Quiet Revolution,* 29.

515 "Philadelphia Plan": Thomas J. Sugrue, "Affirmative Action from Below: Civil Rights, the Building Trades, and the Politics of Racial Equality in the Urban North, 1945–1969," *Journal of American History* 1 (June 2004): 145–73.

515 Electoral college reform: Alexander Keyssar, "Peculiar Institution," *Boston Globe,* October 17, 2004.

516 *"Our ability to change this system":* PPP 289, September 11, 1970.

516 *"If Nixon don't give us back":* Reeves, *President Nixon,* 229.

516 U.S. News & World Report *noted:* USNWR, June 22, 1970.

516 *The advisory council worked in secret:* Jonathan Schell, *The Time of Illusion* (New York: Alfred A. Knopf, 1975), 103, 190. See also Reeves, *President Nixon,* 230. Vetting by Huston: Schell, *Time of Illusion,* 117.

517 Environmental Protection Agency: Reeves, *President Nixon,* 238.

517 Jane Fonda surveillance and harassment: Hershberger, *Jane Fonda's War,* 50–74. White Panthers: Jeff A. Hale, "The White Panthers' 'Total Assault on the Culture,'" in Peter Braunstein and Michael William Doyle, eds., *Imagine Nation: The American Counterculture of the 1960s and '70s* (New York: Routledge, 2001), 124–56.

518 *"We are now confronted":* Reeves, *President Nixon,* 229.

518 *Huston prepared a forty-three-page outline:* Ibid., 235–36; Stanley Kutler, *The Wars of Watergate: The Last Crisis of Richard Nixon* (New York: W. W. Norton, 1992), 97; Schell, *Time of Illusion,* 114.

518 *"He would prefer that the thing":* Reeves, *President Nixon,* 236.

518 *Another unusual function:* Ibid., 153, 231, 244–45.

519 *A team formed to carry:* Ibid., 258.

519 *"rather weak handshake":* Dean, *Blind Ambition,* 20. On the twenty-third Nixon met: Ibid., 258; Anthony Lukas, *Nightmare: The Underside of the Nixon Years* (New York: Viking, 1976), 79. *The next day Nixon raged to Haldeman:* Reeves, *President Nixon,* 237; Jefferson Cowie, "Nixon's Class Struggle: Romancing the New-Right Worker, 1969–1973," *Labor History* 43 (Summer 2002): 257–83. *The next day Nixon savaged:* Schell, *Time of Illusion,* 108; Lyle Johnston, *"Good Night, Chet": A Biography of Chet Huntley* (Jefferson, NC: McFarland & Co., 2003), 110.

519 *Jane Fonda saw it in a jailhouse:* Fonda, *My Life So Far,* 261.

519 *In* Joe, *Peter Boyle:* "Joe, an East Village Tale, Arrives," NYT, July 16, 1970.

520 *The filmmakers' thesis resembled:* Philip Slater, *The Pursuit of Loneliness: American Culture at the Breaking Point* (Boston: Beacon Press, 1970).

520 *In real life, Peter Boyle:* "A Bigot Named Joe," *Life,* October 16, 1970.

520 *Congresswoman Patsy Mink called:* Statement of Judith Resnik, Judiciary Committee hearings, John G. Roberts Supreme Court appointment, September 9, 2005, http://judiciary.senate.gov/testimony.cfm?id=1611&wit_id=4630; Weaver and Gulliver, *Southern Strategy,* 135. *Five thousand demonstrated in New York:* Debra Michals, "From 'Consciousness Expansion' to 'Consciousness Raising': Feminism and the Countercultural Politics of the Self," Braunstein and Doyle, eds., *Imagine Nation,* 59. *Two hundred feminists took over the offices:* Ibid.; *Ladies' Home Journal,* August 1970. Time *put leader Kate Millett:* "Who's Come a Long Way, Baby?" *Time,* August 31, 1970.

520 *"I became a feminist":* Sally Kempton, "Cutting Loose: A private view of the women's uprising," *Esquire,* July 1970.

521 *The lead letter in response:* Letters, *Time,* September 14, 1970. *The Women's Board of the West Virginia GOP:* Fleshman to Margaret Chase Smith, June 2, 1970, "Second Declaration of Conscience" file, Margaret Chase Smith Library, Skowhegan, Maine.

521 *Jane Fonda arrived at the set:* Fonda, *My Life So Far,* 254. *Wrote William F. Buckley:* Ibid., 234.

521 *"Soledad Brothers" raid:* Charles R. Ashman, *The People vs. Angela Davis: The Trial of the Century* (New York: Pinnacle, 1972); *Herbert's Hippopotamus* (dir. Paul Alexander Juutilainen, 1996); Carroll, *It Seemed Like Nothing Happened,* 52; "Angela Davis, Black Revolutionary," *Newsweek,* October 26, 1970; Channel 45 six o'clock news, August 24, 1970, http://www.clas.ufl.edu/users/ssmith/davisbio.html. Sixteen most wanted list: Hale, "The White Panthers' 'Total Assault on the Culture.'" *Philadelphia police raided Black Panther:* Jefferson Decker, "Frank Rizzo, Richard Nixon, and Law-and-Order" (master's thesis, Department of History, Columbia University, 2003).

521 *Chatting with the press in Denver:* PPP 245, August 3, 1970; Schell, *Time of Illusion,* 121.

522 *The Popular Front for the Liberation of Palestine:* "Pirates in the Sky," *Time,* September 21, 1970. *In Madison, radicals bombed:* Tom Bates, *Rads: The 1970 Bombing of the Army Math Research Center at the University of Wisconsin and Its Aftermath* (New York: Harper Perennial, 1992). *In November, on the other side:* "Bomb Damages Russian Offices Here," NYT, November 26, 1970; "Superjew," *Esquire,* August 1970.

522 *Harris reported that 76 percent:* Godfrey Hodgson, *America in Our Time: From World War II to Nixon—What Happened and Why* (New York: Doubleday, 1976), 364. *The* New York Times *revealed:* Dutton, *Changing Sources of Power,* 42. *The University of Tennessee's new president:* Wills, "How Nixon Used the Media."

522 *On September 1 Senator McGovern:* Gordon L. Weil, *The Long Shot: George McGovern Runs for President* (New York: W. W. Norton, 1973), 13–16.

523 *"What these young radicals need":* Scranton files, Series 12, Box 58, MIP.

CHAPTER TWENTY-FIVE: AGNEW'S ELECTION

524 *"I will be urging the election":* Jules Witcover, *White Knight: The Rise of Spiro Agnew* (New York: Random House, 1972), 350–60. *"Pirates in the Sky":* Time, September 21, 1970. Springfield appearance: Witcover, *White Knight,* 359; John R. Coyne, ed., *The Impudent Snobs: Agnew vs. the Intellectual Establishment* (New Rochelle, NY: Arlington House, 1972), 360–65. *Buchanan and Safire had worked hard:* Whitcover, *White Knight,* 357–58.

525 *AFL-CIO president George Meany:* Jefferson Cowie, "Nixon's Class Struggle: Romancing the New-Right Worker, 1969–1973," *Labor History* 43 (Summer 2002): 257–83. *Their "supreme venerable" told the press:* Richard Reeves, *President Nixon: Alone in the White House* (New York: Simon & Schuster, 2001), 266. *At a Stevenson rally, DNC chair:* "O'Brien Excoriates Party 'Extremists,'" NYT, September 11, 1970. *He had Agnew, in Casper, Wyoming:* Coyne, ed., *Impudent Snobs,* 365–69.

525 *At the California Republican convention:* Whitcover, *White Knight,* 363. *After Ted Kennedy told students:* Ibid.

526 *Next, it was Las Vegas:* Ibid., 365.

526 *Nixon reinforced Agnew's message:* PPP 295, September 16, 1970; Jonathan Schell, *The Time of Illusion* (New York: Alfred A. Knopf, 1975), 120; Reeves, *President Nixon,* 247. Life *put Spiro Agnew on the cover:* "Agnew on the Warpath," *Life,* October 16, 1970.

526 *IMPUDENT SNOBS UNITE HERE:* Ibid.
526 *John Mitchell, drunk at a party:* Reeves, *President Nixon,* 246. *"If the vice president were slightly roughed":* Ibid., 265.
527 Gore/Ellington primary: Reg Weaver and Hal Gulliver, *The Southern Strategy* (New York: Scribner, 1971), 107–10.
527 *Gore hopped on a tree stump:* Ibid., 108.
527 *On September 22 Spiro Agnew:* Ibid., 118–200.
528 Agnew in Indianapolis, Salt Lake City, North Dakota: "Agnew on the Warpath."
528 *President Nixon was in Europe:* Reeves, *President Nixon,* 244. *The president was handling the crisis:* Ibid., 255. *soccer field:* Ibid., 251–52. *"If there is anything I want to do":* "I Don't Want the Hot Words of TV," *Time,* October 5, 1970. Rome, Yugoslavia: Reeves, *President Nixon,* 258. *"Facing the Middle East":* **Time,** October 5, 1970.
528 Charles Goodell: Tom Wells, *The War Within: America's Battle over Vietnam* (Berkeley: University of California Press, 1994), 365; "Bipartisan Senate Group Maps A 3-Pronged Antiwar Strategy," NYT, May 9, 1970; Mary Hershberger, *Jane Fonda's War: A Political Biography of an Antiwar Icon* (New York: New Press, 2005), 21.
529 *"Isn't that something!":* Reeves, *Richard Nixon,* 171.
529 *When his group Los Hijos de Tormenta:* Patrick Allitt, *Catholic Intellectuals and Conservative Politics in America, 1950–1985* (Ithaca, NY: Cornell University Press, 1995), 54–55. Jim Buckley and Bill Rusher: George J. Marlin, *Fighting the Good Fight: A History of the New York Conservative Party* (South Bend, IN: St. Augustine Press, 2002), 166.
529 *In June, Jim Buckley traveled:* Ibid., 171. *At a July 22 White House meeting:* Reeves, *President Nixon,* 245.
529 *A commission on pornography:* Carroll, *It Seemed Like Nothing Happened,* 28; David M. Edwards, "Politics and Pornography: A Comparison of the Findings of the President's Commission and the Meese Commission and the Resulting Response," http://home.earthlink.net/~durangodave/html/writing/Censorship.htm.
530 *"Earlier today, I was asked":* Whitcover, *White Knight,* 372–78. *Goodell was the "Christine Jorgensen":* Reeves, *Richard Nixon,* 267. *"Miss Jorgensen Asks Agnew for Apology":* NYT, October 11, 1970.
530 *He took up the cudgels:* Reeves, *Richard Nixon,* 268.
530 *The next leg:* Ibid.
530 Hijacking and drug abuse statements: PPP 344, 345, October 14, 1970. *On Tuesday he had signed:* PPP 346, October 15, 1970. *A concrete chip or three:* Schell, *Time of Illusion,* 128. *In Green Bay, Wisconsin:* Reeves, *Richard Nixon,* 268; PPP 358, October 17, 1970.
531 *He wound up Tuesday in Kansas:* PPP 368, October 19, 1970.
531 Rockford Star, *October 20–November 3, 1970: Rockford Star* morgue files, Rockford, Illinois.
532 *On Tuesday the twenty-seventh:* PPP 389, October 27, 1970; "Nixon Toughens Drug Laws," *Rockford Star,* October 28, 1970. *Bush's opponent was the conservative:* Weaver and Gulliver, *Southern Strategy,* 124. *"George Walker Bush is one member":* James Moore, *Bush's War for Reelection: Iraq, the White House, and the People* (New York: Wiley, 2004), appendix.
534 *In Life, Hugh Sidey reported: Rockford Star,* October 25, 1970. *Thursday night in San Jose:* Schell, *Time of Illusion,* 130; Reeves, *President Nixon,* 270; Fawn Brodie, *Richard Nixon: The Shaping of His Character* (New York: W. W. Norton, 1981), 375; *Rockford Star,* October 30, 1970 (AP report).
534 Phoenix speech: *Rockford Star,* November 1, 3, 1970; Reeves, *President Nixon,* 271.
535 Election results: Ibid., 272–73; "GOP Shocked, Baffled by Election Losses," *Rockford Star,* November 5, 1970.
535 John Wayne commercial for James Buckley: Bob Greene, *Running* (Chicago: Regnery, 1973), 80. Bill Brock ads: Weaver and Gulliver, *Southern Strategy,* 124. *Forty-six-year-old Senator William Saxbe:* Ibid., 41.
535 *Publicly the president claimed victory:* Witcover, *White Knight,* 396.
535 *"Don't keep saying that, John":* Reeves, *President Nixon,* 274.
536 *It came out in that election-eve broadcast:* Ibid., 271; Schell, *Time of Illusion,* 131; *Rockford Star,* November 3, 1970; "Excerpts from Senator Muskie's Nationwide TV Broadcast on Election Eve," NYT, November 3, 1970, 40.
537 Economic statistics: Reeves, *President Nixon,* 269–70.
537 *In August, Congress had handed:* Allen J. Matusow, *Nixon's Economy: Booms, Busts,*

Dollars, and Votes (Lawrence: University Press of Kansas, 1998), 67. *The* New York Times *found a typical blue-collar:* Reeves, *President Nixon*, 264, 271.

537 *"I really want the economy to boom":* Ibid., 264. *On November 7 in Key Biscayne:* Ibid., 273.

538 *He began seeing 1972 in apocalyptic terms:* Matusow, *Nixon's Economy*, 84. *"America has only two more years":* Ibid.

CHAPTER TWENTY-SIX: HOW TO SURVIVE THE DEBACLE

541 *Steve Roberts of the* New York Times: "Earthquakes as Artform," in Steven V. Roberts, *Eureka* (New York: Quadrangle/New York Times Books, 1974), 27–33.

541 *In February, forty-eight students: Chicago Sun-Times,* February 15, 1971.

541 *"a plan that shows how to survive the debacle":* Harold Brown, *How You Can Prophet from the Coming Devaluation* (New York: Avon, 1971). *"The rebirth of Israel":* Hal Lindsey, *The Late Great Planet Earth* (New York: Bantam, 1971). *"While you are reading these words":* Paul Ehrlich, *The Population Bomb* (New York: Ballantine, 1971).

542 *"If all of modern science and technology":* B. F. Skinner, *Beyond Freedom & Dignity* (New York: Bantam, 1971). *"In the neural system as now constituted":* Alvin Toffler, *Future Shock* (New York: Bantam, 1971).

542 *"There is a revolution coming":* Charles Reich, *The Greening of America* (New York: Bantam, 1971); "The Graying of *The Greening of America,*" *Weekly Standard,* December 19, 2005; Michael Barone, *Our Country: The Shaping of America from Roosevelt to Reagan* (New York: Free Press, 1990), 468.

542 McGovern *and Greening of America:* Robert Sam Anson, *McGovern: A Biography* (New York: Holt, Rinehart, and Winston, 1972), 146n.

543 *A comforting thought:* Robert Christgau, "A Slender Hope for Salvation," LAT, November 29, 1970.

543 *Turnouts for elections:* Edward Luttwak, "A Scenario for a Military Coup d'État in the United States," *Esquire,* July 1970.

543 *At the University of Nebraska:* PPP 12, January 14, 1971.

544 *The State of the Union:* PPP 26, January 22, 1971.

544 *He put it a little differently:* Bruce J. Schulman, *The Seventies: The Great Shift in American Culture, Society, and Politics* (New York: De Capo Press, 2002), 30. *In a strategy meeting:* Richard Reeves, *President Nixon: Alone in the White House* (New York: Simon & Schuster, 2001), 274.

544 *Jetting to Nebraska:* John W. Dean, *Blind Ambition: The White House Years* (New York: Simon & Schuster, 1976), 66.

544 Colson's staff, approval rating: Reeves, *President Nixon,* 297.

545 Colson and Chotiner intelligence: Ibid., 279, 281. *"Opponents List":* Ibid., 297–98; Stanley Kutler, *The Wars of Watergate: The Last Crisis of Richard Nixon* (New York: W. W. Norton, 1992), 175.

545 *On January 31, 1971, the* New York Times: "U.S. Silent on Speculation About an Invasion of Laos," NYT, January 31, 1971. *"The president is aware":* "The Nondenial Denier," NYT, February 16, 2003.

545 Laos operation: Jonathan Schell, *The Time of Illusion* (New York: Alfred A. Knopf, 1975), 142–44, 208; Reeves, *President Nixon,* 299–304.

545 *On February 4:* Ibid., 301.

546 *Then the subject turned to Governor Wallace:* H. R. Haldeman, *The Haldeman Diaries: Inside the Nixon White House* (New York: G. P. Putnam's Sons, 1994), 243–44.

546 *When he traveled to the Midwest:* Bruce Oudes, ed., *From: The President: Richard Nixon's Secret Files* (New York: HarperCollins, 1989), 226. Nixon and Quaker pacifism: "Excerpts from the Interview Granted by President Nixon on Foreign Affairs," NYT, March 10, 1971; "Quakers Assail Nixon War Stand," NYT, April 8, 1971.

547 Selling of the Pentagon: "Police, Protesters Clash as Agnew Vilifies Media," *Harvard Crimson,* March 19, 1971, http://www.thecrimson.com/article.aspx?ref=355478; "The Year Archie Bunker Came In and Lawrence Welk Went Out," NYT, January 2, 1972. *TV critic Jack Gould:* "TV: CBS Explores Pentagon Propaganda Costs," NYT, February 24, 1971.

547 *The* Washington Post *took Agnew's side:* "Mr. Agnew versus CBS versus the DOD," WP, March 26, 1971. *Unconvinced, one group of Republican:* James Mann, "Close Up:

Young Rumsfeld," *Atlantic Monthly*, November 2003. Bob Dole on "new Chamberlains": "Democrats Scored by Dole on Vietnam," NYT, March 7, 1971.

547 *Pat Buchanan, in a March 24 memo:* Schell, *Time of Illusion*, 180. *"Another Stormy Spring Foreseen":* NYT, March 26, 1971, 20.

548 *"Sinatra has the makings":* Oudes, ed., *From: The President*, 225.

548 *Senator Sam Ervin was on the case:* Karl E. Campbell, "Senator Sam Ervin and the Army Spy Scandal of 1970–1971: Balancing National Security and Civil Liberties in a Free Society," Charlotte-Mecklenburg Historic Landmarks Commission, http://www.cmhpf.org/senator%20sam%20ervin.htm.

549 *Weather Underground bomb:* "Capitol Rich in History Where Bomb Exploded," NYT, March 2, 1971.

549 *"self-discipline on the part of the executive branch":* Schell, *Time of Illusion*, 155.

549 Dairy industry scandal: Ibid., 146; Fawn Brodie, *Richard Nixon: The Shaping of His Character* (New York: W. W. Norton, 1981), 34; *United States v. John Connally*, CR 74-440, 349, Exhibit 1, full transcript of conversations.

CHAPTER TWENTY-SEVEN: CRUELEST MONTH

551 *On March 20, alongside Route 9:* David Cortright, *Soldiers in Revolt: GI Resistance During the Vietnam War* (Chicago: Haymarket Books, 2005), 37–38.

551 *"I just work hard at surviving":* Ibid., 33. *At Fort Bliss, soldiers:* Christian Appy, *Working Class War: American Combat Soldiers and Vietnam* (Chapel Hill: University of North Carolina Press, 1993), 93. *AWOLs went up fivefold:* Jane Fonda, *My Life So Far* (New York: Random House, 2005), 224. *But if MPs did that now:* Mary Hershberger, *Jane Fonda's War: A Political Biography of an Antiwar Icon* (New York: New Press, 2005), 19. *"The unwilling, led by":* Appy, *Working Class War*, 43, 30. *"What are you going to do":* Ibid., 253.

551 *The Student Mobilization Committee started:* Jerry Lembcke, *The Spitting Image: Myth, Memory, and the Legacy of Vietnam* (New York: NYU Press, 1998), 41. New York Times *columnist:* "A Whiff of Mutiny in Vietnam," NYT, August 27, 1969.

552 *A sergeant wrote on behalf:* Lembcke, *Spitting Image*, 47. Life *interviewed one hundred soldiers: Life*, October 24, 1969.

552 *Vietnamese-speaking psy-ops:* Tom Wells, *The War Within: America's Battle over Vietnam* (Berkeley: University of California Press, 1994), 340. *Aircraft carrier crews grounded:* "Pentagon Papers Chase," *Nation*, July 9, 2001. Amphetamines, marijuana, heroin: Appy, *Working Class War*, 283–85.

552 *FTA:* Hershberger, *Jane Fonda's War*, 42–46; *F.T.A.* (dir. Francine Parker, 1972).

552 *One officer walked around:* Wells, *War Within*, 297.

552 The *Post quoted an audience member:* "GI Movement: A Show to Call Its Own," WP, March 15, 1971.

553 *In public hearings, Vietnam Veterans Against the War:* Lembcke, *Spitting Image*, 57. *They marched eighty-six miles:* Ibid., 57–58.

553 *"Winter Soldier" hearings:* Hershberger, *Jane Fonda's War*, 27–34; Gerald Nicosia, *Home to War: A History of the Vietnam Veterans Movement* (New York: Carroll & Graf, 2004), 79–92. *A* Times *dispatch:* "'War Crimes' Testimony," April 7, 1971.

553 *Hugh Hefner donated:* Nicosia, *Home to War*, 91. Vietnam Veterans Against the War press conference: Ibid., 103.

553 *Their press release was devastating* : Wells, *War Within*, 480.

554 Dentists fitting draft-avoiders with orthodontics: Appy, *Working Class War*, 33.

554 *"It seemed like the silliest":* "Confessions of Lieutenant Calley," *Esquire*, November 1970.

554 My account of Lieutenant Calley's court-martial and aftermath is drawn from Michal R. Belknap, *The Vietnam War on Trial: The My Lai Massacre and Court-Martial of Lieutenant Calley* (Lawrence: University Press of Kansas, 2002); James Stuart Olson and Randy Roberts, eds., *My Lai: A Brief History with Documents* (New York: Bedford/St. Martin's, 1998); Wayne Greenshaw, *The Making of a Hero: The Story of Lieut. William Calley Jr.* (New York: Touchstone, 1971); and William Greider, "Calley's Trial: The Moral Question and Battlefield Laws," WP, April 5, 1971.

557 *On April 5 Senator Hatfield read:* "No Pentagon Study on Viet Civilian Deaths," LAT, April 6, 1971. The *Times, did, however:* NYT, April 8, 1971, 7.

557 Before you go on tonight: Richard Reeves, *President Nixon: Alone in the White House* (New York: Simon & Schuster, 2001), 185.

558 *The speech was the usual:* PPP 135, April 7, 1971, with audio.

559 *"We've thrown the best":* NLT, conversation 476–16.

560 *Colson had "the balls":* Reeves, *President Nixon,* 321.

561 *On Sunday, April 18, Vietnam Veterans Against:* Nicosia, *Home to War,* 108. VVAW march to Arlington: Ibid., 109.

561 *Haldeman called Daniel Patrick Moynihan:* NLT, conversation 481–21.

561 *"Someone has to demolish McCloskey":* NLT, conservation 483–7.

561 *"Goddamn gook VC!":* Nicosia, *Home to War,* 114.

562 *"quite a job keeping his people":* NLT, conversation 482–27.

562 *"shit cans filled with blood":* Nicosia, *Home to War,* 100.

562 *The next day, at the Old Executive:* NLT, conversation 486–1.

562 *That night Senator Phil Hart:* Nicosia, *Home to War,* 124.

563 *Nixon was livid:* NLT, conversation 486–1.

563 *Ron Ziegler told the press:* Nicosia, *Home to War,* 125. *"Leave the sons of bitches":* NLT, conversation 484–13. *John Mitchell visited the president's:* NLT, conversation 484–2.

563 *"'Goddamn it, forget the law!'":* NLT, conversation 484–13.

563 Clark, Supreme Court vote, camping: Nicosia, *Home to War,* 125–31.

564 *"That'll fix the veterans":* NLT, conversation 484–4.

564 *The next day John Kerry testified:* Nicosia, *Home to War,* 137–38; transcript at http://www.richmond.edu/~ebolt/history398/JohnKerryTestimony.html.

564 *The next day, solemn and respectful:* Nicosia, *Home to War,* 141–43.

565 *The organizers of the second, Haldeman briefed:* NLT, conversation 484–13.

565 *But it was organized:* "Inside Report: Muskie and the Trotskyites," WP, April 19, 1971. *"We had a great break":* NLT, conversation 482–8.

565 *"There's a separate organization":* NLT, conversation 477–1.

565 *"If the government won't stop":* NLT, conversation 486–5.

565 May Day Tribes' demonstration: Reeves, *President Nixon,* 319–22.

566 *I WAS AN AMERICAN POW:* Jeremy Varon, *Bringing the War Home: The Weather Underground, the Red Army Faction, and Revolutionary Violence in the Sixties and Seventies* (Berkeley: University of California Press, 2004), 131.

566 *When the polls arrived:* Reeves, *President Nixon,* 322.

566 "EAU CLAIRE, Wis. (AP)": "Al Capp Accused of Morals Offense," NYT, May 8, 1971.

566 *"The allegations are entirely":* "Coed Charges Al Capp with Morals Offense," LAT, May 8, 1971. See also Margo Howard, *A Life in Letters: Ann Landers' Letters to Her Only Child* (New York: Warner Books, 2003), 45–46.

566 *Either way, Chuck Colson sent:* Seymour Hersh, "Nixon's Last Coverup," *New Yorker,* December 14, 1992. *"The shock is not that there's":* NYDN, January 23, 1972.

567 *"I believe in white supremacy":* Playboy, May 1971, quoted by J. Hoberman in *Village Voice,* May 8, 2001.

567 *Robert D. Heinl argued that:* Hershberger, *Jane Fonda's War,* 39–40. *On May 24 at Travis Air Force Base:* Fonda, *My Life So Far,* 273–74; "30 Airmen Held as Base Erupts," WP, May 25, 1971.

567 *"Mr. President, what are you":* PPP 189, June 1, 1971.

568 *The next week's Gallup:* "Muskie, Kennedy and HHH Crowd Nixon in New Count," WP, June 4, 1971. *Two days later:* "61 Pct. of Americans Now Believe Entry in Vietnam War Was Mistake," WP, June 6, 1971. *"What we assumed":* Timothy Crouse, *The Boys on the Bus* (New York: Ballantine Books, 1974), 242.

CHAPTER TWENTY-EIGHT: PING-PONG

569 *Nixon had told his patron:* Leonard Garment, *Crazy Rhythm: From Brooklyn and Jazz to Nixon's White House, Watergate, and Beyond* (New York: Crown, 1997), 86. *Nixon's diplomatic mentor:* A. J. Langguth, *Our Vietnam: The War, 1954–1975* (New York: Touchstone, 2000), 80. *President Kennedy's people had talked:* "Tit for Tat: Two Prophesies," *Time,* August 2, 1971.

569 *"Within the next decade":* "Riding the Tiger," *Time,* October 27, 1967. Time, *whose founder:* "River of Aid," *Time,* April 21, 1967. *A 1966 Harris poll found:* "Harris Poll

Reports the Voters Prefer Wage and Price Curbs," NYT, October 12, 1966. *a right-wing publicist:* Rick Perlstein, *Before the Storm: Barry Goldwater and the Unmaking of the American Consensus* (New York: Hill & Wang, 2001), 104. China *was the word Nixon: Seattle Times,* October 28, 1966.

569 *"Our leader has taken leave":* Richard Reeves, *President Nixon: Alone in the White House* (New York: Simon & Schuster, 2001), 283.

570 *That first summer, Kissinger:* Ibid., 105–7. *That August the president met:* Ibid., 121.

570 *When Ceauşescu visited:* Ibid., 269.

570 *That November, Pakistan's:* Ibid., 282. East Pakistan slaughter: Christopher Hitchens, *The Trial of Henry Kissinger* (New York: Verso, 2001), 44–71.

570 *"The overworked term genocide":* Ibid., 45. Time *managed to get an Australian:* "A Visit to Canton," *Time,* October 6, 1967.

571 *Now, in 1971, team member Tim Boggan:* "The Play and the Meals Are Tough on U.S. Team," NYT, April 12, 1971.

571 *"Because it's their bag":* NLT, conversation 481–7, April 17, 1971.

571 *Editorialized the* New York Times: "Brave New World for Ping-Pong," NYT, April 16, 1971. *The most Scotty Reston:* "China Beyond Vietnam," NYT, April 16, 1971. *"Ping-Pong diplomacy":* Jules Witcover, *The Making of an Ink-Stained Wretch: Half a Century Pounding the Political Beat* (Baltimore: Johns Hopkins University Press, 2005), 150–51.

571 *"The Chinese government reaffirms":* Reeves, *President Nixon,* 319. *Kissinger relayed a message:* Hitchens, *Trial of Henry Kissinger,* 47.

572 *"The thing is okay!":* Reeves, *President Nixon,* 325.

572 *On May 31 Kissinger got word:* Ibid., 327.

572 *He'd attended the White House Correspondents':* Ibid., 321. *"We'll get them on the ground":* Ibid., 325–26. *"They couldn't oblige us fast enough":* "Nixon Hoped Antitrust Threat Would Sway Network Coverage," WP, December 1, 1997.

572 *according to one estimate 350,000:* Iwan Morgan, *Nixon* (London: Hodder Arnold, 2002), 118.

572 *He had read the economic tea leaves:* John Judis, *Grand Illusions: Critics and Champions of the American Century* (New York: Farrar, Straus & Giroux, 1992), 190–224.

573 *Nixon outlined all this:* PPP 222, July 6, 1971.

573 *Kissinger's stomachache:* Jonathan Schell, *The Time of Illusion* (New York: Alfred A. Knopf, 1975), 175.

573 *The June 13 Sunday* New York Times: "Tricia Nixon Takes Vows in Garden at White House," NYT, June 13, 1971.

574 *The next day's* Times: "Vietnam Archive: A Consensus to Bomb Developed Before '64 Election, Study Says," NYT, June 14, 1971.

575 *The third day revealed:* "McNaughton Draft for McNamara on 'Proposed Course of Action,'" NYT, June 15, 1971.

575 *That was written two weeks before:* PPP 172, April 7, 1965.

575 *In its customary spot:* "Argument Friday; Court Here Refuses to Order Return of Documents," NYT, June 16, 1971.

575 *Reported the* Post: "FBI Checking All Having Access to Known 15 Copies of Viet Study," WP, June 16, 1971.

575 Nixon-Kissinger response to Pentagon Papers: Reeves, *President Nixon,* 331–35.

576 John O'Neill and Veterans for a Just Peace: "After Decades, Renewed War on Old Conflict," WP, August 28, 2004.

576 *By the next day, they had:* Reeves, *President Nixon,* 332. *Once was for his 1950 wedding:* "Carol Cummings' Troth," NYT, December 3, 1950. *"bridegroom was":* "Daniel Ellsberg of M.I.T. Marries Patricia Marx," NYT, August 9, 1970. *"to paraphrase H. Rap Brown":* "Victory in the Ashes of Vietnam?" NYT, February 4, 1969.

577 *November 1970 letter . . . from MIT faculty:* Letters, NYT, November 30, 1970. Ellsberg biography: Tom Wells, *The War Within: America's Battle over Vietnam* (Berkeley: University of California Press, 1994), 359–63. *"best platoon leader":* "Pentagon Papers Chase," *Nation,* July 9, 2001. *"You guys have been conned":* Tom Wicker, *On Press* (New York: Viking, 1978), 180.

577 *Ellsberg had lectured Henry Kissinger:* Daniel Ellsberg, *Secrets: A Memoir of Vietnam and the Pentagon Papers* (New York: Viking, 2002), 236–49. *"I'm just not in a position":* PPP 104, March 9, 1967, press conference.

577 *American Legion counterprotesters:* "Moratorium, Mets Stir New Yorkers," WP, October 16, 1969.

578 *"Tony, can you get ahold":* Wells, *War Within,* 364.

578 *McGovern told him:* "McGovern Cites Advice to Ellsberg on Papers," NYT, August 1, 1972.

578 *Kissinger figured out by the seventeenth:* Reeves, *President Nixon,* 332. *"Go back and read the chapter":* Ibid., 338.

578 *Chuck Colson—who had:* "The Man Who Converted to Softball," *Time,* June 17, 1974.

579 *Ellsberg, he told Haldeman:* Bruce Oudes, ed., *From: The President: Richard Nixon's Secret Files* (New York: HarperCollins, 1989), 283. *the Justice Department's Robert Mardian:* R. W. Apple, ed., *The Watergate Hearings: Break-in and Coverup* (New York: Viking, 1973), 511.

579 *"We have the Democrats on a marvelous":* Oudes, ed., *From: The President,* 283–84.

579 *Provide top-secret documents:* Stanley Kutler, *The Wars of Watergate: The Last Crisis of Richard Nixon* (New York: W. W. Norton, 1992), 4–5. *likely to get lost:* Ibid.

579 *Nixon called the majority leader:* Reeves, *President Nixon,* 336.

580 *Said Haldeman: "Huston swears":* Ibid., 334–35.

580 "I want Brookings": Reeves, *President Nixon,* 339. Mardian and Hoover: Ibid., 372. Recruiting for Ellsberg project: Stanley Kutler, *Abuse of Power: The New Nixon Tapes* (New York: Free Press, 1997), 10–12; Oudes, ed., *From: The President,* 261; Staffs of United Press International and the *World Almanac, The Impeachment Report: A Guide to Congressional Proceedings in the Case of Richard M. Nixon, President of the United States* (New York: Signet, 1974), 160; John W. Dean, *Blind Ambition: The White House Years* (New York: Simon & Schuster, 1976), 47.

580 *Colson suggested E. Howard Hunt:* Kutler, *Abuse of Power,* 13.

581 *"He told me a long time ago":* Christopher Matthews, "New Tapes Debunk Oliver Stone's 'Nixon,'" *San Francisco Chronicle,* January 1, 1998.

581 *Nixon asked Colson and Haldeman:* Kutler, *Abuse of Power,* 16.

581 *"Every moment's continuance":* New York Times Co. v. United States, Black concurrence, 403 U.S. 713.

581 Gravel Pentagon Papers hearing: Norman Mailer, *St. George and the Godfather* (New York: New American Library, 1972), 79–80; Reeves, *President Nixon,* 334–35; "Gravel Calls Night 'Hearing,' Reads Pentagon Documents," WP, June 30, 1971; "Gravel Unlikely to Be Disciplined by Senate," WP, July 1, 1971.

581 *"another Senator McCarthy":* Kutler, *Abuse of Power,* 11.

582 *the* Times *had predicted a constitutional:* "Voting Bill Ready for House Action," NYT, June 5, 1970. *Samuel Lubell, the prescient:* "The 18-year-old Vote Could Beat Nixon in '72," *Look,* July 13, 1971.

582 *Haldeman started worrying:* Dean, *Blind Ambition,* 40.

582 *"Jesus Christ, John!":* Ibid., 44.

582 *"I have requested this television time":* PPP 231, July 15, 1971. Nixon calling conservatives "the animals": Margaret MacMillan, *Nixon and Mao: The Week That Changed the World* (New York: Random House, 2007), 259.

583 Birth of White House secret police: Kutler, *Wars of Watergate,* 112–14; Reeves, *President Nixon,* 349; Anthony Lukas, *Nightmare: The Underside of the Nixon Years* (New York: Viking, 1976), 68–108.

583 *An acquaintance described Krogh:* Ibid., 73.

583 G. Gordon Liddy: Ibid., 86; Reeves, *President Nixon,* 349; G. Gordon Liddy, *Will: The Autobiography of G. Gordon Liddy* (New York: St. Martin's Press, 1980). *"I enjoyed the mass salute":* Ibid., 4.

584 *Furnished with a red wig:* Lukas, *Nightmare,* 81. *"The art of espionage":* Ibid., 90.

584 *FBI agents visited Dr. Fielding:* Ibid., 93. *"Krogh should, of course":* Ibid., 94.

584 *Young and Krogh filed the action:* Reeves, *President Nixon,* 353.

584 *Hunt approached a Cuban friend:* Lukas, *Nightmare,* 95.

584 *"I think we have a perfect":* Ibid., 98.

CHAPTER TWENTY-NINE: THE COVEN

585 *A pulp thriller of relevance:* David St. John, *The Coven* (New York: Weybright & Talley, 1972).

586 *George Gordon Battle Liddy suspected:* G. Gordon Liddy, *Will: The Autobiography of G. Gordon Liddy* (New York: St. Martin's Press, 1980), 217. *Liddy gave over twelve pages:* Ibid., 147–59. *restraining hold:* Ibid., 193. *For, "To permit the thought":* Ibid., 268.

586 *It was like one of the agents:* Anthony Lukas, *Nightmare: The Underside of the Nixon Years* (New York: Viking, 1976), 77.

587 *The International Association of Chiefs:* "91 Policemen Reported Kill in First 9 Months of 1971," NYT, January 2, 1972. *In Philadelphia, former police chief:* Jefferson Decker, "Frank Rizzo, Richard Nixon, and Law-and-Order" (master's thesis, Department of History, Columbia University, 2003).

587 *In New York vigilantes shouting:* "Fire Bomb Kills Woman, Hurts 13 in Hurok Office," NYT, January 27, 1972. *A cabdriver in Queens rammed:* "Cab Rams Protesters; 5 Hurt," NYDN, January 25, 1972. *Two attempts on his life followed:* "Author Shot," WP, January 16, 1972; "Violence Besets Newsman After Book on Newark Riots," WP, January 19, 1972. *Newark Boys Chorus School:* "Vandalized Buses Bring an Inquiry," NYT, January 5, 1972.

587 *"What burns me to the bottom":* "A Wallace Backer Stirred by Busing," NYT, May 14, 1972. *Then one hot evening:* "Irene McCabe and Her Battle Against Busing," *Detroit News* Web site, http://info.detnews.com/history/story/index.cfm?id=161&category =people.

588 *In Washington, D.C., feminist Ti-Grace:* Patrick Allitt, *Catholic Intellectuals and Conservative Politics in America, 1950–1985* (Ithaca, NY: Cornell University Press, 1995), 153. *In Mountain Home, Idaho:* "The Covered Wagon," *New York Review of Books* 17, no. 11 (December 30, 1971). *In New Mexico, in the rugged:* "Dying Young in New Mexico," WP, January 16, 1972. See also "State Aides Scored in Albuquerque Riots," NYT, June 16, 1971; "Albuquerque Divided over Cause of First Major Riot," NYT, June 20, 1971.

588 *The federal commissioner of public services: Philadelphia Inquirer*, February 9, 1972. *In January, police in New York:* "Police in 3 Cities Defuse Bombs Placed in 8 Banks," NYT, January 8, 1972; "FBI Seeking Soldier in Bank Bombs Case," WP, January 14, 1972; "U.S. Extends Hunt for Bomber to Europe," CT, January 15, 1972. Stanford and H. Bruce Franklin: "Radical Professor Firing Approved," WP, January 10, 1972; "Stanford Fire Laid to Arson," WP, January 18, 1972. *The next day, in Miami:* "Addenda," WP, January 19 1972, A9. *That same day, Mayor Daley:* "Chicago Water Called Safe from Poisons," "Poison Plot Story Stuns Friends of Two Suspects," "Tighten Water Plant Guard After Poison Scare Arrests," CT, January 19, 1972.

589 *"Typical of the group":* Richard Reeves, *President Nixon: Alone in the White House* (New York: Simon & Schuster, 2001), 322. *"The show was a total glorification":* Ibid.

589 *Two University of Michigan English professors:* Christopher Russell Reaske, ed., *Student Voices on Political Action, Culture, and the University* (New York: Random House, 1971). Black Viewpoints, *a Signet paperback: Black Viewpoints* (New York: Signet, 1971). Michigan, BU, Princeton gynecological clinics: "Colleges Expand Modern Psychiatric Aid," NYT, January 1, 1972.

589 *"after reading this book":* Julius Lester, "Blacks Rage to Live," *New York Times Book Review,* November 22, 1970. *On August 21, Jackson was shot:* "'Soledad Brother' and 5 Are Killed in Prison Battle," NYT, August 22, 1971; Charles R. Ashman, *The People vs. Angela Davis: The Trial of the Century* (New York: Pinnacle, 1972). *A black crime wave broke out:* "Anti-Negro Group Vexing Police in Wilmington, N.C.," NYT, October 1, 1971. *In Baton Rouge, Louisiana:* "Muslims Blamed as Four Die in Baton Rouge Racial Disorder," LAT, January 11, 1972. *In upstate New York:* "Syracuse Seeks a Truce Between White and Black Youths," NYT, August 8, 1971.

590 Attica riot: Tom Wicker, *A Time to Die* (New York: Quadrangle/New York Times Books, 1975).

592 *The* Chicago Tribune *ran:* "What Do You Think of the Handling of the Attica Prison Riot," CT, September 15, 1971.

592 Lindsay, Agnew, Attica responses: WP, January 20, 1972. *Nelson Rockefeller shocked his liberal:* "Agitation at Attica: Rockefeller," NYT, September 25, 1971. Muskie response: Richard Scammon and Ben Wattenberg, *The Real Majority: An Extraordinary Examination of the American Electorate* (New York: Coward McCann, 1980), 15.

592 *"Sometimes when I see those columns":* PPP 222, July 6, 1971.

593 Fielding break-in: Lukas, *Nightmare,* 99–101; Liddy, *Will,* 163–69.

593   *The Plumbers sketched out possible:* Ibid., 170.
594   *On September 8 the president:* Reeves, *President Nixon*, 368; NLT, conversation 274–42.
594   "We have the power": Stanley Kutler, *Abuse of Power: The New Nixon Tapes* (New York: Free Press, 1997), 29.
594   *"Bob,* please *get me the names":* Ibid., 31.
594   *In truth, the responsible:* Francis X. Winters, *The Year of the Hare: America in Vietnam, January 25, 1963–February 15, 1964* (Athens: University of Georgia Press, 1999).
595   *At a September 16 press conference:* PPP 292, September 16, 1971.
595   *Indeed, none of his briefers:* Lukas, *Nightmare*, 83.
595   AT THE HIGHEST LEVEL: Reeves, *President Nixon*, 371; Lukas, *Nightmare*, 84.
595   *"Five million might finance McCarthy":* NLT, Colson and Nixon conversation, December 23, 1971. *Another was to secretly push a black:* "Nixon's Fateful Reversal," WP, October 30, 1997; Reeves, *President Nixon*, 371. *by January McCarthy announced:* "White House Discounts Bid by Ashbrook," NYT, January 2, 1972.
596   *also in January, Colson:* Reeves, *President Nixon*, 424.
596   Antonin Scalia and White House OTP: Public Broadcasting PolicyBase, "Nixon Administration Public Broadcasting Papers: Summary of 1971," http://www.current.org/pbpb/nixon/nixon71.html. *"all funds for Public Broadcasting":* Ibid.
596   *The News Twisters:* David Brock, *The Republican Noise Machine: Right-Wing Media and How It Corrupts Democracy* (New York: Crown, 2004), 26–33; Jonathan Aitken, *Charles W. Colson: A Life Redeemed* (New York: Continuum, 2006), 143–44.
596   Bestseller lists: See, for example, *Time*, December 27, 1971.
597   *"They're using any means":* Kutler, *Abuse of Power*, 8.
597   *The* New Yorker *ran a cartoon:* "Lessons from Watergate: A Derivative for Psycho-analysis," *Psychoanalytic Quarterly* 45 (1976): 37–61.
597   *"I thought your delegation":* Joseph Persico, *The Imperial Rockefeller: A Biography of Nelson A. Rockefeller* (New York: Simon & Schuster, 1982), 80.
597   *"The Carpenters are hardly":* "Those Reassuring Carpenters," CT, August 16, 1971.
597   *in a 1966* Esquire *profile:* Gay Talese, "Frank Sinatra Has a Cold," *Esquire*, April 1966. *"I'll do anything to defeat that bum":* Kitty Kelley, *His Way: The Unauthorized Biography of Frank Sinatra* (New York: Bantam Books, 1987), 424.
598   "Okie from Muskogee" and "Welfare Cadillac": "Love It or Leave It: New Patriotic Music Wins Fans, Enemies," WSJ, August 18, 1970.
598   Polling on economy: Reeves, *President Nixon*, 351. *He had excoriated:* PPP 250, August 4, 1971.
599   *"That little Jew cocksucker":* Reeves, *President Nixon*, 343.
599   My account of Connally hiring and New Economic Policy is drawn from Allen J. Matusow, *Nixon's Economy: Booms, Busts, Dollars, and Votes* (Lawrence: University Press of Kansas, 1998). An added source on Nixon's conviction of America's economic limits comes from John Judis, *Grand Illusions: Critics and Champions of the American Century* (New York: Farrar, Straus & Giroux, 1992), 190–224.
600   *Colson explained the bottom line:* Jefferson Cowie, "Nixon's Class Struggle: Romancing the New-Right Worker, 1969–1973," *Labor History* 43 (Summer 2002): 257–83.
601   *"Nobody asked," a historian observed:* Matusow, *Nixon's Economy*, 154.
602   *The speech began with a boast:* PPP 264, August 15, 1971.
603   *"Nixon Stuns Democrats":* Nick Thimmesch, WP, September 2, 1971.
603   *"In all the years":* Matusow, *Nixon's Economy*, 156. *The stock market joined:* Daniel Yergin and Joseph Stanislaw, *The Commanding Heights: The Battle Between Government and the Marketplace That Is Remaking the Modern World* (New York: Touchstone Books, 1999), 63. Time *once more rhapsodized:* "Nixon's Grand Design for Recovery," *Time*, August 30, 1971.
603   *"New Score Is Dow 32":* Matusow, *Nixon's Economy*, 156.
603   *"Robin Hood in reverse":* Ibid., 158. *The only national politician:* Gordon L. Weil, *The Long Shot: George McGovern Runs for President* (New York: W. W. Norton, 1973), 129.
603   *On August 17 he became:* PPP 268.
604   *"clearly this divides the Democrats":* Jonathan Schell, *The Time of Illusion* (New York: Alfred A. Knopf, 1975), 183.
604   *By the standards set by HEW:* Allen J. Matusow, *The Unraveling of America: A History of Liberalism in the 1960s* (New York: HarperCollins, 1984), 193. *Joe Kraft hoped:* "Holding Line on Busing," WP, January 20, 1972. *But the "fanatics" spoke for:* George

Gallup, "76% of Public Opposes Busing," WP, November 1, 1970. *Nixon ordered Ehrlichman:* H. R. Haldeman, *The Haldeman Diaries: Inside the Nixon White House* (New York: G. P. Putnam's Sons, 1994), 328.

604 *John Mitchell proposed Richard Poff:* John W. Dean, *Blind Ambition: The White House Years* (New York: Simon & Schuster, 1976), 49–50.

605 *"He's a real reactionary":* Reeves, *President Nixon*, 376. *"Fuck him":* Ibid., 383. *"The simple fact is that":* Ibid.

605 *Powell was the author of a memo:* The full text of the August 23, 1971, memo is at http://www.mediatransparency.org/story.php?storyID=22. *Rehnquist had reportedly:* Letter to the editor, *Newsday*, March 9, 1972. This quote was in circulation at the time, but I have not been able to verify its authenticity.

605 *"Rehnquist is pretty far right":* Reeves, *President Nixon*, 387.

605 *"Conservatives," he complained:* Reeves, *President Nixon*, 294–95.

605 Buchanan strategy memos: Schell, *Time of Illusion*, 180–81.

606 *Even the most conservative:* "5 Democrats Ask Nixon to Set Date for Pullout," NYT, April 23, 1971.

606 *"The sooner we get the hell":* Reeves, *President Nixon*, 382.

CHAPTER THIRTY: THE PARTY OF JEFFERSON, JACKSON, AND GEORGE WALLACE

607 *There might be five serious parties:* "Splinter Politics," NYT, January 2, 1972. *Wicker's more sober colleague:* "Reporting the Campaign," NYT, January 7, 1972.

607 *The president's approval rating:* "President Holds Firm at 49 Pct.," WP, January 20, 1972. *The January 17 Harris:* "Sen. Muskie Pulls Up Even with Nixon in Trial Heat," WP, January 17, 1972. *The day after the Harris poll:* "Selling of the President Will Be Musical," NYT, January 19, 1972; see also "Ads in 'Selling of President' Musical Irk McGinniss," NYT, March 3, 1972, 28: ironically the play of McGinniss's anti–Madison Avenue book included a product placement for a pesticide company owned by one of the investors. *When the president sat down:* "Nixon Shows He Is an Old Hand at TV Techniques," NYT, January 5, 1972. *The "Anderson papers":* See, for instance, "A Look at How Foreign Relations Are Conducted Now," WP, January 20, 1972, and Art Buchwald's humor column "Another Secret Document," the same day. *The* New York Times *editorialized:* "The President in 1971," NYT, January 2, 1972.

608 *in real life, during its run:* "Pet Slayer Strikes Again," CT, January 14, 1972.

608 *In the entertainment pages:* These films are from NYT, January 4, 7, 1972; LAT, January 12, 1972; and CT, January 15, 1972. *Rex Reed called the new western:* "Blood Bath for Sadists," NYDN, January 21, 1972. Two reviews of *Clockwork Orange:* "'Orange'—'Disorienting but Humane Comedy'"; ". . . Or 'A Dangerous, Criminally Irresponsible Horror Show'?"; both in NYT, January 9, 1972, Arts and Leisure section.

608 Topps trading cards of 1972 presidential candidates are occasionally available on eBay. *Democrats hoped he would not:* "Democrats Spin Wheel to Allocate Hotels, Seats at Miami," WP, January 20, 1972.

609 *Only one thing was certain:* "Kennedy Ties Viet Deaths, Nixon Policies," WP, January 18, 1972.

609 *California Democrats announced:* "Kennedy to Appear at Democratic Rally in L.A. Next Month," LAT, January 12, 1972. *then the next day:* "Kennedy Plans to Inform Florida That He Won't Seek Nomination," NYT, January 12, 1972.

609 *Five days later his friend:* NYDN, January 23, 1972.

609 Patsy Mink and Secret Service protection: NYDN, January 23, 1972. Edward T. Coll: "Benefit Is Minimal; N.H. Debate Has Minimal Benefit," WP, March 6, 1972. *Sam Yorty, the Los Angeles mayor:* Hunter S. Thompson, *Fear and Loathing on the Campaign Trail '72* (New York: Popular Library, 1973), 52, 80.

610 *"Moscow Muskie":* "Muskie Scores N.H. Publisher," WP, February 11, 1972. *Wilbur Mills, the powerful chairman:* Thompson, *Fear and Loathing*, 208; poll is "Democrats, in Debt, Turn Down Fund-Raising Idea," NYT, January 9, 1972. *Senator Vance Hartke made a:* Ibid.

610 Pete McCloskey: "Simon to Auction About 70 Works," NYT, March 30, 1971; "McCloskey's Campaign: Truth-in-Government Issue Is Key Hope," NYT, January 6, 1971. John Ashbrook: "Nixon's Too Left-Wing for William Loeb," NYT, Decem-

ber 12, 1971; "White House Discounts Bid by Ashbrook," NYT, January 2, 1972. *"end as all previous attempts":* Matusow, *Nixon's Economy: Booms, Busts, Dollars, and Votes* (Lawrence: University Press of Kansas, 1998), 157. *Nixon moved to buy off:* PPP 387, December 9, 1971; NYDN, January 25, 1972, on Otepka. *It worked:* National Review: Garry Wills, *Nixon Agonistes: The Crisis of the Self-Made Man* (New York: Mariner Books, 2002), preface, xv.

610 Henry "Scoop" Jackson: Richard J. Whalen, "Will the Real Majority Stand Up for Scoop Jackson?" NYTM, October 3, 1971. *The* New York Times *reported, "He hopes":* "Jackson Believes He Must Win Florida Primary or Forget Presidential Bid," NYT, September 30, 1971.

611 *He switched parties for a presidential:* Vincent J. Cannato, *The Ungovernable City: John Lindsay and the Battle to Save New York* (New York: Basic Books, 2003), 500. *"a combination of decadence and barbarism":* Ibid., 146. *even though the welfare population:* Kenneth S. Baer, *Reinventing Democrats: The Politics of Liberalism from Reagan to Clinton* (Lawrence: University Press of Kansas, 2000), 25. *even though the Knapp Commission:* "The Knapp Commission Didn't Know It Couldn't Be Done," NYTM, January 9, 1972. *A survey by the Addicts Rehabilitation Center:* Charles Rangel, "Do You Know Any 12-Year-Old Junkies?" NYT, January 4, 1972. *"City Restrooms May Be Razed": New York Post,* January 30, 1972. *"42d Street Crowd Helps Robber Flee":* NYT, January 5, 1972.

611 Forest Hills and scatter-site housing: Paul Cowan, *Tribes of America: Journalistic Discoveries of Our People and Their Cultures* (New York: New Press, 2008), 113–31; Jack Newfield, *Bread and Roses, Too* (New York: Dutton, 1971), 188.

612 *Lindsay's presidential strategy:* "Running Against 'Washington,'" NYT, January 1, 1972; Cannato, *Ungovernable City,* 516–18.

612 *"I will not tolerate gang rule":* "Rizzo Takes Post in Philadelphia," NYT, January 4, 1972; Jefferson Decker, "Frank Rizzo, Richard Nixon, and Law-and-Order" (master's thesis, Department of History, Columbia University, 2003). *Nixon received Rizzo in the Oval Office:* Ibid.; H. R. Haldeman, *The Haldeman Diaries: Inside the Nixon White House* (New York: G. P. Putnam's Sons, 1994), 401.

612 *"I'm tired of those kooks":* Richard Reeves, *President Nixon: Alone in the White House* (New York: Simon & Schuster, 2001), 324. Wallace in Florida: Dan T. Carter, *The Politics of Rage: George Wallace, the Origin of the New Conservatism, and the Transformation of American Politics* (Baton Rouge: Louisiana State University Press, 1996), 412–25; Reeves, *President Nixon,* 424; Thompson, *Fear and Loathing,* 429.

613 Shirley Chisholm: *Chisholm '72: Unbought and Unbossed* (documentary, Shola Lynch, dir., 2004).

613 *"I would announce on Inauguration Day": Playboy,* August 1971.

614 *Dutton insisted that "some of":* Frederick G. Dutton, *Changing Sources of Power: American Politics in the 1970s* (New York: McGraw-Hill, 1971), 28. *"the growing edge of the present":* Ibid., xi.

614 *Scotty Reston was one of Dutton's:* "Reporting the Campaign," NYT, January 7, 1972. *It brought in an immediate eighty-five thousand:* Rick Perlstein, "Ms. Magazine: Feminist Fighter," *Columbia Journalism Review,* November 2001.

614 *All he had to show for it:* "Muskie Has Lead Among Democrats," WP, January 23, 1972.

615 George McGovern background: Robert Sam Anson, *McGovern: A Biography* (New York: Holt, Rinehart, and Winston, 1972); documentary *One Bright Shining Moment* (Stephen Vittoria, dir., 2005).

616 *Jimmy the Greek, the Vegas oddsmaker:* Jack Anderson, "Jimmy the Greek Calls Election Shots," WP, January 19, 1972.

616 *McGovern had faced his first:* Shirley MacLaine, *You Can Get There from Here* (New York: W. W. Norton, 1975), 63. *When McGovern had announced:* Wicker, *On Press,* 61.

616 McGovern in Paris: Gordon L. Weil, *Long Shot: George McGovern Runs for President* (New York: W. W. Norton, 1973), 22–27; "McGovern Meets Vietcong as War-Study Trip Begins," NYT, September 10, 1971.

617 *Then he flew to Saigon:* "McGovern Begins a Fact-Finding Tour of Vietnam," NYT, September 14, 1971; "McGovern Says Pullout Would Topple Thieu," WP, September 16, 1971.

617 *Nixon had held a November:* PPP 356, November 12, 1971. *Then, on Christmas Day:* Jonathan Schell, *The Time of Illusion* (New York: Alfred A. Knopf, 1975), 203.

617 *After that, Nixon made:* PPP 12, January 12, 1972.

617 *The only real antiwar action:* Reeves, *President Nixon*, 314. *On New Year's Eve in Times Square:* "Revelers by Thousands Usher in Frosty New Year," NYT, January 1, 1972.

618 POWS NEVER HAVE A NICE DAY: Steven V. Roberts, *Eureka* (New York: Quadrangle/New York Times Books, 1974), 20. *"Following the President's lead":* Schell, *Time of Illusion*, 231. *Dan Rather asked the president:* PPP 1, January 2, 1972.

618 *"It is simply not true":* "McGovern Bids U.S. Set Pullout Date," NYT, January 9, 1972.

619 *"They're out on a limb there":* Reeves, *President Nixon*, 426.

619 *The president stepped up to the TV:* PPP 21, January 25, 1972.

620 *A New York Times editorial:* "President's Peace Proposals," NYT, January 26, 1972. *"After really listening":* NYDN, January 27, 1972. Hugh Scott and Sybil Stockdale: Ibid.

621 *"Mr. President, stop the bombing":* Reeves, *President Nixon*, 429; January 30, 1972, *Saturday News* clipping in BBP, Box 259.

621 *The Digest had responded: Reader's Digest*, June 1967. Philip Berrigan and Harrisburg 7 trial origins: Chronological clippings in BBP; Cowan, *Tribes of America*, 275–99.

623 *After all, Bob Haldeman had:* "Nixon's Aide Says Peace-Plan Foes Help the Enemy," NYT, February 8, 1972; "Chief of Staff in the White House," NYT, February 8, 1972; James Reston, "The Haldeman Case," NYT, February 9, 1972.

623 *The first Democratic presidential contest:* NYDN, January 26, 1972. *"The Muskie bandwagon": One Bright Shining Moment* (Stephen Vittoria, dir., 2005).

623 Dirty tricks: Schell, *Time of Illusion*, 218–22, 289; Robert Novak, *The Prince of Darkness: 50 Years of Reporting in Washington* (New York: Crown Forum, 2007), 218; Reeves, *President Nixon*, 413.

624 China trip: Margaret MacMillan, *Nixon and Mao: The Week That Changed the World* (New York: Random House, 2007); Reeves, *President Nixon*, 432–57; Julie Nixon Eisenhower, *Pat Nixon: The Untold Story* (New York: Kensington Publishing, 1987), 133–37; William Burr, ed., *The Kissinger Transcripts: The Top-Secret Talks with Beijing and Moscow* (New York: New Press, 1998), 59–65. *Another detail of timing:* Reeves, *President Nixon*, 432.

626 *"Let there be freedom of choice!":* PPP 1, January 2, 1972. *"last summer, a woman":* "In Small Town, U.S.A., Women's Liberation Is Either a Joke or a Bore," NYT, March 22, 1972. *Phyllis Schlafly Report:* Peter B. Levy, ed., *America in the Sixties—Left, Right, and Center: A Documentary History* (Westport, CT: Praeger, 1998), 154–55.

627 *"Mrs. Nixon's presence in Peking": Chicago Today*, February 22, 1972.

627 *Ronald Reagan explained to a Philadelphia:* Douglas Brinkley, "The President's Pen Pal," *New Yorker*, July 26, 1999. *The next Gallup poll affirmed:* "Nixon Favored by 83% of Republicans," WP, March 2, 1972.

628 *"I'd like to rearrange a front page":* Reeves, *President Nixon*, 650. *And at breakfast the day before:* Ibid., 454.

628 *Agnew, not unconvincingly:* "UAW Defers Stand on Presidential Race," WP, January 16, 1972. *"His caution and prudence":* Jules Witcover, *The Making of an Ink-Stained Wretch: Half a Century Pounding the Political Beat* (Baltimore: Johns Hopkins University Press, 2005), 148. *"Muskie Campaign Still Lacks Spark":* NYT, November 21, 1971.

628 "Canuck" letter and response: David Broder, "Muskie Denounces Publisher," WP, February 27, 1972; Witcover, *Making of an Ink-Staind Wretch*, 154–56.

628 *The next day a lacerating front-page:* Schell, *Time of Illusion*, 218–19.

629 *A White House staffer:* "FBI Finds Nixon Aides Sabotaged Democrats," WP, October 20, 1972; Jules Witcover, "'Canuck' Episode: A '72 Dirty Trick," WP, September 13, 1973.

629 For overview of Don Segretti and his activities: "Sabotage by Segretti: Network of Amateurs," NYT, July 10, 1973; Schell, *Time of Illusion*, 221; Stanley Kutler, *The Wars of Watergate: The Last Crisis of Richard Nixon* (New York: W. W. Norton, 1992), 199; Reeves, *President Nixon*, 424; Lukas, *Nightmare*, 152–60.

629 *"Now, get a massive mailing":* "Kennedy, Muskie, Jackson Eyed for Nixon Dirty Tricks in '71," WP, October 30, 1997.

631 *"I don't want him in":* Reeves, *President Nixon*, 301.

631 *He had been on a flight:* Ibid., 324. *A few days later Wallace drawled casually:* Ibid., 324.

632 *Three months later, Evans and Novak:* "The Nixon-Wallace Détente," WP, January 19, 1972.

632 *On January 2, 1972, when Dan Rather:* PPP 1, January 2, 1972. *John Mitchell funneled $10,000:* Schell, *Time of Illusion,* 217.

632 *"Harlem for Muskie Committee":* Ibid., 218; Lukas, *Nightmare,* 162.

632 *it was McGovern's "straight, decent":* Thompson, *Fear and Loathing.*

633 *McGovern's was the only viable campaign:* Lukas, *Nightmare,* 165 (Buchanan: "We must do as little as possible at this time to impede McGovern's rise").

633 Florida commercials: James Moorehead Perry, *Us & Them: How the Press Covered the 1972 Election* (New York: Crown, 1973). *Muskie whistle-stopped:* Thompson, *Fear and Loathing,* 112. *Muskie's publicity man:* Ibid., 97.

633 *On "Citizens for Muskie" letterhead:* Schell, *Time of Illusion,* 220; Kathleen Hall Jamieson, *Packaging the Presidency: A History and Criticism of Presidential Campaign Advertising,* 3rd ed. (New York: Oxford University Press, 1996), 279.

633 *"Muskie is a rat fink";* "Mothers Backing Muskie": Ibid.; Lukas, *Nightmare,* 157.

634 Florida results: Thompson, *Fear and Loathing,* 129.

634 *"As Gene McCarthy made America": Saturday Review,* March 11, 1972.

634 *He spoke to the nation—on St. Patrick's Day:* PPP 90, March 16, 1972. *Wallace, thrilled, took it:* "Call for a Curb on Busing," CT, March 18, 1972.

CHAPTER THIRTY-ONE: THE SPRING OFFENSIVE

635 *Deliverymen and limousines kept:* Anthony Lukas, *Nightmare: The Underside of the Nixon Years* (New York: Viking, 1976), 158–59.

635 International Telephone & Telegraph scandal: Jonathan Schell, *The Time of Illusion* (New York: Alfred A. Knopf, 1975), 169–71; Lukas, *Nightmare,* 182–84; "Tricky Dick Redux," *San Diego Reader,* January 9, 1997; Richard Reeves, *President Nixon: Alone in the White House* (New York: Simon & Schuster, 2001), 323–24.

636 *"Who exactly do you represent?":* Ibid., 461.

636 *Harry Dent had wanted:* Stanley Kutler, *The Wars of Watergate: The Last Crisis of Richard Nixon* (New York: W. W. Norton, 1992), 193. *And what the general counsel suggested:* G. Gordon Liddy, *Will: The Autobiography of G. Gordon Liddy* (New York: St. Martin's Press, 1980), 209.

636 Liddy's presentation to Mitchell: Ibid., 196–201.

637 *Running a campaign plane and a press plane:* Bob Greene, *Running* (Chicago: Regnery, 1973), 117.

637 *"Ethics in the sausage casings business":* Maurice Stans, *The Terrors of Justice: The Untold Side of Watergate* (New York: Everest House, 1978), 88.

637 *In October of 1971:* Lukas, *Nightmare,* 128–29.

638 *On January 19, the House:* "Election Fund Bill Is Voted," WP, January 20, 1972.

638 *Nixon signed it with a flourish:* PPP 46, February 7, 1972.

638 *A shakedown frenzy preceded:* Reeves, *President Nixon,* 462–63; Schell, *Time of Illusion,* 211. *Gulf Chemical sent $100,000:* New York Times, ed., *The Watergate Hearings: Break-in and Cover-up Proceedings of the Senate Select Committee on Presidential Campaign Activities* (New York: Bantam, 1973), chronology section.

638 *"Mr. President," one reporter asked:* PPP 324, March 24, 1972.

638 *"They are out to defeat us":* Reeves, *President Nixon,* 464.

639 NIXON... GODFATHER IN THE WHITE HOUSE: This button is occasionally available on eBay.

639 *"Muskie has been working":* "McGovern Rejects 13 Slates," CT, January 13, 1972. *"It's the populism of the prairies":* "McGovern Gibes at 'Park Ave. Populism,'" NYT, February 26, 1972.

639 Morris Dees: Gordon L. Weil, *The Long Shot: George McGovern Runs for President* (New York: W. W. Norton, 1973), 38; "Mail for McGovern," NYT, July 18, 1972; Richard Viguerie, *America's Right Turn: How Conservatives Used New and Alternative Media to Take Power* (Los Angeles: Bonus Books, 2004), 146–48. *In his 1968 Senate race:* Ibid., 147.

639 *It was why he announced:* Weil, *Long Shot,* 31. *"I will not change my beliefs":* Rick Perlstein, *Before the Storm: Barry Goldwater and the Unmaking of the American Consensus* (New York: Hill & Wang, 2001), 260.

640 *McGovern sallied forth at Keene State:* Hunter S. Thompson, *Fear and Loathing on the Campaign Trail '72* (New York: Popular Library, 1973), 370–78; Theodore H. White,

The Making of the President 1972 (New York: Atheneum, 1973), 76. *(Eleanor McGovern, pointing out:* Weil, *Long Shot,* 99. *In Florida he came out for busing:* Thompson, *Fear and Loathing,* 81. Space shuttle: NYDL, January 21, 1972. *He toured Chicago without:* "Huglies, 3 Others Back Muskie Drive," WP, January 18, 1972; "McGovern Rejects 13 Slates."

640 *In January, DNC chair O'Brien:* Thompson, *Fear and Loathing,* 93.

640 *Maybe what Dutton told Scotty:* Frederick G. Dutton, *Changing Sources of Power: American Politics in the 1970s* (New York: McGraw-Hill, 1971), 246. *Front-runner Muskie was sounding:* "Snowfall Disrupts Wisconsin Primary Schedules," NYT, March 30, 1972.

640 Lordstown strike: Stanley Aronowitz, *False Promises: The Shaping of American Working Class Consciousness* (New York: McGraw-Hill, 1974), 21–50.

641 *"humanistic, critical of big business":* "Reporting the Campaign," NYT, January 7, 1972.

641 Harrisburg 7 trial and outcome: Chronological clippings in BBP; Cowan, *Tribes of America,* 275–99.

641 *The AFL-CIO revealed a poll:* Thompson, *Fear and Loathing,* 154.

644 *The McGovern campaign had begun:* Ibid., 174–75; White, *Making of the President 1972,* 98

644 *By locking up the left-wing activist:* Weil, *Long Shot,* 34. *"to have an opportunity to educate":* Ibid., 37. *McGovern wrote ingratiating letters:* McGovern to Chip Berlet, in author's possession.

645 *At McGovern's Washington headquarters:* Thompson, *Fear and Loathing,* 407. McGovern Wisconsin organization: Ibid., 169–74; "Wisconsin Team Keeps April Faith in McGovern," NYT, August 25, 1972.

645 *Teddy White compared them:* White, *Making of the President 1972,* 125. *Timothy Crouse in* Rolling Stone: Thompson, *Fear and Loathing,* 171.

645 *McGovern started dropping in on bowling:* Weil, *Long Shot,* 65.

645 *a press conference in the home:* "McGovern Gibes at 'Park Ave. Populism.'"

645 *George Wallace called a press conference:* "Wallace Plans to Step Up Drive for Nomination," NYT, March 16, 1972.

646 *He called Wallace's Florida:* Peter N. Carroll, *It Seemed Like Nothing Happened: America in the 1970s* (New Brunswick, NJ: Rutgers University Press, 1990), 84; George S. McGovern, *An American Journey: The Presidential Campaign Speeches of George McGovern* (New York, Random House, 1974), 186.

646 *The Wednesday before the election:* "McGovern Says Nixon Ignored Kin of P.O.W.'s," NYT, March 29, 1972; "Snowfall Disrupts Wisconsin Primary Schedules," NYT, March 30, 1972; "Economy Is Key in Wisconsin," NYT, April 1, 1972.

646 Vietnam spring offensive: Schell, *Time of Illusion,* 230; Reeves, *President Nixon,* 465.

646 *It was, in a way, his Gulf of Tonkin:* A. J. Langguth, *Our Vietnam: The War, 1954–1975* (New York: Touchstone, 2000), 597.

647 *The president ordered a fleet:* Ibid.

647 *Jackson, Wallace, and Humphrey massed:* "3 Democrats Back U.S. Right to Renew Raids in the North," NYT, April 5, 1972. *Since Muskie didn't mention:* H. R. Haldeman, *The Haldeman Diaries: Inside the Nixon White House* (New York: G. P. Putnam's Sons, 1994), 435.

647 *At 9:40 Frank Mankiewicz:* Weil, *Long Shot,* 66. *"Archie Bunker's street":* Thompson, *Fear and Loathing,* 174. *Reporters, having missed the story:* Ibid., 177.

647 *Lindsay's press secretary lost $102:* Ibid., 142.

647 *The next day McGovern people:* Thompson, *Fear and Loathing,* 160.

647 *His janissaries made calls:* Ibid., 165. Time *started planning:* "Here Comes the Prairie Populist," *Time,* May 8, 1972. *Evans and Novak noted the emergence:* "Anyone But McGovern," WP, April 6, 1972.

647 *"The P wanted to be sure":* Haldeman, *The Haldeman Diaries.*

648 *On April 6, B-52 strikes pushed:* "A Big New Phase of War Is Opening," NYT, April 6, 1972. *"The simple truth is that this test":* Congressional Record 118, pt. 19, 11,560.

648 *Ten-dollar, twenty-dollar, fifty-dollar checks:* "Mail for McGovern," NYT, July 18, 1972. *The Federal Elections Campaign Act:* Schell, *Time of Illusion,* 211.

648 *"Every great power must":* PPP 115, April 10, 1972.

649 *"What the enemy seeks":* Reeves, *President Nixon,* 468.

649 *On April 16, five behemoth:* Ibid., 469. *Three days later, Kissinger proceeded:* Schell, *Time of Illusion,* 236–37.

649 *He embarked on a series of photo ops:* PPP 120, 121, 122, April 14, 1972; PPP 123, April 15, 1972; PPP 125, April 18, 1972; PPP 126, April 19, 1972.

649 *"Our draft calls now average":* PPP 129, April 26, 1972.

649 *"I still think we ought to take":* "Nixon Proposed Using A-Bomb in Vietnam War," NYT, March 1, 2002; NLT, conversation 23–70.

650 *Massachusetts's plentiful antiwar Democrats:* Thompson, *Fear and Loathing*, 74.

650 *"If we don't fight them there":* Peter B. Levy, ed., *America in the Sixties—Left, Right, and Center: A Documentary History* (Westport, CT: Praeger, 1998).

650 *This was nasty politics:* Weil, *Long Shot*, 107, 129–31.

651 *Evans and Novak were reporting:* "Kennedy's Fatalistic Mood," WP, April 12, 1972. Humphrey heckling in Pennsylvania: Thompson, *Fear and Loathing*.

651 *"The only logical explanation":* "John Mitchell's Democrats," NYT, April 30, 1972.

651 *"The sudden surge in Senator Hubert Humphrey's":* "Behind Humphrey's Surge," WP, April 27, 1972.

651 *One "liberal senator":* "Behind Humphrey's Surge," WP, April 27, 1972, A23.

652 *"George McGovern has run":* "John Mitchell's Democrats."

652 National Commission on Marijuana and Drug Abuse: "National Commission to Propose Legal Private Use of Marijuana," NYT, February 13, 1972. *"a crushing burden for law enforcement":* Weil, *Long Shot*, 100. *Nixon hoped it would help:* See Michael Massing, *The Fix: Solving the Nation's Drug Problem* (Berkeley: University of California Press, 2000). *"You can't just let anybody walk":* "Society: Loosening Up," *Time*, June 26, 1972; Shirley MacLaine, *You Can Get There from Here* (New York: W. W. Norton, 1975), 62. *Pat Nixon, in one of her rare:* "Mrs. Nixon Asserts Jane Fonda Should Have Bid Hanoi End War," NYT, August 9, 1972.

652 *"I'd vote for him if he'd turn Christian":* Thompson, *Fear and Loathing*, 171.

653 *"Jesus, we won the fucking city":* Ibid., 74.

653 *On April 23, "in a spontaneous act":* Abbie Hoffman, Jerry Rubin, and Ed Sanders, *Vote!: A Record, a Dialogue, a Manifesto—Miami Beach, 1972 and Beyond* (New York: Warner Paperbacks, 1972), 42–44.

653 *"We feel the colored element":* Evans and Novak, "The McGovern Phenomenon," WP, April 20, 1972.

653 *"Is this Wallace Country?":* "Controlling the Crowds; a Wallace Campaign Rally," WP, May 1, 1972, A1.

654 *Across the border:* "Running Hard 'Extremism,'" WP, April 30, 1972, A1.

654 *The* Washington Post *featured him:* "Running Hard on 'Extremism,'" WP, May 1, 1972. *The man who'd been offered two cabinet posts:* Richard J. Whalen, "Will the Real Majority Stand Up for Scoop Jackson?" NYTM, October 3, 1971. *Then, the day before the Ohio:* Thompson, *Fear and Loathing*, 199.

654 *who kept columnist Joseph Alsop:* Taylor Branch, *Pillar of Fire: America in the King Years, 1963–1965* (New York: Simon & Schuster, 1998), 294.

654 *"Jesus Christ! That old cocksucker!":* Curt Gentry, *J. Edgar Hoover: The Man and the Secrets* (New York: Norton, 2001), 28.

654 *"The good J. Edgar Hoover has done":* PPP 140, May 4, 1972.

655 *A squad of Cuban operatives:* Lukas, *Nightmare*, 195.

655 Howard Johnson's reservation: Ibid., 193.

655 *McGovernites charged election fraud:* Thompson, *Fear and Loathing*, 189–92. *"McGovern and Humphrey Running Even":* NYT, May 7, 1972.

655 *The next contest was in . . . Nebraska:* "Nebraska," WP, May 11, 1972, A1. *Everywhere he went:* "'Radical' Issue Hits McGovern," WP, May 9, 1972, A1; Thompson, *Fear and Loathing*, 202, 218.

655 *The panicked campaign distributed:* "'Radical' Issue Hits McGovern," WP, May 9, 1972.

656 *The* Washington Post *patiently explained:* "McGovern's 'Radical Views' Attacked," WP, May 6, 1972. *The Republican National Committee's monthly magazine:* First Monday, June 1972, courtesy of Howard Park.

656 *On May 8, amid:* PPP 147. *Connally urged him:* NLT, conversation 722–11.

656 *They code-named it Operation Linebacker:* Reeves, *President Nixon*, 472.

656 *"I cannot emphasize too strongly":* Ibid., 474.

657 *George Wallace's line on Vietnam:* "Wallace Begins Busy Md. Campaign," WP, May 7, 1972.

657 *"General, why haven't we bombed":* Liddy, *Will*, 223. *On May 9 the Senate Democra-*

tic: "President Rebuffed by Democrats," WP, May 10, 1972. *But David Broder spoke:* "Most Politicians Privately Cautious," WP, May 10, 1972. *Broder also cited an unnamed:* "Most Politicians Privately Cautious," WP, May 10, 1972, A11. *The* New York Times, *for its:* "Mr. Nixon's Brinkmanship," NYT, May 10, 1972. *Chuck Colson spent $4,400:* Jeb Stuart Magruder, *An American Life: One Man's Road to Watergate* (New York: Atheneum, 1974), 208.

657 *The campuses once more exploded:* "Hundreds Are Arrested in Antiwar Demonstrations," NYT, May 11, 1972. *This is to advise you:* Reeves, *President Nixon,* 476. *The question every political analyst:* "Leaders of Organized Labor Remain Largely Hostile to McGovern's Candidacy," NYT, May 14, 1972, 38.

658 *when the president spoke at the AFL-CIO:* Ibid., 393; Fawn Brodie, *Richard Nixon: The Shaping of His Character* (New York: W. W. Norton, 1981), 51; "President Asks Labor's Support; Reception Is Cool," NYT, November 20, 1971. *"Some wrote in those days":* PPP 364, November 19, 1971. *The January convention pronounced:* NYDN, January 26, 1972. *In March, Meany resigned:* PPP 102, March 23, 1972. *On April 20 he testified:* "Meany Asks Nixon to Act on Prices," NYT, April 21, 1972.

658 *Meany said all Americans:* "President Entitled to Public Support," CT, May 14, 1972.

659 *One of the canvassers back in Wisconsin:* Thompson, *Fear and Loathing,* 171.

CHAPTER THIRTY-TWO: CELEBRITIES

660 *Arthur Bremer wanted to be famous:* Arthur Bremer, *An Assassin's Diary* (New York: Harper's Magazine Press, 1973).

660 *Celebrities in Wisconsin:* "Celebrities Rally Behind McGovern," April 2, 1972.

661 *In March, Pontiac housewife:* "Irene McCabe and Her Battle Against Busing," *Detroit News* Web site, http://info.detnews.com/history/story/index.cfm?id=161&category =people. *He drew over six thousand:* Dan T. Carter, *The Politics of Rage: George Wallace, the Origin of the New Conservatism, and the Transformation of American Politics* (Baton Rouge: Louisiana State University Press, 1996), 434.

662 *My reconstruction of the day George Wallace was shot comes from a dossier assembled* by the Laurel, Maryland, Historical Society, esp. WP, May 16, 1972.

662 *Five nights earlier, busing dominated:* "Busing Top Issue in 4th District," WP, May 12, 1972.

663 *Richard Nixon's reaction:* Richard Reeves, *President Nixon: Alone in the White House* (New York: Simon & Schuster, 2001), 478–79.

664 *He called for Chuck Colson:* Stanley Kutler, *The Wars of Watergate: The Last Crisis of Richard Nixon* (New York: W. W. Norton, 1992), 38.

664 *Nixon and Colson planning is from NLT,* tape 24–124, 24–134.

664 *Nixon met with his secretary of the treasury:* Reeves, *President Nixon,* 478; "Mr. Connally Resigns," NYT, May 17, 1972. See also *Supplement Appropriations Bill, 1973: Hearings Before Subcommittee of the Committee on Appropriations, House of Representatives, Ninety-second Congress, Second Session* (Washington: U.S. Government Printing Office, 1972), 1058.

665 *Life happened to have:* "Ted Kennedy Hears the News," *Life,* May 26, 1972.

665 *"McGovern and HHH Abreast vs. Nixon":* WP, May 21, 1972, A2.

665 *Democratic county chairmen:* "Democratic Chairmen Pessimistic," WP, May 14, 1972.

665 *A behind-the-scenes figure:* "Party Chief Pays Visit to Wallace," WP, May 24, 1972; "O'Brien Deplores Attempts to Curb Wallace Delegates," WP, May 25, 1972.

666 *There had already, on May 16:* Tad Szluc, *Compulsive Spy: The Strange Career of E. Howard Hunt* (New York: Viking Press, 1974), 146. *On May 22, as the president:* PPP 168, May 22, 1972. My account of the first Watergate break-in attempts is drawn from Anthony Lukas, *Nightmare: The Underside of the Nixon Years* (New York: Viking, 1976), 197–200; New York Times, ed., *The Watergate Hearings: Break-in and Cover-up Proceedings of the Senate Select Committee on Presidential Campaign Activities* (New York: Bantam, 1973), chronology section.

666 *A second group, led by Liddy:* G. Gordon Liddy, *Will: The Autobiography of G. Gordon Liddy* (New York: St. Martin's Press, 1980), 229.

667 *As G. Gordon Liddy wrote:* Ibid., 194. *On the twenty-eighth, the president:* PPP 176, May 28, 1972.

667 *In the next Gallup poll:* "Nixon Popularity Hit 2-Year Peak on Soviet Trip," WP,

June 4, 1972. *Inflation was down:* Bruce Miroff, *The Liberals' Moment: The McGovern Insurgency and the Identity Crisis of the Democratic Party* (Lawrence: University Press of Kansas, 2007), 230.

668 *whose children left their handprints:* Ibid., 177. *"Dirty politics,"* Hunter S. Thompson wrote: Thompson, *Fear and Loathing,* 202.

668 *McGovernites were convinced:* Abbie Hoffman, Jerry Rubin, and Ed Sanders, *Vote!: A Record, a Dialogue, a Manifesto—Miami Beach, 1972 and Beyond* (New York: Warner Paperbacks, 1972), 73. *Now, Humphrey shifted to dirty pool:* Thompson, *Fear and Loathing,* 217–18. *His adviser the old Kennedy hand:* Ibid. *Pamphlets circulated signed by Lorne Greene:* Gordon L. Weil, *The Long Shot: George McGovern Runs for President* (New York: W. W. Norton, 1973), 102–5; "Calif. Rivals Woo Jewish Vote," LAT, June 1, 1972; American Jewish Committee, "The Politics of American Jews: The Election of 1972," New York Public Library Oral History Collection, 1972–1975, oral histories of Charlie Guggenheim and Anne Wexler; Humphrey; and McGovern Israel pamphlets in possession of author, courtesy of Ryan Hayes. *But the Field poll showed McGovern:* "California Poll Gives McGovern 46–26 Pct. Lead Over HHH," WP, June 2, 1972.

668 *"acid, abortion, and amnesty":* "McGovern Called 'Triple A' Candidate," WP, May 26, 1972.

668 California Humphrey/McGovern debates: Weil, *Long Shot,* 90–127.

669 McGovern and *"demogrant":* Weil, *Long Shot,* 69–90.

670 *Humphrey got a $300,000 cash:* Herbert E. Alexander, *Financing the 1972 Election* (Lexington, MA: Lexington Books, 1976), 153. *the doyen of the "Democratic Party's":* "McGovern on the Defensive," WP, May 28, 1972.

670 Angela Davis trial: Charles R. Ashman, *The People vs. Angela Davis: The Trial of the Century* (New York: Pinnacle, 1972).

671 *His spokesmen lied Wednesday:* Thompson, *Fear and Loathing,* 377.

671 *He cleverly argued that winner-take-all:* Byron E. Shafer, *Quiet Revolution: The Struggle for the Democratic Party and the Shaping of Post-Reform Politics* (New York: Russell Sage Foundation, 1983), 143.

671 *"Oh, my goodness, no":* Thompson, *Fear and Loathing,* 261; "McGovern Setback Held Serious, Not Fatal," NYT, June 30, 1972.

671 *"One of the factors that brought Goldwater":* Reeves, *President Nixon,* 497.

672 *Hours later, Berl Bernhard called back:* "Muskie Balks at Yielding to McGovern," WP, June 10, 1972.

672 *Armed with his 176 delegates:* "Muskie Refuses to Back McGovern; Remains in Race," NYT, June 10, 1972.

672 *"I'm not dropping out":* Timothy Crouse, *The Boys on the Bus* (New York: Ballantine Books, 1974), 160. *The Lorne Greene flyer:* "McGovern, in City, Says Humphrey Distorts Stand," NYT, June 10, 1972.

672 *The* New York Times *and Daniel Yankelovich:* "Times Survey: Defections in Party Face McGovern," NYT, June 9, 1972. *On June 14 Ted Kennedy:* "Muskie's New Goal: 'Viable Alternative,'" NYT, June 15, 1972. *That same day Edmund Muskie:* Ibid.

672 *McGovern battled back with Warren Beatty:* J. Hoberman, *The Dream Life: Movies, Media, and the Mythology of the Sixties* (New York: New Press, 2003), 345–49; "Rock 'n' Rhetoric Rally in the Garden Aids McGovern," NYT, June 15, 1972; "Love Is Hell, Warren," NYT, June 25, 1972.

674 *It was partially a Camelot thing:* Interview with Garry Wills. *"Why does McCarthy need you?":* Lewis Chester, Bruce Page, and Godfrey Hodgson, *American Melodrama: The Presidential Campaign of 1968* (New York: Viking, 1969), 97.

674 *Shirley MacLaine's alienation:* Shirley MacLaine, *You Can Get There from Here* (New York: W. W. Norton, 1975), 72.

675 *Her brother Warren was politically undisciplined:* Thompson, *Fear and Loathing,* 199.

675 *Chris Mitchum, the liberal son of Robert:* "Love Is Hell, Warren."

676 *In place of cynics, McGovern had Fred Dutton:* "A Reporter's Notebook: McGovern and Youth," NYT, June 20, 1972.

676 *"the only alternative to the supreme politician":* Ibid. Nixon's approval rating: "60 Pct. Approval Puts Nixon at 2-Year High," WP, June 25, 1972.

676 Second Watergate burglary: Lukas, *Nightmare,* 204–15.

677 *The president said much the same:* Kutler, *Wars of Watergate,* 190.

677 *Sunday morning Richard Nixon:* H. R. Haldeman, *The Haldeman Diaries: Inside the Nixon White House* (New York: G. P. Putnam's Sons, 1994), 471.

677 *It was in the* New York Times: "5 Charged with Burglary at Democratic Quarters," NYT, June 18, 1972.

678 My account of the immediate Watergate cover-up efforts is drawn from New York Times, ed., *Watergate Hearings,* chronology section; Reeves, *President Nixon,* 499–512; Kutler, *Wars of Watergate,* 187–211; Jonathan Schell, *The Time of Illusion* (New York: Alfred A. Knopf, 1975); Lukas, *Nightmare;* and Stanley Kutler, *Abuse of Power: The New Nixon Tapes* (New York: Free Press, 1997).

681 *the* Post, *back on page 9:* "Employer of 2 Tied to Bugging Raised Money for Nixon," WP, June 22, 1972.

682 *That afternoon the president held:* PPP 207, June 22, 1972.

683 Martha Mitchell caper: Lukas, *Nightmare,* 219–20.

684 *The* Post *kept on coming up with annoying little scoops:* "Architect Says 'Bug' Suspect Tried to Acquire Miami Plans," June 25, 1972, D1. *"For the last week, the Republican Party":* "GOP Hits *Post* for 'Hearsay,'" WP, October 17, 1972. *"They think that political parties":* Kutler, *Abuse of Power,* 59.

684 *A typical Watergate story:* "Did G.O.P. Need Supersecurity?" WP, June 29, 1969, 16.

685 *"Mr. Rather, we have checked":* PPP 207, June 22, 1972.

685 *Reported David Broder:* "McGovern, Democrats Divided, Reeling After Weeks of Crisis," LAT, July 2, 1972.

685 *"In Chicago in 1968":* "Delegates: Those Reforms Are Coming Home to Roost," NYT, June 25, 1972.

685 *Harris was out with a new poll:* "Post-Summit Advance Also Made by Kennedy," WP, June 26, 1972.

CHAPTER THIRTY-THREE: IN WHICH PLAYBOY BUNNIES, AND BARBARELLA, AND TANYA INSPIRE THEORETICAL CONSIDERATIONS UPON THE NATURE OF DEMOCRACY

686 Robert Redford: J. Hoberman, *The Dream Life: Movies, Media, and the Mythology of the Sixties* (New York: New Press, 2003), 353. *Abbie Hoffman and Jerry Rubin set up housekeeping:* Abbie Hoffman, Jerry Rubin, and Ed Sanders, *Vote!: A Record, a Dialogue, a Manifesto—Miami Beach, 1972 and Beyond* (New York: Warner Paperbacks, 1972), 28, 42–44. *"McGovern Backer No Longer Thinks":* Bob Greene, *Running* (Chicago: Regnery, 1973), 56.

686 *"Fellas, I don't believe":* Hoffman, Rubin, and Sanders, *Vote!,* 9–10. *"Call me Chuck":* Ibid., 16–21.

686 *At McGovern headquarters:* Norman Mailer, *St. George and the Godfather* (New York: New American Library, 1972), 69.

687 *Not at the Doral's rooftop:* Greene, *Running,* 4. *Germaine Greer, the women's liberationist:* Hoffman, Rubin, and Sanders, *Vote!,* 75–76.

687 *Presidential candidates arrived:* Mailer, *St. George and the Godfather,* 9–20.

687 Fontainebleau lobby: Hoffman, Rubin, and Sanders, *Vote!,* 181.

687 Playboy Plaza party: Ibid., 75; Mailer, *St. George and the Godfather,* 32.

688 For California procedural decision see ibid., 35–37, 44–66; Shirley MacLaine, *You Can Get There from Here* (New York: W. W. Norton, 1975), 66; Hunter S. Thompson, *Fear and Loathing on the Campaign Trail '72* (New York: Popular Library, 1973), 261.

688 *"Will there be another Chicago?":* Hoffman, Rubin, and Sanders, *Vote!,* 73.

688 *The Happy Warrior gave a press conference:* Greene, *Running,* 21. *"If we lose California":* Victory Navasky, "A Funny Thing Happened on the Way to the Coronation," NYT, July 23, 1972.

689 *"Daley used to call us together":* "Primary Reform Sharply Curtails Daley Role," WP, January 20, 1972. Daley at vacation house: "Report Daley Ducks Parley," CT, July 11, 1972.

689 *This melodrama had been building:* "Plea for 'Soft-Stand' by McGovern Is Refused by Daley," CT, June 8, 1969; "McGovern and Daley Open Old Wounds," WP, June 8, 1969; McGovern-Daley Clash Spotlights Civil War Raging Among Democrats," WP, June 11, 1969.

689 *Forty were Daley's:* "Challenge to Daley's Slate Upheld," CT, June 28, 1972; "'Seething' Daley Delegates Vow Floor Fight to Regain Seats," CT, July 5, 1972.

689 *A former officer of the Chicago League of Women Voters:* "City Hall Forces Refuse Help in Delegate Hearing," CT, June 2, 1972.

689 *A reform alderman later testified:* "Charges by Challengers; Daley Delegate Abuse Told," CT, June 7, 1972. *One who was naive enough to try:* Hoffman, Rubin, and Sanders, *Vote!*, 62.

689 Decline of Daley machine: Adam Cohen and Elizabeth Taylor, *American Pharaoh: Mayor Richard J. Daley: His Battle for Chicago and the Nation* (Boston: Little, Brown, 2000), 515–21.

690 Singer-Jackson challenge background: Ibid., 521–23; "Mayor Assails Action; Daley Delegates Dumped," CT, July 1, 1972; "Democratic Rules Reform Ending Favorite Son Bids," NYT, January 10, 1972; "Daley Is Challenged in Delegate Races for National Convention," CT, January 14, 1972; "Primary Reform Sharply Curtails Daley Role," CT, January 20, 1972. *The hearings officer returned to Washington:* "Daley Delegates Suffer Challenge Hearing Setback," CT, June 1, 1972; "Challenge to Daley's Slate Upheld," CT, June 28, 1972. State Democratic convention: "Singer Hits Increase in Delegates," CT, June 13, 1972; "Daley Will Lead State Delegation," CT, June 17, 1972. *"What are we, for God's sake":* "Primary Reform Sharply Curtails Daley's Kingmaker Role," WP, January 20, 1972.

690 Disrupted challengers' meetings: "Caucuses to Elect Delegates," CT, June 21, 1972; "Battle over Delegates; Daley Men Raid Caucuses," CT, June 23, 1972; "Daley Raiders Again Raise Voices at Rump Caucus," CT, June 25, 1972. *"What divine authority":* "Daley Denies Use of Rough Tactics," CT, June 27, 1972. See also full-page ad, CT, June 30, 1972, B16: "Since we were legally elected, we are entitled to be part of the Illinois delegation at the national convention."

691 *Daley traveled to Washington:* "Seek Accord on Delegates," CT, June 29, 1972.

691 *"This is like Soviet Russia":* "'Seething' Daley Delegates Vow Floor Fight to Regain Seats," CT, July 5, 1972. *"The mayor has to understand":* "Daley Will Keep Fighting," CT, July 1, 1972. *The full Supreme Court:* "Fears Suit If Challenges Seated; Court Ruling Helps Daley: Attorney," CT, July 8, 1972. *In Chicago, circuit court judge:* "Singerites Could Face Jail Terms," CT, July 10, 1972. On Covelli and Daley machine, see Cohen and Taylor, *American Pharaoh*, 413. *"One reform alderman said she would gladly go to jail:* "Would Risk Jail; Ald. Langford," CT, July 10, 1972.

692 McGovern suite for uncommitted delegates: Hoffman, Rubin, and Sanders, *Vote!*, 100.

692 *Jesse Jackson suggested a compromise:* "Tower Ticker," CT, July 9, 1972.

692 *"I hate Daley's guts!":* Hoffman, Rubin, and Sanders, *Vote!*, 71. *"I just don't see where your delegation":* Bruce Miroff, *The Liberals' Moment: The McGovern Insurgency and the Identity Crisis of the Democratic Party* (Lawrence: University Press of Kansas), 193.

692 List of challenges and procedure: Mailer, *St. George and the Godfather*, 204.

692 *Jesse Jackson showed a ticket:* "Report Daley Ducks Parley."

693 *"What kind of pleasure":* Greene, *Running*, 24.

693 *"I'm the first, man!":* Hoffman, Rubin, and Sanders, *Vote!*, 79–80.

693 South Carolina challenge: Mailer, *St. George and the Godfather*, 42–46.

693 National Women's Political Caucus: Byron E. Shafer, *Quiet Revolution: The Struggle for the Democratic Party and the Shaping of Post-Reform Politics* (New York: Russell Sage Foundation, 1983), 460–92. *One of the NWPC's most aggressive:* "Mrs. Romney Rebuts Story," WP, February 18, 1972, A17.

693 *"If you people had your way":* Brenda Feigen, *Not One of the Boys: Living Life as a Feminist* (New York: Knopf, 2000), 59.

694 WE'RE HERE TO MAKE POLICY: Hoffman, Rubin, and Sanders, *Vote!*, 68. *"Unequivocal does not mean":* Mailer, *St. George and the Godfather*, 45.

694 *"The streets of '68 are the aisles of '72!":* Hoffman, Rubin, and Sanders, *Vote!*, 71.

694 *"Wrote the Chicago Daily News's:* Ibid., 114.

694 *The next day the business:* "McGovern Obtains a Platform He Can Reshape to Meet Needs," WP, July 13, 1972.

694 Gay rights resolution: Dudley Clendinen and Adam Nagourney, *Out for Good: The Struggle to Build a Gay Rights Movement in America* (New York: Simon & Schuster, 1999), 133–36.

695 *one week later, George Meany:* Ibid., 147; Stanley Kutler, *The Wars of Watergate: The Last Crisis of Richard Nixon* (New York: W. W. Norton, 1992), 192. *At a Steelworkers' convention:* Miroff, *Liberals' Moment*, 187.

695 Abortion rights resolution: "Sisters vs. Sisters; Abortion Battle Turns Bitter," WP, July 13, 1972; Feigen, *Not One of the Boys*, 63–64; Mailer, *St. George and the Godfather*, 61; MacLaine, *You Can Get There from Here*, 66.

696 McGovern campaign as "morgue patrol": Timothy Crouse, *The Boys on the Bus* (New York: Ballantine Books, 1974), 68.

696 McGovern confrontation in Doral lobby: Robert Sam Anson, "Miami Beach," *Atlantic Monthly,* September 1972; Greene, *Running*, 66; Mailer, *St. George and the Dragon*, 66; Hoffman, Rubin, and Sanders, *Vote!*, 122; "Viet Stand Brings Headaches for McGovern," WP, July 13, 1972; "McGovern Yields to Foes of War," CT, July 13, 1972.

696 McGovern nomination: Greene, *Running*, 19. *"There are two reasons that we are going to win":* Ibid., 22.

696 *Humphrey, who was flashing peace signs:* Ibid., 23. MCGOVERN SUCKS!: Mailer, *St. George and the Godfather*, 66.

697 Vice-presidential selection: Ibid., 11, 77; Thompson, *Fear and Loathing*, 370–78; Theodore H. White, *Making of the President 1972* (New York: Atheneum, 1973), 193–99.

697 *Thomas Eagleton's name had appeared:* ProQuest Historical Newspapers search. Secretary Laird on Eagleton: NBC News, July 17, 1972, indexed at http://openweb.tvnews .vanderbilt.edu/1972–7/1972–07–17-NBC-5.html.

698 Endicott "Chub" Peabody: Mailer, *St. George and the Dragon*, 11, 77. Frances "Sissy" Farenthold: Ibid.; Feigen, *Not One of the Boys*, 62; "Marathon Session Sifted Long Roster of Candidates," NYT, July 14, 1972, 1; "Eagleton Is Nominated on First Ballot," WP, July 14, 1972.

698 seventy-nine vice-presidential candidates: Ibid.; Kutler, *Wars of Watergate*, 195.

698 *Only 3 million people:* Richard Reeves, *President Nixon: Alone in the White House* (New York: Simon & Schuster, 2001), 523. *an eighteen-year-old California delegate:* Hoffman, Rubin, and Sanders, *Vote!*, 103. *"By 1976," wrote Abbie and Jerry:* Ibid., 70. Allen Ginsberg: Ibid., photo plates. *"girls in patched jeans":* "Sisters vs. Sisters." *black man and white woman kissing:* Hoffman, Rubin, and Sanders, *Vote!*, photograph section. *Interracial marriage had been illegal: Loving v. Virginia*, 388 U.S. 1 (1967).

698 *Gus Tyler, old-line leader:* American Jewish Committee, "The Politics of American Jews: The Election of 1972," New York Public Library Oral History Collection, 1972–1975.

699 *"I made Harry Reasoner's bed":* Greene, *Running*, 30.

699 *The press studied the latest Gallup:* Mailer, *St. George and the Godfather*, 101. *Nineteen-year-old hotel maids:* Greene, *Running*, 30.

699 Custer, South Dakota, press conference: Ibid., 30–33; Crouse, *Boys on the Bus*, 344–45; Thompson, *Fear and Loathing*, 430–36. See also Gordon L. Weil, *The Long Shot: George McGovern Runs for President* (New York: W. W. Norton, 1973), 156–94.

699 *"In political campaigning it is":* "Excerpts from Eagleton News Parley," NYT, July 26, 1972, 20.

700 *The Knight newspaper chain:* "Knight v. Eagleton," *Time*, August 7, 1972.

701 AFTER MONTHS OF PRECINCT WORK: Greene, *Running*, 30.

701 *McGovern himself told an AP:* Crouse, *Boys on the Bus*, 347. *"one thousand percent for Tom Eagleton":* Ibid., 348.

701 *That was why, back in the 1950s:* Fawn Brodie, *Richard Nixon: The Shaping of His Character* (New York: W. W. Norton, 1981), 331.

701 *That evening at a buffalo-meat:* Greene, *Running*, 36. *(The week's funniest:* "The Eagleton Affair: McGovern's First Crisis," *Time*, August 7, 1972. *Then, Friday afternoon:* Crouse, *Boys on the Bus*, 348.

702 Eagleton toughing out crisis: "The Eagleton Affair," *Time*.

702 *The liberal* St. Louis Post-Dispatch: Mailer, *St. George and the Godfather*, 100.

703 *all three networks refused:* Ibid., 104.

703 *"In the Democratic primaries":* "The McGovern Image; Candor of Democratic Nominee Viewed as Chief Casualty of Eagleton Affair," NYT, July 31, 1972, 12.

703 *"Bug Suspect Got Campaign Funds":* WP, August 1, 1972.

703 *"Miss Army Recruiter":* Jane Fonda, *My Life So Far* (New York: Random House, 2005), 196.

703 POW mail: Mary Hershberger, *Jane Fonda's War: A Political Biography of an Antiwar Icon* (New York: New Press, 2005), 77–80.

704 *In one case parents only learned:* "U.S. Held Up Letter by P.O.W. Two Years," NYT, October 12, 1972; letter to the editor, "Exploiting P.O.W.'s," NYT, October 24, 1971.

704 *Valerie Kushner, wife of an imprisoned major:* "McGovern Says Nixon Ignored Kin of P.O.W.'s," NYT, March 29, 1972. Mrs. Kushner seconded: "A Stunning Sweep," NYT, July 13, 1972.

704 Fonda Vietnam trip: Hershberger, *Jane Fonda's War,* 76–108; Fonda, *My Life So Far,* 299–319.

705 *While Fonda was in Vietnam:* "Rules on Air Strikes in South Vietnam Allow Leeway," NYT, July 17, 1972.

705 *"It is impossible for this visitor":* "Signs of War Everywhere in North Vietnam Capital," NYT, May 15, 1972. *"Nixon's flying":* Hershberger, *Jane Fonda's War,* 83. *Ramsey Clark, former attorney general:* "Ramsey Clark Airings Called 'Contemptible,'" WP, August 12, 1972.

706 *"Miss Fonda made a speech":* WP, July 17, 1972, B2.

706 *Fonda arrived in Paris:* Fonda, *My Life So Far,* 319–20; Hershberger, *Jane Fonda's War,* 104.

706 *The same day, the State Department:* Ibid.

707 *Then the sex kitten was joined:* "Dikes Hit, Waldheim Says; Rogers Quickly Denies It," NYT, July 25, 1972.

707 *Of a sudden, on July 27:* PPP, July 27, 1972.

707 *Then Nixon sent his UN ambassador:* Hershberger, *Jane Fonda's War,* 106.

707 *They did report that:* "Fonda on Vietnam," WP, July 25, 1972; "The District Line," WP, July 31, 1972; "End War Amendment Is Revived in Senate," WP, July 26, 1972. *The* Post *also reported the attempts:* "U.S. Won't Prosecute Fonda," WP, August 26, 1972; "Skip Fonda Films, NY Official Asks," July 31, 1972. *Also, the paper printed a letter:* M. J. Smith, "Jane Fonda to North Vietnam," WP, August 1, 1972.

708 *Nixon had privately been maintaining:* Leonard Garment, *Crazy Rhythm: From Brooklyn and Jazz to Nixon's White House, Watergate, and Beyond* (New York: Crown, 1997), 86. *"peace with honor":* See, for example, PPP, April 26, 1972.

708 *As the president put it to Kissinger:* "Tape: Nixon Mulled Vietnam Exit in 1972," Associated Press, August 8, 2004. See also Jeffrey Kimball, conference presentation, "Vietnam and the Presidency: Vietnam and Presidential Tapes," John F. Kennedy Presidential Library and Museum, March 10, 2006.

709 *Back in February, Nixon had:* PPP, February 9, 1972. *"We had a lot of success with that":* Maureen Dowd, "Hey, What's That Sound?" NYT, August, 20, 2005.

709 *McGovern returned to his hometown:* Greene, *Running,* 39. *In between stops he worked:* Mailer, *St. George and the Godfather,* 101. *Muskie didn't merely decline:* Miroff, *Liberals' Moment,* 97. *Even Ralph Nader, the consumer:* Ralph Nader, *Crashing the Party: How to Tell the Truth and Still Run for President* (New York: St. Martin's Press, 2002), 37.

709 *They unveiled him:* Greene, *Running,* 45–46. *The day before, on August 7:* Thompson, *Fear and Loathing,* 374. *"Come January," the glad-handing:* Greene, *Running,* 39.

710 *In other news, Arthur Bremer's:* "Bremer Guilty in Shooting of Wallace, Gets 63 Years," NYT, August 5, 1972. *In New York, police:* "Obscenity Issue Pending Before the Supreme Court Slows Drive on Smut in Times Square," NYT, August 20, 1972, 33. *In Paris, the Vietnam:* "Dike Charges Snag Progress in Paris Talks," WP, August 10, 1972, A20. Pat Nixon press conference: "Mrs. Nixon Asserts Jane Fonda Should Have Bid Hanoi End War," NYT, August 9, 1972; "First Lady's Campaign," WP, August 9, 1972. *More or less, that was true:* James T. Patterson, *Grand Expectations: The United States, 1945–1965* (New York: Oxford University Press, 1995), 762.

710 *The* Los Angeles Times *reported:* Hershberger, *Jane Fonda's War,* 121.

710 *Two policemen watched her:* Hoffman, Rubin, and Sanders, *Vote!,* 188

710 *Thirteen candidates in primary elections:* "Issues Vary as Four States Vote," WP, August 7, 1972. *And on his first full day:* "Schmitz Details Theory on Plots," NYT, August 6, 1972.

710 *On August 15 the House Internal:* Hershberger, *Jane Fonda's War,* 115–21.

711 *Larry O'Brien made the incredible:* "O'Brien Asserts Bugging of Offices Preceded Raid," NYT, August 16, 1972, 20. O'Brien, of course, was correct. Martha Mitchell "political prisoner": Crouse, *Boys on the Bus,* 104.

711 *McGovern spoke at the headquarters:* Greene, *Running,* 54; "McGovern Says Nixon

Will Cut Pay Guideline," WP, August 16, 1972, A4; "McGovern Bars Briefings by Kissinger as Unhelpful," NYT, August 16, 1972, 1.

711 *John Mitchell had resigned:* "Mitchell Quits Post, Putting Family First," NYT, July 2, 1972, 1.

711 *Haldeman reported of the seven:* Stanley I. Kutler, *Abuse of Power: The New Nixon Tapes* (New York: Free Press, 1997), 111.

712 *Then it was off:* Greene, *Running,* 61.

712 *It specified the exact timing:* Crouse, *Boys on the Bus,* 176; Jonathan Schell, *The Time of Illusion* (New York: Alfred A. Knopf, 1975), 278–79.

712 *Young Voters for the President:* Ibid., 274–75; Greene, *Running,* 84, 131, 146; Mailer, *St. George and the Godfather,* 158, 163, 182.

712 *Don Riegle, an antiwar:* Ibid., 127–29.

713 *Billboards were everywhere:* Greene, *Running,* 55. PEACE POT PROMISCUITY: Reeves, *President Nixon,* 531.

713 *"Lennon, formerly with the group":* Jon Wiener, *Gimme Some Truth: The John Lennon FBI Files* (Berkeley: University of California Press, 1999).

714 Vietnam Veterans Against the War convoy: "Large Auto Convey of War Foes Is Set," NYT, July 29, 1972; "War Foes Jailed in Florida for Refusal to Testify," NYT, July 14, 1972; "Six War Foes Indicted in a Plot to Disrupt G.O.P. Convention," NYT, July 15, 1972, 1; "Veterans Assert Testimony Was False," NYT, July 16, 1972; "U.S. Court Orders War Foes Freed," NYT, July 19, 1972; "Vietnam Veteran Gives Up in Texas," NYT, July 20, 1972, 15; "3 Vietnam Veterans Are Freed on Bond," NYT, July 21, 1972; "6th Antiwar Veteran Freed," NYT, July 29, 1972; "Vietnam Veterans Jailed in Florida Contempt Case," NYT, August 10, 1972. *The charges came of tape recordings:* "Informer Appears Key to U.S. Case Against 6 Antiwar Veterans," NYT, August 14, 1972, 16. See Bud Schultz and Ruth Schultz, eds., *It Did Happen Here: Recollections of Political Repression in America* (Berkeley: University of California Press, 1989), 319–33.

714 *What VVAW was actually planning:* "War Protesters Vow No Violence," August 5, 1972, 12. VVAW lawsuit: "Wiretaps on Antiwar Units Laid to Federal Agencies," NYT, August 12, 1972, 20.

714 *Their way was strewn with eggs:* Mailer, *St. George and the Godfather,* 166. Puke-in: Ibid., 212; Hoffman, Rubin, and Sanders, *Vote!,* 183. *"This is crazy":* Greene, *Running,* 71.

715 *"I want to fuck Pat Nixon":* Ibid., 59. *Another faction—the "Zippies":* Mailer, *St. George and the Godfather,* 211. *"Attica means fight back!":* Gerald Nicosia, *Home to War: A History of the Vietnam Veterans Movement* (New York: Carroll & Graf, 2004), 237. *"Sisterhood means fight back!":* Mailer, *St. George and the Godfather,* 215. *"Zippie Free Women":* Nicosia, *Home to War,* 236; Hoffman, Rubin, and Sanders, *Vote!,* 171–72. *"Pot People's Party":* Joseph Califano Jr., *Inside: A Public and Private Life* (New York: Public Affairs Books, 2005), 257.

715 *Until, that is, an armada:* Joe Bangert, "'Hanoi Jane' and 'Thanh Phong Bob,'" *The Veteran* 31, no. 1 (2001); Hoffman, Rubin, and Sanders, *Vote!,* 171–72. *The vets also discovered:* Mailer, *St. George and the Godfather,* 213. *They tried to ask John Wayne:* Thompson, *Fear and Loathing,* 383–84.

715 *On Monday as the conventioneers:* Greene, *Running,* 70–71.

716 *A North Carolina delegate observed:* Mailer, *St. George and the Godfather,* 222.

716 *Inside, a train of keynoters:* Republican National Committee, *Official Proceedings of the Republican National Convention* (Washington, 1972). Republican convention podium: Hoffman, Rubin, and Sanders, *Vote!,* 179, 174; Mailer, *St. George and the Godfather,* 204; Schell, *Time of Illusion,* 275.

716 *"You can even eat a lettuce":* Ibid.; Greene, *Running,* 62.

716 *84 percent of them were public officeholders:* Mailer, *St. George and the Godfather,* 206. *In Texas, only one:* Ibid., 151.

717 *On Tuesday evening:* Hoffman, Rubin, and Sanders, *Vote!,* 206–9; Greene, *Running,* 69; Thompson, *Fear and Loathing,* 385. *"To a Republican lady":* Mailer, *St. George and the Godfather,* 166.

717 *On Wednesday, as delegates:* Ibid., 222. *Then came the big VVAW march:* Thompson, *Fear and Loathing,* 382–92.

717 *A security guard gripped:* Ron Kovic, *Born on the Fourth of July* (New York: Akashic Books, 2005), 174–81.

718 *Ron Kovic started confronting delegates:* Kovic, *Born on the Fourth of July,* 181.

718 Police buses, Mace in air-conditioning: Mailer, *St. George and the Godfather,* 221. Jimmy Stewart, John Wayne: Ibid., 190.

718 *A train of nominators and seconders:* RNC, *Official Proceedings.*

718 *During the nomination roll call:* Mailer, *St. George and the Godfather,* 209; Greene, *Running,* 68. *Gerald Ford read his line:* Schell, *Time of Illusion,* 279.

718 *He arrived for his acceptance:* RNC, *Official Proceedings. Some wore buttons:* Hoffman, Rubin, and Sanders, *Vote!,* 164–66.

719 *"Her name"—his voice broke:* Audio at PPP 226, August 23, 1972.

719 *At 1 a.m. police stood:* Mailer, *St. George and the Godfather,* 202; "Police Seize 900 in Miami Beach," NYT, August 24, 1972. *Though one was disappointed:* Greene, *Running,* 58.

CHAPTER THIRTY-FOUR: NOT HALF ENOUGH

720 *Nixon was twenty-six points ahead:* Richard Reeves, *President Nixon: Alone in the White House* (New York: Simon & Schuster, 2001), 523. *But on September 1, Harris:* "Nixon Given Edge in Alienated Vote," WP, September 1, 1972.

720 *George McGovern started in New England:* Bob Greene, *Running* (Chicago: Regnery, 1973), 48–51. *On September 10, George Gallup:* "Youth Vote Moves Toward GOP Camp," WP, September 10, 1972, A3. *"far and away the most fiercely":* Frederick G. Dutton, *Changing Sources of Power: American Politics in the 1970s* (New York: McGraw-Hill, 1971).

721 *the twenty-six-year-old Bob Haldeman:* Fawn Brodie, *Richard Nixon: The Shaping of His Character* (New York: W. W. Norton, 1981), 424; Stanley Kutler, *The Wars of Watergate: The Last Crisis of Richard Nixon* (New York: W. W. Norton, 1992), 82. *"Youth Against McGovern":* Greene, *Running,* 49, 87.

721 *In Youngstown, Ohio:* Greene, *Running,* 52. *In Philadelphia:* Ibid., 108.

722 *"Kennedy in '76!":* Ibid., 103. Daley parade for first lady: Julie Nixon Eisenhower, *Pat Nixon: The Untold Story* (New York: Simon & Schuster, 1979), 349. *One of his more indiscreet ward bosses:* Walter Karp, *Indispensable Enemies: The Politics of Misrule in America* (New York: Franklin Square Press, 1993), 78.

722 *The Democratic leaders of Essex County:* "Shriver Campaigns at Picnic in Jersey," NYT, September 18, 1972, 16.

722 *On the sixteenth:* "Jury Bares New Details of Break-in," WP, September 16, 1972, A1. *The next morning's story:* "Spy Funds Linked to GOP Aides," WP, September 17, 1972, A1.

722 *McGovern started using the word* Watergate: See, for instance, George S. McGovern, *An American Journey: The Presidential Campaign Speeches of George McGovern* (New York, Random House, 1974), 53, 65.

723 *Larry O'Brien, reported:* "Charge by O'Brien," NYT, August 25, 1972. *The report found eleven:* "G.A.O. Report Asks Justice Inquiry into G.O.P. Funds," NYT, August 27, 1972. *Nixon responded that both:* "Stans Demands G.A.O. Fund Audit for Democrats," NYT, August 28, 1972.

723 *One article, "McGovern Mail Lottery":* "McGovern Mail Lottery Charges Being Studied," WP, August 30, 1972.

723 *Walter Cronkite got wind:* Timothy Crouse, *The Boys on the Bus* (New York: Ballantine Books, 1974), 184–85. *It came too late to affect:* "Nixon More Believable, 59% to 20%," WP, September 28, 1972.

724 *On September 30, the Post's:* "Mitchell Controlled GOP Secret Fund," WP, September 30, 1972. *Three days later:* "McGovern Lost Credibility Asset," WP, October 2, 1972.

724 McGovern UPI editors speech: Crouse, *Boys on the Bus,* 115; McGovern, *American Journey,* 52.

724 *"What kind of lead":* Greene, *Running,* 161–62.

724 *Persistently, Jules Witcover:* Crouse, *Boys on the Bus,* 257–58.

724 Nixon on Liberty Island: Ibid., 258–60; Greene, *Running,* 136.

725 Nixon at Americana Hotel: Greene, *Running,* 139–40; Crouse, *Boys on the Bus,* 263, 266; PPP, September 26, 1972.

725 Nixon in California: Hunter S. Thompson, *Fear and Loathing on the Campaign Trail '72* (New York: Popular Library, 1973), 400–404; Crouse, *Boys on the Bus,* 267; Greene, *Running,* 143.

725 *"Why not mutiny?":* Crouse, *Boys on the Bus,* 240.

726 *Jules Witcover, after McGovern's UPI speech:* Ibid., 115–16.

726 *The president did say:* PPP, October 5, 1972.

726 *On October 8, Republican:* Jonathan Schell, *The Time of Illusion* (New York: Alfred A. Knopf, 1975), 288.

726 *October 10, a scoop:* "FBI Finds Nixon Aides Sabotaged Democrats," WP, October 10, 1972; Jules Witcover, "The Canuck Episode," WP, September 13, 1973.

727 October 10 Ron Ziegler briefing: "White House: No Comment," WP, October 11, 1972.

727 *The* Post *reported yet more fishiness:* "Muskie Demands Personal Response to Charges," WP, October 10, 1972; "Muskie Details 'Sabotage' Incidents," WP, October 16, 1972; "Lawyer for Nixon Said to Have Used GOP's Spy Fund," WP, October 16, 1972. *A* New Republic *reporter bugged:* Crouse, *Boys on the Bus,* 221–23.

728 *Bernstein and Woodward didn't attend:* Crouse, *Boys on the Bus,* 307–14.

728 *The* New York Times *filled in:* "Segretti Is Linked to Calls to White House in Spring," NYT, October 18, 1972. *Time had added a data point:* "More Fumes from the Watergate Affair," *Time,* October 23, 1972.

728 *McGovern later put out:* "McGovern: Newspapers," http://livingroomcandidate .movingimage.us.

728 *attack three Tuesdays before the election:* "GOP Hits *Post* for 'Hearsay,'" WP, October 17, 1972, A1; "Clark MacGregor's Statement on the *Washington Post,* " WP, October 18, 1972.

729 Clark Mollenhoff: Crouse, *Boys on the Bus,* 250–56.

729 For Oval Office strategizing on using attacks on Nixon campaign offices, see October 13, 1972, conversation between the president and Colson in Stanley I. Kutler, *Abuse of Power: The New Nixon Tapes* (New York: Free Press, 1997), 157.

730 Post *editor Ben Bradlee:* "GOP Hits *Post* for 'Hearsay.'"

730 *The* New York Times *reported:* "McGovern Discloses Large New Loans," NYT, October 26, 1972.

730 McGovern *"skinny cats" and "people's fund-raisers":* McGovern, *American Journey,* 29.

731 Direct mail: "Money Pours In; Mail-Order Money Raises Morale of McGovern Staff," WP, October 20, 1972. *"Mr. Nixon has described the Vietnam War":* McGovern, *American Journey,* 110. *McGovernophobic organs:* "2 Million Loaned to McGovern by Unions, Rich Contributors," CT, September 13, 1972; "$4.5 Million in Loans," CT, July 14, 1972; "Secrecy Preferred by Some McGovern Moneymen," WSJ, September 1, 1972.

731 *Reporters got so used to:* Greene, *Running,* 160. For McGovern campaign disarray generally, see Kristi Witker, *How to Lose Everything in Politics* (Chicago: Academy Publishers Chicago, 1988), passim. *Mexican-American regional coordinator:* "McGovern Mexican Aide Quits," CT, September 14, 1972, 8. *One day Vermont's popular:* Bruce Miroff, *The Liberals' Moment: The McGovern Insurgency and the Identity Crisis of the Democratic Party* (Lawrence: University Press of Kansas, 2007), 155.

732 *"Thirty-nine percent of the delegates":* Ibid., 189.

732 *De Mau Mau:* "'Mau Mau' Gang Blamed," CT, October 16, 1972.

732 Nixon in Philadelphia: H. R. Haldeman, *The Haldeman Diaries: Inside the Nixon White House* (New York: G. P. Putnam's Sons, 1994), 518; Greene, *Running,* 220–24; Jefferson Decker, "Frank Rizzo, Richard Nixon, and Law-and-Order" (master's thesis, Department of History, Columbia University, 2003).

732 Nixon Camp David address: PPP, October 21, 1972.

733 *Then he watched the seventh game:* Reeves, *President Nixon,* 537.

733 Nixon in New York: Crouse, *Boys on the Bus,* 285–88; Greene, *Running,* 231–35; PPP, October 23, 1972.

733 *It began with the piercing blast:* "Nixon: McGovern Welfare," http://livingroomcandidate.movingimage.us/.

734 *Officially, the organization:* Miroff, *Liberals' Moment,* 228–29.

734 *"They're payin' people":* "McGovern: Welfare," http://livingroomcandidate.movingimage.us/.

735 *The in-house ad agency shot that down:* Jamieson, *Packaging the Presidency,* 308. *"They don't realize how rough":* Kutler, *Abuse of Power,* 173.

735 *"And whenever the war is over":* "McGovern: Defense Spending," ibid.

735 *A four-minute spot:* "McGovern: Convention," ibid.

736 *In his law-and-order ad:* "McGovern: Crime and Drugs," ibid.

736 McGovern speech to VFW conference: McGovern, *American Journey,* 103.

736 *"The McGovern defense plan":* "Nixon: Defense," http://livingroomcandidate .movingimage.us/.

737 *Nixon radio ads:* Kathleen Hall Jamieson, *Packaging the Presidency: A History and Criticism of Presidential Campaign Advertising,* 3rd ed. (New York: Oxford University Press, 1996), 305.

737 *Two Republican consultants' research:* Ibid., 309; Walter DeVries and V. Lance Tarrance, *The Ticket-Splitters: A New Force in American Politics* (Grand Rapids, MI: Eerdmans, 1972). *A four-minute one:* "Nixon: Nixon the Man," http://livingroomcandidate .movingimage.us.

737 *In another ad, he was once more at his desk:* "Nixon: Busing," ibid.

737 *The most compelling ad:* "Nixon: Passport," ibid.

738 *"We have now heard from both Vietnams":* Reeves, *President Nixon,* 539–40.

738 *Nixon took a campaign turn:* Theodore H. White, *Making of the President 1972* (New York: Atheneum, 1973), 332.

738 Cronkite Watergate broadcast: Crouse, *Boys on the Bus,* 185–87; "American Masters: Walter Cronkite," PBS special, http://www.pbs.org/wnet/americanmasters/database /cronkite_w.html.

738 *"Paley was pleading":* "Nixon Hoped Antitrust Threat Would Sway Coverage," WP, December 1, 1997.

739 *Indeed, even before "peace is at hand":* "President Is Favored on Vietnam," WP, October 15, 1972.

739 *At one appearance at the University of Minnesota:* Miroff, *Liberals' Moment,* 99.

739 *"In a recent month":* Jamieson, *Packaging the Presidency,* 317.

740 *"I've come here with some good news":* Greene, *Running,* 107.

740 *A strange little book appeared:* Arthur Tobier, *How George McGovern Won the Presidency, and Why the Polls Were Wrong* (New York: Ballantine Books, 1972).

740 For the mood of McGovern optimistm see full-page ad, NYT, November 5, 1972, E5.

741 *Anne Wexler, one of McGovern's whiz-kid:* "Could Everyone Be Wrong?" NYT, October 29, 1972.

741 *In Ohio, a microcosm:* Ibid. *McGovern people talked about:* Ibid.

742 *"If I ever find out you're a Communist, Jane":* Jane Fonda, *My Life So Far* (New York: Random House, 2005), 225.

742 Nixon's final televised speech: PPP, November 2, 1972.

742 *The Sunday before the election, McGovern:* Reeves, *President Nixon,* 540. *"the harshest rhetoric of any campaign":* Crouse, *Boys on the Bus,* 380.

742 *"Mr. Nixon will not end the war":* Jamieson, *Packaging the Presidency,* 316. *"The more the McGovern side":* Ibid.

743 *Election eve, and the president gathered:* Kutler, *Wars of Watergate,* 195.

743 *"Stop that! Stop that!":* Reeves, *President Nixon,* 557.

743 *He called George Allen:* Election-night conversations on tape 33, available online at http://nixon.archives.gov/forresearchers/find/tapes/tape033/tape033.php. George Allen is conversation 41.

744 *Sixteen minutes later, Colson:* Conversation 47.

744 *An hour and a half later, Colson:* Conversation 52.

744 *"Mr. President, you've done the impossible!":* Conversation 59.

744 *Henry Kissinger oozed:* Conversation 60.

744 *Then, in an astonishing:* Conversation 62.

745 *One night in April of 1971:* "5 Democrats Ask Nixon to Set Date for Pullout," NYT, April 23, 1971.

745 Election results: Reeves, *President Nixon,* 541; White, *Making of the President 1972,* 341–45.

746 *Harry Dent comforted him:* Conversation 69. *"Freeze them!":* Reeves, *President Nixon,* 543.

746 *"The opposition line will be":* Reeves, *President Nixon,* 541–42.

SELECTED BIBLIOGRAPHY

Ambrose, Stephen. *Nixon, Vol. 2: The Triumph of a Politician, 1962–1972.* New York: Simon & Schuster, 1989.

Anderson, Totton J., and Eugene C. Lee. "The 1966 Election in California." *Western Political Quarterly* 20 (June 1967).

Angel, D. Duane. *Romney: A Political Biography.* New York: Exposition Press, 1967.

Anson, Robert Sam. *McGovern: A Biography.* New York: Holt, Rinehart, and Winston, 1972.

Apple, R. W., ed. *The Watergate Hearings: Break-in and Coverup.* New York: Viking, 1973.

Appy, Christian. *Working Class War: American Combat Soldiers and Vietnam.* Chapel Hill: University of North Carolina Press, 1993.

Ashman, Charles R. *The People vs. Angela Davis: The Trial of the Century.* New York: Pinnacle, 1972.

Barone, Michael. *Our Country: The Shaping of America from Roosevelt to Reagan.* New York: Free Press, 1990.

Bass, Jack, and Marilyn Thompson. *Ol' Strom: An Unauthorized Biography of Strom Thurmond.* Atlanta: Longstreet Press, 1998.

Battle, Jason J. "Racial Politics and the 1966 Alabama Gubernatorial Election." *Alabama Review* 49:2 (1996).

Belknap, Michal R. *The Vietnam War on Trial: The My Lai Massacre and Court-Martial of Lieutenant Calley.* Lawrence: University Press of Kansas, 2002.

Biles, Roger. *Richard J. Daley: Politics, Race, and the Governing of Chicago.* De Kalb: Northern Illinois University Press, 1995.

Bopp, William J., ed. *The Police Rebellion: A Quest for Blue Power.* Springfield, IL: Charles H. Thomas, 1971.

Boyarsky, Bill. *The Rise of Ronald Reagan.* New York: Random House, 1968.

Braunstein, Peter, and Michael Doyle, eds. *Imagine Nation: The American Counterculture of the 1960s and '70s.* New York: Routledge, 2001.

Breasted, Mary. *Oh! Sex Education.* New York: Praeger, 1969.

Broder, David, and Stephen Hess. *The Republican Establishment: The Present and Future of the GOP.* New York: Harper & Row, 1967.

Brodie, Fawn. *Richard Nixon: The Shaping of His Character.* New York: W. W. Norton, 1981.

Brown, Charles Sumner. "Negro Protest and White Power Structure: The Boston School Controversy, 1963–1966." Ph.D. diss., Department of Sociology, Boston University, 1973.

Burr, William, and Jeffrey Kimball. "Nixon's Nuclear Ploy." *Bulletin of the Atomic Scientists* 59, no. 1 (January/February 2003).

Cannato, Vincent J. *The Ungovernable City: John Lindsay and the Battle to Save New York.* New York: Basic Books, 2003.

Cannon, Lou. *Governor Reagan: His Rise to Power.* New York: Public Affairs, 2005.

Carmine, Edward G., and James A. Stimson. *Issue Evolution: Race and the Transformation of American Politics.* Princeton, NJ: Princeton University Press, 1990.

Carroll, Peter N. *It Seemed Like Nothing Happened: America in the 1970s.* New Brunswick, NJ: Rutgers University Press, 1990.

Carter, Dan T. *The Politics of Rage: George Wallace, the Origin of the New Conservatism, and the Transformation of American Politics.* Baton Rouge: Louisiana State University Press, 1996.

Chester, Lewis, Bruce Page, and Godfrey Hodgson. *American Melodrama: The Presidential Campaign of 1968.* New York: Viking, 1969.

Cohen, Adam, and Elizabeth Taylor. *American Pharaoh: Mayor Richard J. Daley: His Battle for Chicago and the Nation.* Boston: Little, Brown, 2000.

Cowan, Paul. *Tribes of America: Journalistic Discoveries of Our People and Their Cultures.* New York: New Press, 2008.

Cowie, Jefferson. "Nixon's Class Struggle: Romancing the New-Right Worker, 1969–1973." *Labor History* 43 (Summer 2002).

Crouse, Timothy. *The Boys on the Bus.* New York: Ballantine Books, 1974.

Dallek, Matthew. *The Right Moment: Ronald Reagan's First Victory and the Decisive Turning Point in American Politics.* New York: Free Press, 2000.

Dallek, Robert. *Flawed Giant: Lyndon Johnson and His Times, 1961–1973.* New York: Oxford University Press, 1999.

Dean, John W. *Blind Ambition: The White House Years.* New York: Simon & Schuster, 1976.

Decker, Jefferson. "Frank Rizzo, Richard Nixon, and Law-and-Order." M.A. thesis, Department of History, Columbia University, 2003.

De Groot, Gerald J. "Ronald Reagan and Student Unrest in California, 1966–1970." *Pacific Historical Review* 65, no. 1 (1996).

Dent, Harry. *The Prodigal South Returns to Power.* New York: Wiley, 1978.

Dionne, E. J. *Why Americans Hate Politics.* New York: Simon & Schuster, 1991.

Downs, Donald Alexander. *Cornell '69: Liberalism and the Crisis of the University.* Ithaca: Cornell University Press, 1969.

Draper, Alan. "Labor and the 1966 Elections." *Labor History* 30 (1989).

Dutton, Frederick G. *Changing Sources of Power: American Politics in the 1970s.* New York: McGraw-Hill, 1971.

Edsall, Thomas Byrne, and Mary Edsall. *Chain Reaction: The Impact of Race, Rights, and Taxes on American Politics.* New York: W. W. Norton, 1991.

Farber, David. *Chicago '68.* Chicago: University of Chicago Press, 1988.

——, ed. *The Sixties: From Memory to History.* Chapel Hill: University of North Carolina Press, 1994.

Feeney, Mark. *Nixon at the Movies: A Book About Belief.* Chicago: University of Chicago Press, 2004.

Flamm, Michael. *Law and Order: Street Crime, Civil Unrest, and the Crisis of Liberalism in the 1960s.* New York: Columbia University Press, 2005.

Fonda, Jane. *My Life So Far.* New York: Random House, 2005.

Garment, Leonard. *Crazy Rhythm: From Brooklyn and Jazz to Nixon's White House, Watergate, and Beyond.* New York: Crown, 1997.

Garrow, David J. *Bearing the Cross: Martin Luther King and the Southern Christian Leadership Conference.* New York: Harper Perennial, 1999.

Gillon, Steven M. *Politics and Vision: The ADA and American Liberalism, 1947–1985.* New York: Oxford University Press, 1987.

Goldwater, Barry. *Conscience of a Majority.* New York: Prentice Hall, 1970.

Greenberg, David. *Nixon's Shadow: The History of an Image.* New York: W. W. Norton, 2004.

Greene, Bob. *Running.* Chicago: Regnery, 1973.

Greenshaw, Wayne. *The Making of a Hero: The Story of Lieut. William Calley Jr.* New York: Touchstone, 1971.

Haldeman, H. R. *The Haldeman Diaries: Inside the Nixon White House.* New York: G. P. Putnam's Sons, 1994.

Hersh, Seymour. *My Lai 4: A Report on the Massacre and Its Aftermath.* New York: Random House, 1970.

Hershberger, Mary. *Jane Fonda's War: A Political Biography of an Antiwar Icon.* New York: New Press, 2005.

Hoberman, J. *The Dream Life: Movies, Media, and the Mythology of the Sixties.* New York: New Press, 2003.

Hodgson, Godfrey. *America in Our Time: From World War II to Nixon—What Happened and Why.* Garden City, NY: Doubleday, 1976.

Hoffman, Abbie, Jerry Rubin, and Ed Sanders. *Vote!: A Record, a Dialogue, a Manifesto— Miami Beach, 1972 and Beyond.* New York: Warner Paperbacks, 1972.

Irvine, Janice M. *Talk About Sex: The Battles over Sex Education in the United States.* Berkeley: University of California Press, 2002.

Jacoby, Tamar. *Someone Else's House: America's Unfinished Struggle for Integration.* New York: Free Press, 1998.

Jamieson, Kathleen Hall. *Packaging the Presidency: A History and Criticism of Presidential Campaign Advertising.* 3rd ed. New York: Oxford University Press, 1996.

Johns, Andrew L. "A Voice from the Wilderness: Richard Nixon and the Vietnam War, 1964–1966." *Presidential Studies Quarterly* 29 (1999).

Judis, John. *Grand Illusions: Critics and Champions of the American Century.* New York: Farrar, Straus & Giroux, 1992.

Kalman, Laura. *Abe Fortas: A Biography.* New Haven: Yale University Press, 1990.

Keogh, James. *President Nixon and the Press.* New York: Funk & Wagnalls, 1972.

Klinkner, Philip A. *The Losing Parties: Out-Party National Committees, 1956–1993.* New Haven: Yale University Press, 1995.

Kutler, Stanley. *The Wars of Watergate: The Last Crisis of Richard Nixon.* New York: W. W. Norton, 1992.

——. *Abuse of Power: The New Nixon Tapes.* New York: Free Press, 1997.

Langguth, A. J. *Our Vietnam: The War, 1954–1975.* New York: Touchstone, 2000.

Lembcke, Jerry. *The Spitting Image: Myth, Memory, and the Legacy of Vietnam.* New York: NYU Press, 1998.

Levy, Peter B., ed. *America in the Sixties—Left, Right, and Center: A Documentary History.* Westport, CT: Praeger, 1998.

Lewis, John. *Walking with the Wind: A Memoir of the Movement.* New York: Simon & Schuster, 1998.

Liddy, G. Gordon. *Will: The Autobiography of G. Gordon Liddy.* New York: St. Martin's Press, 1980.

Lukas, Anthony. *The Barnyard Epithet and Other Obscenities: Notes on the Chicago Trial.* New York: HarperCollins, 1970.

——. *Don't Shoot—We Are Your Children!* New York: Random House, 1971.

——. *Nightmare: The Underside of the Nixon Years.* New York: Viking, 1976.

Lurie, Leonard. *The Running of Richard Nixon.* New York: Coward, McGann, and Geoghegan, 1972.

MacMillan, Margaret. *Nixon and Mao: The Week That Changed the World.* New York: Random House, 2007.

Maier, Thomas. *Dr. Spock: An American Life.* New York: Basic Books, 2003.

Mailer, Norman. *St. George and the Godfather.* New York: New American Library, 1972.

Mason, Robert. *Richard Nixon and the Quest for a New Majority.* Chapel Hill: University of North Carolina Press, 2004.

Matthews, Chris. *Kennedy and Nixon: The Rivalry That Shaped Postwar America.* New York: Free Press, 1997.

Matusow, Allen J. *The Unraveling of America: A History of Liberalism in the 1960s.* New York: HarperCollins, 1984.

——. *Nixon's Economy: Booms, Busts, Dollars, and Votes.* Lawrence: University Press of Kansas, 1998.

McGinniss, Joe. *The Selling of the President.* New York: Penguin, 1970.

McGovern, George S. *An American Journey: The Presidential Campaign Speeches of George McGovern.* New York: Random House, 1974.

Michener, James. *Kent State: What Happened and Why.* New York: Random House, 1971.

Miroff, Bruce. *The Liberals' Moment: The McGovern Insurgency and the Identity Crisis of the Democratic Party.* Lawrence: University Press of Kansas, 2007.

Newfield, Jack. *Bread and Roses, Too.* New York: Dutton, 1971.

Newton, Michael. *Bitter Grain: Huey Newton and the Black Panther Party.* Los Angeles: Holloway House, 1980.

Nicosia, Gerald. *Home to War: A History of the Vietnam Veterans Movement.* New York: Carroll & Graf, 2004.

Nixon, Richard. *Six Crises.* New York: Doubleday, 1962.

Novak, Robert. *Nixon in the White House: The Frustration of Power.* New York: Random House, 1971.

Olson, James Stuart, and Randy Roberts, eds. *My Lai: A Brief History with Documents.* New York: Bedford/St. Martin's, 1998.

Oudes, Bruce, ed. *From: The President: Richard Nixon's Secret Files.* New York: Harper-Collins, 1989.

Patterson, James T. *Grand Expectations: The United States, 1945–1965.* New York: Oxford University Press, 1995.

Pearson, Hugh. *Shadow of a Panther: Huey Newton and the Price of Black Power in America.* New York: Addison-Wesley, 1994.

Perlstein, Rick. *Before the Storm: Barry Goldwater and the Unmaking of the American Consensus.* New York: Hill & Wang, 2001.

Persico, Joseph. *The Imperial Rockefeller: A Biography of Nelson A. Rockefeller.* New York: Simon & Schuster, 1982.

Porambo, Ron. *No Cause for Indictment: An Autopsy of Newark.* New York: Melville House, 2007.

Quinn, Edward, and Paul J. Doyle, eds. *The Sense of the Sixties.* New York: Free Press, 1968.

Reeves, Richard. *President Nixon: Alone in the White House.* New York: Simon & Schuster, 2001.

Rice, Bradley R. "The 1966 Gubernatorial Elections in Georgia." Ph.D. diss., Department of History, University of Southern Mississippi, 1982.

Roberts, Steven V. *Eureka.* New York: Quadrangle/New York Times Books, 1974.

Royko, Mike. *Boss: Richard J. Daley of Chicago.* New York: New American Library, 1971.

Safire, William. *Before the Fall: An Inside View of the Pre-Watergate White House.* New York: Ballantine, 1977.

Scammon, Richard, and Ben Wattenberg. *The Real Majority: An Extraordinary Examination of the American Electorate.* New York: Coward McCann, 1980.

Schell, Jonathan. *The Time of Illusion.* New York: Alfred A. Knopf, 1975.

Schultz, John. *No One Was Killed: Convention Week, Chicago—August 1968.* Chicago: Big Table Publishing Co., 1989.

——. *The Chicago Conspiracy Trial.* New York: De Capo Press, 1993.

Shadegg, Stephen C. *Winning's a Lot More Fun.* New York: Macmillan, 1969.

Shafer, Byron E. *Quiet Revolution: The Struggle for the Democratic Party and the Shaping of Post-Reform Politics.* New York: Russell Sage Foundation, 1983.

Shesol, Jeff. *Mutual Contempt: Robert Kennedy, Lyndon Johnson, and the Feud That Defined a Decade.* New York: W. W. Norton, 1998.

Shogan, Robert. *Bad News: Where the Press Goes Wrong in the Making of the President.* Chicago: Ivan R. Dee, 2001.

Stans, Maurice. *The Terrors of Justice: The Untold Side of Watergate.* New York: Everest House, 1978.

Thompson, Hunter S. *Fear and Loathing on the Campaign Trail '72.* New York: Popular Library, 1973.

Turner, William. *The Police Establishment.* New York: G. P. Putnam's Sons, 1968.

United States Congress. *Civil Rights: Hearings Before a Subcommittee on the Judiciary, United States Senate, Eighty-ninth Congress, Second Session, on S. 3296.* Washington, DC: U.S. Government Printing Office, 1966.

United States Congress. *Civil Rights, 1966: Hearings Before Subcommittee No. 5, Eighty-ninth Congress, Second Session.* Washington, DC: U.S. Government Printing Office, 1966.

U.S. Commission on Civil Rights. *Hearings Before the United States Commission on Civil Rights: Hearing Held in Cleveland, Ohio, April 1–7, 1966.* Washington, DC: The Commission, 1966.

Varon, Jeremy. *Bringing the War Home: The Weather Underground, the Red Army Faction, and Revolutionary Violence in the Sixties and Seventies.* Berkeley: University of California Press, 2004.

Weaver, Reg, and Hal Gulliver. *The Southern Strategy.* New York: Scribner, 1971.

Weil, Gordon L. *The Long Shot: George McGovern Runs for President.* New York: W. W. Norton, 1973.

Wells, Tom. *The War Within: America's Battle over Vietnam.* Berkeley: University of California Press, 1994.

Whalen, Richard. *Catch the Falling Flag: A Republican's Challenge to His Party.* Boston: Houghton Mifflin, 1972.

White, F. Clifton, and William J. Gill. *Why Reagan Won.* Washington: Regnery Gateway, 1981.

White, Theodore H. *Making of the President 1960.* New York: Atheneum, 1961.

———. *Making of the President 1968.* New York: Atheneum, 1969.

———. *Making of the President 1972.* New York: Atheneum, 1973.

Wicker, Tom. *A Time to Die.* New York: Quadrangle/New York Times Books, 1975.

Wills, Garry. *The Second Civil War: Arming for Armageddon.* New York: New American Library, 1968.

———. *Nixon Agonistes: The Crisis of the Self-Made Man.* Boston: Houghton Mifflin, 1970.

Witcover, Jules. *The Resurrection of Richard Nixon.* New York: G. P. Putnam's Sons, 1970.

———. *White Knight: The Rise of Spiro Agnew.* New York: Random House, 1972.

———. *The Making of an Ink-Stained Wretch: Half a Century Pounding the Political Beat.* Baltimore: Johns Hopkins University Press, 2005.

ACKNOWLEDGMENTS

My debts stretch before me, numberless and interminable. In part that's because this project began aeons ago. In fact, it was conceived before I even began my first book—when I realized, reviewing Stanley Kutler's 1997 collection of Nixon White House transcripts, *Abuse of Power,* my hypothesis that America awarded Richard Nixon with a landslide victory in 1972 not in spite of the paranoia and dreads that produced Watergate, but in some ways because of them.

Or maybe it was conceived when I was sixteen years old, taking advantage of my new driver's license to trek to the cavernous Renaissance Bookstore in downtown Milwaukee, burrowing in the smelly basement where they kept the old magazines from the sixties stacked higgledy-piggledy in mountainous piles.

That said, let me begin by thanking, in addition to the Renaissance Bookstore, whose basement I still haunt, Stanley Kutler as first among the scholars and writers who were so generous with their time, insights, and support. The list also includes Larry Berman, Sidney Blumenthal, Bill Boyarsky, Vincent Cannato, Jefferson Cowie, John Dean (that guy really knows a thing or two about Nixon), Angela Dillard, David Farber (whose paper "The Silent Majority and Talk About Revolution" somehow didn't end up in the endnotes, but which influenced every chapter of this book), Michael Flamm, David Greenberg, Maurice Isserman, Laura Kalman, Michael Kazin (whose *America Divided: The Civil War of the 1960s* blazed an important trail), Phil Klinkner, A. J. "Jack" Langguth, Jerry Lembcke, Scott Lemieux, Steve Miller, Kim Phillips-Fein, Richard Reeves (whose *President Nixon: Alone in the White House* was probably my most consulted source), Jeff Shesol, Sam Tanenhaus, Elizabeth Taylor, Jeremy Varon, and Garry Wills.

Phil Klinkner and Maurice Isserman are in the above list, but I want to recognize them again for their extraordinary generosity in sharing carefully compiled documentary files (Richard Jensen, Howard Park, Ryan Hayes, and Chip Berlet generously did so as well). Phil and Maurice are also among the scholars who hosted me for wonderful visits to their schools, in their case Hamilton College; others include Nelson Lichtenstein of the University of California–Santa

Barbara, Michael Kazin of Georgetown, Matthew Lassiter and Robert Mickey of the University of Michigan, Kenton Worcester of Marymount Manhattan College, John Tresch formerly of the Columbia University Society of Fellows in the Humanities, Adam Goodheart and Ted Widmer of Washington College, the Ashbrook Center for Public Affairs at Ashland University, and Nick Salvatore and Jefferson Cowie of Cornell University. And at Princeton University Press, Sean Wilentz and Peter Dougherty afforded me the extraordinary opportunity of publishing an edition of Richard Nixon's speeches and writings. I am deeply honored and humbled that scholars such as these have seen fit to accept me into their professional company.

Those are folks I have the pleasure of knowing. There are others whose debt I must acknowledge simply because their work—sometimes work almost forty years old—has profoundly influenced me and/or was especially useful. These include Robert Sam Anson, Christian Appy, Stanley Aronowitz, Michael Barone, Michal R. Belknap, Taylor Branch, Mary Breasted, Karl E. Campbell, Dan T. Carter, Adam Cohen, Timothy Crouse, Matthew Dallek, Michael William Doyle, Mary Edsall and Thomas Byrne Edsall, Leonard Garment, David J. Garrow, Bob Greene, Mary Hershberger, Christopher Hitchens, J. Hoberman, Godfrey Hodgson, Janice M. Irvine, Tamar Jacoby, Kathleen Hall Jamieson, John Judis, Paul Alexander Juutilainen, Jeffrey Kimball, Allen J. Matusow, Joe McGinniss, the late Jack Newfield, Michael Newton (who published a quickie "pulp" paperback on the Black Panthers in 1980 that stands the test of time), Gerald Nicosia, Robert Novak, James Stuart Olson, Bruce Oudes, the late Ron Porambo, Randy Roberts, Richard Scammon, Jonathan Schell, John Schultz (whose books on the Chicago convention and the Chicago conspiracy trial are invaluable), Byron Shafer, Benjamin Wattenberg, Gordon Weil, Tom Wells, Richard J. Whalen, Tom Wicker, and Jules Witcover (this towering first-drafter of history is surely the most cited author herein)—and, of course, my two dedicatees, the late Anthony Lukas and the late Paul Cowan (and the long-defunct blog Noosphere Blues that introduced me to hero Cowan). I owe a special debt to Chris Matthews for inspiring the Orthogonian/Franklin thread that runs throughout the book, and also to Peter B. Levy for compiling in *America in the Sixties—Left, Right, and Center* the perfect collection of sixties documents.

The recollections of the actual actors in this drama add much, I hope, to the drama of this story. So I thank those who were forthcoming with their memories, from just answering an emailed question to tucking into a long meal while I harassed them about how and why they did or said this, that, or the other thing on a particular day thirty-five or forty years ago: Terry Anzur, Frank Aukofer, Senator Birch Bayh, William F. Buckley, Geoffrey Cowan, Rachel Cowan, Lee Edwards, Alan Eisenberg, Daniel Ellsberg, Richard Flacks, Ryan Hayes, Tim Hill, the late Molly Ivins, Lewis Z. Koch, Jay Larkey, Jesse Lemisch, Don Luce, David Moberg, Bill Moyers, Don Oberdorfer, John

O'Donnell, Leon Panetta, Heather Parton, Kevin Phillips, David Roediger, Don Rose, Marshall Sahlins, Nick Salvatore, John Schmidhauser, the late Neal Shine, and David Walther.

I live in a very special neighborhood. This book is fueled by the coffee talk of its citizens. In Hyde Park on the South Side of Chicago, in the shadow of the University of Chicago, a month hardly passes when you don't meet some random citizen who knows more on your own subject of "expertise" than you do—most often at the Third World Café on Fifty-third Street. Among my fine *Nixonland* interlocutors there have been David Berrier, Curtis Black, Heather Blair, Matt Frizzell, Bob Hodge, Aaron Lav, the late Bill Maddox, Doug Mitchell, Adrian Montague, Christina Siun O'Connell, Erika Schmidt, Jon Stokes, and Bill and Barbara Wimsatt. Steve Chapman, Emil Jorgensen, and Amanda Cage have the misfortune of not residing in Hyde Park, but what the hell, I'll throw them in here too. And, in between composing paragraphs, I greatly enjoyed and benefited from my sometimes contentious online colloquies with my friends Jameson Campaigne, Orrin Judd, and Chris Nunneley.

I was served by the professionalism of the archivists and staffs at the Chicago Museum of History (thank you, box 722!), the Regenstein Library at the University of Chicago (especially Ray Gadke in microforms), the Nixon Project of the National Archives and Records Administration, the Richard Nixon Library and Birthplace, and Cornell University Special Collections. Special thanks, too, to Bruce Dumont and Chicago's Museum of Broadcast Communications for opening their archives for me as they transition between buildings. And Rick Shenkman's work fostering a community space for historians at HistoryNewsNetwork.com has been marvelous.

I received generous support for the project from Dave Block, Dan Cantor, George Chauncey, Kevin Drum, Tom Frank, Frank Geier, Hank and Pat Geier, David Glenn, Michael Kazin, Mark and Carol Leff, Stanley Kutler, John Palattella, my parents Jerry and Sandi Perlstein, Aaron Swartz, the late James Weinstein, Eric Wunderman, and the White House Historical Association. Thanks, too, to Eric Alterman and Rick MacArthur for their quiet advocacy.

When I wrote my first book, my ability to reconstruct the mental world of activists working for political change was profoundly enhanced by my work as a participant-observer with the New York Working Families Party. This time, I enjoyed a privileged perch within a sui generis movement for political change and media accountability as extraordinary in its way as the rise of the CIO in the 1930s and the Moral Majority and Christian Coalition in the 1980s and '90s: the progressive blogosphere, or "netroots." Here's where the paring gets pretty ruthless, but I'd at least like to recognize John Amato, John Aravosis, Duncan Black, the late Steve Gilliard, Jane Hamsher, Ezra Klein, Howie Klein, Josh Marshall, Markos Moulitsas, Max Sawicky, Pastor Dan Schultz, Matt Stoller—and, first among equals, the one person besides my wife with whom I've enjoyed my most important intellectual partnership, Heather

"Digby" Parton. Along the way, I also benefited greatly from the interval I spent covering the 2004 presidential election for the *Village Voice;* much thanks to Laura Conaway and Doug Simmons. And I'm exceptionally proud to now be working as a senior fellow with Campaign for America's Future, my new institutional home.

Brilliant friends have read chunks, and more than chunks, of this manuscript in various states of undress and improved it considerably. These include Thomas Geoghegan, Christopher Hayes, Paul Krugman, Allison Xantha Miller (thanks for *Punishment Park*!), Aaron Swartz (thanks for the website!), Jason Vest (thanks for the inspired and inspiring grouchiness!), Kyle Westphal (thanks for the author photo!), and the Washington, D.C., reading group whose members include Charlie Cray, David Glenn (thanks for the *Rolling Stone* cache!), Henry Farrell, David Frum, Scott McLemee, Krist Raab, Jim McNeill, and Rich Yeselson.

My professional partners in this adventure have been agent Chris Calhoun and editor Colin Harrison. I don't think I could have done better, and I thank them both so gratefully for their faith and investment in me. And Laura Wise's production team was exceptionally efficient and meticulous.

I signed the contract for this book in November 2001. It's been a long road, and I've surely missed some landmarks along the way in these acknowledgments. No way, though, of missing the continual rewards brought by the renewal of perhaps my oldest friendship, with Anil Mudholkar—though, scratch that, my richly sustaining friendship with my sister Linda Perlstein dates back far further—and with my new brother from another mother, Lewis Z. Koch.

And finally there is Kathy Geier. Kathy Geier. Kathy Geier. To *conspire* means to "breathe together." This book is our conspiracy.

INDEX